Dedicated to our families, who have provided unwavering support throughout the whole process of writing this book.

We are especially grateful to our children—Andy, Will, Rachel, and Lily— for their patience and understanding.

Child Development

PRINCIPLES AND PERSPECTIVES

Joan Littlefield Cook

University of Wisconsin–Whitewater

Greg Cook

University of Wisconsin–Whitewater

Boston   New York   San Francisco
Mexico City   Montreal   Toronto   London   Madrid   Munich   Paris
Hong Kong   Singapore   Tokyo   Cape Town   Sydney

EXECUTIVE EDITOR: Karon Bowers

DEVELOPMENT MANAGER: Judith H. Hauck

DEVELOPMENT EDITOR: Mary Piper Hansen

SENIOR MARKETING MANAGER: Wendy Gordon

EDITORIAL-PRODUCTION ADMINISTRATOR: Annette Joseph

EDITORIAL-PRODUCTION SERVICE AND ELECTRONIC COMPOSITION: Omegatype Typography, Inc.

TEXT DESIGNERS: Lidija Tomas Design; MediaLynx Design Group, Inc.

PHOTO RESEARCHER: Sarah Evertson, Imagequest

ELECTRONIC ART: Imagineering Media Services and Omegatype Typography, Inc.

COMPOSITION AND PREPRESS BUYER: Linda Cox

MANUFACTURING BUYER: Megan Cochran

COVER ADMINISTRATOR: Linda Knowles

COVER DESIGNER: Studio Nine

For related titles and support materials, visit our online catalog at www.ablongman.com.

Between the time website information is gathered and then published, it is not unusual for some sites to have closed. Also, the transcription of URLs can result in typographical errors. The publisher would appreciate notification where these errors occur so that they may be corrected in subsequent editions.

Library of Congress Cataloging-in-Publication Data

Cook, Joan Littlefield.
    Child development : principles and perspectives / Joan Littlefield Cook, Greg Cook.
        p. cm.
    Includes bibliographical references and index.
    ISBN 0-205-31411-2 (alk. paper)
        1. Child development. I. Cook, Greg (Greg L.) II. Title.

    HQ772.C596 2005
    305.231—dc22

                                                                    2003062695

Printed in the United States of America

10 9 8 7 6 5 4 3 2 1   VHP   09 08 07 06 05 04

Chapter 3

Prenatal Development and Birth   86

Chapter 4

Physical Development: Body, Brain, and Perception   128

SECTION 2:
COGNITIVE DEVELOPMENT

Chapter 5

*Cognitive Development:
Piagetian and
Sociocultural Views   170*

Chapter 6

*Information Processing:
The Development of Memory
and Thought* 206

Chapter 7

Intelligence and Academic Skills 248

Chapter 8

Language Development   284

SECTION 3:
SOCIAL DEVELOPMENT

Chapter 9

Attachment, Temperament, and Emotion   328

SECTION 4:
CHILDREN IN CONTEXTS

Chapter 12

Families   460

Chapter 13

Schools, Media, and Culture   506

Our students often ask us at the beginning of the term why they should study child development and how it will be useful in their lives. Our mission in writing this textbook was to ensure we answered the "why" and "how" clearly throughout. As a result, you'll notice our two primary goals as you read this book:

- To illustrate how child development principles and concepts are useful from many different *perspectives*—from the perspectives of different careers, different personal situations, different social policy issues—and how child development directly impacts all of our lives. By exploring different perspectives, students are better able to understand both the "why" and "how."

- To provide students with the best (and most integrated) *active learning system* on the market. Our book's features work together and support learning that is contextualized, meaningful, and motivating. The active learning system works to ensure that students learn and retain useful material—and can apply it to their own interactions with children, now and in the future.

Child Development: Principles and Perspectives is not a comprehensive encyclopedia of everything known about child development. Instead we focused on the topics that research has suggested are most important in telling the story of where the field has been and where it is today. Our research and our teaching expertise provide a strong foundation for our approach to telling the story of the *principles* of child development.

Exploring Different Perspectives

Individuals, theorists, even entire professions see things differently—they notice different details, frame issues and problems differently, and propose different solutions. This field contains many different theories, research findings, ideas, and viewpoints. What we have come to appreciate over our years of teaching is that this diversity is a wonderful learning tool. Trying to take others' points of view broadens and deepens students' comprehension of information, helping them develop a richer understanding of the content and issues in child development. Thinking about different perspectives also helps students see the many ways in which child development information is useful, both to others and to their own lives. By looking from different perspectives, students come to understand more completely and more personally—and, ironically, this approach may help students appreciate the many *similarities* in development across children as well. In *Child Development: Principles and Perspectives* we introduce students to people involved in child development in all walks of life: from parents, teachers, and social workers to scholars, researchers, and therapists. Weaving together and understanding the many perspectives on how to raise children, how best to work with children, and how to effect change in our society to better accommodate children is, in our opinion, the best tool any of us can have.

Each chapter begins this process with a feature called **A Perspective to Think About.** This feature not only explains the perspective of someone who is in a difficult or vulnerable situation, but also provides a way for students to think about that particular situation in relation to the chapter's topic. Yet we want students to go beyond one person and explore the views and

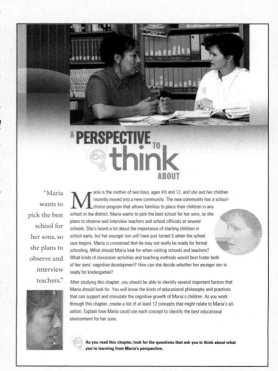

A PERSPECTIVE TO think ABOUT

"Maria wants to pick the best school for her sons, so she plans to observe and interview teachers."

Maria is the mother of two boys, ages 4½ and 12, and she and her children recently moved into a new community. The new community has a school-choice program that allows families to place their children in any school in the district. Maria wants to pick the best school for her sons, so she plans to observe and interview teachers and school officials at several schools. She's heard a lot about the importance of starting children in school early, but her younger son will have just turned 5 when the school year begins. Maria is concerned that he may not really be ready for formal schooling. What should Maria look for when visiting schools and teachers? What kinds of classroom activities and teaching methods would best foster both of her sons' cognitive development? How can she decide whether her younger son is ready for kindergarten?

After studying this chapter, you should be able to identify several important factors that Maria should look for. You will know the kinds of educational philosophy and practices that can support and stimulate the cognitive growth of Maria's children. As you work through this chapter, create a list of at least 12 concepts that might relate to Maria's situation. Explain how Maria could use each concept to identify the best educational environment for her sons.

As you read this chapter, look for the questions that ask you to think about what you're learning from Maria's perspective.

experiences others bring to the issues—including their own. As such, one of the most valuable features of our book is **Your Perspective Notes.** Each of these marginal notes asks students to think about how the material they just read applies to their own lives and reinforces the importance of different opinions and ideas. These questions are designed not only to stimulate inner thought and actually involve the student with the material but also to ignite classroom discussion.

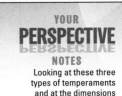

YOUR PERSPECTIVE NOTES

Looking at these three types of temperaments and at the dimensions listed in Table 9.5, how would you rate your temperament?

Three boxed features appear in each chapter and further explore various perspectives on child development: **A Professional Perspective, A Personal Perspective,** and **A Social Policy Perspective.**

A Professional Perspective

In **A Professional Perspective** a real professional discusses how he or she uses child development information. Using an interview format, each of these features introduces students to a different career; by the end of the book, students have explored 14 different career paths (among them social work, genetic counseling, clinical and counseling psychology, school psychology, and marketing) that involve work with children, adolescents, and development. Students should get plenty of career ideas from these boxes.

A Personal Perspective

Also presented as an interview, **A Personal Perspective** allows students to connect with the personal feelings of an actual parent, child, or adolescent who is experiencing something discussed in the chapter. For example, in the chapter where we discuss ethnic identity, an African American adult gives an insightful explanation of how her childhood and early experiences influenced the formation of her own ethnic identity. This feature allows students to see how real people of all backgrounds relate to child development issues.

A Social Policy Perspective

We designed **A Social Policy Perspective** to give students an understanding of how work in the field of child development can inform government officials, community service agencies, and others who have wide-ranging effects on the lives of children. This feature focuses on many of the controversial issues in society, examining the perspectives of both sides of each debate. It highlights the ways in which programs, laws, regulations, and other factors can affect children and asks students to think about the impact of social policies.

Taken together, these different *perspective* features help students see how child development information is useful in a wide variety of professional, personal, and controversial situations. They also help students understand the real-life challenges faced by professionals, parents, volunteers, and policy makers whose work relates to the field of child development.

Features of the Active Learning System

Another primary goal of ours was to create an *active learning system* to help students better understand, apply, and retain key concepts. We want students to take an active role in understanding the principles of child development—because the more involved they become, the more they will think about what they are learning on different levels. Our book engages students in the critical thinking process from the very first page. We employed the principles of constructivism, active learning, and the importance of context in learning to provide students with several opportunities to apply and reinforce key concepts throughout each chapter.

One thing we have learned from educational research and personal experience is that people tend to learn better when they can see clear relationships between facts and real life. Students can read and memorize facts and theories, but seeing how information relates to everyday life adds a critical dimension to the learning process and, ultimately, a deeper understanding of the material. This *active approach* to learning is similar in many ways to how a child develops. Just as children are immensely active in their own process of physical development—by jumping, climbing, and running, their muscles grow stronger and more coordinated—learning is more effective when students are actively involved in the process.

All of our active learning system features work together to support learning that is contextualized, meaningful, and motivating. Additionally, several features encourage students to connect the chapter material to real-life scenarios and activate their critical thinking skills. One of the strengths of these features is that the situations we describe are realistic—they are the typical kinds of problems that people face when they work with or raise children and adolescents. Strengthened by MyPsychLab, a powerful interactive program that provides multimedia tools all in one place online, *Child Development: Principles and Perspectives* offers students many opportunities to practice and master what they're learning. MyPsychLab's unique, Individualized Study Plan works together with these features as part

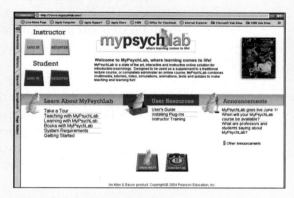

of the active learning system. This personalized study and review strategy allows students to actively track their progress in a topic and to prepare for the end-of-chapter test.

A Perspective to Think About

We begin each chapter with **A Perspective to Think About,** as we described earlier. Then, throughout the chapter, **Thinking of** questions in the margins ask students to provide advice or solutions in response to the opening situation, actively applying what they have learned thus far. To tie it all together, at the end of each chapter, **Thinking Back to** offers suggestions on how the chapter content could be used to advise the characters described in that chapter's **A Perspective to Think About.** We don't give hard-and-fast answers, but we do summarize some key connections.

Preview Questions

Each major section of a chapter begins with several preview questions that will orient students' thinking toward the material and provide a framework

secure attachment

In Ainsworth's classification, the healthy type of attachment between infant and caregiver. Indicated when the infant in distress seeks contact with the caregiver, clings, and is soothed by the caregiver; and when the infant uses the caregiver as a safe base for exploring unfamiliar environments. Other indicators include *separation anxiety* and *stranger anxiety*.

LET'S REVIEW . . .

1. Which of the following is *true* about early childhood education programs such as Head Start, High/Scope Perry Preschool, and the Abecedarian Project?

   a. These programs are not cost-effective.
   b. These programs regularly produce permanent gains in IQ scores.
   c. These programs produce improved academic progress and higher graduation rates.
   d. These programs have little effect on social measures like arrest records or employment.

Jacqueline, a fourth grader, said, "I like to try things that are a little hard for me, because when I finally can do them, it makes me smarter!" Jacqueline has:

   a. a mastery orientation.
   b. a helpless orientation.
   c. an entity view of ability.
   d. performance goals.

Compared to students in other countries, academic scores of students in the United States:

   a. are the best.
   b. are lower than most other countries.
   c. have improved since 1995.
   d. have declined since 1995.

students can use for learning. The questions help students recognize the important points and see the organization of the section in advance.

Key Terms

Key vocabulary terms are highlighted in **bold print** in the text and are repeated, with their definitions, in the margins. An alphabetical list of these terms also appears at the end of the chapter so students can review any terms that are still unfamiliar. These key terms include both the concepts that are most important and the vocabulary most likely to be unfamiliar to anyone studying child development for the first time.

Let's Review Questions

Each of the major sections in the chapters ends with a set of **Let's Review** questions, which include multiple-choice and true/false questions concerning the material. These questions are meant to be relatively general and moderately easy—not brain-busters, which students usually learn to avoid. We provide the answers nearby, printed upside down, so in just a few seconds this feature can give students quick feedback on their understanding of the material.

Chapter Summary

A **Chapter Summary** in a question-and-answer format appears at the end of each chapter. It reminds students about the main questions addressed in the chapter and gives a quick summary of the most important concepts. It is by no means a substitute for reading the chapter, but it is an effective review tool.

Topics Covered

This book covers the main topics related to the physical, cognitive, and social development of children and adolescents. We explore genetics and heredity; physical growth before and after birth; the development of thought, intelligence, and language; the emergence of self-identity, gender concepts, and morality; and how children interact with parents, caregivers, siblings, and friends. We emphasize influences within families, but we also explore the influences of schools, the media, and the culture that surrounds the child.

Although most of the book is about development that progresses in a normal or typical fashion, we do point out many of the ways that development can go awry. And unlike most textbooks on child development, this book devotes an entire chapter to atypical paths in development. Chapter 14 covers behavioral, emotional, developmental, and learning problems and abuse and neglect. On the other end of the spectrum, it also covers gifted, talented, and resilient children. Rather than limiting these topics to add-on coverage spread across many chapters, we give them full treatment in their own chapter. By doing so, we provide a better context for understanding the common origins, influences, and treatments for various problems, and we emphasize how problems often co-occur within the same children. Chapter 14 also juxtaposes the two ends of the developmental spectrum, allowing students to compare (for example) developmental problems with giftedness and showing how children at both ends need special consideration.

History versus Contemporary Science

Most of this book focuses on contemporary science and on what is happening in the field today, but we include selected historical background and classic studies; often these have influenced how we think about the field of child development and explain how particular scientific approaches emerged. We want to remind students that just as adults are influenced by childhood experiences, the science of child development has been shaped by its own past. In Chapter 1 we describe many of the people who helped form the field during its infancy: Sigmund Freud, Erik Erikson, and B. F. Skinner, to name a few. The remainder of the book emphasizes contemporary science but sometimes presents historical information about how a topic emerged in the field. We focus on what researchers currently understand about child development, and we raise the questions that are yet to be answered.

Focus on Diversity

We all know that differences in gender, ethnicity, religion, culture, and language can affect what each of us defines as our everyday experience. In the study of child development, we face the tremendous challenge of describing the commonalities of development while at the same time recognizing all of the potential differences that can exist. In this book we embrace diversity, drawing upon research studies that capture statistics and results from many cultures and discussing the influences of culture and ethnicity on many aspects of development.

Supporting Material

Instructor Supplements

Instructor's Manual (0-205-39469-8)
Bradley Caskey, *University of Wisconsin–River Falls*

The Instructor's Manual is a wonderful tool for classroom preparation and management. Each chapter includes an At-a-Glance Grid with detailed pedagogical information linking to other available supplements; a detailed chapter outline; teaching objectives covering major concepts within the chapter; a list of key terms with page references; lecture material, including suggested discussion questions and topics; demonstrations and in-depth activities referencing top journals; a comprehensive list of child development and popular video, media, and web resources; and a list of suggested readings. In addition, this manual includes a preface, a sample syllabus, and tables of contents for the Child Development Digital Media Archive and Transparencies; and the appendix includes a comprehensive list of student handouts.

Test Bank (0-205-39449-3)
Carolyn Morgan, *University of Wisconsin–Whitewater*

This thoroughly reviewed test bank helps instructors prepare for exams with challenging questions that target key concepts. Each chapter includes more than 100 questions, including multiple-choice, true/false, short-answer, and essay items, each with an answer justification, page reference, difficulty rating, and type designation. In addition, the appendix includes a sample open-book quiz.

TestGen EQ Computerized Test Bank (0-205-40409-X)

The computerized version of the test bank is available with Tamarack's easy-to-use TestGen EQ 5.0 software, which lets you prepare printed, network, and online tests. It includes full editing capability for Windows and Macintosh.

PowerPoint Presentation (0-205-39611-9)
Gerard Barron, *Mercyhurst College*

An exciting interactive tool for use in the classroom, the presentation package includes key points covered in the textbook and images from the textbook.

Transparencies for Child Development (0-205-40747-1)

This package of full-color acetates helps to enhance classroom lecture and discussion through the use of images from a variety of Allyn & Bacon's child development texts.

Development: Journey through Childhood Video with Video Guide (0-205-40748-X)
Dr. Kelly Welch, *Kansas State University*

This engaging video includes two or three clips per chapter, plus critical thinking questions. Clips include such footage as live birth, babies and language development, differences in personality among toddlers, child and parent interaction, and exceptional children. In addition, the accompanying video guide provides further critical thinking questions and Internet resources for more information.

The Allyn & Bacon Digital Media Archive for Child Development

This collection of media products—charts, graphs, tables and figures, and video clips—enlivens your classroom with resources easily integrated into your lectures.

Student Supplements

MyPsychLab (Available for Fall 2004 classes)

MyPsychLab is a powerful interactive teaching and learning system. In one convenient online location, students can enhance their performance and improve their grades by creating an Individualized Study Plan and practicing with an Electronic Study Guide (Grade Aid). Live tutors in the Tutor Center facilitate increased mastery. Help with assignments and papers is provided by Research Navigator, which combines a powerful search engine (EBSCO) and feeds from the *New York Times*. Classic and contemporary experiments come to life through dynamic animations and simulations. Students navigate to all of these exciting resources from the launching pad of an electronic version of *Child Development: Principles and Perspectives.*

For instructors MyPsychLab offers the time-saving convenience of a complete course management system (CourseCompass) with grade book, testing, and presentation options, and the ease of having all instructional assets aggregated in one place. Students benefit from the endless opportunities to practice and master what they're learning.

Grade Aid with Practice Tests (0-205-39450-7)
Carolyn Morgan, *University of Wisconsin–Whitewater*

A comprehensive and interactive study guide that includes the following for each chapter: "Before You Read," with a brief chapter summary and chapter learning objectives; "As You Read," a collection of demonstrations, activities, and exercises, including activities that correspond to the *Development: Journey through Childhood and Adolescence* CD-ROM (see description below); "After You Read," containing three short practice quizzes and one comprehensive practice test; "When You Have Finished," with short-answer and essay questions to reiterate concepts; and crossword puzzles using key terms from the text.

Companion Website with Online Practice Tests (www.ablongman.com/cook1e)

This website includes flash cards, learning objectives, web links, and online practice tests for each chapter of the text to help students review and retain the material. For additional online resources, please see our **Human Development Supersite** at **http://cwabacon.pearsoned.com/bookbind/pubbooks/humandev_ab/**.

Development: Journey through Childhood and Adolescence CD-ROM (0-205-39568-6)
Dr. Kelly Welch, *Kansas State University*

This multimedia learning tool is available to be packaged with the text or sold separately. It includes eight interactive units that cover prenatal development through adolescence and uses video, audio, and animation to introduce biological, cognitive, and psychosocial changes. Video clips include such footage as a live birth, kids demonstrating new physical and social skills, and a teen mom discussing the realities of pregnancy. Flash and 3-D video animations teach students about the inner workings of the human body, including the reproductive organs, conception, and pregnancy. Several exercises for students are included, such as drag-and-drop activities, multiple-choice quizzes, flash-card glossary terms, journal writing, and quick-response exercises called "Mad Minutes."

Research Navigator for Psychology

This easy-to-read guide helps point students in the right direction as they explore the tremendous array of information on child development on the Internet. The guide also provides a wide range of additional annotated web links for further exploration, and contains an access code to Research Navigator, Allyn & Bacon's online collection of academic and popular journals, at **www.researchnavigator.com**. Research Navigator offers students three exclusive databases of credible and reliable source content (EBSCO's ContentSelect, the *New York Times* on the web, and Link Library) to help students focus their research efforts and get the research process started.

Tutor Center

The Tutor Center at **www.aw.com/tutorcenter** (access code required) provides students free, one-on-one, interactive tutoring from qualified psychology instructors on all material in the text. The Tutor Center offers students help with understanding major principles as well as methods for study. During Tutor Center hours students can obtain assistance by phone, fax, Internet, and e-mail. For more details and ordering information, please contact your Allyn & Bacon publisher's representative.

MyPsychLab aggregates many of these important student supplements (Grade Aid, Research Navigator, and Tutor Center) in one place, helping to facilitate and enhance student learning.

Writing from Experience

In addition to our training and research in child development, we call on our practical experience from raising our own four children. As this book is going into press, our oldest son, Andy, is 13 years old, just crossing the threshold into true adolescence and looking eagerly toward high school. Our second son, Will, is 9. He looks up to his older brother, loves sports, and excels in most school topics. Our twin daughters, Rachel and Lily, are 7. They are fraternal twins and couldn't be more different from each other. Rachel is quite active and loves to climb, run, and jump. Lily prefers to play house and produce artwork, and she thinks homework is the best part of school. We have thoroughly enjoyed watching our children's first steps, first words, first days of school, and all the many hugs and other benefits of living with young children. Like most families, we have also struggled as we try to balance home life with work, and we have dealt with premature infants, speech and physical therapy, school problems, sibling rivalry, and many of the other challenges that can appear in family life. Through our children we have learned the practical side of child development. We know that even the grandest theories fail to capture the complexities and practicalities of real life with children. We have used these experiences to inform our writing—they helped us focus on the practical applications of what we teach and what we write. We encourage students to bring their personal perspective to the study of child development; and we do the same thing, including our personal perspective at times throughout the book. Although the book is not about "the Cook children," we hope that our own experiences will offer students another perspective to consider.

Acknowledgments

Bringing a new textbook from the initial concept to the printing press is the most exciting and overwhelming project we have ever attempted. We are indebted to a great many generous people for their creativity, support, and practical advice. Carolyn Merrill, our executive editor early in the project, got the ball rolling by providing a vision and focus that was truly exciting for us. Her enthusiasm is contagious, and she was brilliant at helping us shape our knowledge of the field and our ideas about teaching and learning into an integrated and useful product. Director of Development Judy Hauck and Executive Editor Karon Bowers took on key roles later in the project with skill, grace, and enthusiasm—they have been invaluable in seeing us through the final stages. All of the folks at Allyn & Bacon were wonderful. They firmly supported our desire to create a book that would be scientifically sound but also practical and readable for a diverse college audience.

Our developmental editor, Mary Hansen, provided the daily support and guidance we needed. She had a special knack for finding humane ways to push us over the finish line as the many deadlines loomed. Tom Pauken, Jeff Lasser, and Jodi Devine also provided valuable editorial support. Annette Joseph, Richard Morel, Karla Walsh and all of their colleagues in the production department at Allyn & Bacon and at Omegatype have helped bring the book to life with a beautiful layout design, colorful artwork and photography, and an overall package that we believe will really help students learn. Brad Parkins, Taryn Wahlquist, and Wendy Gordon in marketing; Laura Coaty in market research; Marcie Mealia in sales; and many others in the sales and marketing division have helped us tremendously throughout the process. A special thanks goes to Greg Bell, the Allyn & Bacon representative in our area, for his support and encouragement over the years. Under the guidance of Erin Liedel, all of the authors of our ancillary materials have enhanced the teaching value of our book by creating excellent student guides, test materials, instructor aids, and a great many audiovisual and Internet supports.

Of course, the most important part of the book is the content, and we want to express our deep appreciation for all of the time and effort provided by the faculty and instructors who reviewed our manuscript pages and offered feedback:

Janette Benson	University of Denver
Elizabeth Blunk	Texas State University–San Marcos
Jim Bodle	College of Mt. St. Joseph
Neil Bohannon	Butler University
Michelle Boyer-Pennington	Middle Tennessee State University
Albert Bugaj	University of Wisconsin–Marinette
Cari Cannon	Santiago Community College
Mark Chapell	Rowan University
Audrey Clark	California State University–Northridge
Luis Cordon	Eastern Connecticut State University
K. Laurie Dickson	Northern Arizona University
John Dilworth	Kellogg Community College
Claire Etaugh	Bradley University
Oney D. Fitzpatrick, Jr.	Lamar University
James Forbes	Angelo State University
Alisha Ford	Minot State University
Janet Fuller	Mansfield University
Tresmaine Grimes	South Carolina State University
Michael Hackett	Westchester Community College
Karen Hartlep	California State University–Bakersfield
Steven Hayduk	Southern Wesleyan University
Marite R. Haynes	Clarion University of Pennsylvania
Christina Holmes	Anna Maria College
Sherri Horner	Bowling Green State University
Katherine Kerns	Kent State University
Marcel Kerr	Tarleton State University
Beverly King	South Dakota State University
Melvyn King	SUNY–Cortland
David Kovach	University of Toledo
Cynthia Legin-Bucell	Edinboro University of Pennsylvania
Gary Levy	University of Utah
Cathy Litty	Western Carolina University
Rebecca Lochrer	Blinn College
Kevin MacDonald	California State University–Long Beach
Pamela Manners	Troy State University
K. Michael McPherson	San Diego Miramar College
Carolyn Mebert	University of New Hampshire
Sharon Seidman Milburn	California State University–Fullerton
Ronald Mulson	Hudson Valley Community College
Dara Musher-Eizenman	Bowling Green State University
Barbara J. Myers	Virginia Commonwealth University
Janna Oetting	Louisiana State University
John Otey	Southern Arkansas University
Robert Pasnak	George Mason University

Warren Phillips	Iowa State University
Sandra Portko	Grand Valley State University
Ratna Raj	Cerro Coso Community College
Brenda Riemer	California State University–Chico
Tisha Rivera	California State University–Los Angeles
Jenny Roberts	Temple University
John Schell	Kent State University
Krista Schoenfeld	Colby Community College
Pam Schwetze	Buffalo State College
Susan Siaw	California State University–Pomona
John Spencer	University of Iowa
Tam Spitzer	St. John Fisher College
Mary Tisak	Bowling Green State University
Thomas Tobey	Indiana State University
Mary Wilson	Northern Essex Community College
Karen Yanowitz	Arkansas State University
Joan Zook	SUNY–Geneseo

Focus group participants:

C. Francoise Acra	University of Miami
Richard Marshall	University of South Florida
Elizabeth Nawrot	Minnesota State University–Moorhead
Jeffery Parker	Pennsylvania State University
Robert Pasnak	George Mason University
David Saarnio	Arkansas State University
Pam Schuetze	Buffalo State University
Sharon Stringer	Youngstown State University
Donna Thompson	Niagara University
Keri Weed	University of South Carolina–Aiken

We also would like to thank the following students at colleges and universities across the country who reviewed materials:

Sara Barton	Emerson College
Liz Bazos	Northeastern University
Gregory Burton	University of Texas–Austin
Sharon Feder	SUNY–New Paltz
Jimmy Ficaro	George Mason University
Shannan Goff	University of New Hampshire
Gabe Gutierrez	Northwestern University
Jamay Liu	Brown University
Jennette Merwin	Emerson College
Eileen Monaghan	Temple University
Allison Murphy	The American University
Sarah Orem	Rice University
Sara Owen	University of Vermont
Michael Popper	Brandeis University
Danielle Stead	University of Rhode Island
Adam Whitehurst	Emerson College

Feedback from all our reviewers was honest, critical, and very informative. The comments helped us understand what instructors really need in the classroom, and we hope we have done justice to the good counsel we received. Scyatta Wallace reviewed our whole book and advised us on diversity issues. Her contribution was truly invaluable.

We thank all of the psychology professors who stimulated our interest in psychology and child development as we learned about this field, especially John Rieser, Richard Odom, John Bransford, Barry Stein, Ron Katsuyama, and Frank DaPolito. A great many of their lessons are woven through this book. We also thank our colleagues in the Psychology Department and the administrators at the University of Wisconsin–Whitewater. Their support and encouragement are deeply appreciated.

Finally, we would like to acknowledge all of the love and support we received from our family and friends. They were there to share our joys and also to support us when things were difficult. We were too busy, too often, but their understanding and compassion allowed us to push on with a project we truly loved. We are especially indebted to our children, Andy, Will, Rachel, and Lily. They have helped us understand child development with our hearts as well as our minds.

About the Authors

Joan Littlefield Cook and Greg Cook

Joan Littlefield Cook teaches in the Psychology Department at the University of Wisconsin–Whitewater. As an undergraduate she majored in psychology at Tennessee Technological University. She earned a Ph.D. in psychology and human development at Vanderbilt University. Since 1986 she has taught courses related to child and adolescent development, educational psychology, and cognitive psychology at the University of Wisconsin–Whitewater, the University of Wisconsin–Madison, and Middle Tennessee State University. Her classes have ranged from huge lecture courses to small seminars. Students have always appreciated her knowledge of the field and her ability to present information in a way that is useful, motivating, and friendly. The Student Association at the University of Wisconsin–Madison voted her as one of their most outstanding professors. Joan's research is on mathematical problem solving and cognitive development. She and her colleagues have published papers in the *Journal of Educational Psychology, Intelligence, Cognition and Instruction, Memory & Cognition,* the *Gifted Child Quarterly,* and the *Journal of Experimental Psychology.* She has coauthored two other books and numerous instructional materials.

Greg Cook also teaches psychology at the University of Wisconsin–Whitewater. He majored in psychology at the University of Dayton and later received his Ph.D. in psychology at Vanderbilt University. Since 1986 he has taught courses in child development, research methods, statistics, and related topics at Whitewater as well as at the Madison and Richland Center campuses in the University of Wisconsin system and at Vanderbilt University. At Whitewater he received a teaching award in his department. Students consistently comment on his ability to present difficult information in a clear and understandable way. His research on cognitive development has been published in scholarly journals such as *Child Development, Developmental Psychology,* and the *Journal of Experimental Child Psychology.* He has also collaborated with colleagues in the College of Education on studies published in the *Journal of Experimental Education,* the *Journal of Research and Development in Education,* and the *Journal of Reading Education.*

How to Use This Book

When reading textbook chapters, students often ask: "Why should I know this material?" or "How is it useful in real life?" We will show you. Every chapter in this book begins with a story of life from another person's perspective—a realistic, often challenging situation that shows you how child development relates to you or to the people around you. Each of these stories, called **A Perspective to Think About,** is linked to **Thinking of** margin questions placed at critical points throughout the chapter. The **Thinking of** questions ask you how you might advise the characters described in **A Perspective to Think About,** based on what you have learned thus far. By the time you

finish studying the chapter, you should have a good idea about how to answer all of those questions. At the end of the chapter, **Thinking Back to** summarizes some of the possibilities for how you could have answered the margin questions—but try answering the questions yourself before checking our summary!

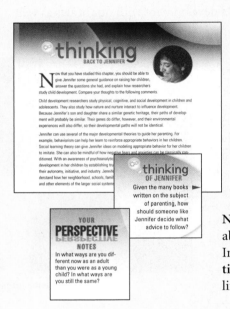

We include several other perspectives as well, to help you think about the content from personal, professional, and social points of view. To support the personal perspective, we offer **Your Perspective Notes** in the margins where you can stop and think about how the chapter material relates to *your own life.* In addition, each chapter contains **A Personal Perspective,** an interview feature that introduces you to real-life parents and children.

To help you understand the professional side of this field, every chapter has **A Professional Perspective,** a one-on-one interview with someone whose job is related to child development. These professional interviews will not only allow you to understand how professionals view children, but will also show you many of the career options that are out there. Working with children is extremely rewarding, and we are excited to be able to show you numerous ways in which you can contribute to children's healthy development.

To demonstrate the importance of child development information for current social issues and policies, we include **A Social Policy Perspective.** This feature highlights many specific controversies and debates surrounding children in our society. After reading these, you will see that different perspectives and opinions are everywhere. What's your take on the issues?

There are many tools in this book to help check your learning. As you begin each major section of every chapter, you'll find preview questions designed to help you recognize the important points as you read.

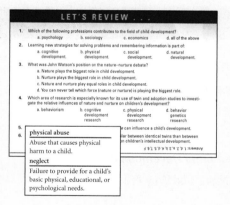

Then, at the end of each section, you'll find **Let's Review** questions to help you make sure you've mastered the material. The answers to these questions accompany them, printed upside down.

The marginal glossary offers you a quick way to find definitions. Because the glossary terms are set apart from the text, you can study the important vocabulary and definitions for each chapter without having to hunt for them.

Finally, the **Chapter Summary** reminds you about the main questions addressed in the chapter and gives you a quick review of the most important concepts. This summary is not a replacement for reading the chapter, but it is an effective tool for studying.

All of these features work together as a learning system, designed to be educational, enlightening, thought-provoking, and memorable. Take what you learn here with you in life: It could help you in your next job, could improve your relationships at home, and surely will influence how you look at every child you meet.

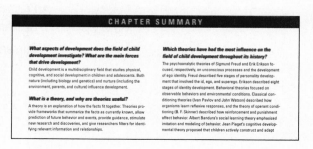

Chapter 1

Exploring Child Development

CHAPTER PREVIEW

Defining the Field

- What Develops?
- What Drives Development? Nature *and* Nurture

Theories about Child Development

- What Is a Theory, and Why Are Theories Useful?
- Psychoanalytic Theories
- Behavioral and Social Learning Theories
- Cognitive Theories
- Biological Theories
- Systems Theories

Using the Scientific Method: Research in Child Development

- Descriptive Research Methods
- Correlational Research Methods: Measuring Associations
- Experimental Research Methods: Determining Cause and Effect
- Methods for Assessing Development
- Ethics in Research with Children

Applications of Child Development Research and Careers Related to Children

- Practical Applications of Child Development Research
- Careers Related to Children

A **PERSPECTIVE** TO **think** **ABOUT**

"What kinds of people will her children become?"

Jennifer, who recently gave birth to a baby girl, is also raising her 6-year-old son, Diego. As she watched Diego grow, Jennifer was amazed at his progress. He was crawling at 7 months and walking independently by 1 year. Also around his first birthday, he began speaking his first real words, including "Momma," "Dadda," "cup," and "ball." Diego's progress was typical for children during their first year, but Jennifer was still amazed to see how quickly he was developing. By 3 years Diego was holding fluent conversations and had a vocabulary of more than 1,000 words. By age 5 he was beginning to read and work with numbers, he was riding a bicycle, and he was beginning to make new friends in his kindergarten class. Now Diego is in first grade, and Jennifer continues to be amazed at the progress of his academic, social, and physical development.

With the birth of her new daughter, Jennifer has the chance to watch another child grow through similar phases. As she looks ahead, she wonders if her daughter will follow a similar path. What kinds of people will her children become? How will they be similar to or different from each other? Like most parents, Jennifer wants to help her children as much as possible, and she wonders how she can use her opportunities as a parent to help her children develop to their fullest potentials.

As you read through this introductory chapter, think about the information from Jennifer's perspective. What advice could you give to Jennifer? What do researchers know about children's development that could help Jennifer make decisions? In other words, what develops as children grow and mature, and what are the forces that drive development? After studying this chapter, you should be able to give specific answers to these questions.

As you read this chapter, look for the questions that ask you to think about what you're learning from Jennifer's perspective.

There are few things more amazing to watch than the growth and development of a child. Babies are tiny and helpless at birth, but in just a few short months they are crawling about, feeding themselves, and exploring everything in sight. The day-to-day changes are often undetectable, but some milestones are cause for celebration: when they take their first steps, say their first words, wave good-bye on their first days of school, and go out on their first dates.

Have you had the opportunity to closely watch a child grow and mature? If not, you can still reflect on your own development. You are certainly different now than you were as a young child. You are obviously larger, stronger, and better coordinated. You also have much more factual information and more effective and efficient problem-solving skills than when you were younger. And your social relations are very different, especially if you have moved away from your family or have started a family of your own. Yet in other ways you have kept many of the qualities you started with. For example, maybe you were shy as a child and continue to be reserved and reflective today, or perhaps you were very active as a child and are still energetic and athletic.

This chapter introduces you to the field of child development. We'll give you a thumbnail sketch of some of the most important theories and scientific methods used in the field, and we'll show you how this information applies to the real lives of children. First, however, we will define the field of child development, examining the basic issues and questions addressed in this field.

Differences in physical development are obvious when you compare the children in this photo. Size, strength, and coordination all increase with development.

Defining the Field

In the field of **child development,** researchers from psychology, sociology, anthropology, social work, biology, medicine, economics, and other related fields work together. Their shared purpose is to describe and understand the important changes that take place as children move through childhood and grow into adolescents and then adults. In some ways children are changing every day—growing, gaining knowledge, and learning new skills. Yet in other ways people remain the same throughout life. For example, an individual who is happy and outgoing as a young child may remain happy and outgoing throughout adolescence and adulthood.

Understanding child development is important for everyone who wants to work with or help children. Parents naturally have a personal stake in providing the best environment and support they can. Teachers, counselors, social workers, psychologists, and other professionals who help children also need to understand the fundamental principles of development as well as the various ways that development can be disrupted or affected. Understanding child development can also help you understand your own progression into adulthood: Knowing more about where you came from can help you appreciate your current phase of life and may give you insights about where you are headed.

As you study this section, ask yourself these questions:

- What characteristics and processes do researchers study?
- What are the main forces that drive child development? Do we have influence over these forces? Which ones, and how?
- What is the "nature–nurture" debate, and what positions have prominent figures throughout the ages taken in this debate?
- How has research in behavior genetics contributed to our understanding of nature and nurture?

What Develops?

A child's development is multifaceted. The most obvious component, of course, is **physical development.** Children grow in size, and their muscles become stronger and more coordinated. Many children grow through a "lanky" period, a time when their rapid gain in height outpaces

YOUR
PERSPECTIVE
PERSPECTIVE
NOTES
In what ways are you different now as an adult than you were as a young child? In what ways are you still the same?

child development

Field of study where researchers from many disciplines work to understand the important changes that take place as children grow through childhood.

physical development

Component of development related to growth in size, strength, and muscle coordination.

How do cognitive activities change with development? Researchers study how perception, memory, intelligence, problem solving, language, and other thinking skills develop during childhood and adolescence.

How do social skills change with age? Friendship patterns, play, and cooperation are just a few of the topics in the area of social development that researchers study.

thinking
OF JENNIFER

What examples of physical, cognitive, and social development did you notice in the description of Jennifer's son? What other examples would you expect to see for each type of development?

their gains in weight and muscle mass. During adolescence sexual maturity is attained, and the adolescent's physical appearance becomes more adultlike.

Cognitive development consists of numerous changes in how children think, process information, store and retrieve memories, solve problems, and communicate with language. We see cognitive growth in the progress children make in their academic work in school: learning to read and write and learning mathematics, social studies, science, art, and other topics. Underlying and supporting this growth are gains in information processing, memory, and problem solving.

Children also make rapid progress in **social development.** As infants they depend on their parents and other family members for food, safety, and entertainment. As they grow, they begin to meet and interact with childhood peers, and this helps improve communication skills. Toddlers play readily with mates of both genders, but by middle childhood most playmates are same-sex only. Later, most adolescents will struggle with the problem of meeting potential partners and dating, exploring their own sexual identities, and forming intimate relationships.

What Drives Development? Nature *and* Nurture

What are the forces that govern or drive the processes, characteristics, and behaviors that develop across childhood? Basically, these forces can be divided into two categories: nature and nurture.

The term **nature** refers to the biological forces that govern development. To a certain extent our development is programmed in our genes—traits inherited from our parents and ancestors. In childhood this biological program unfolds. In some respects child development can be compared to the blossoming of a flower: A seed sprouts, grows into a fragile seedling, and eventually becomes a mature flowering plant. Nature provides the genetic program contained in the seed—and in the child.

Nurture consists of the conditions and supports provided by the environment. A flower needs sunlight, water, and proper temperature, and it helps if someone pulls weeds and adds

cognitive development

Component of development related to changes in how children think, remember, and communicate.

social development

Component of development related to changes in how children interact with other people (e.g., family members, peers, and playmates).

nature

The biological forces (e.g., genetics) that govern development.

fertilizer. It is the same way for children. Nurture refers to the conditions that surround the child. Hopefully, the child will have the love and support given by parents, siblings, the extended family, teachers, peers, and other people important in the child's life. Children can be greatly affected by how these important people nurture them.

Other elements of "nurture" include a child's economic and sociocultural environment. Poverty, malnutrition, and a lack of adequate medical care can obviously alter a child's developmental path. Cultural heritage and diversity can enrich a child's life, and the neighborhood where the child lives can determine the type of schooling and peers that the child will have.

Through the ages, philosophers and scientists have debated the relative roles of nature and nurture. John Watson, a renowned American psychologist of the early twentieth century, was a strong proponent of the "nurture" school. He wrote:

> [G]ive me a dozen healthy infants, well formed, and my own specified world to bring them up and I'll guarantee to take any one at random and train him to become any type of specialist I might select—doctor, lawyer, artist, merchant-chief and, yes, even beggar-man and thief, regardless of his talents, penchants, tendencies, abilities, vocations, and race of his ancestors. (1930/1924, p. 104)

Watson argued that experience and learning—nurture—determined what children would become. But other researchers have disagreed, pointing out that characteristics such as personality are determined more by genetics (nature) than by nurture. Today, however, many scientific investigations have shown that nature and nurture actually work together in development (Rutter, 2002). Rather than arguing about which one is most important, we are interested in learning exactly how the two groups of factors interact with each other. The interacting effects of nature and nurture are evident in the field of *behavior genetics.*

In **behavior genetics** researchers study the relative role of nature and nurture in development. By studying twins and adopted children, behavior geneticists have been able to estimate that many psychological traits, including intelligence, emotionality, and basic personality variables, are approximately 40 to 60 percent inherited. For example, researchers have shown that IQ scores of identical twins are much more similar than scores of nonidentical twins (Bouchard & McGue, 1981). Because identical twins come from the same fertilized egg, their genes are exact copies (give or take a few errors in cell division). But nonidentical twins come from separate fertilized eggs, so they are no more alike genetically than any other sibling pairs. Given the fact that both identical and nonidentical twins tend to share similar family and learning environments, scientists attribute the greater similarity in IQ between identical twins to their greater genetic similarity. Adoption studies also show a strong genetic component in IQ. Studies of children who were adopted as young infants have shown that these children's IQs at age 18 are more similar to the IQs of their biological mothers than to the IQs of the adoptive mothers who nurtured them (Loehlin, Horn, & Willerman, 1994; Scarr, Weinberg, & Waldman, 1993).

The impact of nature, or genetic inheritance, is obvious when children are born with genetic disorders such as Down syndrome or cystic fibrosis. Research also has shown genetic links to conditions such as schizophrenia, depression, and severe obesity. The role of *nurture,* however, also emerges in many of these same studies. For example, inheriting genes linked to schizophrenia, depression, or obesity does not guarantee that a person will actually have the condition. Many people who inherit these genes manage to overcome or avoid the problems. Also, nurture certainly has an impact on traits such as IQ. IQ scores for identical twins, for example, are more similar when the twins grow up together than when they are raised in separate families (Bouchard & McGue, 1981). Both identical and nonidentical twins show similar patterns of emotional attachment to their parents, indicating that shared family experiences (nurture) play a larger role than genetics (nature) in establishing attachment patterns (O'Connor & Croft,

YOUR PERSPECTIVE

NOTES

Think back into your own childhood, and identify several examples of nature and nurture and how they influenced your development.

thinking OF JENNIFER

◄ How could you use behavior genetics research to understand how nature and nurture influenced the development of Jennifer's son?

nurture

The conditions and supports that are provided by the environment and contribute to learning and development.

behavior genetics

Field of study that compares the influence of genetics (nature) to the influence of learning and the environment (nurture) and examines how these forces interact to influence development.

2001). In sum, rather than arguing about whether development is controlled completely by nature or completely by nurture, we are now beginning to understand the interactive roles played by both of these forces, thanks to the results from behavior genetics research. We will describe more of this research, and discuss its implications, in Chapter 2.

LET'S REVIEW . . .

1. Which of the following professions contributes to the field of child development?
   a. psychology   b. sociology   c. economics   d. all of the above

2. Learning new strategies for solving problems and remembering information is part of:
   a. cognitive   b. physical   c. social   d. natural
   development.   development.   development.   development.

3. What was John Watson's position on the nature–nurture debate?
   a. Nature plays the biggest role in child development.
   b. Nurture plays the biggest role in child development.
   c. Nature and nurture play equal roles in child development.
   d. You can never tell which force (nature or nurture) is playing the biggest role.

4. Which area of research is especially known for its use of twin and adoption studies to investigate the relative influences of nature and nurture on children's development?
   a. behaviorism   b. cognitive   c. physical   d. behavior
                         development   development   genetics
                         research   research   research

5. **True or False:** Genetics is an example of how *nature* can influence a child's development.

6. **True or False:** The fact that IQ scores are more similar between identical twins than between nonidentical twins shows the influence of *nurture* on children's intellectual development.

Answers: 1. d, 2. a, 3. b, 4. d, 5. T, 6. F

Theories about Child Development

Over the years researchers have gathered countless observations and facts about all facets of children's development. There are data on everything from average heights and weights to IQ scores to friendship and play patterns to the effects of discipline and divorce. This vast array of facts would be incomprehensible if the data were not organized in some coherent fashion. In this section we explain why researchers develop *theories* to organize the facts. We also describe some of the most important theories that have influenced the field of child development.

As you study this section, ask yourself these questions:

- What do researchers mean when they use the word *theory*? How are theories useful in a field such as child development?

- Which theories have been most important in the field, and what were their main ideas?

- How would your view of children change if you adopted each of the theories described in this section?

- How could you use each of these theories to guide you when working with children? What research questions might each theory suggest?

What Is a Theory, and Why Are Theories Useful?

A **theory** is an explanation of how facts fit together. Theories provide frameworks that show how the facts are organized and related, and these frameworks can serve several useful functions (Thomas, 2000):

▶ Theories *summarize the facts as currently known.* By understanding contemporary theories you can see what researchers currently know about child development. Also, by tracing important theories through history, you can see what experts once thought and how knowledge and ideas have changed.

▶ Theories also *allow prediction of future behavior and events.* Theories tell us how the facts tend to be related in most situations; so if we know some of the facts in a particular case, then we can predict the related facts. For example, an accurate theory of discipline should tell us how children tend to respond to harsh versus nurturing forms of punishment. Then, if we know that a particular child is receiving harsh punishment, we can predict what the child's response may be.

▶ By allowing prediction, theories *provide guidance* to parents, teachers, counselors, therapists, social workers, and others who work with children.

▶ Theories also *stimulate new research and discoveries.* By definition theories cannot be directly verified—so researchers test theories by drawing specific inferences, or *hypotheses,* from the general theories and then collecting scientific observations to find out if the hypotheses are valid. In the course of testing hypotheses, researchers collect many new facts and observations and may make new discoveries. This process often leads to revisions in the theories or perhaps to the development of new theories.

▶ Finally, you should also understand that theories *act as filters for identifying relevant information, observations, and relationships.* Theories influence how we look at children and their development, and they even influence the kinds of questions researchers ask about development. A researcher will see the simple act of a child's helping his or her father, for example, very differently depending on whether the researcher has a psychoanalytic, behavioral, or ecological orientation.

Table 1.1 provides an overview of some of the major theories about child development. Psychoanalytic theories were among the earliest in the field; they had a major influence in shaping our early notions of child development. The development field has largely discarded these theories, however, as later theories have proved to be more accurate and useful. The behavioral and social learning theories were prominent in the mid-twentieth century. Although newer approaches have emerged since, professionals who work with children still rely on these theories in designing programs to modify children's behavior. Neuropsychology and dynamic systems theories are relatively new, and we are still exploring their potential.

As you read about these various theories, keep in mind that each one offers a summary of what researchers knew and suspected about child development at a given time. Theories change as science progresses. Also, don't expect any one theory to explain everything about child development. Most theories are targeted at certain aspects of child development—such as how children learn, how they think about things in the world, or how they interact with the people around them. But no theory, by itself, is sufficient to explain all the myriad processes and changes that occur as children grow and develop. With these thoughts in mind, consider the following theories. We'll begin with the earliest and end with the most recent.

Psychoanalytic Theories

Psychoanalytic theories focus on the structure of personality and on how the conscious and unconscious portions of the self influence behavior and development. The two most prominent psychoanalytic theories were developed by Sigmund Freud and Erik Erikson.

theory

An explanation of how facts fit together, allowing us to understand and predict behavior.

psychoanalytic theories

Theories that focus on the structure of personality and on how the conscious and unconscious portions of the self influence behavior and development.

TABLE 1.1 An Overview of Major Developmental Theories

PSYCHOANALYTIC	BEHAVIORAL AND SOCIAL LEARNING	COGNITIVE	BIOLOGICAL	SYSTEMS
Focus on personality development and effects of conscious and unconscious mind on behavior and development	Focus on observable conditions in environment and how they relate to observable behaviors	Focus on how children learn to think	Focus on biological and physical explanations of development	Focus on the rich network of systems that operate in and around the child. Development emerges from complex interactions among multiple levels or systems
Psychoanalytic (Sigmund Freud) • Mind contains the id, ego, and superego; all are in constant conflict • Five stages of psychosexual development • Personality is well developed by end of adolescence	**Classical Conditioning (Ivan Pavlov; John Watson)** • Behavior controlled by stimulus–response connections • Unconditioned stimulus reflexively elicits unconditioned response; unconditioned stimulus is paired with neutral stimulus; conditioned stimulus comes to elicit conditioned response • Explains the development of many fears	**Cognitive Developmental Theory (Jean Piaget)** • Children actively construct their own understanding • Children develop mental schemes to represent their understanding • Children assimilate and accommodate their schemes • Four major stages of cognitive development	**Ethology (Konrad Lorenz)** • Based on Darwin's theory of evolution and natural selection • Researchers study behaviors that help animals (including humans) compete and survive	**Ecological Systems Theory (Urie Bronfenbrenner)** • Layers of systems affect the development of the child • Layers include interactions among family, friends, schools, neighborhoods, government agencies, parents' workplace, and the values, laws, and customs of the larger society • These interactions change over time
Psychosocial (Erik Erikson) • Focus on development of healthy ego identity • Series of eight psychosocial crises • More positive or more negative crisis resolution dependent on interactions with other people • Personality development is lifelong	**Operant Conditioning (B. F. Skinner)** • Behavior influenced by the consequences of actions • Reinforcement increases probability that a behavior will be repeated; punishment decreases probability that a behavior will be repeated • Children adjust behavior to gain reinforcement and avoid punishment	**Sociocultural Theory (Lev Vygotsky)** • Emphasizes roles of culture and social interaction in cognitive development • Children adopt the psychological tools created and encouraged by their culture • Social speech is internalized as private speech; eventually becomes inner speech	**Neuropsychology** • Direct observation of brain and nervous system structures and functions during thought • Uses technological advances to identify specific areas of brain activity during cognitive tasks	**Dynamic Systems Theories** • Theories based on models used by mathematicians and physicists to understand complex systems • Complex interactions of multiple factors can appear chaotic, but stable patterns (attractor states) can emerge as the system self-organizes • Patterns change over time
	Social Learning Theory (Albert Bandura) • Children learn by observing and imitating others' behavior; they do not always need reinforcement or punishment • Reinforcement and punishment give information to help children think about which behaviors to imitate	**Information-Processing Theory** • Detailed analysis of processes used in thinking • Emphasis on roles of basic processing efficiency and prior knowledge base		

Sigmund Freud, the originator of psychoanalysis, proposed five stages of personality development.

Sigmund Freud (1856–1939) was an Austrian physician specializing in neurology who treated patients for a variety of ailments. Some of his patients experienced symptoms (e.g., paralysis) that seemed to be caused by neurological abnormalities—but when Freud carefully examined these patients, he found no evidence of physical problems. After puzzling over these cases, Freud concluded that the symptoms sprang from unconscious psychological conflict. They were similar to what we might today call psychosomatic illnesses. Over several decades, Freud used hypnosis, free association, dream interpretation, and detailed clinical interviews with his patients to explore their unconscious desires and conflicts. In the process he created his famous (and controversial) theory of psychoanalysis and child development.

According to Freud, the mind contains three basic components: the id, ego, and superego.

▶ The *id* lies completely below the level of conscious awareness and represents the primitive sexual and aggressive instincts that humans inherited from their primate ancestors.

▶ The *ego* is the rational branch of personality; it tries to negotiate realistic ways to satisfy the id's impulses.

▶ The *superego* represents the moral branch of personality and contains our ethical principles, ideals, and conscience.

These three components are in a perpetual state of conflict. When arguing with another person, for example, you might experience an impulse (from the id) to shove the person. At the same time you would recall (thanks to the superego) that it is not polite to assault people. You might arrive at a compromise (negotiated by the ego): to let fly a few angry words and then avoid seeing the person for a while. To have a healthy personality, we need the morality of the superego to balance the primitive instincts of the id. We also need an ego that is strong, realistic, and able to conduct swift and delicate negotiations among the id, the superego, and the demands of the world at large.

FIGURE 1.1 Freud's Five Stages of Psychosexual Development

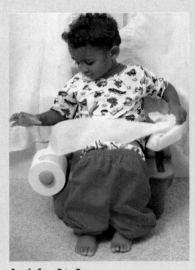

Oral: Age 0 to 2

Infant seeks oral gratification by sucking, biting, and babbling.

Anal: Age 2 to 3

Potty training helps toddlers balance their need for anal gratification with society's demand to be clean and neat.

Phallic: Age 3 to 7

In early childhood an unconscious desire for the opposite-sex parent is controlled by identification with the same-sex parent.

How do these components develop during childhood? Freud believed that we are born with the id, inherited from our ancestors. He then proposed five stages of psychosexual development to explain how the ego and superego emerge to tame the id. Figure 1.1 summarizes these stages. During the *oral and anal stages,* feedback from parents helps infants and toddlers curb their instincts for oral and anal gratification. Freud believed that children need an appropriate amount of stimulation in these *erogenous zones* (pleasure-sensitive zones). Receiving too much or too little stimulation can cause a fixation, setting the child on a negative developmental path. As young children learn to delay gratification—for example, to use the bathroom appropriately and to wait until morning to eat—the ego gradually begins to emerge to help keep the id in check.

Freud's most controversial proposal involved the *phallic stage.* He proposed that children have unconscious sexual desires for their opposite-sex parent. Eventually they realize that they cannot have the parent for themselves, in part because the other parent is too big and powerful to remove. Children then accept a compromise solution: They identify with their same-sex parent. Boys begin to mimic their fathers, and girls their mothers. This way, they avoid confrontation (which the child would surely lose) and "join ranks" with the same-sex parent (who is having sex with their opposite-sex parent—the true object of their desires). Through identification, the child acquires the superego of the same-sex parent. In other words, to be like these parents, children copy their morals, ideals, and values; these become the conscience of the child. Along with children's new sense of morality come feelings of shame and guilt for the incestuous feelings they have had. So the phallic stage is followed by a period of *latency,* or dormancy. During the *latency stage* children's sexual feelings are repressed, and they prefer to play with same-sex peers and to engage in pursuits that are not sexually threatening. Sexual desires will reawaken in the *genital stage* as children mature into adolescents and begin to explore their sexual identities.

Freud proposed his theory to account for his patients' difficulties—many of which involved anxieties about sexuality or about sexual disturbances from childhood. Critics of Freud

thinking
OF JENNIFER

From a Freudian perspective, what would you want to know about the dynamics in Jennifer's family in order to understand her son's development?

Latency: Age 7 to 11
Sexual urges are repressed, and the child prefers same-sex companions.

Genital: Age 11 to adult
With puberty sexual urges reappear, and the adolescent learns about mature relationships.

have argued that his theory focuses too much on the unconscious mind and sexual impulses, and many experts today do not view his theory as an adequate explanation for normal development in children. Still, Freud was one of the earliest thinkers to propose an elaborate theory of child development. Many of Freud's concepts have become permanent fixtures in our popular culture, and there is no question about his enormous impact on how we think about child development and psychology.

Erik Erikson (1902–94) offered a revision of Freud's psychoanalytic theory. Erikson focused more on healthy child development, especially the development of ego identity. Erikson's *psychosocial theory* involves

> conflicts, inner and outer, which the vital personality weathers, re-emerging from each crisis with an increased sense of inner unity, with an increase of good judgment, and an increase in the capacity to "do well" according to his own standards and to the standards of those who are significant to him. (Erikson, 1968, p. 92)

Erikson believed that our identity develops as we pass through a series of psychosocial stages. He proposed eight stages, representing eight major crises (Table 1.2). As children interact with significant other people in their social environment, they resolve the stage at hand by adopting an identity oriented more toward one pole of the crisis than the other. For example, in stage one infants struggle with trust versus mistrust. If they have positive interactions with nurturing parents or caretakers, infants learn that the world is dependable and that people are basically trustworthy. If their parents are rejecting or neglecting, however, infants learn to mistrust them. These children then tend to mistrust almost everyone they meet. Erikson also believed that resolutions in earlier stages affect later stages. For example, a child who develops a basic sense of trust in stage one is more likely to develop a healthy sense of autonomy in stage two, and so forth. Unlike Freud, Erikson believed that personality development continued long after adolescence, and he proposed stages that covered early, middle, and later adulthood periods.

YOUR PERSPECTIVE NOTES

Where are you currently located in Erikson's series of psychosocial stages? How have the resolutions of the previous stages gone for you? How might those resolutions influence the remaining stages for you?

TABLE 1.2 Erikson's Eight Stages of Psychosocial Development

STAGE (CRISIS)	AGE	POSITIVE RESOLUTIONS	NEGATIVE RESOLUTIONS
Basic trust versus mistrust	0 to 1 year	With responsive caregiving, infant learns to trust parents or primary caregivers; acquires basic sense that the world and other people are trustworthy; develops self-confidence.	If caregiving is unresponsive or neglectful, infant can develop a basic sense of mistrust in caregivers, other people, and self.
Autonomy versus shame and doubt	2 to 3 years	Child gains independence from caregivers by walking, talking, toilet training; learns pride in independence ("Me do it!").	When independence is stifled or punished, child can develop basic sense of shame in self and doubt about his/her abilities.
Initiative versus guilt	4 to 5 years	Child initiates activities to meet larger goals; learns to take initiative to set own goals, design projects, interact with peers.	When initiative is stifled, child can learn guilt that own desires conflict with those of parents.
Industry versus inferiority	6 to 12 years	School years involve frequent comparisons with peers; confidence and sense of industry emerge when comparisons are favorable.	When comparisons are unfavorable, a sense of inferiority can develop; children feel their work and abilities do not measure up.
Identity versus role confusion	Adolescence	Sense of central identity emerges through sexual, emotional, educational, ethnic/cultural and vocational exploration.	Sense of self can be confused or diffuse if a core identity does not solidify.
Intimacy versus isolation	Early adulthood	One or more intimate relationships form; may lead to marriage and family.	Without intimate relationships, feeling of isolation can develop; sense of being alone.
Generativity versus stagnation	Middle adulthood	Individual makes a positive contribution to the next generation by raising children, teaching, volunteering.	Without a positive connection to others, can feel sense of stagnation, fear that life is wasted on selfish pursuits.
Integrity versus despair	Later adulthood	When other stages are resolved positively, an integrated sense of self has emerged; positive view of life and healthy attitude about death.	When other stages are resolved negatively, a negative sense of self emerges; despair that life was wasted, goals unfulfilled; fear of death.

Behavioral and Social Learning Theories

A major criticism of psychoanalytic theories is that these theories' important concepts are difficult, if not impossible, to test scientifically. How do we observe, measure, or verify the existence of the id, for example? **Behaviorism** began as an American movement aimed at developing a more objective and scientific psychology. John Watson (1878–1958) was the "father of American behaviorism." Watson argued that psychology needed to focus on observable conditions in the environment and how they are related to overt, or observable, behaviors.

Watson began by adopting Ivan Pavlov's work on **classical conditioning.** Pavlov, a Russian physiologist, conducted experiments on the digestive system in dogs. He showed that when a dog tastes or smells meat powder, which in this case is the *unconditioned stimulus,* the dog automatically salivates, which is the *unconditioned response.* Further, when a researcher repeatedly pairs a previously neutral stimulus, like the sound of a bell, with the meat powder, the bell can begin to elicit salivation even when the meat powder is no longer present. The bell has become a *conditioned stimulus* and elicits salivation as a *conditioned response.*

Watson studied how children learn stimulus–response connections by classical conditioning. In his most famous demonstration, Watson conditioned an 11-month-old named Albert to fear a white rat (Watson & Rayner, 1920). At first Albert showed no fear and would readily reach out to touch the rat. When Albert was holding the rat, however, Watson clanged a steel bar loudly with a hammer behind Albert's head, frightening little Albert. As a result, Albert would not touch the rat and began to cry whenever he saw it. Albert's fear was a conditioned response. Later, Albert generalized, or extended, this fear to a white rabbit, a fur coat,

behaviorism

An American movement to develop a psychology that was objective and scientific, focusing on the principles of classical conditioning and operant conditioning.

classical conditioning

Process where neutral stimuli are paired with unconditioned stimuli until they come to evoke conditioned responses.

a dog, and even a Santa Claus mask! Watson warned that children might learn a great many fears through classical conditioning. He argued that parents and others should harness the powers of conditioning to set children on positive developmental paths. If environments could be controlled properly, children had unlimited potential. Remember Watson's guarantee about "a dozen healthy infants," quoted earlier?

Whereas Watson focused on children's reflexive responses to stimuli, B. F. Skinner (1904–90) pointed out that children also learn through the consequences of their actions. He called this process **operant conditioning.** As an example, consider a girl who happens to clean her room. Her father, seeing the great deed, gives her a big hug and says, "What a great job—thanks for being so helpful!" After receiving such praise, the child may be more likely to clean her room again in the future. If so, Skinner would say that the child's helpful behavior has been "reinforced" by the hug and praise. In operant conditioning terms, *reinforcement* is any characteristic in the environment that serves to *increase* the probability that a person will repeat a behavior in the future. Punishment, on the other hand, is any characteristic that *decreases* the probability that a person will repeat a behavior. When a 17-year-old boy comes home late, missing his curfew, his parent may ground him or suspend his driving privileges. If these punishments are effective, the boy will be less likely to come home late in the future. According to Skinner, children "operate" on their environments (hence the term "operant" conditioning), adjusting their behaviors to attract more reinforcements and to avoid punishments.

Adding to the theories of classical and operant conditioning, Albert Bandura (1925–) demonstrated that children also learn by **social learning**—by *observing* and *imitating* the behaviors of other people. For example, when Theresa's father smiles at a visitor, young Theresa smiles too. After watching a television superhero battle with evil villains, Jamie solves his problem at school the next day by picking a fight. After seeing another girl drop a coin into a donation box, Sara asks her mother for a coin that she can donate. Bandura emphasized that children do not always need reinforcements or punishments to shape their behavior; sometimes they act in imitation of the behaviors that they observe around them. In more recent years, Bandura's social learning theory has evolved into a social cognition theory. The social cognition approach emphasizes how children *think* about the behaviors and interactions they observe. In this view, reinforcements and punishments provide information that can help the child decide which behaviors to imitate. If children see someone receive reinforcement for a behavior, they are more apt to imitate that behavior themselves in the future. This emphasis on how children think about events is part of a trend away from behavioral theories and toward cognitive theories of development.

Cognitive Theories

Jean Piaget (1896–1980), a Swiss psychologist, created a **cognitive developmental theory** to explain how children actively adjust their own understandings as they learn about the world. Piaget proposed that children represent what they understand about the world in cognitive structures he called "mental *schemes.*" For example, the infant in Figure 1.2 understands how to grasp the ball—he has a "grasping scheme." As the baby acquires new experiences, however, his grasping scheme may be challenged. What would happen, for example, if he tried to grasp a larger ball? Most likely, he would first try to grasp the larger ball with one hand, as he had grasped the smaller ball before. But the one-hand-grasp scheme would not work. To hold the larger ball successfully, the infant would need to use trial-and-error practice to learn to use two hands.

In this scenario Piaget would say that the infant tried to assimilate the larger ball into his grasping scheme.

operant conditioning

Process where reinforcing or punishing consequences of actions affect behaviors.

social learning

Process where children learn by observing and imitating the behaviors of other people.

cognitive developmental theory

A theory that focuses on how children adjust their own understanding as they explore and learn about the world.

FIGURE 1.2 Assimilation and Accommodation
This infant seems pleased to be able to grasp and hold the ball. How would he adjust his grasping scheme to assimilate a larger ball?

▶ *Assimilation* is the process of bringing new objects or information into a scheme that already exists in the mind. If the assimilation is not successful (e.g., if the infant drops the ball), then the scheme needs to be accommodated.

▶ *Accommodation* is the process of adjusting or adapting a scheme so it better fits the new experience. Through accommodation the infant would learn that grasping sometimes requires two hands. Now the infant has a more powerful and flexible grasping scheme. He understands how to grasp smaller objects with one hand and larger ones with two hands.

As children continue to gain new experiences, they adapt their cognitive structures, or schemes, through a continual cycle of assimilation and accommodation. Piaget also believed that children's cognitive structures develop through four major stages or phases of development: *sensorimotor, preoperational, concrete operational,* and *formal operational* thought. We'll look more closely at these stages, and at the rest of Piaget's cognitive developmental theory, in Chapter 5.

Another cognitive theory that we'll discuss in Chapter 5 is Lev Vygotsky's **sociocultural theory.** Vygotsky (1896–1934) was a Russian psychologist and a contemporary of Piaget. Vygotsky's theory emphasized how children adopt the thought structures represented in the language and culture that surround them. Cultures create *psychological tools* to solve problems and handle information, and these tools become reflected in the language of the culture. As children acquire the language, they also adopt the psychological tools embedded in it. Children in the United States, for example, often hear the words *freedom* and *democracy.* As they learn and internalize these words, they may become optimistic that they can shape their own destinies and make contributions to society. Contrast this with an experience one of us had in East Germany (formerly a Communist country). It was 1990, just months after the Communist government fell. I frequently heard citizens say, "It's not possible," as in "It's not possible to go there" (because the store was closed) or "It's not possible to do that" (because a sign was posted prohibiting parking, smoking, or loitering). The phrase sounded odd to me. As a U.S. citizen, I of course knew that it was "possible" to do those things: I could break in, park illegally, smoke, or loiter anywhere I wanted! Under Communism, however, citizens had

sociocultural theory

A theory that focuses on how language and culture influence the development of thought in children.

learned that government regulations were not mere requests—they were absolute requirements. Through language, cultures communicate expectations and influence how people think about society and the larger world.

Children take the *social speech* spoken by people around them and turn it into their own *"private speech."* At first children speak private speech aloud, as in "Now I cross the laces, then make a bow." Later this private speech becomes silent *"inner speech,"* or what most of us would consider true mental thinking. Our inner thoughts therefore derive from the social speech that we hear in the culture around us. Vygotsky's theory reminds us about the important impacts that culture and society have on the cognitive growth of children.

Piaget and Vygotsky had a tremendous impact on our understanding of child development. Piaget, in particular, wrote hundreds of books and articles on children's cognitive development, and his work stimulated countless investigations by other researchers. Since Piaget, researchers have continued investigating cognitive development, often using an **information-processing approach.** This approach focuses on how children perceive information in the world, store and retrieve information from their memory systems, and learn and use strategies to solve complex problems. Information-processing psychologists often emphasize the roles of *basic processing efficiency,* or a child's speed and accuracy in carrying out cognitive processes, and of *changes in the knowledge base,* or changes in the knowledge a child already has. Researchers also have studied how children process academic information such as spelling, science, and mathematics. Although this newer research has not always supported Piaget's theory (see criticisms of Piaget's theory in Chapter 5), the field is indebted to Piaget, the founder of cognitive developmental theory.

Biological Theories

Another group of child development theories focuses on biological explanations. One important biological theory is **ethology,** which examines the adaptive significance or survival value of behaviors. Ethology has its roots in Charles Darwin's (1809–1882) theory of evolution and his concept of natural selection ("survival of the fittest"). Ethologists often study animals in their natural environments, carefully observing behavior patterns and instincts that help the animals compete and survive. Two European zoologists, Konrad Lorenz and Niko Tinbergen, were especially important in formulating the basic tenets of ethology. Lorenz (1973/1977) is most known for his work on *imprinting.* Lorenz showed that baby goslings become attached to the first guardian figure they observe after hatching from their eggs. In his famous demonstration, Lorenz himself served as the guardian, and the goslings imprinted on him and followed him everywhere. Ethologists believe that the purpose of imprinting is to create a bond of attachment between goslings and mother geese so that goslings will be more likely to remain close to their mothers for protection. Extending ethology to humans, researchers have investigated bonding between human infants and their mothers. Some have speculated that the first hours after birth represent a critical period for developing a healthy bond (Klaus & Kennell, 1976). Other researchers believe that attachment bonds develop more gradually in humans, extending across the first year or so of life. We have much more to say about attachment in Chapter 9.

Beyond bonding and attachment, ethologists have wondered if other behavior patterns have adaptive significance for humans. Aggression, dating rituals, and emotional responses are just a few of the areas they have studied. Sociobiology, a subarea within ethology, focuses on the evolutionary development of social interactions among humans and among animals. *Behavior genetics* is another area related to ethology. As we discussed earlier in this chapter, behavior genetics asks to what degree particular behaviors are genetic (inherited) as opposed to learned. Each of these areas of study contributes to our knowledge by helping us understand the biological origins and history of important traits and behaviors.

information-processing approach

A theoretical approach focusing on how children perceive, store, and retrieve information, and on the strategies they use to solve problems.

ethology

Area of study focusing on the adaptive significance or survival value of behaviors.

Konrad Lorenz is one of the "fathers of ethology." In this demonstration of imprinting, these baby geese follow him like he is their father too!

Technological advances in recent decades have allowed more direct observation of the brain and nervous system than was ever possible before. **Neuropsychology,** a growing field in which psychologists, biologists, and other scientists are studying the structure and function of the brain and nervous system, has especially benefited from these advanced technologies. *Computerized tomography (CT)* scans can give computer-enhanced three-dimensional X-ray images of the brain. With *positron emission tomography (PET),* clinicians inject radioactive markers in a person's bloodstream and then trace them through the brain as the person engages in certain cognitive tasks. For example, with PET scans researchers can tell which areas of the brain are most active when a student is reading versus speaking, or doing math versus trying to recall vocabulary words. One problem with PET scans is that they are not precise—they only indicate which gross areas are involved in processing. A newer technology is *functional magnetic resonance imaging (fMRI),* which can detect changes in the rate of metabolism, or energy consumption, in

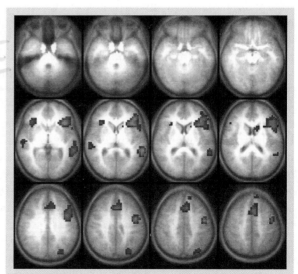

This fMRI/PET scan shows a composite image of brain activity taken as children think about a problem. Notice how the frontal lobe is especially active in this task. Neuropsychologists use technologies like this to study how the brain functions and changes as children grow and learn new skills.

neuropsychology

An area of study that focuses on the study of the brain and nervous system; researchers often observe brain function using technology such as CT scans, PET, and fMRI.

smaller areas of the brain. With fMRI researchers can precisely identify the specific parts of the brain that become more active as people process different types of information. With these and other technologies, researchers are gaining a better understanding of the biological substrate of cognitive processing. Knowledge gained in neuropsychology will undoubtedly both inform and challenge the various theories of cognitive development.

Systems Theories

As children develop, their behaviors are complex. Clearly, development cannot be explained by a single concept such as genes, instinct, reinforcement, or the id. The newest wave of theories attempt to capture the complexity of child development by focusing on the rich network of systems that operate in and around the child. According to *systems theories,* development emerges from complexity; we cannot understand development by reducing the world into a small set of simple terms. Urie Bronfenbrenner's (1989, 1995) *ecological systems theory* is an excellent example of this type of theory. Several other researchers also have used *dynamic systems theories* that take a similar approach.

■ **Ecological Systems Theory.**   About 70 years ago, Lev Vygotsky taught us about the important role that cultural context plays in children's cognitive development. More recently, experts in child development have begun looking at culture and the environment as a complex set of systems and interacting social layers. Urie Bronfenbrenner (1989, 1995) proposed an **ecological systems theory** to explain how the systems and interrelationships that surround a child affect all aspects of a child's development. Figure 1.3 shows the layers of systems described in Bronfenbrenner's theory:

▶ The *microsystem,* or inner layer, represents the direct relationships and interactions children have with people in their immediate environment (parents, siblings, friends, teachers, etc.). Parents who are warm and nurturing have a different effect on a child's development than do parents who are cold and distant. Aggressive friends have a different effect than friends who are more peaceful. These relationships are also bidirectional, because a child's own characteristics can influence how others respond to him or her. An easygoing child, for example, may elicit increased warmth and affection from parents. Parents may respond to a child with a difficult temperament by becoming more harsh and punitive.

▶ The *mesosystem* represents the connections among home, neighborhood, school, day care, and other elements in the larger social environment. Parental involvement in school and increased communication between home and school can have a positive effect on children's school performance. Although children may not take part directly in such communications, the interactions among these larger elements certainly affect their development.

▶ The *exosystem* represents even larger social settings and networks. Extended family networks, friendship networks, governmental regulations, social service programs, and even workplace rules regarding family leave and flexible hours are examples of elements in the larger social milieu that have bearings on child development.

▶ At the widest level, the *macrosystem* represents the values, customs, laws, and resources of the culture at large. Cultures that are more individualistic (e.g., that of the United States) tend to stress early independence in children and competition with peers. In collectivist cultures (e.g., those of China and Japan), however, the emphasis is on community and cooperation. In impoverished countries malnutrition and inadequate health care can compromise children's development. Affluent nations, where resources abound, can offer more support for optimal development (provided that children have access to the resources).

▶ The *chronosystem* represents how the effects of these systems, and the interrelationships among them, change over time. The birth of a new sibling can significantly alter the

thinking
OF JENNIFER

◀ How could Jennifer use Bronfenbrenner's ecological systems theory to better understand her children's development? What factors within this theory will be the same for both of her children? What factors might differ?

ecological systems theory

Theory focusing on the complex set of systems and interacting social layers that can affect a child's development.

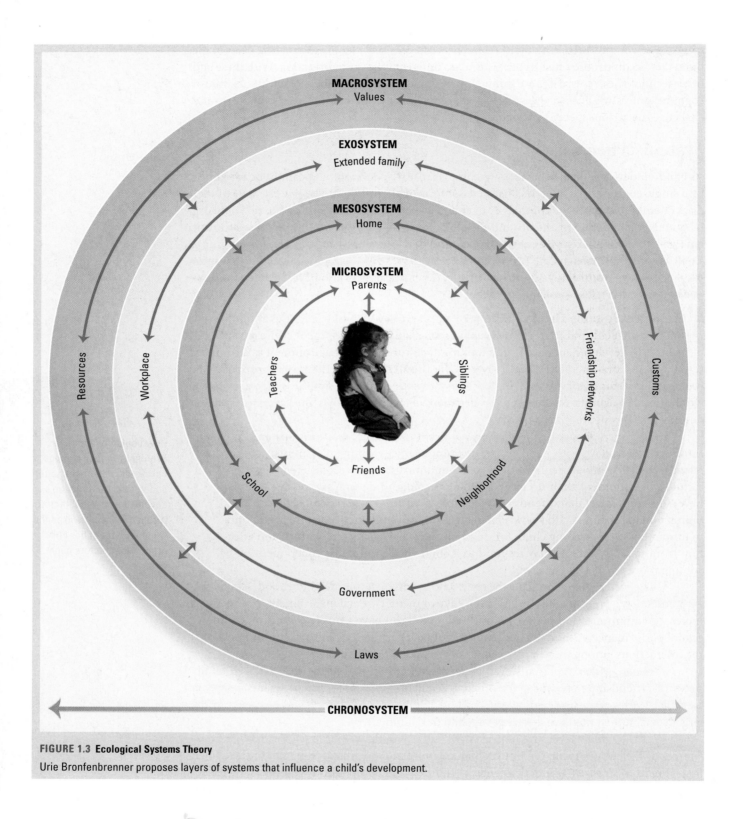

FIGURE 1.3 Ecological Systems Theory

Urie Bronfenbrenner proposes layers of systems that influence a child's development.

relationship between child and parents. When families move, children must deal with new schools, neighborhoods, and peer groups. And economies change, moving through cycles of boom and bust and rising and falling employment rates. Any of these changes can influence child development. Bronfenbrenner's theory serves as an important reminder about the variety of forces that can alter a child's developmental path in both positive and negative ways.

■ **Dynamic Systems Theories.**   **Dynamic systems theories** also focus on how layers of systems interact with one another and change over time. These theories, however, are based on models mathematicians and physicists use to understand complex and dynamic systems (Thelen & Smith, 1998). As you know, human behavior is extraordinarily complex and rich in variety. It is virtually impossible to predict exactly how any one child will respond to a given situation, and we can rarely explain any specific behavior by pointing to a single cause. As an example, think about how children respond to the divorce of their parents. We can make general statements about how *most* children become sad or depressed, or how *many* children's grades drop in school, but obviously these statements are not true for all children whose parents divorce. (You can read much more about the effects of divorce in Chapter 12.) Some children may seem unaffected by the divorce; a few others may even become more happy or successful after the divorce. When effects do occur, can we ever identify their precise cause? Usually not. For example, suppose a boy shows an increase in aggressiveness (fighting at school and arguing with friends) following his parents' divorce. The reason could be the loss of his father figure, his mother's depression, a reduction in family income, a move to a rougher neighborhood, a shift to a new school, or a whole host of other variables. In reality, it was likely some combination of multiple variables and conditions that caused the increase in aggression, not any single variable alone.

According to dynamic systems theory, then, the boy's response to divorce emerges from the complex interaction of elements from multiple layers both in and around the child. Inside the child we would consider his self-esteem, his ability to cope with intense emotions, and his skills in interacting with peers. Outside the child, factors might include the proximity of a network of extended family, the aggressiveness of his peers, the quality of his school interactions, and the types of interactions he has with his parents. At the broadest level, the prevailing attitudes about divorce in his culture and society may be important. And at the most elemental levels, we could look at genetic tendencies toward aggression and at how the child's emotions relate to biochemical changes in his brain and nervous system. At first, combining all of these variables may yield a picture that is too chaotic to interpret. But eventually patterns begin to emerge out of the chaos. For example, soon after the divorce, the child may be confused and his behavior may be erratic. Later, as he digests the various pushes and pulls from all of these levels of variables, he may settle into a stable pattern of behavior—such as meeting common frustrations with acts of aggression. Other children, experiencing different combinations of pushes and pulls, may settle into different patterns, such as withdrawal or depression.

In dynamic systems theories, the stable patterns that emerge are called *attractor states.* That is, these states represent the preferred mode of behavior or the dominant psychological attitude or emotion. These attractor states tend to emerge as the whole system *self-organizes* dynamically around the whole field of inputs. It isn't any one variable that causes the aggression to emerge—it isn't the loss of the father alone, or the mother's depression alone. Rather, the aggression emerges as a relatively stable and persistent response to the complex interaction of inputs. The system is also dynamic because it *changes with time.* The father may begin to visit the child more frequently, the mother may gradually become less depressed, the child may learn more effective ways of coping with frustration, and even societal attitudes may change (albeit slowly). A change in any variable may affect the system, and in the real world it is common to see complex changes along multiple variables. Strong influences also can disrupt the system, causing a move out of one stable state and into another. An intense instance of racial injustice or an assault by a bully, for example, might push a child's reaction pattern from mild aggression to outright hostility and physical violence. On the other hand,

dynamic systems theories

Theories that use models from mathematics and physics to understand complex systems of development.

an intimate friendship or the warmth of a caring adult role model could move the pattern in a more positive direction.

Researchers are interested in how systems become stable, when they change, and what makes them change. As Thelen and Smith (1998) put it,

> all components of the system are continually linked and mutually interactive within the individual, and between the individual and the environment . . . mental and physical activity are assembled in the moment, but always as a function of the system's history. Actions done in this moment, in turn, set the stage for behavior in the next second, minute, week, and year. With this formulation, it makes no sense to ask what part of behavior comes from stages, mental structures, symbol systems, knowledge modules, or genes, because these constructs do not exist in timeless, disconnected form. There is no time and no level when the system ceases to be dynamic. (p. 625)

In recent years dynamic systems theories have helped us understand how infants learn to walk, reach for objects, and perceive forms, as well as how children learn new word meanings, understand emotions, and move across Piaget's stages of cognitive development (Fischer & Bidell, 1998; Thelen & Smith, 1998). Dynamic systems theories also have helped explain the complex effects that antipoverty and welfare programs have on children (Yoshikawa & Hsueh, 2001). Researchers are just beginning to use dynamic systems thinking to model the complexity of child development. Rather than arguing about nature versus nurture, we now have the opportunity to consider how all of the elements affecting development work in complex interaction. In the coming years it will be interesting to see how well this type of theory performs.

As you can see, theorists have proposed a wide variety of ideas to explain how children and adolescents develop. We hope that these brief sketches have let you glimpse the different theories' usefulness in explaining what is (or was) known about children. Each theory offers some degree of prediction and guidance for people working with children. These theories also guide future research efforts by suggesting new factors and variables that need to be explored. As you consider these theories, don't expect any single approach to be the only one that is "right" or "correct." Many theories address narrow or specific aspects of child development. For example, Piaget's cognitive developmental theory focused on how children think, whereas Bronfenbrenner's ecological systems theory focuses more on how children interact with other people. So it wouldn't make sense to pit these two theories against each other and ask which one "wins." Each theory offers at least some valuable insight about children and adolescents, yet no single theory captures all of the complexities of human development.

As research continues, we will continue to gain information that favors (or discredits) one or another line of thought, and new theories will continue to emerge. In the next section we will describe the most important research techniques used to study child development.

LET'S REVIEW . . .

1. Which of the following is *not* one of the useful functions served by theories?
   a. Theories summarize the facts as currently known.
   b. Theories allow prediction of future behavior and events.
   c. Theories contradict the facts gathered by scientific observation.
   d. Theories stimulate new research and discoveries.

2. Who proposed that an important component of personality forms when children identify with their same-sex parent?
   a. Sigmund Freud b. Erik Erikson c. B. F. Skinner d. Urie Bronfenbrenner

3. A focus on how observable conditions in the environment relate to observable behaviors in people was the emphasis of:

    a. behaviorism.   b. cognitive theory.   c. contextual theory.   d. psychoanalytic theory.

4. The microsystem, mesosystem, and macrosystem are parts of:

    a. Erikson's psychoanalytic theory.

    b. Bandura's social learning theory.

    c. Bronfenbrenner's ecological systems theory.

    d. Vygotsky's cognitive–developmental theory.

5. True or False: The CT scan, PET scan, and fMRI are tools used in neuropsychology to study brain development.

6. True or False: Dynamic systems theories are useful in isolating variables like nature and nurture and determining which one has the most influence on development.

Answers: 1. c, 2. a, 3. a, 4. c, 5. T, 6. F

Using the Scientific Method: Research in Child Development

How do researchers identify patterns in child development? How do we know what types of behaviors are typical of children at different ages? How do we gather information to test theories and to generate solutions to the practical problems faced by children and families? In the field of child development, we rely on scientific research methods to gather data, test hypotheses, and generate new ideas.

As you study this section, ask yourself these questions:

- What are some examples of descriptive research methods, and how are they useful in studying development?

- What is the proper way to interpret a correlation, and what are the advantages and disadvantages of correlational research?

- How do researchers determine cause and effect? How is the experimental method different from correlation? Why don't all research studies employ the experimental method?

- How do cross-sectional, longitudinal, and hybrid research designs differ in how they assess developmental effects?

- What steps do researchers take to protect the rights and privacy of children who participate in their studies?

Descriptive Research Methods

Descriptive methods attempt to describe something about a behavior, such as how often and under what conditions it occurs. One way to describe a behavior is simply to observe it. In *naturalistic observation* researchers watch children in their natural environment (such as at home, in school, or on the playground) and record what they do, when, and with whom, or other details. For example, if you want to know how often preschoolers look at books and engage

descriptive methods

Research methods that attempt to describe something about a behavior of interest, such as how often it occurs and under what conditions.

in "prereading" activities, you can go to a day care center and watch the children. But what if the children never show the behavior? Or what if the particular setting or the activities going on while you observe aren't conducive to reading (such as nap time or Play-Doh play)? The biggest advantage of naturalistic observation is that a researcher can gather information about real-life behaviors—but a major disadvantage is that the researcher cannot control the situation to ensure that the behavior of interest will occur. In *structured observation,* in contrast, the researcher creates a suitable situation, arranges for children to be placed there (often in a laboratory or in a specially prepared space within the home or school), and observes their behavior. For example, to observe reading interest and prereading activities, you could set up a room with a variety of toys, including many interesting books. You could watch children and see if they chose to look at the reading materials, for how long, and in what ways. So in structured observation the researcher has more control than in naturalistic observational settings. However, this method does not answer questions about the real-life occurrence and form of the behavior. In both types of observation, it's very important that the person collecting the information not know what the expected results are. Otherwise, that person's knowledge could influence his or her observations and the outcome of the research—a situation called *observer bias.*

Researchers can also ask children to give *self-reports,* or direct answers to questions about a topic or process. For example, you could ask children how much they like to read, how often they look at books, and the like. You could do this in face-to-face interviews or through written questionnaires. The major drawback of self-reports involves participants' abilities to remember accurately and to verbalize their answers. Some children are stronger in these abilities than others, and these differences can lead to inaccurate conclusions. In addition, children will sometimes give the answers they think the interviewer wants to hear, rather than answers that are more accurate but that they believe are less desirable in some way. Interviewers must also be very careful to not lead children to give certain kinds of responses. This kind of unintentional prompting can occur through the kinds of questions asked, through the phrasing of questions, or through unconscious nonverbal signals such as body movements or facial expressions.

Finally, researchers can do *case studies*—intensive studies of one child or a small number of children. The goal of a case study is to create a detailed description of the individual(s), usually focusing on some particular behaviors. Case studies often focus on children who are exceptional in some way, such as children with some sort of developmental delay or unusually high level of competence or achievement. These studies may employ a variety of different measures. Examples include detailed and repeated observations (both naturalistic and structured); standardized tests and informal assessments; self-reports; and/or physiological measures such as brain activity, heart rate, or respiration patterns during specific activities. For example, you could study a child who is clearly advanced in reading skill so as to understand why and how the skill is developing, or a child who is delayed in reading in order to identify factors that might be contributing to the delay.

Descriptive research methods are valuable in providing information about a behavior, and they are often a useful starting point for understanding some aspect of development. These methods often help researchers develop *hypotheses,* or specific predictions about what causes or affects a given behavior. But these methods do not answer questions about relationships among variables; other methods are needed for this.

Correlational Research Methods: Measuring Associations

Suppose we wanted to answer this question: Is reading ability in the early grade school years related to the amount of time parents spend reading to children during the preschool years? What

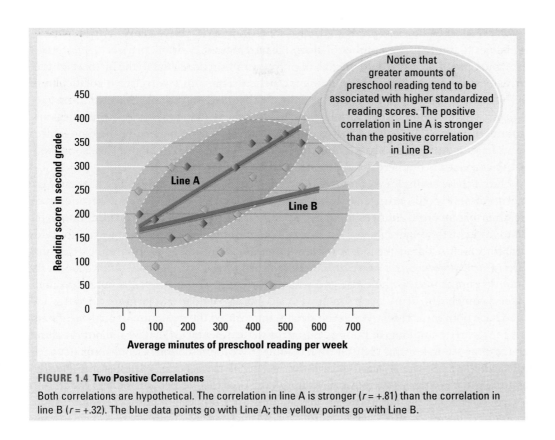

Notice that greater amounts of preschool reading tend to be associated with higher standardized reading scores. The positive correlation in Line A is stronger than the positive correlation in Line B.

FIGURE 1.4 Two Positive Correlations

Both correlations are hypothetical. The correlation in line A is stronger ($r = +.81$) than the correlation in line B ($r = +.32$). The blue data points go with Line A; the yellow points go with Line B.

kinds of observations would we need to make? One approach we might take would be to ask parents of preschoolers to keep careful notes (reading logs) on the number of minutes they spent each time they read to their child. After 6 weeks we could collect the logs and calculate the average number of minutes per week that each child was read to by a parent. Later, when the children were in second grade, we could take each child's score on a standardized reading test and match it with his or her average number of minutes of preschool reading. Figure 1.4 presents hypothetical data like those that we might collect if we actually conducted this study. The graph shows that the children who were read to most in preschool tended to have higher reading scores in second grade. The children read to least tended to have lower scores. With the **correlational method,** researchers measure the degree to which two or more variables are related or associated.

A *correlation coefficient* is a number that indicates the direction and strength of an association between two or more variables. In our example, we could compute a correlation coefficient for the association between average minutes of preschool reading and second-grade reading scores. Correlation coefficients (symbolized by the letter r) can range from -1.0 to $+1.0$. *Positive coefficients* ($r = 0.0$ to $+1.0$) indicate that the scores on the two variables tend to run in the same direction. In other words, higher scores on one variable tend to be linked with higher scores on the other variable, and lower with lower. Line A in Figure 1.4 clearly shows a positive correlation, and we calculated the coefficient to be $+.81$. The *magnitude* of the coefficient indicates the strength of the correlation. Line A shows a fairly strong positive relationship ($+.81$)—a fairly strong tendency for greater preschool reading time to be linked with higher second-grade reading scores. Contrast this with the data in line B of Figure 1.4. Here, the correlation coefficient is $+.32$. That is, second-grade reading scores still tend to rise along with preschool reading (i.e., the correlation is still a positive one), but the relationship is weaker than in line A (i.e., the numerical value is smaller).

correlational method

Research method that measures the degree to which two or more variables are related or associated.

Now consider an example of a negative correlation. What if we asked mothers of newborn babies to estimate the number of alcoholic beverages they drank per week, on average, during their pregnancies? Would their alcohol consumption be related to the birth weights of their babies? Line A in Figure 1.5 shows hypothetical data with a correlation coefficient of −.74. *Negative coefficients* ($r = 0.0$ to $−1.0$) indicate that the two variables have an inverse relationship: Higher scores on one variable tend to be linked with lower scores on the other variable, and vice versa. You can see that there is a relatively strong pattern in the data—birth weights tend to decrease as alcohol consumption increases. Line B in Figure 1.5 also shows a negative correlation, but here the relationship is weaker ($r = −.28$).

From these examples you can see the usefulness of correlational studies. If these were actual studies, we could learn that children tend to score higher in reading in second grade when their parents read more to them as preschoolers, and that alcohol consumption is related to lower birth weight in newborn babies. Both of these results would suggest important advice for parents. But at this point we need to emphasize a key limitation of correlational studies: *Correlation does not prove causation!* On the basis of correlational studies alone, we cannot determine what is the cause and what is the effect. For example, compared to nondrinkers, women who drink larger amounts of alcohol also tend to smoke more cigarettes and tend to have poorer nutrition. Was it the alcohol that caused the reduction in birth weight, or was it the cigarette smoking, or poor nutrition, or some other factor that we did not measure? In the reading study, it seems plausible that reading more to preschoolers would enhance their reading ability—but the real causal direction might be the reverse. For example, children might inherit "reading aptitude," with some children destined to become better readers and some poorer readers. Children with greater "reading aptitude" might be more fun to read to; they might be more attentive, ask more interesting questions, and otherwise behave in ways that would encourage their parents to spend more time reading to them. If so, then increased

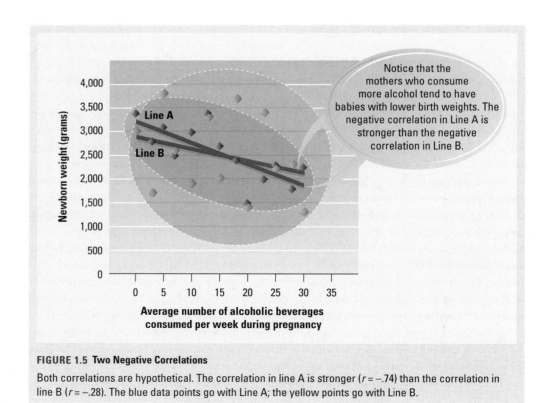

FIGURE 1.5 Two Negative Correlations

Both correlations are hypothetical. The correlation in line A is stronger ($r = −.74$) than the correlation in line B ($r = −.28$). The blue data points go with Line A; the yellow points go with Line B.

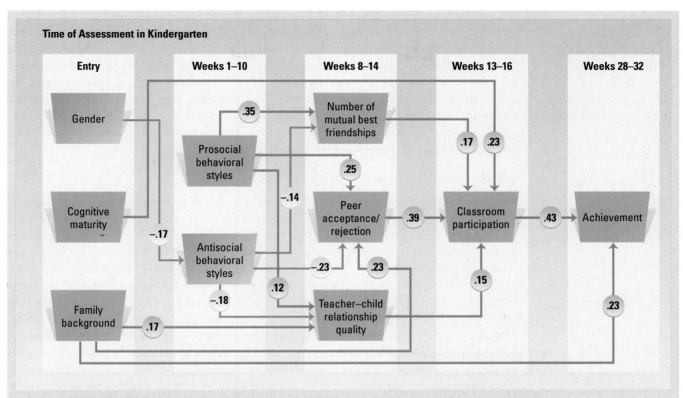

Time of Assessment in Kindergarten

| Entry | Weeks 1–10 | Weeks 8–14 | Weeks 13–16 | Weeks 28–32 |

FIGURE 1.6 Path Analysis Model

This diagram shows correlations among several variables that are related to greater achievement in kindergarten.

Note: Correlations ≤ .12 are not statistically significant.

Source: G. W. Ladd, S. H. Birch, & E. S. Buhs. (1999). Children's social and scholastic lives in kindergarten: Related spheres of influence? *Child Development, 70,* 1373–1400. Reprinted with permission.

"reading aptitude" (as measured in the second-grade standardized tests) would be the cause, not the effect, of increased parental reading time.

Researchers recognize the complex ways that variables can interrelate to influence the behavior and development of children. As we mentioned in our discussion of systems theories, more and more research is trying to describe this complexity by measuring multiple variables. Sometimes researchers compute *path analyses* to see how multiple variables are intercorrelated. Ladd, Birch, and Buhs (1999), for example, investigated a large group of kindergarten children. First they assessed the children's cognitive maturity and family background when they entered kindergarten. As the school year progressed, the researchers took measures of prosocial (helpful) behaviors, antisocial (harmful) behaviors, relationships with peers and teachers, classroom participation, and achievement (measured by a kindergarten readiness test). Figure 1.6 shows correlations among these variables. For example, prosocial behavior relates positively with mutual friendships ($r = .35$), and antisocial behavior relates negatively with mutual friendships ($r = -.14$). The strongest relationship is between classroom participation and achievement ($r = .43$). But classroom participation is itself related to several other variables such as cognitive maturity and mutual friendships. As you can see, children's success in kindergarten involves a whole array of interrelated factors.

Even when we measure an array of complicated relationships, we still cannot be sure which are the causes and which are the effects. Do children participate more in kindergarten

thinking
OF JENNIFER

◄ How would correlational research help you understand the factors involved in the development of Jennifer's children? Given that this research method cannot determine cause and effect, is this type of research still useful?

Using the Scientific Method: Research in Child Development | 25

YOUR PERSPECTIVE

NOTES

What other factors can you think of that might have direct or indirect relationships with school achievement in kindergarten? How would a path analysis help you understand the relative contributions of these factors, and their interactions?

because they have more friends in class, or do they have more friends because they participate more? Do children achieve more because they participate more in class, or do they participate more because they are performing well and already feel confident? We can hypothesize several different ways to explain the same correlation. So again, correlation in itself is not sufficient for determining cause and effect. But ultimately, of course, researchers would like to determine cause and effect. To accomplish this they use the experimental method.

Experimental Research Methods: Determining Cause and Effect

How could we demonstrate that alcohol consumption during pregnancy actually *causes* a reduction in birth weight? Consider the hypothetical experiment diagrammed in Figure 1.7. Experimenters randomly assign 50 pregnant rats either to an experimental group or to a control group. The 25 rats in the experimental group have water bottles that contain a mixture of water and pure grain alcohol. The 25 rats in the control group have bottles with pure water. Other than this difference, the researchers treat all 50 rats as much alike as possible. They provide identical cages, offer the same food, and follow the same feeding schedules with all the rats. Their aim is to have the two groups differ systematically along only one variable: alcohol versus pure water. This variable is the *independent variable*—the variable that the researchers systematically manipulate in the experiment. The idea is to manipulate this variable independently of other factors (e.g., diet) that might affect pregnancy. In the hypothetical experiment, after the rat pups are born, we can weigh each pup and compare the average birth weights in the experimental and control groups. Birth weight is the *dependent variable*. That is, it represents the outcome that we measure, an outcome that is *dependent* on the manipulation of the independent variable.

With the **experimental method,** then, researchers systematically manipulate the independent variable to determine if it causes a difference in the dependent variable. If we conduct this experiment properly, the only systematic difference between the two groups will be exposure to alcohol: The experimental group is exposed to alcohol, and the control group is not. If we observe that the pups in the groups differ reliably in birth weight (e.g., if the birth weights in the experimental group are substantially lower than those in the control group), then we can conclude alcohol exposure caused this difference. What else could be the cause? Rats in both groups got the same diet, were on the same feeding schedules, and had the same experience in every way possible other than alcohol exposure.

Of course, researchers cannot perfectly control every factor in the experiment. Individual rats will differ in their metabolisms and appetites, for example. And each mother rat will weigh a different amount even before pregnancy. Because these factors may affect the birth weights, we use *random assignment to groups* to prevent such factors from differing systematically between the groups. With random assignment, each participant (in this case, each rat) has an equal chance of being assigned to any of the groups in an experiment. It is therefore unlikely that all of the heavier mother rats would be assigned to the control group or that all of the rats with lighter appetites would be assigned to the experimental group.

If experimenters can show a systematic relationship between an independent variable and a dependent variable, then they can demonstrate cause and effect. In our example, we might be able to show that alcohol consumption during pregnancy actually *causes* reduced birth weight in rat offspring. But of course, we experimented on rats, not humans. It would obviously be unethical for us to require that some women consume alcohol during pregnancy just so we could observe the effect on human newborns.

experimental method

Research method where investigators systematically manipulate an independent variable to determine if it causes a difference in a dependent variable.

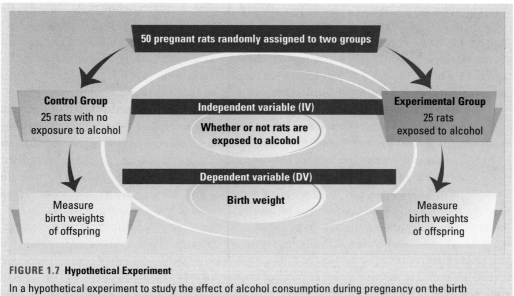

FIGURE 1.7 Hypothetical Experiment

In a hypothetical experiment to study the effect of alcohol consumption during pregnancy on the birth weight of newborns, the researcher systematically manipulates the independent variable (IV) to determine its effect on the dependent variable (DV). If the only difference between the control and experimental groups is alcohol exposure versus nonexposure, then any reliable difference in birth weights can be attributed to the alcohol exposure. Experiments are the only method that can determine cause–effect relationships. Why would this experiment never be conducted with human participants?

This points out the main disadvantage of the experimental method: Researchers always must ask whether it is ethical to manipulate the independent variable that is of interest in the experiment. For example, think back to the discussion of a correlation between preschool reading and second-grade reading scores. The correlation was not sufficient to establish cause and effect. Would it be appropriate or ethical to conduct an experiment in this situation? Could we, for example, require that some parents read more to their preschool children and that some parents read only a little or not at all? Could we, ethically, randomly assign parents and their children to these two experimental conditions? If any of the experimental conditions might conceivably have a negative effect on a child's development, then ethically it is difficult to justify the experiment. Sometimes we turn to animal research to study variables that would be unethical to manipulate with humans. Research on the effect of alcohol consumption on pregnancy, for example, has utilized rats and other animal species. (Animal rights activists have argued that those types of experiments are also unethical, and there are now strict guidelines for conducting research using animals.) In other situations, however, there is no analogue with animals. For example, it wouldn't make sense to study the effects of preschool reading with monkeys. And it surely wouldn't make sense to study how mutual friendships affect class participation and school achievement in a rat colony! With these types of questions, on which it would be unethical or impractical to conduct human experiments, we have to stick to correlational research methods.

In summary, correlational methods have the advantage of demonstrating and measuring associations among variables, even for variables that we cannot ethically manipulate in experiments. The main disadvantage of correlational research is that correlations alone cannot prove causation. A major advantage of the experimental method is that experiments, if conducted properly, can demonstrate cause-and-effect relationships. A disadvantage is that it is sometimes unethical or impractical to conduct experiments in child development research.

Methods for Assessing Development

One of the main objectives in child development research is to determine how children do and do not change as they grow through childhood and into adolescence and adulthood. Researchers primarily use two types of methods for assessing developmental patterns: the cross-sectional method and the longitudinal method.

With the **cross-sectional method,** researchers compare groups of children of different ages against one another at the same point in time. As an example, consider a cross-sectional study conducted by Cowan, Nugent, Elliott, Ponomarev, and Saults (1999). These researchers investigated developmental changes in short-term memory for single-digit numbers. Their participants were groups of first graders, fourth graders, and young adults. Each participant heard recordings of lists of single-digit numbers (e.g., 3, 7, 5, 9). Later the researchers asked them to recall the lists as accurately as possible. At the time the participants heard the lists, the researchers also asked them to play a game on a computer screen; this activity was intended to distract them from verbally repeating, or rehearsing, the series of digits. The goal was to see how well the participants could remember the digits when they couldn't rehearse them. On average, the first graders recalled approximately 3.6 digits correctly, the fourth graders 4.5 digits, and the adults 5.4. Using this cross-sectional study design, these researchers were able to demonstrate short-term memory gains from first grade into early adulthood.

Another approach is to use a longitudinal design. **Longitudinal methods** compare performance or observations across ages by taking repeated measurements from the same people across time. Researchers can then compare the measurements or observations to see how they are changing (or remaining the same) as the participants age. Consider, for example, a longitudinal study conducted by Nancy Eisenberg and her colleagues (1999). These researchers used a variety of measures to assess how frequently children engaged in prosocial, or helping, behaviors. They followed a group of 32 children, taking measurements approximately every 2 years from the time the children were 4 years old until they reached 24 years. The results? Individual differences in prosocial behavior tended to be relatively consistent and stable across development. The children who tended to be the most helpful during preschool (age 4) also tended to show more prosocial behaviors and attitudes during later childhood, in adolescence, and even into early adulthood.

The cross-sectional and longitudinal methods offer different advantages and disadvantages to researchers. The longitudinal method allows a more direct test of development. By following the same children as they age, researchers can observe how behaviors, attitudes, and other dispositions change or remain the same in those children. A disadvantage, however, is that it is difficult to get participants to remain in a study across long periods of time. For example, Eisenberg and her colleagues actually began their study with 37 children. Over the years a few children moved away and could not be contacted; one person participated all the way through adolescence and then refused to complete the study as an adult. You can imagine that participants might drop out of a study for a variety of reasons—from simple boredom and loss of interest, to a lack of time due to expanding responsibilities as participants mature, to illness or even death.

This factor, called *differential dropout,* poses an especially serious problem with longitudinal studies. If the reason for the dropout is related to the nature of the study itself, then the validity of the results is compromised. If the least prosocial participants were the ones who dropped out of Eisenberg's study, for example, then the results would represent an overestimate of how prosocial most people tend to be. Further, some people might start out being helpful (and agree to participate as children) but then become less helpful (and therefore drop out of the study). If this happened, then the researchers would end up with an overestimate of the stability of prosocial behaviors: The participants who would have demonstrated

cross-sectional method

A type of research design that studies development by comparing groups of children of different ages against one another at the same point in time.

longitudinal method

A type of research design that studies development by measuring or observing the same children across time as they grow and mature.

the most instability would have removed themselves from the study. Clearly, the longer it takes to conduct a longitudinal study, the more likely it is that participants will drop out. Also, the sheer time that it takes to conduct this type of study can make it impractical. Can most researchers really wait 20 years to finish their study? Will they (or the field) even be interested in the same developmental questions 20 years in the future?

The main advantage of the cross-sectional study is that it can be completed in a relatively short period of time. Instead of waiting until participants grow and develop, researchers using the cross-sectional approach take a "cross section" of different ages at one point in time. A disadvantage of this approach, however, is that the participant groups will differ not only in age but also in intelligence, physical strength, and many other qualities that make people unique—and these differences could affect the study results. In the short-term memory study we described, obviously the first graders were not the same children as the fourth graders, and the adults were still another group of people. When we compare the groups on memory performance, how can we be sure that the differences were due to differences in age rather than simply to differences among individuals?

When the age groups differ substantially, as they did in the short-term memory study, there also can be a problem with cohort effects. *Cohort effects* are differences in behavior or other attributes that result from the unique experiences of people who grow up in different periods. Changes in education, technology, medicine, the economy, and the cultural climate are just a few of the factors causing children growing up today to have a different developmental experience than did children several decades ago. For example, we cannot assume that the first graders of today will grow up in the same way as children did during the Great Depression of the 1930s or during the Vietnam War era. Consider the terrorist attacks on the United States on September 11, 2001. Some claim that September 11 was "the day the world changed forever" or the day that freedom and innocence were lost. Would it be fair to compare children raised after the attacks to children raised before? In what ways might their experiences differ?

Some researchers try to balance the advantages and disadvantages of cross-sectional and longitudinal research by using *hybrid designs*. Figure 1.8 shows an example. When the study begins (in the year 2002), groups of 4-, 8-, 12-, and 16-year-olds are all studied at the same time. This part of the study is cross-sectional. Then the researchers track the children's progress by repeating the study with the same children every 4 years. Notice that the children who were 4 years old in 2002 are 8 years old in 2006, and so on. This is the longitudinal component. These types of designs are sometimes called *cross-lag* or *sequential designs*.

Whether researchers use the correlational or experimental methods, and whether they use cross-sectional, longitudinal, or hybrid designs, they need to carefully protect the rights of every child who participates in their studies. Let's turn now to the ethical treatment of children in research.

thinking
OF JENNIFER

◄ How might cross-sectional and longitudinal research help Jennifer understand her children's development? What cautions should she be aware of with these methodologies?

Ethics in Research with Children

Researchers who work with children must follow the ethical guidelines of the American Psychological Association and the Society for Research in Child Development. The full text of their guidelines can be found at the following websites: www.apa.org/ethics and www.srcd.org/about.html. Here is a summary of the most important ethical standards:

▶ *Risks versus benefits.* Researchers should conduct studies only when the potential benefits outweigh any known risks. Research designs and procedures must be sound enough that the information to be gained has sufficient value to outweigh any harm, stress, or inconvenience that participants might experience. In some cases participants even receive compensation or other benefits for taking part in the study.

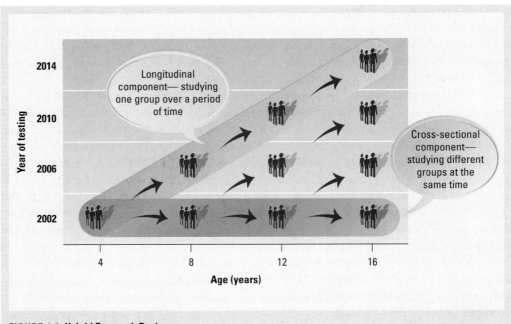

FIGURE 1.8 Hybrid Research Design
In a hybrid design to assess development, researchers study children of different ages at the same time (the cross-sectional component), then follow and retest the same children as they age (the longitudinal component). These research designs are rare in developmental research, in part because they are complicated and time-consuming.

▶ *Nonharmful procedures.* Researchers may not use procedures that could harm a child either physically or psychologically. They must use the least stressful research procedures at all times. If there is any question about possible harm to a child, researchers must consult with appropriate authorities or colleagues.

▶ *Informed consent.* Researchers must explain the purposes, procedures, and all known risks and benefits of their studies to the potential participants. When working with minors, researchers must obtain informed consent from both the children and their parents or guardians. Parents and children over 6 must give written consent. Younger children give oral consent.

▶ *Unforeseen consequences.* If a research procedure results in any negative consequence for a child, the researcher must do whatever is necessary to correct the situation. Also, if during the study the researcher collects information that could have a bearing on a child's well-being, the researcher must discuss this with the child's parents or guardians and with appropriate experts who might be able to assist the child.

▶ *Privacy.* Researchers must keep all information obtained from participants confidential. They must never reveal participants' names or other identifying information to anyone else, and they may not include this information in any written research reports unless the participants have given prior consent. Most research reports give only group averages or scores accumulated across many participants. Reports that give data from individuals must be anonymous.

▶ *Implications of research.* Researchers must be aware of social, political, and human implications—not only of their research but also of how it is presented to colleagues and to the public. Research on sensitive topics is certainly not forbidden, but researchers must take special care when the results may be alarming to groups or individuals.

**YOUR
PERSPECTIVE
NOTES**
Regarding the ethics of conducting research with children, do you think these guidelines provide enough protection to child participants? Why or why not?

To ensure compliance with these ethical guidelines, all researchers must get advance approval for their projects from an *institutional review board (IRB)*. At most universities, for example, IRBs of trained professionals review research proposals. Before approving any study, the IRB must be satisfied that the potential benefits outweigh any potential risks and that the researchers will follow proper procedures for obtaining informed consent, protecting participants' privacy, and adhering to all other ethical standards. Ethical guidelines also exist for research conducted with animals.

LET'S REVIEW . . .

1. Attendance in school tends to decline as drug use increases. This is an example of:
   - a. a positive correlation.
   - b. a negative correlation.
   - c. lack of a correlation.
   - d. a cohort effect.

2. Which of the following is the most important limitation of correlational research?
   - a. It is difficult to obtain positive correlations.
   - b. Correlation does not prove causation.
   - c. Correlational research cannot describe the complex relations among three or more variables.
   - d. Correlation coefficients do not tell you anything about the strength of the relationship between variables.

3. Dr. Jorgenson conducted an experiment to test the effectiveness of a new parent training program. She randomly assigned 40 parents to two groups. One group received the new parent training program, and the other group received the old standard program. After the training programs were finished, Dr. Jorgenson asked each parent to rate their interactions with their children. In this scenario, what is the *independent variable*?
   - a. The two parent training programs (new versus standard).
   - b. The interaction rating given by each parent after the training.
   - c. The number of parents assigned to each training program.
   - d. The amount of time each parent spent in the training program.

4. Which of the following research methods is capable of demonstrating a cause-and-effect relationship?
   - a. correlational methods
   - b. experimental methods
   - c. path analysis methods
   - d. all of the above

5. **True or False:** Differential dropout is a problem that plagues the cross-sectional method of assessing development.

6. **True or False:** Before working with children, all researchers must have their studies approved by an institutional review board so that the rights and privacy of the children will be protected.

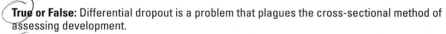

Answers: 1. b, 2. b, 3. a, 4. b, 5. F, 6. T

Applications of Child Development Research and Careers Related to Children

One goal of science is to advance knowledge for its own sake, but another important goal is to provide information that can help people with practical challenges in life. And we can't think of any practical challenge that is more important than raising and educating children! You may already have a clear idea about the work you would like to do, perhaps as a teacher, counselor, psychologist, social worker, or researcher. If you have not yet chosen a career but do have an interest in working with children, then we hope that this section will give you several interesting ideas. What could be more rewarding than a job in which you have the opportunity to help the next generation attain a healthy and satisfying life?

As you study this section, ask yourself these questions:

- What kinds of child development research could help parents and families with the practical problems involved in raising children?
- What is *social policy,* and how can child development research influence it?
- How can psychologists, counselors, educators, and other professionals use child development research to guide their work with children?
- What career opportunities are available for people who want to work with or for children?

Practical Applications of Child Development Research

■ **Family and Parenting.**   How do you discipline children while at the same time showing that you love and care for them? Should parents have special concerns about raising an only child or about raising a large number of children? How does divorce affect children? And what about children in blended stepfamilies or with single parents? There are an infinite number of questions and concerns related to family life and parenting. Parenting a child is the most important responsibility that any of us will ever have, and most parents want to improve their knowledge and skills. Almost all of the topics in this book can offer some advice to parents. Researchers continue to collect new data to answer the latest questions (e.g., how to protect children from the dangers of the Internet) and to continue to probe the age-old issues (e.g., whether genes or upbringing influences children more). To get a feel for the types of advice experts have offered parents over the years, look at Table 1.3, where we list a few examples of authoritative books written for parents. Also, in each chapter of this book, a box called A Personal Perspective will present an interview with a parent or other person about his or her real-life experiences with children. These boxes give examples of how people think about child development or of how people can use topics in child development to improve their understandings of or work with children. For your first box, look at the Personal Perspective box called "Meet First-Time Parents."

thinking
OF JENNIFER

Given the many books ▶ written on the subject of parenting, how should someone like Jennifer decide what advice to follow?

■ **Social Policy.**   Although it has been 40 years since President Lyndon Johnson launched our nation's "War on Poverty," the sad fact is that 1 out of every 6 children still lives in poverty (Children's Defense Fund, 2002a). How does poverty affect children's development, and how can society ameliorate the negative effects? In 1993 President Clinton signed the Family and Medical Leave Act, which allows parents to take up to 12 weeks of unpaid leave from work to care for a newborn or adopted child. Are families benefiting from this law? In 1996 Congress passed a major welfare reform act. Among other things, this law dissolved the federal government's Aid to Families with Dependent Children (AFDC) entitlement program (Gennetian & Miller, 2002; Smith, Brooks-Gunn, Kohen, & McCarton, 2001). The newer laws favor job training and back-to-work programs for adults living in poverty; but statistics indicate that when welfare reform took effect, nearly two-thirds of the people receiving monthly AFDC payments were children (Zaslow, Tout, Smith, & Moore, 1998). How have children and families fared under the newer welfare programs?

In the area of **social policy,** officials at the federal, state, and local levels try to use knowledge provided by child development research to improve the lives of children and fam-

social policy

Attempts to improve the lives of children and families by using child development research to affect laws, regulations, and programs.

TABLE 1.3 A Sampling of Books Written by Child Development Experts

Psychological Care of Infant and Child by John B. Watson	Published in 1928, this was one of the first authoritative books written by a professional psychologist to help parents raise children. Owing perhaps to the harsh realities of the Great Depression, Watson did not believe that parents should shelter young children from the difficulties of life:
	Treat them as though they were young adults. . . . Let your behavior always be objective and kindly firm. Never hug and kiss them, never let them sit in your lap. If you must, kiss them once on the forehead when they say good night. Shake hands with them in the morning. Give them a pat on the head if they have made an extraordinarily good job of a difficult task. Try it out. In a week's time you will find how easy it is to be perfectly objective with your child and at the same time kindly. You will be utterly ashamed of the mawkish, sentimental way you have been handling it. (pp. 81–82)
	Would you be willing to take Watson's advice today?
Infancy and Human Growth by Arnold Gesell	Also written in 1928, Gesell's book offered a detailed scientific record of the milestones and trends in infant growth and development. Gesell was a professor in the Institute of Psychology at Yale University and directed Yale's "Psycho-Clinic," which later became one of the nation's leading institutes for the study of child development. Reaching, crawling, walking, feeding, stacking blocks, climbing, playing with peers, reactions to adults, and recognition of the self are just a few of the skills Gesell traced through infancy. Prematurity, twins, retardation, giftedness, and comparisons to other animal species are also included. From the 1920s through the 1950s, most educated parents took advice from this or one of Gesell's many other books on child development, including *The Mental Growth of the Preschool Child* (1925), *The Guidance of Mental Growth in Infant and Child* (1930), and *Youth: The Years from Ten to Sixteen* (1956).
Baby and Child Care by Benjamin Spock (with Steven J. Parker)	Benjamin Spock was a renowned pediatrician who first published this landmark book in 1946. After 17 editions, this book is still published in 39 languages and has sold more than 50 million copies worldwide. Spock provides practical advice on nearly every major and minor problem faced by parents. Feeding, diapering, illnesses, medical care, sibling rivalry, and nightmares are just a few of the topics covered. Over the decades Spock did an impressive job keeping his book current with knowledge in child development, and *Baby and Child Care* remains an indispensable aid to any parent. Spock's other books include *A Teenager's Guide to Life and Love* (1971) and *A Better World for Our Children: Rebuilding American Family Values* (1994).
How to Parent so Children Will Learn: Clear Strategies for Raising Happy, Achieving Children by Sylvia Rimm	Published in 1996, this book is one of many practical guides written by educational psychologist Sylvia Rimm. Rimm offers commonsense practical solutions on a variety of topics about raising children from preschool through college. Parents enjoy her straightforward and often humorous advice. Rimm directs the Family Achievement Clinic in Cleveland, Ohio where she is also a clinical professor at Case Western Reserve University's School of Medicine. Rimm also is widely known through public radio, network television, and a nationally syndicated newspaper column. Her other books include *Raising Preschoolers: Parenting for Today* (1997) and *See Jane Win: The Rimm Report on How 1,000 Girls Became Successful Women* (1999).
The Black Parenting Book by Anne C. Beal, Linda Villarosa, and Allison Abner	This 1999 book offers practical advice geared specifically toward parents of African American preschool children. The authors discuss topics such as cultural pride, self-esteem, handling racism, health and nutrition, fostering spirituality and family traditions, and discipline. Dr. Beal is a pediatrician at Massachusetts General Hospital, teaches at Harvard Medical School, and offers parenting advice in *Essence* magazine. Villarosa is an editor for the *New York Times* and *Body & Soul: The Black Women's Guide to Physical Health and Emotional Well-Being*. She and Abner are coauthors of *Finding Our Way: The Teen Girls' Survival Guide*.
Raising Nuestros Niños: Bringing Up Latino Children in a Bicultural World by Gloria G. Rodriguez	This practical reference offers advice and ideas on preserving Latino cultural pride and heritage while dealing with the practical day-to-day issues of child rearing. Rodriguez addresses ways to enhance Latino children's self-esteem, and discusses the important role of family and community in fostering children's development. Gloria Rodriguez, Ph.D., an award-winning expert in early childhood education, is the founder and CEO of Avance, a program that provides help and training to Latino families in the United States and Latin America.

ilies. Private organizations and individuals can also affect social policy. In 1999, for example, Bill Gates, the founder of Microsoft, donated $750 million to the Global Alliance for Vaccines and Immunizations (GAVI). As many as 4 million children die each year from diseases that timely vaccinations could prevent. With the help of Gates's donation, GAVI teamed with the World Bank, the World Health Organization, and the Rockefeller Foundation to try to double the number of children worldwide who survive each year thanks to vaccinations (Society for Research in Child Development, 2000).

Research in child development affects social policy in two ways. First, research findings can stimulate changes in social policy. Research showing that children from

Meet First-Time Parents

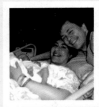

Carolyn and Bob Landers
Dallas, Texas
New parents

What is the biggest question that you have about your child's future and development?
We wonder what we can do on a daily basis that will enhance our son's development. We want to offer a variety of new experiences without creating a rigid schedule or "to do" list for him. It seems like children get overcommitted and spread very thin at an early age—it seems to start shortly after birth. But we also worry we'll miss something that everyone else is doing that gives their child an advantage, and as a result, our son will be behind in some way. It's all of the short-term things that can have very long-term consequences that concern us.

What are the main hopes and worries you have for your child?
Above everything, we wish good health for our son. That is the foundation that makes everything else possible. We also hope to impart to him at an early age a love of learning and an understanding of the importance of a good education that ultimately results in a fulfilling career. We also hope that he'll find his own path (even if it's different from our vision) so he'll know real happiness and be true to himself. We hope to give him a happy childhood full of wonderful memories and the knowledge that he is very loved and cherished. This will hopefully give him a sense of self-worth and confidence and help him make his own decisions and develop true friendships. A friend sent a beautiful blessing which sums it up nicely: "May love be the first awareness of Connor's life, and the last. And may all that lies between be filled with discovering its many faces."

Our son's personal safety and health are our main worries. Childhood is a more dangerous time now than it was for both of us. We didn't worry (much) about abduction, molestation, weapons at school, et cetera. I hope we can give him enough information to be aware and to protect himself without taking away the innocence of his childhood or making him afraid of everyone he meets.

Where will you go for answers to practical questions about raising your child?
We'll go mainly to family and friends who have children. We'll do a lot of reading, too, but there's nothing like those who have gone before for getting the real scoop about what to expect and how to solve problems. I know we'll rely on our gut instincts a lot, too. ■

thinking
OF JENNIFER

◄ What similarities do you see between Jennifer's concerns and the concerns these first-time parents are having? What would you say to reassure these parents?

disadvantaged families fared poorly in school, for example, stimulated the creation of Project Head Start, an enrichment program designed to give disadvantaged preschoolers the skills they will need in the classroom. Second, after public policies and programs have come into being, child development researchers play an important role in evaluating their effectiveness.

Child health, welfare programs, child and foster care, juvenile delinquency, and educational reform are just a few of the social policy areas that relate directly to child development. Every chapter of this textbook includes a Social Policy Perspectives box that highlights an important social policy issue relevant for that chapter. For this chapter, take a look at the Social Policy Perspective box called "Every Day in America." As you will see, our nation needs to do much more to protect the lives and healthy development of children.

A Social Policy PERSPECTIVE...

Every Day in America

Every day in the United States,

- 5 children or adolescents commit suicide
- 9 children or adolescents are victims of homicide
- 34 children or adolescents die from accidents
- 77 babies die
- 180 children are arrested for violent crimes
- 401 babies are born to mothers who had late or no prenatal care
- 825 babies are born low in birth weight (weighing less than 5½ pounds)
- 1,310 babies are born without health insurance
- 1,329 babies are born to teen mothers
- 2,019 babies are born into poverty

- 2,861 teens drop out of high school
- 3,585 babies are born to unwed mothers
- 4,248 children are arrested
- 7,883 children are reported abused or neglected
- 9.2 million children are without health insurance
- 11.6 million children live in poverty

Think about how these statistics are reflected in the city, neighborhood, or area where you live. Which of these problems is most significant in your area? Why do you think these problems exist? Have welfare reforms or any other changes in social policy been effective? What government programs, policies, or laws would you enact to address these problems?

SOURCE: Data from Children's Defense Fund (2002a). ∎

■ **Psychology, Counseling, Education, and Other Uses.** Child development research also has many practical uses in therapeutic, educational, and other settings. Child therapists and counselors need to have a thorough understanding of the normal (and abnormal) pathways that child development can take. They must be able to tailor their interventions and therapy techniques to the developmental needs of the individual child. Teachers need to understand development so they can help all children maximize their learning potential. It is important that teachers know how children learn new information, how they work independently and in groups, and how they relate with friends and peers. Day care providers, nurses, camp counselors, and anyone else who works professionally with children can benefit by studying what researchers have learned about children and their development.

Careers Related to Children

Another feature you will encounter in each chapter is a box called A Professional Perspective in which we present an interview with a professional who works with children. For this chapter, see the Professional Perspective box "Career Focus: Meet a Child Social Worker." A great many career opportunities allow you to work with children or on behalf of children. In *therapeutic settings,* psychiatrists, clinical psychologists, school psychologists, counselors, and clinical social workers help children who suffer from mental illness or from the abuse or stress they face in life. *Social service agencies* also employ people to work with children—for example, in domestic violence shelters, at boys and girls clubs, in halfway houses, and in criminal justice or delinquency programs. *Teachers* work on a daily basis with children, and *day care providers* help families manage the balance between work and child care. Many *corporations* also hire people to work with children or to help inform the corporation about children. Marketing, advertising, and the development of children's products are a few examples of business applications. *Government agencies* hire people trained in child development to direct, manage, or supervise projects designed to help children and families. And of course, to keep

YOUR PERSPECTIVE NOTES

When you vote in elections, do you consider the impact of social policy on children's lives? What political issues now being debated in your local area might have an impact on children?

Pamela Talbot
Flat Rock, Michigan

Social worker who evaluates foster homes for licensing in the state of Michigan

Career Focus: Meet a Child Social Worker

What do you do in your work to help children and families?
I review the financial stability, safety, and suitability of homes of people who want to be foster parents. This involves social history interviews, getting state and local criminal clearances and medical clearances, then making a recommendation as to whether the person should receive a foster care license. I also provide training to potential foster parents to prepare them for the children, birth parents, court system, and our agency. I investigate allegations of abuse, neglect, or rule non-compliance and make a recommendation about what to do if the allegation is true.

What aspects of child development do you use in your work?
I use information on family structures, discipline, abuse and neglect, separation and attachment, and the effects of drug and alcohol abuse as I train prospective foster parents, with a strong emphasis on discipline. We also address how all of the factors within the family affect the child's stage of development so foster parents can be better prepared to deal with the children's behaviors and needs. Most foster children are not at an average stage of development, because of environmental, educational and/or emotional neglect and physical abuse. Many people expect the children to adjust to their home with no problems and be just like their kids were. They don't understand the life the kids were exposed to.

From what you see, what is the most important problem faced by children and families?
Drug and alcohol abuse, physical abuse, and neglect. Kids come into care for a lot of different reasons, usually more than one. It's not uncommon for a drug-addicted parent to be physically abusing a child and leaving them home alone. Educational and environmental neglect are also issues, as the kids aren't going to school and the house is unsafe (for example, with excessive roaches, no heat or lights, and no furniture). Sexual abuse is also fairly common, but not nearly as common as the other areas.

What advice do you have for students who are considering a career in your field?
First you have to clear up any unresolved personal issues. A lot of people are not able to work effectively with all parties involved because of biases, and some even end up in therapy themselves. Also, you can't personalize the things that are going on, and you can't expect to save the world. But it is very rewarding when you are able to make that difference! To know that you have helped to break the cycle and hopefully made the future better for many generations is wonderful. It's just a long road to get there.

What education and training is needed to work in your area?
You need at least a bachelor's degree in a related area (social work, psychology, child development, etc.). State-mandated training (in Michigan, about 24 hours for caseworkers and 16 hours for licensing workers) and ongoing yearly training is required, and there is also training at the agency. ■

the field up to date, *scientists and researchers* conduct new studies and develop and test new theories of child development. Research scientists provide the database that all of the other professionals can use to decide how best to help children.

In this chapter we introduced the field of child development. We described the basic issues and theories that have shaped the field, and we explained how researchers use the scientific method to study child development. In the remaining chapters you will learn about many of the important trends and research findings in this exciting field. Along the way you will discover many interesting things that can guide your work with children—and can also, as a bonus, help you understand your own development.

LET'S REVIEW . . .

1. Research findings about child development have been used:
   a. to offer practical advice to parents about raising children.
   b. to stimulate new laws, government regulations, and other social policies.
   c. to help professionals work with children in therapeutic, educational, and other settings.
   d. all of the above.

2. Which book has been used the most widely as a practical guide to help parents raise children?
   a. *Psychological Care of Infant and Child,* by John Watson
   b. *Infancy and Human Growth,* by Arnold Gesell
   c. *Baby and Child Care,* by Benjamin Spock
   d. *How to Parent So Children Will Learn,* by Sylvia Rimm

3. **True or False:** Child development researchers are often responsible for evaluating how changes in social policy affect children.

4. **True or False:** People interested in working with children, or working to improve the lives of children, can find employment in social service agencies, government agencies, and many corporations.

Answers: 1. d, 2. c, 3. T, 4. T

Students: Now that you have finished the chapter, look back to the questions we posed in the "A Perspective to Think About" scenario at the beginning. You should be able to use a large amount of the chapter material to answer the questions. Use the "Thinking Of" notes in the margin as a guide to help you. After you have considered your own answers, check them against the "Thinking Back" summary that follows.

thinking
BACK TO JENNIFER

Now that you have studied this chapter, you should be able to give Jennifer some general guidance on raising her children, answer the questions she had, and explain how researchers study child development. Compare your thoughts to the following comments.

Child development researchers study physical, cognitive, and social development in children and adolescents. They also study how nature and nurture interact to influence development. Because Jennifer's son and daughter share a similar genetic heritage, their paths of development will probably be similar. Their genes do differ, however, and their environmental experiences will also differ, so their developmental paths will not be identical.

Jennifer can use several of the major developmental theories to guide her parenting. For example, behaviorism can help her learn to reinforce appropriate behaviors in her children. Social learning theory can give Jennifer ideas on modeling appropriate behavior for her children to imitate. She can also be mindful of how negative fears and anxieties can be classically conditioned. With an awareness of psychoanalytic theories, Jennifer can encourage positive ego development in her children by establishing trust in infancy and allowing her children to express their autonomy, initiative, and industry. Jennifer can draw on ecological systems theory to understand how her neighborhood, schools, family and friendship networks, ethnic background, and other elements of the larger social systems affect her children's development.

CHAPTER SUMMARY

What aspects of development does the field of child development investigate? What are the main forces that drive development?

Child development is a multidisciplinary field that studies physical, cognitive, and social development in children and adolescents. Both nature (including biology and genetics) and nurture (including the environment, parents, and culture) influence development.

What is a theory, and why are theories useful?

A theory is an explanation of how the facts fit together. Theories provide frameworks that summarize the facts as currently known, allow prediction of future behavior and events, provide guidance, stimulate new research and discoveries, and give researchers filters for identifying relevant information and relationships.

Which theories have had the most influence on the field of child development throughout its history?

The psychoanalytic theories of Sigmund Freud and Erik Erikson focused, respectively, on unconscious processes and the development of ego identity. Freud described five stages of personality development that involved the id, ego, and superego. Erikson described eight stages of identity development. Behavioral theories focused on observable behaviors and environmental conditions. Classical conditioning theories (Ivan Pavlov and John Watson) described how organisms learn reflexive responses, and the theory of operant conditioning (B. F. Skinner) described how reinforcement and punishment affect behavior. Albert Bandura's social learning theory emphasized imitation and modeling of behavior. Jean Piaget's cognitive developmental theory proposed that children actively construct and adapt their own structures of thought and logic through four stages of cognitive growth. Lev Vygotsky described how the internalization of language brings the culture's psychological tools to the developing minds of children. Ethologists study the adaptive and survival values of behaviors, and neuropsychologists use modern technology to study the structure and function of the brain and nervous system. Urie Bronfenbrenner's ecological systems theory identifies layers of systems that influence the child, from the child's interaction with immediate family members to the larger context of culture and society. Other dynamic systems theories use math and physics models to understand the complex systems that affect child development.

What are descriptive research methods, and how do they help us understand development?

Descriptive research methods include observation, self-reports, and case studies. The goal of descriptive methods is to provide information and describe some aspect of development. These methods help researchers gather information and develop hypotheses, but they do not answer questions about relationships among variables.

What is the correlational research method, and what are its main strengths and weaknesses?

With the correlational method, researchers measure the degree to which two or more variables are related or associated. Correlation is especially useful in situations in which it would be unethical to manipulate an independent variable experimentally (e.g., to investigate the effects of prenatal alcohol consumption on the development of the fetus). This method also can be used to describe the complex array of interactions among many variables. Its main weakness is that correlation alone does not prove causation.

What is the experimental research method, and what are its main strengths and weaknesses?

With the experimental method, researchers manipulate an independent variable to test its effect on a dependent variable. The main strength of experimentation is that, if conducted properly, experiments can determine cause-and-effect relationships. The main weakness is that it would be unethical to manipulate many of the variables that are of interest in child development. We cannot randomly assign families to live in poverty, children to suffer abusive forms of punishment, or women to use alcohol or drugs during pregnancy, for example. To investigate these types of situations, researchers usually use correlational methods.

What methods do researchers use to assess development, and what are these methods' main strengths and weaknesses?

The cross-sectional method compares groups of children of different ages against one another at the same point in time. With the longitudinal method, researchers follow the same children across time and retest or evaluate them as they age. The longitudinal method provides a more direct test of development, but it can be very time-consuming and is compromised when participants drop out of the study. The cross-sectional method is more efficient, and participants are less likely to drop out, but cohort effects can be a problem when the groups differ substantially in age. Hybrid designs try to use the strengths of both types of methods.

What steps must researchers take to protect the rights and privacy of children who participate in their studies?

All researchers must get approval for their studies from an institutional review board. The IRB evaluates proposals to determine if the potential benefits outweigh the risks. Researchers must use non-harmful procedures, obtain informed consent from participants (and from parents or guardians of minor participants), report unforeseen consequences, protect the privacy of information, and consider the implications of their research.

What are some of the areas of practical application for child development research and theory?

The knowledge provided by child development research can help people deal with family and parenting concerns. It also has important implications for all social policy involving children. It also improves the services offered to children in therapeutic, educational, and medical settings.

What are some careers related to children?

A wide variety of careers involve work with children. Therapy, social service, education, and day care are examples of settings that involve direct work with children and families. Corporations and government agencies hire people to develop products or programs that affect children. Scientists and researchers investigate child development and evaluate the impact that social policies have on children and families.

KEY TERMS

behavior genetics (5)

behaviorism (12)

child development (2)

classical conditioning (12)

cognitive development (4)

cognitive developmental
  theory (13)

correlational method (23)

cross-sectional method (28)

descriptive methods (21)

dynamic systems theories (19)

ecological systems theory (17)

ethology (15)

experimental method (26)

information-processing
  approach (15)

longitudinal method (28)

nature (4)

neuropsychology (16)

nurture (4)

operant conditioning (13)

physical development (3)

psychoanalytic theories (7)

social development (4)

social learning (13)

social policy (32)

sociocultural theory (14)

theory (7)

Chapter 2

Genes and Heredity

CHAPTER PREVIEW

A PERSPECTIVE TO think ABOUT

"Daniel and Teri wonder if their baby will grow up to be more like them or more like his biological parents."

Daniel and Teri have been married for 6 years and have tried desperately to have their own baby. Two years ago Teri found out that she is not able to conceive children, so she and Daniel decided to try to adopt a baby. Last month their adoption came through, and they now have a baby boy! He is perfectly healthy and has a huge smile, and Daniel and Teri are showering him with love and attention. Because the adoption agency keeps adoption information confidential, Daniel and Teri don't have much information about the baby's background. They know only that he came from a teenage single mother who gave the baby up so she could go back to school. Someday, Daniel and Teri may be able to meet the baby's biological mother, if both sides agree to meet. Until then, Daniel and Teri wonder if their baby will grow up to be more like them or more like his biological parents.

Already they can see that their baby's physical features—his traits—will be different from theirs. The baby has blue eyes and light-colored hair, whereas Daniel and Teri both have brown eyes and darker hair. But what about the baby's psychological features? Will his temperament, personality, and level of intelligence resemble Daniel and Teri's? Or will he grow up to be more like his biological parents in these characteristics? What influence will Daniel and Teri have on the development of their baby?

As you read through this chapter, think about the information from Daniel and Teri's perspective. What would you tell Daniel and Teri to help them understand how their new baby will be influenced by the nurturing care that they provide and by the genes inherited from his biological parents? What roles will both nature and nurture play in determining the baby's developing temperament, personality, and intelligence? After studying this chapter, you should be able to give Daniel and Teri a relatively detailed and concrete explanation of how genetics and the environment will influence their baby's physical and psychological traits. You should be able to use at least a dozen specific concepts in your answer.

 As you read this chapter, look for the questions that ask you to think about what you're learning from Daniel and Teri's perspective.

YOUR
PERSPECTIVE
NOTES

To what degree do you believe that your level of intelligence was inherited versus learned? What about the basic components of your personality? In general, do you believe that traits like these are more inherited or more learned? Why do you believe this?

The questions Daniel and Teri face cut to the very core of child development research. How much of a child's behavior, personality, intellectual functioning, and other characteristics depends on genes inherited from the child's biological parents? How much are these characteristics learned or modified from experiences with the parents who raise the child or with teachers, peers, and other elements of the environment? In Chapter 1 we introduced this as the nature–nurture question—a question that philosophers have debated for centuries and that is still one of the most fundamental questions scientists research today. We begin this second chapter by reviewing what we know about genes, chromosomes, cell division, and human reproduction. Understanding these basic biological structures and processes will help you appreciate human inheritance and the important interactions between genes and the environment.

Genes and Human Reproduction

Each one of us began as a single cell—a fertilized egg cell. By the time we reach adulthood, that cell has multiplied into several trillions of cells. Genes are molecules that govern the structure and function of every cell in the body. They dictate how our cells coordinate to form the basic tissues that we need. These genes exist in every cell in the body. We inherit some of these genes from our mother and some from our father, but the combination of genes that govern our cells is unique to each one of us and distinguishes us from all other human beings. What are genes, and how are they passed down from one generation to the next?

As you study this section, ask yourself these questions:

- What are chromosomes, DNA, and genes? How are these structures different, and how do they function to determine our genetic codes?
- What is the Human Genome Project? What are the potential benefits of the project? What are the potential dangers?
- What is the difference between mitosis and meiosis? How do these processes ensure that every cell in our body has the same genes and that each person inherits genes that are different from everyone else's?
- What is the difference between identical and nonidentical twins?

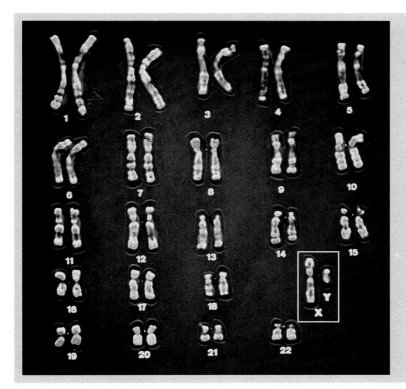

FIGURE 2.1 Karyotype Showing 46 Paired Chromosomes
In this karyotype (or picture of chromosomes), there are 22 similar pairs and 1 with different X and Y chromosomes (the boxed pair).

Genes and the Magical Four-Letter Code

Inside the nucleus of most any cell in the human body, there are 46 chromosomes. **Chromosomes** are structures made of long strands of deoxyribonucleic acid (DNA). Chromosomes operate in pairs, so we have 23 pairs of chromosomes, as you can see in Figure 2.1. Twenty-two of the pairs are the same across males and females, and these are called *autosomes*. The remaining pair are the *sex chromosomes,* and they differ across the sexes. Females have two X chromosomes and males have one X and one Y chromosome.

As Watson and Crick (1953) first discovered, **DNA** consists of two strands of sugar and phosphate molecules that twist around each other like a spiral staircase. In Figure 2.2 you can see the staircase and the "steps" that connect the two sides. The steps are made out of four different varieties of a *nucleotide base* molecule. The four varieties are adenine (A), thymine (T), guanine (G), and cytosine (C). The different nucleotide bases on one side of the staircase pair with specific bases on the other side to form each step. As you can see in the figure, the DNA strand is simply a repeating series of these connecting steps or base pairs. Also notice that *adenine always pairs with thymine, and guanine always pairs with cytosine.* Thus, if you have a sequence of ACCACT on one side of the staircase, the complementary sequence on the other side will be TGGTGA.

Within the 46 chromosomes in each human cell, there are approximately 3 billion pairs of nucleotide bases (Human Genome Program, 1992, 2001). It is the specific sequence of these base pairs that makes up our *genetic code.* The entire code is divided up into smaller pieces called *genes.* A **gene** is a segment of the DNA strand that provides an instruction for a particular structure, function, or trait. There are approximately 30,000 genes aligned along the 46 chromosomes in each human cell. It is also important to note that only about 10 percent of the nucleotide base pairs actually provide active instructions. Some of the inactive sequences play a role in cell division, but the function of many of the remaining sequences is not yet known.

chromosomes

Strands of deoxyribonucleic acid (DNA) molecules that contain the genetic codes.

DNA

Two strands that twist around each other like a spiral staircase. Connected by a series of nucleotide bases (adenine, thymine, guanine, and cytosine).

gene

A segment of DNA that provides an instruction for a particular structure, function, or trait.

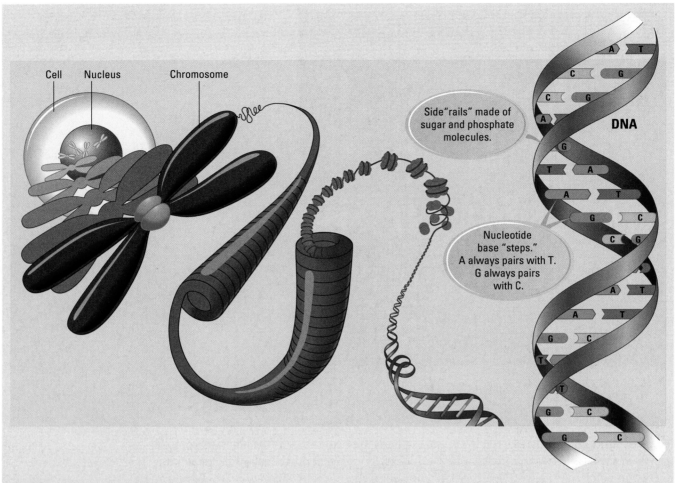

Cell Nucleus Chromosome

Side "rails" made of sugar and phosphate molecules.

DNA

Nucleotide base "steps." A always pairs with T. G always pairs with C.

FIGURE 2.2 Chromosomes, DNA, and Genes

The nucleus of each cell contains the chromosomes. Chromosomes are made up of tightly twisted strands of DNA. The DNA is constructed like a staircase, with each side of the staircase connected by "steps" made of pairs of nucleotide bases. Adenine (A) always pairs with thymine (T), and guanine (G) always pairs with cytosine (C). Genes are shorter segments of chromosomal DNA, usually several thousand base pairs in length.

Finding specific genes and discovering their functions are hugely complicated tasks. For example, Figure 2.3 shows part of the sequence of bases on one side of the DNA strand that makes up just one of the genes related to one form of mental retardation. This form of mental retardation is associated with fragile-X syndrome, a genetic disorder we'll discuss later in the chapter. This particular gene contains 39,057 bases. And remember, this is only one side of the DNA strand! To complete the picture, you need to add the complementary strand where each A connects to a T, each G to a C, and so on, to result in 39,057 base *pairs*. Can you imagine how complicated it must be to decode this type of sequence for every human gene?

On June 26, 2000, President Clinton gathered with a group of leading scientists to announce a historic milestone: A working draft of the human genome was now complete (Human Genome Program, 2000)! A *genome* is the set of genes that provides the instructions for an entire organism. Perhaps you have heard about the **Human Genome Project**, a multinational effort among governments and scientists to map the order of every nucleotide base (AGCT) and locate the position of every gene in the human genome. This project began in

Human Genome Project

A multinational effort by governments and scientists to map the 3 billion nucleotide bases and 30,000 genes contained in human chromosomes.

```
GGCGTGCGGCAGCGCGGCGGCGGCGGCGGCGGCGGCGGCGGCGGCGGAGGCGGCGGCGGCGGCGGCGGCGGCG
GCGGCTGGGCCTCGAGCGCCCGCAGCCCACCTCTCGGGGGCGGGCTCCCGGCGCTAGCAGGGCTGAAGAG
AAGATGGAGGAGCTGGTGGTGGAAGTGCGGGGCTCCAATGGCGCTTTCTACAAGGTACTTGGCTCTAGGG
CAGGCCCCATCTTCGCCCTTCCTTCCCTCCCTTTTCTTCTTGGTGTCGGCGGGAGGCAGGCCCGGGGCCC
TCTTCCCGAGCACCGCGCCTGGGTGCCAGGGCACGCTCGGCGGGATGTTGTTGGGAGGGAAGGACTGGAC
TTGGGGCCTGTTGGAAGCCCCTCTCCGACTCCGAGAGGCCCTAGCGCCTATCGAAATGAGAGACCAGCGA
GGAGAGGGTTCTCTTTCGGCGCCGAGCCCCGCCGGGGTGAGCTGGGGATGGGCGAGGGCCGGCGGCAGGT
ACTAGAGCCGGGCGGGAAGGGCCGAAATCGGCGCTAAGTGACGGCGATGGCTTATTCCCCCTTTCCTAAA
CATCATCTCCCAGCGGGATCCGGGCCTGTCGTGTGGGTAGTTGTGGAGGAGCGGGGGGGCGCTTCAGCCGG
GCCGCCTCCTGCAGCGCCAAGAGGGCTTCAGGTCTCCTTTGGCTTCTCTTTCCGGTCTAGCATTGGGAC
TTCGGAGAGCTCCACTGTTCTGGGCGAGGGCTGTGAAGAAAGAGTAGTAAGAAGCGGTAGTCGGCACCAA
ATCACAATGGCAACTGATTTTTAGTGGCTTCTCTCTTTGTGGATTTCGGAGGAGATTTTAGATCCAAAAGTT
TCAGGAAGACCCTAACATGGCCCAGCAGTGCATTGAAGAAGTTGATCATCGTGAATATTCGCGTCCCCCT
TTTTGTTAAACGGGGTAAATTCAGGAATGCACATGCTTCAGCGTCTAAAACCATTAGCAGCGCTGCTACT
TAAAAATTGTGTGTGTGTGTTTAAGTTTCCAAAGACCTAAATATATGCCATGAAACTTCAGGTAATTAAC
TGAGAGTATATTATTACTAGGGCATTTTTTTTTTTTAACTGAGCGAAAATATTTTTGTGCCCCTAAGAACTT
GACCACATTTCCTTTGAATTTGTGGTGTTGCAGTGGACTGAATTGTTGAGGCTTTATATAGGCATTCATG
GGTTTACTGTGCTTTTTAAAGTTACACCATTGCAGATCAACTAACACCTTTCAGTTTTAAAAGGAAGATT
TACAAATTTGATGTAGCAGTAGTGCGTTTGTTGGTATGTAGGTGCTGTATAAATTCATCTATAAATTCTC
ATTTCCTTTTGAATGTCTATAACCTCTTTCAATAATATCCCACCTTACTACAGTATTTTGGCAATAGAAG
GTGCGTGTGGAAGGAAGGCTGGAAAATAGCTATTAGCAGTGTCCAACACAATTCTTAAATGTATTGTAGA
ATGGCTTGAATGTTTCAGACAGGACACGTTTGGCTATAGGAAAATAAACAATTGACTTTATTCTGTGTTT
ACCAATTTTATGAAGACATTTGGAGATCAGTATATTTCATAAATGAGTAAAGTATGTAAACTGTTCCATA
CTTTGAGCACAAAGATAAAGCCTTTTGCTGTAAAAGGAGGCAAAAGGTAACCCCGCGTTTATGTTCTTAA
CAGTCTCATGAATATGAAATTGTTTCAGTTGACTCTGCAGTCAAAATTTTAATTTCATTGATTTTATTGA
TCCATAATTTCTTCTGGTGAGTTTGCGTAGAATCGTTCACGGTCCTAGATTAGTGGTTTTGGTCACTAGA
TTTCTGGCACTAATAACTATAATACATATACATATATATGTGTGAGTAACGGCTAATGGTTAGGCAAGAT
TTTGATTGACCTGTGATATAAACTTAGATTGGATGCCACTAAAGTTTGCTTATCACAGAGGGCAAGTAGC
ACATTATGGCCTTGAAGTACTTATTGTTCTCTTCCAGCAACTTATGATTTGCTCCAGTGATTTTGCTTGC
ACACTGACTGGAATATAAGAAATGCCTTCTATTTTTGCTATTAATTCCCTCCTTTTTTGTTTTGTTTTGT
AACGAAGTTGTTTAACTTGAAGGTGAATGAAGAATAGGTTGGTTGCCCCTTAGTTCCCTGAGGAGAAATG
TTAATACTTGAACAAGTGTGTGTCAGACAAATTGCTGTTATGTTTATTTAATTAAGTTTGATTTCTAAGA
AAATCTCAAATGGTCTGCACTGATGGAAGAACAGTTTCTGTAACAAAAAAGCTTGAAATTTTTATATGAC
TTATAATACTGCTGTGAGTTTTAAAAGTAAAGCAAAAGTAAACTGAGTTGCTTGTCCAGTGGGGATGGACA
GGAAAGATGTGAAATAAAAACCAATGAAAAATGAACTGCTGTGGAGAAGTGTTACATTTATGGAAAAAGA
AATAGGAACCTTGTTCATCAAATTGATAGAAAAGCTTTTAAAACTAAACAAATCAAACAACTTGAGTATA
ATGGAATTCAGACTTTGATTTGCCTAACATAACCACCATATTTGCAAGGACAGCTCTCTATCTTCTGGTG
TTTATTCTTAAAAAACTTAAAAGTTAGATTTAGCGATCACCAGAGCCACTACTTTTATGCTTAGGTATTTG
TTTGACTTAGAAAAAATTGGTCACGTGTACCACTTTATAGTGCCCTGCAGGTGTTAAGTATGTGAAGGCAC
TTTGACTTACACCTCATAAAATCTTTACAAAGTATTTTCTAAATGAATAATGATGAAATAAAGTCTTTAT
TCTAGGTGCATCTGCCCCACATAATTTGTTTTCTTTGGACTAGAAGTTTTGATGTGTTGAGAATGGTAAT
GAATTAACTCCATTTTAAATGTAGAATGCGTATCACTCCAATATGAATGCCCTAATGAATCCTAAGATTT
GTAGGTTTTGTGTACTAGTATGAAAATTACTAAAGATGGAAAAATCACATGTTGGAGACATAAGATACAA
ACCTTTTTGTTTTCTGAAAATACAACCTCTGATTTCTGATTCCTTGTTGTAATATGGTGTAATTATACTA
GATTGTAATTTTGTTGTTAGATTATACTTTTTTTAAGTTCAGTGTTTGAGGACAGACTTTCATTTGGTTAG
TAGTATTATGGCAGCTAGCAGCTAAATATGATAAAGTGTACAATCAAAAAGGATATTTTTAATGAAGATAT
TAGTGGTCTAACATGTCATTTCAGATACATAGCTGAAATGTAGTAAAATCAGTTTTACTACAAATAAACT
TGCATAAGGTTTATAAATTTATAAGTTTATAAATCAACTTGGGTAAAGTGTAAATAAACTTGCACTCGTG
GTTTCTCTGAAGTCTCCTGAGCTAACTTTGCATAAAGGTGTTATTCTGTACTTCGAGGAAGTGAATTATT
GGGGTCAACCACATTTTTTTTCCTTCCTACAGTCTGATTGCCCTTTTTAGTTTTTAGGATCTTTGTGGCT
GCATCATTTTTCCCCTTTTGAACTGTGCATTTTCTAACCCCATACTTAAATATTCTCATAACCTCCAAAT
TATTAATTAGATGCAACATTCAGTGGTATATTACTGGAGTTTCTGATTTCTGCCCACTATAGGAATGTGC
TTCCTGAGAAGATTGGGATCGTGATTATAATAATAGTTAACAGGGGATGAGTACTTTCTAGGTGCCAGGC
ACTGTTCTCTCTGATACTTTATTTGATGTATTGTTGTTATTCCCATTCTTTAAATGATGCACAGAGAGGT
TAGGTAAGTGACTTACTACCAAGTGTCAGGGCCATTAAGGGTCAGGATTCTGAATTCCTGAAATGATGAA
ATTTAGCTTGAAGAAATTGGTTTGATTTCCTGCTTAGTTTTTCAATTTCATGGTGGT . . .
```

FIGURE 2.3 One-Tenth of the Sequence of Nucleotide Bases Needed to Form One of the Genes Related to Fragile-X Mental Retardation

The total sequence contains 39,057 bases, and this represents only one side of the DNA strand. Each of these bases would be paired with its complementary mate on the second strand, resulting in 39,057 base *pairs* for the gene.

Note: This is 3,906 bases, approximately one-tenth of the gene code for FMRI1 on Chromosome X.

Source: National Center for Biotechnology Information. (2003). LocusLink: FMRI1: Fragile-X Mental Retardation 1, Locus ID: 2332. Retrieved August 20, 2003, from www.ncbi.nlm.nih.gov/entrez/viewer.fcgi?val=NT_011681.12&from=3380196&to=3419252&txt=on&view=fasta.

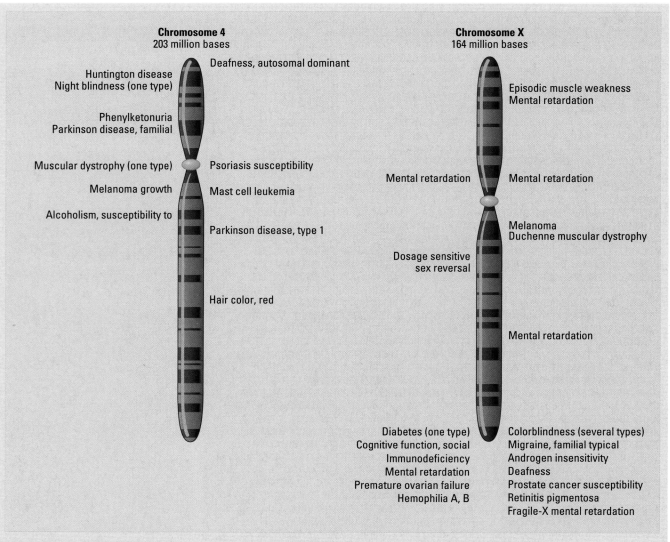

FIGURE 2.4 Human Chromosomes 4 and X Showing a Few of the Many Thousands of Gene Locations That Have Been Identified

Later in the chapter, we will discuss Huntington disease (on chromosome 4) and sex-linked genes (on X). For a more complete catalog, see McKusick (1998) or the online version that is kept up to date through the Genome Data Base at Johns Hopkins University.

Source: U.S. Department of Energy. (2003). Human Genome Project Information website. Retrieved March 20, 2003, from www.ornl.gov/TechResources/Human_Genome/posters/chromosome.

1990 and has been the most ambitious and technically challenging project ever undertaken by scientists. Scientists now have a rough map of the order of 3 billion nucleotide bases in the human genome, but they still don't know what all of the base sequences mean. Scientists still need to determine which sequences of nucleotide bases define most of our 30,000 genes. Figure 2.4 lists a few of the many thousands of genes that have been located on specific chromosomes so far. Researchers are still working hard to identify our remaining genes.

Over the coming decades, the impact of the Human Genome Project will be staggering. When the project is complete, scientists will know the genetic markers for every disease that can be inherited. This information may then help save or prolong millions of lives. For example, if hemophilia runs in your family, you will be able to take a genetic test to find out if you carry the gene (marked in Figure 2.4) associated with this disease. If you do carry the gene, you will know to work with your physician. In addition, physicians might be able to use gene therapy to alter some of your cells' genetic functions. What if they could give you an injection of healthy genes to counteract the destructive effects of disease genes in your body or replace destructive genes entirely? Or what if they could selectively turn off the function of disease genes, preventing you from developing the diseases in the first place?

Already, parents can select the sex of embryos by using certain reproductive technologies. Clinicians can grow embryos in test tubes using the mother's eggs and the father's sperm. The embryos with the preferred set of sex chromosomes (XX for a female or XY for a male) can then be implanted in the mother's uterus. Embryos carrying disease genes can be selected out in a similar manner. Embryos conceived by more "natural" means can also be tested while they are in the mother's womb. Based on the results, couples can decide whether to abort an embryo or allow it to develop until birth. In the future, couples could have their embryos tested for a variety of genetically based diseases and could select the healthiest embryos to carry to birth. Coming generations could potentially escape the devastating effects of a large number of genetically determined diseases.

But where do we draw the line? As you can see, there are profound moral questions in this area that will test our abilities to make sound ethical decisions. Should we selectively abort embryos simply because they are not the sex that we want? And inheriting a disease gene usually just gives us the tendency to develop the disease at some time in our life. It does not guarantee that we will develop the disease, given that the onset of many diseases can depend on additional genetic changes, diet, exposure to risk factors, and other environmental factors. Should parents selectively abort or discard embryos that have *tendencies* toward certain diseases? And how bad does a disease need to be to allow selective abortion? Maybe we can agree that future generations should be spared from diseases that lead to early and painful deaths, but what about diseases—such as colon cancer or Alzheimer's—that tend to emerge late in life? And what about embryos carrying other traits that are not desirable? What if an embryo has genes related to low intelligence or a violent personality? Remember, too, that genetic tests are not foolproof. Will society be able to accept the possibility that some embryos will be aborted because they falsely test positive for a fatal disease? Our growing understanding of genetics raises exciting possibilities but also brings many complicated questions.

Another issue relates to the privacy of individuals after they have had genetic tests. To read more about privacy and ethics in genetic research, read the Social Policy Perspective box called "Protecting the Genetic Privacy of Citizens."

Human Reproduction and Cell Division

A new embryo is formed when a sperm cell from the father fertilizes an egg cell from the mother. When the sperm and egg cells join, chromosomes from the father and mother combine to give the embryo a unique combination of genes. The chromosome from the father has one version of a gene and the chromosome from the mother has another version of the same gene—these versions are called the **alleles** of a particular gene. The alleles determine the unique traits of each individual. It isn't always easy for this unique embryo to develop, however. A variety of problems can cause some couples to have difficulty conceiving babies. Low sperm count in the father and damage to the mother's reproductive system are two of the more common problems. In other situations, single individuals or gay or lesbian couples may want to have children, but they obviously cannot conceive without an opposite-sex parent. In all these cases, artificial insemination and the other alternative techniques described in Table 2.1 (p. 49) can help people conceive babies. To learn about one mother's experience with alternative techniques, read the Personal Perspective box, "Using Artificial Insemination" (p. 50).

YOUR PERSPECTIVE NOTES

Do you know anyone who used an "alternative" method of conception? If so, why do you believe they chose that particular method? How has it worked for them?

allele

An alternative version of a gene.

Protecting the Genetic Privacy of Citizens

Wouldn't it be helpful to know if you were carrying genes linked to a serious disease like diabetes, breast or prostate cancer, or heart disease? If you knew at a young age that you inherited the tendency to develop one or more of these diseases, you could alter your lifestyle to avoid the risk factors that might trigger the onset of the disease. With diet, exercise, and the early use of hypertension medication, for example, you might be able to avoid the heart attack that might otherwise have surprised you at age 48.

But what if your genetic predisposition were revealed to your employer or your health insurance company? Could you be fired from your job, or lose the next big promotion, because your employer was afraid you couldn't take the pressure of the work? Might future employers be reluctant to hire you for fear you would become sick or disabled? Could your health insurance company drop your coverage because it saw you as too great a risk? Would anyone give you health coverage?

These questions are at the center of a national debate about the privacy of genetic information. Even before the first draft of the human genome was complete, the U.S. government issued an order prohibiting federal agencies from using genetic information in any decisions to hire, promote, or dismiss workers.

Legislatures in 23 states quickly followed suit by passing laws against "genetic discrimination" in hiring (Uhlmann, 2000). How should genetic information be used, and what limits are necessary?

From one perspective, many employers and insurance companies already use health-risk assessments when considering applicants. How many times have you been asked about "preexisting conditions" or about your smoking and drinking habits? If cigarette smoking causes health problems, isn't it reasonable to ask smokers to pay more for their health insurance? Who pays more for car insurance, a 20-year-old single male or a 40-year-old married female? So we already classify people into groups based on relative risks. Lacking reliable ways to predict the future for any individual, we lump together all of those who share certain risk-related characteristics. Is it really fair to lump every 20-year-old male into a high-risk driving category? Some argue that genetic testing will allow us to assess risks in a way that is more fair, reliable, and objective. An editorial in the *New York Times* suggested that "as the potential for rational discrimination grows, the space for old-fashioned bias may shrink. Men and women will increasingly be judged not by the color of their skin but by the content of their chromosomes" (Sullivan, 2000).

Francis Collins, the head of the Human Genome Project in the United States, presents the other perspective. Collins predicts that the main legacy of the project will be the use of genetics to tailor and improve health care for individuals (Altman, 2000). But he warns that these benefits will not occur unless we pass effective laws to prevent organizations from denying individuals insurance or jobs based on genetic information. Many people already fear the potential negative effects of genetic testing. One telephone poll found that 63 percent of respondents would not want to take genetic tests if the results would be available to employers and insurers (Uhlmann, 2000). If people avoid genetic tests, they will lose the opportunity for early detection of risks. Millions may suffer or die from diseases that could have been prevented.

Even if every state passes laws preventing genetic discrimination, how effective will the laws be? Will companies have loopholes? Can we really force employers to overlook health risks when choosing among applicants? How will insurance companies remain profitable if they are forced to accept more risky and costly applicants? How do you think we should balance the need for early risk detection against other potential uses and misuses of genetic information? ■

So far, research on artificial insemination and in vitro fertilization does not indicate any particular developmental problems when children are conceived by these methods (Golombok, MacCallum, & Goodman, 2001; Golombok, MacCallum, Goodman, & Rutter, 2002). Children have been studied all the way into adolescence. They are well adjusted in their emotions, friendships, school performance, and other behaviors as rated by themselves, their parents, and their teachers. One difference that has been noted is that mothers who use these

TABLE 2.1 Alternative Techniques for Conception

Artificial insemination	• Sperm are collected from the father and then injected into the mother's reproductive system for fertilization. • If the father cannot produce viable sperm, sperm can be collected from another man or a sperm bank.
In vitro fertilization	• Several eggs are removed from the mother's ovary. • Eggs and sperm are placed in a petri dish for fertilization and initial cell divisions. • Several embryos (each with four to eight cells) are placed in the mother's uterus for further development.
Cryopreservation	• Sperm can be collected and frozen and are still viable if thawed several years later. • Embryos from in vitro fertilization can be frozen and thawed later to be placed in the mother's uterus.
Assisted in vivo fertilization	• Eggs are collected from the mother's ovary. • Sperm are collected from the father. • Eggs and sperm are injected into the fallopian tube of the mother for fertilization and further development.
Surrogate mothers	• In vitro fertilization is used to combine the sperm and egg from a father and mother. • The embryo is placed into the uterus of another woman (a surrogate), who then grows and delivers the baby for the biological parents.

Source: Adapted from Moore & Persaud (1998).

techniques tend to be more warm and involved with their children, compared to other mothers. This may reflect the difficulties they had conceiving children or their strong desire to overcome barriers in having their own children. Most of the parents who have been studied have not told their children about how they were conceived, and many say they regret not telling them. They worry that their children may hear the truth from another source, or they worry that it will only get more difficult for them to reveal the secret as time goes on.

To fully appreciate genetic inheritance, you need to understand a few facts about cell division. First, let's look at how genes are copied into every cell in your body. **Mitosis** ("copy division") occurs when a cell copies its own chromosomes, then divides to form two cells. During cell division the DNA material on each chromosome "unzips." The weak bonds between the nucleotide bases on opposite sides of the staircase break. Figure 2.5 (p. 51) diagrams how the DNA strand first unzips and then replicates itself. It forms two new strands that then link up with the two old strands and wrap up again to make two new chromosomes. When this process is completed, we have a duplicate set of chromosomes. If all goes well, an exact copy of the DNA goes into each cell. Mitosis occurs throughout the body as it grows, functions, and heals. Except in mutations—changes in the order of nucleotide bases—and sex cells, every cell in our body contains an exact copy of the 46 chromosomes that originated from our single fertilized egg cell.

One exception to mitosis occurs with our sex cells, or *gametes*. Gametes are the sperm and egg cells, and these specialized cells form through a different process called *meiosis*. **Meiosis** ("reduction division") occurs when sperm and egg cells form. Meiosis reduces the number of chromosomes in these cells from 46 to 23. The entire process of meiosis is shown in Figure 2.6 (pp. 52–53). At the beginning of meiosis, the cell duplicates all of its DNA. Each of the original 46 chromosomes unzips its DNA, doubles it to make a duplicate chromosome, and remains connected to the duplicate. Now the cell has 46 doubled chromosomes—each

mitosis

"Copy division," the type of cell division that occurs when chromosomes are copied into each new cell.

meiosis

"Reduction division," the type of cell division that occurs during the formation of gametes (sperm and eggs).

Using Artificial Insemination

Lea Adams
Derwood, Maryland
Mother of now 13-year-old conceived through artificial insemination

Why did you decide to use artificial insemination to have your baby?

I was an unmarried professional woman who was 30-something and making more money than most of the men I knew. Only certain agencies would allow single-parent adoption, and many of those would only place at-risk kids with single parents. That didn't make much sense to me, since I couldn't stay home to take care of a child with severe disabilities.

How did the procedure work? Did you want to know who the sperm donor was?

It was very straightforward for me because I got pregnant with the first insemination. I didn't use a sperm bank because the closest one was too far away. I convinced an infertility practice, which had a set of donors, to take me on as a patient. The procedure is like a typical internal exam, only they inject sperm into a little tube that is attached to a cap that fits over the cervix. That tube gets clamped and later you remove it. No big deal. I don't know who the donor was. I had a lawyer work with my doctor to make sure the donor could not track down my child or vice versa. I was fearful some stranger could show up and take away my baby, but I also wanted to protect the donor.

What have you told your child regarding the identity of his father?

I told him I don't know the identity of the donor. I have always been careful to talk about "donor" rather than "father." I have always answered any questions he's asked like, "How did you have a baby if you weren't married?" I told my son that I wanted him so much that I went to the doctor and the doctor gave me some sperm so I could get pregnant and have a baby . . . With the diversity of family types in the world today, I don't think he thinks there is anything unique about his situation. He doesn't tell his friends that he was artificially inseminated. He simply says he doesn't have a father.

What was the typical reaction to your decision from friends, family, and others?

I think most people viewed me as "brave." My divorced friends whose ex-husbands aren't cooperating parents have all said I "did it the right way." Sometimes when I was pregnant and morning sick, or exhausted with a sick baby, or frustrated with a petulant 3-year-old, and so on, people would say, "Well, you asked for it!" It's hard to say whether they were commenting on single parenthood or artificial insemination, but I always retorted, "You mean if I were married and became a parent, I wouldn't have asked for it?" The farther we move away from the point of conception, the fewer of those kinds of things I hear.

Do you have any advice for others considering artificial insemination?

If you want a baby and will love it and be a wonderful mother, then do whatever it will take. Don't focus on the donor or worry about it. Just enjoy your child! ■

thinking
OF DANIEL & TERI

Explain to Daniel and Teri how their son inherited a unique combination of chromosomes from his biological mother and father. What events happened during meiosis to ensure that the genetic material inherited by the baby was unique to him?

has twice the normal amount of DNA. The 46 doubled chromosomes pair up as usual to form 23 pairs of duplicate chromosomes. Each pair then exchanges genetic material in a process called *crossing over*. This will ensure a new and unique shuffling of genes coming from the mother and father. After crossing over, the chromosomes unpair; and as the cell starts to divide in two, one member of each pair, still connected to its duplicate, goes randomly into each new cell. Each of the two new cells then prepares to divide again, and now each chromosome separates from its duplicate. In this next division, each new cell has one version of the single chromosome. Four cells have formed from the original one. Now each sperm or egg contains 23 single-stranded chromosomes (Moore & Persaud, 1998). When a sperm and egg cell unite at fertilization, we again have a single cell with 46 chromosomes: 23 from the father's sperm and 23 from the mother's egg.

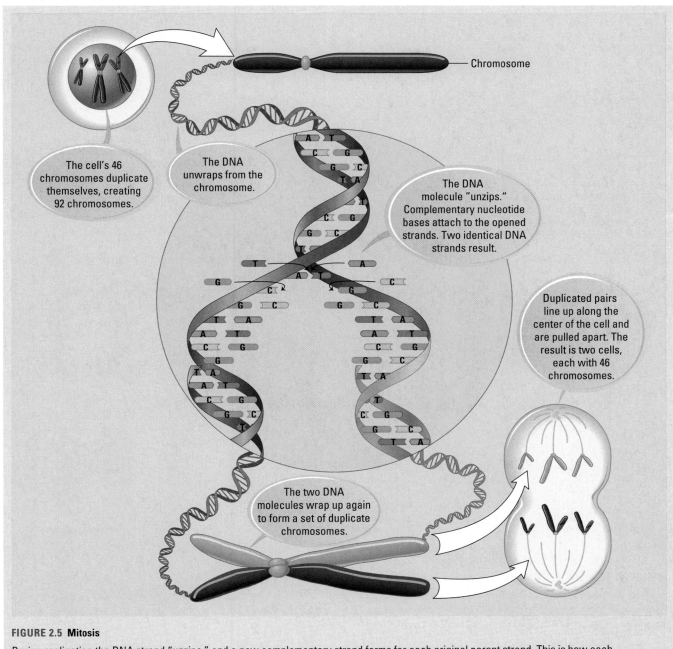

The cell's 46 chromosomes duplicate themselves, creating 92 chromosomes.

The DNA unwraps from the chromosome.

The DNA molecule "unzips." Complementary nucleotide bases attach to the opened strands. Two identical DNA strands result.

Duplicated pairs line up along the center of the cell and are pulled apart. The result is two cells, each with 46 chromosomes.

The two DNA molecules wrap up again to form a set of duplicate chromosomes.

Chromosome

FIGURE 2.5 Mitosis

During replication the DNA strand "unzips," and a new complementary strand forms for each original parent strand. This is how each chromosome duplicates itself (with its genetic code) during cell division.

Meiosis does two things. First, it reduces the number of chromosomes to 23 in each gamete so that the fertilized egg will have the normal number of 46 after conception. Second, it ensures diversity in the gene pool by swapping or crossing over genetic material across chromosome pairs and then randomly distributing chromosomes among the gametes. Even when the same parents have several children, the children will have plenty of genetic differences from one another, because they will not inherit the same combinations of chromosomes or genes.

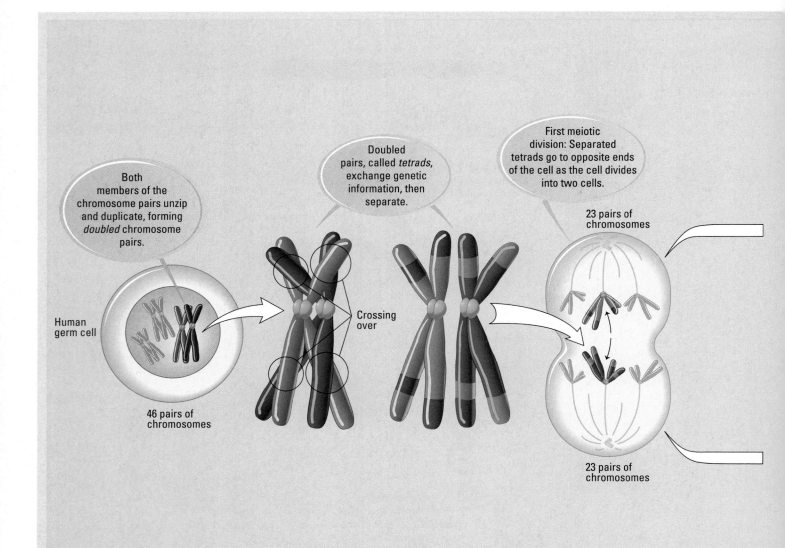

FIGURE 2.6 Meiosis

The gametes (sperm and egg cells) form via meiosis. Meiosis reduces the number of chromosomes from 46 to 23 in each cell. Crossing over of chromosome segments and random shuffling of chromosomes to cells ensure genetic diversity in the species. After fertilization, cell division occurs via mitosis, in which all 46 chromosomes are copied into each new cell.

monozygotic (MZ) twins

Identical twins. These twins form when one zygote divides to make two zygotes.

Identical twins are the one exception—these children do have the same genetic codes. *Identical twins* are twins who grow from the same fertilized egg (called a zygote). After the zygote begins dividing, it separates into two separate zygotes that will develop into two babies. Scientists refer to identical twins as **monozygotic (MZ) twins,** because they come from one zygote. Developing from the same fertilized egg, MZ twins have copies of each other's 46 chromosomes and therefore share the same genetic code. MZ twins are always the same sex and tend to be very similar in appearance. MZ twins occur in about 1 in every 260 births (this rate is virtually the same in all segments of the population), and MZ twins do not seem to run in families (Thompson, McInnes, & Willard, 1991).

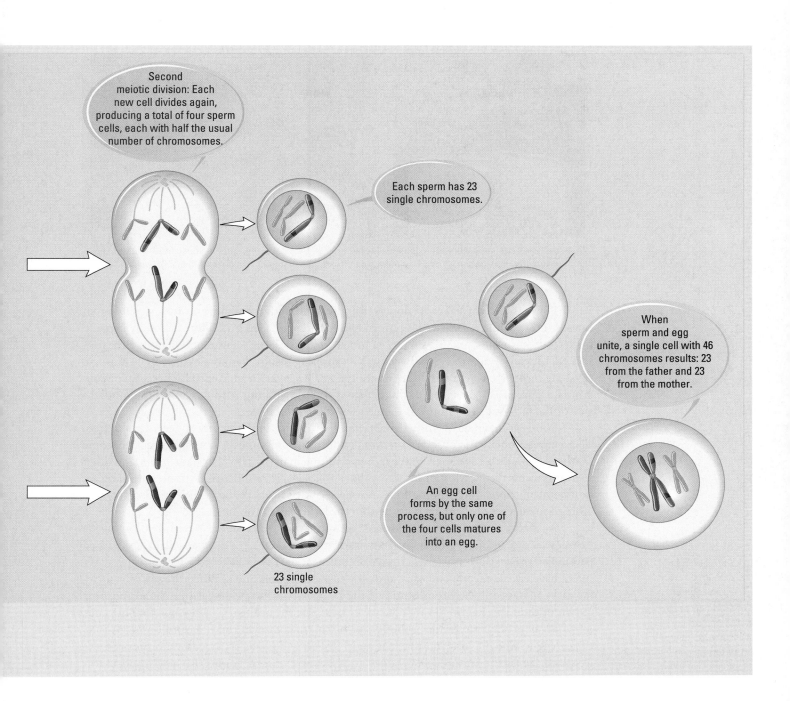

Second meiotic division: Each new cell divides again, producing a total of four sperm cells, each with half the usual number of chromosomes.

Each sperm has 23 single chromosomes.

When sperm and egg unite, a single cell with 46 chromosomes results: 23 from the father and 23 from the mother.

An egg cell forms by the same process, but only one of the four cells matures into an egg.

23 single chromosomes

Nonidentical twins, sometimes called *fraternal twins,* grow from two separate conceptions. That is, the mother releases two eggs, and two different sperm from the father fertilize them. Because they come from two separate conceptions and therefore form two separate zygotes, we refer to nonidentical twins as **dizygotic (DZ) twins.** DZ twins are no more alike genetically than are any other brothers or sisters from the same parents. They can be different sexes, and their appearance can also be very different. Theoretically, they could even have different fathers. How? If the mother has intercourse with two different men within a short span of time, it is possible that two eggs she released could be fertilized by different fathers. Although this doesn't happen very often, it demonstrates just how different nonidentical twins can be.

dizygotic (DZ) twins
Nonidentical twins. These twins form when two eggs are fertilized by two different sperm cells.

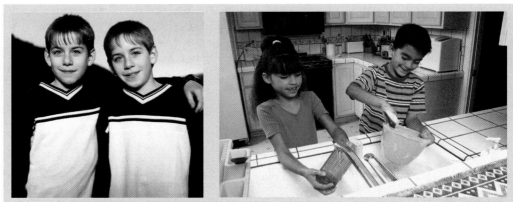

Identical twins are much more alike genetically than are nonidentical twins. Later in the chapter, you will see that these differences are used to estimate how much influence genetics has on traits and behavior.

For reasons that scientists don't yet understand, different ethnic groups have different rates of DZ twinning. DZ twins occur in about 1 in every 500 births for Asians, in 1 in 125 births for Caucasians, and in as many as 1 in 20 births in some African populations (Thompson, McInnes, & Willard, 1991). Because DZ twinning results from the ovulation of multiple eggs, the mother's genetics and the functioning of her ovaries and reproductive system govern its occurrence. Consequently, higher rates of DZ twinning tend to run on the mother's side of the family. DZ twinning also increases as the mother ages.

Some women take fertility drugs when they are having difficulty conceiving children. The drugs stimulate the ovaries to release extra eggs. Sometimes several of the eggs become fertilized by multiple sperm from the father, resulting in twins, triplets, quadruplets, and other sets of multiple births. Most of the babies born this way are nonidentical (nonidentical twins, nonidentical triplets, etc.). Sometimes, however, one or more of the nonidentical zygotes divides to form a set of identical twins within the larger set of multiples.

A final note about cell division and reproduction concerns sex determination. As we have already mentioned, among the 23 pairs of chromosomes in a normal cell is a specialized pair, called the **sex chromosomes.** Sex chromosomes consist of the X and Y chromosomes. Females have two X chromosomes, and males have one X and one Y. When the sex cells form, females can pass only X chromosomes to their eggs. Males, however, pass the X chromosome to half of their sperm and the Y to the other half. The sex of the offspring therefore depends on which type of sperm fertilizes the egg. If the sperm is carrying an X chromosome, the fertilized egg will be XX and will produce a girl. If the sperm is carrying a Y chromosome, the fertilized egg will be XY and will produce a boy. X and Y chromosomes also have implications for genetic defects, as you will see in the next section.

sex chromosomes

The 23rd pair of chromosomes (in humans), specialized to determine the sex of the child and other characteristics. Males are XY and females are XX.

LET'S REVIEW . . .

1. Each cell in the human body typically has 46:

   a. genes.   b. gametes.   c. chromosomes.   d. nucleotide base pairs.

2. If one strand of base pairs has the sequence of A, T, C, C, G, what will the complementary sequence be on the other strand?

   a. A, T, C, C, G   b. G, C, T, T, A   c. C, G, A, A, T   d. T, A, G, G, C

3. Mitosis is the type of cell division that ensures that
   a. almost every cell in the human body has 23 chromosomes.
   b. almost every cell in the human body has 46 chromosomes.
   c. crossover occurs to exchange genes across chromosomes.
   d. random shuffling of chromosomes occurs to increase genetic diversity.

4. What is the name of the type of cell division that creates sperm and egg cells?
   a. meiosis   b. mitosis   c. crossing-over   d. DNA replication

5. **True or False:** Each pair of nucleotide bases forms one gene.

6. **True or False:** The rate of dizygotic (nonidentical) twins varies across ethnic groups and tends to be higher in some family lines.

Answers: 1. c, 2. d, 3. b, 4. a, 5. F, 6. T

How Traits and Genetic Abnormalities Are Inherited

Imagine how complicated the genetic code must be that forms each unique individual human being. More than 3 billion pairs of nucleotide bases must be ordered properly to form 30,000 genes stretched across our 46 chromosomes. And all of this code must be copied accurately into each one of our trillions of cells. Errors, or mutations, do occur, and some of these then get passed down to the next generations. In some cases the errors involve only a few base pairs; sometimes, however, whole chromosomes are damaged, lost, or duplicated too many times.

In this section we describe a few examples of diseases that people can inherit when genetic errors occur. Scientists have identified several thousand such diseases, but here we'll present just a few examples to give you a better understanding of how genetic errors can cause these abnormal conditions. As the Human Genome Project progresses, we continue to learn more about the specific codes involved in these problems. Many hope that someday we will discover treatments or even cures through forms of genetic therapy or other kinds of intervention.

As you study this section, ask yourself these questions:

- How do dominant and recessive disease traits operate? What is the relative likelihood that children will inherit a disease if their parents have the disease or carry the disease gene?

- How do X-linked or sex-linked traits operate? Why are males more likely to inherit some X-linked traits, but females more likely to inherit others?

- What are some of the most common examples of disorders caused by extra or missing chromosomes?

- What are the most common procedures doctors use to test the health of fetuses, and what are the relative advantages and risks of each procedure?

Dominant–Recessive Traits

We have already mentioned that chromosomes come in pairs. Many human traits are governed by **dominant–recessive relationships** between alleles—the two different versions of a gene—acting across pairs of chromosomes. That is, if a person inherits a dominant allele on one chromosome and a recessive allele on the corresponding chromosome, the dominant

dominant–recessive relationship

Relationship between genes where the dominant allele will govern a particular trait, and the recessive allele will be repressed. To express a recessive trait, the individual needs to inherit two recessive alleles—one on each chromosome.

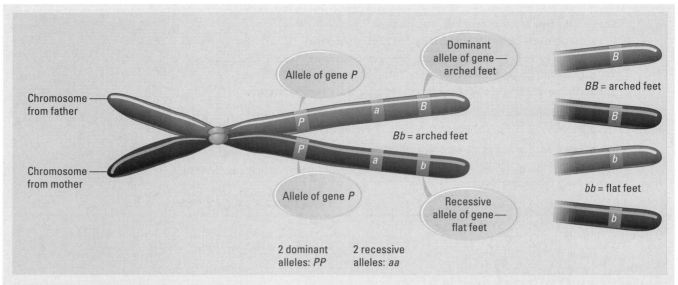

FIGURE 2.7 Alleles Showing Arched and Flat-Feet Genes

The matching pairs of genes on paired chromosomes are called *alleles*. They are not always identical. This illustration shows the alleles of three different genes—one pair of dominant alleles, one pair of recessive alleles, and one dominant–recessive pair.

allele will rule and determine the trait. For example, the allele for arched feet is dominant, and the allele for flat feet is recessive (Starr & Taggart, 1998). If you inherit two dominant alleles, or a mix of one dominant and one recessive allele, your feet will be arched. You can see the alleles in Figure 2.7. To inherit flat feet, you would need to inherit two of the recessive alleles, one on the chromosome that came from your father and one on the chromosome from your mother. Because of this dominant–recessive relationship, traits governed by dominant alleles are much more likely to be expressed than are traits from recessive alleles. Other examples of dominant-allele traits are given in Table 2.2. Which of these traits do you have?

■ **Dominant Gene Diseases.** Huntington disease is the most common example of a genetic disorder that is governed by a dominant allele. Although Huntington disease is genetic, the symptoms usually do not appear until age 30 or after. The disease causes progressive damage to the brain and nervous system, leading to deteriorating intelligence, emotional control, balance, and speech. The gene for Huntington disease has been identified on chromosome 4 (refer back to Figure 2.4). The disease occurs in about 4 to 8 out of every 100,000 births, with

TABLE 2.2 Common Traits Governed by Dominant–Recessive Gene Relationships

DOMINANT TRAITS	RECESSIVE TRAITS
Detached earlobes	Attached earlobes
Ability to roll tongue	Inability to roll tongue
Dimpled cheeks	Nondimpled cheeks
Longer eyelashes	Shorter eyelashes
Larger eyeballs	Smaller eyeballs
Arched feet	Flat feet

Source: Adapted from Starr & Taggart (1998).

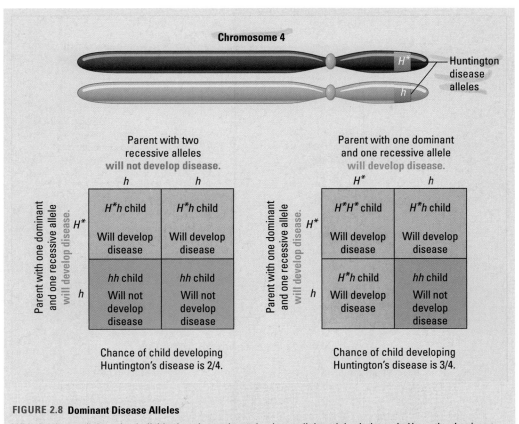

FIGURE 2.8 Dominant Disease Alleles

With dominant allele traits, individuals only need *one* dominant allele to inherit the trait. Here, the dominant allele causes Huntington disease. Dominant alleles are represented by the uppercase H and recessive alleles by the lowercase h. The asterisk is a reminder of which allele causes the disease (H*). On the left, one parent with the disease (H*h) and one healthy parent (hh) have a 50 percent chance of having a child who inherits the disease. On the right, both parents have the disease allele (both are H*h), and they have a 75 percent chance. What would be the odds if one parent carried two dominant disease alleles (H*H*)?

the highest rate among populations from western Europe (Thompson, McInnes, & Willard, 1991). At this time there is no cure for Huntington disease.

Figure 2.8 shows the likelihood that offspring will inherit Huntington disease when one or both parents have the disorder. On the left side of the figure, one parent has the dominant allele for Huntington (H) and also has one recessive allele (h) that is healthy. Because the disease gene is dominant, this parent will develop the disease. The other parent carries two recessive healthy alleles (hh), so this parent will not develop Huntington. When these two parents have children, we would expect half of their offspring (on average) to inherit the dominant allele and therefore the disease. On average, we would expect the remaining half to inherit two recessive alleles and be healthy. On the right side of the figure, you can see that having both parents with the dominant allele dramatically increases the likelihood that their children will inherit the disease.

■ **Recessive Gene Diseases.** Recessive gene diseases are less common, because two recessive alleles need to be inherited before the individual shows the condition. In other words, for a child to inherit a recessive trait, both parents must either have the trait (with two recessive alleles) or at least carry the trait (with one recessive allele). One common recessive disorder is cystic fibrosis. This disease is controlled by genes on chromosome 7. Cystic fibrosis affects

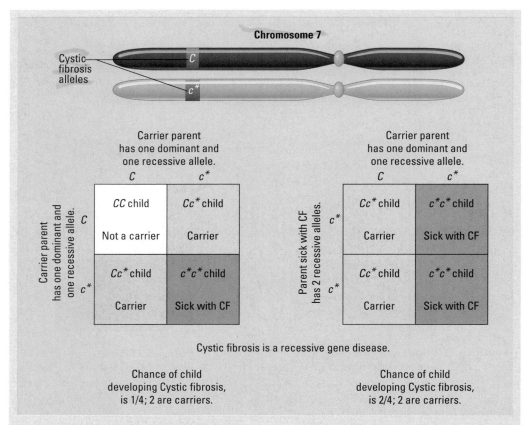

Chromosome 7

Cystic fibrosis alleles

Carrier parent has one dominant and one recessive allele.

Carrier parent has one dominant and one recessive allele.

Carrier parent has one dominant and one recessive allele.

	C	*c**
C	*CC* child Not a carrier	*Cc** child Carrier
c*	*Cc** child Carrier	*c*c** child Sick with CF

Parent sick with CF has 2 recessive alleles.

	C	*c**
c*	*Cc** child Carrier	*c*c** child Sick with CF
c*	*Cc** child Carrier	*c*c** child Sick with CF

Cystic fibrosis is a recessive gene disease.

Chance of child developing Cystic fibrosis, is 1/4; 2 are carriers.

Chance of child developing Cystic fibrosis, is 2/4; 2 are carriers.

FIGURE 2.9 Recessive Disease Alleles

With recessive allele traits, individuals must inherit *two* recessive alleles (one from each parent) to show the trait. Here, inheriting two recessive alleles (c*c*) causes cystic fibrosis. On the left, both parents are carriers (Cc*), but neither has the disease because they both have the dominant healthy allele. Their children, however, have a 25 percent chance of inheriting two recessive alleles (c*c*) and developing the disease. On the right, the risk is increased to 50 percent when one parent has the disease. What would the risk be if both parents had the disease? What if one parent carried the disease allele (Cc*) but the other parent did not (CC)?

tissues in the body that produce mucus secretions. The lungs, gastrointestinal tract, pancreas, and liver are often affected. People with cystic fibrosis usually experience serious respiratory problems and lung infections, and without lung transplants most do not live past the age of 30. Cystic fibrosis is the most common recessive disease among Caucasians, occurring in approximately 1 in every 2,000 Caucasian children (Thompson, McInnes, & Willard, 1991). Nearly 1 in every 22 Caucasians carries the recessive allele. The disease is virtually unknown in Asian populations and is very rare among people of African descent. Figure 2.9 shows the inheritance patterns for recessive traits such as cystic fibrosis.

Sickle-cell disease (SCD) is the most common genetic disorder worldwide (Embury, Hebbel, Mohandas, & Steinberg, 1994). SCD is actually a group of diseases involving defective hemoglobin, the substance in all red blood cells that carries oxygen from the lungs to the rest of the body. The best-known form of the disease is sickle-cell anemia. SCD is most common in people of African and Hispanic descent. About 1 in 500 African American babies and 1 in 1,000 Hispanic babies are affected. It also occurs in people with Mediterranean, Middle Eastern, and Native American backgrounds. In SCD a gene on chromosome 11 causes the production of a defective form of hemoglobin. Unlike normal red blood cells, which are soft and round, red blood cells with the defective form of hemoglobin become stiff and distorted after they deliver oxygen, curving into the shape of a sickle (the tool used to cut wheat). Sickled cells are sticky and can form clots in small blood vessels throughout the body, causing damage to the tissues. In many states hospitals routinely test for SCD among newborns using a simple blood test, and the condition can even be detected through prenatal genetic testing. As of now there is no cure; but many treatments are available to manage the disease, and genetic researchers hope to develop a cure through gene therapy (Kaslow et al., 2000; "Sickle Cell Anemia," 2002).

Tay–Sachs disease is another recessive allele disorder. Tay–Sachs is controlled by a gene on chromosome 15 that causes damage to the brain and central nervous system. The disease begins in infancy and causes mental retardation, blindness, and loss of muscle control; it is usually fatal by the age of 2 or 3 years (McKusick, 1998; Starr & Taggart, 1998). At present there is no effective cure or treatment. This disease is extremely rare except among certain segments of the Jewish population. Because this disease is fatal in childhood, people with Tay–Sachs do not live to reproductive age. Parents who carry the recessive gene, however, can pass it along to their children. If both parents are carriers, there is a 25 percent chance that their children will inherit the disease. If only one is a carrier, their children will not inherit the disease, but they can inherit the recessive allele and therefore become carriers themselves.

■ **X-Linked Traits.** Dominant and recessive alleles on the X and Y sex chromosomes cause **X-linked (sex-linked) traits,** or differences between males and females. Recall that females have two X chromosomes (XX), but males have one X and one Y (XY). The Y chromosome is very small and does not contain much genetic material (look back at Figure 2.1 and find the Y chromosome). Most of the alleles on the X chromosome therefore do not have a corresponding allele on the Y chromosome, and this causes males to be much more likely than females to suffer recessive disease traits.

A well-known example is hemophilia (Type A, or classic hemophilia). People with hemophilia lack a clotting agent in their blood, and they can bleed to death from cuts and serious bruises. When males inherit the recessive hemophilia allele on their X chromosome, they do not have an opportunity to mask the disease with the dominant allele for healthy blood clotting on the Y, so they develop the disease. Females are more fortunate. Even if they inherit the recessive hemophilia allele on one X, they almost always have the dominant allele for normal blood clotting on their other X. These females will not get the disease, although they can pass the allele to their children. To have hemophilia, a female would need to inherit the recessive allele on both X chromosomes—a very rare occurrence. One famous case of hemophilia involved the Russian Prince Alexis. His father, Czar Nicholas II, did not carry the disease allele, but his mother, Czarina Alexandra, did. She was a descendant of England's Queen Victoria, who was also a carrier. (It is estimated that 18 members of the British royal family had hemophilia or carried the allele.) Prince Alexis and his family were eventually executed in the Russian Revolution of 1917.

Other examples of X-linked recessive traits include Duchenne muscular dystrophy, color blindness, and some forms of retinitis pigmentosa (a major form of blindness). All of these conditions are more common among males than females.

Dominant disease alleles on the X chromosome are another matter. Females have two chances to inherit these disease alleles (having two X chromosomes), but males have only one chance (one X chromosome). Because the allele is dominant, having the allele on either X can cause the disease in females. Females are twice as likely to show these diseases as males. Dominant X-linked diseases are very rare, however. Vitamin D–resistant rickets is one example, occurring twice as often among females as among males (Thompson, McInnes, & Willard, 1991). With this form of rickets, children have kidney problems that block the production of calcium for bone growth. By one year of age, infants begin showing limb deformities and

X-linked (sex-linked) traits
Differences between males and females caused by dominant and recessive alleles on the X and Y chromosomes.

decreased growth (D'Alessandro, 2002). Rett syndrome (causing severe mental retardation) is another example; it occurs only among females, because the few males who do inherit the disease die before birth (Smith, 2001). Girls who have the disease allele on one X chromosome usually have the recessive (nondisease) allele on their other X chromosome. The nondisease allele operates enough to allow survivability for female fetuses. With male zygotes, however, the small Y chromosome does not carry the nondisease allele, so only the disease allele operates. The allele causes such severe damage that these male zygotes are miscarried.

Fragile-X syndrome is another special case involving the sex chromosomes. This syndrome causes facial deformities; it also damages the brain, causing mental retardation. It is linked to a defective part of the X chromosome—the chromosome is weakened at the tip and also contains a defective allele that contributes to the syndrome. Fragile-X syndrome occurs in about 1 in 1,500 males and 1 in 3,000 females (Thompson, McInnes, & Willard, 1991). It is one of the leading inherited causes of mental retardation among males, second only to Down syndrome (described in the next section).

Chromosome Abnormalities

Abnormalities in the structure or number of whole chromosomes are present in 1 of every 160 live births. They also account for the majority of all miscarriages (Thompson, McInnes, & Willard, 1991). Normally, each sperm and egg have 23 chromosomes. As the gametes form during meiosis, however, errors can occur that cause the sperm or egg to have a missing or extra chromosome. In most cases, this causes a miscarriage early in pregnancy. Nature seems to have a way of weeding out these serious genetic defects. One exception is with chromosome 21, one of the smallest chromosomes (look back to Figure 2.1).

Down syndrome occurs when babies are born with an extra 21st chromosome. Another name for Down syndrome is *trisomy 21*, as the disorder is due to the presence of three ("tri") chromosomes ("somy") at location 21. Individuals with Down syndrome typically have the facial characteristics shown in Figure 2.10. They are short in stature, have short and broad hands, and tend to have heart problems and a shortened life span. Also, people with Down syndrome have mental retardation, with IQs typically around 25 to 50. Down syndrome is the most common genetic cause of mental retardation, accounting for 40 percent of the moderate to severe cases of retardation in the general population (Pennington, Moon, Edgin, Stedron, & Nadel, 2003). In adulthood, the average person with Down syndrome has the mental ability of a typical 7- to 8-year-old child.

In about 95 percent of Down syndrome cases, the extra 21st chromosome exists because the 21st chromosome pair did not separate normally when the egg was formed. The mother's age is a strong risk factor. As Figure 2.11 indicates, the risk has increased dramatically by the age of 35. We still do not know the reasons for this increase. Perhaps the eggs have deteriorated in older mothers, leading to problems in chromosome formation. After the mother reaches 35, the risk is high enough that doctors usually recommend genetic testing early in pregnancy to determine if the fetus has the extra chromosome. We'll describe the methods and alternatives for genetic testing later in this chapter. Although most sources emphasize the increased risk for women of "advancing age," you should keep in mind that the birthrate for younger women is so much higher that more than half of all babies with Down syndrome are born to mothers who are actually *younger* than 35 (Thompson, McInnes, & Willard, 1991).

Down syndrome

Trisomy 21, a genetic disorder that occurs when there is an extra 21st chromosome. Lower IQ, facial defects, heart problems, and shortened life span are characteristic problems.

■ **Sex Chromosome Abnormalities.** With the exception of trisomy 21 (Down syndrome), having an extra chromosome usually leads to pregnancy loss or death of the infant within the first few months of life. Another exception, however, involves the X and Y chromosomes. Babies can survive with extra or missing sex chromosomes—and according to Thompson, McInnes, and Willard (1991), abnormalities in the number of sex chromosomes

FIGURE 2.10 Down Syndrome Features

Down syndrome is caused by an extra chromosome at the 21st pair. Flattened nose, tightened eyelids, low-set ears, and short neck are typical features. Lower IQ is one of the main problems faced by children with Down syndrome.

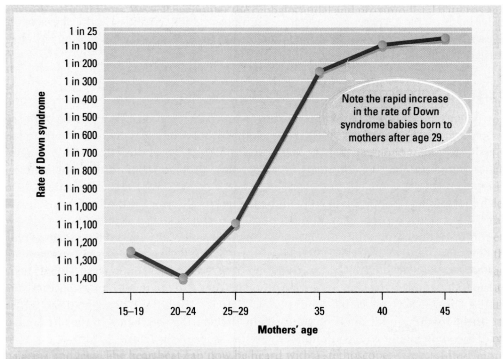

Note the rapid increase in the rate of Down syndrome babies born to mothers after age 29.

FIGURE 2.11 Risk of Down Syndrome due to the Mother's Age

This graph shows that the rate of Down syndrome births increases dramatically as mothers age.

Source: Data from Thompson, McInnes, & Willard (1991), p. 215.

TABLE 2.3 Summary of Sex Chromosome Abnormalities

DISORDER	SEX CHROMOSOME ARRANGEMENT	FREQUENCY	MAJOR CHARACTERISTICS
Klinefelter syndrome (in males)	XXY, extra X chromosome	1/1,000 males	Underdeveloped testes and secondary sexual characteristics, infertility. Slightly reduced IQ, increased risk of learning problems, poor social adjustment.
XYY syndrome (in males)	XYY, extra Y chromosome	1/1,000 males	Tall stature, increased risk of behavioral problems (acting out). Individuals remain fertile.
Trisomy X (in females)	XXX, extra X chromosome	1/1,000 females	Tall stature, lower IQ, learning problems. Individuals remain fertile.
Turner syndrome (individual develops as female)	X, missing chromosome	1/10,000 females	Short stature, webbed neck, broad shoulders, spatial perception and motor skill deficits, infertility.
XX males (reversal)	XX	1/20,000 males	Sex reversal (normally males are XY). A part of the Y chromosome breaks off during meiosis and attaches to one of the X chromosomes. Because this part of the Y chromosome contains the genes that determine male sexual development, the individual develops male sexual characteristics.
XY females (reversal)	XY	1/20,000 females	Sex reversal (normally females are XX). Part of the Y chromosome breaks off and is lost during meiosis. Now the XY individual does not have the genes required for normal male development, and the default is to develop female sexual characteristics.

Source: Adapted from Thompson, McInnes, & Willard (1991).

are among the most common of all human genetic disorders and occur in about one in every 500 live births. Table 2.3 describes several sex chromosome abnormalities. In the next section we describe the most common techniques doctors use to determine if a developing fetus has inherited or developed any of these or other genetic disorders.

Prenatal Screening and Genetic Testing

Many parents are concerned and anxious during pregnancy, especially if a genetic disorder runs in the family or the baby is at risk in some other way. Fortunately, medical experts today can assist expectant parents who have these concerns. Several procedures can detect genetic diseases and abnormalities, and many other potential problems, before the baby is born. *Ultrasonography, amniocentesis,* and *chorionic villus sampling (CVS)* are the procedures used most frequently. An obstetrician may recommend these tests during the mother's prenatal visits, and the obstetrician or another specialist usually performs the procedure.

In **ultrasonography (ultrasound)**, a technician uses an instrument that sends sound waves into the mother's abdomen. By reading the return of the sound waves, the instrument produces an image of the fetus and surrounding structures. Ultrasound measurements help physicians determine if the fetus is growing properly. They also can reveal many structural defects (e.g., heart defects or neural tube or spinal defects). Ultrasound poses no harm to the fetus or the mother, and it can be performed any time during pregnancy. In the ultrasound picture shown in Figure 2.12, you can clearly see the shape of the fetus.

We will never forget the ultrasound session from our third pregnancy (we already had two boys). As the technician moved the instrument over the abdomen, an image of two tiny side-by-side fetuses appeared on the monitor. At first we thought we were seeing an echo of one baby—echoes are common with ultrasounds. But the technician assured us that it was

ultrasonography (ultrasound)

Images, produced by sound waves, of the fetus inside the mother's womb. Help physicians monitor fetal growth and detect physical defects.

amniocentesis

Procedure used to detect chromosomal and genetic abnormalities in the fetus. A needle is inserted through the mother's abdomen and uterus and into the amniotic sac, and fetal cells are withdrawn from the amniotic fluid.

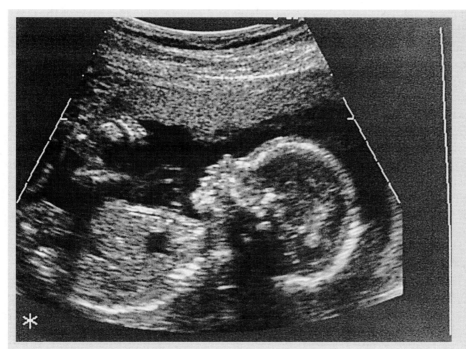

no echo. Instead, we were seeing the first picture of our twin girls, DZ twins. Two boys, and now two girls! Once we knew that both fetuses looked healthy, our thoughts immediately turned to other things . . . like how to feed and diaper two babies at once and how to fit six people into our small car. (We traded it for a van.)

If the parents are at high risk for passing a genetic defect to the baby, or if the mother's age is 35 or more, then the doctor will usually suggest genetic screening. In **amniocentesis** a doctor or technician inserts a needle through the mother's abdomen and uterus and into the amniotic sac that surrounds the fetus. The technician also uses ultrasound during this process to show the position of the fetus and to guide the needle to an open pocket of amniotic fluid. The needle draws a small amount of fluid from the amniotic sac. Cells that the fetus has sloughed off into the fluid are then cultured in a laboratory for genetic testing. Technicians remove the chromosomes from these cultured cells and arrange them by size to form a picture called a *karyotype*. The picture of chromosomes in Figure 2.1 at the beginning of this chapter is a karyotype. By examining the karyotype experts can detect any of several hundred disorders, especially those caused by missing, extra, or broken chromosomes. If a single-gene disease or other genetic disorder runs in the family, specific tests check for DNA markers or other indications of the disease.

Amniocentesis can be conducted after the 14th week of pregnancy, and the results are usually available in 1 to 2 weeks. There is about a 1 in 200 chance that the procedure itself will cause a serious problem. Inserting the needle near the fetus can cause early labor contractions and a miscarriage; or bacteria or injury caused by the needle can lead to serious infections. Because of these risks, doctors usually do not perform amniocentesis unless the fetus is already at a high risk for a serious genetic disorder or other complication.

Chorionic villus sampling (CVS) can be performed earlier, beginning around the 8th week of pregnancy. With CVS the results can be available in just a few days. In this procedure a technician usually inserts a long catheter (tube) through the vagina and into the uterus. Or a needle may be inserted through the abdomen and uterus (similar to amniocentesis). The

thinking
OF DANIEL & TERI

What would Daniel and Teri be able to learn if they had access to a karyotype or other results of genetic tests that may have been performed with their baby? If they knew in advance which diseases or conditions their baby might be susceptible to, what might they be able to do to intervene or to help him?

chorionic villus sampling (CVS)

Procedure used to detect chromosomal and genetic abnormalities in the fetus. A catheter (tube) is inserted into the uterus and cells are taken from the chorionic layer of the placenta around the fetus. Chromosomes are removed to conduct genetic tests.

technician takes a few cells from the chorionic layer of the placenta that surrounds the fetus. As you will see in the next chapter, this layer of cells originated from the zygote, so the chromosomes and genetic codes in these cells will be the same as those in the fetus. By culturing these cells, specialists can construct a karyotype and perform genetic tests as with amniocentesis. The advantage of CVS is that it can be conducted earlier in pregnancy and parents can have results several weeks sooner than with amniocentesis. If parents must decide whether to terminate the pregnancy because of a serious defect found in the fetus, this earlier diagnosis is helpful. A disadvantage of CVS is that the risk of inducing miscarriage is about twice as high as with amniocentesis. Because CVS is performed earlier, the fetus is smaller and more vulnerable to the invasion than with amniocentesis. The risks associated with both procedures are decreasing, however, as the techniques improve and experts gain experience. Figure 2.13 shows how technicians collect cells using CVS and amniocentesis. To learn more about a career that involves working with genetic tests, read the Professional Perspective box called "Career Focus: Meet a Genetic Counselor."

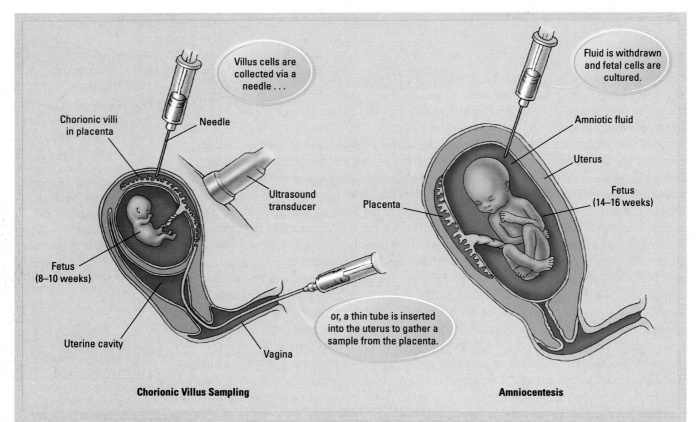

FIGURE 2.13 Two Ways by Which Fetal Cells Are Collected for Genetic Testing during Pregnancy

With chorionic villus sampling (CVS) (left), either a catheter is inserted through the vagina and into the uterus to take placental villus cells for testing, or villus cells are extracted using a needle inserted into the placenta. With amniocentesis (right) a needle is inserted through the mother's abdomen and into the amniotic sac. Amniotic fluid is withdrawn, containing cells from the fetus.

Source: H. Bee & D. Boyd. (2000). *Lifespan development,* 3rd ed., p. 77. Published by Allyn and Bacon, Boston, MA. Copyright © 2004 by Pearson Education. Reprinted by permission of the publisher.

Career Focus: Meet a Genetic Counselor

Robin L. Bennett, MS, CGC
Seattle, Washington

Genetic counselor; president of the National Society of Genetic Counselors (www.nsgc.org); and author of The Practical Guide to the Genetic Family History *(1999), published by John Wiley & Sons*

What are the main roles and job duties of genetic counselors?
We help people at risk for or affected with a genetic disorder. We translate complicated genetic facts into practical information to help clients understand a disorder, the available courses of action, how heredity contributes, and the testing options that are available. During a visit, we create a family *pedigree,* which is a summary of the medical conditions and family relationships over at least three generations. A critical role is discussing the feelings and concerns the clients has about genetic and prenatal testing as well as potential consequences. We also refer clients to community resources and appropriate medical specialties.

When a serious disease or defect is detected, how do counselors inform and assist clients?
The diagnosis is discussed face-to-face, and clients are strongly encouraged to have a support person with them (a partner, relative, or friend). Genetic counselors are trained in grief and crisis counseling. They try to anticipate clients' reactions and refer clients to specialists (such as individual and family therapists) and support groups as needed (see www.geneticalliance.org for information on support groups).

What are the newest techniques and trends in your field?
Presymptomatic or *susceptibility* genetic testing is now available, where people can be tested for the potential of a genetic disorder. Genetic counseling for these individuals is extremely important, because these are healthy individuals at risk of developing the condition, but the tests do not predict when a person will be affected or how their disease will progress. Interpreting these tests is quite complex both medically and emotionally. *Pharmacogenomics,* where people can be tested for a cluster of susceptibilities so that "designer medications" can be prescribed, is also new. This will hopefully significantly reduce the incidence of adverse reactions to drugs, but it's very expensive. Gene therapy continues to be in the news, but these therapies are still a ways off in terms of clinical practice.

What training and education is usually needed to work in your field?
A master's degree in genetic counseling is required, which involves course work in medicine, psychology, and human genetics, as well as over a thousand hours in fieldwork. Genetic counselors work in a variety of settings including medical centers, private practice, medical research, public health and policy, pharmaceutical companies, genetic testing laboratories, and in instructional settings. If they work in clinical practice, they must be certified by the American Board of Genetic Counseling. ■

thinking
OF DANIEL & TERI

◀ How could a genetic counselor help Daniel and Teri identify their adopted baby's risk for various genetic disorders?

LET'S REVIEW . . .

1. Which combination of alleles below is necessary for a person to inherit a disease such as cystic fibrosis? In this example, "C" refers to the healthy allele, and "c" refers to the disease allele.

   a. cc   b. Cc   c. cC   d. CC

2. Hemophilia, Duchenne muscular dystrophy, and color blindness are examples of:

   a. X-linked dominant diseases.   c. diseases caused by missing chromosomes.
   b. X-linked recessive diseases.   d. diseases caused by a broken X chromosome.

3. Which of the following is more common among females than males?
   a. X-linked recessive traits   c. Fragile-X syndrome
   b. X-linked dominant traits   d. Klinefelter syndrome

4. Which test below could be used earliest in pregnancy to identify missing or extra chromosomes?
   a. amniocentesis   c. chorionic villus sampling
   b. ultrasonography   d. human genome mapping

5. **True or False:** Children will inherit Huntington disease if they inherit a disease allele from one parent and a healthy allele from the other parent.

6. **True or False:** Down syndrome is caused by a missing chromosome.

Answers: 1. a, 2. b, 3. b, 4. c, 5. T, 6. F

How Genes and Environments Interact

The first part of this chapter introduced you to some of the basic concepts of genetics and inheritance. Any human behavior requires more than genetics, however: An environment of some kind is necessary for development to occur. In this section we will discuss how genetics and the environment interact to produce complex behaviors and characteristics.

As you study this section, ask yourself these questions:

- How do genetics and the environment act together to determine our traits?
- How do the concepts of reaction range, canalization, and probabilistic epigenesis help explain the interaction of genetics and environment?
- What does niche-picking have to do with genetics? How does it help explain developmental outcomes?

Developmental psychologists call the interaction of genetics and the environment the **G × E interaction.** Pronounced "G by E interaction," this term refers to the ways in which nature (represented by genetics and heredity) combines with nurture (a person's environment) to produce a given outcome. As you learned in Chapter 1, philosophers and scientists have long been interested in the relative roles of nature and nurture. For centuries the emphasis has shifted back and forth between nature and nurture, but it is now clear that both are essential for development to take place (de Waal, 1999). There are several ways to think about how genes and the environment interact. We will describe three common ways—*range of reaction, canalization,* and *niche-picking.* Then we'll introduce one newer approach, *probabilistic epigenesis.*

Range of Reaction

One way to understand the interaction between genes and the environment is to recognize that an individual's genetic material (i.e., the genotype, or actual genetic code) establishes boundaries on the possible phenotype, or observable traits, that can occur. For any individual, the various possible phenotypic outcomes are the **range of reaction** for that genotype (Gottesman, 1963). The key idea is that genes set the boundaries for the range of reaction, but the environment determines which possible outcomes actually materialize. Figure 2.14 illustrates the hypothetical range of reaction for cognitive skills for three hypothetical children.

G × E interaction

The interacting effects of genetics and the environment on the development of traits and behaviors.

range of reaction

The range of possible phenotypes (traits or behaviors) that exist for a particular genotype (genetic code).

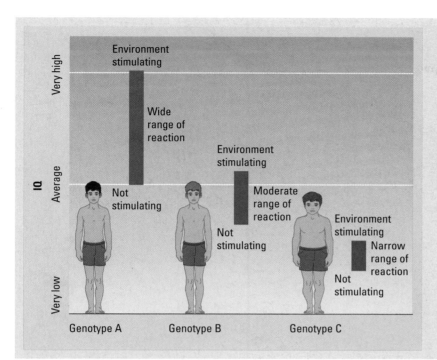

FIGURE 2.14 Range of Reaction for Cognitive Skills (IQ) of Three Hypothetical Children

Child A shows a large range of reaction (RR). When the environment is not stimulating, his IQ is low. As the environment improves, however, this child's IQ shows large improvement. Child C, however, has a very limited range of reaction. The genotype for this child has set rather narrow limits to his range of reaction, so there is little room for changes as the environment changes. A child with Down syndrome might have such a genotype, leading to low IQ. The range for Child B falls in between these two, with more moderate changes as the environment is altered.

Remember that the range of reaction is a theoretical construct. It is useful for helping us think about the way in which genes and the environment interact. We can never know for certain the range of reaction for a specific individual, because it is impossible to know or try all of the environmental possibilities during the limited time of one person's development.

Canalization

A second way to think about G × E interactions emphasizes how genetics can help protect children from the effects of the environment. **Canalization** refers to the way genes limit developmental outcomes (Waddington, 1942, 1957). In other words, genes provide a strong buffer against environmental variations, limiting the effects that the environment can have. The result is that development can proceed along only a few species-specific paths and can produce only outcomes that are typical for that species. Figure 2.15 diagrams this concept. Genetics provides a small number of pathways, or "canals," through the hills and valleys of the developmental landscape. The environment can be thought of as a force (like the wind) that moves the individual around within the developmental landscape. The deeper the canal, the more genes predetermine the developmental pathway. In this model, choice points where one canal splits into two, offering two different developmental directions, represent critical periods in development.

The view of canalization presented in Figure 2.15 emphasizes the protective role of genetics. It explains how an individual can physically and psychologically survive despite fairly extreme environmental conditions. Notice, however, that this theory places a heavy emphasis on genetic determinism—environmental conditions must be strong to change an individual's developmental path.

A more recent interpretation places less emphasis on genetic determination. This newer model gives more weight to the role of the environment, particularly prenatal and early experiences (Gottlieb, 1997). This interpretation is called *experiential canalization*. In this view, genetics provides a fairly wide range of possible developmental outcomes and it is the

YOUR
PERSPECTIVE
NOTES

What are some implications of the range of reaction for programs that attempt to enrich children's environments? Given that we cannot know which children have larger and which have smaller ranges of reaction, what should policy makers do to optimize the developmental outcomes of as many children as possible?

canalization

Genetic limits on the effects of the environment. In experiential canalization, in contrast, it is the environment that limits the expression of genes.

FIGURE 2.15 Canalization

The hills and valleys in the diagram represent the "developmental landscape" through which an individual progresses. The individual's development is represented by the path of the ball moving through this landscape. Genetics determines the shape of the landscape, while forces in the environment move the ball through the critical choice points.

Source: Adapted from C. H. Waddington. (1974). A catastrophe theory of evolution. *Annals of the New York Academy of Sciences, 231*, 32–42. Reprinted by permission.

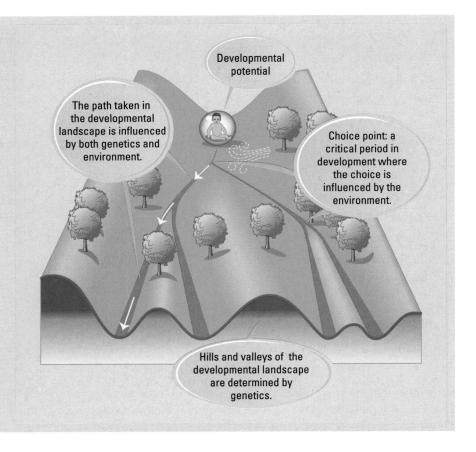

Developmental potential

The path taken in the developmental landscape is influenced by both genetics and environment.

Choice point: a critical period in development where the choice is influenced by the environment.

Hills and valleys of the developmental landscape are determined by genetics.

environment that plays the limiting role. For example, think about speech perception. Until about one year of age, infants respond similarly to the basic sounds used in all languages. After that, they can detect subtle differences in language sounds only in their own native language, the language they experienced during their first year (Werker & Tees, 1984). In other words, genetics endows all humans with the ability to perceive language sounds, but individuals' linguistic environment eventually limits the sounds they can distinguish.

These two views of canalization lead to quite different implications for a variety of practical problems. For example, all parents wonder from time to time if they are having any important impact on their children's developmental outcomes. The view of canalization that emphasizes the protective effects of genetics would say that unless a parent is providing extreme conditions in some way, the child's outcome is going to proceed along a genetically determined path. Small to moderate variations in parenting style, day-to-day living conditions, and the like will have little impact on the child's outcome (Scarr, 1992). The experiential canalization view would offer a different opinion. According to this view, early experiences and opportunities that parents offer would have a significant impact in the child's developmental outcome.

thinking
OF DANIEL & TERI

How would your response to Daniel and Teri be different depending on whether you emphasize canalization or experiential canalization? What would the implications of each concept be for Daniel and Teri?

Niche-Picking: I Gotta Be Me . . .

It may surprise you to learn that one way a child's genes interact with the environment is by affecting the kinds of environments that are available (Bouchard, 1997; Scarr, 1992, 1993; Scarr & McCartney, 1983). In other words, a child's genes make it more or less likely that the child will be placed in, or will select, a certain kind of environment. First, during infancy,

People who inherit high activity levels tend to select activities and environments to suit this disposition. Can you see here how genetics has an influence on the role played by the environment?

genes primarily operate in a *passive* manner. At this stage the infant's environment is almost totally controlled by his or her parents. However, the child and parents share many genes, so the home environment is usually consistent with and supportive of the child's genes. Second, as the child gets older, genes play a more *evocative* role. This means that the child's genetic tendencies evoke certain responses from parents and others. For example, if a child likes to be physically active, parents tend to provide more opportunities for physical activities. They may offer more frequent trips to the playground or encourage the child to join sports teams. These activities are evoked by and tend to support the child's genetic tendencies.

Third, as children get older and have more freedom to choose their own activities, genes work in an *active* way. Older children can actively seek out the specific *niches,* or activities and environments, that suit them best. That is, they engage in **niche-picking.** Given a choice, shy children tend to choose more quiet and passive activities, such as going to movies and reading books. Active children gravitate to physical sports and noisy settings. A child's genetic predisposition toward being shy or active leads the child to pick niches that support his or her tendencies. So genes influence behavior not only by predisposing children to develop certain traits or characteristics, but also by affecting the kinds of environments that surround them.

Our twin daughters offer an example of passive, evocative, and active gene influences. When they were infants, we provided an environment that suited our own interests—we read lots of books to them, played music for them, and held and rocked them. Our interests and skills reflected our own genes, and given that we shared a lot of genes with our daughters, the environment we provided was reasonably consistent with their genetic tendencies. But as the girls grow older, they are clearly evoking different kinds of environments. Rachel is very active and prefers fast-paced physical activities. Lily is much happier playing with computer

thinking
OF DANIEL & TERI

◄ How will the genetics of Daniel and Teri's baby affect the environment they provide for him? What about when their son begins picking his own activities and environments?

niche-picking

The tendency to pick activities and environments that fit with our genetic predispositions.

Identify examples of
passive, evocative, and
active gene influences
on your development.
How have your genes
affected the "niches"
you have picked?

probabilistic epigenesis

The likelihood that specific
environmental conditions
will activate specific genes
that lead to particular traits
or behavioral outcomes.

games or with Barbie dolls, or sitting in someone's lap. We respond to the differences so that Rachel is able to spend more time in physical activities and Lily more time in quieter kinds of play. The girls are not old enough yet to do much active niche-picking, but their different preferences will almost certainly lead them to select different kinds of environments when they begin developing hobbies, choosing friends, and deciding how to spend their spare time.

Probabilistic Epigenesis: Activating Your Genes

Though researchers have investigated G × E interactions for some time now, they continue to discover increasingly complex ways in which genes and environment interact to produce behavior. The concept of *probabilistic epigenesis* provides a good example. The term *epigenesis* refers to the emergence of a trait, characteristic, or behavior over the course of development (as opposed to its presence from the beginning). *Probabilistic* means that there is some probability that a given characteristic or trait will develop depending on certain conditions in the environment (as opposed to a certainty that it will occur regardless of the environment). According to the concept of **probabilistic epigenesis,** the likelihood of a given behavioral outcome depends on the existence of specific genetic potential that must be activated by specific environmental conditions (Gottlieb, 1997). The idea of such an interaction is not new, but awareness of the central role of the environment in activating specific genes is. Researchers agree that only about 10 to 15 percent of an individual's total genome is actually expressed, or made active. This means that every individual has many more potential developmental pathways than are ever realized, and *it is the individual's environment that controls which parts of the genome are activated.* Figure 2.16 illustrates the complex interactions that take place. For example, we know that certain environmental conditions (e.g., light, stress, nutrition, length of the day) affect levels of numerous hormones in the body. Hormones in turn enter the nuclei of cells and affect protein production, which essentially "turns on" or "turns off" certain genes. So not only do our genes affect behavior, as we have long realized (see the upper-left arrow in

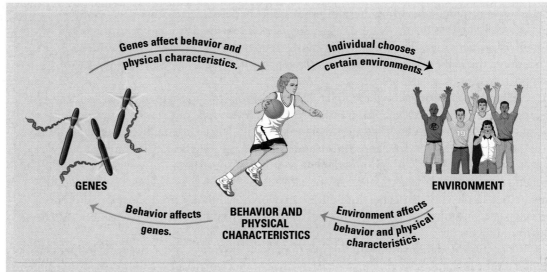

FIGURE 2.16 Probabilistic Epigenesis

Genes can determine physical and behavioral characteristics (such as a high activity level) causing the child to select certain environments (e.g., active and stimulating sports). But the environment also stimulates changes in the body (e.g., in hormones) that selectively turn genes on and off.

Source: Based on Gottlieb (1991).

Figure 2.16), but our environment influences which parts of our vast genetic potential are actually activated and expressed (the lower two arrows in Figure 2.16).

An interesting implication of probabilistic epigenesis is that a *significant change in the environment will change which genes are expressed.* This can create a situation in which characteristics or behaviors not normally seen in a species can develop, even though the actual genetic material has stayed the same. For example, certain changes of the developmental environment of bird embryos can result in the birds' developing teeth, which they normally do not have (Kollar & Fisher, 1980). Because the embryos were already formed, the genetic potential for the abnormal characteristic must already have been present, but the characteristic does not appear in the normal course of development for birds. The environmental changes activated genes that are normally "turned off." In another example, exposure of fruit flies to ether during prenatal development causes them to grow an extra set of wings (Ho, 1984). The altered genetic activation can be passed along to future generations as well—the offspring of fruit flies with extra wings also develop the second set of wings.

What does this mean for human development? Clearly humans have a vast genetic potential, and only a small portion of it is expressed. Which portion is expressed depends on the child's environment. Though researchers continue to make progress, we do not yet have a good understanding of which environmental factors are most important in affecting gene expression. Nor can we pinpoint (yet) precisely how environmental factors shape complex traits like intelligence and personality. But the concept of probabilistic epigenesis makes a strong statement about the relationship between genes and the environment. It emphasizes that this relationship does affect development—that the two factors are truly *interdependent.*

thinking
OF DANIEL & TERI

◄ How can the concept of probabilistic epigenesis explain differences between the outcomes of Daniel and Teri's baby in his adopted environment and potential outcomes in other possible environments?

LET'S REVIEW . . .

1. In the range of reaction concept, which of the following sets the upper and lower boundaries for the range of possible developmental outcomes?

   a. genes   b. environment   c. G × E interactions   d. proximal processes

2. A child likes to draw and sketch pictures whenever she can. This is an example of:

   a. canalization.   c. evocative G × E interaction.

   b. passive G × E interaction.   d. active G × E interaction.

3. Canalization is *different* from experiential canalization in that:

   a. canalization emphasizes that limits are set by the environment.

   b. canalization emphasizes that limits are set by genetics.

   c. experiential canalization emphasizes that limits are set by genetics.

   d. experiential canalization places equal emphasis on both genetics and the environment in setting limits.

4. Which of the following best describes the concept of probabilistic epigenesis?

   a. Genes determine behavior.

   b. Genes do not affect behavior.

   c. Genes activated by the environment affect behavior.

   d. The environment activated by genes affects behavior.

5. **True or False:** The concept of niche-picking is the idea that our genes can influence the kinds of environments that we select for ourselves.

6. **True or False:** We never know what the range of reaction will be for any particular child.

Answers: 1. a, 2. d, 3. b, 4. c, 5. T, 6. T

Behavior Genetics: Measuring the Heritability of Traits

How different are you from your siblings and parents? What accounts for the differences and similarities? Behavior genetics is a field that tries to answer these questions.

As you study this section, ask yourself these questions:

- What is behavior genetics, and how does this field help explain development?
- How do behavior geneticists obtain heritability estimates? What does heritability mean, and what does it *not* mean?
- What are shared and nonshared environments, and how does each contribute to development?
- What are the heritabilities of cognitive skills and personality? What do these heritabilities tell us about the causes and developmental courses of these traits?

Behavior Genetics, Heritability, and the Environment

Behavior genetics is the study of how genetic and environmental factors relate to the behavioral differences we see among people (Plomin, 1990). Behavior geneticists often talk about the *heritability* of certain behavioral outcomes. **Heritability** is a mathematical estimate of the degree of genetic influence for a given trait. Heritability estimates range from 0.00 to 1.00; higher values mean that there is a stronger genetic influence on the trait. For example, the estimated heritability for height is .90, which means that a great deal of the variance in height in a population is due to genetic variance in that population. Contrast this with the estimated heritability of some attitudes, such as religiosity or attitudes toward racial integration. The heritability estimate for religiosity ranges from .04 to .22, depending on how religiosity is assessed; for attitudes on integration it is .06 (Loehlin & Nichols, 1976). These low heritability estimates mean that very little, if any, of the variation in these attitudes is genetic. Instead, the variation is due mostly to learning experiences and other differences in the environment. Though it is theoretically possible for heritability estimates to be as high as 1.0, the complex traits that behavioral geneticists study never show heritabilities this high. In general, heritability estimates over .50 are considered fairly high (Plomin, 1990).

In recent decades behavior geneticists have become more interested in estimating the influence of the environment on development. As you read earlier in this chapter, an actual developmental outcome reflects both a genetic influence and an environmental influence. But there are two types of environment that we must consider when explaining differences in behavioral outcomes. **Shared environment** consists of experiences and aspects of the environment that are common to all individuals living together (Plomin, 1986). These shared experiences tend to produce *similarities* in behavioral outcomes. Within a family, shared environments include such things as the existence of lots of reading materials at home, the cultural or sporting events the family attends, or the overall socioeconomic level of the household.

However, the shared environment cannot explain behavioral *differences* among family members. To explain differences we must examine the aspects of the environment that differ from one person to another. The **nonshared environment** consists of experiences and aspects of the environment that are unique to an individual (Hetherington, Reiss, & Plomin, 1994). Nonshared environments differ across people, and they produce differences in behavioral outcomes. For example, perhaps one child in a family spends lots of time listening to music CDs and playing musical instruments, whereas another spends more time watching and par-

---

behavior genetics

The study of how genetic and environmental factors relate to the behavioral differences among people.

heritability

A mathematical estimate of the degree of genetic influence for a given trait or behavior.

shared environment

Experiences and aspects of the environment that are common across all individuals who are living together.

nonshared environment

Experiences and aspects of the environment that differ across people.

ticipating in sports activities. Although they are growing up in the same family, these children spend much of their time in different types of environments.

Researchers are beginning to realize that environmental aspects that once were believed to be shared by all family members can actually be nonshared. For example, for many years researchers assumed that parents used the same parenting style with all of their children. We now realize, however, that parents often adjust their style to fit the personality or basic temperament of each child. A parent may be more harsh with a child perceived as difficult but more permissive with a child perceived to be easygoing, for example. In this case parenting style is a nonshared feature of the environment—it is not shared among the children. However, there is some disagreement as to how to label certain aspects of the environment, and this leads to confusion when we try to understand the research (Maccoby, 2000; Rose, 1995). For example, if parents use the same parenting style with all of their children, but the different children *respond* to this style in different ways, is parenting style a shared or nonshared feature of the environment? Behavior geneticists categorize it as nonshared in this case (because it leads to differences in the children's behaviors). But others would say that it is shared (because the same treatment was applied to all of the children).

Both shared and nonshared environments are clearly important, but they contribute to different aspects of behavior. Along with shared heredity, shared environmental factors help explain some of the remarkable similarities often seen among family members. However, behavior geneticists are interested primarily in how people come to show different behavioral outcomes, so they have focused more on identifying and understanding nonshared influences. It is easy to see why this information is so important when we consider traits such as intelligence or various kinds of psychopathology. For example, schizophrenia (a severe mental disorder in which irrational thoughts dominate) has a strong genetic component, with an estimated heritability as high as .70. However, many people at risk for schizophrenia never develop the disorder even though a sibling raised in the same family does develop it. A better understanding of the nonshared environmental influences in the families of schizophrenics might help researchers identify specific factors that trigger the development of schizophrenia. This in turn might eventually lead to more effective treatment for and prevention of this serious disorder (Plomin, 1990).

How Is Heritability Estimated?

Two methods that researchers have used to estimate heritability are *twin studies* and *adoption studies*. **Twin studies** estimate the genetic contribution to a given trait by comparing measurements from identical and nonidentical twins. Think about the genetic makeup of these two different kinds of twins and you will see the logic of this method. As you recall from earlier in this chapter, identical twins form when a single fertilized egg splits, resulting in two zygotes. The two individuals that develop from these zygotes are *genetically identical*—they must be, because they came from the same fertilized egg. Nonidentical twins, on the other hand, come from two different eggs fertilized by two different sperm. Therefore, they are no more alike genetically than are any other siblings, having on average 50 percent of their genetic material in common. But both types of twins tend to be raised in similar environments. So the main difference between the two types of twin pairs is the amount of genetic material they have in common (plus nonshared features of their environments). Figure 2.17 illustrates this logic.

In twin studies researchers estimate heritability by taking measurements (e.g., IQ or personality measures) of both kinds of twins. They compute correlations between the members of each pair of twins; then they compare the correlations for identical twins to the correlations for nonidentical twins. (Recall from Chapter 1 that a correlation is a number

twin studies

Comparisons between measurements of identical and nonidentical twins, used to estimate the genetic contribution to traits and behaviors.

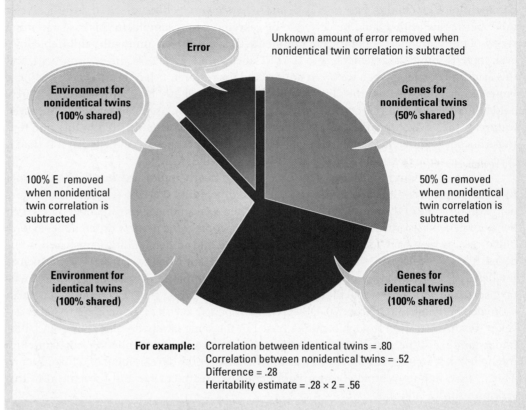

Twin Studies:

When raised together, identical twins share 100% of G and 100% of E. Nonidentical twins share 50% of G and 100% of E. Subtracting the correlation between nonidentical twins from the correlation for identical twins removes 100% of E and 50% of G, leaving 50% of G. An estimate of the full heritability is computed by multiplying the remainder by 2.

Error

Unknown amount of error removed when nonidentical twin correlation is subtracted

Environment for nonidentical twins (100% shared)

Genes for nonidentical twins (50% shared)

100% E removed when nonidentical twin correlation is subtracted

50% G removed when nonidentical twin correlation is subtracted

Environment for identical twins (100% shared)

Genes for identical twins (100% shared)

For example: Correlation between identical twins = .80
Correlation between nonidentical twins = .52
Difference = .28
Heritability estimate = .28 × 2 = .56

FIGURE 2.17 Twin Studies, Heritability, and Correlations

In twin studies, measurements are taken from identical and nonidentical twins, and correlations are computed between the members of each pair of twins. If there is an important genetic influence, the identical twin correlation will be significantly higher than the correlation for the nonidentical twins. A heritability estimate can be computed by doubling the difference between the two correlations. In adoption studies, correlations of the child and his or her biological family members are compared to correlations of the child and his or her adoptive family members. If there is an important genetic influence on the trait, then the correlation with the biological family members will be significantly higher than the correlation with the adoptive family members.

representing the amount of association between two scores.) If there is an important genetic influence on the trait measured, then the correlation for the identical twins should be significantly higher than the correlation for the nonidentical twins. Figure 2.17 shows how researchers calculate a numerical heritability estimate from these correlations.

Adoption studies estimate the genetic contribution to a given trait by studying adopted children. Again, think about the genetic and environmental similarities of these adopted children, their biological families, and their adoptive families to understand the logic of this method. On average, children have about 50 percent of their genetic material in common with each of their biological parents and siblings. Children raised by their biological parents

adoption studies

Comparisons between measurements of children and their adoptive and biological parents used to estimate the genetic contribution to traits and behaviors.

Adoption Studies:

When adopted, children share 50% of G and 0% of E with their biological parents and siblings, but they share 0% of G and 100% of E with their adoptive parents and siblings. Subtracting the correlation between adoptive relatives from the correlation for biological relatives removes 100% of E and 0% of G, leaving 50% of G. An estimate of the full heritability is computed by multiplying the remainder by 2. This can only be considered an estimate. Some error is removed when the correlations are subtracted, but it is impossible to know how much is removed and how much remains.

Error

Unknown amount of error removed when adoptive correlation is subtracted

Environment for adoptive relatives (100% shared)

Genes for biological relatives (50% shared)

Environment for biological relatives (0% shared)

Genes for adoptive relatives (0% shared)

100% E removed when adoptive correlation is subtracted

0% G removed when adoptive correlation is subtracted

For example: Correlation with biological relatives = .80
Correlation with adoptive relatives = .52
Difference = .28
Heritability estimate = .28 × 2 = .56

and with their biological siblings also share the same environment. Adopted children still share 50 percent of their genetic material with their biological parents and siblings, but they do not share the same environment. Finally, adopted children share 0 percent genetic material with their adoptive parents and siblings, but they do share the same environment. Adoption studies take measures of children who were adopted, their biological parents and/or siblings, and their adoptive parents and/or siblings. The researchers compute correlations between the adopted child and his or her biological family members, and between the adopted child and his or her adoptive family members. They then compare the two correlations. If there is an important genetic influence on a given trait, then the correlation with the biological family members should be significantly higher than the correlation with the adoptive family members. Researchers can compute a numerical heritability estimate from the correlations, as shown in Figure 2.17.

These two methods provide a way to estimate heritabilities. They are sometimes combined, as in studies that calculate estimates of heritability from measures of identical twins adopted into different families. But remember that both twin studies and adoption studies, no matter how they are used, provide only *estimates* of heritability. Remember, too, that several factors can affect these estimates. For example, adoption studies have the potential problem of *selective placement,* in which agencies place adopted children in homes that are similar in important ways to those of the biological parents. Agencies may well take into consideration factors such as racial and cultural background, overall socioeconomic status, and level of education when they select adoptive homes for children. What effect do you think selective placement would have on heritability estimates? Some adoption studies have reported that selective placement was not an important factor for the traits under consideration. Many, however, provide no information (Plomin, 1990). In twin studies, there is an assumption of *equal environments.* This means that researchers generally assume the similarity of the environment for identical twins to be the same as for nonidentical twins. Do you think this assumption is valid? Or are identical twins likely to share a more similar environment than nonidentical twins? If identical twins share a more similar environment, then heritability estimates may well be inflated (Kendler, Neale, Kessler, Heath, & Eaves, 1993; Pam, Kemker, Ross, & Golden, 1996).

Finally, remember that in many cases children are exposed to or select certain environments based on their genetic tendencies. This leads to a *correlation between genetics and environment* that current research methods are not able to unravel. It is difficult to say how heritability estimates are affected, because such correlations are not clearly the effect of either heredity or the environment but result from their interaction. Newer statistical techniques such as path analysis, which you learned about in Chapter 1, can help describe these kinds of relations between genetics and heredity and account for the possible effects of selective placement and unequal environments (e.g., Crosnoe & Elder, 2002). We can now obtain more accurate heritability estimates through these techniques than through simple comparison of correlations.

Heritability of Complex Characteristics

Using the methods just described, researchers have studied a wide variety of different human characteristics to understand the influences of genetics and the environment. Table 2.4 summarizes the estimated heritabilities for various characteristics. Almost all show small to moderate heritabilities.

thinking
OF DANIEL & TERI

According to these data, would we expect Daniel and Teri's child to have an IQ that is more similar to Daniel and Teri's or more similar to the IQs of his biological parents?

■ **Heritability of Cognitive Skills.** Probably the most extensively studied behavioral trait is intelligence. Researchers often measure intelligence by means of scores on standardized intelligence tests (e.g., IQ scores). Bouchard and McGue (1981) summarized the results of many family, twin, and adoption studies (Table 2.5). These data indicate that heredity has a significant influence on IQ scores: The correlations for identical twins are consistently higher than those for nonidentical twins, and the correlations for biological relatives are often higher than for adoptive families. The estimated heritabilities of IQ in these studies range from .30 to .72. (Can you figure out how each heritability estimate was computed?) Based on these and numerous other studies, behavior geneticists generally accept that the heritability of IQ is about .50 (see Plomin & DeFries, 1998; Rose, 1995 for reviews). As Table 2.4 showed, there have been similar findings for a variety of specific cognitive skills (such as spatial reasoning, verbal reasoning, and

TABLE 2.4 Heritability Estimates for a Variety of Traits and Behaviors

TRAIT OR BEHAVIOR	HERITABILITY ESTIMATE	SOURCE
Cognitive Skills		
General intelligence	.52	1
Verbal reasoning	.50	1
Reasoning	.48	2
Spatial visualization	.46	2
Perceptual speed	.46	2
Vocational interests (in adolescence)	.42	1
Spatial reasoning	.40	1
Verbal comprehension	.38	2
Scholastic achievement (in adolescence)	.38	1
English usage	.40	3
Mathematics	.40	3
Social studies	.34	3
Natural sciences	.38	3
Memory	.32	2
Verbal fluency	.30	2
Processing speed	.22	1
Divergent thinking	.22	2
Personality and Temperament		
Anxiety	.70	4
Sociability	.64	4
Activity–impulsivity	.62	4
Dominance	.60	4
Emotionality	.54	4
Extraversion	.51	1
Task orientation	.50	4
Conservatism	.50	5
Neuroticism	.46	1
Control	.44	4
Aggression	.40	4
Masculinity/femininity	.32	4
Sexual orientation	.30 to .70	9
Belief in God	.22	3
Attitude toward racial integration	.06	3
Involvement in religious affairs	.04	3
Problem Conditions		
Hyperactivity (adolescent males)	.75	7
Schizophrenia (risk for)	.70	6
Obesity (body mass index)	.50 to .90	8
Alcoholism (risk for)	.50 to .71	9

Sources: (1) Plomin, R., Owen, M. J., & McGuffin, P. (1994). The genetic basis of complex human behaviors. *Science, 264,* 1733–1739. (2) Nichols, R. C. (1978). Twin studies of ability, personality, and interests. *Homo, 29,* 158–173. (3) Loehlin, J. C., & Nichols, R. C. (1976). *Heredity, environment, and personality.* Austin: University of Texas Press. (4) McCartney, K., Harris, M. J., & Bernieri, F. (1990). Growing up and growing apart: A developmental meta-analysis of twin studies. *Psychological Bulletin, 107,* 226–237. (5) Martin, N. G., Eaves, L. J., Heath, A. C., Jardine, R., Feingold, L. M., & Eysenck, H. J. (1986). Transmission of social attitudes. *Proceedings of the National Academy of Sciences, USA, 83,* 4364–4368. (6) Plomin, R. (1990). *Nature and nurture: An introduction to human behavioral genetics.* Pacific Grove, CA: Brooks/Cole. (7) Stevenson, J. (1992). Evidence for genetic etiology in hyperactivity in children. *Behavior Genetics, 22*(3), 337–344. (8) Maes, H. H. M., Neale, M. C., & Eaves, L. J. (1997). Genetic and environmental factors in relative body weight and human adiposity. *Behavior Genetics, 27*(4), 325–351. (9) Rose, R. J. (1995). Genes and human behavior. In J. T. Spence, J. M. Darley, & D. J. Foss (Eds.), *Annual review of psychology* (Vol. 46, pp. 625–654). Palo Alto, CA: Annual Reviews.

TABLE 2.5 Correlations and Associated Heritability Estimates for IQ

	CORRELATION IN IQ SCORE	HERITABILITY ESTIMATE
Family Studies		
Biological relatives, raised together: (0.5G + 1.0Es)		
Parent with offspring	0.42	NA
Sibling with sibling	0.47	NA
Adoption Studies		
Biological relatives, adopted apart: (0.5G + 0Es)		
Parent with offspring	0.22	$0.22 \times 2 = .44$
Sibling with sibling	0.24	$0.24 \times 2 = .48$
Adoptive relatives (0.0G + 1.0Es)		
Adoptive parent with adopted child	0.19	$(0.42 - 0.19) \times 2 = 0.46$
Adopted sibling with adopted sibling	0.32	$(0.47 - 0.32) \times 2 = 0.30$
Identical twins, adopted apart (1.0G + 0Es)	0.72	0.72
Twin Studies		
Identical twins, raised together (1.0G + 1.0Es)	0.86	$(0.86 - 0.60) \times 2 = 0.52$
Nonidentical twins, raised together (0.5G + 1.0Es)	0.60	

Note: G refers to shared genetics; Es refers to shared environment.

Sources: Bouchard & McGue (1981), p. 1057; Plomin (1990), p. 70.

perceptual speed) and achievement scores (such as English usage, mathematics, social studies, and natural sciences).

So it seems that a variety of cognitive skills have a significant hereditary component. Does this component change across age? After all, different genetic systems may become more or less important at different ages. Also, environmental influences change as children age. Several studies have shown that heritability estimates for some cognitive skills do change—they *increase* with age, as shown in Figure 2.18 (Alarcón, Plomin, Fulker, Corley, & DeFries, 1998; Bishop et al., 2003; Boomsma, 1993; McGue, Bacon, & Lykken, 1993; Plomin & DeFries, 1998). In other words, the relative influence of genetics on cognitive skills appears to become stronger the older a person gets! When this result came out, it surprised many researchers. For decades it had been assumed that genes are particularly important in setting an individual's initial developmental path (remember the concept of canalization?), but that the environment exerts more and more influence with age (because we encounter more and more aspects of the environment with age). However, think back to the idea of niche-picking. Niche-picking theory says that individuals' genes affect their environment by guiding the environments they select. This effect then becomes stronger as people become more independent and make more of their own choices of environments. Perhaps the increase in heritability estimates reflects this indirect influence of genetics. It is also possible that the specific genes exerting their effects are different at different points in the life span. In other words, though the overall influence of genetics seems to increase, we do not know which genes are involved. Some may become more influential; others may become less important. Further work is needed to identify the contributions and interactions of specific genes at different points in time. It's also important to understand that research on heritability of cognitive skills is often controversial. There are concerns about issues such as bias in, or inappropriateness of, the measures used to assess the skills. We will return to this controversy when we talk about intelligence in Chapter 7.

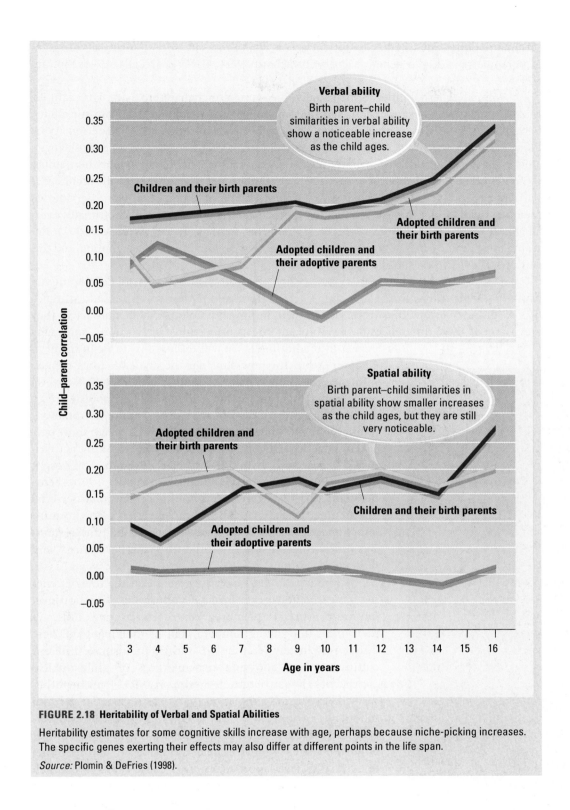

FIGURE 2.18 Heritability of Verbal and Spatial Abilities

Heritability estimates for some cognitive skills increase with age, perhaps because niche-picking increases. The specific genes exerting their effects may also differ at different points in the life span.

Source: Plomin & DeFries (1998).

■ **Heritabilities of Personality.** Behavior geneticists also have studied the heritability of many aspects of personality. As with research on cognitive skills, most studies of personality indicate that genetics are an important influence. Heritability estimates from twin and adoption studies range up to .70, as summarized in Table 2.4. Averaging across the major dimensions of personality, it seems that about 40 to 50 percent of variation in personality is due to genetic factors (Bouchard, 1994; Carey & DiLalla, 1994; Plomin, 1990).

Estimated heritabilities for personality measures also change across age. For example, for such measures as extraversion, neuroticism, emotionality, activity level, and sociability, heritabilities appear to decline after late adolescence (McGue et al., 1993; Pedersen, 1993; Plomin, Emde, Braungart, Campos, Corley, et al., 1993; Viken, Rose, Kaprio, & Koskenvuo, 1994). But note that researchers have calculated the vast majority of personality heritability estimates based on self-report or parent-report questionnaires. Can we trust the accuracy of self-reports, and are they consistent across time? More recent studies that use observational methods yield a wider range of heritability estimates—and lower heritability estimates overall (Emde et al., 1992; Plomin et al., 1993; Robinson, Reznick, Kagan, & Corley, 1992). Research into specific genes or gene markers for aspects of personality is only beginning, and this work has identified no specific markers so far.

One personality characteristic that has received much attention from developmental psychologists is *temperament,* or a child's activity level and pattern of response to stimulation. Children clearly differ from an early age in how irritable, sociable, and active they are. Many of these differences have significant effects on a child's interactions, and many

Could cultural differences in philosophical approaches reflect genetically influenced differences in temperament?

persist into adulthood. We will discuss this topic in detail in Chapter 9, but for now consider the evidence for a genetic influence on temperament. As you saw in Table 2.4, several aspects of temperament show moderate heritabilities (e.g., anxiety, sociability, activity–impulsivity, and emotionality). Studies with children as young as 3 months of age show persistent genetic influence on traits such as attention, activity, involvement, and shyness (Braungart, Plomin, DeFries, & Fulker, 1992; Cherny et al., 1994; Emde et al., 1992). Temperament differences are important for a child's interpersonal interactions. Perhaps you know from experience how your interactions with a child who is easygoing, smiling, and responsive differ from those with a child who is irritable, fussy, and difficult to soothe.

Some researchers have suggested that the role of genes in temperament has even broader, cultural-level implications. Jerome Kagan has proposed that societies may differ in the typical underlying temperament of their people. These differences in temperament may then predispose different cultures toward adopting certain kinds of philosophical approaches (Kagan, Arcus, & Snidman, 1993). This hypothesis leads to Kagan's suggestion that a basic aspect of cultural difference, each culture's underlying philosophical orientation, may reflect genetic factors. For example, Buddhist philosophies place more emphasis on serenity and harmony than do Western approaches, and those traits are much more common in people in Asian cultures than in Western ones. This may seem far-fetched, but consider the fact that Caucasian and Asian babies consistently show cultural differences in aspects of temperament such as activity level and vocalizing—and many aspects of temperament have a clear genetic influence. Kagan is not suggesting that one philosophical orientation is better than the other. Nor is he arguing that the environment is unimportant for temperament or philosophical orientation. But it is interesting to consider that an aspect of culture that has always been assumed to be environmental in origin may actually reflect some basic, genetically influenced tendencies.

thinking
OF DANIEL & TERI
◄ What can you tell Daniel and Teri about the heritability of personality traits and the role played by the environment?

We also find genetic influence when we measure specific manifestations of personality, including such things as voting, traditionalism, divorce, parenting, childhood accidents, exposure to drugs, television viewing, and even your choice of friends in college (Iervolino et al., 2002; Loehlin, 1992; Martin & Heath, 1993; Plomin, 1994; Plomin, Corley, DeFries, & Fulker, 1990; Tellegen et al., 1988). Clearly, there are no specific genes for such things as childhood accidents and TV watching. So why do these measures show a heritable component? Think back to our discussion of niche-picking, and think about what is involved in different kinds of activities, and these results may make more sense. For example, genetic predispositions toward introversion and lower activity levels might lead a child to choose to spend greater amounts of time watching television. But predispositions toward introversion and *higher* activity levels might instead lead the child to choose a solitary but fast-paced activity such as action video games. So the moderate heritabilities of specific activities and attitudes do not mean that they are "coded in the genes." Instead, these findings support the idea that genetics influence some basic aspects of personality, which in turn lead a person to select specific activities and develop certain attitudes from among the available choices.

In Table 2.4 you can see that the heritability estimates for hyperactivity, schizophrenia, obesity, and alcoholism are fairly high. Researchers have reported preliminary evidence for specific genetic markers for a few of these behaviors, but they will have to do much more research before we can draw confident conclusions (Cloninger, Adolfsson, & Svrakic, 1996; Holden, 1995; Rose, 1995).

In this chapter we discussed the basics of how genes work. We considered what genes are composed of, how they are transmitted from one generation to the next, and how they influence complex behaviors like intelligence and personality. The current work in behavioral genetics is exciting, and the astonishing pace of progress on the Human Genome Project virtually ensures that in a few years we will know much more about genetic influences on behavior. We hope you will keep several important points in mind as you think about the information on genes and environment. First, it is becoming increasingly clear that genes and the environment interact in complex ways. The central question for those interested in the development of children has evolved from "Which factor?" to "Which factor has the biggest effect?" to the current "How do the two factors work together to influence complex behaviors and characteristics?" Second, we must reiterate that the fact that a characteristic or a behavior is influenced by genetics does not mean that the environment is unimportant; nor does it take away an individual's free will. As Gottlieb notes, "genes do not make behavior happen, even though behavior won't happen without them" (1997, p. xiii). Finally, much of the work currently under way investigates genetic contributions to controversial attributes and behaviors, such as intelligence, sexual orientation, and aggression. Fully as important as research on the role of genes is the issue of how societies interpret and use the information that researchers discover. Behavior geneticists hope that society will use new discoveries to develop and implement informed and humane policies—but it is the responsibility of thoughtful policy makers and an informed public to make this happen.

1. Mr. Cho consistently treats all of his students in the same way, and all of the students respond in the same way to his classroom structure. In this case, Mr. Cho's classroom treatment is part of his students':

    a. shared environment.

    b. nonshared environment.

    c. neither shared nor nonshared environment.

    d. shared or nonshared environment, depending on how "shared" is defined.

2. In twin studies, correlations for nonidentical twins raised together include the influence of:

    a. only genetics.

    b. only the environment.

    c. half the genetics and half the environment.

    d. half the genetics and all the environment.

3. Suppose researchers estimated the heritability of smoking addiction at 0.95. Based on this heritability estimate, which of the following is true?

    a. There is a "smoking" gene.

    b. Some people have a genetic predisposition to smoking addiction.

    c. If you have the "smoking gene," you will become addicted to nicotine.

    d. The environment has no effect on whether smoking addiction develops.

4. **True or False:** The main goal of behavior genetics is to explain why people are similar to one another in their behaviors.

5. **True or False:** In general, most of the cognitive skills that have been assessed show a moderate degree of heritability.

Answers: 1. a, 2. d, 3. b, 4. F, 5. T

thinking
BACK TO DANIEL & TERI

Now that you have studied this chapter, you should be able to give Daniel and Teri a detailed explanation of how nature and nurture will operate together to influence the development of their adopted son. First, you could review the process of meiosis to explain how crossing-over and the random shuffling of chromosomes ensure that each new baby receives a unique combination of chromosomes and genetic material. The baby will not be a clone of either of his biological parents, but instead will inherit a portion of the genes from each parent. If the biological parents carry any inherited disease, there is a chance that the baby will develop the disease. If Daniel and Teri have access to the results of any genetic tests (e.g., amniocentesis or CVS) that were performed, they could learn if their baby is susceptible to such a disease. With some inherited diseases (e.g., hemophilia) early knowledge and intervention may save the child's life. With others (e.g., Tay–Sachs disease), Daniel and Teri may not be able to help much.

Daniel and Teri will likely be especially interested in the effect that the environment they provide will have on their adopted baby. You can explain the complex kinds of G × E interactions that take place, including the ideas of range of reaction, experiential canalization, and probabilistic epigenesis. Each of these concepts suggests how an enriched environment may help their child realize a greater amount of his genetic potential. In fact, environment can even affect which particular genes are expressed. Yet it also will be important to help Daniel and Teri understand that although the environment they provide is critical, even this environment will be affected in important ways by their baby's genetics. You can describe how evocative G × E interactions and niche-picking work. Finally, you can help Daniel and Teri understand the idea of heritability. Remember that heritability estimates indicate genetic influence but do *not* imply that the environment is unimportant for the development of specific traits or behaviors. By helping Daniel and Teri understand heritabilities in terms of genetic predispositions that might or might not be activated by the environment, you can help them watch for opportunities to foster skills they see in their child. It will be important to communicate that their child's development depends on his genetics *and* his environment—neither factor can operate alone.

What are the differences among chromosomes, DNA, and genes? What is the Human Genome Project, and what can we learn from it?

Most cells in the human body contain 46 chromosomes (23 pairs). DNA molecules are arranged along each chromosome. DNA is a string of nucleotide bases (adenine, thymine, guanine, and cytosine) linked in complementary pairs (A–T and G–C). A gene is a segment of DNA, usually several hundred to several thousands of base pairs long. Each gene provides the code for a trait, tissue, or other structure. It is the aim of the Human Genome Project to identify the full genetic code for human beings. From the project we already know about specific gene codes for a wide variety of diseases and other traits.

What is the difference between mitosis and meiosis? How are identical and nonidentical twins formed?

In mitosis, the 46 chromosomes in the original cell are copied into two cells. With meiosis, however, the number of chromosomes is reduced to 23 in each sex cell (sperm and egg). With crossing-over and the random shuffling of chromosomes to cells, meiosis increases the genetic diversity in offspring. Identical (monozygotic) twins form when one fertilized egg splits later in development to form two zygotes. MZ twins share the same genetic code. Nonidentical (dizygotic) twins come from two separate eggs fertilized by separate sperm. DZ twins are no more alike genetically than are any other sibling pairs.

How do dominant–recessive gene traits work, and what are some of the more common examples?

Chromosomes operate in pairs, and the genes on each member of the pair work to influence our traits. If you inherit one dominant and one recessive allele, the dominant allele will determine the trait. For a recessive allele to be expressed, you need to carry the recessive allele on both chromosomes. Arched feet, dimpled cheeks, and detached earlobes are examples of dominant traits. Flat feet, nondimpled cheeks, and attached earlobes are recessive. Huntington disease is an example of a dominant-gene disease. Cystic fibrosis, sickle-cell disease and Tay–Sachs disease are recessive. Recessive diseases carried on the X chromosome (e.g., hemophilia, Duchenne muscular dystrophy, color blindness, and some forms of retinitis pigmentosa) are more likely to be expressed in males. Dominant X-linked diseases (e.g., vitamin D–resistant rickets, Rett syndrome) occur more in females. Fragile-X syndrome is caused by a weakened tip on the X chromosome and is more likely to occur in males.

What are the major chromosome abnormalities?

Chromosome abnormalities involve missing or extra chromosomes. Down syndrome occurs when children have an extra chromosome at location 21 (trisomy 21); it causes mental retardation and other problems, and the risk of having a baby with Down syndrome increases dramatically as the mother's age passes 35. Klinefelter syndrome usually occurs when males have an extra X chromosome (XXY); males can also have an extra Y (XYY). In trisomy X (XXX) females are born with an extra X chromosome. Females can also have a missing sex chromosome (only one X), leading to Turner syndrome. Sex reversal sometimes occurs when part of the Y chromosome is lost (leading to XY females) or becomes attached to the X chromosome (leading to XX males).

What are the main procedures doctors use to identify structural defects and genetic abnormalities in developing fetuses?

Ultrasonography (ultrasound) sends sound waves through the mother's abdomen to produce images of the fetus. Through ultrasound the doctor can monitor the growth of the fetus and can detect many structural defects and other problems. In amniocentesis fluid is removed from the amniotic sac and fetal cells are retrieved for genetic testing. In chorionic villus sampling (CVS), cells are removed from the chorionic layer of the placenta. Amniocentesis and CVS allow clinicians to detect chromosome abnormalities and several hundred genetic diseases.

In what ways do genes and environment interact to produce behavior?

Several concepts have been proposed to explain how genes and the environment interact. Some concepts, like range of reaction and canalization, emphasize the limits that genes set on possible developmental paths. Others emphasize the role of the environment in limiting outcomes (experiential canalization) or in activating certain genes (probabilistic epigenesis). The interactions are complex: Sometimes the environment works to "turn on" or "turn off" certain genes, and sometimes genes influence the child's environment. Researchers agree that both genes and the environment are essential and that they interact in very complex ways to produce behavior.

What are shared and nonshared environments? How does each contribute to development?

A shared environment involves experiences that are shared by all those who live together, while a nonshared environment is unique to a particular individual. Behavior geneticists conclude that shared environment contributes to behavioral similarities to only a small degree and that most similarity in behavior is due to shared genetics. The major environmental effect comes from nonshared environment, which contributes to differences between people's behaviors.

However, there is disagreement about how to classify aspects of the environment as shared and nonshared.

How is a heritability estimate obtained? What are the heritabilities of cognitive skills and personality?

Heritability is a numerical estimate of the degree of genetic influence on a particular trait. Twin and adoption studies estimate the heritability of human traits by subtracting correlations in various ways. Modern path analyses provide more accurate heritability estimates by statistically accounting for such problems as unequal environments, selective placement, and relations between genes and environments. Many cognitive skills and personality traits show small to moderate heritabilities. Surprising levels of heritability have been found for some very specific behaviors, probably because of genetic influence on more general underlying traits. Even high heritabilities, however, do not mean that the environment does not have an important influence.

KEY TERMS

adoption studies (74)

allele (47)

amniocentesis (63)

behavior genetics (72)

canalization (67)

chorionic villus sampling (CVS) (63)

chromosomes (43)

dizygotic (DZ) twins (53)

DNA (43)

dominant–recessive relationship (55)

Down syndrome (60)

G × E interaction (66)

gene (43)

heritability (72)

Human Genome Project (44)

meiosis (49)

mitosis (49)

monozygotic (MZ) twins (52)

niche-picking (69)

nonshared environment (72)

probabilistic epigenesis (70)

range of reaction (66)

sex chromosomes (54)

shared environment (72)

twin studies (73)

ultrasonography (ultrasound) (62)

X-linked (sex-linked) traits (59)

Chapter 3

Prenatal Development and Birth

CHAPTER PREVIEW

A PERSPECTIVE TO think ABOUT

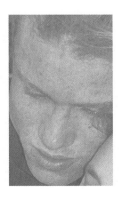

"Not only are Kendra and James too young to have a baby, but they also drink alcohol frequently and may use other drugs as well."

Kendra is 17 years old and has been dating 18-year-old James for 6 months. Last week she learned she is pregnant. Kendra's mom is very worried—not only are Kendra and James too young to have a baby, but they also drink alcohol frequently and may use other drugs as well. In addition, there is a family history of premature babies, and Kendra's mom is worried that Kendra's young age makes this more likely. Kendra seems serious about doing what is best for her baby, but she knows little about prenatal development. James wants to be supportive and help in any way he can after the baby is born, but he believes there isn't much he can do to help during the pregnancy and birth. What concerns should they have about the health of the baby? What are some of the most important risk factors that you see in their situation? What are the potential effects of their behavior on the developing baby? What steps can Kendra and James take now that would improve the chances of the baby being born full-term and healthy?

After reading this chapter, you should be able to identify more than a dozen potential risks, and you should also know how to advise Kendra and James so they can minimize the risks that they might face during pregnancy. What advice would you give to Kendra's mom and the teenage couple?

 As you read this chapter, look for the questions that ask you to think about what you're learning from Kendra's and James's perspectives.

A s in many unplanned pregnancies, Kendra, James, and their families worry about the health and development of the baby. Although Kendra and James are young and did not plan to start a family, they want to do what they can so their baby will be healthy. But many couples do not have much information about how a baby is conceived and develops prenatally, or about how their behavior can affect the developing fetus. In this chapter we will discuss the basics of conception, prenatal development, and birth. We'll also detail a variety of factors that can adversely affect the developing fetus. As you read, it may seem that the odds are stacked against a new baby's ever being born healthy! It's true that many things can harm a developing fetus, but we hope you will also notice that many important influences are controllable. That is a very positive thing in our view, because it means that any woman and her partner can greatly increase their odds of having a healthy baby—by making positive, healthy lifestyle choices. And the truth is that the vast majority of pregnancies do produce healthy, full-term babies.

Prenatal Development

Prenatal development is the development of an organism before ("pre") its birth ("natal"). Prenatal development includes the creation of the organism through fertilization as well as the typical course of development up to birth. In this section we will discuss how conception occurs, then trace the events that take place as the organism develops.

As you study this section, ask yourself these questions:

- What happens during fertilization? What events must precede and follow fertilization for a pregnancy to take place and continue?

- What events mark the beginning and end of each prenatal stage? What kinds of problems can occur in each stage?

- Which stage is most critical for the formation of the baby? Why?

Conception

The female reproductive system, shown in Figure 3.1, contains two ovaries. Each ovary will nourish several hundred egg cells (ova) as they mature and become ready for fertilization. During a woman's reproductive years, an ovum will come to maturity approximately every 28 days. When the ovum has matured, the ovary releases it in a process called **ovulation**. During a typical menstrual cycle, only one ovum matures and is released. But when more than one ovum is released, nonidentical twins or triplets can be conceived. Experts estimate that two ova are emitted 1 in 80 times and that three ova are emitted 1 in 6,500 times (Nathanielsz, 1992).

After ovulation the ovum moves into the fallopian tube adjacent to the ovary. It is in the upper and wider part of the fallopian tube that fertilization normally occurs. As many as 500 million sperm cells can be ejaculated during intercourse, but only a few hundred will survive the journey through the mother's uterus and into the fallopian tube containing the egg. During **fertilization** the 23 chromosomes from one of the father's sperm cells combine with the 23 chromosomes

prenatal development

Development of the organism that occurs before ("pre") its birth ("natal").

ovulation

Release of an egg (ovum) from the female ovary.

fertilization

The union of the father's sperm cell with the mother's egg cell yielding one fertilized cell with a unique combination of genes along 46 chromosomes.

At fertilization, 23 chromosomes from the father's sperm cell join 23 chromosomes from the mother's egg to produce a unique combination.

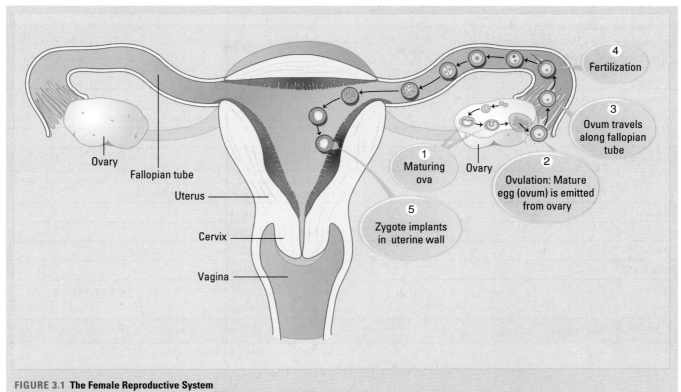

FIGURE 3.1 The Female Reproductive System

When an egg is mature, it is emitted from the ovary and moves down the fallopian tube. If fertilized, the egg will form a zygote that will travel to the uterus and become implanted in the inner lining, where it will continue its development.

Labels in figure:
Ovary
Fallopian tube
Uterus
Cervix
Vagina
Ovary
1 Maturing ova
2 Ovulation: Mature egg (ovum) is emitted from ovary
3 Ovum travels along fallopian tube
4 Fertilization
5 Zygote implants in uterine wall

from the mother's ovum to create one fertilized egg cell. As soon as one sperm cell penetrates the ovum's outer membrane, a reaction immediately seals the membrane, making it impermeable to other sperm. This is nature's way of ensuring that only 23 chromosomes from the father, carried by one sperm, join with 23 chromosomes from the mother.

Following fertilization, prenatal development will proceed according to an intricate schedule of cell division and differentiation. All of the cell divisions throughout prenatal development occur by *mitosis*. As we described in Chapter 2, mitosis is a "copy division" that results in a complete copy of the genetic material in all 46 chromosomes in each cell. The cell then divides and forms two identical cells. During this early phase of cell division researchers refer to the organism as a *zygote*. (Notice that mitosis is different from meiosis, the "reduction division" process we discussed in Chapter 2.) **Differentiation** is the important process whereby each new cell, as it divides, forms a particular structure—such as a muscle cell, a heart cell, or a brain cell—that serves a particular function. How each dividing cell "knows" which structure and function to acquire is one of the great mysteries of life. Geneticists are trying to discover how certain segments of DNA selectively "turn off" and other segments "turn on" to program the cell for its specialized purpose.

Stages of Prenatal Development

Researchers typically organize the major prenatal events into three stages: the *germinal stage*, the *embryonic stage*, and the *fetal stage* (Moore & Persaud, 1998). Table 3.1 provides a summary of the major events and milestones that occur as mitosis and differentiation proceed. Let's look at these stages in more detail.

differentiation
Process that occurs during cell division in which each new cell, as it divides, is committed to becoming a particular structure and serving a particular function.

TABLE 3.1 Major Events and Milestones during Prenatal Development

STAGE AND AGE SINCE CONCEPTION	EVENT OR MILESTONE
Germinal Stage (0 to 14 days)	
12 hours	First cell division of fertilized egg (zygote is now two cells).
3 to 4 days	Zygote enters the uterus.
	First cell differentiation leads to trophoblast and blastocyst.
8 to 12 days	Implantation of zygote in uterine lining.
Embryonic Stage (weeks 3 to 8)	
14 days	Blastocyst differentiates to form ectoderm, mesoderm, endoderm. Major genetic and chromosomal abnormalities can cause miscarriage.
3 weeks	Spinal cord and brain begin to form.
3 to 4 weeks	Placenta and umbilical cord form.
4 weeks	Eyes begin to form, heart flutters, arm buds appear.
5 weeks	Arms developed, leg buds appear.
8 weeks	Organogenesis complete; all major organs and structures have begun.
	Embryo weighs 1/30th of one ounce.
Fetal Stage (weeks 8 to birth)	
8 to 12 weeks	First arm and leg movements, not detected by mother.
	First reflexes appear.
	Sex can be detected with ultrasound.
17 to 20 weeks	Mother feels fetal movements.
	Heartbeat can be heard with stethoscope.
	Fetus weighs about 1 pound.
24 weeks	Fat begins to form; rapid weight gain begins.
26 to 28 weeks	Lungs mature enough to support breathing.
	Fetus weighs approximately 2 pounds.
38 to 40 weeks	Normal gestational age for birth.
	Newborn weighs 7½ pounds on average.

■ **The Germinal Stage: Conception to 2 Weeks.** The **germinal stage** spans the first 2 weeks of pregnancy, beginning at conception and ending when the zygote implants itself in the mother's uterine lining. Approximately 12 hours after conception, the fertilized egg cell divides for the first time, resulting in two identical cells. The zygote will take 3 to 4 days to travel through the fallopian tube before reaching the uterus, where the first cell differentiation takes place. The outer layer of cells divides rapidly and elongates to form an outer layer called the *trophoblast.* The inner cells, or *blastocyst,* remain more rounded in appearance. Over the next few weeks, cells in the trophoblast will differentiate further to become the placenta, umbilical cord, amniotic sac, and other structures that support the developing baby. The blastocyst will later develop into the fetus itself. The fact that the placenta and other support structures develop from cells in the zygote has important implications for genetic counseling. Recall from Chapter 2 that in chorionic villus sampling (CVS), specialists sample cells from the placental membrane. Because these cells originated from the zygote, they have the same genes and chromosomes as the baby.

germinal stage

The first stage of prenatal development, from conception to 2 weeks.

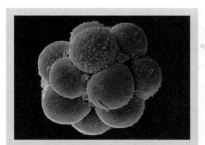

Here is a zygote only 4 days after fertilization. At this point, it contains only about a dozen cells and may still be traveling through the fallopian tube on the way to the mother's uterus.

By 8 to 12 days after conception, **implantation** occurs: The zygote embeds itself in the inner lining of the mother's uterus. After this point in development, we refer to the organism as an *embryo*. To generate energy to support the rapid cell divisions that take place in these early days, the embryo can absorb oxygen and nutrition from direct contact with the mother's blood. The embryo irritates the mother's uterine lining, burrowing into the tissue that lines the inner surface of the uterus. Blood from the mother's tissue covers the embryo, and oxygen and nutrients can then "leak" into the embryo. At this point the embryo does not yet have its own circulatory system (a heart or blood vessels). Even when it does, later in development, the mother's blood never mixes directly with the blood in the fetus; the two blood supplies are kept separate within the placenta. Hormonal changes in the mother have allowed the uterine lining to be most nourishing at about 9 days after conception, so this is the optimal time for implantation. After 9 days hormonal changes cause the lining to be less nourishing. As a result, the risk of pregnancy loss increases rapidly unless the embryo implants by the 9th day (Wilcox, Baird, & Weinberg, 1999).

Of course, once the embryo makes contact with the uterine lining, it becomes vulnerable to any toxins that might exist in the mother's bloodstream. For healthy development to proceed, the mother's blood needs not only to be rich in healthy nutrients and oxygen but also to be free from harmful substances such as alcohol, cocaine, and nicotine. We will discuss the harmful effects of such substances later in this chapter.

■ **The Embryonic Stage: Weeks 3 to 8.** The **embryonic stage** begins after the second week of pregnancy. At this point the blastocyst differentiates into three cell layers: the ectoderm, the mesoderm, and the endoderm. The *ectoderm* is the outer layer of the cell mass, and during the embryonic stage it will give rise to the nervous system (including the brain and spinal cord), sensory receptors, and outer skin layers. The *mesoderm,* or middle layer, will become the circulatory system, skeleton, muscles, excretory system, reproductive system, the outer layer of the digestive tract, and the inner layer of skin. The *endoderm,* or inner layer, will eventually become the respiratory system and the remainder of the digestive system. This differentiation is critically important. If major genetic abnormalities exist at this point in development, miscarriage is likely to occur. Remember, this differentiation occurs early in pregnancy, only 2 weeks or so after conception. A miscarriage at this early stage is unlikely even to be noticed by the mother.

Soon after the first differentiation of cells in the embryo, the embryo becomes elongated and folds over to form a neural tube. During the 3rd week the brain and spinal cord begin to form from the neural tube. At the time when the first brain cells are differentiating from the neural tube, they are extremely vulnerable to toxins in the uterine environment. If the first brain cells are damaged, irreversible alterations can jeopardize normal brain development.

During weeks 3 to 4 the placenta and umbilical cord form. Their function is to provide a more efficient supply of oxygen and nutrition to the growing embryo. The *placenta* is spongy tissue that grows out of the trophoblast layer and into the uterine lining of the mother. After just a few weeks, it surrounds most of the embryo and provides a surface

implantation

Process where the zygote embeds itself into the inner lining of the mother's uterus.

embryonic stage

The second stage of prenatal development, weeks 3 through 8. The embryo forms tissue representing every system and major part of the body.

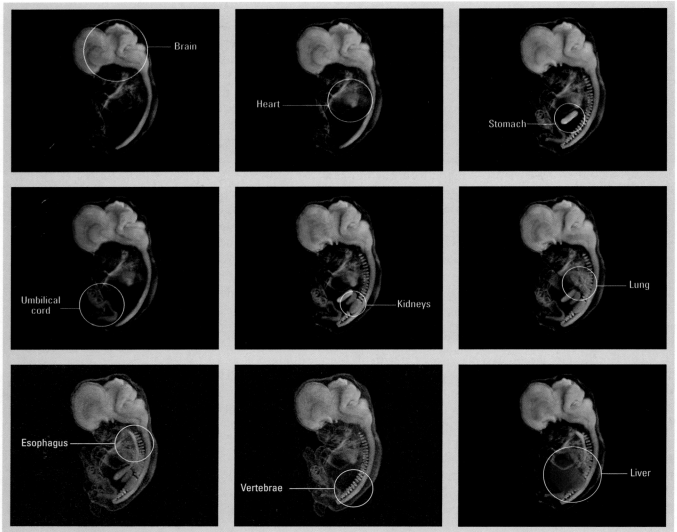

An embryo at 54 days' gestation (about 8 weeks) is seen here. By the end of the embryonic stage of prenatal development, all the major body structures have formed but they are not functional yet.

where the mother's blood comes into very close proximity to the blood cells from the baby. The *umbilical cord* connects the placenta to the developing embryo. It contains two arteries and one vein that carry materials back and forth between the mother and the developing baby.

Now supplied with greater fuel and oxygen, the embryo can undergo even more rapid and complex development. By 4 weeks the eyes begin to form, the torso continues to form, and the heart tissue begins to "flutter" in a primitive heartbeat. Arm buds also appear. By 5 weeks the arms have developed and leg buds begin to form.

If you look back across these early weeks of development, you can see two patterns that describe the formation and growth of the embryo. One of these is the **cephalocaudal pattern.** *Cephalo* refers to head and *caudal* to tail, so the cephalocaudal pattern is the tendency of the areas in the head and upper body to form and grow before the areas in the tail or lower body.

cephalocaudal pattern

A pattern of growth where areas in the head and upper body tend to form and grow before the areas in the lower body.

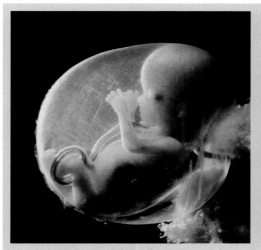

The fetal stage of prenatal development lasts from 8 weeks until birth. These photos show the fetus at 3 months (left side) and at 5 months (right side). Notice the growth in size and amount of detail of body structures.

As you've seen, the brain and eyes form before the arms, and the arms before the legs. The second is the **proximodistal pattern**. *Proximo* refers to nearness (to the body's midline) and *distal* to distance away (from the midline). Heart tissue, for example, is near the midline, and it begins to form before the arms, which are away from the midline. These patterns help us estimate the **critical periods** in development—the times when structures are first forming, and when they are most vulnerable to damage if the initial cell divisions are disrupted by environmental events. We will encounter the cephalocaudal and proximodistal patterns again in Chapter 4, because they also describe the pattern that occurs as infants gain control and coordination over their muscles—first in the upper body and along the midline, and later in the lower body and away from the midline.

By the 8th week after conception, organogenesis is complete. **Organogenesis** is the process through which each important body structure differentiates within the embryo. At the conclusion of this process, each structure is represented by its own unique cellular tissue. Brain, heart, lungs, kidneys, fingers, genitals, and even toenails are now identifiable in the embryo. Although most of the important organs are not yet functioning, all of the major structures now exist. The completion of organogenesis signals the end of the embryonic stage. The embryo is now just over one inch long and weighs only a 30th of an ounce.

■ **The Fetal Stage: Week 8 to Birth (38 to 40 weeks).** Once organogenesis is complete, we refer to the organism as a *fetus*. The **fetal stage** spans a period of about 32 weeks and represents by far the longest period during prenatal development. During this time the fetus grows dramatically in size and weight. Meanwhile, the tissues and organs differentiate further (gaining detail) and gradually become functional. During weeks 8 through 12, the first arm and leg movements begin, although the mother cannot yet feel them. The first reflexes also appear—usually the startle and sucking reflexes—and the sex organs develop enough that an ultrasound examination can reveal the sex of the fetus. During weeks 17 through 20, the mother begins to feel movements as the fetus rolls around within the amniotic sac and moves its arms and legs. The heartbeat can now be heard with a stethoscope.

At 18 weeks the fetus weighs less than 1 pound and is not yet mature enough to survive outside the uterus. By week 24 fat begins to form, and now rapid weight gain begins.

proximodistal pattern
A pattern of growth where areas closer to the center of the body tend to form and grow before the areas toward the extremities.

critical periods
Segments of time when structures are first forming and are most vulnerable to damage.

organogenesis
Organ formation: process where each major organ and system in the body differentiates within the embryo.

fetal stage
The third and final stage of prenatal development, lasting from 8 weeks after conception until birth.

thinking
OF KENDRA & JAMES

Kendra will gain weight ▶ rapidly while her baby is in the fetal stage. Can you explain why it is important for her baby that Kendra gains a healthy amount of weight during this stage?

Weight gain is critically important for survival, as the newborn baby will live off of accumulated fat during the first few days until the mother's breast-milk supply is well established. By 26 to 28 weeks the lungs are mature enough to allow successful breathing. At approximately 2 pounds, the fetus may now be viable if born early; but development that occurs during the final weeks is still important, increasing the chances of survival and vastly improving the health of the newborn baby. During weeks 28 through 40 the fetus typically gains more than 5 pounds. The major organ systems become more functional and strong, and the brain develops very rapidly. At its peak during the fetal stage, the brain produces 250,000 new cells per minute (Kolb, 1999), and it will total 80 billion cells by birth! At the end of a normal gestational period (38 to 40 weeks), the average newborn weighs 7½ lbs. and is approximately 21 inches long.

Even after infants are born, they are dependent on their caregivers for nourishment and support.

LET'S REVIEW . . .

1. The process of fertilization normally occurs in the:
   a. ovary.   b. fallopian tube.   c. uterus.   d. placenta.

2. What is the process whereby each new cell, as it divides and is created, commits to becoming a particular structure and serving a particular function?
   a. organogenesis   b. mitosis   c. implantation   d. differentiation

3. Major genetic abnormalities normally lead to a miscarriage at the beginning of the:
   a. germinal stage.   b. embryonic stage.   c. fetal stage.   d. baby's birth.

4. All of the major organs and tissues in the body have started to form by the _____ week after conception.
   a. 8th   b. 12th   c. 20th   d. 24th

5. **True or False:** The sex organs of the fetus can be detected by ultrasound beginning around 3 to 4 weeks after conception.

6. **True or False:** At around 26 to 28 weeks after conception, the lungs are mature enough to support breathing if the baby is born early.

Answers: 1. b, 2. d, 3. b, 4. a, 5. F, 6. T

Teratogens: Hazardous to the Baby's Health

Each year hundreds of thousands of babies are born with birth defects that threaten their lives or compromise their future development. Most defects occur from unknown causes. About one-third, however, are related to environmental factors that threaten the fetus while it is still developing in the mother's womb (Moore & Persaud, 1998). Because we have some control over mothers' exposure to these factors, we can greatly reduce the incidence of these birth defects. But to do so, we need to know what the factors are and how people can avoid them. This section will explain some of the most important changes that we can make to protect the health of developing babies.

During most of its prenatal development, the fetus is surrounded by structures that support and protect it. The fetus floats within the amniotic sac, where the amniotic fluid buffers it against temperature changes, loud noises, and the mother's sudden movements. The placenta and umbilical cord deliver the oxygen and nutrients that the fetus needs. Blood from the mother and baby does not actually mix, but the smaller molecules (such as oxygen and nutrients) squeeze into the baby's bloodstream in the placenta. Waste products that build up on the baby's side of the placenta are eliminated in the reverse process—they squeeze into the mother's bloodstream, and they are then processed and eliminated by the mother. At one time people believed that these structures fully protected the fetus from harmful elements in the environment. Today, however, we know that the fetus is not fully protected. We have learned this lesson the hard way—by seeing thousands of babies born with serious birth defects.

During the 1960s a new area of research emerged: *teratology*, or the study of teratogens. A **teratogen** is any substance or environmental factor that might cause birth defects. For example, when toxins such as alcohol and cocaine get into the mother's bloodstream, they cross the placenta and damage the developing fetus. Pollution in the environment can build up in the mother's tissues, and many of these harmful chemicals can be transmitted to the fetus. Infectious viruses and diseases in the mother also can reach the fetus.

As you study this section, ask yourself these questions:

- If a mother drinks alcohol, smokes cigarettes, or uses illegal drugs during pregnancy, how does this affect her fetus? Why do these substances have the effects that they do?

- Are there times during pregnancy when these substances are more or less harmful? Why?

- What is the impact on a fetus of any infectious disease that the mother might carry?

- Do teenage mothers, or mothers who delay childbearing until their late 30s or 40s, face special risks?

- What about the roles and responsibilities of men and fathers? Are teratogens matters of concern for them, too, or only for women?

The most common teratogens and risk factors are summarized in Table 3.2. In the next several sections, we highlight a few of these risk factors and describe why their associated birth defects occur.

Alcohol

According to a nationwide survey, 19 percent of all pregnant women drink alcohol during their pregnancies (National Institute on Drug Abuse [NIDA], 2001). Unfortunately, alcohol use during pregnancy can be catastrophic. Numerous studies with both humans and animals have established that alcohol exposure during pregnancy can cause physical deformities, growth retardation, damage to the central nervous system, and even miscarriage and fetal death (Cornelius, Goldschmidt, Day, & Larkby, 2002; Institute of Medicine, 1996).

teratogen

Any substance or condition that might disrupt embryonic development and cause birth defects.

TABLE 3.2 Teratogen and Risk Factors

TERATOGEN OR RISK FACTOR	POTENTIAL EFFECTS
Legal and Illegal Drugs	
Alcohol	The leading known cause of mental retardation. Fetal alcohol syndrome (FAS) includes growth deficiency, head and facial deformities, and central nervous system dysfunction. Fetal alcohol effects (FAE) include retarded growth, microcephaly, hyperactivity, lowered IQ, and other effects occurring alone or in combinations.
Cocaine	Preterm birth. Growth retardation. Malformations in brain, intestines, genital–urinary tract. Hemorrhage, lesions, and swelling in the fetal brain. Irritability, muscle tremors, rigidity, decreased spontaneous movement, visual problems, sleep disturbance in newborns.
Cigarette smoking	Low birth weight is the most common problem. Increased risk of spontaneous abortion, stillbirth, neonatal deaths, hyperactivity, poor school performance.
Marijuana	Low birth weight, muscle tremors, increased startle response, visual problems. Increased risk of leukemia has been reported.
Heroin	Low birth weight, jaundice, respiratory distress in newborns. Also withdrawal symptoms that include restlessness, agitation, muscle tremors, sleep disruption that can continue for 4 to 6 months. Increased fetal and neonatal deaths.
Environmental Pollution	
Mercury	When absorbed by pregnant women, can cause the fetus to develop brain damage, blindness, mental retardation, and cerebral palsy. Found in some industrial settings; accumulates in fish from contaminated waters.
Polychlorinated biphenyls (PCBs)	When consumed during pregnancy can cause prematurity, low birth weight, microcephaly, lower scores on infant measures of neurological health, and visual and short-term memory problems. PCBs come from industrial settings and material such as electric insulators; leach into the groundwater. Many water sources and fish in the industrial midwest are contaminated with PCBs.
Lead	Lower levels are associated with cognitive impairment in infancy; moderate to higher levels are associated with growth retardation and miscarriage. Lead is found in industrial settings, air pollution, and old paint in many homes.
Electromagnetic radiation	No measurable effects have been found for exposure to the small doses associated with computer monitors, microwave ovens, radio waves, or electric blankets, or to medical procedures such as ultrasound, magnetic resonance imaging (MRI), and most medical X rays. Large doses (e.g., as in repeated pelvic X rays) should be avoided.
Maternal Diseases	
Herpes simplex virus (HSV)	Prematurity, microcephaly, eye disorders, and mental retardation.
Cytomegalovirus (CMV)	Embryonic death, growth retardation, microcephaly, blindness, deafness, mental retardation, and cerebral palsy.
Syphilis	Syphilis infection in the infant, deafness, malformations of teeth and bones, facial deformities, excess fluid in the brain, and mental retardation.
Human immunodeficiency virus (HIV)	Effects not clear but include infant HIV infection, growth retardation, microcephaly, and head and facial deformities.
Rubella (German or 3-day measles)	Rubella in the infant, cataracts, heart defects, deafness, glaucoma, and lowered IQ.
Chicken pox	Brain damage; mental retardation; muscle atrophy; skin scarring; and malformations of the eyes, limbs, fingers, and toes.
Other Maternal Conditions	
Stress	Studies are mixed. Some show low birth weight, early labor, and increased labor complications. Animal studies show more serious effects, including pregnancy loss.
Age	Teen pregnancy has been associated with low birth weight, early delivery of the baby, and increased rates of neonatal death. Risks of prematurity, fetal death, and complications during birth increase slightly as women move through their late 30s and into their 40s.
Paternal Considerations	
Alcohol	Studies with rats and mice have shown damage to genetic material in sperm and increased activity levels in offspring.
Cocaine	May bind to sperm cells and be carried to the egg. May disrupt development in the embryo or jeopardize its survival.
Indirect effects	Pregnancies are threatened when fathers or men contribute to the risky behaviors of women. Men must consider the extent to which they encourage or promote women's use of legal or illegal drugs, contribute to environmental pollution, and spread sexually transmitted and other diseases. Healthy pregnancies are the responsibility of men as well as women.

Additional references (others cited in text): *Marijuana:* Dalterio & Fried, 1992; Robison et al., 1989. *Heroin:* Kaltenbach & Finnegan, 1992; Wilson, 1992. *Environmental pollutants:* Bentur, 1994; Bentur & Koren, 1994; Jacobson & Jacobson, 1996; Jacobson, Jacobson, & Humphrey, 1990; Moore & Persaud, 1998. *Maternal diseases:* Moore & Persaud, 1998. *Stress:* Anderson, Rhees, & Fleming, 1985; Barlow, Knight, & Sullivan, 1979; Berkowitz & Kasl, 1983; Burstein, Kinch, & Stern, 1974; Ching & Newton, 1982; Falorni, Fornasarig, & Stefanile, 1979; Istvan, 1986; Newton & Hunt, 1984; Standley, Soule, & Copans, 1979.

Alcohol damages the fetus in several ways. The alcohol in the mother's bloodstream does cross the placenta, and once it reaches the fetus it can disrupt cell division and kill fetal cells. Cells in the brain and nervous system are particularly vulnerable to alcohol—and once destroyed, these cells are not replaced. Alcohol in the mother's bloodstream also causes vessels in the placenta to constrict, reducing the flow of blood through the placenta. This reduced blood flow deprives the developing fetus of the oxygen and important nutrients needed for healthy development.

Alcohol-exposed children are at greater risk for being impulsive, easily distracted, and hyperactive (Mattson & Riley, 1998; Mick, Biederman, Faraone, Sayer, & Kleinman, 2002). Retarded brain growth (microcephaly) and lowered IQ are prominent features of alcohol exposure. In fact, experts now state that prenatal alcohol exposure is the leading known cause of mental retardation in the United States (Abel & Sokol, 1987; Institute of Medicine, 1996). Once a baby is born with mental retardation, there is no cure. Abstinence from drinking, however, would prevent every single case of alcohol-induced mental retardation as well as every case of the even more serious syndrome—fetal alcohol syndrome.

Fetal alcohol syndrome (FAS) was first identified in 1968 (Lemoine, Harousseau, Borteyru, & Menuet, 1968, as cited in Mattson & Riley, 1998). An FAS newborn shows all of the following conditions: (1) overall growth deficiency; (2) head and facial malformations; and (3) dysfunction of the central nervous system (brain and spinal cord), often resulting in some degree of mental retardation (Institute of Medicine, 1996). Babies exposed to alcohol are typically small for their gestational age, indicating a disruption in overall growth during pregnancy. Tight eyelids, flattened midface, short nose, and thin upper lip are typical head and face malformations associated with FAS. Lowered IQ, hyperactivity, and poor motor coordination are examples of deficits that indicate dysfunction of the central nervous system. The combination of these conditions defines the syndrome known as FAS.

In the United States the estimated incidence of FAS is between 2 and 5 in every 1,000 live births, or as many as 12,000 births, each year (Sampson et al., 1997). More frequently, babies are born without the full syndrome but still show one or more of the individual symptoms, such as lowered IQ and hyperactivity, or lowered IQ alone. These conditions are commonly referred to as **fetal alcohol effects (FAE)**. The physical defects and the cognitive and behavioral deficits associated with FAE may be subtle and may not even become apparent until later in childhood. As a result, it is hard to estimate their incidence. Still, researchers believe that as many as 1 in every 100 live births shows FAS or FAE (Sampson et al., 1997). And this estimate does not include the number of miscarriages and fetal deaths attributable to alcohol damage.

FAS and the more severe forms of FAE tend to occur when mothers are chronic alcoholics (consuming at least six drinks per day) or engage in regular binge drinking (consumption of four or more drinks per occasion, at least once per week). The effects depend on a variety of factors. These include the timing of the exposure, the genetic health of the fetus and mother, the alcohol metabolism and tolerance of the mother, and the pattern of drinking during

This child has fetal alcohol syndrome (FAS), a combination of birth defects that includes facial deformities, growth deficiency, and nervous system dysfunctions that can include lower IQ and hyperactivity. FAS is completely preventable if women avoid alcohol consumption during pregnancy.

fetal alcohol syndrome (FAS)

A syndrome of birth defects caused by prenatal exposure to alcohol. Includes growth deficiencies, head and facial malformations, and central nervous system dysfunction.

fetal alcohol effects (FAE)

Individual or multiple birth defects caused by prenatal exposure to alcohol. Lowered IQ, hyperactivity, growth deficiencies, and physical malformations can exist alone or in combinations but not in a way that indicates FAS.

pregnancy. You should be aware, however, that noticeable attention deficits and hyperactivity have been reported with babies whose mothers consumed only three drinks, on average, per week (Mattson & Riley, 1998). When it comes to protecting the health and developmental integrity of the baby, there really is no safe level of alcohol consumption.

Cocaine

About 1 out of every 100 women responding to a nationwide survey reported using cocaine during pregnancy (NIDA, 2001). As you might imagine, however, women tend to underreport use of illegal drugs such as cocaine. When researchers analyzed the fecal material of newborns to detect prenatal cocaine exposure, they found that 6.3 percent of privately insured and 26.9 percent of Medicaid or underinsured babies tested positive for cocaine exposure (Schutzman, Frankenfield-Chernicoff, Clatterbaugh, & Singer, 1991). It is evident that a large number of babies are being exposed to cocaine, especially those born to lower-income mothers.

Fetal exposure to cocaine retards growth, can cause preterm birth, and can cause malformations in the baby's brain, intestines, and genital–urinary tract (Moore & Persaud, 1998). In adults cocaine causes blood vessels to constrict and can dramatically increase blood pressure. Therefore, sudden heart failure, stroke, and brain hemorrhage are possible in any adult who consumes a large dose of cocaine—and the effects are similar in the developing fetus. Cocaine-exposed newborns can show evidence of hemorrhage, lesions, swelling in the brain, and other brain abnormalities. Cocaine also alters the function of neurotransmitters in the brain (this is how it produces the euphoric effect in adults). This can disrupt how the fetus's brain grows and forms connections during the prenatal period. As a result, cocaine-exposed newborns tend to show increased irritability, muscle tremors, rigidity, and decreased spontaneous movement. They also show impaired sensory function, decreased visual attention, and trouble regulating their own state of arousal (asleep, awake, or attentive).

Cigarette Smoking

Approximately 12 percent of pregnant women smoke cigarettes. These rates vary widely by age and race, however. For example, among all of the U.S. births registered in 2000 to mothers who were 18 to 19 years old, 31 percent of Caucasian mothers smoked while pregnant (Martin, Hamilton, Venture, Menacker, & Park, 2002). The rate was only 8 percent among African American mothers and 3 percent for Mexican Americans.

Cigarette smoke contains more than 450 different harmful chemicals, including nicotine, carbon monoxide, carbon dioxide, and cyanide (Martin, 1992). These chemicals damage the placenta and reduce the blood supply to the placenta and uterus, and this cuts down the supply of oxygen and nutrients available to the fetus. In addition, nicotine is an addictive stimulant that tends to suppress appetite, so women who smoke tend to eat less and gain less weight during pregnancy. But pregnant women need to gain sufficient weight to properly support the nutritional needs of the baby. On average, women gain 20 to 25 pounds while pregnant. When they gain less weight, their babies are more likely to be premature and are at greater risk for health complications.

Low birth weight is the most common problem associated with newborns of mothers who smoke. In addition, children born to mothers who smoked during

YOUR PERSPECTIVE

NOTES

Which do you think has more alcohol in it: one mixed drink, one beer, or one glass of wine? Most research shows that they are all equal: one mixed drink is equivalent to a 12-ounce beer or a 5-ounce glass of wine.

YOUR PERSPECTIVE

NOTES

Binge drinking is frequent on college campuses; can you see the danger with this behavior?

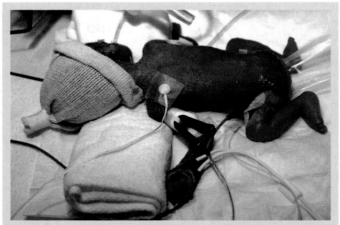

Born to a mother who used cocaine during pregnancy, this tiny baby was born too early. She will be at a very high risk for a variety of health problems, and only time will tell if she can even survive.

The Case of Malissa Ann Crawley

From Anderson, South Carolina: When Malissa Ann Crawley gave birth to her third child, Antwon, his blood tested positive for cocaine. Crawley was arrested for unlawful neglect of a child (Associated Press, 1999). Crawley pleaded guilty to the neglect charge and was sentenced to 5 years in prison. After serving 2 months, she was released to appeal her case.

The South Carolina State Supreme Court upheld Crawley's conviction, stating that a pregnant woman can be charged for harming a viable fetus. The United States Supreme Court refused to hear the case, so Crawley went back to prison. After serving approximately one year and completing a 6-month addiction treatment program, Crawley was released under the conditions that she must find suitable employment and housing and that she must submit to frequent home visits and drug testing.

South Carolina takes a strong stand in prosecuting pregnant women who use illegal drugs, and most other states have passed similar legislation. For example, in Florida, Indiana, Minnesota, Oklahoma, and Utah, mothers can be charged with abuse if their babies are born with FAS or showing addiction to drugs (Tomkins & Kepfield, 1992). These get-tough policies are gaining wide attention—and raising thorny questions. In light of what we know about the harmful effects of teratogens, it seems that there is a growing trend to hold pregnant women responsible for their unhealthy behaviors. But are these laws appropriate? That is, will they protect the health of developing fetuses?

Many are concerned that the burden falls completely on the mother. In Nebraska the laws focus on the entire family as a unit, and it is possible to prosecute fathers who drink alcohol with their pregnant

wives or girlfriends (Tomkins & Kepfield, 1992). Does this seem like an appropriate response? And should men be prosecuted for delivering drugs to "minors" (i.e., fetuses) when they provide pregnant women with illegal substances? Finally, there is also concern about the "slippery slope." After we protect fetuses from the harmful effects of illegal drugs and alcohol, where do we stop? Do we prosecute women for smoking cigarettes, eating contaminated fish, working in stressful environments, eating poorly, or exercising too much?

Do you agree that Malissa Ann Crawley should have served time in prison for delivering cocaine to her unborn baby? If so, how far do you think such legal actions should go? And in the end, will laws be effective in discouraging people from engaging in behaviors that contribute to unhealthy pregnancies? ■

---

pregnancy are more likely to be hyperactive and to have short attention spans, and they tend to score lower in reading, spelling, and math (Fogelman, 1980; Naeye & Peters, 1984). Finally, cigarette smoke can damage the placenta. As a result, women who smoke during pregnancy are at increased risk for spontaneous abortions, stillbirths, and neonatal deaths. The good news is that more women are learning about the dangers of smoking. Since 1989 there has been a 37 percent decrease in the number of women who smoke during pregnancy (Martin et al., 2002).

So far, we have discussed the effects of alcohol, cocaine, and cigarettes. The additional effects from marijuana and heroin are summarized in Table 3.2. All of these are drugs of choice, and if pregnant women chose to avoid these substances, many millions of children could be born without birth defects. As a society, what should we do when women do not choose to avoid drugs during pregnancy? To see how one state tries to protect developing babies, read the Social Policy Perspective box on "The Case of Malissa Ann Crawley."

> **thinking**
> OF KENDRA & JAMES
>
> ◄ What concerns would you have if Kendra and James abuse drugs? What would the potential risks be for the fetus?

Maternal Diseases

If a woman is carrying an infectious disease while pregnant, it can endanger the fetus. The virus or microorganism that causes the disease in the mother will usually cross the placenta to the fetus and can cause birth defects or infectious disease in the baby. For example, some experts believe that up to 30 percent of premature births may be due to vaginal infections (Nathanielsz, 1992). If the mother has *rubella* (German or three-day measles) during the first trimester of pregnancy, there is a 20 percent chance that the infection will harm the baby. Cataracts, heart defects, and deafness are likely, and sometimes glaucoma and lowered IQ also result (Moore & Persaud, 1998). Let's look at three particularly worrisome diseases, all sexually transmitted: herpes, syphilis, and HIV/AIDS.

■ **Herpes.** *Herpes simplex virus (HSV)* is a sexually transmitted disease that, in adults, causes blisters around the mouth and lips ("cold sores") and blisters and sores in the genital areas. HSV is contagious and is passed between partners by oral and genital contact such as kissing, intercourse, and oral sex. The virus spreads most easily when sores are present, but it also can spread before the sores emerge and when there are no noticeable symptoms. About half of the American population is infected with HSV, but two-thirds of those infected are not aware that they have the disease (Herpes.com, 2002). Although HSV is mostly a nuisance disease for adults, it can have serious consequences for developing fetuses and newborn babies. When a woman catches HSV in early pregnancy, her risk of miscarriage increases threefold (Moore & Persaud, 1998).

Babies born with HSV usually contract the virus during delivery rather than through the exchange of blood elements through the placenta during prenatal development. If they receive antiviral medications, about half of HSV-infected newborns will escape permanent damage. The remaining half are at risk for serious neurological damage, mental retardation, and even death (Herpes.com, 2002). When mothers are not showing symptoms (such as open sores) at the time of birth, the risk of infecting the baby is very small (as low as 4 in 10,000 births). The risks are high, however, if the mother is showing symptoms at birth. In these cases doctors recommend *cesarean-section birth* (also referred to as C-section birth). In a cesarean section a surgeon removes the baby through an incision in the mother's abdomen and uterus to avoid exposing the baby to the virus (Herpes.com, 2002).

Cytomegalovirus (CMV), another member of the herpes family of viruses, is carried by 50 to 75 percent of U.S. adults (Mayo Clinic, 2003). Among adults, CMV spreads the same way as HSV: through kissing and other intimate contact. CMV remains dormant in most adults with healthy immune systems, so infected adults rarely experience any symptoms of the virus. For fetuses, however, the virus is very dangerous (Moore & Persaud, 1998). When CMV infection occurs during the embryonic stage of development (weeks 2 to 8), the embryo usually dies. If CMV infects a fetus later in pregnancy, the baby usually is born alive but is at risk for retarded growth, microcephaly (small head circumference, associated with delayed motor, speech, and mental development), blindness, deafness, mental retardation, and cerebral palsy.

■ **Syphilis.** *Syphilis* is another sexually transmitted disease. Fortunately, the incidence rate of syphilis infection has declined steadily since 1997 (Centers for Disease Control and Prevention, 2001a). If the mother contracts syphilis while she is pregnant and does not receive treatment, the baby will almost always be born with birth defects and infected with the disease. It is estimated that 1 in every 10,000 babies born alive in the United States has syphilis. Birth defects include deafness, malformations of teeth and bones, facial deformities, excess fluid in the brain, and mental retardation (Moore & Persaud, 1998). But prompt and adequate treatment of the mother can completely protect the baby from the ill effects of syphilis.

■ **HIV/AIDS.** The teratogenic effects of *HIV,* the virus that causes AIDS, are not yet clear, but they may include growth retardation and head and facial deformities. Babies born with HIV usually contract the virus at or near delivery, and the chances of infecting the baby with HIV increase if the mother breast-feeds the baby. During the early 1990s approximately 3,000 infants were infected with HIV each year in the United States. More than 80 percent of those babies' mothers abused drugs or had sexual partners who abused drugs (Kaltenbach & Finnegan, 1992). More recently, antiviral medications such as zidovudine (ZDV) have dramatically reduced the transmission of HIV from infected mothers to infants. Treatment of infected mothers with ZDV cuts the rate of transmission in half (Centers for Disease Control and Prevention, 2001b).

thinking
OF KENDRA & JAMES

◄ How can Kendra and James reduce the chances of spreading a sexually transmitted disease to their baby?

Maternal Age

In the United States, nearly 900,000 teenagers become pregnant each year, and nearly one-quarter of all first births are to teenage mothers (Ventura, Mosher, Curtin, Abma, & Henshaw, 2001). At the other end of the spectrum, many women delay childbirth to complete their educations and pursue careers. Are infants at greater risk when they are born to younger or older mothers? Is there a biological advantage if a woman gives birth in her 20s or 30s? For the most part, research has indicated that pregnancies tend to proceed in a healthy manner across all of the reproductive years.

As you can see in Figure 3.2, however, the percentage of babies born low in birth weight is highest for mothers under the age of 15 and over 45. Low-birth-weight percentages decline steadily through the teen years and begin to rise again in the 30s. You can also see that non-Hispanic blacks have a greater percentage of low-birth-weight babies across the entire range of ages—a racial and ethnic difference that needs to be addressed with better prenatal care and education.

Many adolescents are not socially and cognitively mature, and this may limit their ability to cope with the stress of an early pregnancy. Low income, poor education, social isolation, drug and alcohol use, and lack of early prenatal care are factors that tend to be associated

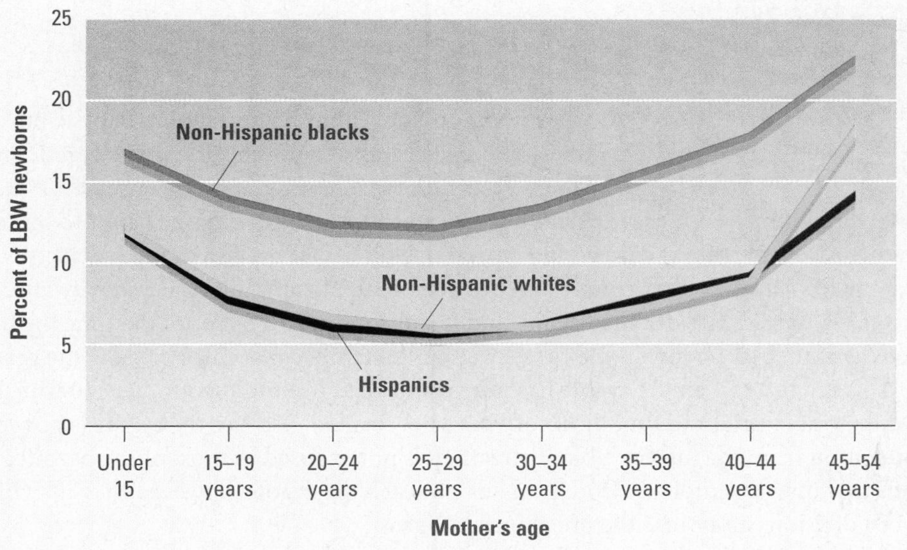

FIGURE 3.2 Percentage of Low-Birth-Weight (LBW) Newborns

The percentage of babies born low in birth weight (less than 5½ pounds) is greatest for mothers under age 15 and over 45. Data are based on all births registered in the United States during the year 2000 for non-Hispanic black, non-Hispanic white, and Hispanic mothers.

Source: Data from Martin et al. (2002), pp. 80–81.

Teenage mothers are at higher risk for giving birth to babies who are premature and low in birth weight. Problems are compounded by factors such as low income, inadequate access to prenatal care, and poor nutrition. Many teens are not psychologically or emotionally prepared for the responsibilities of caring for a new baby.

with teenage pregnancy—and with negative birth outcomes. There is also some question as to whether young teenagers, who may only recently have started menstruation, are biologically ready to carry a pregnancy to full term. Fortunately, the pregnancy rate for younger teens (ages 15 to 17) fell 21 percent during the 1990s, and the rate is now at its lowest point since the government started recording the statistic in 1976 (Ventura et al., 2001).

Women in the later years of their reproductive lives also have concerns. High blood pressure, diabetes, and other health conditions occur more frequently as women age. Whether because of biological health or as a result of other indirect factors (such as increased stress), the risks of prematurity, fetal death, and complications during birth increase slightly as women move through their late 30s and into their 40s (Berkowitz, Skovron, Lapinski, & Berkowitz, 1990; Cnattingius, Forman, Berendes, & Isotalo, 1992; Fretts, Schmittdiel, McLean, Usher, & Goldman, 1995). Among women who give birth in their 40s, mothers who are giving birth for the first time tend to have more problems than those who have already had one or more children. Older mothers have an increased risk of having a baby with Down syndrome (see Chapter 2). (Most of the other known chromosomal abnormalities are not associated with increased maternal age, however.) Yet even with some increased risks, we should emphasize that the vast majority of pregnancies do proceed normally and result in the birth of a happy and healthy newborn, even when the mother is over 40 years of age.

Critical Periods

At what point do you think the developing baby is most vulnerable to toxins such as alcohol, cocaine, and cigarette smoke? Are the defects more severe when the exposure occurs early in prenatal development? Or are they more severe when the baby is exposed closer to birth? You will find answers to these questions in Figure 3.3. Notice that the risk of birth defects is small during the first 2 weeks after conception but rises dramatically and peaks shortly after week 3. By week 8, the risk has declined again, and it will continue to fall until the time the baby is born. Why is the risk so low in the first 2 weeks? Remember that this period is the germinal stage. This is a time when the zygote has not yet attached itself to the mother's uterine lining and when the placenta and umbilical cord have not formed. Because the zygote is not yet getting nutrition from the mother's bloodstream, it is not exposed to most of the harmful compounds that may exist in her blood. If toxins do reach the zygote, however, they may disrupt early cell divisions and cause the pregnancy to be lost.

After week 3, the placenta and umbilical cord provide a conduit through which harmful elements can pass from the mother to the baby. This is also the period when most organs and structures are first forming—remember the concept of organogenesis? Therefore, any disruption at this stage can cause major malformations. After week 8, organogenesis is complete, so exposure now will tend to cause more minor malformations or disturbances in the functions of organs. For example, prolonged exposure to toxins during the fetal stage tends to cause growth retardation and lowered IQ.

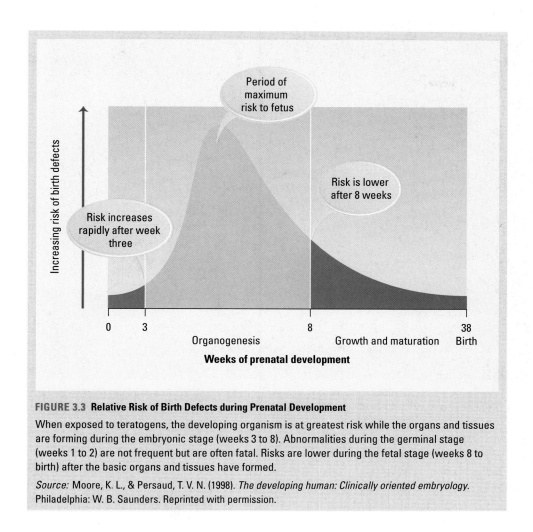

FIGURE 3.3 Relative Risk of Birth Defects during Prenatal Development

When exposed to teratogens, the developing organism is at greatest risk while the organs and tissues are forming during the embryonic stage (weeks 3 to 8). Abnormalities during the germinal stage (weeks 1 to 2) are not frequent but are often fatal. Risks are lower during the fetal stage (weeks 8 to birth) after the basic organs and tissues have formed.

Source: Moore, K. L., & Persaud, T. V. N. (1998). *The developing human: Clinically oriented embryology.* Philadelphia: W. B. Saunders. Reprinted with permission.

By looking at Figure 3.3, you can see that the early weeks of pregnancy are crucial to the baby's health. The problem, of course, is that most women are not even sure that they are pregnant until they are near (or even past) the 8th week of pregnancy. By then the critical periods for the major organ systems have passed. If women want to avoid the harmful effects of teratogens, can they afford to wait until they are sure they are pregnant before they adjust their lifestyles? We hope you can see that, to prevent the harmful effects of teratogens, women with risky habits really need to make changes even before they know that they are pregnant.

What about Fathers?

So far, we have discussed the birth defects that can occur when mothers expose their babies to toxic substances and conditions during pregnancy. Can babies also be born with birth defects because the father used or was exposed to teratogens? In most cases, when toxic substances affect sperm cells, the damaged sperm do not survive the long journey to the egg. Nature often seems to select out unhealthy sperm before they have a chance to fertilize an egg. Still, studies with rats and mice have shown that alcohol damages the genetic material in sperm (Abel, 1992). And in one study with rats, rat offspring showed increased levels of activity when their fathers consumed alcohol before the conception (Abel, 1993). Another study found that cocaine accumulates in the testes and other organs and can bind to human sperm

In many cultures, it is considered a romantic overture to offer a woman an alcoholic drink. Given what we know about the catastrophic effects of alcohol on the developing fetus, can't we think of a better way for people to communicate their interest in each other?

cells (Yazigi, Odem, & Polakoski, 1991). Because cocaine does not destroy the mobility and viability of the sperm cells, this means that cocaine ingested by the father can be carried to the egg cell during fertilization. Although human studies have not yet confirmed the effects, researchers suspect that cocaine can then directly disrupt development in the zygote, probably jeopardizing its survival. The vast majority of birth defects, however, result from the mother's exposure to toxins, because it is elements in the mother's bloodstream that cross the placenta to the developing baby.

Putting aside the direct effects of fathers' exposure to toxins, can fathers be responsible for birth defects in other ways? Think about alcohol, for instance. In the United States, 14 percent of men consume two or more drinks on average per day, but only 3 to 4 percent of women drink at this level (Abel, 1992). Also consider that 69 percent of women who are alcoholics have husbands who are also alcoholic. When men support the alcohol culture and encourage women to drink, don't they share responsibility for the results? Many fathers do reduce their alcohol consumption, or abstain completely, while their wives are pregnant.

thinking
OF KENDRA & JAMES
What can James do to help Kendra have a healthy pregnancy and reduce risks to the developing baby? Are the habits of Kendra's friends and other family members also important?

This is a supportive gesture, but is it sufficient? Remember that the most serious birth defects occur during organogenesis—that is, during weeks 2 to 8 of the pregnancy. Most women are not even aware that they are pregnant until around the second month. So male partners' abstention during pregnancy is not enough.

Men as well as women should realize that many of our exposures to toxins are due to our habits. And these habits develop over the many years before pregnancy occurs. To ensure a healthy pregnancy, a woman of reproductive age needs to avoid harmful substances even before she knows she is pregnant—or plan her pregnancy so she can take precautions ahead of time. Men should ask themselves if they want to encourage or contribute to women's use of alcohol, drugs, and tobacco. In light of what we know about the dangers of secondhand smoke, men should refrain from smoking around pregnant women to avoid harming the developing fetus. Men should also consider how they contribute to other prenatal hazards, from environmental pollution to sexually transmitted diseases. Clearly, healthy pregnancies are the responsibility of both women and men.

The Process of Birth

It's been almost 9 months and the time is nearly here. The baby's room is ready, the hospital bag is packed, and everyone is eagerly awaiting the birth of the new baby. Mom has been feeling a vague tightening in her uterus off and on for weeks or even months now, but these *false labor contractions* are only "practice," not as regular as real labor contractions will be. Eventually the contractions become more regular, closer together, and more intense. Within hours the baby will be born.

As you study this section, ask yourself these questions:

- What are the stages of labor, and what important events take place during each stage?

- What are some of the potential complications of the birth process, and what can be done to avoid or reduce them?

- What is the newborn baby like? What are the common treatments and tests given to the newborn?

- What are some of the psychological adjustments that parents and siblings must make after the birth of a baby?

Stages of Birth

Exactly what triggers the start of the birth process is still a mystery. Researchers believe that when the fetal brain reaches a certain point of maturity, it sends a signal that prompts hormonal changes in the mother (Nathanielsz, 1992). These changes cause the mother's uterine muscles to contract, and the contractions create an ever increasing feedback loop of hormones that stimulate more frequent and more intense contractions until the baby is born. As shown in Figure 3.4, physicians typically divide the birth process into three stages of labor: dilation, delivery, and afterbirth.

Stage 1 of labor is the longest, lasting on average from 6 to 14 hours. The length of this stage is usually longer for first-time mothers but varies significantly from one woman to another. This stage begins when the uterus starts regular contractions. The contractions are gentle and infrequent at first but eventually occur every 2 minutes or so (with each contraction lasting up to 2 minutes) and become much more intense. The contractions cause **dilation**, the gradual opening of the cervix. The *cervix* is a tough ring of tissue that has remained tightly closed throughout pregnancy to keep the fetus securely inside the uterus and help protect it from infection. During Stage 1 of labor, the cervix must dilate to 10 cm, which is about 100 times its normal diameter, to allow for passage of the baby. Contractions also cause the cervix to thin out—a process called *effacement*. In addition, the contractions push the fetus downward so the baby's head presses firmly against the cervical opening.

During Stage 2 of labor, the baby actually moves through the birth canal and is delivered. This stage is much shorter than the first, lasting an average of 30 minutes to 2 hours. Contractions are approximately 2 to 5 minutes apart, and they push the baby through the birth canal for delivery. During this stage the mother feels an overwhelming urge to bear down strongly to help push the baby out. This stage ends with the delivery of the baby.

In Stage 3 the placenta and other membranes emerge through the birth canal in a process referred to as **afterbirth**. During this stage, which usually lasts less than an hour, the mother continues to experience contractions as her uterus expels the placenta. These contractions are much less intense than those of the first and second stages. Mothers are usually quite preoccupied with their newborn baby, so their attention is not on the contractions.

Birthing Complications: Something Isn't Right

The vast majority of pregnancies end happily, producing a healthy infant. Occasionally, however, birthing problems occur—although we have learned a tremendous amount in the last half century about how to deal with these complications.

■ **Malpresentation.**　One complication during birth involves the position of the fetus. The optimal fetal position is head down. This position allows the head to move through the birth canal first and minimizes risk to both mother and baby. About 4 percent of the time, however, the fetus is positioned differently in the uterus, a situation called **malpresentation** (Fogel, 1997). In a *breech position* the buttocks or the feet are lowest in the uterus. In a *transverse position* the baby lies sideways inside the uterus. Both of these positions pose serious dangers during delivery.

Physicians or midwives can easily detect malpresentations before delivery by ultrasound procedures or by physical examination. Experienced obstetricians will often try to "turn" an ill-positioned fetus, though this is not always successful. In some cases the fetus turns on its own, sometimes just as labor begins, but it is impossible to predict whether or when this change will take place. To prevent potentially serious harm to the baby and mother, many practitioners choose a planned *cesarean section (C-section)* delivery for malpresented

YOUR

PERSPECTIVE

NOTES

Do you know someone who gave birth recently? How long was her labor? Was this her first delivery? If not, was her labor shorter this time than it was for her first delivery?

dilation

The gradual opening of the cervix caused by labor contractions during the first stage of birth.

afterbirth

The third and last stage of birth, in which the placenta and other membranes are delivered through the birth canal.

malpresentation

Improper positioning of the fetus in the mother's uterus.

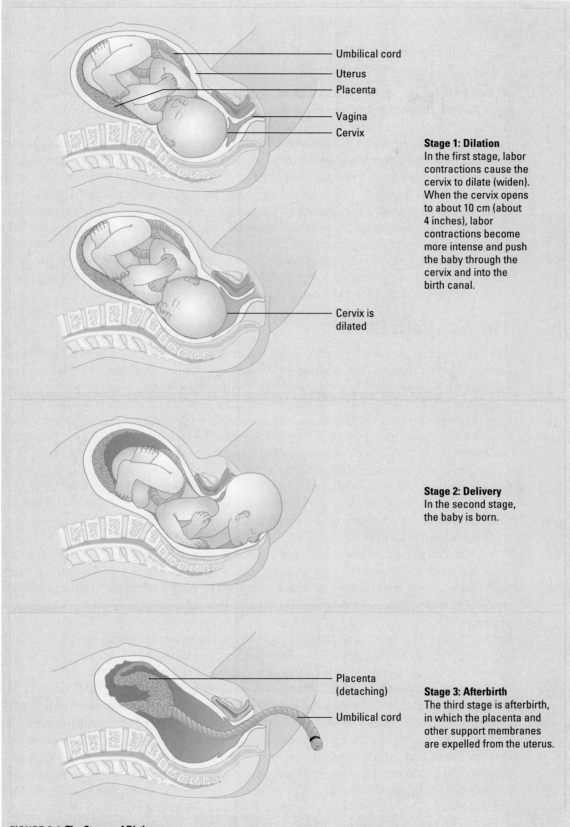

Umbilical cord
Uterus
Placenta
Vagina
Cervix

Stage 1: Dilation
In the first stage, labor contractions cause the cervix to dilate (widen). When the cervix opens to about 10 cm (about 4 inches), labor contractions become more intense and push the baby through the cervix and into the birth canal.

Cervix is dilated

Stage 2: Delivery
In the second stage, the baby is born.

Placenta (detaching)
Umbilical cord

Stage 3: Afterbirth
The third stage is afterbirth, in which the placenta and other support membranes are expelled from the uterus.

FIGURE 3.4 The Stages of Birth

In Stage 1 labor contractions cause the cervix to dilate (widen). When the cervix opens to about 10 cm, labor contractions become more intense and push the baby through the cervix and into the birth canal. In Stage 2 the baby is born. Stage 3 is afterbirth, in which the placenta and other support membranes are expelled from the uterus.

Source: Adapted from Moore & Persaud (1998).

babies. Malpresentation is a complication of birth, but it need not have serious consequences if it is detected and monitored carefully.

■ **Fetal Distress.**   Fetal distress occurs when the fetus experiences a sudden lack of oxygen, change in heart rate, or change in respiration. Any one of these can indicate that the fetus is at risk. Practitioners can identify these conditions by using electrodes or other devices to monitor the fetus during birth. One type of distress that can have very serious consequences is *anoxia,* or deprivation of oxygen. A fetus can withstand brief oxygen deprivation with no ill effects, but more than a few minutes of decreased oxygen can lead to permanent brain damage (Stechler & Halton, 1982). Anoxia can occur for any of several reasons. These include deterioration or premature separation of the placenta, maternal fatigue or hyperventilation during labor, sudden compression of the umbilical cord during labor, or failure of the baby to begin breathing immediately after birth. The possibility of anoxia is one reason why practitioners become concerned during longer labors, and it is a big reason for the increased amount of fetal monitoring currently done during labor. Early identification and prompt treatment of fetal distress is also a common reason for C-section deliveries.

The Newborn Baby

The long-awaited moment has arrived, and the newest member of the family is here! Physicians and nurses immediately examine the newborn to identify any potential problems. They monitor the baby's breathing and temperature regulation, and often treat the newborn's eyes with silver nitrate. This prevents visual problems due to diseases such as gonorrhea that the baby may have contracted from the mother during birth. Hospital or birthing center staffers also monitor the mother to ensure that she does not experience excessive blood loss or develop infections. They often encourage her to nurse the baby very soon after delivery.

The typical newborn baby is not a Gerber-baby look-alike—but is beautiful nonetheless. Infants' heads may seem huge in comparison to their bodies, and their skulls are usually misshapen from being squeezed during birth. Babies are born wet with amniotic fluid, and some may still have remnants of the white, cheesy coating (called vernix caseosa) that protected their skin before birth.

Newborns will turn their heads and eyes toward voices and will gaze into their parents' faces. Although their vision is still a little fuzzy, they can see. They also possess several adaptive reflexes. If you touch newborns' cheeks, they will turn their heads in the direction of the touch. Touch their lips, and they will suck. Both of these reflexes help a newborn find the nipple and begin feeding. And if you put your finger in the newborns' hand, the infant will reflexively grasp your finger and hold on tight. We will give a more complete description of newborns' reflexes and sensory abilities in the next chapter, along with a description of babies' growth and the development of their brains and nervous systems.

The first formal test that almost all newborn babies get right after birth is the **Apgar test,** by far the most widely used newborn screening assessment (Apgar, 1953). Practitioners conduct this brief assessment 1 minute after delivery and again 5 minutes after delivery. The reason for giving the assessment twice is to make sure that changes in a newborn's condition will be noticed—because subtle changes can be overlooked in the bustle surrounding a delivery. The Apgar test gives the infant a score of 0, 1, or 2 (2 being the best) on each of five dimensions: heart rate, respiration, muscle tone, color, and reflex irritability. The newborn's total score indicates overall condition. The maximum score is 10. A score from 7 to 10 means that the baby does not need any immediate assistance or close monitoring. A score of 4 to 6 indicates some potential problems: The baby needs close monitoring and possibly some intervention. A score of 0 to 3 indicates a serious risk and calls for immediate action.

fetal distress

A condition that indicates that the fetus is at risk; usually includes a sudden lack of oxygen (anoxia), a change in fetal heart rate, and/or a change in fetal respiration.

Apgar test

A brief assessment of the newborn conducted at 1 and 5 minutes after birth; used to identify newborns who are at risk and need medical attention.

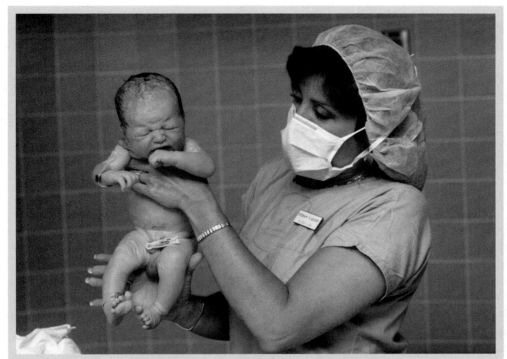

Most newborns are given the Apgar test at 1 and 5 minutes after birth to identify those who need immediate medical attention. This newborn has a healthy pink color.

Becoming a Family: Psychological Adjustments to Having a Newborn

For most families, having a baby is an exciting and happy event. Even so, the addition of a new person to the family requires a great deal of adjustment. Sleeping and eating patterns, family members' amount of free time, and attention to different individuals' needs and desires are all affected. Jealous siblings may even wish that the parents would "take him back"!

■ **The Transition to Parenthood.**   A successful transition to this new phase of family life involves a wide range of factors. Parents who are welcoming their firstborn child must adjust their self-perceptions: They are now a mother and father, not simply a couple. They must learn to share their time, energy, and emotion with this very needy newcomer. Success in this transition does *not* mean that the new parents experience no stress or problems—such a situation is probably impossible. Instead, in a successful transition the couple manages to identify and deal in positive ways with stressors and problems so that all the family members' needs are adequately met. Parents who have a supportive, positive relationship and well-developed coping skills can discuss and solve problems rather than avoiding or denying them (Belsky, Lerner, & Spanier, 1984; Duncan & Markham, 1988; Frosch, Mangelsdorf, & McHale, 1998; Heinicke & Guthrie, 1996). Families that have made a successful transition show more warmth toward one another, greater sensitivity to one another's needs, and more positive interactions with one another than families that have difficulties with the transition. The amount of time needed for this transition varies depending on the family, but it usually takes about 6 months to a year after the baby's birth.

The transition to parenthood also seems to bring to the forefront any issues that a new parent has with his or her own parents. For example, if a new father recalls the relationship with his own parents as cold or rejecting, such feelings can cast a shadow on his attitudes toward his new role as a parent (Belsky & Isabella, 1985). The same is true of identity issues. During the period of adjustment new parents incorporate a parental dimension in their self-concept—sometimes starting this process even before conception if the pregnancy is planned. And the more secure each parent is in who he or she is and in what is important to each person individually and to the family as a whole, the more successful the transition to parenthood seems to be (Diamond, Heinicke, & Mintz, 1996). Finally, the transition is easier if the new parents are realistic in their expectations, both of themselves and of their baby. Having a newborn can certainly be an exciting and joyous experience, but it also involves an incredible amount of hard work and sacrifice. To believe otherwise is to set yourself up for frustration and disappointment. And the bigger the gap between the expectation and the reality, the more difficult the transition will be.

In addition, there are *child factors:* The transition to parenthood can be made more or less difficult by several aspects of the newborn himself or herself. After all, infants arrive with temperaments and needs all their own. Some babies have sweet, compliant, happy temperaments. Some do not. Some babies do not sleep for more than 30 minutes at a time, never nap when the parents would like, do not eat well, spit up their food three times a day, and fuss from 5 to 7 p.m. every night. For the parents of more difficult babies, the transitional period can be easier if the parents (either together or alone) have regular breaks from the infant care. It's also important for them to remember that most families do find a workable routine eventually.

■ **The Transition to Becoming a Sibling.** An older sibling, once the "king of the hill," can have a difficult time coming to grips with the fact that he or she is no longer the center of everyone's concerns after a new baby arrives. Increases in whininess, sleeping difficulties,

The family system changes dramatically with the introduction of a new family member. Factors to consider in the adjustment include issues between the mother and father, and issues involving older siblings who have a new baby (or two!) with whom to share everything. What can this family do to ease their transition?

withdrawal, clinginess, aggressive behaviors, and toileting problems are common in older siblings during the first few months after the birth of a new baby. Most of these changes are short-term, lasting only a few months. Some studies, however, have found correlations between the birth of a sibling and lower levels of verbal development, achievement, and socioemotional adjustment several years later. These findings seem to apply particularly to children in economically disadvantaged families (Baydar & Greek, 1997; Baydar & Hyle, 1997). Such problems are probably due more to changes in the family's overall context and interaction patterns (e.g., poorer parenting strategies, less one-on-one time with the older child, increased financial stress, decreased opportunities for skill development) than to the birth of the newborn as such. And many children adjust quite well to a newborn sibling, showing few negative and even some positive changes. For example, some siblings show greater independence in feeding and toileting habits, improved language abilities, or better peer relations.

Though the transition to being a sibling is not likely to be conflict free, parents can help children adjust. It is important for parents to recognize that becoming a sibling is a major change and can be especially tough for preschool children. It makes sense to prepare the child as much as possible. Talk with the child about changes, acknowledge any negative feelings, and try to provide as much one-on-one time as possible. Help the child develop coping skills by suggesting positive ways to gain attention. Make sure the child has adequate opportunities to play with friends, and encourage more father–child interaction. Point out the many ways in which the older child is needed and can be helpful. And finally, parents should model positive coping skills and positive attitudes themselves, thereby helping the child see that the transition can lead to a new phase of family life that is as happy and secure as the phase before.

LET'S REVIEW . . .

1. What is the purpose of the contractions during Stage 1 of labor?
   a. to open the cervix
   b. to push the baby through the birth canal
   c. to push the placenta and other membranes through the birth canal
   d. to push the baby into a transverse position

2. Which stage of labor is typically the shortest and least intense for the mother?
   a. Stage 1   b. Stage 2   c. Stage 3   d. dilation

3. What is the main event that happens in Stage 2 of labor?
   a. dilation of the cervix
   b. beginning of labor contractions
   c. delivery of the placenta and other membranes
   d. delivery of the baby

4. What condition exists when a fetus is deprived of oxygen during the birth process?
   a. hypoxia   b. anoxia   c. malpresentation   d. breech birth

5. **True or False:** The correct order of events during the birth process is dilation of the cervix, delivery of the baby, and afterbirth.

6. **True or False:** An Apgar score of 5 indicates that the newborn is at serious risk and that immediate attention is needed to save the baby.

Answers: 1. a, 2. c, 3. d, 4. b, 5. T, 6. F

Options in Giving Birth: Choices and Alternatives

When a woman gives birth in the United States today, she has many options available to her that were not possible even 50 years ago. One of the biggest changes in recent decades has been the increasing control that a woman has over the circumstances surrounding the birth. In this section we will discuss many of the options that mothers and their families have for giving birth.

As you study this section, ask yourself these questions:

- What specific things can mothers and fathers do to prepare for labor and delivery? What birthing options are available, and what are the advantages and disadvantages of each?

- What are the advantages and disadvantages of the use of drugs during labor and delivery? What effects do these drugs have on mothers and on babies?

- What can the father do to help during labor and delivery? What are the effects of his presence during labor?

Approaches to Labor and Delivery

In the early 1900s, few babies born in this country were born in a hospital. Women gave birth at home attended by friends, family, and sometimes a midwife. There were few doctors in attendance, no harsh lights, no isolation from those who could offer emotional support. But there were also no drugs for pain relief and no medical assistance in cases of problematic deliveries. By midcentury, hospital births had become the norm. Women labored either alone in a room or in a ward full of other laboring women trying their best to cope with each contraction. Partners and other family members were not allowed to be with the women. Women lay in bed, often flat on their backs. When birth was imminent, hospital staff wheeled a woman to a delivery room and gave her a general anesthetic that rendered her unconscious. Her baby was born in a sterile and brightly lit operating room. Then nurses took the baby to the hospital nursery, where the mother could come and visit. Mother and baby often stayed in the hospital (though not in the same room) for up to a week.

How things have changed! Today, although 99 percent of babies are born in hospitals (Martin, Hamilton, Ventura, Menacker, & Park, 2002), there is much more awareness of the importance of personal support, pain management techniques (both drug- and non-drug-based), and the overall comfort level of the birthing environment. Today's modern *birthing centers* attempt to combine the advantages of a hospital—access to medical expertise and equipment in case of difficulties—with the comforts of a home birth. Rooms have rocking chairs and couches, and partners and family members are encouraged to stay with the laboring woman. Lighting is soft, staffers encourage relaxation techniques and moving around during labor, and even whirlpool baths are available in many places. Unless there are complications, labor and birth take place in the same room. *Rooming-in* lets the baby stay in the same room with the mother so that parents can begin getting to know their newest family member as soon as possible. As a society we have come to realize that having a baby is, in most cases, a normal life event rather than a medical condition. Today's birthing environment often reflects this change in view.

In addition, many births today are attended by *certified nurse–midwives* instead of physicians. To learn more about the midwifery profession, read the Professional Perspective box called "Career Focus: Meet a Certified Nurse–Midwife."

Career Focus: Meet a Certified Nurse–Midwife

Abbi Beuby
Kailua, Hawaii

Certified nurse–midwife working in a private OB/GYN practice

What does a midwife do? Why did you become one?

Delivering babies makes up about 5 percent of a typical midwifery practice. I work with pregnant patients from their first visit to last, and I do all the follow-up visits and postpartum checks. I am able to spend more time with them and do far more teaching than the physician has time for. I usually spend a half hour with them their first visit and then 15 to 20 minutes each subsequent visit. I do the initial ultrasounds and the third-trimester ultrasounds to check fluid and size of the baby. The rest of my day is spent doing annual visits, contraceptive counseling, and some primary care.

I was an RN in labor and delivery for 8 years, working with high- and low-risk patients, and I had my master's degree. I mostly thought this was the next step after being a nurse for so long. The most fun part of my job is when I do the first ultrasound that looks like "something" and the parents see their baby for the first time. (On the first ultrasounds the babies are usually too small to see anything.) I used to love doing deliveries, but that's very stressful. Essentially, you have two lives in your hands. It also requires a lot from your family, being on call all the time and up all night sometimes.

Why do some parents choose midwives? How is the birthing approach different?

Most women choose a midwife because we take a more natural approach to childbirth. Physicians see what can go wrong all the time; we see what is going right. We are taught that giving birth is a natural thing; women have been doing it forever. These days, doctors realize that women want a more natural birth and have been striving to achieve that, but this is relatively new. We spend more time with women in labor, coaching and helping them through, and in the total care, including office visits and postpartum care. We spend more time talking to them rather than at them. A midwife strives to remember not only their names but their other kids, parents, spouse, what they do for a living, vacation, and so on.

Are there situations or conditions in which you're not allowed to or would refuse to serve?

I do not take care of women with pregnancy-induced hypertension (preeclampsia/toxemia). I do not take care of those who go into preterm labor, before 36 weeks, and those who are severe diabetics. There are some women who come into the pregnancy with problems, and those are chosen case by case.

What advice would you give to prospective parents who are considering the midwife option?

Look at their credentials, meet them, and discuss their philosophy. Not all midwives believe the same thing or do things the same. Some are very natural and believe no pain medications should be administered. This works for some, but not everyone can handle that. Some do deliveries at home, others in hospitals, and everything in between, so there are lots of options. I also think it is important for the parents to meet with the midwife's backup physician. If things turn ugly, this is the person who they will need to trust to bring their child into the world.

What training and education is usually needed to work in your field?

There are a number of ways to become a midwife. The classic way is to become an RN first then get a master's degree. Certificate-only programs don't give a master's, but both of these routes give the title "certified nurse–midwife." Some programs don't require a nursing degree; those midwives are "certified midwives." Both of these certifications require a national board examination, and the certification must be renewed every 8 years. There is the "lay" midwife, which is the "learn-on-the-job" midwife. They are illegal in most states; however, they have a big following. In the midwest, many of the Amish use them. Here in Hawaii they are considered "a-legal"—not illegal, but also not legal. ■

thinking
OF KENDRA & JAMES

◄ How might a midwife be especially beneficial to Kendra and James? Conversely, in what ways would a traditional physician be better? Which of the two would you recommend Kendra and James consult?

Many expectant mothers attend prepared childbirth classes to learn about techniques they can use to ease the pain and anxiety of childbirth. The birthing partner seen here is learning how to help the mother relax during labor.

■ **Prepared Childbirth.** One common approach to labor and delivery is **prepared (natural) childbirth.** This approach is largely based on the work of Grantly Dick-Read (Dick-Read, 1933/1972) and of Frederick Lamaze (1958). Dick-Read believed that women become fearful of labor and delivery, partly because they do not know what to expect. This fear increases muscle tension during contractions, and the tension in turn creates pain. It becomes a negative cycle: Increased pain results in more fear and more tension, which increases the pain, and so on. Dick-Read theorized that if women could develop accurate and positive expectations about childbirth, they would experience far less pain.

The *Lamaze method* is one prepared childbirth approach. Lamaze builds both on Dick-Read's theory of pain during childbirth and on the theory of classical conditioning first described by Ivan Pavlov. According to Lamaze, women have been conditioned to believe that labor contractions will be painful. Just the thought of a contraction can cause women to tense up, making the pain of real contractions more intense. To break the conditioning cycle, in Lamaze prenatal classes women learn selective relaxation of muscles and controlled breathing. During labor, obviously the uterine muscles contract strongly—they have to in order to push the baby out. But most women instinctively tense other muscles in the body as the contractions begin. Lamaze training in selective relaxation helps women learn *not* to tense other muscles during uterine contractions. The tension and therefore the pain are reduced. Controlled breathing during contractions helps lessen pain by serving as a distraction from the contractions. Together, these two Lamaze techniques can greatly reduce the fatigue and pain experienced during childbirth.

So prepared childbirth involves education about labor and delivery to reduce fear of childbirth, and it also involves practicing selective relaxation and controlled breathing to reduce muscle tension and pain. The final element in prepared childbirth is the presence of a labor coach or companion. This is often the father of the baby. The coach attends the child-

prepared (natural) childbirth
Use of birthing techniques designed to reduce muscle tension, promote relaxation, and reduce pain during labor and delivery.

birth preparation classes with the woman, helps her practice the relaxation and breathing techniques, and is on hand and ready to offer assistance throughout labor and delivery. The coach can help the woman remember how and when to use the relaxation and controlled breathing she has learned, and can help talk her through the more difficult contractions (hence the name "coach").

Achieving a truly pain-free labor and delivery is not common, but women who use prepared childbirth methods experience less pain during childbirth, especially when they are accompanied throughout labor by husbands or partners (Davenport-Slack & Boylan, 1974; Nettlebladt, Fagerstrom, & Udderberg, 1976). Some studies also indicate that women who engage in prepared childbirth need less pain medication and enjoy childbirth more (Hodnett & Osborn, 1989; Moir, 1986). But it is not clear whether these positive effects are due to increased knowledge of what to expect during birth, to relaxation techniques and controlled breathing, to the presence of a support person—or to existing differences between women who choose to participate in prepared childbirth and those who do not.

■ **The Leboyer Method.** Another interesting approach to childbirth was developed by Frederick Leboyer, who argued that the hospital birth experience is unnecessarily traumatic for the baby (Leboyer, 1975). According to Leboyer, the environment and practices of the surgical-type delivery room (typical prior to Leboyer's time) created a decidedly uncomfortable "first impression" for newborns. There were harsh lights, loud sounds, and cold air; practitioners held the newborn upside down, put drops in his or her eyes, briskly cut the umbilical cord, and promptly removed the baby from the mother. All these events combined to create a highly traumatic experience. The *Leboyer method* carries out any necessary procedures, but in a calmer, quieter, and more respectful way. Typically, the Leboyer delivery room is quiet and softly lit. Helpers place the baby on the mother's abdomen immediately after birth, encourage skin-to-skin contact, and refrain from cutting the umbilical cord until it stops pulsing. They give the baby a bath in warm water (simulating the amniotic fluid that comforted the baby during pregnancy), then return the newborn to the mother and encourage nursing as soon as possible. Leboyer claimed that such practices produce babies who are more relaxed and alert. Research has not supported these advantages for Leboyer-born babies, but these practices do not seem to harm mothers or babies either (Nelson et al., 1980). Leboyer's methods have been extended by those who suggest that *underwater delivery* would be less harmful to both mother and baby. There is no evidence to suggest that this is correct, however (Moir, 1986).

■ **Home Births and Other Helpful Techniques.** More and more women in this country are returning to what was the norm in the early 1900s: giving birth at home rather than in a hospital or birthing center. A *home birth* offers many advantages to both mothers and babies. These include a comfortable and familiar environment, no concern about making it to the hospital in time, often extensive support from the mother's partner and other family members, and immediate and constant infant–family contact. The obvious disadvantage is that if problems develop for mother or baby, the equipment

Today couples have a variety of options to choose from when deciding how to give birth to their babies. This mother has given birth underwater to relieve strain and ease the transition of the baby through the birth canal.

Upright birthing positions have been used for centuries in certain cultures as seen in this Aztec statue. It was not until the early 1900s that hospital procedures required mothers to lie flat on their backs as a way to ease the process for *physicians*.

and personnel to deal with them are not immediately available. Home births can be a satisfying, comfortable, and safe choice if a woman has a trained professional (such as a midwife) on hand, has received thorough screening during pregnancy to identify potential problems, and has quick access to help in case of an emergency (Ackermann-Liebrich et al., 1996; Cohen, 1981; Hazell, 1975).

Whether giving birth in a hospital or at home, women today can move around freely during labor. Moving around and being upright seem to encourage labor to progress more quickly. When a woman stands, sits, or squats during contractions instead of lying down, her pelvis widens. This makes it easier for the baby to enter and move through the birth canal. Pushing is also more effective, because the mother has gravity on her side. Upright positions also seem to increase the blood circulation to the mother's abdominal muscles and increase the supply of oxygen to the baby (Cottrell & Shannahan, 1987; Fogel, 1997). Upright positions have long been the norm in other cultures; they were common even in this country in the early 1900s, when many U.S. obstetrical textbooks recommended upright positions during labor (Fogel, 1997).

Finally, one further source of help during labor and delivery can start long before the contractions begin: physical fitness. Many cultures encourage women to remain active and to get moderate, regular exercise throughout their pregnancies. The traditional reasons for this cultural practice may not be accurate in some cases—for example, some cultures believe that maternal exercise during pregnancy results in a smaller, and therefore easier-to-deliver, baby. Even so, research has provided support for this tradition. The more physically fit a woman is, the fewer complications she is likely to experience, the better she will feel during her pregnancy, and the faster her recovery time is likely to be (Hatch et al., 1993; Khanna, 1998; Stevenson, 1997). The American College of Obstetricians and Gynecologists says that women can benefit from mild to moderate regular exercise during pregnancy, with no apparent ill effects on the fetus, as long as they have no preexisting risk factors or complications (Marble, 1995). Pregnant women should avoid excessive physical exertion, however.

In summary, the alternative approaches to birthing allow families some choice in deciding what their birth experience will be. Simply having some degree of control over the event may help women and their partners develop a more positive attitude and feel more confident going into labor and delivery. This in turn may enable the mother to relax more; may reduce her tension, anxiety, and perhaps her pain; and may contribute to a more positive birth experience for the entire family.

YOUR
PERSPECTIVE
PERSPECTIVE
NOTES

If you are living with your biological parents, ask them about your birth and delivery. Did your mother use prepared childbirth techniques? Did she find them effective?

Drugs during Labor and Delivery

Even with the use of the prepared childbirth techniques we've described, most women experience significant pain and discomfort as labor contractions continue—sometimes for 12 hours or more—and the baby moves through the birth canal. Various studies have documented that anywhere from 68 to 95 percent of all hospital-based deliveries in the United States involve some type of medication for the relief of the mother's pain (Gibbs, Krischer, Peckham, Sharp, & Kirschbaum, 1986; Rosenblith & Sims-Knight, 1985).

During the middle part of the twentieth century, general anesthetics and major tranquilizers were used for pain relief. However, doctors later realized that many of these drugs crossed the placenta and placed the fetus at significant risk. Today there is a focus on minimizing the use of drugs during labor and delivery. Physicians administer the smallest doses possible and as late in labor as possible, and many women use prepared childbirth techniques to eliminate or decrease their need for pain medication. A popular approach is to use *epidural anesthesia,* the injection of a mixture of pain-relieving drugs into spaces along the spine of the mother. Usually physicians give epidurals low in the spine so that the drugs block sensations only from the waist down. Over the years, research studies assessing the effects of pain-relieving drugs on the health of the newborn baby have shown mixed results. Based on several reviews of this work, however, we offer the following general conclusions (Brackbill, McManus, & Woodward, 1985; Coalson & Glosten, 1991; Curran, 1991; Rosenblith & Sims-Knight, 1985):

▶ Many of the drugs tested have short-term effects on the newborn's behavior. These include respiratory distress; abnormal variations in heart rate; increased or decreased activity levels; difficulties in nursing; and difficulties controlling sleeping, waking, and alert states. Most drugs have not shown measurable long-term consequences, however.

▶ Different babies react to medications in different ways. Newborns with preexisting problems (such as premature babies) are at higher risk for detrimental effects of drug exposure.

▶ When long-term effects of medication have been found, they have generally been relatively small—typically, smaller than the effects of other factors such as low birth weight and lower socioeconomic status.

▶ The overall amount of medication administered is important; higher amounts are associated with more adverse outcomes.

▶ For some of the drugs studied, there may be some benefits to the fetus, such as increased oxygenation due to better uterine blood flow.

Epidural administration seems to be a relatively safe and effective way to deliver pain medication during labor. The most commonly used combinations of medications have not shown significant detrimental effects on the newborn. One complication, however, is that a mother who uses epidural medication loses sensation in the pelvic region and therefore cannot feel the normal urge to push. Women can be instructed when to push, of course, but the use of these medications can still prolong labor. Sometimes practitioners have to use forceps to assist the baby through the birth canal.

thinking
OF KENDRA & JAMES

◀ Help Kendra think about the use of pain-relieving drugs during labor. What questions should she ask her doctor about drugs and labor? What can she do to avoid using pain-relieving drugs or to reduce the dosages needed?

The Partner's Role: Helping during Birth

One aspect of the birthing experience that has undergone tremendous change is the family's role, especially the role of the father or partner. Throughout much of the twentieth century, in this country as in many others, the father's traditional role was to wait, pacing anxiously in the hospital halls, and maybe to hand out cigars after the baby's birth was announced. Even back when home births were the norm in this country, the father typically did not assist during labor and delivery—that task was left to midwives and female relatives. Since the advent of prepared childbirth, however, many women's partners have taken more active roles. Today, most partners participate at least to some degree in the birth of their children.

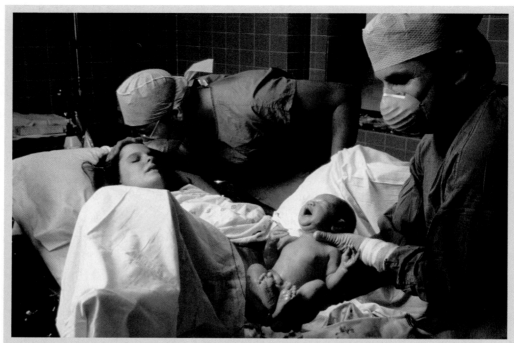

Partners today can be fully involved in the births of their children. This father coached his wife as she delivered their baby.

What do partners do during labor and delivery? Their role typically consists of four tasks. First, they help the expectant mother remain as comfortable as possible during labor, helping her walk around, change positions, and continue slow but normal breathing through contractions as long as possible. Second, partners coach the laboring woman to use the selective relaxation and controlled breathing techniques she has practiced during the pregnancy. This becomes an ever more important job as the contractions increase in frequency and intensity. Toward the end of Stage 1, the mother is often very tired. Perhaps she is a bit disoriented if the labor has been long, and she may feel anxious and unsure if she will be able to make it through the delivery. The coach/partner's help—in reminding her to take one contraction at a time, switch from one form of breathing to another, and relax—can make a tremendous difference in keeping the mother calm and in control. Third, the partner can offer great emotional support simply by being with the mother. Partners often know better than anyone else what kinds of things the laboring woman finds soothing or irritating, and what kinds of encouragement will be effective. Finally, partners often may assist with the actual birth. They sometimes "catch" the baby when he or she is born, and they can even cut the umbilical cord.

Though some partners may worry that they are not really being helpful, mothers report that their presence during labor is comforting and useful. Studies have found that when partners are present during labor, mothers experience less pain, need less pain medication, and enjoy the birth process more. Partners report benefits as well, expressing more positive feelings about the birth and greater emotional closeness to both the baby and the mother (Bondas-Salonen, 1998; Broome & Koehler, 1986; Cronenwett & Newmark, 1974; Davenport-Slack & Boylan, 1974; Dragonas, 1992; Nettlebladt et al., 1976; Szeverenyi, Hetey, Kovacsne, & Muennich, 1995).

Prematurity and Infant Mortality: Infants at Risk

Take a look at the premature baby in Figure 3.5. Prematurity is one of the biggest threats faced by infants in our country. Only 11.4 percent of babies are born preterm, but these babies account for up to 67 percent of infant deaths in the United States (McCormick, 1985; Nathanielsz, 1992). Although the United States ranks first in the world in health technology, we rank 17th among industrialized countries in the rate of low-birth-weight births, often associated with preterm birth (Children's Defense Fund, 2001b). And the rates of both preterm and low-birth-weight births are increasing. The incidence of preterm birth rose from 9.4 percent in 1981 to 11.6 percent in 2000. The rate of low-birth-weight births now stands at 7.6 percent, the highest level since 1973. The statistics for some groups within the U.S. population are even more grim. For example, African American women have a low-birth-weight rate of 13 percent and a prematurity rate of an alarming 17.3 percent; both of these percentages are nearly double those of whites (Matthews, Menacher, & MacDorman, 2002).

Clearly, there is reason for concern. But what do we know about the causes and effects of preterm birth and low birth weight? And, more importantly, what have we learned about how to prevent these serious problems?

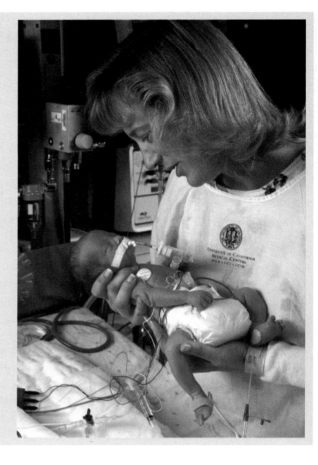

FIGURE 3.5 Premature Infant

This is a baby born at approximately 27 weeks' gestation and weighing only 2 pounds. If you could observe her in real life, you would notice that her limbs jerk and twitch, her breathing is erratic, and she shrinks from human touch as if it hurts. Her tiny body cannot properly regulate its own temperature, and her sucking reflex is not strong enough for breast or bottle feeding.

As you study this section, ask yourself these questions:

- What are the differences among preterm birth, low birth weight, very low birth weight, and the designation "small for gestational age"?
- What are the risk factors and possible effects associated with preterm and low-birth-weight birth?
- What is the relationship between prematurity and infant mortality?
- How can we reduce the rates of prematurity and infant mortality?

What Is Prematurity?

There is sometimes confusion about the meaning of the term *premature*. A normal full-term pregnancy is about 38 to 40 weeks long, and the average weight for full-term babies is 7½ pounds. Birth within 2 weeks of the expected due date (2 weeks early or late) is considered normal and full-term. A **preterm birth** is birth before 37 weeks' gestation, or more than 3 weeks before the expected due date. A baby born weighing less than 5½ pounds is considered to have a **low birth weight**. Newborns weighing less than 3½ pounds are classified as being at **very low birth weight** and are at even greater risk for serious problems. Infants who are **small for gestational age (SGA)** are those who are below the 10th percentile of birth weight for their gestational age (i.e., among the lightest 10 percent of babies born at that number of weeks since conception).

---

preterm birth

Birth that occurs before 37 weeks of gestation, or about 3 weeks earlier than the normal due date.

low birth weight

Weight less than 5½ pounds at birth (2 pounds lighter than average); indicates potential for health risks.

very low birth weight

Weight less than 3½ pounds at birth (4 pounds lighter than average); indicates serious health risks.

small for gestational age (SGA)

Born below the 10th percentile of birth weight for gestational age; indicates serious health risks

Why bother distinguishing among all these classifications? The reason is that their outcomes differ. In other words, different babies face different levels of immediate and long-term risk. Although preterm birth is certainly not good, many babies born preterm are at an appropriate level of development and weight, given their length of gestation. As long as birth weight is not too low and is appropriate for the gestational age—and provided that the infant receives appropriate treatment—many preterm babies go on to develop normally. Babies who are SGA, however, are particularly worrisome. Something has kept them from growing as well as they should have, given how long they've been in the uterus. It is difficult to know what has gone wrong in these cases, but poor prenatal nutrition of the fetus is a likely factor. Perhaps the maternal diet has been poor, or there have been problems with the placenta, or problems in the fetus have prevented it from being able to utilize nutrients. As you read earlier in this chapter, teratogens such as alcohol and cocaine also retard fetal growth, causing babies to be born small for their gestational age. SGA babies fare much worse than preterm infants. They show greater rates of infection, brain damage, and death during their first year and are more likely to show long-term problems in academic achievement (Copper et al., 1993; Korkman, Liikanen, & Fellman, 1996).

In about half of the cases of preterm birth and low birth weight, the causes are not known. Research has identified numerous risk factors, however. Table 3.3 lists some of these along with the most common effects of prematurity.

If you look closely at the list in Table 3.3, one of the most striking things you will notice is that several of the risk factors are controllable. This is good news: It means that our society may be able to reduce the risk of serious birth complications to some extent. That may not be a simple task, however. For example, lack of prenatal care consistently correlates with preterm birth and low birth weight. The reason for this correlation may be that no one detects early warning signs or addresses high-risk behaviors if the pregnant woman is not receiving regular prenatal monitoring. We know how to provide high-quality preventive prenatal care, but many women who stand to benefit from this kind of care either do not have access to it or do not use it. To see what it is like to have a baby who is very premature, read the Personal Perspective box called "Meet the Parents of a Very Premature Baby."

YOUR
PERSPECTIVE
NOTES
Do you know anyone who was or who had a preterm or low-birth-weight baby? What were the suspected causes? What have the effects been?

TABLE 3.3 **Risk Factors for and Effects of Preterm and Low-Birth-Weight Births**

RISK FACTORS	EFFECTS
Lack of prenatal care	Increased risk of infant mortality
Vaginal infection	Increased risk of difficulties in:
Short interval between birth and subsequent pregnancy (less than 3 months)	• respiration (e.g., respiratory distress syndrome, apnea, anoxia)
Malnutrition	• circulation, leading to brain hemorrhage
Cigarette smoking	• feeding, due to poor ability to suck
Drug use (e.g., alcohol, cocaine)	• social interactions (difficult to rouse, difficult to calm, ambiguous interpersonal signals)
Maternal age (especially younger than age 15)	• regulating sleep, awake, alert cycles
Marital status (unmarried)	Increased longer-term risk of:
Maternal illness affecting blood vessels (e.g., diabetes, high blood pressure)	• cerebral palsy • lowered academic achievement, lowered IQ • attentional problems
Membership in certain ethnic groups	• poor language development
Genetic background and family history	• motor and perceptual difficulties • specific learning disabilities
Personal history of miscarriage or preterm labor	
Multiple gestations (i.e., twins, triplets, etc.)	

A Personal PERSPECTIVE...

Meet the Parents of a Very Premature Baby

Kim Powell and Larry Sikkink
Decorah, Iowa

Parents of Senia, born at 28 weeks' gestation weighing 1 pound, 15 ounces

When did you learn that your baby would be premature? What were your first thoughts? Do you know what caused the prematurity?

Kim: I experienced a healthy pregnancy up to my sixth month. Then, at a prenatal exam, the doctor found I had high blood pressure as well as protein in my urine. The next day I was admitted to a hospital with a neonatal intensive care unit (NICU). At 28 weeks' gestation, on the way to my first ultrasound, I began feeling light-headed and felt a sudden pain in my upper abdomen. I began throwing up and had a severe headache. The doctor said I had to have an emergency cesarean section if my baby and I were to live. I had HELLP syndrome (hemolysis, elevated liver enzymes, low blood platelets). There is no known cause or predictor for HELLP syndrome, and some mothers and babies die from the complications. I knew my baby would be born prematurely, but I was too sick to realize what that

meant. Immediately after her birth, Senia was whisked away to the NICU, intubated, placed on a warming table, and connected to an IV feeding tube and breathing and heart monitors. My husband was still on the 90-minute drive from our home. Senia's left lung collapsed after birth, requiring three days of lung massage therapy. At 2 weeks she was moved to an incubator, where she stayed for 4 weeks.

Larry: Senia had been delivered about 15 minutes before my arrival, the NICU team was attending to her, and I would be allowed to see her in about 30 minutes. I was shocked. How could I be the father of a baby girl already? An NICU doctor assured me that given time, care, and love, our daughter's chances for survival were very good.

Has your baby needed or used any special services? What is your baby like today?

Kim: At 4 pounds and 1 ounce, after 7 weeks in the NICU, Senia came home on an apnea and bradycardia monitor. For 2½ months Senia had episodes where her breathing would stop and her heart rate would lower. She also had several bouts of pneumonia in her first year. It took 2 years for Senia to perform like others

her age, but she is now all caught up. She is tall for her age and is at the 50th percentile in weight. Cognitively she tests above age level. Senia started kindergarten at 5 and loves writing, books, music, and dancing.

What advice do you have for other parents who may have a premature or low-birth-weight baby?

Kim: Educate themselves and read about other premature babies. Kim Wilson and I wrote *Living Miracles: Stories of Hope from Parents of Premature Babies* (Griffin Trade Paperbacks) so parents could share their situation. Above all else, though having a preemie is very stressful, parents should try to focus on the baby and enjoy every minute of watching the baby develop. ■

thinking OF KENDRA & JAMES

◀ What can Kendra and James do to reduce their risk of having a premature baby? Given what we know about them and their situation, what do you think are the major risk factors that they face?

Infant Mortality

infant mortality

Deaths that occur between birth and 1 year of age.

The term **infant mortality** refers to deaths that occur before the age of one year. In spite of the medical community's best efforts, many infants die each year. As you can see in Figure 3.6, the United States does not rank well when compared to other industrialized countries with respect to infant mortality, even with our sophisticated medical technology. Again, African American babies fare even worse than babies in the rest of the U.S. population. The African American infant mortality rate in 2000 was 13.5, almost twice the overall rate of 6.9 deaths per 1000 live births (Matthews et al., 2002; Pastor, Makuc, Reuben, & Xia, 2002). Infant

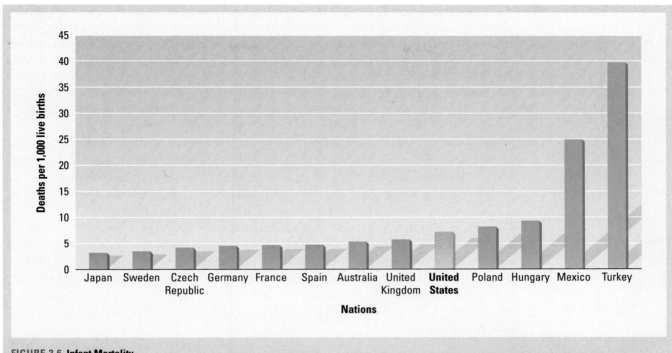

FIGURE 3.6 Infant Mortality

This graph shows infant mortality rates for selected nations. All data are for the year 2000, except for the United States, for which the latest available data were from 1999.

Source: Organisation for Economic Cooperation and Development (2002).

mortality is related to poor or absent prenatal care, teenage pregnancy, poor nutrition, risky health behaviors during pregnancy, and higher rates of prematurity and low-birth-weight births. Experts agree that the same steps that would reduce rates of prematurity and low birth weight would also reduce the rates of infant mortality.

Prenatal Care: Having a Healthy Baby

Although we cannot prevent all of the problems that newborns face, we know one thing for certain: Access to and appropriate use of good-quality prenatal care results in healthier babies. In prenatal visits practitioners can effectively identify and address many risk factors for problems during pregnancy. Again, these include poor nutrition; smoking, alcohol, and drug use; exposure to environmental toxins; and maternal infections, illnesses, and pregnancy-related conditions that put the fetus at risk. Another important component of prenatal care is education. Education can increase the mother's knowledge of how the baby is developing, what she and her partner can do to improve their odds of having a healthy baby, and what options she has for labor and delivery. Participation in prepared childbirth classes and the supportive involvement of the woman's partner and family can enhance this education. Ideally, of course, both men and women should begin making healthy lifestyle choices even before the woman becomes pregnant, for some of these choices clearly have the power to prevent birth complications. Although the medical community has made astonishing strides in the treatment of many problems suffered by newborns, it is far more effective and desirable to prevent such problems from happening in the first place.

thinking
OF KENDRA & JAMES

◄ How would Kendra and James benefit by receiving good prenatal care? List several specific risks that their participation in prenatal care might help them reduce or avoid.

And we have good news to report on this point: More women are now getting prenatal care and the rates of prenatal care have especially increased among ethnic minority women (National Center for Health Statistics, 2002c). Overall, in 2001, 83 percent of women received prenatal care in the first trimester of their pregnancy (up from 76 percent in 1990). During this same time period, the percentage of Hispanic and African American women who received no prenatal care at all dropped from about 4 to 2 percent. Although there is a way to go before all women are served with early prenatal care, rates of care are clearly improving.

In this chapter we have gone from the conception through the birth of a baby. We have discussed the normal course of prenatal development, the stages of labor and delivery, and many of the options and choices that a pregnant woman has. We have also covered problems that can occur during the prenatal and birth period, describing teratogens that can endanger the developing fetus and risk factors for preterm and low-birth-weight birth.

From these details we hope you clearly see two main points. First, pregnant women and their families can greatly increase their odds of having a healthy baby by making healthy lifestyle choices and avoiding risk factors such as teratogens and teenage pregnancy. *Much is under their control!* And second, although problems can occur, most babies develop normally and are born healthy, robust—and ready to proceed with rapid development of their physical, cognitive, and social skills. In the next chapters we'll turn to these exciting realms of postnatal development.

LET'S REVIEW . . .

1. Among industrialized nations, when it comes to low-birth-weight deliveries, the United States ranks:

    a. best. b. worst. c. 3rd. d. 17th.

2. Very low-birth-weight babies are those who are born weighing less than:

    a. 2 pounds. b. 3½ pounds. c. 5½ pounds. d. 7½ pounds.

3. Generally, the babies who are at the greatest risk are those born:

    a. preterm.

    b. low in birth weight.

    c. small for their gestational age.

    d. before 36 weeks of gestation and under 5 pounds.

4. Which of the following are risk factors related to infant mortality?

    a. poor prenatal care

    b. poor nutrition

    c. premature and low-birth-weight births

    d. all of the above

5. **True or False:** In the United States there are no ethnic differences in the rates of prematurity or infant mortality.

6. **True or False:** With good prenatal care, we can control or avoid some of the risk factors associated with infant mortality and preterm and low-birth-weight births.

Answers: 1. d, 2. b, 3. c, 4. d, 5. F, 6. T

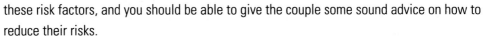

thinking
BACK TO KENDRA & JAMES

Now that you have studied this chapter, you should be able to identify more than a dozen risk factors that Kendra and James might face. You should know the possible effects of these risk factors, and you should be able to give the couple some sound advice on how to reduce their risks.

One factor that you probably noticed is Kendra's age. In her late teens, Kendra's risk of having a low-birth-weight baby is elevated (compared to that of mothers in their 20s and 30s), but it is not as high as it would have been if she were younger than 15. Proper prenatal care and nutrition can diminish the health risks of teenage pregnancy. Also, given that teenagers tend to be less informed about childbirth, babies, and parenting, it would help if Kendra and James would take classes or otherwise prepare themselves for parenthood.

Like all potential parents, both Kendra and James should be concerned about their lifestyles and the teratogens that they may be exposed to. Alcohol, cigarette smoke, and cocaine and other illegal drugs all can harm the developing baby. Sexually transmitted and other infectious diseases can cause the baby to be born infected or with birth defects, so Kendra and James should take precautions to avoid these diseases. If Kendra and James continued drinking alcohol, using drugs, and exposing themselves to other potential teratogens until they knew Kendra was pregnant, the baby may already be damaged.

Kendra should receive good prenatal care. Both parents should also take childbirth classes. There they can learn about the stages of labor and things they can do to control Kendra's experience of pain. By taking active roles in the birth, both parents can have a more satisfying experience and enhance their attachment to the new baby.

Like Kendra and James, all potential parents should consider the risk factors that they might face and take steps to reduce or avoid them. A great many pregnancy problems and birth defects are prevented when parents take the proper precautions.

Where does conception normally take place? What are two of the general processes that occur during prenatal development?

Conception normally occurs when the ovum and sperm meet in the upper part of the fallopian tube. After fertilization, prenatal development proceeds with mitosis (duplication division) and differentiation (in which cells take on new structures and functions).

What are the stages of prenatal development and the major events that take place in each?

The three stages are the germinal, embryonic, and fetal stages. During the germinal stage (0 to 2 weeks), the first cell divisions take place, and the embryo implants in the uterine lining. During the embryonic stage (3 to 8 weeks), the ectoderm, mesoderm, and endoderm form and later give rise to the major organs and parts of the body. The placenta, umbilical cord, and other structures form to support the developing baby. The body forms in a cephalocaudal (head-to-tail) and proximodistal (midline-to-outer) pattern. Organogenesis is complete by the end of the embryonic stage, so this stage includes most critical periods in organ and tissue formation. During the fetal stage the baby grows in size and the body systems gradually become more functional.

What effects do legal and illegal drugs have on the developing baby?

Several legal and illegal drugs can harm the developing baby. Alcohol is the leading known cause of mental retardation. It can also cause growth retardation, facial deformities, and FAS. Cocaine can cause growth retardation; cognitive deficits; and defects in the brain, intestines, and genital–urinary tract. Cigarette smoking is associated with lower birth weight; hyperactivity; poor school performance; and increased risks for miscarriage, stillbirth, and neonatal death.

If a pregnant woman has an infectious disease, will this harm the developing baby?

Several sexually transmitted and other infectious diseases can harm the developing baby. Sometimes the baby is born already infected with the disease; in other cases the disease causes birth defects. If the mother has rubella, the baby can become infected with rubella or can be born with cataracts, heart defects, deafness, or lowered intelligence. Cytomegalovirus can cause embryonic death, retarded growth, microcephaly, blindness, mental retardation, and cerebral palsy. If the mother has HIV, the baby can be born infected with HIV and/or may show growth retardation and head and facial deformities.

Does the age of the mother affect pregnancy?

Infants of teenage mothers are at higher risk for low birth weight, prematurity, and neonatal death, especially when the mother is younger than 15. Risks of prematurity, fetal death, and pregnancy complications increase slightly after the age of 35.

What are critical periods, and why are they important in prenatal development?

Critical periods are times when developing organs and tissues are most vulnerable to defects. They usually occur when the organs and tissues are first forming, differentiating from surrounding cells. Most critical periods occur during the embryonic stage (weeks 3 to 8) and are therefore complete by the time most women know that they are pregnant. Parents should avoid exposure to teratogens during pregnancy.

Can fathers expose developing babies to teratogens?

In most cases, no—or at least not directly. Elements in the father's bloodstream do not pass to the developing baby, but some toxic substances can reduce the mobility and viability of sperm. Research with rats indicates that fathers' alcohol consumption may increase activity level in offspring and that cocaine can bind to sperm cells and be carried to the fertilized egg. Men have a serious ethical responsibility to support healthy pregnancies in women.

What are the stages of labor, and what happens in each?

In Stage 1 the cervix dilates (widens) and effaces (thins), and the fetus moves downward to the birth canal. In Stage 2 the baby moves through the birth canal and is delivered. In Stage 3 the placenta and all membranes are delivered.

What is a newborn baby like?

The newborn baby has a large head and may be covered with a cheesy coating. Newborns can see, but their vision is fuzzy. They have reflexes that help them learn to feed, and they will grasp your finger if you touch their palms. They turn their heads to the sound of voices and gaze into the faces of their parents. The Apgar test, given 1 and 5 minutes after birth, identifies newborns who are at risk and need special medical attention.

What are some complications that can occur during labor and delivery?

In malpresentation the fetus's position in the womb makes delivery difficult and dangerous. In fetal distress the fetus experiences a serious change in vital signs that put it at risk. Anoxia, a serious birth complication in which the fetus does not receive enough oxygen, can lead to permanent brain damage.

What kind of help is available to a woman in labor?

Women usually choose either an obstetrician or a midwife to provide medical help during labor and delivery. The continuous presence of a labor companion, usually the baby's father, has beneficial effects. In prepared childbirth women learn selective relaxation and controlled breathing techniques to help them relax and to reduce the pain of contractions.

Is it safe to use drugs for pain relief during labor and delivery?

Most of the drugs used today to reduce anxiety or pain may have short-term negative effects on the fetus and newborn but have not been shown to have long-term consequences. Epidural anesthesia, in which medications are injected into spaces along the spine, is increasingly common and appears to have few negative effects on the baby.

What role do fathers or other partners play during labor and delivery?

Fathers or partners help during labor and delivery by helping mothers relax, use selective relaxation techniques and controlled breathing, and remain calm. Both mothers and fathers report that fathers' presence during labor and delivery has beneficial effects.

How is prematurity defined, and what are the major risk factors associated with prematurity?

Premature infants can be defined as preterm (born before 37 weeks' gestation), low-birth-weight (weighing less than 5½ pounds), very low-birth-weight (weighing less than 3½ pounds), or small for gestational age (born below the 10th percentile for weight for their gestational age). SGA babies are especially at risk, because something has prevented them from growing as well as would be expected, given the amount of time they spent in the uterus. Numerous risk factors for preterm and low-birth-weight births have been identified. Several, such as lack of prenatal care, malnutrition, smoking, alcohol and drug use, and young maternal age, are controllable.

What is infant mortality, and what might reduce it? How would prenatal care help?

Infant mortality is the death of babies before one year of age. The infant mortality rate is very high in the United States. Increased access to and use of good prenatal care would reduce the rates of preterm and low-birth-weight births, and this in turn would help reduce infant mortality. With prenatal care, practitioners can identify at-risk pregnancies early. Also, parents can learn how to reduce their risks by avoiding teratogens and engaging in healthy behaviors.

KEY TERMS

afterbirth (106)

Apgar test (108)

cephalocaudal pattern (92)

critical periods (93)

differentiation (89)

dilation (106)

embryonic stage (91)

fertilization (88)

fetal alcohol effects (FAE) (97)

fetal alcohol syndrome (FAS) (97)

fetal distress (108)

fetal stage (93)

germinal stage (90)

implantation (91)

infant mortality (122)

low birth weight (120)

malpresentation (106)

organogenesis (93)

ovulation (88)

prenatal development (88)

prepared (natural) childbirth (114)

preterm birth (120)

proximodistal pattern (93)

small for gestational age (SGA) (120)

teratogen (95)

very low birth weight (120)

Chapter 4

Physical Development

Body, Brain, and Perception

A PERSPECTIVE TO think ABOUT

"Beverly wonders what she can do to make sure her baby doesn't miss important opportunities during the first years."

Beverly is 8 months into her first pregnancy, and she is very excited about becoming a new mom! She has been avidly reading magazine articles about infant brain development—she wants to help her baby get off to the best start possible. From what Beverly has read, it seems that the baby's brain gets "wired" during the first 3 years after birth. She wonders how this happens and what she can do to make sure her baby doesn't miss important opportunities during the first years. One of her friends had a baby recently, and she frequently played classical music during the last months of her pregnancy. The friend says that "Mozart is supposed to help babies wire their brains for math and science." Can this be true? Can music and other sounds possibly have any effect on babies' development—even before birth? Also, Beverly has heard that other mothers enroll their infants in "jazzercise" classes where they stretch and exercise their babies' muscles. The sessions sound like a fun way to bond with infants—but will pumping the babies' arms and legs and helping them bend their trunk muscles really help them sit up, crawl, and walk? And what kinds of toys and decorations are best for babies during these early years? Can infants see different colors early on? Do toys that move and make sounds encourage development, or does all of the clamor just confuse the young baby?

Like most new parents, Beverly is eager to support her baby's development. What would you suggest? After studying this chapter, you should be able to give Beverly sound advice. Using at least a dozen research findings or concepts, you should be able to help Beverly sort out the fact from the fiction and get her baby off to a great start.

 As you read this chapter, look for the questions that ask you to think about what you're learning from Beverly's perspective.

We begin this chapter by describing physical growth during infancy, childhood, and adolescence. This discussion carries us up through the years of sexual maturation. Then we turn to motor development, starting back in infancy with babies' first reflexes. As children grow in size, they also learn to control their muscles, and we review some of the major motor development milestones. Next we look at research on brain development. Neurons in the brain form complex networks of interconnections that allow the brain to process information and govern behavior. How important are the early years in the formation of the brain's structure and neural connections? We end the chapter with a summary of perceptual development. What are the sensory capabilities of newborn babies, and how do the perceptual systems progress during the early months? This chapter will introduce you to important aspects of physical development. You will learn about the growth of the body and the nervous system, and about how infants use their perceptual systems to process information from the world around them.

Physical Growth and the Development of Motor Coordination

We begin by focusing on physical growth. We look first at changes in height and weight, then at the transformations that occur during puberty as young adolescents move toward sexual maturity. We continue by looking at motor coordination, from the gross motor developments of sitting, crawling, and walking to developments in the fine motor skills of reaching, grasping, and writing.

As you study this section, ask yourself these questions:

- What changes occur in height and weight during infancy, middle childhood, and adolescence? During which periods are the changes most rapid?

- What changes occur during puberty? Do adolescents who mature earlier respond to puberty differently than those who mature later?

- What kinds of reflexes do infants have soon after birth, and what functions do these reflexes serve?

- What patterns do we see as children learn to control their movements? What factors govern motor development in infancy and childhood?

- What are the main problems that we see in childhood nutrition?

Physical Growth

At birth, the average newborn weighs 7½ pounds, with males weighing about half a pound more than females. Newborns actually lose a slight amount of weight in the first days after birth. During these early days, newborns spend almost all of their time sleeping; also, it takes time for newborns to adjust to the process of feeding. If they are breast-fed, their mothers' milk production is low the first few days. The main benefit of the initial breast feedings is to pass antibodies from the mother's milk to the baby. These antibodies will help the newborn fend off illnesses and infections. After the mother's milk production increases and the newborn adjusts to life outside the womb, weight returns to birth levels—usually by about 2 weeks of age.

By 5 months, birth weight has doubled. Figure 4.1 graphs weight gain through childhood and adolescence. As these growth charts show, girls reach half of their adult body weight by 9 years of age. Boys achieve half of their adult weight by age 11. Changes in height are even

Girls' Average Weight

Boys' Average Weight

On average, girls achieve half of their adult body weight by 9 years of age.

On average, boys achieve half of their adult body weight by age 11.

FIGURE 4.1 Average Body Weight for Girls and Boys Ages 2 to 20 Years

Source: National Center for Health Statistics in collaboration with the National Center for Chronic Disease Prevention and Health Promotion (2000).

Do you recall the age period when the girls in your class stood taller than the boys? After being about equal in height throughout childhood, girls enter their adolescent growth spurt at an earlier age than boys. By the end of adolescence, boys will stand five inches taller (on average) than girls.

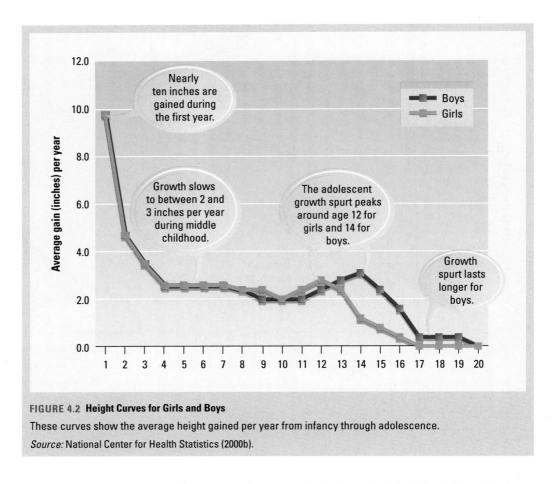

FIGURE 4.2 Height Curves for Girls and Boys

These curves show the average height gained per year from infancy through adolescence.

Source: National Center for Health Statistics (2000b).

more rapid. On average, newborns measure 20 inches in length and add another 50 percent in their first year. By age 2, children have already attained more than half of their adult height! By looking at Figure 4.2, you can see that growth slows to about 2 to 3 inches per year during middle childhood but accelerates again during adolescence. Growth during childhood and adolescence is stimulated primarily by *growth hormones* from the pituitary gland. Interestingly, maximum secretion of growth hormone occurs during periods of deep sleep.

The **adolescent growth spurt** is an increase in growth that begins with the onset of *puberty*. At puberty, or the beginning of adolescence, sex hormones start to trigger the process of sexual maturation. This release of sex hormones also stimulates the release of additional growth hormones from the pituitary gland. As Figure 4.2 indicates, boys and girls grow at about the same rate until adolescence. Then comes the growth spurt, usually peaking around 12 years of age for girls. For boys the growth spurt peaks a few years later, usually around 14 years. This lag in growth spurt means that there is a short period of time, around the ages of 11 to 14, when females are taller than males, on average. The growth spurt lasts longer for boys, however. By the time he reaches 18 years of age, the average male is now about 5 inches taller than the average female. Both sexes have nearly reached their adult height. In both sexes the long bones (e.g., in the arms and legs) may continue to grow slightly until age 25, and minor growth in the vertebral column can continue until age 30 (Tanner, 1978).

Sexual Maturation

The primary factors governing the onset of puberty are genetics and two types of sex hormones: **androgens** (male hormones) and **estrogens** (female hormones). The hypothalamus,

adolescent growth spurt

The increase in growth associated with the onset of puberty.

androgens

One type of sex hormone, released in greater concentration by males.

estrogens

One type of sex hormone, released in greater concentration by females.

Physical Development: Body, Brain, and Perception

part of the lower forebrain, signals the release of sex hormones from the gonads (ovaries in females, and testes in males). The gonads in both males and females secrete both types of sex hormones, but at different concentrations. The male testes secrete higher levels of testosterone (an androgen), and the female ovaries secrete higher levels of estradiol (an estrogen). The sex hormones stimulate the growth and maturation of the reproductive systems as well as secondary sexual characteristics. In males, the most noticeable changes tend to begin in this order: The penis and testicles increase in size, pubic hair appears, the voice begins to deepen, the first ejaculation occurs, hair grows in the armpits, and facial hair begins to grow. In females, changes usually occur as follows: Breasts begin to enlarge, pubic hair appears, hair grows in the armpits, hips enlarge, and the first menstruation occurs.

As with the adolescent growth spurt, sexual maturation tends to occur earlier in girls than in boys. Many girls show noticeable changes by age 10 to 11, but most boys enter puberty a year or two later. For most girls **menarche** (the first menstrual period) occurs at 12 to 13. The average age at menarche, however, has been decreasing. In the United States, for example, the average age at menarche fell from 13.8 in 1920 to 12.8 around 1960 (Marshall & Tanner, 1986; Tanner, 1991). Over the last 100 years, children have grown larger and matured faster than in previous generations. Improved nutrition and overall health have contributed greatly to this long-term pattern, or *secular trend*. As you will see later, weight gain is related to menarche; perhaps improved nutrition and health cause earlier weight gain, signaling the female body to begin the reproductive phase of life. Although the same secular trend has occurred in other industrialized nations, girls in the United States have always reached menarche a bit earlier than girls in other nations. The reasons for this are not known.

Of course, these are just the physical changes associated with puberty and sexual maturation—but what about the psychological effects? For many adolescents puberty is a confusing and awkward time. Their bodies are changing rapidly and in dramatic ways. No longer children, teenagers may look toward late adolescence and adulthood with mixed feelings of excitement and apprehension. Researchers have devoted considerable attention to adolescents' changing body image. During adolescent growth, boys tend to add muscle mass and height, and with these changes they tend to become more satisfied with their bodies (Duncan, Ritter, Dornbusch, Gross, & Carlsmith, 1985; Simmons & Blyth, 1987). In contrast, girls tend to add more fat tissue, and many become less satisfied with their bodies. This is particularly true among girls who reach menarche before age 12, because their build tends to be more short and stocky by late adolescence. A study of nearly 5,000 girls in Scotland, for example, showed that more early-maturing girls perceived their bodies as "too fat." More late-maturing girls saw themselves as "too thin" (Williams & Currie, 2000). Girls with both types of negative body image tended to have lower self-esteem. Early-maturing girls also tend to have older friends, engage in more delinquency, have more problems in school, begin dating at a younger age, and tend to have more problems with depression and substance abuse (Magnusson, 1988; Simmons & Byth, 1987; Stice, Presnell, & Bearman, 2001; Wiesner & Ittel, 2002). You can imagine how the social context can put added pressure on early-maturing girls, as they receive more attention from boys and may feel somewhat alienated from slower-developing girls their own age. For more on this issue, read the Professional Perspective box called "Meet a Young Adolescent."

Early maturation can enhance the self-image of boys, however (Nottelmann et al., 1987; Simmons & Blyth, 1987). Thanks to their size and strength, early-maturing boys have the advantage in sports. Also, peers may see their more developed musculature, facial hair, and deeper voices as being attractive. Late-maturing boys often feel uncomfortable about comparing themselves with their more developed peers. Remember entering the gym showers at this age? On the negative side, however, early-maturing boys tend to engage in more delinquent behavior than do boys who mature later (Duncan et al., 1985; Ge, Brody, Conger,

YOUR PERSPECTIVE

NOTES

Did you begin puberty earlier or later than other adolescents your age? How did your rate of maturation affect your feelings about yourself and about how you compared with your age-mates?

menarche
The first menstrual period for females, usually occurring around 12 to 13 years of age.

Meet a Young Adolescent

Hannah Lee Vestal
Bristol, Tennessee

Age 15, discussing the impact of physical changes during adolescence

Which physical changes do you and your friends notice most? What differences do you notice between early and late "bloomers"?

I notice a lot of physical changes in myself and in others. I notice hair, clothing, body, nails, and much more. But, for some reason, I think I am always looking for faults; I always notice them so much. I think developed girls look at not-so-developed girls and wish they could be that way, and vice versa! I see some late "bloomers" who are very self-conscious and limit their clothing due to the fact that they are not fully developed. But I also see late bloomers who are very comfortable with themselves and their bodies, so they are more willing to wear the clothing of choice. Some early bloomers (like me) are a lot more inclined to cover themselves and hide the fact that they have bloomed. But again, I see some early bloomers who embrace the fact that they are developed. They sometimes wear low-cut shirts or strapless tops, which I guess is good in a way. They are so comfortable with themselves that they *can* wear those clothes.

What do you think are the most exciting, awkward, and stressful aspects of puberty?

Starting to date, friends, and drugs. Starting to date is very difficult because if you don't date, you start to feel like you are ugly and no one wants to date you. Dating makes you feel very critical of yourself. It makes you want to change things about yourself, mainly your looks. If you do date, you might feel pressured to do things you aren't ready for. Friends can also be very stressful. High school is like one big soap opera, one that you can't miss a single episode of. The drama of who's dating who and the "he said, she said" stuff is very aggravating and childish. But pressure from friends is not as bad as TV and politicians make it out to be, at least not at my school. Drugs are readily available, but I have never been asked if I would like to take drugs, smoke anything, or drink. I think to get involved in that stuff you have to go looking for it. Teens can't blame all their mess-ups on pressure, because it's not really there as much as adults think. Most of it is in the individual.

What advice would you give adults about an adolescent's perspective during puberty?

I think parents should be very honest with their children, especially at this age. If you tell your kids about the experiences you had, they'll learn more from that than they would from watching a movie on it or reading a book about it. If you tell your kids if or how your experiences changed your life, for good or bad, they will respect that. They'll tell you more and trust you. I know I can talk to my mom about almost anything. She won't yell at me, but will listen and tell me how she feels, and about her experiences and the effects they had on her. ■

Simons, & Murry, 2002). Being larger and stronger than their age-mates these boys often affiliate with older adolescents. They may get into situations they are not prepared to handle—and get into trouble as a result. One study indicated that early-maturing boys felt more hostile and distressed than other boys (Ge, Conger, & Elder, 2001).

Although G. Stanley Hall (1904) and other theorists have characterized adolescence as a time of "storm and stress," most adolescents manage to work their way through puberty and adolescent transitions in a relatively peaceful manner. On that positive note, let's now turn our attention back to infancy and see how infants and young children develop motor coordination in their growing bodies.

Reflexes: The Infant's First Coordinated Movements

reflexes

Involuntary movements that are elicited by environmental stimuli.

Human infants are equipped at birth with several interesting reflexes. **Reflexes** are involuntary movements that are elicited by environmental stimuli such as sound, light, touch, and body position. If you touch a new-born's cheek, the infant's head will turn in the direction of the touch. This is called the *rooting reflex.* If any-thing touches infants' lips, they auto-matically begin to suck—the *sucking reflex.* As you will see later in this chapter, the cerebral cortex (the upper part of the brain), which governs vol-untary muscle movements, is not well developed at birth. So at first it is the lower brain centers (spinal cord, brain stem, and midbrain) that control in-fants' involuntary reflexes. What pur-poses do these reflexes serve? Some help the infant find nourishment, some help the infant exercise muscles, and still others may be protective mechanisms inherited from our pri-mate ancestors. Let's consider three classes of reflexes: *primitive, postural, and locomotor* (Gabbard, 1992).

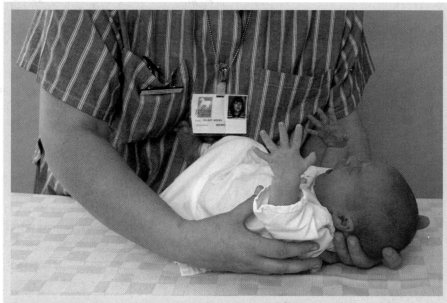

This newborn is demonstrating the Moro reflex. When startled, she extends her arms and legs and spreads her fingers. Why do infants have this reflex?

Primitive reflexes include *rooting* and *sucking.* As we've described, both of these re-flexes help infants find nourishment. When the breast or bottle touches their cheek, they turn their head to the source of nutrition. When the nipple touches their mouth, they begin to suck. Other primitive reflexes are remnants from earlier evolutionary forms in which they may have served protective functions. The startle reflex or *Moro reflex,* for example, occurs when an infant is startled by a loud noise or begins to fall. A sharp bang on the crib will cause infants to extend their arms and legs outward, spread their fingers and toes, then bring their limbs back to their bodies. You will see the same response if you hold an infant in your arms, lying on its back, and then drop your arms suddenly a few inches (be sure to catch the baby!). The *grasping reflex* occurs when an object touches an infant's palm—the baby's fingers will automatically wrap around the object and grip strongly. These reflexes may have helped our primate ancestors hold onto their mothers or catch hold of support when falling. With the *Babinski reflex,* a stroke on the heel causes the toes to fan outward. Most primitive reflexes are functional in the later months of prenatal development (e.g., fetuses suck their thumbs by the fourth prenatal month). They tend to disappear by about 4 months after birth as the higher cortical centers in the brain begin to take over voluntary control of muscle movements.

Several **postural reflexes** help infants keep their heads upright, maintain their postural balance, and roll their heads in the direction of their body lean. One interesting example is the *parachute reflex.* If infants are held upright and then quickly tilted face-down, they will re-flexively extend their arms outward as if to balance and brace against the movement. Postural reflexes emerge by the age of 2 to 4 months and then disappear by 12 months.

During the first few months of life, infants will show "crawling" motions if they are lying on their stomachs and you stroke their feet. If you hold them upright with their feet touching a surface such as a tabletop or the floor, they take small "walking" steps. If held hor-izontal in water with their heads up, infants make "swimming" motions with their arms and legs. These *crawling, walking,* and *swimming reflexes* are examples of **locomotor reflexes.** The locomotor reflexes tend to emerge during the first month or so after birth and then disappear again by 4 months of age.

primitive reflexes
Reflexes that help the infant find nourishment or served protective functions during earlier periods of evolution.

postural reflexes
Reflexes that help infants keep their heads upright, maintain balance, and roll their heads in the direction of their body lean.

locomotor reflexes
Infant reflexes that mimic locomotor movements such as crawling, walking, and swimming.

There has been much debate about the functional significance of infant reflexes. Some theorists have argued that with practice, early reflexes will evolve into coordinated voluntary movements. Infants who are given regular practice with the walking reflex, for example, tend to maintain the reflex longer and tend to show voluntary walking about a month earlier than infants who are not given extra practice (Zelazo, 1983; Zelazo, Zelazo, & Kolb, 1972). Reflexes may provide valuable exercise that strengthens the muscles and helps the nervous system make connections between the brain and the muscle groups. Other researchers contend that the lag between the disappearance of most reflexes and the onset of similar voluntary movements shows that these two phases of motor development are independent. Some even claim that the early reflexes must be suppressed so that the brain can take voluntary control of the muscles (Pontius, 1973). Either way, pediatricians have long used the existence and disappearance of reflexes as early indicators of nervous system function. Remember from Chapter 3 that the Apgar test includes a measure of "reflex irritability" as part of the assessment of early functioning in newborns. The Brazelton Neonatal Behavioral Assessment Scale, designed to assess the health of infants, measures some 20 different reflexes. A lack of reflexive response, or a delay in the emergence or disappearance of certain reflexes, can signal a problem with neurological development.

Voluntary Movements: The Motor Milestones

When our children were newborn babies, we loved the way they wiggled and squirmed when we held and played with them. Many of their movements were jerky and somewhat erratic, but it was a joy to watch them stretch and exercise their tiny muscles. Newborns can typically move their eyes and turn their heads to find your face or track the sound of your voice. Put your finger in the palm of a newborn's hand, and the strength of the infant's grip (from the grasping reflex) is surprising. When babies are awake, their arms and legs seem to be constantly stretching and flexing, their fingers gripping and extending. These early arm and leg movements are spontaneous and involuntary, not directed at reaching at or holding particular objects. It will be several months before the infant can coordinate voluntary and purposeful behaviors like reaching for a toy or dumping out a box of blocks. Over the next months, babies' reflexes, spontaneous movements, and later voluntary movements gradually strengthen their muscles and stimulate neurological development in their brains and nervous systems.

Figure 4.3 illustrates the major milestones in gross-motor development across the first year of life. If you examine these changes, you can clearly see a *cephalocaudal pattern,* or head-to-toe pattern, of development (Frankenburg et al., 1992). By 1 month of age, the muscles in infants' necks are strong enough to allow them to hold their heads upright. Next, the muscles in the trunk become more coordinated. Infants can roll over by 3 months and sit upright without support by 6 months. Around 7 months the legs are strong enough to allow infants to crawl—pushing with their legs and dragging their bodies along the floor. At 7 months babies also can stand by holding onto a table or other form of support. For many parents the most significant milestone is the baby's first step. Most infants take their first unaided steps sometime around their first birthday. But it is important to know that these ages are averages, and the rate of development for individual babies varies considerably. For example, 25 percent of infants are walking well at 11 months; another 25 percent begin walking well at 13 months; and 10 percent do not walk proficiently until 15 months (Frankenburg et al., 1992). Individual genetics, different rates of neurological development, and opportunities to practice muscle movements all contribute to this variability. Pediatricians will, however, see serious delays in motor development as potential indication of neurological or muscular deficits. To learn more about how to identify and treat developmental delays in motor development, read the Professional Perspective box called "Career Focus: Meet a Physical Therapist" (p. 138).

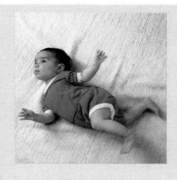

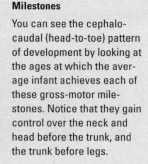

FIGURE 4.3 Gross-Motor Milestones

You can see the cephalo-caudal (head-to-toe) pattern of development by looking at the ages at which the average infant achieves each of these gross-motor milestones. Notice that they gain control over the neck and head before the trunk, and the trunk before legs.

A *proximodistal* or nearer-to-farther (from the body's center) pattern, can be seen in the progress infants make in reaching and grasping. At first they reach with their arms; next come the fine-motor skills of grasping with the hands and fingers (Gabbard, 1992). In Figure 4.4, (p. 139), you can see that voluntary control over the upper arm is shown by 4 to 5 months. The infant has voluntary control over the upper arm and can reach out and pull an object in with both arms. At this age infants wrap all four fingers and their thumbs around the object in what is referred to as the *palmar grasp*. By 10 months infants show the more advanced *pincer grasp*, using the thumb opposite the forefinger. At 15 months they can hold a writing implement (although they begin again with the palmar grasp) and make scribbles by using the large muscles in the upper arm. By 2 to 3 years children begin using the more precise "tripod" grasp for holding pencils and other writing implements. By 4 years they have the fine-motor coordination to print a few recognizable letters in large block print. By 5 years they have more control over their printing, can print in a smaller size, and can usually write their first name. By 6 years they are printing the whole alphabet (capital letters) and numbers to 10. As you can see, precise control over the fine-motor movements of the fingers comes much later than control over the gross-motor movements of the elbows, arms, and shoulders.

The cephalocaudal and proximodistal patterns in motor development mirror the progressive maturation of centers in the brain. As we'll discuss later in this chapter, cells and connections in the part of the brain that controls muscle movements in the head and upper body tend to mature first. Neurological development then spreads, allowing control and coordination of muscles to proceed both downward and outward through the body. The reflexes seen in early infancy are controlled mainly by pathways in the spinal cord, and the actions of these

Career Focus: Meet a Physical Therapist

Deanna Walsh
Madison, Wisconsin
*Physical therapist
at Meriter Hospital*

What ages of children and what types of conditions do you work with? Are families involved in the children's therapy?

The youngest children I treat are premature infants and the oldest may be up to 16 or 17 years old. I see children who are having a variety of movement problems. I see babies and children with torticollis (a tight muscle in their neck that restricts their movement), cerebral palsy, autism with associated movement difficulties, delays in their gross-motor development (difficulty learning to crawl, walk, jump, etc.), spina bifida, muscular dystrophy, Down syndrome, other genetic syndromes that impact movement, and after surgery or fractures. The children I see may have problems with their balance or coordination, muscle weakness, muscle tightness, difficulty with mobility, or difficulty with specific movements. Some children require special equipment to make movement easier. This might include special braces or inserts in their shoes, crutches, walkers, adapted bicycles, or wheelchairs.

Typically, I see a child for 1 or 2 treatments per week, depending on the child and family's needs. A great deal of my job is teaching families what they can do to help their child, since they are the people who are with the child most of the time. By involving families in their child's treatment, greater improvements are seen. Instead of working on an activity for one hour per week, the child will be incorporating it into their day, every day.

How do you determine if a child is exhibiting delayed motor development?

I routinely use many different standardized tests when assessing a child's motor skills. Most tests address certain age groups and look at certain types of skills (e.g., balance, locomotor, coordination, and ball skills). I also observe the quality of a child's movements to determine if she or he is having difficulty with mobility skills.

What education and training is needed to become a physical therapist?

Most physical therapy programs are now master's degree programs, and many are moving toward the doctorate level. Most include extensive clinical experience as part of the

training, and this is typically where most students gain some hands-on experience working with children. Physical therapy is an excellent career for people who like to be involved with patients and their families. There are many practice settings in physical therapy—such as school-based therapy, hospital-based therapy, outpatient clinics, home health agencies, academics, research, nursing homes, and rehab centers. The great thing about all areas of physical therapy is that you get to help people meet their individual goals. Working with great kids and their families is an added benefit of working with pediatrics. ■

thinking
OF BEVERLY

◄ What are some initial signs that Beverly can look for to determine if her new baby needs to see a physical therapist?

nerve pathways become inhibited once the higher cortical centers develop. The stepping reflex, for example, disappears as the motor cortex matures enough to allow coordinated and voluntary movements of the legs.

But is brain maturation the only factor driving motor development? Obviously not. For example, the disappearance of the stepping reflex is also related to weight gain during infancy. Infants who gain weight more rapidly tend to lose the stepping reflex earlier. One group of researchers demonstrated this effect with 1-month-old infants. When they fitted these infants with leg weights that mimicked the amount of weight they would gain in the next few weeks, the stepping reflex diminished (Thelen, Fisher, & Ridley-Johnson, 1984). And when the

FIGURE 4.4 Gross- to Fine-Motor Skills

The proximodistal (from nearer to farther from the body's center) pattern of development can be seen in the progress children make in reaching and grasping. Infants begin by reaching with both arms and using the palm to grasp objects. After gaining more fine-motor control over muscles in the hands and fingers, they can use the more effective pincer grasp. Later, they can hold smaller objects and produce the intricate movements needed to write legibly.

researchers held other infants in water, they showed a more vigorous stepping reflex. The fatty leg tissue was more buoyant under water, so the reflex revived when the muscles were relieved of the extra weight load. Esther Thelen hypothesizes that the normal disappearance of the stepping reflex is affected by the biomechanical load placed on the limbs and not caused entirely by maturation of the higher brain centers. As we mentioned earlier, Philip Zelazo and his colleagues demonstrated that daily practice could strengthen the stepping reflex (Zelazo, Zelazo, & Kolb, 1972). Zelazo has even suggested that motor development may be subservient to cognitive development (Zelazo, 1983). Independent walking, for example, may occur only after infants develop certain information-processing and memory skills. According to this view, babies need to associate balance with stepping and to remember how to coordinate different body movements to walk successfully. So when it comes to motor development, cognitive practice may be as important as physical exercise and the strengthening of muscles.

Esther Thelen and her colleagues have proposed a *dynamic systems theory* (see Chapter 1) to describe the myriad interactive processes involved in motor development (Thelen, 1989; Thelen & Smith, 1998). In this theory coordinated movements like reaching, crawling, walking, and throwing are dynamic actions that emerge from the complex interplay of individual muscles, nerve pathways, physical growth, learning, and motivation:

- *Neurological development* gives infants the ability to exert voluntary control over their muscles.
- *Parental encouragement* and interesting objects in the environment motivate infants to raise their heads, turn their bodies, crawl, and take their first steps.
- *Opportunities to exercise* give babies the muscle strength they need to lift and control their growing limbs.
- As *cognitive systems mature*, babies are able to remember where interesting objects are hidden and how to figure out how to find them.

The brain, the body, and the environment all work in concert to propel the child toward increased strength and coordination. Without the brain, the muscles won't move. Without muscular exercise, the brain won't develop. Without motivation, the child won't exercise. The important question is not which part of the system develops first, but rather how the various components work together to move the infant and child toward higher levels of development.

Because parenting practices differ across cultures, babies in some cultures receive more vigorous physical stimulation than babies in other cultures. In Mali, for example, mothers often suspend the babies by their arms or legs (which stretches the babies' muscles) and encourage babies to sit and stand at an early age (Bril & Sabatier, 1986). Researchers have also noted that some African cultures emphasize physical stimulation, and babies raised in these cultures are typically ahead of North American babies in the major motor milestones (Ainsworth, 1967; Rabain-Jamin & Wornham, 1993; Super, 1976).

In contrast, in some South American cultures mothers are more protective of young infants and tend to limit their babies' opportunities to explore and exercise their motor skills. In Brazil, for example, researchers find that mothers carry their babies or hold them in their laps for a large part of the day. Many Brazilian mothers reportedly believe that sitting and standing positions can cause damage to the legs and spines of young infants, so they rarely allow their babies to sit or play on the floor by themselves (Santos, Gabbard, & Goncalves, 2001). During the first 6 months of infancy, these Brazilian babies lag behind their North American age-mates in motor skills such as sitting up and reaching for objects. By 8 months of age, however, they gain more physical exercise and catch up with babies raised in other cultures. Studies have found similar trends in babies in Chile (Andraca, Pino, LaParra, & Castillo, 1998).

Infants among the Hopi tribe in Arizona and the Tewa of New Mexico take their first steps at about 14 months of age, or 1 to 2 months later than most other infants in North America (Dennis & Dennis, 1939/1991). For their classic study on cultural differences in motor development, Wayne and Marsena Dennis spent two summers living among the Hopi. In some villages, they found, Hopi mothers used the traditional practice of strapping their infants to cradle boards that the mothers then carried on their backs. For the first 9 months of life, these infants spent most of their days restrained tightly on these boards, and they remained on the cradle boards even when they were nursing and when sleeping at night. Other Hopi villages were more "Americanized," and mothers in these villages had given up use of the cradle boards. Did the infants in these villages walk at an earlier age than the cradle-board babies? Interestingly, the answer was *no:* Use of the cradle board delayed the onset of walking by only 2 days on average (Dennis & Dennis, 1939/1991). Whether confined to the board or allowed to play and exercise more freely, all the Hopi infants took their first steps at about 14 months of age. As you can see, studies investigating different cultures do not agree completely about the roles of physical practice and exercise in motor development.

thinking
OF BEVERLY

Based on dynamic systems theory and these cross-cultural studies of infant exercise, what would you advise Beverly about infant "jazzercise" and other similar activities? How does early exercise influence motor development?

Nutrition and Eating-Related Problems

Clearly, adequate nutrition is essential for healthy growth and development. A healthy diet includes the proper balance of several key nutrients (Gabbard, 1992):

- *Proteins* provide our bodies with amino acids, the essential "building blocks" of growth. Proteins from diet are necessary to support new growth in the body, especially in periods of rapid growth—in the last trimester of pregnancy, in infancy, and during the adolescent growth spurt.

- *Carbohydrates* are an important source of fuel for the body, providing energy for muscle activity, the generation of body heat, and the enormous energy demands of the brain and nervous system.

- *Fats* provide a store of energy, and body fat helps insulate the body from fluctuations in environmental temperature. Dietary saturated fat and high blood cholesterol are linked to heart disease and other harmful conditions. However, it is important to know that the body actually produces cholesterol and requires it for many bodily functions, including synthesis of sex hormones (androgens and estrogens).

- *Minerals and vitamins* help maintain normal body growth and functions. Calcium, for example, is important for forming bones and teeth and for the maintenance of healthy bones as we age.

■ **Malnutrition.** Although starvation has become rare in the United States, **malnutrition** (nutritional deficiency caused by an inadequate intake of calories, protein, vitamins, or minerals) still plagues too many infants and children. A national survey taken between 1988 and 1994 indicated that as many as 12 million Americans lived in families that "sometimes" or "often" did not have food or money to buy food (Alaimo, Briefel, Frongillo, & Olson, 1998). Of these, nearly 70 percent went 1 or more days per month without food, and 4 percent went without food 14 or more days per month. An estimated 3 to 4 million were children or adolescents under the age of 17. The survey found food insufficiency in 15 percent of Hispanic families, 8 percent of African American families, and 3 percent of non-Hispanic Caucasian families. This is an alarming record, given the great economic prosperity that our nation as a whole supposedly enjoys.

What are the short- and long-term effects of malnutrition? Children who lack adequate nutrition tend to show stunted growth. Research in 1991 found stunted growth caused by nutritional deficiencies or other health issues in as many as 10 percent of all 2-year-olds in the United States (Parvanta, Sherry, & Yip, 2000). Proper nutrition also is essential to support the adolescent growth spurt and sexual maturation. When malnutrition becomes severe, adolescents can show reduced muscle and body mass, and females can show delayed menarche. Malnutrition during pregnancy can impede fetal growth; babies can be born with low birth weight, smaller brain size, and impaired mental and motor behavior. Inadequate calories or lack of a balanced diet can cause lowered intelligence. Malnourished children perform less well in school. As adults, they can continue to suffer physical and intellectual deficits that often limit their ability to earn a good wage.

In developing countries the rate of malnutrition is even more alarming. According to the World Health Organization, in the developing countries 230 million children under the age of 5 are seriously malnourished (de Onis, Monteiro, Akré, & Clugston, 2002). These children are significantly underweight and show stunted growth. Approximately 80 percent live in Asia, 15 percent in Africa, and 5 percent in Latin America. As Table 4.1 shows, in various regions of the world, large segments of the population are not able to meet their basic nutritional requirements. De Onis and colleagues comment that "to continue to allow underprivileged

YOUR
PERSPECTIVE
NOTES
What government, community, and private programs are you aware of that address the needs of hungry families and pregnant women at risk for malnutrition? What else needs to be done to address this issue?

malnutrition
___

Nutritional deficiency caused by inadequate intake of calories, protein, vitamins, or minerals.

TABLE 4.1 Children under Age 5 in Developing Countries Who Are Significantly Malnourished and Underweight

REGION	EXAMPLE COUNTRIES	NUMBER OF CHILDREN (UNDER AGE 5)	PERCENTAGE OF CHILDREN (UNDER AGE 5)
South Asia	includes Bangladesh, India, Pakistan	101 million	60
East Asia	includes China, Mongolia	26 million	21
Southeast Asia	includes Indonesia, Laos, Vietnam, Philippines	22 million	38
West Africa	includes Ghana, Namibia, Nigeria	12 million	33
East Africa	includes Ethiopia, Rwanda, Uganda	11 million	31
South America	includes Bolivia, Brazil, Colombia	3 million	8
Central America	includes Mexico, Guatemala, Honduras	3 million	18
North Africa	includes Algeria, Egypt	2 million	11
Caribbean	includes Dominican Republic, Haiti, Jamaica	600 thousand	19

Note: "Underweight" is defined as being 2 standard deviations below the median weight for that age.

Source: de Onis, Monteiro, Akré, & Clugston (2002).

environments to affect children's development not only perpetuates the vicious cycle of poverty but also leads to an enormous waste of human potential" (2002, p. 10).

■ **Obesity.**   In the United States, in contrast to the developing nations, the most frequent nutritional problem is *obesity*. As you can see in Figure 4.5, the percentage of U.S. children and adolescents who were obese tripled from the 1960s to 2000. The problem is even worse among adults: A full 64 percent of adults over the age of 20 were obese during the 1999–2000 test

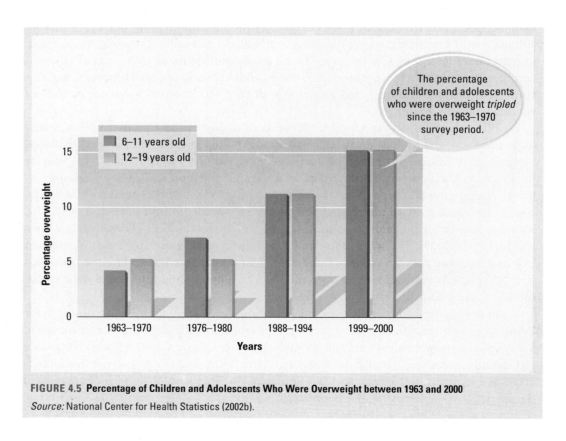

FIGURE 4.5 Percentage of Children and Adolescents Who Were Overweight between 1963 and 2000

Source: National Center for Health Statistics (2002b).

period (National Center for Health Statistics, 2002a). The problem among children and adolescents is especially serious among certain ethnic minorities, with African American and Hispanic children and teens showing higher rates of overweight and obesity than Caucasian Americans. The rate is particularly high for early-maturing minority girls; in 1996, for example, 57.5 percent of early-maturing African American females were overweight (Adair & Gordon-Larsen, 2001; McNutt et al., 1997; National Center for Health Statistics, 2002). Families rely more and more on fast foods and processed foods, and these foods boost children's intake of calories and saturated fat. In addition, it seems that children are becoming less physically active. In a 1992 policy statement, the American Academy of Pediatrics proclaimed that "we are in the midst of a youth fitness crisis" (p. 1002). The academy blamed some of the excessive accumulation of fat among children on low levels of physical activity. As an example, they cited a survey by the A. C. Nielsen Company showing that children aged 2 to 5 years watch an estimated 25.5 hours of television per week. And of course, with more than half of adults now overweight, children today see fewer positive role models for health and fitness than in earlier decades.

An increasing number of children in the United States are overweight. Why is this an increasing trend?

■ **Eating Disorders.** There is pressure toward unhealthy thinness as well, especially for girls and women. For example, consider the story of Sarah. At the age of 13 Sarah was already thinner than most girls her age, but she still believed that she was fat and unattractive. On a typical day Sarah ate a plain piece of toast in the morning and a cup of yogurt and fruit for dinner. She rarely snacked. She exercised vigorously every day, determined to lose another 5 to 10 pounds. By the time she was 15, Sarah weighed only 85 pounds (more than 25 percent less than the average weight for her age). Because of her severe weight loss, she stopped having menstrual periods, but she was still determined to lose more weight. Sarah was never satisfied with how she looked, and she felt that she was losing control of her weight. In despair, Sarah tried to end her life by taking an overdose of sleeping pills. Fortunately, her parents found her before it was too late, and they admitted her to the hospital. Before she was released from the hospital, she gained 14 pounds. Sarah and her parents now attend counseling sessions, and only time will tell if she will be able to recover from her condition.

You have probably recognized that Sarah suffers from **anorexia nervosa.** This serious condition involves a distorted body image, an intense fear of gaining weight, and the refusal to maintain a minimally healthy body weight. People with anorexia, like Sarah, have an irrational view of their own bodies. By objective standards they are already thin, but they are still convinced that they are fat and unattractive. They show a relentless determination to be even more thin. People with anorexia have a very restricted diet, and they attempt to lose additional weight through vigorous exercise or by purging food through self-induced vomiting or the misuse of laxatives or enemas.

Bulimia nervosa, or bulimia, is a related condition that involves cycles of binge eating (consumption of huge amounts of food) followed by purging, fasting, or excessive exercise as a means to compensate for overeating. People with bulimia experience a loss of control during binge episodes: They know they are overeating, but they feel powerless to stop. Afterwards, they feel intense guilt. In contrast to some anorexics, who purge after eating only small amounts of food, bulimics purge after uncontrolled eating binges.

anorexia nervosa

A serious eating disorder involving distorted body image, intense fear of gaining weight, and refusal to maintain a healthy weight.

bulimia nervosa

A serious eating disorder with binge eating followed by purging, fasting, or excessive exercise.

Both types of eating disorders are most common among female adolescents. Approximately 1 out of every 100 female adolescents is anorexic, 2 to 3 times as many are bulimic (Mash & Wolfe, 1999). In the past these disorders were rare in males, but body dissatisfaction and eating disorders may be increasing among male adolescents, along with use of anabolic steroids and other untested supplements to increase muscle mass (Labre, 2002). Anorexia typically appears between the ages of 14 and 18, whereas bulimia usually emerges in later adolescence. There is a mild to moderate genetic link to eating disorders. These disorders tend to run in families, and compared to nonidentical twins, identical twins are 3 to 5 times more likely to share an eating disorder (Hsu, Chesler, & Santhouse, 1990). Researchers believe that adolescents can inherit emotional tendencies that make them vulnerable to eating disorders. Too often, these vulnerabilities can combine with low self-esteem, family pressures, and the strong societal message that "thin is beautiful" to lead to eating disorders (Davison & Birch, 2002; Stice & Whitenton, 2002).

We all know that society places too much emphasis on being thin. The mass media are full of images of attractive women who are significantly thinner than the general population. In fact many models are so thin that they are unhealthy. Very few adolescent girls can "measure up" to these unreasonable standards. Most adolescent girls are not satisfied with their body image, and 80 percent diet to control their weight (Mash & Wolfe, 1999). For ethnic minority teens, the stress of trying to fit into the majority culture adds additional pressures (Perez, Voelz, Pettit, & Joiner, 2002). Striving to be thin, some adolescent girls spiral into a dangerous cycle of anorexia or bulimia. For many anorexics, food is the only thing they feel they can control. And for bulimics, binging and purging is another symptom of their lack of control over life events. Psychological therapy and medications have shown promise in treating adolescent eating disorders (DeAngelis, 2002). Severe cases, like Sarah's, may require hospitalization to force weight gain or to treat other symptoms such as suicidal behavior or chronic depression.

LET'S REVIEW . . .

1. At what point in development are girls generally taller than boys?
   a. During early childhood, ages 6 to 9 years.
   b. During early adolescence, ages 11 to 14 years.
   c. During middle adolescence, ages 16 to 18 years.
   d. None of the above. In general, boys are taller than girls throughout development.

2. Early maturation can be problematic for many girls. One reason is that:
   a. their growth spurt tends to occur at the same time as the growth spurt in boys.
   b. although their secondary sexual characteristics emerge early, they tend to have late menarche.
   c. their hormone production is not sufficient to support the development of secondary sexual characteristics.
   d. they tend to be more short and stocky by late adolescence and are therefore less satisfied with their body image.

3. What should you conclude about a 1-month-old infant who does not show the Moro reflex?
   a. This reflex normally does not emerge until 4 months, so the infant is developing normally.
   b. This reflex disappears by 3 weeks of age, so the infant is developing normally.
   c. Most infants do not show the Moro reflex, so there is no reason to be concerned.
   d. The infant may have a neurological problem or immaturity.

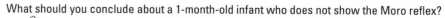

4. Which statement below provides the best summary of the dynamic systems theory of motor development?

    a. Motor skills emerge from the combination of physical growth, learning, and motivation.

    b. Motor development is governed primarily by neurological development as maturation in the brain allows more coordinated motor movements.

    c. Motor development is governed primarily by experience as physical exercise stimulates the formation of neural circuits in the brain.

    d. Cognitive development precedes motor development; infants must first understand how to coordinate individual movements before they can execute complex motor skills.

5. **True or False:** Like most infants, Kelli learned to sit upright on her own before she learned to walk. This is an example of the proximodistal pattern of motor development.

6. **True or False:** Anorexia and bulimia are most likely caused by a combination of genetic, social, and psychological factors.

Answers: 1. b, 2. d, 3. d, 4. a, 5. F, 6. T

Development of the Brain and Nervous System

The brain and nervous system are the structures that give rise to all of our thoughts, emotions, and behaviors. The most complicated organ in the body, the brain gets a quick head start on development. The brain is one of the first structures to form when tissue differentiation begins in the embryo, and at birth the brain and head are already more than half their adult size. In Figure 4.6 you can see that the head represents one-fourth of the newborn's total length but only one-eighth of the adult's height. The cephalocaudal pattern is evident here again. At birth, the brain and head region are much farther along in growth and development than the trunk and legs.

The study of how the brain grows and forms the intricate web of connections necessary to code our thoughts, memories, and motor actions is one of the most fascinating areas of science today. In 1995, for example, scientists and public policy officials met at the White House Conference on Early Childhood and Brain Development to discuss the exciting findings emerging from the research on early brain development (Fox & Leavitt, 1999). Many were touting the critical importance of the first few years of life in the formation of the complex neural circuits that make up the brain. Although there were still many mysteries to solve about how the brain grows and functions, researchers already understood the great importance of early childhood experiences.

If the proper experiences are not available for infants, will their brains develop normally? How does the brain grow and form internal connections? In this section we outline the major structures in the brain and describe how the brain forms in early development. We emphasize the growth of and interconnections among the most important units in the brain—the neurons. We also describe how experience and stimulation in the child's environment affect the growing brain.

As you study this section, ask yourself these questions:

- What are the main parts of the brain, and what are their basic functions?

- What are the main parts of neurons, and how do neurons develop?

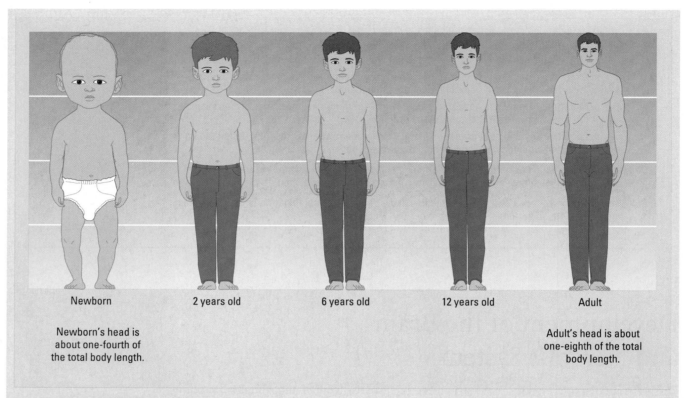

Newborn

2 years old

6 years old

12 years old

Adult

Newborn's head is about one-fourth of the total body length.

Adult's head is about one-eighth of the total body length.

FIGURE 4.6 Changing Head/Body Proportions

The newborn's head is relatively large in proportion to the rest of the body. The cephalocaudal pattern of development is apparent here: the head and brain grow early, and the lower body grows more rapidly later. This gives the brain a head start in forming the complicated circuits that will govern movements, thoughts, and emotions.

- How does the brain shape the complex neural circuits that are necessary to process information and organize behavior?

- In what ways does experience help shape the developing brain? Why is early experience so critical?

Structure of the Brain and Nervous System

The major structures in the human brain are shown in Figure 4.7. The *spinal cord* is the body's "information superhighway"—it allows vast amounts of information to be exchanged between the body and the brain. At the top of the spinal cord, the *brain stem* controls automatic functions (like breathing and heart rate) and regulates the general level of alertness throughout the higher levels of the brain. The *cerebellum,* on the back of the brain, controls posture, body orientation, and complex muscle movements. The *cerebral cortex* is the "gray matter" that forms the top portion of the brain, and it is divided into four major lobes (frontal, temporal, parietal, and occipital). The many convolutions (folds) in the cortex allow a greater amount of surface area to fit within the confines of the skull. The cortex is actually a thin layer of material, less than one-eighth of an inch thick, so it is important that its surface area be maximized.

Many areas within the cortex have specialized functions. The *motor area,* in the middle of the cortex, controls voluntary muscle movements from raising your eyebrows to wiggling your toes. Just behind the motor area is the *somatosensory area,* which registers sensory input

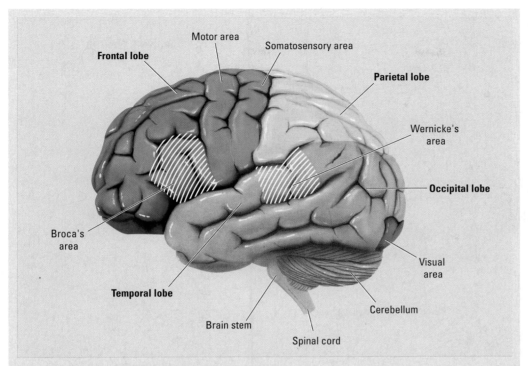

FIGURE 4.7 The Major Structures in the Brain and Spinal Cord

Source: Adapted from R. Fabes & C. L. Martin. (2003). *Exploring child development,* 2nd ed., p. 167. Published by Allyn and Bacon, Boston, MA. Copyright © 2004 by Pearson Education. Reprinted by permission of the publisher.

from all areas of the body. *Wernicke's area* processes speech input, and *Broca's area* organizes articulation for speech output. The *visual area* in the back of the brain receives messages from the eyes for visual processing. The large *frontal lobe* is involved in organizing, planning, and other executive functions important in higher-level thinking, problem solving, and creativity. Although researchers continue to discover specialized functions of various parts of the brain, it is also clear that most of our thoughts, perceptions, emotions, and memories are governed by complex communications occurring throughout the brain.

At the microscopic level, communication throughout the nervous system is controlled by specialized cells called **neurons.** The process involves *neural impulses* (electrical impulses) that travel through the neurons and *neurotransmitters* (chemical messengers) that transmit the impulses from one neuron to another. Neurons have three main parts, as shown in Figure 4.8. *Dendrites* are branchlike structures that receive input from other neurons. The *cell body* contains the nucleus and governs the function of the neuron. The *axon,* a relatively long fiber, carries electrical impulses that send messages to other cells. Mature axons are covered by a *myelin sheath,* a fatty substance that insulates the axon and speeds the axon's transmission of electrical activity. The end of the axon branches out to form *terminal buttons. Synapses* are the open spaces between terminal buttons of one neuron and dendrites of the next neuron. When the electrical impulse reaches the end of the axon, it causes the release of chemical neurotransmitters from the terminal buttons. The neurotransmitters flow across the synapse to the dendrites, where they can stimulate or inhibit the response of the neighboring cells. This process of electrochemical stimulation allows neurons to communicate throughout the nervous system.

neurons

Specialized cells that process information and allow communication in the nervous system.

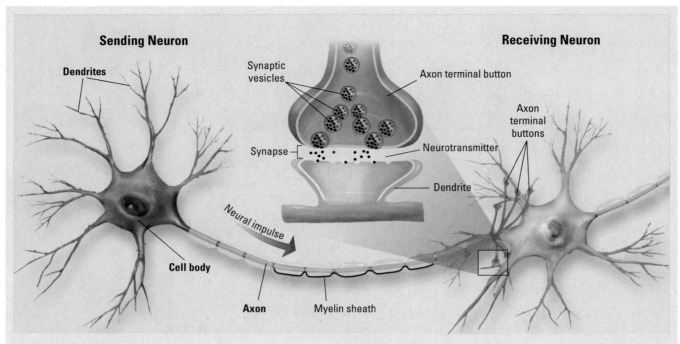

FIGURE 4.8 Parts of a Neuron

Each neuron in the brain and nervous system contains a cell body, dendrites, and an axon. Dendrites receive input from neighboring cells. Messages move down the length of the axon to the terminal buttons, and across the synapses to neighboring cells.

Source: Adapted from R. Fabes & C. L. Martin. (2003). *Exploring child development,* 2nd ed., p. 115. Published by Allyn and Bacon, Boston, MA. Copyright © 2004 by Pearson Education. Reprinted by permission of the publisher.

Forming the Brain and Nervous System

Now that you're familiar with the major parts of the nervous system, let's take a look at how they form and develop. At about 4 weeks after conception, the human embryo folds over to form a *neural tube.* The neural tube will later develop into the central nervous system (the brain and spinal cord). By 7 weeks, neurons have begun to form at the neural tube. By 10 weeks, some of the neurons begin migrating to the top of the tube, where they form the first layer of the cerebral cortex. The cortex will eventually have six layers of neurons. The innermost layers form first. As more neurons grow, they migrate past the first layers to create the outer layers. New neurons form at an enormous pace. "At the peak of neuron production it is estimated that 250,000 are created each minute" (Kolb, 1999, p. 11)! By 20 weeks of gestation, the cerebral cortex has approximately 80 billion neurons, and this is nearly all that the cortex will ever have.

The focus of brain development now shifts from the creation of new neurons to the growth of connections among the neurons. By 20 weeks, axons and dendrites have begun growing (Huttenlocher, 1999). By 23 weeks, the first synapses have formed as the axons and dendrites come into proximity. (Most synapses form after birth, however, as axons and dendrites continue to grow new branches.) By 31 weeks (only 7 to 9 weeks before a full-term birth), the cerebral cortex has grown enough that it begins folding inside the skull, forming the convolutions that characterize this part of the brain. At birth, the newborn's brain has the same outward appearance as an adult's brain—although inside much growth has yet to occur.

After birth the brain shows regular growth spurts (Epstein, 1978; Kolb, 1999; Kolb & Fantie, 1989). The weight of the brain increases 30 percent between the ages of 3 and 18

YOUR PERSPECTIVE NOTES

In your opinion, does brain growth allow children's thought processes to improve, or does exercising thought processes stimulate the brain to grow? What kinds of evidence would you need to address this question?

months. Brain weight increases up to another 10 percent during each period from the years 2 to 4, 6 to 8, 10 to 12, and 14 to 16. As you will see in Chapter 5, these age periods correspond closely with the stages of cognitive development Jean Piaget proposed several decades ago. There is a noticeable gender difference in these brain growth patterns, as we saw with physical growth and sexual maturation earlier in the chapter. Between the ages of 10 and 12, the rate of brain growth for girls is twice that for boys. Boys' brain growth spurt is larger between ages 14 and 16 (Epstein, 1978).

Remember, most neurons are formed midway during pregnancy (by the 20th week of gestation). The rapid brain growth that occurs during postnatal growth spurts is therefore due to the formation of new synapses, an increase in blood vessels to feed the growing brain, and proliferation of *glial cells*. **Glial cells** are specialized cells in the nervous system that support neurons in several ways. First, they provide structural support, holding neurons together. The name *glial* refers to this property of "gluing" neurons together. In addition, glial cells provide nourishment, remove waste products, occupy injured sites in the nervous system, and form the myelin sheaths that insulate axons. There are more than 100 billion glial cells in a mature brain, outnumbering neurons (Kolb, 1999).

After neurons form, they mature in two important ways: *synaptogenesis* and *myelination*. In **synaptogenesis** the dendrites and axons grow longer and branch out to form an enormously large number of synapses with neighboring neurons. Thousands of synapses can form rather randomly as the axons of one neuron come into proximity with dendrites from another (Huttenlocher, 1999). Most synapses form after birth. **Myelination** is the growth of the myelin sheath around the axon. The myelin sheath insulates the axon, which more than triples the speed of transmission of the impulse and communication with other neurons (Bornstein & Arterberry, 1999). Although most axons are myelinated by birth, some areas of the brain are not completely myelinated for several years. For example, the motor and sensory areas in the cortex are still forming myelin until about 4 months after birth. As you'll recall from the section on the development of voluntary movements, is is not until after the motor areas are myelinated (after 4 months) that babies accomplish coordinated motor actions such as sitting, reaching, and standing. Likewise, areas in the parietal and frontal lobes are not completely myelinated until about 15 *years* of age (Kolb & Fantie, 1989). Before the frontal lobe is fully myelinated, children and young adolescents show immaturities in planning, organizing information, and solving complex problems.

Although brain weight increases dramatically with synaptogenesis and myelination, the child's brain is actually *shrinking* in other ways. Synaptogenesis, governed largely by genetics, leads to a tremendous overabundance of synapses by the time the child reaches 2 years of age. But from early childhood into adolescence, heavy **synaptic pruning** *means that many more synapses are lost than gained!* Synapses that are activated by environmental input and brain activity are maintained, but synapses that are not used are lost or "pruned." Figure 4.9 shows the developmental phases of heavy synaptogenesis followed by synaptic pruning. During childhood, as many as 100,000 synapses can be lost every second! About 40 percent of the synapses that existed at 2 years of age are lost by adulthood (Kolb, 1999). A similar pattern exists with the formation and loss of the neurons themselves. Before birth, neurons proliferate at a tremendous rate and migrate to their final destinations, where they form the structures in the brain and the rest of the nervous system. But during migration, and during periods of heavy synaptogenesis, many neurons die. Some researchers refer to this process as **programmed cell death** (Kandel, Schwartz, & Jessell, 2000). As with synaptogenesis, environmental input and neural activity determine which neurons will survive. It is as if genetics provides an overabundance of neurons and synapses, and experience sculpts this "material," chiseling away the excess until the final form is achieved.

thinking OF BEVERLY

◄ What would you tell Beverly about the development of the brain and nervous system? How could this information be useful to her as she strives to enhance her baby's development?

glial cells

Specialized cells in the nervous system that support neurons in several ways.

synaptogenesis

One form of neuron maturation where dendrites and axons branch out to form an enormously large number of connections with neighboring neurons.

myelination

A form of neuron maturation where the fatty insulation (myelin sheath) grows around the axons.

synaptic pruning

Process where unused synapses are lost (pruned).

programmed cell death

Process where many neurons die during periods of migration and heavy synaptogenesis.

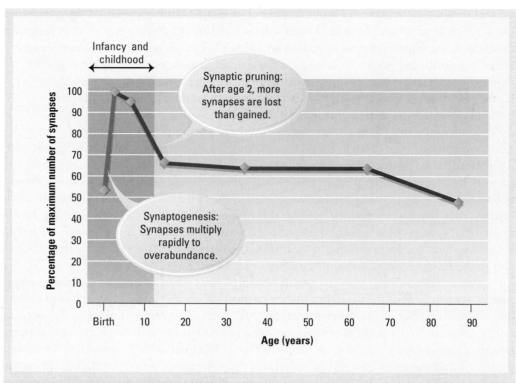

FIGURE 4.9 Synaptogenesis and Synaptic Pruning

New synapses form at an incredible rate during the first 2 years of life. During childhood, synaptic pruning reduces the total number of synapses. Synaptic density then remains relatively stable until the later years of life.

Source: Adapted from P. R. Huttenlocher & A. S. Dabholkar. (1997). Regional differences in human cerebral cortex. *Journal of Comparative Neurology, 387,* 167–178. Copyright © 1997 by Wiley-Liss, Inc. Reprinted by permission of Wiley-Liss, Inc., a subsidiary of John Wiley & Sons, Inc.

The Role of Experience in Brain Development

Researchers describe two types of brain development: *experience-expectant* and *experience-dependent* (Black & Greenough, 1986; Greenough & Black, 1999). With **experience-expectant development,** the brain has evolved to "expect" certain basic experiences or activities that all humans share—such as attachment to caregivers, recognition of human faces, hand–eye coordination, and communication by language (e.g., Nelson, 2001). The foundations for these types of experiences tend to be hardwired in the brain. Their development follows the pattern we've already described: Excess synapses form early in development ("expecting" the experience) and then are pruned throughout childhood (based on the actual experience). Genetics governs the proliferation of synapses; experience determines which synapses survive. Scientists speculate that cycles of synapse overproduction and pruning are staggered across the various activities, yielding a schedule of critical or sensitive periods of development (Greenough & Black, 1999). Synapses related to hand–eye coordination, for example, may be produced and pruned earlier than synapses for language. With experience-expectant development, every human can develop the same set of common processes and tendencies, yet each person can develop his or her own twist on the universal theme.

Experience-dependent development, on the other hand, has to do with experiences that are not universal. Examples include the vocabulary of a particular language (e.g., Portuguese), culture-specific behaviors (e.g., a handshake), and specific motor skills (e.g., skateboarding).

experience-expectant development

Development of universal experiences and activities (such as hand–eye coordination), where excess synapses form and are then pruned according to experience.

experience-dependent development

Development of specific experiences and activities (such as riding a skateboard), where new synapses form to code the experience.

The brain cannot "expect" these particular behaviors, so new synapses must form, stimulated by the experiences themselves, to encode them. As we learn to ride a skateboard, for example, new synapses form to code the motor movements. Later some of these synapses may be pruned as we refine our skills. Experience-dependent development occurs throughout the life span, giving us the potential for lifelong learning and the retention of individualized skills, facts, and knowledge. This type of development contributes to the distinctive character coded into an individual's brain and sets each of us apart from all other humans.

■ **When Less Is More: The Importance of Synaptic Pruning.** With experience-dependent development, additional synapses tend to form to encode the skills and information learned through experience. In that sense, more synapses code more learning. This is not necessarily true, however, with experience-expectant development. Researchers have learned an interesting lesson in studying brain development in children with fragile-X syndrome (Greenough & Black, 1999). Fragile-X syndrome is one of the leading inherited causes of mental retardation among males (see Chapter 2). In this syndrome a defective gene suppresses the normal production of a protein (FMRP) that is important for synaptic pruning. Without FMRP, the synapses overproduced during experience-expectant development cannot be pruned. Maintaining inefficient synapses adds "noise" to the neural circuits, leading to less effective processing in the brain and the mental retardation associated with fragile-X syndrome. As Greenough and Black (1999) put it, "elimination of synapses during development, in other words, is often a good thing that is necessary to proper neurobehavioral development" (p. 35).

■ **Effects of Enriched Environments.** Can parents or caregivers enhance synaptogenesis and synaptic pruning in a child by providing stimulating experiences? Consider one experiment where experimenters randomly assigned laboratory rats to live in "enriched" versus "plain" environments. Rats in the "enriched" environments lived in cages equipped with numerous ramps, tubes, boxes, and other stimulating toys to explore. Rats in "plain" environments lived in drab laboratory cages that lacked the added stimulation. What effect did the added stimulation have on the development of the rats' brains? It depended on the age of the rats (Kolb, Gibb, & Dallison, 1999). With rats in early adulthood, the enriched environment caused neurons to grow longer dendrites and *increased* the number of synapses per neuron. With young, newly weaned rats, however, the enriched environment led to a *decrease* in synapses. That is, for the young rats, the enriched experience facilitated synaptic pruning during *experience-expectant development,* but for the older rats, the experience added synapses in *experience-dependent development.* The effect that experience has on the brain therefore depends on the age of the individual.

Clearly, exposure to stimulating environments is important for forming sophisticated neural networks in the young brain. Children deprived of adequate stimulation lose the positive benefits of synaptic pruning during experience-expectant development, and they lose the opportunity to gain new synapses during experience-dependent development. In both ways, they fail to reach their full cognitive potentials. But how far do we need to go to stimulate the developing brain? What does it take to create appropriately "enriched" environments? For normally developing infants, the answer is found in the everyday environment around them: colorful and varied visual patterns in their toys and books; voices speaking, reading, and singing to the infant; hugs, cuddles, and tickles; and the stimulation of rocking, bouncing, and climbing. Opportunities to interact in rich and meaningful ways with the environment flood the developing brain with input and stimulate its development.

Some years back, a Georgia governor pushed for legislation aimed at enriching the environments of all newborn babies. To see how far his policy went, take a look at the Social Policy Perspective box called "Can Mozart Stimulate Neural Connections in Infants?"

thinking
OF BEVERLY

◄ Describe several examples of experience-expectant and experience-dependent development that might occur with Beverly's baby. How can Beverly encourage each of these forms of development?

thinking
OF BEVERLY

◄ How can this information about enriched environments with rats be useful in Beverly's thinking about her situation?

thinking
OF BEVERLY

◄ What would you tell Beverly about the "Mozart effect"? Were her friend's efforts in playing classical music during pregnancy helpful for her baby's development? Why or why not?

A Social Policy PERSPECTIVE...

Can Mozart Stimulate Neural Connections in Infants?

In his 1999 budget Georgia governor Zell Miller proposed that the state spend $105,000 to send a CD or cassette of classical music home with every baby born in the state. Miller commented that "[n]o one questions that listening to music at a very young age affects the spatial, temporal reasoning that underlies math and engineering and even chess" and that "[h]aving that infant listen to soothing music helps those trillions of brain connections to develop" (Sack, 1998). Does research evidence support Miller's claims? Frances Rauscher and her colleagues published a series of intriguing studies suggesting that extensive music training significantly enhanced the spatial–temporal skills of preschool children. These researchers also found that listening to a Mozart sonata improved college students' spatial-reasoning IQ scores by 8 to 9 points (Rauscher, Shaw, & Ky, 1993, 1995; Rauscher et al., 1997). The spatial-reasoning scores involved were on tests of reasoning about proportions, ratios, and other concepts in mathematics. Improvements in these skills after exposure to classical music has been labeled the "Mozart effect." Reports about the Mozart effect and about how early experience wires the developing brain led the proactive governor of Georgia to propose jump-starting infants' brain development with classical music.

But will it work? For the college students, the benefit of listening to classical music was temporary, lasting only 10 to 15 minutes (Rauscher et al., 1997)—and several other researchers have been unable to replicate the Mozart effect (e.g., Nantais & Schellenberg, 1999; Steele, Bass, & Crook, 1999). Still, the excitement over the initial findings prompted the Florida legislature to pass a law requiring that toddlers in state-run schools hear classical music every day (Goode, 1999). Based on information in this chapter, how would you suggest that state and local governments, other agencies, schools, and parents enhance brain development in infants and toddlers? What information would you use to support new social policies in this area? ◼

Neural Plasticity and Sensitive Periods

The experience-expectant phase of development that occurs early in the life cycle provides *neural plasticity* for the developing brain. **Plasticity** is the brain's tendency to remain somewhat flexible or malleable until synaptogenesis is complete and until the brain's synapses have been pruned and locked into particular functions (Huttenlocher, 2002). For example, an infant born with a cataract in one eye will receive reduced visual stimulation to that eye and consequently less activity through the neural circuits normally connected to it. As a consequence, the synapses that would normally form and connect to the defective eye may instead become devoted to the healthy eye. In this way, the young child's brain maximizes processing from the healthy eye to partially compensate for the loss of processing from the defective eye. This degree of compensation cannot occur when adults develop cataracts, however. Adults' brains lack this degree of plasticity; their neural circuits are already pruned and devoted to processing input from the respective eyes.

As another example, suppose an adult suffers head trauma and brain damage to the left hemisphere. Because the left hemisphere is specialized for language processing in most adults, the person will likely lose a significant amount of language function. With a strong rehabilitation regimen, the person may be able to recoup some language function; but he or she will probably experience lifelong deficits like slurred speech or trouble keeping track of complex sentence segments. Similar damage to the left hemisphere of a young child, however, will not lead to such dramatic lifelong deficits. Thanks to neural plasticity, corresponding areas in the child's right hemisphere can take over the responsibility of language specialization, compensating for the damage in the left hemisphere. Language processing in the right hemisphere

plasticity

The brain's tendency to remain somewhat flexible or malleable until synaptogenesis is complete and until the brain's synapses have been pruned and locked into serving particular functions.

will maintain synapses and neural circuits that, without the accident, would have been pruned away or devoted to other functions.

Plasticity is greatest before the age of 2 years, a period when new synapses are still proliferating and have not yet been pruned. From the age of 2 until adolescence, plasticity gradually declines. With declining plasticity *sensitive periods,* or windows of opportunity, also begin to close. The eyes and visual centers of the brain need sensory input in the first months after birth, or their neural circuits quickly degenerate. Plasticity lasts longer in other areas of the brain. Language centers, for example, maintain some plasticity until around the age of 12. Before age 12, children can learn a second language and speak it with the accent of a native speaker. If we begin learning a new language after 12, however, we can learn the vocabulary and syntax but usually never master the native speaker's intonations and subtle speech sounds. The ability to acquire a new accent has already been "pruned away" in the brain. After adolescence neural circuits in general are less flexible, and brain damage from accidents, stroke, or disease will have more permanent effects.

Larger Developmental Patterns in the Brain

So far, we have described microscopic development in the brain, focusing on individual neurons and synapses. Researchers also track the development of larger areas in the brain, correlating their development with corresponding advances in behavior and thought. The *visual area* in the back of the brain (look back to Figure 4.7, p. 147) develops early. This area reaches its peak in synapse density within 4 months after birth, and synapse density decreases to adult levels by approximately age 10 (Huttenlocher, 1990). As you will see in our next section, on Perceptual Development, newborn babies can fixate their eyes and track moving targets, but the abilities to see three-dimensional depth and to see details in more complex patterns improve dramatically by 4 months. These developments correspond closely with growth and refinement in the visual area of the brain. By middle childhood, plasticity in the visual center has decreased. For example, a doctor can correct amblyopia (one "lazy" eye) in a child under 4 by using a patch to block input to the healthy eye, pushing the other eye to process more input. After the age of 4, intervention is much more difficult.

Heavy growth in the *frontal lobes* occurs between the ages of 3 and 6 years (Thompson et al., 2000). The frontal lobes are responsible for organizing and planning behavior, so by 3 to 6 years this brain growth helps children to participate more fully in group settings like preschool and kindergarten. Between 6 and 13 years, the highest growth rates are in the *temporal* and *parietal lobes* (Thompson et al., 2000), areas associated with language specialization and spatial learning. As we described earlier, the sensitive period for language ends by early adolescence, after this peak in brain growth.

What Does the Future Hold?

With advances in technologies used to scan the brain and measure brain activity, and with our increased understanding of genetics and cell behavior, there is no doubt that brain research will make great strides in coming years. One preliminary study, for example, has demonstrated that high levels of four brain proteins exist in the bloodstreams of newborn babies who later show childhood autism or mental retardation (Nelson et al., 2000). Because these proteins govern the formation of and interconnections among neurons in the brain, it seems that their abnormal levels may lead to malformation of brain structures. If so, early drug treatments or other interventions might correct the imbalance and help prevent the development of these disorders. And even if these four proteins are not the cause of the disorders, they may at least serve as early markers—they may indicate which infants are at risk for developing autism and certain forms of retardation. Armed with this knowledge, researchers may be able to track the true origins of these disorders. Many other extraordinary developments are occurring in brain research. These advances will undoubtedly have a profound impact on the quality of life for millions of children.

1. As the brain develops, which of the following occurs *last*?
   a. The neural tube forms.
   b. Neurons form and migrate to the cortex.
   c. There is a period of heavy synaptic pruning.
   d. Neurons undergo programmed cell death.

2. Which of the following is the best example of experience-expectant development?
   a. An infant learns to walk.
   b. A toddler learns to recite the "ABCs."
   c. A college student studies psychology.
   d. A child learns to buckle a bicycle helmet.

3. What do we learn about brain development by studying children who inherit fragile-X syndrome?
   a. Programmed cell death is a leading cause of mental retardation.
   b. Delayed myelination is a leading cause of mental retardation.
   c. The loss of synapses during childhood reduces "noise" in neural circuits and helps the brain function more efficiently.
   d. Synaptic pruning reduces the brain's ability to process information, and mental retardation can be avoided if pruning is prevented.

4. Which of the following areas of the brain is the *last* to undergo rapid growth and development?
   a. The frontal lobes   c. The temporal and parietal lobes
   b. The visual cortex   d. The neural tube

5. True or False: Research with young rats suggests that providing extra stimulation in the environment tends to facilitate synaptic pruning in the brain.

6. True or False: During childhood and adolescence plasticity in the brain gradually increases.

Answers: 1. c, 2. a, 3. c, 4. c, 5. T, 6. F

Perceptual Development

As we saw in the previous section, the human nervous system is relatively immature at the time of birth. Most of the synapses in the sensory systems have not yet formed. Also, many of the neurons have not yet acquired the myelin sheath that insulates the axons and speeds transmission of neural impulses. Newborns can move their eyes to locate and track objects in their surroundings, but until they gain better control of the intricate muscles in and around their eyes, infants have trouble focusing on a target and coordinating the images coming from each eye. At the back of the eye, specialized neurons called *photoreceptor cells* are aligned along the retina. In adults these photoreceptors are so dense in the center of our vision (the fovea) that they create a depression in the retina—the foveal pit. But in newborns photoreceptors are spread more evenly across the entire retina; there is no foveal pit to provide detail vision. For these and many other anatomical reasons, it is hard to imagine that newborn infants are able to make much sense out of the overwhelming array of input that bombards their eyes and other sensory systems. It is no wonder that John Locke and other early philosophers claimed that the newborn's mind was a "blank slate." According to this view, infants need to learn by trial and error to use their senses to form meaningful perceptions. And one of the founders of psychology, William James (1890/1950), claimed that the mental experience of the infant was "one great blooming, buzzing confusion" (p. 488).

Do infants really begin life this helpless? Clearly not. When researchers began investigating early perceptual development, one of the great challenges they faced was finding a way to get young infants to communicate what (or if) they could perceive. Infants, of course, cannot talk. (The term "infant" is derived from the Latin word *infans,* which means "unable to speak.") In the 1950s the emergence of reliable nonverbal techniques for testing infants opened the floodgates of research. Now, after a half century of systematic research, scientists have learned an impressive amount about the perceptual capabilities of infants. Instead of a "blooming, buzzing confusion," it is apparent that even young infants have a tremendous propensity to organize and use sensory information in a meaningful way.

We begin this section by describing the early breakthroughs in research on infant perception. Then we describe what researchers have learned about perceptual development in the basic sensory modalities: vision, hearing, taste, and smell. We end the chapter with a look at higher-order perceptual abilities, including the abilities to perceive depth and to coordinate information across different modalities.

As you study this section, ask yourself these questions:

- How do researchers know what infants can see and hear?
- What capabilities do newborns have in vision, hearing, taste, and smell?
- What kinds of information do infants prefer?
- When do infants begin to see depth, and how do we know that they can see the distances between surfaces and objects?
- Do infants take a long time to learn to coordinate information across their sensory modalities, or do they show this capability soon after birth?

Robert Fantz and Visual Preferences

As early as 1951, Robert Fantz was conducting experiments to determine if form perception was innate or learned (see Fantz, 1961). At first Fantz worked with newly hatched chickens. On their first exposure to light, Fantz recorded the number of times the baby chicks pecked at objects of various shapes. He reasoned that if they pecked significantly more often at some shapes than at others, then they must have some innate capability to perceive form. And they did. Jumping up the evolutionary scale, Fantz then began testing form perception in infant chimpanzees (Fantz, 1956). He placed different types of patterns in front of their eyes and recorded the amount of time the chimpanzees spent fixating their eyes on each pattern. Did the chimps fixate longer on some patterns than on others? They did, again indicating an early ability to see and distinguish among the visual patterns.

But what about human infants? Fantz and his associates used a *looking chamber* (Figure 4.10) to test infants only a few hours to a few months old (Fantz, 1961). The researchers placed infants on the sliding tray at the bottom. A researcher, standing over the chamber, could slide patterns on cards through slots in the top of the chamber. Peering through a hole, the experimenter could also observe the infants' eyes and use electronic devices to record the

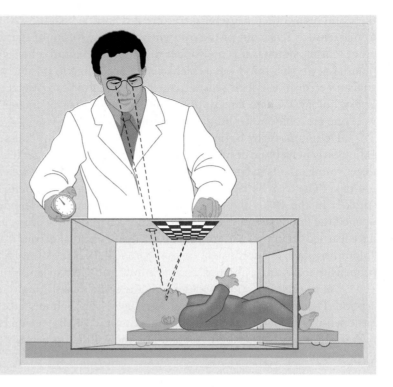

FIGURE 4.10 Looking Chamber

Early researchers used the "looking chamber" to investigate visual preferences in young infants. The infant looked up from the bottom toward stimulus patterns illuminated within the chamber. A researcher monitored the infant's eyes, recording the amount of time the infant's gaze fixated on each stimulus pattern.

Source: Based on Fantz (1961).

time infants spent fixating on each pattern. "If an infant consistently turns its gaze toward some forms more often than toward others, it must be able to perceive form" (Fantz, 1961, p. 67). This became the logic of the **preferential-looking technique,** a simple but powerful procedure that many researchers have since used to investigate infant perception.

Figure 4.11 graphs results from one of Fantz's early experiments. Newborns only 2 to 5 days old preferred a drawing of a face over a bull's-eye or newsprint, but they preferred any of these detailed patterns over plain colored disks (Fantz, 1963). Infants spent approximately equal time looking at the colored disks, especially to the yellow and white disks, so we don't know if they could distinguish these colors. Using this preferential-looking technique, Fantz collected some of the first scientific data that demonstrated conclusively that human infants are able to perceive form and pattern. Hundreds of researchers, in laboratories all around the world, have since followed with their own studies investigating the kinds of visual information human infants can detect and process. And researchers have adapted Fantz's logic and procedures to assess perception in other sensory modalities as well.

■ **Human Faces and Other Preferences.** Using Fantz's preferential-looking technique and other similar techniques, researchers have discovered that newborn babies have the following visual preferences (see Bjorklund, 1989 for a review):

> moving stimuli

> outer contours or edges

> sharp color contrasts (e.g., where black meets white, or where red meets white)

> patterns with some detail or complexity (but not too complex!)

> symmetrical patterns

> curved patterns

> patterns that resemble the human face

preferential-looking technique

Technique used to test infant visual perception. If infants consistently look longer at some patterns than at others, researchers infer they can see a difference between the patterns.

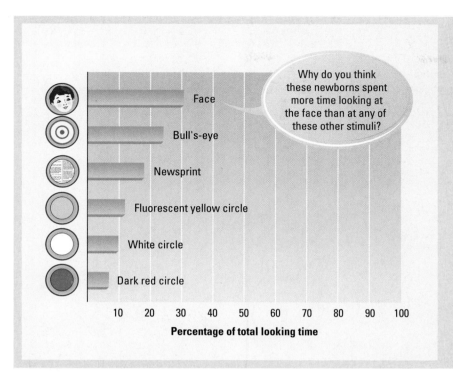

FIGURE 4.11 Preferential-Looking Results

This graph shows results from an early preferential-looking study. Stimuli were presented one at a time in random order to newborns who were only 2 to 5 days old. What types of features caught the newborns' eyes?

Source: Based on Fantz (1963).

Some of these preferences are evident in Figure 4.11; notice that infants preferred the bull's-eye over the plain disks, and they preferred the face most of all. Infants at a young age can obviously see these patterns well enough to choose one over the others. Parents can capitalize on these preferences in shaping their babies' environments. Crib mobiles, baby books, blocks, and other infant toys should feature sharp color contrasts, symmetrical patterns, curves, and even human face patterns. As infants explore these and other patterns, their sensory systems get the input they need to stimulate further growth and development.

One of the more intriguing findings is that infants tend to prefer patterns that resemble the human face. One group of researchers entered the delivery room when babies were born and showed newborns the patterns shown in Figure 4.12 (Goren, Sarty, & Wu, 1975). One at a time, in a random series, they placed the patterns about 6 to 10 inches in front of each newborn's nose, then moved the patterns slowly toward the left or right. Although the newborns were only a few minutes old, they reliably turned their heads farther to follow the pattern that most resembled the human face. Because people in the delivery room were wearing surgical masks, the newborns had had no opportunity to see a real human face before the testing began! Other researchers have replicated this finding about the newborn's preference for the facial pattern (Johnson, Dziurawiec, Ellis, & Morton, 1991). These researchers speculate that at birth babies are already equipped with an innate *schema,* or mental framework, for the structure of the human face. However, other researchers remind us that these newborns may not recognize the patterns as "faces" per se. Instead, they may be responding to particular features that happen to be contained in faces—left-right symmetry and more details in the top than bottom half, for example (Turati, Simion, Milani, & Umiltá, 2002).

The "specialness" of the human face has received much attention in the research literature. By 3 months of age, infants can recognize their own mothers' faces in photographs. In one study, female 3-month-olds looked longer at photographs of their own mothers' faces than at photos of other adult females (Barrera & Maurer, 1981a). Interestingly, 3-month-

thinking
OF BEVERLY

◀ Based on the preferential-looking research reviewed so far, what could you advise Beverly regarding the perceptual abilities of her baby? Are there suggestions here about the types of patterns or decorations her newborn might be able to see or might prefer?

FIGURE 4.12 Face Stimuli

Researchers showed these patterns one at a time to newborns who were only a few minutes old. Although they had yet to see their first real face, the newborns preferred to look at the pattern that most resembled the arrangement of the human face. Why do you think this was so?

Source: C. C. Goren, M. Sarty, & P. Y. K. Wu. (1975). Visual following and pattern discrimination of face-like stimuli by newborn infants. *Pediatrics, 56,* p. 545, Figure 1. Copyright © 1975. Reproduced with permission.

YOUR

PERSPECTIVE
PERSPECTIVE

NOTES

Why do you believe 2-month-olds preferred looking at "attractive" faces? How did they learn or know which faces were more attractive?

old boys did not show the same pattern. Beyond recognizing their mothers' faces, when do you think infants begin to judge the physical attractiveness of faces? Would you believe by 2 months? In an intriguing study, Judith Langlois and her colleagues asked college students to rate the "attractiveness" of photos of female adults. Then they slide-projected the photos in pairs on a large screen in front of infants (Langlois et al., 1987). When an "attractive" photo was paired with an "unattractive" photo, 2-month-olds looked longer at the attractive photo. Langlois and her colleagues (1987) concluded that "the tendency to detect and prefer certain faces over others is present very early in life, long before any significant exposure to contemporary standards, definitions, and stereotypes" (p. 367). If beauty is "in the eye of the beholder," it's there at a surprisingly early age!

Infant scanning of faces changes significantly from 1 to 2 months of age (Maurer & Salapatek, 1976). As Figure 4.13 shows, 1-month-olds tend to fixate more on the external features of faces (the chin and hairline), whereas 2-month-olds tend to focus on the internal features (especially the eyes and mouth). This change may help explain why it is in the 2- to 3-month period that infants begin showing recognition of familiar faces (e.g., their mothers) and a preference for attractive faces: It's the internal features that help us recognize people the most.

Habituation–Dishabituation Research

Recall from Figure 4.11 that young infants preferred to look at the face over the newsprint and any kind of detail over plain colors—but did not show a preference among the plain colored disks. Can infants see the differences among these colors? Based on this test alone, we cannot assume that infants can visually discriminate between the colors. Here lies an important limitation of the preferential-looking technique: To show visual discrimination, infants not only must be able to *see* the difference between the stimuli, but also must have some reason to *prefer* one over the other. What if infants can see the difference, but find both stimuli to be equally interesting?

To solve this problem, a more stringent test of visual discrimination involves the **habituation–dishabituation technique.** This technique capitalizes on infants' tendency to look longer at novel (new) stimuli than at familiar (old) stimuli. As an example, consider the experiment conducted by Cohen, Gelber, and Lazar (1971). Imagine that you show a red circle to a 4-month-old infant for several seconds, and you record the amount of time the infant spent looking at the circle. Then you remove the circle—and then you show it again. Repeat this procedure, each time recording how long the infant looks at the circle. Plotting the looking times, you may notice a trend, as shown in Figure 4.14. That is, the infant's interest in the stimulus has likely decreased across trials. The infant has showed **habituation**—the tendency to reduce a response to a stimulus that is presented repeatedly. Habituation indicates that the infant processed the stimulus and recognized it on its repeated appearances. Now look at what happens during the *dishabituation trials* in Figure 4.14. Here, the same infant sees a series of stimuli with familiar or novel forms and colors. Fixation time for the same familiar red circle remains low, continuing the trend shown in habituation trials. The infant continued to show habituation to the familiar color and form. But a change in color (to a green circle) or a change in form (to a red triangle) produces an *increase* in fixation time. Changing both color and form (to a green triangle) produces an even greater increase. These increases reflect **dishabituation**—the recovery or increase in response when a new stimulus replaces a familiar stimulus. Dishabituation indicates that the infant can see the difference between the novel and familiar stimuli. In this case, the infant can obviously see the difference between colors (red versus green) and forms (circle versus triangle).

Notice that at the outset of the experiment, there was no reason for the infants to prefer green over red or triangle over circle, but that habituating infants to "red" and "circle" induced such preferences. The habituation–dishabituation technique thus avoids one of the problems with the preferential-looking technique because it can demonstrate visual discrimination even when there is no chance that infants might have an already established preference for one stimulus over another. In an additional example, Barrera and Maurer (1981b) habituated 3-month-old infants to a photograph of a female stranger's face. The infants dishabituated when a novel photograph (of another female stranger) was presented—showing an ability to discriminate between strangers' faces. The preferential-looking technique could not have produced this evidence, because without habituation there is no reason for infants to prefer one stranger's face over another (unless, of course, the faces differ greatly in their levels of attractiveness!).

An important practical application of habituation–dishabituation is that an infant's degree of dishabituation response provides a moderately accurate prediction of intelligence later in childhood. Numerous studies have found a correlation of approximately .40 between young infants' degrees of dishabituation and the same children's intelligence test scores at 1

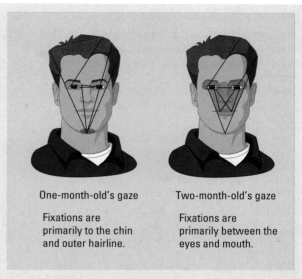

FIGURE 4.13 Infant Visual Fixation on Facial Patterns

Tracking their eye movements, you can see that 1-month-old infants spend most of their time looking at external features of the face—mostly the chin and outer hairline. By 2 months, infants are now looking more at the internal features, especially the eyes and mouth.

Source: Based on Maurer & Salapatek (1976).

habituation–dishabituation technique

Technique used to test infant perception. Infants are shown a stimulus repeatedly until they respond less (habituate) to it. Then a new stimulus is presented.

habituation

The tendency of infants to reduce their response to stimuli that are presented repeatedly.

dishabituation

The recovery or increase in infant's response when a familiar stimulus is replaced by one that is novel.

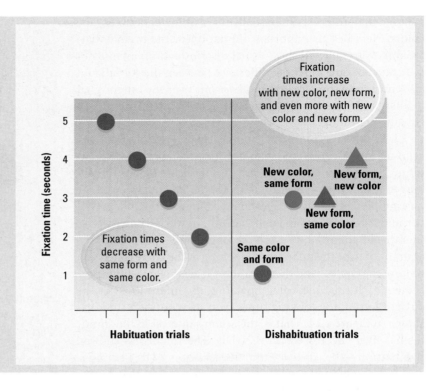

FIGURE 4.14 Habituation–Dishabituation Example

This graph shows hypothetical data from work with a 4-month-old infant using the habituation–dishabituation technique. The infant shows habituation by looking less and less at a red circle that is presented repeatedly—but looking time increases (dishabituation) when novel forms or colors are presented.

Source: Based on Cohen, Gelber, & Lazar (1971).

thinking
OF BEVERLY

Would you expect Beverly's baby to habituate to the decorations, toys, and other stimuli in his or her environment? Knowing about habituation and dishabituation, how would you advise Beverly to enhance the stimulation value of her baby's surroundings? How is this concept related to the research on enriched environments with rats that we discussed earlier in the chapter?

to 8 years of age (McCall & Carriger, 1993). Infants who show more dishabituation tend to score higher in IQ. The memory, discrimination, and recognition skills involved in habituation–dishabituation are related to the kinds of cognitive skills measured in typical intelligence tests. The habituation–dishabituation technique therefore can help researchers assess cognitive functioning in early infancy. Infants who were exposed prenatally to cocaine, for example, show depressed habituation and dishabituation (Mayes, Granger, Frank, Schottenfeld, & Bornstein, 1993). In one study, half of the 3-month-olds who were cocaine exposed failed to achieve habituation at all (Mayes & Bornstein, 1995).

Vision: Acuity, Color, and Depth

■ **How Clear Is Their Sight? Measuring Infant Visual Acuity.**   One of the fundamental questions in perception regards **visual acuity**—the ability to see fine detail. You are probably familiar with the standard eye chart used to measure visual acuity. According to this chart, a person with normal, 20/20 vision can read a certain row of letters on the chart from 20 feet away. A person with 20/40 vision would need to be 20 feet away to read what someone with normal vision could read from 40 feet. But how can researchers test acuity in young infants who don't know the alphabet? To do this, Fantz presented infants with the striped patterns shown in Figure 4.15. The test pairs each striped pattern with a uniform gray square. If an infant does not have sufficient acuity to see the stripes, then the striped pattern blends to gray. As you can see in the figure, it is harder to see the most closely spaced stripes. (Back up several feet from your textbook, and the stripes will fade even more.) When infants can see the stripes, however, they tend to prefer to look at the stripes over the gray square. At a distance of 10 inches, 6-month-olds can see stripes as thin as $^1/_{64}$ inch, but 1-month-olds need the stripes to be at least $^1/_8$ inch thick. Researchers estimate that visual acuity in newborns is somewhere between 20/150 and 20/600. Infants reach 20/20 vision by 6 to 12 months (Cohen, DeLoache, & Strauss, 1979). Even though acuity is poor in the first

visual acuity

The ability to see fine detail.

months, Hainline (1998) reminds us that when "development proceeds normally, infant vision seems perfectly adequate for the things that infants need to do" (p. 42)—for example, locate a caregiver, see a food source, or lock in on a smiling face.

■ How Colorful Is Their Sight? Color Vision in Infancy.

It is unclear how well newborn infants are able to distinguish among various colors. Studies have found that newborns prefer to look at green, yellow, or red over gray (Adams, Maurer, & Davis, 1986). However, other evidence indicates that newborns can distinguish red from white but not blue, green, or yellow from white (Adams, Courage, & Mercer, 1994). Using habituation–dishabituation researchers demonstrated that 4-month-olds distinguish and categorize various hues in much the same way as adults (Bornstein, Kessen, & Weiskopf, 1976). Most of the evidence collected in the last few decades suggests that the photopigments in the eye that are necessary for normal color vision are present by at least 3 months, and it is safe to say that color vision is relatively mature by 6 months (Kellman & Banks, 1998; Suttle, Banks, & Graf, 2002).

■ How Deep Is That Drop? Early Depth Perception.

As soon as our children learned to crawl, they were into everything. They were determined to use their newfound mobility to explore every nook and cranny in the house. The staircase seemed especially intriguing for the babies—but frightening for us as parents.

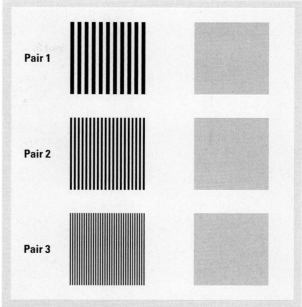

FIGURE 4.15 Patterns Used to Test Visual Acuity in Infants

Researchers use the preferential-looking technique to determine which set of stripes infants differentiate from the plain gray square.

Source: Based on Fantz (1961).

It seemed to us that the babies could see that the stairs fell off into depth: They crawled more slowly at the top and carefully extended their hands or bottoms down the first step. Still, their awkward crawling movements and several near misses prompted us to install a gate across the top of the stairs.

When do infants first begin to perceive depth? Do they need to learn the dangers of deep drops through trial-and-error learning? The classic research on depth perception was Eleanor Gibson and Richard Walk's (1960) *visual cliff* experiment. Similar to the photo in Figure 4.16, a heavy sheet of glass extended across a solid surface and a deep drop-off. Infants from 6 to 14 months of age were tested. The researchers placed each infant in the middle; then the baby's mother called, first from one side and then the other. All of the 6-month-olds crawled out onto the solid side to reach their mothers, but they refused to crawl onto the deep side. Many cried, but still they did not venture over the visual cliff. Gibson and Walk concluded that depth perception is available by the time infants learn to crawl. A decade later, other researchers demonstrated that infants just under 2 months of age could see the difference between the deep and solid sides (Campos, Langer, & Krowitz, 1970). They placed infants face-down on each side of the visual cliff and measured their heart rates. Infants showed significantly more slowing of their heart rates on the deep side. In infants, heart rate deceleration indicates engrossed attention. Although it was clear that these young infants could perceive depth, it seems that they were more intrigued by than afraid of the "cliff."

In the visual cliff experiment, several cues indicate depth. First, there are *pictorial cues*—the relative size and density of the pattern elements shown beneath the glass. Also, there is *motion parallax:* As the head and eyes move, the elements on the solid side move more rapidly across the field of vision. (More recent evidence suggests that infants do not use pictorial cues alone to judge depth until 7 months of age; see Bornstein & Arterberry, 1999, for a review.) By 3 to 4 months of age, infants can judge depth using *binocular disparity*—the

FIGURE 4.16 Visual Cliff

A "visual cliff" like this was used in the classic study of depth perception by Gibson and Walk (1960). How can you tell if the infant can see the deep drop under the glass?

difference between the images projected on the two eyes (Fox, Aslin, Shea, & Dumais, 1980). At an even earlier age, 1-month-olds show avoidance (e.g., blinking their eyes) in the face of approaching objects (Náñez & Yonas, 1994). Developmentally, sensitivity to the different types of depth cues seems to progress from the use of object motion, to binocular disparity, and finally to pure pictorial cues. Neurological development and experience both play important roles in facilitating depth perception. As Bornstein and Arterberry (1999) put it, "no matter how early in life depth perception can be demonstrated, the ability still rests on some experience, and no matter how late its emergence, it can never be proved that only experience has mattered" (p. 238).

Auditory Perception

Research on young infants' auditory capabilities lets us draw several conclusions (Aslin, 1987). First, the auditory system is functional several weeks before birth—researchers have found that auditory stimuli such as loud sounds produce changes in fetal heart rate and brain-wave activity. Second, by 6 months after birth, infants are capable of responding to a broad range of sounds. Even the youngest infants easily distinguish rattles, voices, songs, and many other environmental noises. Still, infants' auditory systems are not completely mature. Infants cannot yet detect very faint sounds, such as the softest of whispers, and they need changes in loudness and frequency (pitch) to be greater before they can detect these changes. For example, infants 6 to 9 months of age can barely detect a frequency change of 2 percent, but adults can detect a .5 percent change.

If you listen to adults speaking to infants, you will notice that we take these developmental differences into account in a special style of speech—*child-directed speech (CDS)*. In **child-directed speech** adults move close to the infant, speaking slowly, clearly, and with exaggerated

child-directed speech

The special singsong way that adults and older children talk to infants, speaking slowly, clearly, and with exaggerated intonation.

changes in intonation. The "singsong" quality of child-directed speech provides greater changes in loudness and frequency, inducing infants to be more attentive.

A third characteristic of early auditory perception is that infants and young children may in fact be more sensitive than adults to higher frequencies of sound (e.g., 20,000 Hz). Sensitivity to higher frequencies evidently begins to decline around the age of 6 years. Again, notice that adults tend to use a higher pitch in child-directed speech. Fourth, infants are able to locate sounds in the environment by turning their head or eyes in the direction of the sound source. Interestingly, this ability declines from birth to 2 months of age; then it improves again around 4 months. Researchers speculate that this trend is due to the loss of the orienting reflex, which is controlled by lower brain centers. Then, as the higher cortex develops, the lower brain centers are overridden; this results in greater voluntary search behaviors (Aslin, 1987).

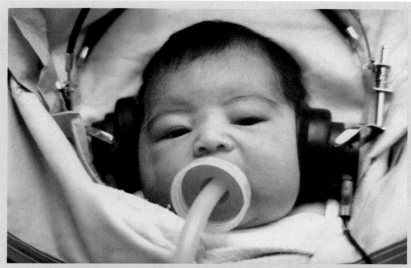

This infant is participating in an experiment on auditory perception. By adjusting how fast he sucks on the pacifier, he can activate one of two tape recordings played into the headphones. If he adjusts his sucking rate, that is evidence that he hears the difference and is working to listen to one sound over the other.

As with faces in visual perception, researchers have devoted extensive study to infant reactions to the human voice. Newborns prefer the voices of their own mothers to voices of unfamiliar females (DeCasper & Fifer, 1980). They do not, however, show a similar preference for the voices of their fathers over those of unfamiliar males (DeCasper & Prescott, 1984). By 2 months infants show a preference for speech with the rising and falling inflections typical of child-directed speech (Sullivan & Horowitz, 1983). At 4 months infants prefer to listen to human voices over silence or white noise (Colombo & Bundy, 1981).

One of the most intriguing experiments we have seen was conducted by DeCasper and Spence (1986). These researchers asked pregnant women to read aloud a particular children's story (e.g., *The Cat in the Hat*) twice each day during the last 6 weeks of pregnancy. Two to 3 days after birth, the experimenters tested the newborns for their recognition of the story. They connected a pacifier to an electronic switch that could activate one of two sound tracks. One sound track was a recording of the newborn's mother reading the familiar story (*The Cat in the Hat*). The other track was a recording of the mother reading a new story (e.g., *The King, the Mice, and the Cheese*). Newborns could choose which story to activate by adjusting their rate of sucking on the pacifier. For some, slower sucking would activate the familiar story; for others, this required faster sucking. In both cases, newborns adjusted their rate of sucking as required to activate the familiar story. Because both sound tracks were recordings of the mother's voice, the infants must have been choosing on the basis of certain qualities (e.g., pace) they heard in the stories. Further, these infants still preferred the familiar story when the stories were recorded by unfamiliar female voices. Based on these results, auditory perception before birth was adequate to process and retain the acoustic qualities of the story—and the newborns' perception and memory were sufficient to differentiate the two sound tracks and recognize which one was familiar. Quite a task for a baby only 2 to 3 days old! Other researchers got similar results when they exposed fetuses to classical or jazz music or to melodies or lullabies sung by their mothers (Panneton, 1985; Satt, 1984; Woodward, 1992). In each case, newborns preferred the familiar sounds over novel ones.

thinking
OF BEVERLY

In light of the DeCasper and Spence (1986) study, can you see why Beverly's friend thought classical music might benefit her fetus? Given what you have learned about prenatal development of the nervous system, explain the myths and realities of providing extra "fetal stimulation."

It is obvious that this child doesn't care for this taste. Reactions to basic categories of smell and taste are controlled in the lower brain centers of babies.

Although auditory perception will continue to develop during infancy and the early childhood years, it is evident that infants enter the world already capable of responding to countless differences in the sounds surrounding them.

Perception of Smell and Taste

Immediately after birth, you can tell from their facial expressions that newborn babies react to certain odors in a manner similar to adults. Newborns show positive facial expressions in response to the aromas of bananas and butter, positive or indifferent responses to vanilla, some rejection to fishy odors, and complete disgust to rotten eggs (Bornstein & Arterberry, 1999; Steiner, 1979). In other experiments Richard Porter and his colleagues studied newborns' recognition of their parents' smells. For example, parents in one study wore gauze pads under their arms for several hours; then researchers used the pads in a "preferential-smelling" test with the parents' newborn babies (Cernoch & Porter, 1985). At the age of 2 weeks, breast-fed babies turned their heads toward the smell of their mothers more than to the smell of unfamiliar females (mothers of other babies). The newborns did not show recognition of the smell of their fathers, however. Also, bottle-fed newborns did not show a preference for the smell of their mothers. From these results we know that infants are capable of discerning small differences in complicated odors, at least when they have close and repeated contact with the odor—as breast-fed infants would have with the smell of their mothers.

Infants show taste preferences immediately after birth, even before their first feedings (Steiner, 1979). When given a sweet solution, newborns smile and make sucking movements. Infants will suck longer to obtain a solution that is sweeter as opposed to less sweet (Crook, 1987). With a sour taste, they purse their lips and wrinkle their noses. A bitter taste causes newborns to spit and make a face indicating disgust and rejection. These early taste preferences seem to be governed by areas in the lower brain, because they appear even in infants born without a cerebral cortex (Steiner, 1979). Reaction to salty flavors develops later, usually by 4 months of age (Beauchamp, Cowart, Mennella, & Marsh, 1994).

Intermodal Perception

Although we have treated the different sensory systems separately so far, in reality most of our experiences are multimodal. As we walk down the sidewalk, we feel the solid surface beneath our feet and the breeze on our faces. We see the colors of the sky and the land, and we hear the voices of people walking around us and the leaves rustling in the trees. When we talk with someone, we also see their body language, gestures, and facial expressions. And we know that smells greatly influence flavors. In short, we experience the world through combined or integrated sensory inputs, or what researchers refer to as **intermodal perception.**

Do we need to learn to combine sensory inputs into unified impressions? According to the *constructivist* view, we do. Jean Piaget (1952b), for example, believed that young infants are not aware that what they see is also what they hear. He hypothesized that infants need to learn,

intermodal perception

The process of combining or integrating information across sensory modalities.

through experience, to coordinate their sensory systems. We will discuss Piaget's constructivist theory of cognitive development in the next chapter. At the other end of the spectrum, T. G. R. Bower (1974) speculated that infants have to learn to *separate* their sensory impressions. In the beginning, infants confuse their sensory impressions—they do not know if they are seeing or hearing, tasting or smelling. Bower concluded that "the initial primitive unity [of the sensory systems] must go, leaving differentiated sensory systems in place of a unitary perceptual world" (p. 151). In a more centrist view, Eleanor Gibson pointed out that important features in the environment (she called them *invariants*) can be detected by multiple sensory systems (Gibson & Walker, 1984; Rose & Ruff, 1987). For example, we can see that the sidewalk is a solid surface (because its texture continues into the distance), and we can also feel its solidity beneath our feet. Similarly, the infant can both smell and taste the sweetness of breast milk or formula, can both see and hear the movement of the rattle. Can infants make connections across these sensory modalities? Research on intermodal, or cross-modal, perception indicates that they can.

One of the classic demonstrations was an experiment conducted by Meltzoff and Borton (1979). These researchers placed a smooth or a "nubby" pacifier in the mouths of 1-month-old infants. They then removed the pacifier and showed both types of pacifiers simultaneously to the infants. The 1-month-olds looked significantly longer at the shape that had been in their mouths—they matched the shape they saw with the one they had felt. Also, Elizabeth Spelke and her colleagues found that infants can match the dynamic features of moving objects across

modalities. In one study, infants saw two films side by side (Spelke, 1979). In one film, a kangaroo (or donkey) puppet bounced up and down at a slower rate, and in the other film it bounced faster. At the same time the researchers played a slow or fast "thump" or "gong" sound synchronized with the bouncing in one of the films. Four-month-old infants looked significantly longer at the film that matched the pace of the sound. Of course, kangaroos don't normally make "thump" or "gong" noises when they jump, and we can assume that the infants had no prior experience with kangaroo activities. Still, these young infants matched the pace of the sound with the pace of the bouncing, showing that infants are quite capable of detecting features shared across sensory modalities. It doesn't appear that infants require a significant amount of learning to connect these sensory impressions, or that they are confused by complex sensory inputs.

In related research, 5-month-old infants matched the sound of an engine increasing or decreasing in volume with a video of an automobile coming toward or moving away from them (Walker-Andrews, & Lennon, 1985). And infants 6 to 8 months old matched the number they heard with the number they saw (Starkey, Spelke, & Gelman, 1983). For example, when they heard two drumbeats, they looked longer at a photo of two household objects; when they heard three drumbeats, they preferred to look at three objects. Also, infants as young as 5 months can match emotional expressions across faces and voices (Walker, 1982). When hearing a tape of a happy voice, for example, infants looked longer at a film of a happy face than at one showing a sad face. By 4 months infants can even match the age of a voice with the age of a face: Hearing the sound of a child reading a nursery rhyme, infants looked longer at a video of a child's face than at a video of an adult's face. When they heard the adult reading, infants looked longer at the adult's face (Bahrick,

Does it take a significant amount of trial-and-error learning for infants to connect the voices they hear with the visual images of faces? Evidently not. Using a variety of interesting stimuli, research on intermodal perception indicates that infants make such connections even when they have had very little experience with the events they are matching.

Netto, & Hernandez-Reif, 1998). Again, these findings demonstrate intermodal perception of a variety of complicated events. Intermodal perception is sufficiently evident during infancy that its strength can serve as a reliable indicator of later cognitive functioning. For infants born preterm, scores on intermodal matching at 12 months of age predict cognitive abilities all the way through 6 years of age (Rose & Wallace, 1985). It takes a healthy nervous system to integrate the information flowing to the infant from multiple perceptual modalities.

As you can see, researchers have learned a lot about the perceptual capabilities of human infants. At birth, newborns can locate and track objects, and they can perceive a variety of forms, colors, sounds, tastes, and smells. As their brains and nervous systems continue to develop, their perceptual abilities will become even more refined. We saw in the previous section that a tremendous number of synapses form in the brain during the first 2 years of life and that experience and learning help shape the synapses into functional communication pathways. As their motor skills advance, toddlers and young children can explore the wider ranges of their environments, becoming exposed to a greater variety of stimuli. With rapidly developing nervous systems and enhanced perceptual capabilities, young children are ready to absorb information and learn amazing amounts about their world. In the next chapter we'll look at two prominent theories that describe how children conceptualize information, form logical thought processes, and learn to think about all of the wonders they encounter.

YOUR **PERSPECTIVE** NOTES

How do you think infants learn to match information across different sensory modalities? Is this ability available at birth? What real-life examples of intermodal perception have you observed in infants you have known?

LET'S REVIEW . . .

1. With the preferential-looking technique, when an infant spends more time looking at a checkerboard pattern than at a plain colored square, we can infer that:
   - a. the infant can see the difference between the checkerboard and the plain square.
   - b. the infant is probably color-blind.
   - c. the infant's visual acuity is very poor.
   - d. the infant has habituated to the checkerboard pattern.

2. Based on research described in this chapter, it seems that infants recognize the configuration of the human face:
   - a. by 3 months of age.
   - b. by 6 months of age.
   - c. by 1 year of age.
   - d. immediately after birth.

3. Which of the following is a correct conclusion regarding the auditory capabilities of infants?
   - a. The auditory system becomes functional by 2 weeks after birth.
   - b. Infants may be more sensitive than adults to higher frequencies of sound.
   - c. Infants can detect subtle differences in the intensity and frequency of a sound.
   - d. The ability to locate a sound increases from birth to 2 months of age.

4. Which of the following is an example of intermodal perception?
   - a. Infants prefer to look at faces over most any other stimulus.
   - b. Infants can perceive the depth on the visual cliff by 2 months of age.
   - c. Newborns can recognize the sound of a story that they heard while they were still in the womb.
   - d. Infants can match the sound of a happy voice with the film of a happy face.

5. **True or False:** Research using the visual cliff indicates that infants as young as 2 months of age can see the depth on the deep side and are intrigued by it, and that by 6 months infants are certainly afraid of the deep side.

6. **True or False:** Reactions to sweet, bitter, and sour flavors can be observed in newborns even before they receive their first feedings, so learning is evidently not required for these flavor perceptions.

Answers: 1. a, 2. d, 3. b, 4. d, 5. T, 6. T

166 | Chapter 4 *Physical Development: Body, Brain, and Perception*
www.ablongman.com/cook1e

thinking
BACK TO BEVERLY

L ike most expectant parents, Beverly is concerned about how to stimulate her baby's development. With all the excitement generated by popular press reports about research on brain development, parents are eager to learn how experience helps to shape the communication pathways in the brain. First, let's help Beverly sort the fact from myth. The popular press has reported that the first 3 years are the most critical for brain development, but this is only partly true. It is a fact that synapses are forming at a tremendous rate during the first 2 years after birth, but "wiring" isn't nearly complete by 3 years. Synaptic pruning shapes the brain's neural circuits. Synapses that are stimulated by experience are maintained, but unused circuits are pruned. From the age of 2 years to adolescence, more synapses are lost than gained, with as many as 100,000 synapses pruned per second! With experience-dependent development, new synapses are added to code new experiences, and this type of wiring continues throughout the lifetime. Beverly should understand that stimulation is important throughout childhood, not just during the first 3 years.

What about playing classical music during pregnancy? Prenatal stimulation may diminish programmed cell death to some extent, as more of the stimulated neurons may survive. Research shows that late-term fetuses are sensitive to noises from the environment, and DeCasper and Spence (1986) even demonstrated that newborns recognize sounds they heard in the womb. There is some slight evidence that classical music can stimulate spatial-reasoning and mathematics skills in preschool children and college students, but there is no evidence yet that this "Mozart effect" has the same impact on fetuses. At this point we can say only that it probably won't hurt. The same goes for "jazzercise" and other exercise for infants. For example, practicing reflexes speeds the emergence of motor skills only slightly, so such classes probably do more for the social interaction between parent and baby than for the motor skills themselves. The infant's nervous system and motor skills will develop well if the normal sources of stimulation are on hand: toys to manipulate, friendly voices and faces, hugs, things to climb on, and encouragement to explore a varied environment.

These are some of the concepts and research findings that you might share with Beverly. Studying the chapter more closely, you can find even more helpful information.

What are the main trends in physical growth during infancy and childhood, and what is the adolescent growth spurt?

At birth newborns average 7½ pounds in weight and 20 inches in length. Weight doubles by 5 months, and children reach half of their adult weight by 9 to 11 years. They reach half of their adult height by 2 years of age and continue to gain about 2 inches per year during childhood. The adolescent growth spurt is the increase in growth observed with the onset of puberty, peaking around the age of 12 for girls and 14 for boys. Between these spurts, girls are taller than boys, on average.

What are the main changes that occur with sexual maturation, and how does early versus late maturation affect adolescents?

With the onset of puberty, sex hormones (androgens and estrogens) initiate increased growth and sexual maturation. In boys, testosterone causes enlargement of the penis and testicles, appearance of pubic hair, deepened voice, first ejaculation, and growth of underarm and facial hair. In girls, estrogens cause breast development, growth of pubic and underarm hair, enlarged hips, and menarche. These changes typically begin earlier for girls than for boys. Early menarche in girls is associated with a more stocky and short build during later adolescence, less satisfaction with body image, lower self-esteem, a tendency to affiliate with older peers, increased delinquency and problems in school, and earlier dating behavior. Early maturation in boys may give them an advantage in sports and social situations but is also associated with increased delinquency.

What reflexes do infants have, and what is their significance?

Newborns show primitive reflexes (rooting, sucking, Moro, grasping, and Babinski) that normally disappear by 4 months of age. Rooting and sucking help newborns obtain nourishment, but the other primitive reflexes are probably remnants from our primate ancestors. Postural reflexes that help the baby maintain balance and head direction emerge by 2 to 4 months and disappear by 12 months. Locomotor reflexes (crawling, walking, swimming) emerge after birth and disappear by 4 months. These and other reflexes may provide exercise that helps form connections between the muscles and brain; these connections will later support voluntary movements. When reflexes do not appear or disappear according to the usual timetable, neurological problems may be present.

What are the main patterns in the development of voluntary movements? What factors influence progress through the motor milestones?

Motor development generally proceeds according to cephalocaudal (head-to-toe) and proximodistal (from-inside-to-outside) patterns. Infants hold their heads up before they can sit alone, and they sit before they walk. They coordinate large muscles in the arms before gaining dexterity in the hands and fingers. Neurological development and opportunities to exercise muscle both contribute. According to dynamic systems theory, motor skills emerge from complex interactions among neurological development, physical growth, learning, and motivation.

What are the main components of a nutritious diet? What are the main eating-related problems we see in childhood and adolescence?

Proteins, carbohydrates, fats, vitamins, and minerals are all important parts of a nutritious diet. Surveys indicate that up to 12 million Americans live in families that sometimes or often have no food to eat. A more frequent problem in this country, however, is obesity. As many as 15 percent of children and adolescents and 64 percent of adults are overweight. The percentage of overweight children tripled from the 1960s to 2000. Anorexia and bulimia are serious eating disorders and are most common among adolescent females.

What are the major patterns we see in the formation of the brain and nervous system?

Development begins with the neural tube, which later forms the brain and spinal cord. Neurons form and migrate to the top of the neural tube to form the cerebral cortex. By 20 weeks of gestation, the cortex has nearly all the neurons it will ever have, and many neurons will later be lost through programmed cell death. Synaptogenesis (formation of synapses between neurons) is rapid until 2 years of age, after which more synapses are lost than gained. Myelination of axons improves the neurons' capability to transmit information.

What are experience-expectant and experience-dependent development? How do "enriched" environments affect these two patterns of development?

In experience-expectant development the brain forms an overabundance of synapses, then prunes excess synapses through experience. This pattern helps form neural circuits that control behaviors that all members of the species "expect" to utilize, such as language function and hand–eye coordination. In experience-dependent development each member of the species grows individualized circuits to code or control more specific experiences, such as the English language and hitting a baseball. New synapses form with new learning and experience. Experiments show that enriched environments stimulate experience-expectant development in younger rats but experience-dependent development in adult rats.

What is meant by the term "neural plasticity"?

Plasticity is the tendency of the brain to remain somewhat flexible until synaptogenesis and pruning lock in most of the brain's circuits. If brain injury occurs at an early age, healthy areas can adjust and compensate for the loss in function of the damaged area. Plasticity decreases throughout childhood and into early adolescence.

How do researchers use the preferential-looking technique to test infant perception?

Researchers show infants two or more stimuli and record the amount of time the infants look at each one. When infants spend more time fixating on some stimuli more than others, we can infer that they can see the difference between the stimuli. Using this technique, Robert Fantz and other researchers have demonstrated that young infants prefer to look at moving stimuli, outer contours and edges, areas of high contrast, detailed or complex patterns, symmetrical patterns, curves, and human face patterns.

How do researchers use the habituation– dishabituation technique to test infant perception?

Researchers present infants with the same stimulus repeatedly until they habituate (show decreased response). When the experimenter then presents a new stimulus, dishabituation (renewed interest and response) indicates that the infant has processed the difference between the "old" and "new" stimuli. This technique is useful when there is no reason for infants to prefer one stimulus over another at the start of the testing procedure.

What do we know about visual acuity, color vision, and depth perception in infants?

Newborn acuity is somewhat limited, with estimates ranging from 20/150 to 20/600. Babies generally attain normal 20/20 vision by 6 months. It is not clear how well newborns are able to distinguish various colors. Evidence suggests that color vision is adultlike by 3 to 6 months. In the "visual cliff" experiment 2-month-olds can see the difference between the deep and solid sides, and babies avoid the deep side by the time they can crawl (around 6 months). By 3 to 4 months, infants use binocular disparity to judge depth. Even 1-month-olds show avoidance of approaching objects, indicating some sensitivity to depth and distance information.

What are the main conclusions about auditory capabilities of infants?

The auditory system is functional before birth, but compared to adults young infants still need sounds to be louder and they need changes in intensity and frequency to be greater in order to detect these changes. Infants may be more sensitive than adults to higher frequencies. Newborns prefer the voices of their own mothers, and they show ability to recognize sounds they heard while in the womb.

Can newborns differentiate major odors and flavors?

Yes. For example, they react positively to the aromas of bananas and butter, but they reject the odors of fish and rotten eggs. Newborns prefer sweeter solutions and reject sour or bitter flavors.

Can infants coordinate information across different sensory modalities?

Yes. Research on intermodal perception indicates that young infants can match what they see with what they hear or feel. One-month-olds look longer at the shape of pacifiers they previously held in their mouths, and older infants can match the sounds of moving objects with films of those objects. At 4 months infants can match the age of the voice they hear with the age of a person on videotape, and at 5 months they can match emotional expressions from voice to face.

KEY TERMS

adolescent growth spurt (132)

androgens (132)

anorexia nervosa (143)

bulimia nervosa (143)

child-directed speech (162)

dishabituation (159)

estrogens (132)

experience-dependent development (150)

experience-expectant development (150)

glial cells (149)

habituation (159)

habituation–dishabituation technique (159)

intermodal perception (164)

locomotor reflexes (135)

malnutrition (141)

menarche (133)

myelination (149)

neurons (147)

plasticity (152)

postural reflexes (135)

preferential-looking technique (156)

primitive reflexes (135)

programmed cell death (149)

reflexes (134)

synaptic pruning (149)

synaptogenesis (149)

visual acuity (160)

Chapter 5

Cognitive Development

Piagetian and Sociocultural Views

CHAPTER PREVIEW

A PERSPECTIVE TO think ABOUT

"Maria wants to pick the best school for her sons, so she plans to observe and interview teachers."

Maria is the mother of two boys, ages 4½ and 12, and she and her children recently moved into a new community. The new community has a school-choice program that allows families to place their children in any school in the district. Maria wants to pick the best school for her sons, so she plans to observe and interview teachers and school officials at several schools. She's heard a lot about the importance of starting children in school early, but her younger son will have just turned 5 when the school year begins. Maria is concerned that he may not really be ready for formal schooling. What should Maria look for when visiting schools and teachers? What kinds of classroom activities and teaching methods would best foster both of her sons' cognitive development? How can she decide whether her younger son is ready for kindergarten?

After studying this chapter, you should be able to identify several important factors that Maria should look for. You will know the kinds of educational philosophy and practices that can support and stimulate the cognitive growth of Maria's children. As you work through this chapter, create a list of at least 12 concepts that might relate to Maria's situation. Explain how Maria could use each concept to identify the best educational environment for her sons.

As you read this chapter, look for the questions that ask you to think about what you're learning from Maria's perspective.

The situation Maria faces is not uncommon. All of us who work with children need to understand cognitive development so that we can be good advocates for children, recognize their strengths and limitations, and provide stimulating academic and intellectual environments. As you learned in Chapter 4, children experience tremendous physical changes from birth through adolescence. Less visible but just as important are the enormous changes in children's thinking during these years. The vast differences between younger and older children's thinking are evident in every aspect of their lives, from the kinds of questions children ask to the kinds of explanations they can understand or offer—and even in the kinds of events and information they will pay attention to. These changes in thinking, in which children's thought gradually becomes more organized and complex, are called *cognitive development*.

In this chapter we explore two of the most influential theories of cognitive development: the stage theory of Jean Piaget, and the sociocultural theory of Lev Vygotsky. Recently, researchers asked 1,500 child development experts to name the "most revolutionary" work published in the last half century (Dixon, 2002). According to the experts, Jean Piaget's 1952 book *The Origins of Intelligence in Children* remained the most revolutionary and influential work published since 1950! The second most important work was Lev Vygotsky's *Mind in Society: The Development of Higher Psychological Processes* (1978). This chapter highlights the central themes of both of these important works as well as newer sociocultural views. As you read, you will see that these theories have had a tremendous impact on how we think about the development of cognition in children.

Piaget's Constructivist View of Cognitive Development

The most influential theorist in the study of cognitive development was Jean Piaget, who was born in 1896 and died in 1980. His prolific career in psychology spanned an astonishing 7 decades. One anonymous writer surmised that

> assessing the impact of Piaget on developmental psychology is like assessing the impact of Shakespeare on English literature or Aristotle on philosophy—impossible. The impact is too monumental to embrace and at the same time too omnipresent to detect. (cited in Beilin, 1994)

As you study this section, ask yourself these questions:

- What influence did Piaget's background in biology have on his theory? What are some specific examples of this biological influence?
- What is constructivism, and why is Piaget considered a constructivist?
- According to Piaget, what processes guide children's interaction with the environment? How do they affect cognitive development?

Piaget as a Child Prodigy

Jean Piaget was no ordinary child. From a very early age, he showed tremendous intellectual talent. Born in Neuchâtel, Switzerland, a small university town, Piaget showed an early interest in nature, particularly in observing wildlife in its natural setting. His observations led to the first of his many scientific publications. He was only 10 years old when he published his first article, a one-page report on an albino sparrow he observed in a park. At the Museum of Natural History in Neuchâtel, Piaget began working with a zoologist who specialized in mollusks (clams, oysters, snails, etc.). Piaget "catalogued and studied adaptation" (Bringuier, 1980, p. 8), detailing how mollusks' shells changed in relation to the movement of the water in which they lived. As you will see, the idea of adaptation came to play a central role in Piaget's later theory of cognitive development. From age 15 to age 18, Piaget published a series of articles on the mollusk research. His work was so noteworthy that a natural history museum in Geneva offered him a position as curator of their mollusk collection. Fortunately for psychology, he had to decline—he hadn't graduated from high school yet!

After earning a Ph.D. degree at 21, Piaget became interested in psychology. He worked for a time at a psychiatric clinic in Zurich, where he learned about Freudian psychoanalysis and how to conduct a clinical interview. Later he moved to Paris to work with Theophile Simon in the Binet Laboratory. Theophile Simon and Alfred Binet were known for their work on intelligence testing, and Piaget's job in the laboratory was to help develop a standardized French version of some reasoning tasks. Piaget later wrote that

Jean Piaget was a pioneer in child development research. His theory revolutionized how we view children's thinking.

> Simon wasn't living in Paris and couldn't oversee what I did—luckily! . . . Simon wanted me to standardize in French the tests that had been devised in English. . . . I became interested immediately in the way the child reasoned and the difficulties he encountered, the mistakes he made, his reasons for making them, and the methods he came up with in order to get to the right answers. From the outset, I did what I've been doing ever since: I made qualitative analyses instead of preparing statistics about right and wrong answers. (cited in Bringuier, 1980, p. 9)

The years in the Binet Laboratory were important in several ways for Piaget and the development of his theory and methods. First, he realized that children were *active* in their thinking, not passive. He found that even very young children made admirable attempts to understand and answer questions, although their reasoning was far from what an adult would see as logical. Drawing on his biological background, he interpreted these attempts as children's efforts to cognitively adapt to the situations they were in, to understand and succeed in their situations. Second, Piaget began to see that children's thinking showed a striking *regularity and consistency,* even though it was often incorrect. Piaget noticed that children of the same age tended to give the same wrong answers, whereas children of a different age tended to give different wrong answers. There seemed to be age-related patterns in the children's thinking. These may not seem to be groundbreaking insights today—but at that time most experts believed that children were passive recipients of information (simply memorizing information without interpreting or modifying it) and did not have coherent or regular ways of thinking. Piaget challenged these well-established views. Finally, Piaget realized that a *clinical method,* in which children are asked to explain the reasons for their answers rather than simply to give an answer, could be an invaluable tool in his efforts to understand children's thinking.

Constructivism and Interaction with the Environment

Piaget combined his background in biology with his interest in understanding how logic and knowledge develop and spent the rest of his career observing children and articulating his theory of cognitive development. He applied several concepts from biology and used them to explain how knowledge develops.

Piaget's theory is often described as a **constructivist view.** According to *constructivists,* people interpret their environments and experiences in light of the knowledge and experiences they already have. People do not simply take in an external reality and develop an unchanged, exact mental copy of objects or events. Instead, they build (or "construct") their own individual understandings and knowledge. For Piaget, the essential building block for cognition is the *scheme.* A **scheme** is an organized pattern of action or thought. It is a broad concept and can refer to organized patterns of physical action (such as an infant reaching to grasp an object), or mental action (such as a high school student thinking about how to solve an algebra problem).

As children interact with the environment, individual schemes become modified, combined, and reorganized to form more complex cognitive structures. As children mature, these structures allow more complex and sophisticated ways of thinking. These, in turn, allow children to interact in qualitatively different ways with their environment. For example, a little girl develops a scheme for noticing similarities between objects (we'll call this a "compare" scheme) and a separate one for noticing differences (a "contrast" scheme). Gradually, she coordinates and combines the two into a single cognitive structure that allows her to compare and contrast objects at the same time. When she encounters a new object, she uses this coordinated cognitive structure to develop a fuller understanding of the object. The first time she encounters an avocado, for example, she can compare and contrast it to other foods. This process will help her determine what kind of food it is and will increase her understanding of the overall category (similar in size to an orange, similar in color to a lime, different in texture from an apple). Cognitive structures not only organize existing knowledge but also serve as filters for all new experiences. That is, we interpret new experiences in light of our already existing cognitive structures. Because no two people ever have exactly the same experiences, no two cognitive structures ever are exactly the same, and no two people ever interpret events in exactly the same way. The way you interpret and understand the information you're learning about Piaget is different (at least slightly) from the way your classmates understand it, because each of you filters and interprets the information through a different cognitive structure.

Piaget believed that extensive interaction with the environment is absolutely essential for each person's cognitive development. Though Piaget acknowledged that biological maturation sets the general limits within which cognitive development occurs, he placed much more emphasis on the role of the environment. Children who have severely limited interactions with their environments simply will not have the opportunities to develop and reorganize their cognitive structures so as to achieve mature ways of thinking. The way

constructivist view

The view that people construct their own knowledge and understanding of the world by using what they already know and understand to interpret new experiences.

scheme

An organized pattern of physical or mental action.

How is this child constructing her own understanding of science concepts?

we interact with the environment is not random, however. Three common processes guide our interactions: *organization, adaptation,* and *reflective abstraction.* If you have studied biology, you will recognize the influence of Piaget's biology background in the first two of these processes. Both concepts originate in the physical sciences, and Piaget used them in his theory of psychological development.

Organization is the tendency of all species to form increasingly coherent and integrated entities. For example, consider the human body. Cells themselves are organized systems of subcellular material. And cells organize into tissues, tissues into organs, organs into organ systems, and organ systems into the body. Piaget believed that the tendency to organize also occurs on the psychological level—that people try to organize their knowledge into coherent systems. In fact, Piaget believed that the tendency to organize is so basic that people cannot keep from trying to organize their knowledge. This explains why you may find yourself thinking about something that didn't make sense to you when you encountered it, even when you don't intend or want to spend time thinking about it! The advantage of this organizational tendency is that it gives us a way to understand and interpret events and objects we encounter; in short, it helps us function more successfully in our psychological environments. The disadvantage is, of course, that the particular way we may organize our knowledge may be completely wrong. If enough mistakes and misinterpretations occur, however, we may reexamine our cognitive organization and perhaps make adjustments. Piaget called this later process adaptation.

In biology the term **adaptation** refers to every species' tendency to make modifications in order to survive and succeed in the environment. (Remember how the mollusks' shells adapted to the water currents?) Applied to cognitive development, *adaptation* means changing one's cognitive structure or one's environment (or both to some degree) in order to better understand the environment. Figure 5.1 diagrams the steps involved in adaptation: A child moves from assimilation through cognitive disequilibrium, accommodation, and cognitive equilibrium, then back to a new assimilation.

Let's explore this process using the example of Lily, a 2-year-old who is learning to name animals, shown in Figure 5.1. Lily has a dog at home, and according to her "doggie scheme," "doggies" are animals that have four feet and fur and that bark and fetch balls. One day, riding in the car with her mother, Lily points to a field with several cows and exclaims, "Look, Mommy, doggies!" She is excited to see so many "doggies," especially ones so large! We can see that Lily is trying to understand these new animals by thinking about them as something she already understands: "doggies." This is an example of **assimilation,** the process of bringing new objects or information into a scheme that already exists.

Thinking of these new animals as "doggies," Lily fully expects that they will also bark and fetch balls. Such misunderstandings are common when we try to force new objects into ill-fitting schemes. Her mother, however, comments, "No, those are cows. They are bigger than dogs. And see the udders underneath? Cows give us milk." These comments place Lily into cognitive disequilibrium—she is confused. Lily realizes that she has never seen udders under dogs and also has never seen dogs that large. To resolve her cognitive conflict, Lily adjusts her understanding of animals. She adds new information about dogs (they are smaller and don't give us milk), and she learns a new animal (cows are like dogs but larger, and they give milk). These adjustments are examples of **accommodation,** the process of modifying old schemes, or creating new ones, to fit better with assimilated information. Now Lily can properly identify dogs and cows, and her new success in naming the animals moves her into cognitive equilibrium. Lily remains in cognitive equilibrium until she visits the zoo and encounters a new animal: an elephant. How will she assimilate this animal?

Piaget, then, claimed that we try to understand new experiences by assimilating them into the schemes or cognitive structures that we already have. If the assimilation does not

YOUR

PERSPECTIVE

NOTES

Can you think of a time when you found yourself wondering about an event, a fact, or a concept that you didn't quite understand, even though you didn't intend to think about it? As you continued to think about it, did it finally "fall into place" as you were able to integrate it into your cognitive structures?

YOUR

PERSPECTIVE

NOTES

Think back over your day so far. Can you identify an example of assimilation in your daily activities? Can you think of an example of accommodation?

organization

The tendency to form increasingly coherent and integrated structures.

adaptation

In cognitive development, the process of changing a cognitive structure or the environment (or both) in order to understand the environment.

assimilation

The process of bringing new objects or information into a scheme that already exists.

accommodation

The process of modifying old schemes or creating new ones to better fit assimilated information.

FIGURE 5.1 Adaptation and Equilibration

In the cycle of adaptation and equilibration, a new experience is first assimilated into an existing scheme. If it doesn't fit properly, cognitive disequilibrium results. Accommodating (adjusting) the scheme brings the child to cognitive equilibrium, until a new assimilation challenges the scheme again.

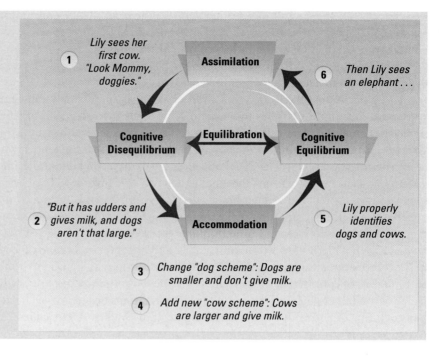

1. Lily sees her first cow. "Look Mommy, doggies."
2. "But it has udders and gives milk, and dogs aren't that large."
3. Change "dog scheme": Dogs are smaller and don't give milk.
4. Add new "cow scheme": Cows are larger and give milk.
5. Lily properly identifies dogs and cows.
6. Then Lily sees an elephant . . .

Assimilation — *Cognitive Equilibrium* — *Accommodation* — *Cognitive Disequilibrium* — *Equilibration*

work completely, there is an imbalance between the new experience and the old scheme. Piaget described this imbalance as a state of *cognitive disequilibrium*. To resolve the disequilibrium, we accommodate, or adjust, our schemes to provide a better fit for the new experience. If we are successful, we achieve *cognitive equilibrium*. **Equilibration** therefore is the dynamic process of moving between states of cognitive disequilibrium and equilibrium as we assimilate new experiences and accommodate schemes.

Because of the process of organization, we are never satisfied with equilibrium. We stretch and extend our cognitive structures by assimilating new and challenging information. According to Piaget, the tendency to seek equilibrium is always present—we are constantly seeking to understand—but equilibration is a dynamic process and is never fully achieved. In other words, although we certainly have periods when we understand and deal effectively with the environment, we never attain perfect, complete, and permanent understanding of everything. Piaget believed that "the normal state of mind is one of disequilibrium—or rather a state of 'moving equilibrium' " (Beilin, 1994, p. 263). There are always new things to learn!

A final process that guides our thinking is reflective abstraction. In **reflective abstraction** we notice something in the environment (e.g., some specific property of an object or action), then reflect on it (Ginsburg & Opper, 1988; Piaget, 1971). That is, we try to relate it to our current cognitive structures. As a result of reflection, we modify our current cognitive structures. For example, a boy playing on the beach may notice that the number of rocks he has is the same regardless of whether he arranges them in a line or a circle or piles them on top of one another. Reflective abstraction in this case involves the child's *noticing* that he has the same number of rocks, then *thinking about the implication* of this fact—that number is not affected by how they are arranged. According to Piaget, we must engage in reflective abstraction in order to learn from our interactions with the environment. The process enables us to isolate and think about specific properties, compare and contrast them, and think about how we understand them. In this way reflective abstraction *leads to* the accommodation of cognitive structures. A child can notice something in the environment, but if he does not think about its meaning or its relation to what he already knows, no cognitive reorganization

YOUR PERSPECTIVE NOTES

Engage in some reflective abstraction. What do you *notice* about Piaget's background in biology, and what do you *think about* how this background relates to his theory of cognitive development?

equilibration

The dynamic process of moving between states of cognitive disequilibrium and equilibrium.

reflective abstraction

The process of noticing and thinking about the implications of information and experiences.

will occur. In our earlier example, Lily would not have accommodated her understanding of "doggies" if she had not (1) *noticed* that the cows were much larger than dogs (and had udders), and (2) reflected or *thought about* what this meant.

The processes of organization, adaptation, and reflective abstraction play important roles in children's development. First, children are naturally curious. They are constantly probing and exploring their environments, looking for ways to challenge their existing schemes, and reflecting on whether the things they encounter make sense to them. But without opportunities for exploration and stimulating experiences, there would be nothing new to assimilate. Second, cognitive disequilibrium is a precursor to learning. When children are confused and perplexed, they are ready to make adjustments—they are ready to make accommodations in their schemes. Although it may be tempting to think of confusion as a sign of failure or as something to avoid, in Piaget's system it is a necessary step toward success. Finally, the concept of constructivism is embedded in the cycle. Faced with disequilibrium, children will accommodate their own schemes, engage in reflective abstraction, and improve and reorganize their cognitive structures. In short, children do not passively absorb structures from the adults and other people around them. They actively create their own accommodations and so construct their own understandings.

thinking OF MARIA

◄ What kinds of teaching practices could Maria look for that would help her find a teacher who uses Piaget's concepts of constructivism, adaptation, organization, and reflective abstraction?

LET'S REVIEW . . .

1. Adaptation is an important concept in Piaget's theory of cognitive development, and this concept can be traced back to Piaget's early work in:

   a. psychology.   b. biology.   c. philosophy.   d. physics.

2. In Piaget's theory, an organized pattern of action or thought is called a(n):

   a. scheme.   b. adaptation.   c. assimilation.   d. organization.

3. Two-year-old David points to a pickup truck and says, "Look, Mommy, a red car!" Calling the truck a car is an example of what Piaget would call:

   a. equilibration.   b. accommodation.   c. abstraction.   d. assimilation.

4. When you consider Piaget's cycle of adaptation, what condition comes immediately before accommodation?

   a. assimilation   b. cognitive equilibrium   c. cognitive disequilibrium   d. organization

5. **True or False:** Piaget is referred to as a "constructivist" because he believed that children learn primarily by copying the cognitive structures that have been constructed by the adults and other more mature people around them.

6. **True or False:** In Piaget's theory, cognitive equilibrium is achieved when children accommodate their schemes so they provide a better fit with new experiences.

Answers: 1. b, 2. a, 3. d, 4. c, 5. F, 6. T

Piaget's Stages of Cognitive Development

We have seen that children adapt individual schemes (like "doggie" and "cow") through equilibration. We might refer to this type of equilibration as *microequilibration*—the equilibration of individual schemes. Piaget also described a process that we might call *macroequilibration,* or the equilibration of larger and more comprehensive cognitive structures. Remember that in biology cells organize into tissues, and tissues form the body. When enough individual cells change or adapt to their environment, the effects can be seen in the tissues and in the body as

TABLE 5.1 Piaget's Four Stages of Cognitive Development

COGNITIVE STAGE	LIMITATIONS	ACHIEVEMENTS
Sensorimotor Thought: Birth to 2 years	• No representational thought; infants cannot form internal symbols early in this stage. • Object permanence is lacking early in this stage.	• Representational, symbolic thought gradually emerges as the stage progresses. • Object permanence develops as the stage progresses.
Preoperational Thought: 2 to 7 years	• Intuitive logic leads to egocentrism, animism, artificialism, and an inability to use more objective forms of logic. • Schemes are not reversible, not operational. • Children fail conservation tasks because of centration, focus on static endpoints, and lack of reversibility.	• Flourishing mental representations and symbols are seen in language, art, and play.
Concrete Operational Thought: 7 to 12 years	• Logic is limited to concrete, tangible materials and experiences.	• Logical thought is more objective, allows skills like class inclusion and transitivity. • Schemes can be reversible, operational. • Children pass conservation problems due to decentration, focus on dynamic transformations, reversibility.
Formal Operational Thought: 12 years and up	• Adolescent egocentrism is seen in the imaginary audience and personal fable.	• Hypothetico-deductive reasoning emerges. • Abstract thought emerges.

a whole. In cognitive development, as individual schemes adapt, larger cognitive structures emerge and change. The microequilibrations eventually lead to macroequilibrations. When these larger structures are modified and reorganized, new and more powerful ways of thinking become possible. According to Piaget, children grow through four *stages* of cognitive development. Each stage involves certain skills and limitations, as summarized in Table 5.1.

As you study this section, ask yourself these questions:

• What are the main limitations in cognitive processing at each of the stages?

• What new cognitive structures, forms of logical thought, or other cognitive advances emerge during each stage?

• What is the practical usefulness of understanding Piaget's stages of cognitive development?

Stage 1: Sensorimotor Thought (Birth to 2 Years)

According to Piaget, infants can engage only in **sensorimotor thought.** That is, they know the world only in terms of their own sensory input (what they can see, smell, taste, touch, and hear) and their physical or motor actions on it (e.g., sucking, reaching, and grasping). They do not have internal mental representations of the objects and events that exist outside their own body. For example, consider what happens when you give 3-month-old Latoya a plastic rattle. Latoya grasps the rattle tightly in her hand, shakes it back and forth, and rubs it against her cheek. Then Latoya brings the rattle to her mouth to explore it in detail by sucking and biting on it. Finally, she flings the rattle to the floor and stares brightly back at you. Now, what does Latoya "know" about the rattle?

According to Piaget, Latoya doesn't know anything about the rattle unless she is having direct sensory or motor contact with it. At the time that she is grasping and shaking the rattle, she knows how it feels in her hand and how it moves and sounds when she shakes it. She can

sensorimotor thought

Thought that is based only on sensory input and physical (motor) actions.

Cognitive Development: Piagetian and Sociocultural Views

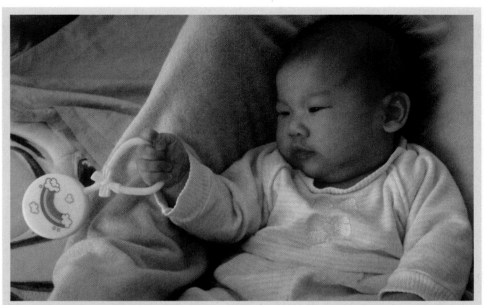

What does this infant understand about her rattle? If she drops the rattle out of sight, will she know that it still exists?

feel its smooth surface against her cheek. She knows more about the detailed bumps, curves, and textures when she has it in her mouth. After she flings it to the floor, however, she has no way of maintaining an internalized representation of the rattle. She therefore cannot "think" about the rattle, and she doesn't know or remember anything about it.

Most adults take mental representation for granted. When we study an object, we form a mental code or image that represents what we know, and we can access this image later when the object is no longer physically available. We are capable of **symbolic (representational) thought**—the ability to form symbols in our mind that represent (or stand for) objects or events in the world. Piaget claimed that young infants cannot form symbols and are therefore stuck in the here-and-now world of their immediate sensory and motor actions. Piaget believed that representational thought gradually emerges as babies develop the ability to form mental symbols. This represents an important achievement, because the emergence of representational thought frees children from the here and now. With representational thought, children can think about past events and anticipate future interactions. Mental representation also allows children to communicate with others using language. By definition, language of any type requires that arbitrary symbols (words) represent actual things. Without mental representation, it is impossible to learn words and understand what they stand for.

Piaget proposed six substages of sensorimotor thought that describe how representational thought emerges during infancy. These substages are summarized in Table 5.2. If you look carefully across the substages, you will notice a general trend in babies' thinking. Infants begin in the early stages as simply *reflexive*—that is, reacting to environmental stimuli via inborn reflexes. They have no voluntary control over objects or events in their environment but can only react to whatever takes place. Gradually, however, infants begin to take more control. These first attempts occur because infants accidentally notice the effects of certain random actions. They begin trying to understand events by using *trial and error*, taking actions and simply observing what happens, then slightly modifying the actions, observing, and so on. Initially these trial-and-error interactions are observations of effects with no anticipation of what the outcomes might be. Eventually, however, babies show evidence of *intentionality.*

symbolic (representational) thought

The ability to form symbols (mental representations) that stand for objects or events in the world.

TABLE 5.2 Piaget's Six Substages of Sensorimotor Thought

SENSORIMOTOR SUBSTAGE	AGE	CHARACTERISTIC	EXAMPLES
1. Basic Reflexes	Birth to 1 month	The first schemes are inborn reflexes.	Rooting, sucking, grasping reflexes.
2. Primary Circular Reactions	1 to 4 months	Infants discover actions involving their own bodies by accident, then learn by trial and error to repeat them until they become habits (schemes).	At first thumb comes to mouth by accident. Through trial and error infants learn to reproduce the event until a thumb-sucking scheme becomes established.
3. Secondary Circular Reactions	4 to 10 months	Infants discover actions involving objects in the environment by accident, then learn by trial and error to repeat them until they become habits (schemes).	Holding a rattle, an infant may accidentally shake the rattle and enjoy the noise. Through trial and error the infant learns to reproduce the event until a shaking scheme becomes established.
4. Coordination of Secondary Schemes	10 to 12 months	Infants intentionally put two schemes together to solve a problem or reach a goal. Intentionality is a new feature—these new behaviors are no longer discovered by accident.	An infant sees a toy behind a box, pushes the box aside, then reaches for the toy. The infant intentionally combined pushing and reaching schemes to reach the goal (the toy).
5. Tertiary Circular Reactions	12 to 18 months	Babies are curious about objects in the world and explore them in a trial-and-error fashion, trying to produce novel reactions.	A baby drops a ball from shoulder height and watches what happens. The baby then explores the "dropping scheme" by dropping the ball from hip height, then from head height, then from knee height, observing each new result.
6. Transition to Symbolic Thought	18 to 24 months	Toddlers begin to form symbolic representations of events, showing the beginnings of mental thought. Representations still tend to be physical (rather than purely mental), as when toddlers use their own body movements to represent movements of objects in the world.	A 1½-year-old girl would like to open the lid of a box, and to think about this she opens and closes her hand repeatedly. Rather than work directly on the box, she first uses her hand motion as a way to "think" about how to open it. She is thinking about the box using a symbolic representation (her hand).

That is, they begin to take actions that they expect to have specific outcomes. Intentionality represents an effort to exert control over the environment because it involves taking actions that are *intended* to produce specific results.

■ **Evidence of Representational Thought.** How do we know when an infant has achieved representational thought? One line of evidence, as we've seen, is the use of language, starting at about one year—because in order to use language, the child must have mental representations to attach labels to. Another line of evidence can be seen in babies' grasp of the concept Piaget called *object permanence*. Piaget made the provocative claim that young infants do not understand **object permanence**—the fact that objects, events, or even people continue to exist when they are not in the infant's direct line of sensory or motor action. Recall Latoya and her rattle. Once Latoya flung the rattle to the floor, Piaget would say that she had no way to think or know about the rattle. Because she couldn't form a mental representation of it, she couldn't consider its continued existence. She couldn't want it or wonder about it. For Latoya, "out of sight" was literally "out of mind."

Piaget traced understanding of object permanence through the substages of sensorimotor thought, from nonexistence at birth to its full achievement at about age 2 (Ginsburg & Opper, 1988; Piaget, 1952a, 1954). In the earliest substages, infants simply do not look for an object once it is out of their immediate experience. They make no attempt to get the object

object permanence

The fact that objects, events, and people continue to exist even when they are out of a child's direct line of sensory input or motor action.

This infant is looking under the blanket for a hidden toy. What does this search behavior tell us about the mental representations formed by infants?

back, though they may continue looking at the place where they last saw the object. Later, they may actively try to retrieve an object, but only if part of it is still visible (e.g., reaching for a toy that is partially hidden under a blanket). By about 1 year, babies will attempt to retrieve an object that is completely hidden. Interestingly, however, if babies watch the object being hidden in one location, then watch as a researcher moves the object to a different location (this is called a visible displacement problem), they will look in the first location rather than the second even though they witnessed the whole sequence. By about 18 months, babies are able to solve these visible displacement problems, but they still cannot find the object when the displacements are invisible. That is, if they watch as the object is hidden in one location, but when the researcher secretly moves the object to a different location, babies look only in the first spot. They don't check other possible places nearby. Finally, by 2 years of age, the child is able to solve invisible displacement problems. Piaget described this ability as evidence of full mental representation.

In summary, there are two major developmental trends as an infant moves through the sensorimotor stage. First, the infant progresses from interacting reflexively with the environment, through a trial-and-error phase, to deliberate and intentional actions on the environment. Second, the child develops the ability to mentally represent objects, events, and concepts. Infants' early thought processes involve reflexes and immediate sensations and motor actions, but toddlers leave the sensorimotor stage with the ability to internalize their thought processes into a purely "mental" form. Internal and intentional thought provides the building blocks for the next stage of cognitive development.

Stage 2: Preoperational Thought (2 to 7 Years)

Piaget's second stage, **preoperational thought,** features the flourishing use of mental representations and the beginnings of logic (intuitive thought). Although logic is emerging, it is based only on personal experience (Piaget called it intuitive). Also, as you will see shortly, children still do not recognize that some logical processes can be reversed.

preoperational thought

Thought characterized by the use of mental representations (symbols) and intuitive thought.

■ **Flourishing Mental Representations.** During the preoperational stage children will practice, and even playfully exaggerate, their new symbolic or mental representation abilities. Let's look at the symbols they use in language, artwork, and play.

Symbols in Language. Talk to a child who is just turning 2, and the conversation will be pretty simple and limited to objects and events currently present. Talk to a 4-year-old, however, and you'll find yourself engaged in a real conversation! As we discuss in Chapter 8, there is an explosive increase in children's vocabulary and grammar (rules for putting words together) after the age of about 18 months. At 18 months, the average vocabulary is about 22 words. By 2 years children use more than 250 words on average, and by 5 years their vocabulary is more than 2,000 words (Anglin, 1993). What makes this rapid escalation of linguistic skill possible? According to Piaget, language development is based on children's mental representational ability—their ability to let a symbol (e.g., a word) stand for an object in the environment. This ability gives children a way to communicate about the objects in the environment, even when the objects are not actually present. Children's use of symbols also allows their thought to become faster and more efficient, because it no longer depends on the actual physical manipulation of objects in the environment. If a child is upset, for example, the child can name the problem, thereby increasing the likelihood that a parent or caregiver can help. The process of construction is also evident in language, as children actively filter what they hear and create their own inventive versions of words and phrases. A young child may call a blanket a "winkie," describe a person with short hair as having "little hair," or say that a criminal is "under arrested."

The ability to form mental representations allows these children to use fantasy and symbolism in their play. Using mental symbols, children can escape the reality of the here and now and pretend to be superheroes on exciting adventures in far-off places.

Symbols in Artwork. Preoperational children's increasing ability to use mental representation is also seen clearly in the artwork they produce. When one of our daughters was 3 years old, she drew a heavy black horizontal line above a bright red horizontal line. "Look, Mom, I made a picture of you!" she said. "See, there's your head, and your hair on top, and that's your favorite red shirt!" What parents have not admired evidence of mental representation in their own child?

To produce such artwork, the child must have mental representations—not only of the mother's face and hair, for example, but also of her favorite red shirt. Though the initial scribbles of 3-year-olds may not resemble any real object to an adult, they are evidence that the child has developed mental representation. In Figure 5.2 are drawings made by children of various ages; you can easily trace the development of more accurate and more complex mental representations.

Symbols in Play. Watch children engaged in play, and you will soon see clear evidence of symbol use. In *symbolic play* children use one object to stand for another, such as when they pretend that a blanket is a magic carpet or a banana is a telephone. Children of 18 months seldom show such symbolic play; for example, they'll pretend to talk on a telephone only when they have in hand a quite realistic-looking toy telephone. By the age of 2, children will use objects far less similar to the real item (such as using a banana for a tele-

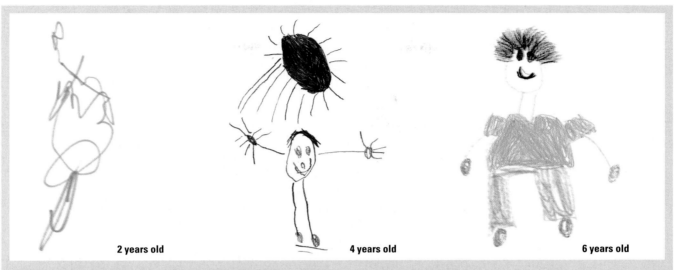

| 2 years old | 4 years old | 6 years old |

FIGURE 5.2 **Artwork Showing the Development of Mental Representation**
The 2-year-old's drawing of a person is just a scribble. At age 4 the child draws the person as a happy head with arms and legs. By age 6, the body is represented more fully, including the neck and torso. What do these drawings tell us about the developing mental representation of what a person is?

phone). Finally, by 5 years children are capable of using practically anything as a pretend "telephone." Their ability to mentally represent objects has progressed to the point that the symbol no longer has to bear any resemblance to the real thing (Corrigan, 1987; O'Reilly, 1995).

Preoperational children also use symbols in *fantasy play,* in which they pretend to be something they are not (like a tiger or a superhero) or to engage in activities that are impossible (like having their teddy bear read them a story). And in *make-believe play* children use toys as props to carry out some procedure, such as using a kitchen set and dishes to pretend to cook dinner, or using a doll to pretend to feed and rock a baby. All these kinds of play require that the child be able to allow one thing to represent another. For Piaget, these types of play indicate children's degree of mental representation. It also allows them to practice and become more skillful in mental representation. We have a lot more to say about the development of play in Chapter 11.

■ **Emergence of Intuitive Thought: "It *Seems* That. . . ."** Another important development during the preoperational stage is the emergence of **intuitive thought,** or reasoning based on personal experience rather than on any formal logical system. Children reason according to what things "seem like," according to their personal experience with the objects and events involved. For example, on the way to preschool one foggy morning, our son, who was about 3½ years old, said, "Better turn your lights on—it's really *froggy* out." When asked what he meant, he explained that he had noticed a lot of this cloudy stuff in the air whenever we drove by ponds. "I know that frogs live in water, so when all the frogs breathe out, they make the air froggy." An admirable attempt, to be sure, but our son's intuitive explanation would not pass the objective tests of true logic. Evidence of intuitive thought can be seen in several characteristics of thinking that are common during the preoperational period, including egocentrism, animism, and artificialism.

Piaget used the term *egocentrism* to refer to the young child's inability to take another person's perspective. To young children it does seem that they are the center of the universe, and it seems that everyone must think about things just the way they do. Preoperational children are not able to understand that other people's perspectives might be different from

thinking
OF MARIA

◀ For Maria's 4½-year-old son, how would language, art, and play activities be important in his cognitive development? Would art and play be important in his preschool and kindergarten classrooms?

intuitive thought
Thought and logic that is based on the child's personal experience rather than on a formal system of rules.

FIGURE 5.3 The Three-Mountains Task

What would the doll see? Can children describe the perspective that would be seen from a different location?

Source: H. Bee & D. Boyd. (2002). *Lifespan development,* 3rd ed., p. 158. Published by Allyn and Bacon, Boston, MA. Copyright © 2004 by Pearson Education. Reprinted by permission of the publisher.

their own. The classic demonstration of egocentrism is the three-mountain task. As pictured in Figure 5.3, experimenters show children a model of three mountains that have landmarks placed among them. A child sits at one location in relation to the mountains, and a doll sits at another location. The experimenter then asks the child to describe what the doll would see from its location. Preschool children typically describe the scene as they view it from their own location. Further, when given photographs depicting the views from each location around the table, children select the photos showing the view from their own locations, not the doll's (Piaget & Inhelder, 1948/1956). In other words, children select views based on their own personal and intuitive experience with the scene. They don't yet take into account the logical necessity that someone viewing the scene from a different place will have a different perspective.

Animism—the idea that inanimate objects have conscious life and feelings—is typical of the preoperational stage (Piaget, 1929, 1930, 1951). For example, children may say that the sun is shining brightly because it is happy, or they may put their pencil down because "it is tired." *Artificialism* is the notion that natural events or objects (e.g., the sun, moon, hurricanes, droughts) are under the control of people or of superhuman agents. A child might say that the sun went down because someone switched it off, or that the moon isn't shining because someone blew it out. As children's cognitive structures encounter more and more instances in which animism and artificialism do not satisfactorily explain events, they begin to move away from these modes of intuitive thought and gradually move toward explanations based on physical facts and on a more objective logic.

YOUR PERSPECTIVE
~~PERSPECTIVE~~

NOTES

Identify examples of egocentrism, animism, or artificialism from your own past, or from your experiences with children you know. What prompted your/their thinking to change?

■ **Conservation Problems.** The most famous examples of preoperational thought come from children's answers to Piaget's *conservation problems.* Piaget used the term **conservation** to refer to the concept that certain basic properties of an object (e.g., volume, mass, and weight) remain the same even if its physical appearance changes (Ginsburg & Opper, 1988; Piaget, 1952b, 1969, 1970; Piaget & Inhelder, 1974). For example, look at the liquid conservation problem shown in Figure 5.4. An experimenter fills two identical beakers with liquid to the same level, as shown on the left. The experimenter asks the child, "Do these two have the same amount of liquid, or does one have more?" The child says that they have the same amount. Then, with the child watching, the experimenter pours the contents of one beaker into a taller and skinnier beaker. When asked if the two beakers "have the same amount, or does one have more?" younger children typically claim that the taller beaker has more liquid than the shorter beaker. When asked why, they usually point to the height of the liquid surface: "See, this one is taller, so it has more." Children using preoperational thought don't seem to understand that the volume of liquid is conserved (remains the same) even though the shape of the container changes. Children give similar responses for tasks involving number and mass (see Figure 5.4).

By looking at Figure 5.4, you can see why preoperational children's tendency to use intuitive thought would lead them astray. At a quick glance, it does "seem that" the taller beaker has more. Piaget, however, analyzed children's responses further and was able to pinpoint other important limitations of preoperational thought. First, young children show marked

conservation

The understanding that some basic properties of objects remain the same even when a transformation changes the physical appearance.

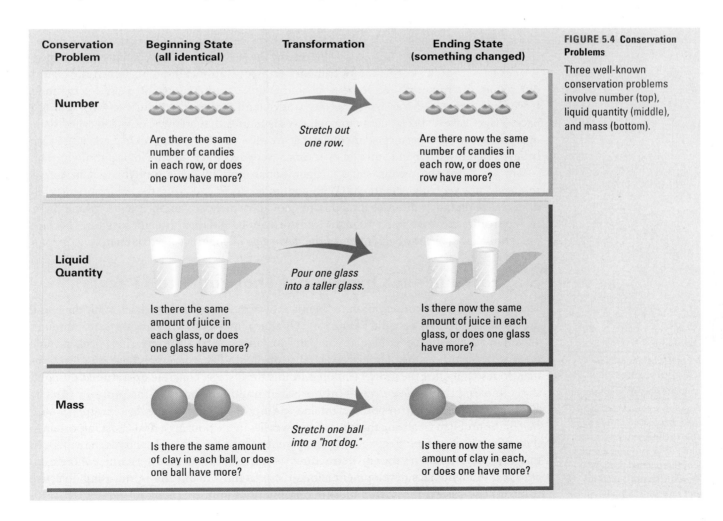

Conservation Problem	Beginning State (all identical)	Transformation	Ending State (something changed)
Number	Are there the same number of candies in each row, or does one row have more?	Stretch out one row.	Are there now the same number of candies in each row, or does one row have more?
Liquid Quantity	Is there the same amount of juice in each glass, or does one glass have more?	Pour one glass into a taller glass.	Is there now the same amount of juice in each glass, or does one glass have more?
Mass	Is there the same amount of clay in each ball, or does one ball have more?	Stretch one ball into a "hot dog."	Is there now the same amount of clay in each, or does one have more?

FIGURE 5.4 Conservation Problems

Three well-known conservation problems involve number (top), liquid quantity (middle), and mass (bottom).

This child thinks the taller container has more liquid in it. What can her answer tell us about the thinking processes of young children?

centration in their thinking. *Centration* is the tendency to focus on only one aspect of a situation at a time instead of taking several aspects into consideration. In the liquid problem, for example, children tend to focus on the height of the liquid, instead of considering that the greater width of one beaker compensates for the taller height of the other. Second, young children focus on the *static endpoints* of the transformation (how things look before and after) rather than considering what happened in the transformation itself. Children look at the beginning state (both levels are equal on the left side of Figure 5.4), then at the ending state (one level is higher on the right side), and they conclude that the higher level must have more. They fail to consider the transformation itself—the act of pouring could show that the amount of liquid did not change. And finally, children at this stage lack a grasp of *reversibility*. That is, they do not imagine what would happen if they reversed the transformation; they don't visualize pouring the liquid back into its original container to demonstrate that the amount would still be the same. When children focus on the height of the liquid, pay attention only to the static endpoints of the problem, and don't imagine pouring the liquid back, you can see why they usually obtain such an intuitive answer as "this one is taller, so it has more."

Piaget saw the lack of mental reversibility as an important hallmark of preoperational thought. To be fully logical, our cognitive structures need to be reversible. Think about the logic of math, for example. If we have 4 and take 2 away, we need to understand that we can return to 4 by adding 2 back. Piaget gave a special name to cognitive structures that are reversible. He called them **operations**—actions performed mentally that are reversible (Ginsburg & Opper, 1988). Piaget believed that these dynamic mental operations were necessary for true logical thought. This is why he called the second stage *pre*operational thought—it is thought that is *not yet reversible*, not yet truly *operational*. With continued experience with the environment, children realize that their intuitive thought does not adequately explain the events around them. As they realize the reversibility of many transformations and their thought structures become operational, we have the beginnings of the next stage of cognitive development.

Stage 3: Concrete Operational Thought (7 to 11 Years)

To an older child the conservation problems shown in Figure 5.4 are trivial. With the liquid problem, a typical 10-year-old would say, "Of course they both still have the same amount; all you did was pour it over here. If you pour the taller one back into the short beaker, you'll see that it's just the same." Or "Sure, the taller one looks like it has more, but it is also skinnier, so it's really just the same." Children in this third stage, **concrete operational thought,** show thinking that is *decentered*—they consider multiple aspects of the problem (understanding the importance of both height and width). They focus on the *dynamic transformation* in the problem (realizing that the true answer lies in the pouring). And, most importantly, they show the *reversibility* of true mental *operations* (just pour it back, and it's the same). In this third stage children's cognitive structures are operational—hence the name, concrete *operational* thought. This development allows them to think about the world using objective rules of logic, freeing them from the misconceptions of intuitive thought.

operations

Mental schemes (actions) that are reversible.

concrete operational thought

Stage of cognitive development in which children are able to think about two or more dimensions of a problem (decentered thought), dynamic transformations, and reversible operations.

Children in the concrete operational stage also show their logical abilities when they solve *class inclusion* and *transitive inference* problems. For example, show a child a set of five dolls and three teddy bears, then ask this question: "Are there more dolls or more toys?" Children in the preoperational stage will typically answer "more dolls," because they tend to focus on only one part of the problem (dolls versus bears) and ignore the fact that all of the objects belong to the general class of toys. Most children in the concrete operational stage, however, understand that both dolls and bears are also toys. To them this is a silly question—of course there are more toys than dolls! In other words, older children understand *class inclusion*—the fact that objects can be classified in different ways and at different levels. Younger children don't understand this. When he was about 4, our younger son heard his mother referred to as "Doctor." He immediately spoke up: "She's not a doctor, she's my mommy!" Our older son just rolled his eyes. To young children, grandmothers can't also be mothers, and firemen can't also be fathers.

Older children also understand *transitive inference*—the process of drawing inferences by comparing relations among objects. Consider the following example. Sue is taller than Jean, and Jean is taller than Lexi. Who is taller, Sue or Lexi? We can draw the inference that Sue is taller than Lexi by comparing the relationships from Sue and Jean to Jean and Lexi. Children in the preoperational stage have trouble following these transitivity problems; they may comment that they can't tell who is taller (after all, they can't see them!) or may just take a guess. With true operational logic, however, children in the concrete operational stage can represent the logical relationships and arrive at the correct answer.

By age 7 most children are capable of using logical thought structures that are increasingly objective and reversible, and they can solve problems that involve class inclusion and transitivity. However, there is still one major limitation in their thinking: Their use of mental operations is still closely tied to *concrete* materials, contexts, and situations. In other words, if children have not had direct experience with the context or situation, or if the material is not tangible, they are not successful in using their mental operations. This is why the stage is called *concrete* operational thought.

Stage 4: Formal Operational Thought (Approximately Age 12 and Above)

According to Piaget, it is during adolescence that cognitive development reaches its fullest potential—**formal operational thought.** Two major changes occur in this stage: Adolescents gradually develop the ability to use hypothetico-deductive reasoning, and they extend their logical thinking to concepts that are abstract (no longer solely to materials that are concrete and tangible).

■ **Hypothetico-Deductive Reasoning.**   For Piaget the culminating achievement of cognitive development is the ability to use hypothetico-deductive reasoning. **Hypothetico-deductive reasoning** is the use of deductive reasoning (reasoning from general principles to particular conclusions) to systematically manipulate several variables, test their effects in a systematic way, and reach correct conclusions. Piaget tested adolescents' developing use of hypothetico-deductive reasoning by using several tasks, many of which involved physics or chemistry (Ginsburg & Opper, 1988; Inhelder & Piaget, 1958). In his famous *pendulum problem,* children and adolescents of different ages were given a set of weights and strings of different lengths. As you can see in Figure 5.5, the weights could be hung from the strings and swung like pendulums. The investigators asked the children and adolescents to determine what caused the pendulums to swing at different rates. Was it the length of the string, the amount of weight, or how high the weight was held before it was released? Children in the

thinking OF MARIA

◀ Would Piaget predict that Maria's 4½-year-old would be able to solve class inclusion and transitivity problems? Would teachers be able to teach such skills to a child this young?

formal operational thought

Piaget's final stage of cognitive development, when an adolescent gradually learns to use hypothetico-deductive reasoning and to extend logical thinking to concepts that are abstract.

hypothetico-deductive reasoning

The ability to use deductive reasoning (reasoning from general to specific facts) to systematically manipulate several variables, test the effects in a systematic way, and reach correct conclusions in complex problems; scientific reasoning.

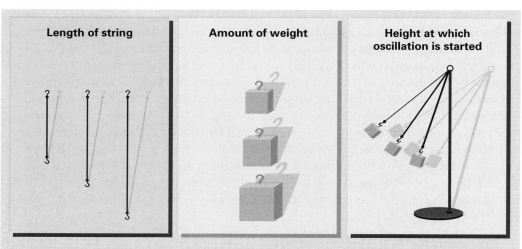

FIGURE 5.5 Piaget's Pendulum Problem

The pendulum problem asks you to figure out what causes the rate of the swing to vary. Is it the length of the string, the amount of weight at the end, or the height from which the weight is dropped? What tests would you conduct to isolate the relevant factor?

concrete operational stage are not good at systematically testing all of the factors; they tend to report whatever answer seems to be correct after conducting only a few tests. Adolescents using formal operations, however, start by considering all of the variables and all of their possible combinations, reasoning that any one factor could be responsible for the pendulum's rate of oscillation. They then systematically test each factor one at a time, holding the other factors constant, until they arrive at the correct solution. The adolescent shows hypothetico-deductive reasoning, or formal scientific reasoning—the ability to plan systematic tests to explore multiple variables.

■ **Abstract Thought.**   The second major development that takes place during the formal operational stage is the adolescent's growing ability to engage in abstract thought. **Abstract thought** is thought about things that are not real or tangible, or things that are only possibilities. You saw an example of this in the pendulum problem. When solving the problem, adolescents took as their starting point *all possible solutions;* this allowed them to reach an accurate solution efficiently. Abstract thought, however, also leads adolescents to spend extraordinary amounts of time speculating on all the possible outcomes of seemingly simple actions—as when they spend 4 hours discussing whether to wear *this* dress or *that* dress to a school social event. Although this behavior may drive parents crazy, it really is a sign of increasing cognitive maturity!

During the stage of formal operations, the adolescent also learns to think logically about such abstract concepts as truth, justice, fairness, and morality. Such concepts are at the heart of many important social, political, and ethical issues faced the world over. Not only are adolescents beginning to comprehend these concepts; they also develop the ability to reason flexibly about them and understand their relativity. For example, adolescents gradually become able to understand that *justice* may mean very different things to different people, depending on the context and intent of an action. They learn that it can be difficult to assess the justness of any particular action without considering these complex factors. The black-and-white meanings of childhood have given way to the grays of adulthood.

Although adolescents are learning formal logical thought and abstract reasoning, Piaget observed that adolescents still show a level of immaturity. He defined **adolescent egocentrism**

thinking
OF MARIA

What kinds of topics and activities could Maria look for that would demonstrate that a school supports hypothetico-deductive reasoning in its teaching?

abstract thought

Thought about things that are not real or things that are only possibilities.

adolescent egocentrism

A cognitive immaturity seen in adolescents—their inability to distinguish between their own abstract reasoning and thoughts and those of others.

as a young person's inability to distinguish between his or her own abstract reasoning and thoughts and those of others (Inhelder & Piaget, 1958). Piaget described two particular forms of adolescent egocentrism. The first is the *imaginary audience*. Adolescents believe that other people are just as concerned with their behavior, feelings, and thoughts as they are themselves. This leads to a sometimes excruciating degree of self-consciousness. Many adolescents feel "on stage," as if everyone else were noticing every embarrassing thing they do. The second adolescent egocentrism is the facet of *personal fable*. Adolescents tend to believe that they and their newly abstract thoughts are unique and that they are invulnerable. Often they believe that no one has ever thought about issues in the same way they do, and that no one else (especially parents!) could ever understand the way they feel. Unfortunately, feelings of invulnerability can lead adolescents to feel that nothing bad will happen to them—even when they engage in very risky behavior, like unprotected sexual activity or drinking and driving.

With the achievement of hypothetico-deductive reasoning and abstract thought, and with the eventual decline of adolescent egocentrism, young adults gradually attain what Piaget considered mature cognition. They become able to reason about anything, real or imagined, and have the capability to use scientific reasoning to solve complex problems. But this does not mean that no further changes in cognition occur. On the contrary, Piaget claimed that we never reach a permanent state of equilibrium. He believed that we are forever adapting and reorganizing our cognitive structures and working "toward *better* equilibrium" (Piaget, 1985, p. 26). Piaget did not, however, envision further major reorganizations of cognitive structure or the development of qualitatively more advanced or different kinds of thought.

Adolescents are fond of discussing deep thoughts and abstract ideas. What kinds of discussions do you remember having with your friends during adolescence?

Evaluation of Piaget's Theory

Cognitive psychologists have done an astounding amount of research to evaluate Piaget's theory. We will not attempt to cover all of this work. Instead, we will discuss the general conclusions about Piaget's most important and well-known claims, and we'll give you an overview of Piaget's legacy today.

Piaget was right about many important aspects of cognitive development. In general, children do seem to move from being more egocentric to less egocentric. They also move from being less systematic and less able to reason logically to being more able to think in these ways. And many studies over many years have replicated Piaget's results on tasks such as object permanence and conservation, if the experimenters conduct the tasks in the same ways as Piaget conducted them. Finally, studies from different cultures indicate that children seem to pass through Piaget's four stages in the same order—although the age brackets of the stages show great variability. Also, whether children ever achieve the formal operational stage depends on several different factors such as educational levels and the kinds of cognitive skills valued in a given culture (Gelman & Baillergeon, 1983; Ginsburg & Opper, 1988; Harris, 1983; Opper, 1977).

Research studies have also, however, highlighted two important weaknesses in Piaget's theory. First, Piaget underestimated the abilities of children, especially during infancy (Gelman & Baillargeon, 1983; Haith & Benson, 1998; Wellman & Gelman, 1998). Research conducted since the 1970s, using techniques and technologies not available back when Piaget was forming his theory, has demonstrated impressive cognitive abilities during infancy. Under the proper conditions, infants as young as 3½ months demonstrate a grasp of object permanence (Baillargeon, 1993; Spelke, 1991). Also, research demonstrates that young infants do code information and store mental representations in the form of memories, as we'll discuss in Chapter 6. Other research shows that preschool children can handle conservation and other problems when the tasks are simple enough and the children have appropriate training (Au, Sidle, & Rollins, 1993; Beilin, 1978; Donaldson, 1982; Gelman, 1972; McCabe & Siegel, 1987). At the same time, it turns out that Piaget may have *overestimated* the abilities of most adolescents and adults. Researchers now believe that only 50 to 60 percent of 18- to 20-year-olds in industrialized countries use formal operations and that the rates are even lower in nonindustrialized countries (Commons, Miller, & Kuhn, 1982; Keating, 1980). Recent research also questions how consistently adolescent egocentrism is found. Studies have suggested that it may indicate more about young adolescents' attempts to develop an identity and psychologically separate from their family than a general cognitive immaturity (Vartanian, 2000, 2001).

A second general criticism addresses the notion of developmental stages. Piaget's theory implies that as children reorganize their cognitive structures, they rise to a higher level of logical thought. Once achieved, these new structures and organizations presumably apply across all contexts. In real life, however, this is not what happens (Gelman, 2000; Gelman & Baillargeon, 1983; Harris, 1983; Larivée, Normandeau, & Parent, 2000). Let's take conservation problems as an example. Research shows that most children pass tests on number conservation problems by age 6 or 7; they pass weight conservation problems by age 9 or 10; but they don't pass volume conservation problems until about age 11 or 12 (Ginsburg & Opper, 1988). If children understand the concept of conservation (showing decentered and reversible thought) in the number problem, why don't they transfer this understanding to the weight and volume problems until years later? And how do we mark the transition from preoperational to concrete operational thought? Does it occur when a child passes the number conservation problem, or do we wait until the child comprehends conservation in all its forms? Not only is it difficult to define these transitions, but children also frequently show evidence of being in two or more stages at once. For these and other reasons, most modern-day researchers reject the concept of broad cognitive developmental stages (Flavell, Miller, & Miller, 1993).

What is least criticized is Piaget's constructivist view of development. Children do seem to be active participants in their own learning and development, assimilating new information into their existing cognitive structures, and modifying or reorganizing their structures when necessary to fit new information. The process of adaptation that Piaget observed in sea mollusks seems a fitting analogy for the adaptive processes children engage in as they achieve cognitive maturity.

Piaget's Legacy

Piaget's theory of cognitive development has left a legacy that no other theory in developmental psychology has even approached. His contributions can be summarized as follows:

▶ Piaget changed *psychology's view of young children*. Before, theorists saw children as passive organisms capable only of reacting to events. After Piaget, they realized that children actively seek to understand their environment and actively initiate events simply to see how things work.

▶ Piaget gave to posterity a *vast store of facts about children* and child development. This knowledge came both directly—from Piaget's own research, observations, and writings—and indirectly, from the research that others conducted attempting to either support or refute his theory.

Career Focus: Meet a Constructivist Teacher

Stacie Anderson
Donnelsville, Ohio

*First grade teacher
at Donnelsville
Elementary School*

How do you use Piagetian concepts in your teaching?
It is critical to have an idea of the preexisting schemes that students already have on a topic or skill area—it sets the stage for how I introduce a lesson. Next, I observe children's thought processes as a new concept, or a new layer of the concept, is introduced. How is it fitting (assimilating) into what they already know? I check to see how the new information is fitting by asking questions and having children evaluate their own thinking and each other's responses.

What specific activities do you use to help children construct knowledge?
Hands-on activities are critical in first grade, and all grades in my estimation. When teaching geometric shapes I have children sort out squares, circles, and triangles and list what they know about each shape (the square has four sides, four cor-

ners, etc.). Then I show a rectangle and ask, "How many sides and angles does it have?" "Is it a square?" Some children will say "Yes." As we take a closer look, they recognize that the sides are different lengths. Now they understand that squares have four equal sides, but rectangles have two side lengths. Then we introduce a parallelogram, rhombus, trapezoid. . . . With counting, students build towers with Unifix cubes to represent each numeral (1 to 10). They observe that "It looks like stairs!" and "Every tower is one taller." They can visually see that each tower is one greater than the other, and this smoothly leads into the concept of adding one.

How do you use Piaget's stages as guidelines for your curriculum or classroom activities?
At the district level, we created benchmarks and indicators of success in critical skill areas. However, based on my experience, it is important to know that a child can exhibit various behaviors that are indicative of several of these stages. Still, first graders do think more concretely and have difficulty thinking beyond their

home, family, and friends. It would be unrealistic to tackle national abstract issues with six-year-olds!

What education and training is required to work in your area?
To be a licensed teacher, you need to have a degree or courses in education, and you need to be supervised as a student teacher for one year. The requirements differ in each state. Many states require teachers to get a master's degree to have a permanent teaching license, and others require an advanced degree to teach above the third grade. A praxis exam is required in most states. ■

thinking
OF MARIA

◀ How could a constructivist teacher help Maria's youngest son if he were to start kindergarten early? In what ways might his schemes be different from the older children in his class?

❱ Piaget's theory has had important *applications in the field of education.* First, the notion of the child as an active and curious organism led to the design of interactive and hands-on curricula in schools. These teaching materials encourage children to make use of their natural curiosity to explore concepts in science, mathematics, and other domains. Second, Piaget's four stages and his concept of cognitive readiness (i.e., the idea that children cannot skip stages but must move from one to another as they are maturationally and cognitively ready) have shaped many guidelines for when to introduce different topics. Third, educators have learned to make use of the notion of cognitive disequilibrium. They do this by deliberately presenting students with puzzles, debates, and conflicting opinions to intentionally upset students' existing cognitive structures and encourage students to grow in understanding. Finally, educators explicitly urge reflective abstraction; they encourage students to think about the implications, usefulness, and limitations of their existing cognitive structures. To learn more about how teachers use Piaget's theory to help children learn, read the Professional Perspective box called "Career Focus: Meet a Constructivist Teacher."

Piaget's work and writing stimulated *vast amounts of research* in a variety of areas of child development. In doing this work, researchers developed new methodologies, tested new ideas of how children think, and opened and pursued new areas of inquiry. There is an old saying in scientific circles that the clear sign of a good theory is not whether the theory is ultimately shown to be right or wrong, but how much research and knowledge it stimulates. Whether or not any aspects of Piaget's theory are ultimately shown to be true, the theory can be considered great by this standard alone.

LET'S REVIEW . . .

1. According to Piaget, infants in the sensorimotor thought stage *cannot:*

   a. use sensory impressions to understand the world.

   b. use motor actions to understand the world.

   c. form symbolic representations to understand the world.

   d. display reflexes during the first month after birth.

2. A major characteristic of preoperational thought is that children tend to use:

   a. reflexes rather than mental symbols.

   b. intuitive thought.

   c. abstract . reasoning

   d. hypothetico-deductive reasoning.

3. Jimmy watches as you take two identical clay balls and roll one into the shape of a hot dog. You then ask him if both pieces of clay now have the same amount, or if one piece has more clay. Jimmy responds, "Of course they have the same amount; all you have to do is roll the hot dog back up into a ball to see that it has the same amount." Jimmy's answer shows that he understands:

   a. reversibility.   b. decentration.   c. static endpoints.   d. transitivity.

4. According to Piaget, the imaginary audience and the personal fable are both parts of:

   a. intuitive thought.

   b. object permanence.

   c. conservation problems.

   d. adolescent egocentrism.

5. **True or False:** When a child gives the correct answer to conservation problems, it is a sign that the child is now in the stage of preoperational thought.

6. **True or False:** One criticism of Piaget's theory is that he overestimated the cognitive abilities of infants.

Answer to the pendulum problem in Figure 5.5: Length of the string is the factor that determines how fast the pendulum swings.

Answers: 1. c, 2. b, 3. a, 4. d, 5. F, 6. F

Vygotsky's Sociocultural View of Cognitive Development

Of course, not everyone was satisfied with Piaget's account of cognitive development. Aside from the evidence against grand stages in cognitive development, some theorists and practitioners have long felt that Piaget's account does not adequately consider one very important influence on cognition: the child's social environment. Lev Semenovich Vygotsky is one theorist who gave the role of social interaction and culture a central place in his account of cognitive development.

- What influence did Vygotsky's own cultural background have on his theory? What historical events were taking place during his time, and how did they affect his theory?

- Why is Vygotsky's theory called a "sociocultural" view? According to this theory, what roles do culture and social interaction play in cognitive development?

- What role does language play in cognitive development, and how can adults facilitate children's development?

Vygotsky's Background: The Sociocultural Context for a New Theory

Vygotsky was born in 1896, the same year as Piaget but in Belorussia (later part of the Soviet Union). Vygotsky's family was Jewish, and they shared a rich cultural background with most of their fellow townspeople. Being Jewish, they also experienced prejudice, discrimination, and strict governmental restrictions. Vygotsky received his early education from a private tutor who taught by means of Socratic dialogue. In this method, the tutor poses questions and helps the student reason through and figure out answers, rather than simply giving the student facts and information. At the University of Moscow, Vygotsky studied law, history, and philosophy. He graduated in 1917, the year of the Russian Revolution, in which the centuries-old tsarist government fell and Lenin came to power at the head of a Marxist government. Vygotsky was a committed Marxist. The new Soviet government seemed to promise an end to ethnic and religious discrimination, promising that everyone would be considered an equal Soviet citizen. Vygotsky also was a firm believer in Marx's emphasis on the importance of social history as an influence on people's behavior and development (Kozulin, 1990; Wertsch, 1985).

In 1924 Vygotsky took a position at Moscow's prestigious Psychological Institute to help restructure the institute and develop a Marxist psychology. Over the next decade this so-called "Mozart of psychology" (Toulmin, 1978) attracted many top Soviet scholars as students and colleagues to assist in developing and testing his theoretical ideas. Unfortunately, in 1934 Vygotsky died from tuberculosis. Although he was only 38, he had already written several important books and other articles, and his brilliance was recognized by all of those who worked around him (Kozulin, 1990; Wertsch, 1985).

It might seem that such a popular figure as Vygotsky would have had an immediate impact on psychology worldwide. He did not. Much of his writing was not published, even in the Soviet Union, until decades after his death. In part this was because the research to support Vygotsky's ideas had to be completed by his students after his death. Also, even as his followers completed the work, the Soviet regime banned much of it. Vygotsky often referenced foreign scientists, philosophers, and literary works. But under Josef Stalin the regime saw the influence of foreigners as undesirable. For 2 decades, therefore, few Soviet psychologists had access to Vygotsky's work. In addition, the cold war meant that there was little hope for dissemination to European and American psychologists. After Stalin's death in 1953, Vygotsky's work again began to be published, and ever since the end of the cold war Vygotsky's influence on psychology has been steadily increasing (Kozulin, 1990; Wertsch, 1985).

Soviet psychologist Lev Vygotsky proposed a sociocultural theory of cognitive development that continues to gain prominence. Can you see the influence of Vygotsky's own cultural background in his theory?

The Role of Speech and Language

The central theme in Vygotsky's theory is that children acquire cognitive structures from their culture and from their social interactions, primarily by listening to the language they hear around them. **Social speech** is the speech that we hear as people talk around us or to us. According to Vygotsky, children adopt important parts of social speech and make it their own **private speech**—the speech children say aloud to themselves. It is the language (speech) that carries the concepts and cognitive structures to the child, and these concepts become the "psychological tools" that the child will use (Vygotsky, 1962).

Consider the simple example of a little girl learning to draw a circle. At first the child has no concept of "circle," so the adult uses social speech to talk her through the process. "Start your mark going around, like this [demonstrating an arc], then bring it all the way around until the marks meet each other." As the child tries to draw her own circle, she repeats the instructions aloud to herself, "I make the mark go 'round, like this, then I bring it 'round until it meets." The concept of "circle" was carried from the social speech (of the adult directing the child) to the private speech of the child. As Vygotsky put it,

> Any function in the child's . . . development appears twice, or on two planes. First it appears on the social plane, and then on the psychological plane. First it appears between people as an interpsychological category, and then within the child as an intrapsychological category. (Vygotsky, 1981, p. 163)

When children are learning new concepts or difficult tasks, they often rely on the support of private speech. "I'll bring the mark around. Oops! I went too far up. Now back down, and around this way. Not too far. Now the marks don't meet. I'll draw it over. There, a circle!" **Internalization** is the process by which external activity and speech become internal and come to be executed mentally. As children master a concept, they need private speech less and less. Eventually they internalize it completely as silent, inner speech.

Private speech is midway between the social interactions in which it originated and the completely internal thought that it will become. Research on the development of private speech shows the progression you might expect: Children go from talking out loud to whispering softly to silently moving their lips before ceasing to show private speech (Bivens & Berk, 1990; Winsler & Naglieri, 2003). Private speech does not simply disappear forever, however. We all revert to some level of private speech when we encounter a difficult problem, or if we make a mistake when working on a task, or when we are confused about a task. Private speech seems to help us focus our attention, regulate our strategies, and plan our problem-solving efforts (Behrend, Rosengren, & Perlmutter, 1992; Berk, 1992; Berk & Spuhl, 1995; Emerson & Miyake, 2003; Schneider, 2002). A considerable body of research indicates that private speech both serves as a step in the internalization process and functions to help people think through problems.

Mediation: With a Little Help from Your Friends

In Vygotsky's theory interpersonal interactions with adults or more skilled peers teach, or *mediate*, the cognitive structures created by the larger culture. **Mediation** is the process of introducing concepts, knowledge, skills, and strategies to the child (Karpov & Haywood, 1998; Vygotsky, 1981). For the mediating adult (or older peer), mediation involves choosing which structures to introduce to the child, deciding when and how to teach them, and helping the child understand their usefulness. For example, think about helping a young child put together a jigsaw puzzle. Many adults encourage specific puzzle-making strategies such as starting with the corners, doing the borders first, or looking for clues (e.g., matching colors,

thinking
OF MARIA

According to Vygotsky's theory, why would it be important for Maria to spend time in schools and classrooms listening to the verbal messages being conveyed? What kinds of messages, or cognitive structures, would she want to hear?

YOUR
PERSPECTIVE
NOTES

Try to remember the last time that you mumbled or talked aloud to yourself when you were trying to do something difficult or challenging. How did your private speech help?

social speech
Speech that we hear as people talk around us or to us.

private speech
Speech that children say aloud to themselves; later internalized to form inner speech and mental activity.

internalization
The process of taking external speech and activity and making it internal and mental.

mediation
The process adults and more skilled peers use to introduce concepts and cognitive structures to less skilled children.

matching shapes). In addition, adults often help children think about more general skills, such as being careful when matching shapes and colors or being systematic when trying a piece in different locations. However, most adults do not try to introduce all of these things at the same time. They mediate by selecting specific strategies and highlighting them; they help the child learn a few skills, then move on to others as the child gains expertise. Gradually the child internalizes all of the strategies, along with the verbal labels for them. In the end the child can use this information as a structure and tackle jigsaw puzzles independently.

Mediation can take place in structured settings (such as during formal schooling) or in informal day-to-day activities (such as when a parent talks about ecology while putting out the trash and recyclables). The key to making mediation effective is to tailor it to an appropriate level for the individual child. The structures being explained should be neither so easy that the child has already internalized them nor so difficult that the child cannot understand them. This optimal level of difficulty lies within what Vygotsky called the child's *zone of proximal development.*

How do adults provide mediation for children's learning?

The Zone of Proximal Development

Vygotsky defined the **zone of proximal development (ZPD)** as the distance between a child's "actual developmental level as determined by independent problem solving" and the child's level of "potential development as determined through problem solving under adult guidance or in collaboration with more capable peers" (Vygotsky, 1978, p. 86). The ZPD refers to the range of problems a child can solve if given some assistance. As shown in Figure 5.6, the bottom boundary of the ZPD consists of the most challenging problems a child can already solve independently. The top boundary of the ZPD consists of problems that the child cannot solve, no matter how much support others may offer. These tasks require higher mental functions that the child has not yet begun to internalize, so even very explicit assistance does not help. The ZPD is the zone between these two boundaries. The tasks within this zone require mental functions that the child is in the process of internalizing but has not yet completely internalized.

An important point to remember about the ZPD is that it is dynamic—the top and bottom boundaries change as the child internalizes more and more mental functions (see Figure 5.6). The boundaries move up as the natural result of effective mediation within the ZPD. An adult interacts with a child, presenting problems that challenge the child. The adult helps the child work through the solution, sometimes needing to offer a great deal of assistance at first. The child gradually learns how to solve these challenging problems. Now the problems that used to be within the child's ZPD are below it.

There is an important implication here for instruction—can you see what it is? According to Vygotsky the most effective instruction involves giving children *challenging material, along with help in mastering it.* Although children may need extensive help at first, Vygotsky said that challenging tasks promote cognitive development, as long as a given task is not beyond the top boundary of a given child's ZPD. And there is a related implication for assessment, or testing. That is, the most informative assessments are not tests of

zone of proximal development (ZPD)

The distance between the current maximum independent performance level of a child and the tasks the child can perform if guided by adults or more capable peers.

FIGURE 5.6 The Zone of Proximal Development

The range of tasks a child is capable of completing with help and guidance defines the zone of proximal development. The bottom boundary is defined by tasks the child already can complete independently. The top is defined by tasks the child cannot complete even with help. The zone changes with development, and both boundaries move up as more mental functions are internalized. As a result, tasks that used to be above the top boundary are within the child's zone; tasks that used to be within the zone become too easy and fall below the bottom boundary.

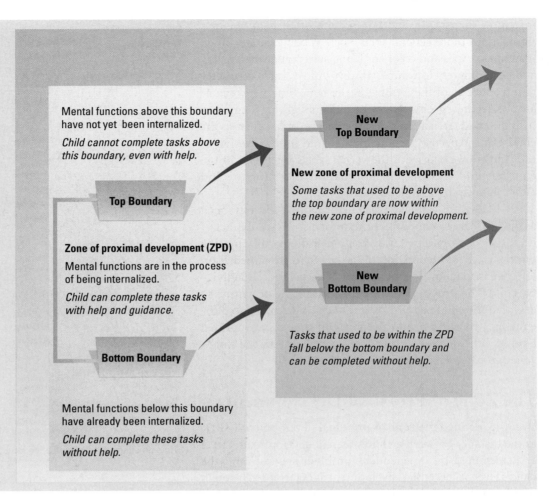

Mental functions above this boundary have not yet been internalized.

Child cannot complete tasks above this boundary, even with help.

Top Boundary

Zone of proximal development (ZPD)

Mental functions are in the process of being internalized.

Child can complete these tasks with help and guidance.

Bottom Boundary

Mental functions below this boundary have already been internalized.

Child can complete these tasks without help.

New Top Boundary

New zone of proximal development

Some tasks that used to be above the top boundary are now within the new zone of proximal development.

New Bottom Boundary

Tasks that used to be within the ZPD fall below the bottom boundary and can be completed without help.

independent performance but tests of assisted performance. Such tests "take stock not only of . . . the processes of maturation that are completed" but also of "processes that are now in the state of coming into being, that are only ripening, or only developing" (Vygotsky, 1956, p. 448).

The contrast between Vygotsky's and Piaget's views of cognitive development is at the heart of a controversy over when children should be allowed to enter school. To learn more about the implications of these theories for thinking about school readiness, read the Social Policy Perspective box called "When Should Children Start School?"

Scaffolding: Support during Learning

If mediation within the ZPD is so important, how do adults and other helpers do it? Scaffolding, a concept that has grown from Vygotsky's theory, helps answer this question. **Scaffolding** is providing supportive help when a child is developing a mental function or learning to do a particular task (Wood, Bruner, & Ross, 1976; Wood & Middleton, 1975; Wood, Wood, & Middleton, 1978). Think about a building being constructed, and picture the supports that the builders set up during the construction process. These scaffolds support the workers until they complete the building. Cognitive scaffolds do exactly the same thing—they provide support for children as they develop the cognitive processes

thinking
OF MARIA

What could Maria look for in schools that would indicate that her sons would be appropriately challenged within their own zones of proximal development? What kinds of mediation might teachers provide?

scaffolding

Support given to a child as he or she develops a new mental function or learns to perform a particular task.

A Social Policy PERSPECTIVE...

When Should Children Start School?

When a child is younger than most of her classmates-to-be, which is better: To delay her entry into school and give her another year to mature and become "ready" for schooling? Or to enroll her, assuming that she will benefit from the activities and interactions and learn just as much as the older children? Most children in the United States today enter kindergarten at 5 years of age, but many states are considering increasing the age of school entry. Schools face increasing pressure to be accountable for their students' performance, so they are looking for ways to increase children's achievement. If older children benefit more from schooling, they should show higher achievement test scores, which often translate into better funding and resources. Parents are increasingly holding their "younger" children (particularly boys) back from entering school for fear that these children may not learn as well or as quickly as their classmates, perhaps might be retained, and then might have behavioral problems.

Those who support older entry ages argue that older children are bi-

ologically, cognitively, and socially more mature, and therefore that they are better able to take advantage of formal instruction. There is also the implicit assumption that the "'gift of time' and general (out of school) experience outweigh the benefits of a school setting" for increasing readiness (Stipek, 2002, p. 4). Others disagree, arguing that there is no single age at which all children will achieve "readiness" across all the biological, cognitive, and social skills involved in schooling. No matter what the cutoff age is, some children will be more and some less ready. More fundamentally, critics argue that holding children back from schooling will only put them *farther behind*, because the school environment is precisely what children need to further their development. Keeping children out of school will only increase the gap between their skills and those of their peers, and it will put them at even higher risk for poor academic achievement. Finally, critics argue that it is not the child's responsibility to be ready for school, but schools' responsibility to be ready for children—no matter what their

level of skills and abilities when they begin.

The research evidence does not argue strongly for older entry ages. Some studies indicate a small advantage for some skills for older children, but the difference fades within the first few years of schooling. For most skills studied, schooling has a significantly stronger effect than age, and younger children at a grade level benefit from schooling as much as older children (Stipek, 2002). There also may be some risks for children who are older than their classmates because of delayed entry. These children show more behavior problems than younger children at the same grade level, with the difference increasing over time (Byrd, Weitzman, & Auinger, 1997; Mayer & Knutson, 1999).

Which sides of this debate would Piaget and Vygotsky likely take, and why? Given the theoretical views and research evidence, how would you advise parents and your local school system to think about the issue of school entry age? And where does the responsibility for readiness lie—with the children being taught, or with the system doing the instruction? ■

needed for a particular task. Cognitive scaffolding can take many different forms. It might include such things as initially doing part of a task for the child, simplifying difficult parts, talking the child through the task, or giving reminders. Any of these actions can help children complete the task and therefore assist them as they develop the necessary processes. Just as with a physical scaffold on a building, however, a cognitive scaffold is not meant to be permanent. It is a *temporary supportive structure*, meant to be gradually removed as the child's mental functions mature. To learn more about how adults provide scaffolds for children's learning, read the Personal Perspective box on page 198 called "How Did I Help My Children Learn?"

The full impact of Vygotsky's ideas cannot be assessed yet, because some of his writings are only now being translated and made widely available. Many aspects of the theory have already proved useful, however—especially in the field of education (Kozulin, 1998). For example, because thought and cognitive development *follow from* language, it is

Kelly Welch
Manhattan, Kansas
Mother of four sons (ages 14, 16, 18, and 20)

How Did I Help My Children Learn?

What kinds of scaffolds did you provide for your children as they learned new things?
Examples of scaffolds are limitless, from helping them learn to make beds, potty training, and even making a bowl of cereal or a peanut butter and jelly sandwich. Typically I would model the behavior and both verbally and physically guide them until I felt they could handle different pieces on their own. For example, I might hold the milk carton while they "poured" the milk, until I eventually let them do it on their own regardless of the spills and messes.

How did you reduce or remove the scaffolds as your child learned?
It's a stepwise process. As I sensed their independence and confidence, I let them do more on their own. I had to refrain from correcting them so I didn't send the message, "Yes, you did it, but not good enough."

Did you use scaffolding differently for your different children? Were the scaffolds removed at a different rate for each child?
Every one of our sons was different. The oldest was a perfectionist, so we had to leave scaffolds in place longer or he would be heartbroken when things didn't work correctly. Our third son became frustrated more easily than the other boys, so we had to remove scaffolds more slowly for him also. He was a hands-on learner. The other two boys learned better from books, so they didn't need as much scaffolding from us.

How do you help your children without doing the work for them?
By making it fun! We modeled the task to the point they wanted to do it. Putting food coloring in the dishwater was a sure way to have them argue over who got to wash the dishes. We also dished up praise whenever we could. We always let them know that it didn't matter what others could do, that they are perfect just the way they are. ■

thinking OF MARIA

◄ What activities could Maria provide at home to encourage her sons' knowledge construction?

---

important to engage children in tasks they cannot yet handle independently, help them work through the tasks, and talk about the process. With mediation more experienced people help children master the cognitive structures they need to succeed in their environment. The role of the parent or teacher shifts from that of an interested observer to that of a fully active participant in a child's development. It is not enough to provide a stimulating environment for the child. We must also make decisions about which aspects of the larger culture to introduce to the child and when to introduce them. We also must find ways to structure these aspects, explain them, and provide scaffolding as the child struggles to master them.

thinking OF MARIA

If Maria observed children working together in groups, with teachers guiding and advising the groups, would this be a sign that the learning environment was conducive to cognitive development? ►

Collaborative learning is a natural outgrowth of Vygotsky's theory. Remember that Vygotsky emphasized that cognitive development is driven by social interaction and that a more capable peer can be an effective mediator. Accordingly, parents and teachers can foster cognitive development by encouraging children to help one another solve problems, share their knowledge and skills, and discuss their strategies and knowledge (Gillies, 2003; Slavin, 1995; Wentzel & Watkins, 2002; Zimbardo, Butler, & Wolfe, 2003). As with any other form of mediation, however, collaborative learning experiences must help each child master the cognitive structures of the larger culture. Also, the mediation must take place within each individual child's ZPD if it is to be effective.

Can you see Vygotsky's sociocultural theory at work in this collaborative learning group? Use the concepts of social speech, mediation, ZPD, and scaffolding to explain why peer collaboration can be an effective way for children to learn.

One lesson to be learned from Vygotsky's theory is the importance of considering the impact of larger cultural systems and experiences on individual cognitive development. For example, in Chapter 1 we described the ecological systems theory developed by Urie Bronfenbrenner, which describes the influence of different systems on development. One recent approach to understanding the development of African American youth builds on both Vygotsky and systems theory. The *phenomenological variant of systems theory* emphasizes the importance of identifying relationships between broader cultural influences and development, but also asks how these influences affect the thinking and cognitive perspectives of the individual. The "focus [is] on the meaning-making processes" (Spencer, 1995, p. 39). For example, experiences of discrimination, racism, and stereotyping affect how minority youth think. The result is that children in minority groups often develop a unique and adaptive set of psychological tools for dealing with the challenges of their specific cultural setting (Spencer, Noll, Stoltzfus, & Harpalani, 2001).

Vygotsky would surely be delighted that his ideas have influenced the way we view cognitive development. And he would be especially glad that his ideas have made a difference in educational practice. Remember that he lived in a tumultuous time, experiencing extraordinary social and intellectual upheavals. He saw firsthand how cultures and societies change over time, and he believed that such changes have a powerful influence on cognitive development. We can see that influence when we compare Vygotsky to Piaget. Piaget grew up in Switzerland, a country that prides itself on autonomy and independence; he theorized that children construct their own cognitive structures as they learn to adapt to the environment. For Piaget the child's own experiences are primary. For Vygotsky, however, the words of the community are primary. Vygotsky believed in the collectivist philosophy of the communist Soviet Union; he proposed that children learn by adopting the cognitive structures offered by the important people—and the larger community—around the child.

YOUR
PERSPECTIVE
PERSPECTIVE
NOTES
Identify some of the scaffolds you have been offered in this textbook or in this class. List them and think about how they have supported your learning.

1. In contrast to Piaget, Vygotsky placed a greater emphasis on the role of _____ in children's cognitive development.

   a. the child's own subjective interpretation   b. math and logic   c. biology and genetics   d. social interaction and language

2. When Jeremy was doing his math homework, he could be heard mumbling aloud: "I carry the six, so that makes this six plus three equals nine." According to Vygotsky, Jeremy just gave us an example of:

   a. social speech.   b. private speech.   c. inner speech.   d. internalized speech.

3. According to Vygotsky's theory, it is best if teachers design educational programs that work:

   a. just below a child's zone of proximal development.

   b. just above a child's zone of proximal development.

   c. within a child's zone of proximal development.

   d. against a child's zone of proximal development.

4. According to Vygotsky, children's thought structures develop from:

   a. the language they hear around them.

   b. their attempts to modify their own internal schemes.

   c. their own experimentation with characteristics in the environment.

   d. the biological maturation of their nervous system.

5. **True or False:** Vygotsky's emphasis on the social transmission of thought and knowledge follows from his belief in Marxist philosophy.

6. **True or False:** In Vygotsky's theory, scaffolds are the support structures that adults and other people provide to help a child learn a difficult task.

Answers: 1. d, 2. b, 3. c, 4. a, 5. T, 6. T

Recent Sociocultural Views of Cognitive Development

Vygotsky's theory served as the foundation for several more recent views of cognitive development. These views emphasize the important influence of social interaction and the larger cultural context on children's cognitive development, and they reveal how Vygotsky's theory has stimulated many researchers to think about cognitive development in new ways.

As you study this section, ask yourself these questions:

- What influence did Vygotsky have on the development of the newer sociocultural views of cognitive development?

- According to these newer views, how do the social context, groups, and the larger culture influence cognitive development?

- What specific ideas can we take from these newer sociocultural views that would help us facilitate children's cognitive development?

Situated Cognition

"If you were selling candy, would you make more profit by selling one piece for 200 cruzeiros or by selling three pieces for 500 cruzeiros?" When Geoffrey Saxe (1988) asked Brazilian schoolchildren questions like this, he found that most were not able to answer correctly. But when he went into city streets in Brazil and asked children who were not attending school at all, he got accurate answers. Why the difference? The children he interviewed in the streets were vendors, children who sold things to support themselves and their families. Although they lacked formal education in mathematics, they had developed their own strategies for solving complicated problems. The street vendors probably would not have succeeded in school math tests, as these tests tend to use problems that are rather abstract and taken out of context. Within their familiar context, however, the vendors were quite adept. Similar results have been found in other cultures, such as Beirut (Jurdak & Shahin, 1999). Their mathematical skills were situation-specific—an example of *situated cognition.*

The **situated cognition** view of cognitive development holds that thinking always takes place within a specific context, and always in relation to a particular problem, situation, or interaction. According to this view you cannot really understand thought or its quality or level without also examining the context in which the thought takes place. For example, suppose you ask a first grader, "What is 4 divided by 2?" He will probably be unable to answer, maybe saying he hasn't "had division yet." But give him four cookies and tell him to make sure that he and his brother both get the same number, and watch how quickly the boy solves the problem. Embedding questions in concrete and meaningful contexts enables children to solve problems that they cannot otherwise understand. The situated cognition view emphasizes that the particular kinds of thinking that occur in different cultures result from adaptations to the particular contexts in which the members of the cultures find themselves. The key factors are the kinds of problems people encounter frequently and the cognitive structures that they find to be effective. In sum, this view reminds us that to properly understand cognitive development, we need also to consider its context. In keeping with this view, many educators strive to teach cognitive skills within contexts—drawing on the types of situations most important within their students' cultures.

Guided Participation

Another recent sociocultural view emphasizes **guided participation.** The central idea here is that development consists of children's gradually increasing participation in sociocultural activity—with gradually decreasing guidance and support from those around them (Lave & Wenger, 1991; Rogoff, 1998, 2003; Rogoff, Mistry, Göncü, & Mosier, 1993). For example, think about a girl learning to read. Initially, she cannot decipher the symbols on the page, so her participation is marginal. But she is a *legitimate peripheral participant* (Lave & Wenger, 1991, 1996), which means that she is involved in the activity to the degree that her current skill allows. She can select the book to be read, listen attentively, ask and answer questions, and examine any pictures that go along with the story. As the child begins to decipher letters and to remember the sounds of different letters, her degree of participation increases and its nature changes. She can now point out specific letters, even recognize and read simple words such as *a* or *an.* Her participation continues to change as she gradually becomes more of a *central participant,* able to do a great deal of the reading herself and even reading simple books to other, less central participants.

The guided participation view is similar to Vygotsky's in that more central participants initially guide the activity, and the child gradually takes on increasing responsibility. But whereas Vygotsky emphasized how children internalize the psychological tools represented in their culture, the guided participation view instead emphasizes how the child's social roles or shared interactions with other people change as the child develops. Also, whereas

Identify an activity in which you have moved from being a legitimate peripheral participant to being a more central participant. What skills and knowledge did you learn as a legitimate peripheral participant, and how did they help you become more of a central participant?

situated cognition

The idea that we cannot fully understand children's thinking and cognition without considering the context within which it occurs.

guided participation

The idea that children are involved in sociocultural activities to the degree that their level of cognitive development allows.

thinking
OF MARIA

What kinds of classroom activities might Maria look for that would indicate that her sons would have opportunities to contribute to socially shared cognition? Why would these opportunities be important?

Vygotsky tended to focus on the internalization of such things as a culture's language or number system, the guided participation view emphasizes participation in more routine, day-to-day activities.

Thinking as Socially Shared Cognition: Two Heads Are Better than One

Vygotsky claimed that even after children internalize cognitive structures, thought is still a social phenomenon, because its roots are in social interaction. Recent work emphasizes this point, describing cognition as a socially shared activity rather than an individual one (Resnick, Levine, & Teasley, 1991; Wertsch, Tulviste, & Hagstrom, 1993). In this view, cognition does not involve an individual's activities alone, or even an individual's contributions to a social interaction. This view holds that thinking extends "beyond the skin" of the individual and includes the "thinking" of pairs and groups of people (Wertsch, Tulviste, & Hagstrom, 1993, p. 337). It does not make sense to ask, "Whose idea is that?" because thought takes place across the members of a group—it is **socially shared cognition.** This theory does not deny that an individual can think independently. But it argues that even "independent" thought is the culmination of many others' input. Thinking resides in the dynamic interactions between individuals within the group, not solely inside the head of any individual.

The three views we have summarized here all draw on different aspects of Vygotsky's theory. These modern sociocultural views of cognition are still in the formative stages. But the key point is that today's sociocultural cognition theorists no longer see thought as something that takes place inside one individual's head and consists of abstract skills applied across many different problems and contexts. Instead, they view cognition as much more complex. They suggest that cognition makes use of specific features and contexts and involves individuals collaborating to create ideas and think in ways that no individual could accomplish alone. In short, they see cognition as a very dynamic, social, and interactive process.

socially shared cognition

The idea that thought is a shared group activity and that the thoughts of any individual child are derived at least in part from dynamic interactions occurring between people and in groups.

LET'S REVIEW . . .

1. Children show more advanced cognitive processing when they are tested within contexts that are familiar and well practiced. This is one of the main points of the:
   a. socially shared cognition view.
   b. guided participation view.
   c. social speech view.
   d. situated cognition view.

2. Which of the following would be an example of development in the guided participation view?
   a. John moves from watching children play basketball to playing in the game himself.
   b. Sue and Lisa work together to solve a problem that neither could solve alone.
   c. Henri can read his favorite books at home but has trouble reading the practice sheets in school.
   d. Tonya needs social scaffolds to help her understand algebra problems.

3. **True or False:** The sociocultural theories are a reaction against Vygotsky's view of cognitive development.

4. **True or False:** According to the sociocultural view, cognition is the product of social interaction more than the private construction of individual thinkers.

Answers: 1. d, 2. a, 3. F, 4. T

thinking
BACK TO MARIA

Now that you have studied this chapter, you should be able to explain how Maria could use concepts from the constructivist and sociocultural theories to identify schools and teachers that would facilitate the cognitive development of her sons, ages 4½ and 12. You should be able to list at least a dozen specific concepts and explain how each would relate to Maria's situation.

Using Piaget's constructivist theory, Maria would want to find classroom environments that promote active learning and look for teachers who use rich hands-on activities. By providing novel materials and concepts in class, teachers provide the environment where children can try to assimilate new information into their existing schemes. If their schemes cannot handle the new information, then children may be puzzled or perplexed. This is not failure; Piaget referred to it as cognitive disequilibrium, and it signals readiness to learn or accommodate schemes. Teachers should encourage reflective abstraction by asking children to look for connections and interrelationships among concepts.

Using Vygotsky's sociocultural theory, Maria should understand that children also learn by adopting the cognitive structures embedded in the language and culture of the classroom and the school. She should spend time observing and listening for the messages contained in the school culture. Are the messages predominantly positive—as in "All students can learn," "Math and science have practical importance," and "Celebrate diversity"? Social speech becomes private speech. Would Maria be proud to see her sons internalize the messages heard in the schools and classrooms she visits? What kinds of mediation and scaffolding do teachers provide? Do teachers properly challenge students within their own zones of proximal development? Maria might observe whether schools offer collaborative learning activities in which less advanced students can learn from their more advanced peers. To decide when to enroll her son in kindergarten, Maria might be interested in finding out the local schools' philosophies on the issue of school readiness: Do they follow Piaget on the need for children to be ready for school? Or, as Vygotsky argued, do they see schools as responsible for mediating within each child's ZPD?

Finally, Maria can consider the newer sociocultural theories. Do schools teach and assess concepts within the context of important real-life situations? Do teachers guide students as they move from being "legitimate peripheral participants" to "central participants"? Do students have opportunities to work collaboratively on projects, creating shared cognitions?

CHAPTER SUMMARY

How does Piaget's theory of cognitive development reflect his background in biology and IQ testing?

Piaget was a young scholar in biology, producing his first scientific publication at the age of 10. In his teens he studied how sea mollusks adapt their shells to changes in water currents, and this image of adaptation formed the core of his theory of cognitive development. Piaget theorized that children create and adapt their own cognitive structures in response to their changing experiences with the world. When he worked in Binet's lab developing IQ tests, Piaget observed that young children's incorrect answers fell into patterns—they were not haphazard. Children of about the same age tended to give the same kinds of wrong answers. Piaget believed that this indicated that young children use a different logic than do older children and adults. His theory proposes four stages of cognitive development that represent changes in the forms of logic and thought children use as they mature.

Why is Piaget's theory considered a constructivist view? What are the main concepts in Piaget's theory about how children develop cognitive structures?

Piaget's is considered a constructivist view because he emphasized that children learn primarily by interpreting their environment and experiences in light of the knowledge and experiences they already have, thus constructing their own schemes and cognitive structures. Adaptation is the process through which children modify their schemes and cognitive structures. In adaptation new experiences are assimilated into existing schemes; if they do not fit adequately, cognitive disequilibrium results. Children can accommodate, or modify, their schemes to provide a better fit with the environment, restoring cognitive equilibrium. Organization is children's tendency to arrange cognitive structures into larger coherent systems. Reflective abstraction involves noticing and thinking about patterns and connections among schemes.

What are Piaget's stages of cognitive development, and what basic changes occur as children progress through these stages?

In the sensorimotor thought stage (birth to 2 years), infants begin by understanding the world through inborn reflexes and through their own direct sensory and motor actions. The ability to represent knowledge internally, in symbolic, mental form, develops gradually. In the preoperational thought stage (2 to 7 years), children can form internal mental representations, and they practice using symbols in their language, art, and play. Thought in this stage is intuitive, based more on personal observation than on objective logic. Egocentrism, animism, and artificialism are prominent features. Children fail conservation

problems because their cognitive schemes are not reversible (not "operational"), they center their thought on only one dimension of the problem, and they focus on the static endpoints of the problem. In the concrete operational stage (7 to 11 years), children can solve conservation problems: Schemes are reversible ("operational"), and children represent multiple dimensions of the problems and the dynamic transformations. Logic is more objective and allows the child to understand class inclusion and transitivity. Logic still requires tangible or concrete material or experience, however. In formal operations (12 years and above), adolescents learn hypothetico-deductive reasoning and abstract thought. They can work systematically through all possible solutions to complex problems. Adolescents maintain a form of adolescent egocentrism, reflected in the imaginary audience and the personal fable.

What are the main criticisms of Piaget's theory? What was Piaget's main contribution to child development?

The two major criticisms are that Piaget underestimated children's abilities, especially during infancy, and that there does not seem to be evidence for the unified stages he proposed. More recent research has demonstrated that infants can form mental representations and demonstrate object permanence at a much earlier age than Piaget predicted. Also, they often show performance indicative of several stages at once, as when a child passes the number conservation task but fails the liquid task. It seems that progress through the stages is not unified: It is not shown simultaneously across tasks and contexts. Still, Piaget left a tremendous legacy for child development. He emphasized the active, constructive nature of children's learning, and many of the cognitive developmental trends he observed have been verified by research. Egocentrism and intuitive thought decline with development as the use of objective logic and abstract thought emerge. Piaget's impact on educational practice, especially his emphasis on active learning processes, has been especially important.

What are the main ideas in Vygotsky's sociocultural view of cognitive development?

Vygotsky proposed that children learn primarily by adopting the cognitive structures embedded in the language and the larger culture around them. As adults and others speak, children adopt their social speech and transform it into their own private speech. Children then internalize their private speech to form internal thought structures. Adults and others mediate cognitive structures for children, often providing scaffolds or supports as children attempt more difficult tasks. The zone of proximal development represents those tasks that the child can perform with mediation or support from more skilled mentors.

What are the more recent sociocultural views stimulated by Vygotsky's theory?

The situated cognition view emphasizes that development involves adaptation to the contexts or situations that are prominent in each child's culture. We cannot properly understand or measure development without considering the situation. The guided participation view stresses how other social agents guide children from being peripheral participants to central participants in important cognitive activities. With socially shared cognition, two heads are better than one: Working together, children can construct more advanced cognitive products than when working alone. All of these views stress the importance of understanding the larger social context when considering children's cognitive development.

KEY TERMS

abstract thought (188)

accommodation (175)

adaptation (175)

adolescent egocentrism (188)

assimilation (175)

concrete operational thought (186)

conservation (185)

constructivist view (174)

equilibration (176)

formal operational thought (187)

guided participation (201)

hypothetico-deductive reasoning (187)

internalization (194)

intuitive thought (183)

mediation (194)

object permanence (180)

operations (186)

organization (175)

preoperational thought (181)

private speech (194)

reflective abstraction (176)

scaffolding (196)

scheme (174)

sensorimotor thought (178)

situated cognition (201)

social speech (194)

socially shared cognition (202)

symbolic (representational) thought (179)

zone of proximal development (ZPD) (195)

Chapter 6

Information Processing

The Development of Memory and Thought

CHAPTER PREVIEW

A PERSPECTIVE TO think ABOUT

"After getting an answer, Angelique writes it down but often forgets what the number refers to in the problem."

Manny is helping Angelique, his 8-year-old daughter, with her math homework. Angelique is having trouble solving the math story problems. Manny asks her to read each problem aloud so he can help her understand it better. Reading the problem takes several minutes because Angelique is not yet a skilled reader. And when she gets to the end of the problem, she seems to have little idea of what she should do next. When Manny asks her simple questions, Angelique seems confused and cannot remember what the problem is asking her to do. Even when Manny sets up the problem for her, Angelique has difficulty doing the computations. After getting an answer, Angelique writes it down but often forgets what the number refers to in the problem. Manny knows that his daughter is intelligent, but both he and Angelique are becoming frustrated. Why is she having such trouble with problems that seem so simple?

After studying this chapter, you should be able to identify several potential reasons for Angelique's difficulties with math story problems. As you work through this chapter, create a list of at least 12 principles of information-processing theory that might relate to Angelique's situation, and think about how Manny could use each concept to help Angelique improve.

As you read this chapter, look for the questions that ask you to think about what you're learning from Angelique's perspective.

A ngelique is struggling to memorize her math facts and to understand how to solve word problems, and her father is struggling to find better ways to help her. Nearly every day, we all find ourselves pushed to our cognitive limits. What strategies do we use to think through complicated problems? When we are overwhelmed with new information, how do we focus on the information that is most important? How can we improve our memory and avoid forgetting important information? As a college student, you are no doubt learning new ways to process and remember the information presented in your classes and textbooks. And although you have had many years to practice learning academic information, it can still be a struggle. Now think about young children. To them, the whole world is new and complex. Simple acts like tying their shoes, reading their first words, and learning basic facts about the world can be just as bewildering to them as physics or calculus might be to you. What kinds of thought processes and memory abilities do young children have? How do these processes change with development?

These are questions that we explore in this chapter. In Chapter 5 we described Piaget's stage theory of cognitive development and looked at some of the more recent views of how culture and social relations influence cognitive development. In this chapter we take a much more detailed look inside the mind of the individual child, using what cognitive psychologists refer to as the *information-processing approach.*

Information Processing and Cognitive Development

Jean Piaget's theory was the dominant view of cognitive development for several decades. As you read in Chapter 5, however, researchers in the 1960s and 1970s began to question some of Piaget's main assumptions, especially the idea that cognitive development proceeded through broad stages. At the same time, developments in computer and information technology offered developmental psychologists an alternative model—the idea that humans process information much the way a computer does. This information-processing view has shaped the majority of the research in cognitive development since the early 1970s.

As you study this section, ask yourself these questions:

- What is the information-processing approach, and what are its basic assumptions? How does the information-processing view differ from other views of cognitive development?

- What is processing capacity, and how does it change with age? How do changes in processing efficiency contribute to cognitive development?

- What is attention? How does it change with age?

What Is the Information-Processing Approach?

information-processing approach

A view of cognitive development that focuses on mental manipulation of symbols, processing capacity and efficiency, and knowledge base.

The **information-processing approach** is a view of cognitive development that focuses on the mental manipulation of coded information, or symbols. Information-processing psychologists have often used the computer as a metaphor for human thought, examining the way a computer stores, moves, and uses information. They have used this as a model to better understand human thinking.

Figure 6.1 compares information processing in computers and humans. Information enters the computer system and is coded so it can be understood by the computer's central

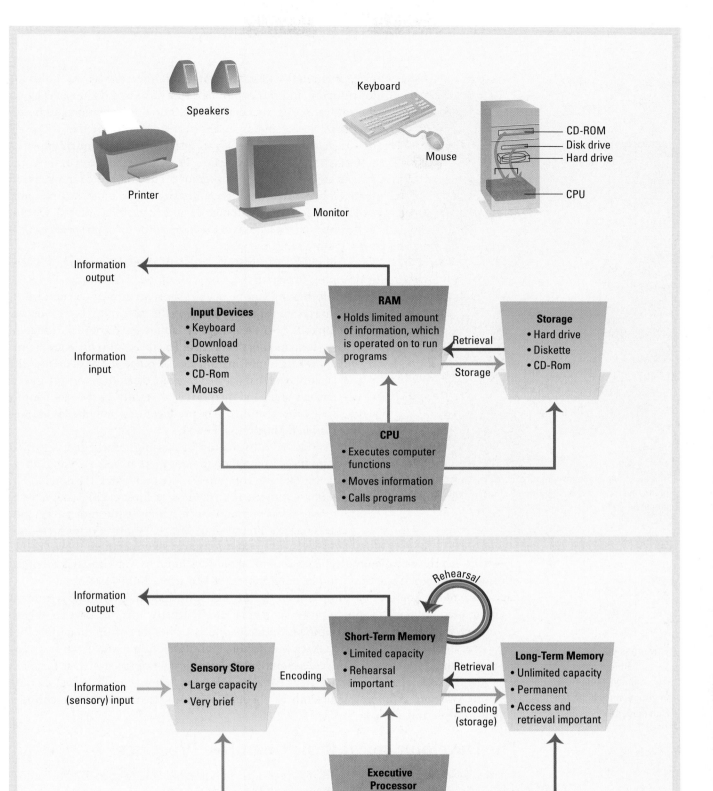

FIGURE 6.1 Information Processing in Computers and Humans

Many information-processing psychologists use the computer as a metaphor for human thinking. This figure shows information flow in a proto-typical computer (in the middle drawing). The bottom drawing depicts an information-processing model of human memory. Can you see the similarities between the computer's processing and that of humans?

Though some people have more processing capacity than others, everyone has a limit. Once the limit is reached, people begin to make errors or forget things.

processing unit (CPU). The computer's memory (RAM) holds the information and can transform it in various ways, depending on the software programs being used. Stored information can be accessed, retrieved, and used. The particular software that will work on the machine, how fast it can operate, and how much information can be processed at one time depend on the speed of the computer's CPU and size of its memory. The amount of information that can be stored depends on the size of the machine's memory and the capacity of any storage devices (e.g., disks or CDs). Output may simply be presented on the monitor or through speakers, or it may be stored in some way.

Similarly, information enters the human system and is encoded into a format that can be understood by the human CPU: the brain. Information can be held in short-term memory and transformed in various ways depending on the "software" (i.e., strategies) the person uses. Also, the person can access and retrieve information from long-term memory as needed. The speed and efficiency of processing, how much information can be processed at once, and the particular strategies that will be successful depend on various aspects of the person's brain and memory. The executive processor coordinates all activities. Output can be produced and presented in various ways, or it can be stored in memory.

Of course, information-processing psychologists would never claim that human thought *is* as mechanized, systematic, logical, and accurate as a computer's—we know that it is not. Nor do computers possess the full richness of human thinking. Clearly computers do not have emotional reactions to the information they are processing. Nor do they have internal motives or desires—not yet, anyway! Regardless of how explicitly we use the computer as a metaphor, however, the information-processing approach helps us think about how humans think and has extended our understanding of cognition and its development (Klahr, 1992; Kuhn, 1992).

One of the important assumptions of the information-processing view is that humans are limited in their capacity to process information. In other words, you can do only so much at once. The specific limit varies tremendously from one person to another, but everybody has one. Once we reach our personal limit, we begin to make errors or forget things. Much of cognitive development consists of developing strategies for making the most of our limited capacity. We develop strategies for learning, remembering, and using information as efficiently as possible so we can free up capacity to consider new information and new problems.

thinking
OF ANGELIQUE

How does the assumption ▶ of limited processing capacity help explain Angelique's difficulties with math story problems?

The Development of Basic Cognitive Processes

A basic fact of cognitive development is that older children are able to process more information and process it faster than younger children. Older children are also better at *attentional allocation*—focusing on some aspects of information and ignoring other aspects. Cognitive capacity, processing efficiency, and attentional allocation are involved in virtually every cognitive act. Let's take a closer look at how developmental changes in these basic processes lead to older children's superior cognitive performance.

■ **Changes in Processing Capacity.** **Processing capacity** is the amount of information a person can remember or think about at one time. Researchers often measure it by presenting

processing capacity

The amount of information a person can remember or think about at one time.

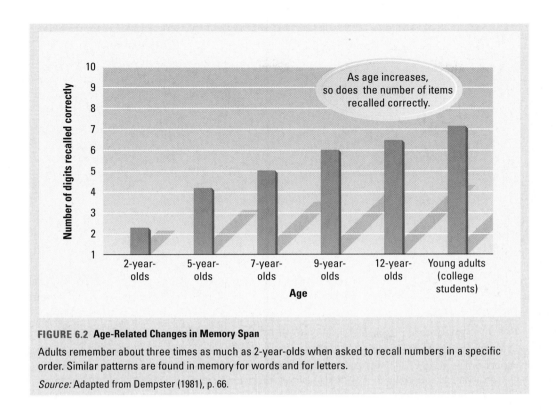

FIGURE 6.2 Age-Related Changes in Memory Span

Adults remember about three times as much as 2-year-olds when asked to recall numbers in a specific order. Similar patterns are found in memory for words and for letters.

Source: Adapted from Dempster (1981), p. 66.

a series of pieces of information very quickly and counting how many items a person can remember in exact order. As you can see in Figure 6.2, measures of processing capacity show consistent and regular increases from the age of 2 years to young adulthood (Case, 1985; Dempster, 1981).

Changes in processing capacity help explain age differences in performance on many kinds of cognitive tasks. For example, do you remember the Piagetian conservation problem we described in Chapter 5? When liquid is poured from a short beaker into a taller and skinnier one, young children often think that the taller one has more liquid. Piaget claimed that younger children center their thinking on only one aspect of the problem (the height of the liquid) but fail to consider the other element (the width of the beakers). Piaget believed that this was part of the child's inability to understand the logical structure of conservation. However, it is also possible that younger children's processing capacity may be too limited to allow them to work with both height and width at the same time. Perhaps younger children can switch their attention back and forth from one dimension to another, but cannot consider all the dimensions at once. As children mature and their capacity grows, they gain the ability to consider several sources of information at the same time, and their cognitive processing therefore becomes more flexible and powerful.

■ **Changes in Processing Efficiency.**   Does processing capacity actually increase with development, or do older children simply learn to use the capacity they have more effectively? Some theorists believe that overall capacity does not really change across age and that, instead, there are changes in **processing efficiency**—the speed and accuracy with which children can process information (Case, 1985; Case, Kurland, & Goldberg, 1982; Demetriou, Christou, Spanoudis, & Platsidou, 2002). Remember that key assumption of the information-processing view: that there is a limited amount of capacity available at any given time. Part of this capacity is believed to be devoted to *operating space,* where the actual manipulation of

processing efficiency
The speed and accuracy with which a person can process information.

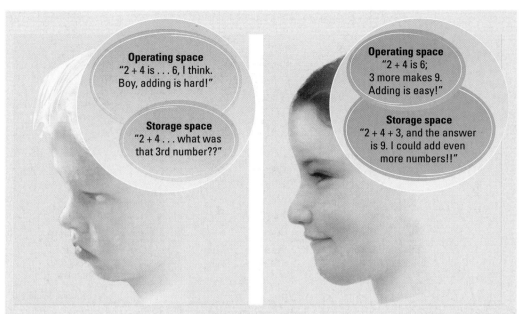

FIGURE 6.3 Storage Space and Operating Space in Working Memory

What is 2 + 4 + 3? Younger children have difficulty with such questions, because they need to use most of their processing capacity to figure out how to add the first two numbers; the capacity left available for storing and remembering other information is minimal. Adding is easy for older children, so more of their capacity is available for storage and other processes.

Source: Based on Bjorklund (1995).

information takes place. The rest is *storage space,* a place for storing and remembering the information we are working with. As shown in Figure 6.3, as children become faster at processing information, they use less of their limited operating space. This frees some of the operating space for other things, like storage of more information. The result is that the older child can remember more information. A child can also use the leftover operating space to do different kinds of processing, such as considering several aspects of a problem simultaneously, relating the current information to other information, and the like.

The automaticity of cognitive skills is important for increasing processing efficiency (Hasher & Zachs, 1979). **Automaticity** is the ability to perform a skill with little or no conscious effort. This frees up more cognitive capacity for other tasks. For example, think about children who are learning to read. At first, the process is very laborious; children recognize individual letters and attempt to combine their sounds to decode words. With practice, their recognition of letters, sounds, and common letter combinations becomes very fast and requires little conscious effort—it has become automatic. Cognitive capacity is now available for other tasks, such as reading with appropriate expression, monitoring comprehension, or wondering what will happen next. Eventually some of these higher-level processes also become more automatic. This allows children to consider additional dimensions as they read, such as comparing and contrasting the current text with others they have read. In this way, automaticity of cognitive skills enables children to move to more sophisticated and complex ways of thinking—it is one of the mechanisms that fosters cognitive development.

Research indicates that increases in processing efficiency depend on extensive experience with specific kinds of information—for example, you cannot develop automaticity in reading unless you read a great deal. In other words, increases in processing efficiency are

thinking
OF ANGELIQUE

How would greater automaticity in reading or in basic math facts help Angelique solve story problems more effectively?

automaticity

The ability to carry out a process with little or no conscious effort, leaving more cognitive capacity to carry out other tasks.

As skills become more automatic, they require less processing capacity. This enables the person to do other things at the same time.

domain-specific and require many hours of practice with specific materials. This research finding conflicts with the idea of age-related increases in overall processing capacity. Age-related overall changes are usually thought of as being **domain-general;** that is, due to general maturation, rather than dependent on experience with specific materials. This argument about domain-general versus domain-specific cognitive development should sound familiar. It is the same one that confronted Piaget's theory, and the accumulation of data demonstrating domain-specificity is what caused many researchers to turn away from Piaget's grand stage theory in the first place. The debate is still not settled. Although much evidence supports the domain-specificity of processing efficiency (Bjorklund, 1987; Kee, 1994), other research shows interesting commonalities across domains. For example, patterns of age differences in processing speed are similar across such different tasks as simple response time, name retrieval, and mental addition, as you can see in Figure 6.4. These commonalities may indicate that there is a domain-general component to changes in processing speed (Catts, Gillispie, Leonard, Kail, & Miller, 2002; Kail, 1988, 1991; Kail & Salthouse, 1994).

What might cause the increases in processing speed that have been found across tasks? One likely possibility is the myelination (growth of the fatty covering) of neurons in the brain. As you read in Chapter 4, sensory and motor areas of the brain are myelinated by early childhood, but myelination of other areas of the brain continues into adolescence or later. This increasing brain maturation may be one factor that contributes to domain-general increases in processing speed (Bjorklund & Harnishfeger, 1990; Kail & Salthouse, 1994).

■ **Changes in Attention.**   **Attention** is the ability to focus on a particular stimulus without becoming distracted by other stimuli. Even very young babies show attention ability, as when newborns look at their mothers' faces while being cuddled. Young infants also show systematic patterns of looking at objects. As you may recall from Chapter 4, younger infants look at the edges of objects and at curved lines; areas of greater contrast, such as the hairline on a person's face, also attract their attention (Haith, 1980). But several aspects of attention improve dramatically across age. Notable among these are children's abilities to sustain attention, to attend selectively, and to use attentional strategies.

As they grow older, children become better at *sustaining their attention,* or keeping focused on a specific stimulus. One important reason for this is their increasing ability to *inhibit* responses to irrelevant stimuli. Such distractions may come from either external sources (e.g., noise outside your window as you try to read) or internal sources (e.g., that silly advertising jingle that keeps playing in your head as you try to take an exam) (Dempster,

domain-specific

Relevant or true for only one topic or task. Domain-specific skills and knowledge develop through extensive practice with a particular task or topic and affect performance on only that task or topic.

domain-general

Relevant or true for a wide range of tasks or topics. Domain-general skills and knowledge develop through maturation and affect performance on many tasks and topics.

attention

The ability to focus on a particular stimulus without becoming distracted by other stimuli.

FIGURE 6.4 Patterns of Age Differences in Processing Speeds for Different Tasks

Processing speed increases at a similar rate across a variety of tasks, suggesting that some aspects of processing efficiency are domain-general. Increasing myelination of neurons in the brain may explain these similar patterns.

Source: Adapted with permission from R. Kail. (1991). Processing time declines exponentially during childhood and adolescence. *Developmental Psychology, 27,* p. 265.

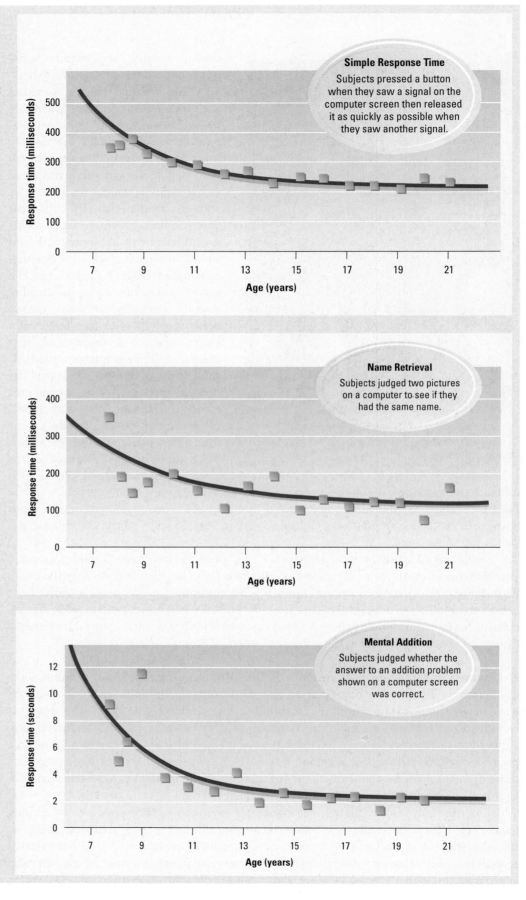

Simple Response Time
Subjects pressed a button when they saw a signal on the computer screen then released it as quickly as possible when they saw another signal.

Name Retrieval
Subjects judged two pictures on a computer to see if they had the same name.

Mental Addition
Subjects judged whether the answer to an addition problem shown on a computer screen was correct.

1992; Harnishfeger, 1995). It is easy to see why the ability to inhibit initial responses is important. How many times have you jumped to a wrong conclusion before you had all the relevant facts? Or have you ever impulsively blurted out a comment only to realize later that you were wrong? Older children are more able to refrain from responding immediately, which enables them to gather additional information, see relationships among information, and offer more thoughtful and appropriate responses. Brain maturation, particularly development of the frontal lobe, plays an important role in this ability to inhibit responses. As you learned in Chapter 4, the frontal lobes develop rapidly during the first year of life and again between ages 3 and 6. The ability to delay or completely inhibit responses increases markedly during these same two time periods (Bell & Fox, 1992; Diamond, 1991; Harnishfeger & Bjorklund, 1994). And research with both animals and humans shows that frontal lobe damage reduces the ability to inhibit responses, even if only a 1- or 2-second delay in responding is required (Fuster, 1989; Goldman-Rakic, 1987).

Another aspect of attention that develops with age is *attentional selectivity*—the ability to pick out the correct stimulus to focus on. Young children are able to attend selectively to some degree. When researchers show 4-year-olds toys and say they will ask them to remember some specific toys later, the children keep their attention focused by saying the names of the toys to be remembered more often than those of the other toys (Baker-Ward, Ornstein, & Holden, 1984). However, selectivity clearly improves as children grow. In one study, researchers told children aged 3 to 8 to remember a subset of items, either toy animals or household objects. All the items were in boxes marked with a picture of either a cage (for the animals) or a house (for the household items). The youngest children were not at all selective, opening all of the boxes regardless of which type of item they were supposed to remember. Older children looked more often in the relevant boxes, although they still spent some time looking in boxes marked with the item type they did not have to remember. The oldest children looked only in the relevant boxes, indicating they were selectively attending to the information they had been asked to remember (DeMarie-Dreblow & Miller, 1988; Miller & Seier, 1994).

One of the most striking changes that occurs with age is children's increasing use of *attentional strategies* to efficiently control and direct their attention. For example, one attentional strategy is to ask yourself periodically if your current thoughts and behaviors are relevant for the task you are supposed to be working on (e.g., is singing along with the radio helping you read the assigned chapter in your child development textbook?). A person can employ several attentional strategies at once; for example, you might try removing distractions (e.g., turning off the radio) and involving yourself more fully in the task at hand (e.g., taking notes on the chapter). Effective use of attentional strategies helps children sustain their attention to selected stimuli. This, in turn, increases the likelihood of more in-depth processing of the selected objects. It also decreases the likelihood that the child will be distracted by irrelevant stimuli. With age, children learn new attentional strategies and become more efficient in applying them. For example, researchers asked young children to compare two dollhouses. The youngest children looked haphazardly from one dollhouse to the other; they compared parts from one house to different parts of the other, and they checked some parts several times but did not check other parts at all. Older children were more efficient and complete, systematically comparing each part of one house to the corresponding part of the other until they had checked them all (Vurpillot, 1968).

Some children find it very difficult to sustain and direct their attention, particularly when they have to inhibit or delay their initial responses. These difficulties can create problems in social interactions and interfere with academic progress. The inability to control attention is a central characteristic in the syndrome called attention-deficit/hyperactivity disorder (ADHD). To learn more about the effects of this disorder, read the Personal Perspective box, "Meet a Child with Attention-Deficit/Hyperactivity Disorder."

YOUR PERSPECTIVE

NOTES

Have you ever been almost asleep when you gradually became aware of the incessant dripping of a leaky faucet? No matter how hard you try to focus on something else, the sound still gets through. What other instances of impaired selective attention have you experienced?

thinking OF ANGELIQUE

◄ How can Manny help Angelique learn to direct her attention more effectively when solving story problems?

Meet a Child with Attention-Deficit/Hyperactivity Disorder

Annie and Tina Gordon
Bristol, Connecticut
A 6-year-old child with ADHD and her mother

Which of the common characteristics of ADHD does Annie tend to show?

Annie is easily distracted and can be impulsive in a group situation, blurting out her thoughts instead of waiting. She has trouble focusing when she is bored, and sometimes she has trouble remaining seated. When Annie was about 4 years old, we noticed she had difficulty speaking complete sentences and pronouncing some word sounds. We had her evaluated by a speech therapist, then by a developmental psychologist who diagnosed her with ADHD.

Is Annie able to sustain her attention for reasonable lengths of time?

When Annie was younger she would go from object to object, not focusing on anything in particular unless it involved something she liked. She had a hard time maintaining a conversation with people and was easily distracted by irrelevant things. For example, if we were outside talking and a butterfly flew by, she might stop talking and try to follow the butterfly, then ask later if we finished our conversation. Annie's ability to focus has improved. She can focus on schoolwork, partly because speech therapy has helped her become a better listener.

How does Annie's ADHD affect your home life?

Annie can get impulsive and interrupt conversations, and her voice volume is loud. We have to remind her to wait to speak and to lower her volume. We don't have her wait too long, because she forgets what she wanted to tell us and it can be quite frustrating for her. She tends to scatter toys around the house, but she's improving on this. She can scatter toys in her bedroom, and then something distracts her to another room, or she forgets what she was doing in her bedroom and pulls more toys out. Sometimes she cannot accept a change in a routine at home, which can be hard on the family.

What interventions have helped Annie?

Speech therapy has been very helpful. This has focused not only on word sounds, but also on understanding and following auditory directions. Behavioral cueing (giving a brief 'signal' to remind her what to do) has also really helped. Annie relies heavily on her visual memory to stay on task, answer questions, read, and write. In kindergarten teachers used a variety of visual materials to help her stay focused. For example, the teacher would put up pictures of the day's activities associated with words. Annie would look at the pictures and words to determine what was going to happen that day. ■

thinking
OF ANGELIQUE

◀ How do Angelique's difficulties compare to Annie's? Could any of the techniques that Annie's mom uses also help Angelique?

LET'S REVIEW . . .

1. According to the information-processing view, humans' ability to process information is:
   a. limited.   c. limited only by their processing speed.
   b. unlimited.   d. limited only by the size of their long-term memory.

2. The term *processing capacity* refers to:
   a. the child's ability to understand math concepts.
   b. the amount of space a child has for storing information from the past.
   c. the amount of information a child can process at one time.
   d. the number of items that a child forgets in a given problem.

3. Which of the following does *not* explain how processing efficiency improves during childhood?

   a. The automaticity of cognitive skills increases with age.

   b. Attentional selectivity decreases with age.

   c. Knowledge and skills within specific domains increase with age.

   d. Myelination of the neurons in the brain increases with age.

4. Compared to the attentional strategies of older children, young children's strategies are:

   a. faster.   c. less systematic.

   b. slower.   d. more flexible.

5. **True or False:** Processing capacity increases with age, but processing efficiency remains the same.

6. **True or False:** Researchers believe that children's processing speed increases as neurons in the brain become myelinated.

Answers: 1. a, 2. c, 3. b, 4. c, 5. F, 6. T

Memory Development

The development of memory is one of the most studied topics in the information-processing literature. No matter what your capacity is for processing new information, and no matter how efficiently you focus your attention, it will do you very little good if you can't store the information and then remember it later. In this section we review many of the most important research studies regarding the development of memory.

As you study this section, ask yourself these questions:

- What are the differences between the stores model and network models of memory?

- What are the characteristics of working memory and long-term memory? What develops in each?

- What are some of the issues in memory development, and why is each important for cognitive development?

Two Models of Memory: Stores and Networks

For decades, variations of the **stores model** of memory guided research on memory development (Atkinson & Shiffrin, 1968). The stores model is the one you saw in the bottom part of Figure 6.1. This model views information as moving through a series of storage locations. Information enters the cognitive system through the *sensory store*, where large amounts of information can be maintained in their original modalities (e.g., visual, verbal, acoustic) for very brief periods of time (approximately half a second). Some of the information in the sensory store is selected and passed along to the *short-term store (STS)*. The STS contains the information that you are consciously aware of at the moment, and its capacity is very limited. It can hold only about five to nine "chunks" of information (Miller, 1956). The size of one chunk can vary tremendously, however. For a young child learning the ABCs, a chunk might consist of a single letter; for an experienced reader, a chunk could be a whole section of text. Information can be maintained in the STS for long periods of time if we actively attend to it, but it will fade and disappear within seconds if we do not. To be stored more permanently, information must be passed along to the *long-term store (LTS)*. The LTS has an infinite storage capacity, and information remains there permanently even when we are not actively attending to it. To see the difference

stores model (of memory)

A model of human memory that views information as moving through a series of storage locations, from the sensory stores to short-term store to long-term store.

between the STS and LTS, notice what happens when you answer this simple question: What is your last name? If you are thinking about your last name and saying it to yourself, then it is now in your STS. But before you saw the question, you probably were not thinking about your last name. Where was your name stored then? In your LTS, the place where we can store information that we are not consciously thinking about right now but might want to use again later. According to the stores model, an *executive processor* controls all three stores and the processes that pass information among them. This processor determines which information will be attended to, and it governs the management of the system's limited capacity from moment to moment.

In recent years, **network models** of memory have largely replaced the stores model. There are several variations of network models, but in general they view memory as an interconnected network of associated information rather than as a series of separate mental storage boxes. Network models consist of *concept nodes* connected by *links*. The links vary in strength, with more heavily weighted links indicating a greater degree of association between the nodes. Rather than thinking of information as moving from STS into LTS, network theorists emphasize that information can be *activated* to different degrees at any point in time. A higher level of activation means that the information is easier to remember. For example, your own name usually has a much higher level of activation than the names of acquaintances. If someone asks your name, you are able to remember and answer much more quickly than if someone asks the name of an acquaintance.

Our son Andy is a skateboarder. Figure 6.5 shows his memory network for topics related to skateboarding. Anytime he thinks about skateboarding, he quickly remembers his local skatepark, all of his skateboarding friends, and the ramps at the park. Trace the nodes of his network to see how the links are connected.

Nodes can be activated from either external sources (e.g., seeing an object in the environment) or internal sources (e.g., thinking about an object). Once started, the activation spreads along the connecting links like ripples on the surface of a pond, increasing the degree of activation of the nodes. The farther the activation travels from the original source, the weaker it becomes, until eventually it dies away. As a child grows, much development takes place in the memory network. The numbers of concept nodes and links increase, and the strengths of links change over time.

Working Memory

In the network model, the term **working memory** (WM) refers to the information that is currently active in the memory system and available for use in any mental task. From this "pool" of activated pieces of knowledge, a person focuses on some pieces for more detailed processing, but all of the activated information is considered to be in working memory (Cowan, 1995, 1997). Working memory is similar to STS in the stores model—both consist of information that a person is consciously processing at the time. But working memory differs from STS in that information is not thought of as being moved from one storage place to another. It is simply made available, as information in a book is made available when you open the book. Another difference between STS and WM is that WM has several distinct components. One component is centrally involved in processing verbal information, another in processing auditory information, and others in allocation and monitoring of cognitive resources as well as rehearsal and temporary storage of information (Baddeley, 1986; Baylis, Jarrold, Gunn, & Baddeley, 2003; Hamilton, Coates, & Herrernan, 2003; Handley, Capon, Copp, & Harper, 2002).

Like STS, working memory has two important characteristics. It is limited in its capacity, and the information in working memory decays over time. In other words, only a certain amount of information can be activated at any given time. If the activation is not maintained in some way, it decays and the piece of information is no longer readily available for use in mental tasks. This information may be permanently lost, or it may simply take more effort to activate it again. As

network models (of memory)
Models of human memory that view memory as an interconnected network of concept nodes connected by links of varying strength.

working memory
The information currently active in your memory system and currently available for use in a mental task.

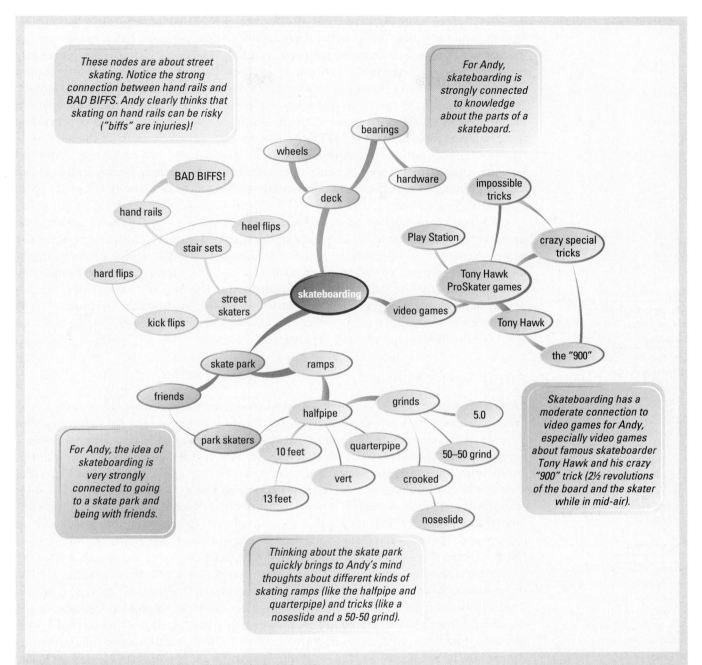

These nodes are about street skating. Notice the strong connection between hand rails and BAD BIFFS. Andy clearly thinks that skating on hand rails can be risky ("biffs" are injuries)!

For Andy, skateboarding is strongly connected to knowledge about the parts of a skateboard.

bearings

wheels

BAD BIFFS!

hand rails

hardware

impossible tricks

heel flips

deck

Play Station

crazy special tricks

stair sets

hard flips

Tony Hawk ProSkater games

kick flips

street skaters

skateboarding

video games

Tony Hawk

the "900"

skate park

ramps

Skateboarding has a moderate connection to video games for Andy, especially video games about famous skateboarder Tony Hawk and his crazy "900" trick (2½ revolutions of the board and the skater while in mid-air).

friends

grinds

5.0

halfpipe

quarterpipe

50–50 grind

For Andy, the idea of skateboarding is very strongly connected to going to a skate park and being with friends.

park skaters

10 feet

vert

crooked

13 feet

noseslide

Thinking about the skate park quickly brings to Andy's mind thoughts about different kinds of skating ramps (like the halfpipe and quarterpipe) and tricks (like a noseslide and a 50-50 grind).

FIGURE 6.5 A Partial Network for "Skateboarding" by Andy, Age 12.

Network models of memory view memory as an interconnected network, with information stored as concept nodes connected by links. In this figure, thicker lines indicate knowledge that is strongly connected; thinner lines indicate weaker connections.

with STS, the amount of information that can be activated in working memory ranges from five to nine chunks of information. The length of time that information can remain activated is short, estimated at approximately 30 seconds, *unless* we do something to keep the information active. For example, we can rehearse the information we are trying to remember or relate it to other pieces of information that are active in working memory. Such strategies help keep the information activated and therefore available in working memory for longer periods of time.

As you learned in our discussion of basic processes, it isn't clear whether the actual capacity of working memory increases with age or whether children simply learn to use their limited capacities more effectively. But you can probably see that the way a child allocates attention has an important effect on working memory. Consciously attending to information maintains activation and keeps the information readily available, which makes it more likely to be permanently stored in the network. In addition, keeping more pieces of information active increases a child's ability to consider several items at the same time. Think back to the example of learning to read. If a child keeps the letters of a word active in working memory (e.g., *c–a–t*), she can begin to chunk them into one word (*cat*). Because she is now processing these letters as one chunk, she can keep other letters and words active at the same time (*cat–in–the–hat*). As these chunk sizes increase, she can activate and process other information about these chunks: She can notice similarities in word structure; she can realize that *cat* and *hat* rhyme; and she can even use some of her working memory capacity to look for other words that might rhyme.

As you might expect, working memory affects practically every cognitive task children undertake. If children could not keep information activated and accessible, they could not use the information to solve problems, answer test questions, or anything else. It is not surprising that scores on tests of short-term and working memory correlate with scores on many other cognitive abilities, including language, intelligence, reading ability, and comprehension ability. In all cases, the better a child's short-term or working memory performance, the higher the child's cognitive ability scores (Cantor, Engle, & Hamilton, 1991; Farmer & Klein, 1995; Gillam, Cowan, & Day, 1995; Montgomery, 1995).

Long-Term Memory

Long-term memory is just that—memory of knowledge or events that endures over a relatively long time period. As you saw in Figure 6.1, the stores model of memory views long-term memory as a separate store. In contrast, network models (Figure 6.5) view long-term memory as the nonactivated part of an integrated memory network. But regardless of how different theorists view the structure of long-term memory, they agree on several fundamental characteristics. First, long-term memory is permanent. Once information is stored in long-term memory, it never decays—it is never truly forgotten. Second, long-term memory is unlimited in its capacity. This means that theoretically you can store an infinite amount of information. This does not mean, however, that you can always remember the information you want, even when you make concentrated efforts to do so. Trying to remember all of the definitions studied in yesterday's class is a prime example for most college students.

Although long-term memory does not suffer from difficulties with decay of information or lack of storage space as working memory does, there can be problems with the initial **encoding** or **storage** of information (i.e., putting it into the LTS or into the network), with **accessing** stored information (i.e., finding the right information at the desired time), and with **retrieval** of stored information (i.e., activating it so that it can become part of working memory or STS and thus available for use). For example, when walking down the sidewalk, do you ever see someone you know but find yourself unable to remember the person's name? The problem may be that you never encoded the person's name; this means you will never be able to remember it, because the name never entered your memory network. Or perhaps you encoded it incorrectly, so you might call the person "Helen" when her name is really "Ellen." Maybe you encoded the name correctly but cannot access it at the moment. We often recognize a person's face (and "know" that we know the person) but fail to access or retrieve the person's names. Finally, you may be able to access the name, but the cues may not be adequate to allow you actually to retrieve it (or, in network model terms, fully activate it). As you might guess, it can be especially difficult to tell whether a memory problem is due to an access or a retrieval problem—access and retrieval tend to be associated, but

long-term memory

Memory of knowledge or events that is permanent.

encoding

The process of placing information in permanent, or long-term, memory. Also called *storage*.

storage

Placing information in permanent, or long-term, memory. Also called *encoding*.

accessing

The process of finding information in memory at the desired time.

retrieval

In the stores model, the process of bringing information from the long-term store to the short-term store. In network models, the process of activating information so that it becomes a part of working memory and thus available for use.

thinking OF ANGELIQUE

How can Angelique's links between basic math facts and their correct answers be strengthened? ▶

they are not the same thing. If you've ever experienced the "tip-of-the-tongue" phenomenon, in which you know for sure that you know something but you just can't remember it at the moment, you've experienced access but an inability to retrieve.

What develops in long-term memory? Clearly, the amount of knowledge in long-term memory grows tremendously with age—older children simply have stored more information. In addition, the organization of the stored information changes with development. Information becomes more interconnected as children understand the relations between concepts. Older children have more connections between stored concepts, and they add different types of links between concepts. For example, Figure 6.6 shows how a child may initially connect an animal such as a dog with its network attributes, in effect representing the things a dog "has" (fur, four legs, a certain color, etc.). Eventually the child will add different kinds of links to this understanding of dogs, such as links that identify the different categories a dog belongs to and represent what a dog "is" (an animal, warm-blooded, etc.). The strengths of associations between concepts also change with development. Some connections become stronger—such as the link between "mammal" and "platypus" when a child learns that a platypus is a mammal. Others become weaker—such as the link between "mammal" and "turtle." Changes in the number, types, and strengths of interconnections of stored information are the things that create change in the organization of long-term memory.

For many years, much of the research on long-term memory concerned *semantic memory*, or knowledge of words and concepts. Children clearly develop semantic memory networks, but their earliest memories seem to be of a different type. *Episodic memory* is memory for events, or episodes, that one experiences in day-to-day life (Tulving, 1972). Some researchers have suggested that children's memories are primarily memories of events and that these episodic memories are organized into **scripts,** mental representations of the

YOUR
PERSPECTIVE
~~PERSPECTIVE~~
NOTES

Have you ever had a "tip-of-the-tongue" experience? How did you finally remember the information? Think of other examples of problems with encoding, access, or retrieval. How would the stores model and the network models explain these problems?

scripts

Mental representations of the way things typically occur in certain settings or for certain events.

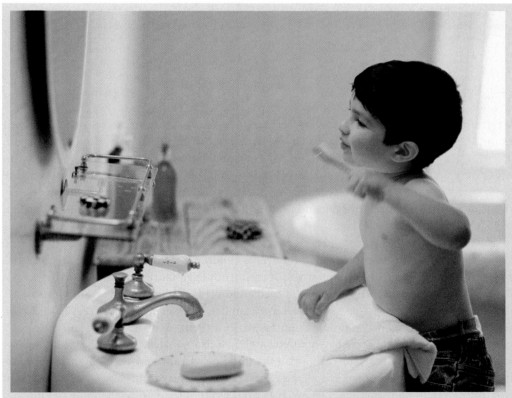

Scripts are formed for events that are encountered repeatedly, like getting ready for bed.

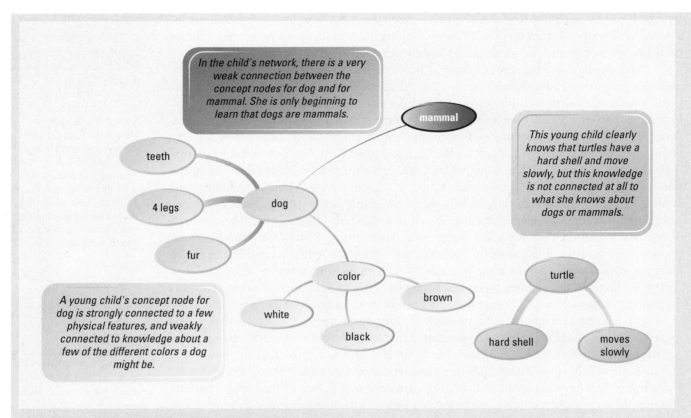

FIGURE 6.6 Developmental Changes in a Long-Term Memory Network

A young child's initial network for the concept of "dog" is shown above; a more elaborated network for "dog" (shown on the facing page) develops as the child learns and grows. Thicker lines indicate stronger connections; thinner lines indicate weaker connections.

way things typically occur in certain settings or for certain events (Nelson, 1986). For example, many children in this country have a script for going to a fast-food restaurant. They know that you go to a counter and tell a person what you want to eat, but that you can order only the foods listed on big signs behind the counter; that you pay for the food before you get it, not after you're done eating; that you take your food to a table and throw everything away when you are finished; and that sometimes there is a playground where you can have fun.

Scripts reflect real-world events, and they indicate what usually happens for a given type of event. They form most readily for events children encounter repeatedly, such as getting ready for bed, going to visit relatives, or eating out in restaurants. Children's first scripts contain only the most central events, and even children as young as one year of age show evidence of scripts (Bauer & Dow, 1994; Bauer & Mandler, 1992; Fivush, Kuebli, & Clubb, 1992). As children grow, they need fewer encounters with an event to form a script, and the scripts become more detailed (Farrar & Goodman, 1992; Hudson, Fivush, & Kuebli, 1992). For example, a 2-year-old's script for eating in a fast-food restaurant may include only the information that first you order your food, then you play on the playground. A 7-year-old's script will likely contain many more details, such as what kinds of food are available, how loud and rowdy you can be, and the fact that food must be paid for before you eat. By organizing knowl-

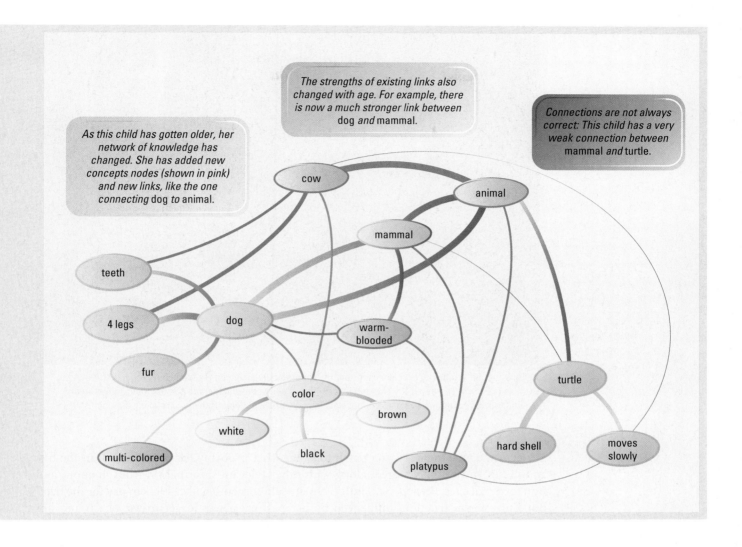

As this child has gotten older, her network of knowledge has changed. She has added new concepts nodes (shown in pink) and new links, like the one connecting dog to animal.

The strengths of existing links also changed with age. For example, there is now a much stronger link between dog and mammal.

Connections are not always correct: This child has a very weak connection between mammal and turtle.

edge, scripts help children predict what will happen next and help them remember events that take place (Hudson & Nelson, 1983; Hudson, Shapiro, & Sosa, 1995).

Issues in Memory Development

■ **Reconstructive Memory.** On an episode of a popular reality television show, two former friends were appearing in small-claims court. One friend (we'll call her Kim) had purchased some expensive airline tickets for a beach vacation. She claimed that her friend "Samantha" had promised to reimburse her for one of the tickets. Kim's mother caught the girls and would not allow them to go (the girls were only 15!), but the tickets could not be returned for a refund. Samantha denied having promised to pay for her ticket, saying that she had stated only that she would help pay for the trip. Because the trip did not take place, Samantha felt she was under no obligation to pay for anything.

Do you think of memory as a mental copy of information and events? Many people do. The story of Kim and Samantha, however, clearly illustrates that memory is anything but a "mental copy." Instead, memory is *reconstructive*. This means that memory stores only some aspects of events and some pieces of knowledge—and when you try to recall the information or event, you retrieve these pieces and then infer the rest. In other words,

Have you and a friend or sibling ever experienced the same event, only to have very different memories of what happened? Explain how this illustrates reconstructive memory.

Reconstruction in memory is vitally important for understanding eyewitness testimony, especially when the witness is a child. The accuracy and detail of children's eyewitness testimony can be good if children are questioned soon after the event in a nonmisleading way and in a comfortable and relaxing atmosphere.

in **reconstructive memory** you patch together what probably happened based on the bits and pieces you actually stored, along with other relevant information from memory and from external cues. Perhaps Samantha actually said something like "I'll help pay for the trip." But Kim's reconstruction, influenced by her past eagerness to get to the beach and her present need to recover some of her lost money, was more like "She said she'd pay for her ticket." Our memory for experiences and knowledge draws on previous knowledge, memories, and the current context, sometimes changed in subtle ways but sometimes altered substantially.

Numerous studies have confirmed that memory can be significantly affected by what people already know, as well as by the way they are asked to recall it. For example, people give very different answers to a question phrased as "How fast was the car going when it crashed into the house?" as opposed to "Can you estimate the car's speed at the time of the accident?" Also—and especially with children—prompted recall, which uses questions like either of the two above, produces more detailed *but more incorrect* recall than unprompted recall (e.g., responses to "Tell me all you can remember about the event") (Ceci & Bruck, 1998; Loftus & Ketcham, 1994).

Why does it matter whether memory is literal or reconstructed? Sometimes it doesn't. It doesn't matter whether you can remember the dialogue from a television show word for word or only the gist of the story. Other times, however, the difference is crucial. For example, read the Social Policy Perspective box, "Children's Eyewitness Testimony."

■ **Infantile Amnesia.**   Most researchers agree that once information reaches long-term memory, it is permanent. It is also clear that even young infants are able to recognize objects and people and can make associations between stimuli (Rovee-Collier & Gerhardstein, 1997). So why is it that most people have no memories of their experiences prior to the age of

What is the earliest memory that you have? Why do you think you cannot remember things that happened when you were 1 or 2 years old?

reconstructive memory

A characteristic pattern in human memory. We store parts of events and knowledge; during recall we retrieve the stored pieces and draw inferences about the rest.

A Social Policy PERSPECTIVE...

Children's Eyewitness Testimony
The Truth, the Whole Truth, and Nothing but the Truth?

In the winter of 1989, a co-owner of the Little Rascals Day Care Center in North Carolina was accused of sexually abusing a child at the school. The following months and years saw a flurry of similar accusations. Few children made accusations early on, but after repeated questioning by parents and police and months of therapy, dozens of children did so. Seven adults were arrested. Juries found two adults guilty at trial, and two pled no contest to the charges. But appeals courts later reversed the convictions, and the prosecutors eventually dropped all charges (Ceci & Bruck, 1998).

Courts are calling on children in ever increasing numbers to provide testimony in legal cases. Often the cases involve serious crimes such as child abuse or homicide. Can children as young as 4 provide reliable and valid information under such circumstances? Are they able to tell the truth, the whole truth, and nothing but the truth? What are the effects of repeated questioning by therapists, police, or lawyers on children's memories?

Growing research literature is looking at these questions. Even preschoolers are *capable* of reporting information accurately, though often they recall less detail than older children and adults and forget more as time passes. Repeated questioning does increase the amount both children and adults recall, but unfortunately the additional information is not necessarily accurate. Preschool children also have difficulty remembering the sources of details, so they are more likely than adults to think that things they were told about or even imagined actually happened to them. And younger children's memories can be affected by the way questions are phrased, the status and attitude of the person asking the questions, and other details of the interview context. If a question is misleading, younger children are more likely to change their answers to include the misleading information. They may even expand on it "in highly productive ways to reconstruct and at times distort reality" (Bruck, Ceci, Francoeur, & Barr, 1995; Ceci & Bruck, 1998, pg. 738; Roebers, 2002; Schneider & Bjorklund, 1998). The false information can be integrated into children's memory and can be repeated as truth in later interviews (Brainerd, Reyna, & Brandes, 1995). In other words, the inaccurate information can essentially *become* the truth for children. And just as important is that experts often cannot tell for certain whether a child is reporting actual or imagined events (Leichtman & Ceci, 1995).

The news is not all bad, however. When questions are asked in a nonmisleading way and in a non-frightening and nondemanding atmosphere, and when children have permission to acknowledge when they do not know the answer, the accuracy and details of children's eyewitness reports can be good (Ceci & Bruck, 1998). Using props during questioning has had mixed results, but asking children to think more deeply by doing things such as drawing pictures can help children remember (Bruck & Ceci, 1999; Butler, Gross, & Hayne, 1995; Steward & Steward, 1996).

If you were a social worker, prosecutor, jury member, or judge in a child sexual abuse case, how would you proceed? What safeguards would you put into place to promote accuracy in children's testimony, and what details of the questioning and therapy processes would you want to know? ■

---

about 3 years? This lack of memory for very early experiences is called **infantile amnesia** and is a consistent finding in the developmental literature. Explaining why infantile amnesia occurs, however, is difficult. It is not due simply to time: People are capable of remembering information for many years. And infants are capable of forming long-term memories—numerous studies have shown that infants can remember events for several weeks even years if they're given specific cues (Myers, Perris, & Speaker, 1994; Rovee-Collier, 1990; Wang, 2003). But people typically do not remember early events on their own, and certainly not easily.

There are several possible explanations for infantile amnesia. Notice that these ideas differ in what they propose as the basis for the problem. The first explanation involves the kinds of memories that an infant is capable of forming (an encoding deficit). The second

infantile amnesia

Inability to recall experiences prior to the age of about 3 years.

involves how knowledge is organized as it is stored (a storage deficit). And the last two focus on how well retrieval cues activate memories stored during infancy (a retrieval deficit).

▶ *Brain maturation* may play a role. As we've noted before, the frontal lobes of the brain show development throughout childhood. The level of development during infancy may support the formation of memories based on motor activities but not verbal stimuli, which means that infants may remember actions but not be able to recall and describe these memories in words later on (Boyer & Diamond, 1992; Rovee-Collier & Gerhardstein, 1997).

▶ Young children may not yet have a well-developed *sense of self* to relate their early memories to. Without some kind of organizing framework such as an understanding of their own thoughts, characteristics, needs, and so forth, they may store information about early experiences as disconnected, unrelated bits of information. They will have few effective cues for accessing and retrieving the information, so their chances of retrieving these memories years later are very small (Fivush & Hammond, 1990; Howe & Courage, 1993).

▶ *Infants' memories can be easily modified.* As you have learned, memory is reconstructive, and young children's memories are even more susceptible to influences from prompting than are older children's and adults' memories. In infants, memory of an event may be mentally recoded in terms of new information each time they remember it until they no longer recognize the original form. In other words, retrieval cues will no longer activate the "original" memory of a given event, though they may activate an updated or modified memory (Boller, Grabelle, & Rovee-Collier, 1995; Rovee-Collier, 1995).

▶ There may be a *mismatch between the initial encoding and retrieval cues.* The way infants encode memories (e.g., based on motor activities, dealing with specific objects and events) and the way they are asked to retrieve them years later (e.g., via verbal cues, often based on general categories of information and activities) may simply not match well. Such a mismatch would result in poor retrieval cues for the early memories and a small likelihood that the memories would be activated (Nelson, 1993).

■ **Autobiographical Memory.** One of us (JLC) had a bicycle accident at about 8 years of age. Whenever I think about it, I can almost feel the pain in my knee, see the bright red of the blood, and remember the words I was thinking: "Just get home, just get home. Dad will help me." I remember remaining reasonably calm until I saw my father standing at the edge of the yard, and then bursting into tears. Do you have any such vivid memories?

Such long-lasting memories of personally experienced events are called **autobiographical memories.** Autobiographical memories are a special subgroup of the episodic memories we discussed earlier. They are memories of events that had a high level of personal significance. Such meaningful memories form the core experiences of a child's "life story." Not surprisingly, autobiographical memories are often quite vivid and detailed, sometimes even including emotions, sights, and sounds. Children begin to form autobiographical memories early in life and begin talking about such past events when they are as young as 2 years of age. Children's descriptions of past events become more organized and detailed between ages 3 and 6. Older children begin adding more background information and providing more of the contexts of the events—such as where they were, what they were thinking and feeling at the time, who was present, and the like. Children learn to describe their autobiographical memories as narratives or stories by interacting with adults; adults elaborate on the information the child provides, ask questions to clarify details or elicit more information, and teach children a cultural format to use in talking about their memories. For example, parents and children often have "remember when you . . ." conversations: "Remember when you had your big bike accident in second grade? Do you remember the bike trick you were trying to do when

YOUR
PERSPECTIVE
NOTES

Are your earliest memories about events? Are they autobiographical? Ask several friends about their earliest memories. Do you see a pattern?

autobiographical memories

Memories of events of great personal importance. They are episodic memories and are often vivid and detailed.

it happened?" Interactions like these teach children a form for describing memories, and they also help children fill in forgotten details. In other words, such conversations strengthen events that might have become inaccessible in memory so that the child is better able to remember them later (Fivush, 1995; Fivush, Haden, & Adam, 1995; Howe, Courage, & Bryant-Brown, 1995).

Autobiographical memories are interesting because they seem so different from our memory for other kinds of information, such as facts and categories. These memories are also important in helping children develop a sense of their own identity, a topic we will discuss in Chapter 10. Given what you've learned about the reconstructive nature of memory, however, can you see a potential problem with autobiographical memories? It can be difficult for a person to figure out how much of an autobiographical memory, particularly one of a traumatic event such as a serious accident or abuse, might be influenced by other people's interpretations of the event or even by imagining an event (Mazzoni & Memon, 2003; Niedzwienska, 2003). To learn about how clinical psychologists deal with autobiographical memories their clients may have, read the Professional Perspective box, "Career Focus: Meet a Child and Family Therapist."

Autobiographical memories are memories of events that are very important to the person. They are often very vivid and can include the emotions, sights, and sounds that were present at the original event.

LET'S REVIEW . . .

1. Which model describes human memory as a set of concept nodes with links that vary in strength?

   a. the stores model   b. the network model   c. the short-term model   d. the autobiographical model

2. According to some researchers, children organize their long-term memories for events into special mental structures called:

   a. scripts.   b. semantic networks.   c. reconstructive stores.   d. autobiographical nodes.

3. Immaturity of the brain, an immature sense of self, and a mismatch between the initial encoding and retrieval cues have all been offered as explanations for:

   a. reconstructive memory.   b. unintentional memory.   c. infantile amnesia.   d. network connection failures.

4. **True or False:** As their processing speed increases, children tend to maintain less information in their working memories.

5. **True or False:** With development the amount of information held in long-term memory increases, and the organization of the information changes.

Answers: 1. b, 2. a, 3. c, 4. F, 5. T

Career Focus: Meet a Child and Family Therapist

Dr. Anne Updegrove
Chicago, Illinois

Licensed clinical psychologist and adjunct faculty at Loyola University

In therapy situations, how do you use research information about autobiographical and reconstructive memory?
Since therapists rely on children's reports, it is important to be familiar with research that explains what factors influence children's memory for their own experiences and events in their lives. Using research gives clinicians a sense of the "big picture" and helps us not to rely solely on our own unique experience, but to be more objective in our evaluation of children.

In your experience, do children seem more prone than adults to making errors when they reconstruct memories in therapy?
I don't think they make more errors. Instead, I think they remember differently and are differentially affected by how questions are asked.

Children's memories tend to be less elaborate, more concrete, and often include details that may seem less relevant or more idiosyncratic. For example, a traumatized child may focus on a stuffed animal that was lost during the traumatic incident or the smell of an individual who has abused them. Also, children are more easily influenced by the way questions are asked if they sense that an adult authority figure wants them to respond in a particular way. The younger the child, the more this seems to be true.

How do you help children recall events accurately, without leading them into inaccurate memories?
It's difficult. We want to help clients remember as much detail as possible but without influencing the nature of their memories. We do several things to enhance accurate recall. First, clients must trust the therapist and feel that he or she is supportive and nonjudgmental. Second, questions should be open-ended. Clients should be asked to "tell me more about that" rather than given leading questions. Good training in assess-

ment and interviewing helps clinicians learn how to ask questions the right way. For example, clinicians learn that using the client's own words when phrasing a question reduces the possibility that you are introducing your own biases into the interview. Third, it can be helpful to ask someone to tell the story in their *own* words. Memories which seem unusually rehearsed or include words that children do not typically know are suspect. Likewise, if a child describes an experience in some detail that is unusual for a child to know about (for example, a sexual act), this lends credibility to the accuracy of the memory.

What kinds of education and training are needed to work as a child or family therapist?
Most therapists have a master's degree or Ph.D. in clinical psychology, counseling, or clinical social work. Course work in child development, family dynamics, assessment, and therapy is needed, with supervised practice in a therapy situation. Most states require a licensing exam. ■

The Development of Knowledge and Strategies

When our two sons were about 9 and 5 years old, they asked me (JLC) to play Pokémon cards with them. Each card had a picture of a different Pokémon character. Different characters had distinctive beginning strength levels and "tricks" they could use to defeat opponents. The object was to defeat the opposing Pokémon and win the card. My sons gave me a few cards to start with and we began our game. Within minutes, I had lost all of my cards. The boys had quickly determined which Pokémon to start with, which trick to use, how much damage they had suffered, and who won the game—all before I could even figure out which of my cards had the highest beginning strength!

What could explain my sons' clear superiority with Pokémon? It wasn't overall level of intelligence. I like to think my sons are intelligent, but so am I. It was not due to their having better memory in general—just ask them about homework or if they've brushed their teeth, and it is as if they have no memory at all! The answer has to do with **knowledge base** (the amount of information a person knows about a particular topic) and **strategies** (the conscious, intentional, and controllable plans we adopt to enhance our performance).

In this section we explore how children develop their knowledge base and how knowledge base affects other cognitive processes. We also look at how children develop strategies to improve their memory and cognitive processing.

As you study this section, ask yourself these questions:

- What effect does knowledge base have on cognitive development?
- How do strategies develop?
- What factors affect strategy use, and how does increasing strategy use foster cognitive development?

Knowledge Base

Though we haven't seen any studies of Pokémon experts (yet), researchers have looked at the effects of knowledge base in many other areas of life. Not surprisingly, the more you know about a particular topic, the more you can remember about it—but that is not the only effect of knowledge base. For example, when you get new information about a topic you already know well, you are more likely to notice details and relationships than someone who has less prior knowledge. You are also better able to group the information in useful ways. So my sons were good at categorizing their Pokémon cards according to the types and overall amount of "powers" they had (a useful category for the card battles), whereas I began by sorting the cards according to color and size (which is not very helpful for the battles). In other words, your knowledge base enables you to encode new information differently. You can also store the new information more effectively. In essence, you are better able to integrate the new information with previous knowledge, which increases the likelihood that you will be able to access and retrieve the new information when you need it. Finally, you are able to carry out all these processes more quickly than someone who does not know much about the topic. And, as you'll recall, the faster you can process information, the less processing capacity you use, and the more of your limited capacity is available for other mental processes. So not only will you be able to remember more of the new information, you will be able to think about it more quickly and at a higher level than someone with less knowledge. Given all this, I suppose it isn't surprising that my sons defeated me so quickly in our Pokémon game.

The influence of prior knowledge is very clear when you study *experts* versus *novices*—that is, when you contrast people who know a lot about a given area with people who know very little about it. Some of the earliest and best-known research on expert–novice differences focused on chess players (Chi, 1978). In one well-known study the chess experts were only 10 years old, whereas the novices were graduate students. The experimenters showed both groups chess pieces in chessboard arrangements that would be likely to occur during a real game. The participants saw the pieces for about one second. Then the researchers asked them to remember the positions and place the pieces on another chessboard in the same arrangements they had viewed. The results are shown in Figure 6.7. Because of their greater knowledge of chess, the children clearly outperformed the adults. This did not happen because the children had better memories in general: When the task was to remember random sequences of numbers, the graduate students did better, as shown in Figure 6.7. In other words, greater

knowledge base

The amount of information a person knows about a particular topic.

strategies

Conscious, intentional, and controllable plans used to improve performance.

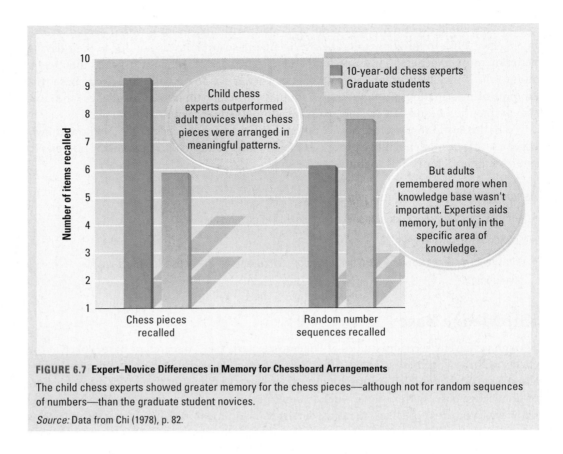

FIGURE 6.7 Expert–Novice Differences in Memory for Chessboard Arrangements

The child chess experts showed greater memory for the chess pieces—although not for random sequences of numbers—than the graduate student novices.

Source: Data from Chi (1978), p. 82.

prior knowledge of chess produced better memory, but only for chess. Expert–novice differences in memory and problem-solving performance are evident in many realms, including academic areas (e.g., mathematics, physics), sports (e.g., soccer, baseball), and even hobbies and entertainment (e.g., dinosaurs, cartoon figures like Superman or Spider-Man, *Star Wars* characters and plots) (Chi, Glaser, & Farr, 1988; Chi & Koeske, 1983; Means & Voss, 1985; Schneider, Gruber, Gold, & Opwis, 1993).

Perhaps the most interesting finding from all the work on expert–novice differences is that experts not only have more information but also mentally organize their knowledge about their topic differently than do novices. Instead of storing information about individual chess pieces as a novice would, chess experts mentally group together entire board configurations (which are made up of many individual pieces). They store the entire thing as a single "chunk" in memory. They sometimes even store common *sequences* of moves as a single chunk! In other words, for a chess expert one chunk may contain dozens of individual pieces arranged in successive moves. In contrast, novices think about, store, and retrieve only a few pieces of information at a time. Experts also mentally categorize information based on general principles instead of according to surface-level characteristics. For example, physics novices mentally store physics information according to the kinds of objects they see in the problem situation (e.g., an inclined plane). In contrast, experts mentally organize their knowledge according to general principles of physics (e.g., the principle of inertia) (Chi, Feltovich, & Glaser, 1981). As a result, physics experts can quickly recognize the underlying principles involved, categorize the general type of problem they are dealing with, and access relevant information and possible solution strategies. Meanwhile, novices are stuck trying to figure out what, if anything, the existence of an inclined plane means. A novice is like a detective who may notice clues but doesn't think about how they fit together to solve a mystery.

thinking
OF ANGELIQUE

What parts of Angelique's knowledge base must improve to help her solve story problems more effectively? How can Manny help with this?

Given that knowledge base affects memory and knowledge organization, how does it help explain cognitive development? Young children are, in essence, "universal novices" (Brown & De-Loache, 1978). They know about fewer topics than older children, and they know less about the topics they have encountered. Because young children have less knowledge, the information in their knowledge bases is less connected than that of older children. Also, it tends to be organized according to surface features rather than according to underlying principles. All these features lead to poorer memory and less efficient cognitive processing. Information-processing psychologists agree that age differences in knowledge base play an important role in explaining cognitive development. In fact, some claim that knowledge base is the *most* important factor in explaining why adults are better than children on most cognitive tasks (Carey, 1985). Notice how different this explanation of cognitive development is from the Piagetian view you studied in Chapter 5!

If a rich knowledge base has such important effects, what does it take for children to acquire one? The few longitudinal studies that have been done confirm what you are probably thinking—lots of practice is absolutely necessary. In studies of both chess experts and tennis experts, it seems that practice, along with motivational factors such as interest and dedication, were more important than general aptitude measures (Renniger, Hidi, & Krapp, 1992; Schneider, 1993). How extensive a knowledge base is necessary? Not surprisingly, it appears that it takes a fairly high degree of knowledge to enhance children's performance and produce changes in the structure of their knowledge (DeMarie-Dreblow, 1991).

No matter what their age, experts have a greater knowledge base and organize their knowledge differently than novices.

Strategy Development

While reading a new book one day, 5-year-old Will encounters the word "museum." He pauses and looks carefully at the pictures on the page, but cannot figure out the word. He tries to sound out the individual letters but still doesn't understand the text. Finally, Will points to the word and asks his mother for help. Will's attempts to understand the book are *strategies*—the conscious, intentional, and controllable plans that people use to improve performance at all stages of information processing (Schneider & Bjorklund, 1998). Will tries three different strategies to encode the new word: using the context, sounding it out, and asking for help. He will probably use several other strategies to understand the story, store it in memory, and recall it later on. Information-processing psychologists have given enormous attention to children's development of cognitive strategies, because they believe that strategies have a strong impact on thinking, remembering, and solving problems.

Research has looked in depth at the development of several specific memory strategies. One strategy is *rehearsal,* or repeating information that you want to remember. Rehearsal can be a very effective memory strategy, because it increases the likelihood that information will be stored in the memory system. As you might expect, the amount of rehearsal is important: More rehearsal tends to produce better memory performance (Flavell, Beach, & Chinsky, 1966). But the style of rehearsal may be even more important (Ornstein, Naus, & Liberty, 1975). Older children tend to use a cumulative (or active) rehearsal style, in which they repeat several items together. In contrast, younger children use a more passive style—they repeat only the last item they are trying to remember. This passive style does not encourage further processing of other items, and it doesn't encourage the child to look for relationships among the items. Younger children can be trained to use cumulative rehearsal and doing so improves their memory performance, but they do not tend to continue using it after training (Naus, Ornstein, & Aivano, 1977).

Two other useful memory strategies are *organization,* in which we use relationships among items to improve our memory for the items, and *elaboration,* in which we create visual or verbal associations to link the items. In general, all three strategies show similar changes across ages:

▶ Younger children are less likely to use these strategies spontaneously than older children, but younger children can easily be taught to use the strategies. And when used, the strategies help their memory performance.

▶ Even after training, younger children usually do not use the strategies as effectively or as consistently as older children. Even when younger children are trained to the point that they use a strategy spontaneously on new information, their memory of the information does not always improve (Bjorklund & Coyle, 1995; Bjorklund, Miller, Coyle, & Slawinski, 1997).

▶ The three strategies typically appear at different ages. Simple forms of rehearsal are found in preschool children, but organization is not common until the elementary school years, and spontaneous use of elaboration does not occur until adolescence or even later (Hasselhorn, 1992; Pressley & Afflerbach, 1995).

▶ Children use strategies more often and more effectively with familiar materials and meaningful, interesting activities (Rogoff & Mistry, 1990).

It is no secret that young children do not learn things as well as older children. For many years it was believed that young children simply could not use strategies. It was quite a surprise when some studies found that even 2-year-olds could use simple strategies. However, strategy use at these young ages is very fragile (Bjorklund, 1995; DeLoache, Cassidy, & Brown, 1985). That is, younger children often do not use a strategy when it would be helpful to do so, and sometimes they do not show improved performance even after they have been taught a strategy.

Although children can spontaneously discover new strategies (Siegler & Jenkins, 1989), they often learn strategies through explicit instruction. Not surprisingly, the specific strategies children learn depend on what they are taught and encouraged to use. Schooling in particular has a powerful effect, and the task demands placed by the school system affect the particular strategies learned (Moely, Santulli, & Obach, 1995; Rogoff, 1990). For example, schools that emphasize recall of facts encourage students to use strategies focused on remembering information quickly and accurately, but not necessarily strategies that elaborate and extend information in novel ways. In contrast, an emphasis on analyzing information or solving problems encourages strategies for comparing, contrasting, and applying information but not necessarily fast recall. These findings would make sense to Vygotsky (recall our discussion in Chapter 5), who believed that the larger culture (in this case, a school) selects and encourages the internalization of specific cognitive skills.

A final and important point to keep in mind is that strategies do not function in isolation. Children do not use only one strategy at a time, and they do not move neatly from less to more sophisticated strategies. Instead, they typically use a variety of different strategies from one problem to the next. In some cases—as with 5-year-old Will and the word "museum"—children even use combinations of multiple strategies on a single problem (Coyle & Bjorklund,

thinking
OF ANGELIQUE

What reading comprehension strategies would help Angelique? What math strategies could she use?

YOUR
PERSPECTIVE
NOTES

Think of a problem you had to solve recently. Did you use only one strategy, or several? How and why have your "favorite" strategies changed over the years?

1997; Siegler, 1995). Children's strategy development can be thought of as a series of *overlapping waves* in which children always use a variety of different strategies, some simpler and some more complex. The particular strategies used most often gradually shift from the simpler to the more complex (Chen & Siegler, 2000; Siegler, 1996). The shift occurs as the child becomes more efficient in using the more complex strategy, which reduces the "cost" in terms of cognitive capacity and provides greater "benefits" in terms of better performance.

LET'S REVIEW . . .

1. Children who were chess experts were compared to adults who were chess novices. What differences were found in their memory for chess pieces?
    a. Child novices remembered as many chess pieces as adult novices.
    b. Child experts remembered fewer chess pieces than adult experts.
    c. Child experts remembered as many chess pieces as adult novices.
    d. Child experts remembered more chess pieces than adult novices.

2. As children's knowledge bases increase, they tend to do all of the following except:
    a. use information-processing strategies more effectively.
    b. organize information into smaller "chunks" or pieces of information.
    c. notice details and relationships among pieces of information.
    d. encode, store, and retrieve information more quickly.

3. Memory researchers have found that older children tend to engage in more _____ rehearsal, but younger children tend to use _____ rehearsal strategies.
    | a. cumulative; passive | b. passive; active | c. useful; irrelevant | d. fast; slow |

4. **True or False:** As a child's knowledge base improves, the child's degree of knowledge organization and strategy use tends to decrease.

5. **True or False:** Rehearsal, organization, and elaboration are strategies that can improve memory performance.

Answers: 1. d, 2. b, 3. a, 4. F, 5. T

The Development of Metacognition

Do you ever think about your own thinking? Do you ever wonder how in the world you will be able to remember a complicated set of information, or even the name or phone number of someone you just met? If so, you have engaged in what psychologists call *metacognition*. **Metacognition** is the understanding or knowledge that people have about their own thought processes and memory. In this section we summarize what researchers know about metacognition. We also introduce you to an area of research called *"theory of mind,"* which is a newer way of looking at metacognition, and we take a brief look at the development of self-regulation in children.

As you study this section, ask yourself these questions:

- What are metacognition and metamemory, and how do they affect cognitive development?
- What do researchers mean by "theory of mind"? Describe the development of children's theory of mind.
- How do self-regulation skills develop during childhood?

metacognition

The understanding or knowledge that people have about their own thought processes.

Metacognition and Metamemory

Several different types of metacognition develop during childhood. These include knowledge about cognitive *tasks* (such as knowing that a long list of words will be more difficult to remember than a short list), knowledge about cognitive *strategies* (such as knowing that simply repeating a telephone number will help you remember it for a short time), and knowledge about *people* (such as knowing that there are limits to what a person can remember).

Much of what we know about metacognition concerns knowledge of memory. **Metamemory,** a subcategory of metacognition, is knowledge about the processes and contents of memory (Flavell, 1971). Metamemory includes knowledge about memory in general, such as the fact that people are limited in how much they can remember. It also includes knowledge of your own specific memory abilities, such as the fact that you remember things better in the morning than in the early afternoon. Metamemory shows significant development from the age of 5 to about 10. Older children are better than younger ones in all three types of metacognitive knowledge: memory tasks, memory strategies, and person variables. For example, older children know that certain kinds of memory tasks (like remembering the gist of a passage or trying to remember something for a short time) will be easier than others (like remembering the exact wording of a passage or trying to remember something for a long time). Older children are also better at selecting and applying appropriate memory strategies, and they are better at modifying an existing strategy to be more effective in different situations. Finally, older children have much more accurate knowledge of their own memory abilities. They are better at estimating how much they will be able to remember and at giving more time and effort to studying harder items than are younger children (Bjorklund, 1995; Kreutzer, Leonard, & Flavell, 1975).

Younger children do have some metamemory knowledge, however. In fact, in some ways, they show quite impressive metamemory skills, especially when tasks are simple and are presented in familiar contexts. For example, preschool children know that:

▶ It is easier to remember a few items than to remember more;

▶ Studying longer should increase the amount remembered;

▶ It is easier to relearn something you knew before but forgot than to learn something completely new; and

▶ It is useful to use external memory devices like writing things down.

Younger children are notoriously optimistic about their own memory abilities: They consistently overestimate how much they will be able to remember. However, they are more accurate when estimating how much someone else will remember on the same task (Flavell, Friedrichs, & Hoyt, 1970; Kreutzer et al., 1975). For example, ask 5-year-old Rachel how many items she thinks she could remember from a list of 50, and she's likely to say, "I could remember them all; I'm a good rememberer!" But ask her how many her twin sister will remember, and the answer is more likely to be "Oh, maybe 15. It's hard to remember all that." This wishful thinking on the part of young children may actually be useful, in that it probably motivates children to keep trying. If young children accurately predicted their own poor memory performance, they might become frustrated and give up. This would reduce their chances to discover and practice memory strategies and gain metamemory knowledge. The general conclusion is that young children do show some impressive metamemory knowledge, but that such knowledge undergoes substantial development, especially after children begin formal schooling (Pressley, 1995). As you probably know from personal experience, school tends to involve many intentional memory tasks. In order to succeed in school, children must develop effective memory skills and metamemory knowledge.

metamemory

Knowledge about the processes and contents of memory.

Theory of Mind

In recent decades work on metacognition has focused on how children develop their own *theory of mind*. A **theory of mind** is a coherent and integrated framework of concepts about the mind, how it works, and why it works that way (Wellman, 1990). Research on children's theory of mind has looked at what children know about thinking in general and at how well they understand the thoughts of other people.

Even young children have some understanding of thinking as a mental activity and know it is different from physical objects and behavior. For example, children as young as 3 know that mental objects are different from real objects (e.g., that an imaginary ice-cream cone is different from the real thing) and that it is possible to carry out mental activities that could not happen in the real world (such as flying to the moon in a cardboard box) (Wellman & Estes, 1986). Three-year-olds can also understand that dreams are not real life, although many young children do believe that different people have the same dreams (Woolley & Wellman, 1992).

However, children's understanding of mental activities undergoes substantial development. For example, young children often do not understand the difference between how a real object *appears* to be and how it actually *is*. This is called the *appearance–reality distinction,* and it is a good indicator of theory of mind. If children are not able to tell the difference between appearance and reality, it means that they are not distinguishing between their beliefs about an object (which are based on how it appears) and how it really exists. For example, in one classic study researchers introduced children to a cat named Maynard (DeVries, 1969). The researchers then put a

Young children have trouble understanding the distinction between appearance and reality. If this cat wears a mask of a dog's face, three-year-olds are likely to believe that it has turned into a dog!

dog mask on Maynard's face. Even though Maynard's body and tail were unchanged and remained visible while the mask was put on, 3-year-olds said that Maynard was now a dog. To them the change in appearance changed the underlying reality. In contrast, 5- and 6-year-olds had no problem understanding that Maynard was still a cat despite his change in appearance. Other work using fake rocks (pieces of sponge painted to look like rocks) and "red milk" (white milk poured into a red cup) also showed that 3-year-olds did not distinguish appearance from reality. This result was consistent even when the tasks were simplified and even after children received explicit training in distinguishing between appearance and reality (Flavell, Green, & Flavell, 1986; Flavell, Green, Wahl, & Flavell, 1987; Taylor & Hort, 1990). In other words, for young children, if it looks like a rock, it is a rock.

Do children understand the beliefs and desires of other people? To be able to do this, children must first understand that other people's thoughts are different from their own. If they can't make this distinction, then they can't understand that other people have their own unique beliefs and desires, and there is no reason even to try to figure out what others are thinking. It's not clear whether young children understand the difference between what they know themselves and what another person knows. Several studies have found that 3-year-olds do not make the distinction even when simple tasks are used, and cross-cultural studies have confirmed this result (Avis & Harris, 1991; Perner, 1991; Sullivan & Wimmer, 1993; Wellman & Bartsch, 1988). However, when the task involves trying to trick another person, some studies

theory of mind

An integrated framework about the mind, how it works, and why it works that way.

have found that even 2½-year-olds can do quite well (Hala, Chandler, & Fritz, 1991; Peskin, 1992; Ruffman, Olson, Ash, & Keenan, 1993; Sullivan & Wimmer, 1993). To "trick" someone requires that you understand what the person is thinking and how that person's thinking is different from your own. It also requires that you have a plan for changing what the other person thinks. Perhaps children are more likely to show their understanding on a "tricking" task because it is fun and motivating. "Tricking" experiments may encourage children to pay more attention and think more carefully about differences between their own and others' beliefs. Or children may get more actively involved because they have to think up ways to trick the other person instead of merely trying to predict what the other person would probably believe.

Recent studies indicate that language seems to play an important role in the development of a theory of mind. Talking to children beginning at a very early age about mental states such as desires, emotions, thinking, knowing, memory, understanding, and the like seems to help them develop a theory of mind (Meins, Fernyhoug, Wainwright, Gupta, Fradley, & Tuckey, 2002; Ruffman, Slade, & Crowe, 2002). And children's performance on several different theory of mind tasks seems to be related to their experience in using language to communicate with those around them (Deak, Ray, & Brenneman, in press; Lohmann & Tomasello, 2003; Nelson, Skwerer, Goldman, Henseler, Presler, & Walkenfeld, 2003). In any case, we still have much to learn about what children understand about others' thoughts and desires.

There is increasing evidence that the lack of a theory of mind may be involved in the serious disorder known as *autism*. Children with autism have great difficulty communicating and interacting with others in socially appropriate ways. Recent work on theory of mind shows that autistic children are often unable to understand other people's thoughts, or even their own mental states, though they often do well on nonsocial tasks. Sometimes called *mindblindness,* such problems may be due to deficits in specific brain structures that have evolved to allow humans to interact socially with others (Baron-Cohen, 1995). Chapter 14 discusses autism in more detail.

Self-Regulation

Of course, even the most complex and well-developed metacognitive knowledge will be useless if the child does not use it in appropriate situations. A key skill is **self-regulation**—the ongoing processes of *monitoring* how well you are doing on a task and *adjusting* your strategies and efforts as needed. Clearly, if you cannot independently assess whether you are making progress and whether your current approach is working, you will not know when to make changes to try to improve. Not surprisingly, self-regulation is a strong predictor of success in school (Zimmerman, 1990).

Even young children show simple forms of self-regulation. If you listen to 2-year-olds talking to babies, you'll notice that they speak in a tone of voice that is higher and slower than usual, and that they use more exaggerated facial expressions and intonations. That is, these young children are monitoring how well others understand them and making adjustments as needed (Clark, 1978).

As with other aspects of metacognition, however, there are vast improvements in self-regulation throughout the childhood years. One task that researchers often use to test self-regulation is the identification of inconsistencies in text passages. For example, read the passages shown in Table 6.1 and see if you can identify any parts that do not make sense or that are inconsistent. Older elementary school children are better at detecting such inconsistencies than are younger students, but even college students and adults can have trouble monitoring their comprehension and detecting inconsistencies. Younger children often fail to notice inconsistencies even in their own writing. However, they can easily correct problems once someone points them out.

Researchers also find differences in comprehension monitoring between children who are strong readers and children the same age who are struggling with reading. Stronger readers tend—often without knowing it—to slow their reading pace and reexamine the difficult

self-regulation

The ongoing processes of monitoring your own task performance and adjusting your strategies and efforts as needed to accomplish a task.

TABLE 6.1 Inconsistencies in Text Passages

Can you identify the inconsistencies in these passages? Younger children and less accomplished readers often have difficulty with tasks like this.

Lily hates broccoli. She thinks it looks, tastes, and smells just awful. She would rather eat dirt than eat broccoli. Last night at dinner, Lily cried because her mom wouldn't let her have any more broccoli to eat.
Some people don't have houses to live in. Instead, they move around from place to place. These people are called *nomads*. Sometimes nomads move around because they are hunters and they have to follow herds of animals so they can get food. After they finish a big hunt, nomads are very tired. They are always happy to get back to their own houses to rest.

parts of the text. Unfortunately, younger and less accomplished readers are the least likely to monitor their own comprehension, even though they need to do this more and would benefit greatly from it (Beal, 1990; Garner & Reis, 1981; Markman, 1977).

When we look at the self-regulation of study skills, research findings are similar. Older children generally show better monitoring and adjustment of study skills, tend to spend more time studying before they say they are ready for a test, and tend to give more attention to items they haven't mastered than to those they already know (Bisanz, Vesonder, & Voss, 1978; Dufresne & Kobasigawa, 1989a).

thinking OF ANGELIQUE

◀ What evidence of metacognitive skills does Angelique show? How will these skills help her improve her math problem-solving skills?

Does Metacognitive Knowledge Improve Cognitive Performance?

After all this, it may surprise you to learn that the relationship between metacognitive knowledge and task performance is modest. Summaries of many different studies show an overall correlation of .41 (recall the discussion of correlation in Chapter 1). The relationship is stronger for older children—as high as .59 for older children and as low as .21 for younger—

Parents, teachers, and the overall culture have a big impact on the metacognitive skills children develop and the beliefs children hold about their effort.

and is higher for some types of tasks than others (Schneider, 1985; Schneider & Pressley, 1989). The relationship between knowledge and performance is complex. Successfully using metacognitive skills and cognitive strategies involves many steps (Siegler, 1998): The child has to recognize the need for the skill, figure out what strategies might be useful, choose a particular strategy and then apply it correctly, make adjustments as needed, and constantly monitor progress to decide whether the strategy is helping or not. This kind of activity requires a variety of skills and pieces of knowledge, not to mention a tremendous amount of processing capacity to oversee and direct it all!

The good news is that metacognitive skills are clearly teachable, and that they can be taught well enough that children will use them in new situations. Parents and teachers play important roles in this process. They teach and encourage children to use many specific metacognitive skills, such as thinking about parts of a task that might be difficult, deciding how a particular strategy might help, checking progress and outcomes, and recognizing and correcting errors (Kurtz, Schneider, Carr, Borkowski, & Rellinger, 1990; Neitzel & Stright, 2003; Pressley, 1995). However, children don't always keep on using these skills after they learn them. It is important for them to see that a given strategy really helps (Siegler, 1998). They must also believe that their *effort* in learning and using the strategy, as opposed to luck, is the cause of better performance. If children do not attribute their successes to their effort, there is no reason for them to work at learning and using metacognitive strategies (Carr, Borkowski, & Maxwell, 1991). How do children develop such beliefs? Again, parents, teachers, and the overall culture have a significant impact on the beliefs children develop as well as on the particular strategies they learn (Butler & Ruzany, 1993; Kurtz et al., 1990; Stetsenko, Little, Oettingen, & Baltes, 1995; Teong, 2003; Thiede, Anderson, & Therriault, 2003).

LET'S REVIEW . . .

1. What does the term *metacognition* refer to?
   a. How people store and retrieve memories.
   b. Thought processes that are unconscious.
   c. Knowledge of one's own thought and memory processes.
   d. The type of cognition used by younger children before they learn more mature forms of thinking.

2. Which of the following is the best example of metamemory?
   a. Rachel can remember what happened yesterday better than what happened two weeks ago.
   b. Susan remembers faces better than names.
   c. Keisha is an expert in dinosaurs, so she remembers a tremendous amount of detail about them.
   d. Carolyn knows that it will be difficult to memorize all of the state capitals.

3. The ongoing process of monitoring how well you are doing and adjusting your strategies and efforts as needed is referred to as:
   a. self-regulation.   b. metacognition.   c. metamemory.   d. theory of mind.

4. **True or False:** Three-year-old children are good at distinguishing appearance from reality.

5. **True or False:** There is a moderate relationship between metacognitive knowledge and performance for most cognitive tasks.

Answers: 1. c, 2. d, 3. a, 4. F, 5. T

Newer Approaches to Understanding Cognitive Development

Research on information processing began in the mid-twentieth century when computers became available on most university campuses and research sites. Since those days computers have obviously become much more powerful and sophisticated. The primitive computers of the 1950s would have been hard pressed to perform the functions of one of today's cheap pocket calculators! And just as computers have grown and developed, so has our understanding of children's cognitive processing. The stores model you saw in Figure 6.1 was first proposed in the 1960s, and it is very simple compared to the models and theories of cognitive processing being developed today. In this last section we will introduce you to some of the ideas that information-processing theorists are exploring today.

As you study this section, ask yourself these questions:

- What are production systems and connectionist models? How do they help us understand cognitive development?

- What are fuzzy traces? How do they explain age differences in memory?

- What are the strengths and weaknesses of the information-processing approach to cognitive development?

Computational Models of Thought

Some information-processing researchers try to map the exact steps that people go through as they solve problems or perform other cognitive tasks. To test their conclusions, these researchers create computer programs that attempt to mimic the thought processes of humans. These theories of cognition that are programmed and tested on computers are known as **computational models** (Klahr & MacWhinney, 1998). Researchers have been developing and testing computational models of adult cognition since the early days of information processing, but we include this as a new approach because of these models' more recent use in work on children's cognitive development. There are two general types of computational models: *production systems* and *connectionist models*.

    Production systems are sets of computerized *if–then statements,* or "productions," that state the specific actions that a person will take under certain conditions. For example, Table 6.2 shows hypothetical productions for solving a Piagetian liquid conservation problem like those you learned about in Chapter 5. Each production specifies a *condition* that must be met before the production will be implemented (this is the *if* part) and a specific *action* that will be taken (the *then* part). When you look closely at Table 6.2, it is easy to see how production systems quickly become complex. The system must specify the many different conditions a person might encounter and the specific actions to be taken under each condition. The system also must include *decision rules* for deciding which productions to implement when the conditions of more than one production are met, when none of the conditions for any existing production are met, or when other complicating situations exist (Klahr & Siegler, 1978).

    Researchers use production systems to clarify and test hypotheses about development. They specify the exact conditions that must be met, the exact actions that will be taken, and the exact input information needed. They then compare the computer-produced output with

computational models

Models of cognition that are programmed on computers; output of the programs is compared to human performance.

production systems

Sets of computerized *if–then* statements that state the specific actions taken under certain conditions.

TABLE 6.2 Examples of Possible Productions for a Piagetian Liquid Conservation Task

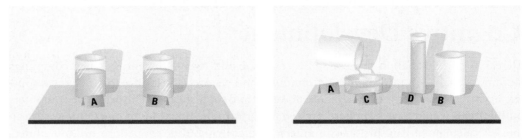

The task is to say whether the two containers still have the same amount of liquid, or if one has more. This hypothetical production system proposes four different ways that children can solve this problem. If these models were run on a computer, the researcher could compare the computer's output to that of real children to see how well the production system matched the children's performance.

Model I	
Considers only the height of liquid in each container.	P1: ((Same Height) → (Say "same"))
	P2: ((Container C more Height) → (Say "C has more"))

Model II	
Considers both the height and the width of the liquid in each container, but only if the height and width information are consistent.	P1: ((Same Height) → (Say "same"))
	P2: ((Container C more Height) → (Say "C has more"))
	P3: ((Same Height) (Container C more Width) → (Say "C has more"))

Model III	
Considers both height and width, but not sure how to coordinate them.	P1: ((Same Height) → (Say "same"))
	P2: ((Container C more Height) → (Say "C has more"))
	P3: ((Same Height) (Container C more Width) → (Say "C has more"))
	P4: ((Container C more Height) (Container C less Width) → (muddle through))
	P5: ((Container C more Height) (Container C more Width) → (Say "C has more"))

Model IV	
Considers both height and width of both containers, coordinating them by estimating volume.	P1: ((Same Height) → (Say "same"))
	P2: ((Container C more Height) → (Say "C has more"))
	P3: ((Same Height) (Container C more Width) → (Say "C has more"))
	P4: ((Container C more Height) (Container C less Width) → (get Volume))
	P5: ((Container C more Height) (Container C more Width) → (Say "C has more"))
	P6: ((Same Volume) → (Say "same"))
	P7: ((Container C more Volume) → (Say "C has more"))

P = An individual production, or *if–then* statement; e.g., *if* both containers have the same height, *then* say "same."

C = The container holding the liquid.

Height = Height of the liquid in the container.

Width = Width of the liquid in the container.

Source: Adapted from Klahr & Siegler (1978), p. 78.

the solutions real children produce for similar problems. This allows the researchers to identify parts of the model that are wrong or vague. Earlier production systems emphasized matching children's performance at different ages. More recently, researchers have focused on developing self-modifying production systems, or systems that "learn," in order to simulate the actual process of developmental change (Halford et al., 1995; Siegler & Shipley, 1995; Simon & Klahr, 1995). These models provide invaluable information about the precise processes that change as a child develops (e.g., exactly what happens when a child generalizes, discriminates, or "chunks" information) and about the conditions under which the changes occur.

Like production systems, **connectionist models** are computational in that they are implemented in a computer simulation and focus on cognitive processes. However, they differ from most other cognitive theories in one important way: Connectionist models hypothesize that knowledge is not "stored" at all. Instead, all knowledge is believed to be reconstructed based on different patterns of activations among interconnected sets of numerous individual components. These models reflect what is known about the workings of neurons in the brain and so are said to be "neurally inspired." They are often referred to as *neural networks*. Figure 6.8 shows a simple connectionist model. The basic elements are its *units,* simple elements that combine to form different patterns. Each unit has a certain *level of activation*—the degree to which it is "turned on" at any given time. The individual units are connected by *links.* The links vary in how strongly they are weighted, with heavily weighted links capable of transmitting activation between two units more easily than lightly weighted links. As shown in the figure, the input layer represents the signals that initially enter the network, the output layer represents the decisions made by the network, and various layers hidden in between enable the network to make a variety of different connections between the input and output layers.

Researchers "train" these connectionist models; that is, they compare a program's output to people's performance, then adjust the program to produce a better match. The main point is to match humans' *developmental changes*—to get the computer model to show the same learning patterns that humans show, including patterns of generalization to new problems. "Learning" occurs through changes in the weights of the links between units. Many different learning rules can be incorporated into the computer program, and each one has different effects on the network. The different learning rules correspond to different hypotheses about how learning takes place, and the different patterns of connections represent different levels of knowledge. By identifying the learning rules and connection patterns that provide the best fit between computer and human learning patterns, we can begin to understand changes in human learning (Bates & Elman, 2002; Thomas & Karmiloff-Smith, 2003).

As you might expect, developing connectionist models is quite complex and time-consuming, and each model must be specific to a single domain. Models have been developed and tested to investigate the learning processes in such diverse areas as learning second languages, acquiring vocabulary, learning word meanings, solving balance-beam problems, and even forming emotional attachments (Klahr & MacWhinney, 1998).

Fuzzy Trace Theory

Think back to something you did yesterday. Now try to remember something interesting that happened several years ago. Do you remember the exact details of the events, or do you instead recall the general gist and then reconstruct the details? The main idea of **fuzzy trace theory** is that memory representations vary on a continuum from very exact and literal memory traces to imprecise, general, and "fuzzy" traces based on the gist of the message (Brainerd & Reyna, 1993, 1995). This view says that people typically do not reason logically from precise, verbatim recollections. Instead, we have a strong tendency toward intuitive reasoning

connectionist models

"Neurally inspired" or neural network models of cognition that view knowledge as based on patterns of activation among interconnected sets of individual units rather than stored as entire concepts.

fuzzy trace theory

The view that memory representations vary on a continuum from exact and literal to imprecise and general memory traces based on the gist of the information or event.

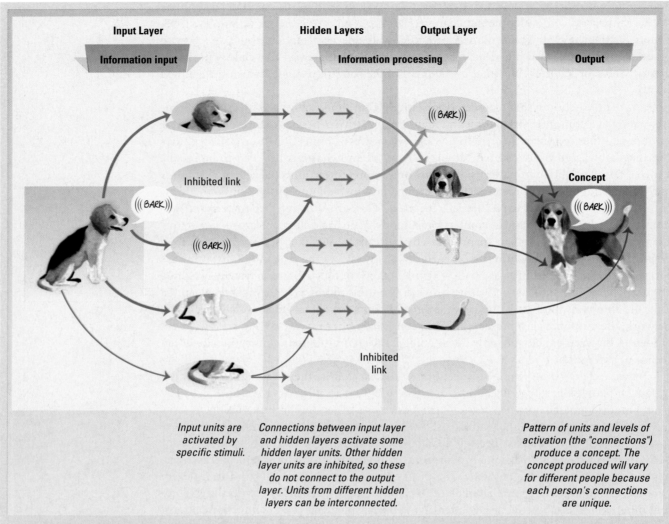

Input Layer

Information input

Hidden Layers

Information processing

Output Layer

Output

Inhibited link

(((BARK)))

(((BARK)))

(((BARK)))

Concept

(((BARK)))

Inhibited link

Input units are activated by specific stimuli.

Connections between input layer and hidden layers activate some hidden layer units. Other hidden layer units are inhibited, so these do not connect to the output layer. Units from different hidden layers can be interconnected.

Pattern of units and levels of activation (the "connections") produce a concept. The concept produced will vary for different people because each person's connections are unique.

FIGURE 6.8 A Simple Connectionist Model

The ovals are the individual units of this model. There are three different layers of units: an input layer, one hidden layer, and an output layer. The lines with arrows represent links between individual units, and the different widths of lines represent degrees of strength between particular units. Notice that the input units can connect to all the output units, but not directly. Their connection is mediated by the hidden layers of units.

Source: Based on Klahr & MacWhinney (1998), p. 649.

based on the main ideas. These fuzzy memory traces are less detailed and are better integrated with our prior knowledge than verbatim traces. Better integration means that there are multiple access and retrieval cues associated with fuzzy traces. As a result, they last longer and are easier to access, less effortful to use, and less susceptible to interference and forgetting than are verbatim traces.

Young children are capable of extracting gist and storing fuzzy memory traces, but they do not do this as consistently as older children and adults. As a result, their memory performance is worse. But it's not clear why younger children rely on verbatim traces. It is not because they can't extract gist and form fuzzy traces; studies have shown that they have this capability and that there is a gradual shift toward more gist processing during the elementary school years (Brainerd & Gordon, 1994; Reyna & Brainerd, 1995). Perhaps this tendency has to do with younger children's relatively limited knowledge base. To extract the main ideas from an encounter, a child must have some way of identifying what the central aspects are. But until the child has at least a basic script for commonly encountered events, there is no solid basis for knowing what is relevant and important and what is not. As children encounter more variations of common events, they build a knowledge base that allows them to identify central aspects and common and important elements. This more developed knowledge base allows children to identify appropriate gists and store them as fuzzy traces. And this in turn improves memory.

What does all this mean for the development of memory? To understand some of the implications, think back to our discussion of children's eyewitness testimony. Young children are more likely to store verbatim memory traces, which might suggest that younger children would have better memory of specific events than older children. But remember that verbatim memory traces decay and become inaccessible more rapidly than fuzzy traces. Unless careful questioning takes place relatively quickly, the specifics are lost from the verbatim traces. And if the questioning is misleading in some way, the likelihood of memory errors increases, because verbatim traces are more susceptible to interference. Older children's memories, on the other hand, have more fuzzy traces. Fuzzy traces are more durable and accessible; they are also less susceptible to interference, so they are less likely to be modified as a result of questioning (Ceci & Bruck, 1998; Robinson & Whitcombe, 2003; Roebers, 2002).

Information Processing: Where Does It Stand?

Since the early 1960s information processing has become the dominant model for understanding cognitive development. Through its emphasis on detailed analysis of specific cognitive processes, the computer metaphor of "thinking as the processing of information" has greatly increased our understanding of developmental change.

There are limits to this approach, however. The most obvious is that despite the detailed information it has provided, the information-processing approach does not offer a comprehensive, overarching structure for explaining cognitive development like that of Piaget's theory. We know a lot about many specific areas of development, and we have many "toy versions" of the real-life cognitive processes we wish to understand (Klahr & MacWhinney, 1998). Yet no comprehensive theory addresses the whole of cognitive development and how it might be related to other areas of development. Second, the information-processing approach has been described as "cold" cognition because of its emphasis on thoughts based on logical reasoning. Information-processing models rarely consider such factors as social interaction, emotional reactions, or motivation, even though these factors are quite important in real-life cognition. In the past, these models have also been slow to incorporate new information about the biological bases of cognitive development, though newer connectionist models are now attempting to do this. And finally, critics have long pointed out that most information-processing models depend on an "executive processor" (something that oversees all processes and determines the allocation of cognitive resources, strategy use, and the like)—but lack details on how the executive works or develops. Both fuzzy trace theory and connectionist models, which explain change without the need for an executive processor, address this criticism.

1. Computational models are:

    a. ideas that children use when they are trying to learn mathematics.

    b. computer programs created to test theories of cognitive development.

    c. theories of memory that show how information passes through the sensory registers, short-term store, and long-term store.

    d. theories of memory that are based on the gist or fuzzy trace of the message being processed.

2. Neural networks are an example of a:

a. production system.	b. connectionist model.	c. stores model.	d. fuzzy trace model.

3. Fuzzy traces tend to be:

    a. remembered longer than memories that are exact and precise.

    b. remembered for less time than memories that are exact and precise.

    c. remembered about as long as memories that are exact and precise.

    d. more effortful to use than memories that are exact and precise.

4. **True or False:** In connectionist models, learning is represented by changes in the weights of the links among units in the model.

5. **True or False:** The connectionist and fuzzy trace theories both say there is an executive processor that directs ongoing cognitive activity.

Answers: 1. b, 2. b, 3. a, 4. T, 5. F

thinking
BACK TO ANGELIQUE

Now that you have studied this chapter, you should be able to list at least a dozen specific information-processing concepts and explain how Manny could use each to help Angelique. You can see the effects of Angelique's limited processing capacity and overloaded working memory. By the time she finishes the effortful task of reading the problem, she doesn't have enough capacity left over to remember what she is supposed to do in the problem! If Manny can help Angelique develop automaticity in reading and basic math facts, she will be able to focus on other aspects of the story problems. Manny can also help Angelique develop her attentional skills by teaching her to identify and attend selectively to the most informative parts of the problem.

Manny can help Angelique's memory for math facts become better organized and easier to access by helping her see the relations among them. Organizing fact "families" that contain complementary addition, subtraction, and (later) multiplication and division facts will strengthen the associations in her memory network, making retrieval faster and more accurate. After more experiences with similar kinds of problems, Angelique will probably develop some scripts for common types of story problems, which will help her figure out the most likely questions and operations. Manny might also identify the strategies that Angelique is using and help her develop more effective ones. The good news is that Angelique is metacognitively monitoring, as her awareness of being confused shows. Manny can build on this, helping Angelique learn how to pinpoint exactly what she doesn't understand. Developing self-regulation skills will help her improve both her math and her reading comprehension skills.

Manny and Angelique's situation provides a good example of how information-processing research helps people solve real-life problems. Teachers and parents alike can benefit from understanding how factors such as processing efficiency, knowledge base, specific strategies, and metacognition contribute to memory and problem solving. The information-processing view offers anyone who works with children specific ideas about what is causing problems for a child; it also offers specific ideas about how to help the child improve.

What is the information-processing approach, and what are its distinctive elements?

The information-processing approach views thinking as the processing of information and often uses the computer as a way to understand how humans think. This approach emphasizes detailed explanations of cognitive processing and the domain-specificity of cognitive skills, and it assumes that processing capacity is limited. It views cognitive development as changes in processing efficiency and knowledge base.

What are basic cognitive processes, and how do they change with development?

Basic cognitive processes are involved in virtually every cognitive act. They include processing capacity, processing efficiency, and attentional allocation. Processing capacity is the amount of information a person can think about at one time. Processing efficiency is a person's speed and accuracy in processing information. With age and experience on a specific topic, processing efficiency improves, and there are also domain-general increases in processing efficiency. As children grow, their attentional strategies become more systematic and controlled; they get better at sustaining their attention and selectively attending to some things while ignoring others.

What are the differences between a stores model of memory and network models?

The stores model proposes a series of storage locations (sensory registers, short-term memory, long-term memory) into which information can be placed. It focuses on the characteristics of each store and on how an executive processor directs the use of processing capacity within the stores. Network models view memory as an interconnected system of concept nodes connected by links. These models focus on how information is organized and on how activation spreads along the links.

What develops in working memory and in long-term memory?

It isn't clear if the actual capacity of working memory changes with age, but its functional capacity does. The size of the chunks that can be kept active in working memory and the speed with which activation spreads within the memory network both increase as children's allocation of attention and speed of processing develop. In long-term memory, the amount of knowledge and its organization change with age. Children get better at encoding information, storing it in long-term memory, and accessing and retrieving it. Children's knowledge begins as scripts for common events.

What are some of the current issues in memory development?

Memory is reconstructive rather than based on mental copies. Younger children's reconstructions are affected more than older children's by several factors. Infantile amnesia, the inability to remember early events in life, may be due to deficits in encoding, storage, access and/or retrieval. Autobiographical memories, or vivid memories of personally important events, help form the basis for a child's sense of self.

How do increases in knowledge base contribute to cognitive development?

Greater knowledge in a given domain leads to more effective and efficient encoding, storage, and retrieval of new information in that domain. Experts organize their knowledge differently than novices, which allows them to quickly identify the important aspects of a situation and focus on problem solutions.

How do strategies change with age?

Young children's strategy use is inconsistent and inflexible and does not always improve their performance. Younger children can be trained to use a strategy, but they often do not generalize it. Parental and cultural expectations and encouragement strongly influence strategy use. Children seem to have a variety of strategies available, and development consists of changes in which strategy is used most often.

What is metamemory, and how does it develop?

Metamemory is knowledge about the processes and contents of memory. Younger children show evidence of metamemory skills in familiar contexts and on simple tasks. Older children have more accurate knowledge of how memory works, and they apply that knowledge to a greater range of tasks and contexts.

Do children have a theory of mind?

A theory of mind is a framework for thinking about the mind and about how and why the mind works as it does. Young children have some understanding of thinking in general, such as the ability to distinguish between dreams and reality, but they are not skilled at distinguishing appearance from reality or their own beliefs from those of others.

How good are children at self-regulation?

Even young children show self-regulation, or the ability to self-monitor and adjust strategies, on some tasks. This ability develops with age, but even older children and adults are not consistent in their use of these metacognitive skills. Also, improved metacognition does not necessarily ensure better performance, because using metacognitive skills involves many steps. Parents and teachers affect metacognitive development by directly teaching and encouraging specific skills, and by teaching children to link success with effort and with specific strategies.

What new approaches have grown out of the information-processing perspective?

New in the developmental sphere are computational models—theories of cognition that are programmed into and run on a computer. Researchers compare the programs' output with that of real children in order to refine the theory. Production systems are sets of computerized *if–then* statements that specify the actions involved in a cognitive task. Connectionist models contain many simple units arranged into layers and connected by links of different weights. Fuzzy trace theory says that memory traces vary from verbatim to imprecise and general. Verbatim traces require more effort to store and use and are more likely to be forgotten or modified. Older children and adults tend to store and reason with fuzzy traces, while younger children tend to use verbatim traces.

What are some of the strengths and weaknesses of the information-processing perspective on cognitive development?

The information-processing view has provided information about the roles of basic processes, memory, knowledge base, strategies, and metacognition in cognitive development. It has emphasized the domain-specificity of cognitive development and highlighted the importance of cognitive efficiency and the knowledge base. However, it does not offer an overarching theory to explain all of cognitive development. Nor does it address social or emotional issues in cognitive development.

KEY TERMS

accessing (220)

attention (213)

autobiographical memories (226)

automaticity (212)

computational models (239)

connectionist models (241)

domain-general (213)

domain-specific (213)

encoding (220)

fuzzy trace theory (241)

infantile amnesia (225)

information-processing approach (208)

knowledge base (229)

long-term memory (221)

metacognition (233)

metamemory (234)

network models (of memory) (218)

processing capacity (210)

processing efficiency (211)

production systems (239)

reconstructive memory (224)

retrieval (220)

scripts (221)

self-regulation (236)

storage (220)

stores model (of memory) (217)

strategies (229)

theory of mind (235)

working memory (218)

Chapter 7

Intelligence and Academic Skills

CHAPTER PREVIEW

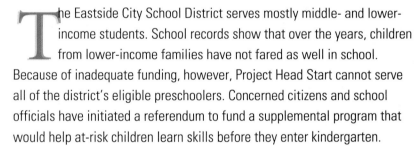

A PERSPECTIVE TO think ABOUT

"Concerned citizens have initiated a referendum to fund a program to help at-risk children"

The Eastside City School District serves mostly middle- and lower-income students. School records show that over the years, children from lower-income families have not fared as well in school. Because of inadequate funding, however, Project Head Start cannot serve all of the district's eligible preschoolers. Concerned citizens and school officials have initiated a referendum to fund a supplemental program that would help at-risk children learn skills before they enter kindergarten.

Lesley and Amanda are taxpayers in the school district, and they have been debating the merits of the referendum. Lesley favors the referendum. She argues, "You know, when parents read to young children, it raises their IQ in school. If the new program gives young children an opportunity to learn, they will have the skills they need when they enter school." Amanda, however, is skeptical: "Intelligence is mostly inherited, so it's a waste to spend so much time and money trying to boost children's IQs." "Well, if we're just talking IQ test results," counters Lesley, "those are mostly based on vocabulary and speed of thinking—and those are things children can improve." Amanda replies, "No way! Intelligence is a depth and quality of thought that some people just have, and I don't see how you can teach it."

After studying this chapter, you should be able to use at least a dozen concepts or research findings to address the debate between Lesley and Amanda. What can you add to improve their definitions of intelligence? What would your thoughts be regarding the school referendum?

 As you read this chapter, look for the questions that ask you to think about what you're learning from Lesley's and Amanda's perspectives.

When defining what it means to be "intelligent," why might a culture such as this one place more emphasis on social interaction than on other qualities such as abstract reasoning?

YOUR
PERSPECTIVE
NOTES
Complete this sentence: "Intelligence is _____." Did you have difficulty? Ask this same question of your friends and classmates. How does your answer differ from theirs?

It's no wonder that Lesley and Amanda define intelligence in different ways. Intelligence is one of the topics studied most often in psychology, yet even the experts disagree on what intelligence is and how to assess it. In this chapter we will describe different definitions and theories of intelligence, and we'll describe various ways of assessing intelligence. However, defining and assessing intelligence gets us only so far. We still must address a fundamental question: How children apply it. So this chapter will also discuss academic skills, one important area in which children put their developing intelligence to practical use.

Theories of Intelligence

Intelligence can be defined in many different ways. Culture has a significant impact on what people think of as intelligence. For example, many industrialized and Western cultures tend to emphasize logical reasoning and abstract thinking and to view mental speed as an indication of higher intelligence. Some nonindustrialized cultures, however, emphasize skill in social interactions instead, and people may see slow and cautious behavior as a sign of higher intelligence (Gardner, Kornhaber, & Wake, 1996). People in the Mashano tribe of Zimbabwe, for example, value prudence and caution in social interactions. Similarly, the Pulawat people of Micronesia respect moderation and diplomacy. People in some Asian cultures, especially those influenced by Confucian philosophy, often emphasize moral behavior and personal effort in defining intelligence.

Most of the psychological research on intelligence comes from the Western, industrialized perspective of Europe and the United States. Theorists within this perspective generally define **intelligence** as the ability to learn, think logically about abstract concepts, and adapt to the environment. Even within this Western perspective, however, there has been great

intelligence

As generally defined in Western cultures, the ability to learn, think logically about abstract concepts, and adapt to the environment.

disagreement about how to define and understand human intelligence. In this section we will introduce you to three different approaches to intelligence: the psychometric approach, Sternberg's triarchic theory, and Gardner's multiple-intelligences approach.

thinking
OF LESLEY & AMANDA

◄ Which cultural perspective fits most closely with Lesley's and Amanda's ideas about intelligence?

As you study this section, ask yourself these questions:

- Is intelligence a general and broad ability, or is it a constellation of many separate skills?

- What are several of the major theories of intelligence? How does each define intelligence?

- What are the major similarities and differences among these theories?

- How does creativity relate to intelligence?

Psychometric Approaches

With the **psychometric approach** to studying intelligence, researchers use paper-and-pencil tests and/or physical measurements in an attempt to quantify people's psychological skills and abilities. This approach originated with Francis Galton (1822–1911) who collected data on physical and perceptual characteristics from almost 10,000 people. Galton measured people's weight, height, muscle strength, lung capacity, skull size, vision, and hearing; he also assessed their reaction times and their ability to make fine discriminations of sensory stimuli. He then used the newly developing methodology of statistics to analyze the measures. Galton failed to show systematic relations between his measures and other indicators of intelligence, such as success in school or business. Even so, this "father of mental testing" was important in establishing the psychometric approach (Boring, 1950; Gardner et al., 1996).

One of the most influential psychometric theorists was Charles Spearman (1863–1945), who gathered information on children in an English village school. Instead of looking

psychometric approach

The attempt to quantify people's psychological skills and abilities, usually by means of paper-and-pencil tests and/or physical measurements.

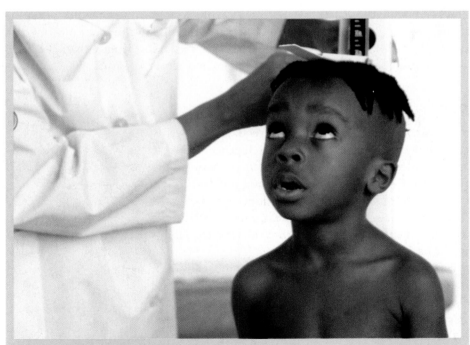

Galton included physical measures such as height, weight, and head circumference among his measures of intelligence. In what way might these measures be expected to relate to a person's general intelligence?

thinking
OF LESLEY & AMANDA

How are Lesley's and Amanda's views of intelligence related to Spearman's concepts of *g* and *s*?

YOUR
PERSPECTIVE
NOTES

Do you agree with the idea of a *g* factor in intelligence that underlies all intellectual accomplishments? Explain why or why not.

only at physical and perceptual measures, Spearman studied the children's cleverness, common sense, and exam scores in various subject areas. Spearman found strong positive correlations among all his measures and proposed a **two-factor theory of intelligence** to explain his results (Spearman, 1904, 1927). The first factor he called **general intelligence** *(g)*. General intelligence is a broad ability that applies to some extent to all intellectual tasks—essentially, the ability to see how things relate and fit together. Spearman thought that *g* was neurologically based, and he saw *g* as providing the driving force behind most intellectual accomplishments (Spearman, 1923, p. 5). Spearman called his second factor **specific intelligence** *(s),* referring to the abilities people have in particular areas, such as reading, verbal, and spatial skills.

The biggest area of disagreement among the different psychometric theories is the question of how many abilities fall under the heading of "intelligence." For example, Louis Thurstone identified 7 mental abilities that he saw as separate and distinct from general intelligence (Thurstone, 1938; Thurstone & Thurstone, 1941). J. P. Guilford identified at least 150 abilities that he thought were important in defining intelligence (Guilford, 1967, 1982). Raymond B. Cattell and John Horn proposed two broad factors, **fluid ability** and **crystallized ability,** along with several other more specific factors (Horn & Cattell, 1966). Fluid ability, much like Spearman's *g,* is a biologically based ability to think. Fluid ability essentially involves the ability to perceive relations among elements, and it peaks by around age 18. In contrast, crystallized ability consists of the knowledge and skills people acquire in a particular culture. Crystallized ability can include such things as number ability, mechanical skills, and vocabulary, and it can increase throughout adulthood.

The important point to remember about these later psychometric theories of intelligence is this: They began to challenge the idea that a *g*-factor theory like Spearman's could adequately explain differences among individuals' intellectual performance. The controversy reminds us that there has always been disagreement about whether each person has a level of "general" intelligence underlying performance across all tasks. Modern cognitive psychologists have argued that psychometric theories place too much stress on static indicators of intelligence (such as facts and vocabulary) and disregard the cognitive processes involved in intelligent thought. These criticisms have led to new theories of intelligence that take more contemporary cognitive and neuropsychological views into account (Garlick, 2002).

Sternberg's Triarchic Theory

Starting in the early 1980s, Yale University psychologist Robert Sternberg developed a **triarchic theory of intelligence.** Sternberg's theory embraces the information-processing concept you read about in Chapter 6. It describes the mental processes involved in intellectual thought as well as the aspects of experience and the environmental context for intelligence. The theory is called "triarchic" because it consists of three interrelated subtheories, as shown in Figure 7.1.

The **componential subtheory** describes how mental processes work together to give us intellectual thought (Sternberg, 1985, 1999). In this subtheory a "component" is a mental process (such as planning, reading, or remembering) that gathers or works with information. Not only does Sternberg's triarchic theory include *three* subtheories (componential, experiential, and contextual); Sternberg also divided the componential subtheory into *three* parts. (Sternberg is famous for doing things in threes!)

Robert Sternberg's triarchic theory describes how mental processes, experience, and the environmental context all interact to produce intelligent thought and behavior.

two-factor theory of intelligence

A theory of intelligence developed by Charles Spearman that emphasized general intelligence *(g)* and specific intelligence *(s).*

general intelligence *(g)*

A broad thinking ability or mental power that underlies all intellectual tasks and functions.

specific intelligence *(s)*

Abilities people have in particular areas, such as reading, verbal, and spatial skills.

fluid ability

A biologically based ability to think and perceive relations among elements.

crystallized ability

The body of specific knowledge and skills acquired in a particular culture.

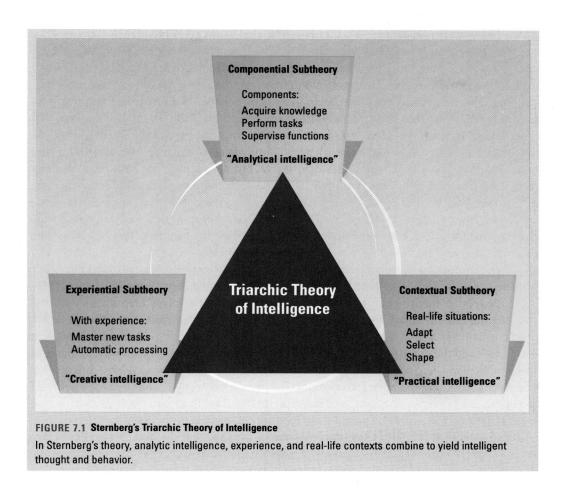

FIGURE 7.1 Sternberg's Triarchic Theory of Intelligence
In Sternberg's theory, analytic intelligence, experience, and real-life contexts combine to yield intelligent thought and behavior.

▶ *Knowledge-acquisition components* bring new information into the mind. These components selectively encode, combine, and compare information, allowing us to acquire new knowledge.

▶ *Performance components* perform tasks such as sorting, classifying, remembering, and otherwise process information. Reading, writing, mathematics computations, and other tasks use performance components.

▶ *Metacomponents* "supervise" the functioning of the other two types of components. Like the metacognitive processes discussed in Chapter 6, they plan, control, and monitor the other processes. These components evaluate how well the other intellectual processes are working.

As an example, Sternberg described how these three components work together when we write a paper (Sternberg, 1988). We use *metacomponents* to define a topic, decide on an organization, monitor the writing progress, and evaluate the finished product. Thanks to *performance components* we can do such things as retrieve appropriate words from memory, remember how to use the word-processing system on our computer, or remember the rules of grammar. *Knowledge-acquisition components* help us during the research phase, allowing us to sift through vast amounts of information and decide what to include in the paper. Because these mental components enable us to analyze information, they are sometimes called *analytical intelligence*. Analytical intelligence is the type of intelligence that is usually measured in typical paper-and-pencils tests.

triarchic theory of intelligence

Theory of intelligence emphasizing how mental processes, experience, and situational contexts relate to intellectual thought. Includes componential, experiential, and contextual subtheories.

componential subtheory

Describes how mental processes work together in intellectual thought ("analytical intelligence").

YOUR PERSPECTIVE

NOTES

Think of a task that you have had to complete, such as taking an exam. Try to identify the aspects of this task that involved the metacomponents, performance components, and knowledge-acquisition components of your intelligence.

YOUR PERSPECTIVE

NOTES

Can you think of someone with especially strong contextual intelligence? Describe the person's abilities to adapt to, select, and shape his or her environment. How have these abilities contributed to the person's intelligence?

experiential subtheory

Describes how we become more intelligent as we master new tasks and learn how to perform them more automatically ("creative intelligence").

contextual subtheory

Describes how intelligent behavior relates to real-life situations as people adapt to, select, and/or shape their environments ("practical intelligence").

The **experiential subtheory** addresses the role of novelty and experience in intelligence. According to this subtheory, we become more intelligent as we master new tasks and learn how to perform them more automatically. For example, think of young children learning to read. At first all of the words are new to children, so they have to think hard to figure out each one. With more experience children begin to recognize more and more words automatically. Eventually the word-recognition process flows smoothly. Now children can begin to deal with other aspects of reading—such as understanding the meaning behind the words, summarizing the gist of a story, and making predictions about what will happen next. As with reading, most complex tasks are difficult to perform at first, but with experience we learn to perform them more automatically. This, in turn, frees up more mental capacity for other aspects of the task. As you can see, this part of Sternberg's theory uses the concept of *automaticity,* which we discussed in Chapter 6. The experiential subtheory ties in with what we typically call *creative intelligence.* That is, some people are quick at figuring out new tasks—they see new patterns easily and find creative new ways to solve problems.

The **contextual subtheory** describes individuals' ability to show intelligent behavior in real-life contexts. That is an aspect of intelligent behavior that Sternberg thought was missing in most other theories of intelligence (Sternberg, 1985). It involves adapting to, selecting, and shaping real-life situations. (Yes, another set of *three.*) When placed in a new situation, people usually try first to *adapt to* their environment: They try to achieve a good fit between themselves and the environment without changing either in any significant way. Sometimes, however, they must do something to improve the fit. One possibility is to *select* a different environment. Another possibility is to attempt to *shape* the existing environment for a better fit. Sternberg (1985) used the example of marriage to illustrate these three processes. If a marriage is not satisfying in some way, a person will try first to adapt by ignoring the negatives and focusing on the marriage's positive aspects. If that does not work, then the person may select a different environment by leaving the marriage—or may try to shape the existing environment by changing its unsatisfactory aspects. Some people are especially good at dealing with their environments. Contextual intelligence is related to what most people call *common sense, street smarts,* or *practical intelligence.*

Sternberg's theory is an ambitious attempt to account for the varied facets of intelligent behavior. His comprehensive explanation is a strength of this theory. Another strength is that empirical research studies have investigated each of the subtheories and have provided at least modest support for many of the ideas (Sternberg, 1985). However, critics charge that although the theory is comprehensive, it is not clear how the three subtheories relate to one another. Nor is it clear why some elements are included but other possible elements are not. Finally, Sternberg does not link his components and processes to the biology of intelligence or to what is known about how the brain functions (Gardner et al., 1996).

Gardner's Theory of Multiple Intelligences

In 1983 Harvard psychologist Howard Gardner proposed a **theory of multiple intelligences.** This theory defines "an intelligence" as a "biopsychological potential to process information that can be activated in a cultural setting to solve problems or create products that are of value in a culture" (Gardner, 1999, p. 34). Notice several important aspects of this definition. First, Gardner is not defining *intelligence;* rather, he is defining *an intelligence.* This is the heart of his theory. Gardner proposes that intelligence is neither a unitary *g* factor, nor a broad factor made up of subcomponents or specific abilities. Instead, he argues that there are several different types of intelligence, each relatively independent of the others. A person's overall level of functioning is determined by his profile of strengths and weaknesses among these different intelligences in interaction with a particular cultural setting. A second important point is that an intelligence is a **biopsychological potential;** this means that there is an underlying biological, and most likely genetic, component. Being genetic, however, does not mean that this potential is unaffected by the environment. A particular biopsychological potential *may or may not be fully realized,* depending on environmental factors. Cultural values, opportunities, and individual choices all affect the developing intelligence. For example, think of a female child born with strong logical–mathematical potential. If she grow up in a culture that does not permit females to be educated, such as under the former Taliban government in Afghanistan, it is very unlikely that the girl will fulfill this particular potential. In other countries girls may go to school, but the culture may steer them toward more "domestic" topics and away from advanced mathematics. Finally, even if the culture is encouraging, a girl herself may decide not to pursue math; again, her mathematics potential is not going to be fully realized.

Gardner identifies eight intelligences (Gardner, 1983, 1999). Clearly, he is not the first to identify several of these areas—all the theorists we have discussed recognize at least two, and sometimes many more, factors. Gardner differs from these other approaches, though, in that he does not base his analysis solely on statistical analysis of a battery of paper-and-pencil tests. Instead, he identified a set of specific criteria to determine whether a given skill qualifies as an intelligence. These criteria include not only psychometric findings but also such things as the potential for isolation by brain damage (which indicates a biological basis for the skill), an evolutionary history (to explain why the intelligence would have evolved), identifiable core operation(s) (to specify the skills involved in the intelligence), and the existence of exceptional people (both those with strength and those with weakness in the particular intelligence). Thus, Gardner's analysis depends on support from more than just psychometric test scores.

Based on his criteria, Gardner discribes the following eight intelligences:

❭ *Linguistic intelligence* involves an especially acute sensitivity to spoken and written language, including the abilities to learn languages and to use language effectively to achieve specific goals. Lawyers, speakers, writers, and poets are all likely to be strong in this intelligence.

❭ *Logical–mathematical intelligence* involves recognizing and using abstract relations to analyze problems logically, carry out mathematical operations, and investigate issues scientifically. Mathematicians, computer programmers, accountants, engineers, and scientists are strong in this intelligence. Gardner believes that Piaget's theory of cognitive development, which you read about in Chapter 5, is predominantly a description of the development of this kind of intelligence.

❭ *Musical intelligence* involves sensitivity to aspects of sound (such as tone, pitch, and rhythm) and skill in creating and communicating with sounds and musical patterns. Composers, conductors, audio engineers, and acousticians are high in musical intelligence.

❭ *Bodily–kinesthetic intelligence* is the ability to use the whole body, or parts of it, to solve problems or make products. This intelligence involves a high degree of control over fine- and gross-motor skills. Dancers and athletes are high in bodily–kinesthetic intelligence; but so are surgeons, craftspeople, actors, and mechanics, as these professions also require a high degree of motor coordination.

❭ *Spatial intelligence* involves the abilities to perceive, transform, and recreate spatial information for large-scale or small-scale projects. Sailors, pilots, engineers, surgeons, sculptors, and painters show high levels of spatial intelligence.

❭ *Interpersonal intelligence* is the capacity to understand and work effectively with other people. This includes understanding other people's motivations, intentions, and desires. Successful salespeople, politicians, teachers, clinicians, and religious leaders show this kind of intelligence.

Howard Gardner believes there is more than one type of intelligence. His theory of multiple intelligences includes eight different types.

thinking
OF LESLEY & AMANDA

◀ How might the supplemental program proposed for the Eastside schools affect children's biopsychological potentials? What should the program do to help all children achieve each of their potentials?

theory of multiple intelligences

Theory of intelligence emphasizing that we all have multiple intelligences that operate relatively independently of one another. Includes eight intelligences.

biopsychological potential

The underlying biological component of each intelligence that may or may not be reached, depending on a person's culture, opportunities, individual choices, and other factors.

What will happen with this girl's biopsychological potential if she has a genetic strength for math and science but grows up in a culture that forbids her from pursuing these topics in school? How has your culture affected your intellectual potential?

▶ *Intrapersonal intelligence* is the ability to understand and regulate your own emotions. It involves a sensitivity to and understanding of your own desires, fears, intentions, and capacities. Examples of this kind of intelligence might include some writers, therapists, and communities' "wise elders." Gardner believes that intrapersonal intelligence allows people to build accurate "mental models" of themselves and to use these models to make good personal decisions (Gardner et al., 1996).

▶ *Naturalist intelligence* is skill in recognizing and classifying plants and animals in the environment. This intelligence includes an ability to distinguish among members of the same and different species and to chart the relations among species. Biologists, environmentalists, hunters, fishermen, farmers, gardeners, and even cooks are all examples of people who may be high in this kind of intelligence.

Gardner emphasizes that all eight intelligences exist to some degree in every individual, because the intelligences are part of being human. However, each person has a different *profile of intelligences*—a different combination of strengths and weaknesses. According to Gardner, it is important that parents and educators recognize each child's individual strengths and weaknesses and provide adequate opportunities for each child to activate his or her own areas of strength. When looking at a school curriculum, for example, we need to recognize that one size doesn't fit all. In addition to covering areas such as reading, math, and science, we need to offer opportunities in art, music, sports, and technical training. Exploring these options lets children activate their unique potentials or strengthen their individual intellectual profiles.

A given intelligence can be activated in many different ways. And children's social context and overall culture will have a strong influence on the particular forms that activated intelligences take—and on whether others or even children themselves view the end results as positive or negative (Furnham, Shahidi, & Baluch, 2002). For example, within a positive context a child with strong interpersonal potential might develop into a skilled counselor or clergyperson. Under less desirable conditions the same child could develop into a con artist or swindler. All these "professions" require a well-developed sensitivity to interpersonal interactions and others' thoughts and feelings. So the particular opportunities provided by the

Howard Gardner proposes that there are several different types of intelligences. What types of intelligences are shown by the children in these photos?

social and cultural context, along with the rest of an individual's profile of stronger and weaker intelligences, help determine how far each intelligence will develop and what form the developed intelligence will take.

Gardner's theory has broadened our view of what constitutes intelligence. Gardner is not without critics, however. One complaint is that his roster of intelligences really does not further our understanding of the concept of intelligence. Critics argue that the theory blurs the distinction between intelligence and other, nonintellectual, human characteristics (Herrnstein & Murray, 1994). Critics also have pointed out that Gardner's measures of the intelligences often correlate with one another, perhaps weakening the argument that the intelligences are independent. Gardner responds that this intercorrelation occurs because of the types of tests that have traditionally been available. If more appropriate measures existed for each of the intelligences, he suggests, we could test their independence more fairly (Gardner et al., 1996; Scarr, 1985). Finally, it is not clear what coordinates the intelligences when they work together on a given task. Gardner says that the intrapersonal intelligence may play this role; but critics claim that such coordination necessarily implies a *g* factor, the very concept that Gardner was reacting against.

What about Creativity?

As you've seen, theorists like Sternberg and Gardner argue that intelligence has numerous important dimensions. There are also other individual attributes that influence how people use their intellectual skills. One of these related attributes is *creativity*. **Creativity** is a capacity for original thinking and problem solving, an ability to do things in new or different ways. For example, try this exercise with a couple of friends: Have each person draw 20 squares on his or her own piece of paper. Using each square as a starting point, have each person create 20 original drawings, each different from the other. Now compare your drawings with those of your friends. How original are the ideas? How easy was it to come up with ideas? In short, how *creative* were you?

Anything can be approached in a creative way, but creative thought is not random or effortless. Creative products are intentional, not accomplished by accident. They also have value in the particular culture in which they emerge, often because they solve an important problem. For example, during the horse-and-buggy-days New York City developed traffic problems. Often several vehicles would arrive at an intersection at the same time, and no one would know whether to stop or proceed. One creative (now infamous?) person, William Eno, came up with the ideas of stop signs, one-way streets, and other traffic guidelines (Bransford & Stein, 1984). Creative thinking is often described as being *divergent*, or coming up with many different ideas, rather than *convergent*, or identifying one answer.

Even though a fortunate accident may inspire an initial creative idea, a creator must recognize the idea's potential and work to develop it to its final form. People tend to be creative in specific areas, usually areas they have rich knowledge about. But some psychologists talk about developing a creative general approach to life. Although this second form of creativity may not produce specific inventions or make you famous, it may be the more important of the two for improving the quality and enjoyability of your life (Csikszentmihalyi, 1990).

What does it take to be creative? An average degree of intelligence seems necessary, but you do not have to have above-average intelligence to think and solve problems creatively (Baer, 1991). However, it does help if you know a lot about the particular topic or problem you're dealing with. This gives you a greater number of basic building blocks to recombine and put together in novel ways. One thing that is essential is the ability to restructure ideas. In other words, you have to be able to think about how to use or combine objects or ideas in original ways. For example, how many things can you do with a tin can? After the first few

YOUR PERSPECTIVE NOTES

For each intelligence proposed by Gardner, identify a person you know who is strong in that intelligence. What would your own profile of intelligences look like across these types of intelligence?

creativity

Original thinking and problem solving that produces a product valued by society.

ideas, you have to break out of the typical ways of thinking about tin cans and come up with novel ideas. Your chances of thinking and problem solving creatively are also greater if you can *incubate* the problem you're dealing with, or stop trying to think about it for a while (Wallas, 1926). Finally, creative thought requires that you keep trying. The famous inventor Thomas Edison reportedly was once asked if he ever felt like a failure when he failed 200 times to make a light bulb. He replied that he didn't fail even once—it was just a 200-step process. Persistence is essential!

How does creativity develop? Dacey (1989) outlines six peak periods in the development of creativity: birth to 5 years of age, 10 to 14 years, 18 to 20 years, 29 to 31 years, 40 to 45 years, and 60 to 65 years. Dacey argues that the peak period from 10 to 14 years is especially important, because at this age youngsters are actively developing a sense of their own individual identities. So children are more likely to be open to thinking of themselves as being creative during this time than when they are younger or older. Regardless of age, however, there are ways to encourage creativity. Supporting experimentation and divergent thinking is important. *Brainstorming,* or producing lots of ideas without subjecting them to evaluation, fosters creativity. Parents and teachers also can model creative thinking, attitudes, and problem solving. This helps children see that anyone can develop creativity—it is not a gift possessed only by a select few. Finally, engaging in play may help increase creativity. Play often involves creating a fantasy world and breaking free from the constraints of reality—a good way for a child (or an adult) to practice the originality, fluency, and flexibility that creativity demands (Woolfolk, 2001).

YOUR PERSPECTIVE NOTES

Think about someone you consider particularly creative. What characteristics of creativity does this person show? If possible, talk to the person and ask how he or she developed this creative ability.

LET'S REVIEW . . .

1. Most experts agree that intelligence involves:
   a. the ability to learn.
   b. the ability to think logically about abstract concepts.
   c. the ability to adapt to the environment.
   d. all of the above.

2. Which theory of intelligence makes the most use of information-processing research to define intelligence?
   a. psychometric theory
   b. Cattell and Horn's fluid versus crystallized abilities
   c. Sternberg's triarchic theory
   d. Gardner's theory of multiple intelligences

3. Now in second grade, Lisa has practiced her addition math facts so thoroughly that she can fly through single-digit flash cards at an impressive speed. Which subtheory in Sternberg's triarchic theory of intelligence would relate most closely to Lisa's speed with math facts?
   a. the componential subtheory
   b. the experiential subtheory
   c. the contextual subtheory
   d. the metacomponent subtheory

4. **True or False:** Culture has a significant impact on how people define intelligence and on the types of skills and abilities that people see as demonstrating intelligence.

5. **True or False:** In Gardner's theory of multiple intelligences, linguistic intelligence is the root of all of the other types of intelligence, and people tend to be intelligent in the other areas only when they are high in linguistic intelligence.

Answers: 1. d, 2. c, 3. b, 4. T, 5. F

Assessing Intelligence

As you can imagine, each of the theories of intelligence we've explored has implications for intelligence *assessment,* or testing. For example, according to Sternberg's triarchic theory, to measure a person's intelligence we need to ask how well that person acquires, processes, and evaluates information. How well does a child or an adult learn from experience? How readily does the person recognize new patterns and solutions? According to Sternberg, we should also measure street smarts, or practical intelligence, to gauge the individual's ability to adapt to or change aspects of real-life situations. Gardner's theory of multiple intelligences advocates the development and use of *intelligence-fair assessments*—testing systems that give children ample opportunities to demonstrate their linguistic, logical–mathematical, musical, bodily–kinesthetic, and other forms of intelligence. Teachers and/or researchers need to observe students on an ongoing basis, and assessment tasks should use familiar materials in realistic contexts (Gardner, 1999; Gardner et al., 1996).

By far the best-known and most frequently used assessments of intelligence, however, grew out of the psychometric perspective. The following section provides a brief history of intelligence testing and describes the main tests used today to assess intelligence in children and adolescents.

As you study this section, ask yourself these questions:

- What was the purpose of the first intelligence scales?

- How did the measurement of intelligence evolve over time?

- Do today's intelligence tests take into account the cultural differences among groups of people?

- What are the differences among the intelligence tests used most frequently today?

History of Intelligence Testing

The first practical intelligence scale came out in France in 1905. Alfred Binet and Theodore Simon devised the scale to help French schools predict which children would perform well in regular education settings and which would benefit from special education. The scale posed a series of increasingly difficult questions or tests, such as pointing to an object in a picture, defining a common word, and explaining the difference between "boredom" and "weariness" (Gregory, 1996). Then each child's progress through the tests was compared to the average pattern shown by other children of the same age. Through these comparisons, Binet and Simon stated, they could determine "how much above or below average" a child was (Simon & Binet, 1905, as quoted in Thorndike & Lohman, 1990, p. 13). Binet and Simon revised the scale in 1908 and 1911. The 1908 version was the first to use the concept of *mental age.* The creators carefully organized the tests according to the average ages at which children passed them. They could then determine each individual child's mental age by the highest level of tests the child could pass. For example, the scale would give an 8-year-old who passed the same tests as the average 10-year-old a mental age of 10. The 1908 scale contained 54 tests (e.g., sentence completion, word definition, repeating digits and sentences, drawing designs from memory), including at least 3 or 4 tests at each mental age from 3 to 13 years. The 1911 scale saw only minor modifications.

In 1916 Lewis Terman, an American psychologist at Stanford University, published his own modified version of the Binet–Simon scale. Terman added his own age norms, which he arrived at by testing more than 1,000 California schoolchildren. Later known as the

Stanford–Binet Scale (because Terman had revised Binet's work at Stanford University), Terman's version stood for several decades as the premier intelligence test in the United States (Gregory, 1996).

Terman's test also popularized the term **intelligence quotient (IQ)**, a concept that was originally developed in Germany by William Stern in 1912. Stern suggested that each child's mental level be adjusted by their chronological age to yield a ratio showing their mental standing. IQ was defined as mental age (MA) divided by chronological age (CA). Later it became popular to multiply the result by 100 to eliminate decimals, giving the formula (MA ÷ CA) × 100. With this formula, a child who shows a mental age of 8 on the test, but who is actually 10 years old, would score an IQ of 80 [(8 ÷ 10) × 100 = 80]. A child who shows a mental age of 10 on the test, but actually has a chronological age of only 8, would score an IQ of 125 [(10 ÷ 8) × 100 = 125]. An 8-year-old who shows a mental age of 8 on the test would have an IQ of 100 [(8 ÷ 8) × 100 = 100]. With this system, 100 is the average IQ for children of a given age. Scores below 100 show performance that is below what is typical for that age, and scores above 100 show above-average performance.

During World War I there was interest in the U.S. military in using intelligence tests. The goals were to weed out "feeble-minded" recruits and to channel the remaining recruits into their most suitable positions (Thorndike & Lohman, 1990). The Germans were already using psychological tests to classify military personnel. Binet had suggested that France follow suit; the French government declined, but officials in the U.S. government liked the idea. Terman and other notable U.S. psychologists served on advisory committees to develop intelligence tests for U.S. Army recruits. By 1917 the "Army Alpha" intelligence test for army recruits was in use. For recruits who did not speak English, were illiterate, or otherwise scored low on the Alpha, a nonverbal test was developed known as "Army Beta" (Thorndike, 1997). Terman's Stanford–Binet scale was also used with military recruits.

One of the most unfortunate outcomes of military intelligence testing occurred when the government made use of test results after the war. Many army recruits had been recent immigrants from southern and eastern Europe who weren't yet fully familiar with the language and culture of the United States. Consequently, they had tended to score lower than other groups on the U.S. intelligence tests. Immigration officials at Ellis Island also administered various intelligence tests and found a similar trend: Mediterranean and Slavic immigrants scored lower on average than English, German, and Scandinavian immigrants (Richardson, 2003). In those days most psychologists and other scientists favored a genetic (nature) explanation for most human traits. Also, they did not fully appreciate the language and cultural biases inherent in the tests. In 1924, partly on the basis of the test results, the U.S. Congress passed an immigration act that limited immigration from certain areas of Europe and even denied Asians the right to apply for U.S. citizenship. As Thorndike and Lohman (1990) observed, "it is unfortunate that psychology became involved in this matter, and it is doubly unfortunate that the data, whatever their quality, should have been so badly misinterpreted" (p. 56). It seems that government officials used the intelligence test data as a convenient and scientific-sounding rationale to justify implementing the ethnocentric agenda of their day.

Intelligence Testing Today

Today, psychologists and other mental health professionals often use intelligence tests to help them diagnose and treat numerous problems in children and adolescents. Measures of intelligence help professionals identify children who have cognitive deficits; learning disabilities; attention deficits; or problems with specific processes such as reading, spatial reasoning, or memory. Test results can also help practitioners determine if a child has an emotional dis-

intelligence quotient (IQ)

Originally computed as (MA ÷ CA) × 100, where the average IQ is 100 for a given age.

turbance, brain disorder, or serious mental illness. Taken alone, intelligence scores don't provide enough information to enable a practitioner to make any of these diagnoses. In combination with clinical interviews (e.g., of the child, parents, and teachers), physical examinations, and results from other psychological tests and observations, however, the scores can add an important piece to the larger puzzle. Educators also use intelligence tests to screen children for entry into special education programs. In addition, the tests can measure children's progress as they receive special programs or other forms of therapy or counseling. Still, we always need to heed the lessons from the past: Any professional who uses intelligence tests (or any other assessment tool) needs to be aware of the tests' potential for cultural bias, misinterpretation, and misuse. We'll discuss this issue more thoroughly later in the chapter.

A variety of tests exist for assessing intelligence across different ages and for different purposes. The most widely used tests are the Stanford–Binet scale and the tests developed by David Wechsler. But before we describe these tests, we need to explain the two essential ingredients that any assessment device needs: *reliability* and *validity*.

The term **reliability** refers to the consistency of scores when a test is repeated under the same or similar conditions. If the same child takes an intelligence test twice, the results should be about the same both times (assuming there has been no intervention between test sessions aimed at improving intelligence). Otherwise, how could we trust that either score was accurate? Researchers measure the reliability of intelligence tests by having the same groups of people retake the test and then computing correlations to determine how similar the scores are across the test and retest sessions. Another way to check reliability is to split a test into two equivalent halves, then see if scores across the two halves are similar. Correlations above .80 usually indicate a high degree of reliability (Sattler, 2001).

A test's **validity** is its ability to measure what it intends to measure—in this case, intelligence. In contrast to the situation with reliability, there are no direct measures of a test's validity. As a result, validity has to be assessed more indirectly. We deem intelligence tests to be valid when the scores accurately predict which children will perform better or worse in school; or when they predict success in other areas of life, such as job performance. That is, we assume that higher intelligence will be related to greater success in school and on the job—so when test scores predict success in these areas, we conclude that the test does indeed measure intelligence. We also have evidence of a test's validity when the scores correlate highly with scores on other tests that are presumed to measure intelligence.

■ The Stanford–Binet Intelligence Scale.

Terman's Stanford–Binet scale has undergone several revisions since its introduction in 1916. A complete restructuring in 1986 created what is now known as the *Stanford–Binet Intelligence Scale: Fourth Edition* (or *SB:IV*). Whereas the earlier Stanford–Binet tests yielded only a single intelligence score, the SB:IV provides an overall intelligence score along with scores in four subareas (verbal reasoning, quantitative reasoning, abstract/visual reasoning, and short-term memory) and on 15 subtests within these subareas. Figure 7.2 shows items like those in the SB:IV. When educators restructured the test in 1986, they tried hard to design test items that were fair to children from diverse cultural backgrounds (Sattler, 2001). A panel of reviewers from different ethnic groups evaluated the test for possible signs of bias, and the standardization process used a sample of more than 5,000 individuals ranging in age from 2 to 24 years and representing all socioeconomic and ethnic groups in the United States. The SB:IV is very reliable, with test–retest and other reliability correlations typically above .90 (Sattler, 2001). The test also shows moderately high correlations with other measures of intelligence, demonstrating a reasonable degree of validity.

■ The Wechsler Scales.

In the 1930s David Wechsler constructed an intelligence test to use with the diverse patients he treated in the psychiatric unit of Bellevue Hospital in New York. Borrowing some of his test items from the U.S. Army Alpha and Beta tests, the Stanford–Binet,

reliability

The consistency of scores when a test is repeated under the same or similar conditions.

validity

The ability of a test to measure what it intends to measure (e.g., intelligence).

Items like those used in the Stanford-Binet Intelligence Scale, Fourth Edition

Verbal   Name pictures. Define *train, dime, taut, cryptography.*

Quantitative   What is the smallest whole number evenly divisible by 1, 2, and 3?

Short-term memory   Recall series of digits (e.g., 4, 6, 9, 0, 3, 2, 5). Recall similar series backwards.

Abstract/visual   Select the picture that shows how a folded and cut piece of paper would look unfolded.

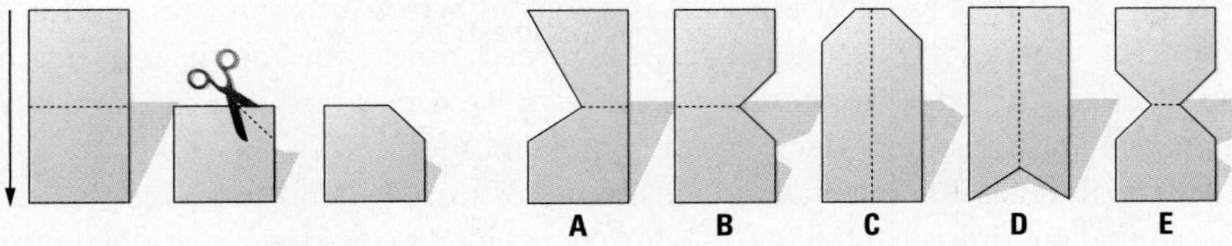

Items like those found in the Wechsler Intelligence Scale for Children, Third Edition

Verbal

Basic information   Who discovered the North Pole? What is the capital of France?

Vocabulary   Define *summer, poet, obstreperous.*

Arithmetic   If a suit sells for ½ of the regular price, what is the cost of a $120 suit?

Comprehension   Why are we tried by a jury of our peers?

Similarities   In what way are *inch* and *mile* alike?

Performance

Picture completion

What is missing from this picture?

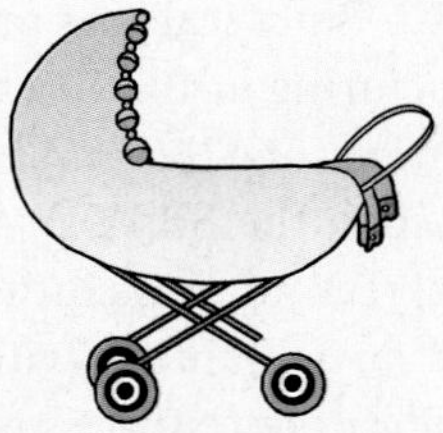

Block design

Reproduce the design below using four or nine blocks.

Object assembly

Arrange the pieces into a meaningful object.

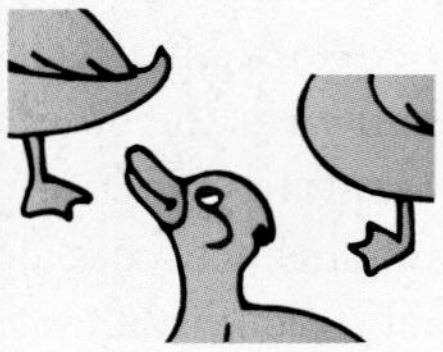

FIGURE 7.2 Sample Intelligence Test Items

The *Stanford–Binet Intelligence Scale: Fourth Edition* and the *Wechsler Intelligence Scale for Children–Third Edition* include items such as the questions shown here.

Source: J. Sattler. (2001). *Assessment of children,* 4th ed. San Diego, CA: Jerome M. Sattler. Reprinted with permission.

and other tests available at the time, Wechsler published the *Wechsler–Bellevue Intelligence Scales* in 1939.

Wechsler began his work with adults, but over the following years he developed a family of intelligence scales designed for people of different ages: the *Wechsler Preschool and Primary*

Scale of Intelligence, Revised (WPPSI–R) for children aged 3 through 7, the *Wechsler Intelligence Scale for Children, Third Edition* (WISC–III) for children 6 to 16, and the *Wechsler Adult Intelligence Scale, Revised* (WAIS–R) for people 16 and up. Each of these scales provides an overall or composite intelligence score and two general subscale scores—verbal and performance. The verbal subscale includes subtests in basic information, vocabulary, arithmetic, comprehension, and similarities. The performance subscale includes picture completion, block design, and object assembly. Additional verbal and performance subtests are available but vary across the WPPSI–R, WISC–III, and WAIS–R. A few sample items like those from the WISC–III appear in Figure 7.2.

As with the SB:IV, standardization of the Wechsler scales used large samples representing all income and ethnic segments of the U.S. population. The tests have reliability correlations around .90 or higher. They also have demonstrated adequate validity (Sattler, 2001). That is, Wechsler scores predict later school success moderately well, with correlations ranging around .50 to .65 in most studies (Kamphaus, 2001). In general, children who score higher on these intelligence tests tend to receive higher grades in school, are more likely to go to college, and tend to receive more favorable job performance ratings.

For some examples of uses of intelligence tests in a professional setting, see the Professional Perspective box called "Career Focus: Meet a School Psychologist."

thinking OF LESLEY & AMANDA

◀ For the intelligence tests described so far, which subscales seem to measure most directly the types of intelligence described by Lesley and Amanda?

Ethnic Differences and Questions about Cultural Bias

Imagine the challenges that faced many immigrants arriving in the United States in the early 1900s. Often malnourished, exhausted, and in poor health after a long journey in a crowded ship, they stepped out on Ellis Island. Anxious to find relatives and explore their new country, they learned that first they must take several tests. One was an intelligence test—perhaps the Stanford–Binet, which was a French test translated into English. If the immigrants didn't speak English, then they would take a version retranslated into their native language. The test administators would then compare their scores to the norms established by U.S.–born citizens who were tested under far more comfortable conditions. Is it surprising that the immigrants' scores were lower? Further, could the questions in the French and American tests adequately measure the general intelligence of people raised in Hungary, Russia, Italy, African nations, or other parts of the world? Did the questions even make sense to people from other cultures? In other words, were the tests culturally fair?

Numerous studies conducted since the 1960s have documented differences in intelligence scores among various U.S. ethnic groups (see Gregory, 1996 and Sattler, 2001 for reviews). Typically, composite scores for non-Hispanic whites are about 100. Asians score slightly higher, African Americans score about 15 points lower, and Hispanics score between Caucasians and African Americans (Suzuki, Vraniak, & Kugler, 1996). You must keep in mind that these are group differences: scores vary much more *within* these groups than *among* them. It is impossible to predict any one

YOUR PERSPECTIVE NOTES

What would it take to develop an intelligence test that was really culturally fair?

Does racial uneasiness between examiner and child affect performance on IQ tests? What other potential problems must we consider when comparing IQ scores across different ethnic groups?

A Professional PERSPECTIVE...

Career Focus: Meet a School Psychologist

Sandy Roland, Ph.D.
Dallas and Richardson, Texas

Licensed specialist in school psychology, Richardson Independent School District

In what circumstances are intelligence tests useful in your practice? Intelligence tests are used to acquire a general level of functioning of the child when considering what strategies may help the child progress in learning. Mainly, we use intelligence tests when determining if a child has mental retardation or a learning disability. Intelligence scores are also sometimes helpful when a child is being screened or evaluated for ADHD [attention deficit/hyperactivity disorder].

How do you decide what tests to use? The child's age, developmental level, special needs, and background are important to consider when choosing an intelligence test. First, the test must have norms for the age of the child. Second, it is important to consider the child's developmental level and if he/she has any special needs, such as a physical disability or speech/language impairment. Finally, the background of the child,

including cultural differences and socioeconomic challenges, need to be considered. We have a wide range of tests to choose from, including developmental screenings, neuropsychological batteries, nonverbal tests, and the typical Wechsler-like tests.

What do scores on intelligence tests tell you about a child? Scores usually tell us a lot about a child, but there are times when the scores are not as useful as the information gained from observation during the testing session. Most tests yield at least one composite score, usually a score to describe the overall cognitive ability of a child. Many tests have subtest scores that tell additional information that can be used when looking at a profile of strengths and weaknesses for the child. Cognitive processing and problem solving can also be gained. During the test, observing the frustration level of the child is also a very important result of the testing situation.

What precautions do you take when interpreting and using scores? It is important to make sure that the most appropriate test is given to the child; and if the most appropriate is unavailable, then the next appropriate test can be used with some precautions. If the child's frustration level is too high and

he/she "shuts down" during the testing session, it should be noted. If the child's attention has to be constantly redirected to the task at hand, if speech/language issues make the testing session difficult, or if there are language or cultural differences to consider, then caution should be used in interpreting those scores.

Describe the education and training required to become a school psychologist. In Texas we need the LSSP (Licensed Specialist in School Psychology) certification. This is a master's-level certification. Practicum and internship are required, as well as a year of post-internship supervision before working independently. Many school psychologists also have a doctorate degree. ■

thinking
OF LESLEY & AMANDA

◄ Do you think educators should use intelligence tests to determine which children qualify for services like the program proposed for the Eastside schools? Why or why not? How should people determine eligibility?

thinking
OF LESLEY & AMANDA

How would you expect ► Lesley and Amanda to respond to these ethnic group differences in IQ scores? How would you expect each of them to explain the differences?

person's score based on the person's ethnic group identity. Still, these group differences have generated a fierce debate about the cultural fairness of intelligence tests. To read more about the social implications of ethnic differences in IQ scores, see the Social Policy Perspective box called "Ethnicity and IQ."

Because of intelligence tests' potential for cultural bias, some critics have argued that these tests should not be used with students from ethnic minority groups. Below are some of the most common arguments *against* testing (Onwuegbuzie & Daley, 2001; Sattler, 2001).

Ethnicity and IQ

How important is intelligence for doing well in school and getting a good job? Do differences in intelligence explain social problems like poverty, unemployment, crime, and poor parenting? Why are there persistent differences in the average IQ scores of different ethnic groups? For decades, heated debate has swirled around these questions and their implications for social policies.

A major flare-up of controversy centered on *The Bell Curve* (Herrnstein & Murray, 1994). This book presents intelligence as a general trait that is significantly influenced by genetics and can be successfully estimated by IQ tests. Herrnstein and Murray argue that differences in intelligence play a central role in many serious problems, including poverty, unemployment, crime, education, and poor home environments. They write that "large proportions of the people who exhibit the behaviors and problems that dominate the nation's social policy agenda have limited cognitive ability" (Herrnstein & Murray, 1994, p. 386).

The biggest controversy centers on *The Bell Curve*'s discussion of ethnic differences in IQ scores.

Although most experts agree that consistent differences exist among the average IQ scores of different ethnic groups, there is deep disagreement as to why. Herrnstein and Murray argue that the differences are due not to poverty, inadequate education, or test bias, but to real differences in cognitive abilities. They acknowledge that the environment undoubtedly plays a role in the development of intelligence, but argue that increasing intelligence has proved to be difficult. Finally, they urge consideration of social policies that recognize the central role of intelligence. For example, they urge a return to emphasizing quality education for gifted students, on the premise that these students will benefit more from good education than less intelligent students. And they advocate a reexamination of affirmative action policies in education and employment, suggesting that disadvantaged individuals should receive preferences only when their qualifications are very similar to those of nondisadvantaged peers.

Critical reaction to *The Bell Curve* was swift and furious. Critics claim that the authors do not acknowledge

problems in the data they use to support their arguments; that newer views of intelligence and cognitive processing have replaced the theories and data on which Herrnstein and Murray rely; and that the book's social policy recommendations are "exotic, neither following from the analyses nor justified on their own terms" (Fraser, 1995; Gardner, 1995, p. 23). Others believe that the authors dismiss the impact of such things as poverty, discrimination, and testing bias far too readily, and that they overemphasize a narrowly defined view of intelligence to explain complex social problems (Fish, 2002; Miele, 1995; Neisser, 1998: Neisser et al., 1996).

What role do you think intelligence plays in the thorny social issues we face? What are the social policy implications of thinking of intelligence as a strongly genetically influenced general factor that is difficult to change? If you were developing social policies to address such things as poverty, crime, and fairness in educational and job opportunities, what role would group differences in intelligence play in your thinking? ■

▶ *Intelligence tests are culturally biased.* The developers of most tests are middle-class whites who bring their own experiences to test construction. If they lack knowledge of other cultures, they may inadvertently create biased instruments. Some test items require knowledge that is specific to middle-class white culture. Cultural bias disadvantages test takers from minority cultures.

▶ *Minorities have less test-taking skill and experience.* Ethnic minority groups tend to focus more on oral skills, so paper-and-pencil tests may not be a good fit with their learning styles. Children from these groups also may have had less practice with standardized tests. Because the tests reflect the values and norms of the dominant majority, these children may be less motivated to perform at their highest level or may not appreciate the importance and implications of doing well on the test.

▶ *Most test examiners are white.* Communication and rapport between white examiners and minority children may be less than optimal, and this may depress scores.

▶ *Test results lead to inadequate and inferior educational placements.* Because of their lower test scores, schools often place minority children disproportionately in special education classes, where curriculum and support may fall short of what other children receive. Special education placements also create negative expectancies in teachers and other school officials—and even in the minds of minority children themselves. In this negative cycle, called *stereotype threat,* the child begins to accept the negative views and expectations; this can lead to poorer intellectual performance (Steele & Aronson, 1995).

In view of these arguments, examiners administering psychological tests need to be sensitive to cultural differences. They should always interpret test results with caution, and they should never base special education placements or other diagnoses solely on the results of a single test. However, it's also important to evaluate criticisms of cultural bias in the light of objective research data. For example, it might seem that the verbal subscales of intelligence tests, which involve vocabulary, factual knowledge, and text comprehension (e.g., define the word *obfuscate*), would reflect more cultural bias than nonverbal subscales involving picture completion, object assembly, and block design (e.g., use blocks to copy a design). However, Taylor and Richards (1991) researched this question and found that African American children actually scored *higher* on the verbal than on the nonverbal subscales of the WISC–R (an earlier version of the WISC–III). Further, when people have identified test items as culturally biased, test statistics have often showed the same ethnic group differences on those items as on the whole test. Sometimes, in fact, results on these "biased" items even favor ethnic minorities (Sattler, 2001).

One factor with a clear link to IQ scores is socioeconomic status, or SES. When SES and other living conditions are the same, IQ differences between non-Hispanic whites and African Americans are far smaller—less than 5 points in some studies (Sattler, 1992). After all, ethnic minority groups make up a disproportionately high percentage of families living in poverty in the United States. And children living in poverty have worse schools and fewer educational opportunities, both leading to lower IQ scores.

Jerome Sattler (1992, 2001), a researcher and expert in childhood assessment, summarized arguments that *favor* using intelligence tests with minority children.

▶ *Tests are useful in evaluating present functioning.* The subscales of intelligence tests can help educators identify the cognitive strengths and weaknesses of children. Some subscale profiles may suggest brain damage or psychological difficulties; more specific tests can then follow up on these potential problems. A significant drop in an IQ score can also signal the need for follow-up. Even if scores do not accurately reflect a given child's overall intelligence, they still can be useful in pointing to significant problems in cognitive functioning.

▶ *Tests help students get access to special programs.* When used properly, test scores can be an important part of the justification for providing the special education programming and other services that some minority children need—services to which they are legally entitled.

▶ *Tests help families, educators, and communities evaluate programs.* By helping to document gains and losses, IQ scores can help us hold schools and programs accountable for benefiting all children. When test scores reveal significant differences among ethnic groups, these findings can stimulate special interventions to address the inequalities. Rather than seeing the tests as marred by bias, we can see them as tools for identifying bias in existing systems.

▶ *Finally, tests are useful in indicating future functioning.* Binet originally designed his scales to predict children's future school performance, and this is still one of the most important uses of intelligence tests today. IQ scores do correlate with academic success and performance in school.

thinking
OF LESLEY & AMANDA

How does this information on socioeconomic status and IQ scores relate to Lesley and Amanda's debate about the Eastside proposal? Whose argument does it favor? Explain.

YOUR
PERSPECTIVE
NOTES

What value do you see in using IQ tests with ethnic minority children? Do you believe the benefits outweigh the potential problems, or not?

Biases that exist in intelligence tests reflect the values and assumptions that operate in the dominant culture. The reality is that educational opportunities, and the likelihood of success in school and work, also reflect the dominant culture. Childhood IQ scores provide early evidence of this effect. They demonstrate the importance of achieving a truly multiethnic and pluralistic society where children of all cultures have an equal chance of success, achievement, and happiness.

LET'S REVIEW . . .

1. The first practical intelligence scale aimed to:
   a. test military recruits during World War I.
   b. determine which schoolchildren needed special education.
   c. test immigrants coming to the United States during the early 1900s.
   d. identify which children were most likely to be geniuses.

2. During the early 1900s, immigration officials gave intelligence tests to people arriving in the United States. One of the lessons learned from this experience was that:
   a. intelligence is mostly inherited.
   b. the intelligence tests were culturally biased.
   c. Mediterranean immigrants had less native intelligence than most other immigrants.
   d. the intelligence tests had very low reliability, because people's scores were nearly random.

3. Which of the following is *not* one of the reasons critics believe that intelligence tests are not fair assessments for ethnic minority children?
   a. Tests can indicate future functioning.
   b. Minorities have less skill and experience in taking standardized tests.
   c. Most test examiners are white.
   d. Tests lead to inadequate and inferior educational placements.

4. **True or False:** The Wechsler series of intelligence scales is the modern version of Terman's Stanford–Binet scale.

5. **True or False:** Even when income levels are the same, average IQ scores for African Americans remain about 15 points lower than those of non-Hispanic whites.

Answers: 1. b, 2. b, 3. a, 4. F, 5. F

Development of Academic Skills

The first two sections of this chapter presented several different ways of thinking about intelligence and surveyed approaches to assessing intelligence. But to understand intelligence, we also need to consider how people put it to use. How do children apply their intellectual abilities? Clearly, intelligence can be applied in many different ways and to solve many different kinds of problems. This section will discuss one important way in which we put intelligence to practical use: the development of academic skills.

As you study this section, ask yourself these questions:

- What are some of the major skills children develop in mathematics? What mathematical competencies and limitations do children of different ages typically show?

- What stages do children go through as they learn to read? What are some important factors that predict reading skill? How can families and schools encourage reading skill?

- What are the major accomplishments that children achieve as they learn to write?

Mathematics

■ **Mathematical Skills in Infancy.** Amazing but true: Researchers have found evidence that even *newborns* have rudimentary mathematical skills. Humans seem to be "born with a fundamental sense of quantity" (Geary, 1994, p. 1). For example, researchers showed newborn infants (less than one week old!) a card with two black dots (Antell & Keating, 1983). The newborns looked at the dots for a bit, then started looking away. Looking away signals boredom; in Chapter 4 we referred to this as *habituation.* When researchers then switched to a card that had three dots, the newborns regained interest in looking at the dots—they *dishabituated.* Newborns also showed dishabituation when the set size was changed from three dots to two. These patterns of habituation and dishabituation show that newborns can see the difference between two and three dots. Because the cards were exactly the same except for the number of dots, these results demonstrate that newborn infants are capable of processing something that is related to the number or quantity of dots located on the cards. In this same experiment, however, the newborns failed to distinguish between cards with four and six dots. Evidently these larger quantities were indistinguishable for newborn infants.

During these early months of life, what do infants understand about quantity and number? Does this infant know how many toys she is looking at?

In the first months after birth, infants can already distinguish among small numbers of objects (e.g., among one, two, and three objects), whether the objects are similar or different, moving or still, or presented at the same time or in sequence. They can even match the number of objects they *see* with the number of sounds they *hear.* For example, when infants hear a sound track of two drumbeats, they prefer to look at a photo of two household objects rather than a photo of three objects. When they hear three drumbeats, however, their preference switches to the photo of three objects (Starkey, Spelke, & Gelman, 1983, 1990). Impressive as these skills are, however, they apply only to very small sets. If researchers increase the number of objects in each set to five or more, then children don't show evidence that they recognize the quantities until they are about 3 or 4 years old (Canfield & Smith, 1996; Simon, Hespos, & Rochat, 1995; Starkey & Cooper, 1980; Strauss & Curtis, 1981; van Loosbroek & Smitsman, 1990; Wynn, 1992, 1995).

How are infants able to show such skills? They clearly cannot count objects. They have no experience with a number system, and they don't have the language skills they need to say the words that go with the numbers. Researchers propose that infants enumerate small sets by **subitizing,** a perceptual process that we all use to quickly and easily determine the basic quantity in a small set of objects. To see how subitizing works, try the following experiment. Have your friend toss three or four pennies onto a table while you have your eyes closed. Now open your eyes and, as quickly as you can, look to see how many pennies there are. Most peo-

subitizing

A perceptual process where people quickly and easily determine how many objects are in a small set without actually counting them.

ple can "see" that there are three pennies, or four pennies, without needing to actually count each penny. There is something about the visual arrangement of the pennies that lets you know immediately how many there are. Of course we can't be sure that infants are subitizing object sets exactly the way we do, but from the experimental evidence it does seem that they use a similar process. Somehow, without actually counting, they can determine that one set of objects has more items than another set, and they can match the number of things they see with the number of sounds they hear. Quite remarkable math skills for such a young age!

■ **Mathematical Skills in Early Childhood.** One of preschoolers' most obvious accomplishments is *learning to count*. Starting at about the age of 2, children begin to associate the counting words used in their language with the correct number of objects. They quickly become quite accurate in their counting and learn to count more and more things.

The structure of number words in children's native language has an impact on some early mathematical competencies. For example, notice how we count in English. We count up through 10 ("one, two, . . . ten"), but then we call the next numbers "eleven" and "twelve." Next come seven numbers with "teen" added to the end ("thirteen, fourteen . . . nineteen"). After the "teens," we count up to 100 by naming the tens place followed by the ones place (as in "twenty-one, twenty-two"). Therefore, as they learn to count to 20 in English and many other Western languages, young children may not recognize the tens-ones system (called the base 10 system) that is the foundation of mathematics. In contrast, many Asian languages follow a much simpler rule (Miller, Smith, Zhu, & Zhang, 1995). After reaching 10 they go straight into naming the tens place followed by the ones place (essentially counting "ten-one, ten-two," and so forth). In these languages children don't need to remember the inconsistent rules of giving special names to 11 and 12, then adding "teen" to the end of a few numbers before finally starting to count with the tens-ones system. As you can see in Figure 7.3, English-speaking children take more time learning to count than their Chinese counterparts. By mastering the counting system at an earlier age, Chinese children get a head start on solving mathematical calculations and problems.

Language differences also affect young children's understanding of *place value*, and this understanding has a bearing on the strategies children use to solve arithmetic problems. For

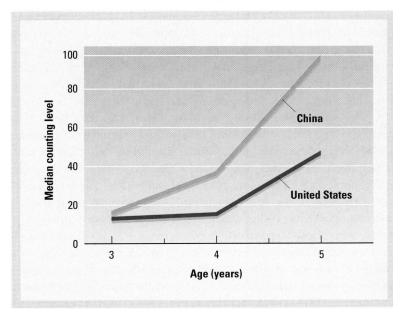

FIGURE 7.3 Preschoolers' Counting Ability in China and in the United States

At 3 years of age, children in both the United States and China have mastered counting up through the number 10. After that age, however, Chinese children learn much more quickly than children in the United States.

Source: K. F. Miller, C. M. Smith, J. Zhu, & Z. H. Zhang. (1995). Preschool origins of cross-national differences in mathematical competence: The role of number-naming systems. *Psychological Science, 6,* 1, p. 57. Reprinted with permission from Blackwell Publishing.

example, a common strategy for simple addition and subtraction problems is "decomposition." In a problem such as 6 + 7, a child might decompose the 7 into 4 + 3, then solve the problem by first adding 6 + 4 to get 10, then adding the remaining 3. Young Korean and Chinese children often use this strategy. But skill in decomposition depends on a solid understanding of the base 10 system, which Asian languages support better than English does (Fuson & Kwon, 1992; Geary, Bow-Thomas, Liu, & Siegler, 1996; Miller et al., 1995). Also, language differences influence how quickly people can pronounce number names, which in turn affects how quickly children memorize basic math facts (Geary, Bow-Thomas, Fan, & Siegler, 1993; Geary et al., 1996). So these seemingly simple differences in number words can contribute to more long-lasting differences in the development of math skills (Beaton et al., 1996; Geary, Liu, Chen, Saults, & Hoard, 1999; Miller et al., 1995; Stevenson, Chen, & Lee, 1993). The effects of language in learning fractions has also been studied (Paik & Mix, 2003).

At about 4 years children combine their developing counting skills with their knowledge of addition and subtraction. At this point they begin to use counting as a tool to solve simple arithmetic problems instead of relying on subitizing. This represents an important advance in their mathematical skills—because a child can use counting with sets of any size and in the absence of concrete objects, whereas subitizing works only with small sets and visible objects. Children quickly begin to use several different **counting strategies,** approaches to solving problems that involve counting of the quantities. For example: A child figures out that 2 + 2 = 4 by first counting to 2 and then counting on (two more steps) to 3 and then 4. Preschoolers learn to solve simple problems whether the change in number is visible to them, screened from their view, or even described verbally in the absence of any concrete objects. Gradually, over the later preschool and elementary school years, children increase the complexity and sophistication of their counting strategies (Baroody, 1992; Groen & Resnick, 1977; Siegler, 1987; Siegler & Robinson, 1982; Starkey & Gelman, 1982).

■ **Mathematical Skills during the Elementary School Years.** Over the course of the elementary school years, the counting strategies children use to solve addition and subtraction problems gradually become more efficient. Table 7.1 shows some of these strategies. Younger children tend to use strategies that require more counting. This is cumbersome and increases the opportunity for errors, but it reduces the burden on their working memory. As children gain experience, they tend to move to strategies that require more memory but can be executed more quickly. Children begin to store basic math facts and simply retrieve them from memory instead of relying on counting strategies. Once a child has memorized a fact, he or she has a tool for deriving the answers to other, nonmemorized problems. For example, given the problem 5 + 8, a child who knows that 5 + 5 = 10 may use this known fact, reason that 8 is three larger than 5, and add 3 to 10 to obtain the answer 13 (Ashcraft, 1992; for reviews, see Geary, 1994, and Ginsburg, Klein, & Starkey, 1998).

How do children memorize and retrieve math facts? One possibility is the **strategy choice model** (Siegler & Jenkins, 1989; Siegler & Shrager, 1984). According to this model, "Children tend to choose the fastest approach that they can execute accurately" (Siegler, 1998, p. 286). Using a fast strategy increases the likelihood that the problem and answer will both be present in working memory, and therefore increases their degree of association. Using the most accurate strategy helps ensure that the association will develop between the problem and its *correct* answer. The more often a correct answer (e.g., 7) is associated with a problem (e.g., 4 + 3), the greater the association between them and the more likely that the child will retrieve this answer on future occasions. If the degree of association is not strong, the child will use a *backup strategy* such as counting, guessing, or deriving an answer based on known facts or rules. According to the strategy choice model, discouraging children from using backup strategies (like counting on their fingers) may actually *delay* their memorizing basic math facts (Siegler, 1998). Can you explain why?

thinking
OF LESLEY & AMANDA

How does the strategy choice model relate to Lesley's comment about the importance of speed of thinking? Do you think she would agree or disagree with this model?

counting strategies

Approaches to solving math problems that involve counting of the quantities.

strategy choice model

The idea that children solve math problems by choosing the fastest approach that they can execute accurately.

TABLE 7.1 Examples of Common Counting Strategies for Addition

STRATEGY	SAMPLE PROBLEM	USE OF STRATEGY
Counting manipulatives	2 + 5	Child counts two manipulatives (e.g., blocks, coins, candies), then counts five more manipulatives, then counts all seven objects.
Counting fingers	2 + 5	Child raises two fingers on one hand, then five on the other hand. Child then counts all seven fingers one at a time, moving each one as it is counted.
Counting all (sum)	2 + 5	Child counts the first number aloud: "One, two." Child then continues counting on by the second number "three, four, five, six, seven"—and then states the answer as "seven."
Counting on first	2 + 5	Child states the first number, "two"; counts on by the second number—"three, four, five, six, seven"; then states the answer as "seven."
Counting on larger (minimum, or min)	2 + 5	Child states the biggest number, regardless of whether it is first or second. Here, child says "five," then counts on by the smaller number ("six, seven"), then states the answer as "seven."
Decomposition (deriving a fact)	7 + 6	Child decomposes the 6 into 3 + 3, adds 7 + 3 and gets 10, adds the other 3 to 10, and gives the answer: 13. (The child could choose to decompose the other number, 7, into 4 + 3, add 4 + 6 to get 10, then add the remaining 3 to 10.)
Fact retrieval	2 + 5	Child retrieves the answer from long-term memory and states the answer as "seven."
Regrouping	16 + 23	Child decomposes both numbers into tens and units (16 = 10 + 6; 23 = 20 + 3), sums the tens and units separately (10 + 20 = 30; 6 + 3 = 9), adds the subtotals (30 + 9 = 39), and gives the answer: 39.

Source: Adapted from D. C. Geary. (1994). *Children's mathematical development: Research and practical applications.* Washington, DC: American Psychological Association. Copyright © 1994 by the American Psychological Association. Adapted with permission.

Though children gradually move from less to more efficient strategies, they do not rely on only a single strategy for solving arithmetic problems. Instead, they consistently use a variety of strategies. The strategy choice model helps explain why. The availability of multiple strategies increases the likelihood that a child can obtain a correct answer quickly. This helps the child succeed in solving problems and helps build strong associations between problems and their correct answers. Researchers have found evidence of multiple strategies for a variety of arithmetic operations and across a wide range of student ages, abilities, and nationalities (Fuson & Kwon, 1992; Geary, 1996; Geary, Fan, & Bow-Thomas, 1992; LeFevre & Bisanz, 1996; Lemaire & Siegler, 1995; Mabbott & Bisanz, in press).

For better or worse, elementary school children spend many hours working mathematical **word problems**, or verbal descriptions of mathematical situations. As you may recall from personal experience, word problems can cause

word problems
Verbal descriptions of mathematical situations that children solve by applying their math skills.

When given addition and subtraction problems, should children be allowed to use back-up strategies such as counting on their fingers?

This street vendor shows a great deal of math skill when he is calculating prices and making change for customers. With the traditional math problems that are used in classrooms, however, he will likely show much less skill. Context has a powerful effect on children's math problem-solving ability.

YOUR

PERSPECTIVE

NOTES

Were word problems difficult for you? How are your mathematical problem-solving efforts affected by problem context and the types of relations in the problem?

even the best math students to groan with dread. Several factors contribute to the difficulty of a word problem—among them the number of words in the problem, the number of required arithmetic operations, and the number of mathematical terms (Jerman & Mirman, 1974; Jerman & Rees, 1972). The context of the problem has an important effect as well. Sometimes problems are difficult because their content is simply not interesting to the child, their wording is confusing, or their context is unfamiliar. In one study, for example, Brazilian children experienced at selling products at street stands were quite good at solving word problems that had a "selling" context, even when the items named in the problems were not ones they had sold. Their performance was much worse when problems did not have the sales context, even though the required computations were identical to those in the other problems (Carraher, Carraher, & Schliemann, 1985). Unfamiliar details and situations may not provide effective cues to help children access and use relevant knowledge, or they may simply overload working memory. With familiar contexts, children have a greater chance of comprehending the situation being described, understanding what they are being asked to figure out, and being motivated to solve the problem (Mayer, Lewis, & Hegarty, 1992; Stern, 1993).

■ **Mathematical Skills during Older Childhood and Adolescence.**   Children continue to increase their knowledge of basic mathematical principles throughout their school years, although some principles take some time to develop (Alibali & Goldin-Meadow, 1993; Goldin-Meadow, Alibali, & Church, 1993). Sometimes misunderstandings about fundamental math principles lead to **bugs,** or systematic errors in children's problem-solving procedures. Table 7.2 presents examples of common bugs in multidigit subtraction (Brown & Burton, 1978; Brown & VanLehn, 1982). Buggy procedures are common in all arithmetic operations, and they can persist well into the late elementary school years.

As children learn about more complex math topics such as fractions, geometry, and algebra, they consistently attempt to build new understanding on what they already know. At

bugs

Systematic errors in children's procedures for solving math problems.

TABLE 7.2 Subtraction Bugs

PROBLEMS AND CORRECT ANSWERS	307 − 49 258	286 − 68 218	293 − 171 122
Bug: Borrow across zero Child decrements first nonzero number correctly but does not alter the zero.	248 (combination of "borrow across zero" and "0 − N = N" bugs)	218	122
Bug: Blank instead of borrow When borrowing is needed, child skips that column and goes to the next.	3	22	122
Bug: Smaller from larger Child always subtracts the smaller number from the larger number.	342	222	122
Bug: Smaller from larger instead of borrow from zero Child does not borrow from zero but instead subtracts the smaller from the larger number.	262	218	122
Bug: Borrow, no decrement Child borrows but does not decrement the number being borrowed from.	368	228	122
Bug: Borrow from zero Child changes zero to a nine but does not decrement the next digit to the left.	358	218	122
Bug: Zero minus N equals N If top digit is a zero, child writes down the bottom number as the answer.	348 (combination of "borrow, no decrement" and "0 − N = N" bugs)	218	122

times this leads to misunderstandings of new principles; but when students recognize their mistakes, they begin to debug their math knowledge and understand the accurate procedures. Instruction that builds on prior knowledge is typically more effective in helping students understand new mathematical concepts. In contrast, instruction that focuses on memorization of facts and rules gives students less opportunity to work out their buggy procedures. As a result, mistakes can take longer to correct (Clement, 1982).

Reading

Reading is perhaps the single most important academic skill we acquire. Western cultures tend to be reading- and writing-based, so we get much of our knowledge and information through books, magazines, newspapers, instruction manuals, print on the Internet and television, and other print media. An expert on reading development, Jeanne Chall, surmised that "the learning and uses of literacy are among the most advanced forms of intelligence, and, compared to other forms, depend more on instruction and practice" (1983, p. 2). Chall (1983) proposed six developmental stages that describe how children typically learn to read, as summarized in Table 7.3. Chall commented that many adults may never reach the most mature stage of reading, even after 4 years of college.

In fact, too many people have trouble reaching even Chall's fourth stage, "Reading for New Learning." Researchers estimate that in the United States 25 percent of people are poor

TABLE 7.3 Chall's Six Developmental Stages in Reading

STAGE AND AGE RANGE	DESCRIPTION OF ACTIVITIES AND SKILLS
Prereading: Birth to kindergarten	Parents "read" to infants and toddlers by pointing to and naming objects and colors in books and reading simple stories. Many 3-year-olds pretend to read—flipping through pages, reciting memorized stories, and creating their own stories as they point to words and pictures. By kindergarten, many children can recite the alphabet, recognize written letters, and print their own name. These and other prereading skills lay the foundation for further development.
Reading/Decoding: Grades 1–2	Children learn to associate letters with their corresponding sounds. Using *phonics,* children sound out letters, decoding the word that is formed when they run the sounds together. With the *whole word method,* children recognize words based on context, pictures, and the shape of the word. Readers at this stage often focus on individual words and phrases and miss the larger meaning of the story.
Fluency: Grades 2–3	Children become more fluent in recognizing or decoding words. Rereading familiar books and reading stories with familiar or stereotyped structures, children gain speed, fluency, and confidence in their reading ability. Chall (1983) commented that children are "learning to read" by associating printed words with stories they already know and understand.
Reading for New Learning: Grades 4–8	Fluency with words allows children to move to less familiar material. With the decoding load reduced, children can focus on meaning and messages, gaining a new way to learn new information. Fourth graders typically begin using printed materials to study subjects like science, history, and geography. Now children are "reading to learn," focusing on fact-based information.
Multiple Viewpoints: High school	Adolescents move beyond basic facts. They begin to appreciate layers of information representing different viewpoints or theories. Examples: History texts might describe events from differing perspectives; biology can be discussed at the cellular, organismic, and ecological levels. School assignments and free reading of more mature fiction and nonfiction facilitate this development.
Construction and Reconstruction: College and adulthood	Mature readers can read multiple sources, opinions, and views and then construct their own understanding. They read to suit their purpose, whether to gain understanding, enjoy entertainment, or consider views of others. They decide how fast or deeply to read and when to gloss, skim, or attend to detail. They know what *not* to read as well as what to read in order to suit their purposes.

readers and 38 percent of fourth graders score below the basic reading level for their grade (Adams, Treiman, & Pressley, 1998; Donahue, Voelkl, Campbell, & Mazzeo, 1999; U.S. Office of Technology Assessment, 1993). To see how volunteers can help children and adults overcome illiteracy, read the Personal Perspective box called "Meet a Literacy Volunteer."

Two of the factors that best predict success in early reading are *familiarity with letters of the alphabet* and *phonemic awareness* (Adams, Treiman, & Pressley, 1998). Preschoolers who show early familiarity with letters tend to be more successful in reading through the primary grades. In contrast, preschoolers who are less familiar with letters tend to have more difficulty learning to read. Children whose primary language is not English tend to be less familiar with letters and have greater difficulty learning to read in English in school. Reading difficulty really emerges, however, when children cannot blend the printed letters together to form whole words.

Phonemic awareness is the understanding that words are made up of smaller units of sound, or *phonemes.* This understanding involves associating printed letters with the sounds that go with them. Phonemic awareness usually begins developing during the first year of formal schooling as children learn to make the speech sounds associated with each letter and with various letter combinations. Success with phonemic awareness is a strong predictor of later reading success—even stronger than the child's overall IQ (Adams, Treiman, & Pressley, 1998; Bradley & Bryant, 1983; MacLean, Bryant, & Bradley, 1987; Vellutino & Scanlon, 1987). A major source of reading weakness is difficulty in decoding (or breaking down) printed words into their individual speech sounds. Instructional activities that emphasize phonemic awareness can facilitate reading growth. Even during the preschool years, play with letters and letter sounds is helpful. Popular TV programs like *Sesame Street* show young children how to link sounds to letters and to blend speech sounds (e.g., "Today's program is brought to you by the letter *T* as in *Toy, Tiger,* and *Teddy*").

phonemic awareness

The understanding that words are made up of smaller units of sound; also, association of printed letters with the sounds that go with them.

Meet a Literacy Volunteer

Kim Davenport
Boston, Massachusetts

Vice president of education and training at Jumpstart Literacy Programs

What do you do to help others learn to read?

Jumpstart Corps members work one-to-one with preschool children to develop language, literacy and social–emotional skills. Corps members are trained on how to read effectively with children using the Dialogic Reading Method, an interactive reading method that encourages children and adults to have conversations about a book.

Why did you decide to become involved with this program?

Literacy is a key component to school success for children. Research tells us that reading with young children builds vocabulary, promotes engagement with books, fosters lifelong reading habits, and develops strong literacy and language skills. Reading with children supports emergent literacy skills such as print awareness, letter knowledge, and phonemic awareness, and builds vocabulary and comprehension skills. My work supports Jumpstart's key mission: to work toward the day that every child succeeds in school. I can think of no more globally pressing issue for children today. It is our responsibility as citizens to support and develop our children. They are our future.

What do you know about the need for programs of this type?

Each year more than 35 percent of children enter school unprepared to succeed. First-grade children from low-income families have an average of 5,000-word vocabularies. In contrast, children from more affluent families enter school with vocabularies of 20,000 words. That difference is startling. We understand how to solve the problem of literacy; now we need a way to reach each child.

How can others become involved with literacy programs?

College students can become involved with Jumpstart through their college campuses. This year Jumpstart hosts programs in 33 communities around the country. You can find a list of cities and programs and ways you can help at www.jstart.org. Across the country there are numerous literacy programs. Check with your local library, child-care resource and referral center, or schools for information about opportunities to read with young children. ■

thinking OF LESLEY & AMANDA

What points from this interview could Lesley use to strengthen her argument against Amanda's views on IQ?

Once children develop phonemic awareness, it is important that they pick up speed in recognizing whole words: They need to *automatize* their recognition of words. Strong readers quickly learn to recognize words, increasing their reading fluency. Reitsma (1983, 1989) studied second graders who were reading at and below grade level. After accomplished readers reread and decoded unfamiliar words a few times, they became significantly faster at recognizing those words. Less accomplished readers, however, showed little or no gain in

By watching educational programs such as *Sesame Street,* preschoolers can practice associating the sights and sounds of the different letters in the alphabet. These early experiences are important in developing phonemic awareness, a very important skill in early reading.

recognition speed. When children fail to automatize word recognition, they must continue to decode words by sounding out the individual letters and speech sounds. The decoding process occupies a great deal of processing capacity, so struggling readers have less capacity available to attend to meaning and get less out of their reading. These kinds of decoding and automaticity difficulties are common in children with learning disabilities in reading. We will discuss learning disabilities in greater detail in Chapter 14.

In sum, when it comes to reading, "the rich get richer." Children with strong decoding skills and phonemic awareness are better able to sound out words. With repeated exposures, they automatize their word recognition. This makes it easier for them to read—and as a result they tend to read more. Increased reading further enhances their reading skills; it also exposes them to a broader array of knowledge and information, which, in turn, facilitates their cognitive development. When you consider all that we can learn through reading, you can see why it is critically important that children get off to a good start in the early reading stages.

Before we leave this topic, we want to discuss briefly the issue of parents' reading aloud to preschool children. In our years as parents and educators, we have heard many times that the best way to promote children's reading and academic success is to read to them frequently. This advice has become so ubiquitous that many parents consider it mandatory to read to their children daily, even beginning in infancy. When we reviewed the research literature, however, we were surprised to find that the evidence on this point is relatively weak. Scarborough and Dobrich (1994) reviewed all of the studies since 1960 that correlated the frequency or quality of parent–child reading with later measures of the children's reading ability. Scarborough and Dobrich concluded that only about 8 percent of the variability in children's reading scores is related to how much they were read to by their parents. Research findings are variable, with some investigators reporting higher correlations, some lower, and some no correlation at all. As much or more of the variability in reading success correlates with such factors as the family's socioeconomic status (SES), the child's own interest in reading, and even the amount of educational television the child watches (Scarborough & Dobrich, 1994).

But although parent–child reading during the preschool years may have only a small *direct* effect on later reading ability, it may have several other *indirect* effects with a more substantial cumulative impact (Lonigan, 1994; Sénéchal & LeFevre, 2002). To see how these interactive effects may occur, consider the path analysis in Figure 7.4. Notice that preschool exposure to print correlates only .35 directly with reading achievement (Lonigan's estimate from his review of the research). Preschool exposure also, however, contributes modest amounts (.23 to .42) to the child's language skills, emergent literacy (prereading skills such as phonemic awareness), and interest in literacy. These factors, in turn, have their own positive association with reading achievement. So taken together, the direct and indirect effects of preschool exposure become substantial. Dunning, Mason, and Stewart (1994) argue further that even if parent–child preschool reading has only a small effect, it is still an effect that parents can control. Factors like family SES and the child's own interest in reading are difficult to change, but parents can choose to exercise their "8 percent" influence on their children's reading ability. And even small effects, when exerted early, can compound into larger differences later in the child's life.

What is more clear is this: Once children begin reading, the amount of time they spend reading is a strong predictor of later strengths in reading, language ability, vocabulary, writing, storytelling, richness of ideas, content area achievement, and overall knowledge (Adams,

thinking
OF LESLEY & AMANDA

◄ How do the low correlations between parent–child reading and later school success relate to Lesley's comments about the Eastside proposal? Do you believe this information would change her opinion of the proposed program?

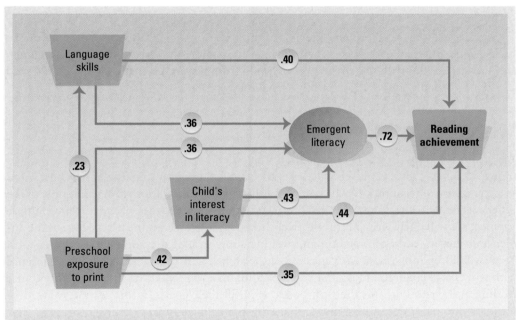

FIGURE 7.4 **Interactive Effects of Parent–Child Reading**

This path analysis shows the direct and indirect effects that parents' reading aloud to preschoolers can have on the children's later reading ability.

Source: "Reading to Preschoolers: Is the Emperor Really Naked?" By C. J. Lonigan in *Developmental Review,* Volume 14, 311, copyright 1994, Elsevier Science (USA), reproduced with permission from the publisher.

Although the direct effects of reading to young children are small, the indirect effects can be substantial. Research suggests that reading to young children can enhance their language ability, interest in books, and their prereading skills. These in turn are related to their ability to learn to read when they enter school.

Treiman, & Pressley, 1998 provide a review of this area of research). Because "practice makes perfect" and "the rich get richer" when it comes to reading, we agree with Adams, Treiman, and Pressley (1998) that "the firmest prescription from research is that children should read as often, as broadly, and as thoughtfully as possible" (p. 336).

Writing

You probably know from experience that reading and writing skills are highly correlated (Spivey & King, 1989). Children who learn the alphabet early, become skilled decoders, and automatize word recognition will later have a strong foundation for spelling and some of the other mechanics of writing. Also, children who can read and synthesize text from multiple perspectives will likely write more effectively because they can keep the perspective of the audience in mind. And both reading and writing show similar developmental progressions. That is, children move from early mastery of the alphabet, to greater fluency and confidence with words and language, to greater sophistication in comprehension and the ability to use reading and writing to suit their purposes or fulfill their goals. In this section we outline some of the major accomplishments that children achieve in the writing process as they move from the early phases of inventive spelling to the more mature phase of successful revision.

■ **Inventive Spelling.**   In the early phases of writing, young children struggle to learn spelling. Before they memorize conventional word spellings, they frequently invent their own made-up versions, a process called **inventive spellings.** For example, a beginner might write *two* as *tu* or *sometimes* as *sumtyms.* We are all painfully aware of the myriad complexities, letter blends, and spelling exceptions that exist in English. Schools today generally accept and encourage inventive spelling, teaching beginners to focus more on their meaning and message than on writing mechanics. Research indicates that inventive spelling does not interfere with children's ability to learn to spell words correctly later on. Instead, as children construct their own spellings, they gain practice with letter sounds and blends, enhancing their phonemic awareness. The use of inventive spelling therefore correlates with later success in conventional spelling, word recognition, and reading fluency (Adams, Treiman, & Pressley, 1998; Uhry & Shepard, 1993).

■ **Mechanics and Intermediate Writing.** During the elementary school years, children gradually learn conventional spellings and begin to form increasingly complex sentence structures. In the earlier grades children must devote most of their processing capacity to the technical requirements of writing: spelling, capitalization, punctuation, and the formation of complete sentences. Children tend to write from an egocentric perspective—they have a difficult time keeping the needs of the reader in mind. Organization also tends to be lacking. Beginning writers tend to engage in **knowledge telling,** a strategy in which children simply add ideas to their essays as they come to mind (Bereiter & Scardamalia, 1987). Even high school and college writers show this strategy, in fact. It seems that many assignments in formal education encourage students to "dump in" all they know about a topic. Few assignments require or encourage students to write creatively, so children often rely on rudimentary and stereotyped structures during this intermediate phase of their writing development.

■ **Planning and Revising.** Young writers have particular difficulty knowing when and what to revise. Once weaknesses are pointed out, however, they do seem capable of correcting most mistakes. As students move into more mature phases of writing, they spend increasing amounts of time on planning and revising. Before writing their first sentence, mature writers spend time gathering facts and sources and organizing their ideas. Their first draft is not their last draft. They realize that good writing evolves through the dynamic process of *recursive revision.* That is, after planning and writing, they reevaluate their plan and rewrite several times. In early revisions accomplished writers attend above all to the meaning and message of their writing. They tend to defer the mechanics of spelling, grammar, and punctuation to later revisions (Adams, Treiman, & Pressley, 1998). Strong writers become skilled at reviewing their own material from the reader's perspective—even reading it aloud—and continually revise their work to meet their writing goals.

In this chapter we have described several theories of intelligence and have surveyed approaches to assessing this important trait. To offer a glimpse of how children put intelligence to use in one important practical setting—school—we have also described the development of three important academic skills. We hope you will remember that although most people agree that understanding intelligence and its development is important, there is little agreement on exactly what intelligence is or how it is best assessed. Changes in theories of cognition, expanding knowledge of biology, and developments in technology and statistics have prompted dramatic changes in our theories of intelligence and methods of measurement. It is certain that as our knowledge continues to grow, our thinking about intelligence, about ways to assess it, and about ways to encourage its application in practical situations will continue to evolve.

YOUR PERSPECTIVE NOTES

When writing, how much time do you spend on planning and revising your text? Looking at one of your most recent writing assignments, can you see revisions that might have improved it?

inventive spelling

Incorrect spellings that children create by sounding out words and writing the associated letters.

knowledge telling

Adding or "dumping" in ideas as they come to mind; a failure to organize ideas selectively in writing.

1. Choong-Youl is a Chinese child who is learning to count. Compared to a child in the United States, Choong-Youl is likely to:

    a. learn the number words for the numbers 1 to 10 more quickly.

    b. learn the number words for the numbers 11 to 20 more quickly.

    c. have a poorer understanding of place value.

    d. start at a later age to use counting as a problem-solving tool.

2. This year Jeremy is able to learn new material by reading textbooks. Before, it was all he could do to understand individual words and sentences. Now, however, Jeremy can process the meaning of text passages and absorb new information. Jeremy's ability to learn by reading shows that he is in Jeanne Chall's stage of:

    a. reading/decoding.

    b. fluency.

    c. reading for new learning.

    d. multiple viewpoints.

3. One important part of learning to read is the understanding that words are made up of smaller units of sound. This is referred to as:

    a. word fluency.

    b. phonemic awareness.

    c. automatizing word recognition.

    d. the prereading component.

4. **True or False:** According to the strategy choice model, children who are discouraged from using counting strategies to solve mathematics problems may take longer to memorize and retrieve basic math facts.

5. **True or False:** The use of inventive spelling in the early elementary school years interferes with children's ability to learn to spell words correctly in the later school years.

Answers: 1. b, 2. c, 3. b, 4. T, 5. F

thinking
BACK TO LESLEY & AMANDA

Now that you have studied this chapter, you should be able to help Lesley and Amanda understand the wide variation in views of intelligence. You can explain that people in different cultures may identify different sets of characteristics, traits, and behaviors as "intelligence." In thinking about the Eastside referendum, Lesley and Amanda might first think carefully about how they and their school system define intelligence. Then you can describe various theories of intelligence. Explain Spearman's *g* factor and contrast it with multifactor theories such as Guilford's or Horn and Cattell's views. Perhaps Amanda and Lesley could use Gardner's theory of multiple intelligences to think about the skills that the supplemental program will target. Will the program focus exclusively on logical–mathematical and linguistic intelligences? Or will it include other intelligences? Discuss Sternberg's theory: Will the proposed program focus on improving specific processing components, or will it attempt to help students deal with novelty and achieve an adaptive fit between their skills and the demands of their environment? Lesley and Amanda might also want to consider what other characteristics, such as creativity, the program might affect.

You can also help Lesley and Amanda better understand the advantages and limitations of IQ tests. You should point out that although IQ is one measure of intelligence, others are possible. Given that predominantly lower-income children are to be served by the proposed program, you might suggest that Lesley and Amanda consider whether using IQ is appropriate, or at least think about whether other measures should be used in addition to IQ. Will the benefits of standardized testing for these children outweigh its possible biases? If so, how will the school system ensure appropriate use of the results of the intelligence tests?

Finally, Lesley and Amanda might benefit from an explanation of the typical skills that children develop in the major academic areas of mathematics, reading, and writing. You could help Lesley think more about the relationship between parents' reading to young children and the children's academic success. She might consider the weak direct, but cumulative indirect, effects of this activity. Will active parent participation be important in helping the children in the program learn to read? How can the program help foster more mature mathematical and writing skills? What about you—would you support the referendum? Why or why not?

CHAPTER SUMMARY

What is the typical definition of intelligence? More specifically, how do the psychometric approaches define intelligence?

Most experts agree that intelligence involves the ability to learn, think logically about abstract concepts, and adapt to the environment. Intelligence is viewed differently in different cultures however. The psychometric approach relies on numerous paper-and-pencil tests and physical measures; the data are analyzed to identify a smaller set of factors that underlie intelligence. Spearman's two-factor theory included general intelligence *(g)* and specific intelligence *(s)*. Guilford identified 150 different factors. Cattell and Horn divided intelligence into fluid ability (thinking ability) and crystallized ability (knowledge and skills).

How is Sternberg's triarchic theory of intelligence different from the psychometric approach?

Sternberg's theory ties in with information-processing theory and involves three subtheories: componential, experiential, and contextual. The componential subtheory describes the mental processes that work with information. Knowledge-acquisition components gain new information, performance components carry out mental strategies, and metacomponents supervise the cognitive system. The experiential subtheory involves the ability to deal with novel tasks and to automatize mental processes. The contextual subtheory describes how people adapt to the real world, select a different environment, or shape the existing environment.

What are the main ideas behind Gardner's theory of multiple intelligences?

Gardner proposed eight independent types of intelligence: linguistic, logical–mathematical, musical, bodily–kinesthetic, spatial, interpersonal, intrapersonal, and naturalist. Gardner believes that people inherit biopsychological potentials to be stronger or weaker in these various intelligences and that people may or may not achieve their potential depending on environmental factors and individual choices. His criteria for identifying a type of intelligence include psychometric data, potential isolation by brain damage, evolutionary history, identifiable core operations, and the existence of exceptional people in that skill area.

What is creativity?

Creativity consists of original thinking and problem solving that produces something valued by society. Creativity is intentional, and it requires a good knowledge base, at least average intelligence, the ability to restructure ideas, and persistence. People develop creativity particularly at certain peak periods, one important period occurring during pre- and early adolescence, and creativity can be increased.

What are the major events in the early history of intelligence testing?

Binet and Simon developed the first practical intelligence test in 1905 to determine which French schoolchildren would benefit from special education. Terman modified the Binet–Simon scale and published the Stanford–Binet scale in 1916. Authorities gave intelligence tests to military recruits during World War I and to immigrants entering the United States during the early 1900s. Because of language and cultural differences, immigrants from certain countries achieved relatively lower scores, and unfortunately the U.S. Congress passed laws limiting immigration from these areas of the world. Concerns regarding cultural bias in testing still exist today.

What are the main intelligence tests used today?

The fourth edition of the Stanford–Binet scale (SB:IV) is the modern version of Terman's Stanford–Binet scale. It provides an overall score with subscores for verbal reasoning, quantitative reasoning, abstract/visual reasoning, and short-term memory, and it includes items appropriate for individuals aged 2 to 24. David Wechsler developed a series of intelligence scales: the WPPSI–R for children 3 to 7 years, the WISC–III for children 6 to 16, and the WAIS–R for ages 16 and up. All three scales provide a composite score and subscores for verbal and performance components.

How do ethnic groups differ, on average, in IQ scores, and what concerns are there about cultural fairness in IQ testing?

Over the years, African Americans have tended to score on average about 15 points lower than non-Hispanic whites, Asian Americans have scored slightly higher than non-Hispanic whites, and Hispanics have scored between non-Hispanic whites and African Americans. There is much more variability within these groups than among them, however. Critics are concerned that test items may contain a middle-class Anglo bias; that minorities may have less test-taking experience; that most examiners are white; and that test results disproportionately place minorities in special education. When socioeconomic levels are equal, ethnic group differences are significantly smaller. Despite concerns about bias, tests can help educators evaluate a child's level of functioning, qualify children for needed special services, evaluate educational programs, and predict students' future functioning in school, providing the tests are used and interpreted properly.

What mathematical skills do children develop as they move from infancy to late childhood?

Even young infants can distinguish between small sets and recognize the effects of addition and subtraction through subitizing. At about age 2, children begin to learn to count. Children begin to use counting strategies in the later preschool years, and they increase the efficiency of these strategies throughout the elementary school years. Children gradually develop associations between problems and correct answers and become able to retrieve answers instead of using counting strategies, though they continue to employ multiple strategies to solve problems. Mathematical word problems are difficult for many students. Problems with unfamiliar contexts are especially difficult during the early elementary school years. Buggy procedures in mathematics can result from the lack of a solid understanding of mathematical principles. Bugs are common in all arithmetic operations and can persist well into the late elementary school years.

What are the main phases that children go through as they learn to read?

Chall identified six stages of reading development: prereading, reading/decoding, fluency, reading for new learning, multiple viewpoints, and construction/reconstruction. In young children familiarity with the alphabet and phonemic awareness predict later reading success. After learning to decode or recognize whole words on sight, children need to automatize word recognition. Although there is little evidence of a direct link between early parent–child reading and later reading success, the potential indirect and cumulative effects of early reading suggest that children should be exposed early and often to reading.

What are the main phases that children go through as they learn to write?

Reading and writing skills are correlated and follow similar developmental pathways. Early writers use inventive spellings. After automatizing proper spellings, children can focus on other technical requirements of writing. Early writers tend to be egocentric, lack organization, and use unsophisticated knowledge-telling strategies. As writers mature, they engage in more planning and revising.

KEY TERMS

biopsychological potential (255)

bugs (272)

componential subtheory (252)

contextual subtheory (254)

counting strategies (270)

creativity (257)

crystallized ability (252)

experiential subtheory (254)

fluid ability (252)

general intelligence (g) (252)

intelligence (250)

intelligence quotient (IQ) (260)

inventive spelling (279)

knowledge telling (279)

phonemic awareness (274)

psychometric approach (251)

reliability (261)

specific intelligence (s) (252)

strategy choice model (270)

subitizing (268)

theory of multiple intelligences (254)

triarchic theory of intelligence (252)

two-factor theory of intelligence (252)

validity (261)

word problems (271)

Chapter 8

Language Development

CHAPTER PREVIEW

A PERSPECTIVE TO think ABOUT

"Diana had not noticed Mariana's lack of words before."

Last week Diana took her 20-month-old daughter, Mariana, to play with some neighborhood friends. Diana watched as Mariana played with 16-month-old Gina. Gina chattered away, claiming and labeling every object she picked up. Over the following days, Diana realized that Mariana, unlike Gina, did not use any real words. When Diana showed Mariana an apple and tried to get her to say the word *apple,* Mariana responded by excitedly saying, "Papapapa!" but was not able to imitate the word. Diana had not noticed Mariana's lack of words before, because she could usually figure out what Mariana wanted or needed; Mariana is good at pointing and using other gestures. Diana remembered that Mariana began cooing when she was 5 months old—she had written this down in Mariana's baby book. Since then, however, Diana hadn't made any further entries about language milestones. Both Diana and her husband are bilingual, speaking both English and Spanish. Diana had hoped that Mariana would learn both languages at once, but some friends have told her that this could be delaying Mariana's language development.

Diana is becoming concerned about her daughter's language development. Should she be? After studying this chapter, you should be able to apply at least a dozen concepts and research findings to Diana and Mariana's situation. What kinds of language skills do most 20-month-old children show? What can Diana do to help encourage Mariana's language development? What kinds of language skills should Mariana show over the months and years to come? Should Diana continue to encourage bilingualism in her daughter, or should she help Mariana learn one language first, then add the second?

 As you read this chapter, look for the questions that ask you to think about what you're learning from Mariana's perspective.

Several years ago, some friends came to our house for dinner, bringing their 4-year-old daughter Kelly. When Kelly asked for a second helping of pasta, she remarked, "This is the bestest, most deliciousest dinner I have *ever* eated!" Kelly's interesting grammatical construction amused us all, but we had no difficulty understanding what she meant. Like Kelly, most children learn very quickly to express their thoughts, desires, and emotions through language—although mastering the specific rules of proper grammar can take much longer. When, like Mariana, some children are slower to develop language, their parents often worry that something is amiss.

What is language, and how does it develop? Is it predominantly a learned skill based on input and feedback from a linguistic environment, or do humans have innate biological predispositions to develop a language? Are grammatical errors such as *bestest* and *eated* a normal part of language development, or do they signify some fundamental problem? Is Mariana's level of language skill appropriate for her age? These are a few of the questions that we will discuss in this chapter.

What Is Language?

Language has long been a fascinating subject for psychologists, perhaps in part because it seems to be one skill that sets humans apart from other species. Members of other species have many different ways to communicate with one another; that is, to send and receive information or messages. But human language has several characteristics that no other species' communication system seems to share. As a way to arrive at a definition of *language*, we'll look at these special properties.

As you study this section, ask yourself these questions:

- What is language? What are the defining characteristics of language?
- How does language differ from communication and from speech?
- What are the five rule systems of language? How does knowledge of each contribute to successful language development?

Characteristics of Language

Three key features distinguish human language (Brown, 1973; Gleason, 1997). First, language has *semanticity*, which means that it represents thoughts, objects, and events through specific and abstract symbols. For example, the word *baby* does not look or sound like a real baby. This word is an abstract symbol: All speakers of the English language agree that the word will refer to a human infant, but *baby* does not share any visual or sound properties with the object it represents. Second, language is *productive*, which means that humans can be amazingly creative in their communication. Unlike most other species, there is no limit to the number or types of utterances that humans can create. As an example, think about the last sentence you spoke or wrote. How many different ways could you express exactly the same meaning? One of the most interesting features of children's language development is that most of the time children don't simply imitate what they hear others say. Even if they're expressing the same meaning as someone else, they don't repeat the words or phrases exactly as they hear them. Instead, children put words together in unique ways from the time they begin to use language. Also, as long as we follow the rules that our particular language has for how to put sounds together, our novel communications are completely understandable by others. Third, language has the quality of

Language uses abstract symbols and allows communication about an infinite number of topics. What fantasies do you think these children might express with their language?

displacement, which means that we can communicate about things that are distant in time or space. We can talk about something that happened long ago (the fall of the Roman Empire) or that might take place far in the future (a manned space flight to Mars). Thanks to displacement we can discuss things that never really happened or that may never happen (a trip to the earth's core)—and even things that are physically or logically impossible or nonexistent (goblins, fairies, and wizards)! Displacement allows humans to communicate about a vast range of things instead of being limited to the immediate circumstances.

So we can define **language** as an arbitrary system of symbols (words) that is rule-governed and allows communication about things that are distant in time or space. Language is more specific than *communication* because we can and do "communicate" without words. And language is more general than *speech,* the oral expression of language. For example, many people communicate by means of American Sign Language, which is a gestural rather than a speech-based language system. And when studying language, it is important to keep in mind the distinction between language *comprehension* and language *production.* Often, young children are able to understand and respond appropriately to spoken language well before they can produce grammatical speech. One point that most researchers agree on is that humans seem to have a very strong instinctive drive to acquire language. Although an impoverished language environment (i.e., one that provides and encourages less language) will affect a child's rate of language acquisition and the quality of the language the child achieves, it is quite difficult to keep humans from developing *any* language (Flavell, 1985; Hulit & Howard, 1997).

The Structure of Language

Language consists of five different rule systems: *phonology, morphology, syntax, semantics,* and *pragmatics.* **Phonology** refers to the important speech sounds of a language and the rules for how to combine these basic sounds into larger units. A *phoneme* is an individual unit of

language

An arbitrary system of symbols (words) that is rule-governed and allows communication about things that are distant in time or space.

phonology

The important speech sounds of a language and the rules for combining basic sounds into larger units.

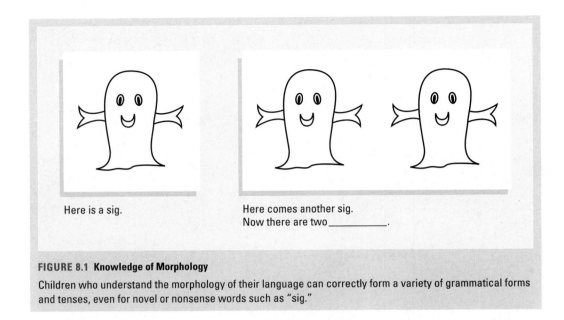

Here is a sig.

Here comes another sig.
Now there are two _____.

FIGURE 8.1 Knowledge of Morphology

Children who understand the morphology of their language can correctly form a variety of grammatical forms and tenses, even for novel or nonsense words such as "sig."

YOUR PERSPECTIVE NOTES

Can you identify some particular rules of syntax that continue to be troublesome for you? Which rules seem to be easier?

morphology

The rules for combining the smallest units of meaning in a language into words.

syntax

The way a language combines words to form phrases and sentences; a system consisting of the rules of grammar for the language.

semantics

The meanings associated with the words in a language.

pragmatics

The use of language to express thoughts and feelings, accomplish things, and communicate effectively with others.

speech sound. Every language consists of a set of specific phonemes. For example, the word "chat" in English consists of three different phonemes: the *chuh* sound in *ch* along with the *a* and *t* sounds. As you might expect, different languages have different numbers of phonemes. English has about 45 phonemes; other languages have as few as 15 or as many as 85 (Solso, 2001). There can be more phonemes than letters in a language's alphabet, because any given letter may have two or more possible speech sounds, and combinations of letters can create additional phonemes. Though there seems to be a bewildering array of phonemes in any given language, one of the most astonishing aspects of language development is that most children master the majority of their native language's phonemes by about 2 years of age.

Children must also master the morphology of their language. **Morphology** consists of the rules for combining a language's smallest units of meaning into words. A *morpheme* is the smallest unit of meaning in a language. Sometimes a morpheme is a single letter. For example, the word *dogs* has two morphemes: the word *dog*, referring to the animal, and the *s*, meaning more than one. A morpheme can be a single syllable, such as the syllable *un* in the word *unclear* (*un* means not; *clear* means easily understood). It can also consist of more than one syllable, as in the word *danger* (neither *dan* nor *ger* has any meaning on its own, so there is only one morpheme). Knowledge of a language's morphology enables children to form different grammatical expressions in their language (e.g., using correct tenses, number, gender, etc.) even if the words are new to them. For example, in one classic study Berko (1958) asked children to generate plurals and past tenses for imaginary creatures like the example in Figure 8.1. Even preschoolers and first graders were able to produce grammatically correct plurals and past tenses with nonsense words like these.

Syntax is the way a language combines words to form phrases and sentences. This system consists of the rules of grammar for the language, and it enables a speaker to generate an almost infinite number of novel sentences. Rules of syntax determine, for example, that it is proper to say *The cowboy ran home* but not *The home ran cowboy*. Syntax allows the speaker to produce grammatically correct sentences about any topic, even when the vocabulary is new or made up of nonsense words. Although children learn the basic rules of syntax fairly early in childhood, it is not until their school years (or even later) that they master some of the more complex rules.

Pragmatics involves using language at a level that's appropriate for a particular listener.

Semantics is the system of meanings associated with words. Clearly, if a child does not learn to associate the correct meaning with a word, then successful language development cannot take place. Developing semantic knowledge is a complicated task that takes many years. Many words have more than one meaning, and these meanings can be subtly different depending on the linguistic and social contexts surrounding a word's use. For example, if a mother says, *Sit here for the present,* she may mean *Sit here for a little while,* but she could also mean *Sit here to get the gift.* Even when a child uses a word in the same way that an adult would in a given context, it does not necessarily mean that the child has the same understanding of the word as the adult.

The final rule system that children must master deals with how to use language to communicate effectively with others. **Pragmatics** has to do with the use of language to express your thoughts and feelings, accomplish things, and communicate effectively with others. Pragmatic knowledge involves such things as how much to talk, when to take turns speaking, and how to use proper manners in communication. Someone who speaks to babies using adult-level vocabulary is not showing good pragmatics. Neither is someone who dominates a conversation, fails to take turns appropriately, or addresses his or her mother or teacher with *"Hey, yo broad!"* Pragmatic knowledge requires a great deal of experience with social interactions as well as semantic and syntactic knowledge, but some aspects of pragmatics develop earlier than you might expect.

thinking
OF MARIANA

◄ Does Mariana show any evidence of early pragmatic knowledge of language?

LET'S REVIEW . . .

1. Which of the following is characteristic of language but *not* of communication?

    a. Information is sent and received.

    b. Information is transmitted using sounds or gestures.

    c. Information about current circumstances can be transmitted.

    d. Information is transmitted using abstract symbols.

2. Which linguistic rule system allows people to produce novel sentences that are grammatically correct?

    a. phonology   b. morphology   c. syntax   d. semantics

3. Which of the following shows a *lack* of pragmatic knowledge of language?
    a. Not allowing others to contribute to a conversation.
    b. Talking to a 2-year-old about a popular children's cartoon.
    c. Using baby talk when speaking to infants and toddlers.
    d. Asking polite questions of a new acquaintance.

4. **True or False:** A morpheme is the same thing as a syllable.

5. **True or False:** The displacement characteristic of language means that communication is not limited to only those things that currently exist.

Answers: 1. d, 2. c, 3. a, 4. F, 5. T

Theories of Language Development

How do children grasp the complex rule systems of language? And more intriguing, how are children able to master them so quickly? Three basic theories attempt to explain language development. The *learning* theory emphasizes the role of the environment, whereas *nativist* theory emphasizes the role of children's genetic and biological inheritance. *Interactionist* perspectives, as you might expect, focus on how various aspects of the environment interact with genetic and biological characteristics.

As you study this section, ask yourself these questions:

- Is language learned, or is it genetically programmed in humans?

- What is the LAD? How does it affect language development?

- What roles do social interaction and general cognitive level play in language development?

- How does child-directed speech (CDS) help children acquire language? Why do adults use CDS?

- What evidence supports each of the three views of language development? What arguments are made against each theory?

Learning Theory: Language as a Learned Skill

The **learning theory** of language development is based on behaviorist theories of learning, particularly B. F. Skinner's principles of operant conditioning and Alfred Bandura's concept of learning through imitation (Bandura & Walters, 1963; Skinner, 1957). Sometimes referred to as the *environmental view*, in this approach language is viewed as a behavior that people learn just like any other skill (Watson, 1924). Learning theorists believe that the specific language training a child receives governs language development and that biological predispositions do not play an important role.

According to the learning theory of language development, *operant conditioning* principles, particularly the procedure of *shaping* (selectively reinforcing certain behaviors while ignoring or punishing others), explain how children come to produce speech. For example, as a child begins to produce verbalizations, parents and others in the child's environment tend to reinforce the sounds that resemble real words (e.g., *dada*) but ignore those that do not (e.g., *gaga*). As a result, the child tends to repeat the reinforced wordlike sounds, and the nonword-

learning theory

Theory that sees language as a skilled behavior that children learn through operant conditioning, imitation, and modeling.

Behaviorists believe that parents teach language through imitation, modeling, and shaping.

like sounds gradually die out. Similarly, caregivers reinforce simple phrases such as "Me want juice" when they meet the child's request. The more clearly the child says the phrase, the more likely an adult is to understand and comply with the request. As the child progresses, parents shift from shaping individual words to shaping longer phrases and sentences (Skinner, 1957).

Imitation and modeling also play important roles. At the same time that parents and others are selectively reinforcing closer approximations to real words and phrases, they also provide models of more advanced language. One way they do this is by repeating the word they think the child means to say. For example, if a little girl says "Mmmm" while looking at her mother, the mother might respond by saying "Mommy, that's right, I'm your mommy." When the child tries to imitate the *mmmaaa* sound in the word *mommy,* the mother reinforces the attempt. Adults also extend words or phrases, elaborating the child's utterances and providing a model of language that is slightly more advanced than the one the child produced on her own. For example, if the child says "Go" as she is walking out the door, her father might say, "That's right, we're going bye-bye." This kind of interaction both reinforces the child's language attempts and provides a model of how to produce more mature words and phrases (Moerk, 1992, 2000).

Numerous studies have established that word meanings can be acquired and altered through conditioning. For example, therapists have successfully used differential reinforcement techniques to improve the language skills of children with mental retardation or autistic disorder. Simply providing models of language and grammar does not appear to affect these children's language skills, but if they are actively encouraged to imitate the model, then their language often improves (Bohannon & Bonvillian, 1997).

However, the learning theory of language development has been criticized for a number of reasons. First, there is continuing debate about how consistently parents "shape" their children's language. Some studies indicate that shaping is inconsistent, and that parents tend to reinforce or punish the accuracy of the content of children's utterances rather than the

YOUR
PERSPECTIVE
NOTES
Have you ever used (or seen someone using) language shaping, modeling, or imitation with young children? What did the adult do, and how did the child respond?

thinking
OF MARIANA
◀ How could Diana use the behaviorist view of language development to improve Mariana's language skills?

grammatical correctness. Also, parents do not appear to explicitly teach their children the rule systems for forming grammatical utterances or understanding language. In fact, these rule systems are quite complex, and most adults would have a great deal of difficulty identifying and describing them for themselves, much less explicitly teaching them to children. Second, critics argue that much of the language children hear in their everyday lives is incomplete, ill formed, and full of errors—far from being a good model from which to learn. Third, learning principles can't really account for the degree of novelty of children's language utterances, or what linguists call *productivity*. From an early age, children regularly say things they have never heard before, such as *I goed to the store*. They also express things they have heard in new and innovative ways. Critics argue that it would be impossible for all of children's utterances to result from imitation and shaping (Brown & Hanlon, 1970; Morgan, Bonamo, & Travis, 1995; Pinker, 1994). Fourth, critics say that children learn language at a very fast pace—too fast to be explained by reinforcement, shaping, and imitation. Finally, critics question the learning theorists' idea that language is "simply another behavior." Research evidence suggests that humans are biologically predisposed to detect language stimuli and to process language differently than other types of information (Eisenberg, 1976).

Nativist Theory: Born to Talk

The famed linguist Noam Chomsky was one of the first to argue that learning theories could not adequately explain how children are able to master so quickly the complex systems of language. Chomsky proposed a **nativist theory,** the idea that language is an innate human capability. Chomsky suggested that humans are born with a **language acquisition device (LAD),** a brain mechanism that is specialized for detecting and learning the rules of language (Chomsky, 1957, 1981; Lenneberg, 1967). Just as humans are born with specialized organs—a heart and lungs—to carry out the complex tasks of circulation and respiration, they are born with a specialized "language organ" in the brain to carry out the complex task of acquiring language (Siegler, 1998, p. 140). Children must hear some amount of language to activate the LAD, but extensive language input is not necessary. Nor is it essential that the language that is heard be completely grammatically correct. Because the LAD is innate, language acquisition does not require great cognitive skill or cognitive effort. This explains why young children, as well as children with mental retardation and other cognitive delays, all develop at least some language ability quickly and easily. Another strength of the nativist view is that it explains both language acquisition patterns that are similar across different languages and patterns that differ. The LAD is innate but does not preprogram a child to learn a specific language.

Chomsky proposed that the LAD contains an innate knowledge of *universal grammar,* or the aspects of language rule systems that are common across all languages. When a child hears language, the LAD analyzes the language to determine its general type of grammatical construction system. Once the basic grammar of the language is recognized, the child can easily abstract important linguistic information and can quickly acquire language. Some theorists propose that innate knowledge of universal grammar is not all available to the child at birth; instead, this knowledge becomes available more gradually as the brain matures, a view called *linguistic maturation* (Wexler, 1999). This approach explains not only how children can learn language when the language they hear is incomplete and poorly structured, but also why they do *not* develop certain language skills until relatively late, even when the language they hear is rich in these linguistic properties (Babyonshev, Ganger, Pesetsky, & Wexler, 2001).

Other nativist theories suggest that rather than containing specific innate knowledge of possible grammar systems, the LAD contains **operating principles**—assumptions and biases that cause children to treat the language environment in special ways (Slobin, 1982, 1985b). In other words, children are predisposed to pay attention to certain aspects of the

nativist theory

Theory that sees language as an innate human capability that develops when language input triggers a *language acquisition device (LAD)* in the brain.

language acquisition device (LAD)

A brain mechanism in humans specialized for acquiring and processing language.

operating principles

Innate assumptions and biases that cause children to pay particular attention to certain features in the language environment such as word endings, order, and intonation.

linguistic environment: the ends of words, word order, differences in intonation, and the like. Because of innate operating principles, children notice the subtle patterns their language uses to express things like plurality, possession, or relationships. Thus, children become progressively more sensitive to the particular features that are most useful in their language (and less sensitive to less useful features). For example, a child learning Russian will gradually focus more closely on word endings to determine relations between words. In contrast, a child learning English will focus more on the order of words. Regardless of the particular kinds of information contained in the LAD, all nativist theorists agree that a physiologically based LAD exists and that the role of the environment is to initiate its maturation. The environment does not shape or train verbal behavior (Bohannon & Bonvillian, 1997).

■ **Is Language Innate?** If language acquisition is biologically programmed, then it should show developmental patterns similar to those of other biologically based systems such as physical maturation. All humans should develop language, and they should develop it in a fairly consistent way. Language should be easy for humans to develop and hard to prevent, but nonhumans should not develop language. Also, there should be physical organs or mechanisms that specialize in language processing. Finally, language development should show *sensitive periods* (times during which a child is particularly sensitive to some aspect of the environment), as happens with many aspects of physical development. Language development shows several of these characteristics.

Do All Humans Develop Language? There is strong evidence from cross-cultural comparisons that all physically intact humans develop language easily and quickly—and that the order and pace of achieving linguistic milestones is remarkably consistent across different languages (Caselli et al., 1995; Slobin, 1982, 1985a). Only extremely impoverished linguistic environments seem to keep children from developing some kind of language skill. Presumably these environments simply don't provide enough language experience to trigger the LAD. Even children with significant cognitive delays develop near normal levels of language usage and syntactic knowledge (Bellugi & St. George, 2001; Fowler, 1998; Tager-Flusberg, Boshart, & Baron-Cohen, 1999).

Can Nonhumans Develop Language? Whether nonhumans develop language has been an issue of some debate. Studies with apes (including the famous apes Washoe and Nim Chimpsky) indicate that apes can understand many semantic relations between linguistic symbols. Through sign language, by manipulating colored plastic tokens, or even by using specially designed computer keyboards, apes can use words to describe things in their environment, ask and answer questions, and make requests (Goodall, 1986; Savage-Rumbaugh, Rumbaugh, & Boysen, 1978). However, the apes in these studies did not seem to learn many aspects of language that come quickly and easily to humans. For example, they did not show knowledge of syntax, rarely included new information in their utterances, and showed little understanding of pragmatics such as conversational turn taking (Gleason, 1997; Terrace, Petitto, Sanders, & Bever, 1980). A bonobo named Kanzi became quite successful at comprehending the semantics and the syntax of verbal instructions, even instructions he had never heard before (Savage-Rumbaugh et al., 1993; Savage-Rumbaugh, Shanker, & Taylor, 1998). Although Kanzi's performance was impressive, nativists argue that it is unclear whether he could *produce* syntactically correct language constructions. They also point out that it took 8 years of intensive training to teach Kanzi these skills. Human children, in contrast, master semantic, syntactic, and pragmatic skills quickly and easily. What explains the difference? Nativists argue that other species lack the specialized brain mechanism common to all humans—the LAD.

Are There Physical Structures Specialized for Language? Humans do possess specific physical structures for producing and processing language. Though you may not

YOUR
PERSPECTIVE
NOTES
Which language features seem most useful in your native language? Have you ever tried to learn a foreign language? If so, were the important features different from or similar to key features of your native language?

Can primates develop true language?

have thought of them this way, the structures of the human mouth and throat are specially suited for producing the complex phonemes of spoken language. Other species are not able to produce these sounds (Lenneberg, 1967). In addition, specific areas within the human brain specialize in processing linguistic information. Figure 8.2 shows some of these areas. In most people, the left hemisphere of the brain is chiefly responsible for processing language information. *Wernicke's area,* located in the left temporal lobe for most people, enables us to comprehend spoken words and produce coherent written and spoken language. *Broca's area,* located in the left frontal lobe, directs the patterns of muscle movements necessary for the production of speech. Other brain areas specialized for language include the *arcuate fasciculus,* a band of fibers that connects Wernicke's area to Broca's area, and the *angular gyrus,* which is involved in processing written language (Gleason, 1997; Maratsos & Matheney, 1994).

So there is evidence of physical organs that are specialized for language processing. However, there does not appear to be a *single* organ that is the LAD proposed by Chomsky. Instead, the LAD may be more correctly thought of as a constellation of several interconnected brain areas (Cornell, Fromkin, & Mauner, 1993; Krishner, 1995). There is still no consensus as to what kinds of innately hardwired information might exist within those structures. Researchers now believe that some aspects of language development may be more domain-specific, whereas others may apply across domains.

Are There Sensitive Periods for Language Development?   Another type of evidence that supports nativist theory is the apparent existence of sensitive periods for language development. According to Lenneberg (1967), we acquire language almost exclusively during childhood, before the brain's organization becomes specialized and fixed. Areas of the brain are predisposed to respond to linguistic input, but children must experience language to activate these mechanisms. If a child does not receive enough linguistic input, the period of heightened sensitivity goes by. The key brain areas become specialized for other types of pro-

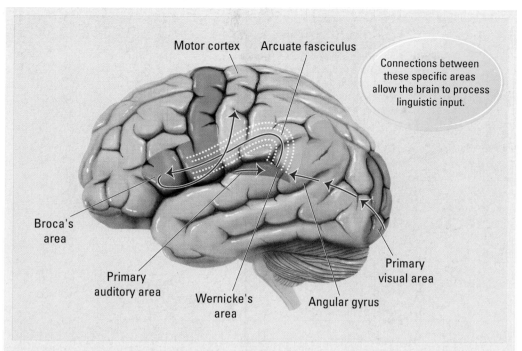

FIGURE 8.2 Brain Structures Involved in Language Processing

Wernicke's area is important in comprehending spoken words and producing coherent written and spoken language. Nerves connect Wernicke's area to the *primary auditory cortex. Broca's area* directs the patterns of muscle movements necessary to produce speech sounds. The *arcuate fasciculus* connects Wernicke's area to Broca's area. The *angular gyrus* processes written language.

Source: Adapted from R. Fabes & C. L. Martin. (2003). *Exploring child development,* 2nd ed. Boston: Allyn & Bacon, p. 167.

cessing, and the opportunity for quick and easy language acquisition is lost. If Lenneberg is correct about sensitive periods, then several things should follow:

▶ Children deprived of language should show poorer language skills since the brain areas will not be activated.

▶ Older children and adults should have greater difficulty learning new languages than young children.

▶ Older children and adults should recover less fully from damage to language areas of the brain, because the brain is already specialized.

There is evidence to support each of these predictions (Locke, 1993). First, case reports indicate that people deprived of linguistic input during childhood do not develop normal linguistic skills, experiencing particular problems with syntax (Curtiss, 1977). Second, learning a new language seems to be more difficult for older children and adults than for younger children. For example, Johnson and Newport examined the English language skills of Chinese and Korean immigrants, focusing on the ages at which immigrants arrived in the United States. Figure 8.3 shows that English proficiency clearly relates to the immigrants' age on arrival. Proficiency was not related to the number of years the immigrants had spoken English or to the amount of formal English instruction they had received (Johnson & Newport, 1989). Other research found the same result in deaf children learning American Sign Language: Proficiency in ASL reflected the age at which children first encountered ASL but not how long they had used ASL (Newport, 1990). And finally, recovery of language functions

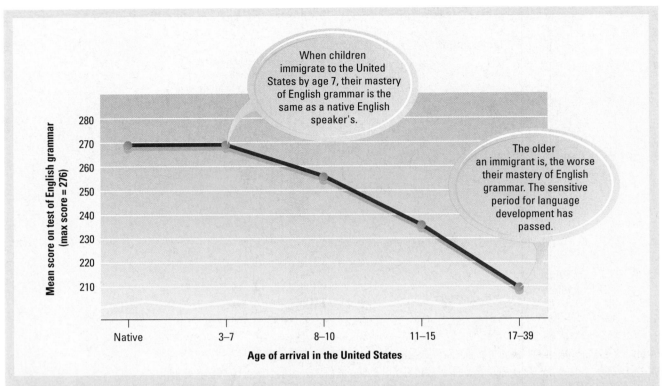

FIGURE 8.3 Support for a Sensitive Period for Language Development

Johnson and Newport (1989) found that Chinese and Korean immigrants' proficiency in English was related to the age at which the immigrants arrived in the United States, but not to the number of years they had spoken English or the amount of formal English instruction the immigrants had received.

Source: J. S. Johnson & E. L. Newport. (1989). Critical period effects in second language learning: The influence of maturational state on the acquisition of English as a second language. *Cognitive Psychology, 21,* p. 79. Copyright © 1989. Reprinted with permission from Elsevier.

after damage to the left hemisphere of the brain is much faster and more complete for younger children (Stiles & Thal, 1993; Witelson, 1987). In fact, if the left hemisphere sustains damage before the age of one year, the language functions can shift into the right hemisphere and "crowd out" the perceptual–spatial skills that usually localize there. The result is that language survives but perceptual–spatial skills suffer. So it seems that language development is biologically very important (Maratsos & Matheny, 1994; Siegler, 1998).

■ **Criticisms of Nativist Theory.** Despite this evidence, disagreement over the nativist approach persists. One of the major criticisms of nativist theory concerns the kind and amount of linguistic input and feedback that children actually receive. Pinker (1994) suggested that language learning according to the behaviorist model could occur only if children received *negative evidence,* or explicit corrections, when they made language errors. Nativists such as Pinker claim that children do not receive this kind of evidence from adults, so they argue that language must be innately driven (Morgan et al., 1995; Pinker, 1994). However, some studies show that adults do provide a great deal of corrective feedback (Bohannon & Bonvillian, 1997; Bohannon & Padgett, 1996; Farrar, 1992; Saxton, 1997). In addition, nativist theory predicts that given any kind of exposure to activate the LAD, children should develop normal language, regardless of the level of complexity, abstraction, or grammatical correctness of the linguistic input. However, children whose language exposure comes only from television do not develop normal language skills (Sachs, Bard, & Johnson, 1981). Other critics point out that nativists have not successfully identified a single universal grammar that can apply to all known languages—a critical element in any theory that proposes a biologically programmed universal grammar (Tomasello, 1995). Finally, there continues to be disagreement about whether other species can develop language.

Interaction Theories: Cognitive and Social Interactionist Approaches

Although both Skinner and Chomsky were right about some aspects of language development, many researchers came to believe that these two opposing theorists were too extreme. Dissatisfaction with both purely learning and purely nativist views led researchers to consider how multiple factors might interact to produce language development. Some interaction approaches emphasize the role of cognitive factors; others emphasize how social interactions contribute to language acquisition.

■ **Cognitive Approaches: Language Depends on Cognition.** Not surprisingly, Jean Piaget, the famous cognitive development theorist you read about in Chapter 5, stressed the role of the general cognitive abilities of the child in language acquisition. **Piaget's cognitive developmental theory** of language development views language as only one of several different abilities that depend on overall cognitive maturation. Proper cognitive development is a necessary prerequisite for normal language development (Piaget, 1954). For example, you may remember that one of the major cognitive achievements by the end of Piaget's first stage of cognitive development—the sensorimotor stage—is object permanence, or the understanding that objects and people continue to exist even when an infant cannot directly experience them. If words are symbols that represent objects, then babies in the sensorimotor stage do not need them. Either babies directly experience objects (and so need no symbols), or objects are out of babies' immediate experience and no longer exist (requiring no symbols). Only when children develop cognitively to the point at which they need symbols to represent things do they have a reason to use words and develop language. Cognitive skills then interact with environmental demands and language experience to produce increasingly mature language skills.

Some correlational evidence is consistent with Piaget's cognitive developmental view. For example, children first begin using words that indicate something disappeared (e.g., *all gone*) at about the same time they develop object permanence. Words that indicate evaluation of effort (e.g., *uh-oh*, or *got it*) appear at around the same time children start using intentional, goal-directed problem-solving strategies (Gopnik, 1984; Gopnik & Meltzoff, 1984). And some research indicates that children do not use grammatical markers for things like past tense or possession in their spontaneous speech until they have some understanding that there is such a thing as the past and that objects can be owned (Slobin, 1982). However, these correlations do not prove that the cognitive skills *caused* the language skills to develop. And interestingly, many children with significant cognitive deficits still show normal language development; this should not occur if Piaget's theory is correct (Bellugi & St. George, 2001; Fowler, 1998). Other work suggests that some specific aspects of language may result from general cognitive development, but not others. For example, Genie, a child deprived of normal language for much of her early childhood, showed reasonably normal semantic and cognitive development but significant delays in syntax and morphology (Curtiss, 1981). In other cases researchers have found normal or advanced development of syntax and morphology, but delays in semantic and cognitive development (Levy, Tennenbaum, & Ornoy, 2000).

One intriguing cognitive approach to understanding language development is **connectionism,** based on the *connectionist models* of cognition you read about in Chapter 6. Recall that connectionist models are neural network models in which links of varying strengths

Piaget's cognitive developmental theory

Theory that sees language as one of several abilities that depend on overall cognitive development. Proper cognitive development is a necessary prerequisite for normal language development.

connectionism

Theory that views language acquisition as the result of changes in the strengths of connections between units. Changes depend on how closely the language produced matches external criteria.

connect simple elements called *units*. Connectionist models of language development say that language acquisition results from changes in the strengths of connections between units based on how closely the language produced matches external criteria. For example, imagine that a little boy sees an animal that looks a lot like the animal he associates with the word *dog*. Units corresponding to characteristics of the input (the dog) stimulate the pattern of connections the child has developed for these input features in the past, so he says "dog." But his father says, "Here, kitty, kitty, kitty. Look at that big kitty." Even though the father is not explicitly correcting his son's utterance, he is providing a model by using a specific word consistently for the new animal. As the boy continues to encounter this type of animal and hear the same name, the links between the units that produce *dog* will decrease in strength, and those that lead to the production of the word *kitty* will increase. Eventually, he will come to call this animal a kitty.

The strongest support for connectionism comes from computer simulations. Researchers presented verbs to a computer with the same frequency that children typically encounter them in everyday language. Even though the computer never received and did not learn any explicit rules, it gradually learned to produce correct past tenses for both regular and irregular verbs, and it showed patterns of acquiring past tenses that were quite similar to those of children (Rumelhart & McClelland, 1986). Even more convincing are the findings that the simulation showed the same kinds of error patterns as children—and that the connectionist model successfully predicts which specific grammatical cues (such as word endings or word order) children will acquire first in specific languages (MacWhinney, 1987, 1999). However, critics argue that language development based on gradual changes in connection strengths would take far longer than it actually does for real children. A related criticism is that children often learn new words after a single exposure to them. Such *one-trial learning* can be difficult for these models to explain.

■ **Social Interactionist Theory.** **Social interactionist theory** says that language development is the result of a complex interaction between the child's biological predispositions and social interactions. Most social interactionists agree with nativists that humans are biologically prepared to develop language, but they believe that simply hearing language is not enough. Instead, interacting with others is critical: To develop language, children must have conversations with other people. This theory also assumes that children have a strong drive to communicate effectively with others. Because humans are social by nature, children *themselves* play a significant role by seeking social interactions and trying to communicate with those around them (Akhtar & Tomasello, 2000).

What role do social interactions play for language development? As we noted earlier, it seems that parents provide much more feedback about language performance than some theorists used to think. They do so in several ways in the course of everyday events & interactions (Hart & Risley, 1995). Children often initiate language interaction by attempting some kind of sound, word, or phrase. If the utterance is grammatically correct, parents may imitate it—repeat or echo it—exactly. But parents also provide implicit feedback. For example, *recasts* are restatements of what the child said but in correct grammatical form. If a child says, "I saw two deers in the yard," her mother might recast this and reply, "You saw two *deer;* that's great!" Parents also use *expansions,* repeating but also correcting and elaborating on the child's utterance. For example, the mother responding to her child's statement about seeing two deers might expand this utterance by saying, "You saw two deer? Remember when we saw the deer at the forest preserve? Did those deer look like the ones in the yard?" Children respond to feedback by correcting their errors (Bohannon & Bonvillian, 1997; Farrar, 1992; Saxton, 1997, 2000).

Bruner (1983) has argued that caregivers typically present language to children quite carefully and in a structured fashion through social interactions. Examples are joint activities

social interactionist theory

Theory proposing that language development results from the interaction of biological and social factors, and that social interaction is required.

Everyday activities and games serve as structured formats that support language development. What language skills is this baby learning?

such as songs with specific accompanying gestures, games such as peekaboo, and common daily activities such as baths and meals. All of these interactions have predictable structures, and all are very common across cultures (Fernald & O'Neill, 1993). These familiar interactions, which Bruner calls **formats,** allow the child to learn specific words, grammatical structures, conversational turn taking (even if the infant's contribution is only a smile or gurgle), and ways to express different intentions and emotions. Because it is so restricted, the format context encourages the child to pay attention and associate the words, structures, and emotions with the correct language elements. As children's language skills improve, caregivers respond by changing the formats to include additional elements or by requiring more complex performance from the child (Bohannon & Bonvillian, 1997; Hart & Risley, 1995; Sokolov, 1993).

But adults support children's language learning in even more specific ways. Adults and older children frequently change their linguistic style when they talk to young children—they use child-directed speech, sometimes called *motherese* (Sachs & Devine, 1976; Snow, 1972). **Child-directed speech** is slower and higher pitched, has more frequent and more extreme ups and downs in pitch, and includes more questions than speech directed to adults. Child-directed speech also exaggerates key words and phrases for emphasis and often repeats such words several times. The sentences are short and simple, and they often focus on objects and activities the child is actively attending to. Child-directed speech occurs in many different cultures and languages (Fernald, 1992; Kuhl et al., 1997). Even deaf mothers use child-directed sign language with their infants, signing more slowly, employing more repetition, and making exaggerated gestures (Masataka, 1996). Infants pay more attention to child-directed speech, and they are more successful in discriminating words with subtle differences in sound when they hear the words in child-directed speech (Cooper & Aslin, 1994; Masataka, 1998; Moore, Spence, & Katz, 1997).

YOUR
PERSPECTIVE
PERSPECTIVE
NOTES
Have you ever used child-directed speech? What is different about it? What prompted you to use it, and what effect did it have on the child?

formats

Common social interactions between infants and caregivers that have a predictable structure and teach words, syntax, and pragmatic skills.

child-directed speech

Special form of speech people often use when speaking to young children; differs in systematic ways from speech to adults and appears to facilitate language development.

Social interactionists believe that child-directed speech is one way that adults directly teach some aspects of language. Caregivers use child-directed speech to introduce and model new vocabulary and proper grammatical structures during social interactions, when the child is most likely to be interested and paying attention. Child-directed speech is also full of recasts and expansions that give children the negative evidence (feedback) they need to alter their own speech (Bohannon & Bonvillian, 1997; Saxton, 1997). And even before they understand the meanings of the simplest words, infants seem to understand the emotional tone of this speech (Fernald, 1992). Thus, child-directed speech may help introduce the pragmatic, nonverbal aspects of language, which are just as important for successful communication as vocabulary and grammar. However, we do not yet fully understand the phenomenon of child-directed speech. Although it seems quite useful, it does not have the same features in all cultures. We do not yet know which particular features are most important or whether the central features are different for younger and older children (Bohannon & Bonvillian, 1997; Fee & Shaw, 1998).

thinking
OF MARIANA

Develop some examples of ▶ how Diana might use imitation, recasts, expansions, formats, and child-directed speech to help Mariana.

LET'S REVIEW . . .

1. According to research findings, which of the following is *true* regarding adult feedback to children about language skills?

    a. Adults do not know how to correct children's language.

    b. Adults do not provide feedback regarding children's language skills.

    c. Adults provide feedback about children's grammar, but children do not learn from the feedback.

    d. Adults provide feedback about children's grammar, and children use this feedback to correct their language.

2. The term *operating principles* refers to:

    a. an innate knowledge of universal grammar.

    b. innate predispositions to notice certain elements of language.

    c. the strategies parents use to shape their children's use of grammar.

    d. rules that govern how connections between units change in response to external feedback.

3. Child-directed speech fosters language development in all of the following ways *except* by:

    a. providing negative evidence about grammar.

    b. drawing an infant's attention to the topic of conversation.

    c. explaining the operating principles for the native language.

    d. emphasizing important features of speech.

4. Which of the following provides the best support for the hypothesis that there are sensitive periods in language development?

    a. The existence of physical organs that are specialized for language processing.

    b. The fact that adults and children are both able to learn second languages.

    c. The fact that children are especially sensitive to child-directed speech.

    d. The greater degree of language recovery shown by children than by adults after damage to the brain's left hemisphere.

5. **True or False:** A child who has significant cognitive deficits will not be able to develop normal language skills.

6. **True or False:** According to connectionist models, the most important factor in language development is having an intact LAD.

Answers: 1. d, 2. b, 3. c, 4. d, 5. F, 6. F

The Development of Language: What Happens When?

We have explored some of the theories of how language develops; but what kinds of changes take place, and when? Most children speak their first word by their first birthday and are quite good at speaking and comprehending their native language by the age of 3 or 4. Although language develops at an astonishing pace during the early years, important changes also continue to occur well into adolescence.

As you study this section, ask yourself these questions:

- What prelinguistic skills help prepare infants for language? How do these skills contribute to language acquisition?

- What is the sequence of vocalizations during the first year of life?

- What are the major developments in semantics, grammar, and pragmatics in early childhood? What are a typical child's language skills like at 2 years? At 5 years?

- What processes underlie the changes in language ability during early childhood?

- In what ways does language continue to develop during middle childhood and adolescence?

Infant Communication: How Language Starts

During the first year of life, important changes take place in three areas relevant to language. First, perceptual skills improve, enabling infants to perceive and discriminate different speech sounds. Second, infants and their caregivers establish a social environment; this encourages babies to turn random vocalizations into words to convey specific meanings. And third, having begun life with sounds that are reflexive and without intentional meaning, by one year babies begin to use real words.

■ **Perceptual Skills.**   It does not take babies long to start recognizing differences between speech sounds. One classic study used a variation of the habituation procedure you learned about in Chapter 4 (Eimas, Siqueland, Jusczyk, & Vigorito, 1971). The researchers gave infants as young as 1 month of age a pacifier that activated a predetermined sound (e.g., *ba*). Babies gradually habituated to the sound, slowing their rate and intensity of sucking. When the sound was changed (e.g., to *pa*), the babies increased their rate of sucking. As you may recall from Chapter 4, this pattern indicates that the babies remembered the first sound and could tell that the second was different. Other studies have shown the same result with a variety of different speech sounds (Aslin, Jusczyk, & Pisoni, 1998). By 6 months, infants are able to discriminate among different sequences of sounds—an important skill, because words are made up of sometimes subtly different sound sequences (Goodsitt, Morse, VerHoeve, & Cowan, 1984). Interestingly, it does not matter whether the speech sounds come from the infant's "native" language or not. Trehub (1976) found that infants with English-speaking parents were just as good at discriminating among Czech sounds as English, but that English-speaking adults were worse than the infants at discriminating among the Czech sounds. Infants quickly lose this ability, however. Werker and Tees (1984) found that English-speaking infants 6 to 8 months old could easily distinguish among non-English speech sounds, whereas older babies had increasing difficulty. In other words, experience with language increases our ability to discriminate among speech sounds in our own language, but we gradually lose the ability to make discriminations that are not required on a regular basis.

TABLE 8.1 Development of Joint Focus of Attention

PHASE	APPROXIMATE AGE	PARENT ACTIONS	CHILD ACTIONS
1	4 weeks to 6 months	• Places object in infant's visual field • Draws infant's attention (moves object, says infant's name)	• Little response initially • Attends to object by 3 months • Recognizes intonation pattern as cue to attend by 6 months
2	7 months	• Responds to baby's attempts by interacting • Reinforces baby's attempts verbally and nonverbally	• Shows intent to communicate, attempts to establish joint reference by pointing • Reaches for object, looks to parent for response
3	8 to 12 months	• Asks about baby's intent • Repeats baby's gestures	• Shows intent through gestures accompanied by vocalizations
4	1 year	• Reduces number of questions • Increases number of labels for objects and events baby is attending to	• Names objects and events • Initiates more interactions

Sources: Hulit & Howard (1997), pp. 117–118; Carpenter, Nagell, & Tomasello (1998).

thinking
OF MARIANA

What phase of joint focus of attention does Mariana seem to show? Does she seem to understand anything about conversational turn taking?

■ **Social Interactions.** During the first year babies are also beginning to understand that they can use sounds to communicate their needs and even to control other people's behavior. Successful communication requires a **joint focus of attention;** that is, it requires that both people focus their attention on the same object or event at the same time. You can imagine what odd "conversations" would take place if each conversational partner were talking about different objects, events, or topics! Joint focus of attention develops gradually over the first year of life. Table 8.1 shows four proposed phases of this development (Carpenter, Nagell, & Tomasello, 1998; Hulit & Howard, 1997). Social interactions during infancy are also essential for the development of important pragmatic language skills. For example, the *formats* you read about earlier in this chapter provide structured frameworks that highlight when and how the infant is expected to contribute to the conversation. These interactions help infants recognize when it is their turn to talk and what kinds of contributions they should make (Bruner, 1983).

■ **From Crying to Words: Speech Production in Infancy.** Table 8.2 summarizes the developmental progression in speech production during the first year. Examine this progression and you will notice that the sounds become increasingly *differentiated,* which means that specific sounds are produced in the presence of specific conditions. The sounds also become increasingly *intentional,* which means that the baby produces them for a specific goal, such as showing a caregiver a toy, getting a caregiver to provide something, or communicating a desire. Both changes, differentiation and intentionality, help lay the groundwork for the infant's first real words around the age of one year.

An infant's first sounds are reflexive, nonintentional sounds such as crying, burping, sneezing, and coughing. Sometimes called *vegetative sounds,* these natural sounds come from many living creatures but are passive and do not convey intentional communicative meaning (Hulit & Howard, 1997). Also, a baby's first cries are undifferentiated; the cry produced because the baby is hungry sounds just like the one produced because the baby is wet, tired, angry, in pain, or the like. By 2 months the baby's cries show much more variation, and by 4 months the baby is producing distinctive cries to signal such things as discomfort and request. *Cooing,* the production of vowel-like sounds such as *o-o-o-o-u-u-u,* is present by 2 months. Cooing communicates an infant's pleasure and comfort; infants often coo during social

joint focus of attention
The situation that occurs when both people in a language interaction are focusing their attention on the same object or event at the same time.

TABLE 8.2 Development of Speech Sounds in Infancy

AGE	TYPE OF SPEECH SOUND
Birth	• Vegetative and undifferentiated sounds: reflexive, nonintentional sounds such as crying, burps, sneezing, coughing
2 months	• Greater variation in cries • Cooing to indicate comfort and pleasure
4 months	• Distinctive cries to signal specific states • Cooing and laughing
5 months	• Transitional babbling: single syllables with one consonant and one vowel sound *(ma)*
6 months	• True babbling: repeated vowel–consonant pair *(mamama)*
8 to 12 months	• Echolalia: immediate imitation of words
9 to 18 months	• Variegated babbling: multiple, differing syllables *(bapadaga)* • Jargon babbling: babbling which includes native language intonation patterns, rhythms, and stresses • Protowords: consistent sound patterns used to refer to specfic objects and events
One year	• First true words, usually accompanied by gestures, babbling, and/or protowords

Source: Adapted from Hulit & Howard (1997), pp. 120–123.

interactions with others, such as when their caregivers talk to or smile at them. By 4 months babies both coo and laugh.

At about 6 months infants show *true babbling,* or repeated consonant–vowel syllables such as *mamama.* True babbling occurs most often when infants are investigating their surroundings or examining objects and when an infant is alone (Stark, Bernstein, & Demorest, 1993). It includes many different sounds, even sounds that are not part of the infant's native language. Gradually the babbling comes to resemble more closely the phonemes of the family's language. This means that all infants have the potential to develop any language. It is the language they experience during the first year or so of life that determines which phonemes they will continue to produce and which will fade away. True babbling is heavily dependent on infants' being able to hear themselves clearly. As a result, it is at this point in development that babies with hearing impairments start to show delays, falling behind infants with normal hearing in the amount and variety of speech produced (Oller & Eilers, 1988; Stoel-Gammon & Otomo, 1986).

Between 8 and 12 months, infants start to show *echolalia,* the immediate imitation of others' sounds or words. Echolalia can be very accurate and may lead adults to believe that an infant has learned words, but infants do not understand the sounds they are producing. From 9 to 18 months, infants start to show *variegated babbling,* which includes syllables that differ from one another (e.g., *badagapa*), and *jargon babbling,* which includes the intonational patterns, rhythms, and stress patterns of the native language. Babies engaging in jargon babbling sound just as if they are carrying on a conversation, but without using real words. This behavior indicates that babies are attending to and beginning to master the rhythmic and intonation characteristics of the language they are hearing but haven't put these aspects together with real words yet.

Finally, around 9 to 10 months, infants begin to use *protowords* (also called *vocables*): consistent patterns of sounds that refer to specific people, objects, or events. For example, one of our sons used the protoword *neenee* to refer to his brother Andy, and many children use the protoword *baba* to refer to a baby bottle. Protowords mark an important transition from the random and nonmeaningful vocalizations of babbling to vocalizations

thinking
OF MARIANA

◄ Does Mariana's language development seem to be progressing at an appropriate pace for her age? At what place in development does she seem to be now?

that are intentional and consistent and have specific meaning. Protowords exist in many languages (Blake & deBoysson-Bardies, 1992). Once a child begins using protowords, it is usually not long until the child begins using true words.

From First Words to Conversation: Language in Early Childhood

The phonological skills that developed so rapidly during the first year continue to improve in early childhood. While even young infants can discriminate among basic speech sounds, some phonemes remain difficult to distinguish, and even more difficult to pronounce, for several more years. The major changes during the early childhood years are in the rule systems of semantics, syntax and morphology (which together constitute the development of grammar), and in pragmatics.

■ **Semantics: Words and Their Meanings.** Somewhere around the age of 1 year, children say their first true adult word. The transition from protowords to real words is gradual, and children continue to use gestures, babbling, and protowords along with real words for several months (Vihman & Miller, 1988). The average child can produce about 50 words by the time she is 18 months old. At this point there is a tremendous increase in the child's rate of learning new words. During this *naming explosion* children can add 10 to 20 new words *each day*! By 2 years, an average child can produce about 200 words, and by age 6 the child will have a vocabulary of about 10,000 words (Anglin, 1993; Nelson, 1973). When you consider that children typically comprehend far more words than they produce, you can appreciate the phenomenal semantic development that takes place during these early childhood years.

Table 8.3 shows the kinds of words that children produce first. As you can see, children's earliest words are usually nouns. They are usually labels for familiar and important objects or people in the environment, such as family members, favorite toys, pets, or favorite foods (Childers & Tomasello, 2002; Nelson, 1973). Children understand and produce nouns earlier than verbs in several languages, and nouns continue to be more frequent throughout language development (Nelson, Hampson, & Shaw, 1993). However, there are some interesting variations in this nouns-first pattern. Nelson (1973) identified two styles of acquiring early words. Most children showed a *referential style,* in which most early words are nouns that label familiar objects and people, as we just described. A subgroup of children, however, showed an *expressive style:* They produced a greater variety of word types and a greater number of social phrases such as "Thank you" or "Stop it." Children with an expressive style seem to use language more to interact socially or to draw attention to their feelings. The structure of a given language probably contributes to style differences, but differences in the language environment a child experiences also seem to play a role. For example, children in cultures that focus on interpersonal harmony (e.g., Japan, China, and Korea) tend to acquire verbs and social words more quickly than American children. Differences in types of play interactions in different cultures also may encourage one style versus the other (Fernald & Morikawa, 1993; Gopnik & Choi, 1995; Tardif, 1996). Firstborn American children are more likely to show a referential style and later-borns an expressive language style, and girls are more likely to have a referential style than boys. Parents have different language interactions with firstborns than with later-borns and with girls than boys, which may encourage style differences (Cherry & Lewis, 1976; Nelson, 1973; Pine, 1995; Shore, 1995).

How Are Early Words Acquired? Regardless of their style, children show amazing semantic development during early childhood. How are they able to learn the meanings of so many words so quickly? Children certainly learn word meanings through their parents' modeling and labeling of objects and events. It is not surprising that the first words children

TABLE 8.3 The Nature of Early Words

TYPE OF WORD	EXAMPLES	PERCENTAGE OF VOCABULARY WORDS
Names for *general examples* of a category	Mother, father, grandparent, doggy, kitty, toy	51
Names for *specific members* of a category	Mommy, Daddy, Grandma, Spot, Fluffy, Teddy	14
Words for *actions*	Go, up, swing, bounce, run, throw, cry	13
Words that *describe* objects or events	Big, little, mine, yummy, cold	9
Words that express *feelings or relationships*	No, sad, please	8
Words that serve *grammatical functions*	What, where, for, is	4

Source: Adapted from Nelson (1973).

acquire are the ones used most frequently by their parents. In addition, the more parents talk to their children, the faster the children's vocabulary grows. But children also use a process called **fast mapping,** in which they acquire at least a partial understanding of a word after only a single exposure (Carey, 1977; Woodward, Markman, & Fitzsimmons, 1994). Children as young as 18 months show fast mapping if both the child and his or her conversational partner are attending to the object being labeled (Baldwin et al., 1996). Despite these impressive abilities, however, children's early words often include errors. Children frequently show *overextensions,* in which they expand a word's meaning to include more objects than it should (Naigles & Gelman, 1995). For example, a young child who is learning the word *parrot* may overextend this label and use it to refer to any feathered creature that flies with wings (what adults would call *birds*) rather than only to a certain type of bird. Children also show *underextensions,* in which they use a word too narrowly. For example, a child may learn that the family's pet is a parrot and believe that this word applies only to this particular parrot, not to parrots in a zoo, on television, or in other places.

Children also use what they know about the grammatical structure of sentences (such as word order and word endings) to figure out the meanings of new words. This process of using syntax as a cue for determining word meaning is called *syntactical bootstrapping* (Gleitman, 1990). For example, if you encountered the sentence "Will is *pidding* his cereal," the placement of the new word along with its *-ing* ending would lead you to infer that *pidding* is an action, not an object. In contrast, the placement and word structure in the sentence "Will threw his *pid*" would lead you to infer that *pid* is an object, not an action (Naigles & Hoff-Ginsburg, 1995).

Finally, as Table 8.4 summarizes, several constraints aid word learning (Golinkoff, Mervis, & Hirsh-Pasek, 1994; Taylor & Gelman, 1988; Woodward & Markman, 1998). **Constraints** are assumptions that children automatically make about the possible meanings of a new word, and constraints can work together to help children determine word meanings. For example, suppose a little girl hears the new word *ostrich* while looking at a big bird with a long neck and legs at the zoo. The *whole object constraint* will lead the child to associate the new word with the whole animal rather than just its long neck, its long legs, or some other part. At the same time, the *mutual exclusivity constraint* will help the child associate only one name, *ostrich,* with this new animal. The *lexical contrast constraint* will bias her toward thinking that this new word has a different meaning from any other word she already knows. This constraint prevents the child from thinking that other animals with long necks (like giraffes or llamas) are also called ostriches. Sometimes, to increase the accuracy of the child's word

fast mapping

A process in language learning in which a child acquires at least a partial understanding of a word after only a single exposure.

constraints

Assumptions that children automatically make about the possible meanings of new words.

TABLE 8.4 Constraints on Early Word Learning

CONSTRAINT	DEFINITION	EXAMPLE
Whole object constraint	The assumption that a new word refers to a whole object rather than its individual parts or features	Child assumes the new word *elephant* refers to the entire animal rather than only its head, ears, trunk, etc.
Mutual exclusivity constraint	The assumption that a new word applies to only one object	Child assumes the new word *elephant* applies to only one object, a large, gray animal
Lexical contrast constraint	The assumption that a new word has a different meaning than previously acquired words	Child assumes the new word *elephant* has a different meaning than other words for large animals, like *cow*
Taxonomic constraint	The assumption that objects that share certain features can have both a common name and more specific individual names	Child assumes that the object called *elephant* can share a label such as *animal* with other objects that possess certain features in common

Sources: Golinkoff, Mervis, & Hirsh-Pasek (1994); Taylor & Gelman (1988); Woodward & Markman (1998).

thinking OF MARIANA

As Mariana starts using words, how can Diana help her use syntactical bootstrapping? How can she help Mariana make the best use of syntactic constraints?

learning, one constraint must overrule another (Savage & Au, 1996; Woodward & Markman, 1998). For example, the mutual exclusivity and lexical contrast constraints keep the child from thinking that a llama can be called *ostrich*, but they also keep the child from understanding that an ostrich can also be called an *animal*. As children get older, the *taxonomic constraint* can overrule these other constraints, helping the child understand that the word *animal* is a category label and that other objects can have that label along with more specific names (such as *ostrich*). Developmental researchers once thought that constraints were innate but recent studies suggest that at least some constraints are learned (Bloom, 1998; Hirsh-Pasek, Golinkoff, & Hollich, 2000).

What word-learning constraints are helping this child learn the word for this animal?

What Is the Function of Early Words?   As you have read, young children's early words are often labels for familiar objects or people. Their early attempts at communication consist of single words, but these words often convey an entire idea or sentence. Words used in this way are called **holophrases.** For example, a young child might say the word *hot* when he sees his father opening the oven door. Depending on the context and accompanying nonverbal cues, this single word might stand for several different and more complex ideas. The child could be saying, "Watch out, Dad! The oven is hot!"; "I need to stay away from that hot oven because it can burn me"; or even "Is the oven hot?" Holophrases cannot communicate the wide range of meanings that the child will be able to express once he starts combining words, but they do serve several communication functions, including demands, requests, desires, and questions. To understand holophrases, the listener needs to pay attention to intonational cues, gestures, and the specific context.

■ **Grammar: Rules for Putting Words Together.**   Between 18 and 24 months of age, children start to produce two- and three-word sentences. Many children's earliest sentences are of the form "familiar word + _____," though the particular familiar word differs from child to child (Bloom, Lightbrown, & Hood, 1975; Maratsos, 1983). For example, a child's early sentences may all consist of the phrase "No + ____," to produce "No *milk*," "No *Mommy*," "No *nap*," "No *kitty*," and so forth. The specific functions served by early sentences (for example, to make demands, ask questions, or claim possession) are very similar across several different languages (Slobin, 1979).

Acquisition of Grammar.   As children expand their language production to sentences, they often use telegraphic speech. Like telegrams, **telegraphic speech** includes the words that are essential to get the meaning across but leaves out nonessential words. Instead of saying, "I'm going to watch my brother Will play baseball," a 2-year-old is likely to say, "I watch Will." Interestingly, even such limited utterances follow certain grammatical rules.

YOUR
PERSPECTIVE
NOTES

Listen carefully to the speech of any 1- to 2-year-olds you know. Do you hear examples of over- or underextension, fast mapping, or holophrases?

holophrases

Single words used to express an entire idea or sentence.

telegraphic speech

Speech that includes only words that are essential to get the meaning across, leaving out nonessential words.

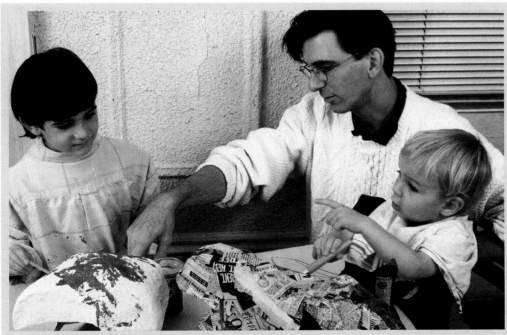

This young child is likely using telegraphic speech to communicate. What do you think he's saying, and what do you think his full meaning is?

Young children do not randomly combine words but chooose certain combinations of words and word orders (de Villiers & de Villiers, 1992; Mandel, Kemler Nelson, & Jusczyk, 1996). For example, children usually place nouns before verbs, as in "Daddy play" rather than "play Daddy"; and they place possessives before nouns, as in "my kitty" instead of "kitty my." Such combinations indicate a beginning understanding that the ordering of words, not just the words themselves, conveys important communication information.

Why do children use telegraphic speech? This pattern seems to reflect limitations in their processing and production capabilities rather than a mistaken belief that the words omitted are unimportant. Even before children begin to produce two-word utterances and telegraphic speech, they respond more appropriately to fully grammatical utterances than to telegraphic utterances. This means that even young children have some understanding that the words they leave out are useful and important, even if not the most essential for meaning (Gerken & McIntosh, 1993; Valian, Hoeffner, & Aubry, 1996). Psychologists used to believe that telegraphic speech was universal, but some now question whether it appears in all languages (de Villiers & de Villiers, 1999; Slobin, 1985a). Children learning languages that emphasize word order and content words (such as English) are likely to show telegraphic speech. Children learning languages such as Turkish or Russian, which emphasize grammatical markers (such as word endings or inflections) but not word order, do not go through an early two-word utterance stage. However, children in these language groups do produce utterances that contain less linguistic information than adult speech, and what they leave out is less important to the message. Perhaps telegraphic speech takes different forms in different languages.

Between the ages of about 2½ and 5 years, children learn the rules of *transformational grammar,* or rules for how to change what you intend to say (the meaning or *deep structure*) into proper grammatical forms for statements, questions, negatives, and commands (the *surface structure* of language). For example, the simplest questions are expressed through a rise in intonation at the end of a declarative sentence. Children begin to produce *wh*- questions (asking *who, what, where, when,* or *why*) by first simply placing the *wh*- word before a noun, as in "Where kitty?" They then begin including a helping verb but not in the correct order, producing such questions as "Where kitty is?" Finally, children acquire the rule for transforming an intended meaning such as "The kitty is here" to a correct question format: "Where is the kitty?" A similar progression takes place as children learn to produce negative sentences. Young children start by simply putting *no* at the beginning of a word or statement, as in "No peas." Next they add improperly ordered helping words, as in "I no peas," before arriving at proper grammatical form—"I don't want peas." By 3 years, children's grammatical knowledge has developed to the point that they are able to produce complex sentences. For example, they can use conjunctions to join simple sentences and can use relative clauses (i.e., clauses that modify preceding nouns, as in "The boy *who lost his dog* is outside") and embedded sentences (i.e., sentences within sentences). By the end of the preschool years, children are quite good at producing complex and grammatically correct sentences (de Villiers & de Villiers, 1999).

Sometime between the ages of 2 and 3, most children begin adding morphemes such as *-s, -ing,* or *-ed* to form plurals, present progressives, and past tenses (Brown, 1973). As children acquire the rules for using morphemes to affect meaning, they sometimes apply them incorrectly and produce incorrect forms of irregular words. This is called **overregularization,** and it often leads children to make mistakes with words they were able to form correctly before they learned the rules. For example, a 3-year-old may be quite capable of saying, "I saw fish in the pond," but at 4 the same child might say, "I seed fishes." These errors occur when children are unable to recall the correct irregular form and so try to express their intent by applying a newly learned rule. Instances of overregularization sometimes cause parents to be concerned that their child is having language problems. However, these errors are nothing to worry about. Although they occur in many different languages, they are really relatively infrequent, occurring in less than 8 percent of the instances when children use irregular words (Marcus et al., 1992; Pinker, 1994). In fact, overregularizations actually indicate children's progress in grammatical knowledge and represent their attempts to use this knowledge to communicate.

How Do Children Acquire Grammar?   As you will recall from our discussion of theories of language development, the question of how children acquire grammar has stirred considerable controversy. Proposed mechanisms have included parental feedback and modeling, imitation, child-directed speech, general cognitive skills, and innate knowledge of grammar. Another model of grammar acquisition, the *competition model,* tries to explain in more detail how children make use of the grammatical cues that are available in their language environment (MacWhinney, 1987; MacWhinney & Chang, 1995). This model suggests that children initially attend to several different types of grammatical cues, such as word endings, word order, and intonation. They then select the one type they believe will be most useful and focus on it. At first, children tend to focus on whichever type of cue is most frequent in their language and therefore most available. In English, for example, this may be the cue of word order, while in other languages intonation may be more available. Then, as children gain more language skill, they begin to select the cue that is most reliable in providing correct information, both for comprehending and for producing correct utterances. Finally, children learn that sometimes the different cues give conflicting information—the cues are in *competition* with one another, hence the name of this model. In these situations children learn to attend to the cue that "wins the competition" most often: the cue that most often gives correct information about correct grammar for that particular language. So in English, children continue to pay more attention to word order, because it is both more frequent and more often a correct guide than intonation (e.g., questions generally put the verb first rather than merely raising the intonation at the end) or even word endings (e.g., it is correct to say *The teachers left* or *The teacher left,* but not *The left teachers* or *Teacher the left*).

Another way children acquire grammar is through *semantic bootstrapping,* or use of their existing knowledge of word meaning to learn grammar (Pinker, 1987). For example, English-speaking children notice that words for objects and people tend to appear in certain positions within sentences—usually just before words for actions, as in the sentence *The dog jumped.* They use this knowledge to infer rules for producing grammatically acceptable sentences and apply the rules to produce complex sentences (e.g., *My dog Rex loves to swim, so he jumped in the pool*).

■ **Pragmatics: Using Language to Communicate with Others.**   During early childhood, children begin to acquire two important aspects of pragmatics: social rules of discourse and referential communication. **Social rules of discourse** are conventions that the speakers of a language follow in conversation. The rules focus on how to initiate and maintain the conversation. The earliest social rule children acquire is *turn taking:* the idea that first one conversational partner makes a contribution to the exchange, then the other, going back and forth until the conversation ends. As you read earlier, parents model this rule in child-directed speech and during countless daily activities, beginning when their offspring are infants. Children develop this knowledge further during early childhood and soon begin to apply it to conversations with other children as well as with adults. Other social rules of discourse, however, cannot be learned until later in childhood—after children have developed some knowledge of the subtleties of semantics, morphology, and syntax. For example, it is only late in their preschool years, at around 5, that children acquire the *answer-obviousness rule.* This rule says that if the answer to a question is obvious given the context and the speaker, then the listener should interpret the question as a request (or even a demand) rather than a true question. For example, suppose a mother finds her 6-year-old son jumping up and down on his bed and says, "Do you have to jump on your bed?" The child, who has acquired the answer-obviousness rule,

social rules of discourse

Conventions that speakers of a language follow when having a conversation, such as taking turns.

What would this parent really mean if she said, "Do you *have* to jump on the bed?!"

understands that his mother is not really interested in whether or not he feels a need to jump on the bed. Instead, the mother's inquiry is an indirect way of commanding him to stop it. Other social rules of discourse involve even more sophisticated knowledge and are usually not acquired until the early school years. These include rules about *saying something relevant to the topic* being discussed, *saying something related to what was just said* in the conversation, and *not repeating something that has already been said* in the conversation.

It is important to remember that there can be substantial cultural differences in rules for social discourse. For example, what constitutes an "obvious" answer depends on the particular culture. African Americans do not use question-demands as frequently as white Americans, so African American children might interpret the question about jumping on the bed as a true request for information rather than a demand. Rules for turn taking differ as well. Many African American children learn at home that they must grab their turn and keep their audience's attention, rather than waiting until someone else finishes and they are given a turn (Delpit, 1995; Saville-Troike, 1986).

Referential communication involves using language to convey a message that the hearer will understand. The child must be able to tailor the message for the intended listener, recognize whether the listener has understood it, and adjust the message if needed to ensure comprehension. Children as young as 2 can adjust their messages when a listener gives clear indication of not understanding, although their skill is limited. They become much more proficient during the school-age years (Shwe & Markman, 1997). By age 4 children are already beginning to show sensitivity to the age of their listener and adjusting their language accordingly. In one study, experimenters asked 4-year-olds to introduce a new toy either to a 2-year-old or to an adult. When talking to the 2-year-olds, the children used shorter sentences and phrases aimed at drawing and maintaining the toddlers' attention. When talking to the adults, the children used complex sentences and more polite speech (Shatz & Gelman, 1973). Preschoolers can recognize and clarify some kinds of ambiguous messages, particularly when they occur in natural contexts that contain a variety of other, nonlinguistic cues. For example,

Think of someone you know who is skilled in social rules of discourse and referential communication, then of someone with less skill. What do the two individuals do differently?

referential communication

The use of language to convey a message that the hearer will understand. It involves tailoring the message for the listener, recognizing whether the listener understood, and adjusting the message if needed.

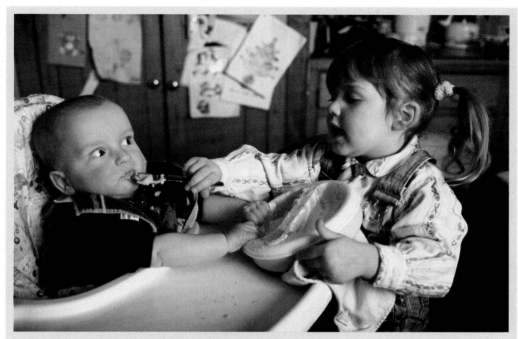
What referential communication skills has this 4-year-old developed?

3-year-olds know they cannot carry out impossible requests (e.g., "Bring me the refrigerator") or unintelligible requests (e.g., requests made by someone who is yawning while speaking). Although preschoolers are able to take steps to clarify ambiguities in messages by asking "what" or "how," they often require prompting to do it. The ability to recognize and clarify ambiguities in messages will become much better during the early school years.

Early childhood is a period of amazing change in language abilities. It is also a time when parents may begin to notice individual differences between their child and others in the pace of language development, and they may worry if their child is not saying words or putting together sentences as quickly as other children of the same age. When should parents worry about their child's pace of language development? What are some common language delays, and which ones signal the need to get help for the child? What kinds of therapy are effective for children who are delayed in language acquisition? The field of *speech–language pathology* helps provide answers to these kinds of questions as well as guidance for worried parents. Table 8.5 presents helpful suggestions for parents. To find out more about this field, read the Professional Perspective box called "Career Focus: Meet a Speech–Language Pathologist."

Perfecting Communication: Language in Middle Childhood and Adolescence

Language development during early childhood is impressive, but the process is far from complete by the time a child enters school. The middle childhood and adolescent years see development in several important areas of language.

■ **Growth in Language Skills.** Vocabulary continues to increase dramatically. The receptive vocabulary of 10-year-olds is about 40,000 words, and it grows to about 80,000 words by high school age (Anglin, 1993; McLaughlin, 1998). The kinds of words that older children and adolescents acquire are more abstract words, such as *irony* or *justice*, because increases in

TABLE 8.5 Facilitating Language Development: Suggestions for Parents

Be an active listener and participant in the conversation the child wants to have
Follow your child's lead.
Ask open-ended questions ("Tell me more").
Encourage your child to elaborate on topics that are important to him or her.

Provide good models
If your child is "misarticulating" sounds, make the sound correctly yourself.
Don't ask your child to repeat the words or the sound he or she is having trouble with.
Correct your child by saying things like "Oh! You want soup?" instead of "Say *soup*, not *thoup*."

Talk, talk, talk about events in the child's life
Talk about these events in a meaningful way.
Don't talk too fast!

Provide a supportive atmosphere
Make sure your child feels free to communicate with you.
Provide lots of good models of speech and language.
Be encouraging and supportive.

Read, read, read to your child
Read to your child during infancy, toddlerhood, preschool years, and beyond.
As you read to older children, point to the words, talk about the pictures.
With older children, talk about words that rhyme, different letters and the sounds they make.

Have the tools of written communication available
Have plenty of crayons, marking pencils, and paper available to your child.
Encourage your child to use these tools to communicate.

Play sound and word games
"How many words are there in the sentence 'I like to go to the store'?"
"How many syllables are there in the word, *baby?* Let's clap it out—*ba* [clap] *by* [clap]."
"Let's play a word game. I'm thinking of *glasses*—kinds that we wear and kinds that we drink from. Can you think of another word that can mean two different things?"

If your child shows "dysfluences" (difficulties)
Let your child finish each communication; don't finish sentences for him/her.
Model easy, slower, less complex speech.
Be patient!

Source: Speech–language pathologist Deena Bernstein (personal communication, March 14, 2003).

cognitive development allow students to understand these abstract concepts (Hulit & Howard, 1997; McGhee-Bidlack, 1991). Phonemic development continues as well. For many children mastery of certain phonemes, such as *j* or *th*, does not come until well into the elementary school years. And though children continue to show increased understanding and use of intonation (or tone of voice) as a cue to meaning, they don't master some aspects of intonation for several years. For example, a sentence such as "Rachel got a bracelet from Mom, and she got a necklace from Lily" can have two different meanings, depending on whether the

Career Focus: Meet a Speech–Language Pathologist

Deena Bernstein, Ph.D.

Lehman College/ City University of New York; Bronx, New York

Certified speech–language pathologist; coauthor with Ellenmorris Tiegerman-Farber of Language and Communication Disorders in Children *(2002), published by Allyn & Bacon*

What are the early signs of problems in language development?
Parents are often the first to suspect that a child might be delayed in acquiring language. They may notice that their infant does not do much babbling ("abbababa"), or stops producing these playful sounds. The child may not interact or make eye contact when parents try to talk and play with him/her. Some young children will have problems learning to produce the sounds of speech. They will be difficult to understand, even beyond the preschool years. Others may be slow to learn new words, word endings (such as "-ing" or "-ed"), small functional words (such as "is," "am," "was"), or to string words together to make sentences. Some may struggle with how to use language to communicate, not knowing how to ask for objects or actions they want. If parents notice these types of problems, they should seek help. Speech–language pathologists will conduct a speech–language

evaluation and work with other professionals to help determine whether a language delay exists, the possible cause(s) for a delay, the skills the child has and/or needs to learn, and intervention strategies that would help the child. It is important that a child receive speech–language therapy as soon as he/she is diagnosed as having a language delay, no matter the cause; the earlier a child receives services, the greater his/her chances for success.

What are other common problems that you see in your practice?
Some parents get concerned when they hear their 3-year-old say things like "I, I, I, I, I want the red car," but this is very common. Three- to 3½-year-olds often repeat not only whole words ("my, my, my, crayon") but also phrases ("Mommy, I want, Mommy I want, Mommy I want a drink") or even parts of words ("play, play, playschool"). However, if a child repeats the sounds of a word ("p, p, p, pot"), shows signs of struggle behaviors (like tics, facial tension, or grimaces), or frequently produces a repetition or prolongation (such as "sssssssit," in more than 1 out of 10 words), then this may indicate a stuttering condition.

Children who have language problems in the first 5 years of life are at risk for reading and writing problems later. When learning to read and write, children must actively think about all the components of the language system, and

this can be difficult for children who have had a difficult time learning the oral language system. Parents should monitor and encourage their child's literacy skills and work with their child's teachers to provide any special help the child might need.

What causes problems in language development?
We often do not know. Some children may have conditions that lead to language problems, such as hearing loss, mental retardation, autism, or attention deficit/hyperactivity disorder. For some children there is a genetic component. Researchers now believe that the "wiring" in the child's brain that is used to learn language is not operating at its optimum capacity, but we don't know why some individuals' "wiring" is less efficient than others.

What training is needed to work as a speech–language pathologist?
You need a master's degree in speech–language pathology or communication disorders. Different states have different requirements, but some kind of certification and/or licensing is needed. ■

thinking OF MARIANA

◀ Should Diana take Mariana for a speech–language evaluation, or is it too soon to take this step?

speaker emphasizes *and* or *she.* The subtly different meanings that intonation can convey often remain difficult for children well into middle childhood.

The school-age years also see increases in children's mastery of grammar and syntax. For example, English-speaking preschoolers rarely use passive verbs and show only incomplete understanding when they hear them. Sentences such as "The toy was chewed up by the puppies" or "Donald was liked by Goofy" are quite difficult for young children, who may understand them as "The toy chewed up the puppies" and "Donald liked Goofy." Children do not produce full passive sentences until ages 8 to 9, and some passive forms remain challenging until the early adolescent years, roughly ages 11 to 13 (Bever, 1970; Horgan, 1978; Maratsos, Kuczaj, Fox, & Chalkley, 1979). However, this sequence of grammatical development is not universal. In languages in which the passive voice is more important and frequent, such as the South African language Sesotho, children understand and use passives much earlier, by ages 2 to 4 (Demuth, 1990). By 9 to 11 years of age, children are also able to draw inferences from what they hear or read and to recognize that the inferred information was not directly stated. This ability to draw inferences is essential for understanding and producing many of the more subtle uses of language, including sarcasm, humor, and metaphor (Casteel, 1993; Dews et al., 1996).

Children's pragmatic language skills continue to build throughout middle childhood and adolescence. Referential communication skills continue to improve until by middle childhood children are able to spontaneously identify and correct ambiguities in their own and others' speech (Beal & Belgrad, 1990; Girbau, 2001; Kemper & Vernoog, 1994). Children of this age are also quite skilled in the social rules of discourse. Not only do they understand how to follow the rules, but they also understand that in certain situations it is acceptable and effective to *violate* them. For example, adolescents know the social rule of not repeating something that someone has already said in a conversation. However, they also understand that intentionally repeating exactly what someone said can be quite funny in some situations, can indicate interest and active listening in others, or can express disrespect and sarcasm in still others.

One of the most notable features of language development during the middle childhood and adolescent years is the increase in **metalinguistic awareness,** or the explicit knowledge about language itself and one's own use of it (Ferreira & Morrison, 1994). Metalinguistic awareness is the ability to shift focus "from the meanings of our utterances to the utterances themselves" (McLaughlin, 1998, p. 369). It results from a great deal of experience with using language as well as increases in cognitive abilities, and it contributes to several linguistic skills. For example, one aspect of metalinguistic awareness is the understanding that a single word can have multiple meanings. This understanding enables children to use language more flexibly and even to create and appreciate humor based on different word meanings. Metalinguistic awareness also helps children self-monitor and self-correct the speech they produce and receive, which means they can communicate more effectively. Further, explicit knowledge of the social rules of discourse helps children engage in more effective and socially acceptable conversations. And finally, studues show a relationship between a higher level of metalinguistic awareness at early ages and higher reading ability in the early elementary school years (McBride-Chang, 1996; Warren-Leubecker & Carter, 1988).

■ **Changes in Uses of Language.**   During middle childhood and adolescence, children not only develop a more complete and explicit understanding of language but also begin to use language in different ways. Preschool children play with language, creating nonsense words that rhyme or adding morphemes to create words that express strong feelings, such as *sicky* or *tippy* (Ely & McCabe, 1994). School-age children continue to create words in this way, and they also develop a great interest in riddles and other forms of verbal humor. These kinds of language play require a more advanced understanding of the five rule systems (phonology, morphology, syntax, semantics, and pragmatics). Especially important is the understanding that language can be ambiguous, particularly word meanings and syntax (Ely & McCabe, 1994; Ely, 1997). For example, our 4-year-old daughters were quite pleased with

metalinguistic awareness

A person's explicit knowledge about language itself and about his or her own use of it.

themselves when they made up a riddle after a night out for pizza: "Why did the chicken cross the road? To get to the other side to eat pizza!" They have told this joke to each other (and to anyone else who will listen) countless times, and they find it just as funny each time. Our older sons simply roll their eyes. They understand that for a joke to be funny, it has to involve an element of ambiguity or surprise (which this joke really never had!). Another reason that older children and adolescents become increasingly sophisticated in the humor they produce and understand is that they have greater understanding of the social and contextual aspects of language (Ely, 1997). For example, after a conversation about the importance of working hard in school, our oldest son remarked, "I know school's important! I don't want to grow up and have a job where you have to say 'You want fries with that?'"

During adolescence children begin to use language as a tool for identifying peer groups and for excluding those outside their peer group. The **adolescent register** is a special form of speech adolescents use to identify themselves as belonging to a particular social, cultural, or generational group (Romaine, 1984). If you have ever overheard a group of adolescents talking with one another, you will recognize that their patterns of language include several distinctive features, including phonemes and syntax that are markedly different from those used by younger and older speakers of the same language. In particular, the adolescent register has an interesting vocabulary that includes many novel slang terms. Think back to movies from or about prior decades—can you recall any of the odd-sounding words and phrases that adolescents used? What was *groovy* in the 1960s, *cool* in the 1970s, and *awesome* in the 1990s became *phat* in the early 2000s; yesterday's *nerds* are today's *posers*. Although adolescent registers exist across social, regional, and ethnic groups, the specific terms, syntax, and phonemes vary widely. Also, because the purpose of an adolescent register is to identify an adolescent as belonging to a particular generation, place, and group, registers change quickly. As adolescents grow to adulthood, the patterns and terms that

adolescent register
Special form of speech adolescents use to identify themselves as belonging to a particular social, cultural, or generational group. It includes distinctive phonemes, syntax, and vocabulary.

What features of their adolescent register do you think these teenagers are using?

marked their groups either fade away or, in some cases, become part of the overall culture. (Pretty cool, huh?)

Genderlects, different ways of talking for males and females, begin in early childhood, probably as a result of differential treatment by adults and peers as well as parent modeling (Gleason, Perlmann, Ely, & Evans, 1994; Kramer, 1974; Perlmann & Gleason, 1994; Sadker & Sadker, 1994). Evidence of developing genderlects has been found in toddlers as young as 2 (Sachs, 1987), but these differences become more pronounced during middle childhood and adolescence. For example, the language of boys playing with other boys includes more verbal conflict, coercive terms, slang terms, and profanity than girls' language (Cheshire, 1982; Jay, 1992; Sheldon, 1990). In contrast, girls' interactions with other girls include more questions, collaborative suggestions, attempts to verbally manage and control interactions, and communications about emotions and feelings (Barth & Kinder, 1988; Goodwin & Goodwin, 1987; Lloyd & Goodwin, 1993; Warren & McCloskey, 1997). Some theorists argue that these genderlects develop because of differences in the goals boys and girls are pursuing when using language. The premise is that boys focus more on gaining power and autonomy, and girls focus more on affiliation or relationship building (Gilligan, 1982). However, genderlect differences seem to be somewhat situation- and culture-specific. More pronounced differences are found in same-sex than in mixed-sex interactions, and some studies have not found female genderlect features among African American adolescent girls (Goodwin, 1990; McCloskey & Coleman, 1992). Chapter 10 will explore in more detail the origins and implications of gender differences in several areas.

Finally, older children begin to use language to describe and understand important aspects of themselves. *Personal narratives* are stories about experiences the storyteller has had. They involve the use of language to inform others about the self, and as a tool for increased self-understanding. Even 2-year-olds can give rudimentary narratives, but it is during middle childhood and adolescence that children become able to provide coherent narratives that fully describe and evaluate their personal experiences. For example, 4-year-olds' personal narratives tend to have a *leapfrog* structure—the narratives jump from one topic to another without giving a complete account of what happened and how they felt about it. Between 4 and 8 years, personal narratives often have more of a *chronological* structure—the storyteller reports a sequence of events without adding details or evaluating the events. By the age of 8 or 9, however, children show a *classic narrative* structure. The story leads up to a main event (the *high point*), the storyteller offers an evaluation of how he or she feels about the event, and the narrative concludes with resolution of the event. The evaluation aspect of personal narratives continues to increase in complexity and variety throughout adolescence (Berman & Slobin, 1994; Engel, 1995; Peterson & McCabe, 1983).

The preferred styles of personal narratives vary depending on the child's overall culture as well as the specific ways in which their parents talk with them (Minami, 2001). In addition to helping children understand themselves, personal narratives serve to help children know and understand their broader culture (Gee, 1992). For example, Hispanic children's narratives focus more on family relationships; Japanese children's narratives include events linked to a central theme rather than to time, place, or family membership. The narratives of middle- and working-class white children in North America typically focus on a single topic, whereas working-class African American children tell personal narratives that are longer and include several different characters and events linked by a general theme (Ely, 1997; Michaels, 1991; Minami & McCabe, 1990). Because these different styles reflect the values and structure of children's respective cultures, personal narratives are one way in which language helps children understand central aspects of their culture in a very personal way.

1. Which of the following is an example of overextension in early word use?
   a. A child calls her mother *mama.*
   b. A child forgets the word for banana.
   c. A child calls her cup *mycup.*
   d. A child calls a duck a *robin.*

2. In word learning the word *constraints* refers to:
   a. the incorrect use of grammatical rules.
   b. assumptions children make about the meaning of new words.
   c. the use of one word to express a whole idea.
   d. the rules for changing declarative sentences to questions.

3. Which of the following is the *best* example of good referential communication skills?
   a. Using simple words when speaking to young children.
   b. Being polite when talking to other people.
   c. Understanding the meaning of words.
   d. Being able to produce grammatically correct sentences.

4. The adolescent register helps adolescents identify themselves as:
   a. being members of adult society.
   b. being popular among peers.
   c. belonging to a particular generation.
   d. being aware of the abstract nature of language.

5. **True or False:** Human newborns are able to discriminate among speech sounds of their native language, but not sounds of other languages.

6. **True or False:** The use of protowords marks the first use of adult language.

Answers: 1. d, 2. b, 3. a, 4. c, 5. F, 6. F

Issues in Language Development

Two practical issues in language development have been controversial for many years: bilingualism and social dialects.

As you study this section, ask yourself these questions:

- What is bilingualism, and how does it develop?

- What are the cognitive effects of bilingualism?

- What are the origins of social dialects? What are the social implications of speaking a social dialect?

Bilingualism: Learning Two Languages

Do you speak more than one language? More than 6 million children in the United States are **bilingual,** or fluent in two languages. In *additive* bilingualism a person learns a second language while maintaining a first language; in *subtractive* bilingualism a person loses fluency in the first language as a result of acquiring a second language (Bialystok & Hakuta, 1994). Different social and cultural conditions usually accompany these two types of bilingualism. When the family and larger community see acquisition of a second language as a positive

bilingual

Fluent in two languages.

asset and highly value both languages, children are more likely to show additive bilingualism. On the contrary, if people see the second language as superior and the first as inferior in some way, children will be more likely to "subtract" the first language (Hamers & Blanc, 2000). A community can send negative messages implicitly, as when the majority of children's settings outside the home use the second language and others in their social and peer groups do not understand the first language. These messages also can be quite explicit, as when a child experiences disapproval and even punishment from others for using the first language. And it is not just children immigrating to the United States who experience conditions that encourage subtractive bilingualism. For example, U.S.-born Hispanic children who learn Spanish as their first language are often at a significant disadvantage when they enter a predominantly English-speaking school system. In past decades teachers actually punished Native American children for speaking their own languages in school.

Children can become bilingual simultaneously or sequentially. *Simultaneous bilingualism* develops when a child learns two languages at the same time, starting from infancy. This situation often occurs when the child has parents who speak two languages. In *sequential bilingualism* a child learns one language first, then later begins learning the second. Children who begin learning a second language by about the age of 3 usually become just as fluent in the second language as in the first. If second-language learning begins later in childhood or adulthood, the person can use the second language effectively for communication but will not attain such complete fluency. The accent of the second language is particularly problematic, and most older learners never acquire a native-sounding accent. However, older learners have a faster rate of acquiring a second language (Krashen, Long, & Scarcella, 1982; Snow, 1987). Some theorists argue that young children are better at acquiring second languages not because of greater language-learning ability but because of the younger child's greater opportunity, longer time period in which to master the second language, and less interference from and less automaticity in the native language (Ekstrand, 1981; MacWhinney, 1992). According to this view, younger children do not have any greater ability to acquire language than older children, but they do have "a less complex task for which [they have] more time" (Hamers & Blanc, 2000, p. 75).

In the early stages of learning two languages, children may occasionally mix words and grammar from both languages. It is not clear why this mixing, or *code switching,* occurs. It may happen because a child doesn't yet understand that the two languages are separate systems, or it may happen simply because the child has acquired words to express a specific thought in one language but not yet in the other language. Parent modeling also seems to play a role. Code switching occurs more often in children whose parents also code-switch. The frequency of code switching decreases as children gain more vocabulary and a stronger grasp of syntax in each language, though even adult bilingual speakers sometimes code-switch intentionally. By the early preschool years, children show clear awareness that the two languages are independent systems and easily differentiate both the vocabulary and grammar of the two languages. At first they may restrict their use of each language to certain contexts—for example, speaking only Spanish at home but speaking only English when outside the home. By the early school years, however, the bilingual child is able to switch automatically and appropriately from one language to another in either context (Cummins, 1991; Hamers & Blanc, 2000; Lanza, 1992; Volterra & Taeschner, 1978). To learn about one family's experience with bilingualism, read the Personal Perspective box called "Meet a Bilingual Family."

In sum, it seems that acquiring two languages is not necessarily a difficult task for children. The rate of language acquisition is slightly slower for bilingual children, but the fact that they are learning two complex and abstract systems may actually provide some cognitive advantages. Studies have found that bilingual children sometimes score higher on measures of such things as concept formation, cognitive flexibility, metalinguistic awareness, ability to correct ungrammatical sentences, verbal and nonverbal creativity, and analogical thinking (Bialystok, Majumder, & Martin, 2003; Diaz & Kinger, 1991; Hamers, 1996; Hamers & Blanc, 2000).

YOUR

PERSPECTIVE

PERSPECTIVE

NOTES

If you are bilingual, would you say your bilingualism is additive or subtractive? Simultaneous or sequential? Was it difficult to learn your languages? How do you understand and use both, and how do you translate between them?

Meet a Bilingual Family

Patrick, David, and Lori Glenn
El Paso, Texas

5-year-old bilingual child and his parents

We understand that Patrick's first language is English. When did he begin learning his second language (Spanish), and how is he progressing?
Patrick was exposed to both English and Spanish from birth. Both grandmothers spoke to Patrick strictly in Spanish. His mother, Lori, read and spoke to him in Spanish most of the time; his favorite book was *Lo que le encanta a Conejito*. His grandmothers sang and recited nursery rhymes to him in Spanish, and they also watched Spanish-language television in his presence.

His paternal grandfather and I [David] always spoke to him in English. Grampa repeated "Grampa" to him whenever he was with him, and Patrick's first word, at four months, was "Grampa!" Lori stopped speaking to him in Spanish when he went to day care (at 2 years, 9 months of age) so that he would better understand English. However,

his maternal grandmother, *Abuela*, spent every afternoon with him. So he continued to be exposed to Spanish, while his day care providers and his parents stressed English. Patrick has progressed well in English, but unfortunately, his Spanish language skills are lacking.

What steps have you taken to help him learn either or both languages?
We speak and read to him in both languages. We have family living in Chihuahua, Mexico, and when we are together, they speak Spanish in his presence, and bring him into conversations. If he does not understand, they will speak to him in English. Funny thing is that we encourage his cousins to speak with him in Spanish, and his cousins' parents encourage them to practice their English around Patrick! It was suggested that we place him in a local magnet school with a bilingual curriculum. We have discussed the possibility of sending Patrick to school in Chihuahua for a semester.

How does your son seem to feel about speaking two languages?
Patrick understands Spanish fairly well, but speaks only a few words. He

has his own imaginary Spanish that is mostly gibberish and sounds like the words being spoken in a conversation. He attempts to join a conversation in Spanish by using his phonetically similar made-up language; so we know he wants to converse, but just does not have the vocabulary. We attribute this to the time spent in school where English is the primary form of communication.

His 11-year-old cousin, Gerardo, is like a brother to Patrick. Gerardo is very articulate, and the Spanish language is melodious, so Patrick loves trying to imitate him. Plus, if Gerardo speaks Spanish, it's got to be cool! Or as Gerardo would say, *"Es bien padre!"* ▪

thinking OF MARIANA

◄ What can Diana and her husband do to make sure Mariana benefits from a bilingual environment without compromising her potential to develop strong English skills?

Because bilingual children must constantly examine and think about the particular language system they are using and the contexts for which each system is appropriate, they may develop an early awareness of the symbolic nature of language systems. This realization may encourage bilingual children to become more reflective about language and about how it can be used both for communication and as a tool for thinking (Mohanty & Perregaux, 1997).

Many early researchers interpreted code switching as an indication of confusion and even developmental delay resulting from learning two languages at the same time. Studies that found large and persistent cognitive deficits in bilingual children seemed to support this belief. However, these early studies had some serious flaws, including selection bias, confounding of bilingualism with lower socioeconomic background, and poor test administration practices (Hamers & Blanc, 2000). More recent research indicates that any negative effects typically occur in children of minority groups in Western societies who are learning a second language in

Will learning two languages be a positive or a negative experience for these bilingual children?

thinking
OF MARIANA

What are the advantages and disadvantages of encouraging Mariana's bilingualism? Does it seem that Mariana is likely to develop additive bilingualism, subtractive bilingualism, or semilingualism?

schools—often the site of the subtractive type of bilingualism. Some authors have even argued that such conditions can result in *semilingualism,* or the failure to achieve a native-level of language proficiency in either language (Romaine, 1995; Skutnabb-Kangas, 1984). Could some common practices of bilingual education be turning a potentially positive attribute into a problem for bilingual children? To learn more about the effects of bilingual educational programs and recent trends in the area, read the Social Policy Perspective box called "Bilingual Education."

Social and Cultural Dialects

Even though people in different geographic regions and cultural groups within a country may all speak the same language, there are often differences in vocabulary, grammar/syntax, pragmatics, and style of language interactions. A **dialect** is a consistent and systematic variety of a single language that is shared by a certain subgroup of speakers (McLaughlin, 1998; Oetting, 2003a). In contrast, an *accent* consists of speech characteristics or differences in how words are pronounced and is one subpart of a dialect. A given language usually has several dialects, some of which are associated with specific geographic regions (e.g., Boston English, Southern English) and others with ethnic and cultural groups (e.g., African American English). A dialect may get its name from a particular ethnic group, but not all members of that ethnic group will necessarily speak the dialect—nor will members of the ethnic group be the only people who can speak it. Dialects develop in response to social and cultural conditions, not according to race, although these factors often go together (Hulit & Howard, 1997).

Dialects are consistent linguistic systems, complete with unique vocabulary terms as well as identifiable linguistic rules that remain consistent over time. Dialects evolve from the distinctive cultural and historical backgrounds of the people who speak them, but researchers do not agree on how dialects originate and develop. One possibility is that dialects incorporate elements of several different languages as people who originally did not share a language try to communicate. For example, the Cajun English dialect found around New Orleans is

dialect

A consistent and systematic variety of a single language that is shared by a certain subgroup of speakers; can be associated with a geographic region or with a specific ethnic or cultural group.

Bilingual Education

In the November 2002 elections, Massachusetts voters elected to end bilingual education as it was then practiced. Both California and Arizona have passed similar voter referenda since 1998, but Colorado's voters rejected such a measure (Zehr, 2002). What is bilingual education, and why is it so controversial?

In the current debate, the term *bilingual education* refers to several different types of programs, all of which have the ultimate goal of helping non-English-speaking children learn English. Ironically, very few of the programs try to help students become truly bilingual—that is, fluent and literate in two languages. Two main types of programs are in contention. In *transitional bilingual education (TBE)*, instruction is mostly in the child's native language. TBE provides some English instruction and gradually increases the use of English as students' English skills increase. In contrast, *structured English immersion (SEI)* teachers instruct mostly in English from the earliest stages, using students' native language only as needed.

Those trying to end TBE forms of bilingual education argue that TBE programs simply do not work. Children spend many years in TBE programs yet still score lower on measures of achievement than students in SEI programs (Baker, 1998).

Critics also claim that TBE programs enroll almost exclusively Spanish-speaking children and Creole-speaking Haitian children, essentially segregating these children from mainstream education (Baker, 1998; Rossell & Baker, 1996). These advocates of reform point to several examples of SEI programs across the country (e.g., in California, Texas, Virginia, and Maryland), and they cite improvements on California test scores under SEI as evidence that these programs work, work better, and work more quickly than TBE (Zehr, 2001). They note the proficiency-level requirement in California's law: Students must be mainstreamed within one year, but must eventually reach the 40th percentile of English mastery on a standardized achievement test. This requirement, they argue, produces an "overdose of English instruction"—exactly what children need if they are to compete in classrooms and the job market (Baker, 1998, p. 203).

Opponents of the reform measures argue that research reviews showing SEI's superiority are flawed, using only a handful of studies, and that critics have misinterpreted the reported changes in test scores in California. In fact, reform opponents claim that rate of test score improvement has been *slower* under SEI, and that changes in other areas (e.g.,

smaller class sizes) could just as well explain improvements. Also, they point out, in some areas scores for students in SEI programs have remained the same or even dropped (Krashen, 1999; Orr & Hakuta, 2000). Some argue that laws ending TBE are discriminatory, equating school underachievement with bilingual education and language difference with cognitive disability (Attinasi, 1998). They also claim that the newly mandated SEI programs follow an inappropriate model. The early studies took place in Canada; their explicit goal was true bilingualism, they used bilingual teachers, and they served students from middle-class backgrounds who were already fluent and literate in one language. Finally, one summary of the research concludes that immersion or early-exit programs (SEI) may keep students where they are in terms of achievement but do not help them catch up (Crawford, 1997).

What do you think of bilingual education? Based on what you know about language and cognitive development, which approach makes the most sense to you? To help children who need to learn English, should schools focus almost exclusively on English, teach the children in their native language, or try to foster true bilingualism? ■

strongly influenced by the French language spoken by the early settlers in this area, as well as by Spanish and several Native American languages (Carver, 1987; Valdman, 1997). However, for other dialects, such as African American English, there is evidence that they used to be *more* similar to the British English of this country's early settlers but have become increasingly different over time. This may be the result of continuing social and economic segregation and/or may be a way to develop and maintain a group's identity. And it is certainly possible that some aspects of a dialect can become more similar to, while other aspects become increasingly different from, Standard English (Wolfram & Thomas, 2002).

The Cajun English dialect this child speaks reflects influences from French, English, Spanish, and several Native American languages.

The most studied social dialect of Standard American English is *African American English (AAE),* also known as *Black English* or *Ebonics.* African American English has a complex history. It may reflect influences from several West African languages, Portuguese, Dutch, and French (Taylor, 1990). AAE is a distinct dialect of English, complete with its own linguistic rules and vocabulary, not a simplistic or incorrect form of Standard English. Depending on the context, there are specific differences in phonetics and grammatical rules between AAE and Standard English (Hulit & Howard, 1997; McLaughlin, 1998; Taylor, 1986). For example, speakers of AAE

▶ make phonetic substitutions, such as *f* for *th* at the end of a word (e.g., *toof* instead of *tooth*) or *d* rather than *th* at the beginning of a word (e.g, *dis* instead of *this*)

▶ reduce final consonants or consonant clusters, as in saying *las'* for *last*

▶ do not require the use of possessives (saying "Billy car" rather than "Billy's car"), plural markers ("two dog" rather than "two dogs"), copula ("he short" instead of "he's short"), past tense markers ("She walk home" instead of "She walked home"), and markers for third person present tense ("He eat too fast" rather than "He eats too fast")

▶ use pronouns differently (e.g., "Jamie called. Jamie he happy you're okay" rather than "Jamie called. He's happy you're okay")

▶ use the verb *was* consistently across person and number, saying "I was running," "You was running," and "They was running" instead of "I was running," "You were running," and "They were running"

▶ express future tense differently, commonly using *be going to, gonna,* or omitting *will* when followed by *be* (e.g., "I be going to come over later," "I gonna come over later," or "I be coming over later" rather than "I'm going to come over later," "I'm gonna come over later," or "I will be coming over later")

▶ express negatives differently, using *ain't* and double or triple negatives (e.g., "I ain't tired" or "Nobody didn't never come to check on me" instead of "I'm not tired" or "Nobody came to check on me"

One interesting feature of AAE that does not have a direct counterpart in Standard English is *aspect*—the use of *be* to indicate whether an action or state of being is ongoing or intermittent (Green, 2002; Warren & McCloskey, 1997). For example, the use of aspect communicates that "He be running" and "He running" mean different things, although Standard English would use "He is running" for both meanings. The first sentence signifies that the person usually or always runs; the second conveys the sense that this person is running right now but usually does not run. Aspect is characteristic of several languages in West Africa (Labov, 1994).

Hispanic English and *Asian English* are other common dialects of Standard English. As with AAE, not all Hispanic American or Asian American children use these dialects. Also, Hispanic and Asian populations in the United States come from a variety of different Spanish and Asian language backgrounds, so these dialects can vary a great deal.

Like AAE, these dialects show consistent differences from Standard English in vocabulary, phonology, and grammar rules. In Hispanic English, for example, phonological differences commonly produce substitutions such as the long *e* sound for a short *e* sound (e.g., saying *beeg* rather than *big*) and *ch* for *sh* (resulting in *choe* instead of *shoe*). Grammatical rules differ as well. In Spanish, comparative terms are created by the addition of modifying words rather than word endings such as *er* or *est*, resulting in sentences such as "My car is more little" instead of "My car is smaller." Plural markers, pronouns, past tense markers, and possessives are optional in Hispanic English, resulting in "two dog" instead of "two dogs"; "Jamie called. Happy you're okay" instead of "Jamie called. He's happy you're okay"; and "She walk home" instead of "She walked home." Negation is indicated by inserting *no* before the verb ("I'm no tired") and questions are marked with a rise in intonation instead of changing word order ("Sue is working?" instead of "Is Sue working?") (Hulit & Howard, 1997; McLaughlin, 1998). Speakers of Asian English dialects also make phonological substitutions (such as saying *lice* instead of *rice*); omit possessive and plural markers producing "Billy book" and "two dog" instead of "Billy's book" and "two dogs"; omit or overgeneralize past tense markers ("She sit down" or "She sitted down" instead of "She sat down"); omit perfective aspect, saying "I have take the car" rather than "I have taken the car"; and form comparatives incorrectly, producing "My house is gooder than yours" or "My doll is more prettier than yours" instead of "My house is better than yours" or "My doll is prettier than yours" (Cheng, 1987).

Different dialects are simply different from one another; no one dialect is inherently better or worse than any other. And even though dialects differ in systematic ways, they also share many similarities (Oetting, 2003a; Oetting & McDonald, 2001). However, the reality is that people often make negative judgments about those who speak a dialect. People may rate dialect speakers as lower in competence, professionalism, intelligence, ambition, education, success, and wealth—even when the raters are themselves speakers of the dialects (Atkins, 1993; Luhman, 1990). Often such judgments affect the treatment of people who speak different dialects in schools or workplaces. There is a tendency to

YOUR PERSPECTIVE

NOTES

Do you speak a dialect of English? What are some examples of its vocabulary and grammar? Do you think your dialect has affected people's judgments about you? If so, in what ways?

thinking OF MARIANA

◀ Is it likely that Mariana will learn a dialect of English? If so, should Diana be concerned about this?

African American English, spoken by many African Americans, includes elements of several western African languages, Portuguese, Dutch, and French. Like other cultural dialects, AAE is a consistent system with its own linguistic rules and vocabulary, not an incorrect form of Standard American English.

treat such individuals as less competent and less intelligent, and speaking a dialect in educational and work settings often brings reprimands or even punishments (Romaine, 1995). Perhaps wider understanding that social dialects have their own complex rule systems and develop as a result of cultural and social circumstances might decrease these negative and unfair judgments (Oetting, 2003b).

In summary, children progress steadily in language. Initially communicating only through gestures and nonlinguistic sounds in infancy, they attain the sophisticated use of language to foster their understanding of themselves and their culture in middle childhood and adolescence. Over the course of a few years, they master an intricate system of linguistic rules that enables them to express their needs and desires—and even to monitor and control their own success in communicating. They accomplish this feat easily, though we still do not completely understand the relative roles played by biology, cognition, and social interaction. It seems that children are capable of learning more than one language from a young age and that doing so may afford cognitive advantages. The concerns surrounding bilingual education and ways to accommodate different dialects in the school and workplace are problems for which we have no ready answers. The deeper understanding of language, its development, and factors that support it that you have gained in this chapter may help you contribute to solutions for these difficult issues.

LET'S REVIEW . . .

1. If a child learning a second language is taught that her first language is an important and valuable part of her cultural heritage, she is likely to develop:

   a. additive bilingualism.
   b. subtractive bilingualism.
   c. semilingualism.
   d. successive bilingualism.

2. Code switching among bilingual children is an indication of:

   a. superior cognitive skills.
   b. inferior cognitive skills.
   c. developmental delay.
   d. developing bilingualism.

3. Aspect:

   a. is an incorrect form of Standard American English.

   b. is a grammatical feature of African American English.

   c. expresses the same information as the verb *is* in Standard American English.

   d. is a consistent substitution for Standard American English word endings.

4. **True or False:** A dialect has consistent linguistic rules and contains its own distinctive vocabulary.

5. **True or False:** Overall, becoming bilingual has a negative effect on children's language development.

Answers: 1. a, 2. d, 3. b, 4. T, 5. F

thinking
BACK TO MARIANA

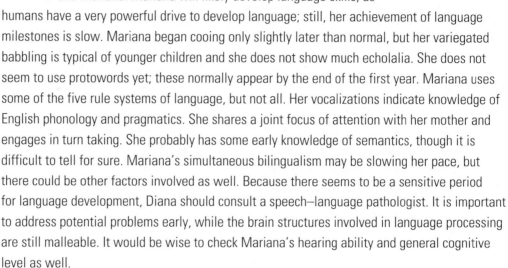

Now that you have studied this chapter, you should be able to identify at least a dozen concepts that might help Diana and Mariana. Mariana will likely develop language skills, as humans have a very powerful drive to develop language; still, her achievement of language milestones is slow. Mariana began cooing only slightly later than normal, but her variegated babbling is typical of younger children and she does not show much echolalia. She does not seem to use protowords yet; these normally appear by the end of the first year. Mariana uses some of the five rule systems of language, but not all. Her vocalizations indicate knowledge of English phonology and pragmatics. She shares a joint focus of attention with her mother and engages in turn taking. She probably has some early knowledge of semantics, though it is difficult to tell for sure. Mariana's simultaneous bilingualism may be slowing her pace, but there could be other factors involved as well. Because there seems to be a sensitive period for language development, Diana should consult a speech–language pathologist. It is important to address potential problems early, while the brain structures involved in language processing are still malleable. It would be wise to check Mariana's hearing ability and general cognitive level as well.

Diana can encourage Mariana's language by reinforcing sounds that are wordlike, recasting and expanding Mariana's utterances, and explicitly using child-directed speech. She can provide formats during everyday activities to provide more structure and predictability for Mariana. Good models of phonology, syntax, and semantics will help Mariana correctly modify the connections in her cognitive units for language. As Mariana acquires more words, Diana can help her use syntactical bootstrapping to learn word meanings and semantic bootstrapping to strengthen her understanding of grammar. Diana may want to continue encouraging Mariana's bilingualism, because learning two languages may offer cognitive benefits such as greater metalinguistic awareness. Mariana may show instances of code switching, but these should decrease over time.

Using these and other concepts and research findings from this chapter, you should be able to provide specific advice to help Diana work with her daughter. You should also be able to adjust the advice to fit the needs of children who are older than Mariana. What might indicate a language delay in a preschooler or a school-age child, and what could a parent do to help?

CHAPTER SUMMARY

What are the defining characteristics and rule systems of language?

Human language has semanticity and displacement and is productive. It consists of arbitrary and abstract symbols and is governed by specific rules for how to communicate. Phonology is the language rule system dealing with speech sounds; morphology is the system for combining sounds to produce meaning; syntax is the knowledge of how to combine words to produce understandable and grammatically correct phrases; semantics involves knowledge of the meanings of words; and pragmatics is an understanding of how to use language to communicate effectively with others.

How do learning theorists explain language development?

Learning theorists say that children acquire language through the process of shaping, imitation, and modeling. Research indicates that differential reinforcement can affect language. Critics of learning theory argue that parents do not provide correct and consistent models of grammatical rules and language use, that learning principles cannot fully explain the degree of novelty in children's utterances, and that the language perception skills shown by newborns do not support this theory.

How do nativists explain language development, and what evidence supports their view?

Nativist theory proposes that humans are endowed with an innate language acquisition device (LAD), which contains either knowledge of universal grammar or operating principles that guide the processing of language information. Across many languages, children develop language quickly and easily and show marked consistency in the achievement of language milestones. There is disagreement as to whether nonhumans develop language, but in any case animal language achievements are slower and require far greater effort than in humans. There are human brain structures that are specialized for language processing, though there does not seem to be a single LAD brain organ. There is some evidence for the existence of sensitive periods in language development. The major criticism of nativist theory is that children receive more detailed and consistent linguistic feedback than nativists once thought.

How do interaction theories view language development?

Cognitive approaches see language as dependent on other, more general cognitive skills. For Piaget the broader ability to represent objects leads to the need for language. According to cognitive connectionist models, language develops as connections among cognitive units gradually change because of matching external criteria.

Social interaction theory emphasizes how interactive formats provide frequent and structured social environments for language learning. Child-directed speech introduces and models new vocabulary, grammatical structures, and pragmatic skills and provides both explicit and implicit feedback.

What abilities of infants help prepare them for language?

Infants have at birth or rapidly develop abilities to discriminate among speech sounds and sequences of sounds, localize sound direction, and recognize voices. Their recognition of speech sounds from their native language rapidly improves, but they lose the ability to distinguish sounds of other languages. Social interaction during the first year of life helps infants learn that sounds can be used to communicate and fosters early pragmatic skills such as turn taking. Child-directed speech and a developing joint focus of attention between infants and caregivers foster prelinguistic skills. Infants begin life making nonspeech sounds with no consistent meaning, then progress through cooing, babbling, echolalia, and protowords during their first year.

What are the major language accomplishments that take place during early childhood?

Semantic, grammatical, and pragmatic knowledge all increase. Most babies speak their first word around age 1. Children go through a naming explosion at around 18 months, adding new words on a daily basis. Early words are often nouns, though researchers have noted two different patterns of early word development. Fast mapping, syntactical bootstrapping, constraints automatically placed on word meaning, and parental modeling and labeling of objects help children to acquire word meanings quickly. Children's early word meanings frequently show overextensions or underextensions, and they often use holophrases and telegraphic speech to express more complex ideas and sentences. First sentences usually appear by about age 2. Children learn to form a variety of sentence types, and they learn (and sometimes overregularize) rules for forming plurals and past tenses. Semantic bootstrapping and gradual recognition of which specific language cues are most often correct for grammatical information are two processes that foster grammar knowledge. Children begin to learn social rules of discourse and referential communication skills.

How does language continue to develop during middle childhood and adolescence?

Vocabulary development continues, and children learn more abstract words. Children become skilled in using the passive voice and making inferences, and they progress in referential communication and social rules of discourse. Metalinguistic awareness improves, which enables children to use language more flexibly and to understand humor. Children become more skilled at language play such as riddles, develop an adolescent register to mark themselves as part of a particular group, and use language as a tool for informing others about themselves and for understanding themselves through personal narratives. Genderlect differences also become more pronounced.

What is bilingualism, and how does it affect language development?

Bilingualism is fluency in two languages. Children may develop additive or subtractive bilingualism, and may develop it simultaneously or sequentially. Code switching often appears when children are in the early stages of learning two languages, but its frequency decreases by the early preschool years. Although bilingualism may slow the rate of language acquisition, it may provide cognitive benefits by encouraging greater reflectiveness about language. Poor bilingual learning conditions may lead to semilingualism. Bilingual education is a controversial and important issue.

What are social dialects?

A social dialect is a consistent and systematic variety of a language shared by a subgroup of speakers that evolves from the group's unique cultural and historical background. Social dialects are not simpler or incorrect forms of a standard dialect, though people who speak social dialects are often subject to negative judgments. African American English, Hispanic English, and Asian English are some common dialects of Standard American English.

KEY TERMS

adolescent register (315)

bilingual (317)

child-directed speech (299)

connectionism (297)

constraints (305)

dialect (320)

fast mapping (305)

formats (299)

holophrases (307)

joint focus of attention (302)

language (287)

language acquisition device (LAD) (292)

learning theory (290)

metalinguistic awareness (314)

morphology (288)

nativist theory (292)

operating principles (292)

overregulation (308)

phonology (287)

Piaget's cognitive developmental theory (297)

pragmatics (288)

referential communication (310)

semantics (288)

social interactionist theory (298)

social rules of discourse (309)

syntax (288)

telegraphic speech (307)

Chapter 9

Attachment, Temperament, and Emotion

CHAPTER PREVIEW

A PERSPECTIVE TO think ABOUT

"Erin had heard about Heartland Children's Daycare through friends and had taken Patrick for a visit."

Erin remembers the first time she left her son Patrick at a day care center. Until then, Erin's mother had been taking care of Patrick during the day, but now it was time for him to spend some time in day care while Erin went to work. Erin had heard about Heartland Children's Daycare through friends and had taken Patrick for a visit during one of their open houses. Patrick was shy at first; he seemed overwhelmed by all of the new faces and things to do. Gradually however, he warmed up and began playing with some of the toys and books. This was a good sign that Patrick might do well in day care.

On the drive over to the center on Patrick's first day, Erin tried to be as cheerful as she could. She mentioned all of the new things Patrick could do at day care: painting, listening to stories, playing outside, and meeting new friends. Patrick was quiet.

At the center, Patrick clung tightly to his mother and peered around. The center was busy, with lots of children running and playing. One of the teachers came over to greet Patrick. She bent down to talk to him but Patrick wouldn't have any of that. Erin again reminded him of all of the fun he would have, but she was barely holding back her own tears. It was hard for her to leave Patrick in this new setting. Finally, Erin kissed Patrick on the cheek. After saying good-bye, she left Patrick with the teacher. When she got back to her car, Erin just sat and worried. Was she doing the right thing? Would Patrick be sad all day? Would he ever adjust to day care?

After studying this chapter, you should be able to use at least a dozen concepts to help Erin understand Patrick's reaction to his new setting. You will be able to explain what researchers know about infant–parent attachment and about when and why young children fear strangers and new settings. Does Patrick seem to have a secure attachment to his mother? What clues can you find in the scenario we've described? How does Patrick's temperament factor into his reaction? What should Erin expect regarding Patrick's adjustment to the new center? Finally, what can Erin do to help Patrick cope with the emotions he feels? Did she handle Patrick's first day well?

 As you read this chapter, look for the questions that ask you to think about what you're learning from Erin's perspective.

Most parents remember the first time they left their child in a day care center or with a baby-sitter. That first time is usually not easy. Some children get very upset, although others react more calmly. In this chapter we explore some of the reasons behind these differences. We begin by looking at how researchers study human attachment and how they classify the various types of attachments that infants form with their parents. Then we look at temperament and at the types of temperament that have been identified. We end with a discussion of emotional development in infancy and childhood. As you would imagine, children's attachment styles, temperaments, and emotions contribute to their varied responses to situations like Patrick's first morning in day care. How important is the initial bond that forms between infants and their caregivers, and what are the long-term effects of this bond? How do children with different temperaments react to their circumstances? How do children learn to cope with strong emotions?

Attachment

In this first section we look at the emotional bond that develops between an infant and his or her primary caretakers. Although most of us would call it "love," researchers refer to this bond by its more technical name—*attachment*. **Attachment** is an emotional tie to a specific person or persons that endures across time and space (Ainsworth, 1973). Infants don't bond with everyone. They reserve this special emotional attachment for the select few who provide their primary care. From its beginnings in the 1950s, most research in this area has focused primarily on the attachments infants form with their mothers. Of course, today many infants receive a substantial amount of care from fathers, older siblings, grandparents, other close relatives, and day care providers, and they can form attachments with whoever provides consistent and loving care. In our discussion we will sometimes refer to "caregivers," though this term sounds too technical for the special emotions and relationships we discuss. We use the term "mother" when describing research that primarily investigated mother attachments, but we hope that fathers and other caregivers will recognize that their relationships follow a similar path.

attachment

An emotional tie to a specific person or persons that endures across time and space.

As you study this section, ask yourself these questions:

- What are the historical roots that gave rise to modern research on attachment? How do these roots affect our thinking about attachment today?

- How do researchers use the "strange situation" to measure infant attachment? What kinds of attachments have investigators identified?

- What primary factors influence healthy attachments? Less healthy attachments? Are certain groups of infants or parents at higher risk for forming unhealthy attachments?

- How do the emotional bonds established early in life influence development throughout childhood?

- What are the main strengths and weaknesses of the different measures that we currently use to assess attachment relationships?

The Story of Attachment Research

Modern-day research on human attachment has two important roots: the ethological theory of John Bowlby and the classic primate experiments conducted by Harry Harlow.

■ **John Bowlby's Ethological Theory.** In John Bowlby's (1958, 1988) ethological theory, attachment emerges from a system of traits and behaviors that have evolved over time to increase the infant's chances of survival. Human infants are dependent on their caregivers for a relatively long period of time. This deep emotional bond increases the amount of attention and the quality of care that an infant receives. Bowlby (1958) commented, "It is fortunate for their survival that babies are so designed by Nature that they beguile and enslave mothers" (p. 367). Smiling, crying, and calling are behaviors infants use to bring adults closer. Newborns follow adults with their eyes. Later, as they learn to reach, crawl, and then walk, they are able to physically find, follow, and cling to their caregivers. Bowlby emphasized the infant's smile as a powerful social releaser of nurturing behavior in adults. And adults have evolved to respond positively to these social cues and to see the infant's round face, bright eyes, and chubby appearance as cute and cuddly. Evolution, then, has provided an interactive system that links nurturing adults to infants who depend on their loving care. Bowlby believed that attachment is especially evident when an infant seeks nearness to a protective adult in moments of distress or fear (Thompson, 1998). The attachment figure provides a "secure base" of emotional comfort for the infant (Ainsworth, 1973).

Bowlby (1969) proposed that infants develop attachments in the following four stages:

Who could resist this smile? Chubby cheeks, soft skin, and big smiles are just some of the features that induce adults to want to cuddle and take care of babies.

1. *Orientation without discrimination* (first 2 to 3 months after birth). Infants signal and respond to any available and caring adult. In this initial stage an attachment to a specific caregiver has not yet formed.

2. *Orientation with discrimination* (2 to 6 months). Infants begin to show a decided preference for their primary caregivers, signaling and responding more to the people who take care of them than to other people.

3. *Safe-base attachment* (6 months to 3 years). Infants and toddlers actively seek to be near their favored caregivers. They follow and cling to them, and they use them as a safe base to explore the environment. Infants, and later toddlers, often

thinking
OF ERIN

Which of Bowlby's four ▶
stages best describes the
attachment behaviors that
Patrick showed on his first
day in day care?

YOUR
PERSPECTIVE
NOTES

What do you think were
the qualities in your
parents or other care-
givers that made you
become attached to
them? Although you
cannot remember back
into your infancy, perhaps
you can reflect back and
think about the things
they did for you that made
you feel comfortable
and attached to them.

become visibly distressed when separated from their attachment figures, indicating that the emotional bond endures across both time and space. Fear of strangers
also emerges.

4. *Goal-corrected partnerships* (3 years and up). Children begin to understand the
feelings and motives of their caregivers. The relationship is more bidirectional
now: Children can adjust or "correct" their behaviors to the changing needs and
desires of their attachment figures, just as attachment figures adapt to children's
changing needs. For example, children learn that sometimes their attachment figures are busy or have other demands that conflict with caregiving. There is now a
more integrated emotional relationship between child and caregiver.

Since the mid-twentieth century, Bowlby's ethological theory has provided the dominant
framework for study of the special bonds between infants and adults.

■ **Harry Harlow's Research with Rhesus Monkeys.** Also during the 1950s, psychologist Harry Harlow conducted one of the most famous series of experiments in child development research. Harlow raised infant rhesus monkeys with the two types of surrogate
(substitute) "mothers" shown in Figure 9.1 (Harlow & Zimmermann, 1959). One surrogate
was bare wire mesh; the other had a soft cloth covering. Would infant monkeys form an attachment to either of these objects? Would the presence of a surrogate provide any emotional
support for the infant? The cloth-covered surrogate did. With his experiments Harlow

**FIGURE 9.1 Surrogate Mothers from
Harlow's Experiment**

Rhesus monkeys became emotionally
attached to the cloth mother that
provided contact comfort but not to
the wire mother that provided food.

provided a convincing demonstration that the critical ingredient in attachment formation is **contact comfort**—the comfortable feeling infants gain by clinging to a soft attachment figure.

Harlow's finding contradicted the predominant psychoanalytic and behavioral theories of the time. These theories predicted that infants would form attachments with the caregiver who provided food. In psychoanalytic theory oral gratification during feeding establishes the initial bond between infant and mother; in behavioral theory food serves as a powerful reinforcer for behaviors related to attachment. Feeding was not what determined attachment for Harlow's monkeys though. Even when the infants received milk from the wire-mesh mother, they spent the great majority of their time clinging to the cloth mother. It seemed that the cloth mother provided the infants with the kind of emotional security John Bowlby had described. When placed in an open room or an unfamiliar setting, infants without their cloth mothers showed extreme anxiety. They typically huddled in the corner, rocking and hugging themselves. But when their cloth mothers were in the room, these same infants showed a very different reaction. They would hug and cling to the mothers—and then, finding security in the mothers' presence, they would explore the room and play freely. When confronted with a fear stimulus (e.g., a clanging robot or a model of a giant insect), the infant monkeys first sought the comfort of their cloth mothers and then turned bravely to face their fears. The mother surrogates that provided contact comfort obviously served as the "secure base" these infant monkeys needed. Mere feeding provided no such benefit.

Taken together, Bowlby and Harlow provided the lens through which subsequent researchers have examined infant–parent attachments. We know that infants have formed an emotional bond to a specific person when they seek closeness to that person as a secure base. When separated, the infant shows distress. When reunited, the infant clings to the attachment figure and becomes emotionally comfortable again.

thinking
OF ERIN

◀ What similarities do you see between the reactions of Harlow's monkeys to strangers and separation and Patrick's responses on his first day in day care? How were Harlow's experiments analogous to situations faced by human children?

contact comfort

The comfortable feeling infants gain by clinging to a soft attachment figure.

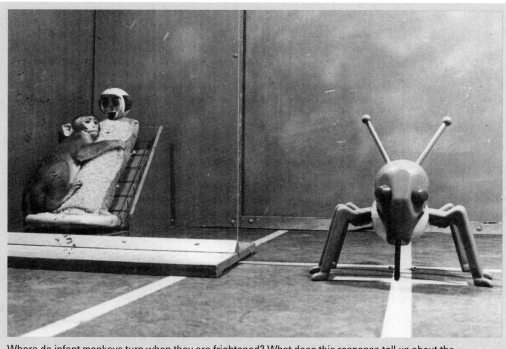

Where do infant monkeys turn when they are frightened? What does this response tell us about the attachment that they have formed with their caregivers?

Mary Ainsworth and the Strange Situation

Now let's look at how researchers have built on Bowlby and Harlow's work to investigate human attachment relationships.

strange situation

A *structured laboratory procedure used to observe attachment behavior in human infants.*

stranger anxiety

Wariness or fear of unfamiliar adults, shown by most infants between 6 and 24 months of age.

separation anxiety

Distress that infants (especially between 6 and 24 months of age) experience when separated from their primary caregivers.

■ **Secure Attachment in the Strange Situation.** To investigate attachment in human infants, Mary Ainsworth developed the *strange situation* test (Ainsworth, 1973; Ainsworth, Blehar, Waters, & Wall, 1978; Ainsworth & Wittig, 1969). Following Bowlby and Harlow, Ainsworth based her procedure on the idea that infants will seek to be near their attachment figure when they are distressed by an unfamiliar setting or an unfamiliar person. The **strange situation** consists of eight episodes strictly scripted to allow researchers to observe attachment behaviors in human infants, as described in Table 9.1. The purpose is to place the infant in a "strange" or unfamiliar setting with the primary caregiver, usually the mother. Does the infant use the mother as a secure base for exploring the new setting? Does the infant become distressed when the mother leaves—and seek her proximity when she returns? Does the infant prefer the mother over an unfamiliar adult?

The procedure begins when the mother brings her infant into a laboratory setting, usually on a university campus. Infants are normally observed at about one year of age. The setting is an average-sized room with a few chairs and interesting toys strewn around.

TABLE 9.1 Mary Ainsworth's Strange Situation Procedure

EPISODE	BEHAVIOR OF INFANT SHOWING SECURE ATTACHMENT
1. Introduction	
Assistant introduces mother and baby to the room. The episode lasts 30 seconds; the other episodes last approximately 3 minutes each.	Baby is held by mother.
2. Unfamiliar room	
Mother places baby on floor with toys and sits in chair. Mother is told not to direct baby's actions, but otherwise to respond normally.	Baby may be wary of room at first, but uses mother as a *safe base* of security. Plays with toys while mother is present. Usually maintains visual contact with mother during play.
3. Stranger enters	
Unfamiliar female adult knocks on door, then enters. Stranger speaks with mother, then approaches baby to play.	Baby may show *stranger anxiety* and clearly prefers mother over stranger. While mother is present, baby may allow stranger to approach and play.
4. Mother leaves	
Mother quietly leaves the room, leaving baby with the stranger. Stranger returns to sit in her chair.	Baby shows *separation anxiety* and renewed *stranger anxiety*. May be somewhat comforted by stranger, but clearly wants mother.
5. Reunion; stranger leaves	
Mother returns and stranger leaves. Mother comforts baby, if baby wishes, and returns baby to play with the toys.	Baby *seeks contact* with mother for joyful reunion. Seeks proximity, clings. May continue playing while mother is present.
6. Mother leaves again	
Mother says "bye-bye" and leaves infant alone in the room.	Baby shows *separation anxiety,* distress.
7. Stranger enters again	
While baby is still alone, the same stranger enters again. Stranger sits in chair, then calls or approaches baby to play.	Baby may show *stranger anxiety* and clearly prefers that mother return.
8. Reunion; stranger leaves	
Mother returns and stranger leaves. Mother picks up baby for a reunion that ends the procedure.	Joy on reunion. Baby *seeks proximity and contact* with mother.

An observation mirror on one wall usually permits observers to videotape the sessions for later analysis. After a 30-second introductory period, the mother places the baby on the floor in the center of the room and sits in one of the chairs. Most infants are wary of the unfamiliar setting and usually situate themselves so they can maintain visual contact with their mothers.

After 3 minutes, an unfamiliar female adult comes in. In a friendly manner, she speaks to the mother and then approaches the infant to play. Most infants show signs of **stranger anxiety,** a wariness or fear of unfamiliar adults. Infants may allow the stranger to approach and play, although most remain wary. Next, the mother calmly leaves the room. Losing their secure base, most infants show renewed stranger anxiety. They are no longer willing to play with the stranger and instead move to the door (or to the mother's chair), where they whine, cry, or show other visible signs of distress that indicate **separation anxiety.** For the next episode, the mother returns and the stranger leaves. Infants joyfully hug and cling tightly to their mothers. Feeling secure once more, infants resume their play. As the episodes continue, the mother exits again, leaving the infant alone; then the stranger reenters. These episodes allow additional opportunities to observe separation and stranger anxiety, respectively. The infant is reunited with the mother in the final episode.

Although we don't normally think of anxieties as being positive, you can see that here *separation anxiety* and *stranger anxiety* both signify that the infant has formed a special emotional attachment to a specific other person. It is the mother, not the stranger, who provides the security the infant needs to feel comfortable in the new setting. The loss of this security is evident when the mother leaves. Wariness of the stranger and preference for the mother both indicate what Ainsworth termed **secure attachment.** The most reliable indicator of secure attachment, however, is the way the infant responds when the mother returns to the room: Securely attached infants seek contact with the mother, cling tightly, and allow the mother to soothe and comfort them. Of the thousands of infant–parent dyads (pairs) observed by Ainsworth and other U.S. researchers in the strange situation procedure, approximately 65 percent show secure attachment. But what about the other 35 percent?

thinking
OF ERIN

How were Patrick's behaviors similar to the ones Ainsworth observed with infants in her strange situation test? Does Patrick seem to have a secure attachment to his mother? How would you help Erin understand that Patrick's crying and other behaviors indicate a healthy attachment with her?

secure attachment

In Ainsworth's classification, the healthy type of attachment between infant and caregiver. Indicated when the infant in distress seeks contact with the caregiver, clings, and is soothed by the caregiver; and when the infant uses the caregiver as a safe base for exploring unfamiliar environments. Other indicators include *separation anxiety* and *stranger anxiety.*

Like this baby, most infants go through a period of time when they are afraid of strangers. What does this behavior tell us about the attachment that has formed between the infant and mother?

thinking
OF ERIN

Do you see any indications ▶ of insecure attachment in Patrick's behavior on his first day at day care? Explain.

insecure–avoidant attachment

In Ainsworth's classification, an unhealthy type of attachment indicated when infants do not use their caregivers as a safe base for exploring unfamiliar environments, do not prefer the caregivers over unfamiliar adults, and are not visibly distressed by separation. Infants ignore or avoid their caregivers when reunited after separation.

insecure–resistant attachment

In Ainsworth's classification, an unhealthy type of attachment indicated when infants seek the proximity of their caregivers but do not seem to gain comfort from the contact.

■ **Insecure Attachment Relationships.** Ainsworth identified two patterns of *insecure attachment*. With **insecure–avoidant attachment,** seen in approximately 20 percent of infants studied in the United States, infants do not seem to use the mother as a secure base. When the stranger enters, these infants do not show a special preference for their mother— they may go directly to the stranger or play with the stranger without first needing to cling to the mother. When the mother leaves, these infants seem undisturbed. They may continue playing rather than going to the door and fussing. When the mother reenters, these infants turn away, ignore her, or avoid her. There is debate about how to interpret this pattern of behavior (Thompson, 1998). Are the infants actively avoiding contact with a parent who has rebuffed them in the past, or are they merely uninterested because they have not developed a special bond?

Insecure–resistant attachment is seen in about 15 percent of infant–parent dyads. These infants usually seek the proximity of their mother, but they do not seem to gain comfort from the contact. Some show exaggerated stranger and separation anxiety or a strong need to stay close to the parent. But when the mother picks the baby up, some of these infants fight off her efforts to provide comfort, often showing signs of anger or heightened distress. Others seem passive when their mothers try to console them. Some researchers label this category *insecure–ambivalent attachment,* because the infant seeks proximity but then shows ambivalence about contact with the caregiver.

More recently, researchers have added a fourth category called **insecure–disorganized (or disoriented) attachment** (Main & Solomon, 1986, 1990). These infants seem confused or dazed, or they may show contradictory behaviors. They may be calm one moment and angry the next. They may remain motionless or may show apprehension as their parent approaches. Their behaviors are not consistently avoidant or resistant, so they do not fall neatly into either of those classifications of insecure attachment. Table 9.2 summarizes the types of attachment that Mary Ainsworth and other researchers have identified.

Other researchers have questioned whether parent–infant attachments should be classified into separate categories at all (Fraley & Spieker, 2003). They note that infants vary so much within these four attachment categories that it may be more informative to rate them all on two continuous scales: degree of avoidance of the parent and degree of hostility or

TABLE 9.2 Different Types of Attachment Identified in the Strange Situation

TYPES OF ATTACHMENT	BEHAVIORS
Secure	• Baby uses mother as safe base for exploring unfamiliar room. • Baby prefers mother over stranger. • Baby may show distress when separated from mother. • Baby seeks proximity and contact with mother on reunion.
Insecure–avoidant	• Baby does not prefer mother over stranger. • Baby avoids contact with mother by turning or looking away.
Insecure–resistant	• Baby shows ambivalent approach–resist behavior: seeks proximity with mother, but then resists contact. • Baby does not avoid mother. • Some infants show anger; others are passive.
Insecure–disorganized/disoriented	• Babies act confused or dazed, or may show contradictory behaviors. • Babies may be calm, then angry. • Babies may be motionless or show apprehension. • Behaviors are not consistently avoidant or resistant as in other categories.

resistance. In the future we will see if this strategy, or some other, provides a better description of the different types or degrees of attachment shown by infants and parents.

Parent, Child, and Cultural Factors in Attachment

What causes these different types of attachments to develop? Parent, child, and cultural factors all are involved.

■ **Parenting Factors Related to Individual Differences in Attachment.** According to Ainsworth, it is the quality of the parent–infant interaction during the first year of life that determines the type of attachment that is formed. Through extensive observation of mother–infant behaviors in the home environment, Ainsworth and others have found that secure attachment relationships tend to be associated with mothers who respond positively, consistently, and warmly to their infants (Ainsworth, 1973; Ainsworth et al., 1978; Thompson, 1998). They hold their babies frequently, tenderly, and for long enough that the infants seem satisfied when they are put back down. When Ainsworth (1973) observed families in their homes, she found that securely attached infants showed very little distress when their mothers left the room briefly. They seemed conscious of their mothers' whereabouts and confident that they would soon return. This was in contrast to the babies' behavior in the strange situation: These same infants showed separation distress when their mothers left them in the unfamiliar laboratory setting. During reunion episodes, securely attached infants gain considerable comfort by being held by their mothers. This response is consistent with Bowlby's view that maternal sensitivity would be most important when an infant was distressed, afraid, or anxious. Cross-culturally, maternal sensitivity was related to infant security in a study of families in the United States and in Bogota, Columbia (Posada et al., 2002).

A particularly important characteristic of secure attachments is the mother's sensitivity to the calls and signals of her baby. These mothers respond quickly when their infants cry or call out. They are not worried that their attention will "spoil" the baby. But it's more than just responding quickly and positively. These mothers show **sensitive responsiveness**—they see things from the baby's point of view and adjust their responses to meet the infant's needs. Consider a one-year-old who opens a book, points to a balloon, and says "dat." The mother responds by smiling and saying, "Yes, that's a balloon and here's another one." The mother has noticed her infant's signal and has responded to it by allowing the infant to initiate a game of pointing and naming. Contrast this to the mother who takes the book from the baby, turns to the beginning, and proceeds to read the book the "right" way. Which mother has shown sensitive responsiveness? Healthy attachments are facilitated when mothers go along with the games, interactions, and other activities that their infants initiate. They adjust their babies' feeding and sleep schedules according to the signals and rhythms of the baby, and they otherwise show sensitivity toward the baby's perspective. With secure attachments, the relationship is mutual rather than being completely dominated by the mother.

Based on her home observations, Ainsworth (1973) believed that indifferent parenting led to insecure–avoidant attachments and that inconsistent parenting led to insecure–resistant (or ambivalent) relationships. Other researchers, however, have produced evidence that avoidant attachments arise more from parenting that is intrusive, overstimulating, or even hostile, and that resistant attachments develop when care is unresponsive (Isabella, 1995; Isabella & Belsky, 1991; Isabella, Belsky, & von Eye, 1989; Lyons-Ruth, Connell, Zoll, & Stahl, 1987). These researchers describe mothers of insecure–avoidant infants as being tense and irritable, showing little interest in their infants, handling them in a mechanical fashion, failing to adjust feedings to the baby's pace, being less responsive to infants' cries and calls, and otherwise reacting to motherhood in a resentful or negative way (Egeland & Farber, 1984). Whether avoidant or resistant, insecurely attached infants learn that their caregivers will not

insecure–disorganized (or disoriented) attachment
An unhealthy type of attachment indicated when infants seem confused or dazed or show contradictory behaviors in the strange situation procedure. Infants may be calm, then become angry; or they may be motionless or apprehensive.

sensitive responsiveness
A quality of infant care where caregivers respond quickly and warmly to the baby's signals and adjust their responses to allow the infant to direct interactions.

YOUR
PERSPECTIVE
~~PERSPECTIVE~~

NOTES

What kinds of parenting
have you observed
that might contribute
to insecure attachment
relationships?

respond sensitively to their needs. Thus, in times of stress, they may reject their parents' attempts to comfort them by looking away or by showing anger and frustration.

Insecure–disorganized (or disoriented) attachments have been associated with parenting that is abusive and/or with parents who themselves have suffered childhood traumas, have unresolved difficulties with their own parents, or are still mourning the death of their attachment figure (Main & Hesse, 1990; Main & Solomon, 1990). Infants who have been frightened by their parents may be confused about how to respond when they are in a stressful situation. They may also be fearful of how their parents will respond under stress. Can they use their parent as a safe base of security, or will their parent be dangerous? You can see how an infant might respond in contradictory ways, such as approaching the parent but also cowering. Or an infant might freeze, immobilized by the dilemma. In less severe cases, disorganized/disoriented attachment behavior can occur when parents display anxiety or send conflicting signals to their infants.

■ **Studies and Interventions with High-Risk Mothers.** To understand how unhealthy attachment relationships form, researchers have observed families at risk. These include families where mothers behave inappropriately toward their infants or in which mothers have serious mental disorders such as schizophrenia and depression. Researchers draw a distinction between neglect and abuse. Neglecting mothers tend to be uninvolved and passive in relation to their infants; abusive mothers interfere more actively and show more hostility (Crittenden & Bonvillian, 1984). In a Swedish study, 60 percent of infants with schizophrenic mothers showed multiple indicators of insecure attachment (avoidance of mother, disruptions in exploration, and/or lack of stranger anxiety). In contrast, only 5 percent of infants with nonpsychotic mothers showed these indicators (Näslund, Persson-Blennow, McNeil, Kaij, & Malmquist-Larsson, 1984). Other researchers have assessed risk factors that might make it difficult for any mother to parent optimally. In a study of low-income families in the United States, the researchers found an increase in insecure attachments when the families suffered three or four of the following stressors: family overcrowding, parental criminality, maternal depression, maternal discord with spouse or significant other, and mothers who were aggressive or feared harm from others (Shaw & Vondra, 1993). If families showed only one or two of these risk factors, however, infants were not at higher risk of insecure attachment.

Of course, most mothers don't want to treat their infants inappropriately. But many parents have difficulty coping with the negative pressures of poverty, mental or physical illness, and stressful marital and other relationships. The already difficult task of parenting can become overwhelming when multiple factors stack up against a mother who has little support from family, neighbors, or community service agencies. Attachment relationships can improve substantially when at-risk mothers receive caring social support, however. One intervention study provided weekly home visits to low-income mothers (Lyons-Ruth, Connell, Grunebaum, & Botein, 1990). Most of the mothers were clinically depressed and had a history of abusive or neglectful parenting. Home visitors helped the mothers interact with their babies in positive and developmentally appropriate ways. They also helped mothers access community resources to meet family needs, and they organized group

How is the attachment relationship affected when parents are frequently hostile or irritable? What if they are abusive?

meetings to reduce the mothers' social isolation. For comparison, another group of high-risk families did not receive the home-visit intervention. In this nonintervention group an alarming 60 percent of the infants exhibited insecure–disorganized attachments. After a year of home visits, however, only 29 percent of the infants in the intervention program showed insecure–disorganized attachments—a figure comparable to the 28 percent the researchers saw in low-risk families from the same neighborhoods. A recent review of 88 different intervention programs found that sensitive parenting improved significantly, and most programs had at least some effect in improving attachment security (Bakermans-Kranenburg, van IJzendoorn, & Juffer, 2003). Programs were most effective when fathers were included in the intervention. These and similar research findings speak to the need to provide positive social supports for at-risk families.

■ **Infant Characteristics Related to Attachment.** Attachment is a two-way relationship, and factors associated with infants themselves also can contribute to their security and insecurity. Infants who become securely attached tend to cry less frequently, greet their mothers more positively, and initiate more bodily contact with their mothers (Ainsworth et al., 1978). Conversely, infants with insecure attachments tend to cry more, often show anger, and show disruptions in bodily contact. Are these differences due to the infant or due to the parenting? Do securely attached infants cry less because their mothers respond more sensitively to them, or do the mothers respond more sensitively because their babies are more pleasant and congenial? It is difficult to determine the cause–effect relationships among these correlational associations. We do know that insecure–disorganized attachments occur at a higher rate among infants with special needs such as high-risk prematurity, Down syndrome, autism, and physical disabilities (Thompson, 1998; van IJzendoorn, Goldberg, Kroonenberg, & Frenkel, 1992). There is also evidence that insecure–resistant infants, in particular, are less alert and active from birth and are more likely to show mental and motor delays throughout infancy (Egeland & Farber, 1984). Infants who are highly irritable are more likely to develop insecure attachments, but only when their mothers receive low levels of social support (Belsky & Isabella, 1988; Egeland & Farber, 1984). Otherwise, the basic personality or temperament of the infant is not a strong predictor of attachment outcome (Goldsmith & Alansky, 1987; Thompson, 1998). We will return to the issue of temperament later in this chapter.

■ **Cultural Differences in Parenting and Attachment Behavior.** Beyond the infant and mother, the values of the larger culture influence parental expectations and behaviors. Table 9.3 shows attachment classifications from the United States and seven other nations. Researchers observed infants in the strange situation, in most cases between 11 and 22 months of age. The newer category of insecure–disorganized/disoriented attachment does not appear in the table because most of the studies cited did not include it. You can see that Great Britain and Sweden registered the highest percentages of secure attachments. Chile and Germany showed the lowest national percentages, although the majority of infants observed in both countries were still securely attached. More variability is seen with insecure attachments. In the European countries (Great Britain, Sweden, the Netherlands, and Germany), nearly all of the insecure infants were classified as avoidant and very few were resistant. The reverse pattern occurred in Japan and Israel. Insecure infants in Chile were evenly divided between the avoidant and resistant categories.

How do our cultural values influence the way we parent? Does the expression of attachment differ across cultures?

TABLE 9.3 Cross-National Attachment Data on Infants Observed in the Strange Situation

COUNTRY OR GROUP	NUMBER OF INFANTS SAMPLED	SECURE ATTACHMENT (PERCENTAGE)	INSECURE–AVOIDANT ATTACHMENT (PERCENTAGE)	INSECURE–RESISTANT ATTACHMENT (PERCENTAGE)
Great Britain	72	75%	22%	3%
Sweden	51	74	22	4
Netherlands	115	68	26	6
Germany	136	57	35	8
Japan	96	68	5	27
Israel	166	64	5	31
Chile	38	53	24	24
U.S.: General population	1,584	67	21	12
U.S.: Chinese Americans	36	50	25	25
U.S.: Low-income Hispanics in South Bronx	50	50	30	20

Source: Data for U.S. general population taken from a review by van IJzendoorn, Goldberg, Kroonenberg, & Frankel (1992). All other data taken from Thompson (1998), who reviewed studies by Beller & Pohl (1986); Durrett, Otaki, & Richards (1984); Fracasso, Busch-Rossnagel, & Fischer (1993); Goossens & van IJzendoorn (1990); Grossmann, Grossmann, Huber, & Wartner (1981); Lamb, Hwang, Frodi, & Frodi (1982); Li-Repac (1982); Sagi et al. (1985); Sagi & Lewkowicz (1987); Sagi, van IJzendoorn, Aviezer, Donnell, & Mayseless (1994); Smith & Noble (1987); Takahashi (1986, 1990); Valenzuela (1990); and van IJzendoorn, Goossens, Kroonenberg, & Tavecchio (1985). We excluded data from high-risk groups.

What cultural factors might underlie these international differences? Japanese culture encourages close physical contact and intimacy between infants and mothers, and Japanese parents rarely leave their infants alone, especially when strangers are present (Takahashi, 1986). Similarly, Israeli infants, particularly those living in communal kibbutz arrangements, are accustomed to close-knit relations and less experience with strangers and separation. When Japanese or Israeli infants encounter the strange situation, many show high levels of distress—sometimes to the point that the researchers need to curtail the separation episodes. Extremely high distress level is one indicator of insecure–resistant attachment. In contrast, German culture stresses early independence in young children (Grossmann, Grossmann, Huber, & Wartner, 1981; Thompson, 1998). German infants learn that their mothers expect independence, so they may be less likely to seek proximity with their mothers in stressful situations. Remember that if infants ignore or avoid contact with their parents in the strange situation, this indicates insecure–avoidant attachment.

Within the United States, attachment patterns show socioeconomic and ethnic variability. Non-Hispanic white mothers tend to value independence and competence in infants and react more negatively to the clingy, dependent behavior typical of insecure–resistant infants (Harwood, 1992; Thompson, 1998). Other ethnic groups have somewhat different values. Puerto Rican mothers, for example, value familial love and respect and look most negatively on the independence shown by insecure–avoidant infants (Harwood, 1992). Many African Americans are raised in extended-family arrangements, with caregiving often shared among the mother, grandmother, aunts, sisters, and other relatives. Might these infants show less fear when their mother leaves? Parent–infant interactions also change in response to the environment in which the family lives. In urban communities where violence is pervasive, for example, some parents may be more restrictive with their children, allowing them less independence and freedom to roam. In these situations young children may be more afraid when their parents leave them and may display this fearfulness in the strange situation.

From this discussion we hope you can see that environmental and cultural differences in mother–infant interactions influence behavior in the strange situation. Ainsworth originally developed her procedure with predominantly middle-class white American infants. Clearly, it is not always appropriate to use the typical behaviors of this group as a normative reference for categorizing infants raised in other circumstances or cultures.

■ **Attachments with Fathers.**   Until now, we have focused exclusively on infant–mother attachments. What about fathers? Summing up the data from 11 studies of attachments with both mothers and fathers, Fox, Kimmerly, and Schafer (1991) concluded that infants were just as likely to form secure attachments with fathers as with mothers. In fact, among the 710 infants studied, the percentages of secure versus insecure attachments were 65/35 for fathers and 65/35 for mothers. Further, the type of infant attachment tended to be consistent from one parent to the other. That is, infants with secure attachments with their mothers tended to also have secure attachments with their fathers; infants with avoidant attachments with their mothers tended to also have avoidant attachments to their fathers; and so on. It is unclear whether this consistency is due to characteristics in the infant that produce a similar attachment with each parent, or whether both parents respond in similar ways to the infant. Either way, it is clear that infants reach beyond their relationships with their mothers. When fathers, older siblings, and other important people provide sensitive care for infants, infants begin to rely on them as a secure base for emotional support.

■ **Day Care and Attachment.**   Many parents worry that their attachment relationships will suffer if they are not with their infants full-time during the early months. Some research conducted during the 1980s suggested that infants who spend more than 20 hours per week in day care centers, family day care homes, or other baby-sitting arrangements are *slightly* more likely to be insecurely attached to their mothers than infants who receive more maternal care or are cared for full-time at home (e.g., Belsky & Rovine, 1988). In these studies, although the majority of infants in day care (even those in day care more than 20 hours a week) were still securely attached to their mothers, the percentages were significantly lower than for infants with mothers at home. More recently, a large-scale nationwide study found that time spent in day care added to the risk of insecure attachment only when it was combined with mothering that was less sensitive and responsive (NICHD Early Child Care Research Network, 1997, 2001). According to this research, day care in itself does not necessarily jeopardize attachment. The combination of parenting problems and full-time day care can have an impact, however.

Yet interpreting these findings is complicated. Many issues enter in when we consider attachment and day care.

▶ First, the attachment relationship of infants in nonmaternal care depends largely on the attitudes the mother has about being at work versus home (Belsky & Rovine, 1988). Career-oriented mothers may resent staying home; other mothers may resent the need to work when they would rather be at home. Either source of resentment can reduce the quality of attachment (Belsky & Rovine, 1988).

▶ Second, the quality of the day care is important. When an infant experiences poor-quality day care combined with lower levels of sensitive responsiveness from the mother, insecure attachments are more likely (NICHD Early Child Care Research Network, 1997).

▶ Third, because researchers cannot randomly assign families to use day care or to care for their infants at home, we do not have controlled experiments that could determine cause and effect. (You can review how experiments establish cause and effect in Chapter 1.) Families who choose to care for infants at home may differ systematically from those who do not, and these differences may affect the attachment relationship more than the type of care (e.g., day care versus home) itself.

▶ Finally, consider that the strange situation may lose its validity when used with infants who spend considerable time outside the home. In the procedure, in order to be classified as securely attached, infants must cling to the parent and show clear evidence that they are joyful when the parent returns. Infants in full-time day care, however, become

Parental Leave Policies in the United States and Other Nations

Many families in the United States face a troublesome dilemma when their new baby is born. Does the mother leave her job to stay at home with the baby? If so, how does the family survive her loss of income? What if she also loses her family's health insurance and other benefits? Will she be able to return to her job later, without penalty or loss of advancement? Or does the father leave his job? As you can imagine, this dilemma is especially acute for single mothers and in two-parent households where neither parent makes a high wage. How do the parents do what is right for their new child without jeopardizing the family's economic security? And when working parents look for someone to care for their infant, they encounter additional trouble. There are very few licensed care arrangements for infants (and children under 2 years of age) in this country. And when a family can find care, it often costs a substantial portion of one parent's wages. Many working parents wonder if it's worth staying at work. But again, can they afford to quit or take substantial time off?

Almost all other industrialized nations have recognized their important role in supporting healthy families. No one benefits when infants are left in substandard care or when families must live in poverty to care for their own children. On average, nations in the European Union provide 36 weeks of *paid leave* to families with new babies (Kamerman, 2000). Most provide similar benefits for adoption. Typically, mothers receive 14 to 16 weeks of maternity leave, paid at a full or substantial rate. An additional 20 or so weeks' leave for the mother (and sometimes for the father or for both parents) is available at a reduced rate of pay. Additional nonpaid time is usually available to one or both parents, if they choose. While on leave parents maintain their job security and full benefits.

Table 9.4 summarizes the family leave policies of several industrialized nations. Out of 29 of the world's most developed nations, only the United States, Australia, and New Zealand have no paid leave benefits (Kamerman, 2000). In the United States, the *Family and Medical Leave Act (FMLA)* was signed into law by President Clinton in 1993. The FMLA requires employers with 50 or more employees to provide up to 12 weeks of *unpaid leave* for the birth or adoption of a child or to care for other family members with serious medical conditions. Leaves are job protected. Employers may require, however, that accumulated sick leave or vacation time be used to cover some or all of the leave. Only about 55 percent of the U.S. workforce is covered by the FMLA (Kamerman, 2000). And although this statute pales in comparison to the provisions made in other nations, passage of the law still met considerable resistance. The impetus for the FMLA began in the 1970s but was not introduced in Congress until 1985. The law passed in Congress twice, in 1990 and 1991, but was vetoed both times by then President George H. W. Bush (Kamerman, 2000). Many employers were concerned that paid leaves would cripple their companies.

Why does the United States, the world's most affluent nation, remain so far behind on family leave policies? Should the care of young infants be left up to the operation of a free-market economy? Or if paid leave were provided, how should it be financed? Should all taxpayers contribute equally, or should employers shoulder most of the burden? These and other difficult questions face us as a society as we struggle to balance the health of our families with our nation's economic prosperity. What do you think is the best policy? ■

accustomed to seeing their parents leave and later return. Their excitement can diminish over time. Is it surprising that these infants show less joy on reunion and less need to cling than infants who stay home full-time? Is their attachment really less secure?

It's important to take these and other issues into account before drawing conclusions about the effects of day care on attachment. We have much more to say about day care in Chapter 12.

Even if day care itself does not disrupt parent–infant attachment, many parents still wish they could spend more time at home during the months after their babies are born. Many parents must return to work sooner than they would like in order to avoid losing their

TABLE 9.4 Family Leave Policies in Selected Countries

COUNTRY	DURATION OF LEAVE	WAGE REPLACED
Sweden	One year of parental leave	80%
	3 months' additional leave	Flat rate
	3 more months	Unpaid
Norway	42 weeks' parental leave	100%
	Parental leave until child is 2	Unpaid
Portugal	6 months' maternity leave	100%
	24 months' additional parental leave	Unpaid
Poland	16–18 weeks' maternity leave	100%
	24 months' additional leave	Flat rate
Spain	16 weeks' maternity leave	100%
	Parental leave until child is 3	Unpaid
Netherlands	16 weeks' maternity leave	100%
	6 months' additional leave per parent	Unpaid
Luxembourg	16 weeks' maternity leave	100%
Mexico	12 weeks' maternity leave	100%
Turkey	12 weeks' maternity leave	Two-thirds
Great Britain	6 weeks' maternity leave	90%
	12 weeks' additional maternity leave	Flat rate
	13 weeks' parental leave	Unpaid
New Zealand	52 weeks maternity leave	Unpaid
United States	12 weeks' maternity leave	Unpaid

Source: Adapted from S. B. Kamerman. (2000). Parental leave policies: An essential ingredient in early childhood education and care policies. *Social Policy Report, 14*(2), pp. 5–6. Adapted with permission.

jobs and the paychecks they need to pay the bills. In some countries generous paid parental leave laws let parents spend more time at home with their new babies. To see how the United States compares, see the Social Policy Perspective box called "Parental Leave Policies in the United States and Other Nations."

thinking OF ERIN

◀ What would you tell Erin regarding the research on day care and attachment?

Early Attachment and Long-Term Outcomes

So far, we've seen that there is a link between the quality of infant attachment and the quality of care an infant receives during the first year of life. Although interesting, this research would be less important if the effects applied only to the first year. They do not. Alan Sroufe, a psychologist and researcher at the University of Minnesota, and his colleagues continue to report on a longitudinal study of a large group of families originally recruited in Minneapolis in the early 1970s (e.g., Elicker, Englund, & Sroufe, 1992; Sroufe, 1990, 1996; Sroufe, Carlson, & Schulman, 1993; Sroufe & Egeland, 1991; see also a review in Thompson, 1998). Researchers observed these families' infants with their mothers in the strange situation when the infants were 12 and 18 months of age. During the preschool years, teachers and observers rated children who had been securely attached as infants as happier and more socially skilled, competent, compliant, and empathetic than children who were insecurely attached as infants. Preschoolers with secure attachments also were more popular with their peers, had higher

This preschool child is being a good friend. How is this type of behavior related to the attachments that children form with their caregivers in the first year of life?

self-esteem, and were less dependent and negative. By age 10, children in the securely attached classification were still less dependent and received higher ratings on self-esteem, self-confidence, social skills, and emotional health. They made more friends than children who had been insecurely attached as infants, and they spent more time with their friends. Adolescents who had been insecurely attached were somewhat more likely to experience psychological problems (Thompson, 1998).

How do these long-term attachment effects work? According to Sroufe, we internalize the significant relationships that we have early in life, and we use those early experiences as interpretive filters when we develop later relationships. We come to expect other people to interact with us in a way that mirrors our early attachment relationships. Securely attached infants, therefore, grow up to seek and expect others to be supportive and positive—and they behave in ways that elicit these qualities in people around them. Insecurely attached infants, however, may later expect and provoke hostility, ambivalence, or rejection in their relationships.

Michael Lamb, a child development researcher at the National Institute of Child Health and Development, provides a slightly different explanation (Lamb, 1987a; Lamb, Thompson, Gardner, & Charnov, 1985). Lamb emphasizes the role of continuities in parenting. In other words, parents who foster secure attachments with their infants often remain sensitive, positive, and supportive through their children's preschool, middle-childhood, and even adolescent years. Warm parenting during childhood may be more important than first-year attachment in helping children maintain positive behavioral, social, and personality characteristics in later years. Support for Lamb's position comes from research showing that early attachment categories do not necessarily correlate with later outcomes if characteristics of the family interactions change. Divorce, illness and other negative circumstances can disrupt relationships even when children were securely attached as infants. Conversely, insecurely attached infants can benefit from later improvements in the quality of their care. Although the quality of the initial attachment is important in getting the infant off to a good start, it is clear that the quality and consistency of parental care after infancy also plays an important role (Thompson, 1998).

Limitations of the Strange Situation Procedure

Ainsworth's strange situation procedure has been a valuable tool for assessing attachment relationships in infants, but unfortunately it is not suitable for use with toddlers older than about 18 months of age. Outward signs of stranger and separation anxiety diminish after 18 months as toddlers become more mobile and cognitively advanced. For example, consider what will happen if a 3-year-old boy is placed in the strange situation. When his mother leaves the room, the 3-year-old can simply open the door and follow. Or he can wait patiently in the room, understanding that his mother will soon return. He has experienced many separations and remembers that his mother has always returned. He has some understanding of time, knowing she will be back "soon." Also, he knows his mother would not leave him in an unsafe situation. Further, his developing language allows him to understand the pleasant conversation between his mother and the stranger, and he too can speak on friendly terms with the stranger. For these and other reasons, separation and stranger anxieties are diminished enough by 2 years of age that the strange situation no longer serves as a reliable indicator of secure and insecure attachment. Consequently, to gauge attachment in children older than 18 months, researchers turn to alternative approaches.

■ **Alternative Measures of Attachment.** The most frequently used alternative to measuring attachment is the **attachment Q-sort (AQS)** method (Waters & Deane, 1985). The AQS can be used with children ages 12 months to 5 years. Parents, teachers, or other adults who have had a chance to observe the child sort through a stack of 90 cards. On each card is a short behavioral description, such as "acts to maintain social interaction." The adult places each card on one of nine piles ranked according to how well the descriptions fit the child—from most to least accurately. Each card then gets a score based on the pile to which it was assigned. Score patterns, when compared to established profiles, then provide measures of security, dependency, sociability, and social desirability in the child. Descriptions related to high scores in security include "greets adult spontaneously" and "actively solicits comforting from adult when distressed." Low scores in security go with descriptions such as "expects adults will be unresponsive" and "does not solicit or enjoy affectionate physical contact with adult." One drawback of the AQS is that it does not involve direct observation of the child in question but rather relies on the observations and judgments of adults who know the child. When adults are well trained in using the AQS, scores show a reasonable, though not perfect, convergence with security as measured in Ainsworth's strange situation (Thompson, 1998; Vaughn & Waters, 1990).

Another alternative is the **adult attachment interview (AAI),** developed by Mary Main and her colleagues (Main, Kaplan, & Cassidy, 1985; also see Thompson, 1998). A structured interview lasting about an hour, the AAI helps an interviewer determine an adult's state of mind regarding attachments with his or her own parents. AAI classifications describe four types of adult attachment:

❯ *Autonomous:* Adults have detailed and thoughtful memories of loving childhood relationships with their parents. Autonomous adults speak about their parents' positive influence on their development. When experiences such as maltreatment or rejection did occur, the adults have convincingly forgiven their parents.

❯ *Dismissing:* Adults minimize negative childhood experiences and dismiss the impact of early attachments on development. Dismissing adults may insist that they cannot remember childhood events, or their memories may be contradictory. They have idealized images of their parents that are not supported by facts or consistent memories.

❯ *Preoccupied:* Adults are still entangled with past family relationships. They remember childhood events, but their stories are not coherent or succinct. Preoccupied adults may still be dependent on their parents or angry about past events.

❯ *Unresolved:* Adults are confused or disoriented when speaking about the loss of a loved one or about past traumas such as sexual or physical abuse.

Researchers consider the autonomous classification the mature form of secure attachment. The other three represent insecure attachment.

The original purpose of the AAI was to predict the types of attachments parents would have with their new infants, and the AAI classifications do correspond well with the types of attachments revealed in Mary Ainsworth's strange situation procedure. Autonomous parents tend to have secure attachments with their infants. Dismissing parents tend to be more rejecting of their infants, leading to insecure–avoidant attachments. Preoccupied adults tend to have insecure–resistant infants, and unresolved parents tend to have insecure–disorganized/disoriented infants. In fact, one study demonstrated a remarkable degree of

YOUR
PERSPECTIVE
NOTES
Based on these AAI descriptions, which type of attachment do you think you have with your parents or other caregivers?

attachment Q-sort (AQS)

A method for classifying attachments in children between 12 months and 5 years of age. Parents or other adults who have observed the child sort through cards with behavioral descriptions and score the selected cards.

adult attachment interview (AAI)

A structured interview used to determine an adult's views regarding attachment to his or her parents.

Style of parenting and attachment can be handed down across generations. As each mother forms an attachment relationship with her baby, the relationship will be influenced by the thoughts and feelings she has about her relationship with her own mother.

consistency in attachments across three generations (Benoit & Parker, 1994). In that study the adult AAI classifications of middle-class and upper-middle-class non-Hispanic white mothers matched the strange situation classifications of their one-year-old infants up to 82 percent of the time. Although less consistent, there was some correlation between the mothers' attachments and the AAI attachments reported by their own mothers. Parents internalize the models of attachment they experienced in their childhoods and use those models to build relationships with their infants (Peck, 2003). To some extent, then, families hand down styles of parenting and attachment across generations. Fortunately, as you read earlier in this section, intervention programs can provide social support and instruction in effective parent–child interactions. When there are problems, such interventions can help establish more positive attachment models and parenting styles, thus breaking negative cycles and improving the quality of attachment in some families.

The AAI has also been used with adolescents. In one study, an ethnically diverse group of 9th and 10th graders completed the AAI (Allen et al., 2003). Secure (autonomous) relationships were observed when mothers and teens were in a supportive relationship where 1) mothers understood how their teens saw themselves (how teens perceived their own strengths and weaknesses); 2) teens felt safe in disagreeing with their mothers; and 3) both sides worked to maintain the relationship even when disagreeing. Parents who are supportive and understanding provide a safe base where teens can explore their independence, developing the type of healthy goal-corrected partnership that John Bowlby described decades ago.

We have described three methods researchers use to classify children's attachments with their caregivers. Each method has its own strengths and weaknesses. A strength of Ainsworth's strange situation test is that it uses direct observation of behaviors of infants and their caregivers. A major weakness, however, is that the procedure works best with infants between about 9 and 18 months of age. The attachment Q-sort and adult attachment interview apply to broader age ranges (strengths), but both rely on subjective perceptions (weaknesses). The AQS relies on adults' perceptions about children; these perceptions depend on the adults' familiarity with detailed behaviors in the child and also may be clouded by personal subjective factors in the adults. The AAI depends on the perceptions and recollections adults have of their own childhoods. Can we completely trust the accuracy of our childhood memories? As you may recall from Chapter 6, memory research gives us reason to doubt the accuracy of early childhood memories. How are our memories of past events shaped by the experiences and relationships we have had since? Still, our perceptions of ourselves and our children may influence the way we parent as much as objective realities do. The AQS and AAI methods therefore provide valuable information and can serve to complement what we have learned from Ainsworth's earlier work.

Beginning with Bowlby and Harlow, attachment research has helped us understand the important link between parenting behavior and childhood development. The comfort and security we drew from our parents forms the model we use to establish secure relationships with our children, thereby transmitting healthy parenting behaviors across generations. When insecure relationships have developed, interventions can sometimes help parents become more sensitive and responsive, perhaps preventing another generation of emotional insecurity. Although there is some evidence that factors related to the infant can affect the attachment relationship, most of the work in this area focuses on the influence of parents and other caregivers in establishing the early emotional bonds. In the next section we look at infant *temperament*, a characteristic that has received considerable attention from researchers who study parent–child interactions.

LET'S REVIEW . . .

1. What is the main point of John Bowlby's ethological theory of attachment?

   a. Infants are attached to the contact comfort they receive from their parents.

   b. Parents have to learn to love and nurture infants.

   c. Attachment behaviors have evolved over time to increase the chances of infant survival.

   d. Evolution has provided a system that causes parents to be attached to infants, but infants must learn to engage in behaviors that support the parents' nurturing tendency.

2. In Ainsworth's strange situation, infants who show stranger anxiety and separation anxiety are most likely to be classified as having:

   a. a secure attachment.

   b. an insecure–avoidant attachment.

   c. an insecure–disorganized/disoriented attachment.

   d. no attachment at all.

3. Which of the following cultures expects infants to show the most independence from parents?

   a. Japanese   b. Israeli   c. German   d. American

4. **True or False:** Infants with secure attachments with their parents tend to grow up to be preschool children who are more happy, competent, and popular with their peers.

5. **True or False:** The adult attachment interview (AAI) identifies secure, insecure–avoidant, and insecure–resistant attachments that adults have with their own parents.

Answers: 1. c, 2. a, 3. c, 4. T, 5. F

Temperament

When our twin girls (nonidentical twins) were about 6 months old, our good friends Steve and Sue volunteered to baby-sit to give us a much needed break. After about 2 hours of quiet dinner and conversation, we returned home to an interesting sight. One of the twins, Lily, was playing on the couch with Steve and Sue. She was bouncing on their laps, giggling, and generally enjoying the attention heaped on her by two loving adults. The other twin, Rachel, was gently rocking back and forth in an infant swing, but the swing was facing the wall!

Although our friends had visited several times before, Rachel was still not comfortable interacting with them without her parents around. She had become upset and cried for quite some time after we left. Our friends are very knowledgeable and experienced with parenting and children. After trying all the standard techniques to comfort Rachel, they came up with a resourceful and effective solution. They settled her in the swing (a familiar and comforting place), turned the swing so Rachel couldn't see these less-familiar adults, and coached our 7-year-old son (Rachel's familiar and comforting older brother) in playing with her. It worked. By the time we got home, Rachel wasn't crying—though she sure seemed glad to see us when we walked in.

How can we explain the extremely different reactions shown by our twin girls? As recently as the 1970s, many child development theorists thought that infants entered the world as "blank slates" and that most of their behaviors and reactions were the result of parenting and other experiences (Foreman, 1995). Had we really treated our daughters so differently in their first few months? Unlikely. Anyone who has spent considerable time with infants recognizes that babies come into the world with their own behavioral styles or dispositions. Some are more sociable and outgoing and smile frequently. Others are more shy, afraid, or reluctant to engage in new situations. Today, researchers refer to the infant and child's behavioral style, or primary pattern of reacting to the environment, as **temperament.** In this section we describe the most widely accepted classifications of temperament and discuss the practical reasons to understand this important characteristic.

As you study this section, ask yourself these questions:

- What are the behavioral dimensions that indicate a person's temperament?
- What main temperamental styles have researchers identified?
- How do different temperaments form? To what extent do nature and nurture influence temperament?
- How can parents, teachers, counselors, and others use information about temperament to interact more effectively with infants and children?

Classifying Infant Temperaments

The most widely accepted method of classifying temperaments is the system developed by two psychiatrists, Alexander Thomas and Stella Chess (1977; Chess & Thomas, 1995). In 1956 Thomas and Chess began an extensive longitudinal study with 141 children from 85 New York families. Later they added several hundred children of working-class Puerto Rican parents and children born prematurely or with physical, neurological, or intellectual handicaps. The study has followed most of these children well into adulthood. Based on detailed interviews with the parents, Thomas and Chess identified nine temperament dimensions that seemed to capture the diverse behavior patterns exhibited among the infants, as shown in Table 9.5. A child can receive a high, medium, or low score on each dimension. Together the scores create a profile of the child's primary pattern of reacting to the environment.

YOUR PERSPECTIVE NOTES

Looking at these three types of temperaments and at the dimensions listed in Table 9.5, how would you rate your temperament?

temperament

The infant or child's behavioral style or primary pattern of reacting to the environment.

TABLE 9.5 Nine Temperament Dimensions

TEMPERAMENT DIMENSION	DEFINITION
1. Activity level	Degree of motor activity during daily activities such as bathing, eating, playing, and dressing: How *active* is the infant?
2. Rhythmicity	Degree of predictability/unpredictability in sleep, feeding, elimination, and other schedules: How *predictable and regular* are the infant's schedules?
3. Approach or withdrawal	Degree of positive or negative response to a new stimulus: When the infant is presented with a new person, situation, or toy, how *positive or negative* is the infant's first response?
4. Adaptability	Ease with which the infant modifies his or her responses in a desirable way when confronted with new or changing situations: How well does the infant *adapt to change*?
5. Threshold of responsiveness	Intensity level of stimulation that is needed to cause a response: How strong does the new situation need to be to *cause a change* in the infant's behavior?
6. Intensity of reaction	Energy level of the response: How *intense* is the infant's response?
7. Quality of mood	Amount of pleasant or unpleasant response: How *joyful or friendly* is the infant's response?
8. Distractibility	Degree to which environmental stimuli interfere with ongoing behavior: How *distracted* is the infant?
9. Attention span and persistence	Degree to which the infant pursues and continues an activity, even in the face of obstacles: How long does the infant *continue activities;* how well does the infant *overcome obstacles* in continuing activities?

Source: Adapted from Thomas & Chess (1977).

Using the nine dimensions, Thomas and Chess (1977) identified three constellations of temperament that are particularly significant:

▶ The **easy child** is primarily positive, smiles easily, has a positive and flexible approach to new situations, adapts to change, and quickly develops regular patterns of eating and sleeping.

▶ The **difficult child** is frequently negative and easily frustrated, withdraws from new situations, is slow to adapt to change, and shows irregular patterns of eating and sleeping.

▶ The **slow-to-warm-up child** displays mildly negative responses to new stimuli and situations, but with repeated exposure gradually develops a quiet and positive interest. Compared to difficult children, these children have less intense emotional reactions and more regular eating and sleeping schedules.

In Thomas and Chess's original longitudinal sample, 40 percent of the children were "easy," 10 percent were "difficult," and 15 percent were "slow to warm up." The remaining 35 percent did not fall neatly into any of these three categories, instead showing their own constellations of temperament dimensions. In some cases a particular dimension—such as an extremely high activity level, high distractibility, or poor attention span—dominated a child's temperament.

■ **How Do Different Temperaments Form?** What shapes temperament? Thomas and Chess (1977) proposed an interactionist model emphasizing the complementary forces of nature and nurture. As we saw in Chapter 2, behavior geneticists have come up with moderately high heritability estimates for temperament and personality. For example, for traits such as activity level, anxiety, emotionality, sociability, task orientation, and control, heritability estimates range from about .40 to .70 (see Table 2.4 in Chapter 2). This means that 40 to 70 percent of the variation in these traits across the population is related to genetics—a substantial contribution. So infants are born with innate tendencies that can be reinforced, channeled, or frustrated by parents, the family, and the larger environment. For example, one family may see a child with a high activity level as "trouble," whereas another family may label such a child

easy child
A child who is primarily positive, smiles easily, is adaptive and flexible, and has regular patterns of eating and sleeping.

difficult child
A child who is frequently negative, is easily frustrated, withdraws from new situations, is slow to adapt to change, and shows irregular patterns of eating and sleeping.

slow-to-warm-up child
A child who shows mildly negative responses to new stimuli and situations but with repeated exposure gradually develops a quiet and positive interest.

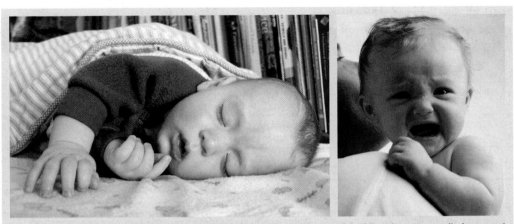

As all parents quickly learn, some infants are more easy-going and peaceful while others are easily frustrated and difficult. Researchers believe that infants are born with a basic temperament—a style of reacting to new situations and stimuli.

"vigorous." With warm and supportive parenting, an active child may learn self-control; harsh and punitive parenting, however, might lead the same child toward aggression (Rubin, Burgess, Dwyer, & Hastings, 2003). Adaptation is bidirectional: Parents adapt to the activity level of the child, and the child adapts to the parents' expectations and constraints. Also recall from Chapter 2 that the philosophical orientation of a whole society may have a relationship to the predominant temperament expressed in that particular gene pool (Kagan, Arcus, & Snidman, 1993; Kagan et al., 1994). The emphasis on serenity and harmony in Asian cultures, for example, may be an expression of a predominant temperament that in turn influences how parents and society treat children. Nature and nurture interact to facilitate some characteristics of temperament and suppress others. "It is a constantly evolving dynamic, as the child and family and society change over time" (Thomas & Chess, 1977, p. 68).

■ **Goodness of Fit.** As children mature, the key factor in their developmental outcomes will be what Thomas and Chess call the **goodness of fit** between their temperaments and their environments (Chess & Thomas, 1995). Healthy development occurs when a child and his or her environment are compatible. Highly active children, for example, will fare better when their parents are on the outgoing side and value physical activity. Conversely, a poor fit can impair development. Parents who are more reserved may not respond well to highly active children, and slow-to-warm-up children may not adapt well with parents who tend to rush them into new situations. When incompatibilities are severe, behavior disorders can emerge in the child (Chess & Thomas, 1995). Characteristics of the child and parent don't necessarily need to match to provide a good fit, however. Sometimes good fits are complementary, as when a highly reactive child benefits from the calming influence of parents who are reflective, flexible, and patient. Good fits are important outside the family as well. Compatibility with peers, teachers, coworkers, and spouses becomes important as the child grows into adulthood. And one culture may approve of active and assertive children, whereas another may view such children as rude and disrespectful.

To see how one parent provided a good fit for her difficult child, read the Personal Perspective box called "Meet the Parent of a Difficult Child."

■ **Consistency over Time.** Measures of temperament are not highly consistent over time. As with most other personality variables, numerous factors can influence temperament (or the behaviors that indicate temperament). With children in their longitudinal study, Thomas

thinking
OF ERIN

How can Erin find a day care setting that will provide a "good fit" for Patrick's temperament? What factors should she and other parents consider?

goodness of fit

The degree to which a child's temperament and environment are compatible or complementary, leading to better developmental outcomes.

Meet the Parent of a Difficult Child

Mary Jane
Portland, Maine

Mother of Maria (15 years old), Rocco (13), John (9), and Maggie (3)

Describe your child's basic temperament (mood, behavior, outlook on life).

My concern is John. John has been challenging since he was 6 or 7 years old. He is quite moody, and mostly my concern is with his anger and lack of self-esteem. It seems to me that he has never quite felt that he is "talented or good at anything." Most concerning to me was John's recent comment that there was nothing on this earth for him; it was boring and he hated it here.

Can you describe recent examples of John's behavior that concern you?
An example is playing family card games. When John loses, he becomes enraged, hitting and kicking everyone else involved. He also has a hard time with sudden changes in schedule. If we announce we are going for ice cream, John will be angry and refuse to go, or if he went he wouldn't have any ice cream because no one asked if that was what he wanted to do. John loves to play computer games, but when we ask him to leave the game he almost always ends up yelling loudly, stomping around, and being sent to his room.

How have you helped John? Can you give specific examples?
We did a little counseling to deal with the anger, and it was beneficial. The only way to get John to talk is to wait and go in with a positive attitude. I sit and talk to him (for over an hour sometimes) and validate that I understand that he feels badly.

During this time I make sure we have complete privacy (no other children barging in!), and it usually ends nicely with him telling me how glad he is that we talked and could we please do it again. I try to plan something special just with him monthly, a hike or going out to a café for cocoa and cookies, etcetera. I really think time with a parent or grandparent once a week can be great therapy. I try to support him by showing him how much he is loved and cared for. ■

thinking
OF ERIN

◄ What would Erin need to do differently if Patrick had a more difficult temperament?

and Chess repeatedly collected measures on each of the nine temperament dimensions listed in Table 9.5. When comparing measures taken 1 year apart, the researchers found reliable correlations for six out of the nine dimensions. But only one dimension (threshold of responsiveness) showed a reliable correlation when measures were taken 4 years apart (Chess & Thomas, 1995). One reason for this variability is that the ways children express temperament can change over time. As children mature, they develop insight into their own temperaments, and they can use this self-awareness to adapt to their environments. A girl may realize, "I'm shy, but I'm not a pushover." She therefore may assert herself more in social situations. A boy may recognize that "I'm excitable, but I know the warning signs" and therefore may show more self-control. In both cases, the children's behavioral output may belie their true internal temperament. In some ways our temperaments change as we adapt to our environments, but in other ways we learn to control how we express our temperaments. Both processes cause the outward measures of temperament to change across time.

Other Approaches to Temperament

In addition to Thomas and Chess's classification system, several other temperament assessment methods exist.

■ **Rothbart's Temperament Dimensions for Infants and Children.** Mary Rothbart (1981) developed an instrument called the *infant behavior questionnaire*, which asks parents

YOUR PERSPECTIVE ~~PERSPECTIVE~~
NOTES
In what ways has your temperament changed over the years? In what ways do you think it is still the same as in your early childhood? How have you shaped the way you express your temperament to adapt to your environment?

to report the frequency of specific behaviors shown by their infants, ages 3 to 12 months. An advantage of this method of assessing temperament is that it yields useful information quickly; it does not require extensive interviews. The questionnaire includes 96 items. One example: "During the past week, when being undressed, how often did your baby smile or laugh?" Parents respond along a six-point scale that ranges from "never" to "always." The original questionnaire scored six dimensions of temperament: *activity level, smiling and laughter, fear, frustration, soothability,* and *duration of orienting.* The revised version now scores 14 dimensions (Rothbart, 2001). If you compare these dimensions to the ones in Table 9.5, you'll see that there is considerable overlap with the Thomas and Chess system. Among Rothbart's dimensions, activity level and smiling and laughter show the greatest stability across the first year of life. The other dimensions show only minimal consistency.

Rothbart developed other questionnaires to measure temperament in children from 18 months to 15 years of age and in adults ("Infant Behavior Questionnaire," n.d.; Rothbart, Ahadi, & Hershey, 1994). The *children's behavior questionnaire,* for example, uses parental reports to measure three broad factors in children ages 3 to 7 years. *Surgency* has to do with activity level, sensation seeking, and approach. *Negative affectivity* involves discomfort, fear, anger, and sadness. *Effortful control* emphasizes children's ability to focus attention, inhibit behavior, and process perceptual information. These measures of childhood temperament have correlations with both positive and negative aspects of social development (Rothbart, Ahadi, & Hershey, 1994). Parents who rate their children high in surgency, for example, also report more aggression in their children. Children rated higher in effortful control, however, seem to show more understanding of others' feelings and to feel more guilt and shame when they commit inappropriate acts.

■ **Kagan's Work with Shy Children.** An aspect of temperament that has received considerable research attention is shyness. Longitudinal research conducted by Harvard University psychologist Jerome Kagan (1994, 1997) provides interesting insights about children who

This child is very shy. How might shyness be related to thresholds of arousal in the brain? How did shy children react to unfamiliar stimuli when they were infants?

are extremely shy. In one study, Kagan presented 16-week-old infants with unfamiliar stimuli such as strong odors, unfamiliar voices, or brightly colored toys waved in front of their faces. About 20 percent of the infants reacted strongly, flailing their arms and legs or crying. By 1 to 2 years of age, one-third of these reactive infants were very fearful in other laboratory situations, and by 4 years they were very shy and inhibited. As adolescents they were at increased risk for developing *social phobia*—an intense and irrational fear of social situations. Kagan surmises that these children had a genetic predisposition to shyness. He points to the limbic system and the hypothalamus, two structures in the brain that process environmental changes and new stimulation. Shy children, Kagan argues, have low thresholds for arousal in these systems (Woodward et al., 2001). In other words, it doesn't take much stimulation to arouse fear states in these children. In the face of unfamiliar situations, their heart rates accelerate more than other children's do. Even when they are asleep, they still show higher heart rates than other children (Kagan, Reznick, & Snidman, 1988). As they grow into childhood, shy children learn to back away from social situations and other events that are highly stimulating for them.

thinking OF ERIN

◄ If Patrick was very shy, what adjustments could Erin and his day care providers make to help Patrick cope with his new situation?

What about the other extreme? In Kagan's study about 40 percent of infants reacted calmly to unfamiliar odors, voices, and colored toys. They remained relatively still and were not distressed. Presumably the new stimuli were not strong enough to arouse fear reactions in these infants—the infants had higher arousal thresholds. At 1 to 2 years of age, these children were not afraid of new laboratory situations, and as 4-year-olds they tended to be sociable and talkative and smiled frequently. Kagan did warn, however, that children with extremely high arousal thresholds might seek intense or dangerous activities. In a small percentage of cases this inclination might lead to problem behaviors, delinquency, or even violence (Kagan, 1997). Proper socialization and positive role models can help steer such children away from thrill seeking with risk-prone peers or in dangerous circumstances.

Appreciating Temperamental Differences

Thomas and Chess, Rothbart, Kagan, and other researchers have provided valuable systems for classifying and understanding temperament in infants and children. From the earliest months, infants show consistent individual differences in how they respond to their surroundings. Some infants approach new things and new people as if they want to explore and learn more. Others withdraw. Some are hesitant at first but gradually warm up. To some extent these early tendencies carry through into childhood, affecting children's social interactions. Some children have a low tolerance for unfamiliar stimuli, and they often become very shy. Others have high arousal thresholds and may seek intense and thrilling experiences.

Children are not all alike, and we cannot treat them all alike. Think back to our twin baby daughters. Lily enjoyed the bouncing, hugs, and kisses showered on her by our friends. With Rachel, however, this same treatment would have been a mistake. Steve and Sue recognized this and adapted their approach to provide a better fit for her temperament, thus demonstrating sensitive responsiveness. Recognizing different temperaments and providing a good fit is important for parents, teachers, day care providers, counselors, and anyone else who works closely with infants and children. Children will react differently to us depending on their own temperaments. Temperament also acts as a filter for processing information. Children who are more outgoing, sociable, and positive in their outlook will differ from children who are more shy and withdrawn in how they process current experiences, how they remember the past, and what they expect from the future. By recognizing these differences and making the appropriate adjustments, we can foster the healthy emotional development of each child.

1. The most widely accepted system for classifying infant temperaments is the one developed by:
   a. Mary Rothbart.   b. Jerome Kagan.   c. John Bowlby.   d. Alexander Thomas and Stella Chess.

2. Healthy development occurs when there is compatibility between the child's temperament and the surrounding environment. This statement summarizes the concept of:
   a. goodness of fit.
   b. genetic–environmental interaction.
   c. longitudinal consistency.
   d. effortful control of temperament.

3. Jerome Kagan believes that extreme shyness in children can be traced to:
   a. fear and anxiety shown by parents in social situations.
   b. the punishments children receive from peers and parents.
   c. low thresholds of arousal in the limbic system and hypothalamus.
   d. a dysfunction in the pituitary gland that causes a lack of energy and enthusiasm.

4. **True or False:** Compared to children with "difficult" temperaments, children who are "slow to warm up" have less intense emotional reactions and more regular eating and sleeping schedules.

5. **True or False:** Surgency, negative affectivity, and effortful control are three of the dimensions that Thomas and Chess use to identify infant temperaments.

Answers: 1. d, 2. a, 3. c, 4. T, 5. F

Emotion

We began this chapter with a discussion of attachment—the first emotional relationship infants form with their caregivers. We now end the chapter by exploring a few of the other topics researchers investigate in the realm of *emotion,* or feelings. How do children develop their ability to understand and express emotions? In this section we look at the beginnings of emotional discrimination: the moment when, for example, infants are first able to see that happy faces look different from sad ones. We also describe the early phases of emotional expression in infants. As children develop further, they begin to understand that their emotions are their own personal reactions to events and that other people's emotions may differ. Finally, we ask how parenting influences emotional development in children. Do children learn positive emotional skills from parents? What happens when parents lack emotional control themselves?

As you study this section, ask yourself these questions:

• What are some of the first emotional reactions of newborn infants?

• When are infants able to tell different emotional expressions apart? How do we know what kinds of information infants get from others' emotional expressions?

• How do children differentiate their own emotions from the emotions of people around them?

• What are the effects on a child's emotional development if the child has depressed or abusive parents?

Infants' Responses to Emotions

Immediately after birth, newborn infants are responsive to certain emotional cues displayed by people around them. Visit any hospital nursery and you will notice that when one newborn starts crying, they all start crying. This phenomenon is referred to as **emotion contagion**— the tendency of the emotional cues displayed by one person to generate similar cues or emotional states in other people. For newborns, some types of cries are more contagious than others. Newborns are more likely to cry when they hear other newborns cry than when they hear recordings of their own cry, of older infants' cries, or of artificially produced crying sounds (Martin & Clark, 1982; Sagi & Hoffman, 1976; Simner, 1971).

Newborns also can produce facial expressions that mimic the expressions of adults who are displaying various emotions. In the photos in Figure 9.2, the young infant imitates the adult's happy, sad, and surprised expressions remarkably well (Field, Woodson, Greenberg,

emotion contagion

The tendency of the emotional cues displayed by one person to generate similar cues or emotional states in other people.

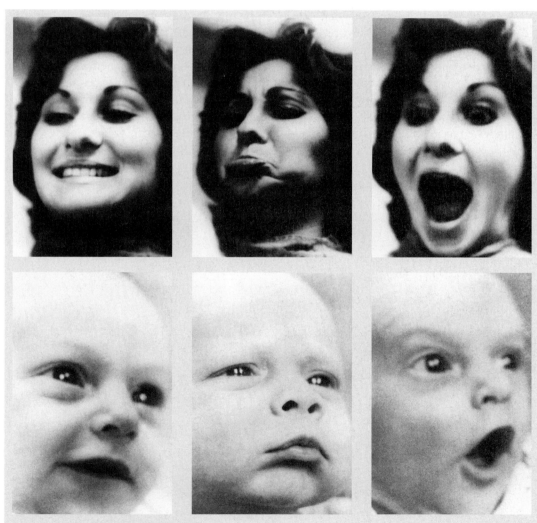

FIGURE 9.2 Adult and Baby Facial Expressions
This newborn baby is imitating the facial expressions made by the adult model. Although they cannot see their own faces, newborns are capable of matching facial movements made by others.

& Cohen, 1982). Newborns can also imitate adults when the adults open their mouths, move their heads, and stick out their tongues (Meltzoff & Moore, 1983, 1989). In one study researchers asked mothers to make facial expressions and speak in ways that showed joy, sadness, and anger (Haviland & Lelwica, 1987). The mothers' 10-week-old infants responded differently to each of these emotions. The infants showed more joy and interest when their mothers were joyful. They made "mouthing" movements when their mothers were sad. They showed less interest and less movement when their mothers showed anger. Other researchers have found that 2-month-olds respond differently to happy faces than to faces showing no emotion at all (Nelson & Horowitz, 1983), and that 5-month-olds can tell the differences among anger, sadness, and fear (Schwartz, Izard, & Ansul, 1985). Infants can discriminate among facial expressions at a young age, however, they seem to rely even more on vocal expressions for determining emotions (Saarni, Mumme, & Campos, 1998).

Even if infants can tell different emotional expressions apart, do they understand what the different expressions mean? Evidence suggests that the answer is yes: Infants as young as 4 months of age can understand the basic emotions behind facial expressions, including joy, anger, surprise, and sadness (Montague & Walker-Andrews, 2001). By 12 months of age, the evidence is even clearer. Consider a clever study that used the visual cliff we described in Chapter 4 (see Figure 4.16) (Sorce, Emde, Campos, & Klinnert, 1985). The researchers placed 12-month-old infants on the shallow side of the cliff and put an attractive toy at the other end of the deep side. As infants approached the deep side, they looked up at their mothers—who had been instructed to show a joyful, interested, sad, angry, or fearful face. As Figure 9.3 shows, none of the infants crossed the deep side when the mothers showed fear. A few crossed when their mothers looked angry or sad, but many more crossed when the mothers appeared interested or joyful. These infants were doing more than just discriminating among various

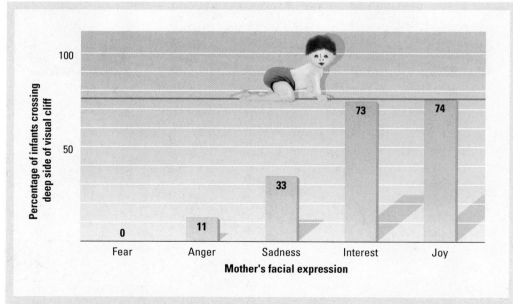

FIGURE 9.3 Infants' Readings of Facial Expressions

When 12-month-old infants were deciding whether to cross the deep side of the visual cliff, they relied on the facial expression made by their mothers. Infants did not cross when their mothers looked afraid, and they were reluctant when mothers looked angry or sad. Most of the infants did cross when mothers looked interested or joyful.

Source: Data from Sorce, Emde, Campos, & Klinnert (1985).

facial expressions: They were using the expressions to get information to guide their behavior. Trusting their mothers, they crossed the deep side when their mothers showed positive emotions, but they were reluctant or refused to cross when the mothers showed negative emotions.

Emotions communicate important information about the environment, and infants learn at an early age to use their parents' emotions as a guide in uncertain situations. When strangers approach, for example, infants often look to their parents for a cue. If the parent speaks to the stranger in a friendly manner, the infant reacts more positively to the stranger (Boccia & Campos, 1989; Feinman & Lewis, 1983). If the parent looks worried, the infant reacts more negatively. And a study conducted more recently showed that 12-month-old infants can even read the negative reactions of people they see on television (Mumme & Fernald, 2003). Researchers created a videotape of an actress viewing two objects (e.g., a bumpy ball and a garden hose connector). The actress showed a negative reaction to one of the objects—turning her head away, gasping, and showing a fearful facial expression. What did the infants do? They showed negative facial expressions when the actress did and, when given both objects to play with, infants avoided the one that the actress seemed to dislike. These and other studies demonstrate that, by the time they reach their first birthdays, infants are capable of reading and understanding something about the emotions expressed by other people. So even before they understand a spoken language, infants are already receiving messages through the language of emotion.

social smile
Smile in which infants show joy in interacting with their caregivers. Emerges at around 6 weeks of age.

self-conscious emotions
Emotions that relate to our self-images or what we think about ourselves; includes shame, embarrassment, pride, and guilt.

Emergence of Basic Emotions

We know infants are happy when we see those beautiful smiles spread across their faces. During their first weeks, newborns' smiles are usually associated with pleasurable physical sensations such as a full tummy, rocking, gentle strokes and touches, and the mother's soft voice. By the first month, interesting sights begin to produce smiles, especially if they involve objects that are eye-catching and fast moving. It's as if the infant's smile means, "Hey, I saw that!" By 6 weeks, the **social smile** emerges—infants smile to show joy in interacting with their caregivers. To see a great social smile, look back at the photo on page 331. Social smiles, cooing, and flailing arms and legs are signs that the infant is having a happy time with you. Laughter usually emerges at around 14 weeks, elicited by activities like tickling and "I'm gonna get you!" or peekaboo games. Anger and sadness follow a similar developmental pattern. They begin with uncomfortable bodily sensations such as hunger, pain, changes in body temperature, or too little or too much sensory stimulation. After about 4 weeks, unpleasant social situations can upset an infant. Taking a toy away, leaving the baby, or putting the baby down for a rest are all examples of interactions that can cause the baby to cry. *Stranger anxiety,* discussed earlier in this chapter, is one of the first fears infants show, usually around 7 months of age.

After the first year **self-conscious emotions** begin to emerge. These are emotions related to our thoughts about ourselves—about how our thoughts and behaviors relate to our images of who we are and who we should be. For example, shame, embarrassment, and pride emerge around 18 to 24 months.

"Oops. I made a mess!" Shame is a self-conscious emotion that emerges around 18 to 24 months of age. Children begin to reflect on who they are and who they should be.

Envy and guilt are evident by 3 years. Because self-conscious emotions relate to moral and ethical values, they show a great deal of cultural variability. Children raised in individualistic cultures such as that of the United States, for example, tend to show pride in their own individual achievements. In collectivistic cultures such as that of Japan, in contrast, individual achievement can be a source of shame or embarrassment; children take pride in group success or in their contributions to the good of the greater group.

Personalized Emotions: Understanding That Feelings Can Differ

During the first 6 months or so of life, infants don't fully understand that they are separate from other people and do not yet reflect on themselves as separate individuals. In research terms, they don't make the *self–other distinction*. Consequently, their emotions often echo the emotional states of their caregivers and other people (Saarni, Mumme, & Campos, 1998); cry contagion and imitation of facial expressions are examples. Later, as children develop the capacity for self-reflection, they begin to appreciate that their emotions are their own personal responses to the situations and events around them. For example, they understand that they can enjoy a toy or TV show even if their friends don't, or that they may be more afraid of thunderstorms than their siblings or friends. We'll explore more about the development of the sense of self in the next chapter, but for now let's look at how personal understanding of emotions emerges in early childhood.

By age 2, children are talking spontaneously about their feelings and the feelings of other people (Saarni, Mumme, & Campos, 1998). They are also becoming aware that their emotional reactions may differ from other people's. A child's emerging *theory of mind* (see Chapter 6) helps the child understand individual differences in emotions. By 2 to 3 years of age, children understand that emotions are connected to our mental appraisals of what we want, like, don't want, and don't like (Wellman, Harris, Banerjee, & Sinclair, 1995). By the age of 5, children's understandings are more dynamic—they understand that events that confirm or disconfirm their beliefs or expectations can trigger emotions. If they think they "should" get a treat, they expect that they will be pleased, happy, or satisfied when they receive one. If they get an unexpected treat, they understand that surprise can result. Anger and sadness, however, can follow when expectations are not met. And because our beliefs, expectations, likes, dislikes, and other mental appraisals differ, we each have our own emotional reactions to events. By middle childhood children understand these individual responses.

As children begin to understand the individualized nature of emotions, they tend to see and report their own positive emotions more than their negative emotions—to show a **positive emotion bias** (Saarni, Mumme, & Campos, 1998). For example, if you describe a hypothetical scenario, 6-year-olds predict a more positive emotional reaction for themselves than for other children (Karniol & Koren, 1987). And 5-year-olds are less likely than 7-year-olds to report being sad (Glasberg & Aboud, 1982). Maybe adults seem to value happiness in children so much that younger children bow to the social pressure, exaggerating their positive emotions and denying or minimizing sadness and other negative emotions. Boys in particular seem to get a message to hide sadness, and they become more skilled at veiling this emotion as they mature. In one study boys and girls expressed sadness about equally at age 6 (Fuchs & Thelen, 1988). By age 9, however, a clear gender difference appeared, and by age 11 boys were only half as likely as girls to express sad feelings. Further, boys reported that they would be less likely to communicate their sadness to their fathers than to their mothers. Boys seem to learn that sadness is not socially accepted for males. Another aspect of the positive emotion

YOUR PERSPECTIVE NOTES

What examples of the positive emotion bias have you seen recently in children or in adults? Why do you think that boys and girls differ in their expression of emotions?

positive emotion bias

Tendency of children to report positive more than negative emotions.

358 | *Chapter 9*   *Attachment, Temperament, and Emotion*   www.ablongman.com/cook1e

bias is that children are more accurate in recognizing other people's positive emotions and less accurate in recognizing negative emotions (Fabes, Eisenberg, Nyman, & Michealieu, 1991; Gross & Ballif, 1991).

Parenting and Emotional Competence

Accuracy in reading emotions is an important social skill. Children who are adept at reading emotions tend to be liked more by their peers (Denham, McKinley, Couchoud, & Holt, 1990). They know when they are making their friends happy, when to back off if their friends become frustrated, and when to console friends who are sad or dejected. Also, children tend to like other children who are happy and know how to control their emotions. As one group of researchers put it, "feeling good . . . makes it easier for a child to enter the peer world" and "greases the cogs of ongoing social interaction" (Denham et al., 2003, p. 251).

Children who learn positive emotional skills from their parents seem to have more success making friends. The children of emotionally expressive mothers tend to receive high regard from their peers (Cassidy, Parke, Butkovsky, & Braungart, 1992). And an interesting longitudinal study linked adults' levels of empathy (ability to feel other people's emotions) with childhood experiences. The study found that when empathetic adults were children, their fathers were more involved in their care and their mothers were more tolerant of dependent behavior, were more likely to restrict the children's aggression, and were more satisfied in their role as mothers (Koestner, Franz, & Weinberger, 1990). You can imagine that parents who fit this description would tend to model positive control of emotions for their children.

This child is happy because he anticipates that he will enjoy what is inside the present. By age 5, children's emotions can be triggered by what they expect or believe will happen.

Of course, the reverse is also true. Children of mothers who are chronically depressed, for example, are prone to feelings of guilt and helplessness. Although they try hard to make their mothers feel happy, they cannot succeed, and they often believe it is their fault (Zahn-Waxler & Robinson, 1995). As one review of the literature on emotional development concluded, "Not surprisingly, depressed parents tend to have children who later also show depressive tendencies" (Saarni, Mumme, & Campos, 1998, p. 269). Even more alarming are the emotional patterns shown by children who are abused. Main and George (1985) observed how toddlers (1 to 3 years old) responded in situations in which other children were crying or showing distress. Nonabused children responded with interest, concern, empathy, or sadness. None of the abused children showed this pattern, however. Instead, abused children tended to react with fear, anger, and sometimes even hostility toward their distressed peers. Rather than comforting crying children, some of the abused children actually attacked them. From the transcripts of their behaviors, it seems that the abused children did not know how to respond effectively to the other children's distress. After making ineffective attempts to interact, they often lashed out. Apparently their interactions with their abusive parents had taught them negative rather than positive ways of dealing with other people's emotions.

Career Focus: Meet a Licensed Counselor Working with Children

Heidi D. Weipert, MA

Muskegon, Michigan

Licensed professional counselor; national certified counselor; Crisis Center Director, Every Woman's Place

Describe the most frequent emotional problems you see in children and adolescents.

I work in a domestic and sexual violence safe haven and also have a private practice where I counsel children and adolescents. When they witness violence, boys often display "batterer" symptoms: anger, aggression, frustration, hyperactivity, unwillingness to share or work with others, and denial. Girls more often show "victim" symptoms: withdrawal, worry, grief, helplessness, sadness, developmental regression, flat affect, and an inability to trust others. Typically, the boys are more likely to assault the counselor or toys and act out violent scenes they have witnessed. Girls are more withdrawn and participate most often in art therapy.

In the shelter, children show sleeplessness, grief for their home or possessions, lack of appetite, or increased need for affection. They are anxious and uncertain of their situa-

tion and futures. In the shelter they can play and interact with their safe parent, siblings, and other families without the threat of physical or emotional violence. The shelter provides a safe place for children to be children . . . and children are sometimes sad to leave their new safe "home."

How do you help children cope with their emotions?

Children in crisis are most afraid of the unknown. The first step is to give them information, so I explain why they are there and what they can expect in the shelter. Then I encourage them to show what their fears or concerns are. From there, we discuss their fears, determine how they have coped in the past, and problem-solve new ways to cope. Then I help the safe parent learn the child's coping tools to support and encourage the child.

The most successful counseling tool I use is the "safe box"—a box of items the child can keep and use as reminders for how to cope. For example, the box can have paper and crayons the child can use to convey thoughts and feelings when talking is difficult, or a special teddy bear to soothe them and help them sleep.

Do you see any common elements in the backgrounds of children who suffer emotional disturbances?

When trauma or crisis occurs, children respond emotionally, and emo-

tional disturbances can affect children of all backgrounds. It is the support, counseling, and unconditional love from safe parents, counselors, family, and friends that aid in repairing emotional disturbances.

What training is necessary to work in your field?

As Crisis Center Director, I am required to have a master's degree in a human service–related field and a state license to conduct counseling sessions.

NOTE: Heidi Weipert's private practice (Children First) is 100 percent donated to the community, providing services for indigent families who cannot afford counseling and advocacy. She also founded the Children's Counseling Interest Network, a special group within the American Counseling Association devoted to professionals working on behalf of children. For more information, go to www.counseling.org. ■

thinking OF ERIN

◄ Describe the positive things that Erin did to help Patrick cope with his emotions on his first morning at the day care center.

As Saarni and colleagues put it, "Young children rely on adults to provide safe environments such that their ability to cope [with negative emotions] is not overwhelmed . . . and caregivers provide direct teaching of coping strategies as well as modeling how to cope" (1998, p. 286). When children do not have these supports, they run the risk of developing emotional disturbances. To learn more about how professionals work to help these children, read the Professional Perspective box called "Career Focus: Meet a Licensed Counselor Working with Children."

Before ending this section, we also want to point out that according to recent research, children sometimes have difficulty reading the emotions expressed by people from ethnic backgrounds other than their own. For example, one group of researchers showed children photographs of adult and child actors who were making happy, sad, angry, and fearful faces (Collins & Nowicki, 2001). Most of the people in the photographs were European American actors. When asked to name the emotions shown in the photographs, African American children (around 10 years of age) made more mistakes than did European American children. African American children also had more difficulty judging emotions from tones of voice when European American adults were speaking. In another study Canadian children (all white and varying in age from about 5 to 10 years) identified the emotion of disgust more accurately when it was shown by white actors than when it was expressed by Asian actors (Gosselin & Larocque, 2000). A surprising finding, however, was that these same children identified the emotions of fear and surprise more accurately when demonstrated by the Asian actors. The researchers speculated that ethnic groups differ somewhat in the extent to which they lower their eyebrows, stretch their lips, wrinkle their noses, and make other facial movements when expressing emotions. Some of these patterns of movement are easier to see in Asian faces, for example; other patterns may be more apparent when expressed by whites of European descent. When interacting with other people, we need to read their emotions accurately so we can respond appropriately. These studies, however, remind us that there may be ethnic group differences in how people express and interpret emotions.

Tying It Together: Attachment, Temperament, and Emotional Development

In their review of the research literature on emotional development, Saarni and colleagues (1998) commented that "the emotional attunement between parent and baby is essentially the crucible in which empathy and concern for others' well-being are forged" (p. 275). In this chapter we have looked at how attachment relationships form early in life between infants and their primary caregivers. The quality of these interactions during the first year of life sets the stage for later emotional development. In their early relationships infants and children form their own understandings of how social relationships should proceed and what to expect from other people. The child's temperament also plays a role, as each child's basic style of interacting with the environment influences the pace and tone of social interactions. Under optimal circumstances, children enjoy the benefits of secure attachment relationships with loving parents, and parents provide a good fit for their child's temperament and positive role models for expressing and coping with emotions. The research evidence suggests that such children will get along well with peers and will have the tools to establish positive and healthy relationships throughout life. Unfortunately, however, a great many children do not experience optimal circumstances. Parents, teachers, counselors, and others who work with children need to understand the many factors that may influence how children respond in social situations. Children with insecure attachments may require extra assurance that adults can be trusted. Children with active temperaments have different needs than children who are extremely shy. And many children may need help in coping with emotions in a positive way rather than reacting with fear, anger, or hostility. Understanding the individual and collective influences of attachment, temperament, and emotion can help each of us work more effectively with the children in our lives.

1. Newborn babies are most likely to start crying when they hear:
    a. another newborn baby cry.
    b. an older child cry.
    c. a recording of their own crying.
    d. a recording of their mother crying.

2. Children tend to predict that their emotional reactions will be more positive than the emotions of other children, and they are better at identifying positive than negative emotions in other people. This pattern is part of the:
    a. positive theory of mind.
    b. positive self-other distinction.
    c. positive emotion bias.
    d. emotional contagion effect.

3. Research conducted with children who have abusive parents indicates that:
    a. children tend to adopt the emotional behaviors they observe in their parents.
    b. children with abusive parents tend to become very shy and withdrawn.
    c. children with abusive parents show increased interest and concern for distress in peers.
    d. these children are prone to developing feelings of guilt and helplessness.

4. **True or False:** Infants cannot imitate the facial expressions that they see in other people until they are approximately 6 months of age.

5. **True or False:** As children develop their "theory of mind," they begin to understand that their emotions are connected to their appraisals of what they like, don't like, want, and don't want.

Answers: 1. a, 2. c, 3. a, 4. F, 5. T

thinking
BACK TO ERIN

Now that you have studied this chapter, you should be able to help Erin understand Patrick's behavior on his first morning at day care. You should begin by explaining how Patrick's reactions reveal his attachment to his mother. By clinging to his mother in his new environment, and by showing both stranger and separation anxiety, Patrick is demonstrating that he is attached to a specific other person—his mother. Erin can help by letting Patrick see her interact in a friendly manner with the staff, signaling to Patrick that they are safe.

You should also discuss with Erin the research on day care and attachment. Many parents worry that day care may disrupt their child's attachment to them. Some research suggests that full-time day care can reduce attachment, but only if it is combined with parenting that is not sensitive or responsive. The majority of infants in day care still show secure attachments to their mothers, and Patrick's attachment to Erin is even more likely to be secure if Erin is sensitive and responsive when caring for Patrick.

Erin should also consider Patrick's temperament. Based on the few details provided in the opening vignette, it does not appear that Patrick is a difficult child. He may be slow to warm up; recall that he did eventually begin to play with toys and books when he visited the day care center's open house. If Patrick is very shy, the day care staff should introduce him gradually to the busy schedule and activities of the day care center, doing what they can to reduce his level of arousal. Erin should also work to find a day care center that provides a good fit for Patrick's temperament.

Erin did several things to try to help Patrick cope with the emotion of his first day. She took Patrick to the open house so he could familiarize himself with the new setting, she spoke cheerfully about day care, and she comforted him as they entered the center. Although she herself was upset, she modeled good emotional control for Patrick. Rather than making a big scene, she eventually just kissed him and said good-bye. Children who are as young as Patrick need considerable help in coping with strong emotions. It seems that Erin handled the first day well, although there is still considerable work to do to help Patrick adjust to his new setting.

How do researchers define attachment? What are the two main roots of modern attachment research?

Attachment is an emotional tie to a specific person or persons that endures across time and space. Modern attachment research is rooted in John Bowlby's ethological theory and Harry Harlow's research with rhesus monkeys. Bowlby theorized that attachment behaviors evolved to increase survivability in infants. He emphasized how smiles and other infant behaviors trigger a nurturing response in adults. He also proposed four stages of attachment: orientation without discrimination, orientation with discrimination, safe-base attachment, and goal-corrected partnerships. Harlow demonstrated that contact comfort was the critical ingredient in attachment formation, not feeding as psychoanalytic and behavioral theorists had proposed. Harlow showed how infant monkeys use their attachment figures as a secure base when they are frightened.

How do researchers use Mary Ainsworth's strange situation procedure to measure attachment relationships? What kinds of attachments does her procedure reveal?

In Ainsworth's strange situation test, eight episodes systematically expose the infant to unfamiliar situations involving a stranger and separation from the caregiver. The episodes reveal secure attachments when infants prefer the caregiver over the stranger, show separation anxiety when the caregiver leaves, and show joy on reunion when the caregiver returns. Other patterns of behavior can reveal insecure–avoidant, insecure–resistant, and insecure–disorganized/disoriented attachments.

Describe the parent, child, and cultural factors associated with individual differences in attachment.

Ainsworth believed that the key to an infant's attachment style was the quality of the infant's interaction with his or her caregiver in the first year of life. When parents are consistently positive and warm in their response, and when they are sensitively responsive to the calls and signals of the baby, secure attachments tend to develop. Indifferent, unresponsive, inconsistent, and abusive parenting often correlates with insecure attachments. Insecure attachments also are more likely when infants have special needs, are highly irritable, cry more, or are less alert and active. Intervention programs can help improve attachments in high-risk families. The prevalence of the different types of insecure attachments varies considerably across nations. Researchers believe that these cross-cultural variations are due to differences in the treatments and expectations of infants. Germans mothers, for example, expect more independence, whereas Japanese mothers rarely leave their infants alone or with other people.

What are the long-term correlates of secure and insecure attachments in infancy?

Infants who are securely attached tend to become preschoolers who are more well liked, happy, competent, compliant, and empathetic. Later in childhood they tend to have higher self-esteem and self-confidence, and they are more sociable and more emotionally healthy. Adolescents who were insecurely attached during infancy tend to have more psychological problems. Early attachment relationships can become internalized models we use to guide our social relations throughout life. Continuities in parenting may also contribute to the correlations between early attachment and later development.

What is the main limitation of using the strange situation to measure attachment? What alternative measures are available?

The strange situation is most appropriate for assessing infants who are younger than 18 months. Stranger anxiety and separation anxiety are not as readily apparent in infants over 18 months, making attachment classifications difficult. The attachment Q-sort can be used with children aged 12 months to 5 years, but it is a more indirect method, relying on the observations and judgments of people who know the child. The adult attachment interview assesses adults' state of mind regarding their own attachments with their parents. It is a retrospective procedure that relies on memories of childhood relationships.

How do researchers define temperament? What is the most popular system for classifying infant temperaments?

Temperament is an infant's or child's behavioral style or primary pattern of reacting to the environment. The most popular method of classifying temperaments is the system developed by Thomas and Chess, who identified three main temperaments (easy, difficult, and slow-to-warm-up) based on nine dimensions of behavior. Thomas and Chess believed that different temperaments result from interactions between genetics, parenting, and culture. They also emphasized the importance of an environment that is a good fit for the temperament of the individual child.

What are some other prominent systems for classifying or understanding temperament?

Mary Rothbart's revised infant behavior questionnaire assesses infant temperament along 14 behavioral dimensions, rated by parents. The original version scored 6 dimensions. The dimensions are similar to those proposed by Thomas and Chess. Rothbart also developed other questionnaires to assess temperament in people ages 18 months to adulthood. Jerome Kagan observed infants who reacted strongly to unfamiliar stimuli. Later, these infants became children who were afraid in other laboratory situations and were very shy and inhibited. As adolescents they were prone to social phobia. Kagan emphasized genetic and biological components involving the limbic system and hypothalamus, brain structures that process changes and new stimulation. Low thresholds of arousal in these systems cause shyness, and high thresholds are related to thrill seeking.

Describe several aspects of emotional development during infancy.

Emotion contagion and imitation of facial expressions are examples of emotional expressivity in newborns. Newborns tend to cry when they hear other newborns cry (contagion), and they can mimic facial expressions posed by adults (imitation). By 2 months infants can discriminate among various facial expressions and respond differently to them. One-year-olds can use their mothers' facial expressions to gain information about how to respond in ambiguous situations.

How does emotional development continue in childhood?

As children begin to distinguish themselves from other people (developing the self–other distinction), their emotions become more individualized or personalized. Two-year-olds spontaneously talk about their own emotions and realize that their emotions can differ from those of other people. With an emerging "theory of mind," children realize that emotions are connected to internal mental states and expectations. Children have a positive emotion bias: They tend to see their own emotions as being more positive than those of other people, and they are more accurate in judging positive than negative emotions in others. Accuracy in judging emotions is related to peer popularity. Children's social skills are related to parenting. Children with depressed or abusive parents are at risk in emotional development. There may be ethnic group differences in how people express emotions and in how they interpret emotions in others.

KEY TERMS

adult attachment interview (AAI) (345)

attachment (330)

attachment Q-sort (AQS) (345)

contact comfort (333)

difficult child (349)

easy child (349)

emotion contagion (355)

goodness of fit (350)

insecure–avoidant attachment (336)

insecure–disorganized/ disoriented attachment (336)

insecure–resistant attachment (336)

positive emotion bias (358)

secure attachment (335)

self-conscious emotions (357)

sensitive responsiveness (337)

separation anxiety (335)

slow-to-warm-up child (349)

social smile (357)

strange situation (334)

stranger anxiety (335)

temperament (348)

Chapter 10

Becoming Who We Are

The Development of Self, Gender, and Morality

A PERSPECTIVE TO think ABOUT

"Rebecca opened up to her aunt: 'I don't get it. It's like all the rules changed when I hit 13!'"

Rebecca is 13, and she is confused. She feels that she doesn't measure up on all the things her friends do so well. Rebecca always earned A's and B's in school, but at junior high her grades have steadily dropped to C's, sometimes even lower in math. Rebecca has always loved to play soccer, but she wouldn't try out for her school team this year—she seems to be afraid of being too "tomboyish." She has become very interested in boys and would rather talk on the phone with her boyfriend than think about homework or sports. A few months ago she wanted to become an archaeologist, but yesterday she said she wants to be a doctor or a dental hygienist instead. Last week Rebecca opened up to her aunt: "I don't get it. It's like all the rules changed when I hit 13! I don't want to be a nerd or jock or anything. The other girls are so mean—they just talk about people all the time and make fun of the least little thing. I used to be good friends with Daniel, the guy next door, but he's really weirded out now too. I heard he got caught stealing cigarettes last week. And at school, it's like a prison! I mean, you have to walk through metal detectors to get in, and people take your stuff from your locker so you can't leave anything out. I dropped a bunch of papers the other day in the hall and people just kept walking by, kicking them and scattering them all over. Nobody even asked if I needed any help! I'd help if it was me walking by—why won't anybody else?"

Is Rebecca going through a normal adolescent "phase," or is there more to her concerns and anxieties? Why are her interests changing so much? How can she better understand the callous behavior of her peers, and can she change it?

As you read this chapter, keep Rebecca's perspective in mind. What information might help Rebecca understand what she is feeling and learning? What can you tell her about

367

why people sometimes do not help others, and what ideas can you offer about how to improve the situation? After studying this chapter, you should be able to give Rebecca some insight into her changing identity, gender concepts, and moral understanding. You should be able to use at least a dozen specific concepts in your answer.

 As you read this chapter, look for the questions that ask you to think about what you're learning from Rebecca's perspective.

How do children come to understand who they are? As Rebecca's situation illustrates, it is not always an easy process. Most children go through periods of questioning their abilities, confidence, even their appearance. How much, if any, of this self-questioning is a necessary part of understanding the self? Rebecca seems to be conforming more and more to her society's expectations about how females are "supposed" to behave, but how important is it for children to have a clear sense of gender and of society's rules about male and female behavior, attitudes, and preferences? And what role does a sense of right and wrong play in the development of a child's self-understanding? In this chapter we will examine development in three different realms: self, gender, and morality. As you read, notice that there are some common themes: Children's developing cognitive skills, their biological makeup, and the parenting they receive all play important parts. These influences affect each child's sense of self, understanding of gender, and developing morality, and so have a significant impact on the complex, integrated person the child becomes.

Who Am I? The Development of Self

Most of us can easily relate to Rebecca's struggle to understand who she is. How does a person develop a sense of self, and when does that process begin? What individual and interpersonal factors influence the development of self-representations? We'll begin this first section by addressing these questions. Then we'll discuss the impact of self-evaluations; finally, we'll look at how children learn to regulate, or control, aspects of the self.

As you study this section, ask yourself these questions:

- What are self-representations and self-evaluations?
- When do children first become aware that they have a separate identity? What self-knowledge do children show during infancy, childhood, and adolescence?
- What factors influence the development of self-evaluations? What impact do positive and negative self-evaluations have on children's emotions and behavior?
- What does it mean to self-regulate? How do children develop this ability?

What Is "Self"?

Based on the pioneering work of William James (1890), psychologists distinguish between two basic aspects of the **self,** or the characteristics, emotions, and beliefs people have about themselves. The first aspect is the **I-self**—the conscious awareness that you exist as a separate, unique person. The I-self involves understanding that you have your own individual thoughts, perceptions, emotions, experiences, and actions, and that you continue to exist across time and contexts. Also part of the I-self is a sense of *personal agency,* the understanding that your actions and emotions can affect the environment, including the behavior and emotions of other people. It may surprise you to learn that very young children do not seem to realize that they are individuals, separate from other people; they have no I-self. The second aspect of the self is the **me-self,** or what you know about yourself. The me-self includes things like the categories by which people define themselves (e.g., gender, age) as well as people's objective knowledge of their own personalities and physical and cognitive characteristics (Harter, 1999; James, 1890; Thompson, 1999). It is to the me-self that we commonly refer when we speak of *self-concepts* or **self-representations**—the ways people describe themselves. Soon after children begin to be able to describe themselves, they start to evaluate their performance and characteristics. **Self-evaluations** are the judgments people make about their own characteristics, the opinions people have of themselves. These evaluations form the basis for **self-esteem,** the emotions people feel about themselves.

There are many different aspects to the self, and a person's self-evaluations may differ depending on the *domain* (i.e., the area or context) being considered (Harter, 1998). For example, a 12-year-old girl might think of herself as highly intelligent in academics, not very creative, painfully inept in social interactions, average in physical attractiveness, and good at swimming. Notice that this girl's self-evaluations are strongly positive in some domains but moderate or negative in others. Research suggests that we ought to speak of an individual's "*profile* of self-evaluations" rather than thinking of the self as a single, unitary concept (Harter, 1998, p. 578). As children get older, they become able to distinguish and evaluate more and more different domains. At the same time, however, they become better at integrating across areas and making global judgments of themselves (Harter, 1998). For example, the girl in our example is evaluating herself in several different domains (academics, creativity, social skills, physical appearance, and athletics). But she also is able to draw an overall conclusion about herself, such as "All in all, I'm a pretty good person." Younger children distinguish fewer domains, and they have difficulty summarizing across domains to form overall self-evaluations.

Most psychologists do not believe that a sense of self is present at birth. Instead, most believe that the I-self and the me-self are cognitive constructions that children create as their cognitive skills develop. From infancy on, children construct *working models of the self,* or increasingly complex cognitive representations of who they are. These working models change as children have more experiences and interact with more people. Their developing cognitive abilities enable children to recognize and integrate their personal characteristics, compare themselves to others, and deal with contradictory information. For example, a boy may think of himself as a nice person but also may realize that sometimes he does not want to do nice things like share his toys. His developing cognitive skills help him understand that there are situations in which it is okay not to share or that there are different ways to be nice other than sharing. He can still think of himself as "nice" even though he is not behaving nicely all the time. Some theorists describe a *looking-glass self* (Cooley, 1902; Mead, 1934)—the idea that in social interactions the child uses others as a "social mirror into which the individual gazes in order to detect their opinions toward the self" (Harter, 1999, p. 17).

YOUR PERSPECTIVE

NOTES

For a moment, think about your "self." Do you think of an integrated, global self, or do you tend to think of several different selves that correspond to different domains? Does each aspect of your self-representation seem accurate, even if some aspects contradict one another?

self

The characteristics, emotions, and beliefs people have about themselves, including an understanding that people are unique individuals.

I-self

The conscious awareness that you exist as a separate person and that you can affect others.

me-self

What you know about and how you describe yourself. Also called self-concept or *self-representation.*

self-representations

The ways people describe themselves; see also *me-self.*

self-evaluations

The opinions people have and judgments they make about their own characteristics.

self-esteem

The emotions people feel about themselves.

Numerous theories attempt to explain the development of the self, and we will describe several of these. Different theories emphasize the influences of different factors, such as the cognitive representation of the self, conflicts among urges and emotions, external reinforcement and punishment, or the impact of caregivers. Interestingly, these theories pay very little attention to roles that genetics or biology might play. To be sure, there is strong evidence that a sense of self is not innate, and social interaction clearly is important in the development of the self. But this does not mean that biological factors play no role at all. In particular, it seems likely that a child's temperament (see Chapter 9) will have an important influence on the self-representation that is constructed. Perhaps future research will explore how interactions between temperament and social factors influence the development of self-representations.

Changes in Self-Representation across Ages

As shown in Table 10.1, a series of events mark the development of self-representation. Let's look at these events in chronological order.

■ **Self-Representation in Infancy and Childhood.** Though there is some disagreement, the traditional belief is that newborns have no sense of themselves as separate individuals; that is, they have no I-self. During the first few months of life, babies move from this state of not knowing they are physically or emotionally separate from other people and objects to an understanding that they are individuals with unique physical sensations and emotions. And not only do they grasp that their own actions and feelings exist separately from those of others, but they also learn that their actions and feelings have an effect on other people. For example, at an early age you learned that throwing your rattle would cause your mother to walk over and pick it up (at least the first five times or so).

When you think about it, this rapid change in understanding is quite remarkable. How does it come about? In order to understand that they are physically and emotionally separate

Young infants do not seem to understand they are physically, emotionally, or behaviorally separate from their parents; they have no I-self.

TABLE 10.1 The Development of Self-Representation

APPROXIMATE AGE	TRENDS
Infancy (Birth to 1 year)	No I-self at birth.
	Use cross-modal perception to develop understanding of self as separate from others; achieve basic understanding of self as separate by 6 to 8 months, but have difficulty distinguishing between their real and ideal selves.
	Begin to understand that own actions affect others' behavior and emotions (personal agency).
	By 1 year, achieve understanding that their emotions and perspective are unique and that others also have their own unique emotions and perspectives.
	Do not compare self to others.
Early childhood (1 to 5 years)	Me-self emerges.
	Self-recognition of mirror image by 21 months.
	Use language to refer to self and possessions and to describe characteristics of self such as emotions and physical characteristics. Personal narratives with caregivers provide labels and descriptions that become included in self-descriptions.
	Ability to mentally represent objects, events, and expectations provides foundation for self-regulation. By 4 to 5 years, begin to internalize others' standards as basis for self-regulation.
	Self-descriptions include concrete and observable characteristics (e.g., physical characteristics), are tied to specific contexts and behaviors, and are unrealistically positive.
	Compare current self to self at a younger age. Social comparison to peers is beginning, but focuses on fairness rather than comparing characteristics of self or levels of performance.
Middle childhood (6 to 10)	Self-descriptions include more internal and interpersonal abilities and traits, more abstract qualities, and are increasingly realistic and accurate.
	Self-representations include increasing number of subdomains, but are able to integrate them into a global self-representation.
	Self-evaluations include both positive and negative aspects, but do not integrate and balance them.
	Compare self to peers to evaluate own qualities and performance.
	Distinguish between real and ideal self.
	Others' opinions and standards are internalized and serve as an important basis for self-regulation.
Early adolescence (10 to 12 years)	Self-descriptions increasingly abstract and differentiated, include increasing reference to social skills and interactions.
	Begin to notice and become concerned with identity issues, including ethnic identity.
	Increasing concern with differences between real and ideal self.
	Self-evaluations include both positive and negative aspects, but still not balanced and integrated. Focus is sometimes on positive and sometimes on negative qualities, which can lead to overgeneralization.
	Social comparison to peers continues but becomes less open.
Adolescence (13 years and older)	Self-descriptions focus mostly on abstract, internal, and more enduring qualities, but also include an understanding that attributes can differ depending on the context and who interactions are with (the relational context).
	Concerns with identity continue. Some aspects are resolved by late adolescence while others will continue into early adulthood.
	Recognize positive and negative aspects of the self, which causes confusion early on. Later in adolescence, these aspects are balanced and lead to a more accurate and stable self-representation with greater knowledge and acceptance of own limitations.
	Self-representations include multiple domains, but are integrated to give a global self-representation that becomes increasingly balanced among all the sub-areas and stable.
	Social comparison decreases by later adolescence, while comparison to own ideals and values increases. Interest in possible future self increases.

Source: Adapted from Harter (1999).

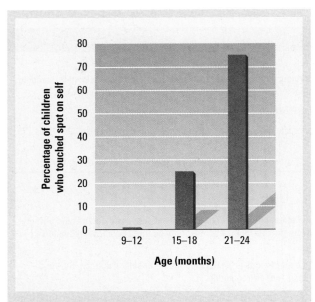

FIGURE 10.1 Development of the Me-Self

Not until approximately 21 months of age do toddlers reliably touch their own faces to wipe off a spot of rouge. Before this age babies tend to touch the mirror, indicating they do not recognize the difference between their physical selves and the mirror image.

Source: Data from Lewis & Brooks (1978), p. 214.

from others, infants have to notice patterns among actions and effects. For example, an infant girl notices that when someone touches or moves her, she feels certain physical sensations. But she also notices that when she sees *other* people or objects touched or moved, she does not have the same physical sensations. Gradually she begins to understand that she feels the sensation of being touched only when *her* body is touched, not when something else is touched, and she begins to understand that her body must be separate from other objects. In other words, the infant develops a physical awareness of her own body. Especially helpful in this process is the ability to psychologically coordinate, or integrate, information across different senses (e.g., across touch and vision). As we discussed in Chapter 4, infant researchers call this *intermodal* (or *cross-modal*) *perception*. Even newborns seem to have this ability to transfer sensory experiences and information from one sense to another (Meltzoff, 1990). Just as cross-modal perception helps infants become aware of their physical selves, it helps them understand that their emotions are distinct from those of others. For example, think about a baby boy happily playing in his crib. This baby watches as another child gets her fingers pinched in a toy and begins to cry loudly. Even though he can see the second child crying, he did not hurt himself, so he feels no impulse to cry. He gradually begins to understand that the other infant must have experienced a physical sensation different from his own and as a result is feeling a different emotion. In other words, he realizes that both his body and his emotions are separate from those of others.

As we noted earlier, infants gradually begin to realize that their actions have an effect on their environment. This concept of *personal agency* gains strength when caregivers respond according to the infant's actions. For example, consider a baby girl who looks at and attempts to reach in the direction of a mobile hanging above her crib. If her mother notices the actions and responds by reaching over and jiggling the mobile, the infant learns that her action (reaching) produced a result (the mobile moved). Consistent interactions of this sort foster a sense of *self-efficacy,* the belief that an individual can accomplish goals. Self-efficacy creates the basis for the child's sense of self-esteem (Bandura, 1997). So even though it can be tiresome for parents, it seems that picking up that rattle time after time can teach an important lesson about a baby's ability to control the environment and accomplish goals!

Between the first and second year, the me-self begins to emerge. One often-cited study demonstrated that toddlers begin to recognize specific properties of their physical selves (Lewis & Brooks, 1978). In the study the researchers placed each baby individually in front of a mirror and allowed the child to play. An experimenter placed a spot of rouge on the baby's face while pretending to wipe it, then put the baby back in front of the mirror. Most babies noticed the spot right away and tried to touch it. But the key question was *where* the children reached to touch the spot. Toddlers who recognized that the features in the mirror were their own touched their own faces rather than the reflection in the mirror. As you can see in Figure 10.1, the majority of children in this study showed this kind of recognition of their physical self by 21 months of age.

Evidence of the development of the me-self also emerges in children's language. Toddlers begin to refer to themselves by name or with pronouns (special favorites are *me* or *mine*). They also begin to use language to describe properties of the self such as physical and emotional states and characteristics: "Me tired," "I'm sad," or "I have big strong muscles." For example, consider the self-descriptions in Table 10.2. You will notice several trends in these descriptions. Across age, children's self-descriptions become *increasingly abstract,* referring more and more to intangible qualities such as responsibility or conscientiousness and less to concrete aspects such as hair color or where they live. Younger children often give actual demonstrations of the things they mention, such as reciting their ABC's or running fast; their concepts are still closely tied to concrete behavior. Also, younger children's descriptions tend to be very disjointed, indicating that their self-representations are not integrated into an overall sense of self. As we noted before, older children show *increasing differentiation* of aspects of the self and yet can integrate the whole picture. Older children also are increasingly *realistic* in their assessments of their abilities, understanding that they can be good in some areas but not so competent in others (Harter, 1999).

Why do children's self-descriptions show such changes? Changes in self-descriptions reflect changes in self-representation, and overall cognitive development plays a very important role. Notice how the changes in self-descriptions in Table 10.2 parallel the changes in cognitive development proposed by theorists such as Piaget. Increasing cognitive development allows children to make more fine-grained distinctions and thus to think about many different aspects of the self. At the same time, cognitive development allows children gradually to coordinate all these aspects into a more global self-concept, putting together all the pieces of the puzzle. Higher levels of cognitive development also enable children to include increasingly abstract aspects in their self-representations. And these parallels make sense: If the self is indeed a cognitive concept, it should show the same trends in development as any other cognitive concept.

Language also plays a role. Most parents and children tell "remember when" stories, and these *personal narratives* help children structure and interpret their knowledge of the self. For example, one of our daughters loves hearing about how she used to "grade papers" just like Mom and Dad—carefully looking over each page in her coloring book, making marks with her pencil, muttering an occasional "hmm" or "intirsting," then closing the book with a flourish and writing a "final grade" on the cover. As children hear and understand the labels and descriptions in personal narratives, they begin to include these as properties of their self-representations.

Another factor in self-representations is **social comparison,** or children's evaluations of their own qualities and performances in relation to those of their peers. Even young children care about how important people, such as parents, view them. But not until middle childhood do most children begin to compare themselves to their peers. As they do so, they begin to realize that they are better at some things than others. In this way social comparison encourages children to think about the self as a collection of different aspects. It also helps children become more realistic in their self-evaluations, because their basis for comparison is now the performance of other children their age instead of their own performance at a younger age. As older children and adolescents gain experience in different social contexts (such as home, school, clubs, and sports activities), they also become aware that they play different social

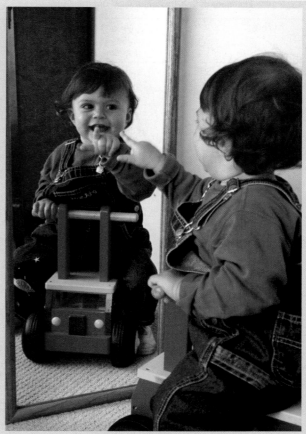

This toddler is reaching toward the mirror. Has he developed a me-self yet?

YOUR

PERSPECTIVE

NOTES

What kinds of personal narratives have you developed throughout your life? How have these helped shape your self-representation?

social comparison

The process of comparing our own qualities and performances to those of our peers.

TABLE 10.2 Examples of Self-Descriptions at Different Ages

3 to 4 years	I live with my mom and my grandma and my sister in a little blue house. I have a big orange fish for a pet. I love ice cream, especially chocolate! I don't have a TV in my room. I have brown hair and I have brown eyes, too. I go to preschool. I can jump really high—watch me! I know all my numbers up to 100, listen; 1, 2, 3. . . .
5 to 7 years	I am really, really great at soccer. I play a lot better than last year when I first started. I have lots of friends, but not girls because girls are yucky. I'm good at doing school stuff. I can read already and I know my numbers. And I'm *very* good at PlayStation! I'm good at a lot of things! So I'm never bad at things, well almost never. I really love it when my dad comes to my soccer games or to my school on field trips. I feel happy when my parents watch me do stuff.
8 to 11 years	I'm in fifth grade this year. I have lots of friends because I'm pretty nice to people, especially to my friends. If I'm really tired or in a bad mood, I might say something mean, but I'm usually nice and in a good mood. Except with my brother, because he bothers me all the time; I'm mean to him a lot. I'm pretty good in some subjects at school like science and social studies but I'm not so good at stuff like math. I feel bad about that, especially since some of my friends are really good at math. But mostly it's okay because I don't really care that much about math. It's more important to me to have a lot of friends and look good. My parents like me and I have a lot of friends, so that's good. It helps me feel good about myself.
Early adolescence	I have a really good sense of humor. I get a little wild sometimes, but I'm usually happy, at least with my friends. I'm pretty nice-looking, at least that's what I've been told! I'm a pretty okay person, most of the time. I *really* like how I am when I'm with my friends! I'm happy, funny, smart, and really cool. My *parents* are a different story . . . I am a lot sadder and madder and whatever with them. I do pretty well in school. I really do like doing new stuff in classes and learning, and I'm pretty creative when I do school projects or papers and stuff like that. I try not to talk about grades too much with my friends because it is *not* cool to get *too* good grades. I know I'm smart, but sometimes I feel like I say things that are really pretty stupid. It makes me hate myself when I do that! I can spend hours trying to figure out what I was thinking, but I still don't know.
Middle adolescence	I am *not* a simple person! I can be really friendly, supportive, helpful, especially with my friends. But I can be mean sometimes too. I know I should be nicer more, and I would really *like* to be, but sometimes I just can't and then I feel kind of bad about myself. In school I can work pretty hard, but I don't like my friends to know when I do because nobody likes a nerdy, pocket-protector guy who studies all the time. It's more important to be popular, but it's also important to me to do at least pretty good in school. My parents make me crazy. They think I should always get the top grade on every test. I can be really sarcastic and mean and, well, maybe even unreasonable to them. But not really unreasonable, because I have to have friends and if I do what they want all the time, I wouldn't have any. They really do not get it! Sometimes it seems like I'm a bunch of different people, even with my friends. At the dance the other night I was being really funny and everything with this one girl, but then this other girl came around and I was maybe kind of mean to her. I didn't mean to, but she was just annoying. I'm kind of confused about it all. I'm not sure what I want to do after high school either. I know my parents are going to want me to be some scientist or doctor or something, but I don't think that's really who I am. But I don't really *know* who I really am yet. It gets very confusing. . . .

Source: Adapted from Harter (1999).

thinking
OF REBECCA

What do you think ▶ Rebecca's self-description might be like? What would this tell you about Rebecca's self-representation?

roles in different contexts (such as son, brother, student, and teammate); these aspects, too, become part of their self-representation. In a similar way, social comparison allows children to understand more fully the different identities they may have (such as African American, Jewish, or middle-class).

■ **Adolescence and the Search for Identity.** Adolescents' developing self-representation becomes an important issue as young people strive to develop their own identities. You may recall Erik Erikson's famous theory of psychosocial development (see Table 1.2 in Chapter 1) (Erikson, 1968). Erikson believed that adolescents' increasing cognitive abilities enable them to think about abstract qualities of the self, to compare their "real selves" to their "ideal selves," and to think about other "possible selves." During adolescence, too, social demands increase rapidly: Teenagers take on different roles and responsibilities in areas such as work, religion, politics, and sexual relationships. Erikson proposed that adolescents must come to a resolution of who they are and what they believe. In other words, they must integrate in some way the many aspects of their self-representation and develop a sense of identity. If adolescents do not resolve the crisis of identity, their unclear sense of self will make it more difficult to deal with the crises that will arise during the adulthood years (i.e., intimacy and integrity).

During middle childhood children begin to compare themselves to their peers. This social comparison helps them differentiate different domains of their self-representation but also makes them aware that they are not as competent in some domains as their peers are.

James Marcia put forth a well-known elaboration of Erikson's theory, as shown in Figure 10.2 (Marcia, 1966). Marcia proposed two components of adolescent identity development. The first component is a *crisis*. In this crisis we question and think about what we know about our self, how it all fits together, and how it compares to the ideal vision we have of our self. Second, after some period of questioning and thought, we may make a *commitment* to an identity, reaching some conclusion or decision about our self. As shown in Figure 10.2, Marcia described four possible identity statuses during adolescence:

▶ *Identity achievement* is the status in which an adolescent has experienced and worked through the crisis and has made a commitment.

▶ *Identity foreclosure* is the status in which an adolescent has experienced very little crisis but has made a commitment based on what others have said he is and should be. The adolescent has taken on an identity without much self-examination or questioning.

▶ *Identity diffusion* is the status in which an adolescent may or may not have experienced a crisis, but is not currently in a state of crisis. The adolescent in identity diffusion either has stopped trying to reach a commitment or for some reason is still unable to do so—there is a clear *lack* of commitment.

▶ *Identity moratorium* is the status of an adolescent who is still in the process of working through the crisis. The experience of the crisis is relatively high, but commitment is low.

As you might expect, adolescents who have experienced the period of crisis before making a commitment show greater complexity in their self-concepts than those in the foreclosed identity status, who have not experienced a period of exploration (Low, 1999).

thinking
OF REBECCA

◀ Which of Marcia's identity statuses do you think Rebecca is in? Does it seem that her changing interests and confusion are normal, or do they indicate a problem? Why or why not?

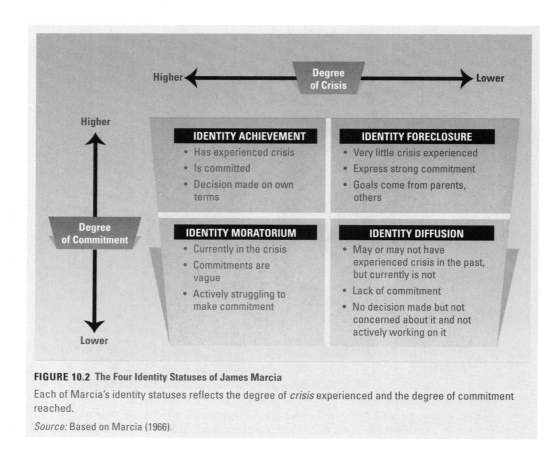

FIGURE 10.2 The Four Identity Statuses of James Marcia

Each of Marcia's identity statuses reflects the degree of *crisis* experienced and the degree of commitment reached.

Source: Based on Marcia (1966).

Adolescents who are members of an ethnic minority in their culture have the additional task of developing an ethnic or racial identity—an understanding of their ethnic background and a feeling of belonging within their minority group. The groundwork for this development occurs during middle childhood, when ethnic children first begin to identify themselves as members of specific ethnic groups. Children as young as five to seven years of age understand the differences between themselves and majority-group children and typically prefer children of their own ethnicity (Aboud & Doyle, 1995; Wright, 1998). According to Phinney (1990), fuller development of ethnic identity then takes place in three stages during adolescence, as shown in Table 10.3. If you examine Phinney's stages, you will notice parallels to Marcia's identity statuses. Minority teens may begin with an *unexamined ethnic identity*. In this stage, as in the foreclosed identity status, adolescents may not have gone through a period of exploration or questioning but may possess clear feelings about their ethnicity that are based on outside sources. These sources may convey a positive image, such as an image held by parents; or they may convey a more negative identity, such as stereotypes communicated by the majority culture (Spencer & Dornbusch, 1990). Alternatively, the unexamined stage may be more of an identity diffusion status, in which adolescents have not really explored identity issues and have no clear sense of ethnicity. The second stage, *ethnic identity search*, is a period of identity moratorium during which teenagers reexamine their ethnic identity and search for what makes sense to them personally. This questioning process occurs when teens apply their growing cognitive abilities to social experiences—typically, experiences that in some way highlight their ethnicity, such as encounters with people of other ethnicities or personal experiences of prejudice. The *resolution of conflict* stage is comparable to Marcia's achieved identity status. In this stage adolescents come to a resolution regarding their

Becoming Who We Are: The Development of Self, Gender, and Morality

TABLE 10.3 **Phinney's Three-Stage Model of Ethnic Identity Development**

STAGE	DESCRIPTION
Unexamined ethnic identity	• Child holds an identity based on outside sources, or has no clear sense of identity • A foreclosed or diffuse identity status • Identity may be based on positive image (e.g., from parents) • Identity may be based on negative image (e.g., stereotypes)
Ethnic identity search	• Increasing cognitive abilities and social experiences combine to prompt reexamination and questioning of ethnic identity • A period of moratorium

Resolution of conflict	• Adolescent settles on an ethnic identity
	
	• Identity achieved status
	
	• Can resolve the crisis by:
	
	  Distancing themselves from their ethnic culture
	
	  Adopting a *blended bicultural identity*, in which aspects of both the majority and ethnic culture are adopted
	
	  Adopting an *alternating bicultural identity*, in which two different identities are created and the individual switches between them depending on the social context
	
	  Making a *complete commitment* to their ethnicity, even if it means loss of acceptance and access to the majority culture

Source: Adapted from Phinney (1989).

ethnicity that is comfortable and makes sense to them. Developing an ethnic identity is often a long and difficult process, however. It is made more difficult because ethnic minority adolescents are often beginning to deal with the stress and conflict created by racial discrimination at the same time (Fisher, Wallace, & Fenton, 2000; Verkuyten, 2003).

Ethnic children progress through three stages as they develop an ethnic identity.

YOUR

PERSPECTIVE
PERSPECTIVE

NOTES

Which identity status do
you believe you are in?
Why? If you are from an
ethnic background, what
stage of ethnic identity
development are you in?

Teens may go about resolving ethnic identity conflicts in a variety of ways, as Table 10.3 indicates. *Acculturation strategies*—the particular strategies a family uses to deal with differences between the customs and beliefs of their ethnic background and the majority culture—affect the development of ethnic identity (Berry, 1993; Phinney, 2003; Saito, 2003). For example, some families emphasize and celebrate their ethnicity as a proud cultural heritage. Such families are likely to encourage their children to learn more about and be proud of their background. The farther minority adolescents progress through the three stages, the better their levels of psychological adjustment and self-esteem (Phinney, Cantu, & Kurtz, 1997). To learn more about how one family has accomplished the task of developing an ethnic identity, read the Personal Perspective box called "Developing an Ethnic Identity."

Remember that identity is multifaceted; an adolescent may reach commitment in some facets well before others. Culture plays an important role in identity development, by suggesting such things as how long it is acceptable to remain in moratorium and what kinds of identities are acceptable to consider. Relationships with parents also affect how adolescents deal with issues of identity. Both younger children and adolescents benefit from parenting that is supportive and accepting, that lets youngsters express themselves, but that also provides reasonable expectations and limits for behavior (Harter, 1998). Contrary to what many people believe, parents continue to be just as important in their children's lives during adolescence as they were during childhood, even though the influence of friends also increases (Lamborn & Steinberg, 1993).

Evaluating the Self

We've seen that self-representation develops over time. What about self-evaluation?

YOUR

PERSPECTIVE
PERSPECTIVE

NOTES

Is your overall self-
evaluation different
when you think about
yourself with your
parents, with teachers,
with male or female
friends? Why do you think
the "relational context"
does or does not matter?

Children first begin to evaluate their performance on individual tasks during the toddler years, but it is not until they are about 7 that children form an overall opinion of themselves, or *global self-evaluation* (Harter, 1998; Stipek, Recchia, & McClintic, 1992). Overall self-esteem tends to be unrealistically high during early childhood. It slowly declines to more realistic and accurate levels as children do more social comparison, become better able to distinguish between how well they would like to perform and how well they actually do perform, and rely increasingly on feedback from others about their performance. As with self-representations, self-evaluations become increasingly differentiated and children gradually come to evaluate each domain independently. Thus, each child develops a self-evaluation profile of relative strengths and weaknesses. Interestingly, beginning as early as sixth grade, children's self-evaluations differ depending on particular *relational contexts* (Harter, Waters, & Whitesell, 1998). Many adolescents report that they like themselves "as a person more in some relationships than in others" (Harter et al., 1998, p. 756).

Self-evaluations typically become much more negative beginning at about age 11 or 12. Puberty may produce stress and dissatisfaction with bodily changes that can lead to a decrease in overall self-esteem, especially for early-maturing girls (Lipka, Hurford, & Litten, 1992). Cognitively, young adolescents become more able to adopt the psychological perspective of others—to think about how others are thinking. They can become so concerned with others' opinions that they are overly critical in their self-evaluations. Social factors are important too. For example, with the move from elementary school to junior high, children experience more emphasis on competition, grades, teacher control, and social comparison, but less individual attention, reduced support from teachers, and fewer opportunities to maintain close friendship networks. These transitions often coincide with physical changes and an already heightened tendency toward self-consciousness and social comparison. The combined effect can create problems (DuBois, Felner, Brand, Phillips, & Lease, 1996; Eccles, Midgley, et al., 1993; Wigfield & Eccles, 1994). However, although self-esteem usually does not rebound

Developing an Ethnic Identity

Angela Watkins
Atlanta, Georgia

African American professor, author, and parent

How did your ethnic identity develop?
I was born during a most promising time for African Americans—the Civil Rights movement was in full motion and it was a time of massive social change. My agents of socialization were African Americans in positions of authority, power, and influence. My family members were key players in the Civil Rights movement. I grew up in Ebenezer Baptist Church in Atlanta, Georgia, the church of the world-renowned Civil Rights leader the Reverend Dr. Martin Luther King Jr. The administrators, teachers, and babysitters that I interacted with in preschool and elementary school were African Americans. Each had a clear sense of ethnicity and an unspoken responsibility to continue the struggle for justice and equality. I remember learning words like *slavery, Jim-Crow, Ku Klux Klan, segregation,* and *discrimination* early in life. I also remember messages of empowerment that counteracted such evil. Throughout my childhood I observed African American pride and dignity firsthand. Although I was keenly aware of racial differences and the evils of racism, I was also aware of the possibilities of active protest.

My teenage years were more challenging, consumed by a personal struggle for ethnic identity congruence. Others' perceptions of me were critically important. I looked for confirmation of my intelligence, my worth, and my potential for success. I remember many positive and affirming experiences, which buffered me for the more difficult ones of prejudice that I often faced. It was clear that society viewed whites as cleaner, better, and smarter and African Americans as less clean, less intelligent, and of lesser value. Fortunately, the buffers I had, coupled with the excellent models in my immediate and extended family, church, and school, saved me from a life of delusion, depression, and defeat.

Now I am married, with a 6-year-old daughter and a flourishing career. Although I am still reminded of the prestige of whites and the subordination of blacks every morning when I turn on the television, now I am more confident, secure, and proud. I have learned to appreciate the history of our resilience, despite slavery and oppression, and I recognize our brilliance and significant inventions. I reject demeaning messages and seek out inspiration and truth. I share these truths in my courses, my writings, and in daily interactions with family and friends. I actively advocate positive social change and participate in acts of protest. Now my own story of survival empowers me. An added benefit is that as I have learned to embrace my own ethnicity, I have a greater appreciation for other cultures of the world.

How have you approached teaching your children about their ethnic heritage?
The task of instilling a healthy sense of ethnic pride in my daughter is a challenging one. At times I wish that I could free her from the evil and the pain. I see her confusion as she notices particular inequalities and tries to understand them. She wants to know why she sees so many white people in magazines, on television, in books, in stores, and in hotels. She ponders the meaning behind her observation of a little white girl who bought a black "Bratz" doll. She has noticed that her skin is light, compared to mine, and wonders if it's okay. I want to give her both the truth of the harsh realities and the richness of our culture. I surround her with symbols of African American culture, black art in our home, a host of books with African American characters and names, black dolls, educational software infused with our cultural flair, black music (spirituals, blues, gospel, and jazz), and greeting cards with African American faces and expressions. I also expose her to lessons of African American history. We watch documentaries that give accurate portrayals of our people. We participate in the Kwanza celebration (a traditional 7-day emphasis on Africentric value systems that occurs around the Christmas holiday season). We attend plays and concerts that highlight the beauty and uniqueness of our culture. We talk a lot. She asks lots of questions and I try to answer them all. I want her to be as equipped as I am to navigate the dominant society and to appreciate the many cultures of the world. I realize that until she develops a love of her own ethnicity she will not be able to accept and appreciate those who are different. She must learn to be multicultural and to respect diversity. In fact, that is a lesson for us all! ■

thinking
OF REBECCA

◀ What are some issues that Rebecca should be sensitive to with her ethnic peers? What could she do to help make their junior high experience less stressful?

The structure and demands of junior high may be a bad match with the physical, cognitive, and social needs of many children at this age. What effect do you think this will have on young adolescents' self-esteem?

to the high levels of early childhood, self-evaluations typically show gradual increases during later adolescence.

■ **Influences on Self-Evaluation.** Most experts agree that positive self-evaluation has its roots in the quality of caregiving an infant receives (Bowlby, 1982). A secure attachment between infant and parent is considered to be "a crucial foundation for the growth of healthy self-regard" (Thompson, 1999, p. 398). Secure attachment helps the baby develop a working model of the self as capable, worthy, and lovable. In interactions with infants, caregivers communicate opinions about the infants' performance and attributes, and the infants internalize these views and incorporate them into their self-evaluations.

A second major influence on self-evaluation comes from the comparisons children draw between their *real selves* and their *ideal selves*—between the performance and attributes children actually have and the qualities they would like to have. Two aspects of this comparison process are important: the actual discrepancy between the ideal and the real in domains that are important to the child, and the degree of social support the child receives from parents and/or peers (Harter, 1999). For example, if a boy would like to be a football star (the ideal self) but is unathletic (the real self), the discrepancy is large. If athletics are not important to the boy, then even a large discrepancy in this domain will have little effect on his self-evaluation. In contrast, if physical skills and athletics are important to the child, his self-evaluation in this domain is likely to suffer. However, if the boy's parents and peers are very supportive of his attempts to play football, focusing on his improvements and praising his efforts, then his self-evaluation will be less negative. Some aspects of his self-evaluation may even become very positive (e.g., "I'm a hard worker," "I'm not afraid to try to learn new things"). The worst cases seem to be situations in which children perceive support as being *contingent on* performance. In other words, if the unathletic boy feels that others will support and accept him only if he plays football well, then he must contend with both a large discrepancy and loss of support—and is likely to develop a very negative self-evaluation.

It is interesting to note that of all the self-evaluation domains researchers have assessed, perceived physical appearance consistently shows the highest correlation with overall self-esteem. Correlations range from .65 to a remarkable .82 (Harter, 1998). This strong relationship is apparent from early childhood on through adulthood; for males and females; across different population groups (e.g., people with learning disabilities, gifted students, behaviorally disruptive adolescents); across different ethnic groups (Gardner, Friedman, & Jackson, 1999; James, Phelps, & Bross, 2001); and in various different cultures (e.g., those of Ireland, Australia, Greece, Japan, and the United States). Concern about physical appearance seems to be especially detrimental for girls, who report significantly greater dissatisfaction with their physical selves than do boys starting at about fourth grade and continuing through adulthood. Although the cultural emphasis on physical appearance is strong for both genders, it appears to take its toll most strongly on girls by presenting unrealistic standards for comparison. Not surprisingly, girls who report that their

thinking
OF REBECCA

How would you describe ▶ Rebecca's self-evaluations? What factors may be contributing to the changes she seems to be experiencing?

self-esteem is based on physical appearance also tend to show especially low levels of self-esteem (Harter, 1993).

■ **Consequences of Positive and Negative Self-Evaluations.** Self-evaluations have important consequences for both behavior and emotions. First, children's evaluations of their own skills and competencies directly affect their choices of activities and their persistence on difficult challenges. For example, if a girl believes that she is a very talented tennis player, she may well choose to spend much of her free time playing tennis and may be willing to work for hours to improve her game. On the other hand, if she believes she is unattractive or is incompetent in social situations, she is not likely to relish parties and school dances. Keep in mind that it is not a child's actual level of competence in a domain but the level that the child *perceives,* together with the discrepancy between the child's real and ideal selves, that determines the consequences. In other words, if others believe that the girl is attractive but she does not, or if she believes that she *should be* more attractive than she feels she really is, her self-evaluations will negatively affect her behavior and motivation (Harter, 1999).

Second, there is a strong relationship between self-evaluations and depression, with correlations ranging from .72 to .80. The direction of the effect is not clear, however. Do low self-evaluations lead to depression? Or does a depressive *affect* (emotional tendency) lead to lower self-evaluations? In one review of the research, two-thirds of the female adolescents showed low self-evaluations followed by depression, but two-thirds of the males showed the reverse direction. Those who reported low self-evaluations first were particularly unhappy with their physical appearance, competence, and behavior in social interactions. In contrast, those who reported depression first had experienced rejection by or conflict with others, especially peers, and loss due to death or the ending of a relationship (Harter, 1999). The relationship between self-evaluations and depression is complicated, showing different paths and influences for different individuals.

How can we help children develop more positive self-evaluations? Table 10.4 presents some suggestions. Parents can establish a sound base by consistently providing sensitively responsive caregiving, as we have discussed in several chapters. Here again we see the crucial importance of high-quality care from infancy. It is important to provide positive support and encouragement for children's activities, but it is also important to offer *honest* feedback on the actual level of accomplishment. Providing honest feedback helps children learn to evaluate their skills realistically, and offering support for their effort along with guidance and instruction helps children improve skills and focus on improvement and progress toward their goals (Damon, 1995). Parents and teachers can help children learn to set realistic and achievable short-term goals; this way, the real-versus-ideal discrepancy is not so large that children become discouraged. It will probably be impossible to eliminate society's emphasis on physical appearance, but caregivers can emphasize other areas of strength to help children think less about appearance in forming their self-evaluations. Finally, it may be especially important for ethnic minority parents to help their children develop positive

If parents are supportive of a child's efforts, even a big discrepancy between the child's real and ideal selves is not necessarily harmful.

thinking
OF REBECCA

◀ Do you think the discrepancy between Rebecca's real and ideal selves is relatively small or large? Is there reason for concern that it may lead to problems such as depression? If so, what could her family do to prevent this from happening?

TABLE 10.4 Fostering Positive Self-Evaluations

Early care-giving promotes a secure emotional attachment.	Learn to read your child's cues. Respond to them, and then watch to see if the need has been met.
	Watch and listen; let the child initiate when feasible. Don't always rush in to start an interaction.
	Provide an environment that is sensitive to your child's temperament. Don't try to push a reluctant child too hard or too fast, or constrain an active child for too long.
	Provide lots of opportunities to play and interact with others, including you.
	Spend time talking with your child, labeling and explaining things in the environment in simple words. Respond to your child's attempts to make things happen (e.g., move the rattle closer to her when she tries to reach it).
	Express delight in your child's early accomplishments; even if every other child also does the same thing, it is a new accomplishment for *this* child!
	Cradle, rock, massage, and otherwise provide comfort to your child when he seeks it from you. Communicate in words, facial and physical gestures, and activities that your child is worthy, lovable, capable.
Provide positive support and encouragement. Outcomes may matter, but also stress effort and improvement.	Praise a good outcome (e.g., "What a beautiful painting! I'm so proud it was chosen for the art show!").
	But also point out the process and the effort (e.g., "Was it fun to come up with those colors? I noticed that you put in a lot of work on that project.").
	Support the *effort* and recognize *progress*, even if the outcome isn't good (e.g., "I know you didn't do as well on the test as you had hoped, but you really tried hard. Keep working hard and you'll get better at it; I know you are disappointed that you didn't make the top team, but all that practice really did help your game.").
	Help your child set realistic goals and sub-goals so the difference between his real and ideal selves is not so great.
	Remind your child that she doesn't have to excel in everything. Some things are truly just for fun!
Provide instruction and guidance to help the child improve.	Make time to help your child with the things you know how to do.
	Work with others (e.g., teachers, coaches, friends) to provide good models for knowledge and skills you do not have.
	Think creatively. Find ways to use your child's strengths to improve her weaknesses (e.g., a child who is not a good reader but is very social might enjoy doing a dramatic reading of a story to her family, friends, stuffed animals, etc.).
	Make teaching interactions as pleasant as possible (e.g., make up card games or money games to practice math skills, play word rhyming games to practice phonics for reading).
Give honest feedback.	Don't lie or exaggerate, especially as children move into elementary school. They usually know when they have not done well, and will simply learn to not believe you. Be honest, but in a gentle and kind way.
	Talk about specific things the child can do to improve, and provide help. Spend time with the child working on the skills, offer guidance, do the activity with the child, and so forth. Different approaches will work with different children.
	Offer balanced feedback. Point out what went well as well as what went poorly.
	Point out examples of both strengths and weaknesses in yourself, other family members, and your child's friends to help them understand that *nobody* is great at *everything*.
Teach goal-setting skills.	Help your child set specific and reasonable goals. Even preschoolers can set and accomplish concrete, short-term goals such as "I have to finish putting my toys away before I go to the park."
	As children get older, model how to set explicit longer-term goals, smaller and more immediate goals, and how to make a plan for accomplishing them. *Example:* Andy wants a new skateboard (longer-term goal). He needs to decide what kind, how much it will cost, and how to get the money (sub-goals). He can check websites and talk to friends to figure out what kind and the cost. He can do extra chores, save birthday money, and not buy snacks after school to save allowance money.
	Help children develop and use a system for tracking progress toward their goals (e.g., a chart, calendar, or written log of progress). Notice and comment on progress toward goals.
Emphasize strengths.	All children do some things well. Remind them of their strengths and offer specific examples of them.

self-evaluations and ethnic identities to counteract negative stereotypes and discrimination. These parents can praise their children's unique attributes, provide positive role models, help the children understand their ethnic history, and expose them to diverse cultures.

Self-Regulation

It is clearly important to develop self-understanding and healthy self-esteem. But one of the most important skills that we develop in childhood is the ability to control aspects of the self. Without this ability we would have great difficulty accomplishing anything, regardless of how good we might feel about ourself! **Self-regulation** is the ability to control our own behavior, emotions, or thoughts, altering them in accordance with the demands of the situation. It includes the abilities to *inhibit* first responses, to *resist interference* from irrelevant stimulation, and to *persist* on relevant tasks even when we don't enjoy them. For example, when our son Will was 7, he liked to play Monopoly Junior with his sisters. Will had developed reasonable self-regulation skills for his age, so he usually did not give in to the temptation to take money from his sisters' piles when they weren't looking (inhibiting first responses). Most of the time, he was able to ignore their incessant singing of "Jingle Bells" as he pondered about whether to buy a property (resisting interference) or distract himself by focusing on the game when he started to feel irritated by the singing (emotional regulation). Though he might not do so on his own, Will did help clean up the game and put it away when we asked, even though he didn't really want to (persisting on less enjoyable tasks). Can you envision what this scene would be like if Will and his sisters had few or no self-regulation skills? We prefer to not think about it!

Mature self-regulation requires several sophisticated cognitive skills. These include awareness of the demands of any given situation; consistent monitoring of our own behavior, thoughts, and strategies; consideration of how successfully we are meeting the demands of the situation; and the ability to change aspects of our current functioning as needed to fit the situation or to accomplish a goal. Aspects of self-regulation correlate with various positive outcomes for children and adolescents—including better academic performance, problem-solving skills, and reading comprehension; more satisfying interactions with peers; higher levels of intrinsic motivation, self-worth, perceived competence, self-efficacy, moral cognition, and moral conduct; fewer behavior problems; and lower levels of psychopathology (e.g., depression) (Brown, Bransford, Ferrara, & Campione, 1983; Eisenberg et al., 2001; Grolnick, Kurowski, & Gurland, 1999; Howse, Lange, Farran, & Boyles, 2003; Kochanska, Murray, & Coy, 1997; Ryan, Connell, & Grolnick, 1992).

■ **When Do Children Develop Self-Regulation Skills?** Precursors of self-regulation appear early in life. Very young babies show no evidence of conscious self-regulation, but they do show primitive control of some aspects of their behavior and reactions. For example, infants will turn away from sources of too much stimulation, such as loud music or voices, within the first few months of life. At 12 to 18 months, children show awareness of social demands in their environment. They are able to comply with simple requests from a caregiver; they can voluntarily initiate, maintain, and stop behaviors, particularly when they are interacting with someone they know well. By 24 months children are able to show aspects of self-control even when a caregiver is not immediately with them. From 3 to 7 years children grow steadily in their ability to inhibit first responses. In one study, for example, older children were better than younger children at not peeking while an experimenter wrapped a gift (Gerstadt, Hong, & Diamond, 1994; Kochanska, Murray, Jacques, Koenig, & Vandegeest, 1996; Kopp, 1982).

Older children and adolescents are increasingly able to self-regulate not only their behavior but also their emotions and problem-solving strategies. For example, across the elementary and middle school years children become much more accurate in monitoring how well they understand what they read, and they gradually learn to modify their study strategies to improve their comprehension. Older children and adolescents are also much more likely to appropriately use strategies to manage negative emotions. If they are angry, they may take a

self-regulation

The ability to control our own behavior, emotions, or thoughts and change them to meet the demands of the situation.

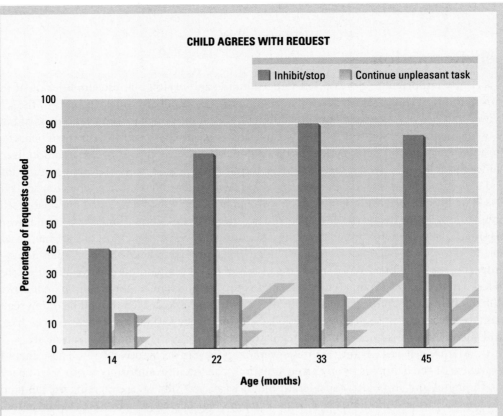

CHILD AGREES WITH REQUEST

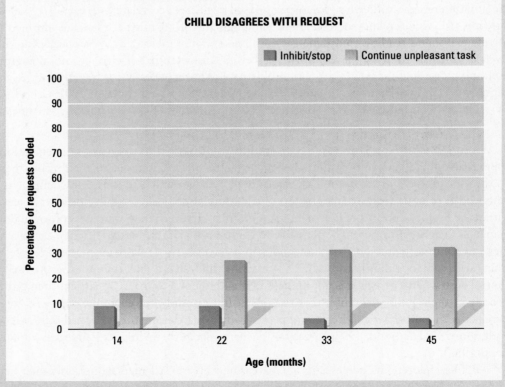

CHILD DISAGREES WITH REQUEST

FIGURE 10.3 Context and Self-Regulation

Even young children show high compliance rates (a common indicator of self-regulation) if they are inhibiting a response and they agree with the request. But if they do not agree, their compliance rates on the easier task of inhibiting a response are even lower than on the harder task of continuing an unpleasant activity.

Source: Data from Kochanska, Coy, & Murray (2001), p. 1099.

walk or hit a pillow; if they're sad, they may engage in a distracting activity, write in a journal, or talk with a friend (Brown et al., 1983; Dufresne & Kobasigawa, 1989b; Thompson, 1994).

Self-regulation is not simply an internal characteristic; the child's context matters too. For example, one recent study looked at young children's compliance with mothers' requests under four different conditions, as shown in Figure 10.3. (Researchers often use compliance as a measure of early self-regulation because it requires children to change their behavior in response to a caregiver's request.) In the experiment mothers asked children either to continue an unpleasant activity (to pick up toys) or to inhibit a desired response (not to play with toys). Not surprisingly, it was easier for children to comply when they agreed with the mother's request than when they did not. Overall, it was harder for children to continue an unpleasant activity than to inhibit a desired one. One reason may be that parents tend to focus on what young children should not do ("Don't touch the stove!") rather than encouraging them to continue an activity ("You must put away all your toys before we have a snack"). It could also be that continuing an undesired activity requires ongoing effort and persistence, whereas a child can inhibit a response more easily—for example, by focusing on a different activity (Kochanska, Coy, & Murray, 2001, p. 1107).

So both the type of self-regulation required and whether the child agreed that the request was a good idea were important. What was more interesting, however, were the interactions of these two factors. As you can see in Figure 10.3, even children as young as 14 months showed a fairly high rate of compliance when they agreed with the request and it involved inhibiting a response (40 percent), and under those circumstances compliance increased to 85 percent by the time children were just over 3½. However, if children disagreed with the request, compliance for inhibiting a response was low at 14 months and later became even worse, dropping to only 4 percent. The lesson here is that self-regulation comes both from internal sources, such as children's developing ability to modify behavior and their opinion of a request, and from external factors, such as the type of self-regulation being requested. The fact that children can self-regulate does not necessarily mean that they will, even on easier tasks. It helps if you can encourage children to see the reasonableness of requests—to understand that the change in behavior makes sense. It's also important to know what level of self-regulation you can reasonably expect at different ages.

■ **What Factors Influence the Development of Self-Regulation?**   Several factors influence the development of self-regulation. Researchers have linked aspects of temperament (see Chapter 9) such as behavioral inhibition, effortful control, and fearfulness to several self-regulatory behaviors in preschool and early school-age children; among these behaviors are emotional regulation, cheating, compliance with adults' requests, and following rules (Kochanska, Murray, & Harlan, 2000; Kochanska et al., 2001; Rothbart & Bates, 1998). Maturation of certain areas of the brain, especially the frontal lobes, enables children to resist interference and inhibit responses. The frontal lobes undergo two periods of rapid growth, one during infancy and another from about 4 to 7 years—and these periods are consistent with the developmental trends in self-regulation we've described (Hudspeth & Pribram, 1990; Luria, 1973).

But these biological links do not mean that self-regulation is completely innate. Aspects of the child's environment have a strong influence. In fact, most psychologists believe that self-regulation, though influenced by biological factors, begins with external control by others and gradually becomes internalized. For example, children learn specific strategies for regulating behavior and emotions by **modeling**—the process of imitating, practicing, and internalizing others' behavior (Schunk & Zimmerman, 1997). And children often use *private speech,* or speech they direct toward themselves (see the discussion of Vygotsky's theory in Chapter 5), to guide their problem-solving efforts and to regulate behavior, cognitive strategies, or emotions.

It also appears that the *way* in which adults try to direct children's behavior and emotions affects how quickly and how well self-regulatory skills develop. For example, we've seen that children are more likely to change their behavior if they agree with a given request. When

modeling

The process of imitating, practicing, and internalizing others' behavior. Also, the process of *providing* the example behavior, as in "her parents are modeling good study skills."

YOUR
PERSPECTIVE
NOTES

How well do you regulate
your behavior and emo-
tions? How could you do
this more effectively?

children comply because they agree with the request, there is a greater chance that they will view the request as being "self-generated and not interfering with" their attempts to be independent (Kochanska et al., 2001, p. 1108). In other words, they may think of the request as being their own idea, or at least regard it as sensible. Compliance under these conditions may ultimately lead to more effective self-regulation. In fact, in the study we discussed earlier, compliance when the children agreed with the request was the only type that predicted compliance when the children were left on their own—which is the goal of developing *self*-regulation. When a child disagrees but is forced to comply anyway, there is less internalization of the parents' standards, and parents tend to resort to more power-based (rather than reason-based) control tactics.

Think for a moment about the implications of this. There will always be times when a child disagrees with parental requests, rules, or decisions. But forcing obedience through the use of power and control may delay the very thing that parents are trying to teach! Strategies that encourage internalization of social standards (e.g., explaining the rationale for a rule, involving children in establishing goals and rules, and so on) require more time and effort from caregivers but are probably more likely to produce voluntary self-regulation. In Chapter 12 we will explore parenting styles, including use of parental power, and their effects on children's cognitive, social, and emotional development.

LET'S REVIEW . . .

1. The I-self is our:
   a. objective knowledge of our own characteristics.
   b. understanding that we exist as a separate person.
   c. ability to understand events from another person's perspective.
   d. feelings about ourself.

2. Andrew has tried three different majors in college. After carefully considering his interests and skills, he believes he has finally found the best major for him. Andrew is probably in which of Marcia's identity statuses?
   a. foreclosure   b. moratorium   c. achievement   d. diffusion

3. If the discrepancy between Diana's real self and ideal self is large and Diana cares about the domain, which of the following is most likely to be true about her self-evaluation?
   a. It will be high.
   b. It will not be affected.
   c. It will be low even if her parents are supportive.
   d. It will be low if her parents are not supportive.

4. Which of the following does *not* explain the negative effect on self-evaluations of the transition to junior high?
   a. Junior high schools usually decrease individual attention but increase the emphasis on competition.
   b. Structural changes in the school setting coincide with an increased tendency for self-consciousness.
   c. Parental monitoring of schoolwork declines when children enter junior high school.
   d. The class structure in junior high schools makes it more difficult to maintain friendship networks.

5. **True or False:** During adolescence, self-evaluations tend to remain stable or increase.

6. **True or False:** Younger children's self-descriptions are more concrete, specific, and nonintegrated than older children's.

Answers: 1. b, 2. c, 3. d, 4. c, 5. F, 6. T

The Development of Gender

Are you male or female? For most people, answering this question may seem simple, because it seems to ask about your **sex** or obvious physical and biological characteristics. Think a little harder about maleness and femaleness, however, and you will begin to appreciate the complexity of our question. What do we really mean? Are we asking about your biologically determined sex? Or are we asking about your **gender**—the whole package of physical, cognitive, and behavioral traits that characterize people of your sex? Or, perhaps we are asking about your **gender role** (also called *sex role*), the social expectations of persons of your sex within your particular culture. If this is the case, we are interested in your cognitive understanding of what it means to be male or female, including how you are *supposed to* behave, think, and feel as well as the jobs, responsibilities, rights, and attitudes that your culture views as appropriate. For example, in your mind, do real men cuddle babies and clean bathrooms, and do real women run banks and build roads? We might be asking about your **gender concept,** your understanding that your gender is a permanent feature that does not alter if you change things like your hair or clothing; but we probably are not, because this understanding should be in place well before your age! But maybe we are asking if you engage in **sex-typed behavior** —that is, if your behavior matches the gender-role expectations of your culture. We could also ask about *gender differences,* or differences between males and females in specific attributes such as cognitive abilities, emotions, aggressiveness, or activity levels. As with many of the topics in this book, researchers have gradually come to realize that gender development in children is a complex process. So our simple question requires a more complicated answer than you might think at first glance (Brannon, 1999; Ruble & Martin, 1998).

As you study this section, ask yourself these questions:

- What are the meanings of the terms *sex, gender, gender role, gender concept, sex typing,* and *gender differences*? What aspects of biology and the environment are important for gender development?

- How big are the gender differences that have been found in behavior, emotions, and cognitive skills? Why do these differences appear, and when are they first apparent?

- At what age do children first show an understanding of gender? How does this understanding develop across childhood and adolescence?

- What factors influence the development of gender knowledge and behavior?

How Do Boys and Girls Differ?

Research has identified consistent gender differences in several specific cognitive skills as well as in a range of social and personal characteristics. Some differences are apparent from infancy; others do not emerge until late childhood or adolescence. Interestingly, in several skills the differences between boys and girls have shrunk over the years since researchers first began studying them. This indicates that socialization and differential experiences play roles in gender differences. The most striking finding is that in most areas the similarities between girls and boys far outweigh the differences. Even when gender differences are significant and consistent over time, we still do not fully understand *why* they exist. Different experiences and socialization are almost certainly involved, but biological factors may also have important effects.

■ **Cognitive Skills.** In cognitive skills the largest and most consistent gender differences are in verbal, language, and certain spatial skills. For example, girls tend to produce words at an earlier age, have a larger vocabulary, and show a higher level of language complexity beginning in early childhood (Feingold, 1993; Halpern, 2000; Hyde & Linn, 1988). The biggest

sex

The male or female physical and biological characteristics of the body.

gender

All the physical, cognitive, and behavioral traits that characterize people of one sex.

gender role

The social expectations for each sex within a particular culture. Sometimes called sex role.

gender concept

The understanding that a person's sex is a permanent feature and cannot be altered through changes in surface features like hair or clothing.

sex-typed behavior

Behavior that matches the gender-role expectations of a culture.

Gender differences in some cognitive abilities exist in childhood, but many do not appear until adolescence. The magnitude of many gender differences has decreased over recent decades.

differences in verbal skills during school-age years—all favoring girls—are in spelling, overall language measures, and writing. Some of these gender differences seem to get smaller during adolescence, whereas differences in other areas (e.g., writing) remain (Halpern, 2000). These differences have remained relatively stable over 30 or more years of research. Differences in other specific skills tend to be small, and some have decreased in magnitude in recent decades (Campbell, Hombo, & Mazzeo, 2000). Clear and consistent gender differences favoring males exist for some spatial skills such as mental rotation (the ability to visualize how an object would look if you viewed it from a different angle). Differences in these areas emerge at around 9 to 13 years and widen throughout adolescence. Gender differences in mental rotation have remained stable over the last few decades (Masters & Sanders, 1993; Voyer, Voyer, & Bryden, 1995).

Is it true that boys are better than girls in mathematics, as so many people seem to believe? It depends on students' ages and skill levels, as well as on the particular area of mathematics being assessed. The only consistent differences found in elementary school favor girls, both for computation and for grades in math (Halpern, 2000). Girls continue to earn higher grades in math throughout the school years, but their superior performance in computation disappears after about age 15. In studies of very talented populations, boys perform better on several mathematics skills. Gender differences favoring boys appear at adolescence and increase during the high school years, but only in areas involving mathematics problem solving. Since the late 1970s boys have consistently scored about 10 percent higher than girls on the math portion of the Scholastic Aptitude Test (the SAT). On national assessments of 4th, 8th, and 12th graders, however, math gender differences have decreased since the early 1980s. The most recent national assessment shows no significant differences at any of these grade levels (Byrnes, 2001a; Campbell et al., 2000). Some studies find that girls hold less positive attitudes toward math, show less interest in math, and receive less encouragement for engaging in math-related activities (Eccles, Wigfield, & Schiefele, 1998; Maccoby, 1998). Schools have

Career Focus: Meet a High School Guidance Counselor

Sara Rodriguez
Houston, Texas

Counselor at Cesar E. Chavez High School

What evidence do you see of gender stereotypes in your students? Do gender stereotypes present problems to teens as they try to define themselves and pursue their goals?

There are things that the girls or boys usually do, and other things they do not usually do. This comes from television, books, their home, and their culture. We do see more openness, especially in what girls are doing, such as playing sports and pursuing careers in math and engineering. Today, it is much easier to pursue one's talents and interests because we are exposed to people who are doing just that. Also, today's colleges and businesses are actively seeking a population that is prepared, has the interest, and at the same time *diverse*. Gender stereotypes may hinder someone initially, but if someone discovers something that they want to do, I believe that the path to their goal opens for them.

What effect does a teen's level of self-esteem have on academic achievement and attitude? Have you noticed whether self-esteem drops during early adolescence?

A student's self-esteem is so important in all aspects. When a student has low self-esteem, the student does not perform well academically, may slack off in class, or feels that he/she cannot do well. Self-esteem is such an individual thing. Many adolescents' self-esteem suffers as they go through their middle school years, while others appear well grounded but hide their insecurities. Others are able to handle this critical period with few problems. This period brings many changes in their lives, and many adolescents are affected. It is important that we treat everyone as worthy individuals, remember everyone is important, and support the individual in their interests and endeavors.

What training does a person need to become a guidance counselor? What advice would you offer someone who is considering this career?

A Master's in Counseling or Master's in Education with Counselor Certification is required. Also, school counselors in our state need 2 years of teaching experience. A general knowledge of counseling and development theories has been most helpful; especially knowing how to adapt our counseling to the individual student, circumstance, or situation.

Guidance counselors enter a very challenging occupation, but a very caring one. You will encounter and work with children who range from being extremely needy to those who are stable and successful. Counselors should be caring and resilient. Remember that sometimes even the little things you say to a student are not forgotten—everything you do will be important. Also, having self-awareness and not forgetting to take care of yourself will help you help others. ■

thinking
OF REBECCA

◄ How could a guidance counselor help Rebecca understand that what she is feeling is normal? How could he or she help Rebecca develop and maintain positive self-esteem?

struggled with these issues for many years, but the stereotypes still exist. To read how one inner-city guidance counselor views these issues, read the Professional Perspective box called "Career Focus: Meet a High School Guidance Counselor."

■ **Social Behavior and Personality Traits.**   Prevailing stereotypes in Western cultures portray boys as more active and aggressive and girls as more emotional and helpful. The research evidence supports some of these images, but not all. On average, boys do show higher activity levels than girls from infancy onward. They are more likely to engage in outdoor play, in rough play, and in activities that cover large areas of physical space (Eaton & Enns, 1986;

Lindsey, Mize, & Pettit, 1997; Maccoby, 1998). Girls, on the other hand, perform better on tasks involving flexibility and fine-motor coordination. These differences increase with age. Both girl and boy infants explore new objects, but they tend to use different strategies for doing so. Boys are more likely to handle a new object physically; girls are more likely to use visual exploration, looking carefully at a novel object without actually touching it. Interestingly, male and female infants show different reactions when left alone to explore. Boys are more likely to explore objects and become more independent, while girls show *less* exploration and greater attempts to establish or maintain contact with their caregiver (Mayes, Carter, & Stubbe, 1993).

What about aggression? Beginning at an early age, boys show more physical aggression, such as hitting or kicking, than girls; this difference continues throughout childhood and into adulthood (Coie & Dodge, 1998). Boys also show higher levels of assertiveness than girls, though the difference is not as large as for physical aggressiveness (Feingold, 1994). Studies have found gender differences in physical aggressiveness and assertiveness across numerous countries (Bettencourt & Miller, 1996; Coie & Dodge, 1998; Maccoby & Jacklin, 1974). But the gender gap may be closing for physical aggression, at least among 10- to 17-year-olds. In 1993 adolescent boys reported 7 times more violent behavior than girls. By 1998 the ratio was 3.5 to 1. Arrest rates showed the same trend—in 2001, females accounted for 18 percent of all arrests of juveniles for violent crimes (Children's Defense Fund, 2002b). This means that adolescent females are engaging in more violent acts than they used to (U.S. Department of Health & Human Services, 2001). It's also important to remember that aggression can take different forms. *Relational aggression* seeks to hurt others through social means such as name-calling or exclusion. Girls are significantly more likely than boys to show relational aggression (Crick & Grotpeter, 1995).

Researchers have not found consistent gender differences in prosocial behavior or emotions. Girls often receive ratings from others, and evaluate themselves, as more helpful, cooperative, and sympathetic, but their actual behavior is not consistently different from that of boys. However, girls are more likely to seek and to receive help than are boys, and some studies indicate that girls are more easily influenced than boys (Eisenberg & Fabes, 1998; Ruble & Martin, 1998). When attempting to influence others, boys are more likely to use threats and physical force. Girls tend to use verbal persuasion or, if that does not work, simply to stop their efforts to influence the other person (Serbin, Moller, Gulko, Powlishta, & Colburne, 1994). Some researchers suggest that male infants are *more* emotionally reactive

Boys show higher levels of physical aggression throughout childhood and adolescence, but girls show higher levels of relational aggression.

than female babies, but that culture socializes boys to express less emotion as they get older (with the possible exception of anger). As a result, according to this theory, boys become less skilled at understanding both their own and others' emotions. By adolescence there are clear gender differences in the expression of emotions, particularly of negative ones. For example, girls are more likely to show symptoms of depression or anxiety and to attempt suicide; boys are significantly less likely to report that they experience sadness, shame, or guilt. However, boys are significantly more likely to actually commit suicide. It seems that adolescent boys learn to bear their negative feelings alone and in silence, with potentially deadly results (Eisenberg, Martin, & Fabes, 1996; Kindlon & Thompson, 2000).

The Development of Gender Concepts and Sex-Typed Behaviors

Table 10.5 summarizes some of what we have learned about the developmental progression of the gender concept, gender roles, and sex-typed behavior. As you can see, some aspects of gender knowledge appear quite early in life. By 12 months infants can tell the difference between male and female voices, visually discriminate between pictures of males and females, and coordinate both types of information. By about 2½ years, children are able to apply gender labels correctly (e.g., *boy, girl, mommy, daddy*). However, they do not identify what seem to be the most obvious cues regarding gender—genital cues. Instead, young children explain whether a person is male or female based on surface features such as hairstyles and clothing. For example, when asked whether she was a girl or a boy and how she knew, 5½-year-old Rachel pointed to her shoulder-length hair and replied without hesitation, "I'm a girl, because my hair is long and sometimes I wear dresses." When asked, "What if you had short hair? Would you still be a girl?" Rachel replied with exasperation, "I wouldn't *have* short hair—I'm a girl!" It is not until about the age of 8 years that most children use genital cues to determine gender (Intons-Peterson, 1988; McConaghy, 1979).

Children begin to show gender-stereotyped *preferences* even before they have a full understanding of their own gender. For example, by age 2 they begin to prefer sex-typed toys (e.g., dolls if they are female, cars if they are male). Boys show a tendency to avoid playing with "girls' toys" as early as 2 to 3 years (Fagot, Leinbach, & Hagan, 1986; Powlishta, Serbin, & Moller, 1993). By the time children are 3 years old, they are already beginning to show *gender segregation* (sometimes called *sex segregation* or *sex cleavage*) in their peer preferences—the tendency to play with peers of their own sex when given a choice. This trend increases significantly, and gender segregation remains quite marked until adolescence. (You can read more about gender segregation and gender differences in play in Chapter 11.) By the time children are 5, their gender stereotypes of activities, toys, behavior, and even personality traits are quite well developed.

Gender stereotypes during the late preschool and kindergarten years are also fairly rigid. For example, kindergartners react quite negatively to cross-gender behavior in peers, especially if it involves cross-gender appearance (e.g., a boy wearing a dress) (Signorella, Bigler, & Liben, 1993; Stoddart & Turiel, 1985). There is some evidence that boys' gender stereotypes develop earlier and are more rigid than girls'. In addition, both boys and girls tend to object particularly to cross-gender behavior and appearance in boys; this may mean that the stereotype for "maleness" is more rigid than the one for "femaleness," at least in our culture (Ruble & Martin, 1998). After about 8 years of age, gender stereotypes start to become more flexible as children begin to understand that most gender norms for behavior, activities, occupations and the like are culturally determined rather than absolute. However, the pendulum swings again in adolescence. In **gender intensification** teenagers often adopt more stereotypical gender-related behavior, emotions, and activities as they try to establish a clear

YOUR
PERSPECTIVE
NOTES
Describe your gender-role beliefs. Is the research on gender differences consistent with your beliefs or not? In what ways does the research surprise you?

thinking
OF REBECCA

◀ Could gender intensification explain the changes in Rebecca's school and extracurricular interests? Why is she showing these changes now rather than when she was younger?

gender intensification

The process of conforming more and more closely to gender stereotypes in behavior, emotions, and activities. It is common at adolescence.

TABLE 10.5 Trends in Gender Development

APPROXIMATE AGE/GRADE	TRENDS
Birth to 12 months	By 7 months, infants can discriminate between male and female voices.
	By 9 months, infants can make visual discriminations of pictures of males and females.
	By 1 year, infants show intermodal coordination of information regarding gender (e.g., match voice with appearance).
12 to 24 months (1 to 2 years)	Males show more aggressive behavior and greater assertiveness than females from an early age. The difference decreases over age, except for relational aggression. These differences are found across many cultures and across ages.
	Beginning around 2 years, children begin to show preferences for same-sex toys. Boys show a tendency to avoid playing with "girls' toys" such as dolls, while girls do not show a consistent avoidance of other-sex toys.
24 to 36 months (2 to 3 years)	By 26 months, children show knowledge of gender differences in adult possessions, roles, physical appearance, and abstract characteristics (e.g., soft, cruel).
	By 30 months, children understand the category labels *boy* and *girl.* They apply gender labels to adults before using them for children. By 36 months, most children understand gender identity (i.e., they can consistently label their own sex), but they rely on hairstyle and clothing cues.
	By 2½ to 3 years, children show knowledge of gender stereotypes regarding objects, activities, and children's toys. Children increasingly play with same-sex toys.
	Both boys and girls have increasing positive contact with same-sex peers and begin to show same-sex peer preferences.
Preschool years (3 to 5 years)	Children show increasing gender differences in toy preferences and play activities.
	By 3 years, most children understand gender stability (i.e., that one's gender is stable over time).
	Children show increasing stereotypes regarding children's toys, activities, colors, traits, and play preferences. Stereotypes increase rapidly and are well-established by 5 years, and are stronger for boys than for girls.
	By 2 to 4 years, there is some evidence of children distinguishing between male and female traits, behavior, and emotions, especially along power/fearfulness dimension (e.g., "boys are strong, fast, and they hit"; "girls cry, need help, and are fearful") and negative/positive evaluation (males as negative; females as positive).
	Preference for same-sex peers and sex-segregation in play groups increases. This preference is found across cultures and even in nonhuman primates.
	Same-sex positive bias develops by age 5. (Girls may develop this positive bias earlier, by age 3.) Same-sex peers are expected to prefer to play together.
	Stereotyped differences in personality/social characteristics begin to develop, especially in aggressive and helping behaviors.
	The late preschool years are a period of high rigidity in gender beliefs and behavior.
Early elementary school (6 to 7 years)	Rigidity in gender-stereotyped beliefs regarding activities, occupations, traits, sports, and school tasks is very high during kindergarten.
	Segregation into same-sex play groups remains high and continues until early adolescence.
	Gender-stereotyped preferences remain high or increase, though preferences are higher for some areas than others. When stereotyped preferences show declines, the decreases are seen only in girls.
	Stable or increasing gender differences are seen in such things as television show preferences (boys view more cartoons and action-adventure shows), sports participation, chores, hobbies, and outdoor/indoor play.
	By entry into school, children have extensive knowledge of gender-related activities, which they use to make inferences about novel tasks, activities, and toys.
	There is a strong negative reaction to cross-gender behavior, especially when it involves cross-gender appearance.

TABLE 10.5 (continued)

APPROXIMATE AGE/GRADE	TRENDS
Elementary school (7 to 9 years)	By 7 years, most children show full understanding of gender constancy (i.e., that gender remains the same despite changes in appearances or clothing).
	By 8 to 9 years, children consistently use genital cues to determine gender. Until now, most children have relied on appearance cues (e.g., hair, dress).
	By first grade, there is evidence of gender-stereotyped patterns of self-concept (e.g., "math is important for boys but not for girls"). These patterns increase across the elementary school years. Self-perceptions (e.g., self-reports of qualities such as kind, gentle, persistent) also become increasingly gender stereotyped.
	Gender stereotypes remain very rigid until 7 to 8 years of age. After this, knowledge of gender stereotypes continues to increase, but stereotype rigidity gradually decreases (i.e., children's gender concepts start to become more flexible). Girls show more and earlier stereotype flexibility than boys.
	Children begin to understand the cultural relativity of gender norms.
	Acceptance of cross-gender behavior and appearance increases during middle elementary school years.
Early adolescence (9 to 11 years)	By 10 years, there is increasing awareness of different cultural values given to traditionally male versus female roles, attributes, etc.
	Flexibility of gender stereotypes increases, at least up to early adolescence. Girls show greater flexibility in stereotyped preferences than do boys.
	There is increasing awareness by both boys and girls of the male-favored status, and girls begin to report dissatisfaction with female status.
	Differences are found or increase in some spatial skills, emotional expressiveness, emotional perceptions, and self-esteem.
Adolescence (11 years and older)	Changes in stereotype flexibility during adolescence are unclear. There is some evidence for increasing flexibility as cognitive development progresses, but conflicting evidence due to increasing pressure toward gender intensification.
	Reactions to cross-gender behavior and appearance become more negative, reversing the trend seen during the later elementary school years.
	Gender intensification increases, especially in girls (e.g., increasing time spent in interpersonal activities, personal care, and doing chores; decreasing time spent in sports activities). High levels of sex-typed activities and interests are seen across contexts for both girls and boys.
	Differences emerge or increase in problem solving, physical skills and performance, and incidence of depression.

gender identity and be accepted by the opposite sex. For example, many adolescent girls become more interested in "female" things like hairstyles, trendy clothes, and shopping, and they may drop tomboyish activities like rough or competitive sports. Gender intensification is stronger in girls than in boys, though sex-typed activities are at high levels in both. At the same time, adolescents' reactions to cross-gender behavior and appearance in peers once again become strongly negative, reversing the trend of the later elementary school years (Ruble & Martin, 1998; Signorella et al., 1993; Stoddart & Turiel, 1985).

■ **The Development of Sexual Orientation.** Most children begin experiencing feelings of sexual attraction sometime during late childhood or early adolescence. The object of their attraction is usually a member of the opposite sex, but some youngsters are attracted to people of the same sex. A person's **sexual orientation** is his or her tendency to be attracted to people of the same sex (homosexual orientation), of the opposite sex (heterosexual orientation), or of both sexes (bisexual orientation). Why an individual develops a specific sexual orientation is a matter of great debate, as you are probably well aware. The basic issue is the same question we have discussed so often: What are the relative influences of nature (genetics and biology) and nurture (the environment in which a child develops), and how do these two factors interact?

sexual orientation

Tendency to be attracted to people of the same sex (homosexual orientation), of the opposite sex (heterosexual orientation), or of both sexes (bisexual orientation).

Researchers estimate that 5 to 10 percent of adults in the United States identify themselves as gay, lesbian, or bisexual (C. J. Patterson, 1995). One study of young homosexual and bisexual men reported that the men experienced feelings of same-sex attraction by the age of 10 and had their first homosexual experiences at around 14 (Savin-Williams, 1995). Some differences between homosexual and heterosexual individuals are apparent during childhood. For example, homosexual men and women report having had cross-gender interests during childhood more often than heterosexuals. Children with *gender identity disorder* (in which a person is dissatisfied and uncomfortable with his or her biological sex) dress and behave in ways that are more typical of the opposite sex. These children are significantly more likely to develop a homosexual orientation than children without the disorder (Bailey & Zucker, 1995; Zucker & Bradley, 1995). One model describes the development of a homosexual identity as progressing through four stages (Troiden, 1988):

▶ *Stage 1: Sensitization.* In this stage, which usually occurs before puberty, a child has a general feeling of being different from his or her same-sex peers.

▶ *Stage 2: Identity confusion.* Usually first experienced during adolescence, this stage involves a conflict between a teenager's prior self-image and his or her current feelings of same-sex arousal (or lack of heterosexual arousal).

▶ *Stage 3: Identity assumption.* This stage often begins during the early 20s. The person defines and accepts himself or herself as homosexual and associates regularly with homosexual peer groups.

▶ *Stage 4: Commitment.* This stage begins when the person enters a same-sex love relationship. The person adopts homosexuality "as a way of life," views a homosexual identity as a valid and satisfying self-identity, and may "come out" to others (Troiden, 1988, p. 110).

Descriptions of different childhood characteristics of heterosexual and homosexual individuals are interesting and indicate that orientations may begin to develop early in life—but they do not explain *why* children have these characteristics. There may be a genetic influence: Twin studies have found higher concordance in homosexuality in identical than in nonidentical twins (Bailey & Pillard, 1991). Prenatal hormone levels may play a role as well. For example, there is a relationship between abnormal prenatal hormone levels and later behavior, personality characteristics, and sexual orientation. Girls exposed to higher than normal prenatal levels of androgens (male hormones) tend to show traits and preferences more typical of males, and males exposed to lower than normal levels of androgens show more female-typical patterns and choices (Berenbaum & Snyder, 1995; Dittman et al., 1990; Meyer-Bahlburg et al., 1995; Money & Ehrhardt, 1972). And autopsy studies have found that some areas of the brains of homosexual men are more similar to those of heterosexual women than to the brains of heterosexual men; remember, however, that differences in brain structure could result from biological factors *or* from differences in experience (Byrnes, 2001b; LeVay, 1993; Swaab, Gooren, & Hofman, 1995).

Research indicates that the environment also plays an important role in the development of sexual orientation. You may have heard of incidents in which families have intentionally and systematically raised boys as girls, or vice versa. When this happens, it is usually because a hormonal problem has produced a child who is genetically of one sex but looks like the other. Many of these children develop as normal members of the gender that they were raised as. This means that the environment can be a powerful force in the development of gender identity and sexual orientation (Money & Ehrhardt, 1972; Zucker & Bradley, 1995). There is also ample evidence that reinforcement, punishment, and observational learning influence gender-related behaviors and preferences, as we will discuss in the next section.

One interesting theory tries to integrate the findings on biological and environmental influences (D. J. Bem, 1996, 2000). According to this *"exotic becomes erotic"* theory, adolescents begin to see "exotic," or very different, attributes and behaviors as erotic, or sexually attractive. In this process biology exerts an indirect influence through temperamental characteristics such as activity level and aggressiveness. First, in the preschool and elementary school years, children who are by nature active and aggressive enjoy more active, rough, and energetic activities and peers—that is, more typically male interests and activities. Children with less active and less aggressive tendencies gravitate toward a more female-typical pattern. The key factor, according to this theory, is not a child's overall activity level and degree of aggressiveness but how different the child feels from his or her own or opposite-sex peers during childhood. During childhood each group will tend to view the other as different ("exotic") and undesirable, and these perceptions will cause arousal. Children interpret this arousal as dislike, discomfort, or sometimes even anger or fear. Puberty then changes things—a lot! At this point youngsters cognitively reinterpret the arousal and gradually come to experience it as attraction. As a result, most adolescents develop sexual attraction toward members of the group they have not identified themselves as belonging to. Notice that this theory tries to explain both heterosexual and homosexual development. The groups that form during early and middle childhood are based not on gender but on traits like activity level and aggressiveness. More active and aggressive girls are more likely to identify with boys early on; less active and less aggressive boys are more likely to identify with girls. Some evidence supports the "exotic becomes erotic" idea. Gender segregation during early and middle childhood is very strong, and young children often describe the opposite sex as undesirable and different ("yucky," to use one 6-year-old's word). And homosexual men and women report higher levels of childhood cross-gender play and preferences, as well as feelings of being different from others of their gender (Bailey & Zucker, 1995; Ruble & Martin, 1998). It's not yet clear if this theory explains sexual orientation better than others, but it raises intriguing possibilities (Nicolosi & Byrd, 2002).

■ **Androgyny.** As with all aspects of development, there are important individual differences in the development of gender concepts and behavior. Traditionally, at least in Western cultures, many people have thought of masculinity and femininity as distinct and mutually exclusive: as opposite extremes of a single dimension. However, researchers during the 1970s began to think of masculinity and femininity as two separate dimensions, as shown in Figure 10.4 (Bem, 1974; Constantinople, 1973). The masculine dimension includes characteristics such as independence, assertiveness, dominance, self-confidence, and ambitiousness. The feminine dimension includes sensitivity to others, compassion, warmth, and emotional expressiveness. In this reconceptualization, individuals can possess masculine or feminine qualities to different degrees—and can possess *both* (or *neither*) at the same time. As you can see in the figure, in **androgyny** a person is strong on both dimensions, having many masculine as well as many feminine psychological characteristics. People who have few qualities of either masculinity or femininity fall into the *undifferentiated* category. It is difficult to reliably categorize children as androgynous until about 10 years of age, but by high school about 25 to 35 percent of students can be categorized as androgynous on the basis of their self-reported characteristics. More girls than boys fit the androgynous definition. This may indicate, once again, that boys' gender concepts and stereotypes are more rigid than girls' (Rose & Montemayor, 1994). Alternatively, society may value masculine characteristics more highly; this would encourage girls toward androgyny but would discourage boys from showing feminine characteristics.

Because androgynous people have both traditionally male and stereotypically female psychological characteristics, researchers theorized that such people would adapt to a wide

thinking
OF REBECCA

◄ Would you describe Rebecca as being strongly masculine, strongly feminine, androgynous, or undifferentiated? What aspects of her behavior or comments influenced your opinion?

androgyny

Possession of many masculine as well as many feminine psychological characteristics.

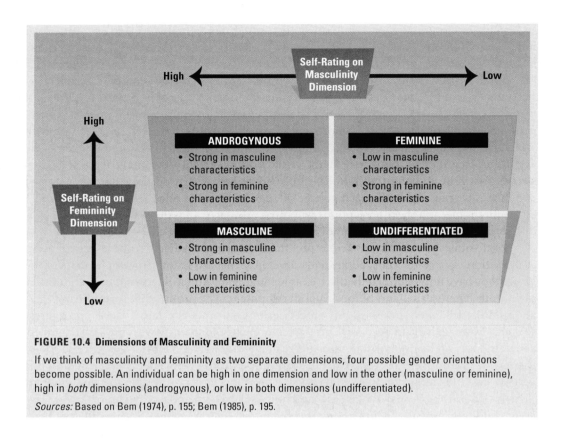

FIGURE 10.4 Dimensions of Masculinity and Femininity

If we think of masculinity and femininity as two separate dimensions, four possible gender orientations become possible. An individual can be high in one dimension and low in the other (masculine or feminine), high in *both* dimensions (androgynous), or low in both dimensions (undifferentiated).

Sources: Based on Bem (1974), p. 155; Bem (1985), p. 195.

range of situations. This should lead to higher self-esteem in androgynous people than in individuals with strongly feminine, strongly masculine, or undifferentiated gender identities. However, research designed to test this theory has had somewhat mixed results (Stake, 1997; Whitely, 1985; Woodhill & Samuels, 2003). The gender identity that produces better psychological adjustment, self-esteem, and well-being probably depends on the values of the culture in which a child develops. If people value traditionally masculine characteristics more highly, as often seems to happen in Western cultures, then having at least some masculine characteristics should have a positive effect. Other cultures may view different patterns more positively.

Theories of Gender Development: A Brief Survey

Much early work on gender development had its roots in the *psychoanalytic perspective* of Sigmund Freud. As you read in Chapter 1, Freud proposed that children go through several stages of psychosexual development. During the phallic stage, Freud proposed, children resolve their unconscious sexual desires for their opposite-sex parent through *identification* with their same-sex parent, imitating and adopting the same-sex parent's approach to behavior, appearance, attitudes, and the like. In this way children form gender concepts and gender roles. A problem with Freud's explanation of gender development is that it says children will not show sex-typed behavior before the phallic stage—that is, before age 4 or 5. In reality, many studies indicate that sex-typed behavior and preferences begin well before age 4. Freud's theory was an important starting point, but it has not received strong research support (Ruble & Martin, 1998). Let's look at more recent ideas about gender development: biological, socialization, and cognitive approaches.

■ Biological Approaches: Born That Way. Current biological theories emphasize a genetic basis for gender differences and focus particularly on the effects of hormones during prenatal development and at puberty. It may surprise you to learn that all embryos, whether genetically male or female, have a female default pattern for development. An embryo remains female or becomes male through a process called *sex differentiation.* The Y chromosome of an XY (i.e., genetically male) embryo contains a substance called *testes-determining factor* (TDF). If TDF is present at 6 to 7 weeks' gestation, then primitive sex organs of the fetus develop into testes. If TDF is not present, then nothing happens until about 10 to 12 weeks' gestation; then the primitive organs develop into ovaries. Hormones direct the formation of external and internal physical structures throughout the body, including the brain, of the developing fetus. In particular, androgens such as testosterone have a significant impact (Ruble & Martin, 1998). For example, girls exposed to higher than normal prenatal levels of androgens are more likely than other females to engage in "tomboyish" behaviors, play with boys' toys, prefer boys as childhood playmates, score higher on visual/spatial tasks at adolescence, and report a bisexual or homosexual orientation. Studies of adolescent boys have linked high androgen levels with aggression and behavior problems (Berenbaum & Snyder, 1995; Buchanan, Eccles, & Becker, 1992; Helleday, 1994; Meyer-Bahlburg et al., 1995).

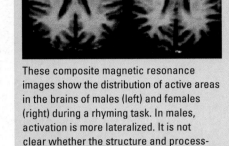

These composite magnetic resonance images show the distribution of active areas in the brains of males (left) and females (right) during a rhyming task. In males, activation is more lateralized. It is not clear whether the structure and processing differences are a *cause* of performance differences or a *result* of environmental and experiential differences.

Researchers using magnetic resonance imaging (MRI) have found gender differences in brain *lateralization,* or the degree to which one hemisphere of the brain is active in a given task. Females show brain activity in both brain hemispheres on language-processing and spatial tasks, so females are less lateralized for these tasks. Boys' brain activity is more lateralized. However, although gender differences in brain structure and functioning do exist, these differences could be the *result* of gender differences in environments and experiences rather than their *cause* (see Ruble & Martin, 1998, for a review).

■ Socialization Approaches: Teaching Gender. Another way to explain gender differences is by examining differences in the social environment boys and girls experience. You do not have to look very hard to find such differences. Boys and girls receive disparate treatment from practically every social agent and in practically every social setting they encounter. But what are the key differences, and how great an impact do they have? The *social learning approach* points to two major influences on gender development: (1) direct and indirect reinforcement and (2) observational learning.

Direct reinforcement consists of consequences the child personally experiences for sex-typed behaviors. You may get praise for wearing a dress if you are a girl ("You look so cute in that pretty dress—what a nice little girl you are!") or for being tough if you are a boy ("That didn't hurt at all, right? You're so tough!"). Direct reinforcement for sex-typed behavior, emotions, and activity preferences can be quite explicit and often starts early in a child's life. One study examined the bedrooms of children aged 5 to 25 months and found that boys' rooms were more likely to be decorated in blue and to contain vehicles and sports equipment, while girls' rooms tended to be pink or yellow and to contain dolls (Pomerleau, Bolduc, Malcuit, & Cossette, 1990).

Differential reinforcement can also be subtle, however. For example, caregivers may limit the choices available to a child, interact with boys and girls in different ways, or hold different expectations for boys' versus girls' abilities and behavior. Parents usually offer different kinds of toys to boys and girls and tend to be more responsive and supportive when children show sex-typed behavior. They also accept different emotional reactions in girls (e.g., fear) than in boys (e.g., anger). Additionally, parents use language differently with boys and girls: They talk more overall to girls and use more supportive and directive language with girls than

Children sometimes receive explicit reinforcement for sex-typed behavior, but reinforcement can also be unspoken and subtle.

with boys (Birnbaum & Croll, 1984; Bradley & Gobbart, 1989; Leaper, Anderson, & Sanders, 1998; Leaper, Leve, Strasser, & Schwartz, 1995). Differential treatment seems to be more noticeable with boys and younger children than with girls and children over 5. Also, fathers exhibit more differential treatment than mothers do (Ruble & Martin, 1998). Studies have revealed that parents' expectations and beliefs about gender differences in abilities correlate significantly with their children's performance and self-perceptions, regardless of the children's actual ability levels. This probably occurs in part because parents provide different experiences for sons and daughters that are consistent with their beliefs (Eccles, Jacobs, et al., 1993).

Children also learn a great deal by observing gender differences. First, of course, they observe "live" models such as parents, teachers, older siblings, and relatives. There is some evidence that children have greater exposure to same-sex models (both adults and peers) and therefore have more opportunity to observe and imitate same-sex behavior and attitudes. This trend increases as children move through adolescence (Crouter, Manke, & McHale, 1995; Hoffman & Teyber, 1985). But children do not need to have direct contact with gender models to learn from watching their behavior. Media sources, too, can promote the development of sex-typed behavior and attitudes. Though recent decades have seen some changes, there is still abundant gender stereotyping in media such as television, movies, books, and music (Huston & Wright, 1998). (We will discuss the impact of the media on several aspects of development in Chapter 13.)

Finally, it is interesting to note that fathers seem to play an especially important role in children's development of gender knowledge and stereotypes. Fathers treat boys and girls more differently than do mothers; men are more effective in encouraging children to engage in non-sex-typed behaviors; and the absence of a father in the home correlates with less traditional gender typing, at least for boys (Katz & Walsh, 1991; Siegal, 1987; Stevenson & Black, 1988). Some of the influence of males probably has to do with the greater power and authority often attributed to men in our society—children tend to follow models they perceive to be powerful. And indeed, boys show more stereotyped gender roles and sex-typed behavior than girls, as we've mentioned. Among boys in father-absent homes, the lack of a male role

model is probably a factor in less traditional gender typing. The impact of fathers on the development of gender typing and sex-typed behavior has led some authors to suggest that men are "custodians of gender-role norms" (Katz & Walsh, 1991, p. 349).

■ **Cognitive Approaches: The Importance of How You Think about It.** Cognitive theories of gender differences emphasize the child's developing understanding of gender and the impact of that understanding on behavior. Based on Piaget's theory, *Kohlberg's cognitive developmental theory* proposed that knowledge of gender and gender-related behavior constitutes a cognitive category and develops in the same way as knowledge of any other cognitive category: through interaction with the world that is filtered through existing cognitive structures. According to Kohlberg, children will not have a mature understanding of gender until they achieve the Piagetian stage of concrete operations, which happens by approximately age 7 (Kohlberg, 1966). The key concept children must grasp in order to understand gender is that of **gender constancy,** or the understanding that an individual's gender remains the same despite changes in outward appearance or behavior (e.g., in hairstyle, clothing, or mannerisms). As you may notice, this idea is simply another form of the Piagetian concept of *conservation* that we described in Chapter 5.

Adherents of Kohlberg's theory have identified three stages of gender understanding (Slaby & Frey, 1975):

Fathers have an important impact on the development of sex-typed behavior, and they tend to treat boys and girls more differently than do mothers.

▶ *Gender identity* (by 2½ years): Children's ability to categorize themselves and others correctly as boys or girls.

▶ *Gender stability* (by 4 to 5 years): The understanding that gender is a stable characteristic over time—that boys continue to be boys, and girls continue to be girls.

▶ *Gender constancy* (also called gender consistency; by 6 to 7 years): The understanding that gender is consistent across changes in outward appearance such as hairstyles or clothing.

Kohlberg proposed that all children progress through these stages in the same order, and studies in several different cultures have supported this sequence of development (Munroe, Shimmin, & Munroe, 1984). According to Kohlberg, children will not show sex-typed behavior until they begin to understand gender constancy; then they will become increasingly interested in and motivated to engage in the behaviors deemed appropriate for their sex. Children do spend more time watching and imitating same-sex models as their knowledge of gender constancy increases, a finding that supports Kohlberg's theory (Frey & Ruble, 1992; Luecke-Aleksa, Andeerson, Collins, & Schmitt, 1995; Slaby & Frey, 1975). But other findings do not support several aspects of Kohlberg's theory. Particularly troublesome is the fact that children consistently show sex-typed behavior long before they have a fully developed understanding of gender constancy. Some studies have even found that *lower* levels of gender understanding relate more strongly to sex-typed behavior than does full understanding (Martin & Little, 1990; Ruble & Martin, 1998). Finally, we know that gender is a very

gender constancy

The understanding that gender remains the same despite superficial changes in appearance or behavior.

Children show preferences for sex-typed toys from an early age; they will even stop playing with a new toy if they learn it is intended for the other sex.

salient characteristic for children, but it is not clear from Kohlberg's theory why children would pay particular attention to gender when developing category knowledge (Bem, 1985).

A more recent cognitive approach, **gender schema theory,** incorporates elements of Kohlberg's theory with the information-processing theory of cognition (see Chapter 6). A gender schema is a cognitive network of gender-related information that organizes gender knowledge and guides expectations and behavior. Gender schemas seem to develop for two main reasons. First, it is usually easy to tell if a person is male or female; this fact makes gender easy for children to use as a basis for categorization. Once the distinction between genders exists, gender serves as an organizing framework for new information. Second, gender is a very salient characteristic for children, because most cultures strongly emphasize it in so many different ways, both physically (e.g., in hair and clothing styles and physical attributes) and psychologically (e.g., through differences in typical male and female activities, occupations, and interaction styles) (Bem, 1985).

Gender schemas affect children in several ways:

▶ As with all schemas, children are more likely to pay attention to and remember information that is consistent with their gender schemas than information that is inconsistent (Welch-Ross & Schmidt, 1996).

▶ Children are more likely to behave according to their gender schemas and to be more accepting of others' behavior when it is consistent with their schemas. This can lead to increasing gender differences as children get older (Byrnes & Takahira, 1993).

▶ Gender schemas affect children's expectations and the inferences they draw in situations in which the gender appropriateness of a behavior or activity is not clear. For example, the gender labels attached to toys significantly affect children's toy choices, even when the toys are novel and it is not obvious why labels designate one gender or the other. In fact, children will stop playing with a novel toy if they learn that the toy's label mentions the opposite sex (Bradbard, Martin, Endsley, & Halverson, 1986; Martin, Eisenbud, & Rose, 1995; Signorella, Bigler, & Liben, 1997).

thinking
OF REBECCA

Describe what you think Rebecca's gender schema might be. How might her gender schema explain her recent behavior?

gender schema theory

The theory that gender knowledge consists of a gender schema, a cognitive network of gender-related information that organizes gender knowledge and guides expectations and behavior.

It is likely that all the theories of gender development we have reviewed are correct to some extent. Ruble and Martin (1998) suggest that gender segregation may play a particularly influential role, describing it as a developmental phenomenon "that increases with age and potentially serves as a mechanism for socializing children into the ways of their own gender group" (Ruble & Martin, 1998, p. 994). Gender segregation reflects biological factors (e.g., arousal levels and temperament differences), social factors (e.g., play styles, interests, and styles of influence), and cognitive factors (e.g., what children understand about and expect from each sex). Thus, gender segregation shows how biological, cognitive, and social factors interact to explain gender development—and it may help drive gender development as well.

1. Young children base their determination of a person's gender primarily on:
   a. genital cues.
   c. behavioral cues.
   b. personality characteristics.
   d. physical appearances.

2. Biological theories of the development of sexual orientation have found that:
   a. differences in brain structure cause sexual orientation.
   b. prenatal hormone levels are associated with later sexual orientation.
   c. differential treatment of boys and girls does not contribute to sexual orientation.
   d. sexual orientation is not genetically based.

3. A 3½-year-old girl refuses to get a haircut because "she doesn't want to turn into a boy." Kohlberg would say that the child:
   a. is suffering from gender identity disorder.
   b. has a gender schema that is based too heavily on information about the opposite sex.
   c. has not yet developed gender constancy.
   d. is likely to show highly sex-typed behavior.

4. Which of the following is *true* regarding gender segregation?
   a. It inhibits the development of mature gender schemas.
   b. It results from biological gender differences and is not affected by social or cognitive factors.
   c. It is an indication of overly sex-typed socialization by parents.
   d. It illustrates the interacting influences of biology, socialization, and cognition on gender development.

5. **True or False:** Boys score higher on measures of mathematical skills beginning in early childhood and continuing through to adulthood.

6. **True or False:** Gender schema theory emphasizes the roles of children's cognitive development and gender knowledge to explain gender differences.

Answers: 1. d, 2. b, 3. c, 4. d, 5. F, 6. T

Moral Development: Thoughts, Emotions, and Behavior

A third important part of becoming who we are is developing morality. **Morality** involves knowing the difference between what is right and wrong and acting on that knowledge. Morality also has an emotional component, in that you feel good about your moral actions and feel guilty or ashamed when you behave in ways that are not moral. So moral development is multifaceted and includes many aspects of reasoning, emotion, and behavior. *Reasoning* about what is morally right in a given situation by no means guarantees moral *behavior*, nor does *emotion* about an action, an event, or another person's situation. In this section we will summarize some of the major theories and findings concerning each of these three components of moral development.

As you study this section, ask yourself these questions:

• What is moral reasoning, and how does it develop?

morality

Knowing the difference between what is right and wrong and acting on that knowledge. Morality includes reasoning, emotions, and behavior.

Moral Development: Thoughts, Emotions, and Behavior   401

- What are the stages of moral reasoning, prosocial reasoning, and empathy? What factors influence a person's movement through these stages?

- How do cognitive development and parenting affect children's moral reasoning, emotions, and behavior?

- What biological and environmental factors affect moral reasoning, emotions, and behavior? How do they interact?

- How can parents and other adults encourage prosocial behavior and decrease aggressive behavior in children and adolescents?

Moral Reasoning: Thinking about Morality

Moral reasoning is the cognitive component of morality and includes the many ways people think about right and wrong. Let's look at Lawrence Kohlberg's work on moral reasoning; then we'll turn to research on prosocial reasoning.

■ **Kohlberg's Stages of Moral Reasoning.** Pretend for a moment that someone dear to you is very sick and will soon die if they do not receive treatment. There is a new drug available that might help, but the pharmacist who developed it is asking a very high price, much more than it cost him to develop the drug. You cannot afford the price, and the druggist will not agree to sell it more cheaply or to let you pay for it later. You are becoming desperate and are considering stealing the drug. Should you? Why, or why not?

Lawrence Kohlberg used hypothetical moral dilemmas like this, which creates a conflict between two values (saving a person's life versus obeying the law), to study the development of moral reasoning (Kohlberg, 1969; Kohlberg, Levine, & Hewer, 1984). Kohlberg based his theory on the work of Jean Piaget, which we described in Chapter 5. Like Piaget, Kohlberg believed that moral development depends on a person's level of cognitive development. You cannot think about moral issues in a sophisticated way if you do not have a fairly high level of overall cognitive development. **Perspective taking**—the ability to understand the psychological perspective, motives, and needs of others—also is essential. To understand a person's intentions and reasons for acting, you have to be able to put yourself in the other person's place and view the situation as the other person might (Selman, 1980).

But cognitive development and perspective-taking ability alone are not enough. That is, they are *necessary but not sufficient* for moral development. Children also must directly experience and think about moral issues and dilemmas in order to understand that their current level of moral reasoning is not adequate. As you may recall, Piaget called this kind of imbalance between experiences and current understanding *cognitive disequilibrium*. Like Piaget, Kohlberg believed that moral development requires us to feel a certain degree of disequilibrium, or discomfort with our current way of thinking, to spur our cognitive construction of more complex and sophisticated reasoning about moral questions.

Kohlberg theorized that children progress through three broad levels of moral reasoning, with each level divided into two specific stages, as shown in Table 10.6. He believed that these stages were universal and invariant—that all children move through the same stages in the same order. However, the pace of development and the final end point will differ depending on specific moral experiences encountered, cognitive maturity, and perspective-taking ability.

Think about the meaning of the word *convention* and you'll understand why Kohlberg's levels are labeled as they are (Table 10.6): A convention is a rule or practice that members of a social group agree to abide by in their behavior, choices, and decisions. At Kohlberg's first level, children have not yet developed the understanding that rules are social conventions, so this is called the *preconventional level*. At this level children accept the rules of powerful others

moral reasoning

The cognitive component of morality; the ways people think about right and wrong.

perspective taking

The ability to understand the psychological perspective, motives, and needs of others; central to the development of moral reasoning, empathy, prosocial reasoning, altruism, and aggression.

TABLE 10.6 Kohlberg's Stages and Levels of Moral Reasoning

Level I: Preconventional

Stage 1: Punishment and obedience orientation

The child decides what is right based on whether the action will be punished or rewarded, but does not consider the interests of others. The child obeys because adults have greater power.

Stage 2: Individualism, instrumental purpose, and exchange

The child follows rules when it serves his own needs or interests. The child is aware that others have interests too, and they may conflict with his own.

Level II: Conventional

Stage 3: Mutual interpersonal expectations, relationships, and interpersonal conformity

The child is concerned with living up to others' expectations. "Being good" is important, and it means having good intentions, being concerned about others, and being loyal and trustworthy.

Stage 4: Social system and conscience

The child defines what is right as what fulfills duties she has agreed to carry out, and abides by laws except in extreme cases. Moral actions are those that the larger society has determined are right.

Level III: Postconventional

Stage 5: Social contract or utility and individual rights

Values and rules are seen as relative to a particular group and can be changed. Rules should be followed for the welfare and protection of all people's rights, and what is moral is what is best for the largest number of people. Some values, such as life and liberty, are recognized as nonrelative and must be upheld regardless of socially agreed upon laws.

Stage 6: Universal ethical principles

A person develops and follows her own self-chosen ethical principles, which are part of an integrated and carefully thought-out system of values. If social laws violate these principles, the person's actions will be consistent with her ethical principles.

Source: Adapted from Kohlberg (1984).

without thinking about where the rules come from, whether they are fixed or flexible, or whether some circumstances could allow changes in the rules. In Stage 1 children determine what is "moral" on the basis of rewards or punishments, regardless of whether the intention was good or not. In Stage 2 children are beginning to understand that others have different perspectives, but they are not able to see a situation from another's perspective. Their moral reasoning at this stage is based on meeting their own needs—what is "good" is what serves their interests.

At the second broad level of moral reasoning, the *conventional level*, children have developed an understanding that rules are social conventions, and they are beginning to be able to understand things from others' perspectives. At this level young people follow rules because they believe this is important to maintain their personal social standing or the social order as a whole. They are becoming able to see how others might view their actions and to understand how their actions can affect other people. In Stage 3 children follow rules in order to gain the approval of their friends and family. In Stage 4 children broaden their understanding and follow rules in order to maintain social order.

Finally, at the *postconventional level*, people move beyond social conventions as the basis for moral reasoning. They no longer obey societal rules without at least questioning them. They understand that others can have opinions that are different from their own, and that different opinions can be equally "right." In Stage 5 they obey rules and laws because this helps protect the rights of individuals. Laws (conventions) can be interpreted and changed for greater fairness, however. In Stage 6 individuals reason about moral issues on the basis of

YOUR PERSPECTIVE
NOTES

For each of Kohlberg's stages, try to think of someone who reasons about moral issues at that level. What has helped some of these people move to higher levels? At what level would you place yourself?

At Stage 6, the highest level of Lawrence Kohlberg's theory of moral reasoning, a person's thinking about moral issues is based on self-chosen abstract ethical principles that apply to all humans. While Mother Teresa clearly achieved Stage 6, few people appear to function consistently at this level.

self-chosen, abstract ethical principles that they apply to all humans and social systems. People at this stage may choose to disobey laws they believe are immoral rather than violating their ethical principles. They accept the legal or social consequences of breaking the rules. Although some adolescents may achieve the postconventional level, people usually do not attain it until adulthood, if ever.

Kohlberg also distinguished between the *structure* of a response to a moral issue, or the way a person reasons about the issue, and the *content* of the response, or the specific choice the person makes. So, in the example of the pharmacist, the *content* of your answer might be that you should steal the drug. But the *structure* of your answer could be either at a lower level (e.g., "my family would be mad if I didn't") or at a higher level (e.g., "it is wrong to let someone die if there is anything I can do to prevent it"). Kohlberg emphasized that the structure, not the content, determines the level of moral reasoning.

Later Work and Research on Kohlberg's Theory. Kohlberg revised his theory several times. In later work Kohlberg said that some aspects of moral development (the levels of reasoning) will be universal, whereas others (the particular moral values developed and choices made) will depend on the specific social conditions in which a child develops. Kohlberg also acknowledged that Stage 6 is rare in real life; it may be more of a theoretical end point than a stage many people actually achieve. However, he also speculated that there may be a seventh stage that goes past the postconventional level. The seventh stage would represent an "ethical orientation arising from . . . existential or religious experience and thinking rather than from moral experience alone" (Kohlberg & Power, 1981, p. 354).

Empirical research supported several aspects of Kohlberg's theory. For example, Figure 10.5 shows some of the results of a 20-year longitudinal study of Kohlberg's original sample. Participants showed the expected sequence of stages from Stage 1 up to Stage 5, with no evidence of skipping stages or of falling back to lower stages once they had reached a higher level. The correlation between age and stage of moral development was .78, indicating a strong positive relationship. Other studies have verified the predicted sequences across several different cultures as well (Colby, Kohlberg, Gibbs, & Lieberman, 1983; Snarey, Reimer, & Kohlberg, 1985; Tietjen & Walker, 1985; Walker, 1989). There is also good support for Kohlberg's ideas about the relationship among cognitive development, perspective-taking skill, and moral development (Krebs & Gillmore, 1982; Selman, 1976; Walker & Hennig, 1997).

Other Moral Orientations. Nevertheless, critics have raised some important questions about Kohlberg's model. Cross-cultural studies support his sequence of stages, but they have also found that people in less technologically advanced and more rural cultures move through the stages more slowly and achieve a lower end stage than those in more advanced and urban cultures (Snarey, 1995). These findings are not necessarily a problem for Kohlberg's theory; to the degree that different cultures provide different kinds of experience with moral issues, the theory would expect differences (Kohlberg, 1969; Snarey et al., 1985). However, these results could be due to a bigger issue: a fundamental difference between the moral orientation of these cultures and the orientation Kohlberg's theory reflects. Critics argue that Kohlberg's stages are based on a *justice orientation* of morality. That is, in Kohlberg's theory morality involves justice, individual responsibility, and preservation of individual rights. In some cultures, however, justice is not the only or the most important factor people consider when making moral judgments. For example, some cultures emphasize a morality based on

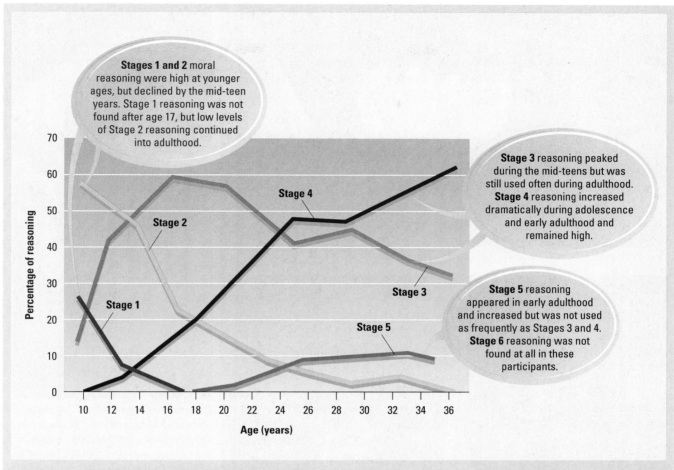

Stages 1 and 2 moral reasoning were high at younger ages, but declined by the mid-teen years. Stage 1 reasoning was not found after age 17, but low levels of Stage 2 reasoning continued into adulthood.

Stage 3 reasoning peaked during the mid-teens but was still used often during adulthood. Stage 4 reasoning increased dramatically during adolescence and early adulthood and remained high.

Stage 5 reasoning appeared in early adulthood and increased but was not used as frequently as Stages 3 and 4. Stage 6 reasoning was not found at all in these participants.

FIGURE 10.5 Follow-Up Research on Kohlberg's Theory of Moral Development

A 20-year follow-up of Lawrence Kohlberg's original participants supported the sequence of stages Kohlberg proposed in his developmental theory of moral reasoning. Ages and stages of moral reasoning showed strong correlations.

Source: Adapted from A. Colby, L. Kohlberg, J. Gibbs, & M. Lieberman. (1983). A longitudinal study of moral judgement. *Monograph of the Society for Research in Child Development, 48* (1–2, Serial No. 200), p. 46. Reprinted with permission of the Society for Research in Child Development.

community, in which social order, status, and duty to others are key. Others emphasize *divinity,* which involves restraint from sinful acts, duty to God, and the sanctity of people, objects, or places. Others, like Kohlberg's, emphasize *autonomy* and focus on justice, preservation of individual rights, and fairness (Shweder, Much, Mahapatra, & Park, 1997). Kohlberg's theory (and the dilemmas used to test it) reflect an orientation that may or may not be relevant in other cultures. Therefore, the theory may apply to only a small or unimportant part of moral development in these cultures. If so, then conclusions about the people's levels of moral reasoning or the universality of moral development will be incomplete or even invalid.

A similar criticism has arisen regarding the validity of Kohlberg's model for women. In 1982 Carol Gilligan proposed that women's moral reasoning derives from a *care ethic,* which emphasizes concern for the welfare of others, preservation of interpersonal relationships, and an obligation to take care of others (Gilligan, 1982). Gilligan said that Kohlberg's emphasis on autonomy, justice, and impartial fairness is more consistent with a traditionally male perspective. She argued that Kohlberg's theory does not fully consider the elements that are central to women's moral reasoning. Was she right? No and yes. There is not much evidence

Cultures differ in their moral orientations. Some emphasize community, others divinity, and others autonomy. Kohlberg's stages of moral reasoning may pertain more to some cultures than to others.

of systematic gender differences in studies using Kohlberg's materials and stages. That is, when participants offer reasons involving care for others, the materials do not systematically score these reasons as being at a lower level (Jadack, Hyde, Moore, & Keller, 1995; Jaffee & Hyde, 2000; Walker, 1995). However, research indicates that a care orientation does exist and that females are somewhat more likely to use it, especially when reasoning about personal and real-life issues (Garmon, Basinger, Gregg, & Gibbs, 1996; Wark & Krebs, 1996). But it is not the case that males do not use a care orientation. Instead, it appears that both men and women can and do use both care and justice orientations. It's just that the typical moral issues encountered by each gender may lead men to use a justice orientation more often and women to use a care orientation more often (Clopton & Sorell, 1993; Gilligan & Attanucci, 1988).

Moral Domains.   Other studies have questioned the degree to which moral reasoning is consistent across contexts. When researchers ask people to think about real-life moral dilemmas rather than hypothetical ones, several interesting findings emerge. People use a "lower" level of moral reasoning, report having strong emotions as they think about the dilemma, and often suggest several different strategies for addressing the dilemma (Walker & Hennig, 1997; Walker, Pitts, Hennig, & Matsuba, 1995). Moral reasoning also seems to be different for different types of moral issues; in other words, moral reasoning is more domain-specific than Kohlberg believed (Nucci, 1996; Turiel, 1998). For example, even 3-year-old children think differently about issues that involve *moral imperatives* (rules that deal with justice, fairness, and the protection of people's rights and welfare) than about those involving *social conventions* (accepted rules or customs that help maintain the order and smooth functioning of a society) or *matters of personal choice* (individual decisions that do not infringe on the rights of others). This means children recognize early in life that some things are morally wrong even if they are not technically illegal (Smetana, 1995; Tisak, 1995). In sum, as with Piaget's theory of cognitive development, it appears that levels of moral reasoning can be influenced significantly by features of the context and are more domain-specific than Kohlberg believed. In addition, as we pointed out earlier, moral reasoning does not guarantee moral behavior.

■ **The Development of Prosocial Reasoning.** Another aspect of moral reasoning involves **prosocial reasoning,** or children's thought processes as they decide whether to help someone. Nancy Eisenberg presented children and young people from preschool through 12th grade with prosocial dilemmas—situations in which helping someone else would require some kind of personal sacrifice. For example, in one scenario a girl on her way to a birthday party was asked to help another child who was hurt. Stopping to help would mean missing the ice cream, cake, and games. Should the girl help, and if so, why? (Eisenberg, 1986; Eisenberg, Carlo, Murphy, & Van Court, 1995).

On the basis of the responses she received, Eisenberg proposed that prosocial reasoning develops through the levels shown in Table 10.7. It is easy to see the parallels between the levels of prosocial reasoning and Kohlberg's levels of general moral reasoning: With age, children move from a sole concern with their own needs to a concern with social approval, and finally to reasoning based on broader principles. As in Kohlberg's theory, Eisenberg's theory views overall cognitive development and perspective-taking ability as important in the development of prosocial reasoning. However, the theory does not assume the levels of prosocial reasoning to be universal. According to Eisenberg both environmental and emotional factors, such as parenting and feelings of empathy, affect the development and use of prosocial reasoning (Eisenberg & Fabes, 1998).

Studies in several different countries have supported the sequence of levels Eisenberg proposed (Eisenberg, 1986; Eisenberg et al., 1995). However, the type of request affects whether children engage in any reasoning at all about whether to help. When a request for help is simple and involves little or no cost, it seems that children give very little thought to what they should do: They simply help (Eisenberg & Shell, 1986; Miller, Eisenberg, Fabes, & Shell, 1996). The social environment also affects prosocial reasoning. For example, children in an Israeli kibbutz, which emphasizes communal values and equality, showed lower levels of needs-oriented reasoning and higher levels of an internalized values orientation (Eisenberg, 1986). In addition, parenting that is warm in emotional tone, communicates expectations of mature behavior, and provides explanations seems to encourage higher levels of prosocial reasoning (Janssens & Deković, 1997).

Guilt and Empathy: The Roles of Emotions in Moral Development

Rather than focusing on reasoning in moral development, some theorists have chosen to examine the roles of emotions in morality, or **moral affect.** Moral affect includes both negative emotions such as guilt and more positive feelings such as empathy.

■ **Freud and Guilt.** Freud's psychoanalytic theory suggests that children internalize from parents a morality consisting largely of the restraint of the sexual impulses of the id.

thinking
OF REBECCA

◄ Might it be helpful to Rebecca to know about Kohlberg's stages of moral reasoning and Eisenberg's stages of prosocial reasoning? How could Rebecca use her knowledge of these stages to make friends or to improve the atmosphere at her school?

prosocial reasoning

Children's thought processes about helping others; specifically, their reasons for deciding whether to help another person.

moral affect

The emotional component of morality, including both negative emotions such as guilt and more positive emotions such as emotional attachment to caregivers, sympathy, and empathy.

TABLE 10.7 Developmental Levels of Prosocial Reasoning

LEVEL	AGES	DESCRIPTION
Hedonistic orientation	Preschool; beginning elementary school	• The child is concerned with his or her own needs and consequences for himself or herself. • Child will help if it benefits himself or herself now or in the future, or if he or she likes or needs the other person. • *Example:* "I'd help because then he'd let me ride his new bike."
Needs-of-others orientation	Some preschool children; many elementary schoolers	• The child is concerned with the needs of others, even if they conflict with his or her own needs. • There is little evidence of sympathy for the other person or of guilt over not helping. • *Example:* "I'd help because he's hurt and needs help."
Approval and/or stereotyped orientation	Elementary school; high school	• The child is concerned with being accepted by others and gaining approval. • Decisions about helping or not are often based on stereotyped views of what "good" or "bad" people do. • *Example:* "I'd help because my dad would be really proud of me."
Empathetic orientation	Older elementary school; high school	• The child shows sympathy for the other person's situation. • The child expresses guilt for not helping and positive feelings for helping. • There are sometimes vague references to internalized values or responsibilities. • *Example:* "I'd help because he must feel really sad. It would help him feel better, and I'd feel good about helping."
Strongly-internalized-values orientation	Small number of high schoolers; no elementary schoolers	• The child is concerned with following his or her own internalized values, norms, beliefs, or duties. • Violating the internal standards can cause loss of self-respect. • *Example:* "It's important to help people who are hurt. If we all did that all the time, our world would be a much better place."

Source: Adapted from Eisenberg, Lennon, & Roth (1983).

According to Freud, children behave in moral ways to avoid the guilty feelings that arise from the superego when the child behaves inappropriately (Freud, 1959). However, most psychologists now believe that although guilt can help motivate moral behavior by helping children focus on the effects of their actions, positive emotions such as attachment to caregivers, sympathy, and empathy can be just as powerful. Shame seems to produce negative self-evaluations, greater preoccupation with the self, and less focus on consequences for other people (Eisenberg & Fabes, 1998; Tangney, 2001). In addition, Freud's theory implies that the way to help children behave morally is to punish their impulses and to threaten to withdraw love and affection. But parenting based on these ideas (i.e., parenting that uses physical control, commands, threats, and withdrawal of affection) actually seems to produce *lower* levels of moral behavior (Denham et al., 2000; Kochanska, 1993; Zahn-Waxler, Iannotti, Cummings, & Denham, 1990). In contrast, parenting that emphasizes in age-appropriate ways the physical and emotional effects of a child's behavior on others fosters more prosocial behavior and moral development. This type of parenting, called *inductive parenting,* tells children how they *should* behave, promotes the development of empathy and sympathy by encouraging children to take the other person's perspective, and helps children understand what the parents' expectations are and why they are appropriate (Krevans & Gibbs, 1996; Turiel, 1998).

empathy

Understanding another person's emotion and feeling the same or similar emotion.

■ **Empathy: Feeling Another's Pain.** One emotion that seems to be very important in moral development is **empathy,** or the ability to understand another person's emotion and feel the same or similar emotion yourself. Empathy sometimes leads to *sympathy*—feeling sorrow or concern for the other person but not feeling the same emotion. However, empathy can also lead to *personal distress,* in which children focus on dealing with their own discomfort or anxiety instead of thinking about what might help the other person (Eisenberg & Fabes, 1998). The roots of empathy can be seen in very young children. Even newborns will cry when they hear another baby cry, and there is some evidence that infants respond more strongly to the sound of other infants' crying than to other similar sounds (Dondi, Simion, & Caltran, 1999; Sagi & Hoffman, 1976). Hoffman (1984, 2001) describes the developmental course of empathy as a series of levels, shown in Table 10.8. As you look at these levels, notice how the growth of empathy involves cognitive development, especially the ability to take others' perspectives both cognitively and emotionally. At the earliest level, infants are not yet aware that they are physically separate from others, but they do show an empathetic response to specific cues such as the sound of crying *(global empathy)*. With development, children come to understand that others are separate and have different emotional states. At first, children try to reduce others' unhappiness by doing things that would help themselves feel better *(egocentric empathy)*. Later, they show clearer understanding of what the other person needs, and they use their developing language skills to affect the other person's emotions and to grasp complex emotions *(empathy for another's feelings)*. Finally, older children and adolescents begin to empathize with others even when the other person is not present. Empathy, no longer tied to a specific experience, can extend to another person's general life situation. Or it can embrace a general group, such as people who are poor, oppressed, or mistreated. Though empathy undergoes substantial development, Hoffman believes that humans are biologically predisposed to respond to the distress of others. Indeed, some evidence from twin studies points to a biological contribution (Hoffman, 1991; Zahn-Waxler, Robinson, & Emde, 1992). However, aspects of the environment also can reinforce and shape empathy—particularly the type of parenting a child experiences (Krevans & Gibbs, 1996).

YOUR PERSPECTIVE NOTES

Think of a time when you felt empathy for someone else. Did your feelings affect your behavior? In what ways?

TABLE 10.8 Developmental Levels of Empathy

LEVEL	DESCRIPTION
1. Global empathy (birth to 1 year)	Strong emotions in others can create similar emotions in the self, but the two are confused since the infant cannot separate the self from others. The infant will behave as if he or she has had the experience (e.g., a baby cries, sucks his thumb, and crawls to his mom when another child is hurt).
2. Egocentric empathy (1 to 2 or 3 years)	The child understands he or she is separate from others. Emotions in others can create similar emotions in the self, but the child understands that he or she did not have the experience. He or she will try to comfort others by doing what would make him or her feel better (e.g., a child offers to let his mother play with his favorite trucks when she is sad or hurt).
3. Empathy for another's feelings (preschool and elementary school years)	The child understands that others' feelings differ from his or her own, is sensitive to cues about others' feelings, and distinguishes a wider range of emotions. He or she feels an emotion similar to another's, but helps by offering what the *other* person finds helpful (e.g., a boy offers a cup of tea to his mother when she is sad).
4. Empathy for another's life conditions (late childhood/early adolescence to adulthood)	The youth begins to understand that emotions can be due to enduring life conditions and situations, such as poverty or discrimination. He or she begins to feel empathy for groups of people such as the poor, ill, or oppressed. He or she still feels a similar emotion to another for specific events, but has an even stronger empathetic emotion for chronic life conditions (e.g., a young man feels especially bad for a peer who is hurt and whose family has struggled with poverty or discrimination).

Source: Adapted from Hoffman (1984).

Are humans biologically predisposed to respond to others' distress? Even young children show empathy.

Moral Behavior: Altruism and Aggression

Of course, the reason that most of us are interested in moral development is our concern with **moral behavior,** or the degree to which a person acts in accordance with moral rules when actually faced with a situation that requires a choice. When we hear reports of officials lying, students cheating, adolescents killing one another, or extremists terrorizing the population, we are not worried about how these individuals are reasoning. Our concerns are about what they will actually *do*. It is useful to understand moral and prosocial reasoning and moral emotions, but how do these elements come together to produce moral behavior?

■ **Watch and Learn: Social Learning Theory.**   Social learning theorists, most notably Albert Bandura, argue that moral (and immoral) behavior is learned in the same way as any other behavior: through reinforcement, punishment, and observational learning (Bandura, 1977). Through operant conditioning and modeling, as discussed in Chapter 1, children gain information about the behaviors that are expected of them as well as acceptable and unacceptable alternatives. A model can be a real person; but it also can be a person on television, a character in a book or a video game, or even a cartoon character. These media models can exert a powerful influence, for better or for worse, on moral behavior. We will talk about the effects of media on children's development in Chapter 13.

Modeling is particularly important, because many of the moral behaviors we wish to encourage in children do not spontaneously occur often enough for reinforcement to be effective. Modeling has a greater impact on younger children, perhaps because they are still in the process of learning what behaviors are acceptable and under what conditions (Peterson, 1982). Models who are emotionally warm and responsive, whom children perceive as being competent and powerful, and whose behavior is consistent with what they say children should do have a greater influence on children's prosocial behavior (Bandura, 1977; Eisenberg & Fabes, 1998). Children also learn aggressive behaviors via modeling. Those who consistently experience higher levels of verbal or physical punishment from parents tend to show higher levels of aggressive behavior and defiance when outside the home (Strassberg, Dodge, Pettit, & Bates, 1994).

moral behavior

The degree to which a person acts in accordance with moral rules when actually faced with a situation that requires a choice.

altruism

Voluntary behavior that is motivated by concern for another or by internal values and goals, not by the expectation of external rewards or punishment.

■ **Altruistic and Prosocial Behavior.** **Altruism** is voluntary behavior motivated by concern for another or by internal values and goals rather than by the expectation of external rewards or punishment (Eisenberg & Fabes, 1998). Self-chosen and internally guided, altruistic behavior occurs simply because a person believes it is the right thing to do. Altruism can be heroic and self-sacrificing, but more often it involves simple acts of sharing, helping, and cooperation. Studying altruism can be difficult, because it is sometimes impossible to determine the motive(s) for a person's action. Researchers often investigate altruism as part of the larger topic of *prosocial behavior* (voluntary behavior intended to help another person), and the terms are sometimes used interchangeably.

Human altruism and prosocial behavior begin very early in life. As we mentioned before, even newborns will cry in response to the cries of another baby; some analysts interpret this as a precursor to prosocial behavior (Dondi et al., 1999). Children as young as one will share toys or food and attempt to help their parents. Young children are more likely to share when there are few toys available and when sharing does not require a great deal of self-sacrifice (e.g., when sharing does not involve a toddler's own *favorite* toy). Sharing is more likely when adults actively encourage it, when other children directly request it, or when another child has recently shared with the child (Hay, Caplan, Castle, & Stimson, 1991). Most forms of prosocial behavior increase across the elementary school years, as researchers have observed in several different countries. Not surprisingly, aspects of the context (e.g., being told that sharing is good, knowing that an adult is watching) and of the child (e.g., level of cognitive development) affect prosocial behaviors such as sharing and cooperation (Eisenberg & Fabes, 1998; Knight, Berning, Wilson, & Chao, 1987).

What factors influence altruistic behavior? The cognitive and emotional factors we've discussed are important contributors: level of moral and prosocial reasoning, empathy, and perspective-taking ability. For example, researchers find that preschoolers who have reached at least the needs-oriented level of prosocial reasoning are more likely to share spontaneously and to help peers than children still at the hedonistic level. In other research investigators asked adolescents to rate their peers with respect to prosocial behavior, then assessed the participants' levels of prosocial reasoning. Teens rated by their peers as more prosocial in behavior showed higher levels of prosocial reasoning (Carlo, Koller, Eisenberg, DaSilva, & Frohlich, 1996; Miller et al., 1996). There is only a modest relationship between empathy and prosocial behavior in younger children, but the relationship becomes stronger with age. Maybe younger children feel empathetic emotions but do not understand why, so they cannot act on their prosocial impulses. As their understanding of their empathetic feelings increases, perhaps children become more able to act on the feelings (Roberts & Strayer, 1996; Underwood & Moore, 1982).

Overall culture and specific family practices also have important effects. For example, children show higher levels of altruism when they live in cultures that expect people to contribute to the welfare of the group and that stress cooperation and avoidance of conflict—cultures such as those of Kenya, Mexico, the Philippines, and some Native American groups. Similarly, families encourage altruism when they regularly expect children to do tasks that benefit the family in some way (e.g., taking out the garbage, caring for siblings) rather than only tasks that benefit themselves (e.g., cleaning their own rooms) (Grusec, Goodnow, & Cohen, 1996; Whiting & Whiting, 1975). Parental teaching also plays a part. When parents use the inductive approach we described earlier, children display higher levels of empathy, prosocial reasoning, and prosocial behaviors. When parents rely on a punitive approach, the outcome is less prosocial behavior (Krevans & Gibbs, 1996; Shure, 2001; Zahn-Waxler et al., 1992). Finally, it is clear that families and other caregivers can encourage altruism through verbal reinforcement, verbal encouragement, and consistent modeling of altruistic behavior. In fact, some studies have found that viewing a model of altruism (e.g., watching an adult donate something of value to a charity) increased children's

thinking
OF REBECCA

◀ What might explain the unhelpful and sometimes mean behaviors of the students at Rebecca's school? Is their behavior typical for youths of this age? What might encourage more helpful behavior?

willingness to contribute to the charity several days or even several months later (Rice & Grusec, 1975; Rushton, 1980). Even *preachings*—verbal explanations that state what a child should do and why without actually telling the child to engage in the behavior—can have some positive effect if they focus on the positive benefits of the prosocial behavior for the person being helped (Eisenberg & Fabes, 1998). In short, families that value, model, expect, and explicitly encourage and discuss altruism are more likely to see such behavior in their children.

■ **Aggressive Behavior.** As you are well aware, aggressive behavior is of increasing concern in our society. The consequences can be extreme for direct victims of aggression, but we all pay a price when our children and youth behave in aggressive ways. **Aggression** is behavior intended to harm people or property (Coie & Dodge, 1998). It is not the outcome that is important, but the intent. Aggression carried out as a means for gaining something, as when a child hits a playmate in order to grab a toy, is called *instrumental aggression.* In contrast, *hostile aggression* is aggressive behavior in which the main goal is to harm someone. *Relational aggression,* which we talked about in our section of gender differences, aims at harming social relationships or self-esteem (Crick & Grotpeter, 1995).

All children show aggressiveness at times, particularly during the early childhood years and most often during conflicts over possessions. Typically, 6-month-olds do not seem to mind when another baby takes their toys. By 12 months, however, toy-grabbing can elicit an aggressive response (Caplan, Vespo, Pedersen, & Hay, 1991). Many peer interactions at this age involve conflict, usually over toys or other objects. Fortunately, most do not involve aggressive behavior and most are short, lasting an average of less than 30 seconds whether an adult intervenes or not (Coie & Dodge, 1998). Physical aggression increases from age 2 to age 3, but decreases by age 5. Verbal aggression (e.g., making threats), on the other hand, increases over this time period as children learn to use language and as parents and peers strongly discourage physical forms of aggression. Instrumental aggression decreases in frequency, in part because children's growing language skills give them other ways of getting what they want, and in part because children are becoming better able to delay their desires and wait their turn. From age 4 to age 7, however, hostile aggression increases. Children's growing cognitive abilities enable them to draw inferences about the intent of others' behavior. If they think another child meant to do harm, they may respond in kind (Coie, Dodge, Terry, & Wright, 1991; Hartup, 1974). As we mentioned in our discussion of gender differences, boys are more physically and verbally aggressive than girls from an early age. In contrast, girls are more likely to engage in relational aggression, as shown in Figure 10.6 (Crick, Casas, & Mosher, 1997; Crick & Grotpeter, 1995).

Patterns of aggressive behavior during adolescence are a bit harder to describe. Hostile and openly aggressive behavior reaches its highest level between ages 13 and 15. Then it decreases, but other forms of aggression continue. Relational aggression in adolescent girls takes more subtle and harmful forms. Adolescent boys are more likely to engage in delinquency: truancy, substance abuse, petty theft, and disorderly conduct (U.S. Department of Justice, 1998). Most boys who get involved in delinquent behavior during adolescence do not continue to behave in antisocial ways. Some, however, show an *early-onset type* (also called *early-starter pattern*) of delinquency. These boys have several things working against them from an early age, including difficult temperaments, subtle cognitive deficits, poor parenting, and high-conflict home environments. This combination leads to school and behavior problems. About half of these boys continue their antisocial behavior throughout adolescence and into adulthood (Brennan, Hall, Bor, Najman, & Williams, 2003; Broidy et al., 2003; Loeber & Stouthamer-Loeber, 1998; Moffitt, Caspi, Dickson, Silva, & Stanton, 1996; Simons, Wu, Conger, & Lorenz, 1994). To date there is little research on the developmental paths of girls who show delinquent or aggressive behavior.

Aggressiveness is a relatively stable characteristic. Figure 10.7 shows the results of one longitudinal study that assessed aggressive behavior over 22 years. As you can see, children

thinking
OF REBECCA

Should Rebecca be concerned about her friend Daniel, or is petty theft a reasonably normal part of adolescence? What might explain his behavior?

aggression

Behavior intended to harm people or property; can be instrumental, hostile, or relational.

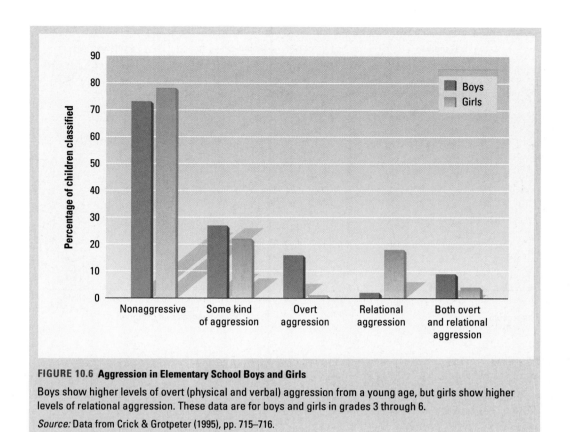

FIGURE 10.6 Aggression in Elementary School Boys and Girls

Boys show higher levels of overt (physical and verbal) aggression from a young age, but girls show higher levels of relational aggression. These data are for boys and girls in grades 3 through 6.

Source: Data from Crick & Grotpeter (1995), pp. 715–716.

who were rated as aggressive at 8 years of age were significantly more likely to be convicted of criminal offenses and of more serious offenses. They were also more likely to commit domestic violence against spouses or children. Other studies have shown similar patterns across early and middle childhood (Hart, Olsen, Robinson, & Mandleco, 1997; Huesman, Eron, Lefkowitz, & Walder, 1984; Newman, Caspi, Moffitt, & Silva, 1997). Twin studies have indicated a genetic predisposition toward aggressive behavior (Plomin, 1990). Clearly some children are at higher risk for aggressive behavior.

What factors influence whether aggressive behavior will continue? As we have seen for the development of prosocial emotions and behavior, the family environment plays a key role. An aggressive, out-of-control child may live in what has been called a *coercive home environment* (G. R. Patterson, 1995, 1997). In such families coercive discipline and conflict resolution strategies such as yelling, threats, orders, and physical punishment are the norm. Both parents and children frequently behave aggressively, and levels of anger and hostility are high. Parents rarely acknowledge or reinforce prosocial behavior, focusing instead on misbehavior. In addition, coercive parents tend to interpret ambiguous events in negative ways, seeing threats where there really aren't any (Dodge, Pettit, & Bates, 1994; G. R. Patterson, 1995, 1997). Even when the home environment is not overtly coercive, parents may indirectly encourage aggression by failing to adequately supervise their children's activities and social relationships or to place appropriate limits on behavior.

The way a child thinks about social situations also affects the likelihood of aggressive behavior. Like coercive parents, some aggressive children seem to interpret social interactions in a negative and hostile way. Researchers have found that these so-called *reactive aggressors* quickly retaliate with aggression to the hostile intent they perceive. As a result, of course, they begin actually having more negative experiences with others, which reinforce their negative

YOUR
PERSPECTIVE
NOTES

Has your home environment affected your level of altruistic or aggressive behavior? In what ways? Looking back, would you change your home situation in any way?

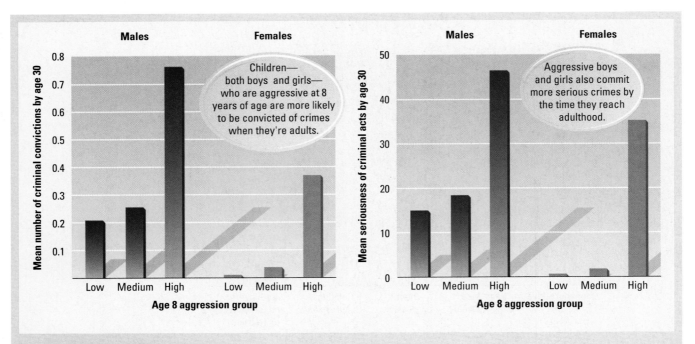

FIGURE 10.7 The Stability of Aggressiveness

One longitudinal study found that children rated as aggressive at 8 years of age continued showing aggressive behaviors more than 20 years later.

Source: L. R. Huesmann, L. D. Eron, M. M. Lefkowitz, L. O. Walder. (1984). Stability of aggression over time and generations. *Developmental Psychology,* *20* (6), p. 1125. Reprinted with permission.

interpretations. Other aggressive children show a different pattern of information processing. *Proactive aggressors* do not jump to the conclusion of intentional harm. Instead, they more slowly form a goal and consciously choose to act aggressively, deciding that this is the most effective strategy for accomplishing their goal. These children believe that aggression will get them what they want and that the personal cost is likely to be low (Crick & Dodge, 1996; Dodge, Bates, & Pettit, 1990; Perry, Perry, & Rasmussen, 1986).

Other researchers have found that aggressive children show lower levels of perspective-taking, moral reasoning, and sympathy than nonaggressive peers, and that they are less likely to see their aggressive behavior as negative (Boldizar, Perry, & Perry, 1989; Gregg, Gibbs, & Basinger, 1994). Perhaps surprisingly, aggressive children tend to have high self-esteem, in spite of the problems their behavior causes with peers and adults. They maintain their self-esteem, and avoid dealing with feelings of empathy, by distorting how they think about their actions. For example, they often blame the victim for a negative outcome instead of their own aggressive behavior (Gibbs, 1993).

Finally, just as cultural conditions can encourage prosocial behavior, they can encourage aggressive behavior. Within the United States some subcultures are clearly more aggressive than others. Poverty is an important factor, however. Males living in large urban areas show higher levels of aggressive behavior, and the rates are especially high for African American males (Atwater, 1992; Graham, Hudley, & Williams, 1992). Poor white children show as much aggressive behavior as African Americans, but a smaller percentage of white children live in poverty. Many factors associated with lower socioeconomic status help explain higher rates of aggressiveness, including higher overall levels of stress, lower-quality education, discipline practices that model aggression, less effective parental monitoring, and a greater like-

Some children tend to interpret ambiguous or innocent events as hostile and to react defensively and with aggression.

lihood of associating with aggressive peers (Dodge et al., 1994; Kupersmidt, Briesler, DeRosier, Patterson, & Davis, 1995; Mason, Cauce, Gonzales, & Hiraga, 1996). Exposure to community, domestic, and peer violence all increase the likelihood of aggressive behavior, and children of all ages are affected (Osofsky, 1999).

How Can Adults Help?

What can parents, teachers, and other concerned adults do to encourage prosocial behavior and decrease aggression in our children? Table 10.9 (p. 416) offers suggestions based on the work we have reviewed and on several successful interventions. It is not difficult to see the general themes we have been highlighting throughout this section. Moral behavior results from a complex interplay of biological tendencies, active thinking about moral situations, interpretations of social situations, and adult and societal guidance. Although some children may be difficult to guide toward prosocial and away from aggressive behavior, parenting practices can make a tremendous difference in determining a child's outcome. Parenting takes place within a cultural context, however. By the messages it conveys in both explicit and subtle ways, a society can do much to reinforce or to undermine parental efforts. Since the appalling school shootings at Columbine High School in Colorado and other places across the country, schools have struggled to confront the issues of aggression, bullies and victims, and school safety. All agree that something must be done, but there is no consensus on what steps to take. For more information about this discussion, read the Social Policy Perspective box (p. 417) called "How Should We Deal with Aggressive Students?"

This chapter has explored development in three broad areas: self, gender, and morality. Though each topic is distinct and different from the others in many ways, all three involve biological tendencies, developing cognitive abilities, and numerous aspects of the social environment—most notably parenting practices. The topics covered in this chapter clearly demonstrate how different areas of development interact to create a child's complex yet integrated sense of *who I am*.

TABLE 10.9 Suggestions for Encouraging Altruistic Behavior and Decreasing Aggression

METHOD	TO ENCOURAGE ALTRUISTIC BEHAVIOR	TO DECREASE AGGRESSIVE BEHAVIOR
Early care-giving	Provide sensitive and responsive care from infancy onward.	Use inductive parenting whenever possible. Take care of yourself and get help from family members and babysitters when needed—it is hard to be kind and sensitive if you are exhausted! With toddlers, structure the environment to decrease conflicts. If your child hits or otherwise conflicts with another child, try using redirection, distracting them with another toy or activity.
Direct reinforcement	Draw attention to and comment on helpful behavior. Point out that helping and being helped makes your child feel good and happy. Reinforce helpful behavior and kind acts with smiles, hugs, and time with you.	Have clear and consistent consequences for aggressive behavior, such as loss of a privilege or timeout. Follow up the consequence with a brief and clear explanation of what the misbehavior was and what the child could do differently next time. Pay attention; comment on and reinforce nonaggressive actions and comments—don't just notice the "bad" things!
Modeling	Help others when you can, in as many ways as you can. When appropriate, describe how you are helping, why, and how it makes you and the other person feel. Help your child when they need it or ask for it.	Use nonaggressive methods for solving problems and dealing with strong emotions. Make nonviolence a clear and consistent family value. Model positive coping strategies for dealing with anger such as taking a walk, calling a friend, writing it down. Teach your child age-appropriate equivalents such as drawing a picture, walking up and down the stairs or around the house, and so on. Remember that children learn from what they observe in the media—monitor and regulate what your child is watching, listening to, and playing.
Perspective-taking	Ask your child how he or she thinks another person feels when someone helps him or her. Ask your child to talk about how he or she feels when someone helps him or her. Encourage your child to "role-play" when playing (e.g., play the part of the hurt puppy and act out how it feels when someone feeds it, pets it, etc.).	If your child is the victim of an aggressive action, encourage him or her to talk about how it makes him or her feel. If your child hurts another physically, socially, or emotionally, encourage him or her to talk about how this makes the other child feel. Talk about how your child can make up for the hurt he or she caused, and encourage him or her to follow through on some of the ideas (e.g., apologizing, offering a toy).
Parental discipline practices	Use inductive parenting as much as possible. When possible, request rather than demand; focus on reinforcing helpfulness rather than punishing misbehavior. Explain what you are doing and why, in words your child can understand. As children get older, involve them in creating family rules and policies. Explain the reasons for the rules, emphasizing how the rules are fair to, protect, and help family members.	Avoid spanking. It models aggression and does not tell your child what they should be doing instead! Avoid socially and psychologically aggressive discipline tactics, such as name-calling, sarcasm, and put-downs. Learn to take a deep breath before talking or acting when disciplining your child. As children get older, ask them what they think an appropriate consequence should be for aggressive behavior, and why. Encourage them to think about what the consequence should help them learn. Establish clear and consistent rules concerning aggression, and enforce them. Make it clear that your home is a safe, supportive place where family members are protected. Develop and use a *specific* plan to help your child change aggressive behaviors. Identify when it is likely to occur, what triggers it, and how your child can "feel it coming." Practice what to do in such a situation. Reinforce the effort as well as the results. You may need help from a professional if the behavior is ongoing or serious.
Discussion of moral issues	Establish a family atmosphere that encourages talking about problems and issues. This requires that your family *spend some relaxed time together* on a regular basis. Listen before talking; sometimes children will talk out a peaceful, helpful, and fair solution all by themselves.	Talk about why your family does not like aggressive behavior, using age-appropriate language. Talk about specific examples as they occur, asking the child what happened, what could have been done differently, and what difference it would have made.
Parental and school expectations	Notice and comment on helpfulness. Some schools establish a "wall of kindness" where children's kind acts are noted on slips of paper and displayed. Work with schools and clubs to involve children in community service projects. Volunteer and help in your child's school and extracurricular activities to communicate that helping is an important value to you.	Don't tolerate bullying or other forms of victimization, either by your child or of your child. Talk to school personnel immediately and insist that the situation be resolved. Support efforts to identify and treat aggressive children in elementary school. "Guidance" programs can include information about what to do if your child is bullied, and they communicate that the school takes it seriously and listens.
Fostering empathy	Emphasize the effects of behavior on the other person to encourage the development of empathy.	Point out the effects of hurtful actions and words on the other child. If your child is hurt, help her think about whether others *intended* to do harm or if it was accidental.

How Should We Deal with Aggressive Students?

■ BURLINGTON, WISCONSIN (November 1998). Five teens were arrested and expelled after their plans to kill school staff and 12 children were reported to police. The boys confessed; three received probation and two were ordered to undergo psychiatric treatment (Kertscher, 1999; Kertscher, Spice, Johnson, Krantz, & Ortiz, 1998).

■ LITTLETON, COLORADO (April 1999). Eric Harris and Dylan Klebold entered Columbine High School carrying two shotguns, a rifle, a pistol, and numerous bombs. They killed 12 students and one teacher, and seriously wounded about 23 others before killing themselves (Luzadder & Vaughan, 1999).

■ BEDFORD, TEXAS (March 2002). A high school junior was expelled from school after a guard found a 10-inch bread knife in the bed of his truck. The student says the knife fell from a box of his grandmother's belongings that he was taking to a thrift shop ("High school expels junior," 2002).

Reports like these have become all too common over the last decade; violence in schools seems to have reached epidemic levels. But how frequent are violent behavior and crime among children and youth? In reality, the rate of many of the most violent school crimes actually decreased across the 1990s. By 2000 fewer students reported carrying a weapon to school, and students reported feeling more secure at school. Children are far more likely to be victims of crime when they are *not* at school. (Kaufman et al., 2001, 2000). However, the rate of threats and injuries with weapons on school property remained constant across the 1990s, as did the number of physical fights not involving weapons. And although horrifying incidents like the Columbine massacre are rare, even one such tragedy is too many.

How should communities and schools deal with aggressive students? The majority of public schools in the United States have adopted some form of *zero tolerance policy* toward firearms, violence, alcohol, and drugs. These policies mandate a specific punishment (often expulsion) for specific offenses. Unfortunately, critics argue, in practice these well-intentioned policies often use suspension and expulsion to punish both serious and trivial incidents. Also, the policies' use is inconsistent across schools and affects minority students disproportionately. Above all, critics say, there is little evidence that zero tolerance policies are effective in reducing student aggression—and they may actually increase students' risk of dropping out of school and engaging in juvenile delinquency (Browne, Losen, & Wald, 2001; Skiba & Knesting, 2001). Other approaches advocate prevention: They focus on early identification and treatment of such things as truancy, bullying (treating both the bullies and the victims), anger, and aggression through school-based group therapy run by trained psychologists or counselors (Larson & Lochman, 2002). School- and districtwide policies and staff training emphasizing conflict resolution skills, effective discipline strategies, and social skills training have helped produce more prosocial environments in some schools (Gagnon & Leone, 2001). Many experts point out that aggression and school violence have multiple causes; schools, parents, and the overall community must coordinate their efforts and resources to deal with these problems effectively.

What policies seem to work best with aggressive students and school violence? How can schools balance the needs and rights of students against the urgency of identifying and dealing with potential problems so as to prevent violence? What social policy suggestions would you make? ■

1. Moral development can be fostered by parenting that:
   a. emphasizes swift and clear punishment of misbehavior.
   b. is coercive.
   c. allows the child to negotiate consequences.
   d. encourages the child to take another's cognitive and emotional perspective.

2. Samuel says it would be wrong to steal a car because his parents would be very upset and disappointed in such a poor choice. Samuel is probably reasoning at which of Kohlberg's stages?
   a. Stage 2   b. Stage 3   c. Stage 4   d. Stage 5

3. Aggressive children who tend to perceive harmful intent when it does not exist are called:
   a. reactive aggressors.   c. coercive aggressors.
   b. proactive aggressors.   d. hedonistic aggressors.

4. Research on Kohlberg's stages of moral reasoning has found that:
   a. the sequence of stages is consistent across many cultures.
   b. both the sequence and the timing of stages is consistent across cultures.
   c. the sequence of stages applies only to Western cultures.
   d. the sequence of stages is evident in men but not in women.

5. **True or False:** The ability to take another's perspective is important for the development of both moral reasoning and moral emotions.

6. **True or False:** The care ethic proposed by Gilligan exists for women but not for men.

Answers: 1. d, 2. b, 3. a, 4. a, 5. T, 6. F

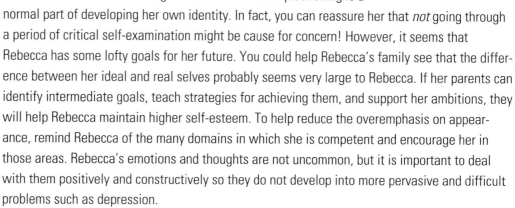

thinking
BACK TO REBECCA

Now that you have studied this chapter, you should be able to give Rebecca some guidance. You can help her understand that some degree of self-doubt and questioning is a normal part of developing her own identity. In fact, you can reassure her that *not* going through a period of critical self-examination might be cause for concern! However, it seems that Rebecca has some lofty goals for her future. You could help Rebecca's family see that the difference between her ideal and real selves probably seems very large to Rebecca. If her parents can identify intermediate goals, teach strategies for achieving them, and support her ambitions, they will help Rebecca maintain higher self-esteem. To help reduce the overemphasis on appearance, remind Rebecca of the many domains in which she is competent and encourage her in those areas. Rebecca's emotions and thoughts are not uncommon, but it is important to deal with them positively and constructively so they do not develop into more pervasive and difficult problems such as depression.

It is also quite normal for Rebecca to be trying to understand her sexual orientation and to show interest in romantic relationships. Her increase in sex-typed behavior reflects her developing gender-role knowledge, gender schema, and sexual orientation. Encourage her to maintain her personal interests and not to quit because of peer pressure or gender stereotypes. Pointing out examples of both men and women who are androgynous or excel in unstereotyped ways might help broaden her gender schema. Rebecca's parents and teachers might consciously work to provide good models of male and female achievement in a variety of areas, both at school and at home.

Finally, Rebecca seems very bothered by the lack of empathy in her peers. Help her understand the different levels of moral and prosocial reasoning and empathy, and the importance of cognitive development and parenting in these areas. It is important for Rebecca's parents to use parenting practices that encourage empathy and altruistic behavior in Rebecca herself if she does not see much of this at school. They can help Rebecca understand why her friend Daniel is engaging in delinquent behavior, explaining that this behavior won't necessarily continue. Finally, Rebecca and her family and friends could work together to build a kinder, more helpful atmosphere. If you can show Rebecca that there are many models of prosocial behavior, as well as suggesting strategies for encouraging empathy and altruism, you may help her understand that aggressive behavior is not inevitable.

What is "self"?

The *self* is a cognitive construction that develops as a child matures cognitively. It includes the I-self and the me-self. With development the self becomes more differentiated but also more integrated, so children become able to describe their performance in different areas but also to give an overall summary of themselves. Some theorists emphasize cognitive aspects as children build more complex working models of the self. Others emphasize social interaction and comparison to others.

How do self-representations change across age?

As children grow, their self-representations become more abstract, domain-specific, and differentiated, but also more integrated. Infants coordinate their experiences across different senses, noticing what changes and what stays the same, to develop an I-self. The quality of caregiving influences the development of the I-self and helps build the foundation for later self-efficacy. The me-self emerges by the second year. Social comparison to peers helps children become more realistic in their self-representations. Adolescents struggle with the crisis of identity versus identity diffusion. Identity statuses can be classified as a foreclosure, moratorium, achievement, and diffusion. Ethnic minority youths go through the additional process of developing an ethnic identity.

When do children begin evaluating themselves? What factors affect self-evaluation?

Toddlers show some signs of self-evaluation, but children do not describe a global self-evaluation until about 7 years of age. Self-evaluations become more realistic through the elementary school years as children increasingly compare themselves to their peers. For several reasons, self-evaluations become much more negative at adolescence. The degree of discrepancy between a child's real and ideal selves, in combination with the supportiveness of parents and peers, affects self-evaluation. Self-evaluation influences choices of activities and persistence, and low self-evaluations can contribute to depression.

What is self-regulation? When and how do children develop it?

Self-regulation is the ability to control and change your behavior, thoughts, or emotions to meet the demands of the situation. Self-regulation develops steadily from infancy onward. Influences on self-regulation include contextual factors such as the type of request made and whether the child agrees with the request or not, biological factors, modeling, private speech, and the nature of interactions between adults and the child.

Do boys and girls show consistent differences in cognitive skills, behavior, and personality?

Similarities far outnumber gender differences. The largest and most consistent gender differences are in verbal, language, and some spatial skills. Differences in mathematics computation and grades favor girls until adolescence, when differences favoring boys in math problem solving appear. Boys show higher activity levels and greater physical aggression than girls, but girls show more relational aggression. Girls are often rated higher in prosocial behavior and empathy, but their actual prosocial behavior is not consistently different.

What do children know about gender? How sex-typed is their behavior?

Children show gender-stereotyped preferences even before they fully understand their own gender. They prefer sex-typed toys and show high levels of gender segregation in their play by the time they are 3 years old. Gender stereotypes become increasingly rigid until early elementary school, then become more flexible until early adolescence. Children's knowledge of gender guides their expectations and behavior. Influences on sexual orientation include genetics and prenatal hormonal levels as well as environmental reinforcement, punishment, and observational learning. Androgynous individuals have both masculine and feminine characteristics.

How do children acquire a gender concept?

According to Freud's psychoanalytic theory, children identify with their same-sex parent and adopt that parent's approach to behavior, emotions, and attitudes. Biological theories of gender development point to the roles of prenatal hormones and brain lateralization. Social learning theories emphasize direct reinforcement for sex-typed behavior and observational learning, both of which may be explicit or more subtle. Fathers seem to play an important role in children's developing gender knowledge. According to Kohlberg's cognitive theory, gender concepts develop in step with cognitive levels in combination with gender-relevant experiences. Gender schema theory portrays the development of a highly connected network of gender-related information that organizes and guides gender-relevant thought and behavior.

How do children think about moral issues?

Kohlberg proposed six stages of development of moral reasoning. Children's movement through the stages depends on their cognitive development, perspective-taking ability, and experiences with moral issues. Gilligan suggested that a care ethic is operative in women's moral reasoning. A problem with Kohlberg's theory is that levels of moral reasoning are not consistent across different moral domains. Theories of prosocial reasoning also have described development as moving through several levels, from egocentrism to concern with social approval to reasoning based on general principles.

How do guilt and empathy affect moral development?

Although guilt can motivate moral behavior, more positive emotions like attachment, sympathy, and empathy also are important. Hoffman suggests that empathy is a biological predisposition in humans and describes four levels of empathy development. Aspects of the environment shape and reinforce empathy. Inductive parenting practices promote higher levels of empathy.

What is the basis for altruistic and for aggressive behavior?

Social learning theorists argue that children learn both altruistic and aggressive behavior through reinforcement, punishment, and model-ing. Levels of moral and prosocial reasoning, empathy and perspective-taking skill, and cultural and family practices, influence both types of behavior. Boys and girls show different types of aggression. Many adolescent boys engage in mildly delinquent forms of behavior. A coercive home environment, in combination with several other risk factors, increases the risk that some boys will persist in antisocial behavior. Some aggressive children also interpret social interactions differently than less aggressive children.

KEY TERMS

aggression (412)	gender intensification (391)	moral behavior (410)	self-evaluations (369)
altruism (410)	gender role (387)	moral reasoning (402)	self-regulation (383)
androgyny (395)	gender schema theory (400)	morality (401)	self-representations (369)
empathy (408)	I-self (369)	perspective taking (402)	sex (387)
gender (387)	me-self (369)	prosocial reasoning (407)	sex-typed behavior (387)
gender concept (387)	modeling (385)	self (369)	sexual orientation (393)
gender constancy (399)	moral affect (407)	self-esteem (369)	social comparison (373)

Chapter 11

Peers, Play, and Popularity

A PERSPECTIVE TO think ABOUT

"After 3 weeks in his new school, Kim still has not made any close friends."

Kim recently moved to the Tampa area with his family. After 3 weeks in his new school, Kim still has not made any close friends. He is beginning to feel lonely and left out, and his parents are a little concerned about him. Kim is shy and quiet and has never made friends easily. In his last school he had only one close friend and just a few casual friends. His parents immigrated to the United States from South Korea before Kim was born; at home his family prefers to speak Korean and maintain other Korean traditions. There are only a few Korean children in Kim's neighborhood and school, however, and Kim is concerned that his schoolmates may exclude him because of his different ethnic and cultural background. How can Kim make friends at his new school? How do peer groups operate, and what does it take to become better liked among peers? What if Kim remains shy and reserved at school—will he be rejected by his classmates?

After studying this chapter, you should be able to apply at least a dozen concepts and research findings to Kim's situation. What advice would you give to Kim and his parents? What helpful information could you offer to help people like Kim understand peer groups, friendships, popularity, and cultural differences in social relationships? What could you add for children who are younger than Kim or for adolescents who are older than Kim?

 As you read this chapter, look for the questions that ask you to think about what you're learning from Kim's perspective.

M any children have problems like Kim's. Learning how to make friends is an important part of growing up. Some children make friends easily, but others struggle. In this chapter we discuss the social relationships that children form with their peers and friends. We begin with the ways infants first react when they see other babies. From there we follow the formation of social relationships up through the intimate friendships and dating relationships that emerge in adolescence. Along the way, we discuss the reasons why children prefer to play with same-sex friends, and we look at pattterns in children's play and ask how play differs across cultures. We end the chapter by discussing the characteristics that distinguish popular from unpopular children and the different ways that children think about social situations. Throughout the chapter you will have many opportunities to reflect on your own childhood friendships and to think about how your social relationships may have differed from those of the other children around you. Whether you were extremely popular or ignored and alone, your childhood social experiences were an influential part of your development. The concepts and research findings presented in this chapter should help you increase your understanding of how you and others fit within the social world of peers, friends, and play.

Peer Relations and Friendships

YOUR
PERSPECTIVE
NOTES

What is your earliest memory of a friend? When did you find your first real friend? Why do you think this person was your friend?

How would you define the terms *peers* and *friendship*? In the child development literature, the term **peers** refers to people who are about the same age as one another. By **friendship** we mean a close, mutual, and voluntary relationship between peers (Rubin, Coplan, Nelson, Cheah, & Lagace-Seguin, 1999). Friendships are reciprocal: Both members of the friendship participate in kind and feel that they are equal partners. Also, friendships are relationships that persist over time; just choosing to play together once doesn't qualify as friendship. Friendships can serve many important functions in a child's development. Friends can provide support, companionship, affection, and stimulation. They help children learn about themselves and teach important social skills. When friends differ in characteristics like ethnicity or religion, they can broaden each other's horizons and help each other see the world from another perspective.

The functions of friendships change as children progress along their developmental paths. When children are younger, they may seek friends primarily for play and amusement. As they mature, however, children begin to value the intimacy and shared companionship offered by their closest friends. From the very beginning, friendships help us shape the internal working models through which we understand our romantic, marital, and parental relationships later in life (Dunn, Cutting, & Fisher, 2002; Furman, Simon, Shaffer, & Bouchey, 2002). In this first section we describe how children's social relationships change across development and how children form and maintain friendships.

As you study this section, ask yourself these questions:

- What kinds of early social interactions are typical among infants and toddlers?
- How do the purposes and functions of friendship change throughout childhood and adolescence?
- Why do boys and girls prefer same-gender playmates? How does this tendency affect their development?
- What are the most prominent trends in adolescent dating and sexual activity?

Social Relations among Infants and Toddlers

If you are like most students, your earliest memory of a friend probably dates back to when you were about 5 or 6. The first foundations of friendship began much earlier, however—when you were a small baby.

peers

People who are about the same age as one another.

friendship

A close, mutual, and voluntary relationship between peers that persists over time.

Mutual gaze is one of the early social interactions in infancy. What do you think these infants think of each other as peers?

■ **Infant Social Interactions.** By the age of only 2 months, infants show a special interest in other people their own size. When placed near each other, young infants show **mutual gaze**—they look intently at each other as if they are taking in all the information they can about this intriguing new peer (Eckerman, 1979; Fogel, 1979). They often express their excitement by flailing their arms and legs. By 6 months of age, infants interact with each other by babbling, smiling, and touching (Vandell, Wilson, & Buchanan, 1980). These are often the infants' first social interactions that involve mutual activity with people other than their family members.

Not surprisingly, infants vary greatly in social responsiveness. Some infants initiate interactions with peers frequently; others do so only rarely. Differences in temperament, in parent–infant relationships, and in opportunities to practice social skills all contribute to this variability. When infants have more exposure to other infants their age, they show more frequency and skill in their social interactions than infants with less exposure to peers (Vandell & Wilson, 1982). By the end of the first year, infants play by imitating each other's actions and by sharing and playing together with toys (Mueller & Silverman, 1989; Rubin, Bukowski, & Parker, 1998).

■ **Toddler Friends and Play.** After 1 year of age, emerging language and motor skills allow toddlers to interact in increasingly complex ways. They can seek each other out, follow each other around, and add verbal dialogue to their play. At the age of 2, **coordinated imitation** becomes much more frequent. Toddler playmates take turns imitating each other and— a new feature—become aware that they are being imitated (Eckerman, 1993; Rubin et al., 1998). Consider Josh and Jalen, two toddlers playing in a sandbox. Josh pours sand on his legs, and Jalen does the same. Josh throws sand at a toy, and Jalen copies again. Then Jalen throws sand straight up in the air, and Josh does too, both giggling and chuckling all the while. The fun in this toddler game is that each boy knows that he is being imitated. Each act becomes an invitation for the other boy to copy. This level of coordination rarely appears in children younger than 2 (Eckerman, 1993).

mutual gaze

Intent eye contact between two people, as when young infants stare at each other.

coordinated imitation

Interaction in which toddler playmates take turns imitating each other and are aware that they are being imitated.

Toddler interactions often evolve around games that children either repeat from prior experiences or create on the spot. Characteristically, these early games include taking turns, playing roles, and engaging in numerous repetitions of the game sequences (Ross, 1982). Common games are stacking and toppling blocks; throwing and catching; putting toys in a pail and pouring; requesting, receiving, and returning items; running and chasing; and climbing and jumping. These early interactions help children acquire important social skills such as learning to play as equals, maintaining fun and interest for both players, and adapting to the characteristics of different playmates.

Toddlers choose playmates based largely on convenience—on who is available for play and who has interesting toys or materials to play with. By 2 years of age, however, pairs of children begin to select each other as mutually preferred playmates (Vandell & Mueller, 1980). That is, although other familiar peers are available for play, these friends pair off and voluntarily choose to play more with each other than with other children. For most children this is the first time that a relationship contains all of the qualities of a true friendship: It is voluntary, mutual, and close, and it persists over time. In a longitudinal study, Howes (1988) followed toddlers for up to 3 years as they maintained friends, lost friends, and made new friends. Her observations suggest that children who are more successful at maintaining friendships tend to enter into peer play more easily and to be more cooperative in social pretend play. For example, they are more likely to join in when asked, "You be the baby and I'll be the mommy, okay?" Children who were less successful in maintaining friendships showed less social skill and were more likely to be rebuffed by peers.

■ **Toddler Conflicts.** Anyone who has spent much time with toddlers knows that conflict is all too common. In one study researchers paired up 2-year-old children who had never met before and allowed them to play together in several sessions that lasted 15 minutes each (Hay & Ross, 1982). After carefully analyzing videotapes of the play sessions, the researchers found that playmates averaged just over 2 instances of conflict for every 15-minute session. Most of

Conflict is common among toddlers. What do you think is the best way to help children of this age handle conflict?

the conflicts (84 percent) were struggles over toys. A few pairs of playmates had no conflicts, but one pair displayed 14 instances of protest, resistance, or retaliation in their 15 minutes of play. Other research suggests that children who are more socially outgoing tend to initiate more conflicts (E. Brown & Brownell, 1990).

Parents, child-care workers, and others who work frequently with young children often need to help toddlers resolve their disputes. Lecturing and moralizing are usually ineffective: Toddlers have difficulty understanding abstract reasoning. The question "How do you think she feels?" is largely nonsensical for the average 2-year-old, who is motivated more by the concrete benefit of getting his or her hands on a friend's colored markers or candy. (Refer back to Chapter 5, where we describe the egocentric forms of thought that are typical for this age.) Distracting the toddlers with another attractive activity is a more practical way to resolve the dispute. Parents and caregivers can then gradually introduce moral reasoning and conflict resolution skills according to the cognitive and emotional maturity of the individual child.

Friendships during the Preschool and Childhood Years

The main ingredients in forming friendships are *opportunity* and *similarity*. To become friends, children need to be available to each other for play and other activities. Children who are neighbors, relatives, or schoolmates spend more time with each other and therefore have more opportunities to form friendships. Children's social contacts increase dramatically when they enter school. In school children encounter a much larger group of peers and tend

What do you think drew these 5-year-olds to each other as best friends? How do children of this age form close friendships?

to have less direct adult supervision when they are together. From the toddler period to the school-aged years, time spent with peers triples (Higgins & Parsons, 1983). Also, like adults, children are drawn to others who are like them. Friendships are more likely to form when children are similar in characteristics such as age, gender, race, attitudes, beliefs, and even play styles (Epstein, 1989; Hartup, 1989; Rubin, Lynch, Coplan, Rose-Krasnor, & Booth, 1994).

"Best friends" are a special category of friends. A child's relationship with a best friend is closer and more exclusive than are relationships with the more casual acquaintances most children refer to as "friends." The number of best friends that children have tends to increase until about age 11; then children become much more selective in whom they designate as their best friends (Epstein, 1986; Rubin et al., 1998). In one study that is often cited, Bigelow (1977) asked Canadian and Scottish schoolchildren what they expected in their best (same-sex) friends. First graders most frequently reported that having common activities was important. By the eighth grade the most important trait was an admirable character, followed by common activities, acceptance, and loyalty/commitment. Only girls mentioned the potential for intimacy (sharing personal thoughts and feelings) as an important feature, and only after the fifth grade. Interestingly, the children rarely mentioned physical attractiveness as an important characteristic in best friends. Also rarely mentioned were shared personal characteristics (such as both friends being shy). On the basis of these findings and of numerous other studies, we can say that children's close friendships typically progress through the following three phases (Berndt, 1986; Bigelow, 1977; Rubin et al., 1998; Smollar & Youniss, 1982):

thinking OF KIM

◄ How could Kim and his parents use the findings from the Bigelow (1977) study to help Kim make new friends?

- *Play-based friends (ages 3 to 7 years):* Play-based friendships are the most common for younger children. Children are good friends when they spend a lot of time playing together, sharing toys, and enjoying the same games and activities.

- *Loyal and faithful friends (ages 8 to 11 years):* Loyalty, faithfulness, and generosity define close friendships during middle childhood. "He shares his best things with me," "She sticks by me when other kids tease me," and "She doesn't ignore me when her other friends are around" are common descriptions of best friends during this second phase.

- *Intimate friends (adolescence and beyond):* Intimate friends share their most personal thoughts and feelings. They trust each other to keep personal secrets, and they use each other as a safe base for exploring issues and problems that they may not discuss with anyone else—including parents, teachers, or close siblings. During adolescence intimacy and self-disclosure distinguish best friends from other friends. Intimacy emerges in early adolescence for girls but only in later adolescence for most boys (e.g., Berndt, 1986).

Gender Segregation among Childhood Friends

Another prominent feature of children's friendships is **gender segregation**—the tendency of children to associate with others of their same sex. Consider the situation that one of us (GC) observed while testing 4-year-old children in a preschool. As the children returned from their outside play period, a new boy in class took a seat in a circle of chairs. Several other boys ran immediately to him, yelling, "Get up, that's where the girls sit!" Hearing this, the new boy leaped up and began to furiously dust off the back of his pants! What did he think was on the chair? Girl germs? Cooties?

There is no doubt that gender segregation exists. In fact, it is nearly universal, occurring in every cultural setting where children have choice in selecting social groups (Fabes, Martin, & Hanish, 2003; Whiting & Edwards, 1988). But how does it begin, and why? There are no clear answers to these questions, but we can learn more by looking at how gender segregation evolves across childhood and adolescence.

By 2 to 3 years of age, children are beginning to show a clear preference for playing with other children of their own sex (Serbin, Moller, Gulko, Powlishta, & Colburne, 1994). At this age children are more interactive and sociable when playing with same-sex friends. When they are with the opposite sex, they tend to watch or play alongside the other child rather than interact directly. Gender segregation is very prominent after the age of 3. As you can see in Figure 11.1, preschool children spend very little time playing one-on-one with the opposite sex. They spend some time in mixed-sex groups but spend most of their time, by far, playing with same-sex peers. By 6 years, segregation is so firm that if you watch 6-year-olds on the playground, you should expect to see only 1 girl–boy group for every 11 boy–boy or girl–girl groups (Maccoby & Jacklin, 1987).

■ **Reasons for Gender Segregation.**   Why does gender segregation exist? Let's consider the most prominent theories.

Play Compatibility.   Some researchers believe that gender segregation occurs because children seek partners whose play styles match or complement their own (Serbin et al., 1994). Among the youngest children, the first to segregate tend to be the most active and disruptive boys and the most socially sensitive girls (Fabes, 1994; Serbin et al., 1994). Both types of children prefer to play with others like them. Children between these extremes can still find compatible play partners of either sex, so they remain longer in mixed-sex groups. Differences in arousal thresholds may play a role. Some evidence suggests that boys are more easily aroused

YOUR
PERSPECTIVE
NOTES
Thinking back to your childhood, did you have more same-sex friends or more opposite-sex friends? Why do you think that was the case?

gender segregation

The tendency for children to associate with others of their same sex.

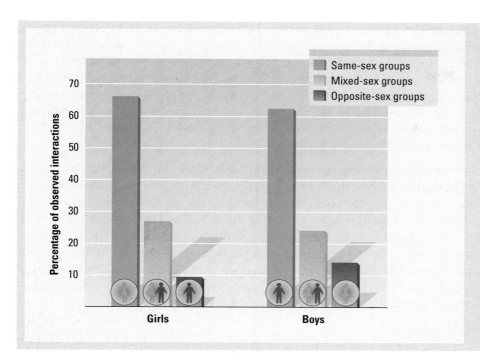

FIGURE 11.1 Gender Interactions among Preschoolers

In free play preschoolers (ages 3 to 6 years) choose to play with same-sex peers most often. When they do cross gender lines, they spend twice as much time playing in mixed-sex groups as with the opposite sex one-on-one.

Source: Data from Fabes (1994).

by situations that involve physical activity and danger (Fabes, 1994). Girls, on the other hand, show more physiological arousal in response to sympathy and interpersonal distress. Gender segregation in play may therefore evolve as children seek playmates with compatible arousal systems and thresholds.

Cognitive Schemas.   According to the cognitive schemas view, children develop concepts or ideas (schemas) about what boys and girls are typically like. (Refer back to Chapter 10 for a discussion of gender schemas.) These concepts include stereotyped, and often exaggerated, notions about gender differences. Examples: "Boys are rough and like to fight and play with trucks" and "Girls are nice and like to talk and play with dolls." Children use these cognitive schemas as filters when they judge themselves and observe other children (Martin, 1994). "I am a boy, so I like to play with trucks" is a concept that may lead boys to seek each other as playmates. Schemas can also cause children to filter out or misremember instances that contradict the schema. Children discount the number of times they've seen girls play ball and boys play with dolls, for example. As children learn gender-based schemas, their play and playmate preferences become more segregated.

Operant Conditioning.   Reward and punishment also contribute to gender segregation. Boys in particular tend to incur harsh criticism when they cross gender lines to play with girls (Fagot, 1977, 1994; Fagot & Patterson, 1969). For most boys, being called a "sissy" is a major insult. Although some girls revel in being "tomboys," others can feel conflicted about being associated with stereotypically masculine activities. Whether consciously or only inadvertently, parents, teachers, peers, the media, and others contribute to gender segregation by reinforcing, or rewarding, sex-typed behaviors in boys and girls. Recall our discussion of operant conditioning theory (reward and punishment) in Chapter 1. We went into much more detail on sex typing and gender formation in Chapter 10.

Psychoanalytic Theory.   One of the oldest views on gender segregation was the theory formulated by Sigmund Freud (see Chapter 1). Although Freud's view isn't given much

thinking
OF KIM

Do you think Kim will be ▶ reluctant to make friends with girls at his school? Explain how the different theories of gender segregation might work for or against his forming opposite-sex friendships.

credence today, he offered the explanation that gender segregation occurs as children repress their sexual feelings during the "latency" stage of development. That is, children avoid interactions with the opposite sex so as to avoid the guilty feelings they associate with sexuality. During the latency stage children channel their energies into less threatening pursuits, such as collecting trading cards or dolls. When they play with opposite-sex friends, children often get teased about being "in love" or "going with" their friend. "No boys allowed!" is the warning posted on many girls' playhouses, and boys reciprocate—at least until the onset of puberty changes things.

■ **Effects of Gender Segregation.** Regardless of why gender segregation occurs, one of its consequences is that boys and girls grow up in different **gender cultures**— different spheres of social influence that are based on the differences between male and female groups and affiliations (Leaper, 1994; Maccoby & Jacklin, 1987). Rough-and-tumble play, chase, keep-away games, superhero warrior games, and competitive sports are more common among boys. Physical aggression, independence, and dominance are common themes in boys' play. Girls' play, however, tends to emphasize social closeness and sensitivity. Doll play and playing house, for example, involve role playing, turn taking, nurturance, and affection. Also, boys tend to play in larger groups; girls develop closer ties in smaller groups. As a consequence, girls may learn to share thoughts and feelings and practice being good listeners in intimate friendships. Boys, however, may see intimate sharing as a sign of weakness that would make them more vulnerable within their dominance hierarchies (Leaper, 1994).

The effects of these differing styles of social interaction carry over into adolescence and adulthood. Consider, for example, a study in which researchers audiotaped college friends (ages 18 to 21) during one-on-one conversations (Leaper, 1994). Analyses of the taped conversations showed no gender differences in the amount of personal self-disclosure the college students made. There were, however, significant differences in how females and males responded to their friends' self-disclosures. As Figure 11.2 shows, females were more likely to support each other with responses that involved active understanding. They actively processed or reflected on their friends' personal comments. In male conversations, however, self-disclosures were most often ignored—males abstained from commenting on their friends' comments. Active understanding was not predominant in mixed-sex conversations either, so females evidently learned to reserve their responses when they were with their male friends.

These differences in conversational styles set up an imbalance in intimate cross-gender relationships: Females expect to give and receive more emotional support, and males tend to withhold or abstain. Numerous studies have linked this imbalance to marital dissatisfaction, divorce, and even domestic violence (Leaper, 1994). Although we cannot blame all these prob-

gender cultures

Different spheres of influence based on the differences between male and female groups and affiliations.

As you can see in these photos, boys and girls grow up in different gender cultures. Boys tend to engage in more rough and physical play while girls spend more time practicing interpersonal sensitivity. How do these experiences influence boys and girls differently?

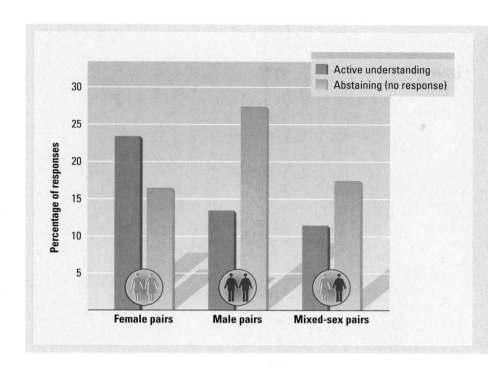

FIGURE 11.2 College Students' Responses to Peers' Self-Disclosure

How do female and male students respond when their friends share a personal comment? Females are more likely to respond with active listening, but males are more likely to ignore the comment (abstain from response).

Source: Data from Leaper (1994).

lems on gender segregation during childhood, you can see how segregated gender cultures provide different social models for boys than girls.

What can adults do to lessen the effects of childhood gender segregation? Leaper (1994) provided several practical suggestions. For example, parents can model egalitarian roles at home, arrange more situations in which children can play and cooperate across genders, and reinforce and support children when they do cross stereotypical gender lines in their play. Teachers can arrange cooperative activities among boys and girls, and they can avoid grouping children by gender when they arrange seating and form lines. Teachers also should avoid using gender as a way to address students; for example, they shouldn't shout "Boys, sit down and be quiet!" unless all of the boys were indeed being loud. Of course, it would not be prudent or practical to try to eliminate all gender differences. Nevertheless, helping children develop more flexible expectations and skills in interacting with the opposite sex would clearly be beneficial.

Friends and Peers in Adolescence

Adolescents spend twice as much time with their friends (outside of the classroom) as with their parents, siblings, and other adults (Csikszentmihalyi & Larson, 1984). As Savin-Williams and Berndt (1990) put it:

> Adolescents typically report that they enjoy their activities with friends more than any other. With friends, they feel that they are understood and can fully be themselves. Friends spend much time together simply talking about themselves, other adolescents, or events in the wider world. They relax, joke, watch television or videos, and participate in sports. These moments of enjoyment and companionship contribute to a generational sense of belonging with others who are respected and liked. (p. 279)

In their review of the research literature on adolescent friendships and peer relations, Savin-Williams and Berndt (1990) found that adolescents who have close and supportive friendships tend to have higher self-esteem, to understand other people's feelings better, and to be

Beginning in adolescence, our closest friends are the people we can trust and with whom we share our personal thoughts and feelings. A shared sense of intimacy bonds best friends together.

more generally popular among their peers. In school they are better behaved, receive higher grades, and score higher on tests of intelligence. Adolescents who do not have close friendships don't fare as well. Keep in mind, however, that these findings are correlational. In other words, we don't know the direction of the causal link between friendships and adolescent development. Do close and supportive friendships facilitate social and academic growth, or do adolescents who are more socially and academically skilled attract more close friends?

When it comes to forming friendships, *similarity* is still the rule in adolescence. Adolescents who become close friends tend to share similar attitudes; educational aspirations; religious and political orientations; and patterns of drinking, drug use, and delinquency (Savin-Williams & Berndt, 1990). As we mentioned earlier, shared intimacy is an important feature of adolescent friendships. Strong bonds form when intimate friends share personal stories and help each other work through difficult problems. Although it can be difficult to maintain friendships as adolescents move through the transitions from middle school to high school and later into the worlds of college or work, many lifelong friends trace their relationships back to their adolescent years.

■ **Cliques and Crowds.**   Another aspect of adolescent peer relations is the emergence of *cliques* and *crowds*. **Cliques** are small groups, usually including three to nine friends, who hang out together on a voluntary basis (Rubin et al., 1998). Friends in cliques are almost always of the same sex and race. By the age of 11, most children report being a member of a clique, and this social group forms the context for the majority of their peer interactions (Crockett, Losoff, & Petersen, 1984). Most cliques are closed circles—members tend to put down or exclude people outside their clique, although adolescents do understand that excluding peers is sometimes wrong and harmful (Horn, 2003). Between the ages of 11 and 18, however, bonds within individual cliques begin to loosen and adolescents begin associating simultaneously with several loosely defined cliques (Rubin et al., 1998).

thinking
OF KIM

Given that similarity is important in forming new friendships, how could you help Kim recognize and emphasize the similarities he shares with his classmates?

cliques

Small groups, usually including three to nine friends, who hang out together on a voluntary basis.

Crowds are larger groups made up of individuals who have similar reputations or share primary attitudes or activities (B. Brown, 1990). When asked to describe the different groups of students that make up their schools, teenagers typically identify crowds such as *jocks, brains, nerds, druggies, toughs, populars, normals, nobodies,* and *loners.* Specific names given to the crowds vary across geographic locations and individual schools, but they tend to fall into these general categories.

Individual students usually can't pick their favorite crowd to join. Instead, they acquire crowd "membership" based on stereotyped perceptions held across the school population. Your crowd designation has to do mostly with what other people think about you and who they think you are like. In one study researchers asked students to guess which crowd their peers had assigned them to. Although 75 percent of the "jocks" and "druggies" correctly guessed their crowd assignment, only 15 percent of the "nobodies" and "loners" were accurate (B. Brown, Clasen, & Niess, 1987). In many schools students see members of ethnic minority groups as separate crowds—the Hispanic crowd, the African American crowd, and so on. Because of the prejudice and discrimination they experience, ethnic minority students may feel more comfortable associating with other members of their racial or ethnic group. In other cases, ethnic groups are segregated because of cultural differences in behavior, dress, religion, or other characteristics.

Many parents worry that by "hanging out with the wrong crowd" their adolescents will become involved with such things as alcohol or illegal drugs. How prevalent are these problems? A large nationwide survey of U.S. high school students indicated that the majority of 9th graders had tried alcohol, and more than one-third had tried marijuana (Centers for Disease Control and Prevention, 2000). As Figure 11.3 shows, smaller percentages of 9th graders had tried cocaine and other drugs. Just over 20 percent of 9th graders admitted that they still used marijuana, and approximately 40 percent still used alcohol. Although the percentages were somewhat higher for 12th graders, you can see that the patterns of alcohol and drug use were already well established by the first year of high school. Use of inhalants (sniffing glue, paint, or aerosols) seemed to be a more recent phenomenon. More 9th graders than 12th graders had ever tried inhalants; and among those still using inhalants, 9th graders outnumbered 12th graders 3 to 1. Table 11.1 shows ethnic differences in substance abuse from the same nationwide survey. Use of alcohol, cocaine, and inhalants was lower among African Americans than among non-Hispanic whites or Hispanics. Hispanics reported the highest use of cocaine and inhalants. Peers with similar drinking and drug use patterns tend to associate together in the same school crowds (Cleveland & Wiebe, 2003; Dishion & Owen, 2002).

Another concern is that some adolescent crowds can put pressure on peers to engage in violence or aggression (Espelage, Holt, & Henkel, 2003). A recent report from the Surgeon General indicated that having antisocial or delinquent peers was one of the strongest risk factors for adolescent violence (U.S. Department of Health and Human Services, 2001). At greatest risk are adolescents who are aggressive and also unpopular. These rejected teens often seek the company of other aggressive and rejected adolescents, sometimes forming gangs or coalescing into small crowds that promote violence and aggression. These findings, together with the data on drug and alcohol use, suggest that parents are justified in worrying about the negative forms of peer pressure exerted within adolescent crowds.

Surprisingly, however, research also indicates that for most adolescents the strongest peer pressures actually tend to be positive. Adolescents claim that the greatest peer pressures they experience are to get along with others, get good grades, graduate from high school, and attend college (B. Brown, 1990). This is certainly good news for parents and teens! Yet even though peers can and do exert a positive influence, many adolescents still struggle to maintain a balance between their own individual development and their desire to be accepted

YOUR PERSPECTIVE
NOTES
Describe the different "crowds" that you recall from your high school. Which crowd did you fit best with? Were ethnic minorities in their own crowds in your school?

thinking OF KIM
◀ As Kim moves into the teenage years, you can imagine he might be tempted to try alcohol or illegal drugs as a way to "belong" with a crowd in school. What advice would you give Kim regarding this temptation?

crowds
Groups of adolescent peers who have similar reputations or share primary attitudes or activities.

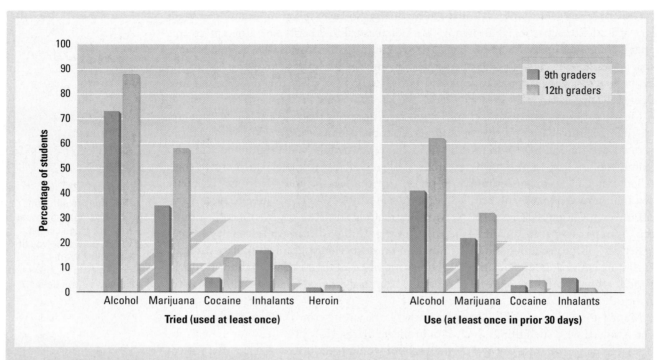

FIGURE 11.3 Alcohol and Drug Use in 9th and 12th Grades

The data graphed here come from a nationwide survey of high school students. Compare the percentages of students in the 9th and 12th grades who reported trying and using alcohol and other drugs.

Note: "Tried" means used the substance at least once; "use" means used the substance at least once during the 30 days prior to the survey. Cocaine includes powder, "crack," and "freebase"; inhalants include sniffing glue or breathing aerosols, paints, or sprays; heroin includes "smack," "junk," and "China white."

Source: Data from Centers for Disease Control and Prevention (2000).

among a group of peers. Crowd membership can restrict adolescents' social contacts, channeling their relationships and dating, and it can limit their exploration of other identities and lifestyles (Rubin et al., 1998).

TABLE 11.1 High School Students' Alcohol and Drug Use by Ethnic Group

	GROUP		
	Non-Hispanic White (percentage)	**African American (percentage)**	**Hispanic (percentage)**
Use alcohol	53	40	53
Use marijuana	26	26	28
Use cocaine	4	1	7
Use inhalants	4	2	5
Tried heroin	2	1	2

"Use" means the students used the substance at least once during the 30 days prior to the survey.

"Tried" means the students ever used heroin, "smack," "junk," or "China White."

Source: Centers for Disease Control and Prevention. (2000, June 9). *Morbidity and Mortality Weekly Report, 49* (No. SS-5; Tables 20, 22, 24), 1–78.

Research has shown a link between self-esteem and membership in particular crowds. In one midwestern community, students in junior and senior high schools rank-ordered five crowds that they identified in their schools (B. Brown & Lohr, 1987). Most admired were the jocks, followed (in order) by populars, normals, druggies/toughs, and nobodies. Not surprisingly, self-esteem scores were highest among students who were jocks and populars, moderate among normals and druggies/toughs, and lowest for nobodies. For outsiders (students who were not associated with any of the crowds), self-esteem depended on the importance they attributed to crowd membership. Self-esteem was relatively high among outsiders who gave little importance to crowd membership, but it was low among students who wanted to—but didn't—belong to a crowd.

Just as clique memberships loosen by midadolescence, crowd affiliations begin to soften by the end of high school. Researchers have commented on the cohesiveness that often develops among high school seniors (Larkin, 1979; Rubin et al., 1998). Differences and animosities seem to fade a bit as members of the different crowds reflect back on their years together and look ahead to what awaits them after they leave school.

Dating and Sexual Activity

Although most cliques form among same-sex peers in early adolescence, many relationships do form across the sexes by midadolescence. Sexual activity, both across and within genders, often follows.

■ **From Gender Segregation to Dating.**　The classic study of the transition from gender segregation to dating is a naturalistic field study that Dexter Dunphy (1963) performed in Sydney, Australia. Dunphy observed that young adolescents (around age 13) congregated in same-sex cliques containing about three to nine close friends. Then group-to-group interactions began to occur between male and female cliques. As you probably recall from your own adolescence, these interactions often begin as teasing and chasing. Eventually, however, they evolve into more cooperative relationships. In Dunphy's study the cross-sex interactions occurred almost exclusively between cliques in the same larger crowd (between male jocks and female jocks, for example), so the cross-sex relationships were among adolescents who had similar attitudes, values, and economic status. When asked to choose partners in social situations, adolescents picked members of their own clique most often. They chose other members of their crowd (not in their clique) less frequently. Only rarely (6 percent of the time) did they select partners outside their crowd. In the next phase, the higher-status members of each clique began heterosexual dating. Gradually, the boundaries between cliques dissolved as more members began dating. Now the most recognizable social unit was the crowd, in which some members were dating and some were not. By late adolescence (ages 18 to 21), Dunphy reported, crowd boundaries also began to dissolve as more couples paired off for dating. This pattern echoes the trends we described earlier, with clique boundaries softening earlier in adolescence and crowds blending by high school graduation.

The trends Dunphy (1963) found in Australia seem to apply worldwide. For example, researchers asked Israeli students to rate the degree of intimacy (sharing of personal thoughts and feelings) they perceived in their closest same- and opposite-sex friendships (Sharabany, Gershoni, & Hofman, 1981). Intimacy among same-sex friends remained constant across adolescence, but intimacy among opposite-sex friends increased substantially over the teen years. Overall, girls reported more intimacy than boys, and the intimacy girls reported in their opposite-sex relationships increased faster than the opposite-sex intimacy reported by boys. By late adolescence the intimacy of cross-sex couples was comparable to the intimacy shared between same-sex friends. As you can see from these studies, children share their personal thoughts and feelings first with the friends who are most like them—their closest same-sex

In early adolescence, members of the same larger crowd begin pairing off for dating. Cross-sex intimacy (the ability to share personal thoughts and feelings with a member of the opposite sex) typically develops faster in girls than in boys.

friends. Later, adolescents gradually begin sharing intimacy with opposite-sex friends, first from within the safe confines of common cliques and crowds, and later in more individualistic dating patterns.

■ **Sexual Activity.** The majority of adolescents in the United States have had sexual intercourse by the time they finish high school. Figure 11.4 shows the percentages of adolescents who reported ever having had sexual intercourse. These data from a nationwide survey of high school students show that more than one-third of adolescents have had intercourse by 9th grade, and nearly two-thirds by 12th grade. African Americans are much more likely than Hispanics of non-Hispanic whites to have engaged in sexual intercourse. In other data from the survey, 30 percent of African American males reported that they had sexual intercourse before the age of 13. By contrast, among all high school students (including male African Americans), 12 percent of males and 4 percent of females reported sexual intercourse before age 13. Males are more likely to engage in casual sex; 37 percent of males versus 17 percent of females reported having their first sexual intercourse with a casual acquaintance (Coles & Stokes, 1985).

Why do some adolescents become sexually active at an early age whereas others wait? The reasons obviously vary, but several tendencies do exist. In general, adolescents who engage in earlier sexual activity are also more likely to perform poorly in school, to achieve lower intelligence-test scores, to lack clear educational goals, to have single parents, to report poor parental communication and lack of parental support, to be more impulsive, and to use alcohol and other drugs (Katchadourian, 1990). The top reasons teens give for being sexually active are peer pressure, curiosity, and the idea that "everyone does it." Girls also cite pressure from boys as a top reason. In addition, many teens report that they were forced to have sex.

YOUR
PERSPECTIVE
NOTES

Do these patterns of sexual activity match what you remember from high school? What were the main pressures at that age for engaging in sexual activity? Why do you think some students abstained from sexual activity?

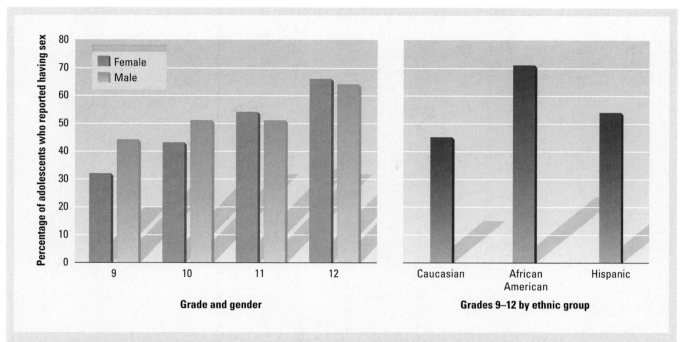

FIGURE 11.4 Percentages of High School Students Who Ever Had Sexual Intercourse

This graph shows the percentages of male and female high school students who reported in a nationwide survey that they had ever had sexual intercourse. The bars at the right show percentages by ethnic group.

Source: National Center for Health Statistics (2000a).

Among sexually active girls, for example, 14 percent reported being victims of rape, and a quarter of these rapes occurred before the girl was even 10 years old (Coles & Stokes, 1985). In about half of the cases, the rapist was a boyfriend or casual friend. In other cases the rapists included relatives and family friends. Among teens who had so far abstained from sex, 65 percent told researchers that they abstained because they feared sexually transmitted diseases; 62 percent feared pregnancy, 50 percent feared parents, and 29 percent feared they would lose their reputations among friends (Katchadourian, 1990).

One result of adolescent sexual activity is that each year nearly one million U.S. teenagers become pregnant (National Center for Health Statistics, 2000a). Increased use of contraception has led to a slight decline in teen pregnancy rates in recent years, but the U.S. rates are still twice as high as in England and Canada and 8 times higher than in Japan. As you can see in Figure 11.5, pregnancy rates are higher for African Americans, and for all teens more pregnancies end in live births than in induced abortions. Unintended pregnancies can place severe strains on adolescent mothers. These girls may not be physically or emotionally ready to bear children. Also, teenage mothers often face reduced educational achievement, limited employment opportunities, and poorer health and developmental outcomes for their babies (National Center for Health Statistics, 2000a).

Sexually transmitted diseases (discussed in Chapter 3) constitute another major concern in connection with teenagers' sexual activity. Adolescents are more likely to engage in casual sex and less likely to use protection than adults. For both these reasons, sexually active teens are a high risk for STDs.

Almost all public school systems provide sex-education programs. Churches and community organizations such as Planned Parenthood, the YMCA, Boy Scouts, and Girl Scouts also offer these programs. Most teens are not willing to talk openly with their parents about sex, and

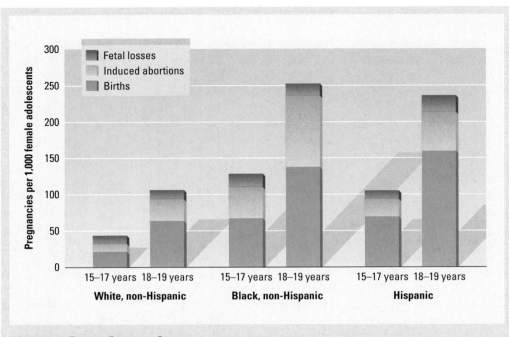

FIGURE 11.5 Teenage Pregnancy Rates

Pregnancy rates and pregnancy outcomes among 15- to 19-year-olds in the United States vary at different ages and among different ethnic groups. The data here come from a 1996 survey.

Source: National Center for Health Statistics (2000a).

YOUR

PERSPECTIVE

NOTES

Was the sex-education program in your school system adequate and effective? How do you think it could be improved?

homosexual orientation

Sexual attraction primarily to people of the same sex.

homosexual experience

Sexual activities with some-one of the same sex.

heterosexual assumption

The erroneous idea that all adolescents are heterosexual at first and "discover" their homosexuality only after having several failed relation-ships with members of the opposite sex.

they don't have independent access to health care or their own health insurance. Without school and community programs, where would they get reliable information? Almost everyone agrees that it is essential to provide sex education in schools, but there is heated debate about what to teach in sex-ed classes. Read about the debate between *abstinence-only* and *comprehensive* sex-ed programs in the Social Policy Perspective box called "The Sex-Education Debate."

■ **Homosexuality.**   We discussed the formation of gay, lesbian, and bisexual identities in Chapter 10, so in this section we will focus on adolescents' early sexual behaviors and feelings. We'll think particularly about how these experiences affect teenagers during this important phase of identity formation.

When studying sexual behavior, we need to distinguish between *homosexual orienta-tion* and *homosexual experiences*. **Homosexual orientation** is a sexual identity in which the person is sexually attracted primarily to people of the same sex. Homosexuals include *gay males* and *lesbian females*. *Bisexuals* have an attraction to both sexes. A **homosexual experi-ence,** however, is simply a sexual encounter with someone of the same sex. When experi-menting with sexuality, many adolescents have some type of *homosexual experience*. For many teens these same-sex experiences are exploratory and do not lead to a *homosexual orientation* in adulthood. For example, in a large national survey, 22 percent of men and 17 percent of women reported that they had had some type of homosexual experience at some point in their lives (Janus & Janus, 1993). In the same survey, only 9 percent of men and 5 percent of women reported that they were currently actively engaged in same-sex relationships. As you can see, most of the people who had homosexual experiences were not gay or lesbian, or at least did not report being in a homosexual relationship at the time.

One of the myths about homosexuality is what researchers call the **heterosexual assumption**—the idea that all adolescents are heterosexual at first and "discover" their

The Sex-Education Debate

In 2001 the surgeon general of the United States, David Satcher, released a report about sex education in U.S. schools. After reviewing hundreds of scientific studies of teenage pregnancy, teen rates of sexually transmitted disease, and adolescent sexual activity, Satcher recommended that sex-education programs teach the importance of abstaining from sex but also teach teens who are already sexually active how to prevent STDs and unintended pregnancies (Alan Guttmacher Institute, 2002).

The issue of teaching teens how to use condoms and other methods of pregnancy and disease prevention has been hotly debated since the federal government began playing a role in sex education in the 1980s. In 1981 Congress passed the Adolescent Family Life Act (AFLA), creating a federally funded program to prevent teen pregnancy by teaching abstinence and self-discipline in the schools. Later, a welfare reform law passed in 1996 and a maternal and child health block grant passed in 2000 began providing additional federal funds to promote *abstinence-only* programs in schools. Abstinence-only programs condemn all sex outside of marriage (for people of any age), and they completely prohibit any positive discussion of contraception. Abstinence-only programs may discuss condoms and other contraceptive methods only in order to explain how often they fail in preventing pregnancy and disease in adolescents.

Since the 1980s U.S. schools overall have shifted toward the abstinence-only approach. They have moved away from giving teens detailed information about how to obtain and use condoms and other contraceptive methods. According to a nationwide survey published in 1999, out of the school districts with sex-education programs, 35 percent mandated the abstinence-only approach; 51 percent required that abstinence be taught as the preferred method but allowed some discussion of contraception in preventing pregnancy and STDs; and only 14 percent offered the kind of comprehensive approach recommended by Satcher (Alan Guttmacher Institute, 2002).

Conservative lawmakers and some religious groups worry that teaching about condoms and contraception sends the wrong moral message—the message that premarital sex is acceptable. Satcher and others argue that the reality is that most teens *are* sexually active and need accurate and unbiased information about how to protect themselves. In a 1995 survey fewer than 60 percent of teenage males (ages 15 to 19) said they received information in school about birth control and STDs before their first sexual intercourse (Lindberg, Ku, & Sonenstein, 2000). Less than half had instruction on how to say no to sex, and fewer than 40 percent were taught how to put on a condom. Only half said they spoke to their parents about these issues. Girls are more likely to get these messages, with about 70 percent reporting formal education about birth control, AIDS, STDs, and abstinence before their first intercourse. Other surveys indicate that 81 percent of parents want their children's schools to provide comprehensive sex education that includes abstinence as well as condom use, birth control, abortion, and disease prevention. About half of all teens say they want more information about these and other sex-related topics (Kaiser Family Foundation, 2002).

Satcher's report pointed out that there was no available research evidence that abstinence-only programs work in preventing or delaying teen sex. Comprehensive programs that teach abstinence and contraception, however, have been associated with slight delays in the onset of sexual activity, reductions in the numbers of sexual partners, and increase contraceptive use among sexually active teens. The teenage pregnancy rate did decline slightly during the 1990s, with most of the decline due to increased use of contraception (Alan Guttmacher Institute, 2002).

The debate still rages. Abstinence promotion was a prominent feature of George W. Bush's 2000 presidential campaign (Alan Guttmacher Institute, 2002). During the early part of the Bush administration, information about condom use, ways to reduce sex among teenagers, and abortion were removed from government websites (Clymer, 2002). On the other side, a federal judge in New Orleans ordered Louisiana to change its federally funded abstinence programs because some programs used the federal funds to advance religious beliefs (Liptak, 2002).

The battle over sex education in schools involves conflicting views on government control, religious morals, family and personal values, and the reality of teen sex. The stakes are obviously high, given our nation's high rate of teen pregnancy and the devastating consequences of HIV infection and other STDs. What should schools do? What role should the federal government play? What kinds of information and values do you think should be taught in sex-education classes? ■

homosexuality only after having several failed relationships with members of the opposite sex (Hunter & Mallon, 2000). For most gay people this assumption couldn't be farther from the truth. After extensive interviews with gay and bisexual men aged 17 to 23, for example, Savin-Williams (1995) reported that most of the men experienced homosexual sex first. If they tried heterosexual relations at all, they did so later and with much less frequency. On average these gay and bisexual men had their first homosexual experience at age 14 and their first heterosexual experience later. Most did not try heterosexual sex until after they graduated from high school. Across their sexual histories the men reported having sex with an average of eight male partners and only one female partner. Most of the men noticed at an early age that they were attracted to the same sex. Some reported having same-sex attractions from their earliest memories; the average was at 8 years of age, although a few had their first male attraction as late as age 16. Individuals obviously differ, but it is clear that in most of these men their attraction to other males emerged at an early age and before any attraction they may have had to the opposite sex.

Although homosexuality is becoming more widely accepted in today's culture, gay men and lesbians still experience tremendous discrimination and harsh treatment from peers and family. Most homosexuals are keenly aware that heterosexuals view their same-sex attraction as "different" or "deviant." When they reveal their feelings, gay males and lesbians typically suffer intense social isolation (Hunter & Mallon, 2000). The vast majority of lesbian and gay adolescents report that they feel separated and emotionally isolated from their peers (Savin-Williams, 1994). Many are victims of violent physical attacks, and you may be surprised to learn that most of these attacks actually come from members of the teenagers' own families (Hunter, 1990; Savin-Williams, 1994). The verbal and physical abuse that many homosexual students receive from peers, parents, and others is very harmful to their sense of self-worth and mental health. Compared to their heterosexual peers, homosexual youths are at a much higher risk of failing a grade in school, skipping school, dropping out of school, running away from home, being kicked out of their own homes, and/or engaging in substance abuse and prostitution. In a review of the research in this area, Savin-Williams (1994) reported that "suicide is the leading cause of death among lesbian, gay male, and bisexual youths, primarily because of the debilitating effects of growing up in a homophobic society" (p. 266). The suicide rate is 2 to 3 times higher among homosexual than among heterosexual youths. And when gay and lesbian adolescents try to take their own lives, family conflict is the reason cited most often.

Many adolescents try to avoid family conflict by hiding their homosexual feelings. This strategy may succeed to some degree. However, it takes a tremendous toll, and it prevents developing adolescents from expressing their true identities in the environment that counts the most—their own families. As one adolescent put it:

> Hiding was so exhausting. I always had to watch myself. I always had to make sure that I was not acting too butch or dressing too much like a dyke. I always felt like I was trying to be someone I wasn't, always trying to fit in where I knew I didn't fit. It was really hard. I really felt alone, I thought I was the only person in the world who felt this way. (Mallon, 1998, p. 119)

Among gay and lesbian youths who do show positive development, self-acceptance is the best predictor of positive growth (Hershberger & D'Augelli, 1995). A general sense of personal worth and a positive view of their sexual orientation are critical for these adolescents' healthy development. Strong family support is also important: It can provide a buffer against the harsh treatment the adolescent receives at school and elsewhere (Hershberger & D'Augelli, 1995). And many homosexuals report that they find great comfort in having good friends who understand and appreciate their sexual orientations (Hunter & Mallon, 2000).

The teenage years are a critical time for identity formation in all adolescents. Regardless of sexual orientation, all teens benefit from understanding and affection from peers, parents, teachers, and the other people who touch their lives. As cultural attitudes continue to change, we hope that larger numbers of developing youths will receive these positive supports.

1. One of the important features of *coordinated imitation* in toddler play is that:

    a. the imitation is coordinated by parents or other adults.

    b. the toddlers are aware that they are being imitated by their playmates.

    c. toddlers use mutual gaze to coordinate the acts of imitation in their play.

    d. toddlers imitate each other's physical actions in play, but they have difficulty imitating verbal dialogue.

2. During childhood the main ingredients that promote friendships are similarity and:

    a. intimacy.   b. loyalty.   c. opportunity.   d. generosity.

3. Which statement below best summarizes the type of friendships children have around the age of 9?

    a. "He is my friend because he sticks by me when other kids make fun of me."

    b. "She is my friend because she is my neighbor and we play together a lot."

    c. "She is my friend because we are in the same class in school."

    d. "He is my friend because we can talk about things that bother me, and he will keep it secret."

4. Research on adolescent crowds indicates that self-esteem is highest among:

    a. druggies/toughs.   b. nobodies.   c. normals.   d. jocks.

5. **True or False:** According to cognitive schema theory, girls and boys avoid playing with each other because their styles of play do not match.

6. **True or False:** Most gay men and lesbians had sexual relations with the opposite sex during their teenage years, then discovered their true attraction to the same sex during early adulthood.

Answers: 1. b, 2. c, 3. a, 4. d, 5. F, 6. F

Play

Developmental psychologists define **play** as a *pleasurable* activity that is *actively engaged in* on a *voluntary* basis, is *intrinsically motivated,* and contains some *nonliteral* element (Hughes, 1999). In plain words, play is something children (and older people) choose to do, on their own, for fun. They do it for the enjoyment of the play itself, not for outside rewards or in response to outside pressures. When children are truly "playing" baseball, for example, they are doing it because they enjoy the game. If they are doing it only to win a trophy or only because their parents made them do it, then it doesn't qualify as play. Finally, most play involves a nonliteral component—some element of make-believe, pretend, or symbolism. When children are playing, they pretend that dolls can talk, toy cars can zoom around imaginary racetracks, and a stick can become a powerful sword or a magic wand.

Play allows children to explore beyond the boundaries of reality. With imagination, fantasy, and creativity, children transform the objects and people in the real world to suit their own playful purposes. Through play children have opportunities to develop muscle coordination, social interaction skills, logical reasoning and problem-solving skills, and the ability to think about the world as it really is and as it could be. In this next section we describe how researchers look at children's play and look at how the structure and function of play change from infancy through adolescence. We end this section by discussing how play differs among children who grow up in different cultures.

play

A pleasurable activity that is actively engaged in on a voluntary basis, is intrinsically motivated, and contains some nonliteral element.

As you study this section, ask yourself these questions:

- How does play change as infants grow into the toddler and preschool age? How does play evolve in middle childhood and adolescence?

- What are the relationships among changing patterns of play, the child's growing understanding of the world, and the way the child thinks about the world?

- How does the culture in which children live affect their play? What are some of the main differences in children's play around the world?

The Social Levels of Play: Parten's Classic Study

In one of the classic studies of play, Mildred Parten (1932) made extensive observations of 42 children as they engaged in free play at their preschool. The children were 1 to 5 years of age, and Parten observed them repeatedly over a period of nearly 8 months. Parten was particularly interested in the social nature of children's play. She identified six levels of play that ranged from completely nonsocial to highly integrated social play, as follows:

1. *Unoccupied behavior:* The child is not playing and not watching anyone or anything in particular. He may momentarily play with his own body, stand around, follow a teacher, or just sit alone. Example: Joey is sitting alone in the play area, apparently not playing with or watching anyone else.

2. *Onlooking:* The child spends most of his time watching other children play. He talks to the children he is watching and asks questions, but he does not engage in the play himself. He focuses on the play of a particular child or group of children, and he stays near them so he can hear and observe. Example: Joey follows Sam around as Sam plays; Joey asks questions and talks to Sam, but he does not play directly with Sam.

3. *Solitary play:* The child plays alone, and he makes no apparent connection between his play and the play of other children around him. Although he may play close to other children, he makes no attempt to make a connection with them. Example: Joey is playing in the sandbox; Sam is playing nearby, but Joey is not talking or sharing with him, and he is not watching Sam.

4. *Parallel play:* The child plays alone but with toys that are like those used by other children around him. His play may be similar to the play of nearby children, but he plays *beside* the other children, not *with* them. Example: Joey is pouring sand into his bucket and dumping it; Joey is sitting near Sam, who is also pouring and dumping sand, but they are not playing together.

5. *Associative play:* The child plays among other children, but his play is not well coordinated with their play. He may talk with the other children and share toys and materials, but his play is still relatively independent of theirs. The primary interest is in associating with other children but not in coordinating their play activity. Example: Joey and Sam are playing in the sandbox together; they talk, exchange buckets, and give sand to each other, but they are still pouring and dumping their own sand.

6. *Cooperative play:* The child plays with other children, and his play is integrated or coordinated with theirs. Play of this type often involves a group of children who are creating a common product, striving for a competitive goal, acting out adult situations, or playing formal games. There is a division of labor: Children play different roles, and their individual efforts contribute to a larger whole. Example:

Several children are building a sand castle together. Joey is shoveling the sand into buckets while Sam dumps the sand to form spires and Sarah carefully pats and smoothes the spires. Together they build a large and beautiful castle.

Parten found a connection between children's ages and their types of play. She observed the lower levels of play primarily among younger children. Unoccupied behavior, the lowest level, rarely occurred; when it did, it was always in 1- and 2-year-olds, never with older children. Onlooking and solitary play, the next two levels, occurred mostly in the younger children and rarely among the 3- to 5-year-olds. Parallel play was the most common type of play overall, but it was still more characteristic of the 1- and 2-year-olds than of the older children. The 3- to 5-year-olds split their playtime about evenly among the upper three levels: parallel, associative, and cooperative play. The 1- and 2-year-olds rarely engaged in cooperative play. When this highest level occurred, it was almost always among children who were 3 to 5 years of age. Similar trends emerged in a study of young children in Taiwan (Pan, 1994).

Parten's observations highlighted the social nature of play. When children are young and lack social skills, they tend to play alone or beside other children—they rarely can coordinate their play with peers or in a larger group. As children gain social skills, they tend to move toward more integrated play—they play with other children, and eventually they learn to coordinate their play roles to accomplish a larger group goal. Clearly, play evolves and changes as children acquire social skills. Parten's work, however, has some limitations. She observed only children who were relatively young (1 to 5 years old), and her descriptions don't tell us much about what the children were doing in their play. To have a more complete understanding of the developmental trends in children's play, we need to look at a larger age range and to include the cognitive and physical aspects of play. We'll do this in the next section.

Types of Play from Infancy through Adolescence

Play is more than just a social enterprise. Through play children learn a lot about the world and about themselves. By pouring, stacking, banging, and throwing, infants and young children explore the qualities of objects in their environments and learn concepts associated with gravity, solidity, and motion. By learning and following the rules of formal games, children can develop and apply their skills in logic. In play children also have opportunities to be creative, solve problems, and explore language. In addition to fostering these cognitive advances, play also can help children develop physical skills such as running, jumping, climbing, and throwing. Children can explore their own limits in play, a process that facilitates the formation of self-concepts. Additionally, they learn how to get along with others, solve disputes, and make and keep friends. In all of these ways, play provides a rich context that drives the development of cognitive, physical, and social skills. Across time, children's play becomes more sophisticated, reflecting an increasing maturity in all of these areas.

In this section we outline some of the main trends that occur in the play of children from infancy through adolescence. We will use Jean Piaget's stages of cognitive development as a basic framework. You may find it helpful to take a quick look back to Chapter 5 to review the major features of these stages.

■ **Sensorimotor Play in Infancy.** During the first year of life, play evolves mostly around the practice of sensory activity and the development of new motor actions. Researchers refer to this period of play as **sensorimotor play,** based on the sensorimotor stage in Piaget's theory. For the first few months, infants spend most of their awake time lying on their backs and looking around at the world. They seem to be soaking up their new environments by staring at objects and colors and listening intently to the various sounds around them. The first noticeable signs of play involve activities they discover with their own bodies. After accidentally

sensorimotor play

Play that evolves mostly around the practice of sensory activity and the development of new motor actions.

bringing his fist to his mouth, for example, an infant may work to repeat this action. When he succeeds, the repetitive motion becomes a game that the infant repeats for several minutes, smiling and squirming with glee at his new discovery. Spitting bubbles and kicking their feet are other similar games that infants discover and playfully repeat.

By 3 months of age, infants can reach out and grasp small objects. Now the world of play expands from actions involving infants' own bodies to interactions with objects in the world. Rattles, balls, pieces of cloth, and other small objects can now be grasped, mouthed, banged, and dropped. Infants repeat these playful actions as they develop new motor actions and explore new objects in their environments.

An interesting development occurs between the ages of 6 and 9 months. At 6 months infants usually treat all objects that are about the same size in the same way. Give a 6-month-old a spoon, for example, and the baby will bang it on the table. Now give the baby a ball, and they bang it too, and the same with a rattle or a small doll (Hughes, 1999). At 6 months, in other words, babies incorporate every object into the action pattern they prefer at the moment (e.g., banging). At 9 months, however, infants pay more attention to the specific features of objects and begin treating objects differently (Hughes, 1999; Ruff, 1984). Now they bring the spoon to their mouth, throw the ball, shake the rattle, and hug the doll. Rather than forcing all objects into a fixed action pattern, 9-month-olds can adjust their play to fit the unique features of each object. At this point infants appreciate having a variety of playthings with different shapes, sounds, textures, and actions. Toys that respond to babies' actions are especially interesting. When babies realize that pushing a particular button produces an exciting sound or flash of light, a smile of recognition spreads across their faces. They recognize that they are having an influence on their environment and that the environment is now responding to them. It is exciting for parents to watch their infants form these early connections. And the infants derive self-confidence and a general sense of self from the realization that they can influence the environment (Hughes, 1999).

■ **Symbolic and Sociodramatic Play in Toddlers and Preschoolers.** As you'll recall from Chapter 5, the major change in the transition to preoperational thought involves the emergence of symbolic thinking—the ability to form mental representations of objects or events in the world. In **symbolic play** children use make-believe and pretend to embellish the objects and actions in their play. Early symbols begin to emerge between 12 and 14 months as toddlers pretend to act out common activities. They may lie on the floor with a small blanket and pretend to go to sleep or use toy dishes to pretend to eat. By 2 to 3 years of age, toddlers pretend that an object is something else: A wooden block is a car, a spoon is an airplane, or the family cat is their baby. Still later, children integrate multiple objects and actions into dramatic play activities. Their bed becomes a castle, their pillow is a magic shield, and they engage in mythical duels with the Evil Knight of Doom (really a chair, or their sister).

Another type of play that becomes common by 3 years of age is **sociodramatic play**—acting out different social roles and characters. Sociodramatic play may be realistic ("I'll be the daddy and you be the baby") or may involve a high degree of fantasy ("I'm queen of the empire; behold my castle!"). Sociodramatic play can serve any of the following functions for young children (Hughes, 1999):

▶ *Imitation of adults:* Children can act out adult roles they have observed, such as the role of a parent, teacher, cook, waiter, doctor, dentist, or veterinarian. Exploring these roles in play lets young children explore the activities of people in the larger world.

▶ *Reenactment of family relationships:* Children often reenact events from their family lives. Most often, sociodramatic play involves simple, everyday activities: "Say good-bye to Mommy; she's going to work now." Sometimes, however, children use sociodramatic play to process larger and more traumatic events:

YOUR PERSPECTIVE NOTES

Describe the kinds of sensorimotor play you have observed in infants. Where do these kinds of play fit within the sequence we present?

symbolic play

Play where children use make-believe and pretend to embellish objects and actions.

sociodramatic play

Play that involves acting out different social roles or characters.

"Daddy and Mommy don't love each other anymore; now we have to move to another house."

▶ *Expression of needs:* Sociodramatic play gives children a chance to express unmet needs. For example, an only child may pretend to have a brother, or a child who misses his or her father may pretend to be playing ball with him.

▶ *Outlet for forbidden impulses:* Sociodramatic play gives children a safer outlet for exploring roles and activities that would not be appropriate for them in real life. Children can pretend to be highly aggressive ("Beware, I'm going to smash down your whole house!"), and they can playact love, marriage, and aspects of sexuality.

▶ *Reversal of roles:* Finally, in sociodramatic play children who usually feel helpless can act out more powerful roles, like those of parent, teacher, and superhero. They can turn the tables by disciplining their dolls or playmates ("Bad behavior—now you go to timeout!"), or they can be the ones giving the commands at preschool ("Now it's time to go to nap, children"). This type of play helps children experience the more powerful perspective, and it can help them confront their anxieties about being the smaller and less powerful person in real life.

Of course, children often engage in sociodramatic play for the pure fun of acting out roles with playmates. Sometimes "You be the Mommy and I'll be the baby" is simply fun, and there doesn't have to be any deeper meaning to the play.

Young children enjoy pretending to be superheroes and other powerful characters. What are the potential benefits of this type of sociodramatic play?

The ages from 3 to 5 years are an especially imaginative period of pretend play. The creativity that children show in their symbolic and sociodramatic play reflects the new symbolic thinking skills they are developing. As children exercise and explore the limits of their symbolic thought, their play becomes ever more imaginative. This imaginativeness, however, will yield to an increasing realism as children move into the next stage of cognitive development.

■ **Focus on Logic and Physical Skills in Middle Childhood.** By 6 years of age, most children have entered the stage of concrete operational thought. Their thought processes become more logical and realistic, and fantasy and pretend tend to give way to seeing the world more as it really is. Children now enjoy play activities and games that involve structured rules. Children can follow the rules in board games; counting games like "one potato, two potato" take on a real logical force; the rules and strategies of video games can occupy some children for hours. Although elements of fantasy can still be fun, it is now the logic in the games that becomes the focus of interest. Children's collections give more evidence of their new sense of logic, order, and organization. At this age children collect sports cards, action figures, Barbie dolls, and other toys more for the interest in acquiring and organizing them than for the fun of playing with them. Negotiating trades and developing strategies for improving such collections are important exercises in logical thought (Hughes, 1999).

During middle childhood play often involves acquiring and improving physical skills. Hitting a baseball, jumping rope, climbing trees, riding bicycles, and skateboarding are

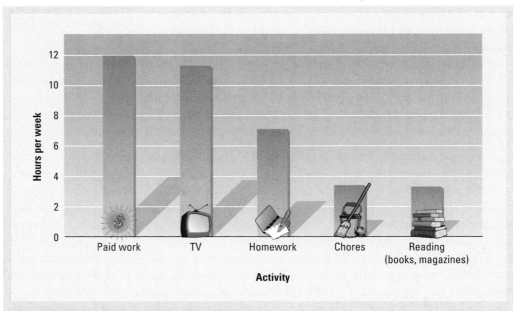

common examples of skill-based play. Mastery of skills is important to children—they often push the limits of their skills and demonstrate their mastery by performing stunts that become increasingly complex and dangerous. Jumping a ramp on a skateboard or hanging by a knee from a tree limb can alarm parents but impress peers. During the grade school years, children demonstrate their skills in order to establish their positions in peer groups (Hughes, 1999). Many children, too, become involved in organized sports. When the fun of participating in the game is children's main motivation, then involvement in sports can rightly qualify as play. If, however, children participate in sports because parents or coaches pressure them, or for the sake of winning alone, then their activity has moved out of the proper realm of play.

■ **Leisure Time in Adolescence.** Adolescence brings a shift from the concrete and realistic thought of the grade school child to the more hypothetical and idealistic thought characteristic of the formal operational stage. In some sense this represents a return to the fantasy of earlier years, but this time adolescents use their imaginations to speculate about how the world could be or should be (Hughes, 1999). Movies, TV, music, and video games are popular; they give adolescents opportunities to escape the realities of life and explore more exciting possibilities. A teenage girl can enjoy a movie with her best friend, for example, or use the movie expedition as a way to meet attractive guys in her peer group. Activities that enable adolescents to be around one another, sharing their ideas and interests, often lead to dating and other intimate contacts. Even when alone, adolescents use music, TV, and similar activities as ways to explore their own interests, examine how they fit with peers, and reflect on where they are going in their lives. Self-understanding, sexual attraction, and intimate communication are important aspects of leisure-time activities in adolescence (Hughes, 1999).

As Figure 11.6 shows, adolescents devote more time to TV than to homework, and their hours spent watching TV outnumber hours spent reading books and magazines by more than

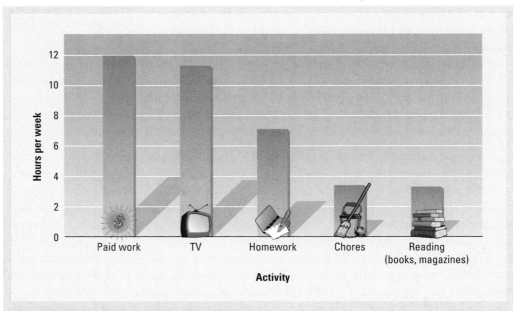

FIGURE 11.6 Common Activities in Adolescence

Shown here are average hours per week U.S. adolescents spend in various activities, based on reports from students mostly 16 to 18 years old.

Source: Data from Anderson, Huston, Schmitt, Linebarger, & Wright (2001).

TABLE 11.2 Trends in Play and Appropriate Toys and Materials for Different Age Groups

AGE	TRENDS IN PLAY	APPROPRIATE TOYS AND MATERIALS
Birth to 3 months	Sensorimotor play focused on seeing, touching, hearing. Infant is not yet crawling or grasping objects.	Toys should provide varied sensory stimulation: colorful pictures, wallpaper, crib ornaments, mobiles, musical toys, rattles. Protect infant from small objects that are choking hazards.
3 to 12 months	Infants can now reach and grasp, so sensorimotor play expands to include these motor activities.	Add toys that infants can grab and manipulate with their hands, squeeze, drop, stack, and put in their mouths (avoid choking hazards!): teething toys, balls, blocks, picture books, and toys with buttons and dials that make sounds and motions.
1 to 2 years	Walking and climbing extend motor activities. Symbolic play emerges with make-believe and pretend.	Provide riding toys, small climbing structures, push and pull toys, stacking blocks, simple puzzles, sandbox and water toys, dolls, stuffed animals, toy dishes, storybooks.
3 to 5 years	Sociodramatic play emerges as children playact roles and characters. Imaginative play is important.	Add props for playacting such as clothes and costumes for dress-up. Offer art materials for coloring, painting, molding. Children enjoy puzzles and simple games (Candyland, Trouble, Old Maid) as well as swing sets, climbing structures, tricycles, and small bicycles.
6 to 10 years	Logical rules, reality-based play, physical skills, and sports become more predominant.	Games with structured rules (Monopoly, Stratego, card games) have appeal; also things that can be collected and organized (sports cards, action figures, dolls). Children master bicycles, skateboards, jump ropes, and sports equipment.
11 years and older	Leisure activities are central. Fantasy involves hypothetical and idealistic scenarios. Affiliation with peers is key.	Video and computer games, adventure games, movies, and music are popular. Teens tend to focus on a few sports in which they excel.

3 to 1. Adolescents don't spend all of their time watching TV, of course. They put a considerable amount of time into paid employment and some time into household chores. Adults often complain that adolescents waste too much time watching TV, but research data suggest that their criticism may be misdirected. According to one British study, for example, 12- to 15-year-olds and 16- to 24-year-olds spent approximately 2.7 hours per day watching TV, but adults (25 to 54 years old) spent 3.5 hours glued to the tube (Gunter & McAleer, 1997). Older adults (ages 55 and up) watched nearly 5 hours per day! We'll examine the effects of TV, video games, computers, and other media in more detail in Chapter 13.

Many adolescents also engage in more active pursuits, such as organized sports, skateboarding, or dancing. At this age, however, they tend to focus selectively on the one or two activities in which they excel (Hughes, 1999). Even in adolescence, these activities still meet the definition of play we introduced at the beginning of this section: They are pleasurable, and the adolescent engages in them actively, voluntarily, and for intrinsic motivations. Such activities even take on a nonliteral characteristic when adolescents speculate about hypothetical possibilities or how life could or should be.

Table 11.2 provides a summary of these and other trends in play, along with suggestions for toys and other playthings for different ages. For some children's and adolescents' personal thoughts about play, read the Personal Perspective box called "Play at Different Ages."

Cultural Differences in Play

Play is a dominant activity of children in cultures all around the world, and play is in some sense both a cause and an effect of culture (Roopnarine & Johnson, 1994). The developmental progression we have described probably occurs in all cultures. Infants around the world engage in sensorimotor play; symbolic and sociodramatic play emerge in early childhood; later, play becomes more logical and realistic and often focuses on the physical skills that are

A Personal PERSPECTIVE...

Play at Different Ages

Sam Blumenfeld
Arlington,
Massachusetts
6½-year-old boy

We asked several children and adolescents what they like to play the most or what they prefer to do during their free time. How do their answers compare with the developmental trends described in this chapter?

What is your favorite thing to play?
[**Scout, age 5**] I like to play restaurant with my friends because we get to make chocolate pudding out of mud and water. I also like to play checkers and Legos.

What do you and your friends play most?
[**Sam, age 6½**] Each time we play different games. Um, we like to dress up to spy. And we also like to scare Charlotte [his little sister].

What do you do in your free time?
[**Laura, age 13**] I like to make things with my friends, like when we made our own dollhouse. I love cooking food, especially desserts. I like going places with my friends, like the movies or the pool, and I like to play the computer. I used to be into dressing up with my friends and playing with dolls. I love reading and pottery also.

How do you spend your free time?
[**Robbie, age 16**] While together my friends and I like to go out to eat, cruise around downtown, play pool, set up bike jumps in construction sites, go to the pool, and sometimes go to the movies. Anything to get your heart rate up is fun, but relaxing and doing something like playing pool is enjoyable as well. ■

thinking
OF KIM

◄ How could Kim use leisure-time activities as a way to form new friendships? Describe two or three activities Kim might try in order to meet and socialize with his peers.

important in the child's culture. However, the culture in which children live can influence where they play, whom they play with, and the main themes in their play. So play helps transmit the culture's important values and attitudes to the child—who will then pass them along to the next generation.

The opportunity to play, and the central themes and styles of social interactions that occur during play, however, vary substantially across diverse cultures. As an example, consider how different cultures value work and play. Children in the United States and Britain spend most of their after-school time in play, but children in Japan and Korea are more likely to spend time studying for school (Takeuchi, 1994). Japanese and Korean cultures place a high value on hard work, sacrifice, and educational achievement. In Japan, for example, students study hard in hopes of getting into the best universities and professional schools. After graduation, Japanese citizens devote enormous time and energy to their occupations. Men work long hours, and children have little opportunity to play or interact with their fathers (Takeuchi, 1994). Among the Hazda people of Tanzania, children are expected to forage for their own food by age 3; by age 10 they are expected to be productive hunters and gatherers (Lancy, 2002). Hazda children learn to work at a young age, and their parents have very little tolerance for play.

Spaces available for play also differ across cultures. In Japan there is little open space, so children typically play indoors and in small groups (Takeuchi, 1994). In the West African nation of Senegal, children tend to live in communal "compounds" containing numerous households, all related to the eldest male in the compound (Bloch & Adler, 1994). Children play outdoors, roaming the compound in larger groups consisting mostly of siblings and cousins. Because of the extended family arrangement of the compounds, all available adults take responsibility for watching the children, and by the age of 4, children roam the compounds rather freely. As in most cultures, gender typing is clear in these children's sociodramatic play. Senegalese girls tend to playact family roles, nurturing younger children and doing domestic chores like cooking and carrying

Cultural values regarding work and play have an enormous influence on how children develop. Japanese children, for example, spend much more time studying than do their U.S. counterparts.

water. Senegalese boys playact farming, herding animals, fishing, and working with machines and automobiles (Bloch & Adler, 1994). Through their play these children learn the skills that are important in their culture.

Other effects of culture are apparent in the social themes and interactions in children's play. In one cross-cultural study, researchers gave 4-year-olds toy figurines to play with and asked the children to talk aloud and tell a story as they played with the figurines (Farver & Welles-Nystrom, 1997). Children in the United States incorporated significantly more aggressive words, unfriendly characters, and physical aggression in their play than did German, Swedish, or Indonesian children. U.S. children tended to solve the problems in their stories with force and violence. In contrast, Indonesian children's story characters were the most friendly, tended to be the most helpful, and solved problems in peaceful ways. In all four cultures the children who showed the most aggression in their play were also the most aggressive with their peers in school and were rated by teachers as performing less well in school.

U.S. culture teaches children to stand up for themselves, get ahead, and "watch out for number one." By contrast, Indonesians emphasize group harmony, emotional restraint, and cooperation. Indonesian children learn to treat all members of the community as family (Farver & Welles-Nystrom, 1997). Are these lessons reflected in the larger society? Consider the fact that the rate of serious crime (homicide, sex offenses, assault, theft, breaking and entering, and fraud) in the United States is higher than in most other industrialized nations (Farver & Welles-Nystrom, 1997). Children's play in this country reflects our society's permissiveness toward aggression. It doesn't take much imagination to see how childhood aggressiveness may translate into increased aggression among American teens and adults. Of course, U.S. society is itself diverse, and attitudes about aggression differ among subcultures. Korean American children, for example, show more cooperation, harmony, and social sensitivity in their play; European American children are more aggressive and antagonistic (Farver, 2000; Farver & Shin, 1997). These cultural values pass from one generation to the next in children's activities as they play.

thinking
OF KIM

Explain how cultural differences in play might relate to Kim's difficulties in making friends in a culture that is predominantly Euro-American. In what ways might these cultural differences affect how Kim reacts in social settings and how other children react to Kim?

1. Karen and Tasha are both jumping rope. Although they sometimes talk to each other and try tricks they see each other perform, they are jumping their own ropes and are not engaged with each other in any coordinated way. According to Parten's classification of social play, Karen and Tasha are engaged in:

   a. onlooking.   b. parallel play.   c. associative play.   d. cooperative play.

2. Between 6 and 9 months of age, most infants begin to:

   a. grasp small toys with their hands.

   b. discover new play activities that involve actions with their own bodies.

   c. discover new play activities by interacting with parents and other adults.

   d. adjust their play activities to fit the specific features of different objects.

3. Which of the following examples of symbolic play is *least* mature?

   a. pretending that a toy car is food

   b. pretending that a plastic apple is food

   c. pretending to feed one doll while another doll is washing dishes

   d. having a pretend tea party with several dolls and toy dishes

4. Compared to children in Germany, Sweden, and Indonesia, children in the United States show more _____ in their play.

   a. aggression   b. cooperation   c. group harmony   d. symbolic pretend

5. **True or False:** Structured rules and logic become the focus of play during middle childhood.

6. **True or False:** Idealism, self-understanding, and intimate communication are important components of the social and leisure-time activities of adolescents.

Answers: 1. c, 2. d, 3. b, 4. a, 5. T, 6. T

Popular and Unpopular Children

Picture yourself as a child in a third-grade classroom. A researcher comes in and explains to the whole class that she would like to know how children pick their friends. She then gives each child a list of all of the children in the class. She asks you to look down the list of names and select the children you "like best" and the ones you "like least." Whom do you pick?

As you can imagine, when the researcher collects the lists, some names will have received a lot of positive nominations (many selections for "like best"). There will be other children, unfortunately, with a lot of negative nominations (many selections for "like least"). Others will get a mixture of positive and negative nominations or practically no nominations at all. This **peer nomination technique** is the method researchers employ most often to measure social status in childhood. Using this rather simple polling technique, researchers have identified numerous characteristics that distinguish popular and unpopular children. In this next section, we will describe the differences between popular and unpopular children, and we will also consider some of the important consequences that occur when some children are rejected by their peers.

peer nomination technique

Polling technique used to identify categories of popular and unpopular children.

As you study this section, ask yourself these questions:

- Why are some children more popular than others? What are the characteristics associated with more and less popular children?

- How do children who are less popular perceive and interpret social events differently from those who are more popular?

- How do children respond when they are rejected or neglected by their peers?

Categories of Popular and Unpopular Children

Figure 11.7 shows how researchers typically categorize children using the peer nomination technique. As you can see in the figure, five categories of children emerge from the nomination patterns: *popular, rejected, controversial, average,* and *neglected.*

Popular children are the ones who receive a large number of "like best" nominations. These children are well liked. In general, popular children are friendly, cooperative, sociable, and sensitive to the needs of others (Rubin et al., 1998). They like to interact with other children, they are helpful, and they show good leadership skills. Popular children also have good communication skills: They speak clearly and are good listeners. Although they can be assertive, popular children are usually not aggressive in a way that interferes with the other children's happiness.

One of the special characteristics researchers have noted in popular children is their easy and nondisruptive manner when joining activities or new groups of children (Dodge, Pettit, McClaskey, & Brown, 1986; Putallaz, 1983). If, for example, they come to the playground at recess and find that other children are already playing kickball, popular children are likely to find an easy and friendly way to join the game. They may begin by hanging around other children who are waiting for a turn to kick, then gradually move onto the team as other children accept them. They are sensitive to social cues from other children, and they back away if others seem offended by their presence. Rather than being overbearing, popular children find a way to join activities without drawing a lot of attention to themselves. They

thinking
OF KIM

◀ How could Kim develop some of the characteristics that popular children possess? Are there specific skills or other areas of improvement that you could suggest for someone like Kim who is trying to make new friends?

popular children

In the peer nomination technique, children whom a large number of peers have chosen as classmates they "like best."

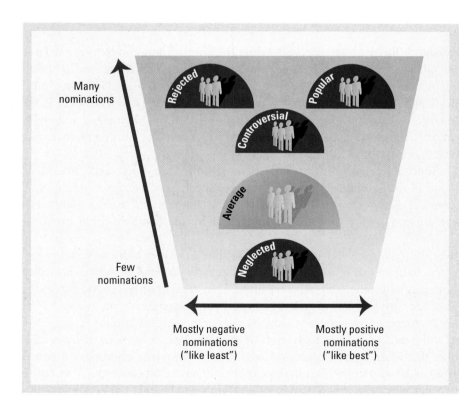

FIGURE 11.7 Peer Nomination Categories

In the peer nomination technique, researchers ask children to name peers they "like best" and "like least." The number and types of nominations (positive and negative) determine categories. For example, "rejected" children are those who receive a large number of negative nominations; "neglected" children are those who receive few nominations of either type.

ease in gradually without disrupting the game for others. Later, after they have gained acceptance from the other children, they may take on a leadership role or may become more of the center of attention.

Rejected children also receive a large number of nominations—but the nominations are of the "like least" variety. These children are actively disliked. This category typically includes two subtypes that are very different from each other. On the one hand, researchers classify about half of all rejected children as *rejected–aggressive* (French, 1988; Rubin et al., 1998). Rejected–aggressive children are physically aggressive (they often hit, push, and bully other children), and they are also verbally abusive (they threaten and tease others). To join the kickball game, for example, they may grab the ball, declare that "it's my turn to kick!" and threaten violence against anyone who challenges them. Alternatively, rejected–aggressive children may disrupt the game and try to start a new game of their own: "C'mon, this game's for sissies; let's go play some real football!" Girls are less likely to use physical aggression or direct verbal assaults. Instead, they use more **relational aggression**—withdrawing friendship or otherwise disrupting or threatening social relationships as a way to hurt other people. For example, girls are more likely to force their way into a game by saying, "If you don't let me play, I won't be your best friend anymore!"

Another 20 percent or so of rejected children are withdrawn and timid, and they fall under the *rejected–withdrawn* heading. Not all withdrawn children are rejected; out of the children who are most withdrawn in a class, only about one-quarter actually receive "like least" nominations (Rubin et al., 1998). When children are younger, they are less likely to dislike classmates who are withdrawn. By later childhood, however, some withdrawn children become outcasts and experience considerable disdain from their peers. In many cases there is something about rejected–withdrawn children that puts off or annoys other children. For example, they may dress or behave oddly, or they may blatantly refuse to participate or cooperate with other children.

The remaining children in the rejected category fall between the aggressive and withdrawn subtypes. It is not clear how these children differ from other peers who may simply be considered "shy."

Controversial children are an especially intriguing group. These children receive large numbers of both positive and negative nominations: A lot of children pick them as "like best," but just as many pick them as "like least." This category tends to be very small in most groups of children, and researchers have not studied it in great detail. In one study, however, it appeared that although controversial boys were more aggressive, active, disruptive, and angry than average children, they were also more helpful and cooperative and showed more leadership than average (Coie & Dodge, 1988).

Average children receive moderate numbers of both "like best" and "like least" nominations. That is, unlike children in the controversial category, average children don't receive a large number of either type of nomination. These children tend to show good social skills, but some are more aggressive than popular children and others are a bit more withdrawn.

Neglected children receive very few "like best" or "like least" peer nominations. Instead, these children seem to be mostly ignored by other children. As you might imagine, neglected children don't interact with other children very often. They tend to be less sociable than the average child, but they are also less negative, disruptive, and aggressive than average. They seem to actively avoid aggressive confrontations (Coie & Dodge, 1988; Rubin et al., 1998). Most neglected children do not show high levels of social anxiety or wariness of other children. (Remember that when social withdrawal becomes more extreme, children sometimes receive enough "liked least" nominations to place them in the rejected category.) Also, membership in the neglected category is not very stable (Rubin et al., 1998). When researchers

---

rejected children

In the peer nomination technique, children who are actively disliked; a large number of peers have chosen them as classmates they "like least."

relational aggression

Withdrawing friendship or otherwise disrupting or threatening social relationships as a way to hurt other people.

controversial children

In the peer nomination technique, children who receive large numbers of both "like best" and "like least" nominations.

average children

In the peer nomination technique, children who receive moderate numbers of both "like best" and "like least" nominations.

neglected children

In the peer nomination technique, children who have very few peers who like them best or least.

wait just a few months and repeat the peer nomination process, they often find that many names in the previous neglected group have moved into other categories. Finally, note carefully how children in the neglected category differ from rejected children. *Neglected children* don't receive many nominations at all—they are mostly ignored. In contrast, *rejected children* are actively disliked and receive a large number of negative nominations.

The peer nomination technique reveals clear associations between levels of popularity and certain personality characteristics. Popular children tend to be sociable and friendly and to enter groups easily. Children who are less popular tend to be more aggressive or withdrawn. Looking at this research, you might infer that a sociable and friendly manner causes some children to become popular, and that aggression and withdrawal lead to unpopularity. However, we must again caution that these associations are merely correlational. We don't know for certain what is the cause and what is the effect. Children who are already popular have an easier time being friendly with other children. On the other hand, children who are rejected at a young age tend to become more hostile and aggressive as the years pass (Dodge et al., 2003). Although we assume that it is the social characteristics of children that lead, at least in part, to their peer nomination category, in the end we cannot be sure. It is logically possible that the popularity or unpopularity comes first and the social characteristics (like friendliness or aggressiveness) come afterward.

A Social Cognition Model of Peer Relations

It is clear that children differ in how they behave in social situations. Some children are more friendly, generous, and cooperative; others tend to be more aggressive or withdrawn. By looking at how children process information in social settings, we can shed light on some of these differences. Drawing on information-processing theory and cognitive psychology (see Chapter 6), Ken Dodge and his associates have developed a **social cognition model** to explain some of the important differences in how different children perceive, interpret, and respond to information in social settings (Crick & Dodge, 1994; Dodge, 1986). To understand how this model works, imagine how you would respond in the following situation. You walk into the campus lunchroom and approach a table where two of your classmates are talking and having lunch. As you sit down at their table, one classmate leans to the other and whispers something in her ear. What do you do? According to Dodge's model of social cognition, your response will depend on the cognitive steps that you take when you process this social event:

▶ First, you *perceive the information.* How did the event look and sound from your perspective? Did the classmate lean over very far to whisper? Was the whisper very soft, or could it be heard across the table?

▶ Next, you *interpret the information* that you perceived. Your interpretation may be suspicious ("She's whispering something bad about me") or more relaxed ("The lunchroom is noisy, and she's just trying to say something so the other friend can hear over the noise").

▶ Finally, you *consider potential responses and enact one.* If your interpretation is suspicious, you may hang your head in embarrassment, or you may get angry and yell, "What are you saying about me?!" If you incline toward the innocent interpretation, you may instead wait until they finish whispering and then find a polite way to join the conversation.

So, according to Dodge's model, your end response will depend on how you perceive and interpret the social information. Also, as you'll recall from Chapter 6, your concepts and expectations can color your perception. Did your classmate smile jokingly when she whispered,

social cognition model

A model that explains how different children perceive, interpret, and respond to information in social settings.

or was that a more menacing sneer? If you expect the classmate to be friendly, it may look more like a smile. If, however, you think she dislikes you, it may look more like a sneer. The perception then leads to an interpretation, which in turn leads to a positive or negative response.

Now consider how this model relates to peer popularity. Research suggests that popular children have a positive bias—they tend to perceive and interpret social situations as being comfortable and friendly (Rubin et al., 1998). When negative events do happen, these children are likely to interpret them as being innocent. In our lunchroom example, a popular child would likely think, "They're just playing a joke on me—that's funny" or "I can tell them a secret too." Rejected children, however, tend to have negative biases that lead to negative interpretations. Rejected–aggressive children tend to see even innocent events as threats. "What are you whispering about me?!" might be their first thought or reaction in our example. Their negative interpretations lead to aggressive responses—to revenge, attack, or self-defense. Because these children are overly negative and aggressive, their peers tend to reject them. Other research indicates that rejected–withdrawn children have difficulty acting out social responses (Stewart & Rubin, 1995). Although they may know how to respond appropriately, they are reluctant to take the risk. In turn, other children may misinterpret their withdrawal as a sign of disinterest or contempt. In the lunchroom example, rejected–withdrawn children might know a polite way to join the conversation but might fear rejection and instead just sit quietly. In turn, their classmates might conclude that they don't like them. By interpreting events negatively or by failing to act out positive responses, some children create circumstances that lead to social failure. Their maladaptive social cognitions cause these children to become unpopular among their peers.

How do these positive and negative patterns of social cognition begin? In reviewing this area of research, Rubin and colleagues (1998) point out that factors such as infant temperament and attachment relationships may be involved. Infants with difficult temperaments (see Chapter 9) are more likely to frustrate parents, who in turn may treat the infants more harshly or with less patience. The infants then learn that negative things happen during social interactions. They may come to expect other people to disapprove of them, setting up a negative bias in their social cognition. Infants who are slow to warm up or behaviorally inhibited may avoid situations that are highly arousing for them.

Many social interactions are somewhat ambiguous. When her friends are whispering, how will the girl in this photo interpret the situation? According to the social cognition model, her interpretation will determine the type of response she gives.

thinking
OF KIM

How might other children misinterpret Kim's shyness? What advice could you give Kim to help him avoid the self-defeating social cognitions of rejected–withdrawn children?

As they become reluctant to act in social situations, they may grow withdrawn. Similar effects flow from infant–parent attachments. Securely attached infants develop positive working models of social relationships. They expect to be safe interacting with other people, so they develop a positive bias in their social cognitions. Infants with avoidant, resistant, or disorganized/disoriented attachments, however, learn that others cannot be trusted, and they form negative biases. Although infant temperament and attachment types are not the whole story, you can see how expectations and cognitive biases can begin to develop in the early years as children form internal working models of how social relationships should proceed.

Consequences of Peer Rejection

Unfortunately, the negative social experiences some children face in their early years can continue in the later years. Compared to popular children, rejected children are 7 times more likely to fail a grade in school and nearly 4 times more likely to drop out of school before 10th grade (Kupersmidt & Coie, 1990; Ollendick, Weist, Borden, & Greene, 1992). Correlations also exist between peer rejection and higher rates of delinquency, arrest, violent behavior, and substance abuse (Kupersmidt & Coie, 1990; Ollendick et al., 1992). Children who are withdrawn in the early school years are at a greater risk for depression, loneliness, and feelings of negative self-worth in the later school years (Hymel, Rubin, Rowden, & LeMare, 1990; Renshaw & Brown, 1993; Rubin, Chen, McDougall, Bowker, & McKinnon, 1995). Reviewing the research in this area, one pair of authors concluded that "childhood peer relations have been identified as one of the most powerful predictors of concurrent and future mental health problems, including the development of psychiatric disorders" (Mueller & Silverman, 1989, p. 529).

Accounts of peer rejection often emerge when communities try to understand incidents of school violence. Consider the case of Charles "Andy" Williams, a 15-year-old high school freshman. Williams opened fire on students and teachers from the bathroom of Santana High School near San Diego, California, in March 2001. In an 8-minute shooting spree, Williams killed 2 students and wounded 11 other students, a security guard, and a student teacher. Some students described Williams as an "outsider," a "nerd," and a "dork." Others reported being close friends with Williams. One friend commented that Williams was the most trustworthy friend he ever had, and a prior girlfriend described him as "real nice" and "very popular" (ABC News, 2001; *New York Times,* 2001). Nevertheless, peer rejection was the focus of the early investigation into the shootings. Some witnesses reported that Williams was smiling as he shot, as if he was getting back at people who had rejected him. Classmates and witnesses told similar stories after the tragic shootings at Columbine High School and at schools in Jonesboro, Arkansas, and Paducah, Kentucky.

Peer rejection is a powerful force in adolescent life, especially when the person being rejected is also ridiculed, harassed, or bullied. Although rejection leads to murder and suicide only in rare instances, it is associated with countless other acts of lesser violence, delinquency, isolation, and loneliness. Fortunately, intervention programs have shown some promise in helping children and adolescents gain acceptance among peers (Asher, Parker, & Walker, 1996). School psychologists, counselors, and other professionals can now use videotapes, adult and peer coaching, role playing, and direct instruction to help rejected and neglected children develop the social skills they need. By successfully making and keeping friends, these children and adolescents may be able to avoid despair and its destructive effects. To learn more about how professionals provide interventions to forestall school violence, read the Professional Perspective box called "Career Focus: Meet a School Violence Counselor."

thinking
OF KIM

◄ What consequences should Kim's family be concerned about if Kim is not able to make friends at his new school?

YOUR
PERSPECTIVE
NOTES

Do you recall any school friends or peers who acted out in a violent way or who had the potential to act violently? How would you characterize them in terms of the peer nomination categories? How did their popularity or unpopularity contribute to the situation? What could have been done to help?

Career Focus: Meet a School Violence Counselor

**Jim Larson,
Ph.D., NCSP**
Whitewater,
Wisconsin

Coordinator, School Psychology Graduate Program, University of Wisconsin–Whitewater; scientific board member, The Melissa Institute for Violence Prevention and Treatment, Miami, Florida; coauthor with John E. Lochman of Helping Schoolchildren Cope with Anger: A Cognitive–Behavioral Intervention (2002), published by Guilford Press

What are the early signs of the potential for violence in children or adolescents?

Young children who hit, kick, and shove are highly likely to continue to use aggression and get in fights as they get older. Bully behavior in young children is highly predictive of bully behavior in adolescents. On the other hand, attempting to identify early signs for extreme violence, such as the multiple homicides at Columbine and elsewhere, is much more problematic. The personal histories and behavior profiles of those shooters were very similar to thousands of other kids who did not commit homicides. Consequently, the likelihood of acting on a reliably predictive early warning sign when they were young was next to impossible. Research in this area continues.

What factors cause or contribute to extreme violence?

They are many, but two of the most important are alienation or rejection from a positive peer culture and poor coping skills. Many of the recent perpetrators of extreme violence in schools believed they were rejected from the dominant peer culture, and most recounted years of harassment and bullying by their more popular classmates. Of course, many kids—including some reading this right now—were bullied and harassed in school, but they managed to cope with it. Perpetrators of extreme violence, however, seem to lack this coping ability. Responsible schools are now watching for students who show these difficulties and are reaching out to help them.

Describe the kind of violence prevention program that you think is most helpful in schools.

An effective violence prevention program has something for everyone. Think of it as having three levels: (1) "Primary prevention" programs for all students teach anger management, conflict resolution, diversity understanding, and effective problem solving; (2) "secondary prevention" programs identify high-risk children and work closely with them to give them more effective coping skills; and (3) "tertiary prevention" programs address school security and protect already aggressive students from further hurting themselves or others.

What should other students do if they recognize the potential for violent behavior in a peer?

Tell someone! Of the very few common elements in all of the school shootings, the most striking was the fact that all of the shooters communicated their intentions to someone before the event. One even told an adult! Since that period, alert students who chose to inform a responsible school official have thwarted some potentially deadly outcomes.

What education and training is needed to work in the area of school violence counseling?

School psychologists have taken leadership in this area. To become a school psychologist, you must earn a master's or an Education Specialist degree consisting of at least 60 graduate credits. For more information about school violence counseling, visit the National Association of School Psychology website at www.nasponline.org. ■

thinking
OF KIM

◄ Is Kim at risk for being alienated or rejected by his peers? How can Kim's parents help him maintain a healthy attitude toward his peers and develop good skills for coping with peer problems?

1. A lot of children in Jenny's class really like her, but many other children strongly dislike her. The *peer nomination technique* would categorize Jenny as:

   a. rejected.   b. neglected.   c. average.   d. controversial.

2. Rejected children tend to be _____ while neglected children are more _____.
   a. disliked; ignored
   b. withdrawn; aggressive
   c. liked; disliked
   d. passive; aggressive

3. Research using the social cognition model of peer popularity suggests that rejected–withdrawn children have difficulty:
   a. perceiving social cues in a positive way.
   b. interpreting social cues in a positive way.
   c. enacting appropriate social responses.
   d. understanding the difference between their perception and interpretation of social cues.

4. Data show high rates of school failure, delinquency, and violence among children who are:
   a. neglected by their peers.
   b. rejected by their peers.
   c. withdrawn from their peers.
   d. popular among their peers.

5. **True or False:** An important skill that many popular children have is an ability to join groups without disturbing the group or drawing too much attention to themselves.

6. **True or False:** Children who are popular among their peers tend to have a positive bias when interpreting cues in social situations.

Answers: 1. d, 2. a, 3. c, 4. b, 5. T, 6. T

thinking
BACK TO KIM

Now that you have studied this chapter, you should be able to apply at least a dozen concepts and research findings to Kim's situation. First, opportunity and similarity are two important elements in making new friends. Kim's main opportunities to meet friends come at school and with close neighbors his age. He could expand his opportunities by participating in extracurricular activities, sports, clubs, and other activities that would bring him in close contact with peers.

Kim's *popularity* may increase if he develops better communication skills; if he is helpful, generous, and sensitive to the needs of others; and if he learns to enter groups in an easy and nondisruptive manner. Using the social cognition model of peer relations, you could help Kim appreciate how his perception and interpretation of social information may influence his behavior and thus his popularity. He could learn to avoid a negative bias in processing social cues, and he could learn to be more confident in enacting appropriate responses in social situations.

Finally, Kim should understand how cultural differences may influence his ability to make friends. Korean American children tend to emphasize harmony, cooperation, and social sensitivity in their play, but European Americans tend to be more aggressive. Children from different backgrounds may misinterpret each others' signals in play. Classmates may think that Kim is aloof and uninterested in their play, for example, whereas Kim may feel afraid or ashamed to play aggressively. Understanding these and other cultural differences can improve communication and understanding and allow children to enjoy sharing each others' cultural heritage.

CHAPTER SUMMARY

How do social relationships evolve from infancy through adolescence?

Infants show mutual gaze when they are around other infant peers, though infants also show individual variability in their responsiveness to peers. Coordinated imitation emerges around 2 years of age, and toddlers enjoy repeating familiar games; they also begin selecting mutually preferred playmates at this age. Opportunity and similarity are important bases for friendships in childhood. Friends tend to evolve from play-based friends in early childhood, to loyal and faithful friends in middle childhood, and to intimate friends in adolescence.

What are the principal theories about why children are so reluctant to play with opposite-sex peers?

The prominent theories for explaining gender segregation involve play compatibility, cognitive schemas, operant conditioning, and psychoanalytic theory. There is concern that boys and girls grow up in different gender cultures, making it more difficult for them to learn to communicate effectively across genders.

What are the differences between cliques and crowds during adolescence, and how do these groups influence social relationships during this period?

Cliques are groups of three to nine friends who hang out together, whereas crowds (e.g., jocks, populars, druggies) are larger groups of adolescents who share similar reputations, attitudes, activities, or other characteristics. Although parents worry about the use of alcohol and illegal drugs among crowd members, adolescents report that they feel more positive peer pressure for school achievement and getting along with others. Self-esteem is related to crowd membership or the perception of the value of belonging to particular crowds.

What are the prominent trends in adolescent dating and sexual activity?

As Dunphy (1963) described the pattern, adolescents in same-sex cliques tend to begin to associate with members of other cliques of the opposite sex. Next, clique boundaries gradually dissolve and teenagers affiliate mainly with the larger crowd. Eventually crowd memberships erode as more dating couples pair off. In nationwide surveys more than one-third of 9th graders and nearly two-thirds of 12th graders report having had sexual intercourse. Sexual activity varies by ethnicity and gender. Teen pregnancy rates are higher in the United States than in other industrialized nations. Gay, lesbian, and bisexual teens usually face severe discrimination, social isolation, and the negative effects of a culture that is largely homophobic.

How do researchers define "play"? Describe the levels of social play that Parten identified.

Play is defined as a pleasurable activity that is actively engaged in by the child on a voluntary basis, is motivated intrinsically, and contains some nonliteral element. In her classic study Parten (1932) identified six levels of social play: unoccupied behavior; onlooking; and solitary, parallel, associative, and cooperative play.

How does play change as children develop from infancy through adolescence?

Sensorimotor play in infancy gives way to symbolic and socio-dramatic play in toddlers and preschoolers. During middle childhood play focuses on logic and physical skills. In adolescence hypothetical and idealistic thought, self-understanding, sexual attraction, and intimate communication occupy much of teenagers' leisure time.

Describe some of the cultural differences in the play of children around the world.

The opportunity to play and the central themes and styles of play differ across cultures. Some examples: Compared to U.S. and British children, Japanese and Korean children spend more time studying for school and less time playing. Japanese children tend to play more indoors and in smaller groups; children in Senegal play outside in large compounds where they are watched by any member of their large extended family. Indonesians and Korean Americans tend to be cooperative and socially sensitive in their play, whereas European American children often are more aggressive.

How do researchers measure peer social status, and what are the different categories of popular and unpopular children?

Researchers typically use the peer nomination technique, asking children to pick the peers they "like best" and "like least." Popular children receive the most positive peer nominations and tend to be friendly, cooperative, sociable, and sensitive to the needs of others. Popular children also tend to join groups in an easy and nondisruptive manner. Rejected children are actively disliked and get the most negative nominations. About half of rejected children are rejected–aggressive, and another one-fifth are rejected–withdrawn. Controversial children get many positive nominations and many negative ones. Average children receive a moderate number of both positive and negative nominations. Neglected children receive very few nominations of either type.

What is the social cognition model of peer relations, and how does it relate to peer popularity?

According to Dodge's (1986) social cognition model, our responses in social situations flow from our perceptions and interpretations of social information and from the way we consider and enact potential responses. Some children have a positive bias and tend to perceive and interpret events positively. Others have a negative bias. These biases can lead to responses that contribute to popularity or unpopularity among peers.

KEY TERMS

average children (452)

cliques (432)

controversial children (452)

coordinated imitation (425)

crowds (433)

friendship (424)

gender cultures (430)

gender segregation (428)

heterosexual assumption (438)

homosexual experience (438)

homosexual orientation (438)

mutual gaze (425)

neglected children (452)

peer nomination technique (450)

peers (424)

play (441)

popular children (451)

rejected children (452)

relational aggression (452)

sensorimotor play (443)

social cognition model (453)

sociodramatic play (444)

symbolic play (444)

Chapter 12

Families

A PERSPECTIVE TO think ABOUT

> "Occasionally Jeremy is well behaved and pleasant, but most of the time he is out of control."

Cassandra has been a lead teacher at the Rising Horizons Child Care Center for 4 years, but she has never had a child as challenging as Jeremy. Jeremy, a second grader, attends Rising Horizons after school. He started in full-time day care when he was 8 months old and has attended Rising Horizons since he was 4. Jeremy has been having problems for quite some time in school, at day care, and at home. He is aggressive, is disruptive in class, has trouble interacting with other children, and often simply does not do what teachers and other adults request. Understandably, other children do not like to play with him, so he has few friends. Academically, first grade was difficult for Jeremy, but he was able to do well enough to move on to second grade.

Jeremy's mother recently told Cassandra that Jeremy is falling behind in his schoolwork again this year; he is in danger of having to repeat second grade if his work does not improve. She asked Cassandra for advice, saying that things have become overwhelming for her. She is recently divorced from Jeremy's father and is trying hard to settle into a new job, a new apartment, and a new neighborhood. Because of tight finances, Jeremy's mother hoped to be able to let Jeremy take care of himself after school a couple of days a week next year, but now she is concerned about whether he is ready for this. Jeremy's behavior seems worse than ever, and his mother says she simply does not know what to do to control him.

Cassandra would like to help, but what can she do? Occasionally Jeremy is well behaved and pleasant, but most of the time he is out of control. What parenting styles or discipline techniques might Jeremy's parents consider? What kinds of reactions are normal for a child experiencing a divorce, and how can his parents help him cope? What can Cassandra do to encourage more appropriate behavior when Jeremy is in day care? After studying this chapter, you should be able to apply at least a dozen concepts and research findings to help improve this situation.

 As you read this chapter, look for the questions that ask you to think about what you're learning from Jeremy's perspective.

What is your family like? What is its structure and cultural setting? What kinds of parenting practices and approaches to discipline did you experience? Children experience a wide variety of family structures. As Cassandra in the opening story has seen, parenting practices and changes in a child's family structure have important effects on children's behavior and developmental outcomes. And as Jeremy's difficulties indicate, discipline can be especially challenging for parents, teachers, and child-care providers. In this chapter we will discuss the research on parenting styles, with particular emphasis on appropriate and effective methods of discipline. We will also discuss a variety of different family cultures and structures to find out how these factors influence children's development. Finally, we will talk about the effects of child care, a setting that increasing numbers of children experience from an early age.

Parenting

Years ago, before we had children, we visited a friend who had two young children. As David served a quick post-swimming-pre-baseball-game summer dinner of hot dogs and canned green beans, he commented, "You got kids, you gotta serve a vegetable." Then he added thoughtfully, "You know, having kids is great, but it's the hardest thing I have ever done in my whole life."

We don't know any parent who would disagree with David's assessment. In this section, however, we hope to shed some light on parenting practices that can support the development of happy and well-adjusted children. Although parenting is never an easy task, this information should be helpful for parents or anyone else who works daily with children.

As you study this section, ask yourself these questions:

- How do parental warmth and parental control affect children's outcomes?
- What are the four parenting styles described by Baumrind? What outcomes are associated with each style? What cautions should we keep in mind when thinking about parenting styles?
- What is the difference between *discipline* and *punishment*? Why is spanking ineffective as a method of discipline? How can parents use discipline effectively?
- What differences exist between the child-rearing roles and practices of mothers and fathers?

Parents high in warmth are supportive, nurturing, and caring, and pay close attention to their children's needs.

Dimensions of Parenting

In studying characteristics of parenting, researchers have identified two dimensions that are especially important: *warmth* and *control*. **Parental warmth** is the degree to which parents are accepting, responsive, and compassionate with their children. Parents who are high in warmth are very supportive, nurturant, and caring. They pay close attention to their children's needs, and their parenting behaviors tend to be child centered (focused on the needs of the child rather than on the convenience or demands of the parents). Researchers see parental warmth as existing on a broad continuum—from parents who show a high degree of warmth to those who show little or no warmth. At the lower end of the continuum are parents who are rejecting, unresponsive to their children, and more parent centered than child centered. This *cold* type of parenting is obviously detrimental to the child's development. Numerous studies have shown that children who experience cold parenting are more aggressive, are less popular, and perform more poorly in school (see Maccoby & Martin [1983] and Parke & Buriel [1998] for reviews). When parenting is high in warmth, children show better social and academic skills, and they show more love and respect for their parents and other people.

Parental control is the degree to which the parents set limits, enforce rules, and maintain discipline with children. There are two types of parental control: *behavioral control*, or using firm and consistent methods of discipline to regulate children's behavior, and *psychological control*, using negative means such as love withdrawal or inducing guilt to control behavior (Barber, 1996, 2002). Have you heard the question "It's eight p.m., do you know where your children are?" Parents who are high in control can answer that question with an emphatic *yes!* They set firm limits on their children's behavior and they enforce rules consistently. They are involved in their children's lives and use discipline to provide structure for their children's behaviors. Parents low in control, however, are lax, permissive, or uninvolved with their children. Their answer might be, "Eight p.m.? I'm not sure. Check his room, or maybe he's out with his friends." Like parental warmth, control is on a continuum: Some

parental warmth

The degree to which parents are accepting, responsive, and compassionate with their children.

parental control

The degree to which parents set limits, enforce rules, and maintain discipline with children.

YOUR
PERSPECTIVE
NOTES

What levels of parental warmth and control did your parents show? What effects do you think their levels had on your development?

parents show a high degree of control, some only a moderate degree, and others very little control or involvement with their children. Appropriate parental control has important effects on children. For example, appropriate behavioral control helps reduce problems such as drug use and delinquency, even in adolescents with deviant peers. In contrast, higher psychological control has been linked to such problems as depression, drug use, and delinquency (Barber, 2002; Galambos, Barker, & Almeida, 2003).

When we look at *parental warmth* and *parental control,* it is important to consider their combined effects. When warm parents use firm control, for example, discipline tends to be child centered, age appropriate, and positive. When cold and rejecting parents use firm control, however, discipline can be very harsh, punitive, and even abusive. By itself, neither warmth nor control is sufficient for explaining the effects of parenting on children's developmental outcomes.

Parenting Styles: Research on the Dos and Don'ts of Raising Children

In the mid-1960s Diana Baumrind began a longitudinal study investigating the effects of different styles of parenting. Her follow-up studies, and the many similar studies conducted by other researchers, have strongly influenced how parents and professionals think about parenting. The research has identified four distinct styles of parenting that represent the different combinations of high and low parental warmth combined with high and low parental control (Baumrind, 1973, 1991; Maccoby & Martin, 1983). Figure 12.1 shows these four parenting styles in a 2 × 2 matrix of warmth and control. Let's look more closely at these styles. As we describe each style, consider what might happen if a 14-year-old stayed out past his curfew. And ask yourself as well—what would you (or your parents) do in a situation like this?

Authoritative parents are warm and exert firm control. They monitor their children closely and have clear standards and high expectations for their behavior. They tend to use disciplinary methods that are supportive rather than punitive. There is clear communication between parent and child, and the lines of communication go both ways. Authoritative parents listen carefully to their children, and they allow give-and-take on disciplinary matters in

authoritative parents

Parents who are warm and exert firm control.

FIGURE 12.1 Parental Warmth and Control Matrix

Two dimensions of parenting (parental warmth and parental control) produce four styles of parenting: authoritarian, authoritative, permissive, and rejecting/neglecting. Research has associated the four styles with different outcomes for children.

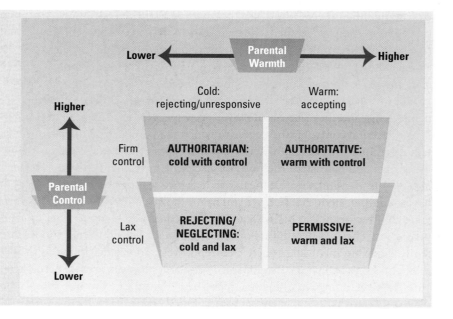

a way that is age appropriate for the child. If their 14-year-old comes in after curfew, their first response is likely to sit with the child and have a calm discussion about the incident. "Your father and I were very worried about you being out so late, and we want you to explain why you missed your curfew." If the child has a reasonable explanation (e.g., a friend just had a bicycle accident and needed help getting home), authoritative parents are understanding and supportive ("It was important for you to help your friend, so we understand why you were late"). They will, however, make sure the child understands the importance of curfew and will institute appropriate consequences if the child does not have a valid excuse. The important point is that authoritative parents are rational, consistent, and child centered in their approach to discipline. They give children a reasonable amount of freedom, but they set and enforce limits as a way to teach children to be responsible. They go beyond simply explaining *why* the rules are in place; they work with the child in age-appropriate negotiation to set reasonable rules. They also often help their children understand the effects of their behavior on others—a tactic sometimes called *inductive parenting*. Over time, authoritative parents expect their children to develop the ability to regulate their own behavior. Compared to other children, children raised by authoritative parents perform better in school, are less hostile and more popular among friends, have greater self-esteem, show more purpose and independence in their activities, and as adolescents are more accurate in understanding their parents' values (Baumrind, 1973, 1991; Knafo & Schwartz, 2003; Parke & Buriel, 1998).

Authoritarian parents also exert firm control, but they do it in a way that is rejecting or unresponsive to the child. "Why are you so late getting home?!" they might yell. "You know you're supposed to be home by nine p.m.; now you're grounded for two weeks!" Authoritarian parents set firm limits and expect that their children will behave. Unlike authoritative parents, however, their disciplinary methods tend to be harsh and punitive. Rather than having a rational discussion of an incident, they are more inclined to lower the boom immediately without regard for the child's perspective. They are obedience oriented and expect that their orders will be followed, often without explanation and certainly without the negotiation that is characteristic of authoritative parents. "My way or the highway" represents the extreme form of authoritarianism. Children raised in an authoritarian environment may feel trapped and angry but afraid to confront their parents (Parke & Buriel, 1998). They perform less well in school, are more hostile and aggressive and less popular with peers, and are less independent than children reared by authoritative parents (Baumrind, 1973).

Permissive parents are warm but have little control. They fail to set or enforce appropriate limits for their children. Permissive parents avoid confrontation with their children. Being too lenient they do not require that their children behave in a mature and responsible manner. Sometimes permissive parents justify their style by saying they'd rather be a friend than a parent to their children. A permissive parent might say, "It's okay that you missed curfew again; just let me know next time when you're going to be late." At the extreme, permissive parents can become *indulgent*—beyond merely allowing their children to misbehave, they may actually encourage or foster their misbehavior: "What curfew? Get out there and enjoy your friends!" Permissive–indulgent parents may encourage or condone inappropriate behaviors such as skipping school, vandalism, alcohol or drug abuse, or sexual promiscuity. Compared to authoritatively raised children, children from permissive homes are more impulsive, perform less well in school, and are less self-assured, independent, and confident in their activities (Parke & Buriel, 1998).

Rejecting/neglecting parents don't set limits and are unresponsive to their children's needs. This category of parenting has two substyles: *Rejecting parents* are harsh and actively reject their children, whereas *neglecting parents* ignore their children and fail to fulfill their responsibilities as parents. Neither subtype would likely have a curfew at all—these types of parents may neither know nor care where their children are. Rejecting/neglecting parents may be

authoritarian parents
Parents who exert firm control but are rejecting or unresponsive to their children.

permissive parents
Parents who are warm but have little control over their children.

rejecting/neglecting parents
Parents who don't set limits and are unresponsive to their children's needs.

Authoritarian parents exert firm control, but demonstrate little warmth and respect for the child's point of view. They tend to use harsh and punitive disciplinary methods. Permissive parents do not set or enforce limits, avoid confrontation with their children, and do not require their children to behave maturely or responsibly. Rejecting/neglecting parents ignore or actively reject their children. They do not discipline their children, or do so harshly and inconsistently. Authoritative parents set limits and have appropriate control over children's behavior; they are warm, supportive, and respectful.

YOUR PERSPECTIVE NOTES

For each of the four parenting styles, think of a parent you know who uses (or did use) the style. Describe what these parents do, and think about how these different styles affect (or affected) the children involved.

under too much stress to parent appropriately; they may not be committed to the task of raising children; or they may be depressed or otherwise psychologically or emotionally unavailable to their children. Children raised by rejecting/neglecting parents fare the worst of all. Compared to other children, rejected/neglected children show higher rates of delinquency, alcohol and drug use, and early sexual activity. They perform more poorly in school and show other disruptions in peer relations and cognitive development (Parke & Buriel, 1998).

In her later work Baumrind expanded the number of parenting styles to seven: *authoritative, democratic, nondirective, authoritarian–directive, nonauthoritarian–directive, unengaged,* and *good enough.* She also added two dimensions in addition to parental warmth and parental control. *Maturity demands* are parents' expectations that the child will show age-appropriate behavior, self-reliance, and self-control. *Democratic communication* is the degree to which parents ask for and consider the child's feelings and opinions. Research in this area also highlights the importance of *intrusiveness,* or control that parents maintain by psychologically manipulating and inhibiting children. Studies have linked higher levels of intrusiveness with poorer outcomes for children and adolescents. Researchers have confirmed this finding in several different cultures, although children of "unengaged" parents still seem to fare worst of all (Barber, 2002; Baumrind, 1991).

■ **Factors to Keep in Mind.** Baumrind's classification of parenting styles has intuitive appeal. Most of us can recognize one or more of these types of parenting from our own childhood histories or from families that we know. And it is easy to agree that firm but warm and supportive parenting would lead to the best childhood outcomes. As you think about research on parenting styles, however, you should keep several cautions in mind.

First, research in this area is largely *correlational*. Parents who are authoritative may have children who become popular and academically successful, but how do we know whether this association is caused by the parenting or instead caused by characteristics in the child? For example, a child born with an easy temperament and friendly personality is easier to parent, and parents may be more inclined to give this child more freedom and responsibility. If a child has a difficult temperament, on the other hand, parents may be warm and responsive at first; but when their child doesn't respond appropriately, their parenting may gradually become more harsh or more permissive or neglectful. Relationships between parents and children are complex: Parents influence how children think and behave, and at the same time children influence how parents parent. It is much too simple to say that a certain style of parenting leads to a particular type of developmental outcome, as if the relationship runs only one way.

Second, the "effects" of parenting styles that are typically reported are not as dramatic as you might expect. Baumrind (1973) studied children's IQ scores and ratings on measures such as hostility, dominance, and independence, but on none of these measures were there overwhelming differences among the parenting styles. That is, from Baumrind's findings, you certainly couldn't conclude that one style led to complete success or that other styles led only to failure. In a more recent and larger-scale study, researchers surveyed 10,000 high school students to learn about the styles used by their parents and about outcomes such as school performance, psychological symptoms, drug use, and delinquency (Lamborn, Mounts, Steinberg, & Dornbusch, 1991). Based on the results, the researchers classified the parents of 4,100 of the students as authoritative, authoritarian, permissive, or neglectful. Students' grade point averages did not differ significantly between the authoritative and authoritarian groups, but GPAs were higher in the authoritative (2.86) than in the permissive (2.68) or neglectful (2.57) groups. Still, you can see from these averages that none of the styles led to straight A's or to all failing grades. Patterns were similar for the other outcomes measured in the study.

Third, the correlations of outcomes with parenting styles are not universal. In Baumrind's (1973) original sample, boys raised authoritatively were less hostile and resistive and had significantly higher IQs than boys raised by authoritarian parents, but there were no significant differences on these traits for girls. Authoritatively reared girls were more assertive and purposive than those raised by authoritarian parents, but the same pattern did not hold for boys. Baumrind (1973) also reported that the African American daughters of authoritarian parents were "exceptionally independent and at ease" (p. 30) and scored higher in dominance and independence than did white girls with authoritarian parents. Baumrind and other researchers have surmised that increased parental restrictiveness may help minority children avoid delinquency, school failure, early pregnancy, and drug use (Baldwin, Baldwin, & Cole, 1990; Baumrind, 1973). So although harsh and restrictive control may offer less adaptive advantage for middle-class white children, it may serve an important survival function for many minority children, who may face poverty, racial discrimination, and violence in their communities. Can we really say that one parenting style is more effective than the others when the associations vary so much depending on the sex and race of the child? We will have more to say about ethnic differences among families later in this chapter.

Finally, how often do we see a pure style of parenting? Parents are rarely warm and supportive all of the time or harsh and cold all of the time. Again, in Baumrind's (1973) original sample, nearly one-third of the parents did not fit neatly into any one style but showed a

thinking OF JEREMY

◄ What characteristics of Jeremy or his home environment might make it harder for his parents to use an authoritative parenting style?

mixture of behaviors. What is the developmental outcome when parents use a blend of styles or parenting behaviors? What if parents are warm and supportive under most circumstances but more rigid and restrictive on certain larger issues, such as dating and choice of peers? Or more warm and supportive with one child than with the others in the family? We know that parents treat siblings differently—particularly when experiencing stresses such as marital problems, single parenthood, economic difficulties, and larger family size—and that the differences can be large (Jenkins, Rasbash, & O'Conner, 2003). Keep all of these complexities in mind when you try to classify the parenting style of any particular parent.

Quality parenting is an issue of great interest and concern to all who work with children, but there is little agreement on how to improve it. One recent proposal involves requiring people to get a license before they can become parents. To read more about the pros and cons of this idea, read the Social Policy Perspective box called "Should Parents Have to Be Licensed?"

Discipline: Spare the Rod and Spare the Child?

The most important issue most parents face is how to provide appropriate discipline for their children. Psychologists use the word **discipline** to refer to the techniques parents and care-givers use to teach children appropriate behavior. Unfortunately, when most people think of *discipline,* they think immediately about **punishment,** or techniques used to eliminate or re-duce undesirable behavior. Unless people have had special training in parenting or child de-velopment, they often overemphasize punishment when disciplining children. Too often, parents end up spanking, hitting, or yelling at children. These forms of behavior control are called *power-assertive methods.* Most parents don't want to be harsh with their children, but over time parents may lose their patience. They may feel that their problems are endless as young children fuss, fight, and get into things. Researchers who have observed parents inter-acting with young children have reported that on average, parent–child conflicts occur 3 to 15 times per hour. Parents interrupt their children, on average, every 7 minutes to get them to change their behavior (Baumrind, 1996; Lee & Bates, 1985; Minton, Kagan, & Levine, 1971). With 2-year-olds, 65 percent of parent–child interactions involve the parent's telling the toddler *not* to do something, as in "Don't touch that!" "Get down!" or "Don't do that!" (Baumrind, 1996; Hoffman, 1975).

What is a parent to do? One thing parents should *not* do is spank, hit, grab, or yell harshly at children. Although parents in this country generally treat children more humanely today than they did 50 or 100 years ago, spanking and other power-assertive forms of pun-ishment are still common. In surveys, 84 percent of American adults state that "it is sometimes necessary to discipline a child with a good hard spanking" (Lehman, 1989; Straus, 1994). Also, 65 percent of parents report that they slap, hit, or spank their infants; 90 percent spank 3-year-olds; and 35 percent are still hitting or spanking their adolescents at age 16 (Straus, 1994). According to data from the National Longitudinal Study of Youth, two-thirds of moth-ers reported hitting or spanking their 6-year-old children, and they administered this form of punishment an average of 150 times per year—almost every other day (Straus, 1994). One out of every four parents uses a belt, wooden paddle, or other object to spank his or her children (Straus & Stewart, 1999). Sociologist Murray Straus (1991, 2001) has studied family violence for more than 20 years. His studies indicate that hitting and spanking is most widespread among parents who are relatively young, parents who themselves were hit or spanked as chil-dren or adolescents, and mothers whose partners hit them. Straus also reports that a greater percentage of middle-income parents use spanking, but that the lower-income parents who do use spanking do so with more frequency.

In the short run, spanking does seem to work. For example, if a child runs into the street or is jumping up and down on the sofa, a quick swat usually terminates the misbehavior. After

discipline
Techniques used to teach chil-dren appropriate behavior.

punishment
Techniques used to eliminate or reduce undesirable behavior.

Should Parents Have to Be Licensed?

We know a lot about different parenting styles and the child outcomes associated with them. As you've seen, however, it isn't always easy to identify the "best" style. Different families' backgrounds, cultures, contexts, and temperaments may require different kinds of parenting behaviors. But have you ever seen a particularly troubling parent behavior and thought, "You ought to need a license to be a parent"?

Some are taking this idea very seriously (Lykken, 2000, 2001; Westman, 1994). They argue that parenting is a privilege and a responsibility, not a right. Requiring parents to obtain a license would communicate that parenting is just as important as all the other activities that we license, such as getting married, driving, or voting. Proponents of licensing also argue that people who wish to become foster or adoptive parents already must obtain official authorization; only parents raising their biological children need not be licensed. According to advocates of this idea, licensing would:

- Provide a way to determine parental competence "*before* rather than *after* damage to a child" (Westman, 1997, p. 201).
- Save millions of children the pain of neglect and abuse.
- Save society tremendous amounts of pain, suffering, and money. Advocates argue that incompetent

parenting is a major cause of crime and violence, because it allows children to grow up unsocialized.

- Establish minimum parenting requirements, such as two parents "committed enough to be married to each other, who are mature and self-supporting, neither criminal nor incapacitated by mental illness" (Lykken, 2000, p. 599).
- Require that others who wish to raise a child (such as never-married women, divorced individuals, or gay and lesbian couples) obtain permission from a judge in family court.

As you might expect, this proposal is quite controversial. No one argues with the claim that it is better to have good parents than to have neglectful or abusive ones, but there are serious constitutionality questions about parental license requirements (Redding, 2002). In addition, licensing proponents clearly favor two-parent families, claiming that *both* biological parents should be present and committed to child rearing. Although a higher percentage of troubled youth do come from single-parent than from two-parent homes, opponents argue that the percentage is not nearly high enough to justify denying licenses to single parents (Scarr, 2000). Others point out that factors other than parenting (such as characteristics of a child's neighborhood culture,

poverty, and discrimination) also have important effects on children's outcomes. Opponents also maintain that it is only parents at the extremes who really cause better or worse outcomes. "[P]retty good parents do not produce better children than average parents or pretty bad parents" (Harris, 2000, p. 630), and "very, very bad parents" are already addressed via (admittedly imperfect) social and child protective services. Perhaps most troubling to critics is the licensing scheme's distinct scent of social engineering. Would low-income parents be denied licenses? If so, ethnic minorities would be disproportionately affected, because they are more likely to be poor. Might not such a program limit the reproductive rights of certain groups to a greater degree than those of other segments of the population (Grigg, 1995)?

What do you think of parent licensing? Would it be a good way to reduce child neglect, child abuse, and violent crime? How could it be structured so as not to discriminate unfairly against lower-income and minority individuals, against single adults or gay and lesbian couples, against those with less education? Who would implement it? How would policies be enforced? If parents lost their license, would the authorities remove their children from the home? Perhaps the idea of parent licensing is more complicated than it first appears. ■

the spanking the child usually sits and cries, and refrains from repeating the offending behavior immediately. In the long run, however, spanking is not effective (Holden, 2002). When children are spanked, they eventually return to the misbehavior or replace it with other inappropriate behaviors. Why else would parents "need" to spank so often? Hitting and spanking can cause children to fear their parents. If children try to run, or if they strike back or talk

Spanking is an ineffective method of discipline in the long term, and it can have a variety of negative side effects.

back to their parents, the hitting usually becomes more severe. Although most spanking is not legally considered physically abusive, it is true that most physical abuse begins as physical punishment—punishment that then gets out of hand (Straus, 1994). Another thing to consider is the message that spanking sends to children. Do we want them to learn that "might makes right" or that it's appropriate for larger people to use physical force to get smaller people to obey? Ironically, "hitting other children" is the misbehavior that parents most often identify as calling for a spanking (Lehman, 1989; Straus, 1994). What message does the child get when the parent slaps them on the hand (or swats them on the behind) and says, "Don't hit other people!"?

Studies show that children who are spanked more often are more physically violent and aggressive; are twice as likely to attack their siblings; are more likely to steal property, commit assaults, and commit other delinquent acts; and have lower moral standards and lower self-esteem (Straus, 1994; Straus, Sugarman, & Giles-Sims, 1997). These studies also show that adolescents who are hit by their parents are more likely to be depressed and have suicidal thoughts, and that these problems worsen the more often they are hit. Adults who were spanked or hit during adolescence are 3 times more likely to hit their spouses; they are more likely to physically abuse their children; and they are more likely to link pain and violence with sexual activity. Analyzing the results of 88 different studies, Gershoff (2002) found consistent correlations between physical punishment and increases in child aggression, delinquency, and antisocial behavior; increased rates of child abuse by parents; and poorer relationships between children and parents. Children whose parents physically punished them were less likely to internalize moral values, and later in life they were more likely to suffer from mental health problems such as low self-esteem, depression, and alcoholism. As adults they were more likely to be aggressive, commit crimes, and abuse their own children and spouses.

Of course, all of these findings are correlational. It could be that children and adolescents who are more violent and engage in more misbehavior simply are spanked and hit more often. To find out whether spanking actually causes negative outcomes for children, we would need to conduct an experiment: We'd need to randomly assign some children to a group that received spankings for misbehavior and other children to a group that did not. (Refer back to Chapter 1 to see how experiments determine cause and effect.) Obviously, we cannot ethically conduct this type of experiment, so we must rely on the suggestive evidence provided by correlational studies.

To be fair, too, we want to point out that other research suggests that the negative effects associated with spanking may be due to the style of parenting rather than to the spanking itself (Baumrind, Larzelere, & Cowan, 2002). As you can imagine, parents who rely heavily on spanking and hitting also tend to be less warm and affectionate, less involved, and less consistent in their parenting than parents who use more positive forms of discipline. When researchers control for differences in warmth and involvement, the correlations between spanking and aggression or delinquency sometimes disappear (Simons, Johnson, & Conger, 1994). In one study, children showed increases in misbehavior when they were spanked by mothers who were rated as less warm and supportive toward their children (McLoyd & Smith, 2002). Spankings by more warm and supportive mothers didn't seem to increase misbehavior, although they didn't decrease it either. These results were similar across African American, non-Hispanic white, and Hispanic families.

Even when used by warm and loving parents, spanking obviously doesn't work as well as most American parents would like to believe. In our opinion, the potential for negative side effects is too great to justify spanking and hitting as appropriate forms of discipline. We can think of no misbehavior that would justify these forms of punishment. Austria, Croatia, Cyprus, Denmark, Finland, Germany, Israel, Italy, Latvia, Norway, and Sweden have all banned parents from using physical punishment with their children (Bitensky, 1998). Sweden was the first country to pass such a bill (in 1979). The Swedish statute states:

> Children are entitled to care, security, and a good upbringing. Children are to be treated with respect for their person and individuality and may not be subjected to physical punishment or other injurious or humiliating treatment. (Durrant, 1999, p. 436)

Under the Swedish law spanking or hitting children carries a civil penalty, but the law also provides considerable educational and social service support to help families learn more appropriate methods of discipline.

Appropriate Discipline

So, once again, what should parents do for discipline? There are many good books on the subject (see Chapter 1 for a few suggestions), and local community colleges and social service agencies usually offer excellent parent-education programs on effective discipline. We present here a basic positive program of discipline that is consistent with guidelines endorsed by the American Academy of Pediatrics (1998) and most parenting experts. First, remember that the term *discipline* refers to techniques used to *teach* children appropriate behavior. The emphasis is on *teaching* rather than on *punishing*. Also recognize that there is no technique that works all of the time and right away. With patience and a calm and positive approach to discipline, parents can set firm limits and help children learn to regulate their behavior in a way that is appropriate for their age. We recommend that parents try the following steps:

1. *Manage the situation:* Parents should be aware of the situations their children are in and should try to manage each situation to reduce the temptations for misbehavior. Begin by childproofing the home. If there are items you don't want your toddler to touch or break, put them out of reach. Notice other infractions that occur at home, and try to rearrange things so the misbehaviors are less tempting. For example, if you don't want siblings pushing and poking at each other during dinner, try seating them on opposite sides of the table. Simple adjustments can make a big difference. Make sure there are plenty of positive things for children to do and appropriate objects to explore. Too often, parents set up situations in which the most interesting thing to do is misbehave. Whose fault is that?

2. *Set clear rules and limits:* Parents need to communicate clearly to children the dos and don'ts that are

YOUR PERSPECTIVE NOTES

Were you spanked as a child? What is your opinion of the research findings regarding spanking? For every type of misbehavior for which you believe a child "deserves a good spanking," try to think of two specific alternatives for handling (or preventing) the misbehavior.

Preventing misbehavior through situation management is one of the most effective ways to teach children appropriate behavior.

most important. Don't have too many rules, or it will be difficult for you and your child to keep up with them all. Pick the issues that are most important for the child's age. "No hitting" and "No biting" might be important rules to teach toddlers, for example, along with other safety rules like "Stay in the yard" and "Don't touch the stove." For older children there can be clear rules about homework, expectations for household chores, and safety issues like wearing a helmet while biking or skateboarding. Try to state rules positively so children know what they *should* do (instead of "Don't run," say "Please walk"). As children mature, parents and children should have cooperative discussions about rules and limits. The two sides should listen to each other's concerns; and parents should give children and adolescents room to negotiate rules as appropriate for their level of maturity and responsibility, keeping in mind issues of safety. How else will youngsters learn to control their own behavior?

3. *Praise good behavior:* Have you heard the slogan "Catch them being good"? It's important to let children know when they are behaving appropriately. Work on strengthening the positive behaviors in your children. "I notice you finished your homework early today—great job!" Behaviors tend to be repeated when they are reinforced or rewarded. When children are busy behaving, they have less time to misbehave. Rewarding good behavior also helps parents keep a positive focus in their discipline.

4. *Use explanation and reasoning:* When misbehavior occurs, parents need to explain the rules and provide good reasons for compliance. A calm and reasoned discussion gives parents an opportunity to express warmth and compassion to the child and an opportunity to demonstrate positive ways to handle conflict. As always, tailor your approach to the developmental level of the child. For toddlers and young children, keep the explanations simple: "The road is dangerous because cars can hurt you." Make adjustments as children mature: "You need to be home by curfew because we worry about you and we want you rested for school tomorrow." Also realize the importance of laying a foundation of trust and care in early childhood so you will have your child's respect as he or she grows into adolescence. If you rely on spanking, hitting, or other physical force in the early years, what are you going to do when your child becomes too big to push around? You and your child will both benefit by learning to use explanation and reasoning early in the relationship.

5. *If you must punish, try removing privileges or using timeouts.* If you have followed all of the preceding steps and an unwanted behavior still persists, you might consider imposing an appropriate punishment. Remember, *punishment* is a technique that reduces the frequency of an undesirable behavior, but it doesn't mean that you have to resort to hitting or yelling. It's best to tie the punishment to the infraction as much as possible. If children are fighting over video games, for example, they could lose the privilege of playing the games the rest of the day. Any such disciplinary action should begin with the mildest form and should take the child's age into account. For a toddler, losing a favorite toy for a few minutes may make a big impact, whereas an 8-year-old may need to lose a privilege for several hours or a day to get the point.

   As an alternative, try a mild **timeout.** Remove the child from the situation and from anything that is encouraging the misbehavior to continue, and place him in a safe, quiet environment. A short timeout (about one minute per year of the child's age) gives children a few minutes to collect themselves and reflect on what

timeout

A disciplinary technique that involves removing the child from the situation and anything that is encouraging the misbehavior to continue, placing the child in a safe and quiet environment.

they have done. It also gives you time to gather your thoughts—and reduces the likelihood that you will lash out in anger and say or do something you will regret. After the brief timeout, try explanation and reasoning again. Always be sure to praise children when their behavior improves. Timeouts are most effective with young children; for older children and adolescents, a loss of privilege or some type of grounding would be more appropriate.

You may feel that the steps we have outlined are not enough; you may believe that children need to "pay a price" for misbehavior. Keep in mind, however, that the focus should be on teaching good behavior. Misbehavior can be very aggravating for parents, especially when they are dealing with difficult children and trying to balance multiple stresses at work and at home. Most parents want to have positive relationships with their children; but it takes time, effort, and considerable emotional control to maintain a warm and caring attitude when children are continually misbehaving. It's just plain easier to lash out, yell, or strike the child. If you find yourself in this situation, we hope that you will take some time to reflect on your own behavior and the potentially negative impact that it may have.

What if children's misbehaviors become severe? The examples we have given have been rather innocent, but we all know that some children and teens engage in behavior that is truly dangerous, violent, and even criminal. By using positive principles of discipline from an early age, we hope that parents can prevent or at least reduce severe misbehavior. If not, the same principles still apply: Try to be supportive first, keep the lines of communication open, and maintain firm rules and limits. If a child's behaviors continue to deteriorate, families should enforce limits with appropriate consequences but without hitting or otherwise contributing to family violence. If the situation continues to worsen, families should seek assistance from school counselors, psychologists, social workers, or other professionals. The point is that regardless of the situation, harsh physical punishment sends the wrong message and is simply not an effective teaching tool. To read more about how some parents deal with the everyday situations requiring discipline, read the Personal Perspective box called "Carrots or Sticks?"

Parents can use a timeout to remove a child from a situation when he is misbehaving. A safe, quiet place gives the child a chance to settle down and think about the rules.

YOUR

PERSPECTIVE

NOTES

Think of a real-life situation in which a child you know misbehaved. Give a specific example of how each of the discipline methods suggested could have helped control the misbehavior and might have taught more appropriate actions.

Mothers and Fathers: Cooperating through Thick and Thin?

Having children can be a great joy, and most parents report that if they could start over, they would do it again (Cowan & Cowan, 1992). Raising children, however, does put a great strain on most marriages. Although couples tend to think that having a baby will bring them closer together, the reality is that new forms of tension accompany the transition to parenthood (Cowan & Cowan, 1992). After the birth of a new baby, parents are on call 24 hours a day and 7 days a week. Infants need attention all day and even through the night, and their feedings, crying, and illnesses can be very disruptive. Parents struggle to meet their own sleep needs and maintain their daily routines. As children mature, the nights return to normal, but then come the challenges of keeping up with school schedules, homework, extracurricular activities, and

Carrots or Sticks?

Matos family
Lawrence, Massachusetts
Hispanic family

What methods of discipline do you use regularly? Are they effective? Are there any methods that you have tried, but found they did not work?

Iris and Manuel Matos: Hispanic family We like to talk to our children about what they did wrong. It lets them know how we feel and how the situation reflects on who they are as a person. Yelling did not work at all. They could handle 5 minutes of yelling, and that was that. Spanking also did not work. When a child thinks about their mom and dad it should be wonderful thoughts about being safe, comfort, trust, and guidance. With spanking, our children would not have the bond with us we have today because we would have instilled fear in them. To us, the most effective way is communicating with our children.

Sharon Buenaventura: Asian family (three boys, ages 12, 9, and 20 months) My discipline methods are

based on their personalities. My eldest son, Michael, fits the mold of the "first born." On the rare occasion that I've had to discipline him, it was really more of a discussion pointing out various reasons why I did not want him to repeat his actions. Michael is quite open to our discussions and will correct his behavior willingly once the reasons are spelled out to him. My second son, Nicky, responds to timeouts and the taking away of privileges (e.g., soccer practice). Discussions do not work for Nicky. He tends to be more free-spirited and not as concerned about following the rules. Christian is still quite young, and I haven't figured out what method of discipline will work best for him. At this time, he may want to touch something that he shouldn't, and simply telling him to "look, not touch" will suffice.

One method I have discovered over the years is that "screaming" or "yelling" is definitely the least effective method for any of my boys. I find that they tend to shut me out and not really listen to anything I may be saying.

Kristin and Marc Petraluzzi: French family (two boys, ages 2½ and 4½) We use timeouts. This has not been really effective, because they have quite a few timeouts daily (the older child). When we had nowhere else to go, we tried a spanking, but that did not seem to

help either. I think we just have strong characters that we are dealing with!

Kim Miller: African American family (two girls, ages 11 and 14) The 14-year-old got a poor grade on a history test because she spent more time instant-messaging her friends than studying for the test. I restricted her access to instant messaging and other unsupervised uses of the computer until she had another test and got a better grade. The key is not ever wavering from the imposed punishment—which in this case meant over 3 weeks of no instant messaging. To encourage getting in bed on time, I instituted a policy that for every minute they are late for bed, they are charged $1. The money goes in a top dresser drawer and can be earned back each night the appropriate behavior is achieved (i.e., 5 consecutive nights of going to bed on time will recoup $5). ■

thinking OF JEREMY

◄ What discipline techniques described here might be effective for getting Jeremy's behavior under control?

the children's time with friends. It may surprise you (or may not, if you have children) to learn that the vast majority of couples report a significant decline in marital satisfaction in the first year after the births of their first babies. One-quarter of all divorces occur before the babies are 18 months old (Cowan & Cowan, 1992).

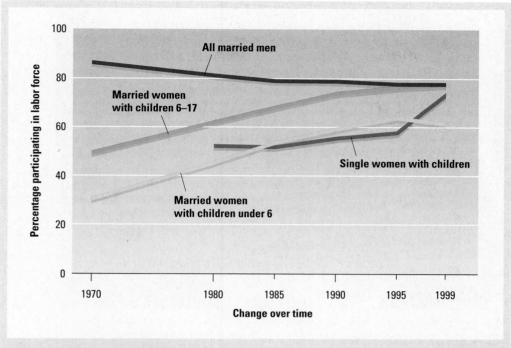

FIGURE 12.2 Workforce Trends, 1970–1999

The percentage of married men working outside the home has decreased since 1970, while the percentage of women working full-time has increased dramatically.

Source: U.S. Census Bureau (2000b).

Another complication for new parents is that today most parents work outside the home. As you can see in Figure 12.2, married women with children ages 6 to 17 years are now as likely to work outside the home as married men. Single women with children and married women with children under 6 years don't lag far behind. In recent decades more women have entered the workforce, while the percentage of men working has decreased slightly. The decrease for men is due mostly to the fact that the overall population is aging, so a larger percentage of men are now over the age of 65 and retired.

When children are born, couples tend to move toward more *traditional* gender roles, with new fathers spending less time on household chores and mothers spending more (Cowan & Cowan, 1992). At the same time, new fathers usually increase the number of hours they work outside the home. The result: Mothers must decrease their paid work time, quit altogether, or struggle to maintain their job while also providing most of the family care at home. An Australian study showed how large the discrepancy in time spent with children can be. On average, mothers spent 23 hours per week alone with children, whereas fathers spent only 2 hours! And mothers were available 55 hours per week for their children, but fathers were on hand only 35 hours (Russell & Russell, 1987). Another study showed that adolescents aged 14 to 18 spent twice as much time alone with their mothers as with their fathers (Montemayor & Brownlee, 1987). Other researchers have documented this predominance of mother involvement in U.S. families of African, Asian, Hispanic, and European descent and in families in Great Britain, Australia, France, and Belgium (Hossain, Field, Malphus, Valle, & Pickens, 1995; Hossain & Roopnarine, 1993; Lamb, 1987b).

The *types* of time children spend with mothers and fathers also differ. Fathers spend a greater percentage of their interaction time playing with children (Hossain et al., 1995).

After their children are born, fathers and mothers tend to move toward more traditional gender roles in such areas as household chores, paid work outside the home, caring for children, and interaction with children.

YOUR

PERSPECTIVE

NOTES

Do these gender differences describe your family or anyone you know? What effects have the stalled revolution, guilt gap, and wage gap had on you or your family?

stalled revolution

The fact that although mothers now work more outside the home, they still shoulder most of the responsibility for day-to-day care of children.

guilt gap

The tendency of mothers to worry more than fathers about the negative impact their work may have on their children and families.

wage gap

The fact that on average, women are still not paid as much as men for comparable work.

Because mothers spend more total time with children, however, they still end up playing with children more than fathers do. Fathers' play tends to be more physical and rough-and-tumble, and mothers' play tends to be more toy oriented and verbal (Parke, 1996; Russell & Russell, 1987). Fathers' physical play is greatest when children are around 2 or 3 years of age, and it declines in frequency after that (MacDonald & Parke, 1986). Interestingly, male monkeys also engage in the rough-and-tumble style of play with their offspring, so there may be a biological component for this type of play in human fathers (Parke & Suomi, 1981). Culture also plays a role, however: Physical play is not frequent among fathers in Sweden, traditional Israeli communities, China, Malaysia, India, or the Aka people of central Africa (Parke & Buriel, 1998).

In sum, although fathers in the United States have become more involved with their children in recent decades, the reality is that mothers still shoulder most of the responsibility for the day-to-day care of the children. Men's involvement in family work has simply not kept pace with women's increasing roles in work outside the home. Sociologists refer to this phenomenon as the **stalled revolution** (Hochschild & Machung, 1989; Newman, 1999). There is also a **guilt gap** in most families—working mothers tend to be more worried than fathers about the negative impact their work may have on their children and families (Hays, 1996; Newman, 1999). Because society has traditionally viewed men as the breadwinners, people tend to see men's increased work time as showing commitment and support for their families. In contrast, women, traditionally viewed as the homemakers, often feel that they must justify each hour they spend away from their children. And when women do work, they face the added indignity of the **wage gap,** earning (on average) only 71 cents for every dollar earned by men for comparable work (Newman, 1999).

As most parents know, one of the toughest challenges families face is how to cooperate in balancing work and home life. Working out the rights and responsibilities of mothers and fathers can be very difficult. Is it any wonder that researchers find that parenting tends to increase feelings of anger, especially in women (Ross & Van Willigen, 1996)?

1. Which of the following parent comments would best illustrate an *authoritative* parenting style?

   a. You said you'd clean your room! You never follow through—you're grounded for three weeks!

   b. You didn't clean your room? Well, it's not that dirty. You can do it some other time.

   c. Go ahead and live in a pigsty—it's your room.

   d. No movies tonight. We agreed you would clean your room by Friday or you wouldn't go to the movies.

2. Research on parenting styles has found that:

   a. the authoritative style is most effective for all children.

   b. the differences in child outcomes between styles are large and consistent.

   c. children whose parents use a rejecting/neglecting style show the worst outcomes.

   d. the authoritarian parenting style has particularly bad effects for low-income ethnic minorities.

3. Children who are frequently spanked tend to be:

   a. more aggressive, more depressed, and lower in self-esteem than other children.

   b. better behaved than other children.

   c. less likely to use physical means to get what they want.

   d. less likely to use physical punishment with their own children.

4. Research shows that fathers today spend

   a. just as much time as mothers taking care of children.

   b. more time than mothers playing with children.

   c. more time than mothers taking care of children but less time playing with children.

   d. less time than mothers caring for children.

5. **True or False:** One of the best techniques for child discipline is the use of situation management to prevent misbehavior in the first place.

6. **True or False:** The term *the stalled revolution* refers to the lack of progress women have made in keeping up with work inside and outside of the home.

Answers: 1. d, 2. c, 3. a, 4. d, 5. T, 6. F

Changing Family Structures

Today, for the first time since the United States began taking a census of its population, married couples living with their own biological children represent less than one-fourth of U.S. households—only 23.5 percent, compared to 25.6 percent in 1990 and 45 percent in 1960 (U.S. Census Bureau, 2000a). Many married couples have no children, or have children who have grown up and left home. The number of children in single-parent homes and in step-families has skyrocketed over the last few decades. And millions of families have adopted children. What are the effects on children of these varying family structures? Is family structure itself the overriding factor in a child's experience, or are other factors more important? In this section we explore several different family structures and consider how they relate to children's emotional, social, and cognitive development.

As you study this section, ask yourself these questions:

- What are the social, emotional, and cognitive outcomes associated with divorce? What factors explain these outcomes? How can parents and professionals help children deal with divorce?

- What are the effects on children of living in never-married households or in stepfamilies? Are the factors that explain these effects similar to those for children of divorced parents?

- How do adopted children fare compared to nonadopted children?

- What does the research evidence indicate about children raised by gay or lesbian parents?

- What are some of the main characteristics researchers have found in families of different ethnic backgrounds, and how might these characteristics affect children's development?

Children and Divorce

Have you experienced a divorce in your family? Even if you have not, chances are very good that you know several people who have. In 1998 14.4 percent of all children under the age of 18 in the United States (more than 10 million children) were living in a home in which the parents were divorced or separated (U.S. Census Bureau, 1998). Contrary to the impression many people have, the majority of children in the United States do live in two-parent households (68.2 percent in 1998) (U.S. Census Bureau, 1998). However, many of these households consist of children living with one biological parent and a stepparent rather than with both biological parents. Bumpass (1984) predicted that 38 percent of all white children and 75 percent of African American children whose parents were married when they were born would experience divorce before they were 16 years old. Given these statistics, it is imperative that parents, teachers, child-care workers, developmental psychologists, clinicians, and legal professionals understand the effects divorce has on children. All of us who work with children need to know how best to help children cope with the changes and emotions that occur when parents divorce.

■ **The Divorce Process.**   Experts agree that it's important to see divorce as a process rather than as a single event. This process can begin years before parents actually separate, and it may not end until long after the legal end of the marriage. From the **divorce-stress-adjustment perspective,** the divorce process initiates many events that parents and children find stressful. It is these stressors that increase the risk of negative outcomes for both parents and children (Amato, 2000; Emery, 1999b; Hetherington, Bridges, & Insabella, 1998). As Figure 12.3 shows, according to this model the overall effect of divorce depends on several factors. Mediating events and processes, such as the effectiveness of parenting or the degree of parental conflict, affect the child's emotions and behavior. The individual child's specific vulnerabilities, such as a difficult temperament or a genetic predisposition to psychological problems like depression, may make it harder for the child to cope with the stresses of divorce. The existence of protective factors, such as social support or good coping skills, help ease the transition. Keep in mind that for some children divorce *relieves* stress. Some children have been enduring their parents' chronic conflict, abuse, or psychological disorders. In these situations, divorce may produce new stresses, such as financial hardships, but the overall effect may be decreased stress and a more positive outcome for the child.

   Some researchers do not agree with the idea that the stresses and mediating factors of the divorce process as such are the main causes of negative outcomes for children. Instead, the **selection model** says that certain characteristics of the parents, such as antisocial personality traits or poor parenting skills, cause *both* the divorce and children's problems (Amato, 2000; Harris, 1998). This perspective is called the *selection model* because negative traits cause certain parents to be "selected" out of marriage, and the same traits have negative effects on

---

divorce-stress-adjustment perspective

A model used to understand divorce outcomes; emphasizes that a complex interaction of stressors, specific vulnerabilities, and protective factors determine the individual child's adjustment to divorce.

selection model

A model used to understand divorce outcomes; emphasizes that certain characteristics of parents (e.g., abusiveness) rather than the divorce itself cause children's negative outcomes.

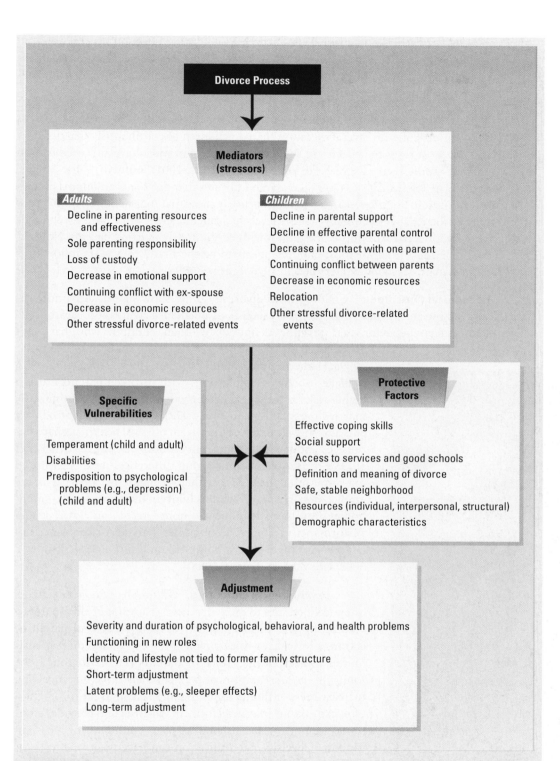

FIGURE 12.3 The Divorce-Stress-Adjustment Perspective

The divorce-stress-adjustment perspective views divorce as a process affected by many different mediators, specific vulnerabilities, and protective factors. All of these factors interact and affect a child's developmental outcomes.

Source: Adapted from Paul R. Amato. (2000). The consequences of divorce for adults and children. *Journal of Marriage and the Family, 62,* pp. 1269–1287. Copyrighted 2000 by the National Council on Family Relations, 3989 Central Ave. NE, Suite 550, Minneapolis, MN 55421. Adapted with permission.

thinking
OF JEREMY

How can the divorce-stress-adjustment perspective help Jeremy's parents and Cassandra understand Jeremy's difficulties? The selection model?

their children. For example, an abusive father can have a negative effect on his children, and he is more likely to be divorced by his wife. If the children show negative effects after the divorce (e.g., aggression or poor school performance), the effects may result more from having lived with the abusive father than from the divorce itself.

■ **Outcomes Associated with Divorce.** As a group, children of divorced parents show lower scores on several measures than do children of continuously married parents. In most cases the effects are small to moderate, but most have appeared consistently in studies across several decades (Amato, 2000, 2001; Reifman, Villa, Amans, Rethinam, & Telesca, 2001). Overall, research indicates that divorce is an important risk factor for children. But the research results also clearly show that most children of divorced parents are resilient: They eventually achieve levels of academic, behavioral, and psychological functioning on a par with those of children with continuously married parents. Not surprisingly, the hardest time for most children seems to be the first 2 to 4 years following a divorce (Buchanan, Maccoby, & Dornbusch, 1996; Emery, 1999a).

Behavioral Outcomes. Children from divorced homes show significantly more *externalizing* (acting-out) problems—behaviors such as disobedience, aggression, lack of self-control, antisocial behavior, and juvenile delinquency—than children who have not experienced divorce (Amato, 2001; Amato & Keith, 1991; Emery, 1999a; Hetherington & Stanley-Hagan, 1995; Wallerstein, Lewis, & Blakeslee, 2000). Adolescents with divorced parents are at a higher risk for teenage pregnancy than those with continuously married parents (McLanahan, 1999). Children of divorced parents also show less robust long-term physical health, perhaps because of enduring differences in economic resources (Tucker et al., 1997). However, ethnic group differences have been found for some outcomes (McLanahan & Sandefur, 1994). For example, non-Hispanic white children living in single-parent homes show more delinquency, more drug use, and lower school performance in single-parent homes than do African American children in single-parent homes (Dunifon & Kowaleski-Jones, 2002; Gil, Vega, & Biafora, 1998).

Psychological Outcomes. Children of divorced parents often feel pressure to grow up faster as a result of their parents' divorce. In part, this feeling may develop because of **parentification,** a reversal of roles in which the child takes on responsibilities usually taken care of by parents (Hetherington, 1999; Johnston, 1990). Parentification can be *instrumental,* involving increased responsibility for household tasks and care of siblings. Or it can take an *emotional* form, in which a child provides emotional support or acts as an advisor or confidant for a parent. Moderate levels of parentification can have positive effects for both boys and girls. However, high levels can create problems such as depression, anxiety, compulsive caretaking, anger, and irritation, especially for girls. Girls receive such treatment from both mothers and fathers more often than do boys. But emotional parentification precipitated by fathers seems especially difficult for boys to deal with; it can lead to anxiety, depression, rebellion, resistance, and withdrawal from the family. Parentifi-

With parentification, children feel pressure to grow up faster and assume responsibilities that are normally reserved for parents. Moderate levels of parentification can have positive effects on children, but higher levels can create problems.

TABLE 12.1 Psychological Distress among Well-Adjusted College Students with Divorced Parents

ITEM TO BE RATED	PERCENTAGES OF YOUNG ADULTS WHO AGREED OR STRONGLY AGREED WITH THE STATEMENT	
	Divorced Parents	Continuously Married Parents
My father caused most of the trouble in my family.	60	19*
I feel like I might have been a different person if my father/mother had been a bigger part of my life.	51	20*
I worry about big events like graduations or weddings, when both my parents will have to come.	50	10*
I had a harder childhood than most people.	48	14*
I wish I had more time with Dad/Mom.	47	19*
My childhood was cut short.	34	17*
I have not forgiven Dad.	30	6*
I have not forgiven Mom.	7	4
I sometimes wonder if my father even loves me.	29	10*
I feel doomed to repeat my parents' problems in my own relationships.	18	15
My father is still in love with my mother.	14	78*
My mother is still in love with my father.	11	82*
My parents' divorce still causes struggles for me.	49	Not applicable
I really missed not having my father around as much after my parents' separation.	48	Not applicable
Even though it was hard, divorce was the right thing for my family.	81	Not applicable
I probably would be a different person if my parents had not gotten divorced.	73	Not applicable

*Difference between children of divorced and married parents is significant, $p < .01$.

Source: Adapted from Laumann-Billings & Emery (2000).

cation occurs not only in divorced families but in situations of maternal depression and in families experiencing high levels of marital conflict (Emery, 1999a; Hetherington, 1999).

Children of divorced parents are 2 to 3 times more likely than others to receive some form of psychological treatment, but they do not show clinical depression or other major psychological disorders any more often than do children of continuously married parents (Emery, 1999a; Howard et al., 1996; Zill, Morrisen, & Coiro, 1993). Children and adolescents in divorced families often report higher levels of depressive symptoms or depressed mood, but these seem to indicate shorter-term separation distress rather than enduring clinical depression (Conger & Chao, 1996). Self-esteem is lower in children of divorced parents, but the effects are typically small (Amato & Keith, 1991; Emery, 1999a). Even though children of divorced parents do not show psychological disorders, it seems that many experience significant psychological and emotional pain and distress. Fear of abandonment, grief, feelings of responsibility for the divorce, anger, and anxiety about their own relationships and about continuing parental conflict occur frequently (Emery, 1999a; Wallerstein et al., 2000). Table 12.1 shows the "agree" responses to various statements of well-functioning college students with divorced parents and of students with continuously married parents. As you can see, students still seem to harbor painful feelings about their parents' divorces, even though more than 80 percent felt that divorce was the right thing for their families. Compared to students with continuously married parents, children with divorced parents had significantly higher ratings of distress on 10 of the items (Laumann-Billings & Emery, 2000).

Some studies suggest that more subtle effects of divorce may not become apparent until children reach adolescence or young adulthood and begin attempting to form intimate and

parentification

Role reversal in which a child assumes responsibilities usually taken care of by parents.

stable relationships. Sometimes called the **sleeper effect of divorce**, this finding may indicate that children deal with issues stemming from their parents' divorce at each developmental stage they pass through (Bray, 1999; Hetherington, Cox, & Cox, 1982; Sun & Li, 2002). Adult children of divorced parents are less likely to marry than children of continuously married parents; and when they do marry, their marriages are more likely to end in divorce. Some suggest that this may happen partly because children of divorced parents have not learned interpersonal skills that are important for maintaining a happy marriage—skills such as communicating effectively, building trust, and managing emotions. If divorced parents are able to rebuild a happy life that includes their children, either as committed single parents or in stable remarriages, children experience fewer problems establishing successful relationships (Amato, 1999a; Wallerstein et al., 2000). The postdivorce quality of the relationship between parents and children is also important—children with higher quality relationships with their parents show better levels of trust in their adult relationships (King, 2002).

Academic and Occupational Outcomes.   Divorce is negatively related to a variety of academic and occupational outcomes, according to many studies (Amato, 1999b; Amato & Keith, 1991; McLanahan, 1999; Teachman, Paasch, & Carver, 1996). Children with divorced parents are about twice as likely to drop out of high school as those with continuously married parents. Children of divorced parents are less likely to attend college, graduate from college (especially women), or find and keep a steady job. They tend to have lower grade point averages in school, lower test scores, lower college expectations, and worse school attendance records. These findings may indicate decreased motivation to achieve academically as well as decreased access to quality education and enriching educational opportunities. The effect of divorce on educational outcomes is greater for non-Hispanic white children than for African American or Hispanic children. For example, white children from single-parent homes are 2.4 times more likely to drop out of high school than those from two-parent homes, compared to 1.8 times for African American children and 1.9 times for Hispanic children (though the overall high school dropout rate is higher for African Americans and Hispanics than for non-Hispanic whites) (McLanahan, 1999). Both men and women from divorced homes are about 1.5 times more likely to be occupationally idle (i.e., not in college but not working) during the teen and early adult years, especially African Americans (McLanahan, 1999). Finally, offspring of divorced parents reach adulthood with a lower annual income and fewer accumulated financial assets, probably because of lower levels of educational attainment (Amato, 1999b). Though many of the effects of divorce on educational and occupational measures are small to moderate in size, they are consistently evident in study results (Amato, 2000; Amato & Keith, 1991; McLanahan, 1999).

Positive Outcomes Associated with Divorce.   Divorce does have some positive outcomes. For both boys and girls, the ending of a high-conflict marriage can produce beneficial effects, provided that the divorce reduces the degree of conflict. Children in high-conflict intact families score significantly *lower* on measures of psychological adjustment and self-esteem than children in divorced families (Amato & Keith, 1991; Booth & Amato, 2001; Hanson, 1999; Hetherington, 1999; Hetherington & Kelly, 2002; Jekielek, 1998). Some children, especially daughters, benefit from the development of very close relationships with their mothers after divorce (Amato & Booth, 1997; Arditti, 1999). Following a divorce, moderate demands on children to take more responsibility for household tasks, care for siblings, and provide emotional support to parents and other family members can lead to greater social responsibility, competence, and empathy during adulthood. As we mentioned before, however, excessive demands of this type lead to parentification and are detrimental to both boys and girls (Hetherington, 1999). And when a parent shows high levels of antisocial behavior such as aggression, emotional and financial impulsivity, drug and alcohol problems, and coercive

sleeper effect of divorce

Subtle effects of divorce that may not become apparent until children reach adolescence or young adulthood and have difficulty forming intimate and stable relationships.

discipline, children fare better the less time they spend with the parent (Jaffee, Moffitt, Caspi, & Taylor, 2003).

It is important to keep in mind that most of the negative outcomes we have discussed represent only small to moderate differences between children from divorced and intact families. For example, Amato (1999a) asked young adults to rate how happy and satisfied they were with their lives, jobs, homes, neighborhoods, and leisure activities. Adults from intact families rated themselves as somewhat happier and more satisfied than adults from divorced families. The differences in ratings were consistent and reliable, but they were still small enough that there was considerable overlap between the groups. Based on the findings, Amato (1999a) speculated that about 42 percent of children from divorced homes grow up to be happier than the average person from an intact family, and about 42 percent of children from intact homes grow up to be less happy than people from divorced families. So although divorce increases the risk for negative outcomes, many children from divorced families still graduate from college and have successful careers and happy marriages. And as you have no doubt observed, there are plenty of people who have significant troubles and worries even when their parents remain happily married.

Unanswered Questions. Are there consistent gender differences in the effects of divorce? It is unclear. Some studies report that boys show greater difficulty in social adjustment, more behavior problems, and more problems with emotional parentification by fathers (Amato & Keith, 1991; Hetherington, 1999; McLanahan & Sandefur, 1994; Mott, Kowaleski-Jones, & Menaghan, 1997). Some report that girls are at greater risk of not finishing college and of becoming "competent at a cost" as a result of high levels of emotional parentification (Hetherington, 1999, p. 113; McLanahan, 1999). In other words, they become socially and behaviorally high functioning, but they also show higher levels of depression and lower self-worth. Other studies find few if any gender differences (Amato & Keith, 1991).

Are the effects of divorce greater for younger or for older children? This answer, too, is unclear. Some studies report larger effects on children in the primary and high school years than on college students. Others find that divorce has a more negative effect on very young children (e.g., children below 6 years of age at the time of divorce) (Allison & Furstenberg, 1989; Amato & Keith, 1991; Wallerstein et al., 2000). Still others have concluded that the child's age at the time of a divorce does not matter, or that age may be more important for some outcomes than for others (Furstenberg & Kiernan, 2001; McLanahan & Sandefur, 1994). To complicate things further, some effects may not become apparent until late adolescence and early adulthood, as we noted earlier (Amato, 1999a; Wallerstein et al., 2000). On a more positive note, it does seem that some of the problems observed immediately after a divorce do get better over time. This finding is certainly a comfort to parents and children going through this experience (McLanahan, 1997).

Finally, what kind of residential arrangement is best for children following divorce? Again, we do not have a definitive answer. The majority of children have their primary residence with their mothers. This is true even if there is **joint legal custody,** an agreement in which both parents are responsible for decisions regarding their children's education, medical treatment, general support, and well-being. Currently, only about 5 to 10 percent of divorced parents share **joint physical custody** (or joint residences), in which children spend approximately equal amounts of time living in both their parents' homes. Joint custody (legal or physical) seems to offer advantages. Children in these custody settings are comparable to those of intact families and show better adjustment than children in sole custody on a number of behavioral, emotional, and relationship measures (Bauserman, 2002). Joint legal custody has become commonplace over the past 2 decades, though some judges still show a maternal preference for custody even when custody laws are specifically written to be gender neutral (Stamps, 2002). Joint physical custody is becoming increasingly popular.

joint legal custody

Legal agreement that grants both divorced parents the responsibility for decisions regarding their children.

joint physical custody

Arrangement in which children of divorced couples spend approximately equal amounts of time living with each parent.

Supporters argue that this arrangement helps children maintain meaningful relationships with both parents. They believe that this benefit compensates for the possible disadvantages of going back and forth between homes and increased exposure to parents' disagreements. Some studies find little or no difference in children's adjustment as a function of where they live; others find that joint residence offers some advantages unless there is high conflict between parents (Buchanan et al., 1996; Emery, 1999a; Johnston, 1995; Maccoby, 1999). It is difficult to draw firm conclusions yet, however. First, the number of children in joint residential arrangements is still small. Second, those parents who are able to maintain a joint arrangement (legal or physical) may differ in important respects from those who try this arrangement but find it unworkable. For example, they may be more cooperative; have better and more consistent parenting skills; and/or be older, better educated, and more financially secure. Regardless of residence arrangements, children who maintain a close relationship with both parents show better adjustment than those who become estranged from one parent. This seems to be especially true for girls who live with their fathers—estrangement from noncustodial mothers is associated with more adjustment problems (Buchanan et al., 1996; Emery, 1999a).

■ **What Factors Explain the Effects of Divorce?**   Knowing what the effects of divorce are does not explain why they occur. Three intervening factors seem to be especially important: *money, parenting quality,* and *community connections.* Lack of money has far-reaching effects. Aside from diminishing children's access to leisure activities, clothes, toys, and the like, lack of money often limits the quality and quantity of health care a child receives. It also limits the quality of education children have access to, and this in turn affects children's later occupational opportunities and lifelong earning potential (Clarke-Stewart, Vandell, McCartney, Owen, & Booth, 2000; McLanahan, 1999; Sun & Li, 2002).

A decline in both the quantity and quality of parenting also accounts for a significant portion of the effects of divorce (Clarke-Stewart et al., 2000; Fisher, Leve, O'Leary, & Leve, 2003; Hilton, 2002; McLanahan, 1999). Even people with good parenting skills can become overwhelmed by the emotional and financial stresses of divorce. In addition, children often become more difficult to manage during this time of change in routines, residences, and rules. Parenting frequently becomes more authoritarian, neglecting, or permissive (Hetherington et al., 1982). If custodial parents are able to maintain good parenting practices, remaining involved with and responsive to their children, their children fare much better (Buchanan et al., 1996; DeGarmo, Forgatch, & Martinez, 1999). Experts agree that open conflict between parents is very detrimental. It results in worse outcomes for children whether the parents divorce or stay married, especially if the conflict is angry or violent or places the child in the middle (El-Sheikh & Harger, 2001; Emery, 1982; Katz & Woodin, 2002). Sadly the amount of conflict experienced by a child may actually increase after a divorce as parents fight over money, resources, custody, and other issues.

Finally, divorce often requires children and their custodial parent to move, sometimes more than once. Residential mobility involves leaving familiar friends, neighborhoods, schools, day care settings and community resources. The result is often a decrease in community connections. This reduces the family's knowledge of and access to community

YOUR
PERSPECTIVE
NOTES

Are you, or is a close friend, a child of divorced parents? What effects has the divorce had? What factors do you think account for the effects of the divorce? Do the research findings we've described accurately portray your/your friend's experience?

Open conflict between parents is very detrimental for children, whether parents divorce or remain married. Unfortunately, conflict does not necessarily decrease following a divorce.

TABLE 12.2 How Can Adults Minimize the Negative Effects of Divorce on Children?

Minimize conflict during and after divorce. Place children's needs above your own when negotiating custody, finances, schooling, and so on. Do not belittle your ex-spouse to children. Do not place children in the middle of parental disputes and ask them to (or imply that they should) take sides.

Minimize the number of changes children must experience at one time. Avoid moving if possible; in any case, make as few residence changes as you can. Help the child maintain contact with familiar friends, teachers, schools, and other community resources. Introduce necessary changes gradually whenever possible.

Prevent children from becoming the family caretakers. Join a support group for divorced parents or call on friends and family for emotional and practical support rather than burdening children with adult responsibilities.

Develop and maintain an effective parenting style. Remain involved and affectionate, but make certain to provide appropriate supervision.

Seek help and support. Ask for help from friends and family, as well as counseling from a professional with training in child development. Try family and/or parent-based therapies to improve parenting skills and the quality of parent–child relationships.

Develop consistent rules for behavior and expectations. Try to agree on your expectations of the child, on consequences for not meeting expectations, and on routines for monitoring the child's behavior and activities. Ideally, both parents should implement the same rules and should support each other.

Help children maintain consistent contact with both parents. Maintain a regular schedule of visits with the noncustodial parent, but adjust the schedule as the child's needs and interests change. Maintain regular telephone, e-mail, or letter contact, especially if a parent lives too far away for frequent visitation. Make sure to remember special events like the child's birthday or holidays. Demonstrate interest in and support for the child's activities by attending recitals, athletic events, and the like at least occasionally.

Seek professional help for children in pain and distress. Try school-based group interventions to help reduce distress or change children's beliefs about divorce. Seek individual therapy for children suspected of having more serious problems, such as conduct disorders or depression. Teach children active coping skills, like problem solving and seeking support from others, and help them establish the belief that they can deal effectively with the stresses they are experiencing. Try to provide a model of effective, positive, and proactive problem solving before, during, and after a divorce.

Help youngsters develop positive interpersonal skills. Work to develop the skills necessary to establish and maintain intimate relationships, then model these skills for your children through your own healthy interpersonal relationships. Counselors and therapists can include interpersonal skills training in their therapy with children. Parents can request that these issues be addressed.

Minimize financial decline as much as possible. Find out about legal or social programs that support families in transition (e.g., programs that help parents obtain child support payments or find housing, job placement, or educational training assistance).

Prevent divorce when possible and appropriate. When possible and appropriate, try to prevent divorce by strengthening a weak marriage and by learning how to deal with conflicts in constructive ways. Try to resolve or minimize conflicts between family and other obligations (e.g., workplace demands).

Sources: Amato (2000); Buchanan, Maccoby, & Dornbusch (1996); Emery, Kitzman, & Waldron (1999); Hetherington (1999); Meyer (1999); Sandler, Tein, Mehta, Wolchik, & Ayers (2000); Wallerstein, Lewis, & Blakeslee (2000).

resources, just at a time when parents and children need support and help more than ever (McLanahan, 1999).

Divorce is a complicated process that individual children experience in individual ways. It is clearly a risk factor for children's well-being; no one argues that children are unaffected by parental divorces. However, it also is clear that most children show great resilience. Psychologists and others who work with divorcing families have identified many things parents and other adults can do to minimize negative effects and ease children's transitions (Pedro-Carroll, 2001; Wallerstein, 2001). Table 12.2 summarizes some of their suggestions. As you will notice, some of these suggestions may be very difficult for divorcing parents to implement, but when parents are able to follow them, they will help children and adolescents make more positive adjustments. To read more about how these suggestions can be put into practice, read the Professional Perspective box called "Career Focus: Meet a Psychotherapist Who Works with Divorced Parents and Children."

thinking OF JEREMY

◄ Which of the suggestions in Table 12.2 might be helpful for Jeremy and his parents? How could Cassandra and Jeremy's parents implement the suggestions?

Career Focus: Meet a Psychotherapist Who Works with Divorced Parents and Children

Barbara Beaver, Ph.D.

Whitewater, Wisconsin

Psychotherapist, licensed clinical psychologist

What do you consider to be "normal" behavioral and emotional changes in children during and after a divorce? What are some signs that indicate a more serious problem might be developing?

I'd consider it *normal* to see some increases in anxiety and need for reassurance. Children might also exhibit mild behavior problems, such as noncompliance and testing of parental limits, or an increase in negative emotions, such as sadness and irritability. In considering if more serious problems are developing we'd need to look at the duration of the problem behaviors (are they going on longer than is typical or expected?); the intensity of the reactions; and the extent to which the problems are interfering with the child's daily functioning, including schoolwork, friendships, appetite and sleep changes. It is also important to consider what the child's behavior was

like before the divorce issues began, to know what may be typical for a particular child.

What kinds of therapy do you use, and how effective are they?

I base the intervention on the problems and needs of the child/family. With some families I may work more with the parent, helping him or her establish consistent rules and behavior management strategies. This can be particularly helpful if the problem is disruptive behavior. I've often used family therapy to help the family's communication skills and improve the parent–child relationship. Bibliotherapy, or using books about divorce, can be helpful to both parent and child. Working individually with the child can help children to express their emotions, including grief and feelings of anger toward both parents. The research also shows that group interventions providing support for children in school can be helpful.

What can parents do to help their children adapt to divorce?

Parents should try to keep the child's life as stable as possible. Familiar routines are especially important for

younger children. Parents should also take care to behave civilly with each other and not put the child in the middle of their relationship.

What education and training is needed to work in your field?

An advanced degree is necessary to be a psychotherapist with children or families, and some type of licensing or certification is required. I have a Ph.D. in clinical psychology and I'm a licensed psychologist, but others may have a master's degree in counseling or social work. ∎

 thinking OF JEREMY

◄ Based on what is considered a "normal" reaction to divorce, does Jeremy's behavior seem normal or does it seem more serious? What are some things that Jeremy's parents could do to help Jeremy work through these emotions?

Never-Married Households

In 1998, 11 percent of all children in the United States lived in households in which the parents had never married (U.S. Census Bureau, 1998). The rates of childbearing outside of marriage vary widely by ethnic group; for example, one study showed a higher percentage of births outside of marriage for African American (70 percent) and Hispanic mothers (41 percent) than for non-Hispanic white mothers (26 percent) (Ventura, Peters, Martin, & Maurer, 1997). Most of the outcomes associated with divorce also hold true for children whose parents never married. In some cases, in fact, the risks to children of never-married parents are somewhat greater. For example, the risk of dropping out before finishing high school is slightly greater for children of never-married parents (37 percent) than for those of divorced parents (31 percent). In contrast, the dropout risk for children of widowed parents is 15 percent, and for children in intact two-parent families it is 13 percent. The risk patterns are the same for teen births. It does not appear to matter how long a child lives in a single-parent household; the effects are similar whether children spend less than 5 years or more than 5 years in a father-absent household (McLanahan, 1999).

The reasons for the increased risks for children in never-married households also are similar to those for children of divorced parents. Financial security is a particularly important factor. Single women head the vast majority of never-married households. Unmarried mothers tend to have relatively low incomes, and they are less likely to receive child support from the fathers of their children than are divorced mothers (Meyer, 1999). Like divorced single parents, never-married single parents tend to have fewer parenting resources and thus show less effective parenting. They also tend to move more frequently, which reduces their access to supportive community connections.

Today increasing numbers of well-educated and financially secure women are becoming single mothers by choice. These women are better off in terms of education and financial resources, but little is known about whether these children fare better than those of other never-married parents. There is also little research on never-married households headed by fathers. Early work on these households shows inconsistent findings. Some research indicates that children have similar levels of well-being regardless of whether they live in single-father or in single-mother homes (Downey, Ainsworth-Darnell, & Dufur, 1998). Other studies have found that children in single-father homes are more troubled, but it is possible that their problems are the reason for, not the result of, these children's being placed with their fathers (Buchanan et al., 1996).

What is the effect on a child of living in a household without a father? The absence of a father is clearly associated with lower family income, which makes an important difference in children's outcomes. But money, of course, is not the only thing that fathers contribute to children's development. Research shows that active involvement by fathers has positive effects on children's adjustment and that the father's presence in itself matters more than income for a child's overall health, degree of behavioral problems, and degree of psychological problems (Lamb, 1999; McLanahan, 1997, 1999). Surprisingly, it is not how often children see their nonresidential fathers that affects children's outcomes. Instead, feelings of closeness between fathers and children and authoritative parenting by the fathers are both related to better academic achievement and fewer psychological problems in children (Amato & Gilbreth, 1999). Fathers contribute additional parenting resources, balance in overall parenting style, additional monitoring and behavioral control, support for children's emotional and psychological growth, and (together with mothers) a model of how to maintain long-term relationships.

Starting Over: Stepfamilies

What happens to children when parents remarry? Just as with children of divorced and never-married parents, the picture is complicated. When mothers remarry, the family's financial status may improve, which in turn increases the quality of services and educational opportunities available to the children. However, some groups of children experience greater benefits of remarriage than others. For example, living with a stepfather can increase a boy's chances of finishing high school, attending and graduating from college, and finding subsequent job opportunities. If the stepfamily remains stable over many years and provides appropriate care for the children, it can have a positive effect on children's intimate relationships when they reach adulthood. If children are able to maintain good relationships with both biological parents and stepparents, they can end up with even *more* access to parenting resources than children with continuously married biological parents (Amato, 1999a; Hetherington et al., 1998;

McLanahan, 1999; Wallerstein et al., 2000). Most stepchildren seem to have reasonably positive views of their stepfathers. Close relationships between stepchildren and stepparents have positive effects on children's academic achievement and psychological well-being, and introducing a stepparent even in adolescence can be beneficial to children's adjustment (Amato, 1999a; Buchanan et al., 1996; Hetherington & Jodl, 1994). In general, stepparents can have a positive impact on their stepchildren's lives.

But stepfamilies also present special challenges. Although remarriage has the potential to increase financial security, there is also the risk that it may worsen children's financial circumstances. Some experts argue that remarried parents, particularly remarried fathers, may feel pressure to provide first for their new spouse's children from a prior marriage or for biological children they have with their new spouse. As a consequence, these parents may decrease financial and/or emotional support to their biological children from a previous marriage, especially if these biological children do not live with them (Wallerstein et al., 2000). Additionally, although this is not inevitable, the quality of parenting is often even lower in remarried families than in single-mother households. The rules change, family members take on different roles, and it takes time to sort things out and establish new routines and responsibilities. There may be competition between children and stepfather for the mother's time and attention, leaving the mother with less time than before to parent effectively. Such competition may be more stressful for girls than for boys, especially if daughters have been providing friendship and close emotional support to their divorced mothers. Stepfathers tend to be less involved and less emotionally supportive than continuously married biological fathers, and they provide less discipline and supervision of children (Hetherington & Clingempeel, 1992). There is some evidence that establishing a successful relationship between stepparent and stepchildren may be more difficult when the children are adolescents than when they are younger, but this finding is not consistent (Bray, 1999; Buchanan et al., 1996). All in all, even though stepparents have the potential to positively affect their stepchildren's development, children in remarried families are typically no better off in their behavioral and psychological outcomes, and sometimes show worse outcomes, than children of single-parent families (Amato, 1994).

Adopted Children

Millions of children grow up in adoptive families, whether adopted by relatives, stepparents, nonrelated adults, or adults of a different country or ethnicity. Not surprisingly, adopted children do much better on many psychological, educational, social, and emotional measures than children cared for in residential institutions, long-term foster care, or returned from foster care to parents who are unable or unwilling to parent effectively (Morgan, 1998; Triseliotis & Hill, 1990). Greater financial resources and stability, higher-quality parenting, highly motivated parents, significant parental emotional involvement and support, and a clear long-term parental commitment help adopted children develop a stronger sense of identity and enable them to take advantage of available financial and community resources. Studies of transracial adoptions, in which parents of one racial group adopt a child of a different race, have found no differences between transracial adoptees and children adopted by same-race parents in terms of their racial self-identity, general adjustment, or self-esteem (Baden, 2002; Feigelman, 2000; Silverman & Feigelman, 1990; Vroegh, 1997). As with children of divorced or single parents, it seems that the majority of adopted children adjust well and function normally.

At the same time, however, adopted children face special challenges. Overall, these challenges put adopted children at greater risk for negative outcomes than biological offspring, particularly when the problems become more severe (Miller, Xitao, Christensen, Grotevant, & van Dulmen, 2000). Adopted children and adolescents are more likely than other children to be referred for psychological treatment and more likely to show aggressive and delinquent behavior, learning disabilities, drug use, and school adjustment problems. In general, adopted children have greater difficulty when they are older (e.g., over 5 years of age) at the time of adoption, perhaps more because of negative early experiences than because of adoption. Adopted boys seem to have more difficulty than adopted girls. Sometimes problems do not emerge during infancy or early childhood but seem to emerge as children move through middle childhood and adolescence. However, adopted children show *better* scores on measures such as participation in academic clubs, prosocial behavior, self-reports of social problems, and self-reported withdrawal. The majority of adopted children report being satisfied with their adoptive status and report feeling emotionally attached to their adoptive parents (Brodzinsky, 1990, 1993; Howe, 1998; Kirschner, 1995; Miller et al., 2000; Morgan, 1998; Sharma, McGue, & Benson, 1996, 1998; Stams, Juffer, Rispens, & Hoksbergen, 2000; Triseliotis, 2000).

Despite the fact that adoption is clearly better for children than institutional care, long-term foster care, or shuttling between a troubled home and foster placements, some authors argue that adolescence is particularly difficult for adopted children. One of an adolescent's major developmental tasks is to define his or her identity. If adolescents know little about their biological backgrounds, this task becomes far more complicated. Adolescents who spend a lot of time wondering about their birth parents may have strained relations with their adoptive parents (Kohler, Grotevant, & McRoy, 2002). Proponents of **open adoption,** in which children are given a great deal of information about their biological parents, argue that such information will help adolescents deal with identity development more successfully. So far, however, research has not yet determined whether open adoption has this effect (Baran & Pannor, 1990; Chapman, Dorner, Silber, & Winterberg, 1987; Lifton, 1994).

Families with Lesbian or Gay Parents

Researchers estimate that as many as 14 million children in the United States have lesbian or gay parents (Patterson, 1992). The majority of these children were born while their biological parents were still in heterosexual marriages, and then one parent came out as gay or lesbian. An increasing number of lesbians, however, are using donor insemination to conceive biological children or are adopting or providing foster care for children. More gay men are also adopting children, providing foster care, or fathering their own biological children. Estimates of the numbers of children with gay or lesbian parents are probably low, because many parents conceal their homosexual orientation out of fear that they will lose custody, visitation, or adoption rights. Although different sexual orientations are becoming more widely accepted, many people still worry about whether gay and lesbian parents can give growing children a healthy environment. Discrimination also exists in the judicial system. In divorces the gay or lesbian parent often loses primary custody of the children, and most states still discourage adoption by gay and lesbian adults.

Does exposure to a gay or lesbian lifestyle disrupt the child's developing sense of identity or cause any other negative developmental outcomes? Charlotte Patterson (1992) conducted a thorough review of the research and concluded that "not a single study has found children of gay or lesbian parents to be disadvantaged in any significant respect relative to children of heterosexual parents" (p. 1036). Recent work has also found that children with lesbian parents are well adjusted and show positive relationships with their parents (Golombok et al., 2003). In her review Patterson found that children raised by lesbian or gay parents showed no disturbances in gender identity. Compared to children raised by heterosexual parents, they were just as happy with the gender to which they belonged and had no wish to be the opposite sex. Children showed no differences in their toy preferences, activities, interests, or occupational goals. They also showed no differences in favorite television programs, TV

open adoption

Arrangement in which adopted children have open access to information about their biological parents.

Lesbian and gay parents can provide just as healthy and caring an environment for raising children as heterosexual parents. Children raised in this family structure are not significantly different in any important way from children raised by heterosexual parents.

characters, or games. One study did suggest that children of lesbian mothers showed more "psychological femininity" than did children of heterosexual mothers (Rees, 1979).

Sexual orientation also did not differ. Children raised by gay or lesbian parents were not more likely to become homosexuals themselves. This finding is particularly interesting in view of the fact that these children received significant portions of their genes from gay or lesbian parents and grew up in environments created in part by those same parents. Still, as the children entered adolescence and early adulthood, their sexual fantasies were primarily heterosexual, and they were no more likely than other children to report being homosexual.

Like other children, children of gay or lesbian parents play mostly with same-sex peers. They show no differences in terms of popularity or other social skills. Other research has found no significant differences in sociability, hyperactivity, emotional difficulty, behavior problems, moral maturity, or measures of intelligence. In one study children with lesbian mothers saw themselves as more lovable, and parents and teachers rated them as more affectionate, responsive, and protective of younger children than children raised by heterosexual parents (Steckel, 1987). Differences between the groups of children were slight, however, and the findings were based solely on self-reports and subjective impressions.

Lesbian mothers also seem to do a better job of fostering contact between their children and their children's fathers. Children with lesbian mothers are 6 times more likely to have weekly contact with their fathers than children of divorced and other single heterosexual mothers (Golombok, Spencer, & Rutter, 1983). When heterosexual mothers do arrange visits with fathers, they report significantly more conflict surrounding the visit than do lesbian mothers. Even beyond the fathers, lesbian mothers arrange more visits with other adult males and relatives for their children. This holds true especially when they live in committed relationships with lesbian partners (Kirkpatrick, 1987).

Finally, although courts often award child custody on condition that the homosexual parent *not* live with his or her romantic partner, the research evidence actually shows advantages for children whose gay or lesbian parents live with committed partners (Patterson, 1992). One study documented higher self-esteem in daughters of lesbian mothers living with partners than in girls whose lesbian mothers lived alone (Huggins, 1989). We have already mentioned that mothers in lesbian partnerships are more likely to arrange male role models for their children. And in other research lesbian couples who conceived children by donor insemination showed as much awareness of parenting skills as heterosexual mothers and more awareness than heterosexual fathers, and both lesbian partners were equally involved in the child's activities (Flaks, Ficher, Masterpasqua, & Joseph, 1995; Vanfraussen, Ponjaert-Kristoffersen, & Brewaeys, 2003). In short, it is evident that lesbian and gay parents are perfectly capable of providing a healthy and caring environment for raising children.

Ethnically Diverse Families

Ethnic minority families are the fastest growing segment of the U.S. population. The census figures shown in Table 12.3 indicate that from 1990 to 2000 the rate of growth in minority populations was much faster than it was in the Euro-American population. It is clear that American families are becoming increasingly diverse. In earlier decades most of the research on family ethnicity focused on negative factors and outcomes. As you are no doubt aware, the rates of poverty, crime, homicide, incarceration, and other such problems are higher among minority groups than among white European Americans. By comparing ethnically diverse families to white families, researchers tended to emphasize the things that were "going wrong" in America's minority-group families. This **cultural deficit perspective** assumed negative outcomes were due to ways in which minority families were not "measuring up" to the standards of the majority white population. According to this perspective, progress occurs mostly when minorities become "more like whites."

Recently, however, researchers have learned that many of the negative outcomes associated with minority families are due more to poverty and difficulties in the neighborhoods that many minority families live in than to ethnic culture itself (Caspi, Taylor, Moffitt, & Plomin, 2000; Leventhal & Brooks-Gunn, 2000; McLoyd, 1998; Pinderhughes, Dodge, Bates, Pettit, & Zelli, 2000). A more positive approach to looking at minority families, the **strength and resilience perspective,** has emerged(Parke & Buriel, 1998). From this newer perspective, researchers are beginning to explore the ways in which minority families have survived, and

cultural deficit perspective
Research perspective that assumed the problems associated with minority-group families were due to the ways that these families were not "measuring up" to the standards of majority white families.

strength and resilience perspective
Research perspective that explores ways in which minority families have survived and even thrived in spite of historical patterns of racism, bigotry, and inequality.

TABLE 12.3 **Growth in U.S. Ethnic Diversity 1990–2000 (figures in millions)**

RACE OR LATINO ORIGIN	1990	2000	PERCENT INCREASE FROM 1990	GROWTH RATE VS. WHITE GROWTH RATE
Whites (non-Latino)*	188.9	194.6	3	—
Latinos (of any race)*	22.4	35.3	58	19.3 times faster
African Americans	30.0	34.7	16	5.3 times faster
Asian Americans and Pacific Islanders	7.3	10.6	45	15 times faster
Native Americans and Alaskans	2.0	2.5	25	8.3 times faster
Other races	9.8	15.4	57	19 times faster
More than one race*	NA	6.8	—	—

*The total U.S. population in the year 2000 was 281.4 million. The U.S. Census considers race separately from Latino origin. In the 2000 census 48 percent of Latinos identified themselves as white. In this table we present the number of whites who did not identify themselves as Latino (estimated by subtracting 48 percent of the Latinos totals from the 1990 and 2000 census totals for whites). The 2000 census was the first to allow respondents to identify themselves as belonging to more than one race (e.g., white *and* Asian).

Source: U.S. Census Bureau (2001).

in some cases even thrived, in spite of historical patterns of racism, bigotry, and inequality in this country. For example, slavery completely stripped basic human rights from African Americans; the federal government interned Japanese Americans in prison camps during the Second World War; settlers and pioneers forcibly removed Native American children from their families and taught them to deny the beliefs and traditions of their home cultures. Because of language and other cultural differences, many Mexican American and Asian American immigrants still have great difficulty being accepted in their new homeland. Many minority-group families struggle with how to blend their cultural background with that of the majority culture. This process, called *acculturation,* often takes several generations. Along the way it can produce conflicts between parents and children and misunderstandings between ethnic minority families and the majority culture (Arcia & Johnson, 1998; Contreras, Mangelsdorf, Rhodes, Diener, & Brunson, 1999; Gutierrez, Sameroff, & Karrer, 1988). The challenges and stresses of poverty, neighborhood disadvantage, and acculturation have widespread effects on families and children's outcomes (we will discuss these effects in Chapter 13). It is amazing how well most families have fared under such adverse conditions.

What characteristics of ethnic families have contributed to their strength and resilience? Table 12.4 summarizes some of the characteristics of several ethnic groups identified by researchers. One important factor seems to be the central role that the family often plays, particularly the extended family. For example, Latino parents teach children that their personal identity is inseparable from the larger identity of the family *(la familia).* In many ethnic groups, people value family and group cooperation over competition and personal achievement. Researchers have noted that African American families tend to show a strong sense of family and family obligation, fluid household boundaries (and great willingness to have relatives move into and out of the household), frequent interaction with relatives, frequent extended-family gatherings for holidays and special occasions, and a strong system of

Asian American parents tend to be strict, but they are generally caring and loving rather than harsh and punitive. Their *chiao shun* and *guan* styles are linked to superior school performance in their children.

TABLE 12.4 Sources of Ethnic Groups' Strength and Resilience

ETHNIC GROUP	ORIGINS	FAMILY FACTORS	CULTURAL TRADITIONS
Latino	Primarily immigrants from Mexico, Central and South America, Puerto Rico, and Cuba, and descendants of Spanish settlers	Personal identity connected to family identity Emphasis on extended-family systems First few years following immigration often spent living with extended-family members	Cooperation Group harmony Respect Obedience and respect for elders Traditional gender roles
African American	Primarily descendants of slaves, originally from West African tribes	Emphasis on extended-family systems Strong sense of family and family obligation Frequent interactions with relatives Grandmothers play important role in moral and religious focus, provide sense of family solidarity Emphasis on strict discipline, especially in working-class and poor families	West African traditions of spirituality, harmony, and communalism Emphasis on ethnic pride
Asian American	Immigrants from 28 countries or ethnic groups from Far East and Southeast Asia, including India, China, Philippines, Vietnam, Cambodia, Laos, Japan, Korea, Pakistan, Thailand, Hmong	Father dominant but emotionally distant Emphasis on *chiao shun* and *guan* styles of strict discipline among some groups	Religious traditions of respect for elders and family harmony Obedience and loyalty to parents Family needs placed above individual needs Traditional gender roles
Native American and Alaskan	Numerous peoples including 450 different tribal units with more than 100 different languages, among them Cherokee, Navajo, Chippewa, Sioux, Pueblos, Aleuts, Eskimos	Emphasis on extended-family systems, communal village structure Grandparents play important official and symbolic role Prior U.S. government policies disrupted family structure, producing lack of cultural and family role models	Cooperation Partnership Respect for elders Increasing emphasis on ethnic pride

Sources: Boykin & Toms (1985); Chao (1994); Parke & Buriel (1998); Reed (1982); Trimble & Medicine (1993).

mutual aid and support among family members (Hatchett & Jackson, 1999; Parke & Buriel, 1998). Asian American families teach their children to be obedient and loyal to their parents and to place the family above individual needs. Extended-family systems have also been crucial in helping Native Americans cope with the discrimination and many forms of adversity they have faced. Even when living in urban areas, American Indians often organize around several households of relatives that operate like a communal village (Parke & Buriel, 1998).

An emphasis on strict discipline is also characteristic of many ethnic groups. Both working-class African American parents and Latino families tend to rely on physical punishment, power assertion, and obedience to authority in their efforts to control their children (Parke & Buriel, 1998). This approach to discipline, however, seems to correlate more with poverty and dangerous neighborhoods than with ethnic identity as such. Lower-income whites also tend to use strict authoritarian discipline, and African American parents in the middle class tend to use a more child-centered and authoritative approach. Researchers are now recognizing that lower-income parents may use physical discipline in an attempt to protect their children from being victims or perpetrators of violence in dangerous communities, and as a way to emphasize the importance of performing well in school (Kelley, Sanchez-Hucles, & Walker, 1993; Parke & Buriel, 1998).

Mothers in China are more restrictive and controlling than Euro-American mothers (Chiu, 1987). As Chinese Americans adapt to life in the United States, they tend to take on parenting styles that lie between these two extremes. In her cross-cultural studies, Chao (1994, 2001) has pointed out that the strict control used by Chinese parents is not the same as the harsh and punitive style used by authoritarian parents in the United States. Chinese parents practice the concepts of *chiao shun* (meaning "training" or "teaching") and *guan* ("to govern" or "to care for or love"). They model appropriate behaviors for their children, and they govern their children firmly but with great care and love. Whereas harsh and punitive parenting (the authoritarian style) correlates with poor school performance in Euro-American students, children raised in the strict *chiao shun* and *guan* style used by many Asian American parents show superior school performance (Chao, 1994; Dornbusch, Ritter, Leiderman, Roberts, & Fraleigh, 1987). This type of cross-cultural research provides us with the important reminder that we cannot always view other cultures through the same lenses that we develop using Euro-American research samples.

A sense of ethnic pride can help buffer some of the hardships that ethnic children often face. Many African American families foster ethnic pride in their children as a way to help them confront the discrimination they will face in U.S. society (Parke & Buriel, 1998). In a national study of African American families, the children who were eventually more successful and upwardly mobile were the ones whose parents had emphasized ethnic pride, the importance of self-development, and an awareness of the racial barriers that they would face (Bowman & Howard, 1985). Similarly, Native Americans are increasingly working to build ethnic pride in their children, both to reconnect with the traditions of their cultures and to support their children's development. We all benefit by recognizing the unique strengths demonstrated by other cultures and diverse ethnic groups.

YOUR
PERSPECTIVE
NOTES

Are you from an ethnic family? Do the descriptions in the text and in Table 12.4 seem accurate to you?

LET'S REVIEW . . .

1. In thinking about the effects of different family structures, which of the following seems to be the most important in determining children's developmental outcomes?
   a. financial resources of the family
   b. whether the father has regular contact with the children
   c. the age at which the child experienced a parental divorce
   d. whether the parents were ever married to each other

2. The divorce-stress-adjustment model says that the overall effect of a divorce on children's outcomes depends on:
   a. genetically based parental traits.
   b. differences in the family's financial resources before and after the divorce.
   c. the emotional health and parenting skills of the parents.
   d. children's vulnerabilities in combination with stressors and protective factors.

3. Most children living in stepfamilies:
   a. have relatively negative views of their stepparents.
   b. experience a higher quality of parenting than children in single-parent households.
   c. are similar in outcomes to children in single-parent households.
   d. have significantly worse outcomes than children living in single-parent households.

4. Which of the following is *not* true of adopted children?
   a. Most adopted children adjust well, function normally, and are emotionally attached to their adoptive parents.

b. Adopted children are at greater risk for a number of negative outcomes than nonadopted children.

c. Children who were older when they were adopted are at greater risk for negative outcomes than those adopted at a younger age.

d. Transracial adoptees have significantly more difficulty developing a sense of self-identity than adoptees with same-race parents.

5. The cultural deficit perspective on ethnic families tends to focus on which of the following?

   a. the negative outcomes experienced by ethnic families

   b. various ways in which ethnic families have survived and succeeded despite adversities

   c. the role of the extended family in ethnic families

   d. differences in parenting styles between ethnic and nonethnic families

6. **True or False:** Moderate parentification can have positive effects on children's responsibility and competence.

7. **True or False:** Children raised by gay or lesbian parents are no more likely to be homosexuals themselves than are children raised by heterosexual parents.

Answers: 1. a, 2. d, 3. c, 4. d, 5. a, 6. T, 7. T

Child Care: Who's Watching the Kids?

It may surprise you to learn that **nonparental child care** (care provided by someone other than a child's parents), especially non*maternal* child care, is not new. In fact, exclusive maternal care of children has been the exception rather than the norm throughout most cultures and in most time periods (Lamb, 1998). It has been quite commonplace for aunts, grandmothers, other relatives, or family friends (usually women) to care for children. What has changed dramatically in this country over recent decades is the number of children cared for by paid care providers who are nonrelatives. This approach to child care has stimulated fierce debate as to the short- and long-term effects of nonparental care on children's development. Parents, development and education experts, and politicians and policy makers have all weighed in.

As you study this section, ask yourself these questions:

- What effect does nonparental child care have on children's attachment to parents? Should parents be concerned or relieved if their children show attachment to their nonparental caregiver, and why?

- Are children in full-time nonparental care more aggressive than other children? What effect does child care have on other social interactions and on cognitive skills?

- What are the components of quality child care? What effect does quality of care have on children's developmental outcomes?

- What are latchkey kids, and how does being a latchkey kid affect a child's development?

The Effects of Nonparental Child Care

Figure 12.4 shows changes in child-care arrangements for preschool children over recent decades. As you can see, the percentage of children in nonrelative family care settings and in child-care centers has increased dramatically; meanwhile, the percentage in the care of a

nonparental child care

Care provided for a child by someone other than the child's parents. Examples are family day care, child-care centers, and care provided by relatives and friends. Nonmaternal care (care provided by people other than mothers) includes care provided by fathers.

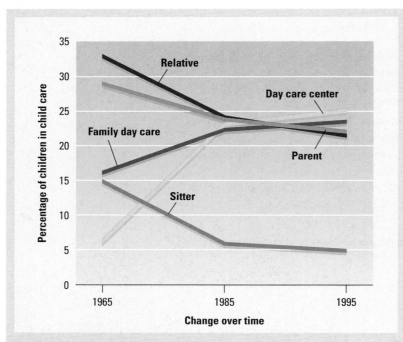

FIGURE 12.4 Changes in Child-Care Arrangements since 1965

Arrangements for child care have changed significantly over recent decades. Although parents and other relatives still care for many children, the number of children in family day care settings has increased 1.5 times and the number in child care centers is 4 times higher

Sources: Hofferth (1996); Smith (2000).

parent or other relative has decreased. The percentage in center-based care was more than 4 times higher in 1995 than in 1965, and these numbers do not include the millions of school-age children who are in some form of adult- or self-supervised care before and after school. Given that so many children receive nonparental care, what are the effects of this kind of care on children's emotional, social, and cognitive development?

This question is more difficult to answer than it might seem. Research since the 1960s has made it clear that numerous important factors must be taken into account—including the quality of the home environment, the quality of the care received, broader social conditions such as socioeconomic status, the age of the child when placed in care, the length of time the child spends in care, and specific vulnerabilities the child may have. By now, it should not surprise you to find that there are no simple or clear-cut answers!

■ **Effects on Attachment.** One of the most controversial issues surrounding nonparental child care is its possible effect on children's attachment. As you will recall from Chapter 9, infant–parent attachment is very important for a child's psychological and emotional health. There was widespread distress when early research showed a significantly increased risk for insecure attachment when children received extensive nonmaternal care during their first year. Studies rated 41 percent of such children as insecurely attached, versus 26 percent of children in maternal care at home (Belsky, 1988; Blehar, 1974). However, more recent studies with larger, more representative samples and using a variety of attachment measures have led experts to conclude that the majority of infants and preschoolers receiving nonparental care do form secure attachments to their parents. Day care by itself evidently does not affect attachment (Lamb, 1998).

Other recent reports, however, indicate the complexity of this issue and the need to consider multiple risk factors. A longitudinal study sponsored by the U.S. National Institute of Child Health and Human Development collected information on many aspects of development in more than 1,000 children across nine states (NICHD Early Child Care Research Network, 1997, 2001). This study indicated that child-care experiences alone did not significantly affect attachment, even when the quality, amount, stability, type of care, or age of entry into care were considered. However, attachment security was lower when low levels of maternal sensitivity and responsiveness *combined with* other risk factors such as poor-quality child care, greater amounts of child care, or lack of stability in care arrangements. Mothers' attitudes toward work and child care are also important. Infants are more likely to show secure attachments when their mothers are more committed to their work, return to their jobs earlier, and are less anxious about child care (Harrison & Ungerer, 2002).

Infants also form significant attachment relationships with their care providers. As with infant–parent attachment, the security of the infant–provider attachment is strongly influenced by the caregiver's sensitivity, responsiveness, and involvement, and by the quality of care he or she provides. The stability of care also is important: Children show greater attachment to caregivers who have provided care for longer periods of time. More secure infant–provider attachments correlate with several positive outcomes for children, including more advanced types of play, more positive relations with peers, and more positive interactions with other adults. Though parents may sometimes worry that a caregiver will replace them in their infant's affections, this does not seem to be the case. There is no evidence that secure infant–caregiver relationships disrupt infant–parent attachments (Lamb, 1998).

■ **Getting Along with Others.** Simply experiencing nonparental care does not in itself help or harm children's social interaction skills and behavior. An important mediating factor is the quality of the care received. Research has found that higher-quality care is associated with such positive outcomes as greater cooperativeness with other children,

Significant attachment to nonparental care providers is associated with positive outcomes and this does not interfere with parent–child attachment. The majority of infants and preschoolers receiving nonparental care show secure attachments to their parents, unless multiple risk factors are present.

more social participation, greater independence, less anxiety, and higher ratings of overall social competence (Andersson, 1992; Clarke-Stewart, Gruber, & Fitzgerald, 1994; Lamb, 1998; NICHD Early Child Care Research Network, 1998, 2002; Peisner-Feinberg et al., 2001; Vandell & Powers, 1983). Quality of care also interacts with other factors, so high quality is more important for some children than for others. For example, children with more socially fearful temperaments developed positive peer relations in high-quality care, but similar children in lower-quality care showed decreases in their social relations (Volling & Feagans, 1995). It is important to remember that child and family characteristics are still major influences, even when children spend a lot of time in child care. The NICHD Early Child Care study found that characteristics such as gender, temperament, infant–mother attachment, and sensitive mothering carried more weight than any child-care factors in explaining children's outcomes (NICHD Early Child Care Research Network, 1998).

Does extensive and/or early child care increase the frequency or intensity of behavior problems in children? Research to date does not offer a clear answer. Some studies show no relationship between nonparental care and behavior problems, but recent large-scale studies indicate that there may be cause for concern (Lamb, 1998). Children who spend more time in child care during their preschool years or who enter child care early show higher levels of teacher-reported behavior problems and more aggressiveness in kindergarten; are rated as getting along poorly with peers, being noncompliant, and having poorer conduct in third grade; have an increased likelihood of being uncooperative with adult requests, especially if the care is of lower quality (Bates et al., 1994; Lamb, 1998; Vandell & Corasaniti, 1990). Data from the NICHD Early Child Care study indicated that children who spend 30 hours or more per week in nonmaternal care are 3 times more likely to show behavioral problems when they reach kindergarten than children cared for primarily by their mothers. Seventeen percent of children in child care showed aggressive behaviors such as demanding attention, speaking

Some studies report greater aggressiveness and other behavior problems among children who spend significant amounts of time in nonparental child care from an early age. More work is needed to fully understand the complex effects of child-care, child, and parent characteristics.

out of turn, pushing, teasing, and fighting; in contrast, only 6 percent of children in maternal care showed such behaviors (Belsky, 2002; Belsky, Weinraub, Owen, & Kelly, 2001). However, earlier reports from this study did not show negative effects of early and extensive child care on the behavior of 2- or 3-year-olds, and the researchers in this study disagree about how to interpret their results (NICHD Early Child Care Research Network, 1998). Some claim the data indicate an important increased risk of behavioral problems. Others say the amount of aggressive behavior by children in child care is normal and that the low levels of aggressive behavior shown by children in maternal care may simply reflect these children's lack of opportunity to show such behaviors (Arnst, 2001). As with attachment and peer relationships, the quality of the child care seems to be an important mediating factor (Lamb, 1998).

■ **Effects on Cognitive Competence.**   Children who participate from a young age in programs specifically designed to improve school readiness, such as Head Start, have consistently shown positive effects on measures of cognitive development and school performance. These children achieve better results than children enrolled in community child-care centers or those who receive minimal nonparental child care (Campbell, Pungello, Miller-Johnson, Burchinal, & Ramey, 2001; Campell, Ramey, Pungello, Sparling, & Miller-Johnson, 2002; Lamb, 1998). Furthermore, the effects are most pronounced for those children whose mothers are least educated, and for children whose parents are more involved in the project. We will describe school readiness programs in more detail in Chapter 13 when we discuss the effects of schools on child development.

What are the cognitive effects of child care that does not aim specifically to enhance school readiness? Family and child background characteristics interact with child-care factors. For example, one study found that children enrolled in nonparental child care before age 1 had higher reading scores at ages 5 and 6 if they were from poor backgrounds, but lower scores if they were from more advantaged backgrounds. Math scores showed a similar pattern when enrollment began before 3 years of age (Caughy, DiPietro, & Strobino, 1994). A longitudinal study of children from advantaged backgrounds showed positive effects of a one-year preschool program for boys, but not for girls. Another showed benefits from preschool attendance for middle-class African American children but not for middle-class white children (Burchinal, Ramey, Reid, & Jaccard, 1995; Larsen & Robinson, 1989).

As with the other outcomes we have considered, the quality of the child care is an important mediating factor. In Sweden, known for its high-quality child care, children who entered day care early showed higher scores on cognitive measures at ages 8 and 13 than those who entered day care later. Children who spent more time in center-based care and received higher-quality care also had better scores (Broberg, Wessels, Lamb, & Hwang, 1997; Hwang & Broberg, 1992). Recent analyses of data from the NICHD Early Child Care study found that the quality of care, especially the degree of language stimulation, had a moderate but consistent effect on children's cognitive and language development scores at 15, 24, and 36 months, even after researchers took into account several family background variables (NICHD Early Child Care Research Network, 2000, 2002, 2003b; Peisner-Feinberg et al., 2001). The effects of quality are evident in middle-class children as well. Middle-class 2- and 4-year olds in child-care centers had higher scores on several measures of cognitive development than those in other care arrangements, including family day care and parental care; bigger differences were evident for centers of higher quality (Clarke-Stewart et al., 1994). In general, then, high-quality nonparental care can have positive effects on several aspects of children's cognitive competence, and children who come from more disadvantaged backgrounds show the greatest improvements. Lower-quality care, however, can have negative effects, especially if children would have received high-quality care at home (Lamb, 1998).

thinking OF JEREMY

◄ What role does being in child care play in Jeremy's behavior? How can Cassandra try to make Jeremy's attendance in child care exert a positive influence?

The Quality Question

As you will have noticed throughout this discussion, the *quality* of care affects many of the outcomes of nonparental child care. This effect has become clear in studies from several countries, and quality seems to be especially important when children come from disadvantaged backgrounds (Lamb, 1998). But what is "quality" in child care? Two components have been identified: *structural quality* and *process quality*. **Structural quality** concerns objective aspects of the child-care environment, such as the adult–child ratio (i.e., the number of children cared for by one caregiver), caregivers' formal education and experience, and the size of the care facility. Structural quality measures are indirect—theoretically, they indicate an environment in which higher-quality care is likely to occur, but they do not guarantee it. In contrast, **process quality** has to do with the interactions between adults and children and children's exposure to materials and activities that support their development (Burchinal, Howes, & Kontos, 2002; Helburn & Howes, 1996; Wishard, Shivers, Howes, & Ritchie, 2003). Process quality is a more direct indication of quality, because it relates to the actual experiences children have in the setting, including their interactions with caregivers. Unfortunately, measures of process quality are also harder to obtain and are more subjective, in that they involve observations and ratings of appropriateness. As a consequence, when states adopt child-care regulations, they usually base quality guidelines on the structural component.

Professional organizations such as the National Association for the Education of Young Children (NAEYC) set standards addressing many elements of both process and structural quality, and care providers must meet these standards in order to receive accreditation from the organization. The standards involve staff–child interactions, curriculum content, involvement of parents, staff training and qualifications, group size, adult–child ratios, and the appropriateness and safety of the physical environment. Governmental requirements for certification as a child-care facility are regulated at the state level, however, and they vary widely. In addition, parents seeking care for their children do not always know which elements experts consider to be

structural quality

In the context of child care, the quality of objective aspects of the child-care environment.

process quality

In the context of child care, the quality of the actual experiences children have in the setting.

TABLE 12.5 Questions to Ask When Seeking Quality Child Care

1. In general, are the children in this setting comfortable, relaxed, and happy? Are they happily involved in play and appropriate activities? Are they enjoying themselves?
2. Do the adults have specialized training in child development and early education?
3. What is the adult-to-child ratio? How many adults are there in all? How many children are there in all? NAEYC recommends that all groups have at least two teachers; that infants' group size not exceed 6 to 8 infants per group; that 2- to 3-year-olds should be in groups of no more than 10 to 14 children; and that group size for 4- to 5-year-olds should not exceed 16 to 20 children.
4. Are the toys, materials, and teachers' expectations different for and appropriate for different ages? Do the caregivers recognize and respect individual differences in the children's abilities, interests, and preferences?
5. Do caregivers address all areas of children's development (e.g., cognitive skills, language skills, social interactions, fine- and gross-motor skills, emotional expression, self-management of positive and negative emotions, behavior self-management)?
6. Does the staff meet on a regular basis to plan and evaluate the program?
7. Do the activities offer a balance between quiet indoor and more vigorous outdoor play; between individual and small group play; between child-initiated and teacher-directed activities?
8. Is the caregiver flexible? Is she or he willing to adjust the daily activities to meet children's individual needs and interests?
9. Are parents welcome to observe, discuss policies or problems, make suggestions, and participate? Is there open and honest communication between the caregiver/staff and parents?
10. Does the caregiver show respect for families' culture, background, and traditions? Does the caregiver offer information about the children's daily activities?

Source: Adapted from National Association for the Education of Young Children (2003). Retrieved January 12, 2003, from www.naeyc.org/accreditation/naeyc_accred/info_general-faq3.asp. Adapted with permission.

important. Or they may disagree with the experts; or other concerns such as cost, accessibility, and reliability of care may take precedence over quality (Scarr, 1998). If good-quality child care is important to you or someone you know, Table 12.5 presents some questions to keep in mind.

Unfortunately, as Figure 12.5 illustrates, the majority of child-care arrangements do not appear to be of high quality—or even of good quality. In fact, one study of center-based care in four different states concluded that an astonishing 86 percent of the assessed centers provided mediocre or poor-quality care. The study judged only 14 percent of the centers to be high enough on process quality measures to foster positive development in children. Infant and toddler care was just as disappointing: The researchers rated 40 percent of care centers as low quality and only 8 percent as high quality. Family day care settings were also mediocre. The study found 56 percent to be at an adequate or custodial level, 35 percent inadequate, and only 9 percent good quality (Helburn & Howes, 1996; Kontos, Howes, Shinn, & Galinsky, 1995).

It is true that better-quality child care costs more than poor-quality care, but perhaps not as much more as you might think. One analysis found that raising the quality of care from good to excellent was indeed expensive, but that improving quality from mediocre to good increased the cost by only about 10 percent. Even so, not all parents can afford the full cost of child care. Currently, families whose annual incomes place them just *above* the poverty level tend to use the poorest-quality care; they cannot afford the full cost of good-quality care, but their income is too high for them to qualify for government child-care assistance (Helburn & Howes, 1996). We know how to improve the quality of child care. The issues are how to pay for the improvements, whether and how to regulate the quality of care, and how much of an improvement is needed. There is ongoing and heated debate about these issues. No one wants children placed in unsafe or detrimental environments, but not everyone agrees that high-quality care has enough of an effect to make the increased cost worthwhile (Helburn & Bergmann, 2002; Scarr, 1998).

thinking OF JEREMY

What aspects of quality child care might be especially important for Jeremy, given his present difficulties and changing family situation?

Latchkey Kids: Children Caring for Themselves

So far we have focused on young children who are cared for by adults other than their parents. What about the increasing number of **latchkey kids,** school-age children who have no adult supervision at all during the hours after school and before their parents get home from work? Numerous forms of child self-care exist. Some children are regularly home alone; some go to unsupervised or poorly supervised friends' homes; some go to public places such as libraries, malls, or parks, where adults are present but not responsible for the children's safety and well-being. Estimates of the number of children in self-care vary widely, from 4 percent of children ages 5 to 12 having self-care as their regular after-school arrangement to as many as 44 percent of third graders who report spending at least some after-school time in self-care. In general, self-care is more common for boys than for girls, for older children than for younger ones, and for upper-income white families than for poorer or for ethnic families (Lamb, 1998; Vandell & Shumow, 1999). It may surprise you to learn that the circumstances of many unsupervised children actually "fit the legal definition of child neglect in most states" (Lamb, 1998, p. 113).

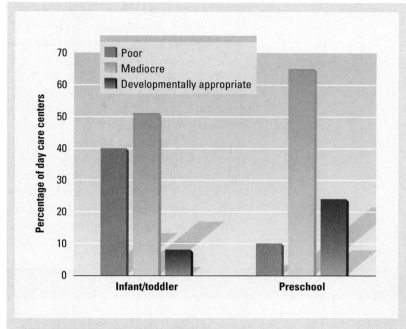

FIGURE 12.5 Quality of Center-Based Child Care

Ratings of the quality of child care show that on average, the care provided in centers and family day care homes is most often mediocre.

Sources: Helburn & Howes (1996); Kontos et al. (1995).

There is much less research on self-care than on adult-supervised care, especially for the youngest of children in self-care. Some researchers report that children in self-care are at increased risk for social, academic, and emotional problems; others have found few short- or long-term differences between the outcomes of children in self-care and those of children being cared for by adults (Rodman, Pratto, & Nelson, 1985; Woods, 1972; Woodward & Fine, 1991). Several authors suggest that if used wisely, self-care can have potential benefits such as greater independence, self-reliance, resourcefulness, and self-confidence (Bryant, 1994; Belle, 1999; Hoffman, 1979). As with adult-supervised care, answers are not straightforward but depend on several factors. Important factors are the type of self-care, how much time is spent in self-care, the age of the child, and family and neighborhood characteristics (Lamorey, Robinson, Rowland, & Coleman, 1999; Vandell & Shumow, 1999). For example, Steinberg (1986) found that fifth through ninth graders who stayed home alone were no more susceptible to harmful peer pressure than those in adult care. However, youngsters who went to unsupervised friends' houses or to public places like shopping malls were more susceptible. The increased exposure to negative peer pressure combined with the absence of nearby adult supervision may be difficult for these young adolescents to withstand. The amount of time spent in self-care also is important. Children who spend more time home alone show more behavior problems, lower social competence, and lower grades than children in adult-supervised care. This is especially true for younger children and for children from lower-income households (Pettit, Laird, Bates, & Dodge, 1997; Vandell & Posner, 1999; Vandell & Shumow, 1999).

When is a child ready for self-care? The answer will certainly depend on the child's degree of cognitive and emotional maturity and on characteristics of the neighborhood. More

latchkey kids

School-age children who have no adult supervision during the hours after school and before their parents get home from work.

authoritative parenting can help make self-care experiences more successful. It is also helpful to have regular parent–child telephone contact, a trusted adult neighbor available nearby, and required rules and routines that children are familiar with (Lamb, 1998; Steinberg, 1986).

As you have seen throughout this chapter, the family environment exerts a powerful influence on children. Parents contribute genetic predispositions and make important choices about environments in which children will spend significant amounts of time, such as day care settings. But parents also shape children's development through their parenting styles, disciplinary practices, cultural and ethnic traditions, and choices of family structure. We began this chapter by prompting you to think about your family and its structure and processes. Return to that question now, and think about the family characteristics and practices that supported you in your development. We hope you will celebrate these positive aspects. At the same time, we hope you will use the information in this chapter to make other family environments (yours or those you work with professionally) even more positive settings for healthy development.

LET'S REVIEW . . .

1. The research on attachment and nonparental child care indicates that:
   a. even lower-quality care has no effect on children's attachment to their parents.
   b. child care can interact with other risk factors to affect attachment.
   c. the stronger the infant–caregiver attachment, the lower the infant–parent attachment.
   d. children who spend more hours in child care show insecure child–parent attachment.

2. The effects of nonparental child care on cognitive skills depend on:
   a. the stability of the child care.
   b. the degree of child–caregiver attachment.
   c. how many hours each day the child spends in care.
   d. care quality combined with family and child characteristics.

3. Process quality in child care has to do with:
   a. objective aspects of the child-care setting.
   b. the experiences and interactions a child has in the child-care setting.
   c. those aspects of the child-care setting that are regulated by the government.
   d. the degree of formal training in child development the caregiver has received.

4. Which of the following is *true* regarding self-care?
   a. Children should not be placed in self-care before the age of 15.
   b. Behavior problems are no more frequent for younger children than for older children in self-care.
   c. Younger children and those who live in less safe neighborhoods show more negative effects of self-care than older children or those in safer neighborhoods.
   d. Self-care in public places or in unsupervised friends' homes is associated with better outcomes than self-care at home alone.

5. **True or False:** Experts agree that children who attend nonparental child care are significantly more aggressive than children who do not.

6. **True or False:** In general, the average quality of nonparental child care in the United States is mediocre.

Answers: 1. b, 2. d, 3. b, 4. c, 5. F, 6. T

thinking
BACK TO JEREMY

Now that you have studied this chapter, you should be able to apply at least a dozen concepts and research findings in understanding Cassandra and Jeremy's situation. Jeremy's parents are clearly showing decreased parenting effectiveness, perhaps because of their changing family structure. Cassandra may be able to help by suggesting some resources for the family, such as support groups, books on parenting during family transitions, and the like. As Jeremy's family adjusts to the new family structure, his parents must try to minimize their conflicts. They need to find ways to help Jeremy talk about his emotions and learn positive coping skills. They also need to make sure that Jeremy's father remains involved with him.

It will be important for Cassandra to offer Jeremy positive interactions and a respectful, positive environment in the child-care setting, as he is already at risk for negative outcomes in several respects. Cassandra should continue to be watchful for instances of aggressive behavior and other inappropriate social interactions on Jeremy's part. At the same time, it's essential that she use appropriate disciplinary techniques so as not to compound Jeremy's difficulties. Perhaps she can try to help Jeremy keep up with his academic work during his time in child care, if he and his parents would like her assistance. Jeremy is clearly not ready for self-care; perhaps Cassandra can help Jeremy's parents think about the potential risks and benefits of self-care and how to determine if Jeremy is ready. She could also provide information about possible child-care programs that might offer appropriate structure and opportunities.

Jeremy's parents might consider professional counseling, which would be helpful as they negotiate the changes ahead. Cassandra might suggest that a counselor help them learn about authoritative parenting practices, and ask how she can help support this effort in the child-care center. Appropriate discipline techniques such as managing the situation, setting clear rules and limits, and praising good behavior will be more effective if Jeremy encounters them both at home and child care. Using these and other concepts and research findings from this chapter, you should be able to offer advice to help Jeremy and his family. You should also be able to adjust the advice to fit the needs of children who are younger or older than Jeremy, or who live in other family structures.

What are Baumrind's four parenting styles? What outcomes are associated with each?

Parental warmth and control combine to create four parenting styles. Authoritative parents are warm and consistent, exert firm control, listen to their children, and use supportive methods of discipline. Their children show the most positive psychological, emotional, and academic outcomes. Authoritarian parents exert firm control but show little warmth or respect and use harsh and punitive disciplinary methods. Their children are more aggressive and hostile and do worse in school. Permissive parents do not set or enforce limits; they avoid confrontation with their children and do not require their children to behave maturely or responsibly. Their children are impulsive, are less self-confident, and do less well in school. Rejecting/neglecting parents ignore or actively reject their children; they do not discipline their children, or do so harshly and inconsistently. Their children show the worst psychological, emotional, and academic outcomes. Research on parenting styles and outcomes is largely correlational, however, and the effects are not as large or consistent across gender or ethnic groups as might be expected.

What are the effects of using spanking for discipline? What are other, more appropriate discipline methods?

Spanking does not improve children's behavior over the long term, nor does it teach children appropriate behavior. Children who are spanked more often are more physically violent and aggressive, more depressed, and more likely to hit others. Alternative methods of discipline include managing the situation, setting clear rules and limits, praising good behavior, using explanation and reasoning, removing privileges, and using timeouts.

How does divorce affect children?

The divorce-stress-adjustment perspective says that the effects of divorce depend on interactions among the stresses produced, specific vulnerabilities of the child, and a variety of protective factors. The selection model says that long-lasting effects are due to parent characteristics rather than to the divorce process as such. Children of divorced parents are at increased risk for several behavioral, emotional, academic, and occupational outcomes. Most experience heightened stress and emotional pain. Some effects may not become apparent until adolescence or young adulthood, but most children adjust reasonably well. Lack of money, ineffective parenting, and a decrease in connections to the community underlie much of the effect of divorce.

What are the developmental outcomes of children whose parents do not marry, and of children in stepfamilies?

Children whose parents do not marry are similar in outcomes to children of divorce, and for similar reasons: problems with finances, parenting quality, and community connections. Father absence has a negative impact on many aspects of children's development, largely because of reduced finances and loss of the contributions fathers make to parenting, behavioral control and monitoring, and emotional and psychological support. Living in a stepfamily can have a positive impact on children's outcomes, but it often does not. There are better outcomes if the stepfamily remains stable and includes and takes responsibility for the children. Parenting quality often declines in stepfamilies, and stepfathers tend to be less involved with and less emotionally supportive of their stepchildren than biological fathers.

What are the developmental outcomes of adopted children and of children raised by lesbian or gay parents?

Most adopted children adjust well, function normally, and report feeling emotionally attached to their adoptive parents. However, they are at increased risk for negative outcomes, especially if problems become more severe and especially during adolescence. Children raised by gay or lesbian parents show no disadvantages across a wide variety of measures.

What are some characteristics of different ethnic families that might contribute to their resilience?

Many ethnic cultures emphasize group harmony, respect, cooperation, connection to family, obedience, traditional gender roles, and an authoritarian parenting style. African American, Latino, and Native American families draw strength from the support of the extended-family system, respect for elders, and ethnic pride. In working and lower-income African American and Latino families, strict discipline may represent an effort to protect children from dangerous neighborhoods.

How does nonparental child care affect children's development?

Nonparental child care by itself does not seem to affect children's attachment, behavior, social interactions, or cognitive development. Effects depend on several factors, including the quality of the nonparental care, parent characteristics, the quality of the home environment, and specific child characteristics. Attachment security is lower if there are multiple risk factors. Noncompliance and aggressive behavior may increase in children who enter care at early ages and spend long hours there, but the quality of nonparental care and other child and home factors seem to be more important. High-quality nonparental care can have positive effects on cognitive skills, especially for children from disadvantaged backgrounds. Lower-quality care can have negative effects, however, especially for children from advantaged backgrounds.

What is "quality" child care?

Structural quality has to do with objective environmental conditions in which higher-quality care is more likely to occur. Process quality, a more direct measure, relates to the interactions and experiences children have in the care setting. The average quality of child care in the United States is mediocre at best. Improving child care from mediocre to good quality would probably cause about a 10 percent cost increase.

What are latchkey kids? How does self-care affect developmental outcomes?

Latchkey kids are school-age children in some form of self-care during nonschool hours. They may have an increased risk for social, academic, and emotional problems, but this result is not consistent. The type of self-care, how much time a child spends in self-care, the child's age, and family and neighborhood characteristics are important factors. More authoritative parenting, regular telephone contact with parents, access to trusted adult neighbors, and established rules and routines can make self-care more successful once children are ready for it.

KEY TERMS

authoritarian parents (465)

authoritative parents (464)

cultural deficit perspective (491)

discipline (468)

divorce-stress-adjustment perspective (478)

guilt gap (476)

joint legal custody (483)

joint physical custody (483)

latchkey kids (501)

nonparental child care (495)

open adoption (489)

parental control (463)

parental warmth (463)

parentification (481)

permissive parents (465)

process quality (499)

punishment (468)

rejecting/neglecting parents (465)

selection model (478)

sleeper effect of divorce (482)

stalled revolution (476)

strength and resilience perspective (491)

structural quality (499)

timeout (472)

wage gap (476)

Chapter 13

Schools, Media, and Culture

A PERSPECTIVE TO think ABOUT

> "How important is it to go to a good school? Is it OK for Michelle to watch so much television? What effect is living in a poor neighborhood likely to have?"

Anna Wong and her daughter Michelle live in a poor Asian neighborhood that is getting worse every year. Anna moved here 15 years ago with her parents when they immigrated from China. Anna has lived here ever since and is now raising her daughter Michelle in this familiar environment. The neighborhood still has many Chinese and Asian American families, including Anna's parents and cousins. Michelle is a very lively and happy 4-year-old, but Anna is having more and more trouble managing the little girl's behavior. Michelle has been having trouble getting along with other children lately, pushing and hitting to get her way instead of waiting her turn or using words to talk about what she wants. Anna finds herself punishing her daughter frequently. She often encourages Michelle to sit still and watch TV, as this keeps her quiet, even though she's pretty sure this isn't good for a child.

Michelle has been attending a federally funded Head Start program four mornings a week. Anna needs to work full-time now, however, so she is thinking of taking Michelle to her cousin's house five days a week for full-time baby-sitting. Although Michelle will soon be old enough for school, Anna is concerned about the quality of the local schools. When Anna herself attended the neighborhood schools, they did little to help her adjust as she progressed into junior high; and their emphasis on competition and public bragging about grades made her very uncomfortable. Lately Anna has been thinking about moving to another city that might have better jobs and schools, but she is concerned about her extended family. She is very close to her family and is afraid that they will all feel very lonely and isolated if she moves.

How worried should Anna be? How important is it for Michelle to go to a good preschool program and local school? Is it OK for Michelle to watch so much television? What effect is living in a poor neighborhood likely to have on Anna and Michelle, and how easy would it be for Anna to leave?

As you read this chapter, think about the information from Anna's perspective. What would you tell Anna to help her think about her situation? Are there differences (or similarities) between your cultural background and Anna's that could make it harder (or easier) for the two of you to understand each other's concerns? After studying this chapter, you should be able to give Anna some insight into how schools, the media, and culture affect her daughter's development. You should be able to use at least a dozen specific concepts in your answer.

 As you read this chapter, look for the questions that ask you to think about what you're learning from Anna's and Michelle's perspectives.

Like Anna, most parents worry about the quality of their children's schools and the effects of television on their children's behavior. Many must also be concerned about the neighborhoods they live in and the economic security of their families. As you may recall from Chapter 1, Bronfenbrenner's ecological systems theory and other dynamic systems theories emphasize the complex interactions of numerous forces and how they affect children's development. In this chapter we will describe three of these forces: schools, media, and the larger cultural context. These factors interact with families and children in complex ways, and the influences are multidirectional. Schools, for example, can have a direct effect on what children learn—but schools also reflect the characteristics and needs of the children they serve. Media sources such as television affect children—and also the interactions that exist between parents and children. Although we cover each main topic separately, please keep in mind that these and many other factors operate simultaneously: Children develop within a complex web of influences and interactions that change over time.

Schools and Development

As you know from experience, children spend many hours in school. As of the year 2000, children in the United States were required to spend about 179 days per year in school (ranging from 173 days in North Dakota to 187 days in Texas), or about 1,250 hours each year. From 1st to 12th grade, this adds up to more than 15,000 hours in school—not including time spent in kindergarten, preschool, or any school-related extracurricular activities. It is easy to see why schools have such an important influence on children's development.

As you study this section, ask yourself these questions:

- How does early childhood education affect development? Who benefits from quality early childhood education programs, and why?

- What are *school readiness* and *achievement motivation*? Why are these important for child development?

- What are some of the important features of effective schooling? How does each feature influence children's school success?

- What differences in school achievement exist between nations and between ethnic groups? What factors explain these differences, and how can schools increase their positive impact on development?

Early Childhood Education

A key theme of this book is that children's early experiences provide a critical foundation for positive cognitive and social development. Unfortunately, some children's early environments do not provide strong foundations, and these children are at risk for numerous academic and social problems. Many are already behind when they enter kindergarten or first grade. Early childhood intervention projects were developed to improve these children's readiness to benefit from formal schooling, increase their success in school, and improve the quality of their lives.

■ **Project Head Start and Other Early Intervention Programs.** Begun in 1965 as part of President Lyndon Baines Johnson's War on Poverty, *Project Head Start* is a federally funded, comprehensive program designed to improve academic achievement and opportunity for children from ages 3 to 5. These children receive health and social services as well as educational support and their parents are included as an integral part of the program (Washington & Oyemade, 1987; Zigler & Styfco, 1993). Interestingly, Urie Bronfenbrenner was a member of the committee that designed the program. As you can imagine, he was a strong supporter of this comprehensive approach! Head Start has changed over the years, going from a part-time-only program to full-time in some places. The age range for services also expanded: In 1994 Congress authorized the Early Head Start program, which assists even younger children, ages newborn to 3 years.

Before Project Head Start expanded to meet the needs of more children, there was the *Abecedarian Project*. Designed to assess the impact of full-time, high-quality intervention beginning in infancy, the Abecedarian Project served primarily African American children living in poverty (Ramey, Campbell, & Blair, 1998). Infants at high risk for problems in cognitive development entered the program at 4.5 months, on average, and continued until at least age 5. Another well-known early intervention program was the High/Scope Perry Preschool program in Ypsilanti, Michigan. This project offered high-quality part-day intervention during the school year (October to May) for poor African American children ages 3 to 5 (Schweinhart, Barnes, & Weikart, 1993; Schweinhart & Weikart, 1998). The program focused on children's active involvement in directing their own learning. It also included weekly home visits to teach parents how to support their children's educational progress.

■ **Effects of Early Intervention Programs.** What effects have early childhood interventions had on children's development? Research reviews have shown the following (Barnett, 1998; McKey et al., 1985; Schweinhart et al., 1993; Zigler, Styfco, & Gilman, 1993):

▶ Compared to children not in such programs, the children in early interventions show an immediate gain of about eight IQ points, but in many cases the difference "fades away" during the elementary school years. The Abecedarian project is an exception, showing IQ differences up to 21 years of age (the oldest age tested so far), as you can see in Figure 13.1 (Campbell, Pungello, Miller-Johnson, Burchinal, & Ramey, 2001).

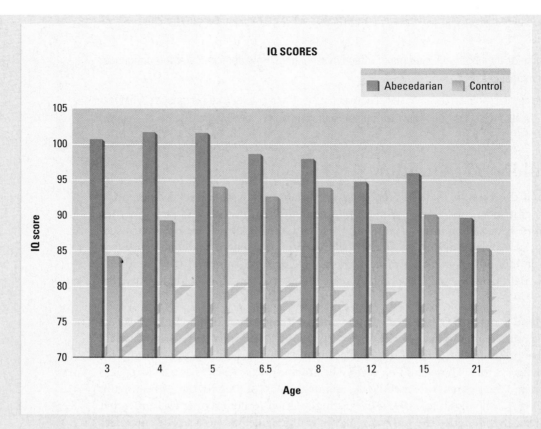

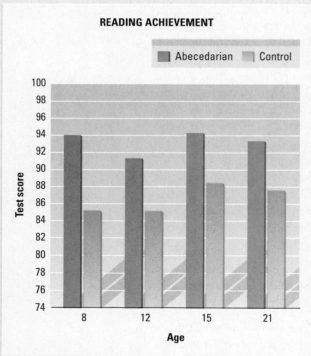

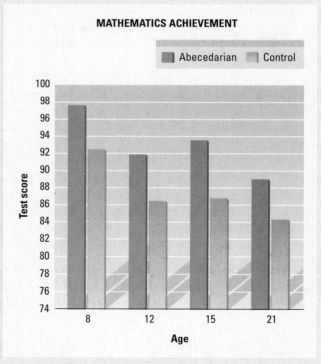

FIGURE 13.1 IQ, Reading, and Math Scores for Children in the Abecedarian Project

Children who participated in the Abecedarian program continued to show higher scores for years after the program ended.

Source: Data from Campbell et al. (2001).

- The children score higher on reading and mathematics achievement tests. Studies of Head Start programs find that these differences fade, but other programs show achievement differences up to adolescence or young adulthood (see Figure 13.1).

- The children show better academic progress on additional measures of academic progress, such as numbers of students placed in special education classes, and rates of graduation from high school, as shown in Figure 13.2.

- The children show other social and health benefits. For example, when surveyed as adults, participants in the High/Scope Perry Preschool intervention were less likely to have been arrested or to have received welfare payments, and more likely to have a better-paying job (for the men), be employed (for the women), and own their own home (see Figure 13.2) (Schweinhart et al., 1993). As a group, children in Head Start have better overall health, immunization rates, and nutrition than non-program children.

Researchers have analyzed the economic benefits of one program, the High/Scope Perry Preschool, although not of the other two (Barnett, 1993). In 1992 dollars the average per-child cost of the program was about $12,356. The average per-child economic benefit—reflecting lower expenses for special education, grade retention, welfare assistance, and

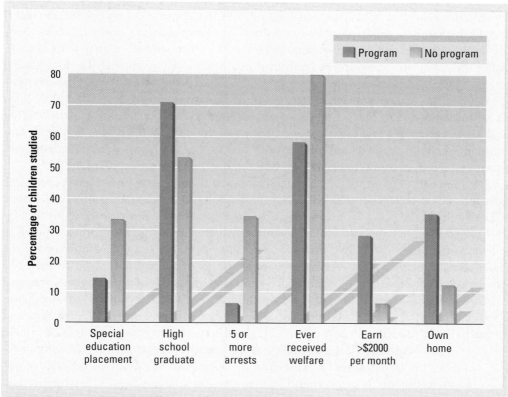

FIGURE 13.2 Results from the High/Scope Perry Preschool Project

Children in the High/Scope Perry Preschool program showed long-lasting benefits on measures of academic progress and of social welfare.

Source: Adapted from L. J. Schweinhart, H. V. Barnes, & D. P. Weikart. (1993). *Significant benefits: The High/Scope Perry Preschool study through age 27* (Monographs of the High/Scope Educational Research Foundation, Number 10), pp. xvi–xvii. Ypsilanti, MI: The High/Scope Press. Adapted with permission.

criminal justice; lower costs to potential crime victims; and higher tax receipts from higher earnings—was about $88,433. That amounted to a return of *$7.16 for every $1.00 spent on the program.* To be sure, this level of economic benefit is probably not typical of all early childhood intervention programs. Still, this impressive outcome is certainly of interest to program developers and policy makers alike.

In general, programs such as the High/Scope Perry Preschool and Abecedarian projects show greater and longer-lasting benefits than Head Start. Why? Several factors probably play a role. Among these may be the quality of the instructional programs, the length of the programs, teacher training and pay, the numbers of at-risk children served and the seriousness of their challenges, and funding differences. However, the first large-scale evaluation of the Early Head Start Program offers encouraging results. The 3-year-old children in the program showed significant benefits on tests of cognitive skills, language development, and socioemotional development such as lower aggression and greater attention skills. There were also positive effects on *parents'* skills and behaviors—including such things as more positive parenting practices and greater support of children's learning by, for example, reading to their child every day (Love et al., 2002).

How do early intervention programs produce long-term effects? It's possible that children's motivation to learn increases; there is also some evidence that parents' behavior and attitudes change in ways that help prepare children for school (Machida, Taylor, & Kim, 2002; Parker, Boak, Griffin, Ripple, & Peay, 1999). But probably most important is a direct improvement in children's cognitive abilities (Abbott-Shim, Lambert, & McCarty, 2003; Barnett, Young, & Schweinhart, 1998; Campbell & Ramey, 1994). Greater cognitive readiness makes it more likely that these children can be successful in academic tasks in their early school years. The overall result may be a sort of snowball effect, in which success in early years leads to greater success in later years, and so on throughout the children's schooling. The long-lasting benefits of the Abecedarian project seem to suggest that it is important to start the intervention early in life—earlier than Head Start programs have traditionally done (Campbell et al., 2001; Fenichel & Mann, 2001). And continuing support from schools seems to help children maintain the gains they make in Head Start. For example, Head Start students fare better academically when the public schools offered both educational and family services support, and encouraged stronger connections between home and school (Mantzicopoulos, 2003).

It's important to remember, however, that even though increased readiness may improve the odds of greater success, it does not guarantee it (Campbell et al., 2001). Look closely at the data from the Abecedarian and High/Scope Perry Preschool projects graphed in Figures 13.1 and 13.2. Though the children who participated in the interventions continued to do better than those who didn't, problems are still evident. For example, 59 percent of the High/Scope participants had received welfare assistance at some point, and 7 percent had been arrested 5 or more times. Other reports show that by age 27 these participants averaged 2.3 arrests—half as many as the nonprogram children, but a relatively high rate nonetheless (Schweinhart et al., 1993). Additionally, although the cognitive scores (IQ, reading, and math) of the Abecedarian participants remained higher than those of controls, all but the reading scores showed a steady decline as the years went by. It is clear that early interventions can be a positive force for child development, but they do not operate in isolation. As systems theories remind us, many additional home, school, community, and cultural factors certainly play a role.

Controversy about the most effective ways to implement early intervention programs is intense. There is no better example of this than the debate that still surrounds Project Head Start almost four decades after its beginning. To find out more about this program, read the Social Policy Perspective box called "Project Head Start: What Lies Ahead?"

thinking
OF ANNA & MICHELLE

Is Michelle's Head Start program likely to help her? Why, and in what ways? What obstacles will Michelle still face when she enters school, despite her participation in Head Start?

Project Head Start: What Lies Ahead?

Project Head Start and Early Head Start provide comprehensive health, nutrition, education, and social services to low-income children from birth to school age. Federal Head Start grants are made directly to agencies that apply for them (often public schools or community agencies). Each program site must meet specific program standards, but sites typically have some freedom in how requirements are met. Head Start programs have positive effects on children's development, but the effects have generally not been as strong or long-lasting as some other programs (Barnett, 1998; McKey et al., 1985; Fenichel & Mann, 2001).

There is continuing debate over Head Start. Some have questioned whether the benefits are worth the immense cost of the program (about $6.5 billion in 2002). Few argue against providing services to needy preschoolers, but many contend that including infants substantially increases the overall program cost while having limited effects. Serious questions have also been raised about whether it is ethical to limit the early educational choices of poor preschoolers. As an alternative to spending billions on a governmentally controlled program, low-income parents could be given vouchers and allowed to select from any early-education or child-care arrangements, including Head Start centers. According to psychologist Sandra Scarr, "Head Start is a dinosaur, a remnant of the government-knows-best philosophy of an earlier era" and "should have to compete in the marketplace" (Scarr, 1999, p. 144). There is vigorous debate over who should control the Head Start program ("Bush Calls for Revamping," 2003). Some policy makers argue that Head Start should be a state government responsibility rather than a federal one. Funding could be provided in block grants to states, with states responsible for administering the funds, developing policies about the program's implementation, overseeing quality, and integrating Head Start services with other state programs. Advocates argue that states are better able to determine the needs of the children living there and coordinate services to meet those needs. Opponents of this change argue that the comprehensive services and community and parent involvement that are hallmark strengths of Head Start would likely be lost. Critics also assert that many states are unprepared to take on the responsibilities that would be involved if this change were made. While some states do an admirable job of providing early childhood intervention to low-income families, programs in other states are poor or nonexistent (Ramey, 1999; Ripple, Gilliam, Chanana, & Zigler, 1999).

Is early intervention worth its cost? How early should intervention begin, and which children should be targeted? Would a voucher system be more fair and effective? Who should control and pay for Head Start? What social policy recommendations would you make? ■

Effective Schooling: What Does It Take?

What were your elementary, middle, and high schools like? Were they places where your intellectual horizons widened, where you enjoyed spending time, where you felt supported and safe? What does it take for schools to have a positive influence on cognitive, social and emotional growth? The research on this topic is vast; this section will offer a brief review of some major topics.

■ **School Readiness.** Although educators have long been interested in fostering children's readiness for schooling, defining readiness is not as easy as you might think. Schools often use chronological age to determine eligibility for entry, but several studies have shown that age is not a good predictor of academic success or learning (Carlton & Winsler, 1999; Morrison, Griffith, & Alberts, 1997). National surveys have asked parents and kindergarten teachers what they think are important readiness indicators. Both parents and teachers emphasize children's overall physical health, verbal communication skills, and enthusiasm. Teachers also emphasize social skills and ability to follow classroom rules and procedures. And parents— but not most teachers—see academic knowledge, such as familiarity with the alphabet or counting skills, as an important prerequisite (Lewit & Baker, 1995). Other educators believe that self-control over behavior and emotions, the ability to keep attention focused, and the ability to avoid impulsive responding are major factors that underlie readiness (Blair, 2002; NICHD Early Child Care Research Network, 2003a). Many school districts use standardized assessments to assess readiness, but these tests show only low to moderate levels of predictive validity. In other words, the tests incorrectly identify many children as not ready for school (Carlton & Winsler, 1999).

How ready are our nation's children? On national surveys in the early 1990s, kindergarten teachers rated approximately 65 percent of their students as ready for kindergarten on all five of the readiness characteristics the surveys assessed—rested, able to verbally communicate clearly, enthusiastic and interested, able to take turns and share, and able to sit still (Lewit & Baker, 1995). The overall health of children entering school, including immunization rates, has improved over the 1990s (National Education Goals Panel, 1999). One study assessed a nationally representative sample of 22,000 children who entered kindergarten in the fall of 1998. The majority of children had basic letter and number knowledge, showed good prosocial skills, persisted at tasks, were eager to learn, and could pay attention (Denton & Germino-Hausken, 2000). However, almost all the measures varied according to factors such as age (older kindergartners score higher); family type (children from single-parent homes tend to score lower); mothers' education (the higher the mothers' level of education, the higher the children's scores); race/ethnicity (non-Hispanic white and Asian children score higher than African American and Hispanic children, especially on teacher ratings of behavior); and/or socioeconomic status (children from higher-income families score higher) (Stipek & Ryan, 1997). So although the majority of children seem reasonably ready for school and there have been important improvements, there is still much room for improvement.

Children old enough for school but identified as not ready present a dilemma for educators. Is it best to "redshirt," or hold back, these children and keep them in their home or in preschool for an additional year, place them in a transition class (either before kindergarten or between kindergarten and first grade), or retain them for an additional year of kindergarten? None of these options has been very successful in helping children catch up to peers who were not kept back. In fact, several studies have found that children recommended for delay, retention, or transition classes but promoted anyway (perhaps at their parents' insistence) score just as well on achievement tests as their classmates (Carlton & Winsler, 1999). Some educators believe we need to rethink the idea of school readiness. They argue that it is *schools* that must be ready, rather than placing the burden of readiness on children (Carlton & Winsler, 1999; Dockett & Perry, 2003). These educators, drawing on Vygotsky's theory of cognitive development (recall Chapter 5), say that holding back unready children deprives them of the "very culture and learning situations [they] need." Also, postponing school entry keeps these children in the environments that created and maintained the unreadiness in the first place (Carlton & Winsler, 1999, p. 346). This view challenges schools to work with children's existing abilities, scaffolding their learning experiences to help them acquire the cognitive skills our culture sees as important for learning and academic achievement. Delaying children will only produce further academic problems, and may well damage both motivation and self-esteem (Rose, Medway, Cantrell, & Marus, 1983).

■ **Achievement Motivation and Learning Orientations.** **Achievement motivation** is the degree to which a person chooses to engage in and keep trying to accomplish challenging tasks. Children's achievement motivation involves a complex interplay between their beliefs about why they do or do not achieve, their values concerning the importance of and expected benefit from achieving, and their psychological goals (Wigfield & Eccles, 2001). Psychologists call children's beliefs about why they succeed or fail **attributions**. Attributions tend to focus on

thinking
OF ANNA & MICHELLE
How ready does Michelle seem for school academically, socially, and emotionally? Should Anna be concerned about Michelle's readiness? What can she do to improve it?

achievement motivation

The degree to which a person chooses to engage in and keep trying to accomplish challenging tasks.

attributions

Individuals' beliefs about why they or others succeed or fail.

mastery orientation

The tendency to attribute success to internal and controllable factors such as hard work and ability, and to attribute failure to controllable or changeable factors such as effort, strategy, or task difficulty.

incremental view of ability

The belief that ability can be improved.

TABLE 13.1 **Mastery versus Helpless Orientations**

MASTERY ORIENTATION	HELPLESS ORIENTATION
Attributes success to hard work and skill	Attributes success to luck
Attributes failure to lack of effort or knowledge	Attributes failure to lack of ability
Sees lack of knowledge and skills as temporary and changeable	Sees lack of knowledge and skills as relatively permanent and unchangeable
Is optimistic about future success, even after failure	Is pessimistic about future success, even after success
Engages in positive self-talk, self-encouragement; holds positive expectations	Engages in negative self-talk, anxiety; holds negative expectations
Asks for help when needed, sees getting help as opportunity to improve skills	Avoids seeking help, sees need for help as confirmation of poor ability
Persists on difficult tasks, tries to find new strategies	Decreases effort on difficult tasks, gives up easily
Seeks challenging tasks, views them as way to increase ability	Avoids challenging tasks, views them as confirmation of poor ability
Has learning goals, seeks to learn new strategies and skills	Has performance goals, seeks to perform well to confirm ability to self and others

Source: Adapted from Alderman (1999).

five factors: ability, effort, luck, task difficulty, and strategy use (Alderman, 1999; Weiner, 1992). Notice how some of these factors are *internal* (ability, effort, strategy use), whereas others are *external* (luck, task difficulty). Some are *stable* over time, whereas others are *unstable* or changeable (such as luck or task difficulty; ability can be viewed as either). And some are more *controllable* (like effort and strategy use), whereas others are *uncontrollable* (like luck).

The attributions a child makes about performance have important effects on the child's behavior and achievement motivation. For example, some children develop a **mastery orientation.** That is, as shown in Table 13.1, they attribute their successes to their own hard work and ability—internal and controllable factors—and their failures to factors that they can either control (such as effort or strategy) or change (such as task difficulty). Furthermore, these children tend to hold an **incremental view of ability,** or the belief that they can improve their ability. They focus on *learning goals,* attempting more difficult tasks because they believe this helps them learn new skills and therefore increase their overall ability. These children tend to be high in achievement motivation, because successes on challenging tasks validate their belief that they are able and work hard. Failures simply mean that they need to work harder or try a different strategy.

Other children, however, develop a more **helpless orientation.** These children attribute their failures to their own basic lack of ability but attribute successes to external and uncontrollable factors such as luck. They also tend to hold an **entity view of ability:** the belief that ability is fixed and unchangeable. They tend to avoid challenging tasks, because failure would tell them they are low in ability. They do not persist on difficult tasks, because to keep trying would be to experience continuous reminders of their lack of ability. In these children's minds, if they were capable, they wouldn't have to try so hard, and continued effort won't help them improve their abilities. So why keep trying? Instead, these children focus on *performance goals,* seeking out tasks they are sure they can do well. Unfortunately, this orientation sets up a negative cycle in which children consistently avoid the very situations that could help them develop important new skills (Dweck & Leggett, 1988; Elliott & Dweck, 1988; Weiner, 2000).

Even children as young as 2½ years of age show different reactions to failure versus success on tasks, and many preschoolers and kindergartners show negative reactions to failure. But children's different views of ability, goals, and overall orientations typically develop in later childhood (Dweck, 2001; Stipek, Recchia, & McClintic, 1992). Parents' and teachers' feedback can strongly influence the specific views that children develop, particularly how

helpless orientation

The tendency to attribute success to external and uncontrollable factors such as luck, and to attribute failure to internal and stable factors such as lack of ability.

entity view of ability

The belief that ability is fixed and unchangeable. People with this view have performance goals; they seek out tasks they are sure they can do well, they avoid challenging tasks, and they do not persist on difficult tasks.

much emphasis adults place on traits versus process when evaluating children's successes and failures. For example, offering praise for intelligence seems to encourage an entity view of ability. In contrast, praise for effort or strategies fosters the more constructive incremental view (Dweck, 2001).

thinking
OF ANNA & MICHELLE

Is it important to encourage ▶ Michelle to develop a mastery orientation and an incremental view of ability? How can Anna do this? Will the family's Asian American cultural background be helpful?

■ **Teachers' Beliefs and Expectations.** Not surprisingly, teachers have an important influence on child development. As we just noted, teachers communicate their beliefs about ability in the kind of feedback they offer. Teachers' beliefs also affect the goals they set for learning (performance versus mastery), classroom activities, grouping practices, and rewards (Ames, 1992). Additionally, teachers' beliefs about learning and teaching shape classroom practice and interactions. For example, teachers who hold a constructivist view of learning (a view based on the theories of Piaget and Vygotsky, as presented in Chapter 5) are more likely than teachers with behavioral views to think of themselves as guides for learning. Constructivist teachers tend to encourage student exploration and questioning, value students' perspectives, adjust the curriculum to fit students' needs, and emphasize thinking processes rather than final answers (Elliott, Kratochwill, Cook, & Travers, 2000). Interestingly, teachers' beliefs about their own teaching effectiveness are correlated with student achievement. Teachers who believe they can teach even the most challenging students work harder to do so, and their students benefit (Tschannen-Moran, Woolfolk Hoy, & Hoy, 1998).

One classic study demonstrated the potential power of teacher beliefs (Rosenthal & Jacobson, 1968). In this study researchers told teachers that certain students would probably show large intellectual gains during the upcoming year. In fact, the researchers had randomly selected the list of "intellectual bloomers." By the end of the year, however, these children showed significantly greater increases in IQ scores than other children in the teachers' classes.

thinking
OF ANNA & MICHELLE

What expectations will ▶ teachers be likely to have of Michelle, and of Anna? How might these expectations affect Michelle's academic progress, comfort in school, and achievement motivation?

This type of change is a **self-fulfilling prophecy:** a prediction that comes true because a person believes it will and behaves in ways that produce the expected outcome. As you might expect, the possibility that self-fulfilling prophecies were at work in school achievement stirred a great deal of interest when the study first came out. However, critics pointed out that the effects were not as substantial as they initially seemed. Significant differences were found only in first and second grades, and they may have occurred because of large gains on the part of only five children. Critics also noted several problems with the design and analysis of the study (Elashoff & Snow, 1971; Snow, 1995). Subsequent work on teacher expectations has shown that the self-fulfilling prophecy effect depends on whether teachers behave differently based on their expectations (e.g., using different classroom activities or interacting differently with low- versus high-expectation students) and whether students notice these differences (Eccles & Roeser, 1999). When both these things happen, teacher expectations can affect academic motivation and achievement. Some researchers have observed negative teacher expectations, differential treatment, and negative effects more often with girls, minority children, and children from poor backgrounds (Causey, Thomas, & Armento, 2000; Jussim, Eccles, & Madon, 1996). However, other studies find that teacher expectations are frequently based on reliable data, such as prior behavior and achievement patterns; are reasonably accurate; and are updated as new information becomes available (Good & Brophy, 1997). Some teachers react to their expectations for poorer performance by working harder to meet students' needs. Others, unfortunately, do not. Children in such teachers' classrooms can get stuck with both lower expectations and lower-quality instruction.

self-fulfilling prophecy

A prediction that comes true because people believe the prediction and behave in ways that produce the expected outcome.

classroom climate

The social and emotional environment within a classroom; the way the classroom feels to those in it.

■ **Classroom Climate.** As you probably know from personal experience, classrooms can differ dramatically in the kind of emotional environment they offer, or **classroom climate.** Classroom climate reflects the general attitudes, social and emotional responses, and perceptions of the individuals in the class; in other words, it is the way the classroom feels to those in

A warm and supportive classroom climate improves students' motivation and achievement. Such an atmosphere requires a supportive teacher who has good classroom management and effective teaching skills.

it (Zahn, Kagan, & Widaman, 1986). Many different factors affect classroom climate, including student characteristics and behaviors (e.g., self-regulation skills, attentional abilities, attitudes, and engagement); teacher characteristics (e.g., levels of warmth and supportiveness, friendliness, expectations, and effectiveness of direction and feedback); and even the physical arrangement of the classroom (Chang, 2003; Eccles & Roeser, 1999; MacAulay, 1990; Wentzel, 2002). A positive classroom climate is associated with higher student motivation and achievement, but simply being a warm and friendly teacher is not enough to produce a positive climate. Good classroom management and effective teaching skills are essential. Teachers must establish and maintain clear procedures and rules for activities and behavior; at the same time, they must allow children to make choices, follow individual interests, and actively participate in class decisions and discussions. These practices help build a classroom climate in which students develop feelings of competence and autonomy—feelings conducive to higher student engagement, motivation, and learning (Ben-Ari & Eliassy, 2003; Deci & Ryan, 1985).

■ **Grouping Practices.** A teacher's or a school's approach to grouping can have an important effect on children's achievement and motivation. There is considerable debate about **ability grouping,** the practice of placing children in instructional groups based on their ability level. Particularly controversial is *between-class ability grouping,* or tracking, in which students within a grade attend separate classes according to ability level. Common in secondary schools, this practice can have positive effects for high-ability students, but the long-term effects for students in lower-ability or noncollege tracks are generally negative (Eccles & Roeser, 1999; Slavin, 1990). Often the quality of instruction in lower-ability classes is not as good as in higher-ability classes. Students' contact with peers of different ability levels is also very limited, which makes it harder for lower-ability students to develop friendships with classmates who might model stronger academic skills and motivation (Garmon, Nystrand, Berends, & LePore, 1995; Slavin, 1990).

YOUR
PERSPECTIVE
NOTES
Think about some "warmer" and "cooler" classroom climates you have experienced. Why did they feel like this to you? What could have made a cooler climate feel warmer?

ability grouping

Placing children in instructional groups based on their ability level, either in different classes (between-class grouping or tracking) or within a single class.

Fortunately, some grouping practices have more positive effects on children's development. In **cooperative learning**, children work together in small groups to learn content or solve problems and earn grades and other rewards based at least in part on the group's performance. In true cooperative learning, students interact with one another and depend on one another to achieve group goals; at the same time, each student is individually accountable for his or her work. Students use collaborative skills such as giving constructive feedback and encouraging all group members to participate, and they monitor themselves to make sure the group is working together well (Johnson & Johnson, 1999). As you can probably guess, true cooperative learning requires a great deal of preparation and monitoring to ensure that all students can and do participate appropriately. When used properly, cooperative learning techniques can have positive effects on students' achievement, academic self-concepts, and acceptance of peers from different ethnic backgrounds, socioeconomic classes, or ability levels (Antil, Jenkins, Wayne, & Vadasy, 1998; Ghaith, 2003; Gillies, 2003; Slavin, 1995).

■ **School Climate and Structure.** Just as classroom climate can encourage certain goals, activities, beliefs, emotions, and behavior, overall school climate influences children and teachers alike (Maehr, 1991; Roeser, Midgley, & Urdan, 1996). Schoolwide practices such as honor roll assemblies, public posting of honor rolls, and class ranking on student report cards and permanent records encourage a schoolwide emphasis on ability, competition, and social comparison. In contrast, recognition of effort and improvement, coupled with instruction that encourages mastery, produces a schoolwide learning orientation (Eccles & Roeser, 1999). Parental involvement both at home (e.g., helping with homework, talking about school) and at school (e.g., volunteering in classes, serving in parent organizations) also contributes to school climate and to better student achievement for both younger and older students (Catsambis, 2001; Keith et al., 1998; Sheldon, 2002). The size of the school also makes a difference. Students and teachers perceive smaller schools as more supportive and safer, and student achievement is better at smaller schools (Klonsky, 2002; Lee & Loeb, 2000; Raywid, 1997; Wasley, 2002). Finally, school climate has an effect on individual children. For example, middle schoolers who felt that their school focused heavily on ability showed decreased achievement and self-esteem and increased anger, truancy, and signs of depression (Roeser & Eccles, 1998).

Class size is an aspect of school structure that has received a great deal of attention. At least for early elementary grades, small class sizes are beneficial. Classes with fewer than 20 students show better academic success (i.e., higher achievement test scores, better grades, lower retention rates, and higher graduation rates) than standard-size classes, particularly for traditionally disadvantaged students such as African American or poor children. These benefits persist even if the children move into standard-size classes in later grades (Biddle & Berliner, 2002). However, reducing class size is quite expensive. There must be enough money to fully staff all classes with well-trained educators and to provide adequate materials and space without cutting into other needed programs and services.

School structure can also make transitions between levels of schooling more or less difficult for children. For example, entering kindergarten or first grade is a big transition. Young children encounter a new social environment and must confront and adjust their own cognitive and social skills. Schools group classes on the basis of age, so children have much more exposure to similar-age children. Within classes teachers conduct formal evaluations of children's skills and often group children for instruction according to their ability levels. All of these structures and procedures highlight ability and increase a child's opportunities for social comparison, which may encourage the child to develop an entity view of ability. Socially, the child must conform to school rules but also become more autonomous and self-regulated. A successful transition into school increases the likelihood of academic success right away, and success in the early grades is one of the best predictors of future school performance and high school graduation (Entwisle & Alexander, 1998).

cooperative learning

A teaching approach in which children work together in small groups to learn content or solve problems. Rewards are based at least in part on the group's performance.

Middle school practices such as publicly posting honor rolls emphasize competition and ability rather than cooperation and effort at a time when students need greater support and chances to maintain friendships. This is an example of a poor stage–environment fit, and it can produce long-lasting negative effects—especially for young adolescents who are at academic risk or psychologically vulnerable.

School structure also has important effects at the transition to middle school or junior high, as we saw in Chapter 10. At this point schools typically increase the emphasis on competition, grades, teacher control, and social comparison. At the same time, middle and junior high schools decrease individual attention and support from teachers and provide fewer opportunities for students to maintain close networks of friendships. Long-lasting declines in students' self-esteem, motivation, and achievement can occur—particularly when school systems require a transition after sixth grade, and particularly for students who are at academic risk or are more psychologically vulnerable (Eccles, Lord, Roeser, Barber, & Jozefowicz, 1997). This mismatch between school structure and children's developmental needs is an example of a poor **stage–environment fit:** a poor match between the environment and the cognitive, social, and emotional needs of a particular stage of development (Eccles & Roeser, 1999). Educators have suggested numerous changes in basic aspects of school structure that could make schools more appropriate for middle school students (Anderman & Maehr, 1994; Eccles, Midgley, et al., 1993; Seidman & French, 1997). Some suggestions:

- Encourage learning-oriented goals (rather than performance-oriented goals) both in the classroom and at the whole school level.

- Use more cooperative learning techniques and less competition-based instruction.

- Restructure honor rolls and school award programs to decrease the emphasis on ability comparisons and to focus more on initiative, effort, and improvement.

- Increase the degree of young adolescents' control in classroom and school decision making.

- Use block schedules: schedules in which students spend longer periods of time on a given subject with a smaller number of teachers, and spend more time with the same peers.

thinking
OF ANNA & MICHELLE
◄ How good was Anna's stage–environment fit as she went through the neighborhood's schools? What can be done either by the schools or by Anna to improve the fit for Michelle?

stage–environment fit

The degree to which the environment is successful in meeting the cognitive, social, and emotional needs of a child in a particular stage of development.

Have teachers conduct regular advisory sessions with students so teachers can get to know individual students, identify potential problems early, and prevent problems.

Some children and families struggle with school transitions on a daily basis. To learn how one adolescent felt about the change to middle school, what helped ease the transition, and what got in the way, read the Personal Perspective box called "Meet a Sixth-Grader Making the Change."

Cross-National and Ethnic Differences in Schooling

As we've seen, the systems that exist within schools have an important impact on children's development. These systems differ tremendously from one culture to another. How do children in the United States compare to those in other countries in their academic achievement? In the latest international assessment of mathematics and science achievement, U.S. eighth-graders

---

 ## A Personal PERSPECTIVE...

Meet a Sixth Grader Making the Change

Johnny Cook
Fort Atkinson, Wisconsin

Sixth grader beginning his first year in middle school

How well do you think you and your friends have adjusted to your new school?
In the 2½ weeks since I started middle school, I think I have adjusted very well. I have already gotten to know all of my teachers, but I have not met many new students yet. It was hard at first, getting to and finding classes on time. My friends have adjusted to school about the same as me. We can all get around now. Middle school is fun and everyone is having a fun time. It gets easier as you go on.

Is your middle school very different from your elementary school? Do you feel comfortable in your middle school?
My elementary school was a fairly small school and not very crowded. My middle school is big, crowded with a lot of kids, and a lot of fun! I

change classes every 47 minutes and go to different ends of the school to get to all of them. My middle school is about the same as my elementary school in terms of being friendly, helpful, encouraging, competitive, and grade-focused, which is good because it helps me stay on track. I feel very comfortable trying new things here and even making a couple of mistakes!

Did your middle school do anything to help you make an easier transition? Did it make the process harder in any way?
Before we actually started middle school we got letters from other sixth-grade students explaining about the school. We also had an orientation all about middle school before we started. Everyone really helped a lot the first week. The teachers made sure everyone got to the right classes and had all the right supplies. They helped me understand my schedule and how it would work. They did not ever make the process harder in any way, but made it easier.

Have you had any difficulties with the transition? What might help?
On the first day we had a little trouble finding our classes on time, but it got easier. Trying to remember locker combinations and getting them open was also hard the first couple times. It might be easier if we came to the school for a whole day and watched students get to their classes and open their lockers. We did visit the school, but only for a while and it all seemed confusing. I think they should show you first how to open your locker. That might make it easier. ■

thinking
OF ANNA & MICHELLE

◄ Does the school experience described in this interview sound like the experience Anna is hoping to provide for Michelle? How do you think this type of environment would affect Michelle's social and academic development, compared to the school environment in their current neighborhood?

---

ranked 19th in math and 18th in science out of 38 countries assessed—significantly above the international average but far below the scores of the top-ranked countries (Martin et al., 2000; Mullis et al., 2000). And when compared to only the countries who participated in assessments in both 1995 and 1999 (a total of 17 countries), the relative performance of U.S. eighth graders declined over those years in both math and science. The decline was especially striking in science: The United States ranked 3rd among the 17 countries in 1995 but fell to 12th by 1999 (U.S. Department of Education, 2000). Twelfth graders have fared even worse than eighth graders in international comparisons, as shown in Figure 13.3 (Mullis et al., 1998).

Findings like these from the late 1990s are very disappointing, particularly because policy makers and educators focused heavily on educational improvement over the preceding decade. Asian countries often lead the world in math and science scores. Researchers have examined educational practices in the United States, Japan, China, and Taiwan and found interesting differences between practices in Asian cultures and in the United States. Some examples:

▶ Children in Asian cultures are actively engaged in learning activities and discussion about the material the majority of the time—more than 80 percent of the time, as opposed to 60 percent engagement of U.S. children in one study of mathematics classes (Lee, 1998).

▶ Asian cultures strongly emphasize academic achievement but also hold a strong belief that effort is more important than ability (Lee, 1998; Stevenson, 1992).

▶ Asian parents have high standards and expectations for their children's achievement and are very involved in helping their children with schoolwork (Stevenson & Lee, 1990).

▶ Lessons in Asian classrooms frequently involve the whole class rather than small groups or individuals, and teachers do not group children by ability during the elementary years.

▶ Asian math classes require students to solve problems and focus on higher-level conceptual knowledge rather than repeating procedural or factual knowledge; they also cover material in greater depth than typical U.S. classes.

▶ Asian students spend more time on academics, and both the school day and the school year are longer. However, children have 10- to 15-minute breaks every 45 minutes or so throughout the day.

▶ Asian teachers spend less time in actual instruction and more time preparing lessons, working with other teachers, and working with individual students. For example, teachers in Beijing teach an average of 2.7 hours per day, compared with 4.7 hours in Taipei and 7.3 hours in Chicago (Lee, 1998; Shen, 2001; Stevenson & Lee, 1995).

It would be unrealistic to propose that the same educational practices that work in Asian cultures be implemented wholesale in the United States; there are quite different cultural systems operating (Shen, 2001). But some school systems have attempted changes inspired by Asian educational practices. For example, one study found that extending the school year by 30 days produced higher achievement scores in several areas (Frazier & Morrison, 1998). It's interesting to note that many of the practices long advocated by educational researchers and developmental psychologists are common in Asian cultures. Examples include active learning by students, emphasis on effort rather than ability, and focus on problem solving and conceptual knowledge. As you're probably well aware, many schools in the United States have made changes to try to improve education, but it will likely take several years before we can see the effects of these changes.

thinking
OF ANNA & MICHELLE

◀ If the schools in Anna's neighborhood tried some of these educational practices, would it help Anna and Michelle feel more comfortable? What problems in implementing the practices might arise?

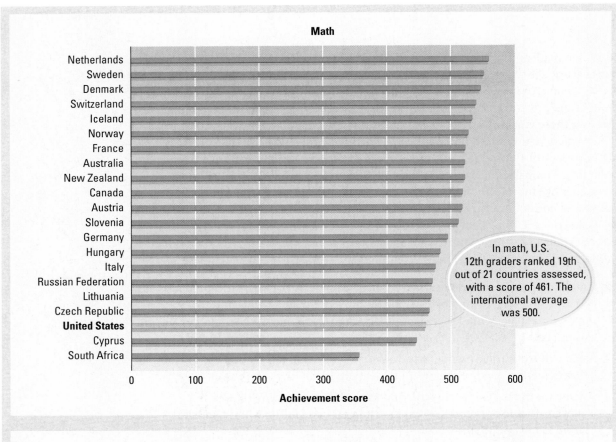

Math

In math, U.S. 12th graders ranked 19th out of 21 countries assessed, with a score of 461. The international average was 500.

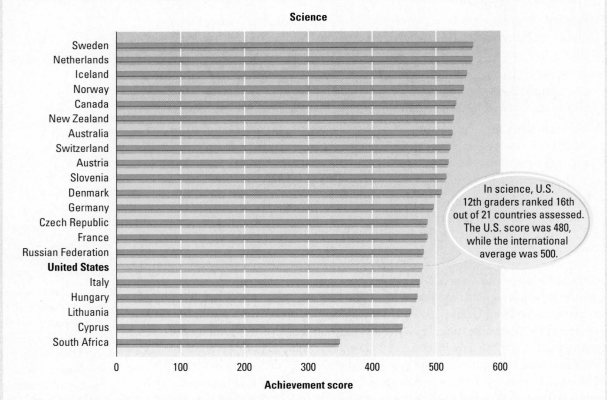

Science

In science, U.S. 12th graders ranked 16th out of 21 countries assessed. The U.S. score was 480, while the international average was 500.

FIGURE 13.3 Cross-National Math and Science Achievement, Grade 12

Twelfth graders in the United States are below the international averages in math and science cross-national comparisons.

Source: Adapted from Mullis et al. (1998).

Asian cultures place a strong emphasis on hard work. In these societies, there are high expectations for children's achievement and active involvement in learning. Teachers have more preparation time than in the United States; children have ample recess time; and parents are very involved in their children's schoolwork.

Policy makers and educators also are keenly interested in monitoring patterns of achievement differences among ethnic groups. (They're interested in gender differences, too, and we discussed these in Chapter 10.) It will come as no surprise to you that children in ethnic groups that have experienced discrimination and prejudice, often living in poor neighborhoods with failing schools, have lower achievement scores. As Figure 13.4 shows, the 2000 National Assessment of Educational Progress found large ethnic group differences in math achievement. Similar differences were found in all the subjects tested. And the gaps do not appear to be narrowing (U.S. Department of Education, 2001b, 2001c, 2002). Differences were stable throughout the 1990s in mathematics, reading, and science, as you can see in Table 13.2. The differences are particularly striking in science, where non-Hispanic white students' scores are 29 percent higher than African Americans' scores and 24 percent higher than those of Hispanic students. Also troubling are the high percentages of ethnic minority students who score below the basic level in reading—the level at which children have the necessary knowledge and skills to allow proficient work at their grade level as judged by professional educators evaluating students' work on the national tests. In 2000 almost *60 percent* of African American, Hispanic, and Native American fourth graders scored below this basic level, compared to 27 percent of non-Hispanic white children and 27 percent of Asian American children (U.S. Department of Education, 2001c). Finally, ethnic differences persist in the school dropout rate. Although the dropout rate declined for all ethnicities during the 1970s and 1980s, the rate of decline was faster for non-Hispanic white students than for African Americans and Hispanics. The dropout rate for Hispanic students as of the year 2000 was 27.8 percent, twice that of African American students (13.1 percent) and four times that of

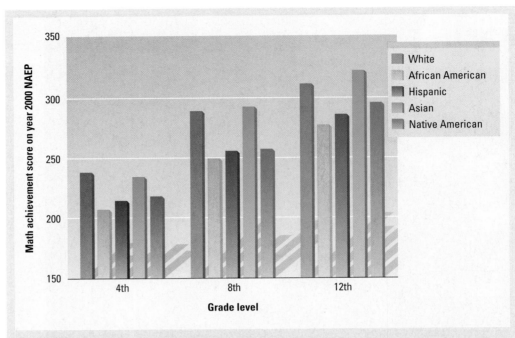

FIGURE 13.4 Ethnic Group Differences in Achievement

This figure shows the ethnic group differences in math. Ethnic group differences in achievement are large in all subject areas tested.

Note: Data for fourth-grade Asian students are from the year 1996. Year 2000 data not available.

Source: U.S. Department of Education (2001b).

non-Hispanic white students (6.9 percent). The fact of these differences, along with their persistence and the overall achievement levels of U.S. students, continue to concern educators (U.S. Department of Education, 2001c).

Why do substantial ethnic differences remain in spite of years of attention and concern? Poverty and its effects are a crucial factor. Ethnic minority children are far more likely to live in poverty than are white children. And poverty affects the quality of schools available, money available for materials and enrichment activities, parents' abilities and opportunities to help, and students' overall health, to name but a few factors (Byrnes, 2003; Skiba, Knesting, & Bush, 2002). Cultural differences also are important, particularly the extent to which schools are compatible with children's home cultures and the degree to which children's cultures value the kinds of skills taught in schools (Byrnes, 2001). School–home compatibility is typically greater for white children than for children of some ethnic minorities. For example, cultural differences in social interaction rules can have subtle but important effects on schooling. African American children learn at home to grab their turn and to entertain to keep others' attention; in contrast, white children learn to wait their turn. Native American children learn that it is disrespectful to look an adult in the eye; white children learn that not meeting the eyes of a person you're talking to can indicate lack of attention or even dishonesty (Delpit, 1995; Gay, 1991; Saville-Troike, 1986). Cultural incompatibility often results in a curriculum that fails to awaken minority students' interest and motivation. As one student reported, "You get tired of learning about the same White people and the same things. . . . I like being in class more when I learn about Blacks and my heritage. It gives me encouragement and lets me know that I have rights . . . and helps improve my grades" (Ford & Harris, 2000, p. 4). And as we saw when comparing Asian to U.S. schools, cultural emphasis on mastering the skills

YOUR PERSPECTIVE NOTES

Have you ever experienced a cultural incompatibility with schooling? Describe how it affected your learning and how it could have been handled.

TABLE 13.2 Ethnic Differences in Achievement Scores across the 1990s

Mathematics	1990	2000
Non-Hispanic white	264	277
African American	232	242
Hispanic	239	249
Asian American	272	280
Native American	250	255
Reading	**1992**	**2000**
Non-Hispanic white	225	226
African American	193	193
Hispanic	201	197
Asian American	214	232
Native American	207	196
Science	**1996**	**2000**
Non-Hispanic white	159	159
African American	123	123
Hispanic	129	128
Asian American	151	155
Native American	146	138
School Dropout Rate	**1990**	**2000**
Non-Hispanic white	9.0%	6.9%
African American	13.2%	13.1%
Hispanic	32.4%	27.8%
Asian American*	—	—
Native American*	—	—

Note: For achievement scores, maximum score is 500 for math and reading, 300 for science.

*Dropout rates not given separately for these two ethnicities.

Sources: U.S. Department of Education (2001b, 2001c, 2001d).

taught in school varies considerably. If parents (or the overall culture) do not believe that learning a certain skill or content is important, they communicate this belief in various ways. The result: Their children are less likely to care about their performance, put in extra effort, or seek help. Schools that are sensitive to the cultures of their students and try to involve parents in their children's schooling can have a positive impact on children's academic achievement (Fan & Chen, 2001; Parker et al., 1999).

How Can We Prevent Problems in Schooling?

What can we do to prevent difficulties in schooling? You yourself may soon be in a position to have a positive impact on children's schooling, whether in the context of work in health and social services of various kinds, in early childhood education, in schools, or in government or private agencies. You may also have children of your own. Table 13.3 presents suggestions for all of us who work with children. It is vital that each child begin school ready to learn, experience early success to gain a solid foundation for learning, and learn that effort and

TABLE 13.3 Preventing Problems with Schooling

STRATEGIES	PARENTS CAN	SCHOOLS CAN
Promote school readiness to help children get off to a good start academically.	Immunize children, encourage good eating and exercise habits, and make sure children get enough sleep. Use quality preschool programs that teach basic skills and encourage positive attitudes toward learning and schooling. Read to children *daily* and encourage them to use descriptive words. Encourage curiosity and questions. Encourage children's efforts, not just their results. Let children know you believe they can learn through effort and persistence.	Offer specific suggestions to parents for increasing school readiness. Thoroughly screen all preschoolers to identify those at highest need of early intervention. Establish an environment that values and encourages curiosity, questioning, and enthusiasm for learning. Develop policies that emphasize effort, persistence, and a mastery orientation. Hold positive expectations for students.
Help create a positive school environment to help children feel comfortable, confident, and happy to be in school.	Be involved in your child's school. Volunteer, and attend school events. Meet with your child's teacher(s) periodically, even if your child is not having any problems. Request teachers who emphasize effort, persistence, and mastery, and who have positive expectations for children. Consider the climate of your child's class—is it warm and supportive or chilly and uninviting?	Encourage meaningful and regular parent involvement. Take steps to eliminate negative classroom environments. Hold regular in-service training on strategies that foster positive classroom climates and mastery learning orientations. Make strong efforts to keep class sizes below 20 students, especially at early grade levels.
Think about the consequences of school structure and policies to provide a good stage–environment fit.	Question school policies that emphasize grades or competition. Ask how learning orientations, effort, and persistence are encouraged. Support programs in middle/junior high schools that make it a friendlier place for students, like block schedules or homeroom "advisory" programs. Watch for signs that your child is having difficulty transitioning to a new school.	Think about whether school policies focus too much on ability. Try to emphasize effort, persistence, and learning orientations more often. Consider having "advisory" programs and/or block-type schedules so teachers and students can get to know one another better. Watch for signs that individual students are having adjustment difficulties. Establish routines that are student-friendly and teach self-management and self-control strategies. Maintain contact with parents to ensure that children's needs are being met.
Understand different cultures to make school more relevant and interesting for students.	Get to know your child's teachers. Help them understand differences between their culture and yours. Help organize a multicultural event in your child's class or school. Try to understand *why* the school curriculum contains the things it does. Try to find reasons that make sense to your child. Point out to your child examples of the content and skills he or she is learning, especially for topics your child thinks are irrelevant.	Plan events that encourage parents and teachers to get to know one another. Offer in-service training to help teachers understand the cultures, expectations, and customs of their students. Encourage teachers to incorporate information about their students' cultural backgrounds into instruction. Ask community members about school topics that seem irrelevant to them or their children. Get suggestions to improve the relevance of the curriculum.
Do more than just teach content so students' nonacademic needs are not an obstacle to learning.	Help children develop positive, supportive friendships. Encourage children to talk about school—about what they're learning, what they like or don't like, and why. Encourage children to develop positive relationships with other trusted adults such as teachers.	Talk with students about attitudes toward learning, strategies for self-control, and how to deal with strong or negative emotions. Provide counseling services or referrals for students having academic, social, or emotional difficulties. Serve as an information resource for academic as well as nonacademic services and issues.

persistence make a difference. Each child must feel that school is relevant and important in his or her life, and each must feel individually known and valued by teachers and schools. These are challenging goals that require the active involvement of all who care about children's academic success and overall quality of life.

LET'S REVIEW . . .

1. Which of the following is *true* about early childhood education programs such as Head Start, High/Scope Perry Preschool, and the Abecedarian Project?
   a. These programs are not cost-effective.
   b. These programs regularly produce permanent gains in IQ scores.
   c. These programs produce improved academic progress and higher graduation rates.
   d. These programs have little effect on social measures like arrest records or employment.

2. Jacqueline, a fourth grader, said, "I like to try things that are a little hard for me, because when I finally can do them, it makes me smarter!" Jacqueline has:
   a. a mastery orientation.
   b. a helpless orientation.
   c. an entity view of ability.
   d. performance goals.

3. Compared to students in other countries, academic scores of students in the United States:
   a. are the best.
   b. are lower than most other countries.
   c. have improved since 1995.
   d. have declined since 1995.

4. Which of the following is *true* about ethnic differences in academic achievement scores?
   a. Ethnic differences in scores have steadily decreased.
   b. Ethnic differences are large and stable.
   c. There are large ethnic differences in a few content areas, but not in all.
   d. Most students of all ethnicities score at least at the *basic* level in reading.

5. **True or False:** A self-fulfilling prophecy is based on reliable information about past behavior and achievement patterns.

6. **True or False:** Smaller class sizes do not guarantee better academic performance.

Answers: 1. c, 2. a, 3. d, 4. b, 5. F, 6. T

Children and the Media

How much time do you spend watching television, listening to CDs, reading for pleasure, playing video games, and surfing the Internet? For many people these activities take up an astonishing amount of time each day. A recent survey of more than 3,000 children from ages 2 to 18 found that each week "American children spend the equivalent of a full-time work week using media" for non-school-related purposes, and that much of this time is not supervised by parents or other adults (Rideout, Foehr, Roberts, & Brodie, 1999, p. 6; Roberts, Foehr, Rideout, & Brodie, 1999). It is no wonder that developmental psychologists have become very interested in the effects of media on children's cognitive, social, and emotional development.

As you study this section, ask yourself these questions:

- What kinds of media do children use most often, and what groups of children use different types of media?

- What effects do television and other media have on children's cognitive skills? How can adults help encourage a positive effect?

- In what ways does media violence affect children's behavior? What can parents do to limit any negative effects?

- How do researchers explain the effects of media on children?

What Kinds of Media Are Children Using?

More kinds of media are available to children today than ever before. Television, movies, radio, CDs, books, and magazines now compete with video games, computer games, and the Internet for children's attention. And many children have virtually unlimited access to various media. One-third of children under the age of 7 have a television in their bedroom, and about 14 percent have a VCR or video-game player as well. The percentages are even higher for older children. One nationally representative study of media use found that television was by far the most commonly used medium at all ages (Roberts et al., 1999). Use of audio media (including radio, CDs, and tapes) is the second most frequent for all but the youngest group of children. Interestingly, at all ages, video-game and computer use occupy *less* time per day than print media (which include any sort of books, magazines, comic books, etc. read for nonschool purposes), though this difference gets smaller for the older groups. Contrary to popular opinion, it appears that children do read outside of school. Watching television, viewing movies, and playing video games all peak by age 13, then decline.

Statistics on overall use of media can mask differences between specific subgroups, however. For example, boys tend to watch more television than girls, and they spend substantially more time playing video games than girls. Some studies report that boys also spend more time on the computer and the Internet from middle childhood on (an average of 34 minutes per day for teen boys versus 13 minutes per day for teen girls), although this difference is smaller than it used to be (Kraut, Scherlis, Mukhopadhyay, Manning, & Kiesler, 1996). Girls, beginning in middle childhood, spend more time than boys reading print media and listening to the radio and music CDs. There are clear gender differences in preferred content: Boys prefer action/adventure, sports, and violent themes more than girls (Griffiths & Hunt, 1995; Huston & Wright, 1998; Roberts et al., 1999; *U.S. Teens & Technology*, 1997).

African American and Hispanic children and teens spend more time using media than do non-Hispanic white children, especially from middle childhood on—about 1 hour a day more for Hispanic youngsters and 2 hours per day more for African Americans. Greater use of television, videotapes, and video games accounts for practically all of the difference. Although African American and Hispanic families are much less likely to have a computer and Internet access at home than non-Hispanic white families, children in all three groups spend equivalent amounts of time on the computer (except preschoolers). It seems that programs to make school computers available before, during, and after school hours have greatly reduced ethnic differences in computer use once children reach school age. Finally, there are consistent differences based on socioeconomic status. Children from lower-income households have less access to and spend less time using computers and the Internet; though again, access to computers at school may be helping reduce this difference. Children in lower-SES households spend more time watching television and are more likely than their higher-SES peers to have a television in their bedroom. Younger children from lower-SES households

Children in the United States watch television an average of almost 36 hours each week, with much of the time unsupervised by adults. Boys, African American children, and Hispanic children watch more than other children. Television can have positive effects on children's cognitive skills but it can also increase aggressive behavior, and heavy television viewing is associated with poorer reading skills.

spend less time with print media, and older children spend more time listening to the radio (Newburger, 2001; Roberts et al., 1999; U.S. Department of Education, 2001a).

Some of these ethnic and SES-group differences probably reflect a lack of opportunity. Lack of money or lack of options available in the community may limit children's access to certain forms of media (such as computers or the Internet) or to alternative activities (such as clubs or recreational sports). There may also be differences in how different groups of children use a medium such as television. For example, there is evidence that Hispanic families sometimes use educational television programs such as *Sesame Street* as a way to increase their skill in English, and that African Americans use television as a source of reliable information about events and culture more than white Americans (Huston & Wright, 1998).

What Are the Effects of Media?

There is no question that the media can have an important influence on children. But how big are the effects, and what are the specific positive and negative effects? It has long been established, for example, that the more a child reads, the better a reader the child becomes (Byrnes, 2001). Although there are certainly differences between reading a novel and reading magazines, comics, or websites, all of these sources do involve reading. If parents and teachers provide guidance, television and movies can even stimulate a greater interest in reading (remember the Harry Potter phenomenon?). The vast majority of research on media and children, however, has focused on the effects of television on cognitive skills, aggression, and prosocial skills.

■ **Television and Cognitive Skills.** Television has mixed effects on cognitive skills and academic achievement. On one hand, studies of TV shows specifically designed to boost reading and math skills indicate positive effects. Both experimental and correlational studies have found that young children who watch programs such as *Sesame Street* score higher on vocabulary, knowledge of colors, math skills, letter recognition, and reading, regardless of factors such as parents' education and income. Teachers rate children who view these shows as having better academic attitudes and skills when they start school, and in this regard some studies report larger effects for children from lower-income families (Huston & Wright, 1998; Wright, Huston, Scantlin, & Kotler, 2001; Zill, 2001). In contrast, toddlers who watch entertainment programs (intended for adults or for children) show lower levels of school-related skills at age 5. However, only TV viewing at ages 2 and 3 affects children's later scores, not viewing at age 4 and older. There may be a "window of opportunity where educational television can have its longest, most powerful effects" (Bickman, Wright, & Huston, 2001, p. 114).

A recent study showed positive relations between educational TV viewing during preschool years and grades in *high school*, especially for boys. However, preschoolers who watched general entertainment programs later earned lower grades in high school, especially girls (Anderson, Huston, Schmitt, Linebarger, & Wright, 2001). Perhaps educational TV shows are effective for the same reason that early childhood interventions seem to be: Children acquire both basic skills, which help them achieve successes early in their school years, and positive attitudes toward school and learning. Early successes and positive attitudes encourage persistence and foster continued success. It's worth remembering, though, that positive effects like these are often stronger when parents and teachers support the skills being presented by watching the shows with their children and/or supplementing the information with additional activities. There has been surprisingly little research on the effects of educational television aimed at older children. Some experimental studies do show positive effects on older children's mathematical problem-solving skills, enjoyment of math, and science knowledge and attitudes (Huston & Wright, 1998).

What is the effect of extensive viewing of noneducational television on academics? There are widely held beliefs that heavy TV use has a significant negative effect on school performance and that it displaces more constructive activities such as reading. It may surprise you to learn that there is not strong evidence to support either of these beliefs (Huston & Wright, 1998):

- Television viewing does not have much effect on the amount of time children spend reading. Children who watch lots of television spend less time reading, but the correlation is reduced or eliminated when researchers take into account factors like SES, age, gender, or parents' educational levels.

- One meta-analysis found that children watching 10 hours of TV per week had *better* achievement scores and grades than those watching less, although scores decreased sharply as TV viewing went beyond 10 hours a week (Williams, Haertel, Walberg, & Haertel, 1982).

- Many studies have associated watching more than about 30 hours per week with worse academic performance. However, the vast majority of these studies are correlational. Although it makes sense to suppose that heavy TV viewing interferes with academics, it could certainly be that children who are already not doing well in school choose TV over academic activities.

- When studies do find negative effects, they tend to be larger for girls and for white, higher-IQ, and higher-SES children. It appears that for these children, heavy TV viewing is taking time away from other activities that would have greater educational value.

■ **Are We Creating Monsters? TV and Aggression.** The amount of violence portrayed on television is staggering. Researchers estimate that by the time the average child in the United States leaves elementary school, that child will have viewed more than 8,000 murders and 100,000 other violent acts on network TV alone. This doesn't include cable channels or videotaped movies! Saturday-morning cartoons and late-afternoon and early-evening programs, all aired at times when children are most likely to be watching, have the highest rates of violent acts (Comstock & Paik, 1991; Huston et al., 1992). In addition, TV often portrays violence as good, without consequence, causing no pain or suffering, and even funny. In short, very different from real-life violence.

But even if children view violence regularly on television, does it affect their behavior? Meta-analyses of the many studies investigating this issue conclude that TV violence has a moderate negative impact on children's behavior. The effect is similar for boys and girls, and it is larger for children than adults (Bushman & Huesmann, 2001; Hogben, 1998; Huston & Wright, 1998; Paik & Comstock, 1994). In general, then, violence on television is related to later aggressive behavior, and the relationship may be of particular concern for children.

One well-known study followed a sample of boys and girls for 22 years. The researchers looked at the relationship between the amount and level of violence of the television they watched as children and their aggressive behavior in adulthood (Eron, Huesmann, Lefkowitz, & Walder, 1972; Huesmann & Miller, 1994). Figure 13.5 graphs results for the boys in their study. For boys, watching TV violence at age 8 was the best predictor of aggressiveness at age 18, and those who watched the most TV at age 8 were most likely to engage in violent criminal behavior by age 30. But couldn't it be that children who had aggressive tendencies chose to watch more violent TV *and* engaged in more violent behavior, so the violence of TV was not a causative factor? Boys who were already aggressive at age 8 did watch more TV. But even among these already aggressive children, the boys who watched more TV had committed more serious criminal offenses by age 30 than those who watched less. It seems there is a bidirectional effect: More aggressive children prefer more violent TV, but TV violence increases their aggression even more. Later studies showed similar relationships between TV violence and later aggression in

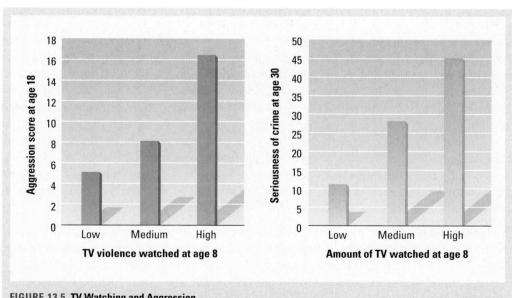

FIGURE 13.5 **TV Watching and Aggression**

Watching violent television shows during childhood predicts aggressiveness during adolescence and amount of violent crime in adulthood. These data are for males, but similar results have been found for females.

Source: Adapted from L. D. Eron. (1987). The development of aggressive behavior from the perspective of a developing behaviorism. *American Psychologist, 42*(5). Adapted with permission. Aggression score data from Eron, Huesmann, Lefkowitz, & Walder (1972), p. 256.

Albert Bandura's experimental studies have shown that children who see violent television content behave more aggressively immediately afterward. This child has just finished watching an aggressive model. Can you see the effect on her behavior?

women and in several countries (though not in all countries studied), even after researchers statistically controlled for the influences of earlier aggression, intelligence level, and social class (Bushman & Huesmann, 2001; Huesmann, Moise-Titus, Podolski, & Eron, 2003).

Establishing a relationship is one thing, but even a strong correlation does not prove a causal link. Experimental studies are needed for this, and there have been many experimental tests of the short-term effects of television violence on children's aggressive behavior. Probably the best-known examples were experiments conducted by Albert Bandura (developer of the social learning theory we described in Chapter 1). Bandura randomly assigned children to view either violent or nonviolent video clips, then observed the children's behavior afterwards while they played with one another or with toys. Children who viewed the violent videos behaved more aggressively with both people and objects. Bandura found this effect across genders, across ethnicities, and regardless of whether children showed preexisting aggressive tendencies (Bandura, 1977). At least in the short term, watching violence on television causes children to behave more aggressively.

Does this mean that any viewing of media violence will create aggressive behavior in all children? No. There are important interactions with other factors. As we saw in the longitudinal study described earlier, TV violence may exert its greatest long-term influence on children who already have aggressive tendencies. The effects are stronger for children who identify more with the TV characters, whose fantasy play and conversation are more centered in television, and whose parents use harsh physical punishment (Anderson et al., 2001; Gunter & McAleer, 1997; Huesmann et al., 2003). One journal article compared the relationship between TV violence and aggression to the link between smoking and lung cancer. Not everyone who smokes develops lung cancer, and not everyone who gets lung cancer is a smoker; smoking is not the only cause of lung cancer. Similarly, not every child who views hours of TV violence becomes aggressive, and not every child who behaves aggressively has watched lots of TV; watching violence on TV is not the only cause of aggressive behavior. But just as smoking is a significant risk factor for lung cancer, watching a steady diet of violent TV during childhood seems to be a risk factor for later aggressive behavior (Bushman & Anderson, 2001).

■ **Other Effects of TV.** If violent television content can affect children's behavior, it is reasonable to think that TV can encourage more positive, or *prosocial,* behaviors as well. In fact, some researchers believe that seeing prosocial behaviors and themes on television ought to be *more* influential than watching negative programming. The argument is that prosocial behaviors are the norm in real life—so when children act out prosocial behaviors learned from television, they are likely to receive reinforcement for their efforts (Rushton, 1979). Meta-analyses support this thesis. These analyses have found moderate to large positive associations between watching prosocial programming such as *Mister Rogers' Neighborhood, Sesame Street,* and *Barney* and behaviors such as helping, sharing, talking about feelings, persisting on tasks, using imagination, donating, offering comfort, and cooperating (Hearold, 1986; Mares & Woodard,

2001). These positive effects are larger among younger children (peaking at about age 7), children from middle- and upper-income homes, and children whose parents watch with them and/or follow up the program with reinforcing activities. Regrettably, children's programs with prosocial content are not nearly as numerous as shows with aggressive content or a mixture of the two. And one analysis indicated that viewing mixed content had a more negative effect on children than viewing content that was purely antisocial (Mares & Woodard, 2001).

What about sexual material? Television exposes children to a great deal of sexual content in everything from entertainment programs, "reality" shows, and music videos to news reports. Whether and how this exposure affects children's attitudes, beliefs, and behavior is unclear. There are no studies of younger children, and studies of older children and adolescents have produced conflicting results. Some evidence suggests that youngsters who watch more TV have less realistic expectations about sexual frequency and satisfaction and have more liberal attitudes toward premarital sex than those who watch less TV (Malamuth & Impett, 2001). But one longitudinal study found that TV's effects on young teens' sexual attitudes are not direct. Also important were family communication style and how actively attentive the teen was to the TV content (Bryant & Rockwell, 1994).

TV viewing can also promote gender and ethnic stereotyping. TV programs and advertisements remain heavily stereotypical in their portrayal of gender and ethnicity (Bang & Reece, 2003). Both correlational and experimental studies indicate that TV encourages stereotypic views of gender and ethnicity (Dixon, 2001). In older adolescents, watching violent (and perhaps even nonviolent) sexual material on TV correlates with negative attitudes toward women and greater acceptance of violence against women (Harris & Scott, 2002). The "ideal" female portrayed in the media can negatively impact adolescent girls' ideas about body image and body weight (Posavac & Posavac, 2002). However, it's important to remember that TV's influence does not have to be negative. Studies of programs such as *Sesame Street* and *Mister Rogers' Neighborhood* show that more positive and realistic portrayals of ethnic minorities and women can have positive effects on children's beliefs. In addition, the presence of African American characters on television can have positive effects on African American children's self-esteem (Bogatz & Ball, 1977; Gorn, Goldberg, & Kanningo, 1976; Huston & Wright, 1998; Signorielli, 2001).

Research also has focused on numerous other effects of TV (Gunter & McAleer, 1997; Huston & Wright, 1998; Singer & Singer, 2001). For example:

- Studies have linked watching educational TV to more positive and intense daydreams—and have found associations between watching violent content and competitive and aggressive daydreams (Harrison & Williams, 1986; Valkenberg & van der Voort, 1994).

- Children as young as 12 months can be affected by what they view and are capable of using the emotional reactions they view to guide their own behavior (Mumme & Fernald, 2003).

- Watching TV does not shorten children's attention span or increase their distractibility, but children's persistence on tasks and willingness to wait is greater after they watch educational programs than after they watch violent cartoons.

- TV advertising definitely affects children's awareness of products, brand name recognition, and positive attitude toward advertised products (Gunter & McAleer, 1997; Strasburger, 2001).

- Advertising affects children's food choices, especially among younger children, and excessive TV watching is linked to obesity in children (Berkey, Rockett, Gillman, & Colditz, 2003; Gortmaker et al., 1996).

- Children who view cigarette advertisements (televised or in print) have more positive attitudes toward smoking.

- Longitudinal studies have found that childhood exposure to alcohol ads predicts alcohol use during adolescence; also, the more TV and music videos children watch, the earlier children begin drinking (Austin & Knaus, 2000; Robinson, Chen, & Killen, 1998).

- Other studies, however, find few consistent relationships between children's TV viewing and later smoking, drinking, or obesity (Anderson et al., 2001).

State of the Art: Newer Forms of Media

New forms of media are constantly emerging, and their developers target many of these products specifically toward children. We have some understanding of the effects of some of these media, such as video games and Internet use. On others, such as virtual reality systems, we have practically no data.

■ **Video Games.** Video games (e.g., Nintendo, PlayStation) are most popular with boys about 8 to 12 years old. Even boys in this age bracket spend less time playing such games than you might expect, with most (79 percent) playing less than one hour per day. As you probably know, the majority of video games are fast-paced, visually based games that demand close attention and fast reactions. In the short term these games improve a variety of skills, including spatial skills (e.g., anticipating and predicting where targets will appear on the screen), the ability to interpret visual images like pictures and diagrams, response times to visual targets, and strategies for keeping track of things happening at several different screen locations (Huston & Wright, 1998; Subrahmanyam et al., 2001). Long-term effects and the transfer of these skills to other contexts aren't clear yet.

Unfortunately, the majority of video games involve at least some aggression and violence. Though this was not true of the earliest games, the amount and severity of aggression (particularly of direct "human" aggression) has increased with each game generation. Experimental studies indicate that playing a violent video game for even a brief time increases aggressive thoughts and behavior. A recent meta-analysis of 35 research reports found a small but significant effect of video game violence on players' aggressive behavior, thoughts, feelings, and physiological arousal (Anderson & Bushman, 2001). The effects were similar in males and females, in children and adults, and in experimental and non-experimental studies. Children who play video games are just as socially involved with peers as those who don't play, but little is known about the social impact of heavy game playing (more than 30 hours per week) on either short-term or long-term outcomes (Subrahmanyam, Kraut, Greenfield, & Gross, 2001).

Boys between the ages of 8 and 12 play video games more often than other children. Video games can improve a variety of spatial skills, but the majority contain violent content that can increase aggressive thoughts and behavior.

■ **Computer Games and the Internet.** Computer software games and CD-ROMs are more education oriented than video games. They typically require more conceptual, logical, and cognitive strategy skills and less fast physical response. These programs can successfully introduce even very young children to computers. They can help teach basic concepts in reading and math; and they can help build children's divergent thinking skills, confidence, and enjoyment in using computers (Huston & Wright, 1998).

Children's access to the Internet is increasing at breakneck speed, but we are only beginning to understand the effects on children of spending time on line. One study found that students aged 10 to 18 used the Internet most frequently for schoolwork, closely followed by entertainment and communicating with friends (both friends they already knew and new friends they "met" through chat rooms, newsgroups, and the like) (Kraut et al., 1996). Ironically, some evidence has associated greater use of the Internet on the part of teens with decreased face-to-face social involvement, greater loneliness, and increases in depression. These effects may lessen over time, however (Kraut et al., 1996). Perhaps these teens substitute online activity for social interactions, or maybe teens who are lonely and have few friends to begin with are more likely to choose Internet over face-to-face involvement (Subrahmanyam et al., 2001). Depending on how young people use the Internet, working on line certainly could affect cognitive skills such as problem-solving ability and information search skills, but no studies have yet explored such effects.

Explaining Media's Effects

Why do media have the effects they do? Let's consider several explanations.

First, children are very capable of **observational learning,** or learning through watching and imitating. And this holds true regardless of whether the child is observing in person or through television (Bandura, 1977). Children often imitate specific behaviors they see in the media, particularly when they actively attend to the behaviors, strongly identify with the characters, and have the opportunity to engage in the behaviors in real life. This opportunity to practice is the reason many researchers are concerned about the prevalence of violence in video games. Not only do these games model aggression, but the game format also gives children chances to *practice* simulated violent acts like kicking, hitting, and shooting. The likelihood that children will imitate the behavior increases even more if parents, teachers, peers, or others provide reinforcement for it (knowingly or not). Children also learn specific strategies, overall problem-solving approaches, and attitudes through observation. If they regularly see helpful and cooperative models solving problems and interacting in prosocial ways, they are getting consistent mental practice in those strategies and are more likely to think of them first when attempting to solve real-life problems. In contrast, if they regularly see aggression being used to address problems, their first inclination is more likely to be an aggressive approach.

Cognitive psychologists propose that children also acquire **cognitive schemas,** as opposed to specific behaviors, through observation (Huston & Wright, 1998). A *schema* is a person's understanding of the objects and sequences of events that are likely to be encountered in a specific situation (see Chapter 5). A steady diet of unrealistic, stereotyped, and perhaps even prejudiced presentations of people and events on television can encourage inaccurate cognitive schemas. Younger children, who have less real-life experience to counter the information, are particularly vulnerable to this effect. Additionally, if children regularly see violent intentions, interpretations, and behavior in the media, they can develop cognitive schemas for social interaction that overemphasize violence. These schemas may lead children to interpret situations as menacing when they really pose no threat.

It is likely that TV produces **desensitization** to emotions and events—a gradual dulling of response that causes more intense stimulation to be needed to produce a reaction. As children get more used to seeing violence on television, they are less shocked by violence, more accepting of it, and more likely to see it as an acceptable way to behave. Desensitization happens to individuals, but it can also happen to a culture as a whole. For example, think about changes over time in audience reaction to movie violence. The 1903 short film *The Great Train Robbery* features a close-up of a cowboy shooting a gun directly into the camera. "The first audiences

observational learning

Learning through watching and imitating others' real or televised behavior.

cognitive schemas

A person's understanding of the objects and sequences of events that are likely to be encountered in specific situations.

desensitization

The gradual decrease of a person's (or culture's) sensitivity to a stimulus; as desensitization increases, more intense stimulation is needed to produce a reaction.

thinking
OF ANNA & MICHELLE

Do you think Michelle may ► be watching too much TV? What effects, good and bad, could this be having? How can Anna increase the benefits of Michelle's TV watching and minimize the negative effects?

arousal

Emotional and physiological activation or alertness. A heightened level of arousal can cause stronger reactions to a stimulus.

who saw the film reacted by running out of the theater screaming" (Bushman & Anderson, 2001, p. 478). What would it take for today's movie audiences to have the same reaction?

Until children become desensitized, however, a media stimulus can increase their level of **arousal.** That is, it can stir them up emotionally and physiologically. Heightened arousal can continue after the media experience ends and can cause the child to react more strongly (positively or negatively) to whatever happens next. For example, a boy in a state of heightened arousal after playing a violent video game may react with much greater anger and aggression when his parents tell him it's time for bed than he would have otherwise (as we know from hard experience!).

When we were teens, our parents despaired over the terrible influence of hard rock music and sci-fi movies like *Star Wars.* In our parents' generation, Elvis was evil. For today's parents, the worry is violent video games and the Internet. Yet in each generation, most children emerge intact and healthy. There is no question that media have an influence—why else would companies continue to pour money into advertising their products in the media? But as systems theories of child development remind us, media constitute *one of several* important influences. Parenting practices, the overall culture, and individual child factors interact with the types of media and media content children regularly experience to influence complex characteristics and behaviors like reading, aggression, prejudice, and helping others. It simply makes sense for parents and other adults to monitor the amount and content of the media children are using. Adults must think carefully about the kinds of influences children are exposed to on a regular basis and make conscious decisions based on the individual children involved. It isn't television per se that has positive or negative effects, but what is portrayed and how families handle it: "The *medium* is not the message. The *message* is the message!" (Anderson et al., 2001, p. 134). To learn more about how people who work in the media utilize knowledge of child development, read the Professional Perspective box called "Career Focus: Meet a Marketing Executive."

LET'S REVIEW . . .

1. Television programs designed to teach academic skills such as reading and mathematics:
   a. have short-term effects, but no long-term benefits.
   b. can help increase children's readiness for school.
   c. have no effect once parents' education and income are considered.
   d. are most effective if children begin watching them after age 4.

2. According to research studies, violence on television:
   a. has no lasting effect on children's behavior.
   b. affects boys' but not girls' aggressive behavior.
   c. has a small immediate effect, but no long-term effects on children.
   d. has a moderate effect on aggressive behavior in children.

3. Based on current research, which of the following is *true* about the effects of playing video games?
   a. They have a greater negative effect on children's behavior than watching violent television.
   b. There is no evidence that they have a negative effect on children's behavior.
   c. They can help children improve several different spatial skills.
   d. They increase the amount of children's social interactions.

4. Jennifer watches a great deal of television. She believes that most women wear size 4 clothes, have beautiful clothes and hair, and go on a date every weekend night. TV seems to have affected Jennifer's:
   a. cognitive schemas about women.
   b. sensitivity to aggressive behavior.
   c. stereotypes about ethnic groups.
   d. tendency to see aggression as a good way to solve problems.

5. **True or False:** African American and Hispanic children spend more time watching television than non-Hispanic white children.

6. **True or False:** Watching even small amounts of television has a negative effect on academic performance.

A Professional PERSPECTIVE...

Career Focus: Meet a Marketing Executive

Jan Craige Singer
Watertown, Massachusetts
President/partner at BIG BLUE DOT

What kind of work do you do?
At BIG BLUE DOT, we work with clients who want to reach children from toddlers to teens and everyone in between. Our services include broadcast design, website design, logos, print and packaging, and branding. We are a mix of graphic designers, producers, brand strategists, and child development specialists dedicated solely to the universe of kids. This blend enables us to deliver fresh, smart, fun, age-appropriate solutions to companies that care about kids. Having an understanding of how kids learn, think, and make sense of the world is at the very core of the work we do. Each time we solve a new design problem, we find a deeper understanding of what kids want at specific stages of development and how our clients can reach children from tots to teens.

What training do you have in development, and how has this knowledge been useful?
My professional background includes TV marketing, promotion, and programming. It wasn't until I had my own children and had the opportunity to develop programming ideas

for the Discovery Channel and the Learning Channel that I realized creating great educational and entertaining stuff for kids was what I enjoyed doing the most. I took a few years off to stay home with my son and daughter and decided to go to graduate school to find out how kids really learn. I now have an Ed.M. from Harvard in child development. I sought out a company where I could combine my love and respect for children with a creative atmosphere. I'm happy to say I found it at BIG BLUE DOT.

Are there many people in your profession who have knowledge and training about development? What's a specific example of how this knowledge affected your work?
Children are the primary target for our clients. They come to us for our knowledge and expertise in reaching kids. It's remarkable how many of the larger entertainment companies have full-time child development experts on staff to help them understand the children they are trying to appeal to. Recently we worked with Suave on a new line of personal care products for tweens (8- to 12-year-olds). Though they hired us for our kid knowledge, the first thing we did was explain the world of tweens by creating a visual tween audit document. This way, our client had something tangible to refer to during the cre-

ative process. The audit explored characteristics of both boys and girls in the 8–12 age group such as the social awareness of the opposite sex, the development of tight groups of friends, caring about how they look, looking for social acceptance, knowing the rules but starting to push the limits a little. We also knew it was important to appeal to both boys and girls, so we searched for a common theme that was rather unisex in nature. We presented several different packaging concepts to Suave. They all reflected the interests and attitudes of tweens in music and dance, adventure and sports, urban cool, ecology and the environment, and mythology and magic.

What advice would you offer to students interested in child development who are considering going into this profession?
I would advise students to think about the incredible opportunity and not forget the responsibility that is unique in marketing to kids. If you love kids, you'll love thinking about them, studying them, designing and creating for them every day. And if you really love kids, you can use your understanding of them to help companies be respectful, honest, playful, educational, and entertaining in the messages and products that they bring to kids. ∎

Cultural Contexts for Development

Throughout this book we have often mentioned the influence of culture when explaining why children behave, think, or feel in certain ways. In every chapter we have pointed out differences among cultures. But what is *culture,* and how does it affect children's development? In this section we will discuss types of cultures and consider their impact on children's development.

As you study this section, ask yourself these questions:

- Why is culture important for our understanding of child development? In what ways does culture affect children?

- What are *individualism* and *collectivism*? In what ways are they different?

- How does poverty affect child development? What differences are there in the effects of urban versus rural poverty?

- What is *acculturation,* and how are children affected by it? Is it good or bad to be a "child cultural broker"?

Cultural Orientations: Individualism and Collectivism

A **culture** is a system of shared customs and meanings that allow individuals to participate as members of a group and that are transmitted from one generation to the next (Cole, 1999; Goodenough, 1994). A culture includes clearly specified rules (such as laws) as well as attitudes, beliefs, goals, values, and traditions. Cultures can be vastly different in their specific customs and meanings, but one important dimension on which people often compare cultures has to do with their emphasis on the group or on the individual. For example, think about how you describe yourself. Do you tend to use terms that emphasize your individuality or your relationships with others? Now think about how responsible you feel for the well-being of your friends and family: Would you readily sacrifice your own desires, independence, and happiness for their sake? Psychologists have posed questions like these to people from a variety of different places. Their responses can be categorized as having an individualistic or collectivistic general cultural orientation.

Individualism involves the general belief that people are independent of each other. Individualistic cultures focus on an individual's "rights above duties, a concern for oneself and immediate family, an emphasis on personal autonomy and self-fulfillment," and an identity based on personal accomplishments (Oyserman, Coon, & Kemmelmeier, 2002, p. 4). In contrast, **collectivism** is the view that individuals are interdependent members of a social group and that the greatest concern is with the group's goals, values, and well-being. In collectivism the emphasis is on fulfilling duties to others, even if it means sacrificing your own desires and happiness; identity has to do with group beliefs, accomplishments, and characteristics rather than individual ones. Group membership in such a culture may be based on kinship, religion, ethnicity, or something else. Researchers often talk about whole countries as having an individualistic or collectivistic cultural orientation, but any specific individual within the country may not have the same orientation. Within a given country there can be large differences in how strictly individuals adhere to the overall cultural orientation or to any of the culture's specific customs or meanings (Chirkov, Ryan, Kim, & Kaplan, 2003; Triandis, 1995).

As you probably have already guessed, researchers often describe Western cultures like that of the United States as individualistic. Within U.S. culture, they typically see European Americans as the most individualistic. And they tend to view East Asian cultures such as those

culture

A system of shared customs and meanings that allow individuals to participate as a member of a group and that are transmitted from one generation to the next.

individualism

A cultural orientation based on the belief that people are independent of each other; emphasizes individual rights, self-fulfillment, and personal accomplishments.

collectivism

A cultural orientation based on the belief that people are interdependent members of a social group; emphasizes duty to others and group goals, values, and well-being.

of China and Japan as more collectivistic. Studies have found differences related to individualism and collectivism in many cultural beliefs and behaviors relevant for child development, including parenting practices, emotional attachment type, attitudes toward academic effort and ability, cognitive styles, school discipline strategies, self-esteem and self-concept, cooperation and competition, conflict resolution, helping behaviors, preferences for working alone versus in groups, and freedom in selecting groups (Greenfield & Suzuki, 1998; Oyserman et al., 2002; Rothbaum, Weisz, Pott, Miyake, & Morelli, 2000). For example, many European Americans (not to mention developmental researchers) view authoritative parenting as effective because it seems to encourage child outcomes such as self-reliance, self-regulation, and exploration—outcomes that an individualistic cultural orientation finds desirable. But this parenting style is not the norm and these outcomes are not the goal in other, less individualistic cultures such as those of East Asian and African countries (Greenfield & Suzuki, 1998).

Recent research is challenging some of the established beliefs about individualistic and collectivistic cultures, however. It appears that some theories and measures may be biased toward one orientation or the other; also, some studies question the traditional beliefs about which cultures show strong tendencies toward one orientation or the other (Oyserman et al., 2002; Rothbaum et al., 2000). One meta-analysis summarized the results of 83 studies conducted since 1980 (Oyserman et al., 2002). As you can see in Figure 13.6, people of European heritage in the United States were more individualistic and less collectivistic than many other groups tested. But the difference in individualism was largest between Euro-Americans and Middle Eastern populations, not between Euro-Americans and East Asian peoples as theorists have often suggested. Also, the difference in individualism between Euro-Americans and African peoples was almost as large as that between Euro-Americans and East Asians. In terms of collectivistic orientations, the largest difference was between European Americans and African populations: The Africans were far more collectivistic than the Euro-Americans.

Other analyses compared European Americans to individual countries—and obtained some surprising results. Euro-Americans were significantly *higher* in collectivism than the Japanese, and they were not significantly different from Koreans. Patterns of differences depended partly on which particular aspects of individualism and collectivism the researchers assessed. For example, Euro-Americans and Japanese were very different in their beliefs about personal uniqueness, personal privacy, directness of communication, and working in groups, but not in their attitudes toward competition. And Euro-Americans rated themselves as quite high in collectivism when it was defined as having a strong sense of *belonging* to a group, but low in collectivism when it was defined as having a strong sense of *duty* to the group. Please note, however, that most of the studies in this meta-analysis surveyed primarily college students, who may differ in some important ways from the general populations of their countries. Perhaps the long-held beliefs about cultural differences in individualism and collectivism are still valid for other segments of the populations. But as you've learned, cultures change. Maybe the college students in the studies reflect changes that members of this younger generation, who probably have broader exposure to other world cultures than prior generations had, bring to their cultures.

What's the Neighborhood Like? Urban and Rural Poverty

In recent years, developmental researchers have focused a great deal of attention on characteristics of the neighborhoods in which children live. Neighborhoods often consist of people who are similar in important ways; for example, in attitudes, beliefs, ethnicity, language, and/or behavior. The resources a community supports, the private and public behavior it encourages, the parenting practices it encourages, and the social activities it organizes and allows can all affect children for better or for worse, directly and indirectly (Furstenberg &

YOUR PERSPECTIVE NOTES

Do you consider your cultural orientation to be individualistic or collectivistic? If you've known anyone with a different cultural orientation, describe any differences you have noticed.

thinking OF ANNA & MICHELLE

Do you see indications of a collectivistic or an individualistic cultural orientation in Anna? In Michelle? How might their orientations affect their beliefs, behaviors, and expectations?

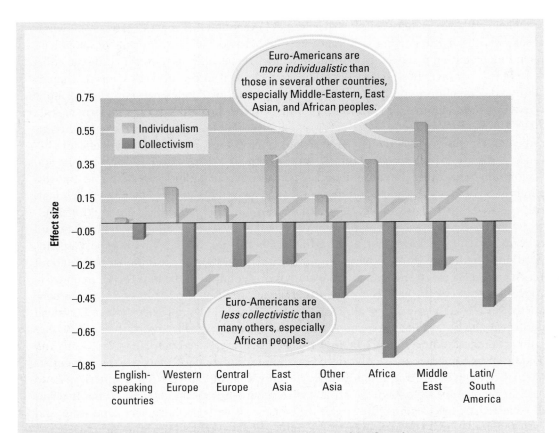

FIGURE 13.6 Individualism and Collectivism: European Americans versus Other Countries

In this graph the positive "effect size" bars indicate that people of European heritage in the United States had higher scores; the negative bars indicate lower Euro-American scores relative to the areas shown.

English-speaking: South Africa, New Zealand, Australia

Western Europe: Spain, Portugal, Norway, Italy, Germany, France, Finland, Denmark, Austria

Central Europe: Slovenia, Russia, Poland, Lithuania, Hungary, Greece, Estonia, Bulgaria

East Asia: Vietnam, Taiwan, Singapore, PR China, Korea, Japan, Hong Kong

Other Asia: Philippines, Pakistan, Nepal, Indonesia, India, Guam

Africa: Zimbabwe, Tanzania, Nigeria, Ghana

Middle East: Turkey, Israel, Egypt, Bahrain

Latin/South America: Venezuela, Puerto Rico, Peru, Mexico, Costa Rica, Colombia, Chile, Brazil, Argentina

Source: Adapted from D. Oyserman, H. M. Coon, & M. Kemmelmeier. (2002). Rethinking individualism and collectivism: Evaluation of theoretical assumptions and meta-analyses. *Psychological Bulletin, 128,* pp. 13, 18. Copyright 2002 by the American Psychological Association. Adapted with permission.

Hughes, 1997). One factor that stands out is the impact of living in a poor neighborhood: Living in poverty has pervasive negative effects on children's development. But does poverty look different depending on where a child experiences it? Researchers have begun to ask whether inner-city ghettos affect children differently than poor rural environments such as those in isolated Appalachian communities or on economically stressed farms.

■ **Poverty: A Culture of Economics.**   As of 2001, the overall poverty rate for U.S. families was 11.7 percent, up from the previous year's rate of 11.3 percent, but still among the lowest in two decades. Poverty rates for all ethnic groups are at record low levels, and the rate for children under the age of 18 is at its lowest level since 1979. However, look carefully at

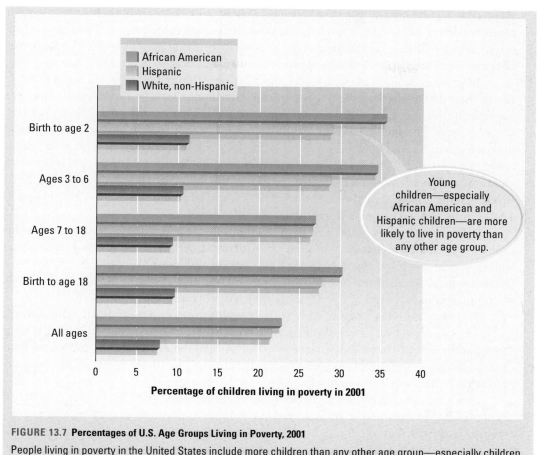

FIGURE 13.7 Percentages of U.S. Age Groups Living in Poverty, 2001

People living in poverty in the United States include more children than any other age group—especially children under the age of 2. African American and Hispanic children are especially at risk.

Source: Proctor & Dalaker (2002).

Figure 13.7 and note what this figure shows about the poverty status of *children* as a group relative to the overall population. Although the situation is improving, the poverty rate of children up to age 18 is still almost 1.5 times higher than the rate for all ages; children from birth to 2 years fare still worse. In other words, children, particularly young children, are more likely to live in poverty than any other age group. This is especially true for African American and Hispanic children; 3 out of 10 children in these ethnic groups live in poverty. Even more striking is the fact that almost half (44.5 percent) of families living in poverty include at least one person who works *full-time.* Indeed, 9 percent of poor families have two or more full-time workers (*Current Population Survey,* 2001; Dalaker, 2001; Proctor & Dalaker, 2002; Song & Lu, 2002).

Think for a moment about what these numbers mean for children. In 2002, the U.S. Census Bureau defined the poverty level as a total annual income of not more than $12,047 for a household of two people ($18,556 for four people). Clearly, in many ways children growing up in households at these income levels live in a different culture than children in wealthier homes. For example, children living in middle-income homes and accustomed to eating out occasionally may be concerned about which restaurant they'll be able to go to for dinner; poor children are more likely to be concerned about whether they will have enough to eat at all. Middle- and upper-income children working on school projects often can take it for

YOUR
PERSPECTIVE
NOTES

Think about the things you've done in the last week or so. How might these activities have been different or more difficult (or easy) if you were poor or if you were wealthy?

granted that someone will supply whatever materials are needed, take them to a library or bookstore to get information, and help them as they complete the project. The same project can present a challenge for children living in poverty for many reasons—lack of transportation, lack of parents' time, and lack of money to buy materials, to name a few.

In general, children living in poverty face seriously limited options and many difficulties in their day-to-day lives. Lack of resources, continuous hassles, and relatively frequent negative life events create high levels of stress for all family members, and the stress never seems to abate. The younger a child is and the longer the child lives in poverty, the larger the impact tends to be. And the more poverty risk factors a child experiences (such as poor health, inadequate parenting, and low social support), the worse the effect. Living in poverty affects children's well-being in numerous ways, including the following (Bradley & Corwyn, 2002; Brooks-Gunn, Klebanov, Liaw, & Duncan, 1995; Duncan & Brooks-Gunn, 1997; Halpern, 1993; Linver, Brooks-Gunn, & Kohen, 2002; Parke & Buriel, 1998):

▶ Poor children are more likely than children who are not poor to suffer physical health problems, including higher rates of preterm birth, low birth weight, illnesses, injuries, poisoning, parental neglect, exposure to toxic substances, and abuse (Pelton, 1989). They have less access to adequate health care and lower rates of immunizations, so illnesses and injuries often progress to more serious levels before they receive treatment.

▶ Poverty correlates significantly with lower IQ scores, lower academic achievement, and lower scores on a variety of cognitive measures (Bradley, Corwyn, & Whiteside-Mansell, 1996; Smith, Brooks-Gunn, & Klebanov, 1997). Poor children are less ready for school than other children in terms of background knowledge, cognitive skills, social skills, and self-regulation of behavior and emotions.

▶ Poor children have less access to quality child care and preschool programs, attend poorer-quality schools, and enjoy far fewer opportunities for positive extracurricular and enrichment activities than other children. They are also more likely to repeat grade levels and eventually to drop out of school (Battin-Pearson et al., 2000; Zill, Moore, Smith, Stief, & Coiro, 1995).

▶ Parents living in poverty rely more often on power-assertive discipline tactics (e.g., issuing commands and using physical punishment) and are less likely to use reasoning, involve the child in decisions, or give praise for proper behavior (Bradley, Corwyn, McAdoo, & Coll, 2001; McLoyd, 1995). Parenting can be less consistent and less child centered, although this often depends on whether other problems or unexpected events arise (Halpern, 1993).

▶ Homelessness is a very real possibility for children living in poverty. One recent survey found that families with children constitute 36 percent of the homeless population, and children under the age of 18 account for almost 26 percent of the total number of homeless people in the United States. Not surprisingly, homeless children have even more health and developmental problems than other poor children (Molnar, Roth, & Klein, 1990; Smith & Smith, 2001; U.S. National Coalition for the Homeless, 2001).

▶ Poor children are more likely than other children to show social and emotional difficulties from an early age. They have higher rates of substance abuse, behavior problems, mental illness, suicide, and personality disorders, and lower self-esteem and self-confidence. Poverty in itself may not directly cause these difficulties, but it creates stressful environmental conditions that make them more likely to develop (McLoyd, 1995).

Children from ethnic minority backgrounds are far more likely to live in poverty and spend longer living in poverty than non-Hispanic white children. Many of the ethnic-group differences we have noted in other chapters (e.g., differences in parenting practices, academic achievement and school completion, early pregnancy, and low birth weight, to

thinking
OF ANNA & MICHELLE ▶

How is poverty affecting Anna and Michelle? What can Anna do to deal more successfully with these effects?

name a few) at least partly reflect the impacts of poverty. For many outcomes, in fact, differences between ethnic groups fade or disappear when analysts take the effects of poverty into account. And innovative ongoing research is showing that moving from a poor neighborhood to an area with little poverty has a multitude of positive effects, including decreased emotional distress, less reliance on harsh parenting practices, and less violent behavior (DeAngelis, 2001).

■ **The Inner City.**   Inner-city poverty is an especially difficult context for children. Almost one-quarter of all children in U.S. inner cities are poor. All of the effects of poverty we've already discussed weigh especially heavily on children living in inner-city poverty, and the vast majority of these children are members of ethnic minorities (Brooks-Gunn, Duncan, & Aber, 1997). There are additional problems as well. Crime, particularly violent crime, is much more frequent in the inner city. Housing is often substandard, crowded, and inconsistent. Positive options for children and adolescents are less available, and negative options like gangs and drug use are more common. Children and parents alike focus more on the present than on the future; "simply surviving in the inner city is viewed by these families as evidence" of success (Brookins, Petersen, & Brooks, 1997, p. 54; Burton, Obeidallah, & Allison, 1996). Parents lack financial and emotional resources, often facing chronic unemployment or inconsistent employment as well as insufficient support and help from the community. Often there is a sense of social isolation from other parts of the city. At the same time, families may not feel connected to the immediate neighborhood but may keep to themselves because of fear for children's safety. Inner-city children achieve far less academic success and graduate from high school at far lower rates than students in other neighborhoods, with a 50 percent dropout rate in some areas. These outcomes limit options for these children even further and serve to perpetuate the cycle of poverty for the next generation.

In addition to the obstacles other poor children face, inner-city children living in poverty must deal with higher levels of violent crime, bad housing, lack of positive options, less support from parents, temptation from gangs and drugs, and a sense of isolation from the community.

Community-bridging families help children find and take advantage of opportunities by closely monitoring their activities and friendships, maintaining social support networks, encouraging their involvement in positive activities, and expecting them to help with family responsibilities.

thinking
OF ANNA & MICHELLE

Do you see any evidence of ► *community-bridging family* characteristics in Anna's family? How could Anna use community-bridging approaches to improve her and Michelle's situation?

YOUR
PERSPECTIVE
~~PERSPECTIVE~~

NOTES

Do you know any community-bridging families? Think about what kinds of things they do differently than other families and how these behaviors affect their children's development.

Are inner-city children doomed to stay in these neighborhoods? Not necessarily. Numerous social programs try to help create economic opportunities and improve the educational success of inner-city youth, with varying degrees of success (Brown & Richman, 1997; Lehman & Smeeding, 1997). Although there is no doubt that neighborhood factors are important, a child's family can overcome the influence of a poor neighborhood. For example, researchers have identified several family behaviors that help inner-city African American adolescents be more successful (Jarrett, 1995). These behaviors characterize *community-bridging families,* which can help children find and take advantage of opportunities within and outside the immediate neighborhood. For example:

▶ Community-bridging families establish and maintain networks among family members (immediate and extended) that provide support and resources.

▶ Such families restrict children's interaction with community members whose lifestyle is inconsistent with the family's goals and values; this reduces children's exposure to negative influences.

▶ These families carefully and consistently monitor their children's activities and friendships.

▶ They encourage children's involvement in positive activities—activities that increase contact with like-minded families and friends and help children develop their skills and talents.

▶ These families expect children to contribute to the family's well-being through chores, responsibilities, part-time jobs, and the like, all of which help increase children's self-esteem and family cohesion.

The poverty rate in rural areas is almost as high as in inner cities, and children in rural poverty suffer many of the same effects as the inner-city poor. The rural poor are from a wide range of ethnicities, background cultures, and geographic regions.

■ **Rural Poverty.** Many people picture growing up in rural America as the ideal childhood, a *Mayberry R.F.D.*–like existence filled with children like Opie Taylor, parents like Andy Griffith, and friends like Aunt Bee and Barney Fife. Urban residents tend to believe that rural people are self-sufficient and friendly; that rural areas are clean, safe, and virtually free from crime; that rural life causes little stress and affords lots of leisure time to enjoy nature and family activities; and that rural families are very traditional in structure, strongly family oriented, and closely connected to friendly communities (Struthers & Bokemeier, 2000; Willits & Luloff, 1995). The reality, of course, is much more complex. Often overlooked is the fact that the poverty rate in rural areas is almost as high as in inner cities. In the year 2000, for example 24.4 percent of children in inner cities and 19.2 percent of children in rural areas were poor, compared to 10.8 percent of children in suburbs (Children's Defense Fund, 2001a). Yet it is only recently that developmental researchers have begun to look at children who grow up in rural areas.

Like all poor children, children living in rural poverty face more limited options, more daily hassles, more negative life events, and an overall higher level of stress than nonpoor children. They experience many of the effects we have reviewed—poorer physical health; lower cognitive skills, school readiness, and academic achievement; higher dropout rates; higher rates of drug use, particularly alcohol and tobacco use; harsher parenting practices; and a greater risk of depression. Children in rural poverty can also suffer from isolation, decreased access to social services and health care, and discrimination. On other measures, however, it's not clear if rural poor children differ from poor urban or nonpoor children. For example, one extensive study of rural Iowa farm children found that family ties are often strong and serve to connect several generations, and that strong social networks connect these farm communities (Elder & Conger, 2000). Strong family loyalty also is frequent in Appalachian poor families. At least for these rural children, poverty does not seem to disrupt social supports as much as it does in the inner city (Crockett, Shanahan, & Jackson-Newsom, 2000; Wilson & Peterson, 2000).

All in all, it is difficult to draw conclusions about rural children who are poor. Researchers have not studied them extensively because of the widespread perception that such children are few in number and that they do not face the same problems as other poor children. Families in rural poverty are also very diverse, representing a wide range of geographic regions, ethnicities, background cultures and values, and occupational histories. Poverty in the mountains of rural Appalachia may be quite different from poverty in small Iowa farming communities, Louisiana bayous, Pennsylvania mining towns, northern Maine fishing villages, or western Native American reservations.

Coming to America: Immigration and Acculturation

acculturation

The process of learning the language, values, customs, and social skills of a new culture.

Throughout the history of the United States, immigrants have coped with the stresses of settling in a new country, usually arriving with few resources and little knowledge of the language and customs. **Acculturation** is the process of learning the language, values, customs, and social skills of a new culture (Chun, Organista, & Marin, 2003; Parke & Buriel, 1998). It is a lengthy process, often spanning several generations. Acculturation can create conflict and stress for parents and children alike, but the difficulty of the overall process varies. For example, one study found greater conflicts between parents' and adolescents' views on specific family values (e.g., obligation to family) in Vietnamese and Armenian immigrant families than among Mexican immigrants. Perhaps this difference occurred because a large Mexican American population lived together in the area studied or because the Mexican families had greater familiarity with mainstream U.S. culture before immigrating (Phinney, Ong, & Madden, 2000). And when adolescents speak different languages than their parents (i.e., the parents talk to their children in the native language, but the children usually respond in English), the teenagers report less communication and closeness with their parents than do teenagers who use the same language as their parents (Tseng & Fuligni, 2000).

Adolescence can be a stressful time for immigrant families. This third-generation immigrant is likely to have adopted American customs faster than her parents, which can lead to conflict. Her first-generation immigrant grandparent is likely to maintain an identity of her country of origin, while the girl and her parents are likely to have an Asian American ethnic identity.

Children of immigrants may find themselves serving as cultural brokers. This son is expected to teach his parents about the majority culture and represent the family to others, but he must also make sure his parents retain status and respect inside and outside the family.

First-generation immigrants—immigrants who are born elsewhere and later immigrate—usually have lower family incomes than later generations. They tend to live with friends or relatives for several years after immigrating, to know less about U.S. customs than their offspring, and to be less proficient in English. *Second-generation immigrants* are the children of immigrant parents. Born in the United States, they are more likely than first-generation immigrants to be *bilingual,* or to speak both English and the language of the country their family came from. They often define their ethnic identity in terms of both their family's country of origin and the United States (e.g., Mexican American, Korean American); in contrast, first-generation immigrants tend to identify with their home country, especially if they were older than adolescence when they immigrated. *Third-generation immigrants* (all subsequent generations of U.S.-born children) tend to have adopted many American customs and to describe themselves as ethnic Americans (Perez & Padilla, 2000). However, they often maintain some aspects of their culture of origin, especially if they continue to live in ethnic neighborhoods and remain in close contact with first- and second-generation immigrants. It's interesting that many third-generation immigrants fare *worse* than their second-generation parents in some ways. For example, even though family income and English proficiency increase with successive generations, educational outcomes are worse for third-generation than for second-generation Hispanic and Asian American children (Bean, Chapa, Berg, & Sowards, 1994; Fuligni, 1997; Kao & Tienda, 1995).

Regardless of their countries of origin, immigrants must develop strategies in order to adapt successfully. For example, studies find that Mexican immigrants emphasize and strengthen family ties; this strategy provides additional sources of economic, emotional, and

thinking
OF ANNA & MICHELLE

How acculturated do Anna, Michelle, and their extended family seem? Do you see evidence of biculturalism? What benefits do they seem to get, and what stresses do they seem to feel, as a result of coming from an immigrant background?

social support. They also cultivate **biculturalism,** or adoption of two cultural orientations at the same time. Biculturalism allows families to maintain the cultural values they have brought from their original homeland but still to understand and function successfully in the new culture. The children of immigrants often find themselves serving as **child cultural brokers**—as interpreters not only of the language but also of the culture of the new country for their parents and other family members (Parke & Buriel, 1998). This can be a difficult position for children. They must try to represent the family to members of the majority culture and to cope with important adult responsibilities like legal matters, tax forms, and insurance claims. Child cultural brokers are supposed to teach their parents about these matters and other subtleties of the new culture, but they must do it in such a way that their parents maintain their status and respect within the family and community. Being a child cultural broker can have some positive effects: These children can develop a greater knowledge of U.S. culture, greater sensitivity to the challenges facing their parents, and stronger bonds with their parents. But this position can also be quite stressful, especially when you remember that even elementary school children sometimes must play this role. Finally, adolescence may present particular problems for second-generation immigrant families. U.S.-born adolescents tend to change their values and beliefs more rapidly than their parents, creating a bigger difference in values between parents and adolescents in these families than in other immigrant or nonimmigrant families. Because many immigrants come from cultures that emphasize respect for and obedience to adults, this difference can create a great deal of family stress and disruption. The more differences there are in the acculturation of parents and children, the more family conflict there tends to be (Farver, Narang, & Bhadha, 2002; Phinney et al., 2000).

Immigrants to the United States gradually acculturate to the mainstream culture, but it's important to remember that mainstream U.S. culture also changes. Latinos and Asian Americans are the fastest-growing ethnic minority groups in the United States, and each of these groups represents a varied collection of home cultures and languages. As the population of the United States becomes more diverse, the mainstream culture will evolve to incorporate new customs and reflect this rich diversity.

Explaining Culture's Influence

In essence, culture gives an individual a "set of lenses for seeing the world" (Triandis, 1994, p. 13). Back in Chapter 1 we described an experience one of us had in East Germany in 1989, months after the fall of the Communist government. The citizens there often said, "It's not possible" when they encountered an impediment, which sounded odd to an American. A lifetime in the United States led to the belief that obstructions can be overcome given enough effort, time, and resources. Being steeped in communist culture led East Germans to the very different belief that trying to remove obstructions was futile and perhaps even dangerous.

Think back to the layers of Bronfenbrenner's ecological systems theory of child development, shown in Figure 1.3, and look at the many different systems that affect children directly or indirectly. All of these systems exist within and are affected by a specific cultural setting. At the broadest levels (the macrosystem and the exosystem), culture affects

biculturalism

Adopting two cultural orientations at the same time.

child cultural brokers

Children of immigrants who serve as interpreters of the language and culture of the new country for their parents and other family members.

the options that are available to children and their families, the resources they have to draw on, the governmental policies and laws that help or hurt them, the types of neighborhoods they live in, and the types of lifestyles they have and wish for. On more individual levels (the microsystem and the mesosystem), culture affects how and with whom children's social interactions take place; what kinds of parenting families consider appropriate; what people see as important or problematic, possible or impossible; what constitutes acceptable versus inappropriate behavior; and what children expect of themselves and others. In short, culture permeates all these levels to affect children's thoughts, emotions, beliefs, and behaviors. Yet most often we aren't even aware of the pervasive effects of our own culture—that is, until we encounter someone else's culture! Because cultural beliefs and customs are so thoroughly ingrained, it's not surprising that we sometimes misconstrue cultural *differences* as *deficits*. We are so accustomed to doing and thinking about things in the ways our own culture considers correct that we forget there are often other, equally correct, ways to go about things. "Like the air one breathes, under ordinary conditions, these values frameworks do not rise to conscious awareness" (Greenfield & Suzuki, 1998, p. 1060).

For a culture to continue, it must be transmitted to new generations. How does this transmission take place? We learn cultural customs and meanings directly, through day-by-day experiences with those around us, as well as indirectly, through the options available (or unavailable) to us, the political and social systems that operate around us, and even the physical environments in which we live. Adults directly and intentionally instruct children in some aspects of culture. For example, in technology-based cultures the ability to read is a highly valued and rewarded skill that adults explicitly teach to children. Through observational learning children pick up many aspects of culture, such as awareness of the conditions under which aggressive or cooperative behavior is considered proper. And when a society withholds certain experiences from certain segments of the population, this too conveys cultural assumptions. For example, when a society refuses to let some of its members go to school, participate in government, own property, or move about freely, this teaches children a clear set of beliefs and rules. The more consistent with one another the lessons of the different modes of transmission are, the more effectively children learn the culture. Cultural transmission is not a one-way street, however. As we've said before, cultures change over time. Children learn their culture's customs and meanings, but they also modify parts of it. Sometimes they experience a strong conflict between the culture of their parents' generation and that of their peers. In striving to adapt, they develop different attitudes, beliefs, or behaviors.

In this chapter we have introduced you to three of the complex systems that affect child development: schools, media, and culture. Though we have discussed each as a separate topic, it's important to keep in mind that these and other systems all interact to create a child's overall social, psychological, and physical environment. One way to think about these systems is by using a "garden metaphor" (Cole, 1999, p. 80). After all, one meaning of the word *culture* is "helping things grow." Our schools, our media sources, our neighborhoods, and our overall cultures can all help children grow and develop in positive ways. We hope that the information in this chapter and throughout this book will help you "culture" the children you spend time with.

YOUR PERSPECTIVE NOTES

Have you experienced any cultural differences that led to misunderstandings or confusions? Describe what happened and how it could have gone more smoothly.

YOUR PERSPECTIVE NOTES

Think about your own culture. How have you learned your culture's beliefs, attitudes, and customs?

1. Andre has been offered a very well-paying job, but it would mean moving far away from his parents and extended family. His family does not want him to leave their town, so Andre does not take the job because he doesn't want to go against his family's wishes. Andre is most likely:

    a. individualistic in his cultural orientation.

    b. collectivistic in his cultural orientation.

    c. neutral in his cultural orientation.

    d. European American.

2. Which of the following is *true* about the effects of poverty on child development?

    a. Poor children have more physical health problems than other children.

    b. Poor children perform just as well in school as other children.

    c. Poor children's parents are just as consistent and child centered as other parents.

    d. Poor children are more likely to attend preschool than other children.

3. Which of the following is one of the main areas of difference between urban poverty and rural poverty?

    a. lack of options

    b. increased daily hassles

    c. high level of stress

    d. strength of family support

4. Nine-year-old Miguel helps his parents with paperwork for their medical forms, translates for them when they must deal with their landlord, and helps them understand which kinds of stores are likely to negotiate prices and which are not. Miguel is a:

    a. first-generation immigrant.

    b. collectivist.

    c. child cultural broker.

    d. community bridger.

5. **True or False:** European Americans rate themselves as high in collectivism when collectivism is defined as having a duty to a group.

6. **True or False:** Ethnic minority children are more likely to live in poverty than nonethnic children.

Answers: 1. b, 2. a, 3. d, 4. c, 5. F, 6. T

thinking

BACK TO ANNA & MICHELLE

Now that you have studied this chapter, you should be able to give Anna some guidance. Her concern over the quality of the local schools is a good sign that she is thinking ahead about Michelle's comfort and success at school. Help Anna understand some of the characteristics of effective schooling. It seems there was a mismatch between Anna's culture and her own schools' climates. Perhaps you can help her find ways to work with the community to improve the schools' understanding of her culture, and vice versa. Better awareness and communication can help both Michelle and Anna feel more comfortable and compatible with the educational system and can increase Michelle's chances for success. Point out the benefits of a mastery orientation in learning and encourage Anna to reinforce this orientation in Michelle. This will be especially important if school practices work against this orientation. Tell Anna about the effects of early childhood education and explain the importance of school readiness. Anna probably cannot afford a better-quality preschool than the Head Start program Michelle attends. Perhaps, however, she can at least take advantage of her family's close relationships to keep Michelle in Head Start while she works more hours.

Although Anna gains free time and seems to have better control of Michelle's behavior by encouraging TV, this tactic may be causing more problems than it is worth. Prompt Anna to think about whether watching inappropriate shows might have triggered any of Michelle's recent behavior problems. If Anna can monitor the programs more closely and watch with Michelle, she may be able to use TV to improve Michelle's school readiness and encourage more helpful and positive behaviors. She can also help Michelle think about the realism of media portrayals of Asian Americans and other ethnicities. The behavior conflicts may also be due partly to differences in acculturation between Anna and Michelle. Perhaps Michelle is trying to balance what she must do to fit in at preschool and what's expected at home. It is also likely that both Anna and Michelle are under a lot of stress because of lack of money and the problems this presents. The stress may be causing Michelle to behave more poorly and Anna to react more negatively. Although you can't solve Anna's money problems, you can help her think about what kinds of neighborhood and family resources might help lighten her burden.

How does early childhood education affect children's development?

High-quality early education can have a positive and long-lasting effect. Gains in IQ sometimes fade away, but other aspects of academic progress persist, such as reduced need for special education and increased graduation rates. Other social benefits of quality preschool education include better employment records, less need for welfare benefits, and fewer arrests. Quality early education may increase children's readiness for school, providing a foundation of skills children can then use to build future success.

What is effective schooling?

Effective schooling helps children develop cognitive, social, and emotional skills and resources. A mastery learning orientation encourages children to try difficult tasks to improve ability, whereas a helpless orientation can produce lower motivation and lead children to avoid challenging tasks. Teachers' beliefs and expectations can affect children's academic motivation and achievement. A positive and supportive classroom climate helps children gain confidence and learn. Classroom grouping practices that emphasize cooperation seem to benefit more children than ability-based grouping. Schoolwide practices that emphasize effort, encourage mastery, and are consistent with children's cognitive, social, and emotional needs help children gain confidence and learn more throughout their school years.

What are some of the major group differences in academic skills?

U.S. students are not international leaders in academic performance. Many differences in educational practices exist between U.S. and Asian cultures, such as emphasis on effort versus ability, expectations about level of performance and active involvement in learning, time spent in school, and parental involvement in schooling. Within the United States, large and enduring ethnic-group differences exist in all subject areas. Poverty and cultural incompatibilities between school and home environments are two explanations for these differences.

How can we prevent problems in schooling?

Quality early childhood education can increase school readiness. Educational practices that encourage mastery orientations can improve achievement motivation, and school structures and practices that fit children's developmental needs can also help. A better understanding of children's cultural backgrounds and family life can help make schooling more relevant and comfortable for all students.

What kinds of media do children use?

TV use outstrips use of other media, and even young children watch many hours per week. African American, Hispanic, and lower-SES children watch more TV than others. Boys are more likely to play video games and use the Internet than girls. Children spend more time reading than playing video games and using computers, especially at younger ages. Older adolescents use audio media more than younger ones.

What effects do the media have on children?

Television has mixed effects on children. Educational TV can improve academic skills and prosocial behavior. Research has linked noneducational TV viewing, particularly heavy viewing, with several negative outcomes, although many of the studies are correlational. Positive effects of prosocial programs are stronger when parents and teachers reinforce the skills being taught. Watching violence on TV causes more aggressive behavior in children in the short term and is correlated with long-term levels of aggressive behavior. Video games can improve spatial skills, but their violent content increases aggression and physiological arousal. Computer software can effectively teach academic skills. Little research is available on the effects of Internet use, but heavy Internet use correlates with poorer social and emotional measures.

How can we explain the effects of media on children?

Children learn by observing and imitating behaviors they encounter in the media, especially when they actively attend, strongly identify with the characters, practice the behaviors, and receive reinforcement from parents or others. Children can develop cognitive schemas based on the way the media depict events and characters. They can experience high levels of physical and emotional arousal, which can lead to more extreme reactions. Over time, children may become desensitized to such things as violence.

What are individualism and collectivism?

Individualism is a cultural orientation that focuses on the individual and the individual's rights, accomplishments, and self-fulfillment. Collectivism focuses on group well-being, values, and accomplishments and emphasizes duty to the group. European Americans are more individualistic and less collectivistic than people in many cultures, but patterns of differences depend partly on the specific aspects of individualism and collectivism considered.

How does poverty affect children?

Poverty limits options, increases daily hassles and negative life events, and creates a persistent high level of stress for children and families. Compared to others, poor children have worse physical health, lower cognitive skills and academic achievement, more stressful home environments, and more social and emotional difficulties. Inner-city poverty is especially difficult for children because of violent crime, poor housing, crowding, lack of parental resources, and easy availability of negative influences like gangs and drugs. Community-bridging families can find ways to provide positive opportunities for their children, however. A substantial number of rural children are poor. They suffer many of the same effects as inner-city poor children, though their social supports may remain stronger.

What is acculturation?

Acculturation is the process of learning about and adopting a new culture. It is a long and potentially stressful process. Children and adolescents often acculturate faster than parents, creating conflict. Children of first-generation immigrants often develop a bicultural identity; they often serve as child cultural brokers, interpreting both the language and the culture of the new country for their parents and other family members.

How can we explain the effect of culture on children's development?

All the systems that influence child development exist within and are affected by a specific cultural setting. We are often unaware of our cultural beliefs and customs unless we encounter conflicts that highlight them.

KEY TERMS

ability grouping (517)

acculturation (546)

achievement motivation (514)

arousal (536)

attributions (514)

biculturalism (548)

child cultural brokers (548)

classroom climate (516)

cognitive schemas (535)

collectivism (538)

cooperative learning (518)

culture (538)

desensitization (535)

entity view of ability (515)

helpless orientation (515)

incremental view of ability (515)

individualism (538)

mastery orientation (515)

observational learning (535)

self-fulfilling prophecy (516)

stage–environment fit (519)

Chapter 14

Children on Different Developmental Paths

CHAPTER PREVIEW

A PERSPECTIVE TO think ABOUT

"How can Krista work effectively with children who have diverse problems and abilities?"

After finishing her education degree at Eastern State University, Krista Capaldi is about to start teaching sixth grade at Shoreland Middle School. She took a course called Exceptional Children and spent a few days on abnormalities in her child development class. Otherwise her education classes focused mostly on children who were normal or typical. Krista knows, however, that she will have several students in her classes who don't fit the typical patterns. She will need to be able to adjust her teaching for children who have behavior problems, learning disorders, or mental disorders, and at the same time she will need to serve students who are gifted and talented. What should Krista expect to see in her classrooms? How often will she encounter children who are following these different developmental paths?

After studying this chapter, you should be able to describe several of the psychological and behavioral disorders, communication and learning disorders, and other problems that are most common among children and adolescents. You should be able to use at least a dozen concepts from this chapter to help Krista understand and work more effectively with the children she will encounter. What kinds of problems might she see in her classroom? How can Krista work effectively with children who have diverse problems and abilities? From their behaviors in school, will she be always able to tell which children are depressed, which have conduct problems, and which are being abused? And what about the children who are gifted and talented? What advice can you give to help Krista support the special talents that these children show?

 As you read this chapter, look for the questions that ask you to think about what you're learning from Krista's perspective.

555

One out of every 5 children suffers from a mental illness or other serious developmental, emotional, or behavioral problem (Mash & Wolfe, 1999). Because children with exceptional needs are mainstreamed in regular classrooms, it is important that teachers like Krista Capaldi understand a wide variety of problems and know how to work effectively with each child. And given the nature of their work, social workers, physicians, and nurses will encounter an even greater percentage of children who have serious problems. So far in this textbook, we have focused mostly on the normal developmental paths that children follow. In previous chapters we sometimes referred to problems that can occur if development goes awry, but we have held the details about serious problems for this chapter. At the end of this chapter we also discuss gifted children, who are more talented than the "normal" or "average" child, and resilient children, who manage to survive and even thrive in the face of incredible adversity.

Before we continue, we want to make a few general points. One point concerns **prevalence rates**—the percentages or numbers of children who show the various problems or conditions. For each condition we discuss, we give the experts' best estimates. There are no hard numbers on prevalence rates, however, because a great many children with serious problems are not diagnosed or treated. Adults often think that a child will "outgrow" a problem, or they simply fail to recognize the child's problem because many children can't communicate their feelings effectively. Often, a child's problems can go unrecognized until the child begins to fail or have problems with peers in school. In instances of abuse, families may intentionally hide what is going on; we will never know precisely how many children suffer maltreatment at the hands of parents and other people.

Another important point is that you can't just add up the various prevalence rates to determine how many children are affected by the total of all of these problems. A high percentage of children with disorders have more than one disorder at once—a situation referred to as **comorbidity**. For example, 40 to 50 percent of children with depression also have an anxiety disorder, conduct disorder, or other psychological disturbance (Kazdin & Marciano, 1998). Children who suffer from mental illnesses are also more likely to experience abuse or neglect. The sad fact is that childhood problems and disorders tend to cluster or co-occur in individual children.

Also, it's important to understand that we rarely can identify the exact cause of any disorder in a particular child. In almost every case multiple causes or multiple conditions contribute to the problem. Today, most experts look at childhood problems from the **developmental psychopathology perspective.** This view emphasizes the wide variety of factors that influence both normal and abnormal paths of development. Among these factors are genetics, the interactions children have with their parents and family, the quality of their education, their peers, and many other elements in their social and cultural environments. The developmental outcome of any particular child is determined by the *transactions* that occur among all of these factors. A child with a genetic predisposition for depression, for example, could develop major depression, have minor symptoms, or possibly experience no symptoms at all, depending on interactions with his or her environment. Children with no genetic predisposition can still develop major depression if they suffer severe traumas or abuse. And some children who have all of the odds stacked against them still manage to escape without serious problems. Again, the point is that for any particular child we usually cannot determine *the* cause of the child's mental illness or other problem. Still, we can report the general tendencies that researchers have discovered—the factors that generally contribute to each type of problem or disorder, and the effects or developmental outcomes that generally result.

prevalence rates

The percentages or numbers of children who show particular problems or conditions.

comorbidity

Situation where a child has more than one psychological disorder or problem at the same time.

developmental psychopathology perspective

The view that a wide variety of factors influences both normal and abnormal paths of development.

Behavioral and Emotional Problems

In this first section we look at the behavioral and emotional problems that are most common or important during childhood and adolescence.

As you study this section, ask yourself these questions:

- What is attention-deficit/hyperactivity disorder (ADHD), and what are the subtypes of this disorder? What do researchers know about the causes of ADHD? Are drugs such as Ritalin really effective in treating ADHD?

- What do we know about children who are aggressive, destructive, and violent? What approaches are used to treat or prevent these problems?

- What are the main types of anxiety disorders among children, and how are they typically treated?

- What do researchers know about depression and suicide among youths?

Attention-Deficit/Hyperactivity Disorder

As a preschooler Tim was always on the go. Whether he was climbing and jumping on the furniture, rocking in his chair, running through the house, banging his toys, or talking constantly and loudly, it seemed that his motor was always running at high speed. When he started kindergarten, he was always interrupting other children, he had a hard time waiting in line, and he was too restless to sit for very long. Although his parents and teachers marveled at his energy and enthusiasm, they were exhausted trying to help him sit still, pay attention, and wait for his turn at home and school.

Most young children prefer to be on the go, and they would rather learn by moving and doing than by sitting and listening quietly. But when their restlessness and high level of activity far exceed the norm for their age level, then they are showing signs of **attention-deficit/hyperactivity disorder (ADHD).** Children with ADHD are excessively active, unable to sustain attention, and deficient in impulse control to a degree that is unusual for their developmental level (Barkley, 1996). The signs of ADHD emerge early, usually before the age of 7, and they persist throughout childhood and often into adolescence and adulthood. Most children with ADHD show two phases with the disorder.

> First, parents and caregivers notice signs of hyperactivity, usually by the time the child is 3 or 4 years of age. Tim, for example, was showing the classic signs of hyperactivity.

> Second, by age 5 to 7, ADHD children begin showing signs of inattentiveness. This side of the disorder usually becomes apparent when children begin formal schooling. They have a hard time finishing assignments, staying on task, and following rules and instructions. They can't concentrate; they seem to daydream; and they are disorganized, forgetful, and easily distracted.

As you can imagine, this combination of inattentiveness and hyperactivity can be challenging. As children grow into middle childhood, the hyperactive symptoms tend to decrease, but the attention problems remain. And adolescents who show more extreme levels of ADHD symptoms report having more negative moods and feeling less alert than those with lower levels of symptoms. They are also more likely to use tobacco and alcohol (Whalen, Jamner,

attention-deficit/ hyperactivity disorder (ADHD)

A condition involving excessive activity, inability to sustain attention, and deficiencies in impulse control that are unusual for the child's developmental level.

If Krista has students
with ADHD, how might
the disorder have
affected the children by
the time they reach her
sixth-grade class? What
symptoms might she
see in her students that
would indicate different
types of ADHD?

Henker, Delfino, & Lozano, 2002). Currently, clinicians recognize three types of ADHD: (1) *ADHD–primarily inattentive,* (2) *ADHD–primarily hyperactive,* and (3) *ADHD–combined.* Although parents and teachers describe as many as one-half of all children as "hyperactive," only 4 to 6 percent of children actually meet the clinical criteria for some type of ADHD. ADHD rates are 3 times higher among boys than among girls. About 85 percent of children with ADHD show either type 2 or type 3: primarily hyperactive or hyperactivity combined with inattentiveness (Barkley, 1996; Biederman et al., 2002).

The causes of ADHD are not known; but most of the research points to a genetic component and problems with areas in the frontal lobes of the brain that are responsible for attention, organization, and the inhibition and control of behavior. Analysts estimate that the heritability of ADHD is as high as .80 (Barkley, 1996). Identical twins share more ADHD symptoms than nonidentical twins, and children and their biological parents share more symptoms than adoptive families. Although genetics seems to play the larger role, research indicates that ADHD rates are slightly higher among children exposed to lead and among those exposed to alcohol and tobacco smoke during prenatal development. ADHD is somewhat more common in lower socioeconomic groups, but it exists at every socioeconomic level and in every country researchers have studied (Barkley, 1996; Linnet et al., 2003).

Family conflict is common when a child has ADHD. ADHD children are more talkative, defiant, and demanding than children without the disorder, and their parents (especially mothers) tend to be more negative and less rewarding (Barkley, 1996). Fathers seem to have less trouble with their ADHD children, perhaps because they spend less time with the children or because they tend to play in a rough-and-tumble style more suitable for highly active children. Parents with ADHD children tend to have more marital conflict; their separation and divorce rates are higher; they tend to consume more alcohol; and mothers are more likely to be depressed. It is not clear whether these family problems are more a cause of ADHD or the result of the stress of dealing with difficult ADHD children, but the evidence seems to suggest more of the latter (Barkley, 1996).

In addition to family problems, children with ADHD have great difficulty in school. By the time they are adolescents, about 40 percent of ADHD children have received some form of special education. One-quarter of ADHD students get expelled from school, 35 percent are retained at least one grade level, and up to 30 percent drop out of school (Barkley, 1996). The majority do not go on to college (Barkley, 1998). Although there is little research on ADHD in adulthood, clinicians believe that nearly half of all children with ADHD carry the symptoms into their adult years—and experience significant problems in their work and social relations as a result.

There is no cure for ADHD, but there are effective treatments. Ironically, the most frequently used and effective treatment seems to consist of stimulant medications. The stimulants Ritalin, Dexedrine, and Cylert seem to activate areas in the brain that relate to the inhibition and self-regulation of behavior. Although one-quarter of ADHD children do not respond to stimulant medication, the remaining three-quarters often show significant improvements in concentration, motor control, cooperation, and the ability to stay on task (Barkley, 1998; Bedard et al., 2003; Rubia et al.,

Stimulant medications are the most effective treatment for most cases of ADHD. Only 4 to 6 percent of children meet the clinical criteria for ADHD, and there are fears that many children are misdiagnosed and treated unnecessarily.

2003). A new stimulant called Adderall also shows promise in treating ADHD. In some cases antidepressant medications also have been effective.

Behavior management programs can be helpful to children with ADHD. These programs train parents and teachers to reward children when they cooperate and stay on task and to remove privileges or give timeouts for disruptive behaviors. Behavior management programs work best when parents and teachers apply them consistently in both home and school settings and combine them with medications such as stimulants (Barkley, 1998; Owens et al., 2003).

Conduct Problems

Almost everyone breaks rules from time to time. A small percentage of children and adolescents, however, engage in frequent or severe forms of acting out. **Conduct problems** are a general category of rule-breaking behaviors that range from frequent bouts of whining, yelling, and throwing temper tantrums to the more severe and dangerous forms of aggression and destructiveness. Two specific types of conduct problems are **oppositional defiant disorder (ODD)** and **conduct disorder (CD)**. Approximately 6 to 10 percent of children and adolescents have *ODD,* defined as a repetitive pattern of defiance, disobedience, and hostility toward authority figures (Kann & Hanna, 2000; McMahon & Wells, 1998). To be diagnosed with ODD, children must show a pattern of behavior, lasting at least 6 months, that includes breaking rules or refusing requests; losing their temper; arguing; deliberately annoying other people; blaming others for their mistakes; or showing anger, resentment, spite, or vindictiveness. For an ODD diagnosis these misbehaviors also must be more frequent than with children of similar age and must cause disruptions in children's school performance and social relationships. Another 2 to 9 percent of children have *CD:* they consistently violate the basic rights of other people or break major societal rules (McMahon & Wells, 1998). Examples include harming people or animals, fighting, bullying, using weapons, being cruel, destroying property, setting fires, stealing, lying, running away from home, and other serious violations. To be diagnosed with CD, a child must show a persistent pattern of serious violations during the past 12 months, with at least one violation within the last 6 months. As many as one-half of all children clinicians see in mental health settings are there because of ODD, CD, or some other type of conduct problem. Conduct problems, then, are the most frequently *reported* category of childhood disorder.

Children who begin defying parents and other authorities at an early age are the most likely to have problems throughout childhood—and eventually to engage in destructive and perhaps criminal activities in adolescence and adulthood (McMahon & Wells, 1998). Researchers have identified an **early-starter pattern** in which preschool children begin by defying parents and throwing tantrums, then move to fighting and aggression during childhood and on to problems such as lying and stealing in adolescence (Loeber & Stouthamer-Loeber, 1998; Patterson, Capaldi, & Bank, 1991; Rubin, Burgess, Dwyer, & Hastings, 2003). Although researchers can't point to a specific "cause" of conduct problems, they have developed an explanatory **coercion model.** This model describes a negative interaction pattern that gets set up early in some families (Patterson & Fisher, 2002; Patterson et al., 1992). Imagine parents who are under stress, have poor parenting skills, and have an infant or toddler who is temperamentally difficult and perhaps hyperactive. Lacking a positive discipline program, the parents tend to become more harsh, punitive, and negative in trying to control their child. A key element in the coercion model is the role that negative reinforcement plays in fostering bad behavior. Parents demand, threaten, or punish; the child whines, refuses, and argues; and the parent eventually gives in. This negatively reinforces the child's bad behavior as well as the parent's own giving in. An uneasy peace may follow, but the long-term consequence is that the child will misbehave even more and the parent will use even more coercive tactics next

conduct problems

A general category of rule-breaking behaviors.

oppositional defiant disorder (ODD)

A conduct problem involving a repetitive pattern of defiance, disobedience, and hostility toward authority figures.

conduct disorder (CD)

A conduct problem involving consistent violations of other people's basic rights or the breaking of major societal rules.

early-starter pattern

A pattern observed in some children who develop conduct problems at an early age.

coercion model

A model describing how negative interactions in some families escalate into cycles of aggression and childhood conduct problems.

Children who follow the early-starter pattern are at the highest risk for delinquency, violence, and other serious conduct problems later in adolescence.

time. These parents also are poor at monitoring their children's behavior and this gets worse over time (Kilgore, Snyder, & Lentz, 2000; Patterson, Reid, & Dishion, 1992). The situation continues to escalate and becomes worse for everyone, creating a stressful and hostile environment and an out-of-control child. This gives the child a negative model of how to handle problems, and as parents' threats and punishments become more extreme, the child acts out even more. An escalating cycle of aggression leads the child to more aggressive and destructive behaviors. As a result, the child has problems forming friendships in school and is also at greater risk for school failure. These factors, combined with the aggressive home environment, lead to delinquent and criminal activity. Look back to Chapter 10 for more information on aggression in childhood and adolescence.

Although the coercion model cannot explain all conduct problems, it does summarize many of the known risk factors for this type of childhood problem. Conduct problems are more likely to develop when infants are premature; have difficult temperaments; or are irritable, hyperactive, or impulsive (McMahon & Wells, 1998). Conduct problems also are more likely when the parents have poor parenting skills; interpret their children's actions in an overly negative way; have marital or other family problems; abuse alcohol or drugs; or engage in aggressive, violent, or antisocial acts themselves. These problems also are more likely to emerge when the mother is depressed or the family is in a lower income group. Genetic factors, exposure to prenatal teratogens, and birthing complications also seem to contribute (Arseneault, Tremblay, Boulerice, & Saucier, 2000; Brennan, Mednick, & Kandel, 1991; Dodge & Pettit, 2003; Hill, Bush, & Roosa, 2003; Shaw, Gillion, Ingoldsby, & Nagin, 2003). Interestingly, although boys are more likely to be diagnosed with CD, a "gender paradox" is that girls with CD tend to show a combination of several different problem behaviors. For example, a girl with CD may engage in stealing, aggression, and substance abuse (Tiet, Wasserman, Loeber, McReynolds, & Miller, 2001).

Practitioners often use parent training and family therapy to treat conduct problems. Especially if the children are still young, teaching parents more effective and positive methods for handling their children's behaviors can help the whole family. Parents can learn to notice and reward more "good" behaviors. They also can learn constructive strategies for dealing with misbehavior in a nonviolent and rational manner (as described in Chapter 12). With older children and adolescents, parents can learn to monitor their child's actions more closely and to give appropriate consequences for misbehavior, such as taking privileges away rather than hitting and yelling. Research shows that discipline that is firm but not harsh can prevent serious behavior problems even when children are running with a deviant peer group (Galambos, Barker, & Almeida, 2003). Therapy is more effective when parents are taught strategies to deal with their own stress, in addition to learning parenting skills (Kazdin & Whitley, 2003).

Through family therapy older children and adolescents can get involved in tackling the problem. They can learn more effective ways of monitoring their own behavior and techniques for managing anger and coping with stress. Additionally, if the conduct problem involves school aggression, teachers (and sometimes even peers) can learn to reinforce appropriate behaviors and help the child avoid aggression (Aber, Brown, & Jones, 2003).

thinking
OF KRISTA

Can the coercion model apply to school also? How could the behaviors of teachers and students interact to generate a cycle of increasing aggression? How can Krista avoid these coercive interactions with her students?

Career Focus: Meet a Juvenile Probation Officer

Nancy Magowan
Philadelphia,
Pennsylvania

*Juvenile probation
officer in the Family
Division of the
Common Pleas
Court, Special
Offender Unit*

What are the most common offenses that youths supervised by the Special Offender Unit commit?

The Special Offender Unit supervises juveniles who are placed in a residential treatment facility for mental therapy and treatment. The offenses include assault, theft, robbery, auto theft, burglary, controlled substance offenses, criminal conspiracy, and sexual offenses such as rape, indecent assault, indecent exposure, and involuntary deviate sexual intercourse.

What do juvenile probation officers do to help youths avoid future offenses?

Once the juvenile completes treatment and is recommended for discharge from the facility, we develop a Probation Supervision Plan. The plan holds the youth accountable for his/her actions, offers some restoration to the victim, protects the community, and develops the youth's competencies. I monitor the youth's progress and success. I often connect the youth with community-based support programs that provide educational or vocational schooling, substance abuse treatment, individual or family therapy, and employment services. We customize the plans to meet the needs of each youth.

What do you think is the most important thing that can be done to prevent behavior problems, violence, and crime among youths?

Preventing youth from entering the juvenile justice system is an ongoing and difficult task. The breakdown of the family seems to affect so many. Family support, guidance, and encouragement are key in a youth's ability to develop positive and appropriate social skills and develop their self-esteem to adjust to the challenges of adolescence and life. Communication between parents, schools, and support programs is essential to maintain continuity and encouragement for the young people in our society in their efforts to succeed. Empowering youth with education and emphasizing their strengths will help reduce the juvenile crime rate.

What education and training is needed to work in your occupation?

After I got my bachelor's degree in Administration of Justice from Penn State University and did an internship at the court where I work now, most of my training was on the job. Additional training and education (40-plus hours) is provided and required by the courts on a yearly basis. My only regret regarding education is not being bilingual. ■

thinking OF KRISTA

◄ How can Krista recognize a potential juvenile offender in her classroom? What can she do to encourage such a student to focus on education and personal talents?

With more dangerous and destructive behaviors, community treatment programs or foster care may become necessary. Because conduct problems often begin with ADHD or co-occur with ADHD, psychiatrists sometimes prescribe stimulants such as Ritalin. In more serious cases, social service agencies or the juvenile justice system may have to deal with adolescents' criminal or violent behaviors (McMahon & Wells, 1998). To learn more about how the juvenile justice system tries to help youths with conduct problems, see the Professional Perspective box called "Career Focus: Meet a Juvenile Probation Officer."

Anxiety Disorders

Almost all children show some type of fear or worry. Younger children tend to be afraid of loud noises, strangers, separation from parents, and being alone in the dark. As they get older, many children still fear thunder and lightning, being injured, and being left alone. For

What fears do you re-
member from your
childhood? Describe two
fears that you have
now that are adaptive
and protective. How are
these fears helpful?

anxiety disorders

Disorders that involve consistent and intense fear, worry,
or anxiety in situations that
pose no real threat or danger.

adolescents, frequent fears include taking tests in school, personal failure, meeting new people, and speaking in public. Normal levels of fear can be beneficial. Fear of heights, for example, can prevent children from climbing out onto dangerous ledges. A healthy amount of test anxiety can motivate you to study hard and try your best on your next exam. The butterflies in your stomach before a big speech, championship ball game, or first job interview tell you that you care about these important events. And it is normal for us to experience even intense levels of fear when our flight-or-fight systems are triggered by the approach of a snarling dog or a dangerous-looking stranger. We can't (and often don't want to) avoid all fear and worry in life—but it's also important not to feel so much anxiety that we panic, freeze, or fail to perform as needed.

Unlike normal childhood fears, **anxiety disorders** involve intense and consistent fear, worry, or anxiety in situations that pose no real threat or danger. Children with anxiety disorders exhibit a degree and type of anxiety that is unusual for their developmental level, and their distress seriously interferes with daily activities such as going to school, making friends, or separating from parents (Mash & Wolfe, 1999). Table 14.1 lists the most frequent types of anxiety disorders. Experts believe that anxiety disorders are the most common types of mental health problems children and adolescents face (Mash & Wolfe, 1999). Unfortunately, however, anxiety disorders are more likely to go unnoticed, undiagnosed, and untreated than other kinds of problems. Most children show fears and worries at some point in their development, so parents and other adults sometimes assume that the anxieties associated with these disorders will pass or fade away with time. Also, children often hide their most intense anxieties. And compared to the destructive conduct problems we looked at earlier, anxiety disorders tend not to be as damaging or as disruptive for other people.

Anxiety disorders have multiple causes. Some, such as posttraumatic stress disorder (PTSD) and acute stress disorder, can be triggered by extreme or traumatic events. Children differ in their degrees of vulnerability to stress, however, because of differences in temperament,

Anxiety disorders can be triggered by severe crises and traumatic events. After the frightening destruction of Hurricane Andrew, as many as 30 percent of the children in the area reported severe levels of PTSD, and 12 percent were still suffering from PTSD one year later (Mash & Wolfe, 1999).

TABLE 14.1 Anxiety Disorders in Childhood and Adolescence

ESTIMATED PERCENTAGES OF CHILDREN AND ADOLESCENTS WITH DISORDER	TYPE OF ANXIETY DISORDER	DESCRIPTION	AVERAGE AGE OF ONSET (YEARS)
6 to 12%	Separation anxiety disorder	Disabling anxiety about being apart from parents or away from home. Excessive for the child's age.	7 to 8
3 to 6%	Generalized anxiety disorder (GAD)	Chronic or exaggerated worry; almost constant and unjustified anticipation of disaster; often includes physical symptoms such as trembling, headache, and nausea.	10 to 14
2 to 4%	Specific phobias	Disabling fears of specific objects or situations that are out of proportion to the real danger. Examples include fear of spiders (arachnophobia) and fear of heights (acrophobia).	7 to 9
1 to 3%	Social phobia	Fear of being the focus of attention or scrutiny, or of doing something intensely humiliating.	12 to 14
2 to 3%	Obsessive–compulsive disorder (OCD)	Repeated, intrusive and unwanted thoughts that cause anxiety; often with ritualized behavior in an attempt to relieve the anxiety. Example: repetitive hand washing with obsessive thoughts about germs.	9 to 12
1 to 5%	Panic disorder (PD)	Panic attacks; sudden feelings of terror that strike without warning; physical symptoms such as chest pain, heart palpitations, shortness of breath; persistent concern about having another attack. Approximately 50% of adolescents have had at least one panic attack.	15 to 19
Not known	Posttraumatic stress disorder (PTSD)	Frightening thoughts that persist after a traumatic event such as witnessing a car accident or suffering sexual abuse.	Any age
Not known	Acute stress disorder	Anxiety and other symptoms after exposure to extreme trauma. May be like PTSD, but symptoms don't last more than 4 weeks past the trauma.	Any age

Sources: American Psychiatric Association (1994); Mash & Wolfe (1999).

the quality of different children's family relations, and the presence or absence of other social supports. Genetics also plays a role. Anxiety disorders are more likely to co-occur in identical than nonindentical twins. The specific type of anxiety, however, tends to differ between members of twin pairs. For example, if one twin suffers from separation anxiety, her twin sister may have a social phobia instead. Genetics may have made both sisters vulnerable to anxiety, but differences in their environments and their specific experiences triggered different types of anxieties. When parents have anxiety disorders, their children's risk of developing anxiety disorders increases fivefold. Again, however, the specific types of anxieties often differ between parents and their children (Mash & Wolfe, 1999). Anxiety disorders are about twice as common in girls as in boys. Many children with anxiety disorders suffer from more than one type, either simultaneously or at different points in their development (Mash & Wolfe, 1999).

When treating children with anxiety disorders, therapists often gradually expose children to the situations they fear while at the same time helping them cope with their intense

It is normal for children to feel intense sadness after experiencing a significant loss. It is considered to be a clinical depression when the symptoms continue after an unusually long time and when they impair the child's ability to perform at school and in social situations.

responses. Suppose a girl has an extreme fear of school, for example. Her therapist may ask her to stand in front of the school building and at the same time coach her to relax and breathe deeply. Gradually, the child may be able to move to the inside of the school, and eventually to the classroom. The therapist may work on the child's cognitions as well, encouraging her to think, "It's a big school, but I can handle it" rather than "Oh God, I'm going to die!" Family therapy also can be helpful. A family therapist can teach parents and siblings to provide better support for the child with the disorder and can address other issues related to family dynamics. With therapy, most children become much better able to deal with their anxieties (Barrett, Dadds, & Rapee, 1996).

Depression

> Teri's father died when she was 11. Since then she has become increasingly withdrawn and moody. Now, at the age of 15, she is disobedient, skips school, and refers to herself as "stupid." As she looks at her life, Teri wonders why she should go on. She tries every day to see the point of living, but there is none. On three occasions she cut her wrists, but the wounds were only superficial. (adapted from Berman & Jobes, 1991, pp. 95–96)

Most of us use the word *depression* to refer to the kind of sadness and loss of energy that occurs periodically in our lives. A diagnosis of **clinical depression,** however, refers to a constellation of symptoms that can include sadness, loss of interest in activities, feelings of worthlessness, sleep problems, and changes in appetite (Kazdin & Marciano, 1998). The symptoms are prolonged, lasting longer than is normal for periods of grief or loss. For example, it is normal for a child to feel intense sadness for several months after losing a parent. But when the symptoms continue for an unusually long time, as with Teri, then clinical depression may have set in. With depression the symptoms cause significant distress and impair the person's ability to perform at school, at work, and in social situations.

Children and adolescents who are depressed tend to have low self-esteem and to have negative thoughts about themselves and the events around them. They are less popular among their peers and more likely to feel rejected and isolated than other youngsters. They tend to perform poorly in school, being likely to miss assignments, miss school, and fail a grade. When they become adults, they are at an increased risk for having marriage problems, being unemployed, abusing drugs, and engaging in criminal activity (Kazdin & Marciano, 1998).

Between 2 and 8 percent of children suffer from major depression; another 1 to 9 percent have a milder form of depression (Kazdin & Marciano, 1998). The rates of depression increase as children mature. Depression is relatively rare (less than 1 percent) among preschoolers. It increases during the elementary school years (up to 2 percent) and increases again during adolescence (to around 2 to 8 percent). There is some evidence that during childhood depression is more common in boys than in girls. By puberty, however, depression is 5 times more common in girls than in boys (Kazdin & Marciano, 1998). When boys are upset, they tend to act out their feelings in physical and sometimes aggressive ways. In contrast, girls from an early age tend to hold these feelings inside. For these reasons, researchers believe that many children and adolescents who don't meet the full criteria for a clinical disorder do suffer from serious symptoms of depression. And the rates of depression seem to be increasing significantly.

The most serious forms of clinical depression run in families. The heritability index for depression is as high as .60, with identical twins much more likely to share symptoms of depression than are nonidentical twins (Nurnberger & Gershon, 1992). Milder forms of depression, however, do not have a consistent genetic link. Clinicians think that depression also is related to faulty cognitive processes (pessimistic and negative thought patterns), learned behaviors, and stressful life events.

One interesting speculation involves the interactions between depressed mothers and their babies (Kazdin & Marciano, 1998). Depressed mothers tend to be more withdrawn, negative, and punitive with their children. As a result, they may not reinforce their infants' emotional responses in healthy ways. When infants are happy, they usually smile, kick their legs, and wiggle around, signaling their parents to come and play. If a depressed mother ignores such signals, then her infant learns to hide feelings of joy (or stops expressing joy because of lack of reinforcement). The infant may feel happy on the inside but has learned that it is no use smiling and wiggling—the mother won't come and play anyway. One of the questions here regards the infant's developing brain. If infants learn to conceal their emotions, how do their brains react? Evidence now suggests that infants with depressed mothers develop abnormalities in the brain regions that regulate and control emotion. Brain-wave activity in their left frontal lobes, for example, tends to be diminished; and activity along other neural pathways looks different than it does in other infants. Researchers are concerned that infants with depressed mothers are having their brains "sculpted" in a faulty manner. As Kazdin and Marciano (1998) conclude, "there is little doubt of the neuropsychological, biological, and physiological significance of early mother–child interactions on children's [emotion] regulation" (p. 218). And—so as not to put all of the blame on mothers—we need to recognize that similar effects may occur when depressed fathers provide a significant portion of their infants' care.

Children and adolescents who suffer from depression tend to improve significantly with psychotherapy. Therapy is especially effective when it focuses on reducing negative and destructive thought processes, improving self-esteem, enhancing social skills, and teaching techniques for relaxation and the management of anxiety (Kazdin & Marciano, 1998). Surprisingly, although antidepressant medications such as Prozac seem to work for adults, these drugs don't work as well with young people. Controlled studies have failed to show that antidepressants work any better with children than placebo (sugar) pills. Researchers are also concerned about the possibility of serious side effects. For example, one study found that children and adolescents taking Prozac for 19 weeks grew more slowly (about .5 inch less in height and 2 pounds less in weight) than those taking a placebo ("FDA Approves Prozac," 2003). The concern is even greater for preschoolers because we know very little about how these drugs affect young children's developing brains or about the effects of long-term use of these medications. Doctors have written millions of prescriptions to provide antidepressants to children and adolescents. (Prozac even comes in peppermint flavor!) The United States Food and Drug Administration approved the use of Prozac for children ages 7 to 17 in January 2003, but there is still much we need to learn (Coyle, 2000; Kazdin & Marciano, 1998; Mash & Wolfe, 1999; "Prozac for Pediatric Use," 2003; Zito et al., 2000, 2002).

Unfortunately, 70 to 80 percent of depressed adolescents do not receive treatment of any kind (Kazdin & Marciano, 1998). Because they are often withdrawn and their symptoms often turn inward, depressed children and adolescents tend to be overlooked. Parents, teachers, and others may expect adolescents to be moody and dramatic and sometimes mistake the symptoms of depression for "a phase that will pass." Some adolescents experience such darkness and despair that they make the ultimate call for help: They attempt to take their own lives.

Suicide

Here is an alarming statistic: Researchers estimate that between 3 and 11 percent of all adolescents in the United States have attempted suicide at some point (Lewinsohn, Rohde, & Seeley, 1994). In one set of studies, researchers interviewed a large representative sample of adolescents in Oregon (Andrews & Lewinsohn, 1992; Lewinsohn, Rohde, & Seeley, 1993; Lewinsohn et al., 1994). When they interviewed the participants again one year later, 26 (out of 1,508) of the teenagers reported that they had attempted suicide since the first interview. That means that in one year alone, 1.7 percent of the adolescents attempted suicide.

What distinguished these 26 adolescents from their age-mates who did not try to kill themselves? Looking back to data from the first interviews, the researchers concluded that adolescents were more likely to attempt suicide if they had been born to teenage mothers, suffered from depression or other psychological disorders, had suicidal thoughts or ideas at the time of the first interview, had a friend who had attempted suicide recently, or had low self-esteem. Other research evidence indicates that adolescents are more likely to attempt suicide if they live in single-parent homes, their parents have less education, they lack support from family and friends, they are suffering from poor health or injury, or they have access to firearms (Fergusson, Beautrais, & Horwood, 2003; Gould, Greenberg, Velting, & Shaffer, 2003; Lewinsohn et al., 1994). Girls are about 3 times more likely than boys to attempt suicide, but boys are more than 4 times more likely to die from their suicide attempts (Lewinsohn et al., 1994; Stillion & McDowell, 1996). Suicide rates are nearly twice as high among Latino American adolescents as among African American or non-Latino white teens. Researchers speculate that in Latino families that immigrated recently to the United States, teens may experience extra stress because of conflicts between their Latino culture and mainstream U.S. culture (Canino & Roberts, 2001). Researchers are still trying to assemble a list of factors that might indicate which adolescents are at especially high risk for trying to take their own lives. As you can tell from our discussion here, however, a great many adolescents fit one or more criteria. It is therefore very difficult to identify in advance which teens will actually make suicide attempts.

Between 1960 and 1990, the rate of suicide death remained about steady for the whole U.S. population, but it steadily increased for young people. For 15- to 24-year-olds, there were about 5 suicides per 100,000 individuals in 1960 and about 13 per 100,000 by 1990 (Stillion & McDowell, 1996). Suicides by children ages 5 to 14 also tripled during that time period, to an annual rate of about 1 out of every 100,000 children. Although it remains rare for these younger children to actually commit suicide, as many as 1 in 5 say that they have seriously thought about killing themselves (Stillion & McDowell, 1996). These numbers should give us all reason to pause and consider how children's lives have changed in recent decades. Researchers have not yet pinpointed specific causes for the increase in youth suicide rates; but as you can imagine, speculation centers on changes in family structure, the increased pace of life, and the loss of family support systems. One way to prevent suicides is to make sure that parents and other adults notice the symptoms of depression (and other psychological disturbances) in children and that depressed youngsters receive treatment at an earlier age. Many parents are unaware that their child is considering suicide (Dhossche, Ferdinand, van der Ende, Hofstra, & Verhulst, 2002). However, one recent review concluded that this situation may be changing. These researchers found that suicide rates have declined since 1990, and the number of prevention strategies implemented increased (Gould, Greenberg, Velting, & Shaffer, 2003). Perhaps awareness of risk factors is increasing and treatment for depression is having an impact.

thinking
OF KRISTA

Are there signs that might suggest to Krista that a student in her class is at high risk for suicide? How reliable are these early indicators?

Developmental and Learning Problems

In this next section we focus on developmental problems that impair a child's ability to process and use information. We cover mental retardation, which is a general deficit that broadly affects thought and language abilities, and several communication and learning disorders with more specific effects. We also cover autism, a condition that can cause severe disruptions in cognitive and social skills.

As you study this section, ask yourself these questions:

• How is mental retardation defined, and what are the different levels of this condition? How do genetic and environmental factors contribute to mental retardation?

• What are the different types of communication and learning disorders? What roles do abnormalities in brain functions play in these disorders?

• What do researchers understand about autism, and what treatment approaches exist for this condition?

Mental Retardation

When compared to other children, children with mental retardation learn more slowly, have more difficulty solving problems, and show language and communication deficits. As a result, they perform less well in school and have more difficulty making friends and engaging in social activities. With special services and support, children with mild to moderate levels of retardation can adjust to many of the normal challenges in life. They can attend regular classrooms, learn to care for themselves, and develop friendships with peers. With more severe levels of retardation, a child may need extensive support merely to negotiate everyday activities such as brushing teeth and getting dressed.

There are three components to the formal definition of **mental retardation (MR)**:

1. *below-normal intellectual functioning* (usually indicated by an IQ of less than 70 or 75);

2. *deficits in adaptive behavior,* the daily activities required for personal and social independence (e.g., communicating needs to others, eating, dressing, grooming, toileting, following rules, and working and playing with others); and

3. *an onset early in life* (before age 18) (Hodapp & Dykens, 1996).

Approximately 2 to 3 percent of the U.S. population has mental retardation, but the numbers vary greatly depending on the specific criteria used to define the condition. Setting the IQ cutoff at 75 rather than 70, for example, doubles the number of children in the MR category (Hodapp & Dykens, 1996). Some experts favor using the higher cutoff (an IQ under 75) so as to qualify more children for special services. Others argue that cultural biases in standardized IQ tests (see Chapter 7) cause too much inaccurate labeling of minority and disadvantaged children as having MR—so proponents of this view favor the lower cutoff score (70). There are also differences in how assessments measure children's adaptive behaviors, and these differences can change the prevalence rates significantly.

Literally thousands of biological and environmental factors can cause mental retardation. The most severe forms of MR tend to result from genetic disorders. Down syndrome and fragile-X syndrome (see Chapter 2) are the two most common types of genetic disorders that cause mental retardation. Together these two disorders alone affect 1 in every 500 children

mental retardation (MR)

A condition characterized by below-normal intellectual functioning, deficits in adaptive behavior, and an onset early in life (before age 18).

This child needs help with many of the self-care activities that most of us take for granted. Deficits in adaptive behavior, low IQ, and early onset (before age 18) are all elements in the definition of mental retardation.

born, and more than 1,000 other genetic diseases also can contribute to MR (Hodapp & Dykens, 1996). Mental retardation can also result from prenatal damage to the brain and nervous system by toxins such as alcohol and drugs. As you read in Chapter 3, prenatal alcohol exposure is the leading *known* cause of mental retardation in the United States (Abel & Sokol, 1987; Institute of Medicine, 1996). And MR can ensue when infants suffer oxygen deprivation or other traumas during birth, and when they are born prematurely.

After children are born, numerous factors in the environment can retard mental development. The best-known environmental causes of MR include exposure to lead and other toxins, poor nutrition, lack of stimulation, and parents who are illiterate or mentally retarded themselves. Rates of mental retardation are higher among children living in poverty, minority children, and males (Hodapp & Dykens, 1996). Mental health researchers often refer to retardation caused by lack of educational opportunity and stimulation as **cultural–familial retardation.** Mental retardation also can have multiple causes. For example, children may inherit low intelligence from their parents; on top of this, they may suffer poor nutrition, and their parents may fail to provide a stimulating learning environment. When both parents have mental retardation, the odds are more than 40 percent that their children also will have MR. The odds drop to 20 percent when only one parent has MR and to less than 10 percent when neither parent has MR (Mash & Wolfe, 1999).

Clinicians typically divide mental retardation into the four levels shown in Table 14.2. Approximately 85 percent of people with mental retardation are in the mild category (Mash & Wolfe, 1999). Toddlers and preschoolers with mild MR usually show only small delays. When they reach early elementary school, however, they fall behind in academic subjects. With some special education and support, these children can learn up to the sixth- or seventh-grade level. They may have only minor problems with peers and other social relationships, and after finishing school they can live and work independently or with a modest amount of supervision. At the other end of the scale, 1 to 2 percent of all people with mental retardation are in the profound category.

TABLE 14.2 Four Levels of Mental Retardation

LEVEL OF MENTAL RETARDATION	APPROXIMATE IQ*
Mild	50 to 70 or 75
Moderate	35 to 50
Severe	20 to 40
Profound	Below 20 or 25

*An IQ score of 100 indicates an "average" level of intelligence.

As infants, they show serious delays in sensory and motor functions, and by the age of 4 they are still responding like typical 1-year-olds (Mash & Wolfe, 1999). These children need considerable training to learn to perform self-care activities such as eating, dressing, and toileting. They will need lifelong care. At present, most people with profound MR in the United States eventually go to live in group homes or residential facilities. Almost all cases of profound MR have a genetic or biological cause.

Researchers who develop prevention and treatment programs for children with mental retardation recommend the following guidelines for helping these children improve the quality of their lives:

▷ Encourage children with MR to explore the environment to learn and gather information.

▷ Work on these children's basic learning skills, such as labeling, sorting, and comparing objects.

▷ Celebrate their developmental advances and accomplishments.

▷ Help them rehearse and extend new skills.

▷ Protect them from the harm of disapproval, teasing, and punishment.

▷ Provide a rich and responsive language environment (Mash & Wolfe, 1999; Ramey & Ramey, 1992).

YOUR PERSPECTIVE

NOTES

Describe any children or adolescents with mental retardation you have known. What level of retardation did they have? What were the possible causes of their condition?

cultural–familial retardation
Retardation caused by lack of educational opportunity and stimulation.

Communication and Learning Disorders

Pretend that you are a child in a second-grade classroom. You have an above-average IQ and you are motivated to learn. When you try to read printed text, however, you can't make sense out of the words and sentences. The print says, "Pam saw the dog play," but you invert the *m* in "Pam" into a *w*, you reverse the letters in "saw" to read "was," and you leave out the *l* in "play." To you, the sentence reads, "Paw was the dog pay." What sense does that make? After struggling day after day, you begin to give up. While other children are reading their books, you just sit and look around. And because so much of the information and instruction given in school involves reading, you are falling behind in most of your subjects. The teacher thinks you have an attention deficit, your classmates call you "stupid," and your parents wonder if you are just lazy. Inside, you know they are all wrong, but you can't figure out why you are having so much trouble. Actually, you are showing signs of a reading disorder—but it may be a long time before you get an official diagnosis and any real help with your difficulties in school.

Unless you have experienced a communication or learning disorder yourself, it is hard to imagine the frustrations that children with these problems feel every day in school. They are just as smart as other children and can learn just as fast as other children, but in some specific area they have significant difficulty with language or learning. They fall behind in school, they may feel rejected by their classmates, and their self-esteem plummets. Many withdraw, show signs of depression or anxiety, or act out in school. Among adolescents with learning disorders, the high school dropout rate is about 40 percent (American Psychiatric Association, 1994).

Table 14.3 describes the main communication and learning disorders. In **communication disorders** children have significant difficulty producing speech sounds, using spoken language to communicate, or understanding what other people say (Mash & Wolfe, 1999). **Learning disorders** involve difficulties with specific skills such as reading, mathematics, or writing. With both types of disorders, children tend to have average to above-average intelligence. They should be capable of learning quickly in school, but their disorder slows them down and disrupts their performance. Communication and learning disorders are also highly connected. Like several other problems we've explored in this chapter, communication and learning disorders are examples of "hidden" problems in childhood—they too often go undiagnosed and untreated. About 5 percent of U.S. students receive official diagnoses of learning disorders, but educators estimate that at least 20 percent of children suffer from reading disorders alone (Mash & Wolfe, 1999). Children with communication and learning disorders already receive half of all of the special education services provided in schools, and even more children could obviously benefit from these programs.

Communication and learning disorders are strongly genetic and related to abnormalities in how the brain functions. When a parent has a communication disorder, about half of that person's children also have communication disorders. Children with phonological disorder (see Table 14.3) show less than normal activation in the left temporal region of their brains, a region strongly related to language function (Wood, Felton, Flowers, & Naylor, 1991). Research has linked expressive language disorder to recurrent ear infections (Lonigan, Fischel, Whitehurst, Arnold, & Valdez-Menchaca, 1992); such infections may lead to hearing loss that reduces input to the developing brain. And children with stuttering, reading, and writing disorders show more than normal activity in the right half of their brains (Mash & Wolfe, 1999). It seems that disruptions in prenatal brain development cause many of these disorders. Even minor defects can change how the brain sorts, organizes, and brings information together from specific brain areas; and these changes in turn hamper the child's ability to interpret and make sense out of the information.

thinking
OF KRISTA

How can school psychologists and teachers such as Krista tell the difference between a child with a learning or communication disorder and a child with mild mental retardation? What are the different adjustments that teachers should make for these different types of problems?

communication disorders

Conditions where children have significant difficulty producing speech sounds, using spoken language to communicate, or understanding what other people say.

learning disorders

Conditions involving difficulties with specific skills such as reading, mathematics, or writing.

TABLE 14.3 Communication and Learning Disorders

CATEGORIES OF DISORDERS	SYMPTOMS AND BEHAVIORS
Communication Disorders	
Phonological disorder	Problems with the articulation or production of language sounds. Most frequent problems involve the *l, r, s, z,* and *th* sounds; e.g., saying "cwy" instead of "cry." Problems persist beyond what is developmentally normal and interfere with school and social activities. About 10% of preschoolers show mild phonological problems. By age 7 years 2 to 3% have a phonological disorder.
Expressive language disorder	Problems using words to communicate thoughts, desires, and feelings. Expression lags significantly behind the child's ability to understand language (receptive language). Speech usually begins late and progresses slowly. Limited vocabulary, short sentences, and simple grammatical structures characterize speech. Affects 2 to 3% of children.
Mixed receptive–expressive language disorder	Problems in expressive language combined with difficulty understanding language. Trouble making sense out of sounds, words, sentences. Seen in less than 3% of children.
Stuttering	Repeating or prolonging speech sounds; e.g., saying "g-g-g-g-g-go" or "Mo-ah-ah-ah-ah-mmy." Child struggles to finish or continue sounds and words, may develop ways to avoid or compensate for problem sounds. Stuttering usually has a gradual onset between ages 2 and 7. Affects 1% of children, 3:1 males. Usually self-correcting; 80% of children who stutter at age 5 no longer stutter by first grade.
Learning Disorders	
Reading disorder	Reading ability substantially below the level expected given the child's age, intelligence, and education. Trouble recognizing basic words; common errors include letter reversals *(b/d; p/q)*, transpositions *(top/pot),* letter inversions *(m/w; u/n),* and omissions (reading *place* instead of *palace.* Trouble decoding (separating the sounds in words). Difficulties with reading comprehension, spelling, and writing. Up to 20% of schoolchildren have significant reading problems.
Mathematics disorder	Math ability substantially below the level expected given the child's age, intelligence, and education. Trouble recognizing numbers and symbols, memorizing basic math facts (e.g., multiplication tables), aligning numbers, and understanding abstract concepts (e.g., place value and fractions). Child may also have problems with visual–spatial abilities. Disorder usually noticed when formal math instruction begins in grade 2 or 3. About 1% of children receive official diagnoses, but 6% score low enough on standardized math tests to be considered as having the disorder.
Writing disorder	Writing ability substantially below the level expected given the child's age, intelligence, and education. Problems with writing, drawing, copying figures, and other fine-motor skills involving hand–eye coordination. Large-motor skills (e.g., running, throwing, climbing) are normal. Written work is low in interest and poorly organized; sentences are short; work contains many errors in spelling, punctuation, and grammar. Disorder affects up to 10% of children.

Source: Adapted from Mash & Wolfe (1999).

In many of these cases, the disorders correct themselves or the children learn ways to compensate for their difficulties. Stuttering and expressive language disorders, for example, often correct themselves by age 6 or 7 (Mash & Wolfe, 1999). Or children who stutter can learn to slow down and breathe deeply before continuing. Speech therapists can train children with phonological disorder in articulation and help them learn to produce correct speech sounds. Children with reading, math, and writing disorders typically receive educational supports in school. They benefit from direct instruction, drill and practice, and learning strategies for breaking problems and assignments into smaller units. Counseling and therapy also can help children improve their self-esteem, deal with peer rejection, and learn how to monitor and control their own learning and thought processes. And with help, families can learn to provide more effective supports for children with communication and learning disorders. On the bright side, most people with these disorders find ways to compensate and go on to live normal lives.

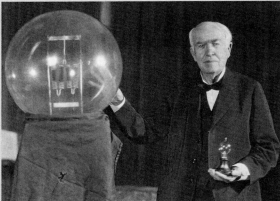

Well-known people such as Albert Einstein, Thomas Edison, and Winston Churchill managed high levels of success even though they were known to have or were suspected of having learning disorders (Mash & Wolfe, 1999).

Autism

At the age of 9, Daniel still didn't speak, read, or write. Although he seemed to understand most of what other people said, he communicated mostly by pointing, grunting, and making nonsense sounds. For his birthday his uncle gave him a cassette tape recorder, which Daniel began using to record short pieces of conversation he heard around him. At night he would lie in bed and replay dozens of times the snippets he had recorded that day. Using these recordings, Daniel began to teach himself to speak. As he learned two-way communication, he became fascinated with birth dates. When meeting you for the first time, he would immediately ask for your birth date and for the names and birth dates of all your pets. If you didn't have a pet, you had to make one up. Daniel insisted. In a split second, Daniel would then tell you *exactly* how old your pet was, down to the very day! Eventually Daniel's skill with birth dates grew into mastery of calendars (give him any date and he could figure out which day of the week it was) and an amazing ability to multiply and divide numbers in his head. Still, Daniel avoided eye contact, didn't respond properly to human emotions, showed little attachment to his family members, and had no reciprocal friendships. He did not attend school, living instead in a group home. This was where one of us (GC) met Daniel and worked with him, along with three other autistic children who lived in the same home.

Autism is a serious developmental disorder characterized by impairments in social interaction and communication. It can take forms ranging from mild to severe. In addition to the problems we've seen in the case of Daniel, most autistic children show repetitive body motions or self-stimulation activities such as rocking their bodies or waving their fingers in front of their eyes. They are inflexible about their daily routines and become upset by changes such as a different bedtime, a new arrangement of furniture, or an attempt to take them shopping at a new store. Autistic children score low on IQ tests (in the range of mental retardation), but a small percentage show exceptional *splinter skills* like Daniel's gift for calculating dates and numbers. Other such skills include exceptional memory for music and speed in building puzzles. Language skills tend to be severely delayed in autistic children. Many of these children simply repeat back words and phrases they hear (a pattern called *echolalia*) without seeming to understand what is said.

Autism is relatively rare, affecting approximately 35 out of every 100,000 children in the United States (Newsom, 1998). It is 4 times more common among boys than girls, and in recent years the number of children identified with autism has increased. Autism has a strong genetic

autism

A serious developmental disorder characterized by impairments in social interaction and communication.

component, being shared much more often between identical than between nonidentical twins (Bailey et al., 1995). Researchers are just beginning to understand the brain mechanisms associated with this disorder. Early evidence indicates immaturity in the limbic system and in the frontal and midbrain areas of the brain (Kabot, Masi, & Segal, 2003; Newsom, 1998). These areas regulate attention, emotion perception, and the control of planning and thought processes. Interestingly, autism is associated with increased neuron density in the hippocampal system (an area related to memory function) and with higher than normal brain weight.

Autism treatment outcomes vary depending on the severity of the disorder in individual children (Newsom, 1998). With severe levels of autism, therapy focuses on teaching self-care skills and helping the child learn to live as independently as possible. Lifelong care and supervision will probably still be essential. With more moderate to mild levels, treatment can be more effective if it starts early and involves intensive one-to-one training and therapy, preferably 20 to 40 hours per week. The work focuses on improving language, teaching social skills, and helping the child learn the skills and behaviors necessary for preschool and early elementary school (Autism Society of America, 2002; Newsom, 1998; Whalen & Schreibman, 2003). Parent education and training are also important parts of effective therapy (Kabot et al., 2003; Whitaker, 2002). With this kind of training and therapy, autistic children can show impressive gains, although most will still not function like their more typical peers.

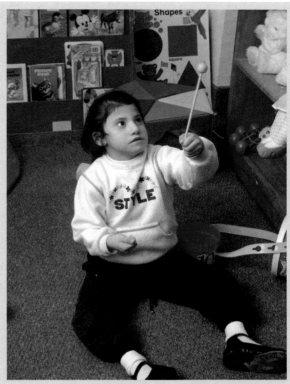
Autistic children suffer from severe deficits in social interaction and communication. This child shows a kind of self-stimulation behavior that is typical for autistic children.

LET'S REVIEW . . .

1. Mental retardation that results from lack of educational opportunity and stimulation is referred to as:
   a. moderate mental retardation.
   b. profound mental retardation.
   c. early-starter retardation.
   d. cultural–familial retardation.

2. Out of all of the people who have mental retardation, what percentage are at the *mild* level?
   a. 25   b. 60   c. 85   d. 98

3. Which of the following contributes *most* to communication and learning disorders?
   a. quality of early parenting
   b. quality of early education
   c. genetic and biological factors
   d. social and cultural factors

4. Robbie is 10 years old, but he hardly speaks. Sometimes he repeats back small bits of what you say to him, but otherwise he doesn't communicate. He has a low IQ and spends a lot of time rocking his body back and forth or waving his fingers in front of his eyes. From this description, Robbie most likely suffers from:
   a. autism.
   b. a communication disorder.
   c. profound mental retardation.
   d. cultural–familial retardation.

5. **True or False:** Almost all cases of profound mental retardation are due to a lack of stimulation and educational experiences at an early age.

6. **True or False:** With expressive language disorder, children have difficulty speaking clearly; they often have difficulty producing the *th* or *r* sounds and say things like "twy" instead of "try."

Answers: 1. d, 2. c, 3. c, 4. a, 5. F, 6. F

Child Maltreatment: Abuse and Neglect

As you saw in Chapter 12, children depend on their parents and other caregivers for the physical, psychological, and emotional support they need for healthy development. Young children in particular are completely dependent on their parents—they can't make it on their own. Unfortunately, there are some parents and caregivers who don't (or can't) live up to their responsibilities, and there are others who exploit the vulnerable and powerless position of children. Child abuse is a tragedy that is very real and all too frequent in the lives of children. Before they grow up, about 1 in every 5 girls and 1 in every 9 boys in the United States will experience some form of sexual abuse (Finkelhor, 1994; Mash & Wolfe, 1999). And each year, 1 in every 10 children endures severe physical violence committed by a parent or caregiver (Mash & Wolfe, 1999; Srauss & Gelles, 1986). Who knows how many others suffer from emotional and psychological abuses that remain hidden in family privacy?

As you study this section, ask yourself these questions:

- What are the different types of abuse and neglect?
- Who is most likely to suffer from abuse or neglect, and who is most likely to commit these harmful actions?
- What are the effects of the different types of abuse on children?

Types and Frequency of Child Maltreatment

Child maltreatment is a general category that includes all situations in which parents or other persons in charge of a child's well-being harm the child or otherwise neglect the child's needs. There are four standard categories of maltreatment:

> **Physical abuse** includes beating, slapping, hitting, kicking, burning, shaking, and otherwise causing physical harm to a child. Most cases are not intentional but result from discipline or physical punishment that got out of hand (Mash & Wolfe, 1999).

> **Neglect** is failure to provide for a child's basic physical, educational, or psychological needs. Neglect includes child abandonment, inadequate supervision, failing to provide proper nutrition or timely medical attention, failing to enroll a child in school, allowing truancy, failing to provide adequate affection, exposing the child to spousal conflict, and permitting drug or alcohol abuse (Mash & Wolfe, 1999).

> **Sexual abuse** includes fondling a child's genitals or breasts, committing intercourse or other sexual acts with a child, exposing the child to indecent acts, and/or involving the child in pornography.

> **Psychological abuse** includes verbal put-downs and other behavior that terrorizes, threatens, rejects, or isolates children or damages their self-esteem, thought processing, or ability to manage social interactions. This is also referred to as *emotional abuse.*

When cases of abuse exist, there is typically considerable overlap among these categories. For example, some degree of psychological abuse is present with every case of neglect or physical or sexual abuse.

In the United States, laws require anyone who comes in contact with children in the course of work or volunteer activities to report any suspected case of child maltreatment to child protection authorities or police (Mash & Wolfe, 1999). This requirement applies to teachers, bus drivers, camp counselors, child-care workers, baby-sitters, physicians, nurses, and anyone else

---

child maltreatment

A general category including all situations where parents or other persons in charge of a child's well-being harm the child or otherwise neglect the child's needs.

physical abuse

Abuse that causes physical harm to a child.

neglect

Failure to provide for a child's basic physical, educational, or psychological needs.

sexual abuse

Abuse that includes fondling a child's genitals or breasts, committing intercourse or other sexual acts with a child, exposing the child to indecent acts, and/or involving the child in pornography.

psychological abuse

Abuse that includes verbal put-downs and other behavior that terrorizes, threatens, rejects, or isolates children.

---

who works with children. They *all* must report *any* credible suspicion they have regarding the abuse or neglect of a child. It is then up to child protection authorities to look into each report, investigate the case if it has merit, and take appropriate actions to protect the child.

To get a feel for the dimensions of the abuse problem in this country, consider that in the year 1999 authorities received nearly *3 million reports* of suspected abuse or neglect (U.S. Department of Health and Human Services, 2001). Out of these, child protection agents investigated 1.8 million cases and verified approximately 826,000 instances of child maltreatment. And this was for one year alone! At that rate, more than 14.8 million cases of maltreatment would occur in the 18 years that it takes for one child to grow up. Keep in mind that these statistics represent only the cases that were actually reported by someone and then verified by child protection agents. How many more cases go unreported in a given year?

As you can see in Table 14.4, neglect is by far the most frequently reported type of maltreatment. The rates of child maltreatment increased significantly during the 1980s, but they started to decline slightly after 1993 (Mash & Wolfe, 1999; U.S. Department of Health and Human Services, 2001). We suspect that a large portion of the increase was due to wider implementation of the mandatory reporting laws through the 1980s, and that the decrease came as helpful services began to reach more at-risk families.

Which children are most likely to be abused? You may find it shocking to learn that overall maltreatment rates are highest for infants under the age of 1 (U.S. Department of Health and Human Services, 2001). Rates tend to decline as children grow older. When it comes to physical abuse, boys are most likely to be abused between the ages of 4 and 11, whereas girls most often suffer abuse between 12 and 15. Girls are 4 times more likely than boys to be sexually abused. The abuse rates are also higher among several ethnic minority groups than they are in non-Hispanic white families, as Figure 14.1 shows.

thinking OF KRISTA

◄ What should Krista do if a child often comes to school with bruises and other injuries? What if the child says that the injuries are due to abuse, but asks Krista not to report it?

TABLE 14.4 Child Maltreatment Cases Reported to U.S. Child Protection Agencies in 1999

Verified cases of child maltreatment, or 1.2% of all children (estimated total)*	826,000
Neglect	482,384
Physical abuse	175,938
Sexual abuse	93,338
Other types (or combinations) of abuse	296,534

*The numbers for neglect, physical abuse, sexual abuse, and other types total more than 826,000 because many cases involved multiple forms of abuse or repeated abuses during the year.

Source: U.S. Department of Health and Human Services (2001). Data collected through the National Child Abuse and Neglect Data System (NCANDS).

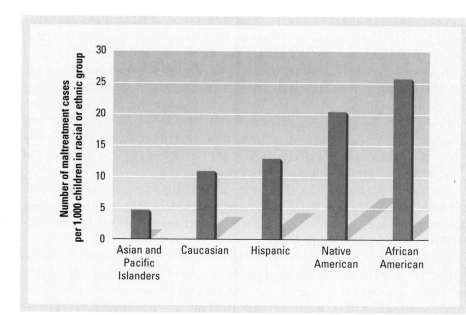

FIGURE 14.1 U.S. Rates of Child Maltreatment by Race and Ethnicity, 1999

Rates of child maltreatment vary across racial and ethnic groups. Shown in this graph are patterns of maltreatment reported to authorities during 1999.

Source: U.S. Department of Health and Human Services (2001).

TABLE 14.5 **Perpetrators of U.S. Child Maltreatment Cases, 1999**

PHYSICAL ABUSE AND NEGLECT	PERPETRATOR	SEXUAL ABUSE
56%	Mothers	15%
16%	Fathers	23%
18%	Both parents	12%
3%	Other relatives	18%
1%	Other care providers (e.g., day care providers, baby-sitters)	3%
6%	Other	29%

Source: U.S. Department of Health and Human Services (2001). Data collected through the National Child Abuse and Neglect Data System (NCANDS).

Who is most likely to commit abuse? When we think of abuse, we may picture a mean father or stepfather yelling, hitting, or giving harsh punishment to children. It may surprise you to know, however, that mothers commit many more acts of physical abuse and neglect than do fathers (see Table 14.5). The reasons is probably that mothers spend so much more time with children than fathers do. Sexual abuse, however, is most likely to be committed by "others" or fathers (refer again to Table 14.5). Isn't it alarming to know that 90 percent of all acts of physical abuse and neglect, and half of all cases of sexual abuse, are committed by parents—the very people who should care most for their children? During 1999 alone there were 1,100 fatalities due to child abuse or neglect (U.S. Department of Health and Human Services, 2001). Out of these, parents caused 81 percent of the deaths and in 86 percent of the cases, the child who died was under 6. A full 43 percent of the deaths were of infants not yet 1 year old.

Effects of Child Maltreatment

It is impossible to determine the exact effect that any form of maltreatment will have on a given child. Cases of maltreatment vary tremendously, differing in severity, length of duration, the age of the child, and other circumstances. In some instances well-meaning parents try to "overprotect" their children but use discipline that is too harsh. In other cases violent parents strike their children in anger. In others, someone violates a child's privacy and sense of self by subjecting the child to sexual abuse. Whenever abuse happens, it breaks the trust that should exist between child and caregiver. Although many abused children still claim love and affection for parents who have harmed them, the abuse often shatters their sense of security and well-being. When abuse occurs early, it threatens the formation of secure bonds of attachment between infants and their parents (recall Chapter 9). According to various studies, 70 to 100 percent of abused infants show insecure attachments with their caregivers (Barnett, Ganiban, & Cicchetti, 1999; Cicchetti, Toth, & Bush, 1988; Wekerle & Wolfe, 1996). When abuse occurs later, it still can cause physical pain, fear, and anxiety; it can lead to feelings of guilt, shame, and embarrassment in children; and it can disrupt children's social interactions as they try to hide their family secrets from their peers. And childhood abuse may have a permanent effect on the brain's structure. The limbic system, important for regulating emotion and memory, seems to be especially affected. "Early stress [is] a toxic agent" that disrupts normal brain development (Teicher, 2002, p. 75).

As we mentioned before, the different types of maltreatment usually overlap. This adds to the difficulty of determining effects. For example, when a child experiences both physical abuse and neglect, any negative effects could result from the physical abuse alone, the neglect alone, the unique combination of both types of maltreatment, or other factors (such as parenting style) that correlate with them. Individual children also have their own individual reactions to the different types of abuse.

Although we can't specify the exact effects for any particular child, we can summarize what researchers have ascertained generally about the effects of each type of maltreatment. We'll outline the main research findings regarding physical abuse, neglect, and sexual abuse. The effects of psychological abuse blend in with those of the other three categories, because this form of maltreatment tends to co-occur with all of the other types. As we describe these outcomes, bear in mind that the abuse is always an act perpetrated by the adult or other caregiver. It is never the fault of the child (Wekerle & Wolfe, 1996).

■ **Effects of Physical Abuse.**   Aside from the deaths and physical injuries that can result from physical abuse, this type of abuse disrupts children's development in many ways. Children who have suffered physical abuse commonly have problems with aggression and hostility themselves. From their abusive parents they learn to use violence as a way to confront conflict, and they also may learn to be unsympathetic about other people's feelings. Recall the study we discussed in Chapter 9 that showed how abused preschoolers reacted when their classmates were crying or in distress (Main & George, 1985). Rather than comforting their peers, the abused children responded with anger, fear, or hostility, sometimes even physically attacking children who were already in distress. Adolescents and adults who were abused as children are twice as likely to commit violent crimes and other criminal offenses as people who were not (McCord, 1983; Wekerle & Wolfe, 1996). Abused children are 3 times more likely to suffer depression, and they are at greater risk for suicide and self-destructive behaviors (Wekerle & Wolfe, 1996). Contrary to popular belief, however, most abused children do *not* grow up to be abusers themselves. It is estimated that only about 30 percent of physically abused or neglected children grow up to abuse or neglect their own children; the remaining 70 percent develop more positive parenting skills (Kaufman & Zigler, 1989).

Children who are physically abused sometimes develop compulsive compliance—they try to avoid severe punishment by complying with their parent's every demand.

An interesting behavior pattern seen among some physically abused children is **compulsive compliance**—ready and quick responses aimed at pleasing adults by complying with their demands and wishes (Crittenden & DiLalla, 1988; Wekerle & Wolfe, 1996). Babies and toddlers who experience physical abuse sometimes become especially watchful of their own behavior, trying hard to avoid doing things that will make their abusive parents angry. Researchers report that this pattern is most noticeable in 1- to 3-year-olds. Most nonabused children this age are testing limits, saying *no,* and developing their own sense of autonomy (you've heard of the "terrible twos"?). Abused children, in contrast, are working to suppress these behaviors. The long-term effects of compulsive compliance are not yet known, but you can imagine the impact on children's sense of well-being, confidence, and self-esteem.

Language delays and poor academic performance also go hand in hand with physical abuse. The expressive language disorders we described earlier in this chapter occur more frequently in abused children. Various studies have shown that physically abused children score an average of 20 points lower than their peers on IQ tests. They also score about 2 years below their grade levels on standardized tests of verbal and math skills, and about one-third fail school subjects or must attend special education classes (Hoffman-Plotkin & Twentyman, 1984; Salzinger, Kaplan, Pelcovitz, Samit, & Krieger, 1984; Wekerle & Wolfe, 1996).

■ **Effects of Neglect.** The cognitive and academic achievement of neglected children is even worse than that of physically abused children (Wekerle & Wolfe, 1996). Parents who neglect their children don't provide as much stimulation for them when they are infants, don't read to them as much when they are preschoolers, and don't become involved or supportive in their schoolwork and other activities. Their children spend a lot of time unsupervised. Language delays, intelligence deficits, and lackluster academic performance are common. Neglected children often show poor impulse control and become highly dependent on their teachers. Some become extremely passive in school. Neglected children tend to be even more socially withdrawn than physically or sexually abused children, often shying away from playing with classmates. One of the difficult decisions child protection authorities often must make is how severe the neglect needs to be before they remove children from their homes. To learn more about this heart-wrenching issue, read the Social Policy Perspective box called "Protecting Children from Neglect."

■ **Effects of Sexual Abuse.** As with other forms of abuse, the effects of sexual abuse depend on the frequency of the abuse and the length of time over which it occurs. In one study of randomly selected cases, more than half of female victims reported more than 50 incidents of abuse. The average number of incidents for the whole sample was 143, and the average age of the first abuse incident was 7 years (Nash, Zivney, & Hulsey, 1993). With sexual abuse, the outcomes are more negative when the abuse begins at an earlier age, the episodes are frequent, physical force is involved, sexual penetration occurs, and the abuser is a close relative such as a father or stepfather (Nash et al., 1993; Wekerle & Wolfe, 1996). Outcomes are less severe when there is a relatively stable two-parent household and the abused child has a warm and supportive relationship with the mother. When mothers show anger, jealousy, or indifference, these responses compound the negative outcomes.

Depression is the symptom most often reported in children and adolescents following sexual abuse. In some studies, two-thirds of female victims showed depression and 42 percent showed evidence of suicidal thoughts in the aftermath of their abuse (Koverola, Pound, Heger, & Lytle, 1993; Wozencraft, Wagner, & Pellegrin, 1991). Another troubling symptom often seen in abused children is an increase in sexual behavior. A study of sexually abused preschoolers found that they engaged in more sexual kissing and used sexual words more often than their peers (Friedrich, 1993). And child sexual abuse correlates with increased sexual activity during adolescence as well as with teenage pregnancy, prostitution, and drug abuse (Wekerle &

compulsive compliance

A behavior pattern seen among some physically abused children: ready and quick responses aimed at pleasing adults by complying with their demands and wishes.

Protecting Children from Neglect

Ana Diaz-DeJesus is a child protection caseworker in Bridgeport, Connecticut. She has a daunting caseload of more than 30 families, including nearly 150 children. Today she is visiting Maria R., a young mother of three children who lives in a filthy apartment with no heat and no food. Maria, a high school dropout and drug user, is raising her children on welfare and all alone. Moving from one cramped apartment to another, she barely stays ahead of eviction. Landlords, neighbors, and even relatives have called authorities to report that she is using drugs, not caring properly for her children, and living with a man who has a record of molesting children. One of the children had to be hospitalized in a coma after falling while unsupervised. At times the family has lived by candlelight because the electricity was turned off. Over many months Ana has often delivered groceries to the apartment and has arranged numerous services for Maria, including drug counseling, domestic violence counseling, and therapy for the children. Maria has never followed through. As she leaves the apartment this time, Ana prays, "God protect this family" (Gross, 1998, p. 1).

Not far from Bridgeport, in New York City, Sabrina Green was found dead several years ago, having suf-

fered untreated burns, gangrene, and blows to the head. Sabrina was only 9 years old. She was living with her half-sister and 10 other children in a small apartment. The half-sister and her boyfriend claimed that Sabrina had lit a fire and tried to put it out, resulting in the burns. Police, however, arrested the half-sister and boyfriend and charged them with manslaughter (Sexton & Swarns, 1997). A few years later in the Bronx, Ahsianea Carzan died of apparent malnutrition. Blind and disabled, she was not able to fend for herself. When she was found, her tiny body weighed only 17 pounds. Ahsianea was 5 years old (Bernstein & Chivers, 2000).

Abuse and neglect are the leading causes of death of children under the age of 4. The former secretary of Health and Human Services, Donna Shalala, reported that "children are being hurt more often and more seriously" (Pear, 1996, p. 1). Both Sabrina Green's and Ahsianea Carzan's families had numerous encounters with child protection agencies, but in neither case did the agencies put the child in foster care. Should the authorities have been more aggressive in protecting these children? Some people think so, and cases like these have prompted many child protection agencies to become more willing to remove children

from their homes. Agencies once tried to keep the family intact as long as possible, but they no longer feel they can allow families so many chances. Other critics, however, believe that child protection agencies remove children too often. In a scathing opinion, one federal judge wrote that agencies are too quick in removing children from homes where mothers suffer domestic violence, and one group of parents in New York City filed a class-action lawsuit claiming that child protection workers routinely violate the law by removing children from families when they are not in real danger (Glaberson, 2002; Swarns, 1999).

Meanwhile, in Bridgeport, Ana Diaz-DeJesus continues to do her best to provide support and services to families, taking heart in the glimmers of improvement she sometimes sees. The problems families face are complex, and the answers are never easy. Speaking about caseworkers like Ana, the deputy director of the Child Welfare League of America commented that "what they do is not rocket science—it's way harder than rocket science" (Gross, 1998, p. 1). Where do you think child protection authorities should draw the line between supporting families and removing children? ■

Wolfe, 1996). About half of abused children show signs of posttraumatic stress disorder (look back to Table 14.1). Despite these and other negative effects of sexual abuse, children and adolescents who have suffered this type of abuse tend to perform better in school than neglected or physically abused youngsters.

As we mentioned before, the outcomes of child maltreatment are as varied as the individual children who suffer the abuse and the individual adults who perpetrate it. Also confusing the issue is the fact that it is virtually impossible to distinguish the effects of the abuse as such from the impacts of all of the other factors that surround these children and families. Abusing families tend to isolate themselves from friends and community, keeping the abuse private. They may move frequently, changing the children's schools and networks of friends. Family conflict and family dysfunction are common, so children may witness other acts of violence or abuse in addition to the maltreatment directed at them. Their homes may be overcrowded, and life may be chaotic and unpredictable. Although most abusers do not have officially diagnosed mental disorders, some do. Often, too, the families live in poverty. By interacting with all of these factors, child abuse and neglect can exact a considerable price.

And consider that the child is usually trapped and powerless to change the environment. As one researcher put it, "She must find a way to preserve a sense of trust in people who are untrustworthy, safety in a situation that is unsafe, control in a situation that is terrifyingly unpredictable, power in a situation of helplessness" (Herman, 1992). Using cognitive and emotional skills that are not yet mature, abused children must struggle to understand their situations and the complex feelings they evoke. When it comes to pointing fingers for the blame of child maltreatment, we need to focus on parents' lack of understanding of their children's needs, on the undue stressors many parents face, and on the failure of the society to offer families enough support.

How can we prevent child maltreatment? Solutions are not easy and must address multiple factors. One program that has been successful in significantly reducing the rate of child maltreatment is the Title I Child–Parent Center program begun in the Chicago public schools in 1967. This program offers preschool education for low-income children as well as a variety of services to support entire families. For example, training is offered in parenting skills and job-related skills, and the program actively encourages family involvement in children's schooling. The services are continued until the child weathers the transition to school (until second or third grade). Compared to other children, those who have participated in this program do better in school, have higher rates of graduation, and have lower arrest rates. Their parents are more involved in the children's schooling and have higher expectations for their children's academic achievement. And, most important for this discussion, the rate of child maltreatment is significantly lower in these families—about 50 percent lower than in similar families not in the program (Reynolds, 2000; Reynolds & Robertson, 2003; Reynolds, Temple, Robertson, & Mann, 2001).

thinking
OF KRISTA

How often do you think teachers like Krista encounter children who are being abused or neglected? What supports can teachers and schools give to families to help prevent maltreatment?

LET'S REVIEW . . .

1. What are teachers, nurses, physicians, child-care workers, and other professionals *required* to do if they suspect that a child has been abused or neglected?

   a. Ignore it; it's a private family matter.

   b. Interview the child to find out what happened.

   c. Contact the parents to find out what happened.

   d. Report it to police or child protection authorities.

2. Who is most likely to be reported for the physical abuse or neglect of a child?

   a. fathers   c. child-care workers

   b. mothers   d. other relatives who care for children

3. Children's IQs and grades in school tend to be *lowest* when they have experienced:

   a. neglect.   b. physical abuse.   c. sexual abuse.   d. psychological abuse.

4. Which symptom is reported most frequently among children and adolescents who have suffered sexual abuse?

   a. depression   b. anxiety disorders   c. conduct problems   d. sexual promiscuity

5. **True or False:** Most of the adults who abuse children have some type of mental disorder.

6. **True or False:** More than half of all abused infants have an insecure attachment with their parents.

Answers: 1. d, 2. b, 3. a, 4. a, 5. F, 6. T

Children Who Thrive: Gifted, Talented, and Resilient Children

After thinking about all these problems and disorders, it is interesting and informative to look at the more positive ways that children can deviate from "average" or "normal." Some children are exceptionally talented, able, or intelligent. How did they get this way? Are geniuses "born" or are they "made"? Parents and teachers need to know how to support gifted and talented children; in addition, by studying these children we can get a more complete picture of the factors that influence development. At the end of this section we discuss children who are *resilient*— they survive, and sometimes thrive, even though the odds seem stacked against them.

As you study this section, ask yourself these questions:

- How are gifted children different from their more typical peers? At what point in development do their exceptional abilities become noticeable?

- How can we help children maintain and strengthen their gifts? Why do some children seem to lose their special talents or exceptional abilities?

- Are child geniuses less healthy than other children, or do they pay a price in other ways as they grow up?

- Why are some children better able to rise above adversity than others? Why do some seem to escape harmful effects even when they grow up in poverty or suffer abuse or other childhood traumas?

Gifted and Talented Children

In her book *Gifted Children,* Ellen Winner (1996) presents biographies of children who have astounding abilities in language, mathematics, music, art, and other realms. One child she interviewed was David, who at the age of only 2 years was already speaking sentences such as "I saw a real ditch digger pick up real dirt and put in dump truck" (p. 15). As you'll recall from Chapter 8, most 2-year-olds are speaking only simple phrases such as "Me do" and "Go bye-bye." David, however, spoke his first words at 8 months, had a vocabulary of 200 words by 15 months, and was reading books on his own at age 3. His mother spent 2 to 3 weeks helping him sound out new words, but otherwise David basically taught himself to read. At 4 he asked for a set of encyclopedias for his birthday. When he entered kindergarten at age 5, he was already reading at the sixth-grade level. David was also advanced in mathematics: He could add and subtract numbers in his head at age 4, and at 5 he understood proportions and percentages. Still, his true love was reading. He devoured books, reading up to a dozen at a time, some in French, Spanish, or other languages.

Winner (1996) also described the amazing talents of Michael Kearney, a child with an IQ over 200. (An IQ that high occurs only once in a million people.) At 4 months Michael was saying things like "Mom, Dad, what's for dinner?" At 10 months he startled people in supermarkets by reading aloud words that he saw on packages and signs. It was as if the voice were coming from somewhere else—who would expect an infant to be reading aloud? Michael entered and finished high school at 5 years of age! At 6 he attended the University of South Alabama; his mother went to classes with him, but she didn't help him with his schoolwork. At 10 Michael Kearney became the youngest person ever to graduate from college. After graduation he spent most of his time watching TV and playing video games, then went on to earn a master's degree in biochemistry at age 14 and is working on a second master's in computer science ("Super-Smart Teen," 1998; "Whiz Kid Worries," 1999). Michael was offered a full scholarship for medical school, but he opted to go to Hollywood for a while after college instead to become a game show host ("Grad, 10, Puts Off More College," 1994). His father said Michael was too young for medical school, and that he could always go when he was older, like 15!

It is easy to see that children like David and Michael are gifted. **Gifted (or talented) children** show achievement that is well above average in one or more areas—usually in language, math, music, art, or athletics. Some children are *globally gifted:* They show exceptional talent in all areas. Other children are *unevenly gifted:* They are exceptional in one or two areas but are at (or below) average levels in others. For example, many children who are gifted in art may actually have reading disorders that make it difficult for them to perform well in most school subjects (Winner, 1996). Educators often use the term *talented* to refer to students with higher abilities in performance subjects such as art, music, dance, and athletics; they tend to use *gifted* to refer to children with special abilities in academic subjects such as mathematics and science. Often, however, the terms are used interchangeably.

Winner (1996) describes three characteristics that are typical of gifted (or talented) children:

▶ Gifted children are *precocious*. They begin learning early, and they progress faster than other children. Like David and Michael, they may begin speaking in infancy and often are already reading before they enter kindergarten.

▶ Gifted children *march to their own drummer*. They don't need much assistance from adults to master information in their favorite subjects. They usually teach themselves with only minimal support, as when parents help them sound out a few words. They often have their own way of learning and unique ways of organizing and sorting information. They don't always conform to the conventional learning methods schools emphasize.

▶ Gifted children have *a rage to master*—an intense craving for information and an obsessive need to make sense out of their favorite topics. They devour information, spend endless hours on their chosen subjects, and rarely engage in any other pursuits. Parents don't push them to achieve; instead, gifted children push their parents for more materials and stimulation.

Many children, if pushed, can achieve at higher than average levels. Their parents can provide them with music lessons, send them to sports camps, and obtain tutors in math or science. With adult help and encouragement, children can learn to do impressive things. But this is not what Winner (1996) means by *gifted*. Gifted children are self-motivated. Their "rage to master" comes from within—it does not originate with eager parents or with teachers or other adults. Parents of gifted children actually often worry that their children are spending too much time on their favorite topics and may encourage them to "go play" or "be a kid."

YOUR
PERSPECTIVE
NOTES

Have you ever had a "rage to master" a particular topic? If so, what was the experience like, and what do you think motivated you? If you haven't experienced this intense level of motivation, what subject comes closest to motivating you to learn at a higher level?

gifted (or talented) children
Children who show extraordinary achievement in one or more areas.

A Longitudinal Study of Gifted and Talented Teens

How do gifted children fare later in development, during the adolescent years? What determines which adolescents maintain their "gifts" while others seem to drop out of their talent areas? These questions were the focus of an interesting longitudinal study that followed gifted and talented adolescents through their 4 years of high school (Csikszentmihalyi, Rathunde, & Whalen, 1997). Teachers from two high schools in Chicago suburbs nominated 208 students who they believed showed exceptional promise in the areas of art, athletics, mathematics, music, and science. These students all achieved at very high levels in their talent areas. The math and science students generally scored in the top 10 percent on national standardized tests; the art and music students won many awards and honors for their performances; the athletes competed at levels up to the state championships. The researchers took several different measures at different times during the 4-year high school period. For a period of 1 week during either the student's freshman or sophomore year, these talented teens carried pagers that beeped at random intervals. When their pagers beeped, the teens filled out detailed questionnaires about their activities at the moment, how they felt, and what they were thinking. Eight years earlier, a group of "average" teens at the same high schools had followed the same procedure. Researchers conducted interviews with both groups of students and their parents, teachers, and coaches at several points, up through their senior years in high school.

How did the talented students differ from the "average" group? Figure 14.2 shows some of the results from the beeper study. As you would expect, the talented teens were more focused in school, and their practice and attention in their talent areas occupied a good deal of their

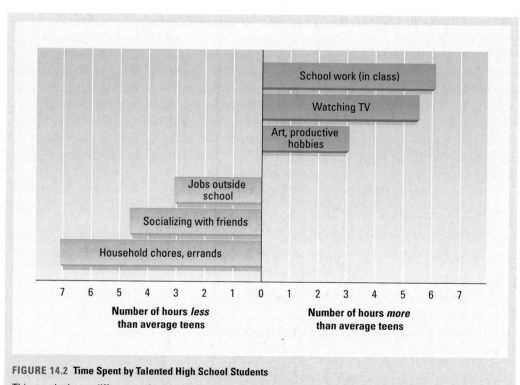

FIGURE 14.2 Time Spent by Talented High School Students

This graph shows differences between talented teens' use of time and "average" high school students' use of time, according to a study in which teens were paged at random moments during their awake hours (approximately 100 hours per week).

Source: Data from Csikszentmihalyi et al. (1997).

Schools and teachers are an important influence on students with special gifts and talents. How will school be for this talented teen today? Exciting and challenging? Or boring?

time outside school. Although as a group they logged more TV hours than average, this result primarily reflected the talented athletes' watching of sports programs. Not shown in the figure is the finding that talented teens also spent more time alone than did their more typical peers.

The talented teens in the study came more often from families with the resources to support their gifted children. Family incomes were higher, and the parents had more education (80 percent had graduated from college). These teens obviously benefited from the money and time their parents invested in tutors, sports camps, music equipment, computers, and other educational resources. Talented teens also benefited from family environments that were, on average, more supportive and positive—the majority had parents who were still married, and they rated their family interactions as more cohesive and flexible than did the other students. If other children had these benefits, how many more would show exceptional talent by the time they reached high school?

Interestingly, the talented teens were more self-critical and rated themselves as being less happy, cheerful, and sociable than their more typical classmates. Across their 4 years of high school, some of the teens remained committed to their talents, but others lost interest or began slipping in their performance. Family income and parental education did not predict which teens would continue to achieve on "talented" levels. Instead, the sheer enjoyment of working in their talent areas determined who continued to excel and who dropped out. The teens who felt cheerful, strong, excited, open, and successful during their talent-related activities were the ones who were most likely to continue performing at high levels. The researchers emphasized the important roles that teachers and parents play in supporting talented teens. When instruction becomes boring and/or parents push too hard, teens are more likely to drop their talents. Strong intrinsic motivation and a desire for challenge are also important variables. Teens with a true "rage to master" are more likely to overcome educational obstacles and family problems in pursuit of their unique talents.

In summarizing their work with the Chicago students, Csikszentmihalyi and his colleagues (1997) concluded that:

thinking
OF KRISTA

How can Krista help her gifted students maintain their interest in school? How can she support their "rage to master"?

▶ No teen can develop talent without both immediate and long-term extrinsic rewards.

▶ No teen will develop a talent unless he or she enjoys working in the talent area.

▶ No teen can avoid conflicts inherent in the development of talent.

▶ Schools are essential for cultivating talent, yet they place peculiar obstacles in the way of its development.

▶ No child succeeds unless he or she receives strong support from adults.

These researchers emphasize the important roles played by parents and schools in fostering talent in young students. Without positive support, many teens become mired in daily hassles and frustrations that distract them from developing their talents. How can they concentrate on math, for example, if they spend most of their time at home arguing with parents or siblings or worrying about their parents' breakup? How do they maintain their enthusiasm at school if their math teachers allow other students to disrupt class, fail to provide positive

A Personal PERSPECTIVE...

Meet a Teen with a Music Talent

Jose Soto
South Central Los Angeles, California

A senior at Idyllwild Arts Academy, a school for talented students

What is your talent or skill area? When do you first remember having a special interest or ability in this area?

The place where I'm the strongest is piano. Specifically, I wish to pursue piano classically, but at the same time I enjoy everything and anything that has to do with jazz. When I was about 10 years old and had been playing for 2 years, I found that it was something I really liked and felt I could do it for a while. Who knew that I might have ended up doing it all of my life?

Why/how do you think you became especially talented in this area?

I went through a lot of programs, including a mariachi course, guitar, flute, theater, and Folklorico, but after a period of time I felt that piano was something that I could connect with.

What supports did you get from family, schools, mentors, or other sources?

My father really wanted me to play to stay out of gangs and away from drugs, and so did my mom. At school, everyone loved the idea and kept pushing me. The place where I first started to learn, which was Plaza de la Raza, really helped me, and the people there kept telling me that I could do anything.

What advice would you give to other teens and their parents to help

them understand the problems and the joys that talented teens have?

The best thing my father and mother did was encourage me and let me be myself. To students, I would say we are not talented but just work hard because of all of the support that we have received. It's our job to try our best but always have fun. ■

thinking
OF KRISTA

◄ How can Krista help to support her gifted and talented students and make sure they have the opportunities and resources they need to flourish?

---

challenges, or are just plain boring? The truly gifted, those with a real "rage to master," may persevere through difficulty, but others may tune out and drop out. How many talented teens do we lose in these ways? To read more about the experiences of one talented teen, see the Personal Perspective box called "Meet a Teen with a Music Talent."

Terman's Kids: The Classic Study of Gifted Individuals

The most ambitious longitudinal study in history was the research project started by Lewis Terman. As you may recall from Chapter 7, Terman popularized IQ testing when he developed the Stanford–Binet Scale in 1916. Around that time Terman began testing thousands of California schoolchildren, using various intelligence tests and detailed interview questionnaires. Beginning in 1921, his research team identified a sample of more than 1,500 children with exceptional intelligence or talent (Terman, 1947). Most of these children scored 140 or higher on IQ tests (nearly three standard deviations above the average score of 100). Others showed unusual talents in particular areas such as music or art. In the beginning Terman referred to his sample as "geniuses," but later he came to prefer the term "gifted" (Shurkin, 1992). Over the years the team tested, retested, and interviewed "Terman's kids" (or "the Termites," as they were often called) at great lengths. Terman's goal was to see how these gifted children fared in life, which children became most successful, and how the Termites differed from more "average" Americans.

thinking
OF KRISTA

How might Krista use ▶
Terman's findings to understand the students in her
classes? How can she help
other students understand
that most really bright
students are not as weak
or socially inept as some
people believe?

Perhaps the most important influence of Terman's study was that it dispelled the common stereotype of geniuses as neurotic, frail, eccentric, and emotionally sensitive individuals (what people call "nerds" today). Overall, the children in Terman's sample were larger, healthier, and better adjusted on average than their peers (Shurkin, 1992; Terman, 1925). They began walking about a month earlier, talked more than 3 months earlier, had fewer headaches and showed less "nervousness" and stuttering, and reached puberty slightly earlier than their average peers. Through childhood, adolescence, and adulthood, they were slightly taller and heavier than average individuals. On average, they tended to live longer, enjoyed better health, had a lower divorce rate, and were happier than most people. Other than the fact that they were about twice as likely to wear eyeglasses (Terman, 1925), you can see that this profile doesn't fit the stereotype that we often associate with brilliant children.

Academically, 85 percent of Terman's kids were accelerated in school, although another 4 percent were held back a grade or more (Shurkin, 1992; Terman, 1925). Half excelled in math. Half could read before they entered school, even though most of their parents reported that they did not push their children to read at an early age. The children's precocity seems to have been self-motivated. On average, the Termites graduated from high school at age 16, and about 90 percent attended college (Shurkin, 1992; Terman 1947, 1959). Although most were 2 years younger than their college peers, they outperformed their classmates in most subjects.

Socially, Terman's kids were just as popular as their peers (Shurkin, 1992). Those with extremely high IQs, however, tended to be somewhat more socially isolated. The boys were not more effeminate than average, but the girls were rated as more masculine than average girls. Families were also an important influence. As you might expect, Terman's kids tended to come from families with higher incomes and more resources. The families of the most successful individuals were more affectionate; their fathers were more involved in raising their children; and their parents provided positive models of success, educational achievement, and happiness.

When it came to success and happiness in life, the Termites who fared best were those who attained the highest levels of education (e.g., Ph.D.'s, M.D.'s, law degrees) and the ones who liked their occupations the most (Shurkin, 1992). As with other correlational findings, of course, it's impossible to know if they did well because they loved their work, or if they loved their work because they did well. Still, Terman's findings seem to support the notion that we can all go farther and be more happy in life when we have the opportunity to study and work in areas we love.

Terman's study also showed that high intelligence can't guarantee success and happiness. The suicide rate among the women in Terman's sample was higher than the national average, perhaps largely because of the societal barriers these intelligent women faced in the mid-1900s. Other men and women in Terman's sample failed to use their special gifts and talents—they became underachievers, dropped out, became alcoholic, or otherwise failed in business and in life. Terman surmised that most failed to succeed because they lacked ambition or the drive to achieve (Shurkin, 1992). Others dropped out by choice. In 1956, just before he died, Terman commented at a meeting of the American Psychological Association:

> We know of several in the group who deliberately chose not to enter the usual American rat-race for material success. Nor can I find it in my heart to criticize those who made this choice; it may well be that fewer honors and lower incomes have been fully compensated by greater contentment and lower incidence of anxiety and ulcers. (quoted in Shurkin [1992], p. 223)

YOUR
PERSPECTIVE
PERSPECTIVE
NOTES

How do you define "suc-
cess" and "achievement"
in life? If you had the
chance to interview the
older adults who are still
living from Terman's
sample and wanted
to find out whether
they became successful
or had high achievements
in life, what would
you ask them?

TABLE 14.6 Notable Figures Who Were Accepted (or Rejected) for Terman's Study

Beatrice Carter	Cited in *Ripley's Believe It or Not* for reading 1,400 books by the age of 10. Carter's IQ of 192 was one of the highest Terman ever tested. A gifted writer and poet, Carter enrolled at Stanford University at the age of 14 and graduated at 17. She seemed smothered by her doting mother, however, who accompanied her everywhere. At the end of World War II Carter married an army private, but they later divorced. Although Carter had some success working with educational radio and TV, she rarely seemed happy.
Harry Harlow	The researcher whose monkey research on contact comfort contributed enormously to the attachment literature. Recall Harlow from Chapter 9? Not only was he one of Terman's kids, but Terman actually gave him his name! Harry Israel (Harlow's original name) was $1/64$ Jewish, and Terman feared that his name might be a barrier in his career. Terman suggested the name Harry Harlow, and the rest is history. Other prominent psychologists from Terman's sample include Robert Sears (who took over the study after Terman's death) and Lee Cronbach.
Jess Oppenheimer	Not a household name, but perhaps the most influential of all of Terman's kids. Oppenheimer created the groundbreaking comedy show *I Love Lucy* in 1951. The show, which launched the career of Lucille Ball, was the first sitcom filmed before a live audience (a model that has carried on since). Ironically, Oppenheimer's childhood file in Terman's office contains a note from a research assistant who interviewed him and concluded, "I could detect no signs of a sense of humor." Later in his life Oppenheimer patented at least 20 inventions, including a laugh-track machine and the original TelePrompTer. His behind-the-scenes work left an indelible impression on American pop culture.
	Some of the Termites were descendants of John Adams, John Quincy Adams, Benjamin Franklin, Samuel Clemens (Mark Twain), Andrew Jackson, William Harrison, Henry Wadsworth Longfellow, Ulysses S. Grant, Harriet Beecher Stowe, Rube Goldberg, Ethan Allen, P. T. Barnum, James Buchanan, and George Washington.
	Two men whom Terman's team had tested and rejected for the study later won Nobel Prizes: William Shockley (coinventor of the transistor) and Luis Alvarez (a physicist). None of Terman's kids won a Nobel Prize.

Sources: Shurkin (1992) and Terman (1925).

And that may be another important lesson from Terman's study—that high academic achievement, business success, and high incomes should not be the highest priorities in life.

More than 80 years after it began, Terman's longitudinal study still continues today (Holahan & Sears, 1995). Researchers have stayed in contact with the Termites who are still living. The study has also continued with the 2,600 offspring of Terman's kids—who, by the way, have IQs that average as high as 133 (Shurkin, 1992). Although the identities of most of Terman's kids have remained confidential, some have become known. Table 14.6 describes a few of the more notable individuals along with two high achievers who were rejected as participants in the original study.

Resilient Children: Thriving through Adversity

It is encouraging to see how well children can do when they have everything working for them, as with the gifted children in Lewis Terman's famous study. We find it even more impressive, however, to see how well some children do when the odds seem to be stacked against them. One family we know provides a good example. The mother had three boys when she was very young. She abused drugs and mostly neglected her children. The father and other relatives provided most of the day-to-day care for the boys. The father, however, was alcoholic himself and was depressed. When the oldest boy was around 12, the mother ran off

Do you know anyone who
has faced serious prob-
lems and managed to
handle them particularly
well? How do you think
they did it? What helped
them cope with adver-
sity? What is the most
difficult challenge that
you have faced?

resilient children

Children who succeed,
achieve, or otherwise have
positive developmental outcomes despite growing up
under negative conditions.

risk factors

Characteristics of children
or aspects of children's
environments that tend to
be associated with developmental problems.

risk chains

Situations where one risk
factor leads to another.

protective factors

Characteristics of children or
aspects of children's environments that block or reduce
the negative impact of risk
factors.

with another man, leaving the boys with their father. The father did his best to care for his sons, but he had a hard time maintaining a job. He had trouble paying the rent, and the family moved frequently as the father tried to find work. Tragically, soon after the oldest son graduated from high school, the father was killed in a car accident. Now the three boys live together, with the oldest boy and his young wife doing their best to finish raising the family.

How do you think the three boys probably turned out? Given what you have learned throughout this book, it would be reasonable to expect the boys to have a difficult time in life. They could be aggressive, have conduct problems, or be depressed. In reality, the oldest son graduated from high school with honors and was an excellent athlete. He is now working to support his wife, who is attending a technical school. When she finishes, he plans to go back to school to become a radiologist. The middle son, still in high school, has excellent grades. He is in the National Honor Society and was an all-conference basketball player last year. The youngest brother doesn't do as well in academics or sports, but he loves to draw and shows special talent in art.

We are sure that these boys' lives have not been easy. All three boys must have endured pain and anxieties that are hard for us to imagine. However, although negative outcomes might still emerge, so far these boys seem to have escaped the severe effects that we see in many children in similar situations. The boys are examples of **resilient children**—children who succeed, achieve, or otherwise have positive developmental outcomes despite growing up under negative conditions (Garmezy, 1985; Luthar, Cicchetti, & Becker, 2000; Rutter, 1987).

Resilient children present some of the most interesting cases in child development. Although they face many hurdles in life, they manage to survive. Some even thrive. When researchers study resilient children, they consider the *risk factors* and the *protective factors* that interact throughout their development. **Risk factors**, as you know, are characteristics of children or aspects of children's environments that tend to be associated with developmental problems. Table 14.7 lists some common risk factors. Poverty is a major risk factor because it correlates with poor nutrition, limited access to medical services, family stress, and reduced educational stimulation. As we've discussed in previous chapters, children also are at risk when they are born prematurely, have difficult temperaments, form insecure attachments with their caregivers, or have any of the other risk factors working against them. These factors often work in **risk chains**, in which one negative factor leads to another. A difficult temperament, for example, can cause stressful interactions between infant and caregiver. Parents with "difficult" infants may learn to be less responsive to their needs and signals, leading to an insecure attachment relationship. As the stressful relationship continues, parents may become more harsh and punitive, leading to increased aggression and lower self-esteem in the child. Later, the aggressive child may have difficulties in school, performing poorly in academic subjects and suffering rejection from peers. It's difficult to tell where these chains begin, but you can see how one negative factor can lead to another and another and another.

Protective factors, also listed in Table 14.7, are characteristics of children or aspects of children's environments that block or reduce the negative impact of risk factors. Having a warm, secure, and supportive relationship with a parent, for example, can protect children from some of the harms they might otherwise suffer. Parents who are attentive to their children's needs are more likely to overcome the strain of a difficult infant temperament; they may insist on more treatment and services for a child with a learning disorder or mental illness; and they can provide positive role models for social interactions. In these and other ways, positive parents can support their children's successes in school and with peers, buffering them

TABLE 14.7 Risk and Protective Factors and Characteristics of Resilient Children

RISK FACTORS	PROTECTIVE FACTORS
Poverty	Adequate or plentiful resources
Premature birth	Healthy birth
Difficult temperament	Easy temperament
Insecure attachment	Secure attachment
Inconsistent, harsh parenting	Warm, supportive parenting
Conflict between parents, divorce, single parenting	Family harmony and cohesion
School failure	School success
Peer rejection and isolation	Peer popularity and support of positive peers
Violent neighborhood	Supportive neighborhood; support of a caring adult
Racial discrimination and injustice; lack of educational and employment opportunities	Absence of discrimination or injustice; many educational and employment opportunities
Other Risk Factors	**Other Characteristics of Resilient Children**
Parents' medical problems, mental illnesses	Humor
Death, divorce, loss of parent	Intelligence
Child's disability, medical problems, or mental illness	Confidence
Child abuse and neglect	Higher self-esteem
	Internal locus of control
	Attractiveness
	Most resilient children have several protective factors in their favor.

Sources: Kirby & Fraser (1997) and Katz (1997).

from the negative effects of poverty, premature birth, and other risk factors. Even if parenting is poor, children can still benefit from a caring and supportive relationship with another adult in their lives.

In the family with the three sons, the father did his best to protect his children from risk factors. Although he was often out of work and battling frequent illnesses, he gave warm and supportive attention to all three boys. He valued education and encouraged good study habits. A network of family supports also helped. The boys' grandparents and other close relatives visited often and provided food, clothing, and school supplies, especially after the father died. The two older boys' sports coaches mentored them, and their teachers recognized and supported their talents. Thanks to these caring relationships and other protective factors, the boys were able to maintain their confidence, self-esteem, and motivation to succeed. Without these supports, the despair of poverty and the loss of both parents might have been too much for them to deal with.

To identify protective factors, researchers study children who have experienced significant trauma or have endured persistent stress in their lives. What separates children with negative outcomes from those who are resilient? In one study researchers investigated female adolescents who had suffered physical or sexual abuse (Moran & Eckenrode, 1992). The adolescents who became depressed after their abuse tended to have lower self-esteem and often failed to take credit for making good things happen in their lives. That is, they lacked what researchers call an *internal locus of control* for good events. Those who suffered abuse

thinking
OF KRISTA

Although some children clearly show the effects of adversity, others are resilient. Given these differences, will Krista always be able to tell which of her students have suffered traumas, abuse, or other stresses? What kinds of support do resilient children need in school?

Children who live in extreme poverty face a great many risk factors. How will this child cope with all of the stress she is likely to encounter in life?

but did not become depressed had higher self-esteem and greater internal locus of control; in fact, these resilient adolescents were no more depressed than adolescents in a control group who had not been abused. The researchers concluded that self-esteem and internal locus of control are two protective factors that can buffer adolescents from the negative effects of childhood abuse. In similar ways, researchers have found that other protective factors listed in Table 14.7 seem to help children and adolescents overcome adversities such as losing parents, having their parents divorce, and living in low-income and high-stress environments (Davey, Eaker, & Walters, 2003; Masten, 2001).

One classic study of resilient children was conducted by Emmy Werner (1989, 2000; Werner & Smith, 2001), a child psychologist who tracked the lives of all children born in 1955 on the island of Kauai, Hawaii. Werner categorized approximately 10 percent of the children as resilient. These children developed into competent, caring, happy adults even though they were born into poverty, had mothers with little education, and grew up in families with considerable distress, alcoholism, or mental illness. Like other researchers, Werner was able to identify several factors that seemed to protect these resilient children from negative developmental outcomes. Pleasant dispositions; average or above-average intelligence; positive ties with family; and external support systems in school, in church, or at work—all these factors helped resilient children avoid the pitfalls and temptations that ensnared their less fortunate peers.

Children demonstrate resilience in different ways (Kirby & Fraser, 1997). Some use their intelligence and coping skills to *play a bad hand well* (Katz, 1997). These children overcome risk by negotiating their way through adversity. For example, they may focus on athletics as a way to compensate for problems at home; or they may emphasize academics, realizing that a college degree is a ticket out of poverty. Other children suffer negative effects from trauma or childhood risks but find a way to *bounce back*. After the loss of a parent, for example, they may suffer from depression, but only for a short time. They use their emotional skills, positive relationships with other adults, or other protective factors to recover their balance. Other children *beat the odds*. Although the risk factors seem to weigh heavily against them, they seem immune to the effects. Some researchers have referred to these children as "invulnerable" (Anthony, 1987), but it's hard to imagine that they are completely free from all negative effects. Although they may seem well adjusted and successful on the outside, they may show signs of trauma on the inside (Luthar et al., 2000). And we must keep in mind that negative outcomes may not become apparent until later adolescence or even adulthood. In other words, children who seem resilient when they are young may harbor problems that will emerge later in life. Also, even if they seem successful and well adjusted as adults, we never know how much better their lives could have been if they had not been exposed to risk factors.

1. At only 4 years of age, David could add and subtract numbers in his head. David's early progress in math is best seen as an example of:

    a. being precocious.

    b. his rage to master.

    c. being globally gifted.

    d. marching to his own drummer.

2. In the beeper study conducted by Csikszentmihalyi and his colleagues (1997), which of the following was *true* of talented teens compared to average high school students?

    a. Talented teens spent less time alone.

    b. Talented teens spent more time watching TV.

    c. Talented teens spent more time on chores at home.

    d. Talented teens spent less time on their work in class.

3. Which of the following did Terman's study of gifted children show to be *false*?

    a. Gifted children were just as popular with their peers as average children.

    b. The majority of gifted children were unhealthy, frail, and emotionally sensitive.

    c. The majority of gifted children were accelerated in their grades and subjects in school.

    d. Some of the gifted children were underachievers or dropped out of the rat race.

4. With resilient children,

    a. there are no risk factors.

    b. there are no protective factors.

    c. the risk factors outweigh the protective factors.

    d. the protective factors outweigh the risk factors.

5. **True or False:** According to Ellen Winner (1996), gifted children are highly self-motivated.

6. **True or False:** Resilient children are invulnerable to stress and trauma.

Answers: 1. a, 2. b, 3. b, 4. d, 5. T, 6. F

A Few Final Thoughts

Throughout this book, we have emphasized many of the different factors that influence children's development. We'd like to leave you with a few general points to keep in mind.

■ **Children's Development Is Complex.** Children develop physically, emotionally, socially, and cognitively—and all these aspects interact with one another as well as with children's overall family and cultural context. As you have seen over and over, it is usually difficult to give one specific answer to the question of why: Why do children do, think, or feel what they do? Why do some children thrive even in the worst of living conditions? Why do others seem to have such difficulty even when they have many advantages? While this complexity may be frustrating at times, it is important to understand that usually there are no quick and easy solutions to the issues that children and their families face.

■ **Think about Children's Development from Several Different Perspectives.** Throughout this book we have emphasized different perspectives—from the different explanations that theorists offer for a developmental phenomenon, to the different professions that deal with children, to different ways to understand and interpret the data from a single experiment. People (and even entire professions) see things differently, focus on different aspects of a situation, and consider different types of solutions. By trying to look at an issue through another person's eyes we can better understand the issue. For example, while taking a walk one day with our 8-year-old skateboarder son, we commented on the remodeling that our neighbors had done to their house. We noticed the inviting front porch and beautifully restored brickwork along the front of the home. Our son had a very different perspective. He exclaimed, "Wow, those steps would be awesome to ollie [meaning, jump over on a skateboard]!" We hadn't even noticed the steps, but our son analyzed them in detail and saw that they offered exciting possibilities. Different people think in different ways; this has a profound impact on what they notice, what they see as a problem, and what they see as possible solutions.

■ **Be Active in Your Thinking about and Analysis of Child Development Information.** As we've pointed out numerous times, sometimes research data can be interpreted in different ways, and often things are more complex than they seem on the surface. Cultivate the habit of asking why the result makes sense and thinking about how the information might be useful to you in your professional and personal life. The more deeply you think about the information you've encountered, the more likely you are to remember it, to use it in the future, and to understand the vast amount of new information you'll encounter in the years to come.

■ **Most Importantly, Be an Active Advocate for Children.** This textbook has given you a start in your knowledge of children's development. You're not an expert on children—no one could be after only one course! But you have gained valuable information that many people you work with, live with, or meet in your life may not have. Build on what you've learned, and use your knowledge to help make children's lives more healthy, positive, and supported. Children depend on caring and supportive adults to help them learn and develop in positive ways. Take the responsibility seriously and help provide the best environment you can for all the children you interact with!

thinking
BACK TO KRISTA

Now that you have studied this chapter, you should be able to give Krista some specific advice about the diverse problems and situations she will see with her students. You could start by describing the main symptoms or indicators of the different behavioral, emotional, developmental, and learning problems she might see. These include the various subtypes of ADHD, conduct problems (including ODD and CD), anxiety disorders, depression, suicide, mental retardation, communication disorders, learning disorders, and autism. You could give her information about some possible causes, effects, and treatments for each of these types of problems. You should do the same with the different types of child maltreatment: physical abuse, neglect, sexual abuse, and psychological abuse. When she encounters students with these problems, Krista will want to work with school psychologists, special education teachers, parents, and others to help the children overcome their difficulties and maximize their learning.

As a professional who works with children, Krista must report any indications of abuse or neglect of a child. You should help her understand the different types of child maltreatment and the indicators for each. Krista will need to know how to contact proper authorities to report maltreatment.

Like any teacher, Krista should provide a classroom environment that supports all children. How can she provide protective factors that can help children cope with adversity? How can she identify the risk factors and risk chains that many of her students will face? By explaining the coercion model of conduct problems, you can help Krista deal more effectively with problem behaviors in class and help her avoid the coercion cycle that develops in so many troubled families.

Finally, you should give Krista advice about working with the gifted and talented children in her classes. She needs to have strategies for supporting their "rage to master." She also needs to understand that many of these self-motivated students have their own ways of learning, which may not conform to traditional classroom routines. As a teacher Krista will be confronted daily with the diverse paths that child development can take. Using these and other concepts from the chapter, you should be able to give her specific advice that can enhance her ability to identify and adjust to the differences her students present.

What symptoms define attention-deficit/hyperactivity disorder? What are the subtypes of ADHD, and what are the most effective treatments?

Children with ADHD are excessively active, unable to sustain attention, and deficient in impulse control to a degree that is unusual for their developmental level. Hyperactivity usually appears at an early age, and inattention becomes evident during the school years. Inability to concentrate, daydreaming, disorganization, forgetfulness, and distractibility are typical signs. Subtypes are ADHD–primarily inattentive, ADHD–primarily hyperactive, and ADHD–combined. Stimulant medications (such as Ritalin) and behavior management programs are the most effective treatments.

What are the most common conduct problems and anxiety problems during childhood and adolescence? What is known about their causes and treatments?

Oppositional defiant disorder (ODD) and conduct disorder (CD) are two major types of conduct problems that involve disobedience, aggression, and violence. Children who show conduct problems early in life (fitting the early-starter pattern) tend to have the most problems later in life. Causes are not known, but coercive family interaction is believed to be a factor. Parent training and family therapy can address these problems. Anxiety disorders include separation anxiety disorder, generalized anxiety disorder, specific phobias, social phobia, obsessive–compulsive disorder, panic disorder, posttraumatic stress disorder (PTSD), and acute stress disorder. Anxiety disorders are the most common types of disorders children face yet often go undetected and untreated. Genetics is believed to be a factor. Clinicians often use psychotherapy and medications to treat anxiety disorders.

What factors are associated with child and adolescent depression? What are the risk factors associated with suicide?

Low self-esteem, negative thoughts, peer rejection and isolation, and school problems are common among depressed children and adolescents. Major depression shows a genetic link, but mild depression does not. Faulty cognitive processes, learned behaviors, and stressful life events all can play roles. According to one study, adolescents who attempted suicide were more likely to have been born to teenage mothers, suffered from depression or other disorders, had previously had suicidal thoughts, had a friend who recently attempted suicide, and had low self-esteem. Suicide attempts are also more likely when teens have single parents, parents with less education, a lack of support from family and friends, and are in poor health.

What kinds of developmental and learning problems can children have?

Mental retardation is apparent early in life and involves below-average intelligence and deficits in adaptive behavior. Cultural–familial retardation results from lack of educational opportunity and stimulation. Most cases of mental retardation are mild. The most severe and profound cases usually have genetic or other biological causes. Communication disorders include phonological disorder, expressive language disorder, and stuttering. Common learning disorders are reading, mathematics, and writing disorders. Communication and learning disorders have strong genetic links and involve problems in brain function. Autism is a serious developmental disorder characterized by impairments in social interaction and communication.

What are the different types of child maltreatment, and how often do they occur?

Physical abuse, neglect, sexual abuse, and psychological abuse are the major categories of child maltreatment. Psychological abuse probably occurs with every case of child maltreatment. In 1999 there were nearly 3 million reports of child maltreatment, and authorities substantiated more than 800,000 cases. Other than psychological abuse, neglect is the most frequent type. Infants suffer the highest rates of maltreatment. Girls are more likely than boys to be sexually abused.

What are the effects of child maltreatment?

It is impossible to predict or determine the effects of maltreatment for any particular child. Among children who suffer physical abuse, common problems include aggression, hostility, conduct problems, depression, compulsive compliance, language and cognitive delays, and poor school performance. With neglect, delays in language, intelligence deficits, and poor academic performance are common. With sexual abuse, there is less impact on school performance, but problems with depression, suicidal thoughts, increased sexual behavior, and PTSD often occur.

What characteristics distinguish gifted and talented students from their "average" peers?

According to Winner (1996), gifted children are precocious, march to their own drummer, and have a "rage to master." Longitudinal studies show that gifted individuals come more often from families with the resources to support giftedness: They are more likely to live with both parents, their parents tend to have more education, and family incomes tend to be higher. Without support and positive role modeling from parents and teachers, children can become disengaged from their academic or other talents. Terman's study showed that most gifted children are healthy, well adjusted, and well liked by peers.

Why are some children more resilient than others?

Resilient children tend to have protective factors that buffer them from the destructive forces of stress and trauma. Supportive adults, easy temperaments, secure attachments with parents, family harmony, school success, positive peers, and supportive neighborhoods are examples of important protective factors. Protective factors help children overcome risks. Resilient children use their resources to play a bad hand well, to bounce back from adversity, and to beat the odds that are stacked against them. Unfortunately, many children do not have enough protective factors to overcome the risks they face, and/or they do not have the personal resources to use the protective factors that are available.

KEY TERMS

anxiety disorders (562)

attention-deficit/hyperactivity disorder (ADHD) (557)

autism (572)

child maltreatment (574)

clinical depression (564)

coercion model (559)

communication disorders (570)

comorbidity (556)

compulsive compliance (578)

conduct disorder (CD) (559)

conduct problems (559)

cultural–familial retardation (569)

developmental psycho-pathology perspective (556)

early-starter pattern (559)

gifted (or talented) children (582)

learning disorders (570)

mental retardation (MR) (568)

neglect (574)

oppositional defiant disorder (ODD) (559)

physical abuse (574)

prevalence rates (556)

protective factors (588)

psychological abuse (574)

resilient children (588)

risk chains (588)

risk factors (588)

sexual abuse (574)

Glossary

ability grouping: Placing children in instructional groups based on their ability level, either in different classes (between-class grouping or tracking) or within a single class.

abstract thought: Thought about things that are not real or things that are only possibilities.

accessing: The process of finding information in memory at the desired time.

accommodation: The process of modifying old schemes or creating new ones to better fit assimilated information.

acculturation: The process of learning the language, values, customs, and social skills of a new culture.

achievement motivation: The degree to which a person chooses to engage in and keep trying to accomplish challenging tasks.

adaptation: In cognitive development, the process of changing a cognitive structure or the environment (or both) in order to understand the environment.

adolescent egocentrism: A cognitive immaturity seen in adolescents—their inability to distinguish between their own abstract reasoning and thoughts and those of others.

adolescent growth spurt: The increase in growth associated with the onset of puberty.

adolescent register: Special form of speech adolescents use to identify themselves as belonging to a particular social, cultural, or generational group. It includes distinctive phonemes, syntax, and vocabulary.

adoption studies: Comparisons between measurements of children and their adoptive and biological parents used to estimate the genetic contribution to traits and behaviors.

adult attachment interview (AAI): A structured interview used to determine an adult's views regarding attachment to his or her parents.

afterbirth: The third and last stage of birth, in which the placenta and other membranes are delivered through the birth canal.

aggression: Behavior intended to harm people or property; can be instrumental, hostile, or relational.

allele: An alternative version of a gene.

altruism: Voluntary behavior that is motivated by concern for another or by internal values and goals, not by the expectation of external rewards or punishment.

amniocentesis: Procedure used to detect chromosomal and genetic abnormalities in the fetus. A needle is inserted through the mother's abdomen and uterus and into the amniotic sac, and fetal cells are withdrawn from the amniotic fluid.

androgens: One type of sex hormone, released in greater concentration by males.

androgyny: Possession of many masculine as well as many feminine psychological characteristics.

anorexia nervosa: A serious eating disorder involving distorted body image, intense fear of gaining weight, and refusal to maintain a healthy weight.

anxiety disorders: Disorders that involve consistent and intense fear, worry, or anxiety in situations that pose no real threat or danger.

Apgar test: A brief assessment of the newborn conducted at 1 and 5 minutes after birth; used to identify newborns who are at risk and need medical attention.

arousal: Emotional and physiological activation or alertness. A heightened level of arousal can cause stronger reactions to a stimulus.

assimilation: The process of bringing new objects or information into a scheme that already exists.

attachment Q-sort (AQS): A method for classifying attachments in children between 12 months and 5 years of age. Parents or other adults who have observed the child sort through cards with behavioral descriptions and score the selected cards.

attachment: An emotional tie to a specific person or persons that endures across time and space.

attention: The ability to focus on a particular stimulus without becoming distracted by other stimuli.

attention-deficit/hyperactivity disorder (ADHD): A condition involving excessive activity, inability to sustain attention, and deficiencies in impulse control that are unusual for the child's developmental level.

attributions: Individuals' beliefs about why they or others succeed or fail.

authoritarian parents: Parents who exert firm control but are rejecting or unresponsive to their children.

authoritative parents: Parents who are warm and exert firm control.

autism: A serious developmental disorder characterized by impairments in social interaction and communication.

autobiographical memories: Memories of events of great personal importance. They are episodic memories and are often vivid and detailed.

automaticity: The ability to carry out a process with little or no conscious effort, leaving more cognitive capacity to carry out other tasks.

average children: In the peer nomination technique, children who receive moderate numbers of both "like best" and "like least" nominations.

behavior genetics: Field of study that compares the influence of genetics (nature) to the influence of learning and the environment (nurture) and examines how these forces interact to influence behavioral differences among people.

behaviorism: An American movement to develop a psychology that was objective and scientific, focusing on the principles of classical conditioning and operant conditioning.

biculturalism: Adopting two cultural orientations at the same time.

bilingual: Fluent in two languages.

biopsychological potential: The underlying biological component of each intelligence that may or may not be reached, depending on a person's culture, opportunities, individual choices, and other factors.

bugs: Systematic errors in children's procedures for solving math problems.

bulimia nervosa: A serious eating disorder with binge eating followed by purging, fasting, or excessive exercise.

canalization: Genetic limits on the effects of the environment. In experiential canalization, in contrast, it is the environment that limits the expression of genes.

cephalocaudal pattern: A pattern of growth where areas in the head and upper body tend to form and grow before the areas in the lower body.

child cultural brokers: Children of immigrants who serve as interpreters of the language and culture of the new country for their parents and other family members.

child development: Field of study where researchers from many disciplines work to understand the important changes that take place as children grow through childhood.

child-directed speech: Special form of speech people often use when speaking to young children; differs in systematic ways from speech to adults and appears to facilitate language development.

child maltreatment: A general category including all situations where parents or other persons in charge of a child's well-being harm the child or otherwise neglect the child's needs.

chorionic villus sampling (CVS): Procedure used to detect chromosomal and genetic abnormalities in the fetus. A catheter (tube) is inserted into the uterus and cells are taken from the chorionic layer of the placenta around the fetus. Chromosomes are removed to conduct genetic tests.

chromosomes: Strands of deoxyribonucleic acid (DNA) molecules that contain the genetic codes.

classical conditioning: Process where neutral stimuli are paired with unconditioned stimuli until they come to evoke conditioned responses.

classroom climate: The social and emotional environment within a classroom; the way the classroom feels to those in it.

clinical depression: A condition that involves sadness, loss of interest in activities, feelings of worthlessness, sleep problems, and changes in appetite that persist for an unusually long time.

cliques: Small groups, usually including three to nine friends, who hang out together on a voluntary basis.

coercion model: A model describing how negative interactions in some families escalate into cycles of aggression and childhood conduct problems.

cognitive development: Component of development related to changes in how children think, remember, and communicate.

cognitive developmental theory: A theory that focuses on how children adjust their own understanding as they explore and learn about the world. Also used to explain language development.

cognitive schemas: A person's understanding of the objects and sequences of events that are likely to be encountered in specific situations.

collectivism: A cultural orientation based on the belief that people are interdependent members of a social group; emphasizes duty to others and group goals, values, and well-being.

communication disorders: Conditions where children have significant difficulty producing speech sounds, using spoken language to communicate, or understanding what other people say.

comorbidity: Situation where a child has more than one psychological disorder or problem at the same time.

componential subtheory: Describes how mental processes work together in intellectual thought ("analytical intelligence").

compulsive compliance: A behavior pattern seen among some physically abused children: ready and quick responses aimed at pleasing adults by complying with their demands and wishes.

computational models: Models of cognition that are programmed on computers; output of the programs is compared to human performance.

concrete operational thought: Stage of cognitive development in which children are able to think about two or more dimensions of a problem (decentered thought), dynamic transformations, and reversible operations.

conduct disorder (CD): A conduct problem involving consistent violations of other people's basic rights or the breaking of major societal rules.

conduct problems: A general category of rule-breaking behaviors.

connectionism: In language development, theory that views language acquisition as the result of changes in the strengths of connections between units. Changes depend on how closely the language produced matches external criteria.

connectionist models: "Neurally inspired" or neural network models of cognition that view knowledge as based on patterns of activation among interconnected sets of individual units rather than stored as entire concepts.

conservation: The understanding that some basic properties of objects remain the same even when a transformation changes the physical appearance.

constraints: Assumptions that children automatically make about the possible meanings of new words.

constructivist view: The view that people construct their own knowledge and understanding of the world by using what they already know and understand to interpret new experiences.

contact comfort: The comfortable feeling infants gain by clinging to a soft attachment figure.

contextual subtheory: Describes how intelligent behavior relates to real-life situations as people adapt to, select, and/or shape their environments ("practical intelligence").

controversial children: In the peer nomination technique, children who receive large numbers of both "like best" and "like least" nominations.

cooperative learning: A teaching approach in which children work together in small groups to learn content or solve problems. Rewards are based at least in part on the group's performance.

coordinated imitation: Interaction in which toddler playmates take turns imitating each other and are aware that they are being imitated.

correlational method: Research method that measures the degree to which two or more variables are related or associated.

counting strategies: Approaches to solving math problems that involve counting of the quantities.

creativity: Original thinking and problem solving that produces a product valued by society.

critical periods: In prenatal development, segments of time when structures are first forming and are most vulnerable to damage.

cross-sectional method: A type of research design that studies development by comparing groups of children of different ages against one another at the same point in time.

crowds: Groups of adolescent peers who have similar reputations or share primary attitudes or activities.

crystallized ability: The body of specific knowledge and skills acquired in a particular culture.

cultural deficit perspective: Research perspective that assumed the problems associated with minority-group families were due to the ways that these families were not "measuring up" to the standards of majority white families.

cultural–familial retardation: Retardation caused by lack of educational opportunity and stimulation.

culture: A system of shared customs and meanings that allow individuals to participate as a member of a group and that are transmitted from one generation to the next.

descriptive methods: Research methods that attempt to describe something about a behavior of interest, such as how often it occurs and under what conditions.

desensitization: The gradual decrease of a person's (or culture's) sensitivity to a stimulus; as desensitization increases, more intense stimulation is needed to produce a reaction.

developmental psychopathology perspective: The view that a wide variety of factors influences both normal and abnormal paths of development.

dialect: A consistent and systematic variety of a single language that is shared by a certain subgroup of speakers; can be associated with a geographic region or with a specific ethnic or cultural group.

differentiation: Process that occurs during cell division in which each new cell, as it divides, is committed to becoming a particular structure and serving a particular function.

difficult child: In temperament research, a child who is frequently negative, is easily frustrated, withdraws from new situations, is slow to adapt to change, and shows irregular patterns of eating and sleeping.

dilation: The gradual opening of the cervix caused by labor contractions during the first stage of birth.

discipline: Techniques used to teach children appropriate behavior.

dishabituation: The recovery or increase in infant's response when a familiar stimulus is replaced by one that is novel.

divorce-stress-adjustment perspective: A model used to understand divorce outcomes; emphasizes that a complex interaction of stressors, specific vulnerabilities, and protective factors determine the individual child's adjustment to divorce.

dizygotic (DZ) twins: Nonidentical twins. These twins form when two eggs are fertilized by two different sperm cells.

DNA: Two strands that twist around each other like a spiral staircase. Connected by a series of nucleotide bases (adenine, thymine, guanine, and cytosine).

domain-general: Relevant or true for a wide range of tasks or topics. Domain-general skills and knowledge develop through maturation and affect performance on many tasks and topics.

domain-specific: Relevant or true for only one topic or task. Domain-specific skills and knowledge develop through extensive practice with a particular task or topic and affect performance on only that task or topic.

dominant–recessive relationship: Relationship between genes where the dominant allele will govern a particular trait, and the recessive allele will be repressed. To express a recessive trait, the individual needs to inherit two recessive alleles—one on each chromosome.

Down syndrome: Trisomy 21, a genetic disorder that occurs when there is an extra 21st chromosome. Lower IQ, facial defects, heart problems, and shortened life span are characteristic problems.

dynamic systems theories: Theories that use models from mathematics and physics to understand complex systems of development.

early-starter pattern: A pattern observed in some children who develop conduct problems at an early age.

easy child: A child who is primarily positive, smiles easily, is adaptive and flexible, and has regular patterns of eating and sleeping.

ecological systems theory: Theory focusing on the complex set of systems and interacting social layers that can affect a child's development.

embryonic stage: The second stage of prenatal development, weeks 3 through 8. The embryo forms tissue representing every system and major part of the body.

emotion contagion: The tendency of the emotional cues displayed by one person to generate similar cues or emotional states in other people.

empathy: Understanding another person's emotion and feeling the same or similar emotion.

encoding: The process of placing information in permanent, or long-term, memory. Also called *storage*.

entity view of ability: The belief that ability is fixed and unchangeable. People with this view have performance goals; they seek out tasks they are sure they can do well, they avoid challenging tasks, and they do not persist on difficult tasks.

equilibration: The dynamic process of moving between states of cognitive disequilibrium and equilibrium.

estrogen: One type of sex hormone, released in greater concentration by females.

ethology: Area of study focusing on the adaptive significance or survival value of behaviors.

experience-dependent development: Development of specific experiences and activities (such as riding a skateboard), where new synapses form to code the experience.

experience-expectant development: Development of universal experiences and activities (such as hand–eye coordination), where excess synapses form and are then pruned according to experience.

experiential subtheory: Describes how we become more intelligent as we master new tasks and learn how to perform them more automatically ("creative intelligence").

experimental method: Research method where investigators systematically manipulate an independent variable to determine if it causes a difference in a dependent variable.

fast mapping: A process in language learning in which a child acquires at least a partial understanding of a word after only a single exposure.

fertilization: The union of the father's sperm cell with the mother's egg cell yielding one fertilized cell with a unique combination of genes along 46 chromosomes.

fetal alcohol effects (FAE): Individual or multiple birth defects caused by prenatal exposure to alcohol. Lowered IQ, hyperactivity, growth deficiencies, and physical malformations can exist alone or in combinations but not in a way that indicates FAS.

fetal alcohol syndrome (FAS): A syndrome of birth defects caused by prenatal exposure to alcohol. Includes growth deficiencies, head and facial malformations, and central nervous system dysfunction.

fetal distress: A condition that indicates that the fetus is at risk; usually includes a sudden lack of oxygen (anoxia), a change in fetal heart rate, and/or a change in fetal respiration.

fetal stage: The third and final stage of prenatal development, lasting from 8 weeks after conception until birth.

fluid ability: A biologically based ability to think and perceive relations among elements.

formal operational thought: Piaget's final stage of cognitive development, when an adolescent gradually learns to use hypothetico-deductive reasoning and to extend logical thinking to concepts that are abstract.

formats: Common social interactions between infants and caregivers that have a predictable structure and teach words, syntax, and pragmatic skills.

friendship: A close, mutual, and voluntary relationship between peers that persists over time.

fuzzy trace theory: The view that memory representations vary on a continuum from exact and literal to imprecise and general memory traces based on the gist of the information or event.

G × E interaction: The interacting effects of genetics and the environment on the development of traits and behaviors.

gender: All the physical, cognitive, and behavioral traits that characterize people of one sex.

gender concept: The understanding that a person's sex is a permanent feature and cannot be altered through changes in surface features like hair or clothing.

gender constancy: The understanding that gender remains the same despite superficial changes in appearance or behavior.

gender cultures: Different spheres of influence based on the differences between male and female groups and affiliations.

gender intensification: The process of conforming more and more closely to gender stereotypes in behavior, emotions, and activities. It is common at adolescence.

gender role: The social expectations for each sex within a particular culture. Sometimes called sex role.

gender schema theory: The theory that gender knowledge consists of a gender schema, a cognitive network of gender-related information that organizes gender knowledge and guides expectations and behavior.

gender segregation: The tendency for children to associate with others of their same sex.

gene: A segment of DNA that provides an instruction for a particular structure, function, or trait.

general intelligence (g): A broad thinking ability or mental power that underlies all intellectual tasks and functions.

germinal stage: The first stage of prenatal development, from conception to 2 weeks.

gifted (or talented) children: Children who show extraordinary achievement in one or more areas.

glial cells: Specialized cells in the nervous system that support neurons in several ways.

goodness of fit: The degree to which a child's temperament and environment are compatible or complementary, leading to better developmental outcomes.

guided participation: The idea that children are involved in sociocultural activities to the degree that their level of cognitive development allows.

guilt gap: The tendency of mothers to worry more than fathers about the negative impact their work may have on their children and families.

habituation: The tendency of infants to reduce their response to stimuli that are presented repeatedly.

habituation–dishabituation technique: Technique used to test infant perception. Infants are shown a stimulus repeatedly until they respond less (habituate) to it. Then a new stimulus is presented.

helpless orientation: The tendency to attribute success to external and uncontrollable factors such as luck, and to attribute failure to internal and stable factors such as lack of ability.

heritability: A mathematical estimate of the degree of genetic influence for a given trait or behavior.

heterosexual assumption: The erroneous idea that all adolescents are heterosexual at first and "discover" their homosexuality only after having several failed relationships with members of the opposite sex.

holophrases: Single words used to express an entire idea or sentence.

homosexual experience: Sexual activities with someone of the same sex.

homosexual orientation: Sexual attraction primarily to people of the same sex.

Human Genome Project: A multinational effort by governments and scientists to map the 3 billion nucleotide bases and 30,000 genes contained in human chromosomes.

hypothetico-deductive reasoning: The ability to use deductive reasoning (reasoning from general to specific facts) to systematically manipulate several variables, test the effects in a systematic way, and reach correct conclusions in complex problems; scientific reasoning.

implantation: Process where the zygote embeds itself into the inner lining of the mother's uterus.

incremental view of ability: The belief that ability can be improved.

individualism: A cultural orientation based on the belief that people are independent of each other; emphasizes individual rights, self-fulfillment, and personal accomplishments.

infantile amnesia: Inability to recall experiences prior to the age of about 3 years.

infant mortality: Deaths that occur between birth and 1 year of age.

information-processing approach: A theoretical approach focusing on how children perceive, store, and retrieve information, and on the strategies they use to solve problems.

insecure–avoidant attachment: In Ainsworth's classification, an unhealthy type of attachment indicated when infants do not use their caregivers as a safe base for exploring unfamiliar environments, do not prefer the caregivers over unfamiliar adults, and are not visibly distressed by separation. Infants ignore or avoid their caregivers when reunited after separation.

insecure–disorganized (or disoriented) attachment: An unhealthy type of attachment indicated when infants seem confused or dazed or show contradictory behaviors in the strange situation procedure. Infants may be calm, then become angry; or they may be motionless or apprehensive.

insecure–resistant attachment: In Ainsworth's classification, an unhealthy type of attachment indicated when infants seek the proximity of their caregivers but do not seem to gain comfort from the contact.

intelligence: As generally defined in Western cultures, the ability to learn, think logically about abstract concepts, and adapt to the environment.

intelligence quotient (IQ): Originally computed as $(MA \div CA) \times 100$, where the average IQ is 100 for a given age.

intermodal perception: The process of combining or integrating information across sensory modalities.

internalization: The process of taking external speech and activity and making it internal and mental.

intuitive thought: Thought and logic that is based on the child's personal experience rather than on a formal system of rules.

inventive spelling: Incorrect spellings that children create by sounding out words and writing the associated letters.

I-self: The conscious awareness that you exist as a separate person and that you can affect others.

joint focus of attention: The situation that occurs when both people in a language interaction are focusing their attention on the same object or event at the same time.

joint legal custody: Legal agreement that grants both divorced parents the responsibility for decisions regarding their children.

joint physical custody: Arrangement in which children of divorced couples spend approximately equal amounts of time living with each parent.

knowledge base: The amount of information a person knows about a particular topic.

knowledge telling: Adding or "dumping" in ideas as they come to mind; a failure to organize ideas selectively in writing.

language: An arbitrary system of symbols (words) that is rule-governed and allows communication about things that are distant in time or space.

language acquisition device (LAD): A brain mechanism in humans specialized for acquiring and processing language.

latchkey kids: School-age children who have no adult supervision during the hours after school and before their parents get home from work.

learning disorders: Conditions involving difficulties with specific skills such as reading, mathematics, or writing.

learning theory: In language development, theory that sees language as a skilled behavior that children learn through operant conditioning, imitation, and modeling.

locomotor reflexes: Infant reflexes that mimic locomotor movements such as crawling, walking, and swimming.

longitudinal method: A type of research design that studies development by measuring or observing the same children across time as they grow and mature.

long-term memory: Memory of knowledge or events that is permanent.

low birth weight: Weight less than 5½ pounds at birth (2 pounds lighter than average); indicates potential for health risks.

malnutrition: Nutritional deficiency caused by inadequate intake of calories, protein, vitamins, or minerals.

malpresentation: Improper positioning of the fetus in the mother's uterus.

mastery orientation: The tendency to attribute success to internal and controllable factors such as hard work and ability, and to attribute failure to controllable or changeable factors such as strategy, or task difficulty.

mediation: The process adults and more skilled peers use to introduce concepts and cognitive structures to less skilled children.

meiosis: "Reduction division," the type of cell division that occurs during the formation of gametes (sperm and eggs).

menarche: The first menstrual period for females, usually occurring around 12 to 13 years of age.

mental retardation (MR): A condition characterized by below-normal intellectual functioning, deficits in adaptive behavior, and an onset early in life (before age 18).

me-self: What you know about and how you describe yourself. Also called self-concept or *self-representation.*

metacognition: The understanding or knowledge that people have about their own thought processes.

metalinguistic awareness: A person's explicit knowledge about language itself and about his or her own use of it.

metamemory: Knowledge about the processes and contents of memory.

mitosis: "Copy division," the type of cell division that occurs when chromosomes are copied into each new cell.

modeling: The process of imitating, practicing, and internalizing others' behavior. Also, the process of *providing* the example behavior, as in "her parents are modeling good study skills."

monozygotic (MZ) twins: Identical twins. These twins form when one zygote divides to make two zygotes.

moral affect: The emotional component of morality, including both negative emotions such as guilt and more positive emotions such as emotional attachment to caregivers, sympathy, and empathy.

moral behavior: The degree to which a person acts in accordance with moral rules when actually faced with a situation that requires a choice.

morality: Knowing the difference between what is right and wrong and acting on that knowledge. Morality includes reasoning, emotions, and behavior.

moral reasoning: The cognitive component of morality; the ways people think about right and wrong.

morphology: The rules for combining the smallest units of meaning in a language into words.

mutual gaze: Intent eye contact between two people, as when young infants stare at each other.

myelination: A form of neuron maturation where the fatty insulation (myelin sheath) grows around the axons.

nativist theory: Theory that sees language as an innate human capability that develops when language input triggers a *language acquisition device (LAD)* in the brain.

nature: The biological forces (e.g., genetics) that govern development.

neglect: Failure to provide for a child's basic physical, educational, or psychological needs.

neglected children: In the peer nomination technique, children who have very few peers who like them best or least.

network models (of memory): Models of human memory that view memory as an interconnected network of concept nodes connected by links of varying strength.

neurons: Specialized cells that process information and allow communication in the nervous system.

neuropsychology: An area of study that focuses on the study of the brain and nervous system; researchers often observe brain function using technology such as CT scans, PET, and fMRI.

niche-picking: The tendency to pick activities and environments that fit with our genetic predispositions.

nonparental child care: Care provided for a child by someone other than the child's parents. Examples are family day care, child-care centers, and care provided by relatives and friends. Nonmaternal care (care provided by people other than mothers) includes care provided by fathers.

nonshared environment: Experiences and aspects of the environment that differ across people.

nurture: The conditions and supports that are provided by the environment and contribute to learning and development.

object permanence: The fact that objects, events, and people continue to exist even when they are out of a child's direct line of sensory input or motor action.

observational learning: Learning through watching and imitating others' real or televised behavior.

open adoption: Arrangement in which adopted children have open access to information about their biological parents.

operant conditioning: Process where reinforcing or punishing consequences of actions affect behaviors.

operating principles: Innate assumptions and biases that cause children to pay particular attention to certain features in the language environment such as word endings, order, and intonation.

operations: Mental schemes (actions) that are reversible.

oppositional defiant disorder (ODD): A conduct problem involving a repetitive pattern of defiance, disobedience, and hostility toward authority figures.

organization: The tendency to form increasingly coherent and integrated structures.

organogenesis: Organ formation: process where each major organ and system in the body differentiates within the embryo.

overregularization: Incorrect application of the linguistic rules for producing past tenses and plurals, resulting in incorrect forms of irregular words such as "goed" or "deers."

ovulation: Release of an egg (ovum) from the female ovary.

parental control: The degree to which parents set limits, enforce rules, and maintain discipline with children.

parental warmth: The degree to which parents are accepting, responsive, and compassionate with their children.

parentification: Role reversal in which a child assumes responsibilities usually taken care of by parents.

peer nomination technique: Polling technique used to identify categories of popular and unpopular children.

peers: People who are about the same age as one another.

permissive parents: Parents who are warm but have little control over their children.

perspective taking: The ability to understand the psychological perspective, motives, and needs of others; central to the development of moral reasoning, empathy, prosocial reasoning, altruism, and aggression.

phonemic awareness: The understanding that words are made up of smaller units of sound; also, association of printed letters with the sounds that go with them.

phonology: The important speech sounds of a language and the rules for combining basic sounds into larger units.

physical abuse: Abuse that causes physical harm to a child.

physical development: Component of development related to growth in size, strength, and muscle coordination.

Piaget's cognitive developmental theory: In language development, theory that sees language as one of several abilities that depend on overall cognitive development. Proper cognitive development is a necessary prerequisite for normal language development.

plasticity: The brain's tendency to remain somewhat flexible or malleable until synaptogenesis is complete and until the brain's synapses have been pruned and locked into serving particular functions.

play: A pleasurable activity that is actively engaged in on a voluntary basis, is intrinsically motivated, and contains some nonliteral element.

popular children: In the peer nomination technique, children whom a large number of peers have chosen as classmates they "like best."

positive emotion bias: Tendency of children to report positive more than negative emotions.

postural reflexes: Reflexes that help infants keep their heads upright, maintain balance, and roll their heads in the direction of their body lean.

pragmatics: The use of language to express thoughts and feelings, accomplish things, and communicate effectively with others.

preferential-looking technique: Technique used to test infant visual perception. If infants consistently look longer at some patterns than at others, researchers infer they can see a difference between the patterns.

prenatal development: Development of the organism that occurs before ("pre") its birth ("natal").

preoperational thought: Thought characterized by the use of mental representations (symbols) and intuitive thought.

prepared (natural) childbirth: Use of birthing techniques designed to reduce muscle tension, promote relaxation, and reduce pain during labor and delivery.

preterm birth: Birth that occurs before 37 weeks of gestation, or about 3 weeks earlier than the normal due date.

prevalence rates: The percentages or numbers of children who show particular problems or conditions.

primitive reflexes: Reflexes that help the infant find nourishment or served protective functions during earlier periods of evolution.

private speech: Speech that children say aloud to themselves; later internalized to form inner speech and mental activity.

probabilistic epigenesis: The likelihood that specific environmental conditions will activate specific genes that lead to particular traits or behavioral outcomes.

processing capacity: The amount of information a person can remember or think about at one time.

processing efficiency: The speed and accuracy with which a person can process information.

process quality: In the context of child care, the quality of the actual experiences children have in the setting.

production systems: Sets of computerized *if–then* statements that state the specific actions taken under certain conditions.

programmed cell death: Process where many neurons die during periods of migration and heavy synaptogenesis.

prosocial reasoning: Children's thought processes about helping others; specifically, their reasons for deciding whether to help another person.

protective factors: Characteristics of children or aspects of children's environments that block or reduce the negative impact of risk factors.

proximodistal pattern: A pattern of growth where areas closer to the center of the body tend to form and grow before the areas toward the extremities.

psychoanalytic theories: Theories that focus on the structure of personality and on how the conscious and unconscious portions of the self influence behavior and development.

psychological abuse: Abuse that includes verbal put-downs and other behavior that terrorizes, threatens, rejects, or isolates children.

psychometric approach: The attempt to quantify people's psychological skills and abilities, usually by means of paper-and-pencil tests and/or physical measurements.

punishment: Techniques used to eliminate or reduce undesirable behavior.

range of reaction: The range of possible phenotypes (traits or behaviors) that exist for a particular genotype (genetic code).

reconstructive memory: A characteristic pattern in human memory. We store parts of events and knowledge; during recall we retrieve the stored pieces and draw inferences about the rest.

referential communication: The use of language to convey a message that the hearer will understand. It involves tailoring the message for the listener, recognizing whether the listener understood, and adjusting the message if needed.

reflective abstraction: The process of noticing and thinking about the implications of information and experiences.

reflexes: Involuntary movements that are elicited by environmental stimuli.

rejected children: In the peer nomination technique, children who are actively disliked; a large number of peers have chosen them as classmates they "like least."

rejecting/neglecting parents: Parents who don't set limits and are unresponsive to their children's needs.

relational aggression: Withdrawing friendship or otherwise disrupting or threatening social relationships as a way to hurt other people.

reliability: The consistency of scores when a test is repeated under the same or similar conditions.

resilient children: Children who succeed, achieve, or otherwise have positive developmental outcomes despite growing up under negative conditions.

retrieval: In the stores model, the process of bringing information from the long-term store to the short-term store. In network models, the process of activating information so that it becomes a part of working memory and thus available for use.

risk chains: Situations where one risk factor leads to another.

risk factors: Characteristics of children or aspects of children's environments that tend to be associated with developmental problems.

scaffolding: Support given to a child as he or she develops a new mental function or learns to perform a particular task.

scheme: An organized pattern of physical or mental action.

scripts: Mental representations of the way things typically occur in certain settings or for certain events.

secure attachment: In Ainsworth's classification, the healthy type of attachment between infant and caregiver. Indicated when the infant in distress seeks contact with the caregiver, clings, and is soothed by the caregiver; and when the infant uses the caregiver as a safe base for exploring unfamiliar environments. Other indicators include *separation anxiety* and *stranger anxiety.*

selection model: A model used to understand divorce outcomes; emphasizes that certain characteristics of parents (e.g., abusiveness) rather than the divorce itself cause children's negative outcomes.

self: The characteristics, emotions, and beliefs people have about themselves, including an understanding that people are unique individuals.

self-conscious emotions: Emotions that relate to our self-images or what we think about ourselves; includes shame, embarrassment, pride, and guilt.

self-esteem: The emotions people feel about themselves.

self-evaluations: The opinions people have and judgments they make about their own characteristics.

self-fulfilling prophecy: A prediction that comes true because people believe the prediction and behave in ways that produce the expected outcome.

self-regulation: The ability to control our own behavior, emotions, or thoughts and change them to meet the demands of the situation. Involves an ongoing process of monitoring your own task performance and adjusting your strategies and efforts as needed to accomplish a task.

self-representations: The ways people describe themselves; see also *me-self.*

semantics: The meanings associated with the words in a language.

sensitive responsiveness: A quality of infant care where caregivers respond quickly and warmly to the baby's signals and adjust their responses to allow the infant to direct interactions.

sensorimotor play: Play that evolves mostly around the practice of sensory activity and the development of new motor actions.

sensorimotor thought: Thought that is based only on sensory input and physical (motor) actions.

separation anxiety: Distress that infants (especially between 6 and 24 months of age) experience when separated from their primary caregivers.

sex: The male or female physical and biological characteristics of the body.

sex chromosomes: The 23rd pair of chromosomes (in humans), specialized to determine the sex of the child and other characteristics. Males are XY and females are XX.

sex-typed behavior: Behavior that matches the gender-role expectations of a culture.

sexual abuse: Abuse that includes fondling a child's genitals or breasts, committing intercourse or other sexual acts with a child, exposing the child to indecent acts, and/or involving the child in pornography.

sexual orientation: Tendency to be attracted to people of the same sex (homosexual orientation), of the opposite sex (heterosexual orientation), or of both sexes (bisexual orientation).

shared environment: Experiences and aspects of the environment that are common across all individuals who are living together.

situated cognition: The idea that we cannot fully understand children's thinking and cognition without considering the context within which it occurs.

sleeper effect of divorce: Subtle effects of divorce that may not become apparent until children reach adolescence or young adulthood and have difficulty forming intimate and stable relationships.

slow-to-warm-up child: In temperament research, a child who shows mildly negative responses to new stimuli and situations but with repeated exposure gradually develops a quiet and positive interest.

small for gestational age (SGA): Born below the 10th percentile of birth weight for gestational age; indicates serious health risks.

social cognition model: A model that explains how different children perceive, interpret, and respond to information in social settings.

social comparison: The process of comparing our own qualities and performances to those of our peers.

social development: Component of development related to changes in how children interact with other people (e.g., family members, peers, and playmates).

social interactionist theory: In language development, theory proposing that language development results from the interaction of biological and social factors, and that social interaction is required.

social learning: Process where children learn by observing and imitating the behaviors of other people.

socially shared cognition: The idea that thought is a shared group activity and that the thoughts of any individual child are derived at least in part from dynamic interactions occurring between people and in groups.

social policy: Attempts to improve the lives of children and families by using child development research to affect laws, regulations, and programs.

social rules of discourse: Conventions that speakers of a language follow when having a conversation, such as taking turns.

social smile: Smile in which infants show joy in interacting with their caregivers. Emerges at around 6 weeks of age.

social speech: Speech that we hear as people talk around us or to us.

sociocultural theory: A theory that focuses on how language and culture influence the development of thought in children.

sociodramatic play: Play that involves acting out different social roles or characters.

specific intelligence *(s)*: Abilities people have in particular areas, such as reading, verbal, and spatial skills.

stage–environment fit: The degree to which the environment is successful in meeting the cognitive, social, and emotional needs of a child in a particular stage of development.

stalled revolution: The fact that although mothers now work more outside the home, they still shoulder most of the responsibility for day-to-day care of children.

storage: Placing information in permanent, or long-term, memory. Also called *encoding*.

stores model (of memory): A model of human memory that views information as moving through a series of storage locations, from the sensory stores to short-term store to long-term store.

stranger anxiety: Wariness or fear of unfamiliar adults, shown by most infants between 6 and 24 months of age.

strange situation: A structured laboratory procedure used to observe attachment behavior in human infants.

strategies: Conscious, intentional, and controllable plans used to improve performance.

strategy choice model: The idea that children solve math problems by choosing the fastest approach that they can execute accurately.

strength and resilience perspective: Research perspective that explores ways in which minority families have survived and even thrived in spite of historical patterns of racism, bigotry, and inequality.

structural quality: In the context of child care, the quality of objective aspects of the child-care environment.

subitizing: A perceptual process where people quickly and easily determine how many objects are in a small set without actually counting them.

symbolic play: Play where children use make-believe and pretend to embellish objects and actions.

symbolic (representational) thought: The ability to form symbols (mental representations) that stand for objects or events in the world.

synaptic pruning: Process where unused synapses are lost (pruned).

synaptogenesis: One form of neuron maturation where dendrites and axons branch out to form an enormously large number of connections with neighboring neurons.

syntax: The way a language combines words to form phrases and sentences; a system consisting of the rules of grammar for the language.

telegraphic speech: Speech that includes only words that are essential to get the meaning across, leaving out nonessential words.

temperament: The infant or child's behavioral style or primary pattern of reacting to the environment.

teratogen: Any substance or condition that might disrupt prenatal development and cause birth defects.

theory: An explanation of how facts fit together, allowing us to understand and predict behavior.

theory of mind: An integrated framework about the mind, how it works, and why it works that way.

theory of multiple intelligences: Theory of intelligence emphasizing that we all have multiple intelligences that operate relatively independently of one another. Includes eight intelligences.

timeout: A disciplinary technique that involves removing the child from the situation and anything that is encouraging the misbehavior to continue, placing the child in a safe and quiet environment.

triarchic theory of intelligence: Theory of intelligence emphasizing how mental processes, experience, and situational contexts relate to intellectual thought. Includes componential, experiential, and contextual subtheories.

twin studies: Comparisons between measurements of identical and nonidentical twins, used to estimate the genetic contribution to traits and behaviors.

two-factor theory of intelligence: A theory of intelligence developed by Charles Spearman that emphasized general intelligence *(g)* and specific intelligence *(s)*.

ultrasonography (ultrasound): Images, produced by sound waves, of the fetus inside the mother's womb. Helps physicians monitor fetal growth and detect physical defects.

validity: The ability of a test to measure what it intends to measure (e.g., intelligence).

very low birth weight: Weight less than 3½ pounds at birth (4 pounds lighter than average); indicates serious health risks.

visual acuity: The ability to see fine detail.

wage gap: The fact that on average, women are still not paid as much as men for comparable work.

word problems: Verbal descriptions of mathematical situations that children solve by applying their math skills.

working memory: The information currently active in your memory system and currently available for use in a mental task.

X-linked (sex-linked) traits: Differences between males and females caused by dominant and recessive alleles on the X and Y chromosomes.

zone of proximal development (ZPD): The distance between the current maximum independent performance level of a child and the tasks the child can perform if guided by adults or more capable peers.

References

Abbott-Shim, M., Lambert, R., & McCarty, F. (2003). A comparison of school readiness outcomes for children randomly assigned to a Head Start Program and the Program's wait list. *Journal of Education for Students Placed at Risk, 8,* 191–214.

ABC News. (2001). An evil smile: Witnesses say suspect looked like he was "getting even." Retrieved March 6, 2001, from http://abcnews.go.com/sections/us/dailynews/shooting_calif010306.html.

Abel, E. L. (1992). Paternal exposure to alcohol. In T. B. Sonderegger (Ed.), *Perinatal substance abuse: Research findings and clinical implications* (pp. 132–160). Baltimore: Johns Hopkins University Press.

Abel, E. L. (1993). Paternal alcohol exposure and hyperactivity in rat offspring: Effects of amphetamine. *Neurotoxicology and Teratology, 15,* 445–449.

Abel, E. L., & Sokol, R. J. (1987). Incidence of fetal alcohol syndrome and economic impact of FAS-related anomalies. *Drug and Alcohol Dependence, 19,* 51–70.

Aber, J. L., Brown, J. L., & Jones, S. M. (2003). Developmental trajectories toward violence in middle childhood: Course, demographic differences, and response to school-based intervention. *Developmental Psychology, 39,* 324–348.

Aboud, F. E., & Doyle, A. B. (1995). The development of in-group pride in black Canadians. *Journal of Cross-Cultural Psychology, 26,* 243–254.

Ackermann-Liebrich, U., Voegeli, T., Gÿunter-Witt, K., Kunz, I., Zÿullig, M., Schindler, C., & Maurer, M. (1996). Home versus hospital deliveries: Follow-up study of matched pairs for procedures and outcome. *British Journal of Medicine, 313,* 1313–1318.

Adair, L. S., & Gordon-Larsen, P. (2001). Maturational timing and overweight prevalence in U.S. adolescent girls. *American Journal of Public Health, 91,* 642–644.

Adams, M. J., Treiman, R., & Pressley, M. (1998). Reading, writing, and literacy. In W. Damon, I. E. Sigel, & K. A. Renninger (Eds.), *Handbook of Child Psychology: Vol. 4* (pp. 275–355) New York: Wiley.

Adams, R. J., Courage, M. L., & Mercer, M. E. (1994). Systematic measurement of human neonatal color vision. *Vision Research, 34,* 1691–1701.

Adams, R. J., Maurer, D., & Davis, M. (1986). Newborns' discrimination of chromatic from achromatic stimuli. *Journal of Experimental Child Psychology, 41,* 267–281.

Ainsworth, M. D. S. (1967). *Infancy in Uganda.* Baltimore: Johns Hopkins University Press.

Ainsworth, M. D. S. (1973). The development of infant–mother attachment. In B. M. Caldwell & H. N. Ricciuti (Eds.), *Review of child development research* (Vol. 3, pp. 1–94). Chicago: University of Chicago Press.

Ainsworth, M. D. S., Blehar, M. C., Waters, E., & Wall, S. (1978). *Patterns of attachment: A psychological study of the strange situation.* Hillsdale, NJ: Erlbaum.

Ainsworth, M. D. S., & Wittig, B. A. (1969). Attachment and exploratory behavior of one-year-olds in a strange situation. In B. M. Foss (Ed.), *Determinants of infant behavior* (Vol. 4, pp. 111–136). London: Methuen.

Akhtar, N., & Tomasello, M. (2000). The social nature of words and word learning. In R. M. Golinkoff, K. Hirsh-Pasek, L. Bloom, L. B. Smith, A. L. Woodward, N. Akhtar, M. Tomasello, & G. Hollich, *Becoming a word learner: A debate on lexical acquisition* (pp. 115–135). Oxford, England: Oxford University Press.

Alaimo, K., Briefel, R. R., Frongillo, E. A., & Olson, C. M. (1998). Food insufficiency exists in the United States: Results from the Third National Health and Nutrition Examination Survey (NHANES III). *American Journal of Public Health, 88,* 419–426.

Alan Guttmacher Institute (2002). State-level policies on sexuality, STD education. Retrieved January 6, 2003, from www.guttmacher.org/pubs/ib_5-01.html.

Alarcón, M., Plomin, R., Fulker, D. W., Corley, R., & DeFries, J. C. (1998). Multivariate path analysis of specific cognitive abilities data at 12 years of age in the Colorado adoption project. *Behavior Genetics, 28*(4), 255–264.

Alderman, M. K. (1999). *Motivation for achievement: Possibilities for teaching and learning.* Mahwah, NJ: Erlbaum.

Alibali, M. W., & Goldin-Meadow, S. (1993). Gesture–speech mismatch and mechanisms of learning: What the hands reveal about a child's state. *Cognitive Psychology, 25,* 468–524.

Allen, J. P., McElhaney, K. B., Land, D. J., Kuperminc, G. P., Moore, C. W., O'Beirne-Kelly, H., & Kilmer, S. L. (2003). A secure base in adolescence: Markers of attachment security in the mother–adolescent relationship. *Child Development, 74,* 292–307.

Allison, P. D., & Furstenberg, F. F., Jr. (1989). How marital dissolution affects children: Variations by age and sex. *Developmental Psychology, 25,* 540–549.

Altman, L. K. (2000, June 27). Reading the book of life: The doctor's world; genomic chief has high hopes, and great fears, for genetic testing. *New York Times.* Retrieved February 15, 2002, from www.nytimes.com.

Amato, P. R. (1994). The implications of research findings on children in stepfamilies. In A. Booth & J. Dunn (Eds.), *Stepfamilies: Who benefits? Who does not?* (pp. 81–87). Hillsdale, NJ: Erlbaum.

Amato, P. R. (1999a). Children of divorced parents as young adults. In E. M. Hetherington (Ed.), *Coping with divorce, single parenting, and remarriage: A risk and resiliency perspective* (pp. 147–163). Mahwah, NJ: Erlbaum.

Amato, P. R. (1999b). The postdivorce society: How divorce is shaping the family and other forms of social organization. In R. A. Thompson & P. R. Amato (Eds.), *The postdivorce family: Children, parenting, and society* (pp. 161–190). Thousand Oaks, CA: Sage.

Amato, P. R. (2000). The consequences of divorce for adults and children. *Journal of Marriage and the Family, 62,* 1269–1287.

Amato, P. R. (2001). Children of divorce in the 1990s: An update of the Amato and Keith (1991) meta-analysis. *Journal of Family Psychology, 15,* 355–370.

Amato, P. R., & Booth, A. (1997). *A generation at risk: Growing up in an era of family upheaval.* Cambridge, MA: Harvard University Press.

Amato, P. R., & Gilbreth, J. G. (1999). Nonresident fathers and children's well-being: A meta-analysis. *Journal of Marriage and the Family, 61,* 557–573.

Amato, P. R., & Keith, B. (1991). Parental divorce and the well-being of children: A meta-analysis. *Psychological Bulletin, 110,* 26–46.

American Academy of Pediatrics. (1992). Fitness, activity, and sports participation in the preschool child. *Pediatrics, 90,* 1002–1004.

American Academy of Pediatrics. (1998). Guidance for effective discipline. *Pediatrics, 101,* 723–728.

American Psychiatric Association. (1994). *Diagnostic and statistical manual of mental disorders* (4th ed.). Washington, DC: Author.

Ames, C. (1992). Classrooms: Goals, structures, and student motivation. *Journal of Educational Psychology, 84,* 261–271.

Anderman, E. M., & Maehr, M. L. (1994). Motivation and schooling in the middle grades. *Review of Educational Research, 64,* 287–309.

Anderson, C. A., & Bushman, B. J. (2001). Effects of violent video games on aggressive behavior, aggressive cognition, aggressive affect, physiological arousal, and prosocial behavior: A meta-analytic review of the scientific literature. *Psychological Science, 12,* 353–359.

Anderson, D. K., Rhees, R. W., & Fleming, D. E. (1985). Effects of prenatal stress on differentiation of the sexually dimorphic nucleus of the preoptic area (SDN–POA) of the rat brain. *Brain Research, 332,* 113–118.

Anderson, D. R., Huston, A. C., Schmitt, K. L., Linebarger, D. L., & Wright, J. C. (2001). Early childhood television viewing and adolescent behavior. *Monographs of the Society for Research in Child Development, 66* (Serial No. 264), 1–156.

Andersson, B. E. (1992). Effects of day care on cognitive and socioemotional competence of thirteen-year-old Swedish school children. *Child Development, 63,* 20–36.

Andraca, I., Pino, P., LaParra, A., & Castillo, F. R. (1998). Risk factors for psychomotor development among infants born under optimal biological conditions. *Revista de Saude Publica, 32,* 138–147. As cited in Santos et al. (2001).

Andrews, J. A., & Lewinsohn, P. M. (1992). Suicidal attempts among older adolescents: Prevalence and co-occurrence with psychiatric disorders. *Journal of the American Academy of Child and Adolescent Psychiatry, 31,* 655–662.

Anglin, J. M. (1993). Vocabulary development: A morphological analysis. *Monographs of the Society for Research in Child Development, 58* (10, Serial No. 238).

Antell, S., & Keating, D. (1983). Perception of numerical invariance in neonates. *Child Development, 54,* 695–701.

Anthony, E. J. (1987). Risk, vulnerability, and resilience: An overview. In E. J. Anthony & B. J. Cohler (Eds.), *The invulnerable child* (pp. 3–48). New York: Guilford Press.

Antil, L. R., Jenkins, J. R., Wayne, S. K., & Vadasy, P. F. (1998). Cooperative learning: Prevalence, conceptualizations, and the relation between research and practice. *American Educational Research Journal, 35,* 419–454.

Apgar, V. (1953). A proposal for a new method of evaluation in the newborn infant. *Current Research in Anesthesia and Analgesia, 32,* 260.

Arcia, E. A., & Johnson, A. (1998). When respect means to obey: Immigrant Mexican mothers' values for their children. *Journal of Child and Family Studies, 7,* 79–95.

Arditti, J. A. (1999). Rethinking relationships between divorced mothers and their children: Capitalizing on family strengths. *Family Relations, 48,* 109–119.

Arnst, C. (2001). Relax, Mom. Day care won't ruin the kids. *Business Week, 3731,* 50.

Arseneault, L., Tremblay, R. E., Boulerice, B., & Saucier, J. (2002). Obstetrical complications and violent delinquency: Testing two developmental pathways. *Child Development, 73,* 496–508.

Ashcraft, M. H. (1992). Cognitive arithmetic: A review of data and theory. *Cognition, 44,* 75–106.

Asher, S. R., Parker, J. G., & Walker, D. L. (1996). Distinguishing friendship from acceptance: Implications for intervention and assessment. In W. M. Bukowski, A. F. Newcomb, & W. W. Hartup (Eds.), *The company they keep: Friendship in childhood and adolescence* (pp. 366–405). New York: Cambridge University Press.

Aslin, R. N. (1987). Visual and auditory development in infancy. In J. D. Osofsky (Ed.), *Handbook of infant development* (2nd ed., pp. 5–97). New York: Wiley.

Aslin, R. N., Jusczyk, P. W., & Pisoni, D. B. (1998). Speech and auditory processing during infancy. In D. Kuhn & R. S. Siegler (Eds.), *Cognitive, language, and perceptual development, Vol. 2* (pp. 147–198) in W. Damon (Gen. Ed.), *Handbook of child psychology.* New York: Wiley.

Associated Press. (1999, January 15). Mom wins parole after drug rehab. *The State* (Columbia, SC), p. B1.

Atkins, C. P. (1993). Do employment recruiters discriminate on the basis of nonstandard dialect? *Journal of Employment Counseling, 30,* 108–118.

Atkinson, R. C., & Shiffrin, R. M. (1968). Human memory: A proposed system and its control processes. In K. W. Spence & J. T. Spence (Eds.), *The psychology of learning and motivation: Advances in research and theory* (Vol. 2, pp. 89–195). New York: Academic Press.

Attinasi, J. J. (1998). English only for California children and the aftermath of proposition 227. *Education, 119,* 263–284.

Atwater, E. (1992). *Adolescence* (2nd ed.). Englewood Cliffs, NJ: Prentice Hall.

Au, T. K., Sidle, A. L., & Rollins, K. B. (1993). Developing an intuitive understanding of conservation and contamination: Invisible particles as a plausible mechanism. *Developmental Psychology, 29,* 286–299.

Austin, E. W., & Knaus, C. (2000). Predicting the potential for risky behavior among those "too young" to drink as a result of appealing advertising. *Journal of Health Communication, 5,* 13–27.

Autism Society of America. (2002). What is autism? Retrieved June 28, 2002, from www.autism-society.org.

Avis, J., & Harris, P. L. (1991). Belief–desire reasoning among Baka children: Evidence for a universal conception of mind. *Child Development, 62,* 460–467.

Babyonyshev, M., Ganger, J., Pesetsky, D., & Wexler, K. (2001). The maturation of grammatical principles: Evidence from Russian unaccusatives. *Linguistic Inquiry, 32,* 1–44.

Baddeley, A. D. (1986). *Working memory.* New York: Oxford University Press.

Baden, A. L. (2002). The psychological adjustment of transracial adoptees: An application of the cultural–racial identity model. *Journal of Social Distress and the Homeless, 11,* 167–191.

Baer, J. (1991). *Creativity and divergent thinking: A task-specific approach.* Hillsdale, NJ: Erlbaum.

Bahrick, L. E., Netto, D., & Hernandez-Reif, M. (1998). Intermodal perception of adult and child faces and voices by infants. *Child Development, 69,* 1263–1275.

Bailey, A., LeCouteur, A., Gottesman, I., Bolton, P., Simonoff, E., Yuzda, E., & Rutter, M. (1995). Autism as a strongly genetic disorder: Evidence from a British twin study. *Psychological Medicine, 25,* 63–77.

Bailey, J. M., & Pillard, R. C. (1991). A genetic study of male sexual orientation. *Archives of General Psychiatry, 48,* 1089–1096.

Bailey, J. M., & Zucker, K. J. (1995). Childhood sex-typed behavior and sexual orientation: A conceptual analysis and quantitative review. *Developmental Psychology, 31,* 43–55.

Baillargeon, R. (1993). The object concept revisited: New directions in the investigation of infants' physical knowledge. In C. E. Granrud (Ed.), *Visual perception and cognition in infancy* (pp. 265–315). Hillsdale, NJ: Erlbaum.

Baker, K. (1998). Structured English immersion: Breakthrough in teaching limited-English-proficient students. *Phi Delta Kappan, 80,* 199–204.

Bakermans-Kranenburg, M. J., van IJzendoorn, M. H., & Juffer, F. (2003). Less is more: Meta-analyses of sensitivity and attachment interventions in early childhood. *Psychological Bulletin, 129,* 195–215.

Baker-Ward, L., Ornstein, P. A., & Holden, D. J. (1984). The expression of memorization in early childhood. *Journal of Experimental Child Psychology, 37,* 555–575.

Baldwin, A. L., Baldwin, C., & Cole, R. E. (1990). Stress-resistant families and stress-resistant children. In J. Rolf, A. S. Masten, D. Cicchetti, K. H. Nuechterlein, & S. Weintraub (Eds.), *Risk and protective factors in the development of psychopathology* (pp. 257–280). Cambridge, England: Cambridge University Press.

Baldwin, D. A., Markman, E. M., Bill, B., Desjardins, R. N., Irwin, R. N., & Tidball, G. (1996). Infants' reliance on a social criterion for establishing word–object relations. *Child Development, 67,* 3135–3153.

Bandura, A. (1977). *Social learning theory* Englewood Cliffs, NJ: Prentice Hall.

Bandura, A. (1997). *Self-efficacy: The exercise of control.* New York: W. H. Freeman.

Bandura, A., & Walters, R. (1963). *Social learning and personality development.* New York: Holt, Rinehart & Winston.

Bang, H., & Reece, B. B. (2003). Minorities in children's television commercials: New, improved, and stereotyped. *The Journal of Consumer Affairs, 37,* 42–67.

Baran, A., & Pannor, R. (1990). Open adoption. In D. M. Brodzinsky & M. D. Schechter (Eds.), *The psychology of adoption* (pp. 316–331). New York: Oxford University Press.

Barber, B. K. (1996). Parental psychological control: Revisiting a neglected construct. *Child Development, 67,* 3296–3319.

Barber, B. K. (2002). *Intrusive parenting: How psychological control affects children and adolescents.* Washington, DC: American Psychological Association.

Barkley, R. A. (1996). Attention-deficit/hyperactivity disorder. In E. J. Mash & R. A. Barkley (Eds.), *Child psychopathology* (pp. 63–112). New York: Guilford Press.

Barkley, R. A. (1998). Attention-deficit/hyperactivity disorder. In E. J. Mash & R. A. Barkley (Eds.), *Treatment of childhood disorders* (pp. 55–110). New York: Guilford Press.

Barlow, S. M., Knight, A. F., & Sullivan, F. M. (1979). Prevention by diazepam of adverse effects of maternal restraint stress on postnatal development and learning in the rat. *Teratology, 19,* 105–110.

Barnett, D., Ganiban, J., & Cicchetti, D. (1999). Maltreatment, negative expressivity, and the development of Type D attachments from 12 to 24 months of age. *Monographs of the Society for Research in Child Development, 64*(3), 97–118.

Barnett, W. S. (1993). Cost–benefit analysis. In L. J. Schweinhart, H. V. Barnes, & D. P. Weikart, *Significant benefits: The High/Scope Perry Preschool study through age 27* (Monographs of the High/Scope Educational Research Foundation, Number 10) (pp. 96–116). Ypsilanti, MI: The High/Scope Press.

Barnett, W. S. (1998). Long-term effects on cognitive development and school success. In W. S. Barnett & S. S. Boocock (Eds.), *Early care and education for children in poverty: Promises, programs, and long-term results* (pp. 11–44). Albany: State University of New York Press.

Barnett, W. S., Young, J. W., & Schweinhart, L. J. (1998). How preschool education influences long-term cognitive development and school success: A causal model. In W. S. Barnett & S. S. Boocock (Eds.), *Early care and education for children in poverty: Promises, programs, and long-term results* (pp. 167–184). Albany: State University of New York Press.

Baron-Cohen, S. (1995). *Mindblindness: An essay on autism and theory of mind.* Cambridge, MA: MIT Press.

Baroody, A. J. (1992). The development of preschoolers' counting skills and principles. In J. Bideaud, C. Meljac, & J. P. Fischer (Eds.), *Pathways to number* (pp. 99–126). Hillsdale, NJ: Erlbaum.

Barrera, M. E., & Maurer, D. (1981a). Recognition of mother's photographed face by the three-month-old infant. *Child Development, 52,* 714–716.

Barrera, M. E., & Maurer, D. (1981b). Discrimination of strangers by the three-month-old. *Child Development, 52,* 558–563.

Barrett, P. M., Dadds, M. R., & Rapee, R. M. (1996). Family treatment of childhood anxiety: A controlled trial. *Journal of Consulting and Clinical Psychology, 64,* 333–342.

Barth, R. J., & Kinder, B. N. (1988). A theoretical analysis of sex differences in same-sex friendship. *Sex Roles, 19,* 349–363.

Bates, E. A., & Elman, J. L. (2002). Connectionism and the study of change. In M. H. Johnson, Y. Munakata, & R. O. Gilmore (Eds.), *Brain development and cognition: A reader* (2nd ed., pp. 420–440). Malden, MA: Blackwell.

Bates, J. E., Marvinney, D., Kelly, T., Dodge, K. A., Bennett, D. S., & Pettit, G. S. (1994). Child-care history and kindergarten adjustment. *Developmental Psychology, 30,* 690–700.

Battin-Pearson, S., Newcomb, M. D., Abbott, R. D., Hill, K. G., Catalano, R. F., & Hawkins, J. D. (2000). Predictors of early high school drop-out: A test of five theories. *Journal of Educational Psychology, 92,* 568–582.

Bauer, P. J., & Dow, G. A. (1994). Episodic memory in 16- and 20-month-old children: Specifics are generalized but not forgotten. *Developmental Psychology, 30,* 403–417.

Bauer, P. J., & Mandler, J. M. (1992). Putting the horse before the cart: The use of temporal order in recall of events by one-year-old children. *Developmental Psychology, 28,* 441–452.

Baumrind, D. (1973). The development of instrumental competence through socialization. In A. D. Pick (Ed.), *Minnesota symposia on child psychology* (Vol. 7, pp. 3–46). Minneapolis: University of Minnesota Press.

Baumrind, D. (1991). Effective parenting during the early adolescent transition. In P. A. Cowan & M. Heatherington (Eds.), *Family transitions* (pp. 111–164). Hillsdale, NJ: Erlbaum.

Baumrind, D. (1996). The discipline controversy revisited. *Family Relations, 45,* 405–414.

Baumrind, D., Larzelere, R. E., & Cowan, P. A. (2002). Ordinary physical punishment: Is it harmful? Comment on Gershoff (2002). *Psychological Bulletin, 128,* 580–589.

Bauserman, R. (2002). Child adjustment in joint-custody versus sole-custody arrangements: A meta-analytic review. *Journal of Family Psychology, 16,* 91–102.

Baydar, N., & Greek, A. (1997). A longitudinal study of the effects of the birth of a sibling during the first six years of life. *Journal of Marriage and the Family, 59*(4), 939–957.

Baydar, N., & Hyle, P. (1997). A longitudinal study of the effects of the birth of a sibling during preschool and early grade school years. *Journal of Marriage and the Family, 59*(4), 957–966.

Bayliss, D. M., Jarrold, C., Gunn, D. M., & Baddeley, A. D. (2003). The complexities of complex span: Explaining individual differences in working memory in children and adults. *Journal of Experimental Psychology: General, 132,* 71–92.

Beal, A. C., Villarosa, L., & Abner, A. (1999). *The black parenting book.* New York: Broadway Books.

Beal, C. R. (1990). The development of text evaluation and revision skills. *Child Development, 61,* 247–258.

Beal, C., & Belgrad, S. (1990). The development of message evaluation skills in young children. *Child Development, 61,* 705–712.

Bean, F. D., Chapa, J., Berg, R. R., & Sowards, K. (1994). Educational and sociodemographic incorporation among Hispanic immigrants to the United States. In B. Edmonston & J. S. Passel (Eds.), *Immigration and ethnicity: The integration of America's newest arrivals* (pp. 73–100). Washington, DC: Urban Institute Press.

Beaton, A. E., Mullis, I. V. S., Martin, M. O., Gonzalez, E. J., Kelly, D. L., & Smith, T. A. (1996). *Mathematics achievement in the middle school years: IEA's third international mathematics and science study (TIMSS).* Chestnut Hill, MA: Boston College.

Beauchamp, G. K., Cowart, B. J., Mennella, J. A., & Marsh, R. R. (1994). Infant salt taste: Developmental, methodological, and contextual factors. *Developmental Psychobiology, 27,* 353–365.

Bedard, A., Ickowicz, A., Logan, G. D., Hogg-Johnson, S., Schachar, R., & Tannock, R. (2003). Selective inhibition in children with attention-deficit hyperactivity disorder off and on stimulant medication. *Journal of Abnormal Child Psychology, 31,* 315–327.

Behrend, D. A., Rosengren, K. S., & Perlmutter, M. (1992). The relation between private speech and parental interactive style. In R. M. Diaz & L. E. Berk (Eds.), *Private speech: From social interaction to self-regulation* (pp. 85–100). Hillsdale, NJ: Erlbaum.

Beilin, H. (1978). Inducing conservation through training. In G. Steiner (Ed.), *Psychology of the twentieth century* (Vol. 7, pp. 260–289). Munich: Kindler.

Beilin, H. (1994). Jean Piaget's enduring contribution to developmental psychology. In R. D. Parke, P. A. Ornstein, J. J. Rieser, & C. Zahn-Waxler (Eds.), *A century of developmental psychology* (pp. 257–290). Washington, DC: American Psychological Association.

Bell, M. A., & Fox, N. A. (1992). The relations between frontal brain electrical activity and cognitive development during infancy. *Child Development, 63,* 1142–1163.

Belle, D. (1999). *The after-school lives of children: Alone and with others while parents work.* Mahwah, NJ: Erlbaum.

Beller, E. K., & Pohl, A. (1986, April). *The strange situation revisited.* Paper presented at the biennial meeting of the International Conference on Infant Studies, Beverly Hills, CA.

Bellugi, U., & St. George, M. (Eds.). (2001). *Journal from cognition to brain to gene: Perspectives from Williams syndrome.* Cambridge, MA: MIT Press.

Belsky, J. (1988). The "effects" of infant daycare reconsidered. *Early Childhood Research Quarterly, 3,* 235–272.

Belsky, J. (2002). Quantity counts: Amount of child care and children's socioemotional development. *Journal of Developmental and Behavioral Pediatrics, 23,* 167–170.

Belsky, J., & Isabella, R. (1985). Marital and parent–child relationships in family of origin and marital change following the birth of a baby: A retrospective analysis. *Child Development, 56,* 342–349.

Belsky, J., & Isabella, R. (1988). Maternal, infant, and social–contextual determinants of attachment security. In J. Belsky & T. Nezworski (Eds.), *Clinical applications of attachment* (pp. 41–94). Hillsdale, NJ: Erlbaum.

Belsky, J., Lerner, R. M., & Spanier, G. B. (1984). *The child in the family.* New York: Random House.

Belsky, J., & Rovine, M. J. (1988). Nonmaternal care in the first year of life and the security of infant–parent attachment. *Child Development, 59,* 157–167.

Belsky, J., Weinraub, M., Owen, M., & Kelly, J. F. (2001, April). *Quantity of child care and problem behavior.* Paper presented at the biennial meeting of the Society for Research in Child Development, Minneapolis, MN.

Bem, D. J. (1996). Exotic becomes erotic: A developmental theory of sexual orientation. *Psychological Review, 103,* 320–335.

Bem, D. J. (2000). Exotic becomes erotic: Interpreting the biological correlates of sexual orientation. *Archives of Sexual Behavior, 29,* 531–548.

Bem, S. L. (1974). The measurement of psychological androgyny. *Journal of Consulting and Clinical Psychology, 42,* 155–162.

Bem, S. L. (1985). Androgyny and gender schema theory: A conceptual and empirical integration. In T. B. Sonderegger (Ed.), *Nebraska symposium on motivation, 1984: Psychology and gender* (pp. 179–226). Lincoln: University of Nebraska Press.

Ben-Ari, R., & Eliassy, L. (2003). The differential effects of the learning environment on student achievement motivation: A comparison between frontal and complex instruction strategies. *Social Behavior and Personality, 31,* 143–166.

Benoit, D., & Parker, K. C. (1994). Stability and transmission of attachment across three generations. *Child Development, 65,* 1444–1456.

Bentur, Y. (1994). Ionizing and nonionizing radiation in pregnancy. In G. Koren (Ed.), *Maternal–fetal toxicology: A clinician's guide* (pp. 515–572). New York: Marcel Dekker.

Bentur, Y., & Koren, G. (1994). The common occupational exposures encountered by pregnant women. In G. Koren (Ed.), *Maternal–fetal toxicology: A clinician's guide* (pp. 425–445). New York: Marcel Dekker.

Bereiter, C., & Scardamalia, M. (1987). *The psychology of written composition.* Hillsdale, NJ: Erlbaum.

Berenbaum, S. A., & Snyder, E. (1995). Early hormonal influences on childhood sex-typed activity and playmate preferences: Implications for the development of sexual orientation. *Developmental Psychology, 31,* 31–42.

Berk, L. E. (1992). Children's private speech: An overview of theory and the status of research. In R. M. Diaz & L. E. Berk (Eds.), *Private speech: From social interaction to self-regulation* (pp. 17–53). Hillsdale, NJ: Erlbaum.

Berk, L. E., & Spuhl, S. T. (1995). Maternal interaction, private speech, and task performance in preschool children. *Early Childhood Research Quarterly, 10,* 145–169.

Berkey, C. S., Rockett, H. R. H., Gillman, M. W., & Colditz, G. A. (2003). One-year changes in activity and in inactivity among 10- to 15-year-old boys and girls: Relationship to change in body mass index. *Pediatrics, 111,* 836–843.

Berko, J. (1958). The child's learning of English morphology. *Word, 14,* 150–177.

Berkowitz, G. S., & Kasl, S. V. (1983). The role of psychosocial factors in spontaneous preterm delivery. *Journal of Psychosomatic Research, 27,* 283–290.

Berkowitz, G. S., Skovron, M. L., Lapinski, R. H., & Berkowitz, R. L. (1990). Delayed childbearing and the outcome of pregnancy. *New England Journal of Medicine, 322,* 659–664.

Berman, A. L., & Jobes, D. A. (1991). *Adolescent suicide: Assessment and intervention.* Washington, DC: American Psychological Association.

Berman, R. A., & Slobin, D. I. (1994). *Relating events in narrative: A crosslinguistic developmental study.* Hillsdale, NJ: Erlbaum.

Berndt, T. J. (1986). Children's comments about their friendships. In M. Perlmutter (Ed.), *Cognitive perspectives on children's social and behavioral development* (pp. 189–212). Hillsdale, NJ: Erlbaum.

Bernstein, N., & Chivers, C. J. (2000, May 19). Disabled girl is found dead, amid signs of malnutrition. *New York Times.* Retrieved August 2, 2002, from www.nytimes.com.

Berry, J. W. (1993). Ethnic identity in plural societies. In M. E. Bernal & G. P. Knight (Eds.), *Ethnic identity: Formation and transmission among Hispanic and other minorities* (pp. 271–296). Albany: State University of New York Press.

Bettencourt, B. A., & Miller, N. (1996). Gender differences in aggression as a function of provocation: A meta-analysis. *Psychological Bulletin, 119,* 422–447.

Bever, T. G. (1970). The cognitive basis for linguistic structure. In J. R. Hayes (Ed.), *Cognition and the development of language* (pp. 279–362). New York: Wiley.

Bialystok, E., & Hakuta, K. (1994). *In other words: The science and psychology of second-language acquisition.* New York: Basic Books.

Bialystok, E., Majumder, S., & Martin, M. M. (2003). Developing phonological awareness: Is there a bilingual advantage? *Applied Psycholinguistics, 24,* 27–44.

Bickman, D. S., Wright, J. C., & Huston, A. C. (2001). Attention, comprehension, and the educational influences of television. In D. G. Singer & J. L. Singer (Eds.), *Handbook of children and the media* (pp. 101–119). Thousand Oaks, CA: Sage.

Biddle, B. J., & Berliner, D. C. (2002). Small class size and its effects. *Educational Leadership, 59,* 12–23.

Biederman, J., Mick, E., Faraone, S. V., Braaten, E., Doyle, A., Spencer, T., Wilens, T. E., Frazier, E., & Johnson, M. A. (2002). Influence of gender on attention deficit hyperactivity disorder in children referred to a psychiatric clinic. *American Journal of Psychiatry, 159*(1), 36–42.

Bigelow, B. J. (1977). Children's friendship expectations: A cognitive–developmental study. *Child Development, 48,* 246–253.

Birnbaum, D. W., & Croll, W. L. (1984). The etiology of children's stereotypes about sex differences in emotionality. *Sex Roles, 10,* 677–691.

Bisanz, G. L., Vesonder, G. T., & Voss, J. F. (1978). Knowledge of one's own responding and the relation of such knowledge to learning. *Journal of Experimental Child Psychology, 25,* 116–128.

Bishop, E. G., Cherny, S. S., Corley, R., Plomin, R., DeFries, J. C., & Hewitt, J. K. (2003). Development genetic analysis of general cognitive ability from 1 to 12 years in a sample of adoptees, biological siblings, and twins. *Intelligence, 31,* 31–50.

Bitensky, S. H. (1998). Spare the rod, embrace our humanity: Toward a new legal regime prohibiting corporal punishment of children. *University of Michigan Journal of Law Reform, 31,* 353–474. As cited in Gershoff (2002).

Bivens, J. A., & Berk, L. E. (1990). A longitudinal study of the development of elementary school children's private speech. *Merrill-Palmer Quarterly, 36,* 443–463.

Bjorklund, D. F. (1987). How age changes in knowledge base contribute to the development of children's memory: An interpretive review. *Developmental Review, 7,* 93–130.

Bjorklund, D. F. (1989). *Children's thinking: Developmental function and individual differences.* Pacific Grove, CA: Brooks/Cole.

Bjorklund, D. F. (1995). *Children's thinking: Developmental functions and individual differences,* 2nd ed. Pacific Grove, CA: Brooks/Cole.

Bjorklund, D. F., & Coyle, T. R. (1995). Utilization deficiencies in the development of memory strategies. In F. E. Weinert & W. Schneider (Eds.), *Memory performance and competencies: Issues in growth and development* (pp. 161–180). Hillsdale, NJ: Erlbaum.

Bjorklund, D. F., & Harnishfeger, K. K. (1990). Children's strategies: Their definition and origins. In D. F. Bjorklund (Ed.), *Children's strategies: Contemporary views of cognitive development* (pp. 309–323). Hillsdale, NJ: Erlbaum.

Bjorklund, D. F., Miller, P. H., Coyle, T. R., & Slawinski, J. L. (1997). Instructing children to use memory strategies: Evidence of utilization deficiencies in memory training studies. *Developmental Review, 17,* 411–422.

Black, J. E., & Greenough, W. T. (1986). Induction of pattern in neural structure by experience: Implications for cognitive development. In M. E. Lamb, A. L. Brown, & B. Rogoff (Eds.), *Advances in developmental psychology* (Vol. 4, pp. 1–50). Hillsdale, NJ: Erlbaum.

Blair, C. (2002). School readiness: Integrating cognition and emotion in a neurobiological conceptualization of children's functioning at school entry. *American Psychologist, 57,* 111–127.

Blake, J., & deBoysson-Bardies, B. (1992). Patterns in babbling: A cross-linguistic study. *Journal of Child Language, 19,* 51–74.

Blehar, M. C. (1974). Anxious attachment and defensive reactions associated with day care. *Child Development, 46,* 801–817.

Bloch, M. N., & Adler, S. M. (1994). African children's play and the emergence of the sexual division of labor. In J. L. Roopnarine, J. E. Johnson, & F. H. Hooper (Eds.), *Children's play in diverse cultures* (pp. 148–178). Albany, NY: State University of New York Press.

Bloom, L. (1998). Language acquisition in developmental contexts. In W. Damon (Series Ed.) & D. Kuhn & R. S. Siegler (Vol. Eds.), *Handbook of child psychology: Vol. 2. Cognitive, language, and perceptual development* (pp. 309–370). New York: Wiley.

Bloom, L., Lightbrown, P., & Hood, L. (1975). Structure and variation in child language. *Monographs of the Society for Research in Child Development, 40* (Serial No. 160).

Boccia, M., & Campos, J. J. (1989). Maternal emotional signals, social referencing, and infants' reactions to strangers. In N. Eisenberg (Ed.), *New directions for child development* (Vol. 44, pp. 25–49). San Francisco: Jossey-Bass.

Bogatz, G. A., & Ball, S. (1977). *The second year of "Sesame Street": A continuing evaluation.* Princeton, NJ: Educational Testing Service.

Bohannon, J. N., & Bonvillian, J. D. (1997). Theoretical approaches to language acquisition. In J. B. Gleason (Ed.), *The development of language* (pp. 259–316). Boston: Allyn & Bacon.

Bohannon, J. N., & Padgett, R. (1996). Useful evidence on negative evidence. *Developmental Psychology, 32,* 551–555.

Boldizar, J. P., Perry, D. G., & Perry, L. C. (1989). Outcome values and aggression. *Child Development, 60,* 571–579.

Boller, K., Grabelle, M. C., & Rovee-Collier, C. K. (1995). Effects of postevent information on infants' memory for a central target. *Journal of Experimental Child Psychology, 59,* 372–396.

Bondas-Salonen, T. (1998). How women experience the presence of their partners at the births of their babies. *Qualitative Health Research, 8,* 784–800.

Boomsma, D. I. (1993). Current status and future prospects in twin studies of the development of cognitive abilities: Infancy to old age. In T. J. Bouchard, Jr. & P. Propping (Eds.), *Twins as a tool of behavioral genetics* (pp. 67–82). West Sussex, England: Wiley.

Booth, A., & Amato, P. R. (2001). Parental predivorce relations and offspring postdivorce well-being. *Journal of Marriage and the Family, 63,* 197–212.

Boring, E. (1950). *A history of experimental psychology.* New York: Appleton-Century-Crofts.

Bornstein, M. H., & Arterberry, M. E. (1999). Perceptual development. In M. H. Bornstein & M. E. Lamb (Eds.), *Developmental psychology: An advanced textbook* (4th ed., pp. 231–274). Mahwah, NJ: Erlbaum.

Bornstein, M. H., Kessen, W., & Weiskopf, S. (1976). The categories of hue in infancy. *Science, 191,* 201–202.

Bouchard, T. J., Jr. (1994). Genes, environment, and personality. *Science, 264,* 1700–1701.

Bouchard, T. J., Jr. (1997). Experience producing drive theory: How genes drive experience and shape personality. *Acta Paediatr Supplement, 422,* 60–64.

Bouchard, T. J., Jr., & McGue, M. (1981). Family studies of intelligence: A review. *Science, 212,* 1055–1059.

Bower, T. G. R. (1974). The evolution of sensory systems. In R. B. MacLeod & H. L. Pick, Jr. (Eds.), *Perception: Essays in honor of James J. Gibson* (pp. 141–165). Ithaca, NY: Cornell University Press.

Bowlby, J. (1958). The nature of the child's tie to his mother. *International Journal of Psycho-Analysis, 39,* 350–373.

Bowlby, J. (1969). *Attachment and loss: Vol. 1. Attachment.* New York: Basic Books.

Bowlby, J. (1982). *Attachment and loss.* New York: Basic Books.

Bowlby, J. (1988). *A secure base: Parent–child attachment and healthy human development.* New York: Basic Books.

Bowman, P. J., & Howard, C. S. (1985). Race-related socialization, motivation and academic achievement: A study of black youth in three-generation families. *Journal of the American Academy of Child Psychiatry, 24,* 134–141.

Boyer, K., & Diamond, A. (1992). Development of memory for temporal order in infants and young children. In A. Diamond (Ed.), *Development and neural bases of higher cognitive function* (pp. 267–317). New York: New York Academy of Sciences.

Boykin, A. W., & Toms, F. D. (1985). Black child socialization: A conceptual framework. In H. P. McAdoo & J. L. McAdoo (Eds.), *Black children: Social, educational, and parental environments* (pp. 33–51). Newbury Park, CA: Sage.

Brackbill, Y., McManus, K., & Woodward, L. (1985). *Medication in maternity: Infant exposure and maternal information.* Ann Arbor: University of Michigan Press.

Bradbard, M. R., Martin, C. L., Endsley, R. C., & Halverson, C. F. (1986). Influence of sex stereotypes on children's exploration and memory: A competence versus performance distinction. *Developmental Psychology, 22,* 481–486.

Bradley, B. S., & Gobbart, S. K. (1989). Determinants of gender-typed play in toddlers. *Journal of Genetic Psychology, 150,* 453–455.

Bradley, L., & Bryant, P. E. (1983). Categorizing sounds and learning to read—a causal connection. *Nature, 301,* 419–421.

Bradley, R. H., & Corwyn, R. F. (2002). Socioeconomic status and child development. *Annual Review of Psychology, 53,* 371–399.

Bradley, R. H., Corwyn, R. F., McAdoo, H. P., & Coll, C. G. (2001). The home environments of children in the United States: Part I. Variations by age, ethnicity, and poverty status. *Child Development, 72,* 1844–1867.

Bradley, R. H., Corwyn, R. F., & Whiteside-Mansell, L. (1996). Life at home: Same time, different places. *Early Development and Parenting, 5,* 251–269.

Brainerd, C. J., & Gordon, L. L. (1994). Development of verbatim and gist memory for numbers. *Developmental Psychology, 30,* 163–177.

Brainerd, C. J., & Reyna, V. F. (1993). Memory independence and memory interference in cognitive development. *Psychological Review, 100,* 42–67.

Brainerd, C. J., & Reyna, V. F. (1995). Learning rate, learning opportunities, and the development of forgetting. *Developmental Psychology, 31,* 251–262.

Brainerd, C. J., Reyna, V., & Brandes, E. (1995). Are children's false memories more persistent than their true memories? *Psychological Science, 4,* 141–148.

Brannon, L. (1999). *Gender: Psychological perspectives.* Boston: Allyn & Bacon.

Bransford, J. D., & Stein, B. S. (1984). *The IDEAL problem solver.* New York: Freeman.

Braungart, J. M., Plomin, R., DeFries, J. C., & Fulker, D. W. (1992). Genetic influence on tester-rated infant temperament as assessed by Bayley's Infant Behavior Record: Non-adoptive and adoptive siblings and twins. *Developmental Psychology, 28,* 40–47.

Bray, J. H. (1999). From marriage to remarriage and beyond: Findings from the developmental issues in stepfamilies research project. In E. M. Hetherington (Ed.), *Coping with divorce, single parenting, and remarriage: A risk and resiliency perspective* (pp. 253–271). Mahwah, NJ: Erlbaum.

Brennan, P. A., Hall, J., Bor, W., Najman, J. M., & Williams, G. (2003). Integrating biological and social processes in relation to early-onset persistent aggression in boys and girls. *Developmental Psychology, 39,* 309–323.

Brennan, P., Mednick, S., & Kandel, E. (1991). Congenital determinants of violent and property offending. In D. J. Pepler & K. H. Rubin (Eds.), *The development and treatment of childhood aggression* (pp. 81–92). Hillsdale, NJ: Erlbaum.

Bril, B., & Sabatier, C. (1986). The cultural context of motor development: Postural manipulations in the daily life of Bambara babies (Mali). *International Journal of Behavioral Development, 9,* 439–453.

Bringuier, J. (1980). *Conversations with Jean Piaget.* Chicago: University of Chicago Press.

Broberg, A. G., Wessels, H., Lamb, M. E., & Hwang, C. P. (1997). Effects of day care on the development of cognitive abilities in 8-year-olds: A longitudinal study. *Developmental Psychology, 33,* 62–69.

Brodzinsky, D. M. (1990). A stress and coping model of adoption adjustment. In D. M. Brodzinsky & M. D. Schechter (Eds.), *The psychology of adoption* (pp. 3–24). New York: Oxford University Press.

Brodzinsky, D. M. (1993). Long-term outcomes in adoption. In R. E. Behrman (Ed.), *The future of children: Adoption* (pp. 153–166). Los Altos, CA: Center for the Future of Children, The David and Lucile Packard Foundation.

Broidy, L. M., Nagin, D. S., Tremblay, R. E., Bates, J. E., Brame, B., Dodge, K. A., Fergusson, D., Horwood, J. L., Loeber, R., Laird, R., Lynam, D. R., Moffitt, T. E., Pettit, G. S., & Vitaro, F. (2003). Developmental trajectories of childhood disruptive behaviors and adolescent delinquency: A six-site, cross-national study. *Developmental Psychology, 39,* 222–245.

Bronfenbrenner, U. (1989). Ecological systems theory. In R. Vasta (Ed.), *Annals of child development* (Vol. 6, pp. 187–251). Greenwich, CT: JAI Press.

Bronfenbrenner, U. (1995). The bioecological model from a life course perspective: Reflections of a participant observer. In P. Moen, G. H. Elder Jr., & K. Lüscher (Eds.), *Examining lives in context* (pp. 599–618). Washington, DC: American Psychological Association.

Brookins, G. K., Petersen, A. C., & Brooks, L. M. (1997). Youth and families in the inner city: Influencing positive outcomes. In H. J. Walberg, O. Reyes, & R. P. Weissberg (Eds.), *Children and youth: Interdisciplinary perspectives* (pp. 45–66). Thousand Oaks, CA: Sage.

Brooks-Gunn, J., Duncan, G. J., & Aber, J. L. (Eds.). (1997). *Neighborhood poverty: Vol. I. Context and consequences for children.* New York: Russell Sage Foundation.

Brooks-Gunn, J., Klebanov, P., Liaw, F., & Duncan, G. (1995). Toward an understanding of the effects of poverty upon children. In H. E. Fitzgerald, B. M. Lester, & B. Zuckerman (Eds.), *Children of poverty: Research, health, and policy issues* (pp. 3–37). New York: Garland.

Broome, M. E., & Koehler, C. (1986). Childbirth education: A review of effects on the woman and her family. *Family and Community Health, 9,* 33–44.

Brown, A. L., Bransford, J. D., Ferrara, R., & Campione, J. (1983). Learning, understanding and remembering. In J. H. Flavell & E. Markman (Eds.), *Handbook of child psychology: Cognitive development,* 4th ed. (Vol. 1). New York: Wiley.

Brown, A. L., & DeLoache, J. S. (1978). Skills, plans, and self-regulation. In R. S. Siegler (Ed.), *Children's thinking: What develops?* (pp. 3–35). Hillsdale, NJ: Erlbaum.

Brown, B. B. (1990). Peer groups and peer cultures. In S. S. Feldman & G. R. Elliott (Eds.), *At the threshold: The developing adolescent* (pp. 171–196). Cambridge, MA: Harvard University Press.

Brown, B. B., Clasen, D. R., & Niess, J. D. (1987, April). *Smoke in the looking glass: Adolescents' perceptions of their peer group status.* Paper presented at the biennial meeting of the Society for Research in Child Development, Baltimore. As cited in B. Brown (1989). The role of peer groups in adolescents' adjustment to secondary school. In T. J. Berndt & G. W. Ladd (Eds.), *Peer relationships in child development* (pp. 188–215). New York: Wiley.

Brown, B. B., & Lohr, M. J. (1987). Peer-group affiliation and adolescent self-esteem: An integration of ego-identity and symbolic-interaction theories. *Journal of Personality and Social Psychology, 52,* 47–55.

Brown, E., & Brownell, C. (1990). Individual differences in toddlers' interaction styles. Paper presented at the International Conference on Infant Studies, Montreal, Canada. As cited in Rubin et al. (1998).

Brown, J. S., & Burton, R. B. (1978). Diagnostic models for procedural bugs in basic mathematical skills. *Cognitive Science, 2,* 155–192.

Brown, J. S., & VanLehn, K. (1982). Towards a generative theory of "bugs." In T. P. Carpenter, J. M. Moser, & T. A. Romberg (Eds.), *Addition and subtraction: A cognitive perspective* (pp. 117–135). Hillsdale, NJ: Erlbaum.

Brown, P., & Richman, H. A. (1997). Neighborhood effects and state and local policy. In J. Brooks-Gunn, G. J. Duncan, & J. L. Aber (Eds.), *Neighborhood poverty: Vol. II. Policy implications in studying neighborhoods* (pp. 164–181). New York: Russell Sage Foundation.

Brown, R. (1973). *A first language: The early stages.* Cambridge, MA: Harvard University Press.

Brown, R., & Hanlon, C. (1970). Derivational complexity and the order of acquisition in child speech. In J. R. Hayes (Ed.), *Cognition and the development of language* (pp. 11–53). New York: Wiley.

Browne, J. A., Losen, D. J., & Wald, J. (2001). Zero tolerance: Unfair, with little recourse. In R. J. Skiba & G. G. Noam (Eds.), *Zero tolerance: Can suspension and expulsion keep schools safe?* (pp. 73–100). San Francisco: Jossey-Bass.

Bruck, M., & Ceci, S. J. (1999). The suggestibility of children's memory. *Annual Review of Psychology, 50,* 419–439.

Bruck, M., Ceci, S. J., Francoeur, E., & Barr, R. J. (1995). "I hardly cried when I got my shot!": Influencing children's reports about a visit to their pediatrician. *Child Development, 66,* 193–208.

Bruner, J. S. (1983). *Child's talk: Learning to use language.* New York: Norton.

Bryant, B. K. (1994). How does social support function in childhood? In F. Nestmann & K. Hurrelmann (Eds.), *Social networks and social support in childhood and adolescence* (pp. 23–35). Berlin: deGruyter.

Bryant, J., & Rockwell, S. C. (1994). Effects of massive exposure to sexually oriented prime-time television programming on adolescents' moral judgment. In D. Zillman, J. Bryant, & A. C. Huston (Eds.), *Media, children, and the family* (pp. 183–195). Hillsdale, NJ: Erlbaum.

Buchanan, C. M., Eccles, J. S., & Becker, J. B. (1992). Are adolescents the victims of raging hormones: Evidence for activational effects of hormones on moods and behaviors at adolescence. *Psychological Bulletin, 111,* 62–107.

Buchanan, C. M., Maccoby, E. E., & Dornbusch, S. M. (1996). *Adolescents after divorce.* Cambridge, MA: Harvard University Press.

Bumpass, L. (1984). Children and marital disruption: A replication and update. *Demography, 21,* 71–82.

Burchinal, M. R., Howes, C., & Kontos, S. (2002). Structural predictors of child care quality in child care homes. *Early Childhood Research Quarterly, 17,* 87–105.

Burchinal, M. R., Ramey, S. L., Reid, M. K., & Jaccard, J. (1995). Early child care experiences and their association with family and child characteristics during middle childhood. *Early Childhood Research Quarterly, 10,* 33–61.

Burstein, I., Kinch, R. A., & Stern, L. (1974). Anxiety, pregnancy, labor, and the neonate. *American Journal of Obstetrics and Gynecology, 118,* 195–199.

Burton, L. M., Obeidallah, D. A., & Allison, K. (1996). Ethnographic insights on social context and adolescent development among inner-city African American teens. In R. Jessor, A. Colby, & R. Schweder (Eds.), *Ethnography and human development: Context and meaning in social inquiry* (pp. 395–418). Chicago: University of Chicago Press.

Bush calls for revamping of Head Start program. (July 7, 2003). Retrieved July 7, 2003, from www.nytimes.com.

Bushman, B. J., & Anderson, C. A. (2001). Media violence and the American public: Scientific facts versus media misinformation. *American Psychologist, 56,* 477–489.

Bushman, B. J., & Huesmann, L. R. (2001). Effects of televised violence on aggression. In D. G. Singer & J. L. Singer (Eds.), *Handbook of children and the media* (pp. 223–254). Thousand Oaks, CA: Sage.

Butler, R., & Ruzany, N. (1993). Age and socialization effects on the development of social comparison motives and normative ability assessment in kibbutz and urban children. *Child Development, 64,* 532–543.

Butler, S., Gross, J., & Hayne, H. (1995). The effect of drawing on memory performance in young children. *Developmental Psychology, 31,* 597–608.

Byrd, R. S., Weitzman, M., & Auinger, P. (1997). Increased behavior problems associated with delayed school entry and delayed school progress. *Pediatrics, 100,* 654–661.

Byrnes, J. P. (2001a). *Cognitive development and learning in instructional contexts* (2nd ed.). Boston: Allyn & Bacon.

Byrnes, J. P. (2001b). *Minds, brains, and education: Understanding the psychological and educational relevance of neuroscientific research.* New York: Guilford Press.

Byrnes, J. P. (2003). Factors predictive of mathematics achievement in White, Black, and Hispanic 12th graders. *Journal of Educational Psychology, 95,* 316–326.

Byrnes, J. P., & Takahira, S. (1993). Explaining gender differences on SAT-math items. *Developmental Psychology, 29,* 805–810.

Campbell, F. A., Pungello, E. P., Miller-Johnson, S., Burchinal, M., & Ramey, C. T. (2001). The development of cognitive and academic abilities: Growth curves from an early childhood educational experiment. *Developmental Psychology, 37,* 231–242.

Campbell, F. A., & Ramey, C. T. (1994). Effects of early intervention on intellectual and academic achievement: A follow-up study of children from low-income families. *Child Development, 65,* 684–698.

Campbell, F. A., Ramey, C. T., Pungello, E., Sparling, J., & Miller-Johnson, S. (2002). Early childhood education: Young adult outcomes from the Abecedarian Project. *Applied Developmental Science, 6,* 42–57.

Campbell, J. R., Hombo, C. M., & Mazzeo, J. (2000). *NAEP 1999 Trends in academic progress: Three decades of student performance.* Washington, DC: U.S. Department of Education, Office of Educational Research and Improvement, National Center for Education Statistics (NCES 2000-469).

Campos, J. J., Langer, A., & Krowitz, A. (1970). Cardiac responses on the visual cliff in prelocomotor human infants. *Science, 170,* 196–197.

Canfield, R. L., & Smith, E. G. (1996). Number based expectation and sequential enumeration by 5-month-old infants. *Developmental Psychology, 32,* 269–279.

Canino, G., & Roberts, R. E. (2001). Suicidal behavior among Latino youth. *Suicide and Life-Threatening Behavior, 31,* 122–131.

Cantor, J. R., Engle, W., & Hamilton, G. (1991). Short-term memory, working memory, and verbal abilities: How do they relate? *Intelligence, 15,* 229–246.

Caplan, M., Vespo, J., Pedersen, J., & Hay, D. F. (1991). Conflict and its resolution in small groups of one- and two-year-olds. *Child Development, 62,* 1513–1524.

Carey, G., & DiLalla, D. L. (1994). Personality and psychopathology: Genetic perspectives. *Journal of Abnormal Psychology, 103*(1), 32–43.

Carey, S. (1977). The child as a word learner. In M. Halle, J. Bresnan, & G. A. Miller (Eds.), *Linguistic theory and psychological reality* (pp. 264–293). Cambridge, MA: MIT Press.

Carey, S. (1985). Are children fundamentally different kinds of thinkers and learners than adults? In S. F. Chipman, J. W. Segal, & R. Glaser (Eds.), *Thinking and learning skills* (Vol. 2, pp. 485–517). Hillsdale, NJ: Erlbaum.

Carlo, G., Koller, S. H., Eisenberg, N., DaSilva, M. S., & Frohlich, C. B. (1996). A cross-national study on the relations between prosocial moral reasoning, gender role orientations, and prosocial behaviors. *Developmental Psychology, 32,* 231–240.

Carlton, M. P., & Winsler, A. (1999). School readiness: The need for a paradigm shift. *School Psychology Review, 28,* 338–352.

Carnegie Task Force on Meeting the Needs of Young Children. (1994, April). *Starting points: Meeting the needs of our youngest children.* New York: Carnegie Corporation.

Carpenter, M., Nagell, K., & Tomasello, M. (1998). Social cognition, joint attention, and communicative competence from 9 to 15 months of age. *Monographs of the Society for Research in Child Development, 63* (4, Serial No. 255).

Carr, M., Borkowski, J. G., & Maxwell, S. E. (1991). Motivational components of underachievement. *Developmental Psychology, 27,* 108–118.

Carraher, T. N., Carraher, D. W., & Schliemann, A. D. (1985). Mathematics in the streets and in the schools. *British Journal of Developmental Psychology, 3,* 21–29.

Carver, C. M. (1987). *American regional dialects: A word geography.* Ann Arbor: University of Michigan Press.

Case, R. (1985). *Intellectual development: Birth to adulthood.* New York: Academic Press.

Case, R., Kurland, M., & Goldberg, J. (1982). Operational efficiency and the growth of short-term memory span. *Journal of Experimental Child Psychology, 33,* 386–404.

Caselli, M. C., Bates, E., Casadio, P., Fenson, J., Fenson, L., Sanderl, L., & Weir, J. (1995). A cross-linguistic study of early lexical development. *Cognitive Development, 10,* 159–199.

Caspi, A., Taylor, A., Moffitt, T. E., & Plomin, R. (2000). Neighborhood deprivation affects children's mental health: Environmental risks identified in a genetic design. *Psychological Science, 11,* 338–342.

Cassidy, J., Parke, R. D., Butkovsky, L., & Braungart, J. M. (1992). Family–peer connections: The roles of emotional expressiveness within the family and children's understanding of emotions. *Child Development, 63,* 603–618.

Casteel, M. A. (1993). Effects of inference necessity and reading goal on children's inferential generation. *Developmental Psychology, 29,* 346–357.

Catsambis, W. (2001). Expanding knowledge of parental involvement in children's secondary education: Connections with high school seniors' academic success. *Social Psychology of Education, 5,* 149–177.

Catts, H. W., Gillispie, M., Leonard, L. B., Kail, R. V., & Miller, C. A. (2002). The role of speed processing, rapid naming, and phonological awareness in reading achievement. *Journal of Learning Disabilities, 35,* 509–524.

Caughy, M. O'B., DiPietro, J. A., & Strobino, D. M. (1994). Day care participation as a protective factor in the cognitive development of low-income children. *Child Development, 65,* 457–471.

Causey, V. E., Thomas, C. D., & Armento, B. J. (2000). Culture diversity is basically a foreign term to me: The challenges of diversity for preservice teacher education. *Teaching and Teacher Education, 16,* 33–45.

Ceci, S. J., & Bruck, M. (1998). Children's testimony: Applied and basic issues. In W. Damon, I. E. Sigel, & K. A. Renninger (Eds.), *Handbook of child psychology: Vol 4. Child psychology in practice* (5th ed., pp. 713–774). New York: Wiley.

Centers for Disease Control and Prevention. (2000, June 9). CDC surveillance summaries. *Morbidity and Mortality Weekly Report, 49* (No. SS-5; Tables 20, 22, & 24), 1–78.

Centers for Disease Control and Prevention. (2001a). Congenital syphilis—United States, 2000. *Morbidity and Mortality Weekly Report, 50* (No. 27, pp. 573–577). Retrieved March 1, 2002, from www.cdc.gov/mmwr/preview/mmwrhtml/mm5027a1.htm.

Centers for Disease Control and Prevention. (2001b). CDC report regarding selected public health topics affecting women's health. *Morbidity and Mortality Weekly Report, 50* (No. RR-6, pp. 15–28). Retrieved March 1, 2002, from www.cdc.gov/mmwr/indrr_2001.html.

Cernoch, J. M., & Porter, R. H. (1985). Recognition of maternal axillary odors by infants. *Child Development, 56,* 1593–1598.

Chall, J. S. (1983). *Stages of reading development.* New York: McGraw-Hill.

Chang, L. (2003). Variable effects of children's aggression, social withdrawal, and prosocial leadership as functions of teacher beliefs and behaviors. *Child Development, 74,* 535–548.

Chao, R. K. (1994). Beyond parental control and authoritarian parenting style: Understanding Chinese parenting through the cultural notion of training. *Child Development, 65,* 1111–1119.

Chao, R. K. (2001). Extending research on the consequences of parenting styles for Chinese Americans and European Americans. *Child Development, 72,* 1832–1843.

Chapman, C., Dorner, P., Silber, K., & Winterberg, T. S. (1987). Meeting the needs of the adoption triangle through open adoption: The adoptee. *Child and Adolescent Social Work, 4,* 7–91.

Chen, Z., & Siegler, R. S. (2000). Across the great divide: Bridging the gap between understanding of toddlers' and older children's thinking. *Monographs of the Society for Research in Child Development, 65*(2); Serial No. 261.

Cheng, L. L. (1987). Cross-cultural and linguistic considerations in working with Asian populations. *ASHA, 29,* 33–38.

Cherny, S. S., Fulker, D. W., Emde, R. N., Robinson, J., Corley, R. P., Reznick, J. S., Plomin, R., & DeFries, J. C. (1994). A developmental–genetic analysis of continuity and change in the Bayley mental development index from 14 to 24 months: The MacArthur Longitudinal Twin Study. *Psychological Science, 5,* 354–360.

Cherry, L., & Lewis, M. (1976). Mothers and two-year-olds: A study of sex differentiated aspects of verbal interaction. *Developmental Psychology, 12,* 278–282.

Cheshire, J. (1982). *Variations in an English dialect.* Cambridge, England: Cambridge University Press.

Chess, S., & Thomas, A. (1995). *Temperament in clinical practice.* New York: Guilford Press.

Chi, M. T. H. (1978). Knowledge structure and memory development. In R. Siegler (Ed.), *Children's thinking: What develops?* (pp. 73–96). Hillsdale, NJ: Erlbaum.

Chi, M. T. H., Feltovich, P. J., & Glaser, R. (1981). Categorization and representation of physics problems by experts and novices. *Cognitive Science, 5*, 121–152.

Chi, M. T. H., Glaser, R., & Farr, M. (Eds.). (1988). *The nature of expertise.* Hillsdale, NJ: Erlbaum.

Chi, M. T. H., & Koeske, R. D. (1983). Network representation of a child's dinosaur knowledge. *Developmental Psychology, 19*, 29–39.

Childers, J. B., & Tomasello, M. (2002). Two-year-olds learn novel nouns, verbs, and conventional actions from massed or distributed exposures. *Developmental Psychology, 38*, 967–978.

Children's Defense Fund. (2001a). Overall child poverty rate dropped in 2000 but poverty rose for children in full-time working families. Retrieved July 19, 2002, from www.childrensdefense.org.

Children's Defense Fund. (2001b). *The state of America's children yearbook 2001.* Washington, DC: CDF Publications.

Children's Defense Fund. (2002a). *Every day in America, Every child deserves a fair start,* and *Every child deserves a healthy start.* Three reports last accessed March 13, 2003, from www.childrensdefense.org.

Children's Defense Fund. (2002b). Fact sheets: Girls & juvenile justice. Retrieved July 19, 2003, from www.childrensdefense.org.

Ching, J., & Newton, N. (1982). A prospective study of psychological and social factors in pregnancy related to preterm and low-birth-weight deliveries. In H. J. Prill & M. Stauber (Eds.), *Advances in psychosomatic obstetrics and gynecology* (pp. 384–385). New York: Springer.

Chirkov, V., Ryan, R. M., Kim, Y., & Kaplan, U. (2003). Differentiating autonomy from individualism and independence: A self-determination theory perspective on internalization of cultural orientations and well-being. *Journal of Personality and Social Psychology, 84*, 97–101.

Chiu, L. H. (1987). Child-rearing attitudes of Chinese, Chinese-American, and Anglo-American mothers. *International Journal of Psychology, 22*, 409–419.

Chomsky, N. S. (1957). *Syntactic structures.* The Hague: Mouton.

Chomsky, N. S. (1981). *Lectures on government and binding.* New York: Foris.

Chun, K. M., Organista, P. B., & Marin, G. (Eds.). (2003). *Acculturation: Advances in theory, measurement, and applied research.* Washington, DC: American Psychological Association.

Cicchetti, D., Toth, S., & Bush, M. (1988). Developmental psychopathology and incompetence in childhood: Suggestions for intervention. In B. B. Lahey & A. E. Kazdin (Eds.), *Advances in clinical child psychology* (Vol. 11, pp. 1–77). New York: Plenum.

Clark, E. V. (1978). Strategies for communicating. *Child Development, 49*, 953–959.

Clarke-Stewart, K. A., Gruber, C. P., & Fitzgerald, L. M. (1994). *Children at home and in day-care.* Hillsdale, NJ: Erlbaum.

Clarke-Stewart, K. A., Vandell, D. L., McCartney, K., Owen, M. T., & Booth, C. (2000). Effects of parental separation and divorce on very young children. *Journal of Family Psychology, 14*, 304–326.

Clement, J. (1982). Algebra word problem solutions: Thought processes underlying a common misconception. *Journal for Research in Mathematics Education, 13*, 16–30.

Cleveland, H. H., & Wiebe, R. P. (2003). The moderation of adolescent-to-peer similarity in tobacco and alcohol use by school levels of substance use. *Child Development, 74*(1), 279–291.

Cloninger, C. R., Adolfsson, R., & Svrakic, N. M. (1996). Mapping genes for human personality. *Nature Genetics, 12*, 3–4.

Clopton, N. A., & Sorell, G. T. (1993). Gender differences in moral reasoning: Stable or situational? *Psychology of Women Quarterly, 17*, 85–101.

Clymer, A. (2002, November 26). Critics say government deleted sexual material from web sites to push abstinence. *New York Times.* Retrieved January 6, 2003, from www.nytimes.com.

Cnattingius, S., Forman, M. R., Berendes, H. W., & Isotalo, L. (1992). Delayed childbearing and risk of adverse perinatal outcome. *Journal of the American Medical Association, 19*, 886–890.

Coalson, D. W., & Glosten, B. (1991). Alternatives to epidural analgesia. *Seminars in Perinatology, 15*, 375–385.

Cohen, L. B., DeLoache, J. S., & Strauss, M. S. (1979). Infant visual perception. In J. D. Osofsky (Ed.), *Handbook of infant development* (pp. 393–438). New York: Wiley.

Cohen, L. B., Gelber, E. R., & Lazar, M. A. (1971). Infant habituation and generalization to differing degrees of stimulus novelty. *Journal of Experimental Child Psychology, 11*, 379–389.

Cohen, R. (1981). Factors influencing maternal choice of childbirth alternatives. *Journal of the American Academy of Child Psychiatry, 20*, 1–15.

Coie, J. D., & Dodge, K. A. (1988). Multiple sources of data on social behavior and social status. *Child Development, 59*, 815–829.

Coie, J. D., & Dodge, K. A. (1998). Aggression and antisocial behavior. In W. Damon & N. Eisenberg (Eds.), *Handbook of child psychology: Vol 3. Social, emotional, and personality development* (pp. 779–862). New York: Wiley.

Coie, J. D., Dodge, K. A., Terry, R., & Wright, V. (1991). The role of aggression in peer relations: An analysis of aggression episodes in boys' play groups. *Child Development, 62*, 812–826.

Colby, A., Kohlberg, L., Gibbs, J. C., & Lieberman, M. (1983). A longitudinal study of moral judgment. *Monographs of the Society for Research in Child Development, 48* (1–2, Serial No. 200).

Cole, M. (1999). Culture in development. In M. H. Bornstein & M. E. Lamb (Eds.), *Developmental psychology: An advanced textbook* (pp. 73–123). Mahwah, NJ: Erlbaum.

Coles, R., & Stokes, G. (1985). *Sex and the American teenager.* New York: Harper & Row.

Collins, M., & Nowicki, S. (2001). African American children's ability to identify emotion in facial expressions and tones of voice of European Americans. *Journal of Genetic Psychology, 162*, 334–346.

Colombo, J., & Bundy, R. S. (1981). A method for the measurement of infant auditory selectivity. *Infant Behavior & Development, 4*, 219–233.

Commons, M. L., Miller, P. M., & Kuhn, D. (1982). The relation between formal operational reasoning and academic course selection and performance among college freshmen and sophomores. *Journal of Applied Developmental Psychology, 3*, 1–10.

Comstock, G. A., & Paik, H. (1991). *Television and the American child.* New York: Academic Press.

Conger, R. D., & Chao, W. (1996). Adolescent depressed mood. In R. L. Simons (Ed.), *Understanding differences between divorced and intact families* (pp. 157–175). Thousand Oaks, CA: Sage.

Constantinople, A. (1973). Masculinity–femininity: An exception to a famous dictum? *Psychological Bulletin, 80*, 389–407.

Contreras, J. M., Mangelsdorf, S. C., Rhodes, J. E., Diener, M. L., & Brunson, L. (1999). Parent–child interaction among Latina adolescent mothers: The role of family and social support. *Journal of Research on Adolescence, 9*, 417–439.

Cooley, C. H. (1902). *Human nature and the social order.* New York: Scribners.

Cooper, R. P., & Aslin, R. N. (1994). Developmental differences in infant attention to the spectral properties of infant-directed speech. *Child Development, 65*, 1663–1677.

Copper, R. L., Goldenberg, R. L., Creasy, R. K., DuBard, M. B., Davis, R. O., Entman, S. S., Iams, J. D., & Cliver, S. P. (1993). A multicenter study of preterm birth weight and gestational age–specific neonatal mortality. *American Journal of Obstetrics and Gynecology, 168*, 78–84.

Cornelius, M. D., Goldschmidt, L., Day, N. L., & Larkby, C. (2002). Alcohol, tobacco and marijuana use among pregnant teenagers: 6-year follow-up of offspring growth effects. *Neurotoxicology and Teratology, 24*(6), 703–710.

Cornell, T. L., Fromkin, V. A., & Mauner, G. (1993). A linguistic approach to language processing in Broca's aphasia: A paradox resolved. *Current Directions in Psychological Science, 2*, 47–52.

Corrigan, R. (1987). A developmental sequence of actor–object pretend play in young children. *Merrill-Palmer Quarterly, 33*, 87–106.

Cottrell, B. H., & Shannahan, M. K. (1987). A comparison of fetal outcome in birth chair and delivery table births. *Research in Nursing and Health, 10*, 239–243.

Cowan, C. P., & Cowan, P. A. (1992). *When partners become parents: The big life change for couples.* New York: Basic Books.

Cowan, N. (1995). *Attention and memory: An integrated framework.* New York: Oxford University Press.

Cowan, N. (1997). The development of working memory. In N. Cowan & C. Hulme (Eds.), *The development of memory in childhood* (pp. 163–200). Hove, East Sussex, England: Psychology Press.

Cowan, N., Nugent, L. D., Elliott, E. M., Ponomarev, I., & Saults, J. S. (1999). The role of attention in the development of short-term memory: Age differences in the verbal span of apprehension. *Child Development, 70,* 1082–1097.

Coyle, J. T. (2000). Psychotropic drug use in very young children. *JAMA: Journal of the American Medical Association, 283,* 1059–1060.

Coyle, T. R., & Bjorklund, D. F. (1997). Age differences in, and consequences of, multiple- and variable-strategy use on a multitrial sort–recall task. *Developmental Psychology, 33,* 372–380.

Crawford, J. (1997). *Best evidence: Research foundations of the Bilingual Education Act.* Washington, DC: National Clearinghouse for Bilingual Education. Retrieved December 24, 2002, from www.ncela.gwu.edu/ncbepugs/reports/bestevidence/

Crick, N. R., Casas, J. F., & Mosher, M. (1997). Relational and overt aggression in preschool. *Developmental Psychology, 33,* 579–588.

Crick, N. R., & Dodge, K. A. (1994). A review and reformulation of social information-processing mechanisms in children's social adjustment. *Psychological Bulletin, 115,* 74–101.

Crick, N. R., & Dodge, K. A. (1996). Social information-processing mechanisms in reactive and proactive aggression. *Child Development, 67,* 993–1002.

Crick, N. R., & Grotpeter, J. K. (1995). Relational aggression, gender, and social–psychological adjustment. *Child Development, 66,* 710–722.

Crittenden, P. M., & Bonvillian, J. D. (1984). The relationship between maternal risk status and maternal sensitivity. *American Journal of Orthopsychiatry, 54,* 250–262.

Crittenden, P. M., & DiLalla, D. L. (1988). Compulsive compliance: The development of an inhibitory coping strategy in infancy. *Journal of Abnormal Child Psychology, 16,* 585–599.

Crockett, L. J., Shanahan, M. J., & Jackson-Newsom, J. (2000). Rural youth: Ecological and life course perspectives. In R. Montemayor, G. R. Adams, & T. P. Gullotta (Eds.), *Adolescent diversity in ethnic, economic, and cultural contexts* (pp. 43–74). Thousand Oaks, CA: Sage.

Crockett, L., Losoff, M., & Petersen, A. C. (1984). Perceptions of the peer group and friendship in early adolescence. *Journal of Early Adolescence, 4,* 155–181.

Cronenwett, L. R., & Newmark, L. L. (1974). Fathers' responses to childbirth. *Nursing Research, 23,* 210–217.

Crook, C. K. (1987). Taste and olfaction. In P. Salapatek & L. B. Cohen (Eds.), *Handbook of infant perception* (Vol. 1, pp. 237–264). New York: Academic Press.

Crosnoe, R., & Elder, G. H., Jr. (2002). Adolescent twins and emotional distress: The interrelated influence of nonshared environment and social structure. *Child Development, 73,* 1761–1774.

Crouter, A. C., Manke, B. A., & McHale, S. M. (1995). The family context of gender intensification in early adolescence. *Child Development, 66,* 317–329.

Csikszentmihalyi, M. (1990). *Flow: The psychology of optimal experience.* New York: Harper & Row.

Csikszentmihalyi, M., & Larson, R. (1984). *Being adolescent: Conflict and growth in the teenage years.* New York: Basic Books.

Csikszentmihalyi, M., Rathunde, K., & Whalen, S. (1997). *Talented teenagers: The roots of success and failure.* Cambridge, England: Cambridge University Press.

Cummins, J. (1991). Interdependence of first- and second-language proficiency in bilingual children. In E. Bialystok (Ed.), *Language processing in bilingual children* (pp. 70–89). Cambridge, England: Cambridge University Press.

Curran, M. J. A. (1991). Options for labor analgesia: Techniques of epidural and spinal analgesia. *Seminars in Perinatology, 15,* 348–357.

Current Population Survey. (2001). Annual demographic survey, March supplement. Retrieved July 19, 2002, from www.bls.census.gov/cps.

Curtiss, S. (1977). *Genie: A psycholinguistic study of a modern-day "wild child."* New York: Academic Press.

Curtiss, S. (1981). Dissociations between language and cognition: Cases and implications. *Journal of Autism and Developmental Disorders, 11,* 15–30.

D'Alessandro, M. P. (2002). Rickets, vitamin-D resistant. Retrieved March 1, 2002, from www.vh.org.

Dacey, J. (1989). *Fundamentals of creativity.* Lexington, MA: D. C. Heath.

Dalaker, J. (2001). *Poverty in the United States: 2000* (U.S. Census Bureau, Current Population Reports, Series P60-214). Washington, DC: U.S. Government Printing Office.

Dalterio, S. L., & Fried, P. A. (1992). The effects of marijuana use on offspring. In T. B. Sonderegger (Ed.), *Perinatal substance abuse: Research findings and clinical applications* (pp. 161–183). Baltimore: Johns Hopkins University Press.

Damon, W. (1995). *Greater expectations: Overcoming the culture of indulgence in America's homes and schools.* New York: Free Press.

Davenport-Slack, B., & Boylan, C. H. (1974). Psychological correlates of childbirth pain. *Psychosomatic Medicine, 36,* 215–223.

Davey, M., Eaker, D. G., & Walters, L. H. (2003). Resilience processes in adolescents: Personality profiles, self-worth, and coping. *Journal of Adolescent Research, 18,* 347–362.

Davison, K. K., & Birch, L. L. (2002). Processes linking weight status and self-concept among girls ages 5 to 7 years. *Developmental Psychology, 38*(5), 735–748.

Deak, G. O., Ray, S. D., & Brenneman, K. (in press). Children's perseverative appearance-reality errors are related to emerging language skills. *Child Development.*

DeAngelis, T. (2001, July/August). Movin' on up? *Monitor on Psychology,* pp. 70–73.

DeAngelis, T. (2002). Promising treatments for anorexia and bulimia. *Monitor on Psychology, 33,* 38–41.

DeCasper, A. J., & Fifer, W. P. (1980). Of human bonding: Newborns prefer their mothers' voices. *Science, 208,* 1174–1176.

DeCasper, A. J., & Prescott, P. (1984). Human newborns' perception of male voices: Preference, discrimination, and reinforcing value. *Developmental Psychobiology, 17,* 481–491.

DeCasper, A. J., & Spence, M. J. (1986). Prenatal maternal speech influences newborns' perception of speech sounds. *Infant Behavior and Development, 9,* 133–150.

Deci, E. L., & Ryan, R. M. (1985). *Intrinsic motivation and self-determination in human behavior.* New York: Plenum.

DeGarmo, D. S., Forgatch, M. S., & Martinez, C. R. (1999). Parenting of divorced mothers as a link between social status and boys' academic outcomes: Unpacking the effects of socioeconomic status. *Child Development, 70,* 1231–1245.

DeLoache, J. S., Cassidy, D. J., & Brown, A. L. (1985). Precursors of mnemonic strategies in very young children's memory. *Child Development, 56,* 125–137.

Delpit, L. (1995). *Other people's children: Cultural conflict in the classroom.* New York: New Press/Norton.

DeMarie-Dreblow, D. (1991). Relation between knowledge and memory: A reminder that correlation does not imply causality. *Child Development, 62,* 484–498.

DeMarie-Dreblow, D., & Miller, P. H. (1988). The development of children's strategies for selective attention: Evidence for a transitional period. *Child Development, 59,* 1504–1513.

Demetriou, A., Christou, C., Spanoudis, G., & Platsidou, M. (2002). The development of mental processing: Efficiency, working memory, and thinking. *Monographs of the Society for Research in Child Development, 67*(1); Serial No. 268.

Dempster, F. N. (1981). Memory span: Sources of individual and developmental differences. *Psychological Bulletin, 89,* 63–100.

Dempster, F. N. (1992). The rise and fall of the inhibitory mechanism: Toward a unified theory of cognitive development and aging. *Developmental Review, 12,* 45–75.

Demuth, K. (1990). Subject, topic and Sesotho passive. *Journal of Child Language, 17,* 67–84.

Denham, S. A., Blair, K. A., DeMulder, E., Levitas, J., Sawyer, K., Auerbach-Major, S., & Queenan, P. (2003). Preschool emotional competence: Pathway to social competence? *Child Development, 74,* 238–256.

Denham, S. A., McKinley, M., Couchoud, E. A., & Holt, R. (1990). Emotional and behavioral predictors of preschool peer ratings. *Child Development, 61,* 1145–1152.

Denham, S. A., Workman, E., Cole, P. M., Weissbrod, C., Kendziora, K. T., & Zahn-Waxler, C. (2000). Prediction of externalizing behavior problems from early to middle childhood: The role of parental socialization and emotion expression. *Development & Psychopathology, 12,* 23–45.

Dennis, W., & Dennis, M. G. (1939/1991). The effect of cradling practices upon the onset of walking in Hopi children. *Journal of Genetic Psychology, 152,* 563–573. Note: This article was published in 1991 but was first received by the journal editor in 1939.

Denton, K., & Germino-Hausken, E. (2000). *America's Kindergartners.* Washington, DC: U.S. Department of Education, National Center for Education Statistics.

de Onis, M., Monteiro, C., Akré, J., & Clugston, G. (2002). *The worldwide magnitude of protein–energy malnutrition: An overview from the WHO Global Database on Child Growth.* Retrieved March 22, 2002, from www.WHO.int/whosis/cgrowth/bulletin.htm.

de Villiers, J. G., & de Villiers, P. A. (1999). Language development. In M. H. Bornstein & M. E. Lamb (Eds.), *Developmental psychology: An advanced textbook* (4th ed.) (pp. 313–373). Hillsdale, NJ: Erlbaum.

DeVries, R. (1969). Constancy of generic identity in the years three to six. *Monographs of the Society for Research in Child Development, 34* (Serial No. 127).

de Waal, F. B. M. (1999). The end of nature versus nurture. *Scientific American, 281*(6), 94–99.

Dews, S., Winner, E., Kaplan, J., Rosenblatt, E., Hunt, M., Lim, K., McGovern, A., Qualter, A., & Smarsh, B. (1996). Children's understanding of the meaning and functions of verbal irony. *Child Development, 67,* 3071–3085.

Dhossche, D., Ferdinand, R., van der Ende, J., Hofstra, M. B., & Verhulst, F. (2002). Diagnostic outcome of adolescent self-reported suicidal ideation at 8-year follow-up. *Journal of Affective Disorders, 72,* 273–279.

Diamond, A. (1991). Neuropsychological insights into the meaning of object concept development. In S. Carey & R. Gelman (Eds.), *The epigenesis of mind: Essays on biology and knowledge* (pp. 67–110). Hillsdale, NJ: Erlbaum.

Diamond, D., Heinicke, C., & Mintz, J. (1996). Separation–individuation as a family transactional process in the transition to parenthood. *Infant Mental Health Journal, 17*(1), 24–42.

Diaz, R. M., & Kinger, C. (1991).Towards an explanatory model of the interaction between bilingualism and cognitive development. In E. Bialystok (Ed.), *Language processing in bilingual children* (pp. 167–192). Cambridge, England: Cambridge University Press.

Dick-Read, G. (1972). *Childbirth without fear: The original approach to natural childbirth.* (Rev. ed., H. Wessel & H. Ellis, Eds.). (Originally published 1933.) New York: Harper & Row.

Dishion, T. J., & Owen, L. D. (2002). A longitudinal analysis of friendships and substance use: Bidirectional influence from adolescence to adulthood. *Developmental Psychology, 38*(4), 480–491.

Dittman, R. W., Kappes, M. H., Kappes, M. E., Borger, D., Stegner, H., Willig, R. H., & Wallis, H. (1990). Congenital adrenal hyperplasia: I. Gender-related behavior and attitudes in female patients and sisters. *Psychoneuroendocrinology, 15,* 401–420.

Dixon, T. L. (2001). Social cognition and racial stereotyping in television. In V. Milhouse, M. K. Asante, & P. O. Nwosu (Eds.), *Transcultural realities: Interdisciplinary perspectives on cross-cultural relations* (pp. 215–224). Thousand Oaks, CA: Sage.

Dixon, W. E. (2002). Twenty studies that revolutionized child psychology. *SRCD Developments: Newsletter of the Society for Research in Child Development, 45,* 1, 4.

Dockett, S., & Perry, B. (2003). The transition to school: What's important? *Educational Leadership, 60*(7), 30–33.

Dodge, K. A. (1986). A social information processing model of social competence in children. In M. Perlmutter (Ed.), *Minnesota symposium on child psychology* (Vol. 18, pp. 77–125). Hillsdale, NJ: Erlbaum.

Dodge, K. A., Bates, J. E., & Pettit, G. S. (1990). Mechanisms in the cycle of violence. *Science, 250,* 1678–1683.

Dodge, K. A., Lansford, J. E., Burks, V. S., Bates, J. E., Pettit, G. S., Fontaine, R., & Price, J. M. (2003). Peer rejection and social information-processing factors in the development of aggressive behavior problems in children. *Child Development, 74*(2), 374–393.

Dodge, K. A., & Pettit, G. S. (2003). A biopsychosocial model of the development of chronic conduct problems in adolescence. *Developmental Psychology, 39,* 349–371.

Dodge, K. A., Pettit, G. S., & Bates, J. E. (1994). Socialization mediators of the relation between socioeconomic status and child conduct problems. *Child Development, 65,* 649–665.

Dodge, K. A., Pettit, G. S., McClaskey, C. L., & Brown, M. W. (1986). Social competence in children. *Monographs of the Society for Research in Child Development, 51*(2), 1–80.

Donahue, P. L., Voelkl, K. E., Campbell, J. R., & Mazzeo, J. (1999). *NAEP 1998 reading report card for the nation and the states.* Washington, DC: U.S. Department of Education, Office of Educational Research and Improvement.

Donaldson, M. (1982). Conservation: What is the question? *British Journal of Psychology, 73,* 199–207.

Dondi, M., Simion, F., & Caltran, G. (1999). Can newborns discriminate between their own cry and the cry of another newborn infant? *Developmental Psychology, 35,* 418–426.

Dornbusch, S. M., Ritter, P. L., Leiderman, P. H., Roberts, D. F., & Fraleigh, M. J. (1987). The relation of parenting style to adolescent school performance. *Child Development, 58,* 1244–1257.

Downey, D. B., Ainsworth-Darnell, J. W., & Dufur, M. J. (1998). Sex of parent and children's well-being in single-parent households. *Journal of Marriage and the Family, 60,* 878–893.

Dragonas, T. G. (1992). Greek fathers' participation in labour and care of the infant. *Scandinavian Journal of Caring Sciences, 6,* 151–159.

DuBois, D. L., Felner, R. D., Brand, S., Phillips, R. S. C., & Lease, A. M. (1996). Early adolescent self-esteem: A developmental–ecological framework and assessment strategy. *Journal of Research on Adolescence, 6,* 543–579.

Dufresne, A., & Kobasigawa, A. (1989a). Children's spontaneous allocation of study time: Differential and sufficient aspects. *Journal of Experimental Child Psychology, 47,* 274–296.

Dufresne, A., & Kobasigawa, A. (1989b). Children's utilization of study time: Differential and sufficient aspects. In C. B. McCormick, G. E. Miller, & M. Pressley (Eds.), *Cognitive strategy research: From basic research to educational applications* (pp. 64–82). New York: Springer.

Duncan, G. J., & Brooks-Gunn, J. (Eds.). (1997). *Consequences of growing up poor.* New York: Russell Sage Foundation.

Duncan, G. J., Brooks-Gunn, J., & Klebanov, P. K. (1994). Economic deprivation and early childhood development. *Child Development, 65,* 296–318.

Duncan, P. D., Ritter, P. L., Dornbusch, S. M., Gross, R. T., & Carlsmith, J. M. (1985). The effects of pubertal timing on body image, school behavior, and deviance. *Journal of Youth and Adolescence, 14,* 227–235.

Duncan, S. W., & Markham, H. J. (1988). Intervention programs for the transition to parenthood: Current status from a preventive perspective. In G. Y. Michaels & W. A. Goldberg (Eds.), *The transition to parenthood: Current theory and research* (pp. 227–310). Cambridge, England: Cambridge University Press.

Dunifon, R., & Kowaleski-Jones, L. (2002). Who's in the house? Race differences in cohabitation, single parenthood, and child development. *Child Development, 73,* 1249–1264.

Dunn, J., Cutting, A. L., & Fisher, N. (2002). Old friends, new friends: Predictors of children's perspective on their friends at school. *Child Development, 73*(2), 621–635.

Dunning, D. B., Mason, J. M., & Stewart, J. P. (1994). Reading to preschoolers: A response to Scarborough and Dobrich (1994) and recommendations for future research. *Developmental Review, 14,* 324–339.

Dunphy, D. (1963). The social structure of urban adolescent peer groups. *Sociometry, 26,* 230–246.

Durrant, J. E. (1999). Evaluating the success of Sweden's corporal punishment ban. *Child Abuse and Neglect, 23,* 435–448.

Durrett, M. E., Otaki, M., & Richards, P. (1984). Attachment and the mother's perception of support from the father. *International Journal of Behavioral Development, 7,* 167–176.

Dweck, C. S. (2001). The development of ability conceptions. In A. Wigfield & J. S. Eccles (Eds.), *Development of achievement motivation* (pp. 57–88). San Diego, CA: Academic Press.

Dweck, C. S., & Leggett, E. L. (1988). A social–cognitive approach to motivation and personality. *Psychological Review, 95,* 256–273.

Eaton, W. O., & Enns, L. R. (1986). Sex differences in human motor activity level. *Psychological Bulletin, 100,* 19–28.

Eccles, J. S., Jacobs, J., Harold, R., Yoon, K. S., Arbreton, A., & Freedman-Doan, C. (1993). Parents' and gender-role socialization during the middle childhood and adolescent years. In S. Oskamp & M. Costanzo (Eds.), *Gender issues in contemporary society* (pp. 59–83). Newbury Park, CA: Sage.

Eccles, J. S., Lord, S. E., Roeser, R. W., Barber, B. L., & Jozefowicz, D. M. H. (1997). The association of school transitions in early adolescence with developmental trajectories through high school. In J. Schulenberg, J. Maggs, & K. Hurrelmann (Eds.), *Health risks and developmental transitions during adolescence* (pp. 283–320). New York: Cambridge University Press.

Eccles, J. S., Midgley, C., Wigfield, A., Buchanan, C. M., Reuman, D., Flanagan, C., & MacIver, D. (1993). Development during adolescence: The impact of stage–environment fit on young adolescents' experiences in schools and in families. *American Psychologist, 48,* 90–101.

Eccles, J. S., & Roeser, R. W. (1999). School and community influences on human development. In M. H. Bornstein & M. E. Lamb (Eds.), *Developmental psychology: An advanced textbook* (pp. 503–554). Mahwah, NJ: Erlbaum.

Eccles, J. S., Wigfield, A., & Schiefele, U. (1998). Motivation to succeed. In W. Damon & N. Eisenberg (Eds.), *Handbook of child psychology: Vol 3. Social, emotional, and personality development* (pp. 1018–1095). New York: Wiley.

Eckerman, C. O. (1979). The human infant in social interaction. In R. Cairns (Ed.), *The analysis of social interactions: Methods, issues, and illustrations* (pp. 163–178). Hillsdale, NJ: Erlbaum.

Eckerman, C. O. (1993). Imitation and toddlers' achievement of co-ordinated action with others. In J. Nadel & L. Camaioni (Eds.), *New perspectives in early communicative development* (pp. 116–138). London: Routledge.

Egeland, B., & Farber, E. A. (1984). Infant–mother attachment: Factors related to its development and changes over time. *Child Development, 55,* 753–771.

Eimas, P. D., Siqueland, E. R., Jusczyk, P., & Vigorito, J. (1971). Speech perception in infants. *Science, 71,* 303–306.

Eisenberg, N. (1986). *Altruistic emotion, cognition, and behavior.* Hillsdale, NJ: Erlbaum.

Eisenberg, N., Carlo, G., Murphy, B., & Van Court, P. (1995). Prosocial development in late adolescence: A longitudinal study. *Child Development, 66,* 1179–1197.

Eisenberg, N., Cumberland, A., Spinrad, T. L., Fabes, R. A., Shepard, S. A., Reiser, M., Murphy, B. C., Losoya, S. H., & Guthrie, I. K. (2001). The relations of regulation and emotionality to children's externalizing and internalizing problem behavior. *Child Development, 72,* 1112–1134.

Eisenberg, N., & Fabes, R. A. (1998). Prosocial development. In W. Damon & N. Eisenberg (Eds.), *Handbook of child psychology: Vol 3. Social, emotional, and personality development* (pp. 701–778). New York: Wiley.

Eisenberg, N., Guthrie, I. K., Murphy, B. C., Shepard, S. A., Cumberland, A., & Carlo, G. (1999). Consistency and development of prosocial dispositions: A longitudinal study. *Child Development, 70,* 1360–1372.

Eisenberg, N., Lennon, R., & Roth, K. (1983). Prosocial development: A longitudinal study. *Developmental Psychology, 19,* 846–855.

Eisenberg, N., Martin, C. L., & Fabes, R. A. (1996). Gender development and gender effects. In D. C. Berliner & R. C. Calfee (Eds.), *The handbook of educational psychology* (pp. 358–396). New York: Simon & Schuster.

Eisenberg, N., & Shell, R. (1986). The relation of prosocial moral judgment and behavior in children: The mediating role of cost. *Personality and Social Psychology Bulletin, 12,* 426–433.

Eisenberg, R. (1976). *Auditory competence in early life: The roots of communicative behavior.* Baltimore: University Park Press.

Ekstrand, L. H. (1981). Theories and facts about early bilingualism in native and migrant children. As cited in J. F. Hamers & M. H. A. Blanc (2000), *Bilinguality and bilingualism* (2nd ed.). Cambridge, England: Cambridge University Press.

Elashoff, J. D., & Snow, R. E. (1971). *Pygmalion reconsidered.* Worthington, OH: Charles A. Jones.

Elder, G. H., Jr., & Conger, R. D. (2000). *Children of the land: Adversity and success in rural America.* Chicago: University of Chicago Press.

Elicker, J., Englund, M., & Sroufe, L. A. (1992). Predicting peer competence and peer relationships in childhood from early parent–child relationships. In R. D. Parke & G. W. Ladd (Eds.), *Family–peer relationships: Modes of linkage* (pp. 77–106). Hillsdale, NJ: Erlbaum.

Elliott, E. S., & Dweck, C. S. (1988). Goals: An approach to motivation and achievement. *Journal of Personality and Social Psychology, 54,* 5–12.

Elliott, S. N., Kratochwill, T. R., Cook, J. L., & Travers, J. F. (2000). *Educational psychology: Effective teaching, effective learning* (3rd ed.). Boston: McGraw-Hill.

El-Sheikh, M., & Harger, J. (2001). Appraisals of marital conflict and children's adjustment, health, and physiological reactivity. *Developmental Psychology, 37,* 875–885.

Ely, R. (1997). Language and literacy in the school years. In J. B. Gleason (Ed.), *The development of language* (pp. 398–439). Boston: Allyn & Bacon.

Ely, R., & McCabe, A. (1994). The language play of kindergarten children. *First Language, 14,* 19–35.

Embury, S., Hebbel, R., Mohandas, N., & Steinberg, M. (Eds.). (1994). *Sickle cell disease: Basic principles and clinical practice.* New York: Raven Press.

Emde, R. M., Plomin, R., Robinson, J., Corley, R., DeFries, J., Fulker, D. W., Reznik, J. S., Campos, J., Kagan, J., & Zahn-Waxler, C. (1992). Temperament, emotion, and cognition at fourteen months: The MacArthur Longitudinal Twin Study. *Child Development, 63,* 1437–1455.

Emerson, M. J., & Miyake, A. (2003). The role of inner speech in task switching: A dual-task investigation. *Journal of Memory & Language, 48,* 148–168.

Emery, R. E. (1982). Interparental conflict and the children of discord and divorce. *Psychological Bulletin, 92,* 310–330.

Emery, R. E. (1999a). *Marriage, divorce, and children's adjustment* (2nd ed.). Thousand Oaks, CA: Sage.

Emery, R. E. (1999b). Postdivorce family life for children: An overview of research and some implications for policy. In R. A. Thompson & P. R. Amato (Eds.), *The postdivorce family: Children, parenting, and society* (pp. 3–27). Thousand Oaks, CA: Sage.

Emery, R. E., Kitzman, K. M., & Waldron, M. (1999). Psychological interventions for separated and divorced families. In E. M. Hetherington (Ed.), *Coping with divorce, single parenting, and remarriage: A risk and resiliency perspective* (pp. 323–344). Mahwah, NJ: Erlbaum.

Engel, S. (1995). *The stories children tell: Making sense of the narratives of children.* New York: Freeman.

Entwisle, D. R., & Alexander, K. L. (1998). Facilitating the transition to first grade: The nature of transition and research on factors affecting it. *The Elementary School Journal, 98,* 351–364.

Epstein, H. T. (1978). Growth spurts during brain development: Implications for educational policy and practice. In J. S. Chall & A. F. Mirsky (Eds.), *Education and the brain: The seventy-seventh yearbook of the national society for the study of education* (pp. 343–370). Chicago: University of Chicago Press.

Epstein, J. L. (1986). Friendship selection: Developmental and environmental influences. In E. Mueller & C. Cooper (Eds.), *Process and outcome in peer relationships.* New York: Academic Press.

Epstein, J. L. (1989). The selection of friends: Changes across the grades and in different school environments. In T. J. Berndt & G. W. Ladd (Eds.), *Peer relationships in child development* (pp. 158–187). New York: Wiley.

Erikson, E. H. (1968). *Identity: Youth and crisis.* New York: Norton. As cited in Thomas, R. M. (1992), *Comparing theories of child development.* Belmont, CA: Wadsworth, pp. 163–164.

Eron, L. D., Huesmann, L. R., Lefkowitz, M. M., & Walder, L. O. (1972). Does television violence cause aggression? *American Psychologist, 27,* 253–263.

Espelage, D. L., Holt, M. K., & Henkel, R. R. (2003). Examination of peer-group contextual effects on aggression during early adolescence. *Child Development, 74*(1), 205–220.

Fabes, R. A. (1994). Physiological, emotional, and behavioral correlates of gender segregation. In W. Damon (Ed.), *New directions for child development* (No. 65, pp. 19–34). San Francisco: Jossey-Bass.

Fabes, R. A., Eisenberg, N., Nyman, M., & Michealieu, Q. (1991). Young children's appraisals of others' spontaneous emotional reactions. *Developmental Psychology, 27*, 858–866.

Fabes, R. A., Martin, C. L., & Hanish, L. D. (2003). Young children's play qualities in same-, other-, and mixed-sex peer groups. *Child Development, 74*(3), 921–932.

Fagot, B. I. (1977). Consequences of moderate cross-gender behavior in preschool children. *Child Development, 48*, 902–907.

Fagot, B. I. (1994). Peer relations and the development of competence in boys and girls. In W. Damon (Ed.), *New directions for child development* (No. 65, pp. 53–65). San Francisco: Jossey-Bass.

Fagot, B. I., Leinbach, M. D., & Hagan, R. (1986). Gender labeling and the adoption of sex-typed behaviors. *Developmental Psychology, 22*, 440–443.

Fagot, B. I., & Patterson, G. R. (1969). An in vivo analysis of reinforcing contingencies for sex-role behaviors in the preschool child. *Developmental Psychology, 1*, 563–568.

Falorni, M. L., Fornasarig, A., & Stefanile, C. (1979). Research about anxiety effects on the pregnant woman and her newborn child. In L. Carenza & L. Zichella (Eds.), *Emotion and reproduction: Proceedings of the Serono Symposium* (Vol. 20B, pp. 1147–1153). London: Academic Press.

Fan, X., & Chen, M. (2001). Parental involvement and students' academic achievement: A meta-analysis. *Educational Psychology Review, 13*, 1–22.

Fantz, R. L. (1956). A method for studying early visual development. *Perceptual Motor Skills, 6*, 13–15.

Fantz, R. L. (1961). The origin of form perception. *Scientific American, 204*, 66–72.

Fantz, R. L. (1963). Pattern vision in newborn infants. *Science, 140*, 296–297.

Farmer, M. E., & Klein, R. M. (1995). The evidence for a temporal processing deficit linked to dyslexia: A review. *Psychonomic Bulletin and Review, 2*, 460–493.

Farrar, J. (1992). Negative evidence and grammatical morpheme acquisition. *Developmental Psychology, 28*, 90–98.

Farrar, M. J., & Goodman, G. S. (1992). Developmental changes in event memory. *Child Development, 63*, 173–187.

Farver, J. M. (2000). Within cultural differences. *Journal of Cross-Cultural Psychology, 31*, 583–602.

Farver, J. M., Narang, S. K., & Bhadha, B. R. (2002). East meets West: Ethnic identity, acculturation, and conflict in Asian Indian families. *Journal of Family Psychology, 16*, 338–350.

Farver, J. M., & Shin, Y. L. (1997). Social pretend play in Korean- and Anglo-American preschoolers. *Child Development, 68*, 544–556.

Farver, J. M., & Welles-Nystrom, B. (1997). Toy stories. *Journal of Cross-Cultural Psychology, 28*, 393–420.

FDA approves prozac for pediatric use to treat depression and OCD (January 3, 2003). *FDA Talk Paper T03-01*. Retrieved July 14, 2003, from www.fda.gov/bbs/topics/ANSWERS/2003/ANS01187.html.

Fee, E. J., & Shaw, K. (1998). Pitch modifications in Mi'kmaq child-directed speech. In E. V. Clark (Ed.), *The proceedings of the twenty-ninth annual child language research forum* (pp. 47–54). Chicago: Center for the Study of Language and Information.

Feigelman, W. (2000). Adjustments of transracially and inracially adopted young adults. *Child and Adolescent Social Work Journal, 17*, 165–183.

Feingold, A. (1993). Cognitive gender differences: A developmental perspective. *Sex Roles, 29*, 91–112.

Feingold, A. (1994). Gender differences in personality: A meta-analysis. *Psychological Bulletin, 116*, 429–456.

Feinman, S., & Lewis, M. (1983). Social referencing at ten months: A second-order effect on infants' responses to strangers. *Child Development, 54*, 878–887.

Fenichel, E., & Mann, T. L. (2001). Early Head Start for low-income families with infants and toddlers. *Reports from the Field, 11*(1), 135–141.

Fergusson, D. M., Beautrais, A. L., & Horwood, L. J. (2003). Vulnerability and resiliency to suicidal behaviours in young people. *Psychological Medicine, 33*, 61–73.

Fernald, A. (1992). Human maternal vocalizations to infants as biologically relevant signals: An evolutionary perspective. In J. H. Barkow, L. Cosmides, & J. Tooby (Eds.), *The adaptive mind: Evolutionary psychology and the generation of culture* (pp. 391–428). New York: Oxford University Press.

Fernald, A., & Morikawa, H. (1993). Common themes and cultural variation in Japanese and American mothers' speech to infants. *Child Development, 64*, 637–656.

Fernald, A., & O'Neill, D. K. (1993). Peekaboo across cultures: How mothers and infants play with voices, faces and expectations. In K. Macdonald (Ed.), *Parent–child play* (pp. 259–285). Albany: State University of New York Press.

Ferreira, F., & Morrison, F. J. (1994). Children's metalinguistic knowledge of syntactical constituents: Effects of age and schooling. *Developmental Psychology, 30*, 663–678.

Field, T. M., Woodson, R., Greenberg, R., & Cohen, D. (1982). Discrimination and imitation of facial expressions by neonates. *Science, 218*, 179–181.

Finkelhor, D. (1994). The international epidemiology of child sexual abuse. *Child Abuse and Neglect, 18*, 409–417.

Fischer, K. W., & Bidell, T. R. (1998). Dynamic development of psychological structures in action and thought. In W. Damon (Series Ed.) & R. M. Lerner (Vol. Ed.), *Handbook of child psychology: Vol. 1. Theoretical models of human development* (5th ed., pp. 467–561). New York: Wiley.

Fish, J. M. (2002). *Race and intelligence: Separating science from myth*. Mahwah, NJ: Erlbaum.

Fisher, C. B., Wallace, S. A., & Fenton, R. E. (2000). Discrimination distress during adolescence. *Journal of Youth and Adolescence, 29*, 679–695.

Fisher, P. A., Leve, L. D., O'Leary, C. C., & Leve, C. (2003). Parental monitoring of children's behavior: Variation across stepmother, stepfather, and two-parent biological families. *Family Relations, 52*, 45–52.

Fivush, R. (1995). Language, narrative, and autobiography. *Consciousness and Cognition, 4*, 100–103.

Fivush, R., Haden, C., & Adam, S. (1995). Structure and coherence of preschoolers' personal narratives over time: Implications for childhood amnesia. *Journal of Experimental Child Psychology, 60*, 32–56.

Fivush, R., & Hammond, N. R. (1990). Autobiographical memory across the preschool years: Toward reconceptualizing childhood amnesia. In R. Fivush & J. A. Hudson (Eds.), *Knowing and remembering in young children* (pp. 223–248). Cambridge, England: Cambridge University Press.

Fivush, R., Kuebli, J., & Clubb, P. A. (1992). The structure of events and event representations: A developmental analysis. *Child Development, 63*, 188–201.

Flaks, D. K., Ficher, I., Masterpasqua, F., & Joseph, G. (1995). Lesbians choosing motherhood: A comparative study of lesbian and heterosexual parents and their children. *Developmental Psychology, 31*, 105–114.

Flavell, J. H. (1971). Stage-related properties of cognitive development. *Cognitive Psychology, 2*, 421–453.

Flavell, J. H. (1985). *Cognitive development* (2nd ed). Englewood Cliffs, NJ: Prentice Hall.

Flavell, J. H., Beach, D. R., & Chinsky, J. H. (1966). Spontaneous verbal rehearsal in a memory task as a function of age. *Child Development, 37*, 283–299.

Flavell, J. H., Friedrichs, A. G., & Hoyt, J. D. (1970). Developmental changes in memorization processes. *Cognitive Psychology, 1*, 324–340.

Flavell, J. H., Green, F. L., & Flavell, E. R. (1986). Development of knowledge about the appearance–reality distinction. *Monographs of the Society for Research in Child Development, 51* (Serial No. 212).

Flavell, J. H., Green, F. R., Wahl, K. E., & Flavell, E. R. (1987). The effects of question clarification and memory aids on young children's performance on appearance–reality tasks. *Cognitive Development, 2*, 127–144.

Flavell, J. H., Miller, P. H., & Miller, S. A. (1993). *Cognitive development* (3rd ed.). Englewood Cliffs, NJ: Prentice Hall.

Fogel, A. (1979). Peer- vs. mother-directed behavior in 1- to 3-month-old infants. *Infant Behavior and Development, 2*, 215–226.

Fogel, A. (1997). *Infancy: Infant, family, and society* (3rd ed.). Minneapolis/St. Paul, MN: West.

Fogelman, K. (1980). Smoking in pregnancy and subsequent development of the child. *Child Care Health and Development, 6*, 233–249.

Ford, D. Y., & Harris, J. J. (2000). A framework for infusing multicultural curriculum into gifted education. *Roeper Review, 23*, 4–10.

Foreman, M. A. (1995). Foreword. In S. Chess & A. Thomas, *Temperament in clinical practice* (pp. v–viii). New York: Guilford Press.

Fowler, A. E. (1998). Language in mental retardation: Associations with and dissociations from general cognition. In J. A. Burack, R. M. Hodapp, & E. Zigler (Eds.), *Handbook of mental retardation and development* (pp. 290–333). New York: Cambridge University Press.

Fox, N. A., Kimmerly, N. L., & Schafer, W. D. (1991). Attachment to mother/attachment to father: A meta-analysis. *Child Development, 62*, 210–225.

Fox, N. A., & Leavitt, L. A. (1999). Introduction. In N. A. Fox, L. A. Leavitt, & J. G. Warhol (Eds.), *The role of early experience in infant development* (pp. x–xvii). Johnson & Johnson Pediatric Institute.

Fox, R., Aslin, R. N., Shea, S. L., & Dumais, S. T. (1980). Stereopsis in human infants. *Science, 207*, 323–324.

Fracasso, M. P., Busch-Rossnagel, N. A., & Fisher, C. B. (1993). The relationship of maternal behavior and acculturation to the quality of attachment in Hispanic infants living in New York City. *Hispanic Journal of Behavioral Sciences, 16*, 143–154.

Fraley, R. C., & Spieker, S. J. (2003). Are infant attachment patterns continuously or categorically distributed? A taxonomic analysis of strange situation behavior. *Developmental Psychology, 39*, 387–404.

Frankenburg, W. K., Dodds, J., Archer, P., Bresnick, B., Maschka, P., Edelman, N., & Shapiro, H. (1992). *Denver II: Training manual.* Denver, CO: Denver Developmental Materials.

Fraser, S. (1995). *The bell curve wars: Race, intelligence, and the future of America.* New York: Basic Books.

Frazier, J. A., & Morrison, F. J. (1998). The influence of extended-year schooling on growth of achievement and perceived competence in early elementary school. *Child Development, 69*, 495–517.

French, D. C. (1988). Heterogeneity of peer rejected boys: Aggressive and nonaggressive subtypes. *Child Development, 59*, 976–985.

Fretts, R. C., Schmittdiel, J., McLean, F. H., Usher, R. H., & Goldman, M. B. (1995). Increased maternal age and the risk of fetal death. *New England Journal of Medicine, 333*, 953–957.

Freud, S. (1959). Some psychological consequences of the anatomical distinction between the sexes. In S. Freud (Ed.), *Collected papers* (pp. 186–197). New York: Basic Books.

Frey, K. S., & Ruble, D. N. (1992). Gender constancy and the "cost" of sex-typed behavior: A test of the conflict hypothesis. *Developmental Psychology, 28*, 714–721.

Friedrich, W. N. (1993). Sexual behavior in sexually abused children. *Violence Update, 3*, 1–7.

Frosch, C. A., Mangelsdorf, S. C., & McHale, J. L. (1998). Correlates of marital behavior at six months postpartum. *Developmental Psychology, 34*, 1438–1449.

Fuchs, D., & Thelen, M. H. (1988). Children's expected interpersonal consequences of communicating their affective state and reported likelihood of expression. *Child Development, 59*, 1314–1322.

Fuligni, A. J. (1997). The academic achievement of adolescents from immigrant families: The roles of family background, attitudes, and behavior. *Child Development, 68*, 351–363.

Furman, W., Simon, V. A., Shaffer, L., & Bouchey, H. A. (2002). Adolescents' working models and styles for relationships with parents, friends, and romantic partners. *Child Development, 73*(1), 241–255.

Furnham, A., Shahidi, S., & Baluch, B. (2002). Sex and culture differences in perceptions of estimated multiple intelligence for self and family: A British–Iranian comparison. *Journal of Cross-Cultural Psychology, 33*, 270–285.

Furstenberg, F. F., & Hughes, M. E. (1997). The influence of neighborhoods on children's development: A theoretical perspective and a research agenda. In J. Brooks-Gunn, G. J. Duncan, & J. L. Aber (Eds.), *Neighborhood poverty: Vol. II. Policy implications in studying neighborhoods* (pp. 23–47). New York: Russell Sage Foundation.

Furstenberg, F. F., & Kiernan, K. E. (2001). Delayed parental divorce: How much do children benefit? *Journal of Marriage and the Family, 63*, 446–457.

Fuson, K. C., & Kwon, Y. (1992). Korean children's single-digit addition and subtraction: Numbers structured by ten. *Journal for Research in Mathematics Education, 23*, 148–165.

Fuster, J. M. (1989). *The prefrontal cortex: Anatomy, physiology, and neuropsychology of the frontal lobe.* New York: Raven Press.

Gabbard, C. P. (1992). *Lifelong motor development* (2nd ed.). Madison, Wisconsin: Brown & Benchmark.

Gagnon, J. C., & Leone, P. E. (2001). Alternative strategies for school violence prevention. In R. J. Skiba & G. G. Noam (Eds.), *Zero tolerance: Can suspension and expulsion keep schools safe?* (pp. 101–126). San Francisco: Jossey-Bass.

Galambos, N. L., Barker, E. T., & Almeida, D. M. (2003). Parents *do* matter: Trajectories of change in externalizing and internalizing problems in early adolescence. *Child Development, 74*, 578–594.

Gardner, H. (1983). *Frames of mind: The theory of multiple intelligences.* New York: Basic Books.

Gardner, H. (1995). Cracking open the IQ box. In S. Fraser (Ed.), *The bell curve wars: Race, intelligence, and the future of America* (pp. 23–35). New York: Basic Books.

Gardner, H. (1999). *Intelligence reframed: Multiple intelligences for the 21st century.* New York: Basic Books.

Gardner, H., Kornhaber, M. L., & Wake, W. K. (1996). *Intelligence: Multiple perspectives.* Fort Worth, TX: Harcourt Brace College.

Gardner, R. M., Friedman, B. N., & Jackson, N. A. (1999). Body size estimations, body dissatisfaction, and ideal size preferences in children six through thirteen. *Journal of Youth and Adolescence, 28*, 603–618.

Garlick, D. (2002). Understanding the nature of the general factor of intelligence: The role of individual differences in neural plasticity as an explanatory mechanism. *Psychological Review, 109*, 116–136.

Garmezy, N. (1985). Stress-resistant children: The search for protective factors. In J. E. Stevenson (Ed.), *Recent research in developmental psychopathology* (pp. 213–233). Oxford, England: Pergamon Press.

Garmon, A., Nystrand, M., Berends, M., & LePore, P. C. (1995). An organizational analysis of the effects of ability grouping. *American Education Research Journal, 32*, 687–715.

Garmon, L. C., Basinger, K. S., Gregg, V. R., & Gibbs, J. C. (1996). Gender differences in stage and expression of moral judgment. *Merrill-Palmer Quarterly, 42*, 418–437.

Garner, R., & Reis, R. (1981). Monitoring and resolving comprehension obstacles: An investigation of spontaneous text lookbacks among upper-grade good and poor comprehenders. *Reading Research Quarterly, 16*, 569–582.

Gay, G. (1991). Culturally diverse students and social studies. In J. P. Shaver (Ed.), *Handbook of research on social studies teaching and learning* (pp. 144–156). New York: Macmillan.

Ge, X., Brody, G. H., Conger, R. D., Simons, R. L., & Murry, V. M. (2002). Contextual amplification of pubertal transition effects on deviant peer affiliation and externalizing behavior among African American children. *Developmental Psychology, 38*, 42–54.

Ge, X., Conger, R. D., & Elder, G. H. (2001). The relation between puberty and psychological distress in adolescent boys. *Journal of Research on Adolescence, 11*, 49–70.

Geary, D. (1994). *Children's mathematical development: Research and practical applications.* Washington, DC: American Psychological Association.

Geary, D. C. (1996). International differences in mathematical achievement: Their nature, courses, and consequences. *Current Directions in Psychological Science, 5*, 133–137.

Geary, D. C., Bow-Thomas, C. C., Fan, L., & Siegler, R. S. (1993). Even before formal instruction, Chinese children outperform American children in mental addition. *Cognitive Development, 8*, 517–529.

Geary, D. C., Bow-Thomas, C. C., Liu, F., & Siegler, R. S. (1996). Development of arithmetical competencies in Chinese and American children: Influence of age, language, and schooling. *Child Development, 67*, 2022–2044.

Geary, D. C., Fan, L., & Bow-Thomas, C. C. (1992). Numerical cognition: Loci of ability differences comparing children from China and the United States. *Psychological Science, 3,* 180–185.

Geary, D. C., Liu, F., Chen, G-P., Saults, S. J., & Hoard, M. K. (1999). Contributions of computational fluency to cross-national differences in arithmetical reasoning abilities. *Journal of Educational Psychology, 9,* 716–719.

Gee, J. P. (1992). *The social mind: Language, ideology and social practice.* New York: Bergin & Garvey.

Gelman, R. (1972). Logical capacity of very young children: Number invariance rules. *Child Development, 43,* 75–90.

Gelman, R. (2000). Domain specificity and variability in cognitive development. *Child Development, 71,* 854–856.

Gelman, R., & Baillargeon, R. (1983). A review of some Piagetian concepts. In P. H. Mussen (Series Ed.) & J. H. Flavell & E. M. Markman (Vol. Eds.), *Handbook of child psychology: Vol. 3. Cognitive development* (pp. 163–230). New York: Wiley.

Gennetian, L. A., & Miller, C. (2002). Children and welfare reform: A view from an experimental welfare program in Minnesota. *Child Development, 73,* 601–620.

Gerken, L. A., & McIntosh, B. J. (1993). The interplay of function morphemes and prosody in early language. *Developmental Psychology, 29,* 448–457.

Gershoff, E. T. (2002). Corporal punishment by parents and associated child behaviors and experiences: A meta-analytic and theoretical review. *Psychological Bulletin, 128,* 539–579.

Gerstadt, C. L., Hong, Y. J., & Diamond, A. (1994). The relationship between cognition and action: Performance of children 3.5–7 years old on a Stroop-like day–night test. *Cognition, 53,* 129–153.

Gesell, A. (1928). *Infancy and human growth.* New York: Macmillan.

Ghaith, G. (2003). The relationship between forms of instruction, achievement and perceptions of classroom climate. *Educational Research, 45,* 83–93.

Gibbs, C. P., Krischer, J., Peckham, B. M., Sharp, H., & Kirschbaum, T. H. (1986). Obstetric anesthesia: A national survey. *Anesthesiology, 65,* 298–306.

Gibbs, J. C. (1993). Moral–cognitive interventions. In A. P. Goldstein & C. R. Huff (Eds.), *The gang intervention handbook* (pp. 159–185). Champaign, IL: Research Press.

Gibson, E. J., & Walk, R. D. (1960). The "visual cliff." *Scientific American, 202,* 64–71.

Gibson, E. J., & Walker, A. S. (1984). Development of knowledge of visual–tactual affordances of substance. *Child Development, 55,* 453–460.

Gil, A., Vega, W., & Biafora, F. (1998). Temporal influences of family structure and family risk factors on drug use initiation in a multiethnic sample of adolescent boys. *Journal of Youth and Adolescence, 27,* 373–393.

Gillam, R. B., Cowan, N., & Day, L. S. (1995). Sequential memory in children with and without language impairment. *Journal of Speech and Hearing Research, 38,* 393–402.

Gillies, R. M. (2003). The behaviors, interactions, and perceptions of junior high school students during small-group learning. *Journal of Educational Psychology, 95,* 137–147.

Gilligan, C. (1982). *In a different voice: Psychological theory and women's development.* Cambridge, MA: Harvard University Press.

Gilligan, C., & Attanucci, J. (1988). Two moral orientations: Gender differences and similarities. *Merrill-Palmer Quarterly, 34,* 223–237.

Ginsburg, H. P., Klein, A., & Starkey, P. (1998). Development of children's mathematical thinking: Connecting research with practice. In W. Damon, I. E. Sigel, & K. A. Renninger (Eds.), *Handbook of child psychology: Vol. 4* (pp. 401–476). New York: Wiley.

Ginsburg, H. P., & Opper, S. (1988). *Piaget's theory of intellectual development* (3rd ed.). Englewood Cliffs, NJ: Prentice Hall.

Girbau, D. (2001). Children's referential communication failure: The ambiguity and abbreviation message. *Journal of Language & Social Psychology, 20,* 81–89.

Glaberson, W. (2002, March 5). Judge rebukes city officials for removing children from homes of battered women. *New York Times.* Retrieved August 2, 2002, from www.nytimes.com.

Glasberg, R., & Aboud, F. (1982). Keeping one's distance from sadness: Children's self-reports of emotional experience. *Developmental Psychology, 18,* 287–293.

Gleason, J. B. (1997). The development of language: An overview and a preview. In J. B. Gleason, *The development of language* (pp. 1–39). Boston: Allyn & Bacon.

Gleason, J. B., Perlmann, R. Y., Ely, D., & Evans, D. (1994). The babytalk register: Parents' use of diminutives. In J. L. Sokolov & C. E. Snow (Eds.), *Handbook of research in language development using CHILDES* (pp. 50–76). Hillsdale, NJ: Erlbaum.

Gleitman, L. (1990). The structural sources of verb meanings. *Language Acquisition, 1,* 3–55.

Goldin-Meadow, S., Alibali, M. W., & Church, R. B. (1993). Transitions in concept acquisition: Using the hand to read the mind. *Psychological Review, 100,* 279–297.

Goldman-Rakic, P. S. (1987). Development of cortical circuitry and cognitive function. *Child Development, 58,* 601–622.

Goldsmith, H. H., & Alansky, J. A. (1987). Maternal and infant temperamental predictors of attachment: A meta-analytic review. *Journal of Consulting and Clinical Psychology, 55,* 805–816.

Golinkoff, R. M., Mervis, C., & Hirsh-Pasek, K. (1994). Early object labels: The case for a developmental lexical principles framework. *Journal of Child Language, 21,* 125–155.

Golombok, G., Perry, B., Burson, A., Murray, C., Mooney-Somers, J., Stevens, M., & Golding, J. (2003). Children with lesbian parents: A community study. *Developmental Psychology, 39,* 20–33.

Golombok, S., MacCallum, F., & Goodman, E. (2001). The "test-tube" generation: Parent–child relationships and the psychological well-being of in vitro fertilization children at adolescence. *Child Development, 72,* 599–608.

Golombok, S., MacCallum, F., Goodman, E., & Rutter, M. (2002). Families with children conceived by donor insemination: A follow-up at age twelve. *Child Development, 73,* 952–968.

Golombok, S., Spencer, A., & Rutter, M. (1983). Children in lesbian and single-parent households: Psychosexual and psychiatric appraisal. *Journal of Child Psychology and Psychiatry, 24,* 551–572.

Good, T. L., & Brophy, J. E. (1997). *Looking in classrooms* (7th ed.). New York: Longman.

Goodall, J. (1986). *The chimpanzees of Gombe: Patterns of behavior.* Cambridge: Harvard University Press.

Goode, E. (1999, August 3). Mozart for baby? Some say, maybe not. *New York Times.* Retrieved September 14, 2000, from www.nytimes.com.

Goodenough, W. H. (1994). Toward a working theory of culture. In R. Borotsky (Ed.), *Assessing cultural anthropology* (pp. 262–273). New York: McGraw-Hill.

Goodsitt, J., Morse, P., VerHoeve, J., & Cowan, N. (1984). Infant speech recognition in multisyllabic contexts. *Child Development, 55,* 903–910.

Goodwin, M. H. (1990). *He-said-she-said: Talk as a social organization among black children.* Bloomington, IN: Indiana Unversity Press.

Goodwin, M. H., & Goodwin, C. (1987). Children's arguing. In S. U. Philips, S. Steele, & C. Tanz (Eds.), *Language, gender, and sex in comparative perspective* (pp. 200–247). New York: Cambridge University Press.

Goossens, F. A., & van IJzendoorn, M. H. (1990). Quality of infants' attachments to professional caregivers: Relation to infant–parent attachment and day-care characteristics. *Child Development, 61,* 832–837.

Gopnik, A. (1984). The acquisition of "gone" and the development of the object concept. *Journal of Child Language, 11,* 273–292.

Gopnik, A., & Choi, S. (1995). Names, relational words, and cognitive development in English and Korean speakers: Nouns are not always learned before verbs. In M. Tomasello & W. E. Merriman (Eds.), *Beyond names for things* (pp. 63–80). Hillsdale, NJ: Erlbaum.

Gopnik, A., & Meltzoff, A. (1984). Semantic and cognitive development in 15- to 21-month-old children. *Journal of Child Language, 11,* 495–513.

Goren, C. C., Sarty, M., & Wu, P. Y. K. (1975). Visual following and pattern discrimination of face-like stimuli by newborn infants. *Pediatrics, 56,* 544–549.

Gorn, G. I., Goldberg, M. E., & Kanningo, R. N. (1976). The role of educational television in changing intergroup attitudes to children. *Child Development, 47,* 277–280.

Gortmaker, S. L., Must, A., Sobol, A. M., Peterson, K., Colditz, G. A., & Dietz, W. H. (1996). Television viewing as a cause of increasing obesity among children in the United States, 1986–1990. *Archives of Pediatrics and Adolescent Medicine, 150,* 356–362.

Gosselin, P., & Larocque, C. (2000). Facial morphology and children's categorization of facial expressions of emotions: A comparison between Asian and Caucasian faces. *Journal of Genetic Psychology, 161,* 346–358.

Gottesman, I. I. (1963). Genetic aspects of intelligent behavior. In N. Ellis (Ed.), *Handbook of mental deficiency.* New York: McGraw-Hill.

Gottlieb, G. (1991). *Individual development and evolution: The genesis of novel behavior.* New York: Oxford University Press.

Gottlieb, G. (1997). *Synthesizing nature–nurture: Prenatal roots of instinctive behavior.* Mahwah: NJ: Erlbaum.

Gould, M. S., Greenberg, T., Velting, D. M., & Shaffer, D. (2003). Youth suicide risk and preventive interventions: A review of the past 10 years. *Journal of the American Academy of Child and Adolescent Psychiatry, 42,* 386–405.

Grad, 10, puts off more college for TV show. (1994, September 6). *Birmingham News,* sec. 4, p. 1.

Graham, S., Hudley, C., & Williams, E. (1992). Attributional and emotional determinants of aggression among African-American and Latino young adolescents. *Developmental Psychology, 28,* 731–740.

Green, L. J. (2002). *African American English: A linguistic introduction.* New York: Cambridge University Press.

Greenfield, P. M., & Suzuki, L. K. (1998). Culture and human development: Implications for parenting, education, pediatrics, and mental health. In W. Damon, I. E. Sigel, & K. A. Renninger (Eds.), *Handbook of child psychology: Vol. 4. Child psychology in practice* (pp. 1059–1109). New York: Wiley.

Greenough, W. T., & Black, J. E. (1999). Experience, neural plasticity, and psychological development. In N. A. Fox, L. A. Leavitt, & J. G. Warhol (Eds.), *The role of early experience in infant development* (pp. 29–40). Johnson & Johnson Pediatric Institute.

Gregg, V., Gibbs, J. C., & Basinger, K. S. (1994). Patterns of developmental delay in moral judgment by male and female delinquents. *Merrill-Palmer Quarterly, 40,* 538–553.

Gregory, R. (1996). *Psychological testing: History, principles, and applications* (2nd ed.). Boston: Allyn & Bacon.

Griffiths, M. D., & Hunt, N. (1995). Computer game playing in adolescence: Prevalence and demographic indicators. *Journal of Community and Applied Social Psychology, 5,* 189–193.

Grigg, W. N. (1995). Are you fit to be a parent? *The New American, 11*(2). Retrieved January 9, 2003, from www.thenewamerican.com.

Groen, G., & Resnick, L. B. (1977). Can preschool children invent addition algorithms? *Journal of Educational Psychology, 69,* 645–652.

Grolnick, W. S., Kurowski, C. O., & Gurland, S. T. (1999). Family processes and the development of children's self-regulation. *Educational Psychologist, 34,* 3–14.

Gross, A. L., & Ballif, B. (1991). Children's understanding of emotion from facial expressions and situations: A review. *Developmental Review, 11,* 368–398.

Gross, J. (1998, January 18). On the case: A special report. Child welfare foot soldier treads fine line. *New York Times.* Retrieved August 2, 2002, from www.nytimes.com.

Grossmann, K. E., Grossmann, K., Huber, F., & Wartner, U. (1981). German children's behavior towards their mothers at 12 months and their fathers at 18 months in Ainsworth's strange situation. *International Journal of Behavioral Development, 4,* 157–181.

Grusec, J. E., Goodnow, J. J., & Cohen, L. (1996). Household work and the development of concern for others. *Developmental Psychology, 32,* 999–1007.

Guilford, J. P. (1967). *The nature of human intelligence.* New York: McGraw-Hill.

Guilford, J. P. (1982). Cognitive psychology's ambiguities: Some suggested remedies. *Psychological Review, 89,* 48–59.

Gunter, B., & McAleer, J. (1997). *Children and television* (2nd ed). London: Routledge.

Gutierrez, J., Sameroff, A. J., & Karrer, B. M. (1988). Acculturation and SES effects on Mexican-American parents' concepts of development. *Child Development, 59,* 250–255.

Hainline, L. (1998). The development of basic visual abilities. In A. Slater (Ed.), *Perceptual development: Visual, auditory, and speech perception in infancy* (pp. 5–50). Hove, East Sussex, England: Psychology Press.

Haith, M. M. (1980). *Rules that babies look by: The organization of newborn visual activity.* Hillsdale, NJ: Erlbaum.

Haith, M. M., & Benson, J. B. (1998). Infant cognition, In W. Damon (Series Ed.) & D. Kuhn & R. S. Siegler (Vol. Eds.), *Handbook of child psychology: Vol. 2. Cognition, perception, and language* (5th ed., pp. 199–254). New York: Wiley.

Hala, S., Chandler, M., & Fritz, A. S. (1991). Fledgling theories of mind: Deception as a marker of three-year-olds' understanding of false belief. *Child Development, 62,* 83–97.

Halford, G. S., Smith, S. B., Dickson, J. C., Mayberry, M. T., Kelly, M. E., Bain, J. D., & Stewart, J. E. M. (1995). Modeling the development of reasoning strategies: The roles of analogy, knowledge, and capacity. In T. Simon & G. Halford (Eds.), *Developing cognitive competence: New approaches to process modeling* (pp. 77–156). Hillsdale, NJ: Erlbaum.

Hall, G. S. (1904). *Adolescence: Its psychology and its relations to physiology, anthropology, sociology, sex, crime, religion, and education* (Vols. 1 and 2). New York: Appleton.

Halpern, D. F. (2000). *Sex differences in cognitive abilities* (3rd ed.). Hillsdale, NJ: Erlbaum.

Halpern, R. (1993). Poverty and infant development. In C. H. Zeanah, Jr. (Ed.), *Handbook of infant mental health* (pp. 73–86). New York: Guilford Press.

Hamers, J. F. (1996). Cognitive and language development of bilingual children. In I. Parasnis (Ed.), *Cultural and language diversity and the deaf experience* (pp. 51–75). Cambridge, England: Cambridge University Press.

Hamers, J. F., & Blanc, M. H. A. (2000). *Bilinguality and bilingualism* (2nd ed.). Cambridge, England: Cambridge University Press.

Hamilton, C. J., Coates, R. O., & Heffernan, T. (2003). What develops in visuo-spatial working memory development? *European Journal of Cognitive Psychology, 15,* 43–70.

Handley, S. J., Capon, A., Copp, C., & Harper, C. (2002). Conditional reasoning and the Tower of Hanoi: The role of spatial and verbal working memory. *British Journal of Psychology, 93,* 501–518.

Hanson, T. L. (1999). Does parental conflict explain why divorce is negatively associated with child welfare? *Social Forces, 77,* 1283–1316.

Harlow, H. F., & Zimmermann, R. R. (1959). Affectional responses in the infant monkey. *Science, 130,* 421–432.

Harnishfeger, K. K. (1995). The development of cognitive inhibition: Theories, definitions, and research evidence. In F. Dempster & C. Brainerd (Eds.), *New perspectives on interference and inhibition in cognition* (pp. 175–204). New York: Academic Press.

Harnishfeger, K. K., & Bjorklund, D. F. (1994). Individual differences in inhibition: Implications for children's cognitive development. *Learning and Individual Differences, 6,* 331–335.

Harris, J. R. (1998). *The nurture assumption: Why children turn out the way they do.* New York: Free Press.

Harris, J. R. (2000). The outcome of parenting: What do we really know? *Journal of Personality, 68,* 625–637.

Harris, P. L. (1983). Infant cognition. In P. H. Mussen (Series Ed.) & M. M. Haith & J. J. Campos (Vol. Eds.), *Handbook of child psychology: Vol. 2. Infancy and developmental psychobiology* (pp. 689–782). New York: Wiley.

Harris, R. J., & Scott, C. L. (2002). Effects of sex in the media. In J. Bryant & D. Zillman (Eds.), *Media effects: Advances in theory and research* (2nd ed., pp. 307–331). Mahwah, NJ: Erlbaum.

Harrison, L. F., & Williams, T. M. (1986). Television and cognitive development. In T. M. Williams (Ed.), *The impact of television: A natural experiment in three communities* (pp. 87–142). Orlando, FL: Academic Press.

Harrison, L. J., & Ungerer, J. A. (2002). Maternal employment and infant–mother attachment security at 12 months postpartum. *Developmental Psychology, 38,* 758–773.

Hart, B., & Risley, T. R. (1995). *Meaningful differences in the everyday experience of young American children.* Baltimore: Paul H. Brookes.

Hart, C. H., Olsen, S. F., Robinson, C. C., & Mandleco, B. L. (1997). The relation of childhood personality types to adolescent behavior and development: A longitudinal study of Icelandic children. *Developmental Psychology, 33,* 195–205.

Harter, S. (1993). Causes and consequences of low self-esteem in children and adolescents. In R. F. Baumeister (Ed.), *Self-esteem: The puzzle of low self-regard* (pp. 87–116). New York: Plenum.

Harter, S. (1998). The development of self-representations. In W. Damon & N. Eisenberg (Eds.), *Handbook of child psychology: Vol 3. Social, emotional, and personality development* (pp. 553–617). New York: Wiley.

Harter, S. (1999). *The construction of the self: A developmental perspective.* New York: Guilford Press.

Harter, S., Waters, P., & Whitesell, N. R. (1998). Relational self-worth: Differences in perceived worth as a person across interpersonal contexts among adolescents. *Child Development, 69,* 756–766.

Hartup, W. W. (1974). Aggression in childhood: Developmental perspectives. *American Psychologist, 29,* 336–341.

Hartup, W. W. (1989). Behavioral manifestations of children's friendships. In T. J. Berndt & G. W. Ladd (Eds.), *Peer relationships in child development* (pp. 46–70). New York: Wiley.

Harwood, R. L. (1992). The influence of culturally derived values on Anglo and Puerto Rican mothers' perceptions of attachment behavior. *Child Development, 63,* 822–839.

Hasher, L., & Zachs, R. T. (1979). Automatic and effortful processes in memory. *Journal of Experimental Psychology: General, 108,* 356–388.

Hasselhorn, M. (1992). Task dependency and the role of category typicality and metamemory in the development of an organizational strategy. *Child Development, 63,* 202–214.

Hatch, M. C., Shu, X. O., McLean, D. E., Levin, B., Begg, M., Reuss, L., & Susser, M. (1993). Maternal exercise during pregnancy, physical fitness, and fetal growth. *American Journal of Epidemiology, 137*(10), 1105–1114.

Hatchett, S. J., & Jackson, J. S. (1999). African American extended kin systems: An empirical assessment in the National Survey of Black Americans. In H. P. McAdoo (Ed.), *Family ethnicity: Strength in diversity* (2nd ed., pp. 171–190). Thousand Oaks, CA: Sage.

Haviland, J. M., & Lelwica, M. (1987). The induced affect response: 10-week-old infants' responses to three emotion expressions. *Developmental Psychology, 23,* 97–104.

Hay, D. F., Caplan, M., Castle, J., & Stimson, C. A. (1991). Does sharing become increasingly "rational" in the second year of life? *Developmental Psychology, 27,* 987–993.

Hay, D. F., & Ross, H. S. (1982). The social nature of early conflict. *Child Development, 53,* 105–113.

Hays, S. (1996). *The cultural contradictions of motherhood.* New Haven, CT: Yale University Press.

Hazell, L. (1975). A study of 300 elective home births. *Birth and the Family Journal, 2,* 11–18.

Hearold, S. (1986). A synthesis of 1043 effects of television on social behavior. In G. Comstock (Ed.), *Public communication and behavior* (Vol. 1, pp. 65–133). New York: Academic Press.

Heinicke, C. M., & Guthrie, D. (1996). Prebirth marital interactions and postbirth marital development. *Infant Mental Health Journal, 17*(2), 140–151.

Helburn, S. W., & Bergmann, B. R. (2002). *America's child care problem: The way out.* New York: Palgrave.

Helburn, S. W., & Howes, C. (1996). Child care cost and quality. *The Future of Children, 6,* 62–82.

Helleday, J., Bartfai, A., Ritzen, E. M., & Forsman, M. (1994). General intelligence and cognitive profile in women with congenital adrenal hyperplasia (CAH). *Psychoneuroendocrinology, 19,* 343–356.

Herman, J. L. (1992). *Trauma and recovery: The aftermath of violence—from domestic abuse to political terror.* New York: Basic Books. As cited in Werkerle & Wolfe (1996), p. 508.

Herpes.com. (2002). "Good" virus/ "Bad" virus: The truth about HSV-1 and HSV-2; Herpes and Pregnancy; Transmission. Retrieved March 1, 2002, from www.Herpes.com.

Herrnstein, R. J., & Murray, C. (1994). *The bell curve: Intelligence and class structure in American life.* New York: Free Press.

Hershberger, S. L., & D'Augelli, A. R. (1995). The impact of victimization on the mental health and suicidality of lesbian, gay, and bisexual youths. *Developmental Psychology, 31,* 65–74.

Hetherington, E. M. (1999). Should we stay together for the sake of the children? In E. M. Hetherington (Ed.), *Coping with divorce, single parenting, and remarriage: A risk and resiliency perspective* (pp. 93–116). Mahwah, NJ: Erlbaum.

Hetherington, E. M., Bridges, M., & Insabella, G. M. (1998). What matters? What does not? *American Psychologist, 53,* 167–184.

Hetherington, E. M., & Clingempeel, W. G. (1992). Coping with marital transitions. *Monographs of the Society for Research in Child Development, 57* (No. 2–3). Chicago: University of Chicago Press.

Hetherington, E. M., Cox, M., & Cox. R. (1982). Effects of divorce on parents and children. In M. E. Lamb (Ed.), *Nontraditional families: Parenting and child development* (pp. 233–288). Hillsdale, NJ: Erlbaum.

Hetherington, E. M., & Jodl, K. M. (1994). Stepfamilies as settings for child development. In A. Booth & J. Dunn (Eds.), *Stepfamilies: Who benefits? Who does not?* (pp. 55–79). Hillsdale, NJ: Erlbaum.

Hetherington, E. M., & Kelly, J. (2002). *For better or for worse: Divorce reconsidered.* New York: W. W. Norton.

Hetherington, E. M., Reiss, D., & Plomin, R. (Eds.). (1994). *Separate social worlds of siblings: The impact of nonshared environment on development.* Hillsdale, NJ: Erlbaum.

Hetherington, E. M., & Stanley-Hagan, M. M. (1995). Parenting in divorced and remarried families. In M. H. Bornstein (Ed.), *Handbook of parenting: Vol. 3. Status and social conditions of parenting* (pp. 233–254). Mahwah, NJ: Erlbaum.

Higgins, E. T., & Parsons, J. E. (1983). Social cognition and the social life of the child: Stages as subcultures. In E. T. Higgins, D. N. Ruble, & W. W. Hartup (Eds.), *Social cognition and social development* (pp. 15–62). Cambridge, England: Cambridge University Press.

High school expels junior after guard finds knife in truck. (2002, March 21). *New York Times.* Retrieved August 7, 2002, from www.nytimes.com.

Hill, N. E., Bush, K. R., & Roosa, M. W. (2003). Parenting and family socialization strategies and children's mental health: Low-income Mexican-American and Euro-American mothers and children. *Child Development, 74,* 189–204.

Hilton, J. M. (2002). Children's behavior problems in single-parent and married-parent families: Development of a predictive model. *Journal of Divorce and Remarriage, 37,* 13–36.

Hirsh-Pasek, K., Golinkoff, R. M., & Hollich, G. (2000). An emergentist coalition model for word learning. In R. M. Golinkoff, K. Hirsh-Pasek, L. Bloom, L. B. Smith, A. L. Woodward, N. Akhtar, M. Tomasello, & G. Hollich, *Becoming a word learner: A debate on lexical acquisition* (pp. 136–164). Oxford, England: Oxford University Press.

Ho, M.-W. (1984). Environment and heredity in development and evolution. In M.-W. Ho & P. T. Saunders (Eds.), *Beyond neo-Darwinism: An introduction to the new evolutionary paradigm* (pp. 267–289). London: Academic Press.

Hochschild, A. R., & Machung, A. (1989). *The second shift: Working parents and the revolution at home.* New York: Viking.

Hodapp, R. M., & Dykens, E. M. (1996). Mental retardation. In E. J. Mash & R. A. Barkley (Eds.), *Child psychopathology* (pp. 362–389). New York: Guilford Press.

Hodnett, E. D., & Osborn, R. W. (1989). Effects of continuous intrapartum professional support on childbirth outcomes. *Research in Nursing and Health, 12,* 289–297.

Hofferth, S. L. (1996). Child care in the United States today. *The Future of Children, 6,* 41–61.

Hoffman, C. D., & Teyber, E. C. (1985). Naturalistic observations of sex differences in adult involvement with girls and boys of different ages. *Merrill-Palmer Quarterly, 31,* 93–97.

Hoffman, L. (1979). Maternal employment. *American Psychologist, 34,* 859–865.

Hoffman, M. L. (1975). Moral internalization, parental power, and the nature of parent–child interaction. *Developmental Psychology, 11,* 228–239.

Hoffman, M. L. (1984). Empathy, its limitations, and its role in a comprehensive moral theory. In W. M. Kurtines & J. L. Gewirtz (Eds.), *Morality, moral behavior, and moral development: Basic issues in theory and research* (pp. 283–302). New York: Wiley.

Hoffman, M. L. (1991). Empathy, social cognition, and moral action. In W. M. Kurtines & J. L. Gewirtz (Eds.), *Handbook of moral behavior and development: Vol. 1. Theory* (pp. 275–301). Hillsdale, NJ: Erlbaum.

Hoffman, M. L. (2001). Toward a comprehensive empathy-based theory of prosocial moral development. In A. C. Bohart & D. J. Stipek (Eds.), *Constructive and destructive behavior: Implications for family, school, & society* (pp. 61–85). Washington, DC: American Psychological Association.

Hoffman-Plotkin, D., & Twentyman, C. T. (1984). A multimodal assessment of behavioral and cognitive deficits in abused and neglected preschoolers. *Child Development, 55*, 794–802.

Hogben, M. (1998). Factors moderating the effect of televised aggression on viewer behavior. *Communication Research, 25*, 220–247.

Holahan, C. K., & Sears, R. R. (1995). *The gifted group in later maturity.* Stanford, CA: Stanford University Press.

Holden, C. (1995). More on genes and homosexuality. *Science, 268*, 1571.

Holden, G. W. (2002). Perspectives on the effects of corporal punishment: Comment on Gershoff (2002). *Psychological Bulletin, 128*, 590–595.

Horgan, D. (1978). The development of the full passive. *Journal of Child Language, 5*, 65–80.

Horn, J., & Cattell, R. B. (1966). Refinement and test of the theory of fluid and crystallized general intelligences. *Journal of Educational Psychology, 57*(5), 253–270.

Horn, S. S. (2003). Adolescents' reasoning about exclusion from social groups. *Developmental Psychology, 39*(1), 71–84.

Hossain, Z., Field, T., Malphus, J., Valle, C., & Pickens, J. (1995). *Fathers' caregiving in low-income African-American and Hispanic American families.* Unpublished manuscript. As cited in Parke & Buriel (1998).

Hossain, Z., & Roopnarine, J. L. (1993). Division of household labor and child care in dual-earner African-American families with infants. *Sex Roles, 29*, 571–583.

Howard, K. I., Cornille, T. A., Lyons, J. S., Vessey, J. T., Lueger, R. J., & Saunders, S. M. (1996). Patterns of service utilization. *Archives of General Psychiatry, 53*, 696–703.

Howe, D. (1998). *Patterns of adoption: Nature, nurture, and psychosocial development.* Oxford, England: Blackwell Science.

Howe, M. L., & Courage, M. L. (1993). On resolving the enigma of infantile amnesia. *Psychological Bulletin, 113*, 305–326.

Howe, M. L., Courage, M. L., & Bryant-Brown, L. (1995). Reinstating preschoolers' memories. *Developmental Psychology, 29*, 854–869.

Howes, C. (1988). Peer interaction of young children. *Monographs of the Society for Research in Child Development, 53* (Serial No. 217), pp. 1–78.

Howse, R. B., Lange, G., Farran, D. C., & Boyles, C. D. (2003). Motivation and self-regulation as predictors of achievement in economically disadvantaged young children. *Journal of Experimental Education, 71*, 151–174.

Hsu, L. K. G., Chesler, B. E., & Santhouse, R. (1990). Bulimia nervosa in eleven sets of twins: A clinical report. *International Journal of Eating Disorders, 9*, 275–282.

Hudson, J. A., Fivush, R., & Kuebli, J. (1992). Scripts and episodes: The development of event memory. *Applied Cognitive Psychology, 6*, 483–505.

Hudson, J. A., & Nelson, K. (1983). Effects of script structure on children's story recall. *Developmental Psychology, 19*, 625–635.

Hudson, J. A., Shapiro, L. R., & Sosa, B. B. (1995). Planning in the real world: Preschool children's scripts for familiar events. *Child Development, 66*, 984–998.

Hudspeth, W. J., & Pribram, K. H. (1990). Stages of brain and cognitive maturation. *Journal of Educational Psychology, 82*, 881–884.

Huesman, L. R., Eron, L. D., Lefkowitz, M. M., & Walder, L. O. (1984). Stability of aggression over time and generations. *Developmental Psychology, 20*, 1120–1134.

Huesmann, L. R., & Miller, L. S. (1994). Long-term effects of repeated exposure to media violence in childhood. In L. R. Huesmann (Ed.), *Aggressive behavior: Current perspectives* (pp. 153–186). New York: Plenum.

Huesmann, L. R., Moise-Titus, J., Podolski, C., & Eron, L. D. (2003). Longitudinal relations between children's exposure to TV violence and their aggressive and violent behavior in young adulthood: 1977–1992. *Developmental Psychology, 38*, 201–221.

Huggins, S. L. (1989). A comparative study of self-esteem of adolescent children of divorced lesbian mothers and divorced heterosexual mothers. *Journal of Homosexuality, 18*, 123–135.

Hughes, F. P. (1999). *Children, play, and development.* Boston: Allyn & Bacon.

Hulit, L. M., & Howard, M. R. (1997). *Born to talk: An introduction to speech and language development.* Boston: Allyn & Bacon.

Human Genome Program, U.S. Department of Energy. (1992). *Primer on molecular genetics.* Washington, DC: Author. Retrieved March 20, 2003, from www.ornl.gov/hgmis/publicat/primer/intro.html.

Human Genome Program, U.S. Department of Energy. (2000). Human Genome Project milestones celebrated at White House. *Human Genome News, 11*(1–2). Retrieved January 18, 2002, from www.ornl.gov/hgmis/publicat/hgn/v11n1/04draft.html.

Human Genome Program, U.S. Department of Energy. (2001). *Human Genome Project information.* Retrieved January 18, 2002, from www.ornl.gov/hgmis.

Hunter, J. (1990). Violence against lesbian and gay male youths. *Journal of Interpersonal Violence, 5*, 295–300.

Hunter, J., & Mallon, G. P. (2000). Lesbian, gay, and bisexual adolescent development: Dancing with your feet tied together. In B. Greene & G. L. Croom (Eds.), *Education, research, and practice in lesbian, gay, bisexual, and transgendered psychology: A resource manual* (pp. 226–243). Thousand Oaks, CA: Sage.

Huston, A. C., Donnerstein, E., Fairchild, H., Feshbach, N. D., Katz, P. A., Murray, J. P., Rubinstein, E. A., Wilcox, B. L., & Zuckerman, D. (1992). *Big world, small screen: The role of television in American society.* Lincoln: University of Nebraska Press.

Huston, A. C., & Wright, J. C. (1998). Mass media and children's development. In W. Damon, I. E. Sigel, & K. A. Renninger (Eds.), *Handbook of child psychology: Vol. 4. Child psychology in practice* (pp. 999–1058). New York: Wiley.

Huttenlocher, P. R. (1990). Morphometric study of human cerebral cortex development. *Neuropsychologia, 28*, 517–527.

Huttenlocher, P. R. (1999). Synaptogenesis in human cerebral cortex and the concept of critical periods. In N. A. Fox, L. A. Leavitt, & J. G. Warhol (Eds.), *The role of early experience in infant development* (pp. 15–28). Johnson & Johnson Pediatric Institute.

Huttenlocher, P. R. (2002). *Neural plasticity: The effects of environment on the development of the cerebral cortex.* Cambridge, MA: Harvard University Press.

Huttenlocher, P. R., & Dabholkar, A. S. (1997). Regional differences in synaptogenesis in human cerebral cortex. *Journal of Comparative Neurology, 387*, 167–178.

Hwang, C. P., & Broberg, A. G. (1992). The historical and social context of child care in Sweden. In M. E. Lamb, K. J. Sternberg, C. P. Hwang, & A. G. Broberg (Eds.), *Child care in context: Cross-cultural perspectives* (pp. 27–54). Hillsdale, NJ: Erlbaum.

Hyde, J. S., & Linn, M. C. (1988). Gender differences in verbal ability: A meta-analysis. *Psychological Bulletin, 104*, 53–69.

Hymel, S., Rubin, K. H., Rowden, L., & LeMare, L. (1990). Children's peer relationships: Longitudinal predictions of internalizing and externalizing problems from middle to late childhood. *Child Development, 61*, 2004–2021.

Iervolino, A. C., Pike, A., Manke, B., Reiss, D., Hetherington, E. M., & Plomin, R. (2002). Genetic and environmental influences in adolescent peer socialization: Evidence from two genetically sensitive designs. *Child Development, 73*, 162–174.

Inhelder, B., & Piaget, J. (1958). *The growth of logical thinking from childhood to adolescence: An essay on the construction of formal operational structures.* New York: Basic Books.

Institute of Medicine. (1996). *Fetal alcohol syndrome: Diagnosis, epidemiology, prevention, and treatment.* Washington, DC: National Academy Press.

Intons-Peterson, M. J. (1988). *Children's concepts of gender.* Norwood, NJ: Ablex.

Isabella, R. A. (1995). The origins of infant–mother attachment: Maternal behavior and infant development. *Annals of Child Development, 10,* 57–81.

Isabella, R. A., & Belsky, J. (1991). Interactional synchrony and the origins of infant–mother attachment: A replication study. *Child Development, 62,* 373–384.

Isabella, R. A., Belsky, J., & von Eye, A. (1989). Origins of infant–mother attachment: An examination of interactional synchrony during the infant's first year. *Developmental Psychology, 25,* 12–21.

Istvan, J. (1986). Stress, anxiety, and birth outcomes: A critical review of the evidence. *Psychological Bulletin, 100,* 331–348.

Jacobson, J. L., & Jacobson, S. W. (1996). Intellectual impairment in children exposed to polychlorinated biphenyls in utero. *New England Journal of Medicine, 335,* 783–789.

Jacobson, J. L., Jacobson, S. W., & Humphrey, H. E. B. (1990). Effects of in utero exposure to polychlorinated biphenyls (PCBs) and related contaminants on cognitive functioning in young children. *Journal of Pediatrics, 116,* 38–45.

Jadack, R. A., Hyde, J. S., Moore, C. F., & Keller, M. L. (1995). Moral reasoning about sexually transmitted diseases. *Child Development, 66,* 167–177.

Jaffee, S. R., Moffitt, T. E., Caspi, A., & Taylor, A. (2003). Life with (or without) father: The benefits of living with two biological parents depend on the father's antisocial behavior. *Child Development, 74,* 109–126.

Jaffee, S., & Hyde, J. S. (2000). Gender differences in moral orientation: A meta-analysis. *Psychological Bulletin, 126,* 703–726.

James, K. A., Phelps, L., & Bross, A. L. (2001). Body dissatisfaction, drive for thinness, and self-esteem in African American college females. *Psychology in the Schools, 38,* 491–495.

James, W. (1890/1950). *The principles of psychology.* New York: Dover. (Originally published in 1890.)

Janssens, J. M. A. M., & Dekovic, M. (1997). Child rearing, prosocial moral reasoning, and prosocial behavior. *International Journal of Behavioral Development, 20,* 509–527.

Janus, S. S., & Janus, C. L. (1993). *The Janus report on sexual behavior.* New York: Wiley.

Jarrett, R. L. (1995). Growing up poor: The family experiences of socially mobile youth in low-income African American neighborhoods. *Journal of Adolescent Research, 10,* 111–135.

Jay, T. (1992). *Cursing in America.* Philadelphia: J. Benjamins.

Jekielek, S. M. (1998). Parental conflict, marital diruption and children's emotional well-being. *Social Forces, 76,* 905–935.

Jenkins, J. M., Rasbash, J., & O'Conner, T. G. (2003). The role of the shared family context in differential parenting. *Developmental Psychology, 39,* 99–113.

Jerman, M., & Mirman, S. (1974). Linguistic and computational variables in problem solving in elementary mathematics. *Educational Studies in Mathematics, 5,* 317–362.

Jerman, M., & Rees, R. (1972). Predicting the relative difficulty of verbal arithmetic problems. *Educational Studies in Mathematics, 4,* 306–323.

Joad, C. (1960). *Classics in philosophy and ethics.* Nottingham, England: Cultural Publications.

Johnson, D. W., & Johnson, R. (1999). *Learning together and alone: Cooperation, competition, and individualization* (5th ed.). Boston: Allyn & Bacon.

Johnson, J. S., & Newport, E. L. (1989). Critical period effects in second language learning: The influence of maturational state on the acquisition of English as a second language. *Cognitive Psychology, 21,* 60–99.

Johnson, M. H., Dziurawiec, S., Ellis, H., & Morton, J. (1991). Newborns' preferential tracking of face-like stimuli and its subsequent decline. *Cognition, 40,* 1–19.

Johnston, J. (1990). Role diffusion and role reversal: Structural variations in divorced families and children's functioning. *Family Relations, 39,* 405–413.

Johnston, J. (1995). Children's adjustment in sole custody compared to joint custody families and principles for custody decision making. *Family and Conciliation Courts Review, 33,* 415–425.

Jurdak, M., & Shahin, I. (1999). An ethnographic study of the computational strategies of a group of young street vendors in Beirut. *Educational Studies in Mathematics, 40,* 155–172.

Jussim, L., Eccles, J. S., & Madon, S. (1996). Social perception, social stereotypes, and teacher expectations: Accuracy and the quest for the powerful self-fulfilling prophecy. In L. Berkowitz (Ed.), *Advances in experimental social psychology* (pp. 281–388). New York: Academic Press.

Kabot, S., Masi, W., & Segal, M. (2003). Advances in the diagnosis and treatment of autism spectrum disorders. *Professional Psychology: Research and Practice, 34,* 26–33.

Kagan, J. (1994). *Galen's prophecy.* New York: Basic Books.

Kagan, J. (1997). Temperament and the reactions to unfamiliarity. *Child Development, 68,* 139–143.

Kagan, J., Arcus, D., & Snidman, N. (1993). The idea of temperament: Where do we go from here? In R. Plomin & G. E. McClearn (Eds.), *Nature, nurture, and psychology* (pp. 197–210). Washington, DC: American Psychological Association.

Kagan, J., Arcus, D., Snidman, N., Feng, W. Y., Hendler, J., & Greene, S. (1994). Reactivity in infants: A cross-national comparison. *Developmental Psychology, 30,* 342–345.

Kagan, J., Reznick, J. S., & Snidman, N. (1988). Biological bases of childhood shyness. *Science, 240,* 167–171.

Kail, R. (1988). Developmental functions for speeds of cognitive processes. *Journal of Experimental Child Psychology, 45,* 339–364.

Kail, R. (1991). Processing time declines exponentially during childhood and adolescence. *Developmental Psychology, 27,* 259–266.

Kail, R., & Salthouse, T. A. (1994). Processing speed as a mental capacity. *Acta Psychologica, 86,* 199–225.

Kaiser Family Foundation. (2002, March). Sex education in the U.S.: Policy and politics. Retrieved January 7, 2003, from www.kff.org/content/2002/3224.

Kaltenbach, K., & Finnegan, L. (1992). Methadone maintenance during pregnancy: Implications for perinatal and developmental outcome. In T. B. Sonderegger (Ed.), *Perinatal substance abuse: Research findings and clinical applications* (pp. 239–253). Baltimore: Johns Hopkins University Press.

Kamerman, S. B. (2000). Parental leave policies: An essential ingredient in early childhood education and care policies. *Social Policy Report, 14*(2). Ann Arbor, MI: Society for Research in Child Development.

Kamphaus, R. W. (2001). *Clinical assessment of child and adolescent intelligence* (2nd ed.). Boston: Allyn & Bacon.

Kandel, E. R., Schwartz, J. H., & Jessell, T. M. (2000). *Principles of neural science* (4th ed.). New York: McGraw-Hill.

Kann, R. T., & Hanna, F. J. (2000). Disruptive behavior disorders in children and adolescents: How do girls differ from boys? *Journal of Counseling and Development, 78,* 267–274.

Kao, G., & Tienda, M. (1995). Optimism and achievement: The educational performance of immigrant youth. *Social Science Quarterly, 76,* 1–19.

Karniol, R., & Koren, L. (1987). How would you feel? Children's inferences regarding their own and others' affective reactions. *Cognitive Development, 2,* 271–278.

Karpov, Y. V., & Haywood, H. C. (1998). Two ways to elaborate Vygotsky's concept of mediation. *American Psychologist, 53,* 27–36.

Kaslow, N. J., Collins, M. H., Rashid, F. L., Baskin, M. L., Grifith, J. R., Hollins, L., & Eckman, J. E. (2000). The efficacy of a pilot family psychoeducational intervention for pediatric sickle cell disease (SCD). *Families, Systems, & Health, 18,* 381–404.

Katchadourian, H. (1990). Sexuality. In S. S. Feldman & G. R. Elliott (Eds.), *At the threshold: The developing adolescent* (pp. 330–351). Cambridge, MA: Harvard University Press.

Katz, L. F., & Woodin, E. M. (2002). Hostility, hostile detachment, and conflict engagement in marriages: Effects on child and family functioning. *Child Development, 73,* 636–652.

Katz, M. (1997). *On playing a poor hand well.* New York: Norton.

Katz, P. A., & Walsh, V. (1991). Modification of children's gender-stereotyped behavior. *Child Development, 62,* 338–351.

Kaufman, J., & Zigler, E. (1989). The intergenerational transmission of child abuse and the prospect of predicting future abusers. In D. Cicchetti & V. Carlson (Eds.), *Child maltreatment: Research and theory on the causes and consequences of child abuse and neglect* (pp. 129–150). New York: Cambridge University Press.

Kaufman, P., Chen, X., Choy, S. P., Peter, K., Ruddy, S. A., Miller, A. K., Fleury, J. K., Chandler, K. A., Planty, M. G., & Rand, M. R. (2001). *Indicators of school crime and safety, 2001*. Washington, DC: U.S. Departments of Education and Justice. NCES 2002-113/NCJ-190075. Retrieved August 8, 2002, from http://nces.ed.gov.

Kaufman, P., Chen, X., Choy, S. P., Ruddy, S. A., Miller, A. K., Fleury, J. K., Chandler, K. A., Rand, M. R., Klaus, P., & Planty, M. G. (2000). *Indicators of school crime and safety, 2000*. Washington, DC: U.S. Departments of Education and Justice. NCES 2001-017/NCJ-184176. Retrieved August 8, 2002, from http://nces.ed.gov.

Kazdin, A. E., & Marciano, P. L. (1998). Childhood and adolescent depression. In E. J. Mash & R. A. Barkley (Eds.), *Treatment of childhood disorders* (pp. 211–248). New York: Guilford Press.

Kazdin, A. E., & Whitley, M. K. (2003). Treatment of parental stress to enhance therapeutic change among children referred for aggressive and antisocial behavior. *Journal of Consulting and Clinical Psychology, 71*, 504–515.

Keating, D. P. (1980). Thinking processes in adolescence. In J. Adelson (Ed.), *Handbook of Adolescent Psychology* (pp. 211–246). New York: Wiley.

Kee, D. W. (1994). Developmental differences in associative memory: Strategy use, mental effort, and knowledge-access interactions. In H. W. Reese (Ed.), *Advances in child development and behavior* (Vol. 25, pp. 7–32). New York: Academic Press.

Keith, T. Z., Keith, P. B., Quirk, K. J., Sperduto, J., Santillo, S., & Killings, S. (1998). Longitudinal effects of parent involvement on high school grades: Similarities and differences across gender and ethnic groups. *Journal of School Psychology, 36*, 335–363.

Kelley, M. L., Sanchez-Hucles, J., & Walker, R. (1993). Correlates of disciplinary practices in working- to middle-class African-American mothers. *Merrill-Palmer Quarterly, 39*, 252–264.

Kellman, P. J., & Banks, M. S. (1998). Infant visual perception. In W. Damon (Ed.), *Handbook of child psychology* (5th ed., Vol. 2, pp. 103–146). New York: Wiley.

Kemper, R. L., & Vernoog, A. R. (1994). Metalinguistic awareness in first graders: A qualitative perspective. *Journal of Psycholinguistic Research, 22*, 41–57.

Kendler, K. S., Neale, M. C., Kessler, R. C., Heath, A. C., & Eaves, L. J. (1993). A test of the equal-environment assumption in twin studies of psychiatric illness. *Behavior Genetics, 23*(1), 21–27.

Kertscher, T. (1999, April 6). Burlington teenager gets probation. *Milwaukee Journal Sentinel*. Retrieved July 19, 2002, from http://proquest.umi.com.

Kertscher, T., Spice, L., Johnson, M., Krantz, C., & Ortiz, V. (1998, November 19). Pewaukee High student arrested after threat. In separate case, three Burlington teens charged with planning killings. *Milwaukee Journal Sentinel*. Retrieved July 19, 2003, from http://proquest.umi.com.

Khanna, N. (1998). Effects of exercise on pregnancy. *American Family Physician, 57*(8), 1764–1768.

Kilgore, K., Snyder, J., & Lentz, C. (2000). The contribution of parental discipline, parental monitoring, and school risk to early-onset conduct problems in African American boys and girls. *Developmental Psychology, 36*, 835–845.

Kindlon, D. J., & Thompson, M. (2000). *Raising Cain: Protecting the emotional life of boys*. New York: Ballantine.

King, V. (2002). Parental divorce and interpersonal trust in adult offspring. *Journal of Marriage and Family, 64*, 642–656.

Kirby, L. D., & Fraser, M. W. (1997). Risk and resilience in childhood. In M. W. Fraser (Ed.), *Risk and resilience in childhood: An ecological perspective* (pp. 10–33). Washington, DC: National Association of Social Workers Press.

Kirkpatrick, M. (1987). Clinical implications of lesbian mother studies. *Journal of Homosexuality, 13*, 201–211.

Kirschner, D. (1995). Adoption psychopathology and the "adopted child syndrome." In *The Hatherleigh guide to child and adolescent therapy* (pp. 103–123). New York: Hatherleigh Press.

Klahr, D. (1992). Information processing approaches to cognitive development. In M. H. Bornstein & M. E. Lamb (Eds.), *Developmental psychology: An advanced textbook* (3rd ed., pp. 273–335). Hillsdale, NJ: Erlbaum.

Klahr, D., & MacWhinney, B. (1998). Information processing. In W. Damon, D. Kuhn, & R. S. Siegler (Eds.), *Handbook of child psychology: Vol 2. Cognition, perception, and language* (5th ed., pp. 631–678). New York: Wiley.

Klahr, D., & Siegler, R. S. (1978). The representation of children's knowledge. In H. W. Reese & L. P. Lipsitt (Eds.), *Advances in child development and behavior* (Vol. 12, pp. 61–116). New York: Academic Press.

Klaus, M. H., & Kennell, J. H. (1976). *Maternal–infant binding*. St. Louis: Mosby.

Klonsky, M. (2002). How smaller schools prevent school violence. *Educational Leadership, 59*, 65–69.

Knafo, A., & Schwartz, S. H. (2003). Parenting and adolescents' accuracy in perceiving parental values. *Child Development, 74*, 595–611.

Knight, G. P., Berning, A. L., Wilson, S. L., & Chao, C. (1987). The effects of information-processing demands and social–situational factors on the social decision making of children. *Journal of Experimental Child Psychology, 43*, 244–259.

Kochanska, G. (1993). Toward a synthesis of parental socialization and child temperament in early development of conscience. *Child Development, 64*, 325–347.

Kochanska, G., Coy, K. C., & Murray, K. T. (2001). The development of self-regulation in the first four years of life. *Child Development, 72*, 1091–1111.

Kochanska, G., Murray, K. T., & Coy, K. C. (1997). Inhibitory control as a contributor to conscience in childhood: From toddler to early school age. *Child Development, 68*, 263–277.

Kochanska, G., Murray, K. T., & Harlan, E. T. (2000). Effortful control in early childhood: Continuity and change, antecedents, and implications for social development. *Developmental Psychology, 36*, 220–232.

Kochanska, G., Murray, K. T., Jacques, T. Y., Koenig, A. L., & Vandegeest, K. A. (1996). Inhibitory control in young children and its role in emerging internalization. *Child Development, 67*, 490–507.

Koestner, R., Franz, C., & Weinberger, J. (1990). The family origins of empathetic concern: A 26-year longitudinal study. *Journal of Personality and Social Psychology, 58*, 709–717.

Kohlberg, L. (1966). A cognitive–developmental analysis of children's sex role concepts and attitudes. In E. E. Maccoby (Ed.), *The development of sex differences* (pp. 82–173). Stanford, CA: Stanford University Press.

Kohlberg, L. (1969). Stage and sequence: The cognitive–developmental approach to socialization. In D. Goslin (Ed.), *Handbook of socialization theory and research* (pp. 347–480). Chicago: Rand McNally.

Kohlberg, L. (1984). Moral stages and moralization: The cognitive-developmental approach. In L. Kohlberg, *Essays on moral development: Vol. II. The psychology of moral development: The nature and validity of moral stages* (pp. 170–211). San Francisco: Harper & Row.

Kohlberg, L., Levine, C., & Hewer, A. (1984). The current formulation of the theory. In L. Kohlberg, *Essays on moral development: Vol. II. The psychology of moral development: The nature and validity of moral stages* (pp. 212–319). San Francisco: Harper & Row.

Kohlberg, L., & Power, C. (1981). Moral development, religious thinking, and the question of a seventh stage. In L. Kohlberg, *Essays on moral development: Vol. I. The philosophy of moral development: Moral stages and the idea of justice* (pp. 311–372). San Francisco: Harper & Row.

Kohler, J. K., Grotevant, H. D., & McRoy, R. G. (2002). Adopted adolescents' preoccupation with adoption: The impact on adoptive family relationships. *Journal of Marriage and Family, 64*, 93–104.

Kolb, B. (1999). Neuroanatomy and development overview. In N. A. Fox, L. A. Leavitt, & J. G. Warhol (Eds.), *The role of early experience in infant development* (pp. 5–14). Johnson & Johnson Pediatric Institute.

Kolb, B., & Fantie, B. (1989). Development of the child's brain and behavior. In C. R. Reynolds & E. F. Janzen (Eds.), *Handbook of clinical child neuropsychology* (pp. 17–40). New York: Plenum.

Kolb, B., Gibb, R., & Dallison, A. (1999). Early experience, behavior, and the changing brain. In N. A. Fox, L. A. Leavitt, & J. G. Warhol (Eds.), *The role of early experience in infant development* (pp. 41–63). Johnson & Johnson Pediatric Institute.

Kollar, E. J., & Fisher, C. (1980). Tooth induction in chick epithelium: Expression of quiescent genes for enamel synthesis. *Science, 207*, 993–995.

Kontos, S., Howes, C., Shinn, M., & Galinsky, E. (1995). *Quality in family child care and relative care*. New York: Teachers College Press.

Kopp, C. B. (1982). Antecedents of self-regulation: A developmental perspective. *Developmental Psychology, 18,* 199–214.

Korkman, M., Liikanen, A., & Fellman, V. (1996). Neuropsychological consequences of very low birth weight and asphyxia at term: Follow-up until school-age. *Journal of Clinical and Experimental Neuropsychology, 18,* 220–233.

Koverola, C., Pound, J., Heger, A., & Lytle, C. (1993). Relationship of child sexual abuse to depression. *Child Abuse and Neglect, 17,* 393–400.

Kozulin, A. (1990). *Vygotsky's psychology: A biography of ideas.* Cambridge, MA: Harvard University Press.

Kozulin, A. (1998). *Psychological tools: A sociocultural approach to education.* Cambridge, MA: Harvard University Press.

Kramer, C. (1974). Women's speech: Separate but unequal? *Quarterly Journal of Speech, 60,* 14–24.

Krashen, S. (1999). What the research really says about structured English immersion. *Phi Delta Kappan, 80,* 705–706.

Krashen, S., Long, M., & Scarcella, R. (1982). Age, rate, and eventual attainment in second language acquisition. In S. Krashen, R. Scarcella, & M. Long (Eds.), *Child–adult differences in second language acquisition* (pp. 161–174). Rowley, MA: Newbury House.

Kraut, R., Scherlis, W., Mukhopadhyay, T., Manning, J., & Kiesler, S. (1996). The HomeNet field trial of residential Internet services. *Communications of the ACM, 39,* 55–63.

Krebs, D., & Gillmore, J. (1982). The relationship among the first stages of cognitive development, role-taking abilities, and moral development. *Child Development, 53,* 877–886.

Kreutzer, M. A., Leonard, C., & Flavell, J. H. (1975). An interview study of children's knowledge about memory. *Monographs of the Society for Research in Child Development, 40* (Serial No. 159).

Krevans, J., & Gibbs, J. C. (1996). Parents' use of inductive discipline: Relations to children's empathy and prosocial behavior. *Child Development, 67,* 3263–3277.

Krishner, H. S. (1995). *Classical aphasia syndromes.* New York: Marcel Dekker.

Kuhl, P. K., Andruski, J. E., Christovich, I. A., Christovich, L. A., Kozhevnikova, E. V., Ryskina, V. L., Stolyarova, E. I., Sundberg, U., & Lacerda, F. (1997). Cross-language analysis of phonetic units in language addressed to infants. *Science, 277,* 684–686.

Kuhn, D. (1992). Cognitive development. In M. H. Bornstein & M. E. Lamb (Eds.), *Developmental psychology: An advanced textbook* (3rd ed., pp. 211–272). Hillsdale, NJ: Erlbaum.

Kupersmidt, J. B., Briesler, P. C., DeRosier, M. E., Patterson, C. J., & Davis, P. W. (1995). Childhood aggression and peer relations in the context of family and neighborhood factors. *Child Development, 66,* 360–375.

Kupersmidt, J. B., & Coie, J. D. (1990). Preadolescent peer status, aggression, and school adjustment as predictors of externalizing problems in adolescence. *Child Development, 61,* 1350–1362.

Kurtz, B. E., Schneider, W., Carr, M., Borkowski, J. B., & Rellinger, E. (1990). Strategy instruction and attributional beliefs in West Germany and the United States: Do teachers foster metacognitive development? *Contemporary Educational Psychology, 15,* 268–283.

Labov, W. (1994). *The social stratification of English in New York City.* Washington, DC: Center for Applied Linguistics.

Labre, M.-P. (2002). Adolescent boys and the muscular male body ideal. *Journal of Adolescent Health, 30* (4, supplement), 233–242.

Ladd, G. W., Birch, S. H., & Buhs, E. S. (1999). Children's social and scholastic lives in kindergarten: Related spheres of influence? *Child Development, 70,* 1373–1400.

Lamaze, F. (1958). *Painless childbirth.* London: Burke.

Lamb, M. E. (1987a). Predictive implications of individual differences in attachment. *Journal of Consulting and Clinical Psychology, 55,* 817–824.

Lamb, M. E. (1987b). *The father's role: Cross-cultural perspectives.* Hillsdale, NJ: Erlbaum.

Lamb, M. E. (1998). Nonparental child care: Context, quality, correlates, and consequences. In W. Damon, I. E. Sigel, & K. A. Renninger (Eds.), *Handbook of child psychology: Vol 4. Child psychology in practice* (pp. 73–133). New York: Wiley.

Lamb, M. E. (1999). Noncustodial fathers and their impact on the children of divorce. In R. A. Thompson & P. R. Amato (Eds.), *The postdivorce family: Children, parenting, and society* (pp. 105–125). Thousand Oaks, CA: Sage.

Lamb, M. E., Hwang, C. P., Frodi, A., & Frodi, M. (1982). Security of mother– and father–infant attachment and its relation to sociability with strangers in traditional and non-traditional Swedish families. *Infant Behavior and Development, 5,* 355–367.

Lamb, M. E., Thompson, R. A., Gardner, W., & Charnov, E. L. (1985). *Infant–mother attachment: The origins and developmental significance of individual differences in strange situation behavior.* Hillsdale, NJ: Erlbaum.

Lamborn, S. D., Mounts, N. S., Steinberg, L., & Dornbusch, S. M. (1991). Patterns of competence and adjustment among adolescents from authoritative, authoritarian, indulgent, and neglectful families. *Child Development, 62,* 1049–1065.

Lamborn, S. D., & Steinberg, L. (1993). Emotional autonomy redux: Revisiting Ryan and Lynch. *Child Development, 64,* 483–499.

Lamorey, S., Robinson, B. E., Rowland, B. H., & Coleman, M. (1999). *Latchkey kids: Unlocking doors for children and their families.* Thousand Oaks, CA: Sage.

Lancy, D. F. (2002). Cultural constraints on children's play. In J. L. Roopnarine (Ed.), *Conceptual, social-cognitive, and contextual issues in the fields of play. Play & Culture Studies, Vol. 4* (pp. 53–60). Westport, CT: Ablex.

Langlois, J. H., Roggman, L. A., Casey, R. J., Ritter, J. M., Rieser-Danner, A., & Jenkins, V. Y. (1987). Infant preferences for attractive faces: Rudiments of a stereotype? *Developmental Psychology, 23,* 363–369.

Lanza, E. (1992). Can bilingual two-year-olds code-switch? *Journal of Child Language, 19,* 633–658.

Larivée, S., Normandeau, S., & Parent, S. (2000). The French connection: Some contributions of French-language research in the post-Piagetian era. *Child Development, 71,* 823–839.

Larkin, R. W. (1979). *Suburban youth in cultural crisis.* New York: Oxford University Press.

Larsen, J. M., & Robinson, C. C. (1989). Later effects of preschool on low-risk children. *Early Childhood Research Quarterly, 4,* 133–144.

Larson, J., & Lochman, J. E. (2002). *Helping schoolchildren cope with anger.* New York: Guilford Press.

Laumann-Billings, L., & Emery, R. E. (2000). Distress among young adults from divorced families. *Journal of Family Psychology, 14,* 671–688.

Lave, J., & Wenger, E. (1991). *Situated learning: Legitimate peripheral participation.* Cambridge, England: Cambridge University Press.

Lave, J., & Wenger, E. (1996). Practice, person, social world. In H. Daniels (Ed.), *An introduction to Vygotsky* (pp. 143–150). London: Routledge.

Leaper, C. (1994). Exploring the consequences of gender segregation on social relationships. In W. Damon (Ed.), *New directions for child development* (No. 65, pp. 67–86). San Francisco: Jossey-Bass.

Leaper, C., Anderson, K. J., & Sanders, P. (1998). Moderators of gender effects on parents' talk to their children: A meta-analysis. *Developmental Psychology, 34,* 3–28.

Leaper, C., Leve, L., Strasser, T., & Schwartz, R. (1995). Mother–child communication sequences: Play activity, child gender, and marital status effects. *Merrill-Palmer Quarterly, 41,* 307–321.

Leboyer, F. (1975). *Birth without violence.* New York: Knopf.

Lecanuet, J. (1998). Foetal responses to auditory and speech stimuli. In A. Slater (Ed.), *Perceptual development: Visual, auditory, and speech perception in infancy* (pp. 317–355). Hove, East Sussex, England: Psychology Press.

Lee, C. L., & Bates, J. E. (1985). Mother–child interactions at age two years and perceived difficult temperament. *Child Development, 56,* 1314–1325.

Lee, S. (1998). Mathematics learning and teaching in the school context: Reflections from cross-cultural comparisons. In S. G. Paris & H. M. Wellman (Eds.), *Global prospects for education: Development, culture, and schooling* (pp. 45–77). Washington, DC: American Psychological Association.

Lee, V. E., & Loeb, S. (2000). School size in Chicago Elementary Schools: Effects on teachers' attitudes and students' achievements. *American Educational Research Journal, 37,* 3–31.

LeFevre, J., & Bisanz, J. (1996). Multiple routes to solution of single-digit multiplication problems. *Journal of Experimental Psychology: General, 125,* 284–307.

Lehman, B. A. (1989, March 13). Spanking teaches the wrong lesson. *Boston Globe,* p. 27.

Lehman, J. S., & Smeeding, T. M. (1997). Neighborhood effects and federal policy. In J. Brooks-Gunn, G. J. Duncan, & J. L. Aber (Eds.), *Neighborhood poverty: Vol. I. Context and consequences for children* (pp. 251–278). New York: Russell Sage Foundation.

Leichtman, M. D., & Ceci, S. J. (1995). The effect of stereotypes and suggestions on preschoolers' reports. *Developmental Psychology, 31,* 568–578.

Lemaire, P., & Siegler, R. S. (1995). Four aspects of strategic change: Contributions to children's learning of multiplication. *Journal of Experimental Psychology: General, 124,* 83–98.

Lemoine, P., Harousseau, H., Borteyru, J. P., & Menuet, J. C. (1968). Les enfants de parents alcooliques: Anomalies observies à propos de 127 cas. [Children of alcoholic parents: Abnormalities observed in 127 cases.] *Ouest Medicine, 21,* 476–482. As cited in Mattson & Riley (1998).

Lenneberg, E. H. (1967). *Biological foundations of language.* New York: Wiley.

LeVay, S. (1993). *The sexual brain.* Cambridge, MT: MIT Press.

Leventhal, T., & Brooks-Gunn, J. (2000). The neighborhoods they live in: The effects of neighborhood residence on child and adolescent outcomes. *Psychological Bulletin, 126,* 309–337.

Levy, Y., Tennenbaum, A., & Ornoy, A. (2000). Spontaneous language of children with specific neurological syndromes. *Journal of Speech, Language, and Hearing Research, 43,* 351–365.

Lewinsohn, P. M., Rohde, P., & Seeley, J. R. (1993). Psychosocial characteristics of adolescents with a history of suicide attempt. *Journal of the American Academy of Child and Adolescent Psychiatry, 32,* 60–68.

Lewinsohn, P. M., Rohde, P., & Seeley, J. R. (1994). Psychosocial risk factors for future adolescent suicide attempts. *Journal of Consulting and Clinical Psychology, 62,* 297–305.

Lewis, M., & Brooks, J. (1978). Self-knowledge and emotional development. In M. Lewis & L. A. Rosenblum (Eds.), *The development of affect* (pp. 205–226). New York: Plenum.

Lewit, E. M., & Baker, L. S. (1995). School readiness. *The Future of Children, 5,* 128–139.

Lifton, B. J. (1994). *Journey of the adopted self: A quest for wholeness.* New York: Basic Books.

Lindberg, L. D., Ku, L., & Sonenstein, F. (2000). Adolescents' reports of reproductive health education, 1988 and 1995. *Family Planning Perspectives, 32*(5), 220–226.

Lindsey, E. W., Mize, J., & Pettit, G. S. (1997). Differential play patterns of mothers and fathers of sons and daughters: Implications for children's gender role development. *Sex Roles, 17,* 643–661.

Linnet, K. M., Dalsgaard, S., Obel, C., Wisborg, K., Henriksen, T. B., Rodriguez, A., Kotimaa, A., Moilanen, I., Thomsen, P. H., Olsen, J., & Jarvelin, M. (2003). Maternal lifestyle factors in pregnancy risk of attention deficit hyperactivity disorder and associated behaviors: Review of the current evidence. *American Journal of Psychiatry, 160,* 1028–1040.

Linver, M. R., Brooks-Gunn, J., & Kohen, D. E. (2002). Family processes as pathways from income to young children's development. *Developmental Psychology, 38,* 719–734.

Lipka, R. P., Hurford, D. P., & Litten, M. J. (1992). Self in school: Age and school experience effects. In R. P. Lipka & T. M. Brinthaupt (Eds.), *Self-perspectives across the life span* (Vol. 3, pp. 93–115). Albany: State University of New York Press.

Liptak, A. (2002, July 26). Judge orders abstinence program changed. *New York Times.* Retrieved January 6, 2003, from www.nytimes.com.

Li-Repac, D. C. (1982). *The impact of acculturation on the child-rearing attitudes and practices of Chinese-American families: Consequences for the attachment process.* Unpublished doctoral dissertation, University of California–Berkeley.

Lloyd, B., & Goodwin, R. (1993). Girls' and boys' use of directives in pretend play. *Social Development, 2,* 122–130.

Locke, J. L. (1993). *The child's path to spoken language.* Cambridge, MA: Harvard University Press.

Loeber, R., & Stouthamer-Loeber, M. (1998). Development of juvenile aggression and violence: Some common misconceptions and controversies. *American Psychologist, 53,* 242–259.

Loehlin, J. C. (1992). *Genes and environment in personality development.* Newbury Park, CA: Sage.

Loehlin, J. C., Horn, J. M., & Willerman, L. (1994). Differential inheritance of mental abilities in the Texas Adoption Project. *Intelligence, 19,* 325–336.

Loehlin, J. C., & Nichols, R. C. (1976). *Heredity, environment, and personality.* Austin: University of Texas Press.

Loftus, E. F., & Ketcham, K. (1994). *The myth of repressed memory.* New York: St. Martin's Press.

Lohmann, H., & Tomasello, M. (2003). Language and social understanding: Commentary on Nelson et al. *Human Development, 46,* 47–50.

Lonigan, C. J. (1994). Reading to preschoolers exposed: Is the emperor really naked? *Developmental Review, 14,* 303–323.

Lonigan, C. J., Fischel, J. E., Whitehurst, G. J., Arnold, D. S., & Valdez-Menchaca, M. C. (1992). The role of otitis media in the development of expressive language disorder. *Developmental Psychology, 28,* 430–440.

Lorenz, K. Z. (1973/1977). *Behind the mirror: A search for a natural history of human knowledge.* New York: Harcourt Brace Jovanovich.

Love, J. M., Kisker, E. E., Ross, C. M., Schochet, P. Z., Brooks-Gunn, J., Paulsell, D., Boller, K., Constantine, J., Vogel, C., Fuligni, A. A., & Brady-Smith, C. (2002). *Making a difference in the lives of infants and toddlers and their families: The impact of Early Head Start.* Department of Health and Human Services Document, Retrieved July 11, 2003, from www.headstartinfo.org/cgi-bin/pubcatstore.cfm.

Low, J. M. (1999). Differences in cognitive complexity of adolescents with foreclosed and achieved identity status. *Psychological Reports, 85,* 1093–1099.

Luecke-Aleksa, D., Andeerson, D. R., Collins, P. A., & Schmitt, K. L. (1995). Gender constancy and television viewing. *Developmental Psychology, 31,* 773–780.

Luhman, R. (1990). Appalachian English stereotypes: Language attitudes in Kentucky. *Language in Society, 19,* 331–348.

Luria, A. R. (1973). *The working brain: An introduction to neuropsychology.* New York: Basic Books.

Luthar, S. S., Cicchetti, D., & Becker, B. (2000). The construct of resilience: A critical evaluation and guidelines for future work. *Child Development, 71,* 543–562.

Luzadder, D., & Vaughan, K. (1999, December 12). Inside the Columbine investigation. Retrieved January 3, 2003, from http://denver.rockymountainnews.com.

Lykken, D. T. (2000). The causes and costs of crime and a controversial cure. *Journal of Personality, 68,* 559–605.

Lykken, D. T. (2001). Parental licensure. *American Psychologist, 56,* 885–894.

Lyons-Ruth, K., Connell, D. B., Grunebaum, H. U., & Botein, S. (1990). Infants at social risk: Maternal depression and family support services as mediators of infant development and security of attachment. *Child Development, 61,* 85–98.

Lyons-Ruth, K., Connell, D. B., Zoll, D., & Stahl, J. (1987). Infants at social risk: Relations among infant maltreatment, maternal behavior, and infant attachment behavior. *Developmental Psychology, 23,* 223–232.

Mabbott, D. J., & Bisanz, J. (in press). Developmental change and individual differences in children's multiplication. *Child Development.*

MacAulay, D. J. (1990). Classroom environment: A literature review. *Educational Psychology, 10,* 239–253.

Maccoby, E. E. (1998). *The two sexes: Growing up apart, coming together.* Boston: Harvard University Press.

Maccoby, E. E. (1999). The custody of children of divorcing families: Weighing the alternatives. In R. A. Thompson & P. R. Amato (Eds.), *The postdivorce family: Children, parenting, and society* (pp. 51–70). Thousand Oaks, CA: Sage.

Maccoby, E. E. (2000). Parenting and its effects on children: On reading and misreading behavior genetics. In S. T. Fiske, D. L. Schacter, & C. Zahn-Waxler (Eds.), *Annual Review of Psychology* (Vol. 51, pp. 1–27). Palo Alto, CA: Annual Reviews.

Maccoby, E. E., & Jacklin, C. N. (1974). *The psychology of sex differences.* Stanford, CA: Stanford University Press.

Maccoby, E. E., & Jacklin, C. N. (1987). Gender segregation in childhood. In E. H. Reese (Ed.), *Advances in child development and behavior* (Vol. 20, pp. 239–287). New York: Academic Press.

Maccoby, E. E., & Martin, J. A. (1983). Socialization in the context of the family: Parent–child interaction. In P. H. Mussen (Ed.), *Handbook of child psychology* (Vol. 4, pp. 1–101). New York: Wiley.

MacDonald, K. B., & Parke, R. D. (1986). Parent–child physical play: The effects of sex and age of children and parents. *Sex Roles, 15,* 367–378.

Machida, S., Taylor, A. R., & Kim, J. (2002). The role of maternal beliefs in predicting home learning activities in Head Start families. *Family Relations, 51,* 176–184.

MacLean, M., Bryant, P., & Bradley, L. (1987). Rhymes, nursery rhymes, and reading in early childhood. *Merrill-Palmer Quarterly, 33,* 255–281.

MacWhinney, B. (1992). Transfer and competition in second language learning. In R. J. Harris (Ed.), *Cognitive processing in bilinguals* (pp. 371–390). Amsterdam: Elsevier.

MacWhinney, B. (Ed.). (1987). *Mechanisms of language acquisition.* Hillsdale, NJ: Erlbaum.

MacWhinney, B. (Ed.). (1999). *The emergence of language.* Hillsdale, NJ: Erlbaum.

MacWhinney, B., & Chang, F. (1995). Connectionism and language learning. In C. A. Nelson (Ed.), *Minnesota symposium on child psychology: Vol 28. Basic and applied perspectives on learning, cognition, and development* (pp. 33–57). Mahwah, NJ: Erlbaum.

Maehr, M. L. (1991). The "psychological environment" of the school: A focus for school leadership. In P. Thurstone & P. Zodhiats (Eds.), *Advances in educational administration* (Vol. 2, pp. 51–81). Greenwich, CT: JAI Press.

Maes, H. H. M., Neale, M. C., & Eaves, L. J. (1997). Genetic and environmental factors in relative body weight and human adiposity. *Behavior Genetics, 27*(4), 325–351.

Magnusson, D. (1988). *Individual development from an interactional perspective: A longitudinal study.* Hillsdale, NJ: Erlbaum.

Main, M., & George, C. (1985). Responses of abused and disadvantaged toddlers to distress in agemates: A study in the day care setting. *Developmental Psychology, 21,* 407–412.

Main, M., & Hesse, E. (1990). Parents' unresolved traumatic experiences are related to infant disorganized attachment status: Is frightened and/or frightening parental behavior the linking mechanism? In M. T. Greenberg, D. Cicchetti, & E. M. Cummings (Eds.), *Attachment in the preschool years: Theory, research, and intervention* (pp. 161–182). Chicago: University of Chicago Press.

Main, M., Kaplan, N., & Cassidy, J. (1985). Security in infancy, childhood, and adulthood: A move to the level of representation. In I. Bretherton & E. Waters (Eds.), *Growing points of attachment theory and research. Monographs of the Society for Research in Child Development, 50* (Serial No. 209), 66–104.

Main, M., & Solomon, J. (1986). Discovery of an insecure–disorganized/disoriented attachment pattern. In T. B. Brazelton & M. W. Yogman (Eds.), *Affective development in infancy* (pp. 95–124). Norwood, NJ: Ablex.

Main, M., & Solomon, J. (1990). Procedures for identifying infants as disorganized/disoriented during the Ainsworth strange situation. In M. T. Greenberg, D. Cicchetti, & E. M. Cummings (Eds.), *Attachment in the preschool years: Theory, research, and intervention* (pp. 121–182). Chicago: University of Chicago Press.

Malamuth, N. M., & Impett, E. A. (2001). Research on sex in the media: What do we know about effects on children and adolescents? In D. G. Singer & J. L. Singer (Eds.), *Handbook of children and the media* (pp. 269–287). Thousand Oaks, CA: Sage Publications, Inc.

Mallon, G. P. (1998). Gay, lesbian and bisexual childhood and adolescent development: An ecological perspective. In G. Appleby & J. Anastas (Eds.), *Not just a passing phase: Social work with gay, lesbian, and bisexual persons.* New York: Columbia University Press. As cited in Hunter & Mallon (2000), pp. 232–233.

Mandel, D., Kemler Nelson, D. G., & Jusczyk, P. W. (1996). Infants remember the order of words in a spoken sentence. *Cognitive Development, 11,* 181–196.

Mantzicopoulos, P. (2003). Flunking kindergarten after Head Start: An inquiry into the contribution of contextual and individual variables. *Journal of Educational Psychology, 95,* 268–278.

Maratsos, M. (1983). Some current issues in the study of the acquisition of grammar. In J. H. Flavell & E. M. Markman (Eds.), *Handbook of child psychology: Vol. 3. Cognitive development* (pp. 707–786). New York: Wiley.

Maratsos, M., Kuczaj, S. A., Fox, D. E. C., & Chalkley, M. A. (1979). Some empirical studies in the acquisition of transformational relations: Passives, negatives and the past tense. In W. A. Collins (Ed.), *Children's language and communication* (pp. 1–45). Hillsdale, NJ: Erlbaum.

Maratsos, M., & Matheney, L. (1994). Language specificity and elasticity: Brain and clinical syndrome studies. *Annual Review of Psychology, 45,* 487–516.

Marble, M. (1995, January 4). Guidelines for pregnant women. *Women's Health Weekly,* pp. N10–12.

Marcia, J. E. (1966). Development and validation of ego identity status. *Journal of Personality and Social Psychology, 38,* 551–558.

Marcus, G. F., Pinker, S., Ullman, M., Hollander, M., Rosen, T. J., & Xu, F. (1992). Overrregularization in language acquisition. *Monographs of the Society for Research in Child Development, 57* (4, Serial No. 228).

Mares, M., & Woodard, E. H. (2001). Prosocial effects on children's social interactions. In D. G. Singer & J. L. Singer (Eds.), *Handbook of children and the media* (pp. 183–203). Thousand Oaks, CA: Sage.

Markman, E. M. (1977). Realizing that you don't understand: A preliminary investigation. *Child Development, 48,* 986–992.

Marshall, W. A., & Tanner, J. M. (1986). Puberty. In F. Falkner & J. M. Tanner (Eds.), *Human Growth* (2nd ed., Vol. 2, pp. 171–209). New York: Plenum.

Martin, C. L. (1994). Cognitive influences on the development and maintenance of gender segregation. In W. Damon (Ed.), *New directions for child development* (No. 65, pp. 35–51). San Francisco: Jossey-Bass.

Martin, C. L., Eisenbud, L., & Rose, H. (1995). Children's gender-based reasoning about toys. *Child Development, 66,* 1453–1471.

Martin, C. L., & Little, J. K. (1990). The relation of gender understanding to children's sex-typed preferences and gender stereotypes. *Child Development, 61,* 1427–1439.

Martin, G. B., & Clark, R. D. (1982). Distress crying in neonates: Species and peer specificity. *Developmental Psychology, 18,* 3–9.

Martin, J. A., Hamilton, B. E., Ventura, S. J., Menacker, F., & Park, M. M. (2002, Feb. 12). Births: Final data for 2000. *National vital statistics reports, 50*(5), 1–102. Retrieved March 27, 2003, from www.cdc.gov/nchs/data/nvsr50/nvsr50_05.pdf.

Martin, J. C. (1992). The effects of maternal use of tobacco products or amphetamines on offspring. In T. B. Sonderegger (Ed.), *Perinatal substance abuse: Research findings and clinical applications* (pp. 279–305). Baltimore: Johns Hopkins University Press.

Martin, M. O., Mullis, I. V. S., Gonzalez, E. J., Gregory, K. D., Smith, T. A., Chrostowski, S. J., Garden, R. A., & O'Conner, K. M. (2000). *TIMSS 1999: International science report.* Chestnut Hill, MA: International Study Center, Lynch School of Education, Boston College.

Martin, N. G., Eaves, L. J., Heath, A. C., Jardine, R., Feingold, L. M., & Eysenck, H. J. (1986). Transmission of social attitudes. *Proceedings of the National Academy of Sciences, USA, 83,* 4364–4368.

Martin, N. G., & Heath, A. C. (1993). The genetics of voting: An Australian twin-family study. *Behavior Genetics, 23,* 558.

Masataka, N. (1996). Perception of motherese in a signed language by 6-month-old deaf infants. *Developmental Psychology, 32,* 874–879.

Masataka, N. (1998). Perception of motherese in Japanese sign language by 6-month-old hearing infants. *Developmental Psychology, 34,* 241–246.

Mash, E. J., & Wolfe, D. A. (1999). *Abnormal child psychology.* Belmont, CA: Brooks/Cole.

Mason, C. A., Cauce, A. M., Gonzales, N., & Hiraga, Y. (1996). Neither too sweet nor too sour: Problem peers, maternal control, and problem behavior in African American adolescents. *Child Development, 67,* 2115–2130.

Masten, A. S. (2001). Ordinary magic: Resilience processes in development. *American Psychologist, 56,* 227–238.

Masters, M. S., & Sanders, B. (1993). Is the gender difference in mental rotation disappearing? *Behavior Genetics, 23,* 337–341.

Matthews, T. J., Menacher, F., & MacDorman, M. F. (2002). Infant mortality statistics from the 2000 period linked birth/infant death data set. *National Vital Statistics Reports, 50*(12). Hyattsville, MD: National Center for Health Statistics.

Mattson, S. N., & Riley, E. P. (1998). A review of the neurobehavioral deficits in children with fetal alcohol syndrome or prenatal exposure to alcohol. *Alcoholism: Clinical and Experimental Research, 22,* 279–294.

Maurer, D., & Salapatek, P. (1976). Developmental changes in the scanning of faces by young infants. *Child Development, 47,* 523–527.

Mayer, R. E., Lewis, A., & Hegarty, M. (1992). Mathematical misunderstandings: Qualitative reasoning about quantitative problems. In J. I. D. Campbell (Ed.), *Advances in psychology: Vol. 91. The nature and origins of mathematical skills* (pp. 137–153). Oxford, England: North-Holland.

Mayer, S., & Knutson, D. (1999). Does the timing of school affect how much children learn? In S. Mayer & P. Peterson (Eds.), *Earning and learning: How schools matter* (pp. 79–102). Washington, DC: Brookings Institution Press.

Mayes, L. C., & Bornstein, M. H. (1995). Information processing and developmental assessments in 3-month-old infants exposed prenatally to cocaine. *Pediatrics, 95,* 539–545.

Mayes, L. C., Carter, A. S., & Stubbe, D. (1993). Individual differences in exploratory behavior in the second year of life. *Infant Behavior and Development, 16,* 269–284.

Mayes, L. C., Granger, R. H., Frank, M. A., Schottenfeld, R., & Bornstein, M. (1993). Neurobehavioral profiles of infants exposed to cocaine prenatally. *Pediatrics, 91,* 778–783.

Mayo Clinic. (2003, March 17). HIV/AIDS. Retrieved March 21, 2003, from www.MayoClinic.com.

Mazzoni, G., & Memon, A. (2003). Imagination can create false autobiographical memories. *Psychological Science, 14,* 186–188.

McBride-Chang, C. (1996). Models of speech perception and phonological processing in reading. *Child Development, 67,* 1836–1856.

McCabe, A. E., & Siegel, L. S. (1987). The stability of training effects in young children's class inclusion reasoning. *Merrill-Palmer Quarterly, 33,* 187–194.

McCall, R. B., & Carriger, M. S. (1993). A meta-analysis of infant habituation and recognition memory performance as predictors of later IQ. *Child Development, 64,* 57–79.

McCartney, K., Harris, M. J., & Bernieri, F. (1990). Growing up and growing apart: A developmental meta-analysis of twin studies. *Psychological Bulletin, 107,* 226–237.

McCloskey, L. A., & Coleman, L. (1992). Difference without dominance: Children's talk in mixed- and same-sex dyads. *Sex Roles, 27,* 241–257.

McConaghy, M. J. (1979). Gender permanence and the genital basis of gender: Stages in the development of constancy of gender identity. *Child Development, 50,* 1223–1226.

McCord, J. (1983). A forty year perspective on effects of child abuse and neglect. *Child Abuse and Neglect, 7,* 265–270.

McCormick, M. C. (1985). The contribution of low birth weight to infant mortality and childhood morbidity. *New England Journal of Medicine, 312,* 82–90.

McGhee-Bidlack, B. (1991). The development of noun definitions: A metalinguistic analysis. *Journal of Child Languages, 18,* 417–434.

McGue, M., Bacon, S., & Lykken, D. T. (1993). Personality stability and change in early adulthood: A behavioral genetic analysis. *Developmental Psychology, 29,* 96–109.

McKey, R., Condelli, L., Ganson, H., et al. (1985). *The impact of Head Start on children, families, and communities* (Final report of the Head Start Evaluation, Synthesis, and Utilization Project). Washington, DC: U.S. Department of Health and Human Services.

McKusick, V. A. (1998). *Mendelian inheritance in man: A catalog of human genes and genetic disorders* (12th ed., Vols. 1–3). Baltimore: Johns Hopkins University Press.

McLanahan, S. S. (1997). Parent absence or poverty: Which matters more? In G. J. Duncan & J. Brooks-Gunn (Eds.), *Consequences of growing up poor* (pp. 35–48). New York: Russell Sage Foundation.

McLanahan, S. S. (1999). Father absence and the welfare of children. In E. M. Hetherington (Ed.), *Coping with divorce, single parenting, and remarriage: A risk and resiliency perspective* (pp. 117–145). Mahwah, NJ: Erlbaum.

McLanahan, S. S., & Sandefur, G. (1994). *Growing up with a single parent: What hurts, what helps.* Cambridge, MA: Harvard University Press.

McLaughlin, S. (1998). *Introduction to language development.* San Diego, CA: Singular Publishing Group.

McLoyd, V. C. (1995). Poverty, parenting, and policy: Meeting the support needs of poor parents. In H. E. Fitzgerald, B. M. Lester, & B. Zuckerman (Eds.), *Children of poverty: Research, health, and policy issues* (pp. 269–299). New York: Garland.

McLoyd, V. C. (1998). Socioeconomic disadvantage and child development. *American Psychologist, 53,* 185–204.

McLoyd, V. C., & Smith, J. (2002). Physical discipline and behavior problems in African American, European American, and Hispanic children: Emotional support as a moderator. *Journal of Marriage and the Family, 64,* 40–53.

McMahon, R. J., & Wells, K. C. (1998). Conduct problems. In E. J. Mash & R. A. Barkley (Eds.), *Treatment of childhood disorders* (pp. 111–207). New York: Guilford Press.

McNutt, S. W., Hu, Y., Schreiber, G. B., Crawford, P. B., Obarzanek, E., & Mellin, L. (1997). A longitudinal study of the dietary practices of black and white girls 9 and 10 years old at enrollment: The NHLBI Growth and Health study. *Journal of Adolescent Health, 20,* 27–37.

Mead, G. H. (1934). *Mind, self, and society from the standpoint of a social behaviorist.* Chicago: University of Chicago Press.

Means, M., & Voss, J. (1985). Star wars: A developmental study of expert and novice knowledge structures. *Memory and Language, 24,* 746–757.

Meins, E., Fernyhough, C., Wainwright, R., Gupta, M. D., Fradley, E., & Tuckey, M. (2002). Maternal mind-mindedness and attachment security as predictors of theory of mind understanding. *Child Development, 73,* 1715–1726.

Meltzoff, A. N. (1990). Foundations for developing a concept of self: The role of imitation in relating self to other and the value of social mirroring, social modeling, and self practice in infancy. In D. Cicchetti & M. Beeghly (Eds.), *The self in transition: Infancy to childhood* (pp. 139–164). Chicago: University of Chicago Press.

Meltzoff, A. N., & Borton, R. W. (1979). Intermodal matching by human neonates. *Nature, 282,* 403–404.

Meltzoff, A. N., & Moore, M. K. (1983). Newborn infants imitate adult facial gestures. *Child Development, 54,* 702–709.

Meltzoff, A. N., & Moore, M. K. (1989). Imitation in newborn infants: Exploring the range of gestures imitated and the underlying mechanisms. *Developmental Psychology, 25,* 954–962.

Meyer, D. R. (1999). Compliance with child support orders in paternity and divorce cases. In R. A. Thompson & P. R. Amato (Eds.), *The postdivorce family: Children, parenting, and society* (pp. 127–157). Thousand Oaks, CA: Sage.

Meyer-Bahlburg, H. F. L., Ehrhardt, A. A., Rosen, L. R., Gruen, R. S., Veridiano, N. P., Vann, F. H., & Neuwalder, H. F. (1995). Prenatal estrogens and the development of homosexual orientation. *Developmental Psychology, 31,* 12–21.

Michaels, S. (1991). The dismantling of narrative. In A. McCabe & C. Peterson (Eds.), *Developing narrative structure* (pp. 303–351). Hillsdale, NJ: Erlbaum.

Mick, E., Biederman, J., Faraone, S. V., Sayer, J., & Kleinman, S. (2002). Case-control study of attention-deficit hyperactivity disorder and maternal smoking, alcohol use and drug use during pregnancy. *Journal of the American Academy of Child and Adolescent Psychiatry, 41*(4), 378–385.

Miele, F. (1995). *Skeptic Magazine* interview with Robert Sternberg on *The Bell Curve. Skeptic, 3,* 72–80.

Miller, B. C., Xitao, F., Christensen, M., Grotevant, H. D., & van Dulmen, M. (2000). Comparisons of adopted and nonadopted adolescents in a large, nationally representative sample. *Child Development, 71,* 1458–1473.

Miller, G. A. (1956). The magical number seven, plus or minus two: Some limits on our capacity for processing information. *Psychological Review, 63,* 81–97.

Miller, K. F., Smith, C. M., Zhu, J., & Zhang, H. (1995). Preschool origins of cross-national differences in mathematical competence: The role of number-naming systems. *Psychological Science, 6,* 56–60.

Miller, P. A., Eisenberg, N., Fabes, R. A., & Shell, R. (1996). Relations of moral reasoning and vicarious emotion to young children's prosocial behavior toward peers and adults. *Developmental Psychology, 32,* 210–219.

Miller, P. H., & Seier, W. L. (1994). Strategy utilization deficiencies in children: When, where, and why. In H. W. Reese (Ed.), *Advances in child development and behavior* (Vol. 25, pp. 107–156). New York: Academic Press.

Minami, M. (2001). Maternal styles of narrative elicitation and the development of children's narrative skill: A study on parental scaffolding. *Narrative Inquiry, 11,* 55–80.

Minami, M., & McCabe, A. (1990). Haiku as a discourse regulation device: A stanza analysis of Japanese children's personal narratives. *Language in Society, 20,* 577–599.

Minton, C., Kagan, J., & Levine, J. (1971). Maternal control and obedience in the two-year-old. *Child Development, 42,* 1873–1894.

Moely, B. E., Santulli, K. A., & Obach, M. S. (1995). Strategy instruction, metacognition, and motivation in the elementary school classroom. In F. E. Weinert & W. Schneider (Eds.), *Memory performance and competencies: Issues in growth and development* (pp. 301–322). Hillsdale, NJ: Erlbaum.

Moerk, E. L. (1992). *A first language taught and learned.* Baltimore: Paul H. Brooks.

Moerk, E. L. (2000). *The guided acquisition of first language skills.* Stamford, CT: Ablex.

Moffitt, T. E., Caspi, A., Dickson, N., Silva, P., & Stanton, W. (1996). Childhood-onset versus adolescent-onset antisocial conduct problems in males: Natural history from ages 3 to 18 years. *Development and Psychopathology, 8,* 399–424.

Mohanty, A. K., & Perregaux, C. (1997). Language acquisition and bilingualism. In J. W. Berry, P. R. Dasen, & T. S. Saraswathi (Eds.), *Handbook of cross-cultural psychology: Vol 2. Basic processes and human development* (2nd ed., pp. 217–253). Boston: Allyn & Bacon.

Moir, D. D. (1986). *Pain relief in labour: A handbook for midwives* (5th ed.). Edinburgh: Churchill Livingstone.

Molnar, J., Roth, W., & Klein, T. (1990). Constantly compromised: The impact of homelessness on children. *Journal of Social Issues, 46,* 109–124.

Money, J., & Ehrhardt, A. A. (1972). *Man and woman: Boy and girl.* Baltimore, MD: Johns Hopkins University Press.

Montague, D. P. F., & Walker-Andrews, A. S. (2001). Peekaboo: A new look at infants' perception of emotion expressions. *Developmental Psychology, 37,* 826–838.

Montemayor, R., & Brownlee, J. (1987). Fathers, mothers and adolescents: Gender-based differences in parental roles during adolescence. *Journal of Youth and Adolescence, 16,* 281–291.

Montgomery, J. W. (1995). Sentence comprehension in children with specific language impairment: The role of phonological working memory. *Journal of Speech and Hearing Research, 38,* 187–199.

Moore, D. S., Spence, M. J., & Katz, G. S. (1997). Six-month-olds' categorization of natural infant-directed utterances. *Developmental Psychology, 33,* 980–989.

Moore, K. L., & Persaud, T. V. N. (1998). *The developing human: Clinically oriented embryology* (6th ed.). Philadelphia: W. B. Saunders.

Moran, P. B., & Eckenrode, J. (1992). Protective personality characteristics among adolescent victims of maltreatment. *Child Abuse and Neglect, 16,* 743–754.

Morgan, J., Bonamo, K. M., & Travis, L. L. (1995). Negative evidence on negative evidence. *Developmental Psychology, 31,* 180–197.

Morgan, P. (1998). *Adoption and the care of children.* London: IEA Health and Welfare Unit.

Morrison, F. J., Griffith, E. M., & Alberts, D. M. (1997). Nature–nurture in the classroom: Entrance age, school readiness, and learning in children. *Developmental Psychology, 33,* 254–262.

Mott, F. L., Kowaleski-Jones, L., & Menaghan, E. G. (1997). Parental absence and child behavior: Does a child's gender make a difference? *Journal of Marriage and the Family, 59,* 103–118.

Mueller, E., & Silverman, N. (1989). Peer relations in maltreated children. In D. Cicchetti & V. Carlson (Eds.), *Child maltreatment: Theory and research on the causes and consequences of child abuse and neglect* (pp. 529–578). New York: Cambridge University Press.

Mullis, I. V. S., Martin, M. O., Beaton, A. E., Gonzalez, E. J., Kelly, D. L., & Smith, T. A. (1998). *Mathematics and science achievement in the final year of secondary school: IEA's third international mathematics and science study (TIMSS).* Chestnut Hill, MA: Center for the Study of Testing, Evaluation, and Educational Policy, Boston College.

Mullis, I. V. S., Martin, M. O., Gonzalez, E. J., Gregory, K. D., Garden, R. A., O'Conner, K. M., Chrostowski, S. J., & Smith, T. A. (2000). *TIMSS 1999: International mathematics report.* Chestnut Hill, MA: International Study Center, Lynch School of Education, Boston College.

Mumme, D. L., & Fernald, A. (2003). The infant as onlooker: Learning from emotional reactions observed in a television scenario. *Child Development, 74,* 221–237.

Munroe, R. H., Shimmin, H. S., & Munroe, R. L. (1984). Gender understanding and sex role preferences in four cultures. *Developmental Psychology, 20,* 673–682.

Myers, N. A., Perris, E. E., & Speaker, C. (1994). Fifty months of memory: Longitudinal study in early childhood. *Memory, 2,* 385–415.

Naeye, R., & Peters, E. (1984). Mental development of children whose mothers smoked during pregnancy. *Obstetrics and Gynecology, 64,* 601–607.

Naigles, L., & Gelman, S. A. (1995). Overextensions in comprehension and production revisited: Preferential-looking in a study of *dog, cat,* and *cow. Journal of Child Language, 22,* 19–46.

Naigles, L., & Hoff-Ginsburg, E. (1995). Input to verb learning: Evidence for the plausibility of syntactic bootstrapping. *Developmental Psychology, 31,* 827–837.

Náñez, J. E., & Yonas, A. (1994). Effects of luminance and texture motion on infant defensive reactions to optical collision. *Infant Behavior and Development, 17,* 165–174.

Nantais, K. M., & Schellenberg, E. G. (1999). The Mozart effect: An artifact of preference. *Psychological Science, 10,* 370–373.

Nash, M. R., Zivney, O. A., & Hulsey, T. (1993). Characteristics of sexual abuse associated with greater psychological impairment among children. *Child Abuse and Neglect, 17,* 401–408.

Näslund, B., Persson-Blennow, I., McNeil, T. F., Kaij, L., & Malmquist-Larsson, A. (1984). Deviations on exploration, attachment, and fear of strangers in high-risk and control infants at one year of age. *American Journal of Orthopsychiatry, 54,* 569–577.

Nathanielsz, P. W. (1992). *Life before birth: The challenges of fetal development.* New York: Freeman.

National Association for the Education of Young Children. (2003). Retrieved January 12, 2003, from www.naeyc.org/accreditation/naeyc_accred/info_general-faq3.asp.

National Center for Biotechnology Information. (2003). Retrieved March 21, 2003, from www.ncbi.nlm.nih.gov.

National Center for Children in Poverty. (1996). *One in four: America's youngest poor.* New York: Columbia University School of Public Health.

National Center for Health Statistics. (2000a). *Adolescent health chartbook (DHHS publication No. 2000-1232-1).* Hyattsville, MD: U.S. Department of Health and Human Services.

National Center for Health Statistics. (2000b). *National health and nutrition examination survey: Clinical growth charts.* Retrieved October 21, 2002, from www.cdc.gov/nchs/about/major/nhanes/growthcharts/clinical_charts.htm#clin1.

National Center for Health Statistics. (2002a). *Overweight prevalence.* Retrieved March 28, 2003, from www.cdc.gov/nchs/fastats/overwt.htm.

National Center for Health Statistics. (2002b). *Prevalence of overweight among children and adolescents: United States, 1999–2000.* Retrieved March 28, 2003, from www.cdc.gov/nchs/products/pubs/pubd/hestats/overwght99.htm.

National Center for Health Statistics. (2002c, December 18). New birth report shows more moms get prenatal care. *Health & Human Services News.* Retrieved March 27, 2003, from www.cdc.gov/nchs/releases/02news/precare.htm.

National Center for Health Statistics in collaboration with the National Center for Chronic Disease Prevention and Health Promotion. (2000). *CDC Growth Charts: United States.* Retrieved from www.cdc.gov/nchs/about/major/nhanes/growthcharts/charts.htm.

National Education Goals Panel. (1999). *The National Education Goals report: Building a nation of learners.* Washington, DC: U.S. Government Printing Office.

National Institute on Drug Abuse. (2001). Pregnancy and drug use trends. *NIDA InfoFax.* Retrieved March 3, 2002, from www.nida.nih.gov/infofax/pregnancytrends.html.

Naus, M. J., Ornstein, P. A., & Aivano, S. (1977). Developmental changes in memory: The effects of processing time and rehearsal instructions. *Journal of Experimental Child Psychology, 23,* 237–251.

Neisser, U. (1998). *The rising curve: Long-term gains in IQ and related measures.* Washington, DC: American Psychological Association.

Neisser, U., Boodoo, G., Bouchard, T. J., Boykin, A. W., Brody, N., Ceci, S. J., Halpern, D. F., Loehlin, J. C., Perloff, R., Sternberg, R. J., & Urbina, S. (1996). Intelligence: Knowns and unknowns. *American Psychologist, 51,* 77–101.

Neitzel, C., & Stright, A. D. (2003). Mothers' scaffolding of children's problem solving: Establishing a foundation of academic self-regulatory competence. *Journal of Family Psychology, 17,* 147–159.

Nelson, C. A. (2001). The development and neural bases of face recognition. *Infant and Child Development 10*(1–2), 3–18.

Nelson, C. A., & Horowitz, F. D. (1983). The perception of facial expressions and stimulus motion by two- and five-month-old infants using holographic stimuli. *Child Development, 54,* 868–877.

Nelson, K. (1973). Structure and strategy in learning to talk. *Monographs of the Society for Research in Child Development, 38* (Serial No. 149).

Nelson, K. (1986). *Event knowledge: Structure and function in development.* Hillsdale, NJ: Erlbaum.

Nelson, K. (1993). The psychological and social origins of autobiographical memory. *Psychological Science, 4,* 7–14.

Nelson, K. B., Grether, J. K., Dambrosia, J. M., Croen, L. A., Dickens, B. F., Hansen, R. L., & Phillips, T. M. (2000, May). Neuropeptides and neurotrophins in neonatal blood of children with autism, mental retardation, or cerebral palsy. Abstract published in the proceedings of the annual meeting of the American Association of Neurology, San Diego, CA.

Nelson, K., Hampson, J., & Shaw, L. K. (1993). Nouns in early lexicons: Evidence, explanations and implications. *Journal of Child Language, 20,* 61–84.

Nelson, K., Skwerer, D. P., Goldman, S., Henseler, S., Presler, N., & Walkenfeld, F. F. (2003). Entering a community of minds: An experiential approach to "theory of mind." *Human Development, 46,* 24–46.

Nelson, N. M., Enkin, M. W., Saigel, S., Bennett, K. J., Milner, R., & Sackett, D. L. (1980). A randomized clinical trial of the Leboyer approach to childbirth. *New England Journal of Medicine, 299,* 655–660.

Nettlebladt, P., Fagerstrom, C., & Udderberg, N. (1976). The significance of reported childbirth pain. *Journal of Psychosomatic Research, 20,* 215–221.

New York Times. (2001). Shooting at California school leaves 2 dead and 13 hurt. Retrieved March 6, 2001, from www.nytimes.com/2001/03/06/national/06SHOO.html.

Newburger, E. C. (2001). Home computers and Internet use in the United States: August 2000. *Current Population Reports.* Washington, DC: U.S. Census Bureau. Retrieved July 8, 2002, from www.census.gov.

Newman, D. L., Caspi, A., Moffitt, T. E., & Silva, P. A. (1997). Antecedents of adult interpersonal functioning: Effects of individual differences in age 3 temperament. *Developmental Psychology, 33,* 206–217.

Newman, D. M. (1999). *Sociology of families.* Thousand Oaks, CA: Pine Forge Press.

Newport, E. L. (1990). Maturational constraints on language learning. *Cognitive Science, 14,* 11–28.

Newsom, C. (1998). Autistic disorder. In E. J. Mash & R. A. Barkley (Eds.), *Treatment of childhood disorders* (2nd ed., pp. 416–467). New York: Guilford Press.

Newton, R. W., & Hunt, L. P. (1984). Psychosocial stress in pregnancy and its relation to low birth weight. *British Medical Journal, 288,* 1191–1194.

NICHD Early Child Care Research Network. (1997). The effects of infant child care on infant–mother attachment security: Results of the NICHD study of early child care. *Child Development, 68,* 860–879.

NICHD Early Child Care Research Network. (1998). Early child care and self-control, compliance, and problem behavior at twenty-four and thirty-six months. *Child Development, 69,* 1145–1170.

NICHD Early Child Care Research Network. (2000). The relation of child care to cognitive and language development. *Child Development, 71,* 960–980.

NICHD Early Child Care Research Network. (2001). Child-care and family predictors of preschool attachment and stability from infancy. *Developmental Psychology, 37,* 847–862.

NICHD Early Child Care Research Network. (2002). Child-care structure → process → outcome: Direct and indirect effects of child-care quality on young children's development. *Psychological Science, 13,* 199–206.

NICHD Early Child Care Research Network. (2003a). Do children's attention processes mediate the link between family predictors and school readiness? *Developmental Psychology, 39,* 581–593.

NICHD Early Child Care Research Network. (2003b). Does quality of child care affect child outcomes at age 4½? *Developmental Psychology, 39,* 451–469.

Nichols, R. C. (1978). Twin studies of ability, personality, and interests. *Homo, 29,* 158–173.

Nicolosi, J., & Byrd, A. D. (2002). A critique of Bem's "exotic becomes erotic" theory of sexual orientation development. *Psychological Reports, 90,* 931–946.

Niedzwienska, A. (2003). Distortion of autobiographical memories. *Applied Cognitive Psychology, 17,* 81–91.

Nottelmann, E. D., Susman, E. J., Blue, J. H., Inoff-Germain, G., Dorn, L. D., Loriaux, D. L., Cutler, G. B., & Chrousos, G. P. (1987). Gonadal and adrenal hormone correlates of adjustment in early adolescence. In R. M. Lerner & T. T. Foch, *Biological–psychosocial interactions in early adolescence.* Hillsdale, NJ: Erlbaum.

Nucci, L. P. (1996). Morality and the personal sphere of action. In E. Reed, E. Turiel, & T. Brown (Eds.), *Values and knowledge* (pp. 41–60). Hillsdale, NJ: Erlbaum.

Nurnberger, J. I., & Gershon, E. S. (1992). Genetics. In E. S. Paykel (Ed.), *Handbook of affective disorders* (2nd ed., pp. 131–148). New York: Guilford Press.

O'Connor, T. G., & Croft, C. M. (2001). A twin study of attachment in preschool children. *Child Development, 72,* 1501–1511.

O'Reilly, A. W. (1995). Using representations: Comprehension and production of actions with imagined objects. *Child Development, 66,* 999–1010.

Oetting, J. B. (2003a). Dialect speakers. In R. Kent (Ed.), *MIT encyclopedia of communication sciences and disorders.* Cambridge, MA: MIT Press.

Oetting, J. B. (2003b). Dialect vs. disorder. In R. Kent (Ed.), *MIT encyclopedia of communication sciences and disorders.* Cambridge, MA: MIT Press.

Oetting, J. B., & McDonald, J. L. (2001). Nonmainstream dialect use and specific language impairment. *Journal of Speech, Language, and Hearing Research, 44,* 207–223.

Olds, D. (1997). Tobacco exposure and impaired development: A review of the evidence. *Mental Retardation and Developmental Disabilities Research Reviews, 3,* 257–269.

Ollendick, T. H., Weist, M. D., Borden, M. G., & Greene, R. W. (1992). Sociometric status and academic, behavioral, and psychological adjustment: A five-year longitudinal study. *Journal of Consulting and Clinical Psychology, 60,* 80–87.

Oller, D. K., & Eilers, R. E. (1988). The role of audition in infant babbling. *Child Development, 59,* 441–449.

Onwuegbuzie, A. J., & Daley, C. E. (2001). Racial differences in IQ revisited: A synthesis of nearly a century of research. *Journal of Black Psychology, 27,* 209–220.

Opper, S. (1977). Concept development in Thai urban and rural children. In P. R. Dasen (Ed.), *Piagetian psychology: Cross-cultural contributions* (pp. 89–122). New York: Gardner Press.

Organisation for Economic Cooperation and Development. (2002). OECD health data 2002: Frequently asked data (Table 2). Retrieved March 27,

2003, from www.oecd.org/EN/document/0,,EN-document-684-5-no-1-29041-0,00.html.

Ornstein, P. A., Naus, M. J., & Liberty, C. (1975). Rehearsal and organizational processes in children's memory. *Child Development, 46,* 818–830.

Orr, J. E., & Hakuta, K. (2000). Inadequate conclusions from an inadequate assessment: What can SAT-9 scores tell us about the impact of Proposition 227 in California? *Bilingual Research Journal, 24,* 141–155.

Osofsky, J. D. (1999). The impact of violence on children. *The Future of Children, 9,* 33–49.

Owens, E. B., Hinshaw, S. P., Arnold, L. E., Cantwell, D. P., Elliott, G., Hechtman, L., Jensen, P. S., Newcorn, J. H., Severe, J. B., Vitiello, B., Kraemer, H. C., Abikoff, H. B., Conners, C. K., Greenhill, L. L., Hoza, B., March, J. S., Pelham, W. E., Swanson, J. M., & Wells, K. C. (2003). Which treatment for whom for ADHD? Moderators of treatment response in the MTA. *Journal of Consulting and Clinical Psychology, 71,* 540–552.

Oyserman, D., Coon, H. M., & Kemmelmeier, M. (2002). Rethinking individualism and collectivism: Evaluation of theoretical assumptions and meta-analyses. *Psychological Bulletin, 128,* 3–72.

Paik, H., & Comstock, G. (1994). The effects of television violence on antisocial behavior: A meta-analysis. *Communication Research, 21,* 516–546.

Paik, J. H., & Mix, K. S. (2003). U.S. and Korean children's comprehension of fraction names: A reexamination of cross-national differences. *Child Development, 74,* 144–154.

Pam, A., Kemker, S. S., Ross, C. A., & Golden, R. (1996). The "equal environments assumption" in MZ–DZ twin comparisons: An untenable premise of psychiatric genetics? *Acta Geneticae Medicae et Gemellologiae, 45*(3), 349–360.

Pan, H. W. (1994). Children's play in Taiwan. In J. L. Roopnarine, J. E. Johnson, & F. H. Hooper (Eds.), *Children's play in diverse cultures* (pp. 31–50). Albany, NY: State University of New York Press.

Panneton, R. K. (1985). *Prenatal auditory experience with melodies: Effects on postnatal auditory preferences in human newborns.* Unpublished doctoral dissertation, University of North Carolina at Greensboro. As cited in Aslin (1987).

Parke, R. D. (1996). *Fatherhood.* Cambridge, MA: Harvard University Press.

Parke, R. D., & Buriel, R. (1998). Socialization in the family: Ethnic and ecological perspectives. In W. Damon & N. Eisenberg (Eds.), *Handbook of child psychology: Vol. 3. Social, emotional, and personality development* (pp. 463–552). New York: Wiley.

Parke, R. D., & Suomi, S. (1981). Adult male–infant relationships: Human and nonhuman primate evidence. In K. Immelman, G. Barlow, M. Main, & L. Petrinovitch (Eds.), *Behavioral development: The Bielefeld Interdisciplinary Project* (pp. 700–725). New York: Cambridge University Press.

Parker, F. L., Boak, A. Y., Griffin, K. W., Ripple, C., & Peay, L. (1999). Parent–child relationship, home learning environment, and school readiness. *School Psychology Review, 28,* 413–425.

Parten, M. B. (1932). Social participation among pre-school children. *Journal of Abnormal and Social Psychology, 27,* 243–269.

Parvanta, I., Sherry, B., & Yip, R. (2000). Nutrition: Public health importance. *Child Health* (no volume number), 321–333. Retrieved March 28, 2003, from www.cdc.gov/nccdphp/drh/datoact/pdf/Chlt6.pdf.

Pastor, P. N., Makuc, D. M., Reuben, C., & Xia, H. (2002). Chartbook on trends in the health of Americans. *Health, United States, 2002.* Hyattsville, MD: National Center for Health Statistics. Retrieved October 15, 2002, from www.cdc.gov/nchs/hus.htm.

Patterson, C. J. (1992). Children of lesbian and gay parents. *Child Development, 63,* 1025–1042.

Patterson, C. J. (1995). Sexual orientation and human development: An overview: *Developmental Psychology, 31,* 3–11.

Patterson, G. R. (1995). Coercion—a basis for early age of onset for arrest. In J. McCord (Ed.), *Coercion and punishment in long-term perspective* (pp. 81–105). New York: Cambridge University Press.

Patterson, G. R. (1997). Performance models for parenting: A social interactional perspective. In J. E. Grusec & L. Kuczynski (Eds.), *Parenting and children's internalization of values* (pp. 193–226). New York: Wiley.

Patterson, G. R., Capaldi, D., & Bank, L. (1991). An early starter model for predicting delinquency. In D. J. Pepler & K. H. Rubin (Eds.), *The develop-*

ment and treatment of childhood aggression (pp. 139–168). Hillsdale, NJ: Erlbaum.

Patterson, G. R., & Fisher, P. A. (2002). Recent developments in our understanding of parenting: Bidirectional effects, causal models, and the search for parsimony. In M. H. Bornstein (Ed.), *Handbook of parenting* (2nd ed., pp. 59–88). Mahwah, NJ: Erlbaum.

Patterson, G. R., Reid, J. B., & Dishion, T. J. (1992). *Antisocial boys.* Eugene, OR: Castalia.

Pear, R. (1996, March 17). Many states fail to fulfill child welfare. *New York Times.* Retrieved August 2, 2002, from www.nytimes.com.

Peck, S. D. (2003). Measuring sensitivity moment-by-moment: A microanalytic look at the transmission of attachment. *Attachment & Human Development, 5,* 38–63.

Pedersen, N. L. (1993). Genetic and environmental continuity and change in personality. In T. J. Bouchard, Jr. & P. Propping (Eds.), *Twins as a tool of behavioral genetics* (pp. 147–162). West Sussex, England: Wiley.

Pedro-Carroll, J. (2001). The promotion of wellness in children and families: Challenges and opportunities. *American Psychologist, 56,* 993–1004.

Peisner-Feinberg, E. S., Burchinal, M. R., Clifford, R. M., Culkin, M. L., Howes, C., Kagan, S. L., & Yazejian, N. (2001). The relation of preschool child-care quality to children's cognitive and social developmental trajectories through second grade. *Child Development, 72,* 1534–1553.

Pelton, L. (1989). *For reasons of poverty: A critical analysis of the public child welfare system in the United States.* New York: Praeger.

Pennington, B. F., Moon, J., Edgin, J., Stedron, J., & Nadel, L. (2003). The neuropsychology of Down syndrome: Evidence for hippocampal dysfunction. *Child Development, 74,* 75–93.

Perez, M., Voelz, Z. R., Pettit, J. W., & Joiner, T. E., Jr. (2002). The role of acculturative stress and body dissatisfaction in predicting bulimic symptomology across ethnic groups. *International Journal of Eating Disorders, 31,* 442–454.

Perez, W., & Padilla, A. M. (2000). Cultural orientation across three generations of Hispanic adolescents. *Hispanic Journal of Behavioral Sciences, 22,* 390–398.

Perlmann, R. Y., & Gleason, J. B. (1994). The neglected role of fathers in children's communicative development. *Seminars in Speech and Language, 14,* 314–324.

Perner, J. (1991). *Understanding the representational mind.* Cambridge, MA: MIT Press.

Perry, D. G., Perry, L. C., & Rasmussen, P. (1986). Cognitive social learning mediators of aggression. *Child Development, 57,* 700–711.

Peskin, J. (1992). Ruse and representations: On children's ability to conceal information. *Developmental Psychology, 28,* 84–89.

Peterson, C., & McCabe, A. (1983). *Developmental psycholinguistics: Three ways of looking at a child's narrative.* New York: Plenum.

Peterson, L. (1982). An alternative perspective to norm-based explanations of modeling and children's generosity: A reply to Lipscomb, Larrieu, McAllister, and Bregman. *Merrill-Palmer Quarterly, 28,* 283–290.

Pettit, G. S., Laird, R. D., Bates, J. E., & Dodge, K. A. (1997). Patterns of after-school care in middle childhood: Risk factors and developmental outcomes. *Merrill-Palmer Quarterly, 43,* 515–538.

Phinney, J. (1989). Stages of ethnic identity in minority group adolescents. *Journal of Early Adolescence, 9,* 34–49.

Phinney, J. S. (1990). Ethnic identity in adolescents and adults: Review of research. *Psychological Bulletin, 108,* 499–514.

Phinney, J. S. (2003). Ethnic identity and acculturation. In K. M. Chun, P. B. Organista, & G. Marín (Eds.), *Acculturation: Advances in theory, measurement, and applied research* (pp. 63–81). Washington, DC: American Psychological Association.

Phinney, J. S., Cantu, C. L., & Kurtz, D. A. (1997). Ethnic and American identity as predictors of self-esteem among African American, Latino, and white adolescents. *Journal of Youth and Adolescence, 26,* 165–185.

Phinney, J. S., Ong, A., & Madden, T. (2000). Cultural values and intergenerational value discrepancies in immigrant and non-immigrant families. *Child Development, 71,* 528–539.

Piaget, J. (1930). *The child's conception of physical causality.* New York: Harcourt, Brace & World. (Original work published in 1926.)

Piaget, J. (1951a). *Play, dreams, and imitation in childhood.* New York: Norton.

Piaget, J. (1951b). *The child's conception of the world.* New York: Harcourt, Brace & World.

Piaget, J. (1952a). *The child's conception of number* (C. Gattegno & F. M. Hodgson, Trans.). London: Routledge & Paul.

Piaget, J. (1952b). *The origins of intelligence in children* (M. Cook, Trans.). New York: International Universities Press.

Piaget, J. (1954a). *The construction of reality in the child* (M. Cook, Trans.). New York: Basic Books.

Piaget, J. (1954b). *The origins of intelligence.* New York: Basic Books.

Piaget, J. (1969). *The child's conception of time.* London: Routledge & Kegan Paul.

Piaget, J. (1970). *The child's conception of movement and speed.* London: Routledge & Kegan Paul.

Piaget, J. (1971). *Biology and knowledge* (B. Walsh, Trans.). Chicago: University of Chicago Press.

Piaget, J. (1985). *The equilibration of cognitive structures.* Chicago: University of Chicago Press.

Piaget, J., & Inhelder, B. (1948/1956). *The child's conception of space.* London: Routledge & Kegan Paul. (Original work published in 1948.)

Piaget, J., & Inhelder, B. (1974). *The child's construction of quantities: Conservation and atomism* (A. J. Pomerans, Trans.). London: Routledge & Kegan Paul.

Pinderhughes, E. E., Dodge, K. A., Bates, J. E., Pettit, G. S., & Zelli, A. (2000). Discipline responses: Influences of parents' socioeconomic status, ethnicity, beliefs about parenting, stress, and cognitive–emotional processes. *Journal of Family Psychology, 14,* 380–400.

Pine, J. M. (1995). Variation in vocabulary development as a function of birth order. *Child Development, 66,* 272–281.

Pinker, S. (1987). The bootstrapping problem in language acquisition. In B. MacWhinney (Ed.), *Mechanisms of language acquisition* (pp. 399–441). Hillsdale, NJ: Erlbaum.

Pinker, S. (1994). *The language instinct.* New York: Morrow.

Plomin, R. (1986). *Development, genetics, and psychology.* Hillsdale, NJ: Erlbaum.

Plomin, R. (1990). *Nature and nurture: An introduction to behavior genetics.* Pacific Grove, CA: Brooks/Cole.

Plomin, R. (1994). *Genetics and experience: The interplay between nature and nurture.* Thousand Oaks, CA: Sage.

Plomin, R., Corley, R., DeFries, J. C., & Fulker, D. W. (1990). Individual differences in television viewing in early childhood: Nature as well as nurture. *Psychological Science, 1,* 371–377.

Plomin, R., & DeFries, J. C. (1998). The genetics of cognitive abilities and disabilities. *Scientific American, 278,* 62–69.

Plomin, R., Emde, R. N., Braungart, J. M., Campos, J., Corley, R., et al. (1993). Genetic change and continuity from 14 to 20 months: The MacArthur Longitudinal Twin Study. *Child Development, 64,* 1354–1376.

Pomerleau, A., Bolduc, D., Malcuit, G., & Cossette, L. (1990). Pink or blue: Environmental gender stereotypes in the first two years of life. *Sex Roles, 22,* 359–367.

Pontius, A. A. (1973). Neuro-ethics of "walking" in the newborn. *Perceptual and Motor Skills, 37,* 235–245.

Posada, G., Jacobs, A., Richmond, M. K., Carbonell, O. A., Alzate, G., Bustamante, M. R., & Quiceno, J. (2002). Maternal caregiving and infant security in two cultures. *Developmental Psychology, 38,* 67–78.

Posavac, S. S., & Posavac, H. D. (2002). Predictors of women's concern with body weight: The roles of perceived self–media ideal discrepancies and self-esteem. *Eating Disorders: The Journal of Treatment and Prevention, 10,* 153–160.

Powlishta, K. K., Serbin, L. A., & Moller, L. C. (1993). The stability of individual differences in gender typing: Implications for understanding gender segregation. *Sex Roles, 29,* 723–737.

Pressley, M. (1995). *Advanced educational psychology for educators, researchers, and policymakers.* New York: HarperCollins.

Pressley, M., & Afflerbach, P. (1995). *Verbal protocols of reading: The nature of constructively responsive reading.* Hillsdale, NJ: Erlbaum.

Proctor, B. D., & Dalaker, J. (2002). *Poverty in the United States: 2001* (U.S. Census Bureau, Current Populations Reports, Series P60-219). Washington, DC: U.S. Government Printing Office.

Prozac for pediatric use. (2003). *FDA Consumer, 37,* 3.

Putallaz, M. (1983). Predicting children's sociometric status from their behavior. *Child Development, 54,* 1417–1426.

Rabain-Jamin, J., & Wornham, W. L. (1993). Practices and representations of child care and motor development among West Africans in Paris. *Early Development and Parenting, 2,* 107–119.

Ramey, C. T., Campbell, F. A., & Blair, C. (1998). Enhancing the life course for high-risk children: Results from the Abecedarian Project. In J. Crane (Ed.), *Social programs that work* (pp. 163–183). New York: Russell Sage Foundation.

Ramey, C. T., & Ramey, S. L. (1992). Effective early intervention. *Mental Retardation, 6,* 337–345.

Ramey, S. L. (1999). Head Start and preschool education: Toward continued improvement. *American Psychologist, 54,* 344–346.

Rauscher, F. H., Shaw, G. L., & Ky, K. N. (1993). Music and spatial task performance. *Nature, 365,* 611.

Rauscher, F. H., Shaw, G. L., & Ky, K. N. (1995). Listening to Mozart enhances spatial–temporal reasoning: Towards a neurophysiological basis. *Neuroscience Letters, 185,* 44–47.

Rauscher, F. H., Shaw, G. L., Levine, L. J., Wright, E. L., Dennis, W. R., & Newcomb, R. L. (1997). Music training causes long-term enhancement of preschool children's spatial–temporal reasoning. *Neurological Research, 19,* 2–8.

Raywid, M. A. (1997), Small schools: A reform that works. *Educational Leadership, 55,* 34–39.

Redding, R. E. (2002). The impossibility of parental licensure. *American Psychologist, 57,* 987–988.

Reed, J. (1982). Black Americans in the 1980s. *Population Bulletin, 37,* 1–37.

Rees, R. L. (1979). *A comparison of children of lesbian and single heterosexual mothers on three measures of socialization.* Unpublished doctoral dissertation, California School of Professional Psychology, Berkeley. As cited in Patterson (1992).

Reifman, A., Villa, L. C., Amans, J. A., Rethinam, V., & Telesca, T. Y. (2001). Children of divorce in the 1990s: A meta-analysis. *Journal of Divorce and Remarriage, 36,* 27–36.

Reitsma, P. (1983). Printed word learning in beginning readers. *Journal of Experimental Child Psychology, 36,* 321–339.

Reitsma, P. (1989). Orthographic memory and learning to read. In P. G. Aaron & R. M. Joshi (Eds.), *Reading and writing disorders in different orthographic systems* (pp. 51–73). The Hague, Netherlands: Kluwer Academic.

Renninger, A., Hidi, S., & Krapp, A. (Eds.). (1992). *The role of interest in learning and development.* Hillsdale, NJ: Erlbaum.

Renshaw, P. E., & Brown, P. J. (1993). Loneliness in middle childhood: Concurrent and longitudinal predictors. *Child Development, 64,* 1271–1284.

Resnick, L. B., Levine, J. M., & Teasley, S. D. (Eds.). (1991). *Perspectives on socially shared cognition.* Washington, DC: American Psychological Association.

Reyna, V. F., & Brainerd, C. J. (1995). Fuzzy-trace theory: An interim synthesis. *Learning and Individual Differences, 7,* 1–75.

Reynolds, A. J. (2000). *Success in early intervention: The Chicago child–parent centers.* Lincoln: University of Nebraska Press.

Reynolds, A. J., & Robertson, D. L. (2003). School-based early intervention and later child maltreatment in the Chicago longitudinal study. *Child Development, 74,* 3–26.

Reynolds, A. J., Temple, J. A., Robertson, D. L., & Mann, E. A. (2001). Long-term effects of an early childhood intervention on educational achievement and juvenile arrest: A 15-year follow-up of low-income children in public schools. *JAMA: Journal of the American Medical Association, 285,* 2339–2346.

Rice, M. E., & Grusec, J. E. (1975). Saying and doing: Effects on observer performance. *Journal of Personality and Social Psychology, 32,* 584–593.

Richardson, J. T. E. (2003). Howard Andrew Knox and the origins of performance testing on Ellis Island, 1912–1916. *History of Psychology, 6,* 143–170.

Rideout, V. J., Foehr, U. G., Roberts, D. F., & Brodie, M. (1999). *Kids and media @ the new millennium: Executive summary.* Menlo Park, CA: Kaiser Family Foundation.

Rimm, S. (1996). *How to parent so children will learn: Clear strategies for raising happy, achieving children.* New York: Three Rivers Press.

Ripple, C. H., Gilliam, W. S., Chanana, N., & Zigler, E. (1999). Will fifty cooks spoil the broth? The debate over entrusting Head Start to the states. *American Psychologist, 54,* 327–343.

Roberts, D. F., Foehr, U. G., Rideout, V. J., & Brodie, M. (1999). *Kids and media @ the new millennium.* Menlo Park, CA: Kaiser Family Foundation.

Roberts, W., & Strayer, J. (1996). Empathy, emotional expressiveness, and prosocial behavior. *Child Development, 67,* 449–470.

Robinson, E. J., & Whitcombe, E. L. (2003). Children's suggestibility in relation to their understanding about sources of knowledge. *Child Development, 74,* 48–62.

Robinson, J. L., Reznick, J. S., Kagan, J., & Corley, R. (1992). The heritability of inhibited and uninhibited behavior: A twin study. *Developmental Psychology, 28,* 1030–1037.

Robinson, T. N., Chen, H. L., & Killen, J. D. (1998). Television and music video exposure and risk of adolescent alcohol use. *Pediatrics, 102,* 54–61.

Robison, L. L., Buckley, J. D., Daigle, A. E., Wells, R., Benjamin, D., & Hammond, G. D. (1989). Maternal drug use and risk of childhood nonlymphoblastic leukemia among offspring: An epidemiologic investigation implicating marijuana (a report from the Children's Cancer Study Group). *Cancer, 63,* 1904–1911.

Rodman, H., Pratto, D., & Nelson, R. (1985). Child care arrangements and children's functioning: A comparison of self-care and adult-care children. *Developmental Psychology, 21,* 413–418.

Rodriguez, G. G. (1999). *Raising nuestros niños: Bringing up Latino children in a bicultural world.* New York: Simon & Schuster.

Roebers, C. M. (2002). Confidence judgments in children's and adults' event recall and suggestibility. *Developmental Psychology, 38,* 1052–1067.

Roeser, R. W., & Eccles, J. S. (1998). Adolescents' perceptions of middle school: Relation to longitudinal changes in academic and psychological adjustment. *Journal of Research on Adolescence, 88,* 123–158.

Roeser, R. W., Midgley, C. M., & Urdan, T. C. (1996). Perceptions of the school psychological environment and early adolescents' psychological and behavioral functioning in school: The mediating role of goals and belonging. *Journal of Educational Psychology, 88,* 408–422.

Rogoff, B. (1990). *Apprenticeship in thinking: Cognitive development in social context.* New York: Oxford University Press.

Rogoff, B. (1998). Cognition as a collaborative process. In W. Damon, (Series Ed.) & D. Kuhn & R. S. Siegler (Vol. Eds.), *Handbook of child psychology: Vol. 2. Cognition, perception, and language* (5th ed, pp. 679–744). New York: Wiley.

Rogoff, B. (2003). *The cultural nature of human development.* London: Oxford University Press.

Rogoff, B., & Mistry, J. (1990). The social and functional context of children's remembering. In R. Fivush & J. A. Hudson (Eds.), *Knowing and remembering in young children* (pp. 197–222). Cambridge, England: Cambridge University Press.

Rogoff, B., Mistry, J., Göncü, A., & Mosier, C. (1993). Guided participation in cultural activity by toddlers and caregivers. *Monographs of the Society for Research in Child Development, 58* (8, Serial No. 236).

Romaine, S. (1984). *The language of children and adolescents—the acquisition of communicative competence.* New York: Blackwell.

Romaine, S. (1995). *Bilingualism* (2nd ed.). Oxford, England: Blackwell.

Roopnarine, J. L., & Johnson, J. E. (1994). The need to look at play in diverse cultural settings. In J. L. Roopnarine, J. E. Johnson, & F. H. Hooper (Eds.), *Children's play in diverse cultures* (pp. 1–8). Albany: State University of New York Press.

Rose, A. J., & Montemayor, R. (1994). The relationship between gender role orientation and perceived self-competence in male and female adolescents. *Sex Roles, 31,* 579–595.

Rose, J. S., Medway, F. J., Cantrell, V. L., & Marus, S. H. (1983). A fresh look at the retention–promotion controversy. *Journal of School Psychology, 21,* 201–211.

Rose, R. J. (1995). Genes and human behavior. In J. T. Spence, J. M. Darley, & D. J. Foss (Eds.), *Annual review of psychology* (Vol. 46, pp. 625–654). Palo Alto, CA: Annual Reviews.

Rose, S. A., & Ruff, H. A. (1987). Cross-modal abilities in human infants. In J. D. Osofsky (Ed.), *Handbook of infant development* (2nd ed., pp. 318–362). New York: Wiley.

Rose, S. A., & Wallace, I. F. (1985). Cross-modal and intramodal transfer as predictors of mental development in fullterm and preterm infants. *Developmental Psychology, 21,* 949–962.

Rosenblith, J. R., & Sims-Knight, J. E. (1985). *In the beginning: Development in the first two years.* Belmont, CA: Brooks/Cole.

Rosenthal, R., & Jacobson, L. (1968). *Pygmalion in the classroom: Teacher expectation and pupils' intellectual development.* New York: Holt, Rinehart & Winston.

Ross, C. E., & Van Willigen, M. (1996). Gender, parenthood, and anger. *Journal of Marriage and the Family, 58,* 572–584.

Ross, H. S. (1982). Establishment of social games among toddlers. *Developmental Psychology, 18,* 509–518.

Rossell, C. H., & Baker, K. (1996). The educational effectiveness of bilingual education. *Research in the Teaching of English, 30,* 7–74.

Rothbart, M. K. (1981). Measurement of temperament in infancy. *Child Development, 52,* 569–578.

Rothbart, M. K., Ahadi, S. A., & Hershey, K. L. (1994). Temperament and social behavior in childhood. *Merrill-Palmer Quarterly, 40,* 21–39.

Rothbart, M. K., & Bates, J. E. (1998). Temperament. In W. Damon & N. Eisenberg (Eds.), *Handbook of child psychology: Vol. 3. Social, emotional, and personality development* (pp. 105–176). New York: Wiley.

Rothbaum, F., Weisz, J., Pott, M., Miyake, K., & Morelli, G. (2000). Attachment and culture: Security in the United States and Japan. *American Psychologist, 55,* 1093–1104.

Rovee-Collier, C. K. (1990). The "memory system" of prelinguistic infants. In A. Diamond (Ed.), *The development and neural bases of higher cognitive functions: Vol. 608. Annals of the New York Academy of Sciences* (517–536). New York: New York Academy of Sciences.

Rovee-Collier, C. K. (1995). Time windows in cognitive development. *Developmental Psychology, 51,* 1–23.

Rovee-Collier, C. K., & Gerhardstein, P. (1997). The development of infant memory. In N. Cowan & C. Hulme (Eds.), *The development of memory in childhood* (pp. 5–40). Hove, East Sussex, England: Psychology Press.

Rubia, K., Noorloos, J., Smith, A., Gunning, B., & Sergeant, J. (2003). Motor timing deficits in community and clinical boys with hyperactive behavior: The effect of methylphenidate on motor timing. *Journal of Abnormal Child Psychology, 31,* 301–313.

Rubin, K. H., Bukowski, W., & Parker, J. G. (1998). Peer interactions, relationships, and groups. In W. Damon (Ed.), *Handbook of child psychology* (Vol. 3, 5th ed., pp. 619–700). New York: Wiley.

Rubin, K. H., Burgess, K. B., Dwyer, K. M., & Hastings, P. D. (2003). Predicting preschoolers' externalizing behaviors from toddler temperament, conflict, and maternal negativity. *Developmental Psychology, 39,* 164–176.

Rubin, K. H., Chen, X., McDougall, P., Bowker, A., & McKinnon, J. (1995). The Waterloo Longitudinal Project: Predicting internalizing and externalizing problems in adolescence. *Development and Psychopathology, 7,* 751–764.

Rubin, K. H., Coplan, R. J., Nelson, L. J., Cheah, C. S. L., & Lagace-Seguin, D. G. (1999). Peer relationships in childhood. In M. H. Bornstein & M. E. Lamb (Eds.), *Developmental psychology: An advanced textbook* (4th ed.). Mahwah, NJ: Erlbaum.

Rubin, K. H., Lynch, D., Coplan, R., Rose-Krasnor, L., & Booth, C. L. (1994). "Birds of a feather . . .": Behavioral concordances and preferential personal attraction in children. *Child Development, 65,* 1778–1785.

Ruble, D. N., & Martin, C. L. (1998). Gender development. In W. Damon & N. Eisenberg (Eds.), *Handbook of child psychology: Vol. 3. Social, emotional, and personality development* (pp. 933–1016). New York: Wiley.

Ruff, H. A. (1984). Infants' manipulative exploration of objects: Basic cognitive processes and individual differences. In M. H. Bornstein & A. W. O'Reilly (Eds.), *The role of play in the development of thought* (pp. 5–15). San Francisco: Jossey-Bass.

Ruffman, T., Olson, D. R., Ash, T., & Keenan, T. (1993). The ABCs of deception: Do young children understand deception in the same way as adults? *Developmental Psychology, 29,* 74–87.

Ruffman, T., Slade, L., & Crowe, E. (2002). The relation between children's and mothers' mental state language and theory-of-mind understanding. *Child Development, 73,* 734–751.

Rumelhart, D. E., & McClelland, J. L. (1986). On learning the past tenses of English verbs. In J. L. McClelland, D. E. Rumelhart, & PDP Research Group, *Parallel distributed processing: Explorations in the microstructure of cognition: Vol. 2. Psychological and biological models* (pp. 216–271). Cambridge, MA: MIT Press.

Rushton, J. P. (1979). Effects of prosocial television and film material on the behavior of viewers. In L. Berkowitz (Ed.), *Advances in experimental social psychology* (pp. 321–351). New York: Academic Press.

Rushton, J. P. (1980). *Altruism, socialization, and society.* Englewood Cliffs, NJ: Prentice Hall.

Russell, G., & Russell, A. (1987). Mother–child and father–child relationships in middle childhood. *Child Development, 58,* 1573–1585.

Rutter, M. (1987). Psychosocial resilience and protective mechanisms. *American Journal of Orthopsychiatry, 57,* 316–331.

Rutter, M. (2002). Nature, nurture, and development: From evangelism through science toward policy and practice. *Child Development, 73,* 1–21.

Ryan, R. M., Connell, J. P., & Grolnick, W. S. (1992). When achievement is not intrinsically motivated: A theory of self-regulation in school. In A. K. Boggiano & T. S. Pittman (Eds.), *Achievement and motivation: A social–developmental perspective* (pp. 167–188). New York: Cambridge University Press.

Saarni, C., Mumme, D. L., & Campos, J. J. (1998). Emotional development: Action, communication, and understanding. In W. Damon (Ed.), *Handbook of child psychology* (Vol. 3, pp. 237–309). New York: Wiley.

Sachs, J. (1987). Preschool boys' and girls' language use in pretend play. In S. U. Philips, S. Steele, & C. Tanz (Eds.), *Language, gender, and sex in comparative perspective* (pp. 178–188). New York: Cambridge University Press.

Sachs, J., Bard, B., & Johnson, M. L. (1981). Language learning with restricted input: Case studies of two hearing children of deaf parents. *Applied Psycholinguistics, 2*(1), 33–54.

Sachs, J., & Devine, J. (1976). Young children's use of age-appropriate speech styles in social interaction and role-playing. *Journal of Child Language, 3,* 81–98.

Sack, K. (1998, January 15). Georgia's governor seeks musical start for babies. *New York Times.* Retrieved September 17, 2000, from www.nytimes.com.

Sadker, M., & Sadker, D. (1994). *Failing at fairness: How America's schools cheat girls.* New York: Scribners.

Sagi, A., & Hoffman, M. L. (1976). Empathetic distress in the newborn. *Developmental Psychology, 12,* 175–176.

Sagi, A., Lamb, M. E., Lewkowicz, K. S., Shoham, R., Dvir, R., & Estes, D. (1985). Security of infant–mother, –father, and *metapelet* attachments among kibbutz-reared Israeli children. In I. Bretherton & E. Waters (Eds.), Growing points of attachment theory and research. *Monographs of the Society for Research in Child Development, 50* (Serial No. 209), 257–275.

Sagi, A., & Lewkowicz, K. S. (1987). A cross-cultural evaluation of attachment research. In L. W. C. Tavecchio & M. H. van IJzendoorn (Eds.), *Attachment in social networks* (pp. 427–459). Amsterdam, Netherlands: Elsevier.

Sagi, A., van IJzendoorn, M. H., Aviezer, O., Donnell, F., & Mayseless, O. (1994). Sleeping out of home in a kibbutz communal arrangement: It makes a difference for infant–mother attachment. *Child Development, 65,* 992–1004.

Saito, L. T. (2003). *Ethnic identity and motivation: Socio-cultural factors in the educational achievement of Vietnamese American students.* Levittown, PA: LFB Scholarly.

Salzinger, S., Kaplan, S., Pelcovitz, D., Samit, C., & Krieger, R. (1984). Parent and teacher assessment of children's behavior in child maltreating families. *Journal of the American Academy of Child Psychiatry, 23,* 458–464.

Sampson, P. D., Streissguth, A. P., Bookstein, F. L., Little, R. E., Clarren, S. K., Dehaene, P., Hanson, J. W., & Graham, J. M. (1997). Incidence of fetal alcohol syndrome and prevalence of alcohol-related neurodevelopmental disorder. *Teratology, 56,* 317–326.

Sandler, I. N., Tein, J., Mehta, P., Wolchik, S., & Ayers, T. (2000). Coping efficacy and psychological problems of children of divorce. *Child Development, 71,* 1099–1118.

Santos, D. C. C., Gabbard, C., & Goncalves, V. M. G. (2001). Motor development during the first year: A comparative study. *Journal of Genetic Psychology, 162,* 143–154.

Satt, B. J. (1984). *An investigation into the acoustical induction of intra-uterine learning.* Unpublished doctoral dissertation, California School of Professional Psychology. As cited in Lecanuet (1998).

Sattler, J. (1992). *Assessment of Children* (3rd ed.). San Diego, CA: Jerome M. Sattler.

Sattler, J. (2001). *Assessment of Children* (4th ed.). San Diego, CA: Jerome M. Sattler.

Savage, S. L., & Au, T. K. (1996). What word learners do when input contradicts the mutual exclusivity assumption. *Child Development, 67,* 3120–3134.

Savage-Rumbaugh, E. S., Murphy, J., Sevcik, R. A., Brakke, K. E., Williams, S. L., & Rumbaugh, D. M. (1993). Language and comprehension in ape and child. *Monographs of the Society for Research in Child Development, 58* (3–4, Serial No. 233).

Savage-Rumbaugh, E. S., Rumbaugh, D. M., & Boysen, S. (1978). Symbolic communication between two chimpanzees (*Pan troglodytes*). *Science, 201,* 641–644.

Savage-Rumbaugh, S., Shanker, S. G., & Taylor, T. J. (1998). *Apes, language, and the human mind.* Oxford, England: Oxford University Press.

Saville-Troike, M. (1986). Anthropological considerations in the study of communication. In O. L. Taylor (Ed.), *Nature of communication disorders in culturally and linguistically diverse populations* (pp. 47–72). San Diego, CA: College-Hill Press.

Savin-Williams, R. (1994). Verbal and physical abuse as stressors in the lives of lesbian, gay male, and bisexual youths: Associations with school problems, running away, substance abuse, prostitution, and suicide. *Journal of Consulting and Clinical Psychology, 62,* 261–269.

Savin-Williams, R. (1995). An exploratory study of pubertal maturation timing and self-esteem among gay and bisexual male youths. *Developmental Psychology, 31,* 56–64.

Savin-Williams, R., & Berndt, T. J. (1990). Friendship and peer relations. In S. S. Feldman & G. R. Elliott (Eds.), *At the threshold: The developing adolescent* (pp. 277–307). Cambridge, MA: Harvard University Press.

Saxe, G. B. (1988). The mathematics of child street vendors. *Child Development, 59,* 1415–1425.

Saxton, M. (1997). The contrast theory of negative input. *Journal of Child Language, 24,* 139–161.

Saxton, M. (2000). Negative evidence and negative feedback: Immediate effects on the grammaticality of child speech. *First Language, 20* (60, Pt. 3), 221–252.

Scarborough, H. S., & Dobrich, W. (1994). On the efficacy of reading to preschoolers. *Developmental Review, 14,* 245–302.

Scarr, S. (1985). Constructing psychology: Making facts and fables for our times. *American Psychologist, 40,* 499–512.

Scarr, S. (1992). Developmental theories for the 1990s: Development and individual differences. *Child Development, 63,* 1–19.

Scarr, S. (1993). Biological and cultural diversity: The legacy of Darwin for development. *Child Development, 64,* 1333–1353.

Scarr, S. (1998). American child care today. *American Psychologist, 53,* 95–108.

Scarr, S. (1999). Freedom of choice for poor families. *American Psychologist, 54,* 144.

Scarr, S. (2000). Toward voluntary parenthood. *Journal of Personality, 68,* 615–623.

Scarr, S., & McCartney, K. (1983). How people make their own environments: A theory of genotype–environment effects. *Child Development, 54,* 424–435.

Scarr, S., Weinberg, R. A., & Waldman, I. D. (1993). IQ correlations in transracial adoptive families. *Intelligence, 17,* 541–555.

Schneider, J. F. (2002). Relations among self-talk, self-consciousness, and self-knowledge. *Psychological Reports, 91,* 807–812.

Schneider, W. (1985). Developmental trends in the metamemory-memory behavior relationship: An integrative review. In D. L. Forrest-Pressley, G. E. MacKinnon, & T. G. Waller (Eds.), *Cognition, metacognition, and human performance* (Vol. 1, pp. 57–109). Orlando, FL: Academic Press.

Schneider, W. (1993). Acquiring expertise: Determinants of exceptional performance. In K. A. Keller, F. J. Monks, & A. H. Passow (Eds.), *International handbook of research on and development of giftedness and talent* (pp. 311–324). Oxford, England: Pergamon Press.

Schneider, W., & Bjorklund, D. F. (1998). Memory. In W. Damon, D. Kuhn, & R. S. Siegler (Eds.), *Handbook of child psychology: Vol. 2. Cognition, perception, and language* (5th ed., pp. 467–521). New York: Wiley.

Schneider, W., Gruber, H., Gold, A., & Opwis, K. (1993). Chess expertise and memory for chess positions in children and adults. *Journal of Experimental Child Psychology, 56,* 328–349.

Schneider, W., & Pressley, M. (1989). *Memory development between 2 and 20* (1st ed.). New York: Springer.

Schunk, D. H., & Zimmerman, B. J. (1997). Social origins of self-regulatory competence. *Educational Psychologist, 32,* 195–208.

Schutzman, D. L., Frankenfield-Chernicoff, M., Clatterbaugh, H. E., & Singer, J. (1991). Incidence of intrauterine cocaine exposure in a suburban setting. *Pediatrics, 88,* 825–827.

Schwartz, G. M., Izard, C. E., & Ansul, S. E. (1985). The 5-month-old's ability to discriminate facial expressions of emotion. *Infant Behavior and Development, 8,* 65–77.

Schweinhart, L. J., Barnes, H. V., & Weikart, D. P. (1993). *Significant benefits: The High/Scope Perry Preschool study through age 27* (Monographs of the High/Scope Educational Research Foundation, Number Ten). Ypsilanti, MI: The High/Scope Press.

Schweinhart, L. J., & Weikart, D. P. (1998). High/Scope Perry Preschool program effects at age twenty-seven. In J. Crane (Ed.), *Social programs that work* (pp. 148–162). New York: Russell Sage Foundation.

Seidman, E., & French, S. E. (1997). Normative school transitions among urban adolescents: When, where, and how to intervene. In H. J. Walberg, O. Reyes, & R. P. Weissberg (Eds.), *Children and youth: Interdisciplinary perspectives* (pp. 166–189). Thousand Oaks, CA: Sage.

Selman, R. L. (1976). Social–cognitive understanding: A guide to educational and clinical practices. In T. Likona (Ed.), *Moral development and behavior: Theory, research, and social issues* (pp. 299–316). New York: Holt, Rinehart & Winston.

Selman, R. L. (1980). *The growth of interpersonal understanding.* New York: Academic Press.

Sénéchal, M., & LeFevre, J. (2002). Parental involvement in the development of children's reading skill: A five-year longitudinal study. *Child Development, 73,* 445–460.

Serbin, L. A., Moller, L. C., Gulko, J., Powlishta, K. K., & Colburne, K. A. (1994). The emergence of gender segregation in toddler playgroups. In C. Leaper (Ed.), *Childhood gender segregation: Causes and consequences. New directions for child development* (Vol. 65, pp. 7–17). San Francisco: Jossey-Bass.

Serbin, L. A., Moller, L. C., Gulko, J., Powlishta, K. K., & Colburne, K. A. (1994). The emergence of gender segregation in toddler playgroups. In W. Damon (Ed.), *New directions for child development* (No. 65, pp. 7–17). San Francisco: Jossey-Bass.

Sexton, J., & Swarns, R. L. (1997, November 15). Pictures of Sabrina: A special report. A slide into peril, with no one to catch her. *New York Times.* Retrieved August 2, 2002, from www.nytimes.com.

Sharabany, R., Gershoni, R., & Hofman, J. E. (1981). Girlfriend, boyfriend: Age and sex differences in intimate friendship. *Developmental Psychology, 17,* 800–808.

Sharma, A. R., McGue, M. K., & Benson, P. L. (1996). The emotional and behavioral adjustment of United States adopted adolescents: I. A comparison study. *Children and Youth Services Review, 18,* 77–94.

Sharma, A. R., McGue, M. K., & Benson, P. L. (1998). The psychological adjustment of United States adopted adolescents and their nonadopted siblings. *Child Development, 69,* 791–802.

Shatz, M., & Gelman, R. (1973). The development of communication skills. *Monographs of the Society for Research in Child Development, 38* (Serial No. 152).

Shaw, D., S., Gilliom, M., Ingoldsby, E. M., & Nagin, D. S. (2003). Trajectories leading to school-age conduct problems. *Developmental Psychology, 39,* 189–200.

Shaw, D. S., & Vondra, J. I. (1993). Chronic family adversity and infant attachment security. *Journal of Child Psychology and Psychiatry, 34,* 1205–1215.

Sheldon, A. (1990). Pickle fights: Genderlect talk in preschool disputes. *Discourse Processes, 13,* 5–31.

Sheldon, S. B. (2002). Parents' social networks and beliefs as predictors of parent involvement. *The Elementary School Journal, 102,* 301–316.

Shen, C. (2001). Social values associated with cross-national differences in mathematics and science achievement: A cross-national analysis. *Assessment in Education, 8,* 193–223.

Shore, C. (1995). *Individual differences in language development.* Thousand Oaks, CA: Sage.

Shure, M. (2001). How to think, not what to think: A problem-solving approach to prevention of early high-risk behaviors. In A. C. Bohart & D. J. Stipek (Eds.), *Constructive and destructive behavior: Implications for family, school, & society* (pp. 271–289). Washington, DC: American Psychological Association.

Shurkin, J. N. (1992). *Terman's kids: The groundbreaking study of how the gifted grow up.* Boston: Little, Brown.

Shwe, H. I., & Markman, E. M. (1997). Young children's appreciation of the mental impact of their communicative signals. *Developmental Psychology, 33,* 630–636.

Shweder, R. A., Much, N. C., Mahapatra, M., & Park, L. (1997). The "Big Three" of morality (autonomy, community, and divinity) and the "Big Three" explanations of suffering. In A. Brandt & P. Rozin (Eds.), *Morality and health* (pp. 119–169). Stanford, CA: Stanford University Press.

Sickle cell anemia. Retrieved October 13, 2002, from www.mayoclinic.com.

Siegal, M. (1987). Are sons and daughters treated more differently by fathers than by mothers? *Developmental Review, 7,* 183–209.

Siegler, R. S. (1987). Strategy choices in subtraction. In J. A. Sloboda & D. Rogers (Eds.), *Cognitive processes in mathematics* (pp. 81–106). Oxford, England: Clarendon Press.

Siegler, R. S. (1995). Children's thinking: How does change occur. In W. Schneider & F. E. Weinert (Eds.), *Memory performance and competencies: Issues in growth and development* (pp. 405–430). Hillsdale, NJ: Erlbaum.

Siegler, R. S. (1996). *Emerging minds: The process of change in children's thinking.* New York: Oxford University Press.

Siegler, R. S. (1998). *Children's thinking* (3rd ed.). Englewood Cliffs, NJ: Prentice Hall.

Siegler, R. S., & Jenkins, E. (1989). *How children discover new strategies.* Hillsdale, NJ: Erlbaum.

Siegler, R. S., & Robinson, M. (1982). The development of numerical understandings. In H. W. Reese & L. P. Lipsitt (Eds.), *Advances in child development and behavior.* New York: Academic Press.

Siegler, R. S., & Shipley, C. (1995). Variation, selection, and cognitive change. In T. Simon & G. Halford (Eds.), *Developing cognitive competence: New approaches to process modeling* (pp. 31–76). Hillsdale, NJ: Erlbaum.

Siegler, R. S., & Shrager, J. (1984). Strategy choices in addition and subtraction: How do children know what to do? In C. Sophian (Ed.), *Origins of cognitive skills.* Hillsdale, NJ: Erlbaum.

Signorella, M. L., Bigler, R. S., & Liben, L. S. (1993). Developmental differences in children's gender schemata about others: A meta-analytic review. *Developmental Review, 13,* 147–183.

Signorella, M. L., Bigler, R. S., & Liben, L. S. (1997). A meta-analysis of children's memories for own-sex and other-sex information. *Journal of Applied Developmental Psychology, 18,* 429–445.

Signorielli, N. (2001). Television's gender role images and contribution to stereotyping: Past, present, and future. In D. G. Singer & J. L. Singer (Eds.), *Handbook of children and the media* (pp. 341–358). Thousand Oaks, CA: Sage.

Silverman, A. R., & Feigelman, W. (1990). Adjustment in interracial adoptees: An overview. In D. M. Brodzinsky & M. D. Schechter (Eds.), *The psychology of adoption* (pp. 187–200). New York: Oxford University Press.

Simmons, R. G., & Blyth, D. A. (1987). *Moving into adolescence: The impact of pubertal change and school context.* New York: Aldine De Gruyter.

Simner, M. L. (1971). Newborn's response to the cry of another infant. *Developmental Psychology, 5,* 136–150.

Simon, T. J., Hespos, S. J., & Rochat, P. (1995). Do infants understand simple arithmetic? A replication of Wynn. *Cognitive Development, 10,* 253–269.

Simon, T., & Klahr, D. (1995). A theory of children's learning about number conservation. In T. Simon & G. Halford (Eds.), *Developing cognitive competence: New approaches to process modeling* (pp. 315–354). Hillsdale, NJ: Erlbaum.

Simons, R. L., Johnson, C., & Conger, R. D. (1994). Harsh corporal punishment versus quality of parental involvement as an explanation of adolescent maladjustment. *Journal of Marriage and the Family, 56,* 591–607.

Simons, R. L., Wu, C., Conger, R. D., & Lorenz, F. O. (1994). Two routes to delinquency: Differences between early and late starters in the impact of parenting and deviant peers. *Criminology, 32,* 247–274.

Singer, D. G., & Singer, J. L. (Eds.). (2001). *Handbook of children and the media.* Thousand Oaks, CA: Sage.

Skiba, R. J., & Knesting, K. (2001). Zero tolerance, zero evidence: An analysis of school disciplinary practice. In R. J. Skiba & G. G. Noam (Eds.), *Zero tolerance: Can suspension and expulsion keep schools safe?* (pp. 17–43). San Francisco: Jossey-Bass.

Skiba, R. J., Knesting, K., & Bush, L. D. (2002). Culturally competent assessment: More than unbiased tests. *Journal of Child and Family Studies, 11,* 61–78.

Skinner, B. F. (1957). *Verbal behavior.* Englewood Cliffs, NJ: Prentice Hall.

Skutnabb-Kangas, T. (1984). *Bilingualism or not: The education of minorities.* Clevedon, Avon, England: Multilingual Matters.

Slaby, R. G., & Frey, K. S. (1975). Development of gender constancy and selective attention to same-sex models. *Child Development, 46,* 849–856.

Slavin, R. E. (1990). Achievement effects of ability grouping in secondary schools: A best-evidence synthesis. *Review of Education Research, 60,* 471–499.

Slavin, R. E. (1995). *Cooperative learning* (2nd ed.). Boston: Allyn & Bacon.

Slobin, D. I. (1979). *Psycholinguistics.* Glenview, IL: Scott, Foresman.

Slobin, D. I. (1982). Universal and particular in the acquisiton of language. In E. Wanner & L. Gleitman (Eds.), *Language acquisition: The state of the art* (pp. 128–170). Cambridge, England: Cambridge University Press.

Slobin, D. I. (1985a). *The crosslinguistic study of language acquisition: Vol. 1. The data.* Hillsdale, NJ: Erlbaum.

Slobin, D. I. (1985b). Crosslinguistic evidence for the language-making capacity. In D. I. Slobin (Ed.), *The crosslinguistic study of language acquisition: Vol. 2. Theoretical issues.* (pp. 1157–1249). Hillsdale, NJ: Erlbaum.

Smetana, J. G. (1995). Morality in context: Abstractions, ambiguities, and applications. In R. Vasta (Ed.), *Annals of child development* (Vol. 10, pp. 83–130). London: Jessica Kingsley.

Smith, A. C., & Smith, D. I. (2001). *Emergency and transitional shelter population: 2000* (U.S. Census Bureau, Census Special Reports, Series CENSR/01-2). Washington, DC: U.S. Government Printing Office.

Smith, J. C. (2001). Rett syndrome in boys. Retrieved March 1, 2002, from www.rettsyndrome.org.

Smith, J. R., Brooks-Gunn, J., & Klebanov, P. K. (1997). Consequences of living in poverty for young children's cognitive and verbal ability and early school achievement. In G. J. Duncan & J. Brooks-Gunn (Eds.), *Consequences of growing up poor* (pp. 132–189). New York: Russell Sage Foundation.

Smith, J. R., Brooks-Gunn, J., Kohen, D., & McCarton, C. (2001). Transitions on and off AFDC: Implications for parenting and children's cognitive development. *Child Development, 72,* 1512–1533.

Smith, K. (2000). *Who's minding the kids? Child care arrangements: Fall 1995.* (Current Population Reports, P70-70). Washington, DC: U.S. Census Bureau.

Smith, P. K., & Noble, R. (1987). Factors affecting the development of caregiver–infant relationships. In L. W. C. Tavecchio & M. H. van IJzendoorn (Eds.), *Attachment in social networks* (pp. 93–134). Amsterdam, Netherlands: Elsevier.

Smollar, J., & Youniss, J. (1982). Social development through friendship. In K. H. Rubin & H. S. Ross (Eds.), *Peer relationships and social skills in childhood* (pp. 279–298). New York: Springer.

Snarey, J. R. (1995). In a communitarian voice: The sociobiological expansion of Kohlbergian theory, research, and practice. In W. M. Kurtines & J. L. Gewirtz (Eds.), *Moral development: An introduction* (pp. 109–134). Boston: Allyn & Bacon.

Snarey, J. R., Reimer, J., & Kohlberg, L. (1985). The development of social–moral reasoning among kibbutz adolescents: A longitudinal cross-cultural study. *Developmental Psychology, 20,* 3–17.

Snow, C. E. (1972). Mothers' speech to children learning language. *Child Development, 43,* 549–565.

Snow, C. E. (1987). Relevance of the notion of a critical period to language acquisition. In M. Bornstein (Ed.), *Sensitive periods in development: interdisciplinary perspectives* (pp. 183–209). Hillsdale, NJ: Erlbaum.

Snow, R. E. (1995). Pygmalion and intelligence. *Current Directions in Psychological Science, 4,* 169–171.

Society for Research in Child Development. (2000). *Newsletter, 43*(1), 3.

Sokolov, J. L. (1993). A local contingency analysis of the fine-tuning hypothesis. *Developmental Psychology, 29,* 1008–1023.

Solso, R. L. (2001). *Cognitive psychology* (6th ed.). Boston: Allyn & Bacon.

Song, Y., & Lu, H.-H. (2002, March). Early childhood poverty: A statistical profile. *National Center for Children in Poverty.* Retrieved July 19, 2002, from www.cpmcnet.columbia.edu/dept/nccp.

Sorce, J. F., Emde, R. N., Campos, J., & Klinnert, M. D. (1985). Maternal emotional signaling: Its effect on the visual cliff behavior of 1-year-olds. *Developmental Psychology, 21,* 195–200.

Spearman, C. (1904). General intelligence, objectively determined and measured. *American Journal of Psychology, 15,* 201–293.

Spearman, C. (1923). *The nature of "intelligence" and the principles of cognition.* London: Macmillan.

Spearman, C. (1927). *The abilities of man.* New York: Macmillan.

Spelke, E. S. (1979). Perceiving bimodally specified events in infancy. *Developmental Psychology, 15,* 626–636.

Spelke, E. S. (1991). Physical knowledge in infancy: Reflections on Piaget's theory. In S. Carey & R. Gelman (Eds.), *The epigenesis of mind* (pp. 133–169). Hillsdale, NJ: Erlbaum.

Spencer, M. B. (1995). Old issues and new theorizing about African-American youth: A phenomenological variant of ecological systems theory. In R. L. Taylor (Ed.), *African-American youth: Their social and economic status in the United States* (pp. 37–69). Westport, CT: Praeger.

Spencer, M. B., & Dornbusch, S. M. (1990). Challenges in studying minority youth. In S. S. Feldman & G. R. Elliott (Eds.), *At the threshold: The developing adolescent* (pp. 123–146). Cambridge, MA: Harvard University Press.

Spencer, M. B., Noll, E., Stoltzfus, J., & Harpalani, V. (2001). Identity and school achievement: Revisiting the "acting white" assumption. *Educational Psychologist, 36,* 21–30.

Spivey, N. N., & King, J. R. (1989). Readers as writers composing from sources. *Reading Research Quarterly, 24,* 7–26.

Spock, B., & Parker, S. (1998). *Baby and child care.* New York: Pocket Books.

Sroufe, L. A. (1990). An organizational perspective on the self. In D. Cicchetti & M. Beeghly (Eds.), *The self in transition: Infancy to childhood* (pp. 281–307). Chicago: University of Chicago Press.

Sroufe, L. A. (1996). *Emotional development.* Cambridge, England: Cambridge University Press.

Sroufe, L. A., Carlson, E., & Schulman, S. (1993). Individuals in relationships: Development from infancy through adolescence. In D. C. Funder, R. D. Parke, C. Tomlinson-Keasy, & K. Widaman (Eds.), *Studying lives through time: Personality and development* (pp. 315–342). Washington, DC: American Psychological Association.

Sroufe, L. A., & Egeland, B. (1991). Illustrations of person–environment interaction from a longitudinal study. In T. D. Wachs & R. Plomin (Eds.), *Conceptualization and measurement of organism–environment interaction* (pp. 68–84). Washington, DC: American Psychological Association.

St. Pierre, R. G., & Layzer, J. I. (1998). Improving the life chances of children in poverty: Assumptions and what we have learned. *Society for Research in Child Development Social Policy Report, 12*(4), 1–25.

Stake, J. E. (1997). Integrating expressiveness and instrumentality in real-life settings: A new perspective on the benefits of androgyny. *Sex Roles, 37,* 541–564.

Stamps, L. E. (2002). Maternal preference in child custody decisions. *Journal of Divorce and Remarriage, 37,* 1–11.

Stams, G. J. M., Juffer, F., Rispens, J., & Hoksbergen, R. A. C. (2000). The development and adjustment of 7-year-old children adopted in infancy. *Journal of Child Psychology and Psychiatry, 41,* 1025–1037.

Standley, K., Soule, B., & Copans, S. (1979). Dimensions of prenatal anxiety and their influence on pregnancy outcome. *American Journal of Obstetrics and Gynecology, 135,* 22–26.

Stark, R., Bernstein, L., & Demorest, M. (1993). Vocal communication in the first 18 months of life. *Journal of Speech and Hearing Research, 36,* 548–558.

Starkey, P., & Cooper, R. G. (1980). Perception of numbers by human infants. *Science, 210,* 1033–1035.

Starkey, P., & Gelman, R. (1982). The development of addition and subtraction abilities prior to formal schooling in arithmetic. In T. P. Carpenter, J. M. Moser, & T. A. Romberg (Eds.), *Addition and subtraction: A cognitive perspective* (pp. 99–116). Hillsdale, NJ: Erlbaum.

Starkey, P., Spelke, E. S., & Gelman, R. (1983). Detection of intermodal numerical correspondences by human infants. *Science, 222,* 179–181.

Starkey, P., Spelke, E. S., & Gelman, R. (1990). Numerical abstraction by human infants. *Cognition, 36,* 97–128.

Starr, C., & Taggart, R. (1998). *Biology: The unity and diversity of life.* Belmont, CA: Wadsworth.

Stechler, G., & Halton, A. (1982). Prenatal influences on human development. In B. B. Wolman (Ed.), *Handbook of developmental psychology* (pp. 175–189). Englewood Cliffs, NJ: Prentice Hall.

Steckel, A. (1987). Psychosocial development of children of lesbian mothers. In F. W. Bozett (Ed.), *Gay and lesbian parents* (pp. 75–85). New York: Praeger.

Steele, C. M., & Aronson, J. (1995). Stereotype threat and the intellectual test performance of African Americans. *Journal of Personality & Social Psychology, 69,* 797–811.

Steele, K. M., Bass, K. E., & Crook, M. D. (1999). The mystery of the Mozart effect: Failure to replicate. *Psychological Science, 10,* 366–369.

Steinberg, L. (1986). Latchkey children and susceptibility to peer pressure: An ecological analysis. *Developmental Psychology, 22,* 433–439.

Steiner, J. E. (1979). Human facial expressions in response to taste and smell stimulation. In H. Reese & L. Lipsitt (Eds.), *Advances in child development and behavior* (Vol. 13, pp. 257–295). New York: Academic Press.

Stern, E. (1993). What makes certain arithmetic word problems involving comparison of sets so difficult for children? *Journal of Educational Psychology, 85,* 7–23.

Sternberg, R. J. (1985). *Beyond IQ: A triarchic theory of human intelligence.* Cambridge, England: Cambridge University Press.

Sternberg, R. J. (1988). *The triarchic mind: A new theory of human intelligence.* New York: Viking.

Sternberg, R. J. (1999). The theory of successful intelligence. *Review of General Psychology, 3,* 292–316.

Stetsenko, A., Little, T. D., Oettingen, G., & Baltes, P. B. (1995). Agency, control, and means–ends beliefs about school performance in Moscow children: How similar are they to beliefs of Western children? *Developmental Psychology, 31,* 285–299.

Stevenson, H. W. (1992, December). Learning from Asian schools. *Scientific American, 267*(6), 32–38.

Stevenson, H. W., Chen, C., & Lee, S.-Y. (1993). Mathematics achievement of Chinese, Japanese, and American children: Ten years later. *Science, 259,* 53–58.

Stevenson, H. W., & Lee, S. (1990). Contexts of achievement: A study of American, Chinese, and Japanese children. *Monographs of the Society for Research in Child Development, 55* (1–2, Serial No. 221).

Stevenson, H. W., & Lee, S. (1995). The East Asian version of whole-class teaching. *Educational Policy, 9,* 152–167.

Stevenson, J. (1992). Evidence for genetic etiology in hyperactivity in children. *Behavior Genetics, 22*(3), 337–344.

Stevenson, L. (1997). Exercise in pregnancy: Part 1: Update on pathophysiology. *Canadian Family Physician, 43*(1), 97–104.

Stevenson, M. R., & Black, K. N. (1988). Paternal absence and sex-role development: A meta-analysis. *Child Development, 59,* 793–814.

Steward, M. S., & Steward, D. S. (1996). Interviewing young children about body touch and handling. *Monographs of the Society for Research in Child Development, 61* (Serial No. 248).

Stewart, S. L., & Rubin, K. H. (1995). The social problem-solving skills of anxious–withdrawn children. *Development and Psychopathology, 7,* 323–336.

Stice, E., Presnell, K., & Bearman, S. K. (2001). Relation of early menarche to depression, eating disorders, substance abuse, and comorbid psychopathology among adolescent girls. *Developmental Psychology, 37*(5), 608–619.

Stice, E., & Whitenton, K. (2002). Risk factors for body dissatisfaction in adolescent girls: A longitudinal investigation. *Developmental Psychology, 38*(5), 669–678.

Stiles, J., & Thal, D. (1993). Linguistic and spatial cognitive development following early focal brain injury: Patterns of deficit and recovery. In M. Johnson (Ed.), *Brain development and cognition: A reader* (pp. 643–664). Oxford, England: Blackwell.

Stillion, J. M., & McDowell, E. E. (1996). *Suicide across the life span* (2nd ed.). Washington, DC: Taylor & Francis.

Stipek, D. (2002). At what age should children enter kindergarten? A question for policy makers and parents. *SRCD Social Policy Report, XVI*(2), 3–16.

Stipek, D. J., & Ryan, R. H. (1997). Economically disadvantaged preschoolers: Ready to learn but further to go. *Developmental Psychology, 33,* 711–723.

Stipek, D., Recchia, S., & McClintic, S. (1992). Self-evaluation in young children. *Monographs of the Society for Research in Child Development, 57* (1, Serial No. 226).

Stoddart, T., & Turiel, E. (1985). Children's concepts of cross-gender activities. *Child Development, 56,* 1241–1252.

Stoel-Gammon, C., & Otomo, K. (1986). Babbling development of hearing-impaired and normally hearing subjects. *Journal of Speech and Hearing Disorders, 51,* 33–41.

Strasburger, V. C. (2001). Children, adolescents, drugs, and the media. In D. G. Singer & J. L. Singer (Eds.), *Handbook of children and the media* (pp. 415–445). Thousand Oaks, CA: Sage.

Strassberg, Z., Dodge, K. A., Pettit, G. S., & Bates, J. E. (1994). Spanking in the home and children's subsequent aggression toward kindergarten peers. *Development and Psychopathology, 6,* 445–461.

Straus, M. A. (1991). Discipline and deviance: Physical punishment of children and violence and other crime in adulthood. *Social Problems, 38,* 133–154.

Straus, M. A. (1994). *Beating the devil out of them: Corporal punishment in American families.* New York: Lexington Books.

Straus, M. A. (2001). *Beating the devil out of them: Corporal punishment in American families and its effects on children.* New York: Lexington Books.

Straus, M. A., & Gelles, R. J. (1986). Societal change and change in family violence from 1975 to 1985 as revealed by two national surveys. *Journal of Marriage and the Family, 48,* 465–479.

Straus, M. A., & Stewart, J. H. (1999). Corporal punishment by American parents: National data on prevalence, chronicity, severity, and duration, in relation to child and family characteristics. *Clinical Child and Family Psychology Review, 2,* 55–70.

Straus, M. A., Sugarman, D. B., & Giles-Sims, J. (1997). Spanking by parents and subsequent antisocial behavior of children. *Archives of Pediatric and Adolescent Medicine, 151,* 761–767.

Strauss, M. S., & Curtis, L. E. (1981). Infant perception of number. *Child Development, 52,* 1146–1152.

Struthers, C. B., & Bokemeier, J. L. (2000). Myths and realities of raising children and creating family life in a rural community. *Journal of Family Issues, 21,* 17–46.

Subrahmanyam, K., Kraut, R., Greenfield, P., & Gross, E. (2001). New forms of electronic media. In D. G. Singer & J. L. Singer (Eds.), *Handbook of children and the media* (pp. 73–99). Thousand Oaks, CA: Sage.

Sullivan, A. (2000, July 23). The way we live now: Counter culture; promotion of the fittest. *New York Times*. Retrieved February 15, 2002, from www.nytimes.com.

Sullivan, J., & Horowitz, F. D. (1983). The effects of intonation on infant attention: The role of the rising intonation contour. *Journal of Child Language, 10,* 521–534.

Sullivan, K., & Wimmer, E. (1993). Three-year-olds' understanding of mental states: The influence of trickery. *Journal of Experimental Child Psychology, 56,* 135–148.

Sun, Y., & Li, Y. (2002). Children's well-being during parents' marital disruption process: A pooled time-series analysis. *Journal of Marriage and Family, 64,* 472–488.

Super, C. (1976). Environmental effects on motor development: The case of "African infant precocity." *Developmental Medicine and Child Neurology, 18,* 561–567.

Super-smart teen goes for another world record (October 23, 1998). *Current Science, 84*(4), 13.

Suzuki, L., Vraniak, D., & Kugler, J. (1996). Intellectual assessment across cultures. In L. Suzuki, P. Meller, & J. Ponterotto (Eds.), *Handbook of multicultural assessment: Clinical, psychological, and educational applications* (pp. 141–177). San Francisco: Jossey-Bass.

Swaab, D. F., Gooren, L. J. G., & Hofman, M. A. (1995). Brain research, gender, and sexual orientation. *Journal of Homosexuality, 28,* 283–301.

Swarns, R. L. (1999, January 30). Children go to foster care needlessly, suit charges. *New York Times*. Retrieved August 2, 2002, from www.nytimes.com.

Szeverenyi, P., Hetey, A., Kovacsne, Z. T., & Muennich, A. (1995). Does the father's presence at delivery have an influence on the parental judgement of the father–child relationship? *Magyar Pszichologiai Szemle, 51,* 83–95.

Tager-Flusberg, H., Boshart, J., & Baron-Cohen, S. (1999). Reading the windows to the soul: Evidence of domain-specific sparing in Williams syndrome. *Journal of Cognitive Neuroscience, 10,* 631–639.

Takahashi, K. (1986). Examining the strange-situation procedure with Japanese mothers and 12-month-old infants. *Developmental Psychology, 22,* 265–270.

Takahashi, K. (1990). Are the key assumptions of the "strange situation" procedure universal? A view from Japanese research. *Human Development, 33,* 23–30.

Takeuchi, M. (1994). Children's play in Japan. In J. L. Roopnarine, J. E. Johnson, & F. H. Hooper (Eds.), *Children's play in diverse cultures* (pp. 51–72). Albany: State University of New York Press.

Tangney, J. P. (2001). Constructive and destructive aspects of shame and guilt. In A. C. Bohart & D. J. Stipek (Eds.), *Constructive and destructive behavior: Implications for family, school, and society* (pp. 127–145). Washington, DC: American Psychological Association.

Tanner, J. M. (1978). *Fetus into man: Physical growth from conception to maturity.* Cambridge, MA: Harvard University Press.

Tanner, J. M. (1991). Menarche, secular trend in age of. In R. M. Lerner, A. C. Petersen, & J. Brooks-Gunn (Eds.), *Encyclopedia of adolescence* (Vol. 2, pp. 637–641). New York: Garland.

Tardif, T. (1996). Nouns are not always learned before verbs: Evidence from Mandarin speakers' early vocabularies. *Developmental Psychology, 32,* 492–504.

Taylor, M., & Gelman, S. A. (1988). Adjectives and nouns: Children's strategies for learning new words. *Child Development, 59,* 411–419.

Taylor, M., & Hort, B. (1990). Can children be trained in making the distinction between appearance and reality? *Child Development, 5,* 89–99.

Taylor, O. (1990). Language and communication differences. In G. Shames & E. Wiig (Eds.), *Human communication disorders* (3rd ed., pp. 126–158). Columbus, OH: Merrill/Macmillan.

Taylor, O. L. (1986). *Nature of communication disorders in culturally and linguistically diverse populations.* San Diego, CA: College-Hill Press.

Taylor, R., & Richards, S. (1991). Patterns of intellectual differences of black, Hispanic, and white children. *Psychology in the Schools, 28,* 5–9.

Teachman, J. D., Paasch, K., & Carver, K. (1996). Social capital and dropping out of school. *Journal of Marriage and Family, 58,* 773–783.

Teicher, M. H. (2002). Scars that won't heal: The neurobiology of child abuse. *Scientific American, 286*(3), 68–75.

Tellegen, A., Lykken, D. T., Bouchard, T. J., Jr., Wilcox, K. J., Segal, N. L., & Rich, S. (1988). Personality similarity in twins reared apart and together. *Journal of Personality and Social Psychology, 54,* 1031–1039.

Teong, S. K. (2003). The effect of metacognitive training on mathematical word-problem solving. *Journal of Computer Assisted Learning, 19,* 46–56.

Terman, L. M. (1925). *Genetic studies of genius: Vol. 1. Mental and physical traits of a thousand gifted children.* Stanford, CA: Stanford University Press.

Terman, L. M. (1947). *Genetic studies of genius: Vol. 4. The gifted child grows up.* Stanford, CA: Stanford University Press.

Terman, L. M. (1959). *Genetic studies of genius: Vol. 5. The gifted group at midlife.* Stanford, CA: Stanford University Press.

Terrace, H. S., Petitto, L. A., Sanders, R. J., & Bever, T. G. (1980). On the grammatical capacity of apes. In K. E. Nelson (Ed.), *Children's language.* New York: Gardner Press.

The infant behavior questionnaire (IBQ and IBQ-R). Retrieved August 18, 2003, from the University of Oregon website: http://darkwing.uoregon.edu/~maryroth/:bqdesc.html.

Thelen, E. (1989). The (re)discovery of motor development: Learning new things from an old field. *Developmental Psychology, 25,* 946–949.

Thelen, E., Fisher, D. M., & Ridley-Johnson, R. (1984). The relationship between physical growth and a newborn reflex. *Infant Behavior and Development, 7,* 479–493.

Thelen, E., & Smith, L. B. (1998). Dynamic systems theories. In W. Damon (Series Ed.) & R. M. Lerner (Vol. Ed.), *Handbook of child psychology: Vol. 1. Theoretical models of human development* (5th ed., pp. 563–634). New York: Wiley.

Thiede, K. W., Anderson, M. C. M., & Therriault, D. (2003). Accuracy of metacognitive monitoring affects learning of texts. *Journal of Educational Psychology, 95,* 66–73.

Thomas, A., & Chess, S. (1977). *Temperament and development.* New York: Brunner/Mazel.

Thomas, M., & Karmiloff-Smith, A. (2003). Connectionist models of development, developmental disorders, and individual differences. In R. J. Sternberg, J. Lautrey, & T. Lubart (Eds.), *Models of intelligence: International perspectives* (pp. 133–150). Washington, DC: American Psychological Association.

Thomas, R. M. (1992). *Comparing theories of child development,* 3rd ed. Belmont, CA: Wadsworth.

Thomas, R. M. (2000). *Comparing theories of child development,* 5th ed. Belmont, CA: Wadsworth.

Thompson, M. W., McInnes, R. R., & Willard, H. F. (1991). *Thompson & Thompson genetics in medicine* (5th ed.). Philadelphia: W. B. Saunders.

Thompson, P. M., Giedd, J. N., Woods, R. P., MacDonald, D., Evans, A. C., & Toga, A. W. (2000). Growth patterns in the developing brain detected by using continuum mechanical tensor maps. *Nature, 404,* 190–193.

Thompson, R. A. (1994). Emotion regulation: A theme in search of definition. In N. A. Fox (Ed.), The development of emotion regulation: Biological and behavioral considerations. *Monographs of the Society for Research in Child Development, 59* (2–3, Serial No. 240).

Thompson, R. A. (1998). Early sociopersonality development. In W. Damon (Ed.), *Handbook of child psychology* (Vol. 3, pp. 25–104). New York: Wiley.

Thompson, R. A. (1999). The individual child: Temperament, emotion, self, and personality. In M. H. Bornstein & M. S. Lamb (Eds.), *Developmental psychology: An advanced textbook* (4th ed., pp. 377–409). Mahwah, NJ: Erlbaum.

Thorndike, R. (1997). The early history of intelligence testing. In D. Flanagan, J. Genshaft, & P. Harrison (Eds.), *Contemporary intellectual assessment: Theories, tests, and issues.* New York: Guilford Press.

Thorndike, R., & Lohman, D. (1990). *A century of ability testing.* Chicago: Riverside.

Thurstone, L. L. (1938). *Primary mental abilities.* Chicago: University of Chicago Press.

Thurstone, L. L., & Thurstone, T. G. (1941). *Factorial studies of intelligence.* Chicago: University of Chicago Press.

Tiet, Q. Q., Wasserman, G. A., Loeber, R., McReynolds, L. S., & Miller, L. S. (2001). Developmental and sex differences in types of conduct problems. *Journal of Child and Family Studies, 10*(2), 181–197.

Tietjen, A., & Walker, L. (1985). Moral reasoning and leadership among men in a Papua, New Guinea village. *Developmental Psychology, 21,* 982–992.

Tisak, M. S. (1995). Domains of social reasoning and beyond. In R. Vasta (Ed.), *Annals of child development* (Vol. 11, pp. 95–130). London: Jessica Kingsley.

Tomasello, M. (1995). Language is not an instinct. *Cognitive Development, 10,* 131–156.

Tomkins, A. J., & Kepfield, S. S. (1992). Policy responses: When women use drugs during pregnancy: Using child abuse laws to combat substance abuse. In T. B. Sonderegger (Ed.), *Perinatal substance abuse: Research findings and clinical applications* (pp. 306–345). Baltimore: Johns Hopkins University Press.

Toulmin, S. (1978, September). The Mozart of psychology. *New York Review of Books.* As cited in Wertsch, 1985.

Trehub, S. E. (1976). The discrimination of foreign speech contrasts by infants and adults. *Child Development, 47,* 466–472.

Triandis, H. C. (1994). *Culture and social behavior.* New York: McGraw-Hill.

Triandis, H. C. (1995). *Individualism and collectivism.* Boulder, CO: Westview Press.

Trimble, J. E., & Medicine, B. (1993). Diversification of American Indians: Forming an indigenous perspective. In U. Kim & J. W. Berry (Eds.), *Indigenous psychologies* (pp. 133–151). Newbury Park, CA: Sage.

Triseliotis, J. (2000). Identity formation and the adopted person revisited. In A. Treacher & I. Katz (Eds.), *The dynamics of adoption* (pp. 81–97). London: Jessica Kingsley.

Triseliotis, J., & Hill, M. (1990). Contrasting adoption, foster care, and residential rearing. In D. M. Brodzinsky & M. D. Schechter (Eds.), *The psychology of adoption* (pp. 107–120). New York: Oxford University Press.

Troiden, R. R. (1988). Homosexual identity development. *Journal of Adolescent Health Care, 9,* 105–113.

Tschannen-Moran, M., Woolfolk Hoy, A., & Hoy, W. K. (1998). Teacher efficacy: Its meaning and measure. *Review of Educational Research, 68,* 202–248.

Tseng, V., & Fuligni, A. J. (2000). Parent–adolescent language use and relationships among immigrant families with East Asian, Filipino, and Latin American backgrounds. *Journal of Marriage and the Family, 62,* 465–476.

Tucker, J. S., Friedman, H. S., Schwartz, J. E., Critiqui, M. H., Tomlinson-Keasey, C., Wingard, D. L., & Martin, L. R. (1997). Parental divorce: Effects on individual behavior and longevity. *Journal of Personality and Social Psychology, 73,* 381–391.

Tulving, E. (1972). Episodic and semantic memory. In E. Tulving & W. Donaldson (Eds.), *Organization of memory* (pp. 382–403). New York: Academic Press.

Turati, C., Simion, F., Milani, I., & Umiltá, C. (2002). Newborns' preferences for faces: What is crucial? *Developmental Psychology, 38*(6), 875–882.

Turiel, E. (1998). The development of morality. In W. Damon & N. Eisenberg (Eds.), *Handbook of child psychology: Vol. 3. Social, emotional, and personality development* (pp. 863–932). New York: Wiley.

U.S. Census Bureau. (1998). *Marital status and living arrangements: March 1998 (update).* (Current Population Reports, Series P20-514). Washington, DC: Government Printing Office.

U.S. Census Bureau. (2000a). *Profile of general demographic characteristics for the United States: 2000* (Table DP-1). Washington, DC: Government Printing Office.

U.S. Census Bureau, (2000b). *Statistical abstract of the United States: Labor force, employment, and earnings* (Sec. 13, pp. 11–12). Retrieved May 29, 2001, from www.census.gov/prod/www/statistical-abstract-us.html.

U.S. Census Bureau. (2001). *Overview of race and Hispanic origin: Census 2000 Brief.* Issued March, 2001 by the U.S. Department of Commerce. Also, census data retrieved June 1, 2001: 1990 data from http://homer.ssd.census.gov/cdrom/lookup/991424885 and 2000 data from www.census.gov/Press-Release/www/2001/cb01cn61.html.

U.S. Department of Education. (2000). National Center for Education Statistics. *Pursuing Excellence: Comparisons of international eighth-grade mathematics and science achievement from a U.S. perspective, 1995 and 1999* (NCES 2001-028), by P. Gonzales, C. Calsyn, L. Jocelyn, K. Mak, D. Kastberg, S. Arafeh, T. Wiliams, & W. Tsen. Washington, DC: U.S. Government Printing Office.

U.S. Department of Education. (2001a). National Center for Education Statistics. *Internet Access in U.S. public schools and classrooms: 1994–2000* (NCES 2001-071), by A. Cattagni & E. F. Westat. Washington, DC: U.S. Government Printing Office.

U.S. Department of Education. (2001b). Office of Educational Research and Improvement. National Center for Education Statistics. *The nation's report card: Mathematics 2000* (NCES 2001-517) by J. S. Braswell, A. D. Lutkus, W. S. Grigg, S. L. Santapau, B. S.-H. Tay-Lim, & M. S. Johnson. Washington, DC: U.S. Government Printing Office.

U.S. Department of Education. (2001c). Office of Educational Research and Improvement. National Center for Education Statistics. *The nation's report card: Fourth-grade reading 2000* (NCES 2001-499), by P. L. Donahue, R. J. Finnegan, A. D. Lutkus, N. L. Allen, & J. R. Campbell. Washington, DC: U.S. Government Printing Office.

U.S. Department of Education. (2001d). National Center for Education Statistics. *Dropout rates in the United States: 2000* (NCES 2002-114), by P. Kaufman, M. N. Alt, & C. D. Chapman. Washington, DC: U.S. Government Printing Office.

U.S. Department of Education. (2002). Office of Educational Research and Improvement. National Center for Education Statistics. *The nation's report card: Science highlights 2000* (NCES 2002-452). Washington, DC: U.S. Government Printing Office.

U.S. Department of Energy. (2003). Human Genome Project Information Website. Retrieved March 20, 2003, from www.ornl.gov/TechResources/Human_Genome/posters/chromosome/index.html.

U.S. Department of Health and Human Services. (2001). *Youth violence: A report of the surgeon general.* Rockville, MD: U.S. Department of Health and Human Services.

U.S. Department of Health and Human Services, Administration on Children, Youth, and Families. (2001). *Child maltreatment 1999.* Washington, DC: U.S. Government Printing Office.

U.S. Department of Justice. (1998). *Crime in the United States.* Washington, DC: U.S. Government Printing Office.

U.S. National Coalition for the Homeless. (2001). *Homeless families with children* (NCH fact sheet #7). Retrieved July 19, 2002, from www.national-homeless.org/families.html.

U.S. Office of Technology Assessment. (1993). *Adult literacy and new technologies.* Washington, DC: U.S. Government Printing Office.

U.S. Teens & Technology [on-line]. (1997). Retrieved July 11, 2002, from www.nsf.gov/lpa/nstw/teenov.htm.

Uhlmann, W. R. (2000, February 29). When genes are decoded, who should see the results?: "Every one of us is at risk." *New York Times.* Retrieved February 15, 2002, from www.nytimes.com.

Uhry, J. K., & Shepard, M. J. (1993). Segmentation/spelling instruction as part of a first-grade reading program: Effects on several measures of reading. *Reading Research Quarterly, 28,* 218–233.

Underwood, B., & Moore, B. (1982). Perspective-taking and altruism. *Psychological Bulletin, 91,* 143–173.

Valdman, A. (Ed.). (1997). *French and Creole in Louisiana.* New York: Plenum Press.

Valenzuela, M. (1990). Attachment in chronically underweight young children. *Child Development, 61,* 1984–1996.

Valian, V., Hoeffner, J., & Aubry, S. (1996). Young children's imitation of sentence subjects: Evidence of processing limitations. *Developmental Psychology, 32,* 153–164.

Valkenberg, P. M., & van der Voort, T. H. A. (1994). Influence of TV on daydreaming and creative imagination: A review of research. *Psychological Bulletin, 116,* 316–339.

Vandell, D. L., & Corasaniti, M. A. (1990). Variations in early child care: Do they predict subsequent social, emotional, and cognitive differences? *Early Childhood Research Quarterly, 5,* 555–572.

Vandell, D. L., & Mueller, E. C. (1980). Peer play and friendships during the first two years. In H. C. Foot, A. J. Chapman, & J. R. Smith (Eds.), *Friendship and social relations in children* (pp. 181–208). New York: Wiley.

Vandell, D. L., & Posner, J. (1999). Conceptualization and measurement of children's after-school environments. In S. L. Friedman & T. D. Wachs (Eds.), *Assessment of the environment across the lifespan* (pp. 167–197). Washington, DC: American Psychological Press.

Vandell, D. L., & Powers, C. (1983). Day care quality and children's free play activities. *American Journal of Orthopsychiatry, 53,* 493–500.

Vandell, D. L., & Shumow, L. (1999). After-school child care programs. *The Future of Children, 9,* 64–80.

Vandell, D. L., & Wilson, K. S. (1982). Social interaction in the first year: Infants' social skills with peers versus mother. In K. H. Rubin & H. S. Ross (Eds.), *Peer relationships and social skills in childhood* (pp. 187–208). New York: Springer.

Vandell, D. L., Wilson, K. S., & Buchanan, N. R. (1980). Peer interaction in the first year of life: An examination of its structure, content, and sensitivity to toys. *Child Development, 51,* 481–488.

van den Boom, D. C. (1994). The influence of temperament and mothering on attachment and exploration: An experimental manipulation of sensitive responsiveness among lower-class mothers with irritable infants. *Child Development, 65,* 1457–1477.

Vanfraussen, K., Ponjaert-Kristoffersen, I., & Brewaeys, A. (2003). Family functioning in lesbian families created by donor insemination. *American Journal of Orthopsychiatry, 73,* 78–90.

van IJzendoorn, M. H., Goldberg, S., Kroonenberg, P. M., & Frenkel, O. J. (1992). The relative effects of maternal and child problems on the quality of attachment: A meta-analysis of attachment in clinical samples. *Child Development, 63,* 840–858.

Van IJzendoorn, M. H., Goossens, F. A., Kroonenberg, P. M., & Tavecchio, L. W. C. (1985). Dependent attachment: B4-children in the strange situation. *Psychological Reports, 57,* 439–451.

van Loosbroek, E., & Smitsman, A. W. (1990). Visual perception of numerosity in infancy. *Developmental Psychology, 26,* 916–922.

Vartanian, L. R. (2000). Revisiting the imaginary audience and personal fable constructs of adolescent egocentrism: A conceptual review. *Adolescence, 35,* 639–661.

Vartanian, L. R. (2001). Adolescents' reactions to hypothetical peer group conversations: Evidence for an imaginary audience? *Adolescence, 36,* 347–380.

Vaughn, B. E., & Waters, E. (1990). Attachment behavior at home and in the laboratory: Q-sort observations and strange situation classifications of one-year-olds. *Child Development, 61,* 1965–1973.

Vellutino, F. R., & Scanlon, D. M. (1987). Phonological coding, phonological awareness, and reading ability: Evidence from a longitudinal and experimental study. *Merrill-Palmer Quarterly, 33,* 321–363.

Ventura, S. J., Mosher, W. D., Curtin, S. C., Abma, J. C., & Henshaw, S. (2001). Trends in pregnancy rates for the United States, 1976–97: An update. *National vital statistics reports, 49*(4). Retrieved March 27, 2003, from www.cdc.gov/nchs/data/nvsr/nvsr49/nvsr49_04.pdf.

Ventura, S. J., Peters, K. D., Martin, J. A., & Maurer, J. D. (1997). Births and deaths: United States, 1996. *Monthly Vital Statistics Report, 46*(1), supp. 2. Hyattsville, MD: National Center for Health Statistics.

Verkuyten, M. (2003). Postive and negative self-esteem among ethnic minority early adolescents: Social and cultural sources and threats. *Journal of Youth & Adolescence, 32,* 267–277.

Vihman, M., & Miller, R. (1988). Words and babble at the threshold of language acquisition. In M. Smith & J. Locke (Eds.), *The emergent lexicon: The child's development of a linguistic vocabulary* (pp. 151–184). New York: Academic Press.

Viken, R. J., Rose, R. J., Kaprio, J., & Koskenvuo, M. (1994). A developmental–genetic analysis of adult personality: Extraversion and neuroticism from 18 to 59. *Journal of Personality and Social Psychology, 66,* 722–730.

Volling, B. L., & Feagans, L. V. (1995). Infant day care and children's social competence. *Infant Behavior and Development, 18,* 177–188.

Volterra, V., & Taeschner, T. (1978). The acquisition and development of language by bilingual children. *Journal of Child Language, 5,* 311–326.

Voyer, D., Voyer, S., & Bryden, M. P. (1995). Magnitude of sex differences in spatial abilities: A meta-analysis and consideration of critical variables. *Psychological Bulletin, 117,* 250–270.

Vroegh, K. S. (1997). Transracial adoptees: Developmental status after 17 years. *American Journal of Orthopsychiatry, 67,* 568–575.

Vurpillot, E. (1968). The development of scanning strategies and their relation to visual differentiation. *Journal of Experimental Child Psychology, 6,* 632–650.

Vygotsky, L. S. (1956). *Izbrannye psikhologicheskie issledovaniya. [Selected psychological investigations].* Moscow: Izdatel'stvo Akademii Pedagogicheskikh Nauk. As cited in Wertsch & Tulviste, 1992.

Vygotsky, L. S. (1962). *Thought and language.* New York: Wiley.

Vygotsky, L. S. (1978). *Mind in society: The development of higher psychological processes.* Cambridge, MA: Harvard University Press.

Vygotsky, L. S. (1981). The genesis of higher mental functions. In J. V. Wertsch (Ed.), *The concept of activity in Soviet psychology* (pp. 144–188). Armonk, NJ: M. E. Sharpe.

Waddington, C. H. (1942). Canalization of development and the inheritance of acquired characters. *Nature, 150,* 563–564.

Waddington, C. H. (1957). *The strategy of the genes.* London: Allen & Unwin.

Walker, A. S. (1982). Intermodal perception of expressive behaviors by human infants. *Journal of Experimental Child Psychology, 33,* 514–535.

Walker, L. J. (1989). A longitudinal study of moral reasoning. *Child Development, 60,* 157–166.

Walker, L. J. (1995). Sexism in Kohlberg's moral psychology? In W. M. Kurtines & J. L. Gerwirtz (Eds.), *Moral development: An introduction* (pp. 83–107). Boston: Allyn & Bacon.

Walker, L. J., & Hennig, K. H. (1997). Moral development in the broader context of personality. In S. Hala (Ed.), *The development of social cognition* (pp. 297–327). Hove, England: Psychology Press.

Walker, L. J., Pitts, R., Hennig, K., & Matsuba, M. K. (1995). Reasoning about morality and real-life moral problems. In M. Killen & D. Hart (Eds.), *Morality in everyday life: Developmental perspectives* (pp. 371–407). New York: Cambridge University Press.

Walker-Andrews, A. S., & Lennon, E. M. (1985). Auditory–visual perception of changing distance by human infants. *Child Development, 56,* 544–548.

Wallas, G. (1926). *The art of thought.* New York: Harcourt Brace.

Wallerstein, J. S. (2001). The challenges of divorce for parents and children. In J. C. Westman (Ed.), *Parenthood in America: Undervalued, underpaid, under siege* (pp. 127–139). Madison: University of Wisconsin Press.

Wallerstein, J. S., Lewis, J. M., & Blakeslee, S. (2000). *The unexpected legacy of divorce: A 25-year landmark study.* New York: Hyperion.

Wang, Q. (2003). Infantile amnesia reconsidered: A cross-cultural analysis. *Memory, 11,* 65–80.

Wark, G. R., & Krebs, D. L. (1996). Gender and dilemma differences in real-life moral judgments. *Developmental Psychology, 32,* 220–230.

Warren, A. R., & McCloskey, L. A. (1997). Language in social contexts. In J. B. Gleason (Ed.), *The development of language* (4th ed., pp. 210–258). Boston: Allyn & Bacon.

Warren-Leubecker, A., & Carter, B. W. (1988). Reading and growth in metalinguistic awareness: Relations to socioeconomic status and reading readiness skills. *Child Development, 59,* 728–742.

Washington, V., & Oyemade, U. J. (1987). *Project Head Start: Past, present, and future trends in the context of family needs.* New York: Garland.

Wasley, P. A. (2002). Small classes, small schools: The time is now. *Educational Leadership, 59,* 6–10.

Waters, E., & Deane, K. E. (1985). Defining and assessing individual differences in attachment relationships: Q-methodology and the organization of behavior in infancy and early childhood. In I. Bretherton & E. Waters (Eds.), Growing points of attachment theory and research. *Monographs of the Society for Research in Child Development, 50* (Serial No. 209), 41–65.

Watson, J. B. (1924). *Behaviorism.* Chicago: University of Chicago Press.

Watson, J. B. (1928). *Psychological care of infant and child.* New York: Norton.

Watson, J. B. (1930). *Behaviorism.* Chicago: University of Chicago Press. Original edition published in 1924.

Watson, J. B., & Rayner, R. (1920). Conditioned emotional reactions. *Journal of Experimental Psychology, 3,* 1–14.

Watson, J. D., & Crick, F. H. C. (1953). Molecular structure of nucleic acids: A structure for deoxyribose nucleic acid. *Nature, 171,* 737–738.

Weiner, B. (1992). *Human motivation: Metaphors, theories, and research.* Newbury Park, CA: Sage.

Weiner, B. (2000). Intrapersonal and interpersonal theories of motivation from an attributional perspective. *Educational Psychology Review, 12,* 1–14.

Wekerle, C., & Wolfe, D. A. (1996). Child maltreatment. In E. J. Mash & R. A. Barkley (Eds.), *Child psychopathology* (pp. 492–537). New York: Guilford Press.

Welch-Ross, M. K., & Schmidt, E. R. (1996). Gender-schema development and children's constructive story memory: Evidence for a developmental model. *Child Development, 67,* 820–835.

Wellman, H. M. (1990). *The child's theory of mind.* Cambridge, MA: MIT Press.

Wellman, H. M., & Bartsch, K. (1988). Young children's reasoning about beliefs. *Cognition, 30,* 239–277.

Wellman, H. M., & Estes, D. (1986). Early understanding of mental entities: A reexamination of childhood realism. *Child Development, 57,* 910–923.

Wellman, H. M., & Gelman, S. A. (1998). Knowledge acquisition in foundational domains. In W. Damon (Series Ed.) & D. Kuhn & R. S. Siegler (Vol. Eds.), *Handbook of child psychology: Vol. 2. Cognition, perception, and language* (5th ed., pp. 523–573). New York: Wiley.

Wellman, H., Harris, P. L., Banerjee, M., & Sinclair, A. (1995). Early understanding of emotion: Evidence from natural language. *Cognition and Emotion, 9,* 117–149.

Wentzel, K. R. (2002). Are effective teachers like good parents? Teaching styles and student adjustment in early adolescence. *Child Development, 73,* 287–301.

Wentzel, K. R., & Watkins, D. E. (2002). Peer relationships and collaborative learning as contexts for academic enablers. *School Psychology Review, 31,* 366–377.

Werker, J. F., & Tees, R. C. (1984). Cross-language speech perception: Evidence for perceptual reorganization during the first year of life. *Infant Behavior and Development, 7,* 49–63.

Werner, E. E. (1989). High-risk children in young adulthood: A longitudinal study from birth to 32 years. *American Journal of Orthopsychiatry, 59,* 72–81.

Werner, E. E. (2000). Protective factors and individual resilience. In J. P. Shonkoff & S. J. Meisels (Eds.), *Handbook of early childhood intervention* (2nd ed., pp. 115–132). Cambridge, England: Cambridge University Press.

Werner, E. E., & Smith, R. S. (2001). *Journeys from childhood to midlife: Risk, resilience, and recovery.* Ithaca, NJ: Cornell University Press.

Wertsch, J. V. (1985). *Vygotsky and the social formation of mind.* Cambridge, MA: Harvard University Press.

Wertsch, J. V., & Tulviste, P. (1992). L. S. Vygotsky and contemporary developmental psychology. *Developmental Psychology, 28,* 548–557.

Wertsch, J. V., Tulviste, P., & Hagstrom, F. (1993). A sociocultural approach to agency. In E. A. Forman, N. Minick, & C. A. Stone (Eds.), *Contexts for learning* (pp. 336–356). New York: Oxford University Press.

Westman, J. C. (1994). *Licensing parents: Can we prevent child abuse and neglect?* New York: Insight Books.

Westman, J. C. (1997). Reducing governmental interventions in families by licensing parents. *Child Psychiatry and Human Development, 27,* 193–205.

Wexler, K. (1999). Maturation and growth of grammar. In W. C. Ritchie & T. K. Bhatia (Eds.), *Handbook of child language acquisition* (pp. 55–109). San Diego, CA: Academic Press.

Whalen, C. K., Jamner, L. D., Henker, B., Delfino, R. J., & Lozano, J. M. (2002). The ADHD spectrum and everyday life: Experience sampling of adolescent moods, activities, smoking, and drinking. *Child Development, 73,* 209–227.

Whalen, C. K., & Schreibman, L. (2003). Joint attention training for children with autism using behavior modification procedures. *Journal of Child Psychology & Psychiatry & Allied Disciplines, 44,* 456–468.

Whitaker, P. (2002). Supporting families of preschool children with autism: What parents want and what helps. *Autism, 6,* 411–426.

Whitely, B. E. (1985). Sex role orientation and psychological well-being: Two meta-analyses. *Sex Roles, 12,* 207–225.

Whiting, B. B., & Edwards, C. P. (1988). *Children of different worlds.* Cambridge, MA: Harvard University Press.

Whiting, B. M., & Whiting, J. W. (1975). *Children of six countries: A psychological analysis.* Cambridge, MA: Harvard University Press.

Whiz kid worries. (1999, September 13). Retrieved July 14, 2003, from http://abcnews.go.com/sections/us/DailyNews/whizkid990913.html.

Wiesner, M., & Ittel, A. (2002). Relations of pubertal timing and depressive symptoms to substance use in early adolescence. *Journal of Early Adolescence, 22*(1), 5–23.

Wigfield, A., & Eccles, J. S. (1994). Children's competence beliefs, achievement values, and general self-esteem. *Journal of Early Adolescence, 14,* 107–139.

Wigfield, A., & Eccles, J. S. (2001). Introduction. In A. Wigfield & J. S. Eccles (Eds.), *Development of achievement motivation* (pp. 1–11). San Diego, CA: Academic Press.

Wilcox, A. J., Baird, D. D., & Weinberg, C. R. (1999). Time of implantation of the conceptus and loss of pregnancy. *New England Journal of Medicine, 340,* 1796–1799.

Williams, J. M., & Currie, C. (2000). Self-esteem and physical development in early adolescence: Pubertal timing and body image. *Journal of Early Adolescence, 20,* 129–149.

Williams, P. A., Haertel, E. H., Walberg, H. J., & Haertel, G. D. (1982). The impact of leisure-time television on school learning: A research synthesis. *American Educational Research Journal, 19,* 19–50.

Willits, F. K., & Luloff, A. E. (1995). Urban residents' views of rurality and contacts with rural places. *Rural Sociology, 60,* 454–466.

Wilson, G. S. (1992). Heroin use during pregnancy: Clinical studies of long-term effects. In T. B. Sonderegger (Ed.), *Perinatal substance abuse: Research findings and clinical applications* (pp. 224–238). Baltimore: Johns Hopkins University Press.

Wilson, S. M., & Peterson, G. W. (2000). Growing up in Appalachia: Ecological influences on adolescent development. In R. Montemayor, G. R. Adams, & T. P. Gullotta (Eds.), *Adolescent diversity in ethnic, economic, and cultural contexts* (pp. 75–109). Thousand Oaks, CA: Sage.

Winner, E. (1996). *Gifted children: Myths and realities.* New York: Basic Books.

Winsler, A., & Naglieri, J. (2003). Overt and covert verbal problem-solving strategies: Developmental trends in use, awareness, and relations with task performance in children age 5 to 17. *Child Development, 74,* 659–678.

Wishard, A. G., Shivers, E. M., Howes, C., & Ritchie, S. (2003). Child care program and teacher practices: Associations with quality and children's experiences. *Early Childhood Research Quarterly, 18,* 65–103.

Witelson, S. F. (1987). Neurobiological aspects of language in children. *Child Development, 58,* 653–688.

Wolfram, W., & Thomas, E. R. (2002). *The development of African American English.* Oxford, England: Blackwell Publishers.

Wood, D., Bruner, J. S., & Ross, G. (1976). The role of tutoring in problem solving. *Journal of Child Psychology and Psychiatry, 17,* 89–100.

Wood, D., & Middleton, D. (1975). A study of assisted problem-solving. *British Journal of Psychology, 66,* 181–191.

Wood, D., Wood, H., & Middleton, D. (1978). An experimental evaluation of four face-to-face teaching strategies. *International Journal of Behavioral Development, 2,* 131–147.

Wood, F., Felton, R., Flowers, L., & Naylor, C. (1991). Neurobehavioral definition of dyslexia. In D. D. Duane & D. B. Gray (Eds.), *The reading brain: The biological basis of dyslexia* (pp. 1–25). Parkton, MD: York Press.

Woodhill, B. M., & Samuels, C. A. (2003). Positive and negative androgyny and their relationship with psychological health and well-being. *Sex Roles, 48,* 555–565.

Woods, M. B. (1972). The unsupervised child of the working mother. *Developmental Psychology, 6,* 14–25.

Woodward, A. L., & Markman, E. M. (1998). Early word learning. In W. Damon (Series Ed.) & D. Kuhn & R. S. Siegler (Vol. Eds.), *Handbook of child psychology: Vol. 2. Cognitive, language, and perceptual development,* (pp. 371–420). New York: Wiley.

Woodward, A. L., Markman, E. M., & Fitzsimmons, C. M. (1994). Rapid word learning in 13- and 18-month-olds. *Developmental Psychology, 30,* 553–566.

Woodward, J. L., & Fine, M. A. (1991). Long-term effects of self-supervised and adult-supervised child care arrangements on personality traits, emotional adjustment, and cognitive development. *Journal of Applied Developmental Psychology, 12,* 73–85.

Woodward, S. A., McManis, M. H., Kagan, J., Deldin, P., Snidman, N., Lewis, M., & Kahn, V. (2001). Infant temperament and the brainstem auditory evoked response in later childhood. *Developmental Psychology, 37,* 533–538.

Woodward, S. C. (1992). *The transmission of music into the human uterus and the response to music of the human fetus and neonate.* Unpublished doctoral dissertation, University of Cape Town. As cited in Lecanuet (1998).

Woolfolk, A. (2001). *Educational psychology* (8th ed.). Boston: Allyn & Bacon.

Woolley, J. D., & Wellman, H. M. (1992). Children's conceptions of dreams. *Cognitive Development, 7,* 365–380.

Wozencraft, T., Wagner, W., & Pellegrin, A. (1991). Depression and suicidal ideation in sexually abused children. *Child Abuse and Neglect, 15,* 505–511.

Wright, J. C., Huston, A. C., Scantlin, R., & Kotler, J. (2001). The Early Window Project: *Sesame Street* prepares children for school. In S. M. Fisch & R. T. Truglio (Eds.), *"G" is for growing: Thirty years of research on children and Sesame Street* (pp. 97–114). Mahwah, NJ: Erlbaum.

Wright, M. A. (1998). *I'm chocolate, you're vanilla.* San Francisco: Jossey-Bass.

Wynn, K. (1992). Addition and subtraction by human infants. *Nature, 358,* 749–750.

Wynn, K. (1995). Origins of numerical knowledge. *Mathematical Cognition, 1,* 36–60.

Yazigi, R. A., Odem, R. R., & Polakoski, K. L. (1991). Demonstration of specific binding of cocaine to human spermatozoa. *Journal of the American Medical Association, 266,* 1956–1959.

Yoshikawa, H., & Hsueh, J. (2001). Child development and public policy: Toward a dynamic systems perspective. *Child Development, 72,* 1887–1903.

Zahn, G. L., Kagan, S., & Widaman, K. F. (1986). Cooperative learning and classroom climate. *Journal of School Psychology, 24,* 351–362.

Zahn-Waxler, C., Iannotti, R. J., Cummings, E. M., & Denham, S. (1990). Antecedents of problem behaviors in children of depressed mothers. *Development and Psychopathology, 2,* 271–291.

Zahn-Waxler, C., & Robinson, J. (1995). Empathy and guilt: Early origins of feelings of responsibility. In J. Tangney & K. Fischer (Eds.), *Self-conscious emotions* (pp. 143–173). New York: Guilford Press.

Zahn-Waxler, C., Robinson, J. L., & Emde, R. N. (1992). The development of empathy in twins. *Developmental Psychology, 28,* 1038–1047.

Zaslow, M., Tout, K., Smith, S., & Moore, K. (1998). Implications of the 1996 welfare legislation for children: A research perspective. *Society for Research in Child Development Social Policy Report, 12*(3), 1–35.

Zehr, M. A. (2001). English-language learners post improved California test scores. *Education Week, 21*(1).

Zehr, M. A. (2002). Colorado extends bilingual education, but Massachusetts voters reject it. *Education Week, 22*(11).

Zelazo, P. R. (1983). The development of walking: New findings and old assumptions. *Journal of Motor Behavior, 15,* 99–137.

Zelazo, P. R., Zelazo, N. A., & Kolb, S. (1972). "Walking" in the newborn. *Science, 176,* 314–315.

Zigler, E., & Styfco, S. J. (1993). *Head Start and beyond: A national plan for extended childhood intervention.* New Haven, CT: Yale University Press.

Zigler, E., Styfco, S. J., & Gilman, E. (1993). The national Head Start program for disadvantaged preschoolers. In E. Zigler & S. J. Styfco (Eds.), *Head Start and beyond: A national plan for extended childhood intervention* (pp. 1–41). New Haven, CT: Yale University Press.

Zill, N. (2001). Does *Sesame Street* enhance school readiness? Evidence from a national survey of children. In S. M. Fisch & R. T. Truglio (Eds.), *"G" is for growing: Thirty years of research on children and Sesame Street* (pp. 115–130). Mahwah, NJ: Erlbaum.

Zill, N., Moore, K. A., Smith, E. W., Stief, T., & Coiro, M. J. (1995). The life circumstances and development of children in welfare families: A profile based on national survey data. In P. L. Chase-Lansdale & J. Brooks-Gunn (Eds.), *Escape from poverty: What makes a difference for children?* (pp. 39–59). Cambridge, England: Cambridge University Press.

Zill, N., Morrison, D. R., & Coiro, M. J. (1993). Long-term effects of parental divorce on parent–child relationships, adjustment, and achievement in young adulthood. *Journal of Family Psychology, 7,* 91–103.

Zimbardo, P. G., Butler, L. D., & Wolfe, V. A. (2003). Cooperative college examinations: More gain, less pain when students share information and grades. *The Journal of Experimental Education, 71,* 101–125.

Zimmerman, B. J. (1990). Self-regulation learning and academic achievement: An overview. *Educational Psychologist, 25,* 3–18.

Zito, J. M., Safer, D. J., dosReis, S., Gardner, J. F., Boles, M., & Lynch, F. (2000). Trends in the prescribing of psychotropic medications to preschoolers. *JAMA: Journal of the American Medical Association, 283,* 1025–1030.

Zito, J. M., Safer, D. J., dosReis, S., Gardner, J. F., Soeken, K., Boles, M., & Lynch, F. (2002). Rising prevalence of antidepressants among US youths. *Pediatrics, 109,* 721–727.

Zucker, K. J., & Bradley, S. J. (1995). *Gender identity disorder and psychosexual problems in children and adolescents.* New York: Guilford Press.

Name Index

Subject Index

Photo Credits